Oxford COLOUR ITALIAN Dictionary Plus

First edition

ITALIAN–ENGLISH
ENGLISH–ITALIAN

ITALIANO–INGLESE
INGLESE–ITALIANO

OXFORD
UNIVERSITY PRESS

Great Clarendon Street, Oxford OX2 6DP

Oxford University Press is a department of the University of Oxford.
It furthers the University's objective of excellence in research, scholarship,
and education by publishing worldwide in

Oxford New York

Auckland Cape Town Dar es Salaam Hong Kong Karachi
Kuala Lumpur Madrid Melbourne Mexico City Nairobi
New Delhi Shanghai Taipei Toronto

With offices in

Argentina Austria Brazil Chile Czech Republic France Greece
Guatemala Hungary Italy Japan Poland Portugal Singapore
South Korea Switzerland Thailand Turkey Ukraine Vietnam

Published in the United States
by Oxford University Press Inc., New York

First published as the Oxford Italian Minidictionary, third edition 2005
Supplementary material first published by OUP in 1999, 2005, and 2006
This edition published 2007

British Library Cataloguing in Publication Data

Data available

Library of Congress Cataloging in Publication Data

Data available

Typeset by Interactive Sciences Ltd, Gloucester
Printed in China through Asia Pacific Offset

ISBN 978–0–19–958733–9
ISBN 978–0–19–921892–9 (US edition)

10 9 8 7 6 5 4 3 2

7948613779897933

Contents

Preface

This dictionary is designed primarily for students of Italian. Its clear presentation and use of color make it easily accessible. This new edition contains new material, not found in the previous edition, on texting. In addition, the notes on Italian life and culture have been expanded. It also contains a list of the Italian words you must know, making it even more useful for students who wish to improve their vocabulary.

Contributors

Editors:

Nicholas Rollin
Francesca Logi

Supplementary Material:

Pat Bulhosen
Francesca Logi
Colin McIntosh
Francesca Moy
Loredana Riu
Paola Tite
Lexus Ltd

Introduction

In order to give the maximum information about English and Italian in the space available, this new dictionary uses certain space-saving conventions.

A swung dash ~ is used to replace the headword within the entry.

Where the headword contains a vertical bar | the swung dash replaces only the part of the headword that comes before the |. For example:

efficien|te *adj* efficient. **~za** *f* efficiency (the second bold word reads efficienza).

Indicators are provided to guide the user to the best translation for a specific sense of a word. Types of indicator are:

- field labels, which indicate a general area of usage (commercial, computing, photography etc);
- sense indicators, eg: **bore** *n* (of gun) calibro *m*; (person) seccatore, -trice *mf*;
- typical subjects of verbs, eg: **bond** *vt* (glue:) attaccare;
- typical objects of verbs, placed after the translation of the verb, eg: **boost** *vt* stimolare (sales); sollevare (morale);
- nouns that typically go together with certain adjectives, eg: **rich** *adj* ricco; (food) pesante;

A bullet point means that a headword has changed its part of speech within an entry, eg: **partition** *n* … •vt …
Open, square bullets □ indicate phrasal verbs.

Square brackets are used around parts of an expression which can be omitted without altering its sense.

A new feature for this edition is the list of Italian words you must know, which can be found in the centre section of the dictionary. A ◘ symbol next to a headword means that there is more information on this subject in the A–Z of Italian life and culture found in the centre section. An exclamation mark [!] indicates colloquial language, and a [✖] indicates slang.

Pronunciation of Italian

Vowels

a is broad like *a* in *father*: **casa**.
e has two sounds: closed like *ey* in *they*: **sera**;
open like *e* in *egg*: **sette**.
i is like *ee* in *feet*: **venire**.
o has two sounds: closed like *o* in *show*: **Roma**;
open like *o* in *dog*: **bocca**.
u is like *oo* in *moon*: **luna**.

When two or more vowels come together each vowel is pronounced separately: **buono**; **baia**.

Consonants

b, **d**, **f**, **l**, **m**, **n**, **p**, **t**, **v** are pronounced as in English. When these are double they are sounded distinctly: **bello**.

c before **a**, **o**, or **u** and before consonants is like *k* in *king*: **cane**.
before **e** or **i** is like *ch* in *church*: **cena**.
ch is also like *k* in *king*: **chiesa**.
g before **a**, **o**, or **u** is hard like *g* in *got*: **gufo**.
before **e** or **i** is like *j* in *jelly*: **gentile**.
gh is like *g* in *gun*: **ghiaccio**.
gl when followed by **a**, **e**, **o**, or **u** is like *gl* in *glass*: **gloria**.
gli is like *lli* in *million*: **figlio**.
gn is like *ni* in *onion*: **bagno**.
h is silent.
ng is like *ng* in *finger* (not *singer*): **ringraziare**.
r is pronounced distinctly.
s between two vowels is like *s* in *rose*: **riso**.
at the beginning of a word it is like *s* in *soap*: **sapone**.
sc before **e** or **i** is like *sh* in *shell*: **scienza**.
z sounds like *ts* within a word: **fazione**; like *dz* at the beginning: **zoo**.

The stress is shown by the sign **'** printed before the stressed syllable.

Glossary of grammatical terms

This section explains the basic terms that are used in this dictionary to help you find the information that you need.

Adjective

An adjective is used to add extra information to a noun:

*an **honest** politician, a **black** cat, a **heavy** book*
= un politico **onesto**, un gatto **nero**, un libro **pesante**

Note that in English the adjective usually comes before the noun, whereas in Italian it usually comes after.

Sometimes, of course, the adjective is separated from its noun:

*the flowers are **beautiful***
= i fiori sono **bellissimi**

Adverb

An adverb is used to add extra information to a verb, an adjective, or another adverb. In Italian adverbs often end in *-mente*:

*to walk **slowly**, **extremely** delicate, **fairly** often*
= camminare **lentamente**, **estremamente** delicato, **abbastanza** spesso

Agreement

There are two types of agreement in Italian which you must be careful about.

The first is the agreement of nouns and adjectives. All nouns in Italian have a gender, and most can also be either singular or plural. Any adjective which describes a noun must 'agree' with it in both gender (masculine or feminine) and number (singular or plural). In other words, the adjective must always be masculine or feminine, singular or plural:

un ragazz**o** italian**o**, una ragazz**a** italian**a**, ragazz**i** italian**i**, ragazz**e** italian**e**

The other kind of agreement is that between a verb and its subject. You must always ensure that the ending of the verb is the one which matches the subject, whether the subject is expressed or not:

Renato e Claudio **stanno** bene
= *Renato and Claudio are well*

io e Stefano **abbiamo** litigato
= *Stefano and I had an argument*

When the verb essere (to be) is used as an auxiliary verb, the past participle should agree with the subject:

Monica si è svegliata presto
= *Monica woke up early*

Auxiliary verbs

An auxiliary verb is a verb which is combined with another verb to form a new tense. In Italian auxiliary verbs are used to form the perfect tense, along with the past participle. There are two auxiliary verbs in Italian, *avere* and *essere*, and each is used with a particular group of verbs.

The auxiliary verb *essere* is used first of all to form the compound tenses of all reflexive verbs:

a che ora ti **sei** alzato?
= *what time did you get up?*

It is also used to form the compound tenses of a group of verbs, for example:

il pullman **è** partito = *the bus has gone*

The auxiliary verb *avere* is used to form the compound tenses of all other verbs:

ho dormito bene = *I slept well*

There is a small group of verbs which can take either *essere* or *avere*, sometimes depending on the meaning, sometimes depending on personal preference.

Comparative

The comparative, as its name indicates, is the form of the adjective or adverb which enables us to compare two or more nouns or pronouns. In English this is usually done by putting *more* before the appropriate adjective or adverb:

my book is ***more*** *interesting than yours*

In Italian the equivalent is più:

il mio libro è **più** interessante del tuo

In English, a few adjectives have an irregular comparative form: *good* (comparative *better*), *bad* (comparative *worse*). Some shorter English adjectives have a special comparative ending in *-er* (for example *bigger*, *smaller*, *happier*). In Italian the adjectives which have an irregular comparative form are *buono* (comparative *migliore*) and *cattivo* (comparative *peggiore*), and the adverbs which have an irregular comparative form are *bene* (comparative *meglio*) and *male* (comparative *peggio*). Note that *più buono* rather than *migliore* is used when talking about food.

Conjunction

A word used to join words or sentences together:

David ***and*** *Peter* = David **e** Peter

we didn't go to school ***because*** *there was a strike*
= non siamo andati a scuola **perché** c'era uno sciopero

Determiner

A determiner is used before a noun in order to identify more precisely what is being referred to. Here are some examples of determiners in English:

a *car*, ***the*** *car*, ***my*** *car*, ***this*** *car*, ***these*** *cars*

In Italian:

un panino, **il** conto, **le** scarpe

Exclamation

An exclamation is a word or phrase expressing a strong feeling, such as annoyance or joy:

hi! = *ciao!*

Feminine

One of the two noun genders. In Italian feminine nouns usually end in *-a* or *-e*:

una donna = *a woman*

una stazione = *a station*

Occasionally feminine nouns have another ending:

una radio = *a radio*

Future tense

The future tense of a verb refers to something that happens in the future:

verrò = *I'll come*

Gender

You will see when using the Italian-English half of this dictionary that some Italian words are marked 'm' or 'f'. Unlike English nouns, every Italian noun has a gender: it is either masculine, feminine or both (m,f). For example the Italian words for 'office', 'tree' and 'roof' are masculine (***un*** *ufficio*, ***un*** *albero*, ***un*** *tetto*), and the words for 'car', 'house' and 'wing' are feminine (***una*** *macchina*, ***una*** *casa*, ***un'****ala*). It is important to know the gender of an Italian noun because the ending of many words that go with it will depend on whether the noun is masculine or feminine. You may find it helpful to remember genders by learning new words in the form given in this dictionary, i.e. preceded by *un*/*una*, etc or *il*/*la*, etc:

una vittima = *a victim*
la sabbia = *sand*

Gerund
The gerund is the form of a verb that ends in *-ing* and in Italian ends in *-ando* or *-endo*:

it's ***raining*** = sta **piovendo**

Imperative
The imperative is the form of the verb that expresses a command, for example *go away!* Italian has two forms, depending on whether the informal *tu* form or the more formal *lei* form is being used:

stai zitto! = *shut up!*
si accomodi! = *take a seat!*

There is also a form of the imperative which is used to influence the behaviour of the group one is part of. In English this is shown by using *let's* before the verb. In Italian the form is identical to the first person plural:

andiamo a casa = *let's go home*

Imperfect tense
The imperfect tense of a verb refers to a continuous or habitual action in the past:

andavo = *I was going, I used to go*

Infinitive
The infinitive is the basic form of a verb, and has no indication of person or tense. In English it is often preceded by to: *to walk*, *to run*, *to receive*. In Italian the infinitive ends in *-are*, *-ere*, *-ire* or *-rre*. In the dictionary, you will usually find information about a verb by looking up the infinitive form:

cadere = *to fall*

When an infinitive is immediately followed by another infinitive in Italian, very often the final *-e* of the first infinitive is dropped. This also happens in some fixed phrases and common expressions:

poter dormire = *to be able to sleep*
aver fame = *to be hungry*

Masculine
One of the two noun genders. In Italian masculine nouns usually end in *-o* or *-e*:

un ragazz**o** = *a boy*
un bicchier**e** = *a glass*

Occasionally masculine nouns have another ending:

un problem**a** = *a problem*

Noun
A noun is a word that names a person, place, or thing:

Fellini, granny, Rome, tree
= Fellini, nonna, Roma, albero

It can also name things like concepts, emotions, abstract qualities, or actions:

health, happiness, intelligence, departure
= salute, felicità, intelligenza, partenza

Object
The direct object of a sentence is the word or group of words which is immediately affected by the action indicated by the verb. So, in the sentence:

the dog chewed the bone

dog is the subject, *chewed* is the verb,

and *bone* is the object.

There may also be a second object in the sentence: an indirect object. In general terms the indirect object indicates the person or thing which benefits from the action of the verb upon the direct object. In the sentence

John gave the dog a bone

bone is the direct object and *dog* is the indirect object.

Past historic tense
The past historic is an Italian tense that refers to something that happened in the past. It is generally used to talk about events in the fairly distant past, and is more common in writing than speech, especially in the north of Italy:

pagò il conto = *she paid the bill*

Past participle
The past participle is the form of a verb that is used to form the perfect tense in Italian:

ha mangiato tutto
= *he's eaten everything*

Perfect tense
The perfect tense is an Italian tense that refers to something that happened in the past. The perfect is generally used to talk about events in the fairly recent past, or that have had some kind of effect on the present:

ha finito = *he finished, he has finished*

Phrasal verb
A phrasal verb is a verb combined with a preposition or an adverb which has a particular meaning. For example, *to run away*, meaning 'to flee', or *to see to something*, meaning 'to ensure that something is done'.

Phrasal verbs are much less common in Italian than English, which means that English phrasal verbs usually have to be translated by a single verb. You therefore need to use your dictionary carefully in order to select the correct translation. If you look up *to run away*, for example, you will see that phrasal verbs are listed after all the other meanings of the word *run*, and in alphabetical order of the following adverb or preposition.

Plural
As in English, most nouns in Italian can be singular or plural. Plural nouns are used to refer to more than one example of that object. In Italian, nouns change their ending to show that they are plural. Nouns ending in *-o* or *-e* in the singular usually end in *-i* in the plural, and nouns ending in *-a* in the singular usually end in *-e* in the plural. There are many exceptions to this rule, however, and these are given in the Italian-English part of the dictionary. Unlike in English, adjectives also have plural forms, used whenever the nouns they are describing are plural:

fiori gialli = *yellow flowers*

Preposition
A word that stands in front of a noun or pronoun, relating it to the rest of the sentence:

play with me = gioca con me
I did it for you = l'ho fatto per te

Present tense
The present tense is the tense of a verb that refers to something that is happening now, or round about now:

leggo = *I read, I am reading*

Pronoun
A pronoun is a word that is used instead of a noun to avoid repeating it

unnecessarily:

I, you, he, she, it, we, you (pl), they
= io, tu, lui, lei, esso, noi, voi, loro
these = questi, *those* = quelle
mine = il mio, *yours* = il tuo

Reflexive verb
A reflexive verb is one whose object is the same as its subject. In English reflexive verbs are indicated by the use of reflexive pronouns such as *myself*, *yourself*, *herself*, etc. The Italian reflexive pronouns are *mi*, *ti*, *si*, *ci* and *vi*. These are sometimes joined on to the verb when it occurs in the infinitive, the imperative, or the gerund:

divertir**si** = *to enjoy* ***oneself***
guarda**ti!** = *look at* ***yourself****!*
si divertono = *they enjoy* ***themselves***

Singular
Of nouns, etc, referring to just one:

una sedia = *a chair*

Subject
The subject of a sentence is the noun or pronoun that generally causes the action of the verb:

l'autista ha frenato
= ***the driver*** *braked*

When the subject is already known or is obvious, it can often be omitted in Italian, and the verb ending does the work of showing what the subject is:

ho perso l'autobus = ***I*** *missed the bus*
dicono sempre la stessa cosa
= ***they*** *always say the same thing*

Subjunctive
The subjunctive is a special form of the verb that expresses doubt, unlikelihood or desire:

voglio che tu **venga**
= *I want you to come*

Superlative
The superlative is the form of the adjective or adverb which is used to express the highest degree. In English the adjective or adverb is usually preceded by *most*. Some English adjectives and adverbs have forms ending in *-est* (*slowest*, *biggest*) and some have irregular superlatives (*best*, *worst*).

In Italian the superlative is usually formed by putting *più* before the adjective or adverb. The definite article *il/la* is always used with superlative adjectives. In Italian the adjectives which have an irregular superlative form are buono (*il/la migliore*) and *cattivo* (*il/la peggiore*), and the adverbs which have an irregular superlative form are *bene* (*meglio*) and male (*peggio*).

Tense
The tense is the particular form of the verb that tells us approximately when the action of the verb takes place. Common tenses in Italian are the present, the perfect, the future, and the imperfect.

Verb
A verb is a word or phrase which indicates what is being done or what is happening:

i ragazzi **giocano** a carte
= *the boys* ***are playing*** *cards*
la scala si **è rotta** = *the ladder* ***broke***
scrivi il tuo indirizzo qua
= ***write*** *your address here*

It can also tell us about a state of affairs:

era troppo tardi = *it* ***was*** *too late*
ha quindici anni = *she'****s*** *fifteen*
il computer non **funziona**
= *the computer isn't* ***working***

Abbreviations/Abbreviazioni

adjective	*adj*	aggettivo
abbreviation	*abbr*	abbreviazione
administration	*Admin*	amministrazione
adverb	*adv*	avverbio
aeronautics	*Aeron*	aeronautica
American	*Am*	americano
anatomy	*Anat*	anatomia
archaeology	*Archeol*	archeologia
architecture	*Archit*	architettura
astrology	*Astr*	astrologia
attributive	*attrib*	attributo
automobiles	*Auto*	automobile
auxiliary	*aux*	ausiliare
biology	*Biol*	biologia
botany	*Bot*	botanica
British English	*Br*	inglese britannico
chemistry	*Chem*	chimica
commerce	*Comm*	commercio
computers	*Comput*	informatica
conjunction	*conj*	congiunzione
cooking	*Culin*	cucina
definite article	*def art*	articolo determinativo
et cetera	*ecc*	eccetera
electricity	*Electr*	elettricità
et cetera	*etc*	eccetera
feminine	*f*	femminile
figurative	*fig*	figurato
formal	*fml*	formale
geography	*Geog*	geografia
geology	*Geol*	geologia
grammar	*Gram*	grammatica
humorous	*hum*	umoristico
indefinite article	*indef art*	articolo indeterminativo
interjection	*int*	interiezione
interrogative	*inter*	interrogativo
invariable	*inv*	invariabile
law	*Jur*	legge/giuridico
literary	*liter*	letterario
masculine	*m*	maschile
mathematics	*Math*	matematica
mechanics	*Mech*	meccanica

Abbreviations/Abbreviazioni

medicine	*Med*	medicina
masculine or feminine	*mf*	maschile o femminile
military	*Mil*	militare
music	*Mus*	musica
noun	*n*	sostantivo
nautical	*Naut*	nautica
pejorative	*pej*	peggiorativo
personal	*pers*	personale
photography	*Phot*	fotografia
physics	*Phys*	fisica
plural	*pl*	plurale
politics	*Pol*	politica
possessive	*poss*	possessivo
past participle	*pp*	participio passato
prefix	*pref*	prefisso
preposition	*prep*	preposizione
present tense	*pres*	presente
pronoun	*pron*	pronome
psychology	*Psych*	psicologia
past tense	*pt*	tempo passato
someone	*qcno*	qualcuno
something	*qcsa*	qualcosa
rail	*Rail*	ferrovia
reflexive	*refl*	riflessivo
religion	*Relig*	religione
relative pronoun	*rel pron*	pronome relativo
somebody	*sb*	qualcuno
school	*Sch*	scuola
singular	*sg*	singolare
something	*sth*	qualcosa
technical	*Techn*	tecnico
telephone	*Teleph*	telefono
theatrical	*Theat*	teatrale
television	*TV*	televisione
typography	*Typ*	tipografia
university	*Univ*	università
auxiliary verb	*v aux*	verbo ausiliare
intransitive verb	*vi*	verbo intransitivo
reflexive verb	*vr*	verbo riflessivo
transitive verb	*vt*	verbo transitivo
transitive and intransitive verb	*vt/i*	verbo transitivo e intransitivo
vulgar	*vulg*	volgare
familiar	[!]	familiare
slang	[✖]	gergo
cultural equivalent	≈	equivalenza culturale

Aa

a (**ad** before vowel) prep to; (*stato in luogo, tempo, età*) at; (*con mese, città*) in; (*mezzo, modo*) by; **dire qcsa a qcno** tell sb sth; **alle tre** at three o'clock; **a vent'anni** at the age of twenty; **a Natale** at Christmas; **a dicembre** in December; **ero al cinema** I was at the cinema; **vivo a Londra** I live in London; **a due a due** two by two; **a piedi** on *o* by foot; **maglia a maniche lunghe** long-sleeved sweater; **casa a tre piani** house with three floors; **giocare a tennis** play tennis; **50 km all'ora** 50 km an hour; **4 euro al chilo** 4 euros a kilo; **al mattino/alla sera** in the morning/evening; **a venti chilometri/due ore da qui** twenty kilometres/two hours away

a'bate m abbot

abbacchi'ato adj downhearted

ab'bacchio m [young] lamb

abbagli'ante adj dazzling • m headlight, high beam

abbagli'are vt dazzle. **ab'baglio** m blunder; **prendere un ~** make a blunder

abbai'are vi bark

abba'ino m dormer window

abbando'na|re vt abandon; leave (luogo); give up (piani ecc). **~rsi** vr let oneself go; **~rsi a** give oneself up to (ricordi ecc). **~to** adj abandoned. **abban'dono** m abandoning; fig abandon; (stato) neglect

abbassa'mento m (di temperatura, prezzi ecc) drop

abbas'sar|e vt lower; turn down (radio, tv); **~e i fari** dip the headlights. **~si** vr stoop; (sole ecc:) sink; fig demean oneself

ab'basso adv below • int down with

abba'stanza adv enough; (alquanto) quite

ab'batter|e vt demolish; shoot down (aereo); put down (animale); topple (regime); (fig: demoralizzare) dishearten. **~si** vr (cadere) fall; fig be discouraged

abbatti'mento m (morale) despondency

abbat'tuto adj despondent

abba'zia f abbey

abbel'lir|e vt embellish. **~si** vr adorn oneself

abbeve'ra|re vt water. **~'toio** m drinking trough

abbi'ente adj well-to-do

abbiglia'mento m clothes pl; (industria) clothing industry

abbigli'ar|e vt dress. **~si** vr dress up

abbina'mento m combining

abbi'nare vt combine; match (colori)

abbindo'lare vt cheat

abbocca'mento m interview; (conversazione) talk

abboc'care vi bite; (tubi:) join; fig swallow the bait

abboc'cato adj (vino) fairly sweet

abbof'farsi vr stuff oneself

abbona'mento m subscription; (ferroviario ecc) season-ticket; **fare l'~** take out a subscription

abbo'na|re vt make a subscriber. **~rsi** vr subscribe (**a** to); take out a season-ticket (**a** for) (teatro, stadio). **~to, -a** mf subscriber

abbon'dan|te adj abundant; (quantità) copious; (nevicata) heavy; (vestiario) roomy. **~te di** abounding in. **~te'mente** adv (mangiare) copiously. **~za** f abundance

abbon'dare vi abound

abbor'da|bile adj (persona) approachable; (prezzo) reasonable. **~ggio** m (Mil) boarding. **~re** vt board (nave); approach (persona); ([!]: attaccar bottone a) chat up; tackle (compito ecc)

abbotto'na|re vt button up. **~'tura** f [row of] buttons. **~to** adj fig tight-lipped

a

abboz'zare vt sketch [out]; **~ un sorriso** give a hint of a smile. **ab'bozzo** m sketch

abbracci'are vt embrace; take up (professione); fig include. **ab'braccio** m hug

abbrevi'a|re vt shorten; (ridurre) curtail; abbreviate (parola). **~zi'one** f abbreviation

abbron'zante m sun-tan lotion

abbron'za|re vt bronze; tan (pelle). **~rsi** vr get a tan. **~to** adj tanned. **~'tura** f [sun-]tan

abbrusto'lire vt toast; roast (caffè ecc)

abbruti'mento m brutalization. **abbru'tire** vt brutalize. **abbru'tirsi** vr become brutalized

abbuf'fa|rsi vr [!] stuff oneself. **~ta** f blowout

abbuo'nare vt reduce

abbu'ono m allowance; Sport handicap

abdi'ca|re vi abdicate. **~zi'one** f abdication

aber'rante adj aberrant

a'bete m fir

abi'etto adj despicable

'abil|e adj able; (idoneo) fit; (astuto) clever. **~ità** f inv ability; (idoneità) fitness; (astuzia) cleverness. **~'mente** adv ably; (con astuzia) cleverly

abili'ta|re vt qualify. **~to** adj qualified. **~zi'one** f qualification; (titolo) diploma

abis'sale adj abysmal. **a'bisso** m abyss

abi'tabile adj inhabitable

abi'tacolo m (Auto) passenger compartment

abi'tante mf inhabitant

abi'ta|re vi live. **~to** adj inhabited •m built-up area. **~zi'one** f house

'abito m (da donna) dress; (da uomo) suit. **~ da cerimonia/da sera** formal/evening dress

abitu'al|e adj usual. **~'mente** adv usually

abitu'ar|e vt accustom. **~si a** vr get used to

abitudi'nario, -a adj of fixed habits •mf person of fixed habits

abi'tudine f habit; **d'~** usually; **per ~** out of habit; **avere l'~ di fare qcsa** be in the habit of doing sth

abnegazi'one f self-sacrifice

ab'norme adj abnormal

abo'li|re vt abolish; repeal (legge). **~zi'one** f abolition; repeal

abomi'nevole adj abominable

abor'rire vt abhor

abor'ti|re vi miscarry; (volontariamente) have an abortion; fig fail. **~vo** adj abortive. **a'borto** m miscarriage; (volontario) abortion. **~sta** adj pro-choice

abras|i'one f abrasion. **abra'sivo** adj & m abrasive

abro'ga|re vt repeal. **~zi'one** f repeal

'abside f apse

abu'lia f apathy. **a'bulico** adj apathetic

abu's|are vi **~ di** abuse; over-indulge in (alcol); (approfittare di) take advantage of; (violentare) rape. **~ivo** adj illegal

a'buso m abuse. **~ di confidenza** breach of confidence

a.C. abbr (avanti Cristo) BC

'acca f [!] **non ho capito un'~** I understood damn all

acca'demi|a f academy. **A~a di Belle Arti** Academy of Fine Arts. **~co, -a** adj academic •mf academician

acca'd|ere vi happen; **accada quel che accada** come what may. **~uto** m event

accalappi'are vt catch; fig allure

accal'carsi vr crowd

accal'da|rsi vr get overheated; fig get excited. **~to** adj overheated

accalo'rarsi vr get excited

accampa'mento m camp. **accam'pare** vt fig put forth. **accam'parsi** vr camp

accani'mento m tenacity; (odio) rage

acca'ni|rsi vr persist; (infierire) rage. **~to** adj persistent; (odio) fierce; fig inveterate

ac'canto adv near; **~ a** prep next to

accanto'nare vt set aside; (Mil) billet

accaparra'mento m hoarding; (Comm) cornering

accapar'ra|re vt hoard. **~rsi** vr grab; corner (mercato). **~'tore, ~'trice** mf hoarder

accapigli'arsi vr scuffle; (litigare) squabble

accappa'toio m bathrobe; (per spiaggia) beachrobe

accappo'nare vt **fare ~ la pelle a qcno** make sb's flesh creep

accarez'zare vt caress; fig cherish

accartocci'ar|e vt scrunch up. **~si** vr curl up

acca'sarsi vr get married

accasci'arsi vr flop down; fig lose heart

accata'stare vt pile up

accatti'vante adj beguiling

accatti'varsi vr **~ le simpatie/la stima/l'affetto di qcno** gain sb's sympathy/respect/affection

accatto'naggio m begging. **accat'tone, -a** mf beggar

accaval'lar|e vt cross (gambe). **~si** vr pile up; fig overlap

acce'cante adj (luce) blinding

acce'care vt blind •vi go blind

ac'cedere vi **~ a** enter; (acconsentire) comply with

accele'ra|re vi accelerate •vt accelerate. **~to** adj rapid. **~'tore** m accelerator. **~zi'one** f acceleration

ac'cender|e vt light; turn on (luce, TV ecc); fig inflame; **ha da ~e?** have you got a light?. **~si** vr catch fire; (illuminarsi) light up; (TV ecc:) turn on; fig become inflamed

accendi'gas m inv gas lighter; (su cucina) automatic ignition

accen'dino m lighter

accendi'sigari m cigar-lighter

accen'nare vt indicate; hum (melodia) •vi **~ a** beckon to; fig hint at; (far l'atto di) make as if to; **accenna a piovere** it looks like rain. **ac'cenno** m gesture; (con il capo) nod; fig hint

accensi'one f lighting; (di motore) ignition

accen'ta|re vt accent; (con accento tonico) stress. **~zi'one** f accentuation. **ac'cento** m accent; (tonico) stress

accentra'mento m centralizing

accen'trare vt centralize

accentu'a|re vt accentuate. **~rsi** vr become more noticeable. **~to** adj marked

accerchia'mento m surrounding

accerchi'are vt surround

accerta'mento m check

accer'tare vt ascertain; (controllare) check; assess (reddito)

ac'ceso adj lighted; (radio, TV ecc) on; (colore) bright

acces'sibile adj accessible; (persona) approachable; (spesa) reasonable

ac'cesso m access; (Med: di rabbia) fit; **vietato l'~** no entry

acces'sorio adj accessory; (secondario) of secondary importance •m accessory; **accessori** pl (rifiniture) fittings

ac'cetta f hatchet

accet'tabile adj acceptable

accet'tare vt accept; (aderire a) agree to

accettazi'one f acceptance; (luogo) reception. **~ [bagagli]** check-in. **[banco] ~** check-in [desk]

ac'cetto adj agreeable; **essere bene ~** be very welcome

accezi'one f meaning

acchiap'pare vt catch

acchito m **di primo ~** at first

acciac'ca|re vt crush; fig prostrate. **~to, -a** adj **essere ~to** ache all over. **acci'acco** m infirmity; **acciacchi** pl aches and pains

acciaie'ria f steelworks

acci'aio m steel; **~ inossidabile** stainless steel

acciden'ta|le adj accidental. **~l'mente** adv accidentally. **~to** adj (terreno) uneven

acci'dente m accident; (Med) stroke; **non capisce un ~** [!] he doesn't understand a damn thing. **acci'denti!** int damn!

accigli'a|rsi vr frown. **~to** adj frowning

a

a

ac'cingersi vr **~ a** be about to
acci'picchia int good Lord!
acciuf'fare vt catch
acci'uga f anchovy
accla'ma|re vt applaud; (eleggere) acclaim. **~zi'one** f applause
acclima'tar|e vt acclimatize. **~si** vr get acclimatized
ac'clu|dere vt enclose. **~so** adj enclosed
accocco'larsi vr squat
accogli'en|te adj welcoming; (confortevole) cosy. **~za** f welcome
ac'cogliere vt receive; (con piacere) welcome; (contenere) hold
accol'larsi vr take on (responsabilità, debiti, doveri). **accol'lato** adj high-necked
accoltel'lare vt knife
accomia'tar|e vt dismiss. **~si** vr take one's leave (**da** of)
accomo'dante adj accommodating
accomo'dar|e vt (riparare) mend; (disporre) arrange. **~si** vr make oneself at home; **si accomodi!** come in!; (si sieda) take a seat!
accompagna'mento m accompaniment; (seguito) retinue
accompa'gna|re vt accompany; **~re qcno a casa** see sb home; **~re qcno alla porta** show sb out. **~'tore, ~'trice** mf companion; (di comitiva) escort; (Mus) accompanist
accomu'nare vt pool
acconci'a|re vt arrange. **~'tura** f hair-style; (ornamento) head-dress
accondiscen'den|te adj too obliging. **~za** f excessive desire to please
accondi'scendere vi **~ a** condescend; comply with (desiderio); (acconsentire) consent to
acconsen'tire vi consent
acconten'tar|e vt satisfy. **~si** vr be content (**di** with)
ac'conto m deposit; **in ~** on account; **lasciare un ~** leave a deposit
accop'pare vt [!] bump off
accoppia'mento m coupling; (di animali) mating
accoppi'a|re vt couple; mate (animali). **~rsi** vr pair off; mate. **~ta** f (scommessa) bet on two horses for first and second place
acco'rato adj sorrowful
accorci'ar|e vt shorten. **~si** vr get shorter
accor'dar|e vt concede; match (colori ecc); (Mus) tune. **~si** vr agree
ac'cordo m agreement; (Mus) chord; (armonia) harmony; **andare d'~** get on well; **d'~!** agreed!; **essere d'~** agree; **prendere accordi con qcno** make arrangements with sb
ac'corgersi vr **~ di** notice; (capire) realize
accorgi'mento m shrewdness; (espediente) device
ac'correre vi hasten
accor'tezza f (previdenza) forethought
ac'corto adj shrewd; **mal ~** incautious
accosta'mento m combination
acco'star|e vt draw close to; approach (persona); set ajar (porta ecc). **~si** vr **~si a** come near to
accovacci'a|rsi vr crouch
accoz'zaglia f jumble; (di persone) mob
accoz'zare vt **~ colori** mix colours that clash
accredita'mento m credit; **~ tramite bancogiro** Bank Giro Credit
accredi'tare vt confirm (notizia); (Comm) credit
ac'cresc|ere vt increase. **~ersi** vr grow larger. **~i'tivo** adj augmentative
accucci'arsi vr (cane:) lie down; (persona:) crouch
accu'dire vi **~ a** attend to
accumu'la|re vt accumulate. **~rsi** vr accumulate. **~'tore** m accumulator; (Auto) battery. **~zi'one** f accumulation.
accura'tezza f care
accu'rato adj careful
ac'cusa f accusation; (Jur) charge; **essere in stato di ~** have been charged; **la Pubblica A~** the public prosecutor
accu'sa|re vt accuse; (Jur) charge;

complain of (dolore); **~re ricevuta di** acknowledge receipt of. **~to, -a** mf accused. **~'tore** m prosecutor

a'cerbo adj sharp; (non maturo) unripe

'acero m maple

a'cerrimo adj implacable

a'ceto m vinegar

ace'tone m nail-polish remover

A.C.I. abbr (Automobile Club d'Italia) Italian Automobile Association

acidità f acidity. **~ di stomaco** acid stomach

'acido adj acid; (persona) sour •m acid

a'cidulo adj slightly sour

'acino m berry; (chicco) grape

'acne f acne

'acqua f water; **fare ~** leak; **~ in bocca!** fig mum's the word!. **~ corrente** running water. **~ dolce** fresh water. **~ minerale** mineral water. **~ minerale gassata** fizzy mineral water. **~ naturale** still mineral water. **~ potabile** drinking water. **~ salata** salt water. **~ tonica** tonic water

acqua'forte f etching

ac'quaio m sink

acquama'rina adj aquamarine

acqua'rello m = **acquerello**

ac'quario m aquarium; (Astr) Aquarius

acqua'santa f holy water

acqua'scooter m inv water-scooter

ac'quatico adj aquatic

acquat'tarsi vr crouch

acqua'vite f brandy

acquaz'zone m downpour

acque'dotto m aqueduct

'acqueo adj **vapore ~** water vapour

acque'rello m water-colour

acqui'rente mf purchaser

acqui'si|re vt acquire. **~to** adj acquired. **~zi'one** f attainment

acqui'st|are vt purchase; (ottenere) acquire. **ac'quisto** m purchase; **uscire per ~i** go shopping; **fare ~i** shop

acqui'trino m marsh

acquo'lina f **far venire l'~ in bocca a qcno** make sb's mouth water

ac'quoso adj watery

'acre adj acrid; (al gusto) sour; fig harsh

a'crilico m acrylic

a'croba|ta mf acrobat. **~'zia** f acrobatics pl

a'cronimo m acronym

acu'ir|e vt sharpen. **~si** vr become more intense

a'culeo m sting; (Bot) prickle

acumi'nato adj pointed

a'custic|a f acoustics pl. **~o** adj acoustic

acu'tezza f acuteness

acutiz'zarsi vr become worse

a'cuto adj sharp; (suono) shrill; (freddo, odore) intense; (Gram, Math, Med) acute •m (Mus) high note

ad prep = **a** (davanti a vocale)

adagi'ar|e vt lay down. **~si** vr lie down

a'dagio adv slowly •m (Mus) adagio; (proverbio) adage

adattabilità f adaptability

adatta'mento m adaptation; **avere spirito di ~** be adaptable

adat'ta|re vt adapt; (aggiustare) fit. **~rsi** vr adapt. **~'tore** m adaptor. **a'datto** adj suitable (**a** for); (giusto) right

addebita'mento m debit. **~ diretto** direct debit

addebi'tare vt debit; ascribe (colpa)

ad'debito m charge

addensa'mento m thickening; (di persone) gathering

adden'sar|e vt thicken. **~si** vr thicken; (affollarsi) gather

adden'tare vt bite

adden'trarsi vr penetrate

ad'dentro adv deeply; **essere ~ in** be in on

addestra'mento m training

adde'strar|e vt train. **~si** vr train

ad'detto, -a adj assigned •mf employee; (diplomatico) attaché. **~ stampa** press officer

addiaccio m **dormire all'~** sleep in the open

addi'etro adv (indietro) back; (nel passato) before

a

ad'dio m & int goodbye. **~ al celibato** stag party

addirit'tura adv (perfino) even; (assolutamente) absolutely; **~!** really!

ad'dirsi vr **~ a** suit

addi'tare vt point at; (in mezzo a un gruppo) point out; fig point to

addi'tivo adj & m additive

addizio'nal|e adj additional. **~'mente** adv additionally

addizio'nare vt add [up]. **addizi'one** f addition

addob'bare vt decorate. **ad'dobbo** m decoration

addol'cir|e vt sweeten; tone down (colore); fig soften. **~si** vr fig mellow

addolo'ra|re vt grieve. **~rsi** vr be upset (**per** by). **~to** adj distressed

ad'dom|e m abdomen. **~i'nale** adj abdominal; **[muscoli] addominali** pl abdominals

addomesti'ca|re vt tame. **~'tore** m tamer

addormen'ta|re vt put to sleep. **~rsi** vr go to sleep. **~to** adj asleep; fig slow

addos'sar|e vt **~e a** (appoggiare) lean against; (attribuire) lay on. **~si** vr (ammassarsi) crowd; shoulder (responsabilità ecc)

ad'dosso adv on; **~ a** prep on; (molto vicino) right next to; **mettere gli occhi ~ a qcno/qcsa** hanker after sb/sth; **non mettermi le mani ~!** keep your hands off me!; **stare ~ a qcno** fig be on sb's back

ad'durre vt produce (prova, documento); give (pretesto, esempio)

adegua'mento m adjustment

adegu'a|re vt adjust. **~rsi** vr conform. **~to** adj adequate; (conforme) consistent

a'dempi|ere vt fulfil. **~'mento** m fulfilment

ade'noidi fpl adenoids

ade'ren|te adj adhesive; (vestito) tight • mf follower. **~za** f adhesion. **~ze** pl connections

ade'rire vi **~ a** adhere to; support (petizione); agree to (richiesta)

adesca'mento m (Jur) soliciting

ade'scare vt bait; fig entice

adesi'one f adhesion; fig agreement

ade'sivo adj adhesive • m sticker; (Auto) bumper sticker

a'desso adv now; (poco fa) just now; (tra poco) any moment now; **da ~ in poi** from now on; **per ~** for the moment

adia'cente adj adjacent; **~ a** next to

adi'bire vt **~ a** put to use as

'adipe m adipose tissue

adi'ra|rsi vr get irate. **~to** adj irate

a'dire vt resort to; **~ le vie legali** take legal proceedings

'adito m **dare ~ a** give rise to

adocchi'are vt eye; (con desiderio) covet

adole'scen|te adj & mf adolescent. **~za** f adolescence. **~zi'ale** adj adolescent

adom'brar|e vt darken; fig veil. **~si** vr (offendersi) take offence

adope'rar|e vt use. **~si** vr take trouble

ado'rabile adj adorable

ado'ra|re vt adore. **~zi'one** f adoration

ador'nare vt adorn

adot't|are vt adopt. **~ivo** adj adoptive. **adozi'one** f adoption

adrena'lina f adrenalin

adri'atico adj Adriatic • m **l'A~** the Adriatic

adu'la|re vt flatter. **~'tore, ~'trice** mf flatterer. **~zi'one** f flattery

adulte'ra|re vt adulterate. **~to** adj adulterated

adul'terio m adultery. **a'dultero, -a** adj adulterous • m adulterer • f adulteress

a'dulto, -a adj & mf adult; (maturo) mature

adu'nanza f assembly

adu'na|re vt gather. **~ta** f (Mil) parade

a'dunco adj hooked

ae'rare vt air (stanza)

a'ereo adj aerial; (dell'aviazione) air attrib • m aeroplane, plane

ae'robic|a f aerobics. **~o** adj aerobic

aerodi'namic|a f aerodynamics sg.

~**o** adj aerodynamic

aero'nautic|a f aeronautics sg; (Mil) Air Force. ~**o** adj aeronautical

aero'plano m aeroplane

aero'porto m airport

aero'scalo m cargo and servicing area

aero'sol m inv aerosol

'afa f sultriness

af'fabil|e adj affable. ~**ità** f affability

affaccen'da|rsi vr busy oneself (**a** with). ~**to** adj busy

affacci'arsi vr show oneself; ~ **alla finestra** appear at the window

affa'ma|re vt starve [out]. ~**to** adj starving

affan'na|re vt leave breathless. ~**rsi** vr busy oneself; (agitarsi) get worked up. ~**to** adj breathless; **dal respiro** ~**to** wheezy. **af'fanno** m breathlessness; fig worry

af'fare m matter; (Comm) deal; (occasione) bargain; **affari** pl business; **non sono affari tuoi** it's none of your business. **affa'rista** mf wheeler-dealer

affasci'nante adj fascinating; (persona, sorriso) bewitching

affasci'nare vt bewitch; fig charm

affatica'mento m fatigue

affati'car|e vt tire; (sfinire) exhaust. ~**si** vr tire oneself out; (affannarsi) strive

af'fatto adv completely; **non...** ~ not... at all; **niente** ~**!** not at all!

affer'ma|re vt affirm; (sostenere) assert. ~**rsi** vr establish oneself

affermativa'mente adv in the affirmative

afferma'tivo adj affirmative

affermazi'one f assertion; (successo) achievement

affer'rar|e vt seize; catch (oggetto); (capire) grasp; ~**e al volo** fig be quick on the uptake. ~**si** vr ~**si a** grasp at

affet'ta|re vt slice; (ostentare) affect. ~**to** adj sliced; (maniere) affected • m cold meat.

affet'tivo adj affective; **rapporto** ~ emotional tie

af'fetto[1] m affection

af'fetto[2] adj ~ **da** suffering from

affettuosità f inv (gesto) affectionate gesture

affettu'oso adj affectionate

affezio'na|rsi vr ~**rsi a** grow fond of. ~**to** adj devoted (**a** to)

affian'car|e vt put side by side; (Mil) flank; fig support. ~**si** vr come side by side; fig stand together; ~**si a qcno** fig help sb out

affiata'mento m harmony

affia'ta|rsi vr get on well together. ~**to** adj close-knit; **una coppia** ~**ta** a very close couple

affibbi'are vt ~ **qcsa a qcno** saddle sb with sth; ~ **un pugno a qcno** let fly at sb

affi'dabil|e adj dependable. ~**ità** f dependability

affida'mento m (Jur: dei minori) custody; **fare** ~ **su qcno** rely on sb; **non dare** ~ not inspire confidence

affi'dar|e vt entrust. ~**si** vr ~**si a** rely on

affievo'lirsi vr grow weak

af'figgere vt affix

affi'lare vt sharpen

affili'ar|e vt affiliate. ~**si** vr become affiliated

affi'nare vt sharpen; (perfezionare) refine

affinché conj so that, in order that

af'fin|e adj similar. ~**ità** f affinity

affiora'mento m emergence; (Naut) surfacing

affio'rare vi emerge; fig come to light

af'fisso m bill; (Gram) affix

affitta'camere m inv landlord • f inv landlady

affit'tare vt rent; **'af'fittasi'** 'for rent'

af'fitt|o m rent; **contratto d'**~**o** lease; **dare in** ~**o** let; **prendere in** ~**o** rent. ~**u'ario, -a** mf (Jur) lessee

af'fligger|e vt torment. ~**si** vr distress oneself

af'fli|tto adj distressed. ~**zi'one** f distress; fig affliction

a

a

afflosci'arsi vr become floppy; (accasciarsi) flop down; (morale:) decline

afflu'en|te adj & m tributary. **~za** f flow; (di gente) crowd

afflu'ire vi flow; fig pour in

af'flusso m influx

affo'ga|re vt/i drown; (Culin) poach; **~re in** fig be swamped with. **~to** adj (persona) drowned; (uova) poached. **~to al caffè** m ice cream with hot espresso poured over it

affol'la|re vt, **~rsi** vr crowd. **~to** adj crowded

affonda'mento m sinking

affon'dare vt/i sink

affossa'mento m pothole

affran'ca|re vt redeem (bene); stamp (lettera); free (schiavo). **~rsi** vr free oneself. **~'trice** f franking machine. **~'tura** f stamping; (di spedizione) postage

af'franto adj prostrated; (esausto) worn out

af'fresco m fresco

affret'ta|re vt speed up. **~rsi** vr hurry. **~ta'mente** adv hastily. **~to** adj hasty

affron'tar|e vt face; confront (nemico); meet (spese). **~si** vr clash

af'fronto m affront, insult; **fare un ~ a qcno** insult sb

affumi'ca|re vt fill with smoke; (Culin) smoke. **~to** adj (prosciutto, formaggio) smoked

affuso'la|re vt taper [off]. **~to** adj tapering

afo'risma m aphorism

a'foso adj sultry

'Africa f Africa. **afri'cano, -a** agg & mf African

afrodi'siaco adj & m aphrodisiac

a'genda f diary

agen'dina f pocket-diary

a'gente m agent; **agenti** pl **atmosferici** atmospheric agents. **~ di cambio** stockbroker. **~ di polizia** police officer

agen'zia f agency; (filiale) branch office; (di banca) branch. **~ di viaggi** travel agency. **~ immobiliare** estate agency

agevo'la|re vt facilitate. **~zi'one** f facilitation

a'gevol|e adj easy; (strada) smooth. **~'mente** adv easily

agganci'ar|e vt hook up; (Rail) couple. **~si** vr (vestito:) hook up

ag'geggio m gadget

agget'tivo m adjective

agghiacci'ante adj terrifying

agghiacci'ar|e vt fig **~ qcno** make sb's blood run cold. **~si** vr freeze

agghin'da|re vt [!] dress up. **~rsi** vr [!] doll oneself up. **~to** adj dressed up

aggiorna'mento m up-date

aggior'na|re vt (rinviare) postpone; (mettere a giorno) bring up to date. **~rsi** vr get up to date. **~to** adj up-to-date; (versione) updated

aggi'rar|e vt surround; (fig: ingannare) trick. **~si** vr hang about; **~si su** (discorso ecc:) be about; (somma:) be around

aggiudi'car|e vt award; (all'asta) knock down. **~si** vr win

aggi'un|gere vt add. **~ta** f addition. **~'tivo** adj supplementary. **~to** adj added •adj & m (assistente) assistant

aggiu'star|e vt mend; (sistemare) settle; ([!]: mettere a posto) fix. **~si** vr adapt; (mettersi in ordine) tidy oneself up; (decidere) sort things out; (tempo:) clear up

agglomera'mento m conglomeration

agglome'rato m built-up area

aggrap'par|e vt grasp. **~si** vr **~si a** cling to

aggra'vante (Jur) f aggravation •adj aggravating

aggra'var|e vt (peggiorare) make worse; increase (pena); (appesantire) weigh down. **~si** vr worsen

aggrazi'ato adj graceful

aggre'dire vt attack

aggre'ga|re vt add; (associare a un gruppo ecc) admit. **~rsi** vr **~rsi a** join. **~to** a associated •m aggregate; (di case) block

aggressi'one f aggression; (atto) attack

aggres's|ivo adj aggressive. **~ività** f

aggressiveness. **~ore** m aggressor

aggrin'zare, aggrin'zire vt wrinkle

aggrot'tare vt **~ le ciglia/la fronte** frown

aggrovigli'a|re vt tangle. **~rsi** vr get entangled; fig get complicated. **~to** adj entangled; fig confused

agguan'tare vt catch

aggu'ato m ambush; (tranello) trap; **stare in ~** lie in wait

agguer'rito adj fierce

agia'tezza f comfort

agi'ato adj (persona) well off; (vita) comfortable

a'gibil|e adj (palazzo) fit for human habitation. **~ità** f fitness for human habitation

'agil|e adj agile. **~ità** f agility

'agio m ease; **mettersi a proprio ~** make oneself at home

a'gire vi act; (comportarsi) behave; (funzionare) work; **~ su** affect

agi'ta|re vt shake; wave (mano); (fig: turbare) trouble. **~rsi** vr toss about; (essere inquieto) be restless; (mare:) get rough. **~to** adj restless; (mare) rough. **~'tore, ~'trice** mf (persona) agitator. **~zi'one** f agitation; **mettere in ~zione qcno** make sb worried

'agli = **a + gli**

'aglio m garlic

a'gnello m lamb

agno'lotti mpl ravioli sg

a'gnostico, -a adj & mf agnostic

'ago m needle

ago'ni|a f agony. **~z'zare** vi be on one's deathbed

ago'nistic|a f competition. **~o** adj competitive

agopun'tura f acupuncture

a'gosto m August

a'grari|a f agriculture. **~o** adj agricultural • m landowner

a'gricol|o adj agricultural. **~'tore** m farmer. **~'tura** f agriculture

agri'foglio m holly

agritu'rismo m farm holidays, agro-tourism

'agro adj sour

agroalimen'tare adj food attrib

agro'dolce adj bitter-sweet; (Culin) sweet-and-sour; **in ~** sweet and sour

agrono'mia f agronomy

a'grume m citrus fruit; (pianta) citrus tree

aguz'zare vt sharpen; **~ le orecchie** prick up one's ears; **~ la vista** look hard

aguz'zino m slave-driver; (carceriere) jailer

ahimè int alas

'ai = **a + i**

'aia f threshing-floor

'Aia f **L'~** The Hague

Aids mf Aids

ai'rone m heron

ai'tante adj sturdy

aiu'ola f flower-bed

aiu'tante mf assistant • m (Mil) adjutant. **~ di campo** aide-de-camp

aiu'tare vt help

ai'uto m help, aid; (assistente) assistant

aiz'zare vt incite; **~ contro** set on

al = **a + il**

'ala f wing; **fare ~** make way

ala'bastro m alabaster

'alacre adj brisk

a'lano m Great Dane

'alba f dawn

Alba'n|ia f Albania. **a~ese** adj & mf Albanian

albeggi'are vi dawn

albe'ra|to adj wooded; (viale) tree-lined. **~'tura** f (Naut) masts pl. **albe'rello** m sapling

al'berg|o m hotel. **~o diurno** hotel where rooms are rented during the daytime. **~a'tore, ~a'trice** mf hotel-keeper. **~hi'ero** adj hotel attrib

'albero m tree; (Naut) mast; (Mech) shaft. **~ genealogico** family tree. **~ maestro** (Naut) mainmast. **~ di Natale** Christmas tree

albi'cocc|a f apricot. **~o** m apricot-tree

see A-Z of Italian life and culture

al'bino, -a mf albino

'albo m register; (libro ecc) album; (per avvisi) notice board

'album m album. **~ da disegno** sketch-book

al'bume m albumen

'alce m elk

'alcol m alcohol; (Med) spirit; (liquori forti) spirits pl; **darsi all'~** take to drink. **al'colici** mpl alcoholic drinks. **al'colico** adj alcoholic. **alco'lismo** m alcoholism. **~iz'zato, -a** adj & mf alcoholic

alco'test® m inv Breathalyser®

al'cova f alcove

al'cun, al'cuno adj & pron any; **non ha ~ amico** he hasn't any/has no friends. **alcuni** pl some, a few; **~i suoi amici** some of his friends

alea'torio adj unpredictable

a'letta f (Mech) fin

alfa'betico adj alphabetical

alfabetizzazi'one f **~ della popolazione** teaching people to read and write

alfa'beto m alphabet

alfi'ere m (negli scacchi) bishop

al'fine adv eventually, in the end

'alga f seaweed

'algebra f algebra

Alge'ri|a f Algeria. **a~no, -a** agg & mf Algerian

ali'ante m glider

'alibi m inv alibi

alie'na|re vt alienate. **~rsi** vr become estranged; **~rsi le simpatie di qcno** lose sb's good will. **~to, -a** adj alienated • mf lunatic

a'lieno, -a mf alien • adj **è ~ da invidia** envy is foreign to him

alimen'ta|re vt feed; fig foment • adj food attrib; (abitudine) dietary • m **~ri** pl food-stuffs. **~'tore** m power unit. **~zi'one** f feeding

ali'mento m food; **alimenti** pl food; (Jur) alimony

a'liquota f share; (di imposta) rate

ali'scafo m hydrofoil

'alito m breath

'alla = **a + la**

allaccia'mento m connection

allacci'ar|e vt fasten (cintura); lace up (scarpe); do up (vestito); (collegare) connect; form (amicizia). **~si** vr do up, fasten

allaga'mento m flooding

alla'gar|e vt flood. **~si** vr become flooded

allampa'nato adj lanky

allarga'mento m (di strada, ricerche) widening

allar'gar|e vt widen; open (braccia, gambe); let out (vestito ecc); fig extend. **~si** vr widen

allar'mante adj alarming

allar'ma|re vt alarm. **~to** adj panicky

al'larme m alarm; **dare l'~** raise the alarm; **falso ~** fig false alarm. **~ aereo** air raid warning

allar'mis|mo m alarmism. **~ta** mf alarmist

allatta'mento m (di animale) suckling; (di neonato) feeding

allat'tare vt suckle (animale); feed (neonato)

'alle = **a + le**

alle'a|nza f alliance. **~to, -a** adj allied • mf ally

alle'ar|e vt unite. **~si** vr form an alliance

alle'ga|re¹ vt (Jur) allege

alle'ga|re² vt (accludere) enclose; set on edge (denti). **~to** adj enclosed • m enclosure; **in ~to** attached. **~zi'one** f (Jur) allegation

allegge'rir|e vt lighten; fig alleviate. **~si** vr become lighter; (vestirsi leggero) put on lighter clothes

allego'ria f allegory. **alle'gorico** adj allegorical

allegra'mente adv breezily

alle'gria f gaiety

al'legro adj cheerful; (colore) bright; (brillo) tipsy • m (Mus) allegro

alle'luia int hallelujah!

allena'mento m training

alle'na|re vt, **~rsi** vr train. **~'tore, ~'trice** mf trainer, coach

allen'tar|e vt loosen; fig relax. **~si** vr become loose; (Mech) work loose

aller'gia f allergy. **al'lergico** adj allergic

all'erta f **stare ~** be alert

allesti'mento m preparation. **~ scenico** (Theat) set

alle'stire vt prepare; stage (spettacolo); (Naut) fit out

allet'tante adj alluring

allet'tare vt entice

alleva'mento m breeding; (processo) bringing up; (luogo) farm; (per piante) nursery; **pollo di ~** battery chicken

alle'vare vt bring up (bambini); breed (animali); grow (piante)

allevi'are vt alleviate; fig lighten

alli'bito adj astounded

allibra'tore m bookmaker

allie'tar|e vt gladden. **~si** vr rejoice

alli'evo, -a mf pupil • m (Mil) cadet

alliga'tore m alligator

allinea'mento m alignment

alline'ar|e vt line up; (Typ) align; Fin adjust. **~si** vr fall into line

'allo = **a** + **lo**

al'locco m Zool tawny owl

al'lodola f [sky]lark

alloggi'are vt put up; (casa:) provide accommodation for; (Mil) billet • vi stay; (Mil) be billeted. **al'loggio** m apartment; (Mil) billet

allontana'mento m removal

allonta'nar|e vt move away; (licenziare) dismiss; avert (pericolo). **~si** vr go away

al'lora adv then; (a quel tempo) at that time; (in tal caso) in that case; **d'~ in poi** from then on; **e ~?** what now?; (e con ciò?) so what?; **fino ~** until then

al'loro m laurel; (Culin) bay

'alluce m big toe

alluci'na|nte adj [!] incredible; **sostanza ~nte** hallucinogen. **~to, -a** mf [!] space cadet. **~zi'one** f hallucination

allucino'geno adj (sostanza) hallucinatory

al'ludere vi **~ a** allude to

allu'minio m aluminium

allun'gar|e vt lengthen; stretch [out] (gamba); extend (tavolo); (diluire) dilute; **~e il collo** crane one's neck. **~e le mani su qcno** touch sb up. **~e il passo** quicken one's step. **~si** vr grow longer; (crescere) grow taller; (sdraiarsi) lie down

allusi'one f allusion

allu'sivo adj allusive

alluvio'nale adj alluvial

alluvi'one f flood

al'meno adv at least; **[se] ~ venisse il sole!** if only the sun would come out!

a'logeno m halogen • adj **lampada alogena** halogen lamp

a'lone m halo

'Alpi fpl **le ~** the Alps

alpi'nis|mo m mountaineering. **~ta** mf mountaineer

al'pino adj Alpine • m (Mil) **gli alpini** the Alpine troops

al'quanto adj a certain amount of • adv rather

alt int stop

alta'lena f swing; (tavola in bilico) see-saw

altale'nare vi fig vacillate

alta'mente adv highly

al'tare m altar

alta'rino m **scoprire gli altarini di qcno** reveal sb's guilty secrets

alte'ra|re vt alter; adulterate (vino); (falsificare) falsify. **~rsi** vr be altered; (cibo:) go bad; (merci:) deteriorate; (arrabbiarsi) get angry. **~to** adj (vino) adulterated. **~zi'one** f alteration; (di vino) adulteration

al'terco m altercation

alter'nanza f alternation

alter'na|re vt, **~rsi** vr alternate. **~'tiva** f alternative. **~'tivo** adj alternate. **~to** adj alternating. **~'tore** m (Electr) alternator

al'tern|o adj alternate; **a giorni ~i** every other day

al'tero adj haughty

al'tezza f height; (profondità) depth; (suono) pitch; (di tessuto) width; (titolo) Highness; **essere all'~ di** be on a level with; fig be up to

altezzos|a'mente adv haughtily. **~ità** f haughtiness

a

altez'zoso adj haughty

al'ticcio adj tipsy, merry

altipi'ano m plateau

alti'tudine f altitude

'alto adj high; (di statura) tall; (profondo) deep; (suono) high-pitched; (tessuto) wide; (Geog) northern; **a notte alta** in the middle of the night; **avere degli alti e bassi** have some ups and downs; **ad alta fedeltà** high-fidelity; **a voce alta, ad alta voce** in a loud voice; (leggere) aloud; **essere in ~ mare** be on the high seas. **alta finanza** f high finance. **alta moda** f high fashion. **alta tensione** f high voltage •adv high; **in ~** at the top; (guardare:) up; **mani in ~!** hands up!

alto'forno m blast-furnace

altolà int halt there!

altolo'cato adj highly placed

altopar'lante m loudspeaker

altopi'ano m plateau

altret'tanto adj & pron as much; (pl) as many •adv likewise; **buona fortuna! – grazie, ~** good luck! – thank you, the same to you

altri'menti adv otherwise

'altro adj other; **un ~, un'altra** another; **l'altr'anno** last year; **domani l'~** the day after tomorrow; **l'ho visto l'~ giorno** I saw him the other day •pron other [one]; **un ~, un'altra** another [one]; **ne vuoi dell'~?** would you like some more?; **l'un l'~** one another; **nessun ~** nobody else; **gli altri** (la gente) other people •m something else; **non fa ~ che lavorare** he does nothing but work; **desidera ~?** (in negozio) anything else?; **più che ~, sono stanco** I'm tired more than anything; **se non ~** at least; **senz'~** certainly; **tra l'~** what's more; **~ che!** and how!

altroi'eri m **l'~** the day before yesterday

al'tronde adv **d'~** on the other hand

al'trove adv elsewhere

al'trui adj other people's •m other people's belongings pl

al'tura f high ground; (Naut) deep sea

a'lunno, -a mf pupil

alve'are m hive

al'za|re vt lift; (costruire) build; (Naut) hoist; **~re le spalle** shrug one's shoulders. **~rsi** vr rise; (in piedi) stand up; (da letto) get up; **~rsi in piedi** get to one's feet. **~ta** f lifting; (aumento) rise; (da letto) getting up; (Archit) elevation. **~to** adj up

a'mabile adj lovable; (vino) sweet

a'maca f hammock

amalga'mar|e vt, **~si** vr amalgamate

a'mante adj **~ di** fond of •m lover •f mistress, lover

a'ma|re vt love; like (musica, ecc). **~to, -a** adj loved •mf beloved

ama'rena f sour black cherry

ama'retto m macaroon

ama'rezza f bitterness; (dolore) sorrow

a'maro adj bitter •m bitterness; (liquore) bitters pl

ama'rognolo adj rather bitter

ama'tore, -'trice mf lover

ambasci'a|ta f embassy; (messaggio) message. **~'tore, ~'trice** m ambassador •f ambassadress

ambe'due adj & pron both

ambien'ta|le adj environmental. **~'lista** adj & mf environmentalist

ambien'tar|e vt acclimatize; set (personaggio, film ecc). **~si** vr get acclimatized

ambi'ente m environment; (stanza) room; fig milieu

ambiguità f inv ambiguity; (di persona) shadiness

am'biguo adj ambiguous; (persona) shady

am'bire vi **~ a** aspire to

'ambito m sphere

ambiva'len|te adj ambivalent. **~za** f ambivalence

ambizi'o|ne f ambition. **~so** adj ambitious

ambu'lante adj wandering; **venditore ~** hawker

ambu'lanza f ambulance

ambula'torio m (di medico) surgery;

(di ospedale) out-patients'

a'meba f amoeba

a'meno adj pleasant

A'merica f America. ~ **del Sud** South America. **ameri'cano, -a** agg & mf American

ami'anto m asbestos

ami'chevole adj friendly

ami'cizia f friendship; **fare ~ con qcno** make friends with sb; **amicizie** pl (amici) friends

a'mico, -a mf friend; ~ **del cuore** bosom friend

'amido m starch

ammac'ca|re vt dent; bruise (frutto). **~rsi** vr (metallo:) get dented; (frutto:) bruise. **~to** adj dented; (frutto) bruised. **~'tura** f dent; (livido) bruise

ammae'stra|re vt (istruire) teach; train (animale). **~to** adj trained

ammai'nare vt lower (bandiera); furl (vele)

amma'la|rsi vr fall ill. **~to, -a** adj ill • mf sick person; (paziente) patient

ammali'are vt bewitch

am'manco m deficit

ammanet'tare vt handcuff

ammani'cato adj **essere ~** have connections

amma'raggio m splashdown

amma'rare vi put down on the sea; (nave spaziale:) splash down

ammas'sar|e vt amass. **~si** vr crowd together. **am'masso** m mass; (mucchio) pile

ammat'tire vi go mad

ammaz'zar|e vt kill. **~si** vr (suicidarsi) kill oneself; (rimanere ucciso) be killed

am'menda f amends pl; (multa) fine; **fare ~ di qcsa** make amends for sth

am'messo pp di **ammettere** • conj ~ **che** supposing that

am'mettere vt admit; (riconoscere) acknowledge; (supporre) suppose

ammic'care vi wink

ammini'stra|re vt administer; (gestire) run. **~'tivo** adj administrative. **~'tore, ~'trice** mf administrator; (di azienda) manager; (di società) director. **~tore delegato** managing director. **~zi'one** f administration; **fatti di ordinaria ~zione** fig routine matters

ammi'ragli|o m admiral. **~'ato** m admiralty

ammi'ra|re vt admire. **~to** adj **restare/essere ~to** be full of admiration. **~'tore, ~'trice** mf admirer. **~zi'one** f admiration. **ammi'revole** adj admirable

ammis'sibile adj admissible

ammissi'one f admission; (approvazione) acknowledgement

ammobili'a|re vt furnish. **~to** adj furnished

am'modo adj proper • adv properly

am'mollo m **in ~** soaking

ammo'niaca f ammonia

ammoni'mento m warning; (di rimprovero) admonishment

ammo'ni|re vt warn; (rimproverare) admonish. **~'tore** adj admonishing. **~zi'one** f Sport warning

ammon'tare vi **~ a** amount to • m amount

ammonticchi'are vt heap up

ammorbi'dente m (per panni) softener

ammorbi'dir|e vt, **~si** vr soften

ammorta'mento m (Comm) amortization

ammor'tare vt pay off (spesa); (Comm) amortize (debito)

ammortiz'za|re vt (Comm) = **ammortare**; (Mech) damp. **~'tore** m shock-absorber

ammosci'ar|e vt make flabby. **~si** vi get flabby

ammucchi'a|re vt, **~rsi** vr pile up. **~ta** f (☒: orgia) orgy

ammuf'fi|re vi go mouldy. **~to** adj mouldy

ammutina'mento m mutiny

ammuti'narsi vr mutiny

ammuto'lire vi be struck dumb

amni'stia f amnesty

'amo m hook; fig bait

a'more m love; **fare l'~** make love; **per l'amor di Dio/del cielo!** for heaven's sake!; **andare d'~ e d'accordo** get on like a house on

a

fire; **amor proprio** self-respect; **è un ~** (persona) he/she is a darling; **per ~ di** for the sake of; **amori** pl love affairs. **~ggi'are** vi flirt. **amo'revole** adj loving

a'morfo adj shapeless; (fig) grey

amo'roso adj loving; (sguardo ecc) amorous; (lettera, relazione) love

ampi'ezza f (di esperienza) breadth; (di stanza) spaciousness; (di gonna) fullness; (importanza) scale

'ampio adj ample; (esperienza) wide; (stanza) spacious; (vestito) loose; (gonna) full; (pantaloni) baggy

am'plesso m embrace

amplia'mento m (di casa, porto) enlargement; (di strada) widening

ampli'are vt broaden (conoscenze)

amplifi'ca|re vt amplify; fig magnify. **~'tore** m amplifier. **~zi'one** f amplification

am'polla f cruet

ampu'ta|re vt amputate. **~zi'one** f amputation

amu'leto m amulet

anabbagli'ante adj (Auto) dipped •mpl **anabbaglianti** dipped headlights

anacro'nis|mo m anachronism. **~tico** adj anachronistic

a'nagrafe f (ufficio) register office; (registro) register of births, marriages and deaths

ana'grafico adj **dati** mpl **anagrafici** personal data

ana'gramma m anagram

anal'colico adj non-alcoholic •m soft drink, non-alcoholic drink

analfa'be|ta adj & mf illiterate. **~'tismo** m illiteracy

anal'gesico m painkiller

a'nalisi f inv analysis; (Med) test. **~ grammaticale/del periodo/logica** parsing. **~ del sangue** blood test

ana'li|sta mf analyst. **~tico** adj analytical. **~z'zare** vt analyse; (Med) test

anal'lergico adj hypoallergenic

analo'gia f analogy. **a'nalogo** adj analogous

'ananas m inv pineapple

anar'chi|a f anarchy. **a'narchico, -a** adj anarchic •mf anarchist. **~smo** m anarchism

A.N.A.S. f abbr (Azienda Nazionale Autonoma delle Strade) national road maintenance authority

anato'mia f anatomy. **ana'tomico** adj anatomical; (sedia) contoured

'anatra f duck

ana'troccolo m duckling

'anca f hip; (di animale) flank

ance'strale adj ancestral

'anche conj also, too; (persino) even; **~ se** even if

anchilo'sato adj fig stiff

an'cora[1] adv still, yet; (di nuovo) again; (di più) some more; **~ una volta** once more

'anco|ra[2] f anchor; **gettare l'~ra** drop anchor. **~'raggio** m anchorage. **~'rare** vt anchor

anda'mento m (del mercato, degli affari) trend

an'dante adj (corrente) current; (di poco valore) cheap •m (Mus) andante

an'da|re vi go; (funzionare) work; **~ via** (partire) leave; (macchia:) come out; **~ [bene]** (confarsi) suit; (taglia:) fit; **ti va bene alle tre?** does three o'clock suit you?; **non mi va di mangiare** I don't feel like eating; **~ di fretta** be in a hurry; **~ fiero di** be proud of; **~ di moda** be in fashion; **va per i 20 anni** he's nearly 20; **ma va' [là]!** come on!; **come va?** how are things?; **~ a male** go off; **~ a fuoco** go up in flames; **va spedito [entro] stamattina** it must be sent this morning; **ne va del mio lavoro** my job is at stake; **come è andata a finire?** how did it turn out?; **cosa vai dicendo?** what are you talking about?. **~rsene** go away; (morire) pass away •m going; **a lungo ~re** eventually

'andito m passage

an'drone m entrance

a'neddoto m anecdote

ane'lare vt **~ a** long for. **a'nelito** m longing

a'nello m ring; (di catena) link

ane'mia f anaemia. **a'nemico** adj anaemic

a'nemone m anemone

aneste'si|a f anaesthesia; (sostanza) anaesthetic. **~'sta** mf anaesthetist. **ane'stetico** adj & m anaesthetic

an'fibi mpl (stivali) army boots

an'fibio m (animale) amphibian •adj amphibious

anfite'atro m amphitheatre

'anfora f amphora

an'fratto m ravine

an'gelico adj angelic

'angelo m angel. **~ custode** guardian angel

angli'c|ano adj Anglican.

angli'smo m Anglicism

an'glofilo, -a adj & mf Anglophile

an'glofono, -a mf English-speaker

anglo'sassone adj & mf Anglo-Saxon

ango'la|re adj angular. **~zi'one** f angle shot

'angolo m corner; (Math) angle. **~ [di] cottura** kitchenette

ango'loso adj angular

an'gosci|a f anguish. **~'are** vt torment. **~'ato** adj agonized. **~'oso** adj (disperato) anguished; (che dà angoscia) distressing

angu'illa f eel

an'guria f water-melon

an'gusti|a f (ansia) anxiety; (penuria) poverty. **~'are** vt distress. **~'arsi** vr be very worried (**per** about)

an'gusto adj narrow

'anice m anise; (Culin) aniseed; (liquore) anisette

ani'dride f **~ carbonica** carbon dioxide

'anima f soul; **non c'era ~ viva** there was not a soul about; **all'~!** good grief!; **un'~ in pena** a soul in torment. **~ gemella** soul mate

ani'ma|le adj & m animal; **~li domestici** pl pets. **~'lesco** adj animal

ani'ma|re vt give life to; (ravvivare) enliven; (incoraggiare) encourage. **~rsi** vr come to life; (accalorarsi) become animated. **~to** adj animate; (discussione) animated; (paese) lively. **~'tore, ~'trice** mf leading spirit; Cinema animator. **~zi'one** f animation

'animo m (mente) mind; (indole) disposition; (cuore) heart; **perdersi d'~** lose heart; **farsi ~** take heart. **~sità** f animosity

ani'moso adj brave; (ostile) hostile

'anitra f = **anatra**

annac'qua|re vt water down. **~to** adj watered down

annaffi'a|re vt water. **~'toio** m watering-can

an'nali mpl annals

anna'spare vi flounder

an'nata f year; (importo annuale) annual amount; (di vino) vintage

annebbia'mento m fog build-up; fig clouding

annebbi'ar|e vt cloud (vista, mente). **~si** vr become foggy; (vista, mente:) grow dim

annega'mento m drowning

anne'ga|re vt/i drown

anne'rir|e vt/i blacken. **~si** vr become black

annessi'one f (di nazione) annexation

an'nesso pp di **annettere** •adj attached; (stato) annexed

an'nettere vt add; (accludere) enclose; annex (stato)

annichi'lire vt annihilate

anni'darsi vr nest

annienta'mento m annihilation

annien'tar|e vt annihilate. **~si** vr abase oneself

anniver'sario adj & m anniversary. **~ di matrimonio** wedding anniversary

'anno m year; **Buon A~!** Happy New Year!; **quanti anni ha?** how old are you?; **Tommaso ha dieci anni** Thomas is ten [years old]. **~ bisestile** leap year

anno'dar|e vt knot; do up (cintura); fig form. **~si** vr become knotted

annoi'a|re vt bore; (recare fastidio) annoy. **~rsi** vr get bored; (condizione) be bored. **~to** adj bored

anno'ta|re vt note down; annotate (testo). **~zi'one** f note

annove'rare vt number

annu'a|le adj annual, yearly. **~rio** m year-book

annu'ire vi nod; (acconsentire) agree

a

annulla'mento m annulment; (di appuntamento) cancellation

annul'lar|e vt annul; cancel (appuntamento); (togliere efficacia a) undo; disallow (gol); (distruggere) destroy. **~si** vr cancel each other out

annunci'a|re vt announce; (preannunciare) foretell. **~'tore, ~'trice** mf announcer. **A~zi'one** f Annunciation

an'nuncio m announcement; (pubblicitario) advertisement; (notizia) news. **annunci** pl **economici** classified advertisements

'annuo adj annual, yearly

annu'sare vt sniff

annuvo'lar|e vt cloud. **~si** vr cloud over

'ano m anus

a'nomalo adj anomalous

anoni'mato m **mantenere l'~** remain anonymous

a'nonimo, -a adj anonymous • mf (pittore, scrittore) anonymous painter/writer

ano'ressico, -a mf anorexic

anor'mal|e adj abnormal • mf deviant. **~ità** f inv abnormality

'ansa f handle; (di fiume) bend

an'sare vi pant

'ansia, **ansietà** f anxiety; **stare/essere in ~ per** be anxious about

ansi'oso adj anxious

antago'nis|mo m antagonism. **~ta** mf antagonist

an'tartico adj & m Antarctic

antece'dente adj preceding • m precedent

ante'fatto m prior event

ante'guerra adj pre-war • m pre-war period

ante'nato, -a mf ancestor

an'tenna f (Radio, TV) aerial; (di animale) antenna; (Naut) yard. **~ parabolica** satellite dish

ante'porre vt put before

ante'prima f preview; **vedere qcsa in ~** have a sneak preview of sth

anteri'ore adj front attrib; (nel tempo) previous

antia'ereo adj anti-aircraft attrib

antial'lergico adj hypoallergenic

antia'tomico adj **rifugio ~** fallout shelter

antibi'otico adj & m antibiotic

anti'caglia f (oggetto) piece of old junk

antica'mente adv long ago

anti'camera f ante-room; **far ~** be kept waiting

antichità f inv antiquity; (oggetto) antique

antici'clone m anticyclone

antici'pa|re vt advance; (Comm) pay in advance; (prevedere) anticipate; (prevenire) forestall • vi be early. **~ta'mente** adv in advance. **~zi'one** f anticipation; (notizia) advance news

an'ticipo m advance; (caparra) deposit; **in ~** early; (nel lavoro) ahead of schedule

an'tico adj ancient; (mobile ecc) antique; (vecchio) old; **all'antica** old-fashioned • mpl **gli antichi** the ancients

anticoncezio'nale adj & m contraceptive

anticonfor'mis|mo m unconventionality. **~ta** mf nonconformist. **~tico** adj unconventional

anticonge'lante adj & m anti-freeze

anticostituzio'nale adj unconstitutional

anti'crimine adj inv (squadra) crime attrib

antidemo'cratico adj undemocratic

antidolo'rifico m painkiller

an'tidoto m antidote

anti'droga adj inv (campagna) anti-drugs; (squadra) drug attrib

antie'stetico adj ugly

antifa'scismo m anti-fascism

antifa'scista adj & mf anti-fascist

anti'furto m anti-theft device; (allarme) alarm • adj inv (sistema) anti-theft

anti'gelo m antifreeze; (parabrezza) defroster

antigi'enico adj unhygienic

An'tille fpl **le ~** the West Indies

an'tilope f antelope

antin'cendio adj inv **allarme ~** fire alarm; **porta ~** fire door

anti'nebbia m inv (Auto) **[faro] ~** foglamp

antinfiamma'torio adj & m anti-inflammatory

antinucle'are adj anti-nuclear

antio'rario adj anti-clockwise

anti'pasto m hors d'oeuvre

an'tipodi mpl antipodes; **essere agli ~** fig be poles apart

antiquari'ato m antique trade

anti'quario, -a mf antique dealer

anti'quato adj antiquated

anti'ruggine m inv rust-inhibitor

anti'rughe adj inv anti-wrinkle attrib

anti'scippo adj inv theft-proof

anti'settico adj & m antiseptic

antisoci'ale adj anti-social

antista'minico m antihistamine

anti'stante a prep in front of

anti'tarlo m inv woodworm treatment

antiterro'ristico adj antiterrorist attrib

an'titesi f inv antithesis

'antivirus m inv virus checker

antolo'gia f anthology

'antro m cavern

antropolo'gia f anthropology. **antro'pologo, -a** mf anthropologist

anu'lare m ring-finger

'anzi conj in fact; (o meglio) or better still; (al contrario) on the contrary

anzianità f old age; (di servizio) seniority

anzi'ano, -a adj elderly; (di grado) senior •mf elderly person

anziché conj rather than

anzi'tempo adv prematurely

anzi'tutto adv first of all

a'orta f aorta

apar'titico adj unaligned

apa'tia f apathy. **a'patico** adj apathetic

'ape f bee; **nido di api** honeycomb

C **aperi'tivo** m aperitif

aperta'mente adv openly

a'perto adj open; **all'aria aperta** in the open air; **all'~** open-air

aper'tura f opening; (inizio) beginning; (ampiezza) spread; (di arco) span; (Pol) overtures pl; (Phot) aperture; **~ mentale** openness

'apice m apex

apicol'tura f beekeeping

ap'nea f **immersione in ~** free diving

a'polide adj stateless •mf stateless person

a'postolo m apostle

apostro'fare vt (mettere un apostrofo a) write with an apostrophe; reprimand (persona)

a'postrofo m apostrophe

appaga'mento m fulfilment

appa'ga|re vt satisfy. **~rsi** vr **~rsi di** be satisfied with

appai'are vt pair; mate (animali)

appallotto'lare vt roll into a ball

appalta'tore m contractor

ap'palto m contract; **dare in ~** to contract

appan'naggio m (in denaro) annuity; fig prerogative

appan'nar|e vt mist (vetro); dim (vista). **~si** vr mist over; (vista:) grow dim

appa'rato m apparatus; (pompa) display

apparecchi'a|re vt prepare •vi lay the table. **~'tura** f (impianti) equipment

appa'recchio m apparatus; (congegno) device; (radio, tv ecc) set; (aeroplano) aircraft. **~ acustico** hearing aid

appa'ren|te adj apparent. **~te'mente** adv apparently. **~za** f appearance; **in ~za** apparently.

appa'ri|re vi appear; (sembrare) look. **~'scente** adj striking; pej gaudy. **~zi'one** f apparition

apparta'mento m apartment

appar'ta|rsi vr withdraw. **~to** adj secluded

apparte'nenza f membership

C *see* A-Z of Italian life and culture

a

apparte'nere vi belong

appassio'nante adj (storia, argomento) exciting

appassio'na|re vt excite; (commuovere) move. **~rsi** vr **~rsi a** become excited by. **~to** adj passionate; **~to di** (entusiastico) fond of

appas'sir|e vi wither. **~si** vr fade

appel'larsi vr **~ a** appeal to

ap'pello m appeal; (chiamata per nome) rollcall; (esami) exam session; **fare l'~** call the roll

ap'pena adv just; (a fatica) hardly • conj **[non] ~** as soon as

ap'pendere vt hang [up]

appen'dice f appendix. **appendi'cite** f appendicitis

Appen'nini mpl **gli ~** the Apennines

appesan'tir|e vt weigh down. **~si** vr become heavy

ap'peso pp di **appendere** adj hanging; (impiccato) hanged

appe'ti|to m appetite; **aver ~to** be hungry; **buon ~to!** enjoy your meal!. **~'toso** adj appetizing; fig tempting

appezza'mento m plot of land

appia'nar|e vt level; fig smooth over. **~si** vr improve

appiat'tir|e vt flatten. **~si** vr flatten oneself

appic'care vt **~ il fuoco a** set fire to

appicci'car|e vt stick; **~e a** (fig: appioppare) palm off on • vi be sticky. **~si** vr stick; (cose:) stick together; **~si a qcno** fig stick to sb like glue

appiccica'ticcio adj sticky; fig clingy

appicci'coso adj sticky; fig clingy

appie'dato adj **sono ~** I don't have the car; **sono rimasto ~** I was stranded

appi'eno adv fully

appigli'arsi vr **~ a** get hold of; fig stick to. **ap'piglio** m fingerhold; (per piedi) foothold; fig pretext

appiop'pare vt **~ a** palm off on; (!: dare) give

appiso'larsi vr doze off

applau'dire vt/i applaud. **ap'plauso** m applause

appli'cabile adj applicable

appli'ca|re vt apply; enforce (legge ecc). **~rsi** vr apply oneself. **~'tore** m applicator. **~zi'one** f application; (di legge) enforcement

appoggi'ar|e vt lean (**a** against); (mettere) put; (sostenere) back. **~si** vr **~si a** lean against; fig rely on. **ap'poggio** m support

appollai'arsi vr fig perch

ap'porre vt affix

appor'tare vt bring; (causare) cause. **ap'porto** m contribution

apposita'mente adv especially

ap'posito adj proper

ap'posta adv on purpose; (espressamente) specially

apposta'mento m ambush; (caccia) lying in wait

appo'star|e vt post (soldati). **~si** vr lie in wait

ap'prend|ere vt understand; (imparare) learn. **~i'mento** m learning

appren'di|sta mf apprentice. **~'stato** m apprenticeship

apprensi'one f apprehension; **essere in ~ per** be anxious about. **appren'sivo** adj apprehensive

ap'presso adv & prep (vicino) near; (dietro) behind; **come ~** as follows

appre'star|e vt prepare. **~si** vr get ready

apprez'za|bile adj appreciable. **~'mento** m appreciation; (giudizio) opinion

apprez'za|re vt appreciate. **~to** adj appreciated

ap'proccio m approach

appro'dare vi land; **~ a** fig come to; **non ~ a nulla** come to nothing. **ap'prodo** m landing; (luogo) landing-stage

approfit'ta|re vi take advantage (**di** of), profit (**di** by). **~'tore, ~'trice** mf chancer

approfondi'mento m deepening; **di ~** fig: (esame) further

approfon'di|re vt deepen. **~rsi** vr (divario:) widen. **~to** adj (studio, ricerca) in-depth

appropri'a|rsi vr (essere adatto a) suit; **~rsi di** take possession of. **~to** adj appropriate. **~zi'one** f (Jur) appropriation. **~zione indebita** (Jur) embezzlement

approssi'ma|re vt **~re per eccesso/difetto** round up/down. **~rsi** vr draw near. **~tiva'mente** adv approximately. **~'tivo** adj approximate. **~zi'one** f approximation

appro'va|re vt approve of; approve (legge). **~zi'one** f approval

approvvigiona'mento m supplying; **approvvigionamenti** pl provisions

approvvigio'nar|e vt supply. **~si** vr stock up

appunta'mento m appointment; **fissare un ~** make an appointment; **darsi ~** decide to meet

appun'tar|e vt (annotare) take notes; (fissare) fix; (con spillo) pin; (appuntire) sharpen. **~si** vr **~si su** (teoria:) be based on

appun'ti|re vt sharpen. **~to** adj (mento) pointed

ap'punto[1] m note; (piccola critica) niggle

ap'punto[2] adv exactly; **per l'~!** exactly!; **stavo ~ dicendo...** I was just saying...

appu'rare vt verify

a'pribile adj that can be opened

apribot'tiglie m inv bottle-opener

a'prile m April; **il primo d'~** April Fools' Day

a'prir|e vt open; turn on (acqua ecc); (con chiave) unlock; open up (ferita ecc). **~si** vr open; (spaccarsi) split; (confidarsi) confide (**con** in)

apri'scatole f inv tin-opener

aqua'planing m **andare in ~** aquaplane

'aquil|a f eagle; **non è un'~a!** he is no genius!. **~'lino** adj aquiline

aqui'lone m (giocattolo) kite

ara'besco m arabesque; hum scribble

A'rabia Sau'dita f **l'~** Saudi Arabia

'arabo, -a adj Arab; (lingua) Arabic • mf Arab • m (lingua) Arabic

a'rachide f peanut

ara'gosta f lobster

a'ranci|a f orange. **~'ata** f orangeade. **~o** m orange-tree; (colore) orange. **~'one** adj & m orange

a'ra|re vt plough. **~tro** m plough

ara'tura f ploughing

a'razzo m tapestry

arbi'trar|e vt arbitrate in; Sport referee. **~ietà** f arbitrariness. **~io** adj arbitrary

ar'bitrio m will; **è un ~** it's very high-handed

'arbitro m arbiter; Sport referee; (nel baseball) umpire

ar'busto m shrub

'arca f ark; (cassa) chest

ar'ca|ico adj archaic. **~'ismo** m archaism

ar'cangelo m archangel

ar'cata f arch; (serie di archi) arcade

arche|olo'gia f archaeology. **~o'logico** adj archaeological. **~'ologo, -a** mf archaeologist

ar'chetto m (Mus) bow

architet'tare vt fig devise; **cosa state architettando?** fig what are you plotting?

archi'tet|to m architect. **~'tonico** adj architectural. **~'tura** f architecture

archivi'are vt file; (Jur) close

ar'chivio m archives pl; (Comput) file

archi'vista mf filing clerk

ar'cigno adj grim

arci'pelago m archipelago

arci'vescovo m archbishop

'arco m arch; (Math) arc; (Mus, arma) bow; **nell'~ di una giornata/due mesi** in the space of a day/two months

arcoba'leno m rainbow

arcu'a|re vt bend. **~rsi** vr bend. **~to** adj bent, curved

ar'dente adj burning; fig ardent. **~'mente** adv ardently

'ardere vt/i burn

ar'desia f slate

ar'di|re vi dare. **~to** adj daring; (coraggioso) bold; (sfacciato) impudent

a

ar'dore m (calore) heat; fig ardour

'arduo adj arduous; (ripido) steep

'area f area. ~ **di rigore** (nel calcio) penalty area. ~ **di servizio** service area

a'rena f arena

are'narsi vr run aground; fig: (trattative) reach deadlock; **mi sono arenato** I'm stuck

'argano m winch

argen'tato adj silver-plated

argente'ria f silver[ware]

ar'gento m silver

ar'gil|la f clay. ~**'loso** adj (terreno) clayey

argi'nare vt embank; fig hold in check, contain

'argine m embankment; (diga) dike

argomen'tare vi argue

argo'mento m argument; (motivo) reason; (soggetto) subject

argu'ire vt deduce

ar'gu|to adj witty. ~**zia** f wit; (battuta) witticism

'aria f air; (aspetto) appearance; (Mus) tune; **andare all'**~ fig come to nothing; **avere l'**~**...** look...; **corrente d'**~ draught; **mandare all'**~ **qcsa** fig ruin sth

aridità f aridity, dryness

'arido adj arid

arieggi'a|re vt air. ~**to** adj airy

ari'ete m ram. **A**~ (Astr) Aries

ari'etta f (brezza) breeze

a'ringa f herring

ari'oso adj (locale) light and airy

aristo'cra|tico, -a adj aristocratic • mf aristocrat. ~**'zia** f aristocracy

arit'metica f arithmetic

arlec'chino m Harlequin; fig buffoon

'arma f weapon; **armi** pl arms; (forze armate) [armed] forces; **chiamare alle armi** call up; **sotto le armi** in the army; **alle prime armi** fig inexperienced. ~ **da fuoco** firearm. **armi** mpl **di distruzione di massa** weapons of mass destruction.

armadi'etto m locker, cupboard

ar'madio m cupboard; (guardaroba) wardrobe

armamen'tario m tools pl; fig paraphernalia

arma'mento m armament; (Naut) fitting out

ar'ma|re vt arm; (equipaggiare) fit out; (Archit) reinforce. ~**rsi** vr arm oneself (**di** with). ~**ta** f army; (flotta) fleet. ~**'tore** m shipowner. ~**'tura** f framework; (impalcatura) scaffolding; (di guerriero) armour

armeggi'are vi fig manoeuvre

armi'stizio m armistice

armo'ni|a f harmony. **ar'monica** f ~ [**a bocca**] mouth organ. **ar'monico** adj harmonic. ~**'oso** adj harmonious

armoniz'zar|e vt harmonize • vi match. ~**si** vr (colori:) match

ar'nese m tool; (oggetto) thing; (congegno) gadget; **male in** ~ in bad condition

'arnia f beehive

a'roma m aroma; **aromi** pl herbs. ~**tera'pia** f aromatherapy

aro'matico adj aromatic

aromatiz'zare vt flavour

'arpa f harp

ar'peggio m arpeggio

ar'pia f harpy

arpi'one m hook; (pesca) harpoon

arrabat'tarsi vr do all one can

arrabbi'a|rsi vr get angry. ~**to** adj angry. ~**'tura** f rage; **prendersi una** ~**tura** fly into a rage

arraf'fare vt grab

arrampi'ca|rsi vr climb [up]. ~**ta** f climb. ~**'tore,** ~**'trice** mf climber. ~**'tore sociale** social climber

arran'care vi limp, hobble

arrangia'mento m arrangement

arrangi'ar|e vt arrange. ~**si** vr manage; ~**si alla meglio** get by; **ar'rangiati!** get on with it!

arra'parsi vr [!] get randy

arre'care vt bring; (causare) cause

arreda'mento m interior decoration; (l'arredare) furnishing; (mobili ecc) furnishings pl

arre'da|re vt furnish. ~**'tore,** ~**'trice** mf interior designer. **ar'redo** m furnishings pl

ar'rendersi vr surrender

arren'devo|le adj (persona) yielding. **~'lezza** f softness

arre'star|e vt arrest; (fermare) stop. **~si** vr halt. **ar'resto** m stop; (Med, Jur) arrest; **la dichiaro in [stato d'] arresto** you are under arrest; **mandato di arresto** warrant. **arresti** pl **domiciliari** (Jur) house arrest

arre'tra|re vt/i withdraw; pull back (giocatore). **~to** adj (paese ecc) backward; (Mil: posizione) rear; **numero ~to** (di rivista) back number; **del lavoro ~to** a backlog of work • m (di stipendio) back pay

arre'trati mpl arrears

arricchi'mento m enrichment

arric'chi|re vt enrich. **~rsi** vr get rich. **~to, -a** mf nouveau riche

arricci'are vt curl; **~ il naso** turn up one's nose

ar'ringa f harangue; (Jur) closing address

arrischi'a|rsi vr dare. **~to** adj risky; (imprudente) rash

arri'va|re vi arrive; **~re a** (raggiungere) reach; (ridursi) be reduced to. **~to, -a** adj successful; **ben ~to!** welcome! • mf successful person

arrive'derci int goodbye; **~ a domani** see you tomorrow

arri'vis|mo m social climbing; (nel lavoro) careerism. **~ta** mf social climber; (nel lavoro) careerist

ar'rivo m arrival; Sport finish

arro'gan|te adj arrogant. **~za** f arrogance

arro'garsi vr **~ il diritto di fare qcsa** take it upon oneself to do sth

arrossa'mento m reddening

arros'sar|e vt make red (occhi). **~si** vr go red

arros'sire vi blush, go red

arro'stire vt roast; toast (pane); (ai ferri) grill. **ar'rosto** adj & m roast

arroto'lare vt roll up

arroton'dar|e vt round; (Math ecc) round off. **~si** vr become round; (persona:) get plump

arrovel'larsi vr **~ il cervello** rack one's brains

arroven'ta|re vt make red-hot. **~rsi** vr become red-hot. **~to** adj red-hot

arruf'fa|re vt ruffle; fig confuse. **~to** adj (capelli) ruffled

arruffianarsi vr **~ qcno** fig butter sb up

arruggi'ni|re vt rust. **~rsi** vr go rusty; fig (fisicamente) stiffen up; (conoscenze:) go rusty. **~to** adj rusty

arruola'mento m enlistment

arruo'lar|e vt/i, **~si** vr enlist

arse'nale m arsenal; (cantiere) [naval] dockyard

ar'senico m arsenic

'arso pp di **ardere** • adj burnt; (arido) dry. **ar'sura** f burning heat; (sete) parching thirst

'arte f art; (abilità) craftsmanship; **le belle arti** the fine arts. **arti figurative** figurative arts

arte'fa|re vt adulterate (vino); disguise (voce). **~tto** adj fake; (vino) adulterated

ar'tefice mf craftsman; craftswoman; fig author

ar'teria f artery. **~ [stradale]** arterial road

arterioscle'rosi f arteriosclerosis

'artico adj & m Arctic

artico'la|re adj articular • vt articulate; (suddividere) divide. **~rsi** vr fig **~rsi in** consist of. **~to** adj (Auto) articulated; fig well-constructed. **~zi'one** f (Anat) articulation

ar'ticolo m article. **~ di fondo** leader

artifici'ale adj artificial

arti'fici|o m artifice; (affettazione) affectation. **~'oso** adj artful; (affettato) affected

artigia'nal|e adj made by hand; hum amateurish. **~'mente** adv with craftsmanship; hum amateurishly

artigi|a'nato m craftsmanship; (ceto) craftsmen pl. **~'ano, -a** m craftsman • f craftswoman

artigli|'ere m artilleryman. **~e'ria** f artillery

ar'tiglio m claw; fig clutch

ar'tist|a mf artist. **~ica'mente** adv artistically. **~ico** adj artistic

'arto m limb

ar'trite f arthritis

ar'trosi f rheumatism

a

a

arzigogo'lato adj bizarre

ar'zillo adj sprightly

a'scella f armpit

ascen'den|te adj ascending • m (antenato) ancestor; (influenza) ascendancy; (Astr) ascendant

ascensi'one f ascent; **l'A~** the Ascension

ascen'sore m lift, elevator Am

a'scesa f ascent; (al trono) accession; (al potere) rise

a'scesso m abscess

a'sceta mf ascetic

'ascia f axe

asciugabianche'ria m inv (stenditoio) clothes horse

asciugaca'pelli m inv hair dryer

asciuga'mano m towel

asciu'gar|e vt dry. **~si** vr dry oneself; (diventare asciutto) dry up

asci'utto adj dry; (magro) wiry; (risposta) curt; **essere all'~** fig be hard up

ascol'ta|re vt listen to • vi listen. **~'tore, ~'trice** mf listener

a'scolto m listening; **dare ~ a** listen to; **mettersi in ~** Radio tune in

asfal'tare vt asphalt

a'sfalto m asphalt

asfis'si|a f asphyxia. **~'ante** adj oppressive; fig: (persona) annoying. **~'are** vt asphyxiate; fig annoy

'Asia f Asia. **asi'atico, -a** agg & mf Asian

a'silo m shelter; (d'infanzia) nursery school. **~ nido** day nursery. **~ politico** political asylum

asim'metrico adj asymmetrical

'asino m donkey; (fig: persona stupida) ass

'asma f asthma. **a'smatico** adj asthmatic

asoci'ale adj asocial

'asola f buttonhole

a'sparagi mpl asparagus sg

a'sparago m asparagus spear

asperità f inv harshness; (di terreno) roughness

aspet'ta|re vt wait for; (prevedere) expect; **~re un bambino** be expecting [a baby]; **fare ~re qcno** keep sb waiting • vi wait. **~rsi** vr expect. **~'tiva** f expectation

a'spetto¹ m appearance; (di problema) aspect; **di bell'~** good-looking

a'spetto² m **sala** f **d'~** waiting room

aspi'rante adj aspiring; (pompa) suction attrib • mf (a un posto) applicant; (al trono) aspirant; **gli aspiranti al titolo** the contenders for the title

aspira'polvere m inv vacuum cleaner

aspi'ra|re vt inhale; (Mech) suck in • vi **~re a** aspire to. **~'tore** m extractor fan. **~zi'one** f inhalation; (Mech) suction; (ambizione) ambition

aspi'rina f aspirin

aspor'tare vt take away

aspra'mente adv (duramente) severely

a'sprezza f (al gusto) sourness; (di clima) severity; (di suono) harshness; (di odore) pungency

'aspro adj (al gusto) sour; (clima) severe; (suono, parole) harsh; (odore) pungent; (litigio) bitter

assag|gi'are vt taste. **~'gini** mpl (Culin) samples. **as'saggio** m tasting; (piccola quantità) taste

as'sai adv very; (moltissimo) very much; (abbastanza) enough

assa'li|re vt attack. **~'tore, ~'trice** mf assailant

as'salto m attack; **prendere d'~** storm (città); fig mob (persona); hold up (banca)

assapo'rare vt savour

assassi'nare vt murder, assassinate

assas'sin|io m murder, assassination. **~o, -a** adj murderous • m murderer • f murderess

'asse f board • m (Techn) axle; (Math) axis. **~ da stiro** ironing board

assecon'dare vt satisfy; (favorire) support

assedi'are vt besiege. **as'sedio** m siege

assegna'mento m allotment; **fare ~ su** rely on

asse'gna|re vt allot; award (premio). **~'tario** mf recipient. **~zi'one** f (di alloggio, borsa di studio) allocation; (di premio) award

as'segno m allowance; (bancario) cheque; **contro ~** cash on delivery. **~ circolare** bank draft. **assegni** pl **familiari** family allowance. **~ non trasferibile** non-transferable cheque.

assem'blea f assembly; (adunanza) gathering

assembra'mento m gathering

assen'nato adj sensible

as'senso m assent

assen'tarsi vr go away; (da stanza) leave the room

as'sen|te adj absent; (distratto) absent-minded • mf absentee. **~te'ismo** m absenteeism. **~te'ista** mf frequent absentee. **~za** f absence; (mancanza) lack

asse'r|ire vt assert. **~'tivo** adj assertive. **~zi'one** f assertion

assesso'rato m department

asses'sore m councillor

assesta'mento m settlement

asse'star|e vt arrange; **~e un colpo** deal a blow. **~si** vr settle oneself

asse'tato adj parched

as'setto m order; (Aeron, Naut) trim

assicu'ra|re vt assure; (Comm) insure; register (posta); (fissare) secure; (accertare) ensure. **~rsi** vr (con contratto) insure oneself; (legarsi) fasten oneself; **~rsi che** make sure that. **~'tivo** adj insurance attrib. **~'tore, ~'trice** mf insurance agent • adj insurance attrib. **~zi'one** f assurance; (contratto) insurance

assidera'mento m exposure. **asside'rato** adj (Med) suffering from exposure; 🄵 frozen

assidu|a'mente adv assiduously. **~ità** f assiduity

as'siduo adj assiduous; (cliente) regular

assil'lante adj (persona, pensiero) nagging

assil'lare vt pester

as'sillo m worry

assimi'la|re vt assimilate. **~zi'one** f assimilation

as'sise fpl assizes; **Corte d'A~** Court of Assize[s]

assi'sten|te mf assistant. **~te sociale** social worker. **~te di volo** flight attendant. **~za** f assistance; (presenza) presence. **~za sociale** social work

assistenzi'a|le adj welfare attrib. **~'lismo** m welfare

as'sistere vt assist; (curare) nurse • vi **~ a** (essere presente) be present at; watch (spettacolo ecc)

'asso m ace; **piantare in ~** leave in the lurch

associ'a|re vt join; (collegare) associate. **~rsi** vr join forces; (Comm) enter into partnership. **~rsi a** join. **~zi'one** f association

assogget'tar|e vt subject. **~si** vr submit

asso'lato adj sunny

assol'dare vt recruit

as'solo m (Mus) solo

as'solto pp di **assolvere**

assoluta'mente adv absolutely

assolu'tismo m absolutism

asso'lu|to adj absolute. **~zi'one** f acquittal; (Relig) absolution

as'solvere vt perform (compito); (Jur) acquit; (Relig) absolve

assomigli'ar|e vi **~e a** resemble. **~si** vr resemble each other

assom'marsi vr combine; **~ a qcsa** add to sth

asso'nanza f assonance

asson'nato adj drowsy

asso'pirsi vr doze off

assor'bente adj & m absorbent. **~ igienico** sanitary towel

assor'bire vt absorb

assor'da|re vt deafen. **~nte** adj deafening

assorti'mento m assortment

assor'ti|re vt match (colori). **~to** adj assorted; (colori, persone) matched

as'sorto adj engrossed

assottigli'ar|e vt make thin; (aguzzare) sharpen; (ridurre) reduce. **~si** vr grow thin; (finanze:) be whittled away

assue'fa|re vt accustom. **~rsi** vr **~rsi a** get used to. **~tto** adj (a caffè, aspirina) immune to the effects; (a

a

droga) addicted. **~zi'one** f (a caffè, aspirina) immunity to the effects; (a droga) addiction

as'sumere vt assume; take on (impiegato); **~ informazioni** make inquiries

as'sunto pp di **assumere** • m task. **assunzi'one** f (di impiegato) employment

assurdità f inv absurdity; ~ pl nonsense

as'surdo adj absurd

'asta f pole; (Mech) bar; (Comm) auction; **a mezz'~** at half-mast

a'stemio adj abstemious

aste'n|ersi vr abstain (**da** from). **~si'one** f abstention

aste'nuto, -a mf abstainer

aste'risco m asterisk

astig'ma|tico adj astigmatic. **~'tismo** m astigmatism

'asti|o m rancour; **avere ~o contro qcno** bear sb a grudge. **~'oso** adj resentful

a'stratto adj abstract

astrin'gente adj & m astringent

'astro m star

astrolo'gia f astrology. **a'strologo, -a** mf astrologer

astro'nauta mf astronaut

astro'nave f spaceship

astr|ono'mia f astronomy. **~o'nomico** adj astronomical. **a'stronomo** m astronomer

astrusità f abstruseness

a'stuccio m case

a'stu|to adj shrewd; (furbo) cunning. **~zia** f shrewdness; (azione) trick

ate'ismo m atheism

A'tene f Athens

'ateo, -a adj & mf atheist

a'tipico adj atypical

at'lant|e m atlas. **~ico** adj Atlantic; **l' [Oceano] A~ico** the Atlantic [Ocean]

at'let|a mf athlete. **~ica** f athletics sg. **~ica leggera** track and field events. **~ica pesante** weight-lifting, boxing, wrestling, etc. **~ico** adj athletic

atmo'sfer|a f atmosphere. **~ico** adj atmospheric

a'tomic|a f atom bomb. **~o** adj atomic

'atomo m atom

'atrio m entrance hall

a'troc|e adj atrocious; (terrible) dreadful. **~ità** f inv atrocity

atrofiz'zarsi vr atrophy

attaccabot'toni mf inv [crashing] bore

attacca'brighe mf inv troublemaker

attacca'mento m attachment

attacca'panni m inv [coat-]hanger; (a muro) clothes hook

attac'car|e vt attach; (legare) tie; (appendere) hang; (cucire) sew on; (contagiare) pass on; (assalire) attack; (iniziare) start • vi stick; (diffondersi) catch on. **~si** vr cling; (affezionarsi) become attached; (litigare) quarrel

attacca'ticcio adj sticky

at'tacco m attack; (punto d'unione) junction

attar'darsi vr stay late; (indugiare) linger

attec'chire vi take; (moda ecc:) catch on

atteggia'mento m attitude

atteggi'ar|e vt assume. **~si** vr **~si a** pose as

attem'pato adj elderly

at'tender|e vt wait for • vi **~e a** attend to. **~si** vr expect

atten'dibil|e adj reliable. **~ità** f reliability

atte'nersi vr **~ a** stick to

attenta'mente adv attentively

atten'ta|re vi **~re a** make an attempt on. **~to** m act of violence; (contro politico ecc) assassination attempt. **~'tore, ~'trice** mf (a scopo politico) terrorist

at'tento adj attentive; (accurato) careful; **~!** look out!; **stare ~** pay attention

attenu'ante f extenuating circumstance

attenu'a|re vt attenuate; (minimizzare) minimize; subdue (colori ecc); calm (dolore); soften (colpo). **~rsi** vr diminish. **~zi'one** f lessening

attenzi'one f attention; **~!** watch out!

atter'ra|ggio m landing. **~re** vt knock down • vi land

atter'rir|e vt terrorize. **~si** vr be terrified

at'tes|a f waiting; (aspettativa) expectation; **in ~a di** waiting for. **~o** pp di **attendere**

atte'sta|re vt state; (certificare) certify. **~to** m certificate. **~zi'one** f certificate; (dichiarazione) declaration

'attico m attic

at'tiguo adj adjacent

attil'lato adj (vestito) close-fitting

'attimo m moment

atti'nente adj **~ a** pertaining to

at'tingere vt draw; fig obtain

atti'rare vt attract

atti'tudine f (disposizione) aptitude; (atteggiamento) attitude

atti'v|are vt activate. **~ismo** m activism. **~ista** mf activist. **attività** f inv activity; (Comm) assets pl. **~o** adj active; (Comm) productive • m assets pl

attiz'za|re vt poke; fig stir up. **~'toio** m poker

'atto m act; (azione) action; (Comm, Jur) deed; (certificato) certificate; **atti** pl (di società ecc) proceedings; **mettere in ~** put into effect

at'tonito adj astonished

attorcigli'ar|e vt twist. **~si** vr get twisted

at'tore m actor

attorni'ar|e vt surround. **~si** vr **~si di** surround oneself with

at'torno adv around, about • prep **~ a** around, about

attrac'care vt/i dock

attra'ente adj attractive

at'tra|rre vt attract. **~rsi** vr be attracted to each other. **~t'tiva** f charm

attraversa'mento m crossing. **~ pedonale** crossing, crosswalk Am

attraver'sare vt cross; (passare) go through

attra'verso prep through; (obliquamente) across

attrazi'on|e f attraction. **~i** pl **turistiche** tourist attractions

attrez'za|re vt equip; (Naut) rig. **~rsi** vr kit oneself out; **~'tura** f equipment; (Naut) rigging

at'trezzo m tool; **attrezzi** pl equipment; Sport appliances pl; (Theat) props pl

attribu'ir|e vt attribute. **~si** vr ascribe to oneself; **~si il merito di** claim credit for

attri'bu|to m attribute. **~zi'one** f attribution

at'trice f actress

at'trito m friction

attu'abile adj feasible

attu'al|e adj present; (di attualità) topical; (effettivo) actual. **~ità** f topicality; (avvenimento) news; **programma di ~ità** current affairs programme. **~iz'zare** vt update. **~'mente** adv at present

attu'a|re vt carry out. **~rsi** vr be realized. **~zi'one** f carrying out

attu'tire vt deaden; **~ il colpo** soften the blow

au'dac|e adj audacious;. **~ia** f boldness; (insolenza) audacity

'audience f inv (telespettatori) audience

'audio m audio

audiovi'sivo adj audiovisual

audi'torio m auditorium

audizi'one f audition; (Jur) hearing

'auge m height; **essere in ~** be popular

augu'rar|e vt wish. **~si** vr hope. **au'gurio** m wish; (presagio) omen; **auguri!** all the best!; (a Natale) Happy Christmas!; **tanti auguri** best wishes

'aula f classroom; (università) lecture-hall; (sala) hall. **~ magna** (in università) great hall. **~ del tribunale** courtroom

aumen'tare vt/i increase. **au'mento** m increase; (di stipendio) [pay] rise

au'reola f halo

au'rora f dawn

auscul'tare vt (Med) auscultate

ausili'are adj & mf auxiliary

auspicabile adj **è ~ che...** it is to be hoped that...

auspi'care vt hope for

au'spicio m omen; **auspici** (pl: protezione) auspices

austerità f austerity

au'stero adj austere.

Au'strali|a f Australia. **a~'ano, -a** adj & mf Australian

'Austria f Austria. **au'striaco, -a** agg & mf Austrian

autar'chia f autarchy. **au'tarchico** adj autarchic

autenti'c|are vt authenticate. **~ità** f authenticity

au'tentico adj authentic; (vero) true

au'tista m driver

'auto+ pref self +; auto-

autoabbron'zante m self-tan •adj self-tanning

autoambu'lanza f ambulance

autoartico'lato m articulated lorry

autobio|gra'fia f autobiography. **~'grafico** adj autobiographical

auto'botte f tanker

'autobus m inv bus

auto'carro m lorry

autocommiserazi'one f self-pity

autoconcessio'nario m car dealer

auto'critica f self-criticism

autodi'fesa f self-defence

auto'gol m inv own goal

au'tografo adj & m autograph

autolesio'nis|mo m fig selfdestruction. **~tico** adj self-destructive

auto'linea f bus line

au'toma m robot

automatica'mente adv automatically

auto'matico adj automatic •m (bottone) press-stud; (fucile) automatic

automatiz'za|re vt automate. **~zi'one** f automation

auto'mezzo m motor vehicle

auto'mobi|le f [motor] car. **~'lismo** m motoring. **~'lista** mf motorist. **~'listico** adj (industria) automobile attrib

autonoma'mente adv autonomously

autono'mia f autonomy; (Auto) range; (di laptop, cellulare) battery life. **au'tonomo** adj autonomous

auto'psia f autopsy

auto'radio f inv car radio; (veicolo) radio car

au'tore, -'trice mf author; (di pinti) painter; (di furto ecc) perpetrator; **quadro d'~** genuine master

auto'revo|le adj authoritative; (che ha influenza) influential. **~'lezza** f authority

autori'messa f garage

autori|tà f inv authority. **~'tario** adj autocratic. **~ta'rismo** m authoritarianism

autori'tratto m self-portrait

autoriz'za|re vt authorize. **~zi'one** f authorization

auto'scontro m inv bumper car

autoscu'ola f driving school

auto'stop m hitch-hiking; **fare l'~** hitch-hike. **~'pista** mf hitch-hiker

■ **auto'strada** f motorway

autostra'dale adj motorway attrib

autosuffici'en|te adj self-sufficient. **~za** f self-sufficiency

autotrasporta'|tore, ~'trice mf haulier, carrier

auto'treno m articulated lorry

autove'icolo m motor vehicle

Auto'velox® m inv speed camera

autovet'tura f motor vehicle

autun'nale adj autumn[al]

au'tunno m autumn

aval'lare vt endorse

a'vallo m endorsement

avam'braccio m forearm

avangu'ardia f vanguard; fig avant-garde; **essere all'~** be in the forefront; (Techn) be at the leading edge

a'vanti adv (in avanti) forward; (davanti) in front; (prima) before; **~!** (entrate) come in!; (suvvia) come on!; (su semaforo) cross now; **va' ~!** go ahead!; **andare ~** (precedere) go ahead; (orologio:) be fast; **~ e indietro** backwards and forwards •adj before •prep **~ a** before; (in presenza di) in the presence of

avanti'eri adv the day before yesterday

avanza'mento m progress; (promozione) promotion

avan'za|re vi advance; (progredire) progress; (essere d'avanzo) be left [over] • vt advance; (superare) surpass; (promuovere) promote. **~rsi** vr advance; (avvicinarsi) approach. **~ta** f advance. **~to** adj advanced; (nella notte) late; **in età ~ta** elderly. **a'vanzo** m remainder; (Comm) surplus; **avanzi** pl (rovine) remains; (di cibo) left-overs

ava'ri|a f (di motore) engine failure. **~'ato** adj (frutta, verdura) rotten; (carne) tainted

ava'rizia f avarice. **a'varo, -a** adj stingy • mf miser

a'vena f oats pl

a'vere

! Si può usare **have** o **have got** per parlare di ciò che si possiede. *have got* non si usa nell'inglese americano

• vt have; (*ottenere*) get; (*indossare*) wear; (*provare*) feel; **ho trent'anni** I'm thirty; **ha avuto il posto** he got the job; **~ fame/freddo** be hungry/cold; **ho mal di denti** I've got toothache; **cos'ha a che fare con lui?** what has it got to do with him?; **~ da fare** be busy; **che hai?** what's the matter with you?; **nei hai per molto?** will you be long?; **quanti ne abbiamo oggi?** what date is it today?; **avercela con qcno** have it in for sb

• v aux have; **non l'ho visto** I haven't seen him; **lo hai visto?** have you seen him?; **l'ho visto ieri** I saw him yesterday

• m **averi** pl wealth sg

avia|'tore m flyer, aviator. **~zi'one** f aviation; (Mil) Air Force

avidità f avidness. **'avido** adj avid

avio'getto m jet

'avo, -a mf ancestor

avo'cado m inv avocado

a'vorio m ivory

Avv. abbr avvocato

avva'lersi vr avail oneself (**di** of)

avvalla'mento m depression

avvalo'rare vt bear out (tesi); endorse (documento); (accrescere) enhance

avvam'pare vi flare up; (arrossire) blush

avvantaggi'ar|e vt favour. **~si** vr **~si di** benefit from; (approfittare) take advantage of

avve'd|ersi vr (accorgersi) notice; (capire) realize. **~uto** adj shrewd

avvelena'mento m poisoning

avvele'na|re vt poison. **~rsi** vr poison oneself. **~to** adj poisoned

avve'nente adj attractive

avveni'mento m event

avve'nire[1] vi happen; (aver luogo) take place

avve'ni|re[2] m future. **~'ristico** adj futuristic

avven'ta|rsi vr fling oneself. **~to** adj (decisione) rash

av'vento m advent; (Relig) Advent

avven'tore m regular customer

avven'tu|ra f adventure; (amorosa) affair; **d'~** (film) adventure attrib. **~'rarsi** vr venture. **~ri'ero, -a** m adventurer • f adventuress. **~'roso** adj adventurous

avve'ra|bile adj (previsione) that may come true. **~rsi** vr come true

av'verbio m adverb

avver'sar|e vt oppose. **~io, -a** adj opposing • mf opponent

avversi|'one f aversion. **~tà** f inv adversity

av'verso adj (sfavorevole) adverse; (contrario) averse

avver'tenza f (cura) care; (avvertimento) warning; (avviso) notice; (premessa) foreword; **avvertenze** pl (istruzioni) instructions

avverti'mento m warning

avver'tire vt warn; (informare) inform; (sentire) feel

avvez'zar|e vt accustom. **~si** vr accustom oneself. **av'vezzo** adj **avvezzo a** used to

avvia'mento m starting; (Comm) goodwill

avvi'a|re vt start. **~rsi** vr set out.

a

~to adj under way; **bene ~to** thriving

avvicenda'mento m (in agricoltura) rotation; (nel lavoro) replacement

avvicen'darsi vr alternate

avvicina'mento m approach

avvici'nar|e vt bring near; approach (persona). **~si** vr approach; **~si a** approach

avvi'lente adj demoralizing; (umiliante) humiliating

avvili'mento m despondency; (degradazione) degradation

avvi'li|re vt dishearten; (degradare) degrade. **~rsi** vr lose heart; (degradarsi) degrade oneself. **~to** adj disheartened; (degradato) degraded

avvilup'par|e vt envelop. **~si** vr wrap oneself up; (aggrovigliarsi) get entangled

avvinaz'zato adj drunk

avvin'cente adj (libro ecc) enthralling. **av'vincere** vt enthral

avvinghi'ar|e vt clutch. **~si** vr cling

av'vio m start-up; **dare l'~ a qcsa** get sth under way; **prendere l'~** get under way

avvi'sare vt inform; (mettere in guardia) warn

av'viso m notice; (annuncio) announcement; (avvertimento) warning; (pubblicitario) advertisement; **a mio ~** in my opinion. **~ di garanzia** (Jur) notification that one is to be the subject of a legal enquiry

avvi'stare vt catch sight of

avvi'tare vt screw in; screw down (coperchio)

avviz'zire vi wither

avvo'ca|to m lawyer; fig advocate. **~'tura** f legal profession

av'volger|e vt wrap [up]. **~si** vr wrap oneself up

avvol'gibile m roller blind

avvol'toio m vulture

aza'lea f azalea

azi'en|da f business. **~ agricola** farm. **~ di soggiorno** tourist bureau. **~'dale** adj (politica) corporate; (giornale) in-house

aziona'mento m operation

azio'nare vt operate

azio'nario adj share attrib

azi'one f action; Fin share; **d'~** (romanzo, film) action[-packed]. **azio'nista** mf shareholder

a'zoto m nitrogen

azzan'nare vt seize with its teeth; sink its teeth into (gamba)

azzar'd|are vt risk. **~arsi** vr dare. **~ato** adj risky; (precipitoso) rash. **az'zardo** m hazard; **gioco d'azzardo** game of chance

azzec'care vt hit; (indovinare) guess

azzuf'farsi vr come to blows

az'zur|ro adj & m blue; **il principe ~** Prince Charming. **~'rognolo** adj bluish

Bb

bab'beo adj foolish •m idiot

'babbo m [!] dad, daddy. **B~ Natale** Father Christmas

bab'buccia f slipper

babbu'ino m baboon

ba'bordo m (Naut) port side

baby'sitter mf inv baby-sitter; **fare la ~** babysit

ba'cato adj wormeaten

'bacca f berry

baccalà m inv dried salted cod

bac'cano m din

bac'cello m pod

bac'chetta f rod; (magica) wand; (di direttore d'orchestra) baton; (di tamburo) drumstick

ba'checa f showcase; (in ufficio) notice board. **~ elettronica**

(Comput) bulletin board

bacia'mano m kiss on the hand; **fare il ~ a qcno** kiss sb's hand

baci'ar|e vt kiss. **~si** vr kiss [each other]

ba'cillo m bacillus

baci'nella f basin

ba'cino m basin; (Anat) pelvis; (di porto) dock; (di minerali) field

'bacio m kiss

'baco m worm. **~ da seta** silkworm

ba'cucco adj **un vecchio ~** a senile old man

'bada f **tenere qcno a ~** keep sb at bay

ba'dante mf carer

ba'dare vi take care (**a** of); (fare attenzione) look out; **bada ai fatti tuoi!** mind your own business!

ba'dia f abbey

ba'dile m shovel

'badminton m badminton

'baffi mpl moustache sg; (di animale) whiskers; **mi fa un baffo** I don't give a damn; **ridere sotto i ~** laugh up one's sleeve

baf'futo adj moustached

ba'gagli mpl baggage. **~'aio** m (Rail) baggage car; (Auto) boot

ba'gaglio m baggage; **un ~** a piece of baggage. **~ a mano** hand baggage

baggia'nata f **non dire baggianate** don't talk nonsense

bagli'ore m glare; (improvviso) flash; (fig: di speranza) glimmer

ba'gnante mf bather

ba'gna|re vt wet; (inzuppare) soak; (immergere) dip; (innaffiare) water; (mare:) wash; (fiume:) flow through. **~rsi** vr get wet; (al mare ecc) bathe.

ba'gnato adj wet

ba'gnino, -a mf life guard

'bagno m bath; (stanza) bathroom; (gabinetto) toilet; (in casa) toilet; (al mare) bathe; **bagni** pl (stabilimento) lido; **fare il ~** have a bath; (nel mare ecc) [have a] swim; **andare in ~** go to the toilet; **mettere a ~** soak. **~ turco** Turkish bath

bagnoma'ria m bain marie

bagnoschi'uma m inv bubble bath

'baia f bay

baio'netta f bayonet

'baita f mountain chalet

bala'ustra, balaus'trata f balustrade

balbet't|are vt/i stammer; (bambino:) babble. **~io** m stammering; babble

bal'buzi|e f stutter. **~'ente** adj stuttering • mf stutterer

Bal'can|i mpl Balkans. **b~ico** adj Balkan

balco'nata f (Theat) balcony

balcon'cino m **reggiseno a ~** underwired bra

bal'cone m balcony

baldac'chino m canopy; **letto a ~** four-poster bed

bal'dan|za f boldness. **~'zoso** adj bold

bal'doria f revelry; **far ~** have a riotous time

ba'lena f whale

bale'nare vi lighten; fig flash; **mi è balenata un'idea** I've just had an idea

bale'niera f whaler

ba'leno m **in un ~** in a flash

ba'lera f dance hall

ba'lia f **in ~ di** at the mercy of

'balla f bale; (🅘: frottola) tall story

bal'labile adj good for dancing to

bal'la|re vi dance. **~ta** f ballad

balla'toio m (nelle scale) landing

balle'rino, -a mf dancer; (classico) ballet dancer; **ballerina** (classica) ballet dancer, ballerina

bal'letto m ballet

'ballo m dance; (il ballare) dancing; **sala da ~** ballroom; **essere in ~** (lavoro, vita:) be at stake; (persona:) be committed; **tirare qcno in ~** involve sb

ballonzo'lare vi skip about

ballot'taggio m second count (of votes)

balne'a|re adj bathing attrib. **stagione ~** swimming season. **stazione ~** seaside resort. **~zi'one** f **è vietata la ~zione** no swimming

b

ba'lordo adj foolish; (stordito) stunned; **tempo ~** nasty weather

'balsamo m balsam; (per capelli) conditioner; (lenimento) remedy

'baltico adj Baltic. **il [mar] B~** the Baltic [Sea]

balu'ardo m bulwark

'balza f crag; (di abito) flounce

bal'zano adj (idea) weird

bal'zare vi bounce; (saltare) jump; **~ in piedi** leap to one's feet. **'balzo** m bounce; (salto) jump; **prendere la palla al balzo** seize an opportunity

bam'bagia f cotton wool

bambi'nata f childish thing to do/say

bam'bi|no, -a mf child; (appena nato) baby; **avere un ~no** have a baby. **~'none, -a** mf pej big or overgrown child

bam'boccio m chubby child; (sciocco) simpleton; (fantoccio) rag doll

'bambo|la f doll. **~'lotto** m male doll

bambù m bamboo

ba'nal|e adj banal; **~ità** f inv banality; **~iz'zare** vt trivialize

ba'nan|a f banana. **~o** m banana-tree

'banca f bank. **~ [di] dati** databank

banca'rella f stall

ban'cario, -a adj banking attrib; **trasferimento ~** bank transfer •mf bank employee

banca'rotta f bankruptcy; **fare ~** go bankrupt

banchet'tare vi banquet. **ban'chetto** m banquet

banchi'ere m banker

ban'china f (Naut) quay; (in stazione) platform; (di strada) path; **~ non transitabile** soft verge

ban'chisa f floe

'banco m (di scuola) desk; (di negozio) counter; (di officina) bench; (di gioco, banca) bank; (di mercato) stall; (degli imputati) dock; **sotto ~** under the counter; **medicinale da ~** over the counter medicines. **~ informazioni** information desk. **~ di nebbia** fog bank

C **'bancomat®** m inv cashpoint, ATM; (carta) bank card

ban'cone m counter; (in bar) bar

banco'nota f banknote, bill Am; **banco'note** pl paper currency

'banda f band; (di delinquenti) gang. **~ d'atterraggio** landing strip. **~ larga** broad band. **~ rumorosa** rumble strip

banderu'ola f weathercock; (Naut) pennant

bandi'e|ra f flag. **~'rina** f (nel calcio) corner flag. **~'rine** pl bunting sg

ban'di|re vt banish; (pubblicare) publish; fig dispense with (formalità, complimenti). **~to** m bandit. **~'tore** m (di aste) auctioneer

'bando m proclamation; **~ di concorso** job advertisement (published in an official gazette for a job for which a competitive examination has to be taken)

C **bar** m inv bar

'bara f coffin

ba'rac|ca f hut; (catapecchia) hovel; **mandare avanti la ~ca** keep the ship afloat. **~'cato** m person living in a makeshift shelter. **~'chino** m (di gelati, giornali) kiosk; Radio CB radio. **~'cone** m (roulotte) circus caravan; (in luna park) booth. **~'copoli** f inv shanty town

bara'onda f chaos

ba'rare vi cheat

'baratro m chasm

barat'tare vt barter. **ba'ratto** m barter

ba'rattolo m jar; (di latta) tin

'barba f beard; (**!**: noia) bore; **farsi la ~** shave; **è una ~** (noia) it's boring

barbabi'etola f beetroot. **~ da zucchero** sugar-beet

bar'barico adj barbaric. **bar'barie** f barbarity. **'barbaro** adj barbarous •m barbarian

'barbecue m inv barbecue

barbi'ere m barber; (negozio) barber's

barbi'turico m barbiturate

bar'bone m (vagabondo) vagrant; (cane) poodle

bar'boso adj [!] boring
barbu'gliare vi mumble
bar'buto adj bearded
'barca f boat. ~ **a motore** motorboat. ~ **da pesca** fishing boat. ~ **a remi** rowing boat. ~ **di salvataggio** lifeboat. ~ **a vela** sailing boat. ~**i'olo** m boatman
barcame'narsi vr manage
barcol'lare vi stagger
bar'cone m barge; (di ponte) pontoon
bar'dar|e vt harness. ~**si** vr hum dress up
ba'rel|la f stretcher. ~**li'ere** m stretcher-bearer
'Barents: **il mare di** ~ the Barents Sea
bari'centro m centre of gravity
ba'ri|le m barrel. ~**'lotto** m fig tub of lard
ba'rista m barman •f barmaid
ba'ritono m baritone
bar'lume m glimmer; **un** ~ **di speranza** a glimmer of hope
'barman m inv barman
'baro m cardsharper
ba'rocco adj & m baroque
ba'rometro m barometer
ba'rone m baron; **i baroni** fig the top brass. **baro'nessa** f baroness
'barra f bar; (lineetta) oblique; (Naut) tiller. ~ **spazio** (Comput) space bar. ~ **strumenti** (Comput) tool bar
bar'rare vt block off (strada)
barri'ca|re vt barricade. ~**ta** f barricade
barri'era f barrier; (stradale) road-block; (Geol) reef. ~ **razziale** colour bar
bar'ri|re vi trumpet. ~**to** m trumpeting
barzel'letta f joke; ~ **sporca** o **spinta** dirty joke
basa'mento m base
ba'sar|e vt base. ~**si** vr ~**si su** be based on; **mi baso su ciò che ho visto** I'm going on [the basis of] what I saw
'basco, -a mf & adj Basque •m (copricapo) beret
'base f basis; (fondamento) foundation; (Mil) base; (Pol) rank and file; **a** ~ **di** containing; **in** ~ **a** on the basis of. ~ **dati** database
'baseball m baseball
ba'setta f sideburn
basi'lare adj basic
ba'silica f basilica
ba'silico m basil
ba'sista m grass roots politician; (di un crimine) mastermind
'basket m basketball
bas'sezza f lowness; (di statura) shortness; (viltà) vileness
bas'sista mf bassist
'basso adj low; (di statura) short; (acqua) shallow; (televisione) quiet; (vile) despicable; **parlare a bassa voce** speak in a low voice; **la bassa Italia** southern Italy •m lower part; (Mus) bass. **guardare in** ~ look down
basso'fondo m (pl **bassifondi**) shallows pl; **bassifondi** pl (quartieri poveri) slums
bassorili'evo m bas-relief
bas'sotto m dachshund
ba'stardo, -a adj bastard; (di animale) mongrel •mf bastard; (animale) mongrel
ba'stare vi be enough; (durare) last; **basta!** that's enough!; **basta che** (purché) provided that; **basta così** that's enough; **basta così?** is that enough?; (in negozio) anything else?; **basta andare alla posta** you only have to go to the post office
Basti'an con'trario m contrary old so-and-so
basti'one m bastion
basto'nare vt beat
baston'cino m ski pole. ~ **di pesce** fish finger, fish stick Am
ba'stone m stick; (da golf) club; (da passeggio) walking stick
ba'tosta f blow
bat'tagli|a f battle; (lotta) fight. ~**'are** vi battle; fig fight
bat'taglio m (di campana) clapper; (di porta) knocker
battagli'one m battalion
bat'tello m boat; (motonave) steamer
bat'tente m (di porta) wing; (di finestra)

b

b

shutter; (battaglio) knocker

'batter|e vt beat; (percorrere) scour; thresh (grano); break (record) • vi (bussare, urtare) knock; (cuore:) beat; (ali ecc:) flap; Tennis serve; **~e a macchina** type; **~e le palpebre** blink; **~e le mani** clap [one's hands]; **~e le ore** strike the hours. **~si** vr fight

bat'teri mpl bacteria

batte'ria f battery; (Mus) drums pl

bat'terio m bacterium. **~'logico** adj bacteriological

batte'rista mf drummer

bat'tesimo m baptism

battez'zare vt baptize

battiba'leno m **in un ~** in a flash

batti'becco m squabble

batticu'ore m palpitation; **mi venne il ~** I was scared

bat'tigia f water's edge

batti'mano m applause

batti'panni m inv carpetbeater

batti'stero m baptistery

batti'strada m inv outrider; (di pneumatico) tread; Sport pacesetter

battitap'peto m inv carpet sweeper

'battito m [heart]beat; (alle tempie) throbbing; (di orologio) ticking; (della pioggia) beating

bat'tuta f beat; (colpo) knock; (spiritosaggine) wisecrack; (osservazione) remark; (Mus) bar; Tennis service; (Theat) cue; (dattilografia) stroke

ba'tuffolo m flock

ba'ule m trunk

'bava f dribble; (di cane ecc) slobber; **aver la ~ alla bocca** foam at the mouth

bava'glino m bib

ba'vaglio m gag

'bavero m collar

ba'zar m inv bazaar

baz'zecola f trifle

bazzi'care vt/i haunt

be'arsi vr delight (**di** in)

beati'tudine f bliss. **be'ato** adj blissful; (Relig) blessed; **beato te!** lucky you!

beauty-'case m inv toilet bag

bebè m inv baby

bec'caccia f woodcock

bec'ca|re vt peck; fig catch. **~rsi** vr (litigare) quarrel. **~ta** f peck

beccheggi'are vi pitch

bec'chino m grave-digger

'bec|co m beak; (di caffettiera ecc) spout. **~'cuccio** m spout

🅲 **be'fana** f Epiphany; (donna brutta) old witch

'beffa f hoax; **farsi beffe di qcno** mock sb. **bef'fardo** adj derisory; (persona) mocking

bef'far|e vt mock. **~si** vr **~si di** make fun of

'bega f quarrel; **è una bella ~** it's really annoying

'beige adj & m beige

be'la|re vi bleat. **~to** m bleating

'belga adj & mf Belgian

'Belgio m Belgium

'bella f (in carte, Sport) decider

bel'lezza f beauty; **che ~!** how lovely!; **chiudere/finire in ~** end on a high note

'belli|co adj war attrib. **~'coso** adj warlike. **~ge'rante** adj & mf belligerent

'bello adj nice; (di aspetto) beautiful; (uomo) handsome; (moralmente) good; **cosa fai di ~ stasera?** what are you up to tonight?; **oggi fa ~** it's a nice day; **una bella cifra** a lot; **un bel piatto di pasta** a big plate of pasta; **nel bel mezzo** right in the middle; **un bel niente** absolutely nothing; **bell'e fatto** over and done with; **bell'amico!** [a] fine friend he is/you are!; **questa è bella!** that's a good one!; **scamparla bella** have a narrow escape • m (bellezza) beauty; (innamorato) sweetheart; **sul più ~** at the crucial moment; **il ~ è che...** the funny thing is that...

'belva f wild beast

be'molle m (Mus) flat

ben ▸**bene**

benché conj though, although

'benda f bandage; (per occhi) blindfold. **ben'dare** vt bandage; blindfold (occhi)

🅲 see A-Z of Italian life and culture

'bene adv well; **ben ~** thoroughly; **~!** good!; **star ~** (di salute) be well; (vestito, stile:) suit; (finanziariamente) be well off; **non sta ~** (non è educato) it's not nice; **sta/va ~!** all right!; **ti sta ~!** [it] serves you right!; **ti auguro ogni ~** I wish you well; **di ~ in meglio** better and better; **fare ~** (aver ragione) do the right thing; **fare ~ a** (cibo:) be good for; **una persona per ~** a good person; **per ~** (fare) properly; **è ben difficile** it's very difficult; **come tu ben sai** as you well know; **lo credo ~!** I can well believe it! •m good; **per il tuo ~** for your own good. **beni** mpl (averi) property sg; **un ~ di famiglia** a family heirloom

bene'detto adj blessed

bene'di|re vt bless. **~zi'one** f blessing

benedu'cato adj well-mannered

benefat|'tore, -'trice m benefactor •f benefactress

benefi'care vt help

benefi'cenza f charity

benefici'ar|e vi **~e di** profit by. **~io, -a** adj & mf beneficiary. **bene'ficio** m benefit. **be'nefico** adj beneficial; (di beneficenza) charitable

bene'placito m approval

be'nessere m well-being

bene'stante adj well-off •mf well-off person

bene'stare m consent

be'nevolo adj benevolent

ben'fatto adj well-made

'beni mpl property sg; Fin assets; **~ di consumo** consumer goods

benia'mino m favourite

be'nigno adj kindly; (Med) benign

beninfor'mato adj well-informed

benintenzio'nato, -a adj well-meaning •mf well-meaning person

benin'teso adv of course

benpen'sante adj selfrighteous

benser'vito m **dare il ~ a qcno** fire sb

bensì conj but rather

benve'nuto adj & m welcome

ben'visto adj **essere ~** go down well (**da** with)

benvo'lere vt **farsi ~ da qcno** win sb's affection; **prendere qcno in ~** take a liking to sb; **essere benvoluto da tutti** to be well-liked by everyone

b

ben'zina f petrol, gas Am; **far ~** get petrol. **~ verde** unleaded petrol. **benzi'naio, -a** mf petrol station attendant

'bere vt drink; (assorbire) absorb; fig swallow •m drinking; (bevande) drinks pl

berga'motto m bergamot

ber'lina f (Auto) saloon

Ber'lino m Berlin

ber'muda mpl (pantaloni) Bermuda shorts

ber'noccolo m bump; (disposizione) flair

ber'retto m beret, cap

bersagli'are vt fig bombard. **ber'saglio** m target

be'stemmi|a f swear-word; (maledizione) oath; (sproposito) blasphemy. **~'are** vi swear

'besti|a f animal; (persona brutale) beast; (persona sciocca) fool; **andare in ~a** [!] blow one's top. **~'ale** adj bestial; (espressione, violenza) brutal; [!]: (freddo, fame) terrible. **~alità** f inv bestiality; fig nonsense. **~'ame** m livestock

'bettola f fig dive

be'tulla f birch

be'vanda f drink

bevi|'tore, -'trice mf drinker

be'vut|a f drink. **~o** pp di **bere**

bi'ada f fodder

bianche'ria f linen. **~ intima** underwear

bi'anco adj white; (foglio, pagina ecc) blank •m white; **mangiare in ~** not eat rich food; **in ~ e nero** (film, fotografia) black and white; **passare una notte in ~** have a sleepless night

bian'core m whiteness

bianco'spino m hawthorn

biasci'care vt (mangiare) eat noisily; (parlare) mumble

biasi'mare vt blame. **bi'asimo** m blame

'Bibbia f Bible

bibe'ron m inv [baby's] bottle

'bibita f [soft] drink

'biblico adj biblical

bibliogra'fia f bibliography

biblio'te|ca f library; (mobile) bookcase. **~'cario, -a** mf librarian

bicarbo'nato m bicarbonate

bicchi'ere m glass

bicchie'rino m [!] tipple

bici'cletta f bicycle; **andare in ~** ride a bicycle

bico'lore adj two-coloured

bidè m inv bidet

bi'dello, -a mf janitor

bido'nata f [!] swindle

bi'done m bin; ([!]: truffa) swindle; **fare un ~ a qcno** [!] stand sb up

bien'nale adj biennial

bi'ennio m two-year period

bi'etola f beet

bifo'cale adj bifocal

bi'folco, -a mf fig boor

bifor'c|arsi vr fork. **~azi'one** f fork. **~uto** adj forked

biga'mia f bigamy. **'bigamo, -a** adj bigamous • mf bigamist

bighello'nare vi loaf around. **bighel'lone** m loafer

bigiotte'ria f costume jewellery; (negozio) jeweller's

bigliet't|aio m booking clerk; (sui treni) ticket-collector. **~e'ria** f ticket-office; (Theat) box-office

bigli'et|to m ticket; (lettera breve) note; (cartoncino) card; (di banca) banknote. **~to da visita** business card. **~'tone** m ([!]: soldi) big one

bignè m inv cream puff

bigo'dino m roller

bi'gotto m bigot

bi'kini m inv bikini

bi'lanci|a f scales pl; (Comm) balance; **B~a** (Astr) Libra. **~'are** vt balance; fig weigh. **~o** m budget; (Comm) balance sheet; **fare il ~o** balance the books; fig take stock

'bil|e f bile; fig rage

bili'ardo m billiards sg

'bilico m equilibrium; **in ~** in the balance

bi'lingue adj bilingual

bili'one m billion

bilo'cale adj two-room

'bimbo, -a mf child

bimen'sile adj fortnightly

bime'strale adj bimonthly

bi'nario m track; (piattaforma) platform

bi'nocolo m binoculars pl

bio'chimica f biochemistry

biodegra'dabile adj biodegradable

bio'etica f bioethics

bio'fisica f biophysics

biogra'fia f biography. **bio'grafico** adj biographical. **bi'ografo, -a** mf biographer

biolo'gia f biology. **bio'logico** adj biological; (alimento, agricoltura) organic. **bi'ologo, -a** mf biologist

bi'ond|a f blonde. **~o** adj blond • m fair colour; (uomo) fair-haired man

bio'sfera f biosphere

bi'ossido m **~ di carbonio** carbon dioxide

bioterro'rismo m bioterrorism

biparti'tismo m two-party system

'birba f, **bir'bante** m rascal, rogue. **bir'bone** adj wicked

biri'chino, -a adj naughty • mf little devil

bi'rillo m skittle

'birr|a f beer; **a tutta ~a** fig flat out. **~a chiara** lager. **~a scura** brown ale. **~e'ria** f beer-house; (fabbrica) brewery

bis m inv encore

bi'saccia f haversack

bi'sbetic|a f shrew. **~o** adj bad-tempered

bisbigli'are vt/i whisper. **bi'sbiglio** m whisper

'bisca f gambling-house

'biscia f snake

bi'scotto m biscuit

bisessu'ale adj & mf bisexual

bise'stile adj **anno ~** leap year

bisettima'nale adj fortnightly

bi'slacco adj peculiar

bis'nonno, -a mf great-grandfather; great-grandmother

biso'gn|are vi **~a agire subito** we must act at once; **~a farlo** it is necessary to do it; **non ~a venire** you don't have to come. **~o** m need; (povertà) poverty; **aver ~o di** need. **~oso** adj needy; (povero) poor; **~oso di** in need of

bi'sonte m bison

bi'stecca f steak

bisticci'are vi quarrel. **bi'sticcio** m quarrel; (gioco di parole) pun

bistrat'tare vt mistreat

bi'torzolo m lump

'bitter m inv (bitter) aperitif

bi'vacco m bivouac

'bivio m crossroads; (di strada) fork

bizan'tino adj Byzantine

'bizza f tantrum; **fare le bizze** (bambini:) play up

biz'zarro adj bizarre

biz'zeffe adv **a ~** galore

blan'dire vt soothe; (allettare) flatter. **'blando** adj mild

bla'sone m coat of arms

'blatta f cockroach

blin'da|re vt armour-plate. **~to** adj armoured

blitz m inv blitz

bloc'car|e vt block; (isolare) cut off; (Mil) blockade; (Comm) freeze. **~si** vr (Mech) jam

blocca'sterzo m steering lock

'blocco m block; (Mil) blockade; (dei fitti) restriction; (di carta) pad; (unione) coalition; **in ~** (Comm) in bulk. **~ stradale** road-block

bloc-'notes m inv writing pad

blog'gista mf blogger

blu adj & m blue

blue-'jeans mpl jeans

bluff m inv (carte, fig) bluff

'blusa f blouse

'boa m boa [constrictor]; (sciarpa) [feather] boa •f (Naut) buoy

bo'ato m rumbling

bo'bina f spool; (di film) reel; (Electr) coil

'bocca f mouth; **a ~ aperta** fig dumbfounded; **in ~ al lupo!** [!] break a leg!; **fare la respirazione ~ a ~ a qcno** give sb mouth to mouth resuscitation or the kiss of life

boc'caccia f grimace; **far boccacce** make faces

boc'caglio m nozzle

boc'cale m jug; (da birra) tankard

bocca'porto m (Naut) hatch

boc'cata f (di fumo) puff; **prendere una ~ d'aria** get a breath of fresh air

boc'cetta f small bottle

boccheggi'are vi gasp

boc'chino m cigarette holder; (Mus, di pipa) mouthpiece

'bocc|ia f (palla) bowl; **~e** pl (gioco) bowls sg

bocci'a|re vt (agli esami) fail; (respingere) reject; (alle bocce) hit; **essere ~to** fail; (ripetere) repeat a year. **~'tura** f failure

bocci'olo m bud

boccon'cino m morsel

boc'cone m mouthful; (piccolo pasto) snack

boc'coni adv face downwards

'boia m executioner

boi'ata f [!] rubbish

boicot'tare vt boycott

bo'lero m bolero

'bolgia f (caos) bedlam

'bolide m meteor; **passare come un ~** shoot past [like a rocket]

Bo'livi|a f Bolivia. **b~'ano, -a** agg & mf Bolivian

'bolla f bubble; (pustola) blister

bol'la|re vt stamp; fig brand. **~to** adj fig branded; **carta ~ta** paper with stamp showing payment of duty

bol'lente adj boiling [hot]

bol'let|ta f bill; **essere in ~ta** be hard up. **~'tino** m bulletin; (Comm) list

bol'lino m coupon

bol'li|re vt/i boil. **~to** m boiled meat. **~'tore** m boiler; (per l'acqua) kettle. **~'tura** f boiling

'bollo m stamp

b

bol'lore m boil; (caldo) intense heat; fig ardour

'bomba f bomb; **a prova di ~** bomb-proof

bombarda'mento m shelling; (con aerei) bombing; fig bombardment. **~ aereo** air raid

bombar'd|are vt shell; (con aerei) bomb; fig bombard. **~i'ere** m bomber

bom'betta f bowler [hat]

'bombola f cylinder. **~ di gas** gas cylinder

bombo'lone m doughnut

bomboni'era f wedding keep-sake

bo'naccia f (Naut) calm

bonacci'one, -a mf good-natured person •adj good-natured

bo'nario adj kindly

bo'nifica f land reclamation. **bonifi'care** vt reclaim

bo'nifico m (Comm) discount; (bancario) [credit] transfer

bontà f goodness; (gentilezza) kindness

'bora f bora (cold north-east wind in the upper Adriatic)

'borchi|a f stud. **~'ato** adj studded

bor'da|re vt border. **~'tura** f border

bor'deaux adj inv maroon

bor'dello m brothel; fig bedlam; (disordine) mess

'bordo m border; (estremità) edge; **a ~** (Aeron, Naut) on board

bor'gata f hamlet

bor'ghese adj bourgeois; (abito) civilian; **in ~** in civilian dress; (poliziotto) in plain clothes

borghe'sia f middle classes pl

'borgo m village

'bori|a f conceit. **~'oso** adj conceited

bor'lotto m **[fagiolo] ~** borlotto bean

boro'talco m talcum powder

bor'raccia f flask

'bors|a f bag; (borsetta) handbag; (valori) Stock Exchange. **~a dell'acqua calda** hot-water bottle. **~a frigo** cool-box. **~a della spesa** shopping bag. **~a di studio** scholarship. **~ai'olo** m pickpocket. **~el'lino** m purse. **bor'sista** mf Fin speculator; (Sch) scholarship holder

bor'se|llo m purse; (borsetto) man's handbag. **~tta** f handbag. **~tto** m man's handbag

bo'scaglia f woodlands pl

boscai'olo m woodman; (guardaboschi) forester

'bosco m wood. **bo'scoso** adj wooded

'Bosnia f Bosnia

'bossolo m cartridge case

bo'tanic|a f botany. **~o** adj botanical •m botanist

'botta f blow; (rumore) bang; **fare a botte** come to blows. **~ e risposta** fig thrust and counter-thrust

'botte f barrel

bot'te|ga f shop; (di artigiano) workshop. **~'gaio, -a** mf shopkeeper. **~'ghino** m Theatr boxoffice; (del lotto) lottery-shop

bot'tigli|a f bottle; **in ~a** bottled. **~e'ria** f wine shop

bot'tino m loot; (Mil) booty

'botto m bang; **di ~** all of a sudden

bot'tone m button; (Bot) bud

bo'vino adj bovine; •m bovini pl cattle sg

box m inv (per cavalli) loosebox; (recinto per bambini) play-pen

'boxe f boxing

'bozza f draft; (Typ) proof; (bernoccolo) bump. **boz'zetto** m sketch

'bozzolo m cocoon

brac'care vt hunt

brac'cetto m **a ~** arm in arm

bracci'a|le m bracelet; (fascia) armband. **~'letto** m bracelet; (di orologio) watch-strap

bracci'ante m day labourer

bracci'ata f (nel nuoto) stroke

'bracci|o m (pl f **braccia**) arm; (di fiume, pl **bracci**) arm. **~'olo** m (di sedia) arm[rest]; (da nuoto) armband

'bracco m hound

bracconi'ere m poacher

'brac|e f embers pl; **alla ~e** char-grilled. **~i'ere** m brazier. **~i'ola** f chop

'brado adj **allo stato ~** in the wild

'brama f longing. **bra'mare** vt long for. **bramo'sia** f yearning

'branca f branch

'branchia f gill

'branco m (di cani) pack; (pej: di persone) gang

branco'lare vi grope

'branda f camp-bed

bran'dello m scrap; **a brandelli** in tatters

bran'dire vt brandish

'brano m piece; (di libro) passage

Bra'sil|e m Brazil. **b~i'ano, -a** agg & mf Brazilian

bra'vata f bragging

'bravo adj good; (abile) clever; (coraggioso) brave; **~!** well done!. **bra'vura** f skill

'breccia f breach; **sulla ~** fig very successful, at the top

bre'saola f dried, salted beef sliced thinly and eaten cold

bre'tella f shoulder-strap; **bretelle** pl (di calzoni) braces

'breve adj brief; **in ~** briefly; **tra ~** shortly

brevet'tare vt patent. **bre'vetto** m patent; (attestato) licence

brevità f shortness

'brezza f breeze

'bricco m jug

bric'cone m blackguard; hum rascal

'briciol|a f crumb; fig grain. **~o** m fragment

'briga f (fastidio) trouble; (lite) quarrel; **attaccar ~** pick a quarrel; **prendersi la ~ di fare qcsa** go to the trouble of doing sth

brigadi'ere m (dei carabinieri) sergeant

bri'gante m bandit; hum rogue

bri'gare vi intrigue

bri'gata f brigade; (gruppo) group

briga'tista mf (Pol) member of the Red Brigades

'briglia f rein; **a ~ sciolta** at breakneck speed

bril'lante adj brilliant; (scintillante) sparkling • m diamond

bril'lare vi shine; (metallo:) glitter; (scintillare) sparkle

'brillo adj tipsy

'brina f hoar-frost

brin'dare vi toast; **~ a qcno** drink a toast to sb

'brindisi m inv toast

bri'tannico adj British

'brivido m shiver; (di paura ecc) shudder; (di emozione) thrill

brizzo'lato adj greying

'brocca f jug

broc'cato m brocade

'broccoli mpl broccoli sg

'brodo m broth; (per cucinare) stock. **~ ristretto** consommé

'broglio m **~ elettorale** gerrymandering

bron'chite f bronchitis

'broncio m sulk; **fare il ~** sulk

bronto'l|are vi grumble; (tuono ecc:) rumble. **~io** m grumbling; (di tuono) rumbling. **~one, -a** mf grumbler

'bronzo m bronze

bros'sura f **edizione in ~** paperback

bru'care vt (pecora:) graze

bruciacchi'are vt scorch

brucia'pelo adv **a ~** point-blank

bruci'a|re vt burn; (scottare) scald; (incendiare) set fire to • vi burn; (scottare) scald. **~rsi** vr burn oneself. **~to** adj burnt; fig burnt-out. **~'tore** m burner. **~'tura** f burn. **bruci'ore** m burning sensation

'bruco m grub

'brufolo m spot

brughi'era f heath

bruli'c|are vi swarm

'brullo adj bare

'bruma f mist

b

b

'bruno adj brown; (occhi, capelli) dark

brusca'mente adv (di colpo) suddenly

bru'schetta f toasted bread rubbed with garlic and sprinkled with olive oil

'brusco adj sharp; (persona) brusque; (improvviso) sudden

bru'sio m buzzing

bru'tal|e adj brutal. **~ità** f inv brutality. **~iz'zare** vt brutalize. **'bruto** adj & m brute

brut'tezza f ugliness

'brut|to adj ugly; (tempo, tipo, situazione, affare) nasty; (cattivo) bad; **~ta copia** rough copy; **~to tiro** dirty trick. **~'tura** f ugly thing

'buca f hole; (avvallamento) hollow. **~ delle lettere** (a casa) letter-box

buca'neve m inv snowdrop

bu'car|e vt make a hole in; (pungere) prick; punch (biglietti) •vi have a puncture. **~si** vr prick oneself; (con droga) shoot up

bu'cato m washing

'buccia f peel, skin

bucherel'lare vt riddle

'buco m hole

bu'dello m (pl f **budella**) bowel

bu'dino m pudding

'bue m (pl **buoi**) ox; **carne di ~** beef

'bufalo m buffalo

bu'fera f storm; (di neve) blizzard

buf'fetto m cuff

'buffo adj funny; (Theat) comic •m funny thing. **~'nata** f (scherzo) joke. **buf'fone** m buffoon; **fare il buffone** play the fool

bu'gi|a f lie; **~a pietosa** white lie. **~'ardo, -a** adj lying •mf liar

bugi'gattolo m cubby-hole

'buio adj dark •m darkness; **al ~** in the dark; **~ pesto** pitch dark

'bulbo m bulb; (dell'occhio) eyeball

Bulga'ria f Bulgaria. **'bulgaro, -a** adj & mf Bulgarian

'bullo m bully

bul'lone m bolt

'bunker m inv bunker

buona'fede f good faith

buona'notte int good night

buona'sera int good evening

buon'giorno int good morning; (di pomeriggio) good afternoon

buon'grado: **di ~** adv willingly

buongu'staio, -a mf gourmet. **buon'gusto** m good taste

bu'ono adj good; (momento) right; **dar ~** (convalidare) accept; **alla buona** easy-going; (cena) informal; **buona notte/sera** good night/evening; **buon compleanno/Natale!** happy birthday/merry Christmas!; **buon senso** common sense; **di buon'ora** early; **una buona volta** once and for all; **buona parte di** the best part of; **tre ore buone** three good hours •m good; (in film) goody; (tagliando) voucher; (titolo) bond; **con le buone** gently; **~ sconto** money-off coupon •mf **buono, -a a nulla** dead loss

buontem'pone, -a mf happy-go-lucky person

buonu'more m good temper

buonu'scita f retirement bonus; (di dirigente) golden handshake

burat'tino m puppet

'burbero adj surly; (nei modi) rough

bu'rocra|te m bureaucrat. **buro'cratico** adj bureaucratic. **~'zia** f bureaucracy

bur'ra|sca f storm. **~'scoso** adj stormy

'burro m butter

bur'rone m ravine

bu'scar|e vt, **~si** vr catch

bus'sare vt knock

'bussola f compass; **perdere la ~** lose one's bearings

'busta f envelope; (astuccio) case. **~ paga** pay packet. **~'rella** f bribe. **bu'stina** f (di tè) tea bag; (per medicine) sachet

'busto m bust; (indumento) girdle

but'tar|e vt throw; **~e giù** (demolire) knock down; (inghiottire) gulp down; scribble down (scritto); [!] put on (pasta); (scoraggiare) dishearten; **~e via** throw away. **~si** vr throw oneself; (saltare) jump

butte'rato adj pock-marked

Cc

caba'ret m inv cabaret

ca'bina f (Aeron, Naut) cabin; (balneare) beach hut. ~ **elettorale** polling booth. ~ **di pilotaggio** cockpit. ~ **telefonica** telephone box. **cabi'nato** m cabin cruiser

ca'cao m cocoa

'cacca f [!] pooh

'caccia f hunt; (con fucile) shooting; (inseguimento) chase; (selvaggina) game •m inv (Aeron) fighter; (Naut) destroyer

cacciabombardi'ere m fighter-bomber

cacciagi'one f game

cacci'a|re vt hunt; (mandar via) chase away; (scacciare) drive out; (ficcare) shove •vi go hunting. **~rsi** vr (nascondersi) hide; (andare a finire) get to; **~rsi nei guai** get into trouble. **~'tore, ~'trice** mf hunter; **alla ~'tora** adj (Culin) chasseur. **~tore di frodo** poacher

caccia'vite m inv screwdriver

ca'chet m inv (Med) capsule; (colorante) colour rinse; (stile) cachet

'cachi m inv (albero, frutta) persimmon

'cacio m (formaggio) cheese

'cactus m inv cactus

ca'da|vere m corpse. **~'verico** adj fig deathly pale

ca'dente adj falling; (casa) crumbling

ca'denza f cadence; (ritmo) rhythm; (Mus) cadenza

ca'dere vi fall; (capelli ecc:) fall out; (capitombolare) tumble; (vestito ecc:) hang; **far ~** (di mano) drop; **~ dal sonno** feel very sleepy; **lasciar ~** drop; **~ dalle nuvole** fig be taken aback

ca'detto m cadet

ca'duta f fall; (di capelli) loss; fig downfall

[C] **caffè** m inv coffee; (locale) café. **~ corretto** espresso coffee with a dash of liqueur. **~ lungo** weak black coffee. **~ macchiato** coffee with a dash of milk. **~ ristretto** strong espresso coffee. **~ solubile** instant coffee. **caffe'ina** f caffeine. **caffel'latte** m inv white coffee.

caffetti'era f coffee-pot

cafo'naggine f boorishness

cafo'nata f boorishness

ca'fone, -a mf boor

ca'gare vi [!] crap

cagio'nare vt cause

cagio'nevole adj delicate

cagli'ar|e vi, **~si** vr curdle

'cagna f bitch

ca'gnara f [!] din

ca'gnesco adj **guardare qcno in ~** scowl at sb

'cala f creek

cala'brone m hornet

cala'maio m inkpot

cala'mari mpl squid sg

cala'mita f magnet

calamità f inv calamity

ca'lar|e vi come down; (vento:) drop; (diminuire) fall; (tramontare) set •vt (abbassare) lower; (nei lavori a maglia) decrease •m (di luna) waning. **~si** vr lower oneself

'calca f throng

cal'cagno m heel

cal'care[1] m limestone

cal'care[2] vt tread; (premere) press [down]; **~ la mano** fig exaggerate; **~ le orme di qcno** fig follow in sb's footsteps

'calce[1] f lime

'calce[2] m **in ~** at the foot of the page

calce'struzzo m concrete

cal'cetto m Sport five-a-side [football]

[C] *see* A-Z of Italian life and culture

C

calci'a|re vt kick. **~'tore** m footballer

cal'cina f mortar

calci'naccio m (pezzo di intonaco) flake of plaster

'calcio[1] m kick; (Sport) football; (di arma da fuoco) butt; **dare un ~ a** kick. **~ d'angolo** corner [kick]

'calcio[2] m (chimica) calcium

'calco m tracing; (arte) cast

calco'la|re vt calculate; (considerare) consider. **~'tore** adj calculating •m calculator; (macchina elettronica) computer

'calcolo m calculation; (Med) stone

cal'daia f boiler

caldar'rosta f roast chestnut

caldeggi'are vt support

'caldo adj warm; (molto caldo) hot •m heat; **avere ~** be warm/hot; **fa ~** it is warm/hot

calen'dario m calendar

'calibro m calibre; (strumento) callipers pl; **di grosso ~** (persona) top attrib

'calice m goblet; (Relig) chalice

ca'ligine m fog; (industriale) smog

'call centre m inv call centre

calligra'fia f handwriting; (cinese) calligraphy

cal'lista mf chiropodist. **'callo** m corn; **fare il callo a** become hardened to. **cal'loso** adj callous

'calma f calm. **cal'mante** adj calming •m sedative. **cal'mare** vt calm [down]; (lenire) soothe. **cal'marsi** vr calm down; (vento:) drop; (dolore:) die down. **'calmo** adj calm

'calo m (Comm) fall; (di volume) shrinkage; (di peso) loss

ca'lore m heat; (moderato) warmth; **in ~** (animale) on heat. **calo'roso** adj warm

calo'ria f calorie

ca'lorico adj calorific

calo'rifero m radiator

calorosa'mente adv (cordialmente) warmly

calpe'stare vt trample [down]; fig trample on (diritti, sentimenti); **vietato ~ l'erba** keep off the grass

calpe'stio m (passi) footsteps

ca'lunni|a f slander. **~'are** vt slander. **~'oso** adj slanderous

ca'lura f heat

cal'vario m Calvary; fig trial

cal'vizie f baldness. **'calvo** adj bald

'calz|a f (da donna) stocking; (da uomo) sock. **~a'maglia** f tights pl; (per danza) leotard

cal'zante adj fig fitting

cal'za|re vt (indossare) wear; (mettersi) put on •vi fit

calza'scarpe m inv shoehorn

calza'tura f footwear

calzaturi'ficio m shoe factory

cal'zetta f **è una mezza ~** fig he's no use

calzet'tone m knee-length woollen sock. **cal'zino** m sock

calzo'l|aio m shoemaker. **~e'ria** f (negozio) shoe shop

calzon'cini mpl shorts. **~ da bagno** swimming trunks

cal'zone m folded pizza with tomato and mozzarella or ricotta

cal'zoni mpl trousers, pants Am

camale'onte m chameleon

cambi'ale f bill of exchange

cambia'mento m change

cambi'ar|e vt/i change; move (casa); (fare cambio di) exchange; **~e rotta** (Naut) alter course. **~si** vr change. **'cambio** m change; (Comm, scambio) exchange; (Mech) gear; **dare il ~ a qcno** relieve sb; **in ~ di** in exchange for

'camera f room; (mobili) [bedroom] suite; (Phot) camera; **C~** (Comm, Pol) Chamber. **~ ardente** funeral parlour. **~ d'aria** inner tube. **C~ di Commercio** Chamber of Commerce. **C~ dei Deputati** (Pol) ≈House of Commons. **~ doppia** double room. **~ da letto** bedroom. **~ matrimoniale** double room. **~ oscura** darkroom. **~ singola** single room

came'rata[1] f (dormitorio) dormitory; (Mil) barrack room

came'ra|ta[2] mf (amico) mate; (Pol)

comrade. ~'**tismo** m comradeship

cameri'era f maid; (di ristorante) waitress; (in albergo) chamber-maid; (di bordo) stewardess

cameri'ere m manservant; (di ristorante) waiter; (di bordo) steward

came'rino m dressing-room

'**camice** m overall. **cami'cetta** f blouse. **ca'micia** f shirt; **uovo in ~** poached egg. **camicia da notte** nightdress

cami'netto m fireplace

ca'mino m chimney; (focolare) fireplace

'**camion** m inv truck, lorry Br

camion'cino m van

camio'netta f jeep

camio'nista mf truck driver

cam'mello m camel; (tessuto) camel-hair •adj inv (colore) camel

cam'meo m cameo

cammi'na|re vi walk; (auto, orologio:) go. **~ta** f walk; **fare una ~ta** go for a walk. **cam'mino** m way; **essere in ~** be on the way; **mettersi in ~** set out

camo'milla f camomile; (bevanda) camomile tea

ca'morra f local mafia

ca'moscio m chamois; (pelle) suede

cam'pagna f country; (paesaggio) countryside; (Comm, Mil) campaign; **in ~** in the country. **~ elettorale** election campaign. **~ pubblicitaria** marketing campaign. **campa'gnolo, -a** adj rustic •m countryman •f countrywoman

cam'pale adj field attrib; **giornata ~** fig strenuous day

cam'pa|na f bell; (di vetro) belljar. ~'**nella** f (di tenda) curtain ring. ~'**nello** m door-bell; (cicalino) buzzer

campa'nile m belfry

campani'lismo m parochialism

campani'lista mf person with a parochial outlook

cam'panula f (Bot) campanula

cam'pare vi live; (a stento) get by

cam'pato adj **~ in aria** unfounded

campeggi'a|re vi camp; (spiccare) stand out. ~'**tore,** ~'**trice** mf camper. **cam'peggio** m camping; (terreno) campsite

cam'pestre adj rural

'**camping** m inv campsite

campio'nari|o m [set of] samples •adj samples; **fiera ~a** trade fair

campio'nato m championship

campiona'tura f (di merce) range of samples

campi'on|e m champion; (Comm) sample; (esemplare) specimen. ~'**essa** f ladies' champion

'**campo** m field; (accampamento) camp. **~ da calcio** football pitch. **~ di concentramento** concentration camp. **~ da golf** golf course. **~ da tennis** tennis court. **~ profughi** refugee camp

campo'santo m cemetery

camuf'far|e vt disguise. **~si** vr disguise oneself

'**Cana|da** m Canada. ~'**dese** agg & mf Canadian

ca'naglia f scoundrel; (plebaglia) rabble

ca'nal|e m channel; (artificiale) canal. ~**iz'zare** vt channel (acque). ~**izzazi'one** f channelling; (rete) pipes pl

'**canapa** f hemp

cana'rino m canary

cancel'la|re vt cross out; (con la gomma) rub out; (annullare) cancel; (Comput) delete. ~'**tura** f erasure. ~**zi'one** f cancellation; (Comput) deletion

cancelle'ria f chancellery; (articoli per scrivere) stationery

cancelli'ere m chancellor; (di tribunale) clerk

can'cello m gate

cance'ro|geno m carcinogen •adj carcinogenic. ~'**so** adj cancerous

can'crena f gangrene

'**cancro** m cancer. **C~** (Astr) Cancer

candeg'gi|na f bleach. ~'**are** vt bleach. **can'deggio** m bleaching

can'de|la f candle; (Auto) spark plug. ~**li'ere** m candlestick

candi'da|rsi vr stand as a candidate.

see A-Z of Italian life and culture

~**to, -a** mf candidate. ~'**tura** f (Pol) candidacy; (per lavoro) application

'**candido** adj snow-white; (sincero) candid; (puro) pure

C

can'dito adj candied

can'dore m whiteness; fig innocence

'**cane** m dog; (di arma da fuoco) cock; **un tempo da cani** foul weather. ~ **da caccia** hunting dog

ca'nestro m basket

cangi'ante adj iridescent; **seta** ~ shot silk

can'guro m kangaroo

ca'nile m kennel; (di allevamento) kennels pl. ~ **municipale** dog pound

ca'nino adj & m canine

'**canna** f reed; (da zucchero) cane; (di fucile) barrel; (bastone) stick; (di bicicletta) crossbar; (asta) rod; (!: hascish) joint; **povero in** ~ destitute. ~ **da pesca** fishing rod

can'nella f cinnamon

can'neto m bed of reeds

can'niba|le m cannibal. ~'**lismo** m cannibalism

cannocchi'ale m telescope

canno'nata f cannon shot; **è una** ~ fig it's brilliant

cannon'cino m (dolce) cream horn

can'none m cannon; fig ace

can'nuccia f [drinking] straw; (di pipa) stem

ca'noa f canoe

'**canone** m canon; (affitto) rent; **equo** ~ fair rents act

ca'noni|co m canon. ~**z'zare** vt canonize. ~**zzazi'one** f canonization

ca'noro adj melodious

ca'notta f (estiva) vest top

canot'taggio m canoeing; (voga) rowing

canotti'era f singlet

canotti'ere m oarsman

ca'notto m [rubber] dinghy

cano'vaccio m (trama) plot; (straccio) duster

can'tante mf singer

can't|are vt/i sing. ~**au'tore,** ~**au'trice** mf singer-songwriter. ~**icchi'are** vt sing softly; (a bocca chiusa) hum

canti'ere m yard; (Naut) shipyard; (di edificio) construction site. ~ **navale** naval dockyard

canti'lena f singsong; (ninna-nanna) lullaby

can'tina f cellar; (osteria) wine shop

'**canto**[1] m singing; (canzone) song; (Relig) chant; (poesia) poem

'**canto**[2] m (angolo) corner; (lato) side; **dal** ~ **mio** for my part; **d'altro** ~ on the other hand

canto'nata f **prendere una** ~ fig be sadly mistaken

can'tone m canton; (angolo) corner

can'tuccio m nook

canzo'na|re vt tease. ~'**torio** adj teasing. ~'**tura** f teasing

C **can'zo|ne** f song. ~'**netta** f ! pop song. ~**ni'ere** m songbook

'**caos** m chaos. **ca'otico** adj chaotic

C.A.P. m abbr (Codice di Avviamento Postale) post code, zip code Am

ca'pac|e adj able; (esperto) skilled; (stadio, contenitore) big; ~**e di** (disposto a) capable of. ~**ità** f inv ability; (attitudine) skill; (capienza) capacity

capaci'tarsi vr ~ **di** (rendersi conto) understand; (accorgersi) realize

ca'panna f hut

capan'nello m **fare** ~ **intorno a qcno/qcsa** gather round sb/sth

capan'none m shed; (Aeron) hangar

ca'parbio adj obstinate

ca'parra f deposit

capa'tina f short visit; **fare una** ~ **in città/da qcno** pop into town/in on sb

ca'pel|lo m hair; ~**li** pl (capigliatura) hair sg. ~'**lone** m hippie. ~'**luto** adj hairy

capez'zale m bolster; fig bedside

ca'pezzolo m nipple

capi'en|te adj capacious. ~**za** f capacity

capiglia'tura f hair

ca'pire vt understand; ~ **male** misunderstand; **si capisce!**

....

C *see* A-Z of Italian life and culture

naturally!; **sì, ho capito** yes, I see

capi'ta|le adj (Jur) capital; (principale) main •f (città) capital •m (Comm) capital. **~'lismo** m capitalism. **~'lista** mf capitalist. **~'listico** adj capitalist

capitane'ria f **~ di porto** port authorities pl

capi'tano m captain

capi'tare vi (giungere per caso) come; (accadere) happen

capi'tello m (Archit) capital

capito'la|re vi capitulate. **~zi'one** f capitulation

ca'pitolo m chapter

capi'tombolo m headlong fall; **fare un ~** tumble down

'capo m head; (chi comanda) boss [!]; (di vestiario) item; (Geog) cape; (in tribù) chief; (parte estrema) top; **a ~** new paragraph; **da ~** over again; **in ~ a un mese** within a month; **giramento di ~** dizziness; **mal di ~** headache; **~ d'abbigliamento** item of clothing. **~ d'accusa** (Jur) charge. **~ di bestiame** head of cattle

capo'banda m (Mus) bandmaster; (di delinquenti) ringleader

ca'poccia m ([!]: testa) nut

capocci'one, -a mf [!] brainbox

Capo'danno m New Year's Day

capofa'miglia m head of the family

capo'fitto m **a ~** headlong

capo'giro m giddiness

capola'voro m masterpiece

capo'linea m terminus

capo'lino m **fare ~** peep in

capolu'ogo m main town

capo'rale m lance-corporal

capo'squadra mf Sport team captain

capo'stipite mf (di famiglia) progenitor

capo'tavola mf head of the table

capo'treno m guard

capouf'ficio mf head clerk

capo'verso m first line

capo'vol|gere vt overturn; fig reverse. **~gersi** vr overturn; (barca:) capsize; fig be reversed. **~to** pp di **capovolgere** •adj upside-down

'cappa f cloak; (di camino) cowl; (di cucina) hood

cap'pel|la f chapel. **~'lano** m chaplain

cap'pello m hat. **~ a cilindro** top hat

'cappero m caper

'cappio m noose

cap'pone m capon

cap'potto m [over]coat

cappuc'cino m (frate) Capuchin; (bevanda) white coffee

cap'puccio m hood; (di penna stilografica) cap

'capra f goat. **ca'pretto** m kid

ca'pricci|o m whim; (bizzarria) freak; **fare i capricci** have tantrums. **~'oso** adj capricious; (bambino) naughty

Capri'corno m (Astr) Capricorn

capri'ola f somersault

capri'olo m roe-deer

'capro m [billy-]goat. **~ espiatorio** scapegoat.

ca'prone m [billy] goat

'capsula f capsule; (di proiettile) cap; (di dente) crown

cap'tare vt (Radio, TV) pick up; catch (attenzione)

cara'bina f carbine

carabini'ere m carabiniere; ▣**carabini'eri** pl Italian police

ca'raffa f carafe

Ca'raibi mpl (zona) Caribbean sg; (isole) Caribbean Islands; **il mar dei ~** the Caribbean [Sea]

cara'mella f sweet

cara'mello m caramel

ca'rato m carat

ca'ratte|re m character; (caratteristica) characteristic; (Typ) type; **di buon ~re** good-natured. **~'ristico, -a** adj characteristic; (pittoresco) quaint •f characteristic. **~riz'zare** vt characterize

carbon'cino m charcoal

car'bone m coal

carbu'rante m fuel

▣ *see* A-Z of Italian life and culture

C

carbura'tore m carburettor

car'cassa f carcass; fig old wreck

carce'ra|rio adj prison attrib. **~to, -a** mf prisoner. **~zi'one** f imprisonment. **~zione preventiva** preventive detention

'carcer|e m prison; (punizione) imprisonment. **~i'ere, -a** mf gaoler

carci'ofo m artichoke

cardi'nale adj & m cardinal

'cardine m hinge

cardio|chi'rurgo m heart surgeon. **~lo'gia** f cardiology. **cardi'ologo** m heart specialist. **~'tonico** m heart stimulant

'cardo m thistle

ca'rena f (Naut) bottom

ca'ren|te adj **~te di** lacking in. **~za** f lack; (scarsità) scarcity

care'stia f famine; (mancanza) dearth

ca'rezza f caress

cari'a|rsi vi decay. **~to** adj decayed

'carica f office; (Electr, Mil) charge; fig drive. **cari'care** vt load; (Electr, Mil) charge; wind up (orologio). **~'tore** m (per proiettile) magazine

carica'tu|ra f caricature. **~'rale** adj grotesque. **~'rista** mf caricaturist

'carico adj loaded (**di** with); (colore) strong; (orologio) wound [up]; (batteria) charged • m load; (di nave) cargo; (il caricare) loading; **a ~ di** (Comm) to be charged to; (persona) dependent on

'carie f [tooth] decay

ca'rino adj pretty; (piacevole) agreeable

ca'risma m charisma

carit|à f charity; **per ~à!** (come rifiuto) God forbid!. **~a'tevole** adj charitable

carnagi'one f complexion

car'naio m fig shambles

car'nale adj carnal; **cugino ~** first cousin

'carne f flesh; (alimento) meat; **~ di manzo/maiale/vitello** beef/pork/veal

car'nefi|ce m executioner. **~'cina** f slaughter

carne'va|le m carnival. **~'lesco** adj carnival

car'noso adj fleshy

'caro, -a adj dear; **cari saluti** kind regards • mf darling, dear; **i miei cari** my nearest and dearest

ca'rogna f carcass; fig bastard

caro'sello m merry-go-round

ca'rota f carrot

caro'vana f caravan; (di veicoli) convoy

caro'vita m high cost of living

'carpa f carp

carpenti'ere m carpenter

car'pire vt seize; (con difficoltà) extort

car'poni adv on all fours

car'rabile adj suitable for vehicles; **passo ~** ▸**carraio**

car'raio adj **passo ~** entrance to driveway, garage etc where parking is forbidden

carreggi'ata f roadway; **doppia ~** dual carriageway, divided highway Am

carrel'lata f (TV) pan

car'rello m trolley; (di macchina da scrivere) carriage; (Aeron) undercarriage; (Cinema, TV) dolly. **~ d'atterraggio** (Aeron) landing gear

car'retto m cart

carri'e|ra f career; **di gran ~ra** at full speed; **fare ~ra** get on. **~'rismo** m careerism

carri'ola f wheelbarrow

'carro m cart. **~ armato** tank. **~ attrezzi** breakdown vehicle. **~ funebre** hearse. **~ merci** truck

car'rozza f carriage; (Rail) car. **~ cuccette** sleeping car. **~ ristorante** restaurant car

carroz'zella f (per bambini) pram; (per disabili) wheelchair

carrozze'ria f bodywork; (officina) bodyshop

carroz'zina f pram; (pieghevole) push-chair, stroller Am

carroz'zone m (di circo) caravan

'carta f paper; (da gioco) card; (statuto) charter; (Geog) map. **~ d'argento** ≈ senior citizens' railcard. **~ assorbente** blotting-paper. **~ di**

see A-Z of Italian life and culture

credito credit card. ~ **geografica** map. 🅲~ **d'identità** identity card. ~ **igienica** toilet-paper. ~ **di imbarco** boarding card or pass. ~ **da lettere** writing-paper. ~ **da parati** wallpaper. ~ **stagnola** silver paper; (Culin) aluminium foil. ~ **straccia** waste paper. ~ **stradale** road map. ~ **velina** tissue-paper. ~ **verde** (Auto) green card. ~ **vetrata** sandpaper

cartacar'bone f carbon paper

car'taccia f waste paper

carta'modello m pattern

cartamo'neta f paper money

carta'pesta f papier mâché

carta'straccia f waste paper

cartave'trare vt sand [down]

car'tel|la f briefcase; (di cartone, Comput) folder; (di scolaro) satchel. **~la clinica** medical record. **~'lina** f folder

cartel'lino m (etichetta) label; (dei prezzi) price-tag; (di presenza) time-card; **timbrare il** ~ clock in; (all'uscita) clock out

car'tel|lo m sign; (pubblicitario) poster; (stradale) road sign; (di protesta) placard: (Comm) cartel. **~'lone** m poster; (Theat) bill

carti'era f paper-mill

car'tina f map

car'toccio m paper bag; **al** ~ (Culin) baked in foil

carto'|laio, -a mf stationer. **~le'ria** f stationer's. **~libre'ria** f stationer's and book shop

carto'lina f postcard. ~ **postale** postcard

carto'mante mf fortune-teller

carton'cino m (materiale) card

car'tone m cardboard; (arte) cartoon. ~ **animato** [animated] cartoon

car'tuccia f cartridge

'casa f house; (abitazione propria) home; (ditta) firm; **amico di** ~ family friend; **andare a** ~ go home; **essere di** ~ be like one of the family; **fatto in** ~ home-made; **padrone di** ~ (di pensione ecc) landlord; (proprietario) house owner. ~ **di cura** nursing home. ~ **popolare** council house. ~ **dello studente** hall of residence

ca'sacca f military coat; (giacca) jacket

ca'saccio adv **a** ~ at random

casa'ling|a f housewife. **~o** adj domestic; (fatto in casa) home-made; (amante della casa) home-loving; (semplice) homely

ca'scante adj falling; (floscio) flabby

ca'sca|re vi fall [down]. **~ta** f (di acqua) waterfall

ca'schetto m **[capelli a]** ~ bob

ca'scina f farm building

'casco m crash-helmet; (asciuga-capelli) [hair-]drier; ~ **di banane** bunch of bananas

caseggi'ato m apartment block

casei'ficio m dairy

ca'sella f pigeon-hole. ~ **postale** post office box; (Comput) mailbox

casel'lante mf (per treni) signalman

casel'lario m ~ **giudiziario** record of convictions; **avere il** ~ **giudiziario vergine** have no criminal record

ca'sello [autostra'dale] m [motorway] toll booth

case'reccio adj home-made

ca'serma f barracks pl; (dei carabinieri) [police] station

casi'nista mf 🅸 muddler. **ca'sino** m 🅸 (bordello) brothel; (fig: confusione) racket; (disordine) mess; **un casino di** loads of

casinò m inv casino

ca'sistica f (classificazione) case records pl

'caso m chance; (Gram, Med, fatto, circostanza) case; **a** ~ at random; ~ **mai** if need be; **far** ~ **a** pay attention to; **non far** ~ **a** take no account of; **per** ~ by chance. ~ **[giudiziario]** [legal] case

caso'lare m farmhouse

'caspita int good gracious!

'cassa f till; cash; (luogo di pagamento) cash desk; (mobile) chest; (istituto bancario) bank. ~ **automatica prelievi** cash dispenser, ATM. ~ **da morto** coffin. ~ **toracica** ribcage

🅲 *see* A-Z of Italian life and culture

C

cassa'forte f safe
cassa'panca f linen chest
casseru'ola f saucepan
cas'setta f case; (per registratore) cassette. ~ **delle lettere** letterbox. ~ **di sicurezza** strong-box
cas'set|to m drawer. ~**'tone** m chest of drawers
cassi'ere, -a mf cashier; (di supermercato) checkout assistant; (di banca) teller
'casta f caste
ca'stagn|a f chestnut. **casta'gneto** m chestnut grove. ~**o** m chestnut[-tree]
ca'stano adj chestnut
ca'stello m castle; (impalcatura) scaffold
casti'gare vt punish
casti'gato adj (casto) chaste
ca'stigo m punishment
castità f chastity. **'casto** adj chaste
ca'storo m beaver
ca'strare vt castrate
casu'al|e adj chance attrib. ~**'mente** adv by chance
ca'supola f little house
cata'clisma m fig upheaval
cata'comba f catacomb
cata'fascio m **andare a** ~ go to rack and ruin
cata'litico adj **marmitta catalitica** (Auto) catalytic converter
cataliz'za|re vt heighten. ~**'tore** m (Auto) catalytic converter
catalo'gare vt catalogue. **ca'talogo** m catalogue
catama'rano m (da diporto) catamaran
cata'pecchia f hovel; [!] dump
catapul'tar|e vt eject. ~**si** vr (precipitarsi) dive
catarifran'gente m reflector
ca'tarro m catarrh
ca'tasta f pile
ca'tasto m land register
ca'tastrofe f catastrophe. **cata'strofico** adj catastrophic
cate'chismo m catechism
cate|go'ria f category. ~**'gorico** adj categorical
ca'tena f chain. ~ **montuosa** mountain range. **catene** pl **da neve** tyre-chains. **cate'naccio** m bolt
cate'|nella f (collana) chain. ~**'nina** f chain
cate'ratta f cataract
ca'terva f **una** ~ **di** heaps of
cati'nell|a f basin; **piovere a** ~**e** bucket down
ca'tino m basin
ca'trame m tar
'cattedra f (tavolo di insegnante) desk; (di università) chair
catte'drale f cathedral
catti'veria f wickedness; (azione) wicked action
cattività f captivity
cat'tivo adj bad; (bambino) naughty
cattoli'cesimo m Catholicism
cat'tolico, -a adj & mf [Roman] Catholic
cat'tu|ra f capture. ~**'rare** vt capture
caucciù m rubber
'causa f cause; (Jur) lawsuit; **far** ~ **a qcno** sue sb. **cau'sare** vt cause
'caustico adj caustic
cauta'mente adv cautiously
cau'tela f caution
caute'lar|e vt protect. ~**si** vr take precautions
cauteriz'z|are vt cauterize. **cauterizzazi'one** f cauterization
'cauto adj cautious
cauzi'one f security; (per libertà provvisoria) bail
'cava f quarry; fig mine
caval'ca|re vt ride; (stare a cavalcioni) sit astride. ~**ta** f ride; (corteo) cavalcade. ~**'via** m flyover
cavalci'oni: **a** ~ adv astride
cavali'ere m rider; (titolo) knight; (accompagnatore) escort; (al ballo) partner
cavalle|'resco adj chivalrous. ~**'ria** f chivalry; (Mil) cavalry. ~**'rizzo, -a** m horseman • f horsewoman
caval'letta f grasshopper
caval'letto m trestle; (di macchina

fotografica) tripod; (di pittore) easel

caval'lina f (ginnastica) horse

ca'vallo m horse; (misura di potenza) horsepower; (scacchi) knight; (dei pantaloni) crotch; **a ~** on horseback; **andare a ~** go horse-riding. **~ a dondolo** rocking-horse

caval'lone m (ondata) roller

caval'luccio ma'rino m sea horse

ca'var|e vt take out; (di dosso) take off; **~sela** get away with it; **se la cava bene** he's doing all right

cava'tappi m inv corkscrew

ca'ver|na f cave. **~'noso** adj (voce) deep

'cavia f guinea-pig

cavi'ale m caviar

ca'viglia f ankle

cavil'lare vi quibble. **ca'villo** m quibble

cavità f inv cavity

'cavo adj hollow • m cavity; (di metallo) cable; (Naut) rope

cavo'lata f [!] rubbish

cavo'letto m **~ di Bruxelles** Brussels sprout

cavolfi'ore m cauliflower

'cavolo m cabbage; **~!** [!] sugar!

caz'zo int vulg fuck!

caz'zott|o m punch; **prendere qcno a ~i** beat sb up

cazzu'ola f trowel

c/c abbr (conto corrente) c/a

CD-Rom m inv CD-Rom

ce pers pron (a noi) (to) us • adv there; **~ ne sono molti** there are many

'cece m chick-pea

cecità f blindness

ceco, -a adj & mf Czech; **la Repubblica Ceca** the Czech Republic

'cedere vi (arrendersi) surrender; (concedere) yield; (sprofondare) subside • vt give up; make over (proprietà ecc). **ce'devole** adj (terreno ecc) soft; fig yielding. **cedi'mento** m (di terreno) subsidence

'cedola f coupon

'cedro m (albero) cedar; (frutto) citron

'ceffo m (muso) snout; (pej: persona) mug

cef'fone m slap

ce'lar|e vt conceal. **~si** vr hide

cele'bra|re vt celebrate. **~zi'one** f celebration

'celebr|e adj famous. **~ità** f inv celebrity

'celere adj swift

ce'leste adj (divino) heavenly • agg & m (colore) sky-blue

celi'bato m celibacy

'celibe adj single • m bachelor

'cella f cell

'cellofan m inv cellophane; (Culin) cling film

'cellula f cell. **~ fotoelettrica** electronic eye

cellu'lare m (telefono) cellular phone • adj **[furgone] ~** m police van. **[telefono] ~** m cellular phone

cellu'lite f cellulite

cellu'loide adj celluloid

cellu'losa f cellulose

'Celt|i mpl Celts. **~ico** adj Celtic

cemen'tare vt cement. **ce'mento** m cement. **cemento armato** reinforced concrete

[C] **'cena** f dinner; (leggera) supper

ce'nacolo m circle

ce'nare vi have dinner

'cenci|o m rag; (per spolverare) duster. **~'oso** adj in rags

'cenere f ash; (di carbone ecc) cinders

ce'netta f (cena semplice) informal dinner

'cenno m sign; (col capo) nod; (con la mano) wave; (allusione) hint; (breve resoconto) mention

ce'none m **il ~ di Capodanno/Natale** special New Year's Eve/Christmas Eve dinner

censi'mento m census

cen's|ore m censor. **~ura** f censorship. **~u'rare** vt censor

'cent m inv cent

centelli'nare vt sip

cente'n|ario, -a adj & mf

[C] *see A-Z of Italian life and culture*

centenarian •m centenary. ~'**nale** adj centennial

cen'tesimo adj hundredth •m (di moneta) cent; **non avere un ~** be penniless

cen'ti|grado adj centigrade. **~metro** m centimetre

centi'naio m hundred

'**cento** adj & m one or a hundred; **per ~** per cent

centome'trista mf Sport one hundred metres runner

cento'mila m one or a hundred thousand

cen'trale adj central •f (di società ecc) head office. **~ atomica** atomic power station. **~ elettrica** power station. **~ nucleare** nuclear power station. **~ telefonica** [telephone] exchange

centra'li|na f (Teleph) switchboard. **~'nista** mf operator

centra'lino m (Teleph) exchange; (di albergo ecc) switchboard

centra'li|smo m centralism. **~z'zare** vt centralize

cen'trare vt **~ qcsa** hit sth in the centre; (fissare nel centro) centre; fig hit on the head (idea)

cen'trifu|ga f spin-drier. **centrifuga [asciugaverdure]** shaker. **~'gare** vt centrifuge; (lavatrice:) spin

'**centro** m centre. **~ [città]** city centre. **~ commerciale** mall. **~ di accoglienza** reception centre. **~ sociale** community centre

'**ceppo** m (di albero) stump; (da ardere) log; (fig: gruppo) stock

'**cera** f wax; (aspetto) look. **~ per il pavimento** floor-polish

ce'ramica f (arte) ceramics; (materia) pottery; (oggetto) pot

ce'rato adj (tela) waxed

cerbi'atto m fawn

'**cerca** f **andare in ~ di** look for

cercaper'sone m inv beeper

cer'care vt look for •vi **~ di** try to

'**cerchi|a** f circle. **~'are** vt circle (parola). **~'ato** adj (occhi) black-ringed. **~'etto** m (per capelli) hairband

'**cerchi|o** m circle; (giocattolo) hoop. **~'one** m alloy wheel

cere'ale m cereal

cere'brale adj cerebral

'**cereo** adj waxen

ce'retta f depilatory wax

ceri'moni|a f ceremony. **~'ale** m ceremonial. **~'oso** adj ceremonious

ce'rino m [wax] match

cerni'era f hinge; (di borsa) clasp. **~ lampo** zip[-fastener], zipper Am

'**cernita** f selection

'**cero** m candle

ce'rone m grease-paint

ce'rotto m [sticking] plaster

certa'mente adv certainly

cer'tezza f certainty

certifi'ca|re vt certify. **~to** m certificate

'**certo** adj certain; (notizia) definite; (indeterminativo) some; **sono ~ di riuscire** I am certain to succeed; **certi giorni** some days; **un ~ signor Giardini** a Mr Giardini; **una certa Anna** somebody called Anna; **certa gente** pej some people; **ho certi dolori!** I'm in such pain!. **certi** pron pl some; (alcune persone) some people •adv of course; **sapere per ~** know for certain; **di ~** surely; **~ che sì!** of course!

cer'vello m brain.

'**cervo** m deer

ce'sareo adj (Med) Caesarean

cesel'la|re vt chisel. **~to** adj chiselled. **ce'sello** m chisel

ce'soie fpl shears

ce'spugli|o m bush. **~'oso** adj (terreno) bushy

ces'sa|re vi stop, cease •vt stop. **~te il fuoco** ceasefire

cessi'one f handover

'**cesso** m ☒ (gabinetto) bog, john Am; (fig: locale, luogo) dump

'**cesta** f [large] basket. **ce'stello** m (di lavatrice) drum

cesti'nare vt throw away. **ce'stino** m [small] basket; (per la carta straccia) waste-paper basket. **'cesto** m basket

'ceto m [social] class

'cetra f lyre

cetrio'lino m gherkin. **cetri'olo** m cucumber

cfr abbr (confronta) cf.

chat'tare vi (Comput) chat

che

- pron rel (*persona*: *soggetto*) who; (*persona*: *oggetto*) that, who, whom fml; (*cosa, animale*) that, which; **questa è la casa ~ ho comprato** this is the house [that] I've bought; **il ~ mi sorprende** which surprises me; **dal ~ deduco che...** from which I gather that...; **avere di ~ vivere** have enough to live on; **grazie! - non c'è di ~!** thank you! - don't mention it!; **il giorno ~ ti ho visto** [!] the day I saw you
- adj inter which, what; (*esclamativo*: *con aggettivo*) how; (*con nome*) what a; **~ macchina prendiamo, la tua o la mia?** which car are we taking, yours or mine?; **~ bello!** how nice!; **~ idea!** what an idea!; **~ bella giornata!** what a lovely day!
- pron inter what; **a ~ pensi?** what are you thinking about?
- conj that; (*con comparazioni*) than; **credo ~ abbia ragione** I think [that] he is right; **era così commosso ~ non riusciva a parlare** he was so moved [that] he couldn't speak; **aspetto ~ telefoni** I'm waiting for him to phone; **è da un po' ~ non lo vedo** it's been a while since I saw him; **mi piace più Roma ~ Milano** I like Rome better than Milan; **~ ti piaccia o no** whether you like it or not; **~ io sappia** as far as I know

checché indef pron whatever

chemiotera'pia f chemotherapy

chero'sene m paraffin

cheti'chella: **alla ~** adv silently

'cheto adj quiet

chi

- rel pron whoever; (*coloro che*) people who; **ho trovato ~ ti può aiutare** I found somebody who can help you; **c'è ~ dice che...** some people say that...; **senti ~ parla!** listen to who's talking!
- inter pron (*soggetto*) who; (*oggetto, con preposizione*) who, whom fml; (*possessivo*) **di ~** whose; **~ sei?** who are you?; **~ hai incontrato?** who did you meet?; **di ~ sono questi libri?** whose books are these?; **con ~ parli?** who are you talking to?; **a ~ lo dici!** tell me about it!

chi'acchie|ra f chat; (pettegolezzo) gossip. **~'rare** vi chat; (far pettegolezzi) gossip. **~'rato** adj **essere ~rato** (persona:) be the subject of gossip; **~re** pl chitchat; **far quattro ~re** have a chat. **~'rone, -a** adj talkative • mf chatterer

chia'ma|re vt call; (far venire) send for; **come ti chiami?** what's your name?; **mi chiamo Roberto** my name is Robert; **~re alle armi** call up. **~rsi** vr be called. **~ta** f call; (Mil) call-up

chi'appa f [!] cheek

chiara'mente adv clearly

chia'rezza f clarity; (limpidezza) clearness

chiarifi'ca|re vt clarify. **~'tore** adj clarificatory. **~zi'one** f clarification

chiari'mento m clarification

chia'rir|e vt make clear; (spiegare) clear up. **~si** vr become clear

chi'aro adj clear; (luminoso) bright; (colore) light. **chia'rore** m glimmer

chiaroveg'gente adj clear-sighted • mf clairvoyant

chi'as|so m din. **~'soso** adj rowdy

chi'av|e f key; **chiudere a ~e** lock. **~e inglese** spanner. **~i'stello** m latch

chiaz|za f stain. **~'zare** vt stain

chic adj inv chic

chicches'sia pron anybody

'chicco m grain; (di caffé) bean; (d'uva) grape

chi'eder|e vt ask; (per avere) ask for; (esigere) demand. **~si** vr wonder

C

C

chi'esa f church
chi'esto pp di **chiedere**
'chiglia f keel
'chilo m kilo
chilo'grammo m kilogram[me]
chilome'traggio m (Auto) ≈ mileage
chilo'metrico adj in kilometres
chi'lometro m kilometre
chi'mera f fig illusion
'chimic|a f chemistry. **~o, -a** adj chemical •mf chemist
'china f (declivio) slope; **inchiostro di ~** Indian ink
chi'nar|e vt lower. **~si** vr stoop
chincaglie'rie fpl knick-knacks
chinesitera'pia f physiotherapy
chi'nino m quinine
'chino adj bent
chi'notto m sparkling soft drink
chi'occia f sitting hen
chi'occiola f snail; (Comput) at sign; **scala a ~** spiral staircase
chi'odo m nail; (idea fissa) obsession. **~ di garofano** clove
chi'oma f head of hair; (fogliame) foliage
chi'osco m kiosk
chi'ostro m cloister
chiro'man|te mf palmist. **~'zia** f palmistry
chirur'gia f surgery. **chi'rurgico** adj surgical. **chi'rurgo** m surgeon
chissà adv who knows; **~ quando arriverà** I wonder when he will arrive
chi'tar|ra f guitar. **~'rista** mf guitarist
chi'uder|e vt close; (con la chiave) lock; turn off (luce, acqua); (per sempre) close down (negozio ecc); (recingere) enclose •vi shut, close. **~si** vr shut; (tempo:) cloud over; (ferita:) heal up.
chi'unque pron anyone, anybody •rel pron whoever
chi'usa f enclosure; (di canale) lock; (conclusione) close
chi'u|so pp di **chiudere** •adj shut; (tempo) overcast; (persona) reserved. **~'sura** f closing; (sistema) lock; (allacciatura) fastener. **~sura lampo** zip, zipper Am

ci

- pron (*personale*) us; (*riflessivo*) ourselves; (*reciproco*) each other; (*a ciò, di ciò ecc*) about it; **non ci disturbare** don't disturb us; **aspettateci** wait for us; **ci ha detto tutto** he told us everything; **ce lo manderanno** they'll send it to us; **ci consideriamo...** we consider ourselves...; **ci laviamo le mani** we wash our hands; **ci odiamo** we hate each other; **non ci penso mai** I never think about it; **pensaci!** think about it!
- adv (*qui*) here; (*lì*) there; (*moto per luogo*) through it; **ci siamo** we are here; **ci siete?** are you there?; **ci siamo passati tutti** we all went through it; **c'è** there is; **ce ne sono molti** there are many; **ci vuole pazienza** it takes patience; **non ci vedo/sento** I can't see/ hear

cia'bat|ta f slipper. **~'tare** vi shuffle
ciabat'tino m cobbler
ci'alda f wafer
cial'trone m scoundrel
ciam'bella f (Culin) ring-shaped cake; (salvagente) lifebelt; (gonfiabile) rubber ring
cianci'are vi gossip
cia'notico adj (colorito) puce
ci'ao int [!] (all' arrivo) hello!, hi!; (alla partenza) bye-bye!
ciar'la|re vi chat. **~'tano** m charlatan
cias'cuno adj each •pron everyone, everybody; (distributivo) each [one]; **per ~** each
ci'bar|e vt feed. **~ie** fpl provisions **~si** vr eat; **~si di** live on
ciber'netico adj cybernetic
'cibo m food
ci'cala f cicada
cica'lino m buzzer
cica'tri|ce f scar. **~z'zante** m ointment
cicatriz'zarsi vr heal [up]. **cicatrizzazi'one** f healing
'cicca f cigarette end; ([!]: sigaretta) fag; ([!]: gomma) [chewing] gum
cic'chetto m [!] (bicchierino) nip; (rimprovero) telling-off
'ciccia f fat, flab

cice'rone m guide
cicla'mino m cyclamen
ci'clis|mo m cycling. **~ta** mf cyclist
'ciclo m cycle; (di malattia) course
ciclomo'tore m moped
ci'clone m cyclone
ci'cogna f stork
ci'coria f chicory
ci'eco, -a adj blind •m blind man •f blind woman
ci'elo m sky; (Relig) heaven; **santo ~!** good heavens!
'cifra f figure; (somma) sum; (monogramma) monogram; (codice) code
ci'fra|re vt embroider with a monogram; (codificare) code. **~to** adj monogrammed; coded
'ciglio m (bordo) edge; (pl f **ciglia**: delle palpebre) eyelash
'cigno m swan
cigo'l|are vt squeak. **~io** m squeak
'Cile m Chile
ci'lecca f **far ~** miss
ci'leno, -a adj & mf Chilean
cili'egi|a f cherry. **~o** m cherry [tree]
cilin'drata f cubic capacity; **macchina di alta ~** highpowered car
ci'lindro m cylinder; (cappello) top hat
'cima f top; (fig: persona) genius; **da ~ a fondo** from top to bottom
ci'melio m relic
cimen'tar|e vt put to the test. **~si** vr (provare) try one's hand
'cimice f bug; (puntina) drawing pin, thumbtack Am
cimini'era f chimney; (Naut) funnel
cimi'tero m cemetery
ci'murro m distemper
'Cina f China
cin cin! int cheers!
cincischi'are vi fiddle
'cine m [!] cinema
cine'asta mf film maker
'cinema m inv cinema. **cine'presa** f cine-camera
ci'nese adj & mf Chinese
cine'teca f film collection
'cingere vt (circondare) surround
'cinghia f strap; (cintura) belt
cinghi'ale m wild boar; **pelle di ~** pigskin
cinguet't|are vi twitter. **~io** m twittering
'cinico adj cynical
ci'niglia f (tessuto) chenille
ci'nismo m cynicism
ci'nofilo adj dog-loving
cin'quanta adj & m fifty. **cinquan'tenne** adj & mf fifty-year-old. **cinquan'tesimo** adj fiftieth. **cinquan'tina** f **una cinquantina di** about fifty
'cinque adj & m five
cinquecen'tesco adj sixteenth-century
cinque'cento adj five hundred •m **il C~** the sixteenth century
cinque'mila adj & m five thousand
'cinta f (di pantaloni) belt; **muro di ~** [boundary] wall. **cin'tare** vt enclose
'cintola f (di pantaloni) belt
cin'tura f belt. **~ di salvataggio** lifebelt. **~ di sicurezza** (Aeron, Auto) seat-belt
cintu'rino m **~ dell'orologio** watch-strap
ciò pron this; that; **~ che** what; **~ nondimeno** nevertheless
ci'occa f lock
ciocco'la|ta f chocolate; (bevanda) [hot] chocolate. **~'tino** m chocolate. **~to** m chocolate. **~to al latte/ fondente** milk/plain chocolate
cioè adv that is
ciondo'lare vi dangle. **ci'ondolo** m pendant
ciono'stante adv nonetheless
ci'otola f bowl
ci'ottolo m pebble
ci'polla f onion; (bulbo) bulb
ci'presso m cypress
'cipria f [face] powder
'Cipro m Cyprus. **cipri'ota** adj & mf Cypriot
'circa adv & prep about
'circo m circus
circo'la|re adj circular •f circular; (di

metropolitana) circle line • vi circulate. ~'**torio** adj (Med) circulatory. ~**zi'one** f circulation; (traffico) traffic

'**circolo** m circle; (società) club

circon'ci|dere vt circumcise. ~**si'one** f circumcision

circon'dar|e vt surround. ~**io** m (amministrativo) administrative district. ~**si di** vr surround oneself with

circonfe'renza f circumference. ~ **dei fianchi** hip measurement

circonvallazi'one f ring road

circo'scritto adj limited

circoscrizi'one f area. ~ **elettorale** constituency

circo'spetto adj wary

circospezi'one f **con** ~ warily

circo'stante adj surrounding

circo'stanza f circumstance; (occasione) occasion

circu'ire vt (ingannare) trick

cir'cuito m circuit

circumnavi'ga|re vt circumnavigate. ~**zi'one** f circumnavigation

ci'sterna f cistern; (serbatoio) tank

'**cisti** f inv cyst

ci'ta|re vt quote; (come esempio) cite; (Jur) summons. ~**zi'one** f quotation; (Jur) summons sg

citofo'nare vt buzz. **ci'tofono** m entry phone; (in ufficio, su aereo ecc) intercom

ci'trullo, -a mf [!] dimwit

città f inv town; (grande) city

citta'della f citadel

citta|di'nanza f citizenship; (popolazione) citizens pl. ~'**dino, -a** mf citizen; (abitante di città) city dweller

ciucci'are vt [!] suck. **ci'uccio** m [!] dummy

ci'uffo m tuft

ci'urma f (Naut) crew

ci'vet|ta f owl; (fig: donna) flirt; [**auto**] ~**ta** unmarked police car. ~'**tare** vi flirt. ~**te'ria** f coquettishness

'**civico** adj civic

ci'vil|e adj civil. ~**iz'zare** vt civilize. ~**iz'zato** adj (paese) civilized. ~**izzazi'one** f civilization. ~'**mente** adv civilly

civiltà f inv civilization; (cortesia) civility

'**clacson** m inv (car) horn

clacsonare vi hoot; honk

cla'mo|re m clamour; **fare** ~**re** cause a sensation. ~**rosa'mente** adv (sbagliare) sensationally. ~'**roso** adj noisy; (sbaglio) sensational

clan m inv clan; fig clique

clandestinità f secrecy

clande'stino adj secret; **movimento** ~ underground movement; **passeggero** ~ stowaway

clari'netto m clarinet

'**classe** f class. ~ **turistica** tourist class

classi'cis|mo m classicism. ~**ta** mf classicist

'**classico** adj classical; (tipico) classic • m classic

clas'sifi|ca f classification; Sport results pl. ~'**care** vt classify. ~'**carsi** vr be placed. ~**ca'tore** m (cartella) folder. ~**cazi'one** f classification

clas'sista mf class-conscious person

'**clausola** f clause

claustro|fo'bia f claustrophobia. ~'**fobico** adj claustrophobic

clau'sura f (Relig) enclosed order

clavi'cembalo m harpsichord

cla'vicola f collar-bone

cle'men|te adj merciful; (tempo) mild. ~**za** f mercy

cleri'cale adj clerical. '**clero** m clergy

clic m (Comput) click; **fare** ~ **su** click on; **fare doppio** ~ **su** double-click on

clic'care vi click (**su** on)

cli'en|te mf client; (di negozio) customer. ~'**tela** f customers pl

'**clima** m climate. **cli'matico** adj climatic; **stazione climatica** health resort

'**clinica** f clinic. **clinico** adj clinical • m clinician

clo'na|re vt clone. ~'**zione** f cloning

'**cloro** m chlorine

clou adj inv **i momenti** ~ the highlights

coabi'ta|re vi live together. **~zi'one** f cohabitation

coagu'la|re vt, **~rsi** vr coagulate. **~zi'one** f coagulation

coaliz|i'one f coalition. **~'zarsi** vr unite

co'atto adj (Jur) compulsory

'cobra m inv cobra

coca'ina f cocaine. **cocai'nomane** mf cocaine addict

cocci'nella f ladybird

'coccio m earthenware; (frammento) fragment

cocci|u'taggine f stubbornness. **~'uto** adj stubborn

'cocco m coconut palm; ⚠ love; **noce di ~** coconut

cocco'drillo m crocodile

cocco'lare vt cuddle

co'cente adj (sole) burning

'cocktail m inv (ricevimento) cocktail party

co'comero m watermelon

co'cuzzolo m top; (di testa, cappello) crown

'coda f tail; (di abito) train; (fila) queue; **fare la ~** queue [up], stand in line Am. **~ di cavallo** (acconciatura) ponytail.

co'dardo, -a adj cowardly • mf coward

'codice m code. **~ di avviamento postale** postal code, zip code Am. **~ a barre** bar-code. 🅲 **~ fiscale** tax code. **~ della strada** highway code.

codifi'care vt codify

coe'ren|te adj consistent. **~za** f consistency

coesi'one f cohesion

coe'taneo, -a adj & mf contemporary

cofa'netto m casket. **'cofano** m chest; (Auto) bonnet, hood Am

'cogliere vt pick; (sorprendere) catch; (afferrare) seize; (colpire) hit

co'gnato, -a mf brother-in-law; sister-in-law

cognizi'one f knowledge

co'gnome m surname

'coi = **con + i**

coinci'denza f coincidence; (di treno ecc) connection

coin'cidere vi coincide

coinqui'lino m flatmate

coin'vol|gere vt involve. **~gi'mento** m involvement. **~to** adj involved

'coito m coitus

col = **con + il**

colà adv there

cola|'brodo m inv strainer; **ridotto a un ~brodo** ⚠ full of holes. **~'pasta** m inv colander

co'la|re vt strain; (versare lentamente) drip • vi (gocciolare) drip; (perdere) leak; **~re a picco** (Naut) sink. **~ta** f (di metallo) casting; (di lava) flow

colazi'one f (del mattino) breakfast; (di mezzogiorno) lunch; **prima ~** breakfast; **far ~** have breakfast/lunch. **~ al sacco** packed lunch

co'lei pron f the one

co'lera m cholera

coleste'rolo m cholesterol

colf f abbr (collaboratrice familiare) home help

'colica f colic

co'lino m [tea] strainer

'colla f glue; (di farina) paste. **~ di pesce** gelatine

collabo'ra|re vi collaborate. **~'tore, ~'trice** mf collaborator. **~zi'one** f collaboration

col'lana f necklace; (serie) series

col'lant m inv tights pl

col'lare m collar

col'lasso m collapse

collau'dare vt test. **col'laudo** m test

'colle m hill

col'lega mf colleague

collega'mento m connection; (Mil) liaison; Radio link; **~ ipertestuale** hypertext link. **colle'gar|e** vt connect. **~si** vr link up

collegi'ale mf boarder • adj (responsabilità, decisione) collective

col'legio m (convitto) boarding-school. **~ elettorale** constituency

'collera f anger; **andare in ~** get

🅲 *see* A-Z of Italian life and culture

angry. **col'lerico** adj irascible

col'letta f collection

collet|tività f inv community. **~'tivo** adj collective; (interesse) general; **biglietto ~tivo** group ticket

C

col'letto m collar

collezi|o'nare vt collect. **~'one** f collection. **~o'nista** mf collector

colli'mare vi coincide

col'li|na f hill. **~'noso** adj (terreno) hilly

col'lirio m eyewash

collisi'one f collision

'collo m neck; (pacco) package; **a ~ alto** high-necked. **~ del piede** instep

colloca'mento m placing; (impiego) employment

collo'ca|re vt place. **~rsi** vr take one's place. **~zi'one** f placing

colloqui'ale adj (termine) colloquial. **col'loquio** m conversation; (udienza ecc) interview; (esame) oral [exam]

collusi'one f collusion

colluttazi'one f scuffle

col'mare vt fill [to the brim]; bridge (divario); **~ qcno di gentilezze** overwhelm sb with kindness. **'colmo** adj full • m top; fig height; **al colmo della disperazione** in the depths of despair; **questo è il colmo!** (con indignazione) this is the last straw!; (con stupore) I don't believe it!

co'lomb|a f dove. **~o** m pigeon

co'loni|a[1] f colony; **~a [estiva]** (per bambini) holiday camp. **~'ale** adj colonial

co'lonia[2] f **[acqua di] ~** [eau de] Cologne

co'lonico adj (terreno, casa) farm

coloniz'za|re vt colonize. **~'tore, ~'trice** mf colonizer

co'lon|na f column. **~na sonora** sound-track. **~na vertebrale** spine. **~'nato** m colonnade

colon'nello m colonel

co'lono m tenant farmer

colo'rante m colouring

colo'rare vt colour; colour in (disegno)

co'lore m colour; **a colori** in colour; **di ~** coloured. **colo'rito** adj coloured; (viso) rosy; (racconto) colourful • m complexion

co'loro pron pl the ones

colos'sale adj colossal. **co'losso** m colossus

'colpa f fault; (biasimo) blame; (colpevolezza) guilt; (peccato) sin; **dare la ~ a** blame; **essere in ~** be at fault; **per ~ di** because of. **col'pevole** adj guilty • mf culprit

col'pire vt hit, strike

'colpo m blow; (di arma da fuoco) shot; (urto) knock; (emozione) shock; (Med, Sport) stroke; (furto) raid; **di ~** suddenly; **far ~** make a strong impression; **far venire un ~ a qcno** fig give sb a fright; **perdere colpi** (motore:) keep missing; **a ~ d'occhio** at a glance; **a ~ sicuro** for certain. **~ d'aria** chill. **~ di sole** sunstroke; **colpi di sole** (su capelli) highlights. **~ di stato** coup [d'état]. **~ di telefono** ring; **dare un ~ di telefono a qn** give sb a ring. **~ di testa** [sudden] impulse. **~ di vento** gust of wind

col'poso adj **omicidio ~** manslaughter

coltel'lata f stab. **col'tello** m knife

colti'va|re vt cultivate. **~'tore, ~'trice** mf farmer. **~zi'one** f farming; (di piante) growing

'colto pp di **cogliere** • adj cultured

'coltre f blanket

col'tura f cultivation

co'lui pron inv m the one

'coma m coma; **in ~** in a coma

comanda'mento m commandment

coman'dante m commander; (Aeron, Naut) captain

coman'dare vt command; (Mech) control • vi be in charge. **co'mando** m command; (di macchina) control

co'mare f (madrina) godmother

combaci'are vi fit together; (testimonianze:) concur

combat'tente adj fighting • m combatant. **ex ~** ex-serviceman

com'bat|tere vt/i fight. **~ti'mento** m fight; (Mil) battle; **fuori ~timento** (pugilato) knocked out.

~'**tuto** adj (gara) hard fought

combi'na|re vt/i arrange; (mettere insieme) combine; (!: fare) do; **cosa stai ~ndo?** what are you doing?. **~rsi** vr combine; (mettersi d'accordo) come to an agreement. **~zi'one** f combination; (caso) coincidence; **per ~zione** by chance

com'briccola f gang

combu'sti|bile adj combustible • m fuel. **~'one** f combustion

com'butta f gang; **in ~** in league

'come

• adv like; (*in qualità di*) as; (*interrogativo, esclamativo*) how; **questo vestito è ~ il tuo** this dress is like yours; **~ stai?** how are you?; **~ va?** how are things?; **~ mai?** how come?; **~?** what?; **non sa ~ fare** he doesn't know what to do; **~ sta bene!** how well he looks!; **~ no!** that will be right!; **~ tu sai** as you know; **fa ~ vuoi** do as you like; **~ se** as if

• conj (*non appena*) as soon as

co'meta f comet

'comico, -a adj comic • m funny side • mf (attore) comedian • f (a torte in faccia) slapstick sketch

co'mignolo m chimney-pot

cominci'are vt/i begin, start; **a ~ da oggi** from today.

comi'tato m committee

comi'tiva f party, group

co'mizio m meeting

com'mando m inv commando

com'medi|a f comedy; (opera teatrale) play; fig sham. **~a musicale** musical. **~'ante** mf comedian; fig pej phoney. **~'ografo, -a** mf playwright

commemo'ra|re vt commemorate. **~zi'one** f commemoration

commen'sale mf fellow diner

commen't|are vt comment on; (annotare) annotate. **~ario** m commentary. **~a'tore, ~a'trice** mf commentator. **com'mento** m comment

commerci'a|le adj commercial; (relazioni, trattative) trade; (attività) business. **centro ~le** shopping centre. **~'lista** mf business consultant; (contabile) accountant. **~liz'zare** vt market. **~lizzazi'one** f marketing

commerci'ante mf trader; (negoziante) shopkeeper. **~ all'ingrosso** wholesaler

commerci'are vi **~ in** deal in

com'mercio m commerce; (internazionale) trade; (affari) business; **in ~** (prodotto) on sale. **~ all'ingrosso** wholesale trade. **~ al minuto** retail trade

com'messo, -a pp di **commettere** • mf shop assistant. **~ viaggiatore** commercial traveller • f (ordine) order

comme'stibile adj edible. **commestibili** mpl groceries

com'mettere vt commit; make (sbaglio)

commi'ato m leave; **prendere ~ da** take leave of

commise'rar|e vt commiserate with. **~si** vr feel sorry for oneself

commissari'ato m (di polizia) police station

commis's|ario m [police] superintendent; (membro di commissione) commissioner; Sport steward; (Comm) commission agent. **~ario d'esame** examiner. **~i'one** f (incarico) errand; (comitato ecc) commission; (Comm: di merce) order; **~ioni** pl (acquisti) **fare ~ioni** go shopping. **~ione d'esame** board of examiners. **C~ione Europea** European Commission

commit'tente mf purchaser

com'mo|sso pp di **commuovere** • adj moved. **~'vente** adj moving

commozi'one f emotion. **~ cerebrale** concussion

commu'over|e vt touch, move. **~si** vr be touched

commu'tare vt change; (Jur) commute

comò m inv chest of drawers

comoda'mente adv comfortably

como'dino m bedside table

comodità f inv comfort; (convenienza) convenience

'comodo adj comfortable; (conveniente) convenient; (spazioso) roomy; (facile) easy; **stia ~!** don't get up!; **far ~** be useful •m comfort; **fare il proprio ~** do as one pleases

C

compae'sano, -a mf fellow countryman

com'pagine f (squadra) team

compa'gnia f company; (gruppo) party; **fare ~ a qcno** keep sb company; **essere di ~** be sociable. **~ aerea** airline

com'pagno, -a mf companion; (Comm, Sport, in coppia) partner; (Pol) comrade. **~ di scuola** schoolmate

compa'rabile adj comparable

compa'ra|re vt compare. **~'tivo** adj & m comparative. **~zi'one** f comparison

com'pare m (padrino) godfather; (testimone di matrimonio) witness

compa'rire vi appear; (spiccare) stand out; **~ in giudizio** appear in court

com'parso, -a pp di **comparire** •f appearance; Cinema extra

compartecipazi'one f sharing; (quota) share

comparti'mento m compartment; (amministrativo) department

compas'sato adj calm and collected

compassi'o|ne f compassion; **aver ~ne per** feel pity for; **far ~ne** arouse pity. **~'nevole** adj compassionate

com'passo m [pair of] compasses pl

compa'tibil|e adj (conciliabile) compatible; (scusabile) excusable. **~ità** f compatibility. **~'mente** adv **~mente con i miei impegni** if my commitments allow

compa'tire vt pity; (scusare) make allowances for

compat'tezza f (di materia) compactness. **com'patto** adj compact; (denso) dense; (solido) solid; fig united

compene'trare vt pervade

compen'sar|e vt compensate; (supplire) make up for. **~si** vr balance each other out

compen'sato m (legno) plywood

compensazi'one f compensation

com'penso m compensation; (retribuzione) remuneration; **in ~** (in cambio) in return; (d'altra parte) on the other hand; (invece) instead

'comper|a f purchase; **far ~e** do some shopping

compe'rare vt buy

compe'ten|te adj competent. **~za** f competence; (responsabilità) responsibility

com'petere vi compete; **~ a** (compito:) be the responsibility of

competi|tività f competitiveness. **~'tivo** adj (prezzo, carattere) competitive. **~'tore, ~'trice** mf competitor. **~zi'one** f competition

compia'cen|te adj obliging. **~za** f obligingness

compia'c|ere vt/i please. **~ersi** vr (congratularsi) congratulate. **~ersi di** (degnarsi) condescend. **~i'mento** m satisfaction; pej smugness. **~i'uto** adj satisfied; (aria, sorriso) smug

compi'an|gere vt pity; (per lutto ecc) sympathize with. **~to** adj lamented •m grief

'compier|e vt (concludere) complete; commit (delitto); **~e gli anni** have one's birthday. **~si** vr end; (avverarsi) come true

compi'la|re vt compile; fill in (modulo). **~zi'one** f compilation

compi'mento m **portare a ~ qcsa** conclude sth

com'pire vt = **compiere**

compi'tare vt spell

com'pito[1] adj poilte

'compito[2] m task; (Sch) homework

compi'ut|o adj **avere 30 anni ~i** be over 30

comple'anno m birthday

complemen'tare adj complementary; (secondario) subsidiary

comple'mento m complement; (Mil) draft. **~ oggetto** direct object

comples|sità f complexity. **~siva'mente** adv on the whole. **~'sivo** adj comprehensive; (totale) total. **com'plesso** adj complex; (difficile) complicated •m complex; (di cantanti ecc) group; (di circostanze, fattori) combination; **in ~so** on the whole

completa'mente adv completely

comple'tare vt complete

com'pleto adj complete; (pieno) full [up]; **essere al ~** (teatro:) be sold out; **la famiglia al ~** the whole family • m (vestito) suit; (insieme di cose) set

compli'ca|re vt complicate. **~rsi** vr become complicated. **~to** complicated. **~zi'one** f complication; **salvo ~zioni** all being well

'complic|e mf accomplice • adj (sguardo) knowing. **~ità** f complicity

complimen'tar|e vt compliment. **~si** vr **~si con** congratulate

compli'menti mpl (ossequi) regards; (congratulazioni) congratulations; **far ~** stand on ceremony

compli'mento m compliment

complot'tare vi plot

compo'nente adj & m component • mf member

compo'nibile adj (cucina) fitted; (mobili) modular

componi'mento m composition; (letterario) work

com'por|re vt compose; (ordinare) put in order; (Typ) set. **~si** vr **~si di** be made up of

comporta'mento m behaviour

compor'tar|e vt involve; (consentire) allow. **~si** vr behave

composi|'tore, -'trice mf composer; (Typ) compositor. **~zi'one** f composition

com'posta f stewed fruit; (concime) compost

compo'stezza f composure

com'posto pp di **comporre** • adj composed; (costituito) comprising; **stai ~!** sit properly! • m (Chem) compound

com'pra|re vt buy. **~'tore, ~'trice** mf buyer

compra'vendita f buying and selling

com'pren|dere vt understand; (includere) comprise. **~'sibile** adj understandable. **~sibil'mente** adv understandably. **~si'one** f understanding. **~'sivo** adj understanding; (che include) inclusive. **com'preso** pp di **comprendere** • adj included; **tutto compreso** (prezzo) all-in

com'pressa f compress; (pastiglia) tablet

compressi'one f compression. **com'presso** pp di **comprimere** • adj compressed

com'primere vt press; (reprimere) repress

compro'me|sso pp di **compromettere** • m compromise. **~t'tente** adj compromising. **~ttere** vt compromise

comproprietà f multiple ownership

compro'vare vt prove

compu'tare vt calculate

com'puter m inv computer. **~iz'zare** vt computerize. **~iz'zato** adj computerized

computiste'ria f book-keeping. **'computo** m calculation

comu'nale adj municipal

co'mune adj common; (condiviso) mutual; (ordinario) ordinary • m borough; (amministrativo) commune; **fuori del ~** extraordinary. **~'mente** adv commonly

comuni'ca|re vt communicate; pass on (malattia); (Relig) administer Communion to. **~rsi** vr receive Communion. **~'tiva** f communicativeness. **~'tivo** adj communicative. **~to** m communiqué. **~to stampa** press release. **~zi'one** f communication; (Teleph) [phone] call; **avere la ~zione** get through; **dare la ~zione a qcno** put sb through

comuni'one f communion; (Relig) [Holy] Communion

comu'nis|mo m communism. **~ta** adj & mf communist

comunità f inv community. **C~ [Economica] Europea** European [Economic] Community

co'munque conj however • adv anyhow

con prep with; (mezzo) by; **~ facilità** easily; **~ mia grande gioia** to my great delight; **è gentile ~ tutti** he is kind to everyone; **col treno** by train; **~ questo tempo** in this weather

co'nato m **~ di vomito** retching

'conca f basin; (valle) dell

C

concate'na|re vt link together. **~zi'one** f connection

'concavo adj concave

con'ceder|e vt grant; award (premio); (ammettere) admit. **~si** vr allow oneself (pausa)

concentra'mento m concentration

concen'tra|re vt, **~rsi** vr concentrate. **~to** adj concentrated •m **~to di pomodoro** tomato pureé. **~zi'one** f concentration

concepi'mento m conception

conce'pire vt conceive (bambino); (capire) understand; (figurarsi) conceive of; devise (piano ecc)

con'cernere vt concern

concer'tar|e vt (Mus) harmonize; (organizzare) arrange. **~si** vr agree

concer'tista mf concert performer. **con'certo** m concert; (composizione) concerto

concessio'nario m agent

concessi'one f concession

con'cesso pp di **concedere**

con'cetto m concept; (opinione) opinion

concezi'one f conception; (idea) concept

con'chiglia f [sea] shell

'concia f tanning; (di tabacco) curing

conci'a|re vt tan; cure (tabacco); **~re qcno per le feste** give sb a good hiding. **~rsi** vr (sporcarsi) get dirty; (vestirsi male) dress badly. **~to** adj (pelle, cuoio) tanned

concili'abile adj compatible

concili'a|re vt reconcile; settle (contravvenzione); (favorire) induce. **~rsi** vr go together; (mettersi d'accordo) become reconciled. **~zi'one** f reconciliation; (Jur) settlement

con'cilio m (Relig) council; (riunione) assembly

conci'mare vt feed (pianta). **con'cime** m fertilizer; (chimico) fertilizer

concisi'one f conciseness. **con'ciso** adj concise

conci'tato adj excited

concitta'dino, -a mf fellow citizen

con'clu|dere vt conclude; (finire con successo) achieve. **~dersi** vr come to an end. **~si'one** f conclusion; **in ~sione** (insomma) in short. **~'sivo** adj conclusive. **~so** pp di **concludere**

concomi'tanza f (di circostanze, fatti) combination

concor'da|nza f agreement. **~re** vt agree; (Gram) make agree. **~to** m agreement; (Comm, Jur) arrangement

con'cord|e adj in agreement; (unanime) unanimous

concor'ren|te adj concurrent; (rivale) competing •mf (Comm), Sport competitor; (candidato) candidate. **~za** f competition. **~zi'ale** adj competitive

con'cor|rere vi (contribuire) concur; (andare insieme) go together; (competere) compete. **~so** pp di **concorrere** •m competition; **fuori ~so** not in the official competition. **~so di bellezza** beauty contest

concreta'mente adv specifically

concre|'tare vt (concludere) achieve. **~tiz'zare** vt put into concrete form (idea, progetto)

con'creto adj concrete; **in ~** in concrete terms

concussi'one f extortion

con'danna f sentence; **pronunziare una ~** pass a sentence. **condan'nare** vt condemn; (Jur) sentence. **condan'nato, -a** mf convict

conden'sa|re vt, **~rsi** vr condense. **~zi'one** f condensation

condi'mento m seasoning; (salsa) dressing. **con'dire** vt flavour; dress (insalata)

condiscen'den|te adj indulgent; pej condescending. **~za** f indulgence; pej condescension

condi'videre vt share

condizio'na|le adj & m conditional •f (Jur) suspended sentence

condizio'na|re vt condition. **~to** adj conditional. **~'tore** m air conditioner

condizi'one f condition; **a ~ che** on condition that

condogli'anze fpl condolences; **fare le ~ a** offer condolences to

condomini'ale adj (spese) common. **condo'minio** m joint ownership;

(edificio) condominium

condo'nare vt remit. **con'dono** m remission

con'dotta f conduct, (circoscrizione di medico) district; (di gara ecc) management; (tubazione) piping

con'dotto pp di **condurre** • adj **medico ~** district doctor • m pipe; (Anat) duct

condu'cente m driver

con'du|rre vt lead; drive (veicoli); (accompagnare) take; conduct (gas, elettricità ecc); (gestire) run. **~rsi** vr behave. **~t'tore, ~t'trice** mf (TV) presenter; (di veicolo) driver • m (Electr) conductor. **~t'tura** f duct

confabu'lare vi have a confab

confa'cente adj suitable. **con'farsi** vr **confarsi a** suit

confederazi'one f confederation

confe'renz|a f (discorso) lecture; (congresso) conference. **~a stampa** news conference. **~i'ere, -a** mf lecturer

confe'rire vt (donare) give • vi confer

con'ferma f confirmation. **confer'mare** vt confirm

confes's|are vt, **~arsi** vr confess. **~io'nale** adj & m confessional. **~i'one** f confession. **~ore** m confessor

con'fetto m sugared almond

confet'tura f jam

confezio'na|re vt manufacture; make (abiti); package (merci). **~to** adj (vestiti) off-the-peg; (gelato) wrapped

confezi'one f manufacture; (di abiti) tailoring; (di pacchi) packaging; **confezioni** pl clothes. **~ regalo** gift pack

confic'car|e vt thrust. **~si** vr run into

confi'd|are vi **~are in** trust • vt confide. **~arsi** vr **~arsi con** confide in. **~ente** adj confident • mf confidant

confi'denz|a f confidence; (familiarità) familiarity; **prendersi delle ~e** take liberties. **~i'ale** adj confidential; (rapporto, tono) familiar

configu'ra|re vt (Comput) configure. **~zi'one** f configuration

confi'nante adj neighbouring

confi'na|re vi (relegare) confine • vi **~re con** border on. **~rsi** vr withdraw. **~to** adj confined

con'fin|e m border; (tra terreni) boundary. **~o** m political exile

con'fi|sca f (di proprietà) forfeiture. **~'scare** vt confiscate

con'flitt|o m conflict. **~u'ale** adj adversarial

conflu'enza f confluence; (di strade) junction

conflu'ire vi (fiumi:) flow together; (strade:) meet

con'fonder|e vt confuse; (turbare) confound; (imbarazzare) embarrass. **~si** vr (mescolarsi) mingle; (turbarsi) become confused; (sbagliarsi) be mistaken

confor'ma|re vt adapt. **~rsi** vr conform. **~zi'one** f conformity (**a** with); (del terreno) composition

con'forme adj according. **~'mente** adv accordingly

confor'mi|smo m conformity. **~sta** mf conformist. **~tà** f (a norma) conformity

confor'tante adj comforting

confor't|are vt comfort. **~evole** adj (comodo) comfortable. **con'forto** m comfort

confron'tare vt compare

con'fronto m comparison; **in ~ a** by comparison with; **nei tuoi confronti** towards you; **senza ~** far and away

confusi|o'nario adj (persona) muddle-headed. **~'one** f confusion; (baccano) racket; (disordine) mess; (imbarazzo) embarrassment. **con'fuso** pp di **confondere** • adj confused; (indistinto) indistinct; (imbarazzato) embarrassed

conge'dar|e vt dismiss; (Mil) discharge. **~si** vr take one's leave

con'gedo m leave; **essere in ~** be on leave. **~ malattia** sick leave. **~ maternità** maternity leave

conge'gnare vt devise; (mettere insieme) assemble. **con'gegno** m device

congela'mento m freezing; (Med) frost-bite

conge'la|re vt freeze. **~to** adj (cibo) deep-frozen. **~'tore** m freezer

C

C

congeni'ale adj congenial
con'genito adj congenital
congestio'na|re vt congest. **~to** adj (traffico) congested. **congesti'one** f congestion
conget'tura f conjecture
congi'unger|e vt join; combine (sforzi). **~si** vr join
congiunti'vite f conjunctivitis
congiun'tivo m subjunctive
congi'unto pp di **congiungere** •adj joined •m relative
congiun'tu|ra f joint; (circostanza) juncture; (situazione) situation. **~'rale** adj economic
congiunzi'one f conjunction
congi'u|ra f conspiracy. **~'rare** vi conspire
conglome'rato m conglomerate; fig conglomeration; (da costruzione) concrete
congratu'la|rsi vr **~rsi con qcno per** congratulate sb on. **~zi'oni** fpl congratulations
con'grega f band
congre'ga|re vt, **~rsi** vr congregate. **~zi'one** f congregation
con'gresso m congress
'congruo adj proper; (giusto) fair
conguagli'are vt balance. **congu'aglio** m balance
coni'are vt coin
'conico adj conical
co'nifera f conifer
co'niglio m rabbit
coniu'gale adj marital; (vita) married
coniu'ga|re vt conjugate. **~rsi** vr get married. **~zi'one** f conjugation
'coniuge mf spouse
connessi'one f connection. **con'nesso** pp di **connettere**
con'netter|e vt connect •vi think rationally. **~rsi** vr go online
conni'vente adj conniving
conno'ta|re vt connote. **~to** m distinguishing feature; **~ti** pl description
con'nubio m fig union
'cono m cone
cono'scen|te mf acquaintance. **~za** f knowledge; (persona) acquaintance; (sensi) consciousness; **perdere ~za** lose consciousness; **riprendere ~za** regain consciousness
co'nosc|ere vt know; (essere a conoscenza di) be acquainted with; (fare la conoscenza di) meet. **~i'tore, ~i'trice** mf connoisseur. **~i'uto** pp di **conoscere** •adj well-known
con'quist|a f conquest. **conqui'stare** vt conquer; fig win
consa'cra|re vt consecrate; ordain (sacerdote); (dedicare) dedicate. **~rsi** vr devote oneself
consangu'ineo, -a mf bloodrelation
consa'pevo|le adj conscious. **~'lezza** f consciousness. **~l'mente** adv consciously
'conscio adj conscious
consecu'tivo adj consecutive; (seguente) next
con'segna f delivery; (merce) consignment; (custodia) care; (di prigioniero) handover; (Mil: ordine) orders pl; (Mil: punizione) confinement; **pagamento alla ~** cash on delivery
conse'gnare vt deliver; (affidare) give in charge; (Mil) confine to barracks
consegu'en|te adj consequent. **~za** f consequence; **di ~za** (perciò) consequently
consegui'mento m achievement
consegu'ire vt achieve •vi follow
con'senso m consent
consensu'ale adj consensus-based
consen'tire vi consent •vt allow
con'serva f preserve; (di frutta) jam; (di agrumi) marmalade. **~ di pomodoro** tomato sauce
conser'var|e vt preserve; (mantenere) keep. **~si** vr keep; **~si in salute** keep well
conserva|'tore, -'trice mf (Pol) conservative
conserva'torio m conservatory
conservazi'one f preservation; **a lunga ~** long-life
conside'ra|re vt consider; (stimare) regard. **~to** adj (stimato) esteemed. **~zi'one** f consideration; (osservazione, riflessione) remark

conside'revole adj considerable
consigli'abile adj advisable
consigli|'are vt advise; (raccomandare) recommend. **~'arsi** vr **~arsi con qcno** ask sb's advice. **~'ere, -a** mf adviser; (membro di consiglio) councillor
con'siglio m advice; (ente) council. **~ d'amministrazione** board of directors. **C~ dei Ministri** Cabinet
consi'sten|te adj substantial; (spesso) thick; (fig: argomento) valid
con'sistere vi **~ in** consist of
consoci'ata f associate company
conso'lar|e¹ vt console; (rallegrare) cheer. **~si** vr console oneself
conso'la|re² adj consular. **~to** m consulate
consolazi'one f consolation; (gioia) joy
'console m consul
consoli'dar|e vt, **~si** vr consolidate
conso'nante f consonant
'consono adj consistent
con'sorte mf consort
con'sorzio m consortium
con'stare vi **~ di** consist of; (risultare) appear; **a quanto mi consta** as far as I know; **mi consta che** it appears that
consta'ta|re vt ascertain. **~zi'one** f observation
consu'e|to adj & m usual. **~tudi'nario** adj (diritto) common; (persona) set in one's ways. **~'tudine** f habit; (usanza) custom
consu'len|te mf consultant. **~za** f consultancy
consul'ta|re vt consult. **~rsi con** consult with. **~zi'one** f consultation
consul't|ivo adj consultative. **~orio** m clinic
consu'ma|re vt (usare) consume; wear out (abito, scarpe); consummate (matrimonio); commit (delitto). **~rsi** vr consume; (abito, scarpe:) wear out; (struggersi) pine
consu'mato adj (politico) seasoned; (scarpe, tappeto) worn
consuma|'tore, -'trice mf consumer. **~zi'one** f (bibita) drink; (spuntino) snack
consu'mis|mo m consumerism. **~ta** mf consumerist
con'sumo m consumption; (di abito, scarpe) wear; (uso) use; **generi di ~** consumer goods or items. **~ [di carburante]** [fuel] consumption
consun'tivo m **[bilancio] ~** final statement
conta'balle mf [!] storyteller
con'tabil|e adj book-keeping • mf accountant. **~ità** f accounting; **tenere la ~ità** keep the accounts
contachi'lometri m inv ≈ mileometer, odometer Am
conta'dino, -a mf farm-worker; (medievale) peasant
contagi|'are vt infect. **con'tagio** m infection. **~'oso** adj infectious
conta'gocce m inv dropper
contami'na|re vt contaminate. **~zi'one** f contamination
con'tante m cash; **pagare in contanti** pay cash
con'tare vt/i count; (tenere conto di) take into account; (proporsi) intend
conta'scatti m inv (Teleph) time-unit counter
conta'tore m meter
contat'tare vt contact. **con'tatto** m contact
'conte m count
conteggi'are vt put on the bill • vi calculate. **con'teggio** m calculation. **conteggio alla rovescia** countdown
con'te|gno m behaviour; (atteggiamento) attitude. **~'gnoso** adj dignified
contem'pla|re vt contemplate; (fissare) gaze at. **~zi'one** f contemplation
con'tempo m **nel ~** in the meantime
contempo|ranea'mente adv at once. **~'raneo, -a** adj & mf contemporary
conten'dente mf competitor. **con'tendere** vi compete; (litigare) quarrel • vt contend

see A-Z of Italian life and culture

C

conte'n|ere vt contain; (reprimere) repress. **~ersi** vr contain oneself. **~i'tore** m container

conten'tarsi vr **~ di** be content with

conten'tezza f joy

conten'tino m placebo

con'tento adj glad; (soddisfatto) contented

conte'nuto m contents pl; (soggetto) content

contenzi'oso m legal department

con'tes|a f disagreement; Sport contest. **~o** pp di **contendere** •adj contested

con'tessa f countess

conte'sta|re vt contest; (Jur) notify. **~'tario** adj anti-establishment. **~'tore, ~'trice** mf protester. **~zi'one** f (disputa) dispute

con'testo m context

con'tiguo adj adjacent

continen'tale adj continental. **conti'nente** m continent

conti'nenza f continence

contin'gen|te m contingent; (quota) quota. **~za** f contingency

continua'mente adv (senza interruzione) continuously; (frequentemente) continually

continu|'are vt/i continue; (riprendere) resume. **~a'tivo** adj permanent. **~azi'one** f continuation. **~ità** f continuity

con'tinu|o adj continuous; (molto frequente) continual. **corrente ~a** direct current; **di ~o** continually

'conto m calculation; (Comm) account; (di ristorante ecc) bill; (stima) consideration; **a conti fatti** all things considered; **far ~ di** (supporre) suppose; (proporsi) intend; **far ~ su** rely on; **in fin dei conti** when all is said and done; **per ~ di** on behalf of; **per ~ mio** (a mio parere) in my opinion; (da solo) on my own; **starsene per ~ proprio** be on one's own; **rendersi ~ di qcsa** realize sth; **sul ~ di qcno** (voci, informazioni) about sb; **tener ~ di qcsa** take sth into account; **tenere da ~ qcsa** look after sth. **~ corrente** current account, checking account Am. **~ alla rovescia** countdown

con'torcer|e vt twist. **~si** vr twist about

contor'nare vt surround

con'torno m contour; (Culin) vegetables pl

contorsi'one f contortion. **con'torto** pp di **contorcere** •adj twisted

contrabban|'dare vt smuggle. **~di'ere, -a** mf smuggler. **contrab'bando** m contraband

contrab'basso m double bass

contraccambi'are vt return. **contrac'cambio** m return

contracce|t'tivo m contraceptive. **~zi'one** f contraception

contrac'col|po m rebound; (di arma da fuoco) recoil; fig repercussion

con'trada f (rione) district

contrad'detto pp di **contraddire**

contrad'di|re vt contradict. **~t'torio** adj contradictory. **~zi'one** f contradiction

contraddi'stin|guere vt differentiate. **~to** adj distinct

contra'ente mf contracting party

contra'ereo adj anti-aircraft

contraf'fa|re vt disguise; (imitare) imitate; (falsificare) forge. **~tto** adj forged. **~zi'one** f disguising; (imitazione) imitation; (falsificazione) forgery

con'tralto m countertenor •f contralto

contrap'peso m counterbalance

contrap'por|re vt counter; (confrontare) compare. **~si** vr contrast; **~si a** be opposed to

contraria'mente adv contrary (**a** to)

contrari|'are vt oppose; (infastidire) annoy. **~'arsi** vr get annoyed. **~età** f inv adversity; (ostacolo) set-back

con'trario adj contrary; (direzione) opposite; (sfavorevole) unfavourable •m contrary; **al ~** on the contrary

con'trarre vt contract

contras|se'gnare vt mark. **~'segno** m mark; **[in] ~segno** (spedizione) cash on delivery

contra'stare vt oppose; (contestare) contest •vi clash. **con'trasto** m contrast; (litigio) dispute

contrattac'care vt counterattack. **contrat'tacco** m counter-attack

contrat'ta|re vt/i negotiate; (mercanteggiare) bargain. **~zi'one** f (salariale) bargaining

contrat'tempo m hitch

con'tratt|o pp di **contrarre** •m contract. **~o a termine** fixed-term contract. **~u'ale** adj contractual

contravve'n|ire vi contravene. **~zi'one** f contravention; (multa) fine

contrazi'one f contraction; (di prezzi) reduction

contribu'ente mf contributor; (del fisco) taxpayer

contribu|'ire vi contribute. **contri'buto** m contribution

'contro prep against; **~ di me** against me •m **i pro e i ~** the pros and cons

contro'battere vt counter

controbilanci'are vt counterbalance

controcor'rente adj non-conformist •adv upriver; fig upstream

controffen'siva f counter-offensive

controfi'gura f stand-in

controindicazi'one f (Med) contraindication

control'la|re vt control; (verificare) check; (collaudare) test. **~rsi** vr have self-control. **~to** adj controlled

con'trol|lo m control; (verifica) check; (Med) check-up. **~lo delle nascite** birth control. **~'lore** m controller; (sui treni ecc) [ticket] inspector. **~lore di volo** air-traffic controller

contro'mano adv in the wrong direction

contromi'sura f countermeasure

contropi'ede m **prendere in ~** catch off guard

controprodu'cente adj self-defeating

con'trordin|e m counter order; **salvo ~i** unless I/you hear to the contrary

contro'senso m contradiction in terms

controspio'naggio m counterespionage

contro'vento adv against the wind

contro'vers|ia f controversy; (Jur) dispute. **~o** adj controversial

contro'voglia adv unwillingly

contu'macia f default; **in ~** in one's absence

contun'dente adj (corpo, arma) blunt

contur'ba|nte adj perturbing

contusi'one f bruise

convale'scen|te adj convalescent

con'vali|da f validation. **~'dare** vt confirm; validate (atto, biglietto)

con'vegno m meeting; (congresso) congress

conve'nevol|e adj suitable; **~i** pl pleasantries

conveni'en|te adj convenient; (prezzo) attractive; (vantaggioso) advantageous. **~za** f convenience; (interesse) advantage; (di prezzo) attractiveness

conve'nire vi (riunirsi) gather; (concordare) agree; (ammettere) admit; (essere opportuno) be convenient •vt agree on; **ci conviene andare** it is better to go; **non mi conviene stancarmi** I'd better not tire myself out

con'vento m (di suore) convent; (di frati) monastery

conve'nuto adj fixed

convenzi|o'nale adj conventional. **~'one** f convention

conver'gen|te adj converging. **~za** f fig confluence

con'vergere vi converge

conver'sa|re vi converse. **~zi'one** f conversation

conversi'one f conversion

con'verso pp di **convergere**

conver'tibile f (Auto) convertible

conver'ti|re vt convert. **~rsi** vr be converted. **~to, -a** mf convert

con'vesso adj convex

convin'cente adj convincing

con'vin|cere vt convince. **~to** adj convinced. **~zi'one** f conviction

C

con'vitto m boarding school

convi'ven|te m common-law husband •f common-law wife. **~za** f cohabitation. **con'vivere** vi live together

convivi'ale adj convivial

convo'ca|re vt convene. **~zi'one** f convening

convogli'are vt convey; convoy (navi) **con'voglio** m convoy; (ferroviario) train

convulsi'one f convulsion. **con'vulso** adj convulsive; (febbrile) feverish

coope'ra|re vi co-operate. **~'tiva** f co-operative. **~zi'one** f co-operation

coordina'mento m co-ordination

coordi'na|re vt co-ordinate. **~ta** f (Math) coordinate. **~te bancarie** bank (account) details. **~zi'one** f co-ordination

co'perchio m lid; (copertura) cover

co'perta f blanket; (copertura) cover; (Naut) deck

coper'tina f cover; (di libro) dust-jacket

co'perto pp di **coprire** •adj covered; (cielo) overcast •m (a tavola) place; (prezzo del coperto) cover charge; **al ~** under cover

coper'tone m tarpaulin; (gomma) tyre

coper'tura f covering; (Comm, Fin) cover

'copia f copy; **bella/brutta ~** fair/rough copy; **~ carbone** carbon copy. **~ su carta** hardcopy. **copi'are** vt copy

copi'one m script

copi'oso adj plentiful

'coppa f (calice) goblet; (per gelato ecc) dish; Sport cup. **~ [di] gelato** ice-cream (served in a dish)

cop'petta f bowl; (di gelato) small tub

'coppia f couple; (in carte) pair

co'prente adj (cipria, vernice) covering

copri'capo m headgear

coprifu'oco m curfew

copri'letto m bedspread

copripiu'mino m duvet cover

co'prir|e vt cover; drown (suono); hold (carica). **~si** vr (vestirsi) cover up; fig cover oneself; (cielo:) become overcast

coque f **alla ~** (uovo) soft-boiled

co'raggi|o m courage; (sfacciataggine) nerve; **~o!** come on. **~'oso** adj courageous

co'rale adj choral

co'rallo m coral

Co'rano m Koran

co'raz|za f armour; (di animali) shell. **~'zata** f battleship. **~'zato** adj (nave) armour-clad

corbelle'ria f nonsense; (sproposito) blunder

'corda f cord; (Mus, spago) string; (fune) rope; (cavo) cable; **essere giù di ~** be depressed; **dare ~ a qcno** encourage sb. **corde vocali** vocal cords

cordi'al|e adj cordial •m (bevanda) cordial; **~i saluti** best wishes. **~ità** f cordiality

'cordless m inv cordless phone

cor'doglio m grief; (lutto) mourning

cor'done m cord; (schieramento) cordon

core|ogra'fia f choreography. **~'ografo, -a** mf choreographer

cori'andoli mpl confetti sg

cori'andolo m (spezia) coriander

cori'car|e vt put to bed. **~si** vr go to bed

co'rista mf choir member

corna ▸**corno**

cor'nacchia f crow

corna'musa f bagpipes pl

cor'nett|a f (Mus) cornet; (del telefono) receiver. **~o** m (brioche) croissant

cor'ni|ce f frame. **~ci'one** m cornice

'corno m (pl f **corna**) horn; **fare le corna a qcno** be unfaithful to sb; **fare le corna** (per scongiuro) touch wood. **cor'nuto** adj horned •m (!: marito tradito) cuckold; (insulto) bastard

'coro m chorus; (Relig) choir

co'rolla f corolla

co'rona f crown; (di fiori) wreath; (rosario) rosary. **~'mento** m (di impresa) crowning. **coro'nare** vt crown; (sogno) fulfil

cor'petto m bodice

'corpo m body; (Mil, diplomatico) corps inv; **~ a ~** man to man; **andare di ~** move one's bowels. **~ di ballo** corps de ballet. **~ insegnante** teaching staff. **~ del reato** incriminating item

corpo'rale adj corporal

corporati'vismo m corporatism

corpora'tura f build

corporazi'one f corporation

cor'poreo adj bodily

cor'poso adj full-bodied

corpu'lento adj stout

cor'puscolo m corpuscle

corre'dare vt equip

corre'dino m (per neonato) layette

cor'redo m (nuziale) trousseau

cor'reggere vt correct; lace (bevanda)

corre'lare vt correlate

cor'rente adj running; (in vigore) current; (frequente) everyday; (inglese ecc) fluent •f current; (d'aria) draught; **essere al ~** be up to date. **~'mente** adv (parlare) fluently

'correre vi run; (affrettarsi) hurry; Sport race; (notizie:) circulate; **~ dietro a** run after •vt run; **~ un pericolo** run a risk; **lascia ~!** don't bother!

corre|tta'mente adv correctly. **cor'retto** pp di **correggere** •adj correct; (caffè) with a drop of alcohol. **~zi'one** f correction

cor'rida f bullfight

corri'doio m corridor; (Aeron) aisle

corri'|dore, -'trice mf racer; (a piedi) runner

corri'era f coach, bus

corri'ere m courier; (posta) mail; (spedizioniere) carrier

corri'mano m bannister

corrispet'tivo m amount due

corrispon'den|te adj corresponding •mf correspondent. **~za** f correspondence; **scuola/corsi per ~za** correspondence course; **vendite per ~za** mail-order [shopping]. **corri'spondere** vi correspond; (stanza:) communicate; **corrispondere a** (contraccambiare) return

corri'sposto adj (amore) reciprocated

corrobo'rare vt strengthen; fig corroborate

cor'roder|e vt, **~si** vr corrode

cor'rompere vt corrupt; (con denaro) bribe

corrosi'one f corrosion. **corro'sivo** adj corrosive

cor'roso pp di **corrodere**

cor'rotto pp di **corrompere** •adj corrupt

corrucci'a|rsi vr be vexed. **~to** adj upset

corru'gare vt wrinkle; **~ la fronte** knit one's brows

corruzi'one f corruption; (con denaro) bribery

'corsa f running; (rapida) dash; Sport race; (di treno ecc) journey; **di ~** at a run; **fare una ~** run

cor'sia f gangway; (di ospedale) ward; (Auto) lane; (di supermercato) aisle

cor'sivo m italics pl

'corso pp di **correre** •m course; (strada) main street; (Comm) circulation; **lavori in ~** work in progress; **nel ~ di** during. **~ d'acqua** watercourse

'corte f [court]yard; (Jur, regale) court; **fare la ~ a qcno** court sb. **~ d'appello** court of appeal

cor'teccia f bark

corteggia'mento m courtship

corteggi'a|re vt court. **~'tore** m admirer

cor'teo m procession

cor'te|se adj courteous. **~'sia** f courtesy; **per ~sia** please

cortigi'ano, -a mf courtier •f courtesan

cor'tile m courtyard

cor'tina f curtain; (schermo) screen

'corto adj short; **essere a ~ di** be short of. **~ circuito** m short [circuit]

cortome'traggio m Cinema short

cor'vino adj jet-black

'corvo m raven

'cosa f thing; (faccenda) matter; inter, rel what; **[che] ~** what; **nessuna ~** nothing; **ogni ~** everything; **per prima ~** first of all; **tante cose** so

C

many things; (augurio) all the best

'**cosca** f clan

'**coscia** f thigh; (Culin) leg

cosci'en|te adj conscious. **~za** f conscience; (consapevolezza) consciousness

co'scri|tto m conscript. **~zi'one** f conscription

così adv so; (in questo modo) like this, like that; (perciò) therefore; **le cose stanno ~** that's how things stand; **fermo ~!** hold it; **proprio ~!** exactly!; **basta ~!** that will do!; **ah, è ~?** it's like that, is it?; **~ ~** so-so; **e ~ via** and so on; **per ~ dire** so to speak; **più di ~** any more; **una ~ cara ragazza!** such a nice girl!; **è stato ~ generoso da aiutarti** he was kind enough to help you • conj (allora) so • adj inv (tale) like that; **una ragazza ~** a girl like that

cosicché conj and so

cosid'detto adj so-called

co'smesi f cosmetics

co'smetico adj & m cosmetic

'**cosmico** adj cosmic

'**cosmo** m cosmos

cosmopo'lita adj cosmopolitan

co'spargere vt sprinkle; (disseminare) scatter

co'spetto m **al ~ di** in the presence of

co'spicuo adj conspicuous; (somma ecc) considerable

cospi'ra|re vi conspire. **~'tore, ~'trice** mf conspirator. **~zi'one** f conspiracy

'**costa** f coast; (Anat) rib

costà adv there

co'stan|te adj & f constant. **~za** f constancy

co'stare vi cost; **quanto costa?** how much is it?

co'stata f chop

costeggi'are vt (per mare) coast; (per terra) skirt

co'stei pron ▸**costui**

costellazi'one f constellation

coster'na|to adj dismayed. **~zi'one** f consternation

costi'er|a f stretch of coast. **~o** adj coastal

costi'pa|to adj constipated. **~zi'one** f constipation; (raffreddore) bad cold

costitu'ir|e vt constitute; (formare) form; (nominare) appoint. **~si** vr (Jur) give oneself up

costituzio'nale adj constitutional. 🅘**costituzi'one** f constitution; (fondazione) setting up

'**costo** m cost; **ad ogni ~** at all costs; **a nessun ~** on no account

'**costola** f rib; (di libro) spine

costo'letta f cutlet

co'storo pron ▸**costui**

co'stoso adj costly

co'stretto pp di **costringere**

co'stri|ngere vt compel; (stringere) constrict. **~t'tivo** adj coercive

costru|'ire vt build. **~t'tivo** adj constructive. **~zi'one** f construction

co'stui, co'stei, pl **co'storo** pron (soggetto) he, she, pl they; (complemento) him, her, pl them

co'stume m (usanza) custom; (condotta) morals pl; (indumento) costume. **~ da bagno** swim-suit; (da uomo) swimming trunks

co'tenna f pigskin; (della pancetta) rind

coto'letta f cutlet

co'tone m cotton. **~ idrofilo** cotton wool, absorbent cotton Am

'**cottimo** m **lavorare a ~** do piece-work

'**cotto** pp di **cuocere** • adj done; (!: infatuato) in love; (!: sbronzo) drunk; **ben ~** (carne) well done

'**cotton fi'oc®** m inv cotton bud

cot'tura f cooking

co'vare vt hatch; sicken for (malattia); harbour (odio) • vi smoulder

'**covo** m den

co'vone m sheaf

'**cozza** f mussel

coz'zare vi **~ contro** bump into. '**cozzo** m fig clash

C.P. abbr (Casella Postale) PO Box

'**crampo** m cramp

'**cranio** m skull

🅘 *see* A-Z of Italian life and culture

cra'tere m crater

cra'vatta f tie; (a farfalla) bow-tie

cre'anza f politeness; **mala ~** bad manners

cre'a|re vt create; (causare) cause. **~tività** f creativity. **~'tivo** adj creative. **~to** m creation. **~'tore, ~'trice** mf creator. **~zi'one** f creation

crea'tura f creature; (bambino) baby; **povera ~!** poor thing!

cre'den|te mf believer. **~za** f belief; (Comm) credit; (mobile) sideboard. **~zi'ali** fpl credentials

'creder|e vt believe; (pensare) think • vi **~e in** believe in; **credo di sì** I think so; **non ti credo** I don't believe you. **~si** vr think oneself to be. **cre'dibile** adj credible. **credibilità** f credibility

'credi|to m credit; (stima) esteem; **comprare a ~to** buy on credit. **~'tore, ~'trice** mf creditor

credulità f credulity

'credu|lo adj credulous. **~'lone, -a** mf simpleton

'crema f cream; (di uova e latte) custard. **~ idratante** moisturizer. **~ pasticciera** egg custard. **~ solare** suntan lotion

cre'ma|re vt cremate. **~'torio** m crematorium. **~zi'one** f cremation

'crème cara'mel m inv crème caramel

creme'ria f dairy (also selling ice cream and cakes)

'crepa f crack

cre'paccio m cleft; (di ghiacciaio) crevasse

crepacu'ore m heart-break

crepa'pelle: **a ~** adv fit to burst; **ridere a ~** split one's sides with laughter

cre'pare vi crack; ([!]: morire) kick the bucket; **~ dal ridere** laugh fit to burst

crepa'tura f crevice

crêpe f inv pancake

crepi'tare vi crackle

cre'puscolo m twilight

cre'scendo m crescendo

'cresc|ere vi grow; (aumentare) increase • vt (allevare) bring up; (aumentare) increase. **~ita** f growth; (aumento) increase. **~i'uto** pp di **crescere**

'cresi|ma f confirmation. **~'mare** vt confirm

'crespo adj frizzy • m crêpe

'cresta f crest; (cima) peak

'creta f clay

'Creta f Crete

cre'tino, -a adj stupid • mf idiot

cric m inv jack

cri'ceto m hamster

crimi'nal|e adj & mf criminal. **~ità** f crime. **'crimine** m crime

crimi'noso adj criminal

'crin|e m horsehair. **~i'era** f mane

'cripta f crypt

crisan'temo m chrysanthemum

'crisi f inv crisis; (Med) fit

cristal'lino m crystalline

cristalliz'zar|e vt, **~si** vr crystallize; fig: (parola, espressione:) become part of the language

cri'stallo m crystal

Cristia'nesimo m Christianity

cristi'ano, -a adj & mf Christian

'Cristo m Christ; **un povero c~** a poor beggar

cri'terio m criterion; (buon senso) [common] sense

'criti|ca f criticism; (recensione) review. **criti'care** vt criticize. **~co** adj critical • m critic. **~cone, -a** mf faultfinder

crivel'lare vt riddle (**di** with)

cri'vello m sieve

Cro'azia f Croatia

croc'cante adj crisp • m type of crunchy nut biscuit

croc'chetta f croquette

'croce f cross; **a occhio e ~** roughly. **C~ Rossa** Red Cross

croce'via m inv crossroads sg

croci'ata f crusade

cro'cicchio m crossroads sg

croci'era f cruise; (Archit) crossing

croci'fi|ggere vt crucify. **~ssi'one** f crucifixion. **~sso** pp di **crocifiggere** • adj crucified • m crucifix

crogio'larsi vr bask

C

C

crogi[u]'olo m crucible; fig melting pot

crol'lare vi collapse; (prezzi:) slump. **'crollo** m collapse; (dei prezzi) slump

cro'mato adj chromium-plated. **'cromo** m chrome. **cromo'soma** m chromosome

'cronaca f chronicle; (di giornale) news; (Radio, TV) commentary; **fatto di ~** news item. **~ nera** crime news

'cronico adj chronic

cro'nista mf reporter

crono'logico adj chronological

cronome'trare vt time

cro'nometro m chronometer

'crosta f crust; (di formaggio) rind; (di ferita) scab; (quadro) daub

cro'staceo m shellfish

cro'stata f tart

cro'stino m croûton

crucci'arsi vr worry. **'cruccio** m worry

cruci'ale adj crucial

cruci'verba m inv crossword [puzzle]

cru'del|e adj cruel. **~tà** f inv cruelty

'crudo adj raw; (rigido) harsh

cru'ento adj bloody

cru'miro m blackleg, scab

'crusca f bran

cru'scotto m dashboard

'Cuba f Cuba

cu'betto m **~ di ghiaccio** ice cube

'cubico adj cubic

cubi'tal|e adj **a caratteri ~i** in enormous letters

'cubo m cube

cuc'cagna f abundance; (baldoria) merry-making; **paese della ~** land of plenty

cuc'cetta f (su un treno) couchette; (Naut) berth

cucchia'ino m teaspoon

cucchi'a|io m spoon; **al ~io** (dolce) creamy. **~i'ata** f spoonful

'cuccia f dog's bed; **fa la ~!** lie down!

cuccio'lata f litter

'cucciolo m puppy

cu'cina f kitchen; (il cucinare) cooking; (cibo) food; (apparecchio) cooker; **far da ~** cook; **libro di ~** cook[ery] book. **~ a gas** gas cooker

cuci'n|are vt cook. **~ino** m kitchenette

cu'ci|re vt sew; **macchina per ~re** sewing-machine. **~to** m sewing. **~'tura** f seam

cucù m inv cuckoo

'cuculo m cuckoo

'cuffia f bonnet; (da bagno) bathing-cap; (ricevitore) headphones pl

cu'gino, -a mf cousin

'cui pron rel (persona: con prep) who, whom fml; (cose, animali: con prep) which; (tra articolo e nome) whose; **la persona con ~ ho parlato** the person [who] I spoke to; **la ditta per ~ lavoro** the company I work for, the company for which I work; **l'amico il ~ libro è stato pubblicato** the friend whose book was published; **in ~** (dove) where; (quando) that; **per ~** (perciò) so; **la città in ~ vivo** the city I live in, the city where I live; **il giorno in ~ l'ho visto** the day [that] I saw him

culi'nari|a f cookery. **~o** adj culinary

'culla f cradle. **cul'lare** vt rock

culmi'na|nte adj culminating. **~re** vi culminate. **'culmine** m peak

'culto m cult; (Relig) religion; (adorazione) worship

cul'tu|ra f culture. **~ra generale** general knowledge. **~'rale** adj cultural

cultu'ris|mo m body-building

cumula'tivo adj cumulative; **biglietto ~** group ticket

'cumulo m pile; (mucchio) heap; (nuvola) cumulus

'cuneo m wedge

cu'netta f gutter

cu'ocere vt/i cook; fire (ceramica)

cu'oco, -a mf cook

cu'oio m leather. **~ capelluto** scalp

cu'ore m heart; **cuori** pl (carte) hearts; **nel profondo del ~** in one's heart of hearts; **di [buon] ~** (persona) kind-hearted; **nel ~ della notte** in the middle of the night; **stare a ~ a qcno** be very important to sb

cupi'digia f greed

'cupo adj gloomy; (suono) deep

'cupola f dome

'cura f care; (amministrazione) management; (Med) treatment; **a ~ di** edited by; **in ~** under treatment. **~ dimagrante** diet. **cu'rante** adj **medico curante** GP, doctor

cu'rar|e vt take care of; (Med) treat; (guarire) cure; edit (testo). **~si** vr take care of oneself; (Med) follow a treatment; **~si di** (badare a) mind

cu'rato m parish priest

cura'tore, -'trice mf trustee; (di testo) editor

'curia f curia

curio's|are vi be curious; (mettere il naso) pry (**in** into); (nei negozi) look around. **~ità** f inv curiosity. **curi'oso** adj curious; (strano) odd

cur'sore m (Comput) cursor

'curva f curve; (stradale) bend. **~ a gomito** U-bend. **cur'vare** vti curve; (strada:) bend. **cur'varsi** vr bend. **'curvo** adj curved; (piegato) bent

cusci'netto m pad; (Mech) bearing

cu'scino m cushion; (guanciale) pillow. **~ d'aria** air cushion

'cuspide f spire

cu'stod|e m caretaker. **~e giudiziario** official receiver. **~ia** f care; (Jur) custody; (astuccio) case. **custo'dire** vt keep; (badare) look after

cu'taneo adj skin attrib

'cute f skin

Dd

da prep from; (*con verbo passivo*) by; (*moto a luogo*) to; (*moto per luogo*) through; (*stato in luogo*) at; (*continuativo*) for; (*causale*) with; (*in qualità di*) as; (*con caratteristica*) with; (*come*) like; (*temporale*) since, for

! *da* si traduce con **for** quando si tratta di un periodo di tempo e con **since** quando si riferisce al momento in cui qualcosa è cominciato. Nota che in inglese si usa il passato prossimo progressivo invece del presente: **aspetto da mesi** I've been waiting for months; **aspetto da lunedì** I've been waiting since Monday

····> **da Roma a Milano** from Rome to Milan; **staccare un quadro dalla parete** take a picture off the wall; **i bambini dai 5 ai 10 anni** children between 5 and 10; **vedere qcsa da vicino/lontano** see sth from up close/from a distance; **scritto da** written by; **andare dal panettiere** go to the baker's; **passo da te più tardi** I'll come over to your place later; **passiamo da qui** let's go this way; **un appuntamento dal dentista** an appointment at the dentist's; **il treno passa da Venezia** the train goes through Venice; **dall'anno scorso** since last year; **vivo qui da due anni** I've been living here for two years; **da domani** from tomorrow; **piangere dal dolore** cry with pain; **ho molto da fare** I have a lot to do; **occhiali da sole** sunglasses; **qualcosa da mangiare** something to eat; **un uomo dai capelli scuri** a man with dark hair; **è un oggetto da poco** it's not worth much; **l'ho fatto da solo** I did it by myself; **si è fatto da sé** he is a self-made man; **non è da lui** it's not like him

dac'capo adv again; (dall'inizio) from the beginning

dacché conj since

'dado m dice; (Culin) stock cube; (Techn) nut

daf'fare m work

d

'dagli = **da + gli**. **'dai** = **da + i**
'dai int come on!
'daino m deer; (pelle) buckskin
dal = **da + il**. **'dalla** = **da + la**. **'dalle** = **da + le**. **'dallo** = **da + lo**
'dalia f dahlia
dal'tonico adj colour-blind
'dama f lady; (nei balli) partner; (gioco) draughts sg
dami'gella f (di sposa) bridesmaid
damigi'ana f demijohn
dam'meno adv **non essere ~ (di qcno)** be no less good (than sb)
da'naro m = **denaro**
dana'roso adj ([!]: ricco) loaded
da'nese adj Danish •mf Dane •m (lingua) Danish
Dani'marca f Denmark
dan'na|re vt damn; **far ~re qcno** drive sb mad. **~to** adj damned. **~zi'one** f damnation
danneggi|a'mento m damage. **~'are** vt damage; (nuocere) harm
'danno m damage; (a persona) harm. **dan'noso** adj harmful
'danza f dance; (il danzare) dancing. **dan'zare** vi dance
dapper'tutto adv everywhere
dap'poco adj worthless
dap'prima adv at first
'dardo m dart
'dar|e vt give; take (esame); have (festa); **~ qcsa a qcno** give sb sth; **~ da mangiare a qcno** give sb something to eat; **~ il benvenuto a qcno** welcome sb; **~ la buonanotte a qcno** say good night to sb; **~ del tu/del lei a qcno** address sb as "tu"/ "lei"; **~ del cretino a qcno** call sb an idiot; **~ qcsa per scontato** take sth for granted; **cosa danno alla TV stasera?** what's on TV tonight? •vi **~ nell'occhio** be conspicuous; **~ alla testa** go to one's head; **~ su** (finestra, casa:) look on to; **~ sui** o **ai nervi a qcno** get on sb's nerves •m (Comm) debit. **~si** vr (scambiarsi) give each other; **~si da fare** get down to it; **si è dato tanto da fare!** he went to so much trouble!; **~si a** (cominciare) take up; **~si al bere** take to drink; **~si per** (malato) pretend to be; **~si per vinto** give up; **può ~si** maybe
'darsena f dock
'data f date. **~ di emissione** date of issue. **~ di nascita** date of birth. **~ di scadenza** cut-off date
da'ta|re vt date; **a ~re da** as from. **~to** adj dated
'dato adj given; (dedito) addicted; **~ che** given that •m datum. **~ di fatto** well-established fact; **dati** pl data. **da'tore** m giver. **datore, datrice** mf **di lavoro** employer
'dattero m date
dattilogra'f|are vt type. **~ia** f typing. **datti'lografo, -a** mf typist
dat'torno adv **togliersi ~** clear off
da'vanti adv before; (dirimpetto) opposite; (di fronte) in front •adj inv front •m front; **~ a** prep in front of
da'vanzo adv more than enough
dav'vero adv really; **per ~** in earnest; **dici ~?** honestly?
'dazio m duty; (ufficio) customs pl
d.C. abbr (dopo Cristo) AD
'dea f goddess
debel'lare vt defeat
debili'ta|nte adj weakening. **~re** vt weaken. **~rsi** vr become weaker
debita'mente adv duly
'debi|to adj due; **a tempo ~to** in due course •m debt. **~'tore, ~'trice** mf debtor
'debo|le adj weak; (luce) dim; (suono) faint •m weak point; (preferenza) weakness. **~'lezza** f weakness
debor'dare vi overflow
debosci'ato adj debauched
debut'ta|nte m (attore) actor making his début •f actress making her début. **~re** vi make one's début. **de'butto** m début
deca'den|te adj decadent. **~'tismo** m decadence. **~za** f decline; (Jur) loss. **deca'dere** vi lapse. **decadi'mento** m (delle arti) decline
decaffei'nato adj decaffeinated •m decaffeinated coffee
decan'tare vt (lodare) praise
decapi'ta|re vt decapitate; behead (condannato). **~zi'one** f decapitation; beheading

decappot'tabile adj convertible

de'ce|dere vi (morire) die. **~'duto** adj deceased

decele'rare vt decelerate

decen'nale adj ten-yearly. **de'cennio** m decade

de'cen|te adj decent. **~te'mente** adv decently. **~za** f decency

decentra'mento m decentralization

de'cesso m death; **atto di ~** death certificate

de'cider|e vt decide; settle (questione). **~si** vr make up one's mind

deci'frare vt decipher; (documenti cifrati) decode

deci'male adj decimal

deci'mare vt decimate

'decimo adj tenth

de'cina f (Math) ten; **una ~ di** (circa dieci) about ten

decisa'mente adv definitely

decisio'nale adj decision-making

deci|si'one f decision. **~'sivo** adj decisive. **de'ciso** pp di **decidere** • adj decided

decla'ma|re vt/i declaim. **~'torio** adj (stile) declamatory

declas'sare vt downgrade

decli'na|re vt decline; **~re ogni responsabilità** disclaim all responsibility • vi go down; (tramontare) set. **~zi'one** f declension. **de'clino** m decline; **in declino** on the decline

decodificazi'one f decoding

decol'lare vi take off

décolle'té m inv décolleté

de'collo m take-off

decolo'ra|nte m bleach. **~re** vt bleach

decolorazi'one f bleaching

decom'po|rre vt, **~rsi** vr decompose. **~sizi'one** f decomposition

deconcen'trarsi vr become distracted

deconge'lare vt defrost

decongestio'nare vt relieve congestion in

deco'ra|re vt decorate. **~'tivo** adj decorative. **~to** adj (ornato) decorated. **~'tore, ~'trice** mf decorator. **~zi'one** f decoration

de'coro m decorum

decorosa'mente adv decorously. **decoroso** adj dignified

decor'renza f **~ dal...** starting from...

de'correre vi pass; **a ~ da** with effect from. **de'corso** pp di **decorrere** • m passing; (Med) course

de'crepito adj decrepit

decre'scente adj decreasing. **de'crescere** vi decrease; (prezzi:) go down; (acque:) subside

decre'tare vt decree. **de'creto** m decree. **decreto legge** decree which has the force of law

'dedalo m maze

'dedica f dedication

dedi'car|e vt dedicate. **~si** vr dedicate oneself

'dedi|to adj **~ a** given to; (assorto) engrossed in; addicted to (vizi). **~zi'one** f dedication

de'dotto pp di **dedurre**

dedu'cibile adj (tassa) allowable

de'du|rre vt deduce; (sottrarre) deduct. **~t'tivo** adj deductive. **~zi'one** f deduction

defal'care vt deduct

defe'rire vt (Jur) remit

defezi|o'nare vi (abbandonare) defect. **~'one** f defection

defici'en|te adj (mancante) deficient; (Med) mentally deficient • mf mental defective **~za** f deficiency; (lacuna) gap; (Med) mental deficiency

'defici|t m inv deficit. **~'tario** adj (bilancio) deficit attrib

defi'larsi vr (scomparire) slip away

défilé m inv fashion show

defi'ni|re vt define; (risolvere) settle. **~tiva'mente** adv for good. **~'tivo** adj definitive. **~to** adj definite. **~zi'one** f definition; (soluzione) settlement

deflazi'one f deflation

deflet'tore m (Auto) quarterlight

deflu'ire vi (liquidi:) flow away; (persone:) stream out

de'flusso m (di marea) ebb

d

defor'mar|e vt deform (arto); fig distort. **~si** vr lose its shape. **de'form|e** adj deformed. **~ità** f deformity

defor'ma|to adj warped. **~zi'one** f (di fatti) distortion

defrau'dare vt defraud

de'funto, -a adj & mf deceased

degene'ra|re vi degenerate. **~to** adj degenerate. **~zi'one** f degeneration. **de'genere** adj degenerate

de'gen|te mf patient. **~za** f confinement

'degli = **di + gli**

deglu'tire vt swallow

de'gnare vt **~ qcno di uno sguardo** deign to look at sb

'degno adj worthy; (meritevole) deserving

degrada'mento m degradation

degra'da|re vt degrade. **~rsi** vr lower oneself; (città:) fall into disrepair. **~zi'one** f degradation

de'grado m damage; **~ ambientale** m environmental damage

degu'sta|re vt taste. **~zi'one** f tasting

'dei = **di + i**. **'del** = **di + il**

dela|'tore, -'trice mf [police] informer. **~zi'one** f informing

'delega f proxy

dele'ga|re vt delegate. **~to** m delegate. **~zi'one** f delegation

dele'terio adj harmful

del'fino m dolphin; (stile di nuoto) butterfly [stroke]

de'libera f bylaw

delibe'ra|re vt/i deliberate; **~ su/in** rule on/in. **~to** adj deliberate

delicata'mente adv delicately

delica'tezza f delicacy; (fragilità) frailty; (tatto) tact

deli'cato adj delicate

delimi'tare vt delimit

deline'a|re vt outline. **~rsi** vr be outlined; fig take shape. **~to** adj defined

delin'quen|te mf delinquent. **~za** f delinquency

deli'rante adj (Med) delirious; (assurdo) insane

deli'rare vi be delirious. **de'lirio** m delirium; fig frenzy

de'litt|o m crime. **~u'oso** adj criminal

de'lizi|a f delight. **~'are** vt delight. **~'oso** adj delightful; (cibo) delicious

'della = **di + la**. **'delle** = **di + le**. **'dello** = **di + lo**

delocaliz'zare vt relocate

'delta m inv delta

delta'plano m hang-glider; **fare ~** go hang-gliding

delucidazi'one f clarification

delu'dente adj disappointing

de'lu|dere vt disappoint. **~si'one** f disappointment. **de'luso** adj disappointed

demar'ca|re vt demarcate. **~zi'one** f demarcation

de'men|te adj demented. **~za** f dementia. **~zi'ale** adj (assurdo) zany

demilitariz'za|re vt demilitarize. **~zi'one** f demilitarization

demistificazi'one f debunking

demo'cra|tico adj democratic. **~'zia** f democracy

democristi'ano, -a adj & mf Christian Democrat

demogra'fia f demography. **demo'grafico** adj demographic

demo'li|re vt demolish. **~zi'one** f demolition

'demone m demon. **de'monio** m demon

demoraliz'zar|e vt demoralize. **~si** vr become demoralized

de'mordere vi give up

demoti'vato adj demotivated

de'nari mpl (nelle carte) diamonds

de'naro m money

deni'gra|re vt denigrate. **~'torio** adj denigratory

denomi'na|re vt name. **~'tore** m denominator. **~zi'one** f denomination; ◼**~zione di origine controllata** guarantee of a wine's quality

deno'tare vt denote

densità f inv density. **'denso** adj dense

◼ see A-Z of Italian life and culture

den'ta|le adj dental. **~rio** adj dental. **~ta** f bite. **~'tura** f teeth pl

'dente m tooth; (di forchetta) prong; **al ~** (Culin) slightly firm. **~ del giudizio** wisdom tooth. **~ di latte** milk tooth. **denti'era** f false teeth pl

denti'fricio m toothpaste

den'tista mf dentist

'dentro adv in, inside; (in casa) indoors; **da ~** from within; **qui ~** in here •prep in, inside; (di tempo) within, by •m inside

denu'dar|e vt bare. **~si** vr strip

de'nunci|a, de'nunzia f denunciation; (alla polizia) report; (dei redditi) [income] tax return. **~'are** vt denounce; (accusare) report

denutrizi'one f malnutrition

deodo'rante adj & m deodorant

dépendance f inv outbuilding

depe'ri|bile adj perishable. **~'mento** m wasting away; (di merci) deterioration. **~re** vi waste away

depi'la|re vt depilate. **~rsi** vr shave (gambe); pluck (sopracciglia). **~'torio** m depilatory

deplo'rabile adj deplorable

deplo'r|are vt deplore; (dolersi di) grieve over. **~evole** adj deplorable

de'porre vt put down; lay (uova); (togliere da una carica) depose; (testimoniare) testify

depor'ta|re vt deport. **~to, -a** mf deportee. **~zi'one** f deportation

deposi'tar|e vt deposit; (lasciare in custodia) leave; (in magazzino) store. **~io, -a** mf (di segreto) repository. **~si** vr settle

de'posi|to m deposit; (luogo) warehouse; (Mil) depot. **~to bagagli** left-luggage office. **~zi'one** f deposition; (da una carica) removal

depra'va|re vt deprave. **~to** adj depraved

depre'ca|bile adj appalling. **~re** vt deprecate

depre'dare vt plunder

depressi'one f depression. **de'presso** pp di **deprimere** •adj depressed

deprez'zar|e vt depreciate. **~si** vr depreciate

depri'mente adj depressing

de'primer|e vt depress. **~si** vr become depressed

depu'ra|re vt purify. **~'tore** m purifier

depu'ta|re vt delegate. **~to, -a** mf Member of Parliament, MP

d

deraglia'mento m derailment

deragli'are vi go off the lines; **far ~** derail

'derby m inv Sport local Derby

deregolamentazi'one f deregulation

dere'litto adj derelict

dere'tano m backside, bottom

de'ri|dere vt deride. **~si'one** f derision. **~'sorio** adj derisory

deri'va|re vi **~re da** (provenire) derive from •vt derive; (sviare) divert. **~zi'one** f derivation; (di fiume) diversion

dermato|lo'gia f dermatology. **derma'tologo, -a** mf dermatologist

'deroga f dispensation. **dero'gare** vi **derogare a** depart from

der'rat|a f merchandise. **~e alimentari** foodstuffs

deru'bare vt rob

descrit'tivo adj descriptive. **des'critto** pp di **descrivere**

des'cri|vere vt describe. **~'vibile** adj describable. **~zi'one** f description

de'serto adj uninhabited •m desert

deside'rabile adj desirable

deside'rare vt wish; (volere) want; (intensamente) long for; **desidera?** can I help you?; **lasciare a ~** leave a lot to be desired

desi'de|rio m wish; (brama) desire; (intenso) longing. **~'roso** adj desirous; (bramoso) longing

desi'gnare vt designate; (fissare) fix

de'sistere vi **~ da** desist from

'desktop 'publishing m desktop publishing

deso'la|re vt distress. **~to** desolate; (spiacente) sorry. **~zi'one** f desolation

'despota m despot

de'star|e vt waken; fig awaken. **~si** vr waken; fig awaken

desti'na|re vt destine; (nominare) appoint; (assegnare) assign; (indirizzare) address. **~'tario** m addressee. **~zi'one** f destination; fig purpose

de'stino m destiny; (fato) fate

destitu|'ire vt dismiss. **~zi'one** f dismissal

d

'desto adj liter awake

'destra f (parte) right; (mano) right hand; **prendere a ~** turn right

destreggi'ar|e vi, **~si** vr manoeuvre

de'strezza f dexterity, skill

'destro adj right; (abile) skilful

detei'nato adj tannin-free

dete'n|ere vt hold; (polizia:) detain. **~uto, -a** mf prisoner. **~zi'one** f detention

deter'gente adj cleaning; (latte, crema) cleansing •m detergent; (per la pelle) cleanser

deteriora'mento m deterioration

deterio'rar|e vt deteriorate. **~si** vr deteriorate

determi'nante adj decisive

determi'na|re vt determine. **~rsi** vr **~rsi a** resolve to. **~'tezza** f determination. **~'tivo** adj (Gram) definite. **~to** adj (risoluto) determined; (particolare) specific. **~zi'one** f determination; (decisione) decision

deter'rente adj & m deterrent

deter'sivo m detergent. **~ per i piatti** washing-up liquid

dete'stare vt detest, hate

deto'nare vi detonate

de'tra|rre vt deduct (**da** from). **~zi'one** f deduction

detri'mento m detriment; **a ~ di** to the detriment of

de'trito m debris

'detta f **a ~ di** according to

dettagli'ante mf retailer

dettagli'a|re vt detail. **~ta'mente** adv in detail

det'taglio m detail; **al ~** (Comm) retail

det'ta|re vt dictate. **~to** m, **~'tura** f dictation

'detto adj said; (chiamato) called; (soprannominato) nicknamed; **~ fatto** no sooner said than done •m saying

detur'pare vt disfigure

deva'sta|re vt devastate. **~to** adj devastated

devi'a|re vi deviate •vt divert. **~zi'one** f deviation; (stradale) diversion

devitaliz'zare vt deaden (dente)

devo'lu|to pp di **devolvere** •adj devolved. **~zi'one** f devolution

de'volvere vt devolve

de'vo|to adj devout; (affezionato) devoted. **~zi'one** f devotion

di prep of; (*partitivo*) some; (*scritto da*) by; (*parlare, pensare ecc*) about; (*con causa, mezzo*) with; (*con provenienza*) from; (*in comparazioni*) than; (*con infinito*) to; **la casa di mio padre/dei miei genitori** my father's house/my parents' house; **compra del pane** buy some bread; **hai del pane?** do you have any bread?; **un film di guerra** a war film; **piangere di dolore** cry with pain; **coperto di neve** covered with snow; **sono di Genova** I'm from Genoa; **uscire di casa** leave one's house; **più alto di te** taller than you; **è ora di partire** it's time to go; **crede di aver ragione** he thinks he's right; **dire di sì** say yes; **di domenica** on Sundays; **di sera** in the evening; **una pausa di un'ora** an hour's break; **un corso di due mesi** a two-month course

dia'bet|e m diabetes. **~ico, -a** adj & mf diabetic

dia'bolico adj diabolical

dia'dema m diadem; (di donna) tiara

di'afano adj diaphanous

dia'framma m diaphragm; (divisione) screen

di'agnos|i f inv diagnosis. **~ti'care** vt diagnose

diago'nale adj & f diagonal

dia'gramma m diagram

dia'letto m dialect

di'alogo m dialogue

dia'mante m diamond

see A-Z of Italian life and culture

di'ametro m diameter
di'amine int **che ~...** what on earth...
diaposi'tiva f slide
di'ario m diary
diar'rea f diarrhoea
di'avolo m devil
di'batt|ere vt debate. **~ersi** vr struggle. **~ito** m debate; (meno formale) discussion
dica'stero m office
di'cembre m December
dice'ria f rumour
dichia'ra|re vt state; (ufficialmente) declare. **~rsi** vr **si dichiara innocente** he says he's innocent. **~zi'one** f statement; (documento, di guerra) declaration
dician'nove adj & m nineteen
dicias'sette adj & m seventeen
dici'otto adj & m eighteen
dici'tura f wording
didasca'lia f (di film) subtitle; (di illustrazione) caption
di'dattico adj didactic; (televisione) educational
di'dentro adv inside
didi'etro adv behind •m hum hindquarters pl
di'eci adj & m ten
die'cina = **decina**
'diesel adj & f inv diesel
di'esis m inv sharp
di'eta f diet; **essere a ~** be on a diet. **die'tetico** adj diet. **die'tista** mf dietician. **die'tologo, -a** mf dietician
di'etro adv behind •prep behind; (dopo) after •adj back; (di zampe) hind •m back; **le stanze di ~** the back rooms
dietro'front m inv about-turn; fig U-turn
di'fatti adv in fact
di'fen|dere vt defend. **~dersi** vr defend oneself. **~'siva** f **stare sulla ~siva** be on the defensive. **~'sivo** adj defensive. **~'sore** m defender; **avvocato ~sore** defence counsel
di'fes|a f defence; **prendere le ~e di qcno** come to sb's defence. **~o** pp di **difendere**
difet't|are vi be defective; **~are di** lack. **~ivo** adj defective
di'fet|to m defect; (morale) fault, flaw; (mancanza) lack; (in tessuto, abito) flaw; **essere in ~to** be at fault; **far ~to** be lacking. **~'toso** adj defective; (abito) flawed
diffa'ma|re vt (con parole) slander; (per iscritto) libel. **~'torio** adj slanderous; (per iscritto) libellous. **~zi'one** f slander; (scritta) libel
diffe'ren|te adj different. **~za** f difference; **a ~za di** unlike; **non fare ~za** make no distinction (**fra** between). **~zi'ale** adj & m differential
differenzi'ar|e vt differentiate. **~si** vr **~si da** differ from
diffe'ri|re vt postpone •vi be different. **~ta** f **in ~ta** (TV) prerecorded
dif'ficil|e adj difficult; (duro) hard; (improbabile) unlikely •m difficulty. **~'mente** adv with difficulty
difficoltà f inv difficulty
dif'fida f warning
diffi'd|are vi **~are di** distrust •vt warn. **~ente** adj mistrustful. **~enza** f mistrust
dif'fonder|e vt spread; diffuse (calore, luce ecc). **~si** vr spread. **diffusi'one** f diffusion; (di giornale) circulation
dif'fu|so pp di **diffondere** •adj common; (malattia) widespread; (luce) diffuse
difi'lato adv straight; (subito) straightaway
'diga f dam; (argine) dike
dige'ribile adj digestible
dige|'rire vt digest; [!] stomach. **~sti'one** f digestion. **~'stivo** adj digestive •m digestive; (dopo cena) liqueur
digi'tale adj digital; (delle dita) finger attrib •f (fiore) foxglove
digitaliz'zare vt digitize
digi'tare vt key in
digiu'nare vi fast
digi'uno adj **essere ~** have an empty stomach •m fast; **a ~** (bere ecc) on an empty stomach
digni|tà f dignity. **~'tario** m

d

dignitary. **~'toso** adj dignified

digressi'one f digression

digri'gnare vi **~ i denti** grind one's teeth

dila'gare vi flood; fig spread

dilani'are vt tear to pieces

dilapi'dare vt squander

dila'ta|re vt, **~rsi** vr dilate; (metallo, gas:) expand

dilazio'nabile adj postponable

dilazi|o'nare vt delay. **~'one** f delay

dilegu'ar|e vt disperse. **~si** vr disappear

di'lemma m dilemma

dilet'tante mf amateur

dilet'tare vt delight

di'letto, -a adj beloved • m delight • mf (persona) beloved

dili'gen|te adj diligent; (lavoro) accurate. **~za** f diligence

dilu'ire vt dilute

dilun'gar|e vt prolong. **~si** vr **~si su** dwell on (argomento)

diluvi'are vi pour [down]. **di'luvio** m downpour; fig flood

dima'gr|ante adj slimming. **~i'mento** m weight loss. **~ire** vi slim

dime'nar|e vt wave; wag (coda). **~si** vr be agitated

dimensi'one f dimension; (misura) size

dimenti'canza f forgetfulness; (svista) oversight

dimenti'car|e vt, **~si** vr **~ [di]** forget. **dimentico** adj **dimentico di** (che non ricorda) forgetful of

di'messo pp di **dimettere** • adj humble; (trasandato) shabby; (voce) low

dimesti'chezza f familiarity

di'metter|e vt dismiss; (da ospedale ecc) discharge. **~si** vr resign

dimez'zare vt halve

diminu|'ire vt/i diminish; (in maglia) decrease. **~'tivo** adj & m diminutive. **~zi'one** f decrease; (riduzione) reduction

dimissi'oni fpl resignation sg; **dare le ~** resign

di'mo|ra f residence. **~'rare** vi reside

dimo'strante mf demonstrator

dimo'stra|re vt demonstrate; (provare) prove; (mostrare) show. **~rsi** vr prove [to be]. **~'tivo** adj demonstrative. **~zi'one** f demonstration; (Math) proof

di'namico, -a adj dynamic. **dina'mismo** m dynamism

dinami'tardo adj **attentato ~** bomb attack

dina'mite f dynamite

'dinamo f inv dynamo

di'nanzi adv in front • prep **~ a** in front of

dina'stia f dynasty

dini'ego m denial

dinocco'lato adj lanky

dino'sauro m dinosaur

din'torn|i mpl outskirts; **nei ~i di** in the vicinity of. **~o** adv around

'dio m (pl **'dei**) god; **D~** God

di'ocesi f inv diocese

dipa'nare vt wind into a ball; fig unravel

diparti'mento m department

dipen'den|te adj depending • mf employee. **~za** f dependence; (edificio) annexe

di'pendere vi **~ da** depend on; (provenire) derive from; **dipende** it depends

di'pinger|e vt paint; (descrivere) describe. **~si** vr (truccarsi) make up. **di'pinto** pp di **dipingere** • adj painted • m painting

di'plo|ma m diploma. **~'marsi** vr graduate

diplo'matico adj diplomatic • m diplomat; (pasticcino) millefeuille (with alcohol)

diplo'mato mf person with school-leaving qualification • adj qualified

diploma'zia f diplomacy

di'porto m **imbarcazione da ~** pleasure craft

dira'dar|e vt thin out; make less frequent (visite). **~si** vr thin out; (nebbia:) clear

dira'ma|re vt issue • vi, **~rsi** vr

branch out; (diffondersi) spread. **~zi'one** f (di strada) fork

'dire vt say; (raccontare, riferire) tell; **~ quello che si pensa** speak one's mind; **voler ~** mean; **volevo ben ~!** I wondered!; **~ di sì/no** say yes/no; **si dice che...** rumour has it that...; **come si dice "casa" in inglese?** what's the English for "casa"?; **che ne dici di...?** how about...?; **non c'è che ~** there's no disputing that; **e ~ che...** to think that...; **a dir poco/tanto** at least/ most •vi **~ bene/male di** speak highly/ill of; **dica pure** how can I help you?; **dici sul serio?** are you serious?

diretta'mente adv directly

diret'tissima f **per ~** (Jur) omitting normal procedure

diret'tissimo m fast train

diret'tiva f directive

di'retto pp di **dirigere** •adj direct. **~ a** (inteso) meant for. **essere ~ a** be heading for. **in diretta** (trasmissione) live •m (treno) through train

diret|'tore, -'trice mf manager; manageress; (di scuola) headmaster; headmistress. **~tore d'orchestra** conductor

direzi'one f direction; (di società) management; (Sch) headmaster's/ headmistress's office (primary school)

diri'gen|te adj ruling •mf executive; (Pol) leader. **~za** f management. **~zi'ale** adj managerial

di'riger|e vt direct; conduct (orchestra); run (impresa). **~si** vr **~si verso** head for

dirim'petto adv opposite •prep **~ a** facing

di'ritto¹, dritto adj straight; (destro) right •adv straight; **andare ~** go straight on •m right side; (Tennis) forehand

di'ritt|o² m right; (Jur) law. **~i** pl **d'autore** royalties

dirit'tura f straight line; fig honesty. **~ d'arrivo** Sport home straight

diroc'cato adj tumbledown

dirom'pente adj fig explosive

dirot'ta|re vt reroute (treno, aereo); (illegalmente) hijack; divert (traffico) •vi alter course. **~'tore, ~'trice** mf hijacker

di'rotto adj (pioggia) pouring; (pianto) uncontrollable; **piovere a ~** rain heavily

di'rupo m precipice

dis'abile mf disabled person

disabi'tato adj uninhabited

disabitu'arsi vr **~ a** get out of the habit of

disac'cordo m disagreement

disadat'tato, -a adj maladjusted •mf misfit

disa'dorno adj unadorned

disa'gevole adj (scomodo) uncomfortable

disagi'ato adj poor; (vita) hard

di'sagio m discomfort; (difficoltà) inconvenience; (imbarazzo) embarrassment; **sentirsi a ~** feel uncomfortable; **disagi** pl (privazioni) hardships

disappro'va|re vt disapprove of. **~zi'one** f disapproval

disap'punto m disappointment

disar'mante adj fig disarming

disar'mare vt/i disarm. **di'sarmo** m disarmament

disa'strato, -a adj devastated

di'sastro m disaster; (!: grande confusione) mess; (!: persona) disaster area. **disa'stroso** adj disastrous

disat'ten|to adj inattentive. **~zi'one** f inattention; (svista) oversight

disatti'vare vt de-activate

disa'vanzo m deficit

disavven'tura f misadventure

dis'brigo m dispatch

dis'capito m **a ~ di** to the detriment of

dis'carica f scrap-yard

discen'den|te adj descending •mf descendant. **~za** f descent; (discendenti) descendants pl

di'scendere vt/i descend; (dal treno) get off; (da cavallo) dismount; (sbarcare) land. **~ da** (trarre origine da) be a descendant of

di'scepolo, -a mf disciple

di'scernere vt discern

d

di'sces|a f descent; (pendio) slope; **~a in picchiata** (di aereo) nosedive; **essere in ~a** (strada:) go downhill. **~a libera** (in sci) downhill race. **disce'sista** mf (sciatore) downhill skier. **~o** pp di **discendere**

dis'chetto m (Comput) diskette

dischi'uder|e vt open; (svelare) disclose. **~si** vr open up

disci'oglier|e vt, **~si** vr dissolve; (fondersi) melt. **disci'olto** pp di **disciogliere**

disci'pli|na f discipline. **~'nare** adj disciplinary **~'nato** adj disciplined

'disco m disc; (Comput) disk; Sport discus; (Mus) record; **ernia del ~** slipped disc. **~ fisso** (Comput) hard disk. **~ volante** flying saucer

discogra'fia f (insieme di incisioni) discography. **disco'grafico** adj (industria) recording; **casa discografica** recording company

'discolo mf rascal • adj unruly

discol'par|e vt clear. **~si** vr clear oneself

disconnet'tersi vr go offline

disco'noscere vt disown (figlio)

discontinuità f (nel lavoro) irregularity. **discon'tinuo** adj intermittent; (rendimento) uneven

discor'dan|te adj discordant. **~za** f mismatch

discor'dare vi (opinioni:) conflict. **dis'corde** adj clashing. **dis'cordia** f discord; (dissenso) dissension

dis'cor|rere vi talk (**di** about). **~'sivo** adj colloquial. **dis'corso** pp di **discorrere** • m speech; (conversazione) talk

dis'costo adj distant • adv far away; **stare ~** stand apart

disco'te|ca f disco; (raccolta) record library

discre'pan|te adj contradictory. **~za** f discrepancy

dis'cre|to adj discreet; (moderato) moderate; (abbastanza buono) fairly good. **~zi'one** f discretion; (giudizio) judgement; **a ~zione di** at the discretion of

discrimi'nante adj extenuating

discrimi'na|re vt discriminate. **~'torio** adj (atteggiamento) discriminatory. **~zi'one** f discrimination

discussi'one f discussion; (alterco) argument. **dis'cusso** pp di **discutere** • adj controversial

dis'cutere vt discuss; (formale) debate; (litigare) argue; **~ sul prezzo** bargain. **discu'tibile** adj debatable; (gusto) questionable

disde'gnare vt disdain. **dis'degno** m disdain

dis'dett|a f retraction; (sfortuna) bad luck; (Comm) cancellation. **~o** pp di **disdire**

disdi'cevole adj unbecoming

dis'dire vt retract; (annullare) cancel

diseduca'tivo adj boorish

dise'gna|re vt draw; (progettare) design. **~'tore, ~'trice** mf designer. **di'segno** m drawing; (progetto, linea) design

diser'bante m herbicide • adj herbicidal

disere'da|re vt disinherit • mf **i ~ti** the dispossessed

diser|'tare vt/i desert; **~tare la scuola** stay away from school. **~'tore** m deserter. **~zi'one** f desertion

disfaci'mento m decay

dis'fa|re vt undo; strip (letto); (smantellare) take down; (annientare) defeat; **~re le valigie** unpack [one's bags]. **~rsi** vr fall to pieces; (sciogliersi) melt; **~rsi di** (liberarsi di) get rid of; **~rsi in lacrime** dissolve into tears. **~tta** f defeat. **~tto** adj fig worn out

disfat'tis|mo m defeatism. **~ta** adj & mf defeatist

disfunzi'one f disorder

dis'gelo m thaw

dis'grazi|a f misfortune; (incidente) accident; (sfavore) disgrace. **~ata'mente** adv unfortunately. **~'ato, -a** adj unfortunate • mf wretch

disgre'gar|e vt break up. **~si** vr disintegrate

disgu'ido m **~ postale** mistake in delivery

disgu'st|are vt disgust. **~arsi** vr **~arsi di** be disgusted by. **dis'gusto**

m disgust. **~oso** adj disgusting

disidra'ta|re vt dehydrate. **~to** adj dehydrated

disil'lu|dere vt disenchant. **~si'one** f disenchantment. **~so** adj disillusioned

disimbal'lare vt unpack

disimpa'rare vt forget

disimpe'gnar|e vt release; (compiere) fulfil; redeem (oggetto dato in pegno). **~si** vr disengage oneself; (cavarsela) manage. **disim'pegno** m (locale) vestibule

disincan'tato adj (disilluso) disillusioned

disinfe'sta|re vt disinfest. **~zi'one** f disinfestation

disinfet'tante adj & m disinfectant

disinfe|t'tare vt disinfect. **~zi'one** f disinfection

disinfor'mato adj uninformed

disini'bito adj uninhibited

disinne'scare vt defuse (mina). **disin'nesco** m (di bomba) bomb disposal

disinse'rire vt disconnect

disinte'gra|re vt, **~rsi** vr disintegrate. **~zi'one** f disintegration

disinteres'sarsi vr **~ di** take no interest in. **disinte'resse** m indifference; (oggettività) disinterestedness

disintossi'ca|re vt detoxify. **~rsi** vr come off drugs. **~zi'one** f giving up alcohol/drugs

disin'volto adj natural. **disinvol'tura** f confidence

disles'sia f dyslexia

disli'vello m difference in height; fig inequality

dislo'care vt (Mil) post

dismi'sura f excess; **a ~** excessively

disobbedi'ente adj disobedient

disobbe'dire vt disobey

disoccu'pa|to, -a adj unemployed • mf unemployed person. **~zi'o-ne** f unemployment

disonestà f dishonesty. **diso'nesto** adj dishonest

disono'rare vt dishonour.

diso'nore m dishonour

di'sopra adv above • adj upper • m top

disordi'na|re vt disarrange. **~ta'mente** adv untidily. **~to** adj untidy; (sregolato) immoderate. **di'sordine** m disorder

disorganiz'za|re vt disorganize. **~to** adj disorganized. **~zi'one** f disorganization

disorienta'mento m disorientation

disorien'ta|re vt disorientate. **~rsi** vr lose one's bearings. **~to** adj fig bewildered

di'sotto adv below • adj lower • m bottom

dis'paccio m dispatch

dispa'rato adj disparate

'dispari adj odd. **~tà** f inv disparity

dis'parte adv **in ~** apart; **stare in ~** stand aside

dis'pendi|o m (spreco) waste. **~'oso** adj expensive

dis'pen|sa f pantry; (distribuzione) distribution; (mobile) cupboard; (Jur) exemption; (Relig) dispensation; (pubblicazione periodica) number. **~'sare** vt distribute; (esentare) exonerate

dispe'ra|re vi despair (**di** of). **~rsi** vr despair. **~ta'mente** (piangere) desperately. **~to** adj desperate. **~zi'one** f despair

dis'per|dere vt, **~dersi** vr disperse. **~si'one** f dispersion; (di truppe) dispersal. **~'sivo** adj disorganized. **~so** pp di **disperdere** • adj scattered; (smarrito) lost • m missing soldier

dis'pet|to m spite; **a ~to di** in spite of. **~'toso** adj spiteful

dispia'c|ere m upset; (rammarico) regret; (dolore) sorrow; (preoccupazione) worry • vi **mi dispiace** I'm sorry; **non mi dispiace** I don't dislike it; **se non ti dispiace** if you don't mind. **~i'uto** adj upset; (dolente) sorry

dispo'nibil|e adj available; (gentile) helpful. **~ità** f availability; (gentilezza) helpfulness

dis'por|re vt arrange • vi dispose; (stabilire) order; **~re di** have at one's disposal. **~si** vr line up

disposi'tivo m device

disposizi'one f disposition; (ordine)

order; (libera disponibilità) disposal. **dis'posto** pp di **disporre** • adj ready; (incline) disposed; **essere ben disposto verso** be favourably disposed towards

di'spotico adj despotic

dispregia'tivo adj disparaging

d

disprez'zare vt despise. **dis'prezzo** m contempt

'disputa f dispute

dispu'tar|e vi dispute; (gareggiare) compete. **~si** vr **~si qcsa** contend for sth

dissacra'torio adj debunking

dissangua'mento m loss of blood

dissangu'a|re vt, **~rsi** vr bleed. **~rsi** vr fig become impoverished. **~to** adj bloodless; fig impoverished

dissa'pore m disagreement

dissec'car|e vt, **~si** vr dry up

dissemi'nare vt disseminate; (notizie) spread

dis'senso m dissent; (disaccordo) disagreement

dissente'ria f dysentery

dissen'tire vi disagree (**da** with)

dissertazi'one f dissertation

disser'vizio m poor service

disse'sta|re vt upset; (Comm) damage. **~to** adj (strada) uneven. **dis'sesto** m ruin

disse'tante adj thirst-quenching

disse'tare vt **~ qcno** quench sb's thirst

dissi'dente adj & mf dissident

dis'sidio m disagreement

dis'simile adj unlike, dissimilar

dissimu'lare vt conceal; (fingere) dissimulate

dissi'pa|re vt dissipate; (sperperare) squander. **~rsi** vr (nebbia:) clear; (dubbio:) disappear. **~to** adj dissipated. **~zi'one** f squandering

dissoci'ar|e vt, **~si** vr dissociate

disso'dare vt till

dis'solto pp di **dissolvere**

disso'luto adj dissolute

dis'solver|e vt, **~si** vr dissolve; (disperdere) dispel

disso'nanza f dissonance

dissua|'dere vt dissuade. **~si'one** f dissuasion. **~'sivo** adj dissuasive

distac'car|e vt detach; Sport leave behind. **~si** vr be detached. **di'stacco** m detachment; (separazione) separation; Sport lead

di'stan|te adj far away; fig: (person) detached • adv far away **~za** f distance. **~zi'are** vt space out; Sport outdistance

di'stare vi be distant; **quanto dista?** how far is it?

di'sten|dere vt stretch out (parte del corpo); (spiegare) spread; (deporre) lay. **~dersi** vr stretch; (sdraiarsi) lie down; (rilassarsi) relax. **~si'one** f stretching; (rilassamento) relaxation; (Pol) détente. **~'sivo** adj relaxing

di'steso, -a pp di **distendere** • f expanse

distil'l|are vt/i distil. **~azi'one** f distillation. **~e'ria** f distillery

di'stinguer|e vt distinguish. **~si** vr distinguish oneself. **distin'guibile** adj distinguishable

di'stinta f (Comm) list. **~ di pagamento** receipt. **~ di versamento** paying-in slip

distinta'mente adv individually; (chiaramente) clearly

distin'tivo adj distinctive • m badge

di'stin|to, -a pp di **distinguere** • adj distinct; (signorile) distinguished; **~ti saluti** Yours faithfully. **~zi'one** f distinction

di'stogliere vt **~ da** remove from; (dissuadere) dissuade from. **di'stolto** pp di **distogliere**

di'storcere vt twist

distorsi'one f (Med) sprain; (alterazione) distortion

di'stra|rre vt distract; (divertire) amuse. **~rsi** vr get distracted; (svagarsi) amuse oneself; **non ti distrarre!** pay attention!. **~tta'mente** adv absently. **~tto** pp di **distrarre** • adj absent-minded; (disattento) inattentive. **~zi'one** f absent-mindedness; (errore) inattention; (svago) amusement

di'stretto m district

distribu|'ire vt distribute; (disporre) arrange; deal (carte). **~'tore** m distributor; (di benzina) petrol pump;

(automatico) slot-machine. **~zi'one** f distribution

distri'car|e vt disentangle; **~si da qcsa** vr fig get out of sth

di'stru|ggere vt destroy. **~t'tivo** adj destructive; (critica) negative. **~tto** pp di **distruggere**. **~zi'one** f destruction

distur'bar|e vt disturb; (sconvolgere) upset. **~si** vr trouble oneself. **di'sturbo** m bother; (indisposizione) trouble; (Med) problem; (Radio, TV) interference; **disturbi** pl (Radio, TV) static. **disturbi di stomaco** stomach trouble

disubbidi'en|te adj disobedient. **~za** f disobedience

disubbi'dire vi **~ a** disobey

disugu|agli'anza f disparity. **~'ale** adj unequal; (irregolare) irregular

di'suso m **cadere in ~** fall into disuse

di'tale m thimble

di'tata f poke; (impronta) finger-mark

'dito m (pl f **dita**) finger; (di vino) finger. **~ del piede** toe

'ditta f firm

dit'tafono m dictaphone

ditta'tor|e m dictator. **~i'ale** adj dictatorial. **ditta'tura** f dictatorship

dit'tongo m diphthong

di'urno adj daytime; **spettacolo ~** matinée

'diva f diva

diva'ga|re vi digress. **~zi'one** f digression

divam'pare vi burst into flames; fig spread like wildfire

di'vano m sofa. **~ letto** sofa bed

divari'care vt open

di'vario m discrepancy; **un ~ di opinioni** a difference of opinion

dive'n|ire vi = **diventare**. **~uto** pp di **divenire**

diven'tare vi become; (lentamente) grow; (rapidamente) turn

di'verbio m squabble

diver'gen|te adj divergent. **~za** f divergence; **~za di opinioni** difference of opinion. **di'vergere** vi diverge

diversa'mente adv otherwise; (in modo diverso) differently

diversifi'ca|re vt diversify. **~rsi** vr differ. **~zi'one** f diversification

diver|si'one f diversion. **~sità** f inv difference. **~'sivo** m diversion. **di'verso** adj different; **diversi** adj pl (parecchi) several • pron several [people]

diver'tente adj amusing. **diverti'mento** m amusement

diver'tir|e vt amuse. **~si** vr enjoy oneself

divi'dendo m dividend

di'vider|e vt divide; (condividere) share. **~si** vr (separarsi) separate

divi'eto m prohibition; **~ di sosta** no parking

divinco'larsi vr wriggle

divinità f inv divinity. **di'vino** adj divine

di'visa f uniform; (Comm) currency

divisi'one f division

di'vismo m worship; (atteggiamento) superstar mentality

di'vi|so pp di **dividere.** **~'sore** m divisor. **~'sorio** adj dividing

'divo, -a mf star

divo'rar|e vt devour. **~si** vr **~si da** be consumed with

divorzi'a|re vi divorce. **~to, -a** mf divorcee. **di'vorzio** m divorce

divul'ga|re vt divulge; (rendere popolare) popularize. **~rsi** vr spread. **~'tivo** adj popular. **~zi'one** f popularization

dizio'nario m dictionary

dizi'one f diction

do m (Mus) C

'doccia f shower; (grondaia) gutter; **fare la ~** have a shower

do'cen|te adj teaching • mf teacher; (Univ) lecturer. **~za** f (Univ) lecturer's qualification

'docile adj docile

documen'tar|e vt document. **~si** vr gather information (**su** about)

documen'tario adj & m documentary

documen'ta|to adj well-documented; (persona) well-informed. **~zi'one** f documentation

d

docu'mento m document

dodi'cesimo adj & m twelfth. **'dodici** adj & m twelve

do'gan|a f customs pl; (dazio) duty. **doga'nale** adj customs. **~i'ere** m customs officer

'doglie fpl labour pains

'dogma m dogma. **dog'matico** adj dogmatic. **~'tismo** m dogmatism

'dolce adj sweet; (clima) mild; (voce, consonante) soft; (acqua) fresh •m (portata) dessert; (torta) cake; **non mangio dolci** I don't eat sweet things. **~'mente** adv sweetly. **dol'cezza** f sweetness; (di clima) mildness

dolce'vita adj inv (maglione) rollneck

dolci'ario adj confectionery

dolci'astro adj sweetish

dolcifi'cante m sweetener •adj sweetening

dolci'umi mpl sweets

do'lente adj painful; (spiacente) sorry

do'le|re vi ache, hurt; (dispiacere) regret. **~rsi** vr regret; (protestare) complain; **~rsi di** be sorry for

'dollaro m dollar

'dolo m (Jur) malice; (truffa) fraud

Dolo'miti fpl **le ~** the Dolomites

do'lore m pain; (morale) sorrow. **dolo'roso** adj painful

do'loso adj malicious

do'manda f question; (richiesta) request; (scritta) application; (Comm) demand; **fare una ~ (a qcno)** ask (sb) a question. **~ di impiego** job application

doman'dar|e vt ask; (esigere) demand; **~e qcsa a qcno** ask sb for sth. **~si** vr wonder

do'mani adv tomorrow; **~ sera** tomorrow evening •m **il ~** the future; **a ~** see you tomorrow

do'ma|re vt tame; fig control (emozioni). **~'tore** m tamer

domat'tina adv tomorrow morning

do'meni|ca f Sunday. **~'cale** adj Sunday attrib

do'mestico, -a adj domestic •m servant •f maid

domicili'are adj **arresti domiciliari** (Jur) house arrest

domicili'arsi vr settle

domi'cilio m domicile; (abitazione) home; **recapitiamo a ~** we do home deliveries

domi'na|re vt dominate; (controllare) control •vi rule over; (prevalere) be dominant. **~rsi** vr control oneself. **~'tore, ~'trice** mf ruler; **~zi'one** f domination

do'minio m control; (Pol) dominion; (ambito) field; **di ~ pubblico** common knowledge

don m inv (ecclesiastico) Father

do'na|re vt give; donate (sangue, organo) •vi **~re a** (giovare esteticamente) suit. **~'tore, ~'trice** mf donor. **~zi'one** f donation

dondo'l|are vt swing; (cullare) rock •vi sway. **~arsi** vr swing. **~io** m rocking. **'dondolo** m swing; **cavallo/sedia a dondolo** rocking-horse/chair

dongio'vanni m inv Romeo

'donna f woman. **~ di servizio** domestic help

don'naccia f pej whore

'dono m gift

'dopo prep after; (a partire da) since •adv afterwards; (più tardi) later; (in seguito) later on; **~ di me** after me

dopo'barba m inv aftershave

dopo'cena m inv evening

dopodiché adv after which

dopodo'mani adv the day after tomorrow

dopogu'erra m inv post-war period

dopo'pranzo m inv afternoon

dopo'sci adj & m inv après-ski

doposcu'ola m inv after-school activities pl

dopo-'shampoo m inv conditioner •adj inv conditioning

dopo'sole m inv aftersun cream •adj inv aftersun

dopo'tutto adv after all

doppi'aggio m dubbing

doppia'mente adv doubly

doppi'a|re vt double; Sport lap; Cinema dub. **~'tore, ~'trice** mf dubber

'doppio adj & adv double. **~ clic** m (Comput) double click. **~ fallo** m

Tennis double fault. ~ **gioco** m double-dealing. ~ **mento** m double chin. ~ **senso** m double entendre. **doppi vetri** mpl double glazing •m double; Tennis doubles pl. ~ **misto** Tennis mixed doubles

doppi'one m duplicate

doppio'petto adj double-breasted

dop'pista mf doubles player

do'ra|re vt gild; (Culin) brown. ~**to** adj gilt; (color oro) golden. ~**'tura** f gilding

dormicchi'are vi doze

dormigli'one, -a mf sleepyhead; fig lazy-bones

dor'mi|re vi sleep; (essere addormentato) be asleep; fig be asleep. ~**ta** f good sleep. ~**'tina** f nap. ~**'torio** m dormitory

dormi'veglia m **essere in** ~ be half asleep

dor'sale adj dorsal •f (di monte) ridge

'dorso m back; (di libro) spine; (di monte) crest; (nel nuoto) backstroke

do'saggio m dosage

do'sare vt dose; fig measure; ~ **le parole** weigh one's words

dosa'tore m measuring jug

'dose f dose; **in buona** ~ fig in good measure. ~ **eccessiva** overdose

dossi'er m inv file

'dosso m (dorso) back; **levarsi di** ~ **gli abiti** take off one's clothes

do'ta|re vt endow; (di accessori) equip. ~**to** adj (persona) gifted; (fornito) equipped. ~**zi'one** f (attrezzatura) equipment; **in** ~**zione** at one's disposal

'dote f dowry; (qualità) gift

'dotto adj learned •m scholar; (Anat) duct

dotto|'rato m doctorate. 🅲**dot'tore,** ~**'ressa** mf doctor

dot'trina f doctrine

'dove adv where; **di** ~ **sei?** where do you come from; **fin** ~**?** how far?; **per** ~**?** which way?

do'vere vi (obbligo) have to, must; **devo andare** I have to go, I must go; **devo venire anch'io?** do I have to come too?; **avresti dovuto dirmelo** you should have told me, you ought to have told me; **devo sedermi un attimo** I must sit down for a minute, I need to sit down for a minute; **dev'essere successo qualcosa** something must have happened; **come si deve** properly •vt (essere debitore di, derivare) owe; **essere dovuto a** be due to •m duty; **per** ~ out of duty. **dove'roso** adj only right and proper

do'vunque adv (dappertutto) everywhere; (in qualsiasi luogo) anywhere •conj wherever

do'vuto adj due; (debito) proper

doz'zi|na f dozen. ~**'nale** adj cheap

dra'gare vt dredge

'drago m dragon

'dramm|a m drama. **dram'matico** adj dramatic. ~**atiz'zare** vt dramatize. ~**a'turgo** m playwright. **dram'mone** m (film) tear-jerker

drappeggi'are vt drape. **drap'peggio** m drapery

drap'pello m (Mil) squad; (gruppo) band

'drastico adj drastic

dre'nare vt drain

drib'blare vt (in calcio) dribble

'dritta f (mano destra) right hand; (Naut) starboard; (informazione) pointer, tip; **a** ~ **e a manca** left, right and centre

'dritto adj = **diritto**[1] •mf 🅸 crafty so-and-so

driz'zar|e vt straighten; (rizzare) prick up. ~**si** vr straighten [up]; (alzarsi) raise

'dro|ga f drug. ~**'gare** vt drug. ~**'garsi** vr take drugs. ~**'gato, -a** mf drug addict

drogh|e'ria f grocery. ~**i'ere, -a** mf grocer

'dubbi|o adj doubtful; (ambiguo) dubious •m doubt; (sospetto) suspicion; **mettere in** ~**o** doubt; **essere fuori** ~**o** be beyond doubt; **essere in** ~**o** be doubtful. ~**'oso** adj doubtful

dubi'ta|re vi doubt; ~**re di** doubt; (diffidare) mistrust; **dubito che venga** I doubt whether he'll come. ~**'tivo** adj ambiguous

🅲 see A-Z of Italian life and culture

'duca, du'chessa mf duke; duchess

'due adj & m two

due'cento adj & m two hundred

du'ello m duel

due'mila adj & m two thousand

due'pezzi m inv (bikini) bikini

du'etto m duo; (Mus) duet

'duna f dune

'dunque conj therefore; (allora) well [then]

'duo m inv duo; (Mus) duet

du'omo m cathedral

dupli'ca|re vt duplicate. **~to** m duplicate. **'duplice** adj double; **in duplice copia** in duplicate

dura'mente adv (lavorare) hard; (rimproverare) harshly

du'rante prep during

du'r|are vi last; (cibo:) keep; (resistere) hold out. **~ata** f duration. **~a'turo, ~evole** adj lasting, enduring

du'rezza f hardness; (di carne) toughness; (di voce, padre) harshness

'duro, -a adj hard; (persona, carne) tough; (voce) harsh; (pane) stale •mf tough person

du'rone m hardened skin

'duttile adj (materiale) ductile; (carattere) malleable

DVD m inv DVD

Ee

e, ed conj and

'ebano m ebony

eb'bene conj well [then]

eb'brezza f inebriation; (euforia) elation; **guida in stato di ~** drink-driving. **'ebbro** adj inebriated; (di gioia) ecstatic

'ebete adj stupid

ebollizi'one f boiling

e'braico adj Hebrew •m (lingua) Hebrew. **e'breo, -a** adj Jewish •mf Jew

eca'tombe f **fare un'~** wreak havoc

ecc abbr (eccetera) etc

ecce'den|te adj (peso, bagaglio) excess. **~za** f excess; (d'avanzo) surplus; **avere qcsa in ~za** have an excess of sth; **bagagli in ~za** excess baggage. **~za di cassa** surplus. **ec'cedere** vt exceed •vi go too far; **eccedere nel bere** drink too much

eccel'len|te adj excellent. **~za** f excellence; (titolo) Excellency; **per ~za** par excellence. **ec'cellere** vi excel (**in** at)

ec'centrico, -a adj & mf eccentric

eccessiva'mente adv excessively.

ecces'sivo adj excessive

ec'cesso m excess; **andare agli eccessi** go to extremes; **all'~** to excess. **~ di velocità** speeding

ec'cetera adv et cetera

ec'cetto prep except; **~ che** (a meno che) unless. **eccettu'are** vt except

eccezio'nal|e adj exceptional. **~'mente** adv exceptionally; (contrariamente alla regola) as an exception

eccezi'one f exception; (Jur) objection; **a ~ di** with the exception of

eccita'mento m excitement. **ecci'tante** adj exciting; (sostanza) stimulant •m stimulant

ecci'ta|re vt excite. **~rsi** vr get excited. **~to** adj excited

eccitazi'one f excitement

ecclesi'astico adj ecclesiastical •m priest

'ecco adv (qui) here; (là) there; **~!** exactly!; **~ fatto** there we are; **~ la tua borsa** here is your bag; **~ [lì] mio figlio** there is my son; **~mi** here I am; **~ tutto** that is all

ec'come adv & int and how!

echeggi'are vi echo

e'clissi f inv eclipse

'eco f (pl m **echi**) echo

ecogra'fia f scan

ecolo'gia f ecology. **eco'logico** adj ecological; (prodotto) environmentally friendly

e commerci'ale f ampersand

econo'm|ia f economy; (scienza) economics; **fare ~ia** economize (**di** on). **eco'nomico** adj economic; (a buon prezzo) cheap. **~ista** mf economist. **~iz'zare** vt/i economize; save (tempo, denaro). **e'conomo, -a** adj thrifty • mf (di collegio) bursar

é'cru adj inv raw

ec'zema m eczema

ed conj vedi **e**

'edera f ivy

e'dicola f [newspaper] kiosk

edifi'cabile adj (area, terreno) classified as suitable for development

edifi'cante adj edifying

edifi'care vt build

edi'ficio m building; fig structure

e'dile adj building attrib

edi'lizi|a f building trade. **~o** adj building attrib

edi|'tore, -'trice adj publishing • mf publisher; (curatore) editor. **~to'ria** f publishing. **~tori'ale** adj publishing • m editorial

edizi'one f edition; (di manifestazione) performance. **~ ridotta** abridg[e]ment. **~ della sera** (di telegiornale) evening news

edu'ca|re vt educate; (allevare) bring up. **~'tivo** adj educational. **~to** adj polite. **~'tore, ~'trice** mf educator. **~zi'one** f education; (di bambini) upbringing; (buone maniere) [good] manners pl. **~zione fisica** physical education

e'felide f freckle

effemi'nato adj effeminate

efferve'scente adj effervescent; (frizzante) fizzy; (aspirina) soluble

effettiva'mente adv **è troppo tardi – ~** it's too late – so it is

effet'tivo adj actual; (efficace) effective; (personale) permanent; (Mil) regular • m sum total

ef'fett|o m effect; (impressione) impression; **in ~i** in fact; **~i personali** personal belongings. **~u'are** vt carry out (controllo, sondaggio). **~u'arsi** vr take place

effi'cac|e adj effective. **~ia** f effectiveness

effici'en|te adj efficient. **~za** f efficiency

ef'fimero adj ephemeral

effusi'one f effusion

E'geo m **l'~** the Aegean [Sea]

E'gitto m Egypt. **egizi'ano, -a** agg & mf Egyptian

'egli pers pron he; **~ stesso** he himself

ego'centrico, -a adj egocentric

ego'is|mo m selfishness. **~ta** adj selfish • mf selfish person. **~tico** adj selfish

e'gregio adj distinguished; **E~ Signore** Dear Sir

eiaculazi'one f ejaculation

elabo'ra|re vt elaborate; process (dati). **~to** adj elaborate. **~zi'one** f elaboration; (di dati) processing. **~zione [di] testi** word processing

elar'gire vt lavish

elastici|tà f elasticity. **~z'zato** adj (stoffa) elasticated. **e'lastico** adj elastic; (tessuto) stretch; (orario, mente) flexible; (persona) easygoing • m elastic; (fascia) rubber band

ele'fante m elephant

ele'gan|te adj elegant. **~za** f elegance

e'leggere vt elect. **eleg'gibile** adj eligible

elemen'tare adj elementary; **scuola ~** primary school

ele'mento m element; **elementi** pl (fatti) data; (rudimenti) elements

ele'mosina f charity; **chiedere l'~** beg. **elemosi'nare** vt/i beg

elen'care vt list

e'lenco m list. **~ abbonati** telephone directory. **~ telefonico** telephone directory

elet'tivo adj (carica) elective. **e'letto, -a** pp di **eleggere** • adj chosen • mf elected member

eletto'ra|le adj electoral. **~to** m electorate

e

elet|'tore, -'trice mf voter
elet'trauto m inv garage for electrical repairs
elettri'cista m electrician
elettri|cità f electricity. **e'lettrico** adj electric. **~z'zante** adj (notizia, gara) electrifying. **~z'zare** vt fig electrify. **~z'zato** adj fig electrified
elettrocardio'gramma m electrocardiogram
e'lettrodo m electrode
elettrodo'mestico m [electrical] household appliance
elet'trone m electron
elet'tronico, -a adj electronic •f electronics
ele'va|re vt raise; (promuovere) promote; (erigere) erect; (fig: migliorare) better; **~ al quadrato/cubo** square/cube. **~rsi** vr rise; (edificio:) stand. **~to** adj high. **~zi'one** f elevation
elezi'one f election
'elica f (Aeron, Naut) propeller; (del ventilatore) blade
eli'cottero m helicopter
elimi'na|re vt eliminate. **~'toria** f Sport preliminary heat. **~zi'one** f elimination
é'li|te f inv élite. **~'tista** adj élitist
'ella pers pron she
el'metto m helmet
elogi'are vt praise
elo'quen|te adj eloquent; fig telltale. **~za** f eloquence
e'lu|dere vt elude; evade (sorveglianza). **~'sivo** adj elusive
el'vetico adj Swiss
emaci'ato adj emaciated
'e-mail f inv e-mail; **indirizzo ~** e-mail address. **~ spazzatura** junk e-mail
ema'na|re vt give off; pass (legge) •vi emanate
emanci'pa|re vt emancipate. **~rsi** vr become emancipated. **~to** adj emancipated. **~zi'one** f emancipation
emargi'na|to m marginalized person. **~zi'one** f marginalization
em'bargo m embargo
em'ble|ma m emblem. **~'matico** adj emblematic
embrio'nale adj embryonic. **embri'one** m embryo
emen|da'mento m amendment. **~'dare** vt amend
emer'gen|te adj emergent. **~za** f emergency; **in caso di ~za** in an emergency
e'mergere vi emerge; (sottomarino:) surface; (distinguersi) stand out
e'merso pp di **emergere**
e'messo pp di **emettere**
e'mettere vt emit; give out (luce, suono); let out (grido); (mettere in circolazione) issue
emi'crania f migraine
emi'gra|re vi emigrate. **~to, -a** mf immigrant. **~zi'one** f emigration
emi'nen|te adj eminent. **~za** f eminence
e'miro m emir
emis'fero m hemisphere
emis'sario m emissary
emissi'one f emission; (di denaro) issue; (trasmissione) broadcast
emit'tente adj issuing; (trasmittente) broadcasting •f transmitter
emorra'gia f haemorrhage
emor'roidi fpl piles
emotività f emotional make-up. **emo'tivo** adj emotional
emozio'na|nte adj exciting; (commovente) moving. **~re** vt excite; (commuovere) move. **~rsi** vr become excited; (commuoversi) be moved. **~to** adj excited; (commosso) moved. **emozi'one** f emotion; (agitazione) excitement
'empio adj impious; (spietato) pitiless; (malvagio) wicked
em'pirico adj empirical
em'porio m emporium; (negozio) general store
emu'la|re vt emulate. **~zi'one** f emulation
emulsi'one f emulsion
en'ciclica f encyclical
enciclope'dia f encyclopaedia
encomi'are vt commend. **en'co-mio** m commendation
en'demico adj endemic
endo've|na f intravenous injection.

~'noso adj intravenous; **per via ~nosa** intravenously

ener'getico adj (risorse, crisi) energy attrib; (alimento) energy-giving

ener'gia f energy. **e'nergico** adj energetic; (efficace) strong

enfasi f emphasis

en'fati|co adj emphatic. **~z'zare** vt emphasize

e'nigma m enigma. **enig'matico** adj enigmatic. **enig'mistica** f puzzles pl

E.N.I.T. m abbr (Ente Nazionale Italiano per il Turismo) Italian State Tourist Office

en'nesimo adj (Math) nth; ⓘ umpteenth

e'norm|e adj enormous. **~e'mente** adv massively. **~ità** f inv enormity; (assurdità) absurdity

eno'teca f wine-tasting shop

ente m board; (società) company; (filosofia) being

entità f inv entity; (gravità) seriousness; (dimensione) extent

entou'rage m inv entourage

en'trambi adj & pron both

en'tra|re vi go in, enter; **~re in** go into; (stare in, trovar posto in) fit into; (arruolarsi) join; **~rci** (avere a che fare) have to do with; **tu che c'entri?** what has it got to do with you? **~ta** f entrance; **~te** pl (Comm) takings; (reddito) income sg

entro prep (tempo) within

entro'terra m inv hinterland

entusias'mante adj fascinating

entusias'mar|e vt arouse enthusiasm in. **~si** vr be enthusiastic (**per** about)

entusi'as|mo m enthusiasm. **~ta** adj enthusiastic • mf enthusiast. **~tico** adj enthusiastic

enume'ra|re vt enumerate. **~zi'one** f enumeration

enunci'a|re vt enunciate. **~zi'one** f enunciation

epa'tite f hepatitis

epico adj epic

epide'mia f epidemic

epi'dermide f epidermis

epifa'nia f Epiphany

epi'gramma m epigram

epil|es'sia f epilepsy. **epi'lettico, -a** adj & mf epileptic

e'pilogo m epilogue

epi'sodi|co adj episodic; **caso ~co** one-off case. **~o** m episode

'epoca f age; (periodo) period; **a quell'~** in those days; **auto d'~** vintage car

ep'pure conj [and] yet

epu'rare vt purge

equa'tore m equator. **equatori'ale** adj equatorial

equazi'one f equation

e'questre adj equestrian; **circo ~** circus

equili'bra|re vt balance. **~to** adj well-balanced. **equi'librio** m balance; (buon senso) common sense; (di bilancia) equilibrium

equili'brismo m **fare ~** do a balancing act

e'quino adj horse attrib

equi'nozio m equinox

equipaggia'mento m equipment

equipaggi'are vt equip; (di persone) man

equi'paggio m crew; (Aeron) cabin crew

equipa'rare vt make equal

é'quipe f inv team

equità f equity

equitazi'one f riding

equiva'len|te adj & m equivalent. **~za** f equivalence

equiva'lere vi **~ a** be equivalent to

equivo'care vi misunderstand

e'quivoco adj equivocal; (sospetto) suspicious • m misunderstanding

'equo adj fair, just

'era f era

'erba f grass; (aromatica, medicinale) herb. **~ cipollina** chives pl. **er'baccia** f weed. **er'baceo** adj herbaceous

erbi'cida m weed-killer

erbo'rist|a mf herbalist. **~e'ria** f herbalist's shop

er'boso adj grassy

ⓘ *see A-Z of Italian life and culture*

e

er'culeo adj (forza) herculean

e'red|e mf heir; heiress. **~ità** f inv inheritance; (Biol) heredity. **~i'tare** vt inherit. **~itarietà** f heredity. **~i'tario** adj hereditary

ere'sia f heresy. **e'retico, -a** adj heretical • mf heretic

e're|tto pp di **erigere** • adj erect. **~zi'one** f erection; (costruzione) building

er'gastolo m life sentence; (luogo) prison

'erica f heather

e'rigere vt erect; (fig: fondare) found

eri'tema m (cutaneo) inflammation; (solare) sunburn

er'metico adj hermetic; (a tenuta d'aria) airtight

'ernia f hernia

e'rodere vi erode

e'ro|e m hero. **~ico** adj heroic. **~'ismo** m heroism

ero'ga|re vt distribute; (fornire) supply. **~zi'one** f supply

ero'ina f heroine; (droga) heroin

erosi'one f erosion

e'rotico adj erotic.

er'rante adj wandering. **er'rare** vi wander; (sbagliare) be mistaken

er'rato adj (sbagliato) mistaken

erronea'mente adv mistakenly

er'rore m error; (di stampa) misprint; **essere in ~** be wrong

'erta f **stare all'~** be on the alert

eru'di|rsi vr get educated. **~to** adj learned

erut'tare vt (vulcano:) erupt • vi (ruttare) belch. **eruzi'one** f eruption; (Med) rash

esage'ra|re vt exaggerate • vi exaggerate; (nel comportamento) go over the top; **~re nel mangiare** eat too much. **~ta'mente** adv excessively. **~to** adj exaggerated; (prezzo) exorbitant • m **è un ~to** he exaggerates. **~zi'one** f exaggeration; **è costato un'~zione** it cost the earth

esa'lare vt/i exhale

esal'ta|re vt exalt; (entusiasmare) elate. **~to** adj (fanatico) fanatical • m fanatic. **~zi'one** f exaltation; (in discorso) fervour

e'same m examination, exam; **dare un ~** take an exam; **prendere in ~** examine. **~ del sangue** blood test. **esami** pl **di maturità** ≈ A-levels

esami'na|re vt examine. **~'tore, ~'trice** mf examiner

e'sangue adj bloodless

e'sanime adj lifeless

esaspe'rante adj exasperating

esaspe'ra|re vt exasperate. **~rsi** vr get exasperated. **~zi'one** f exasperation

esat|ta'mente adv exactly. **~'tezza** f exactness; (precisione) precision; (di risultato) accuracy

e'satto pp di **esigere** • adj exact; (risposta, risultato) correct; (orologio) right; **hai l'ora esatta?** do you have the right time?; **sono le due esatte** it's two o'clock exactly

esat'tore m collector

esau'dire vt grant; fulfil (speranze)

esauri'ente adj exhaustive

esau'ri|re vt exhaust. **~rsi** vr exhaust oneself; (merci ecc:) run out. **~to** adj exhausted; (merci) sold out; (libro) out of print; **fare il tutto ~to** (spettacolo:) play to a full house

'esca f bait

escande'scenz|a f outburst; **dare in ~e** lose one's temper

escla'ma|re vi exclaim. **~'tivo** adj exclamatory. **~zi'one** f exclamation

es'clu|dere vt exclude (possibilità, ipotesi). **~si'one** f exclusion. **~'siva** exclusive right; **in ~siva** exclusive **~siva'mente** adv exclusively. **~'sivo** adj exclusive. **~so** pp di **escludere** • adj **non è ~so che ci sia** it's not out of the question that he'll be there

escogi'tare vt contrive

escursi'one f excursion; (scorreria) raid; (di temperatura) range

ese'cra|bile adj abominable. **~re** vt abhor

esecu|'tivo adj & m executive. **~'tore, ~'trice** mf executor; (Mus) performer. **~zi'one** f execution; (Mus) performance

esegu'ire vt carry out; (Jur) execute; (Mus) perform

e'sempio m example; **ad** o **per ~** for example; **dare l'~ a qcno** set sb an example; **fare un ~** give an example

esem'plare m specimen; (di libro) copy

esen'tar|e vt exempt. **~si** vr free oneself. **e'sente** adj exempt. **esente da imposta** duty-free. **esente da IVA** VAT-exempt

esen'tasse adj duty-free

e'sequie fpl funeral rites

eser'cente mf shopkeeper

eserci'ta|re vt exercise; (addestrare) train; (fare uso di) exert; (professione) practise. **~rsi** vr practise. **~zi'one** f exercise; (Mil) drill

e'sercito m army

eser'cizio m exercise; (pratica) practice; (Comm) financial year; (azienda) business; **essere fuori ~** be out of practice

esi'bi|re vt show off; produce (documenti). **~rsi** vr (Theat) perform; fig show off. **~zi'one** f (Theat) performance; (di documenti) production

esibizio'nis|mo m showing off

esi'gen|te adj exacting; (pignolo) fastidious. **~za** f demand; (bisogno) need. **e'sigere** vt demand; (riscuotere) collect

e'siguo adj meagre

esila'rante adj exhilarating

esile adj slender; (voce) thin

esili'a|re vt exile. **~'rsi** vr go into exile. **~to, -a** adj exiled •mf exile. **e'silio** m exile

e'simer|e vt release. **~si** vr **~si da** get out of

esi'sten|te adj existing. **~za** f existence.

e'sistere vi exist

esi'tante adj hesitating; (voce) faltering

esi'ta|re vi hesitate. **~zi'one** f hesitation

'esito m result; **avere buon ~** be a success

'esodo m exodus

e'sofago m oesophagus

esone'rare vt exempt. **e'sonero** m exemption

esorbi'tante adj exorbitant

esorciz'zare vt exorcize

esordi'ente mf person making his/her début. **e'sordio** m opening; (di attore) début. **esor'dire** vi début

esor'tare vt (pregare) beg; (incitare) urge

e'sotico adj exotic

espa'drillas fpl espadrilles

es'pan|dere vt expand. **~dersi** vr expand; (diffondersi) extend. **~si'one** f expansion. **~'sivo** adj expansive; (persona) friendly

espatri'are vi leave one's country. **es'patrio** m expatriation

espedi'ente m expedient; **vivere di ~i** live by one's wits

es'pellere vt expel

esperi|'enza f experience; **parlare per ~enza** speak from experience. **~'mento** m experiment

es'perto, -a adj & mf expert

espi'a|re vt atone for. **~'torio** adj expiatory

espi'rare vt/i breathe out

espli'care vt carry on

esplicita'mente adv explicitly. **es'plicito** adj explicit

es'plodere vi explode •vt fire

esplo'ra|re vt explore. **~'tore, ~'trice** mf explorer; **giovane ~tore** boy scout. **~zi'one** f exploration

esplo|si'one f explosion. **~'sivo** adj & m explosive

es'por|re vt expose; display (merci); (spiegare) expound; exhibit (quadri ecc). **~si** vr (compromettersi) compromise oneself; (al sole) expose oneself

espor'ta|re vt export. **~'tore, ~'trice** mf exporter. **~zi'one** f export

esposizi'one f (mostra) exhibition; (in vetrina) display; (spiegazione ecc) exposition; (posizione, fotografia) exposure. **es'posto** pp di **esporre** •adj exposed; **esposto a** (rivolto) facing •m (Jur) statement

e

espressa'mente adv expressly; **non l'ha detto ~** he didn't put it in so many words

espres|si'one f expression. **~'sivo** adj expressive

es'presso pp di **esprimere** •adj express •m (lettera) express letter; (treno) express train; (caffè) espresso; **per ~** (spedire) [by] express [post]

e

es'primer|e vt express. **~si** vr express oneself

espropri'a|re vt dispossess. **~zi'one** f (Jur) expropriation. **es'proprio** m expropriation

espulsi'one f expulsion. **es'pulso** pp di **espellere**

es'senz|a f essence. **~i'ale** adj essential •m important thing. **~ial'mente** adj essentially

'essere

•vi be; **c'è** there is; **ci sono** there are; **che ora è? – sono le dieci** what time is it? – it's ten o'clock; **chi è? – sono io** who is it? – it's me; **ci sono!** (*ho capito*) I've got it!; **ci siamo!** (*siamo arrivati*) here we are at last!; **siamo in due** there are two of us; **questa camicia è da lavare** this shirt is to be washed; **non è da te** it's not like you; **~ di** (*provenire da*) be from; **~ per** (*favorevole*) be in favour of; **se fossi in te,...** if I were you,...; **sarà!** if you say so!; **come sarebbe a dire?** what are you getting at?

•v aux have; (*in passivi*) be; **siamo arrivati** we have arrived; **ci sono stato ieri** I was there yesterday; **sono nato a Torino** I was born in Turin; **è riconosciuto come...** he is recognized as...; **è stato detto che** it has been said that

•m being. **~ umano** human being. **~ vivente** living creature

essic'cato adj dried

'esso, -a pers pron he, she; (cosa, animale) it

est m east

'estasi f ecstasy; **andare in ~ per** go into raptures over

e'state f summer

e'sten|dere vt extend. **~dersi** vr spread; (allungarsi) stretch. **~si'one** f extension; (ampiezza) expanse; (Mus) range. **~'sivo** adj extensive

estenu'ante adj exhausting

estenu'a|re vt wear out; deplete (risorse, casse). **~rsi** vr wear oneself out

esteri'or|e adj & m exterior. **~'mente** adv externally; (di persone) outwardly

esterna'mente adv on the outside

ester'nare vt express, show

e'sterno adj external; **per uso ~** for external use only •m (allievo) day-boy; (Archit) exterior; (in film) location shot

'estero adj foreign •m foreign countries pl; **all'~** abroad

esterre'fatto adj horrified

e'steso pp di **estendere** •adj extensive; (diffuso) widespread; **per ~** (scrivere) in full

e'stetic|a f aesthetics sg. **~a'mente** adv aesthetically. **~o, -a** adj aesthetic; (chirurgia, chirurgo) plastic. **este'tista** f beautician

'estimo m estimate

e'stin|guere vt extinguish. **~guersi** vr die out. **~to, -a** pp di **estinguere** •mf deceased. **~'tore** m [fire] extinguisher. **~zi'one** f extinction; (di incendio) putting out

estir'pa|re vt uproot; extract (dente); fig eradicate (crimine, malattia). **~zi'one** f eradication; (di dente) extraction

e'stivo adj summer

e'stor|cere vt extort. **~si'one** f extortion. **~to** pp di **estorcere**

estradizi'one f extradition

e'straneo, -a adj extraneous; (straniero) foreign •mf stranger

estrani'ar|e vt estrange. **~si** vr become estranged

e'stra|rre vt extract; (sorteggiare) draw. **~tto** pp di **estrarre** •m extract; (brano) excerpt; (documento) abstract. **~tto conto** statement [of account], bank statement. **~zi'one** f extraction; (sorte) draw

estrema'mente adv extremely

estre'mis|mo m extremism. **~ta** mf extremist

estremità f inv extremity; (di una corda) end •fpl (Anat) extremities

e'stremo adj extreme; (ultimo) last; **misure estreme** drastic measures; **l'E~ Oriente** the Far East •m (limite) extreme. **estremi** pl (di documento) main points; (di reato) essential elements; **essere agli estremi** be at the end of one's tether

'estro m (disposizione artistica) talent; (ispirazione) inspiration; (capriccio) whim. **e'stroso** adj talented; (capriccioso) unpredictable

estro'mettere vt expel

estro'verso adj extroverted •m extrovert

estu'ario m estuary

esube'ran|te adj exuberant. **~za** f exuberance

'esule mf exile

esul'tante adj exultant

esul'tare vi rejoice

esu'mare vt exhume

età f inv age; **raggiungere la maggiore ~** come of age; **un uomo di mezz'~** a middle-aged man

'etere m ether. **e'tereo** adj ethereal

eterna'mente adv eternally

eternità f eternity; **è un'~ che non la vedo** I haven't seen her for ages

e'terno adj eternal; (questione, problema) age-old; **in ~** [!] for ever

eterosessu'ale mf heterosexual

'etica f ethics

eti'chetta[1] f label; price-tag

eti'chetta[2] f etiquette

etichet'tare vt label

'etico adj ethical

eti'lometro m Breathalyzer®

Eti'opia f Ethiopia

'etnico adj ethnic

e'trusco adj & mf Etruscan

'ettaro m hectare

'etto, etto'grammo m hundred grams, ≈ quarter pound

eucari'stia f Eucharist

eufe'mismo m euphemism

eufo'ria f elation; (Med) euphoria. **eu'forico** adj elated; (Med) euphoric

'euro m inv Fin euro

Euro'city m international Intercity

eurodepu'tato m Euro MP, MEP

Eu'ropa f Europe. **euro'peo, -a** agg & mf European

eutana'sia f euthanasia

evacu'a|re vt evacuate. **~zi'one** f evacuation

e'vadere vt evade; (sbrigare) deal with •vi **~ da** escape from

evane'scente adj vanishing

evan'gel|ico adj evangelical. **evange'lista** m evangelist

evapo'ra|re vi evaporate. **~zi'one** f evaporation

evasi'one f escape; (fiscale) evasion; fig escapism. **eva'sivo** adj evasive

e'vaso pp di **evadere** •m fugitive

eva'sore m **~ fiscale** tax evader

eveni'enza f eventuality

e'vento m event

eventu'al|e adj possible. **~ità** f inv eventuality

evi'den|te adj evident; **è ~te che** it is obvious that. **~te'mente** adv evidently. **~za** f evidence; **mettere in ~za** emphasize; **mettersi in ~za** make oneself conspicuous

evidenzi'a|re vt highlight. **~'tore** m (penna) highlighter

evi'tare vt avoid; (risparmiare) spare

evo'care vt evoke

evo'lu|to pp di **evolvere** •adj evolved; (progredito) progressive; (civiltà, nazione) advanced; **una donna evoluta** a modern woman. **~zi'one** f evolution; (di ginnastica, aereo) circle

e'volver|e vt develop. **~si** vr evolve

ev'viva int hurray; **~ il Papa!** long live the Pope!; **gridare ~** cheer

ex+ pref ex+, former

'extra adj inv extra; (qualità) first-class •m inv extra

▣ **extracomuni'tario** adj non-EU

extrater'restre mf extra-terrestrial

▣ *see A-Z of Italian life and culture*

Ff

fa[1] m inv (Mus) F

fa[2] adv ago; **due mesi ~** two months ago

fabbi'sogno m requirements pl

'fabbrica f factory

fabbri'cabile adj (area, terreno) that can be built on

fabbri'cante m manufacturer

fabbri'ca|re vt build; (produrre) manufacture; (fig: inventare) fabricate. **~to** m building. **~zi'one** f manufacturing; (costruzione) building

'fabbro m blacksmith

fac'cend|a f matter; **~e** pl (lavori domestici) housework sg. **~i'ere** m wheeler-dealer

fac'chino m porter

'facci|a f face; (di foglio) side; **~a a ~a** face to face; **~a tosta** cheek; **voltar ~a** change sides; **di ~a** (palazzo) opposite; **alla ~a di** (!: a dispetto di) in spite of. **~'ata** f façade; (di foglio) side; (fig: esteriorità) outward appearance

fa'ceto adj facetious; **tra il serio e il ~** half joking

fa'chiro m fakir

'facil|e adj easy; (affabile) easygoing; **essere ~e alle critiche** be quick to criticize; **essere ~e al riso** laugh a lot; **~e a farsi** easy to do; **è ~e che piova** it's likely to rain. **~ità** f ease; (disposizione) aptitude; **avere ~ità di parola** express oneself well

facili'ta|re vt facilitate. **~zi'one** f facility; **~zioni** pl special terms

facil'mente adv (con facilità) easily; (probabilmente) probably

faci'lone adj slapdash. **~'ria** f slapdash attitude

facino'roso adj violent

facoltà f inv faculty; (potere) power. **facolta'tivo** adj optional; **fermata facoltativa** request stop

facol'toso adj wealthy

'faggio m beech

fagi'ano m pheasant

fagio'lino m French bean

fagi'olo m bean; **a ~** (arrivare, capitare) at the right time

fagoci'tare vt gobble up (società)

fa'gotto m bundle; (Mus) bassoon

'faida f feud

fai da te m do-it-yourself, DIY

fal'cata f stride

'falc|e f scythe. **fal'cetto** m sickle. **~i'are** vt cut; fig mow down. **~ia'trice** f [lawn-]mower

'falco m hawk

fal'cone m falcon

'falda f stratum; (di neve) flake; (di cappello) brim; (pendio) slope

fale'gname m carpenter. **~'ria** f carpentry

'falla f leak

fal'lace adj deceptive

fallimen'tare adj disastrous; (Jur) bankruptcy. **falli'mento** m Fin bankruptcy; fig failure

fal'li|re vi Fin go bankrupt; fig fail • vt miss (colpo). **~to, -a** adj unsuccessful; Fin bankrupt • mf failure; Fin bankrupt

'fallo m fault; (errore) mistake; Sport foul; (imperfezione) flaw; **senza ~** without fail

falò m inv bonfire

fal'sar|e vt alter; (falsificare) falsify. **~io, -a** mf forger; (di documenti) counterfeiter

falsifi'ca|re vt fake; (contraffare) forge. **~zi'one** f (di documento) falsification

falsità f falseness

'falso adj false; (sbagliato) wrong; (opera d'arte ecc) fake; (gioielli, oro) imitation • m forgery; **giurare il ~** commit perjury

'**fama** f fame; (reputazione) reputation

'**fame** f hunger; **aver ~** be hungry; **fare la ~** barely scrape a living. **fa'melico** adj ravenous

famige'rato adj infamous

fa'miglia f family

famili'ar|e adj family attrib; (ben noto) familiar; (senza cerimonie) informal • mf relative, relation **~ità** f familiarity; (informalità) informality. **~iz'zarsi** vr familiarize oneself

fa'moso adj famous

fa'nale m lamp; (Auto) light. **fanali** pl **posteriori** (Auto) rear lights

fa'natico, -a adj fanatical; **essere ~ di calcio** be a football fanatic • mf fanatic. **fana'tismo** m fanaticism

fanci'ul|la f young girl. **~'lezza** f childhood. **~lo** m young boy

fan'donia f lie; **fandonie!** nonsense!

fan'fara f fanfare; (complesso) brass band

fanfaro'nata f brag. **fanfa'rone, -a** mf braggart

fan'ghiglia f mud. '**fango** m mud. **fan'goso** adj muddy

fannul'lone, -a mf idler

fantasci'enza f science fiction

fanta'si|a f fantasy; (immaginazione) imagination; (capriccio) fancy; (di tessuto) pattern. **~'oso** adj (stilista, ragazzo) imaginative; (resoconto) improbable

fan'tasma m ghost

fantasti'c|are vi day-dream. **~he'ria** f day-dream. **fan'tastico** adj fantastic; (racconto) fantasy

'**fante** m infantryman; (nelle carte) jack. **~'ria** m infantry

fan'tino m jockey

fan'toccio m puppet

fanto'matico adj phantom attrib

fara'butto m trickster

fara'ona f (uccello) guinea-fowl

far'ci|re vt stuff; fill (torta). **~to** adj stuffed; (dolce) filled

far'dello m bundle; fig burden

'**fare**

• vt do; make (dolce, letto ecc); (*recitare la parte di*) play; (*trascorrere*) spend; **~ una pausa/un sogno** have a break/a dream; **~ colpo su** impress; **~ paura a** frighten; **~ piacere a** please; **farla finita** put an end to it; **~ l'insegnante** be a teacher; **~ lo scemo** play the idiot; **~ una settimana al mare** spend a week at the seaside; **3 più 3 fa 6** 3 and 3 makes 6; **quanto fa? – fanno 10 000 euro** how much is it? – it's 10,000 euros; **far ~ qcsa a qcno** get sb to do sth; (*costringere*) make sb do sth; **~ vedere** show; **fammi parlare** let me speak; **niente a che ~ con** nothing to do with; **non c'è niente da ~** (*per problema*) there is nothing we/you/etc. can do; **fa caldo/buio** it's warm/dark; **non fa niente** it doesn't matter; **strada facendo** on the way; **farcela** (*riuscire*) manage

• vi **fai in modo di venire** try and come; **~ da** act as; **~ per** make as if to; **~ presto** be quick; **non fa per me** it's not for me

• m way; **sul far del giorno** at daybreak.

• **farsi** vr (*diventare*) get; **farsi avanti** come forward; **farsi i fatti propri** mind one's own business; **farsi la barba** shave; **farsi il ragazzo** [!] find a boyfriend; **farsi male** hurt oneself; **farsi strada** (*aver successo*) make one's way in the world

fa'retto m spot[light]

far'falla f butterfly

farfal'lino m (cravatta) bow tie

farfugli'are vt mutter

fa'rina f flour. **fari'nacei** mpl starchy food sg

fa'ringe f pharynx

fari'noso adj (neve) powdery; (mela) soft; (patata) floury

farma|'ceutico adj pharmaceutical. [C] **~'cia** f pharmacy; (negozio) chemist's [shop]. **~cia di turno** duty chemist. **~'cista** mf chemist. '**farmaco** m drug

[C] *see* A-Z of Italian life and culture

f

'faro m (Auto) headlight; (Aeron) beacon; (costruzione) lighthouse

'farsa f farce

'fasci|a f band; (zona) area; (ufficiale) sash; (benda) bandage. **~'are** vt bandage; cling to (fianchi). **~a'tura** f dressing; (azione) bandaging

fa'scicolo m file; (di rivista) issue; (libretto) booklet

'fascino m fascination

'fascio m bundle; (di fiori) bunch

f

fa'scis|mo m fascism. **~ta** mf fascist

'fase f phase

fa'stidi|o m nuisance; (scomodo) inconvenience; **dar ~o a qcno** bother sb; **~i** pl (preoccupazioni) worries; (disturbi) troubles. **~'oso** adj tiresome

'fasto m pomp. **fa'stoso** adj sumptuous

fa'sullo adj bogus

'fata f fairy

fa'tale adj fatal; (inevitabile) fated

fata'l|ismo m fatalism. **~ista** mf fatalist. **~ità** f inv fate; (caso sfortunato) misfortune. **~'mente** adv inevitably

fa'tica f effort; (lavoro faticoso) hard work; (stanchezza) fatigue; **a ~** with great difficulty; **è ~ sprecata** it's a waste of time; **fare ~ a fare qcsa** find it difficult to do sth; **fare ~ a finire qcsa** struggle to finish sth. **fati'caccia** f pain

fati'ca|re vi toil; **~re a** (stentare) find it difficult to. **~ta** f effort; (sfacchinata) grind. **fati'coso** adj tiring; (difficile) difficult

'fato m fate

fat'taccio m hum foul deed

fat'tezze fpl features

fat'tibile adj feasible

'fatto pp di **fare** •adj done, made; **~ a mano** hand-made •m fact; (azione) action; (avvenimento) event; **bada ai fatti tuoi!** mind your own business; **di ~** in fact; **in ~ di** as regards

fat'to|re m (Math, causa) factor; (di fattoria) farm manager. **~'ria** f farm; (casa) farmhouse

fatto'rino m messenger [boy]

fattucchi'era f witch

fat'tura f (stile) cut; (lavorazione) workmanship; (Comm) invoice

fattu'ra|re vt invoice; (adulterare) adulterate. **~to** m turnover, sales pl. **~zi'one** f invoicing, billing

'fatuo adj fatuous

fau'tore m supporter

'fava f broad bean

fa'vella f speech

fa'villa f spark

'favo|la f fable; (fiaba) story; (oggetto di pettegolezzi) laughing-stock; (meraviglia) dream. **~'loso** adj fabulous

fa'vore m favour; **essere a ~ di** be in favour of; **per ~** please; **di ~** (condizioni, trattamento) preferential. **~ggia'mento** m (Jur) aiding and abetting. **favo'revole** adj favourable. **~vol'mente** adv favourably

favo'ri|re vt favour; (promuovere) promote; **vuol ~re?** (a cena, pranzo) will you have some?; (entrare) will you come in?. **~to, -a** adj & mf favourite

fax m inv fax. **fa'xare** vt fax

fazi'one f faction

faziosità f bias. **fazi'oso** m sectarian

fazzolet'tino m ~ **[di carta]** [paper] tissue

fazzo'letto m handkerchief; (da testa) headscarf

feb'braio m February

'febbre f fever; **avere la ~** have o run a temperature. **~ da fieno** hay fever. **feb'brile** adj feverish

'feccia f dregs pl

'fecola f potato flour

fecon'da|re vt fertilize. **~'tore** m fertilizer. **~zi'one** f fertilization. **~zione artificiale** artificial insemination. **fe'condo** adj fertile

'fede f faith; (fiducia) trust; (anello) wedding-ring; **in buona/mala ~** in good/bad faith; **prestar ~ a** believe; **tener ~ alla parola** keep one's word. **fe'dele** adj faithful •mf believer; (seguace) follower. **~l'mente** adv faithfully. **~ltà** f faithfulness

---

see A-Z of Italian life and culture

'federa f pillowcase

fede'ra|le adj federal. **~'lismo** m federalism. **~zi'one** f federation

fe'dina f **avere la ~ penale sporca/pulita** have a/no criminal record

'fegato m liver; fig guts pl

'felce f fern

fe'lic|e adj happy; (fortunato) lucky. **~ità** f happiness

felici'ta|rsi vr **~rsi con** congratulate. **~zi'oni** fpl congratulations

'felpa f (indumento) sweatshirt

fel'pato adj brushed; (passo) stealthy

'feltro m felt; (cappello) felt hat

'femmin|a f female. **femmi'nile** adj feminine; (abbigliamento) women's; (sesso) female • m feminine. **~ilità** f femininity. **femmi'nismo** m feminism

'femore m femur

'fend|ere vt split. **~i'tura** f split; (in roccia) crack

feni'cottero m flamingo

fenome'nale adj phenomenal. **fe'nomeno** m phenomenon

'feretro m coffin

feri'ale adj weekday; **giorno ~** weekday

'ferie fpl holidays; (di università, tribunale ecc) vacation sg; **andare in ~** go on holiday

feri'mento m wounding

fe'ri|re vt wound; (in incidente) injure; fig hurt. **~rsi** vr injure oneself. **~ta** f wound. **~to** adj wounded • m wounded person; (Mil) casualty

'ferma f (Mil) period of service

fermaca'pelli m inv hairslide

ferma'carte m inv paperweight

fermacra'vatta m inv tiepin

fer'maglio m clasp; (spilla) brooch; (per capelli) hair slide

ferma'mente adv firmly

fer'ma|re vt stop; (fissare) fix; (Jur) detain • vi stop. **~rsi** vr stop. **~ta** f stop. **~ta dell'autobus** bus-stop. **~ta a richiesta** request stop

fermen'ta|re vi ferment. **~zi'one** f fermentation. **fer'mento** m ferment; (lievito) yeast

fer'mezza f firmness

'fermo adj still; (veicolo) stationary; (stabile) steady; (orologio) not working • m (Jur) detention; (Mech) catch; **in stato di ~** in custody

fe'roc|e adj ferocious; (bestia) wild; (dolore) unbearable. **~e'mente** adv fiercely. **~ia** f ferocity

fer'raglia f scrap iron

ferra'gosto m 15th August (bank holiday in Italy); (periodo) August holidays pl

ferra'menta fpl ironmongery sg; **negozio di ~** ironmonger's

fer'ra|re vt shoe (cavallo). **~to** adj **~to in** (preparato in) well up on

'ferreo adj iron

'ferro m iron; (attrezzo) tool; (di chirurgo) instrument; **bistecca ai ferri** grilled steak; **di ~** (memoria) excellent; (alibi) cast-iron; **salute di ~** iron constitution. **~ battuto** wrought iron. **~ da calza** knitting needle. **~ di cavallo** horseshoe. **~ da stiro** iron

ferro'vecchio m scrap merchant

ferro'vi|a f railway. **~'ario** adj railway. **~'ere** m railwayman

'fertil|e adj fertile. **~ità** f fertility. **~iz'zante** m fertilizer

fer'vente adj blazing; fig fervent

'fervere vi (preparativi:) be well under way

'fervid|o adj fervent; **~i auguri** best wishes

fer'vore m fervour

fesse'ria f nonsense

'fesso pp di **fendere** • adj cracked; (!: sciocco) foolish • m ! (idiota) fool; **far ~ qcno** con sb

fes'sura f crack; (per gettone ecc) slot

'festa f feast; (giorno festivo) holiday; (compleanno) birthday; (ricevimento) party; fig joy; **fare ~ a qcno** welcome sb; **essere in ~** be on holiday; **far ~** celebrate. **~i'olo** adj festive

festeggia'mento m celebration; (manifestazione) festivity

festeggi'are vt celebrate; (accogliere festosamente) give a hearty welcome to

fe'stino m party

festività fpl festivities. **fe'stivo** adj holiday; (lieto) festive. **festivi** mpl public holidays

fe'stoso adj merry

fe'tente adj evil smelling; fig revolting •mf [!] bastard

fe'ticcio m fetish

'feto m foetus

fe'tore m stench

'fetta f slice; **a fette** sliced. ~ **biscottata** slices of crispy toast-like bread

fet'tuccia f tape; (con nome) name tape

feu'dale adj feudal. **'feudo** m feud

FFSS abbr (Ferrovie dello Stato) Italian state railways

fi'aba f fairy-tale. **fia'besco** adj fairy-tale

fi'acc|a f weariness; (indolenza) laziness; **battere la ~a** be sluggish. **fiac'care** vt weaken. **~o** adj weak; (indolente) slack; (stanco) weary; (partita) dull

fi'acco|la f torch. **~'lata** f torchlight procession

fi'ala f phial

fi'amma f flame; (Naut) pennant; **in fiamme** aflame. **andare in fiamme** go up in flames. ~ **ossidrica** blowtorch

fiam'ma|nte adj flaming; **nuovo ~nte** brand new. **~ta** f blaze

fiammeggi'are vi blaze

fiam'mifero m match

fiam'mingo, -a adj Flemish •mf Fleming •m (lingua) Flemish

fiancheggi'are vt border; fig support

fi'anco m side; (di persona) hip; (di animale) flank; (Mil) wing; **al mio ~** by my side; **~ a ~** (lavorare) side by side

fi'asco m flask; fig fiasco; **fare ~** be a fiasco

fia'tare vi breathe; (parlare) breathe a word

fi'ato m breath; (vigore) stamina; **strumenti a ~** wind instruments; **senza ~** breathlessly; **tutto d'un ~** (bere, leggere) all in one go

'fibbia f buckle

'fibra f fibre; **fibre** pl (alimentari) roughage. ~ **ottica** optical fibre

ficca'naso mf nosey parker

fic'car|e vt thrust; drive (chiodo ecc); ([!]: mettere) shove. **~si** vr thrust oneself; (nascondersi) hide; **~si nei guai** get oneself into trouble

fiche f inv (gettone) chip

'fico m (albero) fig-tree; (frutto) fig. ~ **d'India** prickly pear

'fico, -a [!] mf cool sort •adj cool

fidanza'mento m engagement

fidan'za|rsi vr get engaged. **~to, -a** mf (ufficiale) fiancé; fiancée

fi'da|rsi vr **~rsi di** trust. **~to** adj trustworthy

'fido m devoted follower; (Comm) credit

fi'duci|a f confidence; **degno di ~a** trustworthy; **persona di ~a** reliable person; **di ~a** (fornitore) usual. **~'oso** adj trusting

fi'ele m bile; fig bitterness

fie'nile m barn. **fi'eno** m hay

fi'era f fair

fie'rezza f (dignità) pride. **fi'ero** adj proud

fi'evole adj faint; (luce) dim

'fifa f [!] jitters; **aver ~** have the jitters

'figli|a f daughter; **~a unica** only child. **~'astra** f stepdaughter. **~'astro** m stepson. **~o** m son; (generico) child. **~o unico** only child

figli'occi|a f goddaughter. **~o** m godson

figli'o|la f girl. **~'lanza** f offspring. **~lo** m boy

'figo, -a ▸**fico, -a**

fi'gura f figure; (aspetto esteriore) shape; (illustrazione) illustration; **far bella/brutta ~** make a good/bad impression; **mi hai fatto fare una brutta ~** you made me look a fool; **che ~!** how embarrassing!. **figu'raccia** f bad impression

figu'ra|re vt represent; (simboleggiare) symbolize; (immaginare) imagine •vi (far figura) cut a dash; (in lista) appear. **~rsi** vr (immaginarsi) imagine; **~ti!** imagine that!; **posso? – [ma] ~ti!** may I? – of course!. **~'tivo** adj figurative

figu'rina f ≈ cigarette card

figu|ri'nista mf dress designer. **~'rino** m fashion sketch. **~'rone** m **fare un ~rone** make an excellent impression

'fila f line; (di soldati ecc) file; (di oggetti) row; (coda) queue; **di ~** in succession; **fare la ~** queue [up], stand in line Am

fi'lare vt spin; (Naut) pay out • vi (andarsene) run away; (liquido:) trickle; **fila!** [!] scram!; **~ con** ([!]: amoreggiare) go out with

filar'monica f (orchestra) orchestra

fila'strocca f rigmarole; (per bambini) nursery rhyme

fi'la|to adj spun; (ininterrotto) running; (continuato) uninterrupted; **di ~to** (subito) immediately • m yarn

fil di 'ferro m wire

fi'letto m (bordo) border; (di vite) thread; (Culin) fillet

fili'ale adj filial • f (Comm) branch

fili'grana f filigree; (su carta) watermark

film m inv film. **~ giallo** thriller. **~ a lungo metraggio** feature film

fil'ma|re vt film. **~to** m short film. **fil'mino** m cine film

'filo m thread; (tessile) yarn; (metallico) wire; (di lama) edge; (venatura) grain; (di perle) string; (d'erba) blade; (di luce) ray; **con un ~ di voce** in a whisper; **fare il ~ a qcno** fancy sb; **perdere il ~** lose the thread. **~ spinato** barbed wire

'filobus m inv trolleybus

filodiffusi'one f rediffusion

fi'lone m vein; (di pane) long loaf

filoso'fia f philosophy. **fi'losofo, -a** mf philosopher

fil'trare vt filter. **'filtro** m filter

'filza f string

fin ▸**fine, fino**[1]

fi'nal|e adj final • m end • f Sport final. **fina'lista** mf finalist. **~ità** f inv finality; (scopo) aim. **~'mente** adv at last; (in ultimo) finally

fi'nanz|a f finance; **~i'ario** adj financial. **~i'ere** m financier; (guardia di finanza) customs officer. **~ia'mento** m funding

finanzi'a|re vt fund, finance. **~'tore, ~'trice** mf backer

finché conj until; (per tutto il tempo che) as long as

'fine adj fine; (sottile) thin; (udito, vista) keen; (raffinato) refined • f end; **alla ~** in the end; **alla fin ~** after all; **in fin dei conti** when all's said and done; **senza ~** endless • m aim. **~ settimana** weekend

fi'nestra f window. **fine'strella** f **di aiuto** (Comput) help box. **fine'strino** m (Auto, Rail) window

fi'nezza f fineness; (sottigliezza) thinness; (raffinatezza) refinement

'finger|e vt pretend; feign (affetto ecc). **~si** vr pretend to be

fini'menti mpl finishing touches; (per cavallo) harness sg

fini'mondo m end of the world; fig pandemonium

fi'ni|re vt/i finish, end; (smettere) stop; (diventare, andare a finire) end up; **~scila!** stop it!. **~to** adj finished; (abile) accomplished. **~'tura** f finish

finlan'dese adj Finnish • mf Finn • m (lingua) Finnish

Fin'landia f Finland

'fino[1] prep **~ a** till, until; (spazio) as far as; **~ all'ultimo** to the last; **fin da** (tempo) since; (spazio) from; **fin qui** as far as here; **fin troppo** too much; **~ a che punto** how far

'fino[2] adj fine; (acuto) subtle; (puro) pure

fi'nocchio m fennel; ([!]: omosessuale) poof

fi'nora adv so far, up till now

'finta f sham; Sport feint; **far ~ di** pretend to; **far ~ di niente** act as if nothing had happened; **per ~** (per scherzo) for a laugh

'fint|o, -a pp di **fingere** • adj false; (artificiale) artificial; **fare il ~o tonto** act dumb

finzi'one f pretence

fi'occo m bow; (di neve) flake; (nappa) tassel; **coi fiocchi** fig excellent. **~ di neve** snowflake

fi'ocina f harpoon

fi'oco adj weak; (luce) dim

fi'onda f catapult

fio'raio, -a mf florist

fiorda'liso m cornflower

fi'ordo m fiord

fi'ore m flower; (parte scelta) cream; **fiori** pl (nelle carte) clubs; **a fior d'acqua** on the surface of the water; **fior di** (abbondanza) a lot of; **ha i nervi a fior di pelle** his nerves are on edge; **a fiori** flowery

fioren'tino adj Florentine

fio'retto m (scherma) foil; (Relig) act of mortification

fio'rire vi flower; (albero:) blossom; fig flourish

f

fio'rista mf florist

fiori'tura f (di albero) blossoming

fi'otto m **scorrere a fiotti** pour out; **piove a fiotti** the rain is pouring down

Fi'renze f Florence

'firma f signature; (nome) name

fir'ma|re vt sign. **~'tario, -a** mf signatory. **~to** adj (abito, borsa) designer attrib

fisar'monica f accordion

fi'scale adj fiscal

fischi'are vi whistle •vt whistle; (in segno di disapprovazione) boo

fischiet't|are vt whistle. **~io** m whistling

fischi'etto m whistle. **'fischio** m whistle

'fisco m treasury; (tasse) taxation; **il ~** the taxman

'fisica f physics

'fisico, -a adj physical •mf physicist •m physique

'fisima f whim

fisio|lo'gia f physiology. **~'logico** adj physiological

fisiono'mia f features, face; (di paesaggio) appearance

fisiotera'pi|a f physiotherapy. **~sta** mf physiotherapist

fis'sa|re vt fix, fasten; (guardare fissamente) stare at; arrange (appuntamento, ora). **~rsi** vr (stabilirsi) settle; (fissare lo sguardo) stare; **~rsi su** (ostinarsi) set one's mind on; **~rsi di fare qcsa** become obsessed with doing sth. **~to** m obsessive. **~zi'one** f fixation; (ossessione) obsession

'fisso adj fixed; **un lavoro ~** a regular job; **senza fissa dimora** of no fixed abode

fit'tizio adj fictitious

fitto[1] adj thick; **~ di** full of •m depth

fitto[2] m (affitto) rent; **dare a ~** let; **prendere a ~** rent; (noleggiare) hire

fiu'mana f swollen river; fig stream

fi'ume m river; fig stream

fiu'tare vt smell. **fi'uto** m [sense of] smell; fig nose

'flaccido adj flabby

fla'cone m bottle

fla'gello m scourge

fla'grante adj flagrant; **in ~** in the act

fla'nella f flannel

'flash m inv Journ newsflash

'flauto m flute

'flebile adj feeble

'flemma f calm; (Med) phlegm

fles'sibil|e adj flexible. **~ità** f flexibility

flessi'one f (del busto in avanti) forward bend

'flesso pp di **flettere**

flessu'oso adj supple

'flettere vt bend

flir'tare vi flirt

F.lli abbr (fratelli) Bros

'floppy disk m inv floppy disk

'florido adj flourishing

'floscio adj limp; (flaccido) flabby

'flotta f fleet. **flot'tiglia** f flotilla

flu'ente adj fluent

flu'ido m fluid

flu'ire vi flow

fluore'scente adj fluorescent

flu'oro m fluorine

'flusso m flow; (Med) flux; (del mare) flood[-tide]; **~ e riflusso** ebb and flow

fluttu'ante adj fluctuating

fluttu'a|re vi (prezzi, moneta:) fluctuate. **~zi'one** f fluctuation

fluvi'ale adj river

fo'bia f phobia

'foca f seal

fo'caccia f (pane) flat bread; (dolce) ≈ raisin bread

fo'cale adj (distanza, punto) focal. **focaliz'zare** vt get into focus (fotografia); focus (attenzione); define (problema)

'foce f mouth

foco'laio m (Med) focus; fig centre

foco'lare m hearth; (caminetto) fireplace; (Techn) furnace

fo'coso adj fiery

'foder|a f lining; (di libro) dust-jacket; (di poltrona ecc) loose cover. **fode'rare** vt line; cover (libro). **~o** m sheath

'foga f impetuosity

'foggi|a f fashion; (maniera) manner; (forma) shape. **~'are** vt mould

'foglia f leaf; (di metallo) foil

fogli'etto m (pezzetto di carta) piece of paper

'foglio m sheet; (pagina) leaf. **~ elettronico** (Comput) spreadsheet. **~ rosa** (Auto) provisional licence

'fogna f sewer. **~'tura** f sewerage

fo'lata f gust

fol'clo|re m folklore. **~'ristico** adj folk; (bizzarro) weird

folgo'ra|re vi (splendere) shine • vt (con un fulmine) strike. **~zi'one** f (da fulmine, elettrica) electrocution; (idea) brainwave

'folgore f thunderbolt

'folla f crowd

'folle adj mad; **in ~** (Auto) in neutral

folle'mente adv madly

fol'lia f madness; **alla ~** (amare) to distraction

'folto adj thick

fomen'tare vt stir up

fond'ale m (Theat) backcloth

fonda'men|ta fpl foundations. **~'tale** adj fundamental. **~to** m (di principio, teoria) foundation

fon'da|re vt establish; base (ragionamento, accusa). **~to** adj (ragionamento) well-founded. **~zi'one** f establishment; **~zioni** pl (di edificio) foundations

fon'delli mpl **prendere qcno per i ~** [!] pull sb's leg

fon'dente adj (cioccolato) dark

'fonder|e vt/i melt; (colori:) blend. **~si** vr melt; (Comm) merge

'fondi mpl (denaro) funds; (di caffè) grounds

'fondo adj deep; **è notte fonda** it's the middle of the night • m bottom; (fine) end; (sfondo) background; (indole) nature; (somma di denaro) fund; (feccia) dregs pl; **andare a ~** (nave:) sink; **da cima a ~** from beginning to end; **in ~** after all; **in ~ in ~** deep down; **fino in ~** right to the end; (capire) thoroughly. **~ d'investimento** investment trust

fondo'tinta m foundation cream

fon'duta f ≈ fondue

fo'netic|a f phonetics. **~o** adj phonetic

fon'tana f fountain

'fonte f spring; fig source • m font

fo'raggio m forage

fo'rar|e vt pierce; punch (biglietto) • vi puncture. **~si** vr (gomma, pallone:) go soft

'forbici fpl scissors

forbi'cine fpl (per le unghie) nail scissors

'forca f fork; (patibolo) gallows pl

for'cella f fork; (per capelli) hairpin

for'chet|ta f fork. **~'tata** f (quantità) forkful

for'cina f hairpin

'forcipe m forceps pl

for'cone m pitchfork

fo'resta f forest. **fore'stale** adj forest attrib

foresti'ero, -a adj foreign • mf foreigner

for'fait m inv fixed price; **dare ~** (abbandonare) give up

'forfora f dandruff

'forgi|a f forge. **~'are** vt forge

'forma f form; (sagoma) shape; (Culin) mould; (da calzolaio) last; **essere in ~** be in good form; **a ~ di** in the shape of; **forme** pl (del corpo) figure sg; (convenzioni) appearances

formag'gino m processed cheese. **for'maggio** m cheese

for'mal|e adj formal. **~ità** f inv formality. **~iz'zarsi** vr stand on ceremony. **~'mente** adv formally

see A-Z of Italian life and culture

f

f

for'ma|re vt form. **~rsi** vr form; (svilupparsi) develop. **~to** m size; (di libro) format; **~to tessera** (fotografia) passportsize

format'tare vt format

formazi'one f formation; Sport line-up. **~ professionale** vocational training

formico'l|are vi (braccio ecc:) tingle; **~are di** be swarming with; **mi ~a la mano** I have pins and needles in my hand. **~io** m swarming; (di braccio ecc) pins and needles pl

formi'dabile adj (tremendo) formidable; (eccezionale) tremendous

for'mina f mould

for'moso adj shapely

'formula f formula. **formu'lare** vt formulate; (esprimere) express

for'nace f furnace; (per laterizi) kiln

for'naio m baker; (negozio) bakery

for'nello m stove; (di pipa) bowl

for'ni|re vt supply (**di** with). **~'tore** m supplier. **~'tura** f supply

'forno m oven; (panetteria) bakery; **al ~** roast. **~ a microonde** microwave [oven]

'foro m hole; (romano) forum; (tribunale) [law] court

'forse adv perhaps, maybe; **essere in ~** be in doubt

forsen'nato, -a adj mad • mf madman; madwoman

'forte adj strong; (colore) bright; (suono) loud; (resistente) tough; (spesa) considerable; (dolore) severe; (pioggia) heavy; (a tennis, calcio) good; (!: simpatico) great; (taglia) large • adv strongly; (parlare) loudly; (velocemente) fast; (piovere) heavily • m (fortezza) fort; (specialità) strong point

for'tezza f fortress; (forza morale) fortitude

fortifi'care vt fortify

for'tino m (Mil) blockhouse

for'tuito adj fortuitous; **incontro ~** chance encounter

for'tuna f fortune; (successo) success; (buona sorte) luck; **atterraggio di ~** forced landing; **aver ~** be lucky; **buona ~!** good luck!; **di ~** makeshift; **per ~** luckily. **fortu'nato** adj lucky, fortunate; (impresa) successful. **~ta'mente** adv fortunately

fo'runcolo m pimple; (grosso) boil

'forza f strength; (potenza) power; (fisica) force; **di ~** by force; **a ~ di** by dint of; **con ~** hard; **~!** come on!; **~ di volontà** will-power; **~ maggiore** circumstances beyond one's control; **la ~ pubblica** the police; **per ~** against one's will; (naturalmente) of course; **farsi ~** bear up; **mare ~ 8** force 8 gale; **bella ~!** ! big deal!. **le forze armate** the armed forces

for'za|re vt force; (scassare) break open; (sforzare) strain. **~to** adj forced; (sorriso) strained • m convict

forzi'ere m coffer

for'zuto adj strong

fo'schia f haze

'fosco adj dark

fo'sfato m phosphate

'fosforo m phosphorus

'fossa f pit; (tomba) grave. **~ biologica** cesspool. **fos'sato** m (di fortificazione) moat

fos'setta f dimple

'fossile m fossil

'fosso m ditch; (Mil) trench

'foto f inv ! photo; **fare delle ~** take some photos

foto'camera f camera

foto'cellula f photocell

fotocomposizi'one f filmsetting, photocomposition

foto'copi|a f photocopy. **~'are** vt photocopy. **~a'trice** f photocopier

foto'finish m inv photo finish

fotogra|'fare vt photograph. **~'fia** f (arte) photography; (immagine) photograph; **fare ~fie** take photographs. **foto'grafico** adj photographic; **macchina fotografica** camera. **fo'tografo, -a** mf photographer

foto'gramma m frame

fotomo'dello, -a mf [photographer's] model

fotoro'manzo m photo story

fou'lard m inv scarf

fra prep (in mezzo a due) between; (in un insieme) among; (tempo, distanza) in;

detto ~ noi between you and me; **~ sé e sé** to oneself; **~ l'altro** what's more; **~ breve** soon; **~ quindici giorni** in two weeks' time; **~ tutti, siamo in venti** there are twenty of us altogether

fracas'sar|e vt smash. **~si** vr shatter

fra'casso m din; (di cose che cadono) crash

'fradicio adj (bagnato) soaked; (guasto) rotten; **ubriaco ~** blind drunk

'fragil|e adj fragile; fig frail. **~ità** f fragility; fig frailty

'fragola f strawberry

fra'go|re m uproar; (di cose rotte) clatter; (di tuono) rumble. **~'roso** adj uproarious; (tuono) rumbling; (suono) clanging

fra'gran|te adj fragrant. **~za** f fragrance

frain'te|ndere vt misunderstand. **~ndersi** vr be at cross-purposes. **~so** pp di **fraintendere**

frammen'tario adj fragmentary

'frana f landslide. **fra'nare** vi slide down

franca'mente adv frankly

fran'cese adj French •mf Frenchman; Frenchwoman •m (lingua) French

fran'chezza f frankness

'Francia f France

'franco[1] adj frank; (Comm) free; **farla franca** get away with sth

'franco[2] m (moneta) franc

franco'bollo m stamp

fran'gente m (onda) breaker; (scoglio) reef; (fig: momento difficile) crisis; **in quel ~** given the situation

'frangia f fringe

fra'noso adj subject to landslides

fran'toio m olive-press

frantu'mar|e vt, **~si** vr shatter. **fran'tumi** mpl splinters; **andare in frantumi** be smashed to pieces

frappé m inv milkshake

frap'por|re vt interpose. **~si** vr intervene

fra'sario m vocabulary; (libro) phrase book

'frase f sentence; (espressione) phrase. **~ fatta** cliché

'frassino m ash[-tree]

frastagli'a|re vt make jagged. **~to** adj jagged

frastor'na|re vt daze. **~to** adj dazed

frastu'ono m racket

'frate m friar; (monaco) monk

fratel'la|nza f brotherhood. **~stro** m half-brother

fra'tell|i mpl (fratello e sorella) brother and sister. **~o** m brother

fraterniz'zare vi fraternize. **fra'terno** adj brotherly

frat'taglie fpl (di pollo ecc) giblets

frat'tanto adv in the meantime

frat'tempo m **nel ~** meanwhile, in the meantime

frat'tu|ra f fracture. **~'rare** vt, **~'rarsi** vr break

fraudo'lento adj fraudulent

frazi'one f fraction; (borgata) hamlet

'frecci|a f arrow; (Auto) indicator. **~'ata** f (osservazione pungente) cutting remark

fredda'mente adv coldly

fred'dare vt cool; (fig: con sguardo, battuta) cut down; (uccidere) kill

fred'dezza f coldness

'freddo adj & m cold; **aver ~** be cold; **fa ~** it's cold

freddo'loso adj sensitive to cold

fred'dura f pun

fre'ga|re vt rub; (!: truffare) cheat; (!: rubare) swipe. **~rsene** ! not give a damn; **chi se ne frega!** what the heck!. **~si** vr rub (occhi). **~ta** f rub. **~'tura** f ! (truffa) swindle; (delusione) letdown

'fregio m (Archit) frieze; (ornamento) decoration

'frem|ere vi quiver. **~ito** m quiver

fre'na|re vt brake; fig restrain; hold back (lacrime) •vi brake. **~rsi** vr check oneself. **~ta** f **fare una ~ta brusca** brake sharply

frene'sia f frenzy; (desiderio smodato) craze. **fre'netico** adj frenzied

'freno m brake; fig check; **togliere il ~** release the brake; **usare il ~** apply the brake; **tenere a ~** restrain. **~ a mano** handbrake

frequen'tare vt frequent; attend

(scuola ecc); mix with (persone)

fre'quen|te adj frequent; **di ~te** frequently. **~za** f frequency; (assiduità) attendance

fre'schezza f freshness; (di temperatura) coolness

'fresco adj fresh; (temperatura) cool; **stai ~!** you're for it! •m coolness; **far ~** be cool; **mettere/tenere in ~** put/keep in a cool place

f

'fretta f hurry, haste; **aver ~** be in a hurry; **far ~ a qcno** hurry sb; **in ~ e furia** in a great hurry. **frettolosa'mente** adv hurriedly. **fretto'loso** adj (persona) in a hurry; (lavoro) rushed, hurried

fri'abile adj crumbly

'friggere vt fry; **vai a farti ~!** get lost! •vi sizzle

friggi'trice f chip pan

frigidità f frigidity. **'frigido** adj frigid

fri'gnare vi whine

'frigo m inv fridge

frigo'bar m inv minibar

frigo'rifero adj refrigerating •m refrigerator

frit'tata f omelette

frit'tella f fritter; (!: macchia d'unto) grease stain

'fritto pp di **friggere** •adj fried; **essere ~** ! be done for •m fried food. **~ misto** mixed fried fish/ vegetables. **frit'tura** f fried dish

frivo'lezza f frivolity. **'frivolo** adj frivolous

frizio'nare vt rub. **frizi'one** f friction; (Mech) clutch; (di pelle) rub

friz'zante adj fizzy; (vino) sparkling; (aria) bracing

'frizzo m gibe

fro'dare vt defraud

'frode f fraud. **~ fiscale** tax evasion

'frollo adj tender; (selvaggina) high; (persona) spineless; **pasta frolla** short[crust] pastry

'fronda f [leafy] branch; fig rebellion. **fron'doso** adj leafy

fron'tale adj frontal; (scontro) head-on

'fronte f forehead; (di edificio) front; **di ~** opposite; **di ~ a** opposite, facing; (a paragone) compared with; **far ~ a** face •m (Mil, Pol) front. **~ggi'are** vt face

fronti'era f frontier, border

fron'tone m pediment

'fronzolo m frill

'frotta f swarm; (di animali) flock

'frottola f fib; **frottole** pl nonsense sg

fru'gale adj frugal

fru'gare vi rummage •vt search

frul'la|re vt (Culin) whisk •vi (ali:) whirr. **~to** m **~to di frutta** fruit drink with milk and crushed ice. **~'tore** m [electric] mixer. **frul'lino** m whisk

fru'mento m wheat

frusci'are vi rustle

fru'scio m rustle; (radio, giradischi) background noise; (di acque) murmur

'frusta f whip; (frullino) whisk

fru'sta|re vt whip. **~ta** f lash. **fru'stino** m riding crop

fru'stra|re vt frustrate. **~to** adj frustrated. **~zi'one** f frustration

'frutt|a f fruit; (portata) dessert. **frut'tare** vi bear fruit •vt yield. **frut'teto** m orchard. **~i'vendolo, -a** mf greengrocer. **~o** m fruit; Fin yield; **~i di bosco** fruits of the forest. **~i di mare** seafood sg. **~u'oso** adj profitable

f.to abbr (firmato) signed

fu adj (defunto) late; **il ~ signor Rossi** the late Mr Rossi

fuci'la|re vt shoot. **~ta** f shot

fu'cile m rifle

fu'cina f forge

'fuga f escape; (perdita) leak; (Mus) fugue; **darsi alla ~** escape

fu'gace adj fleeting

fug'gevole adj short-lived

fuggi'asco, -a mf fugitive

fuggi'fuggi m stampede

fug'gi|re vi flee; (innamorati:) elope; fig fly. **~'tivo, -a** mf fugitive

'fulcro m fulcrum

ful'gore m splendour

fu'liggine f soot

fulmi'nar|e vt strike by lightning; (con sguardo) look daggers at; (con scarica elettrica) electrocute. **~si** vr burn out. **'fulmine** m lightning. **ful'mineo** adj rapid

'fulvo adj tawny

fumai'olo m funnel; (di casa) chimney

fu'ma|re vt/i smoke; (in ebollizione) steam. **~'tore, ~'trice** mf smoker; **non fumatori** non-smoker, non-smoking

fu'metto m comic strip; **fumetti** pl comics

'fumo m smoke; (vapore) steam; fig hot air; **andare in ~** vanish. **fu'moso** adj smoky; (discorso) vague

fu'nambolo, -a mf tightrope walker

'fune f rope; (cavo) cable

'funebre adj funeral; (cupo) gloomy

fune'rale m funeral

fu'nesto adj sad

'fungere vi **~ da** act as

'fungo m mushroom; (Bot) fungus

funico'lare f funicular [railway]

funi'via f cableway

funzio'nal|e adj functional. **~ità** f functionality

funziona'mento m functioning

funzio'nare vi work, function; **~ da** (fungere da) act as

funzio'nario m official

funzi'one f function; (carica) office; (Relig) service; **entrare in ~** take up office

fu'oco m fire; (fisica, fotografia) focus; **far ~** fire; **dar ~ a** set fire to; **prendere ~** catch fire. **fuochi** pl **d'artificio** fireworks

fuorché prep except

fu'ori adv out; (all'esterno) outside; (all'aperto) outdoors; **andare di ~** (traboccare) spill over; **essere ~ di sé** be beside oneself; **essere in ~** (sporgere) stick out; **far ~** [!] do in; **~ luogo** (inopportuno) out of place; **~ mano** out of the way; **~ moda** old-fashioned; **~ pasto** between meals; **~ pericolo** out of danger; **~ questione** out of the question; **~ uso** out of use •m outside

fuori'bordo m speedboat (with outboard motor)

fuori'classe mf inv champion

fuorigi'oco m & adv offside

fuori'legge mf outlaw

fuori'serie adj custom-made •f (Auto) custom-built model

fuori'strada m inv off-road vehicle

fuorvi'are vt lead astray •vi go astray

furbe'ria f cunning. **fur'bizia** f cunning

'furbo adj cunning; (intelligente) clever; (astuto) shrewd; **bravo ~!** nice one!; **fare il ~** try to be clever

fu'rente adj furious

fur'fante m scoundrel

furgon'cino m delivery van. **fur'gone** m van

'furi|a f fury; (fretta) haste; **a ~a di** by dint of. **~'bondo, ~'oso** adj furious

fu'rore m fury; (veemenza) frenzy; **far ~** be all the rage. **~ggi'are** vi be a great success

furtiva'mente adv covertly. **fur'tivo** adj furtive

'furto m theft; (con scasso) burglary; **commettere un ~** steal. **~ d'identità** identity theft

'fusa fpl **fare le ~** purr

fu'scello m (di legno) twig; (di paglia) straw; **sei un ~** you're as light as a feather

fu'seaux mpl leggings

fu'sibile m fuse

fusi'one f fusion; (Comm) merger

'fuso pp di **fondere** •adj melted •m spindle. **~ orario** time zone

fusoli'era f fuselage

fu'stagno m corduroy

fu'stino m (di detersivo) box

'fusto m stem; (tronco) trunk; (recipiente di metallo) drum; (di legno) barrel

'futile adj futile

fu'turo adj & m future

see A-Z of Italian life and culture

Gg

gab'bar|e vt cheat. **~si** vr **~si di** make fun of

'gabbia f cage; (da imballaggio) crate. **~ degli imputati** dock. **~ toracica** rib cage

gabbi'ano m [sea]gull

gabi'netto m consulting room; (Pol) cabinet; (bagno) lavatory; (laboratorio) laboratory

'gaffe f inv blunder

gagli'ardo adj vigorous

gai'ezza f gaiety. **'gaio** adj cheerful

'gala f gala

ga'lante adj gallant. **galante'ria** f gallantry. **galantu'omo** m (pl **galantuomini**) gentleman

ga'lassia f galaxy

gala'teo m [good] manners pl; (trattato) book of etiquette

gale'otto m (rematore) galley-slave; (condannato) convict

ga'lera f (nave) galley; [!] prison

'galla f (Bot) gall; **a ~** adv afloat; **venire a ~** surface

galleggi'are vi float

galle'ria f tunnel; (d'arte) gallery; (Theat) circle; (arcata) arcade. **~ d'arte** art gallery

'Galles m Wales. **gal'lese** adj welsh •m Welshman; (lingua) Welsh •f Welshwoman

gal'letto m cockerel; **fare il ~** show off

gal'lina f hen

gal'lismo m machismo

'gallo m cock

gal'lone m stripe; (misura) gallon

galop'pare vi gallop. **ga'loppo** m gallop; **al galoppo** at a gallop

'gamba f leg; (di lettera) stem; **a quattro gambe** on all fours; **essere in ~** (essere forte) be strong; (capace) be smart

gamba'letto m pop sock

gambe'retto m shrimp. **'gambero** m prawn; (di fiume) crayfish

'gambo m stem; (di pianta) stalk

'gamma f (Mus) scale; fig range

ga'nascia f jaw; **ganasce** pl **del freno** brake shoes

'gancio m hook

'ganghero m **uscire dai gangheri** fig get into a temper

'gara f competition; (di velocità) race; **fare a ~** compete

ga'rage m inv garage

ga'ran|te mf guarantor. **~'tire** vt guarantee; (rendersi garante) vouch for; (assicurare) assure. **~'zia** f guarantee; **in ~zia** under guarantee

gar'ba|re vi like; **non mi garba** I don't like it. **~to** adj courteous

'garbo m courtesy; (grazia) grace; **con ~** graciously

gareggi'are vi compete

garga'nella f **a ~** from the bottle

garga'rismo m gargle; **fare i gargarismi** gargle

ga'rofano m carnation

'garza f gauze

gar'zone m boy. **~ di stalla** stable-boy

gas m inv gas; **dare ~** (Auto) accelerate; **a tutto ~** flat out. **~ lacrimogeno** tear gas. **~** pl **di scarico** exhaust fumes

gas'dotto m natural gas pipeline

ga'solio m diesel oil

ga'sometro m gasometer

gas's|are vt aerate; (uccidere col gas) gas. **~ato** adj gassy. **~oso, -a** adj gassy; (bevanda) fizzy •f lemonade

'gastrico adj gastric. **ga'strite** f gastritis

gastro|no'mia f gastronomy. **~'nomico** adj gastronomic. **ga'stronomo, -a** mf gourmet

'gatta f **una ~ da pelare** a headache

gatta'buia f hum clink

gat'tino, -a mf kitten

'gatto, -a mf cat. **~ delle nevi** snowmobile

gat'toni adv on all fours

gay adj inv gay

'gazza f magpie

gaz'zarra f racket

gaz'zella f gazelle; (Auto) police car

gaz'zetta f gazette

gaz'zosa f clear lemonade

'geco m gecko

ge'la|re vt/i freeze. **~ta** f frost

gela't|aio, -a mf ice-cream seller; (negozio) ice-cream shop. **~e'ria** f ice-cream parlour. **~i'era** f ice-cream maker

gela'ti|na f gelatine; (dolce) jelly. **~na di frutta** fruit jelly.

ge'lato adj frozen • m ice-cream

'gelido adj freezing

'gelo m (freddo intenso) freezing cold; (brina) frost; fig chill

ge'lone m chilblain

gelosa'mente adv jealously

gelo'sia f jealousy. **ge'loso** adj jealous

'gelso m mulberry[-tree]

gelso'mino m jasmine

gemel'laggio m twinning

ge'mello, -a adj & mf twin; (di polsino) cuff-link; **Gemelli** pl (Astr) Gemini sg

'gem|ere vi groan; (tubare) coo. **~ito** m groan

'gemma f gem; (Bot) bud

'gene m gene

genealo'gia f genealogy

gene'ral|e[1] adj general; **spese ~i** overheads

gene'rale[2] m (Mil) general

generalità f (qualità) generality, general nature; ~ pl (dati personali) particulars

generaliz'za|re vt generalize. **~zi'one** f generalization. **general'mente** adv generally

gene'ra|re vt give birth to; (causare) breed; (Techn) generate. **~'tore** m (Techn) generator. **~zi'one** f generation

'genere m kind; (Biol) genus; (Gram) gender; (letterario, artistico) genre; (prodotto) product; **il ~ umano** mankind; **in ~** generally. **generi** pl **alimentari** provisions

ge'nerico adj generic; **medico ~** general practitioner

'genero m son-in-law

generosità f generosity. **gene'roso** adj generous

'genesi f inv genesis

ge'netico, -a adj genetic • f genetics

gen'giva f gum

geni'ale adj ingenious; (congeniale) congenial

'genio m genius; **andare a ~** be to one's taste. **~ civile** civil engineering. **~ [militare]** Engineers

geni'tale adj genital. **genitali** mpl genitals

geni'tore m parent

gen'naio m January

'Genova f Genoa

gen'taglia f rabble

'gente f people pl

gen'til|e adj kind; **G~e Signore** (in lettere) Dear Sir. **genti'lezza** f kindness; **per gentilezza** (per favore) please. **~'mente** adv kindly. **~u'omo** (pl **~u'omini**) m gentleman

genu'ino adj genuine; (cibo, prodotto) natural

geogra'fia f geography. **geo'grafico** adj geographical. **ge'ografo, -a** mf geographer

geolo'gia f geology. **geo'logico** adj geological. **ge'ologo, -a** mf geologist

ge'ometra mf surveyor

geome'tria f geometry

ge'ranio m geranium

gerar'chia f hierarchy

ge'rente m manager • f manageress

'gergo m slang; (di professione ecc) jargon

see A-Z of Italian life and culture

g

geria'tria f geriatrics sg
Ger'mania f Germany
'germe m germ; (fig: principio) seed
germogli'are vi sprout. **ger'moglio** m sprout
gero'glifico m hieroglyph
'gesso m chalk; (Med, scultura) plaster
gestazi'one f gestation
gestico'lare vi gesticulate
gesti'one f management
ge'stir|e vi manage. **~si** vr budget one's time and money

'gesto m gesture; (azione pl f **gesta**) deed
ge'store m manager
Gesù m Jesus. **~ bambino** baby Jesus
gesu'ita m Jesuit
get'ta|re vt throw; (scagliare) fling; (emettere) spout; (Techn), fig cast; **~re via** throw away. **~rsi** vr throw oneself; **~rsi in** (fiume:) flow into. **~ta** f throw
'getto m throw; (di liquidi, gas) jet; **a ~ continuo** in a continuous stream; **di ~** straight off
getto'nato adj popular. **get'tone** m token; (per giochi) counter
'ghetto m ghetto
ghiacci'aio m glacier
ghiacci'a|re vt/i freeze. **~to** adj frozen; (freddissimo) ice-cold
ghi'acci|o m ice; (Auto) black ice. **~'olo** m icicle; (gelato) ice lolly
ghi'aia f gravel
ghi'anda f acorn
ghi'andola f gland
ghigliot'tina f guillotine
ghi'gnare vi sneer
ghi'ot|to adj greedy; (appetitoso) appetizing. **~'tone, -a** mf glutton. **~tone'ria** f (qualità) gluttony; (cibo) tasty morsel
ghir'landa f (corona) wreath; (di fiori) garland
'ghiro m dormouse; **dormire come un ~** sleep like a log
'ghisa f cast iron
già adv already; (un tempo) formerly; **~!** indeed!; **~ da ieri** since yesterday

gi'acca f jacket. **~ a vento** windcheater
giacché conj since
giac'cone m jacket
gia'cere vi lie
giaci'mento m deposit. **~ di petrolio** oil deposit
gia'cinto m hyacinth
gi'ada f jade
giaggi'olo m iris
giagu'aro m jaguar
gial'lastro adj yellowish
gi'allo adj & m yellow; **[libro] ~** thriller
Giap'pone m Japan. **giappo'nese** adj & mf Japanese
giardi'n|aggio m gardening. **~i'ere, -a** mf gardener •f (Auto) estate car; (sottaceti) pickles pl
giar'dino m garden. **~ d'infanzia** kindergarten. **~ pensile** roofgarden. **~ zoologico** zoo
giarretti'era f garter
giavel'lotto m javelin
gi'gan|te adj gigantic •m giant. **~'tesco** adj gigantic
gigantogra'fia f blow-up
'giglio m lily
gilè m inv waistcoat
gin m inv gin
gineco|lo'gia f gynaecology. **~'logico** adj gynaecological. **gine'cologo, -a** mf gynaecologist
gi'nepro m juniper
gingil'larsi vr fiddle; (perder tempo) potter. **gin'gillo** m plaything; (ninnolo) knick-knack
gin'nasio m ≈ grammar school
gin'nast|a mf gymnast. **~ica** f gymnastics; (esercizi) exercises pl
ginocchi'ata f **prendere una ~** bang one's knee
gi'nocchi|o m (pl m **ginocchi** o f **ginocchia**) knee; **in ~o** on one's knees; **mettersi in ~o** kneel down; (per supplicare) go down on one's knees. **~'oni** adv kneeling
gio'ca|re vt/i play; (giocherellare) toy; (d'azzardo) gamble; (puntare) stake; (ingannare) trick. **~rsi la carriera** throw one's career away. **~'tore,**

~'**trice** mf player; (d'azzardo) gambler

gio'cattolo m toy

giocherel'l|are vi toy; (nervosamente) fiddle. ~**one** adj skittish

gi'oco m game; (Techn) play; (d'azzardo) gambling; (scherzo) joke; (insieme di pezzi ecc) set; **fare il doppio ~ con qcno** double-cross sb

giocoli'ere m juggler

gio'coso adj playful

gi'oia f joy; (gioiello) jewel; (appellativo) sweetie

gioiell|e'ria f jeweller's [shop]. ~**i'ere, -a** mf jeweller; (negozio) jeweller's. **gioi'ello** m jewel; **gioielli** pl jewellery

gioi'oso adj joyous

gio'ire vi ~ **per** rejoice at

Gior'dania f Jordan

giorna'laio, -a mf newsagent

gior'nale m [news]paper; (diario) journal. ~ **di bordo** logbook. ~ **radio** news bulletin

giornali'ero adj daily •m (per sciare) day pass

giorna'lino m comic

giorna'lis|mo m journalism. ~**ta** mf journalist

giornal'mente adv daily

gior'nata f day; **in** ~ today

gi'orno m day; **al** ~ per day; **al** ~ **d'oggi** nowadays; **di** ~ by day; **un** ~ **sì, un** ~ **no** every other day

gi'ostra f merry-go-round

giova'mento m **trarre** ~ **da** derive benefit from

gi'ova|ne adj young; (giovanile) youthful •m young man •f young woman. ~'**nile** adj youthful. ~'**notto** m young man

gio'var|e vi ~**e a** be useful to; (far bene a) be good for. ~**si** vr ~**si di** avail oneself of

giovedì m inv Thursday. ~ **grasso** last Thursday before Lent

gioventù f youth; (i giovani) young people pl

giovi'ale adj jovial

giovi'nezza f youth

gira'dischi m inv record-player

gi'raffa f giraffe; Cinema boom

gi'randola f (fuoco d'artificio) Catherine wheel; (giocattolo) windmill; (banderuola) weathercock

gi'ra|re vt turn; (andare intorno, visitare) go round; (Comm) endorse; Cinema shoot •vi turn; (aerei, uccelli:) circle; (andare in giro) wander; ~**re al largo** steer clear. ~**rsi** vr turn [round]; **mi gira la testa** I'm dizzy

girar'rosto m spit

gira'sole m sunflower

gi'rata f turn; (Comm) endorsement; (in macchina ecc) ride; **fare una** ~ (a piedi) go for a walk; (in macchina) go for a ride

gira'volta f spin; fig U-turn

gi'rello m (per bambini) babywalker; (Culin) topside

gi'revole adj revolving

gi'rino m tadpole

'giro m turn; (circolo) circle; (percorso) round; (viaggio) tour; (passeggiata) short walk; (in macchina) drive; (in bicicletta) ride; (circolazione di denaro) circulation; **nel** ~ **di un mese** within a month; **senza giri di parole** without beating about the bush; **a** ~ **di posta** by return mail. ~ **d'affari** (Comm) turnover. **giri** pl **al minuto** rpm. ~ **turistico** sightseeing tour. ~ **vita** waist measurement

giro'collo m choker; **a** ~ crewneck

gi'rone m round

gironzo'lare vi wander about

girova'gare vi wander about. **gi'rovago** m wanderer

'gita f trip; **andare in** ~ go on a trip. ~ **scolastica** school trip. **gi'tante** mf tripper

giù adv down; (sotto) below; (dabbasso) downstairs; **a testa in** ~ (a capofitto) headlong; **essere** ~ be down; (di salute) be run down; ~ **di corda** down; ~ **di lì, su per** ~ more or less; **non andare** ~ **a qcno** stick in sb's craw

gi'ub|ba f jacket; (Mil) tunic. ~'**botto** m bomber jacket

giudi'care vt judge; (ritenere) consider

gi'udice m judge. ~ **conciliatore**

see A-Z of Italian life and culture

g

justice of the peace. ~ **di gara** umpire. ~ **di linea** linesman

giu'dizi|o m judg[e]ment; (opinione) opinion; (senno) wisdom; (processo) trial; (sentenza) sentence; **mettere ~o** become wise. ~**'oso** adj sensible

gi'ugno m June

giu'menta f mare

gi'ungere vi arrive; ~ **a** (riuscire) succeed in •vt (unire) join

gi'ungla f jungle

gi'unta f addition; (Mil) junta; **per ~** in addition. ~ **comunale** district council

gi'unto pp di **giungere** •m (Mech) joint

giun'tura f joint

giuo'care, giu'oco = **giocare, gioco**

giura'mento m oath; **prestare ~** take the oath

giu'ra|re vt/i swear. **~to, -a** adj sworn •mf juror

giu'ria f jury

giu'ridico adj legal

giurisdizi'one f jurisdiction

giurispru'denza f jurisprudence

giu'rista mf jurist

giustifi'ca|re vt justify. **~zi'one** f justification

giu'stizi|a f justice. **~'are** vt execute. **~'ere** m executioner

gi'usto adj just, fair; (adatto) right; (esatto) exact •m (uomo retto) just man; (cosa giusta) right •adv exactly; ~ **ora** just now

glaci'ale adj glacial

gla'diolo m gladiolus

'glassa f (Culin) icing

gli def art mpl (before vowel and s + consonant, gn, ps, z) the; ▸**il** •pron (a lui) [to] him; (a esso) [to] it; (a loro) [to] them

glice'rina f glycerine

'glicine m wisteria

gli'e|lo, -a pron [to] him/her/them; (forma di cortesia) [to] you; ~ **chiedo** I'll ask him/her/them/you; **gliel'ho prestato** I've lent it to him/her/them/you. **~ne** (di ciò) [of] it; **~ne ho dato un po'** I gave him/her/them/you some

glo'bal|e adj global; fig overall. **~izza'zione** f globalization. **~'mente** adv globally

'globo m globe. ~ **oculare** eyeball. ~ **terrestre** globe

'globulo m globule; (Med) corpuscle. ~ **bianco** white corpuscle. ~ **rosso** red corpuscle

'glori|a f glory. **~'arsi** vr **~arsi di** be proud of. **~'oso** adj glorious

glos'sario m glossary

glu'cosio m glucose

'gluteo m buttock

'gnorri m **fare lo ~** play dumb

'gobb|a f hump. **~o, -a** adj hunchbacked •mf hunchback

'gocci|a f drop; (di sudore) bead; **è stata l'ultima ~a** it was the last straw. **~o'lare** vi drip. **~o'lio** m dripping

go'der|e vi (sessualmente) come; **~e di** enjoy. **~sela** have a good time. **~si** vr **~si qcsa** enjoy sth

godi'mento m enjoyment

goffa'mente adv awkwardly. **'goffo** adj awkward

'gola f throat; (ingordigia) gluttony; (Geog) gorge; (di camino) flue; **avere mal di ~** have a sore throat; **far ~ a qcno** tempt sb

golf m inv jersey; Sport golf

'golfo m gulf

golosità f inv greediness; (cibo) tasty morsel. **go'loso** adj greedy

'golpe m inv coup

gomi'tata f nudge

'gomito m elbow; **alzare il ~** raise one's elbow

go'mitolo m ball

'gomma f rubber; (colla, da masticare) gum; (pneumatico) tyre. ~ **da masticare** chewing gum

gommapi'uma f foam rubber

gom'mista m tyre specialist

gom'mone m [rubber] dinghy

'gondol|a f gondola. **~i'ere** m gondolier

gonfa'lone m banner

gonfi'abile adj inflatable

gonfi'ar|e vi swell •vt blow up; pump up (pneumatico); (esagerare) exaggerate. **~si** vr swell; (acque:) rise. '**gonfio** adj swollen; (pneumatico) inflated. **gonfi'ore** m swelling

gongo'la|nte adj overjoyed. **~re** vi be overjoyed

'**gonna** f skirt. **~ pantalone** culottes pl

goo'glare vt/i google

gorgogli'are vi gurgle

go'rilla m inv gorilla; (guardia del corpo) bodyguard

'**gotico** adj & m Gothic

gover'nante f housekeeper

gover'na|re vt govern; (dominare) rule; (dirigere) manage; (curare) look after. **~'tore** m governor

go'verno m government; (dominio) rule; **al ~** in power

gps m gps

gracchi'are vi caw; fig: (persona:) screech

graci'dare vi croak

'**gracile** adj delicate

gra'dasso m braggart

gradata'mente adv gradually

gradazi'one f gradation. **~ alcoolica** alcohol[ic] content

gra'devol|e adj agreeable.

gradi'mento m liking; **indice di ~** (Radio, TV) popularity rating; **non è di mio ~** it's not to my liking

gradi'nata f flight of steps; (di stadio) stand; (di teatro) tiers pl

gra'dino m step

gra'di|re vt like; (desiderare) wish. **~to** adj pleasant; (bene accetto) welcome

'**grado** m degree; (rango) rank; **di buon ~** willingly; **essere in ~ di fare qcsa** be in a position to do sth: (essere capace a) be able to do sth

gradu'ale adj gradual

gradu'a|re vt graduate. **~to** adj graded; (provvisto di scala graduata) graduated • m (Mil) noncommissioned officer. **~'toria** f list. **~zi'one** f graduation

'**graffa** f clip

graf'fetta f staple

graffi'a|re vt scratch. **~'tura** f scratch

'**graffio** m scratch

gra'fia f [hand]writing; (ortografia) spelling

'**grafic|a** f graphics; **~a pubblicitaria** commercial art. **~a'mente** adv graphically. **~o** adj graphic • m graph; (persona) graphic designer

gra'migna f weed

gram'matica f grammar

'**grammo** m gram[me]

gran adj ▸**grande**

'**grana** f grain; (formaggio) parmesan; ([!]: seccatura) trouble; ([!]: soldi) readies pl

gra'naio m barn

gra'nat|a f (Mil) grenade; (frutto) pomegranate. **~i'ere** m (Mil) grenadier

Gran Bre'tagna f Great Britain

'**granchio** m crab; (errore) blunder; **prendere un ~** make a blunder

grandango'lare m wide-angle lens

'**grande** (a volte **gran**) adj (ampio) large; (grosso) big; (alto) tall; (largo) wide; (fig: senso morale) great; (grandioso) grand; (adulto) grown-up; **ho una gran fame** I'm very hungry; **fa un gran caldo** it is very hot; **in ~** on a large scale; **in gran parte** to a great extent; **un gran ballo** a grand ball • mf (persona adulta) grown-up; (persona eminente) great man/woman. **~ggi'are** vi **~ggiare su** tower over; (darsi arie) show off

gran'dezza f greatness; (ampiezza) largeness; (larghezza) width, breadth; (dimensione) size; (fasto) grandeur; (prodigalità) lavishness; **a ~ naturale** life-size

grandi'nare vi hail; **grandina** it's hailing. '**grandine** f hail

grandiosità f grandeur. **grandi'oso** adj grand

gran'duca m grand duke

gra'nello m grain; (di frutta) pip

gra'nita f crushed ice drink

gra'nito m granite

'**grano** m grain; (frumento) wheat

g

gran'turco m maize

'**granulo** m granule

'**grappa** f grappa; (morsa) cramp

'**grappolo** m bunch. ~ **d'uva** bunch of grapes

gras'setto m bold [type]

gras'sezza f fatness

'**gras|so** adj fat; (cibo) fatty; (unto) greasy; (terreno) rich; (grossolano) coarse •m fat; (sostanza) grease. ~'**soccio** adj plump

'**grata** f grating. **gra'tella, gra'ticola** f (Culin) grill

gra'tifica f bonus. ~**zi'one** f satisfaction

grati'na|re vt cook au gratin. ~**to** adj au gratin

grati'tudine f gratitude. '**grato** adj grateful; (gradito) pleasant

gratta'capo m trouble

grattaci'elo m skyscraper

'**gratta e 'vinci** m inv scratch card

grat'tar|e vt scratch; (raschiare) scrape; (grattugiare) grate; (!: rubare) pinch •vi grate. ~**si** vr scratch oneself

grat'tugi|a f grater. ~'**are** vt grate

gratuita'mente adv free [of charge]. **gra'tuito** adj free [of charge]; (ingiustificato) gratuitous

gra'vare vt burden •vi ~ **su** weigh on

'**grave** adj (pesante) heavy; (serio) serious; (difficile) hard; (voce, suono) low; (fonetica) grave; **essere** ~ (ammalato) be seriously ill. ~'**mente** adv seriously

gravi'danza f pregnancy. '**gravido** adj pregnant

gravità f seriousness; (Phys) gravity

gra'voso adj onerous

'**grazi|a** f grace; (favore) favour; (Jur) pardon; **entrare nelle** ~**e di qcno** get into sb's good books. ~'**are** vt pardon

'**grazie** int thank you!, thanks!; ~ **mille!** many thanks!

grazi'oso adj charming; (carino) pretty

'**Grec|ia** f Greece. **g~o, -a** agg & mf Greek

'**gregge** m flock

'**greggio** adj raw •m crude oil

grembi'ale, grembi'ule m apron

'**grembo** m lap; (utero) womb; fig bosom

gre'mi|re vt pack. ~**rsi** vr become crowded (**di** with). ~**to** adj packed

'**gretto** adj stingy; (di vedute ristrette) narrow-minded

'**grezzo** adj = **greggio**

gri'dare vi shout; (di dolore) scream; (animale:) cry •vt shout

'**grido** m (pl m **gridi** o f **grida**) shout; (di animale) cry; **l'ultimo** ~ the latest fashion

'**grigio** adj & m grey

'**griglia** f grill; **alla** ~ grilled

gril'letto m trigger

'**grillo** m cricket; (fig: capriccio) whim

'**grinfia** f fig clutch

'**grin|ta** f grit. ~'**toso** adj determined

'**grinza** f wrinkle; (di stoffa) crease

grip'pare vi (Mech) seize

gris'sino m bread-stick

'**gronda** f eaves pl

gron'daia f gutter

gron'dare vi pour; (essere bagnato fradicio) be dripping

'**groppa** f back

'**groppo** m knot

gros'sezza f size; (spessore) thickness

gros'sista mf wholesaler

'**grosso** adj big, large; (spesso) thick; (grossolano) coarse; (grave) serious •m big part; (massa) bulk; **farla grossa** do a stupid thing

grosso|lanità f inv (qualità) coarseness; (di errore) grossness; (azione, parola) coarse thing. ~'**lano** adj coarse; (errore) gross

grosso'modo adv roughly

'**grotta** f cave, grotto

grovi'era m Gruyère

gro'viglio m tangle; fig muddle

gru f inv (uccello, edilizia) crane

gruccia f (stampella) crutch; (per vestito) hanger

gru'gni|re vi grunt. **~to** m grunt

'grugno m snout

'grullo adj silly

'grumo m clot; (di farina ecc) lump. **gru'moso** adj lumpy

'gruppo m group; (comitiva) party. **~ sanguigno** blood group

gruvi'era m Gruyère

'gruzzolo m nest-egg

guada'gnare vt earn; gain (tempo, forza ecc). **gua'dagno** m gain; (profitto) profit; (entrate) earnings pl

gu'ado m ford; **passare a ~** ford

gua'ina f sheath; (busto) girdle

gu'aio m trouble; **che ~!** that's just brilliant!; **essere nei guai** be in a fix; **guai a te se lo tocchi!** don't you dare touch it!

gu'anci|a f cheek. **~'ale** m pillow

gu'anto m glove. **guantoni** pl [**da boxe**] boxing gloves

guarda'coste m inv coastguard

guarda'linee m inv Sport linesman

guar'dar|e vt look at; (osservare) watch; (badare a) look after; (dare su) look out on •vi look; (essere orientato verso) face. **~si** vr look at oneself; **~si da** beware of; (astenersi) refrain from

guarda'rob|a m inv wardrobe; (di locale pubblico) cloakroom. **~i'ere, -a** mf cloakroom attendant

gu'ardia f guard; (poliziotto) policeman; (vigilanza) watch; **essere di ~** be on guard; (medico:) be on duty; **fare la ~ a** keep guard over; **mettere in ~ qcno** warn sb. **~ carceraria** prison warder. **~ del corpo** bodyguard. **~ di finanza** ≈ Fraud Squad. **~ forestale** forest ranger. **~ medica** duty doctor

guardi'ano, -a mf caretaker. **~ notturno** night watchman

guar'dingo adj cautious

guardi'ola f gatekeeper's lodge

guarigi'one f recovery

gua'rire vt cure •vi recover; (ferita:) heal [up]

guarnigi'one f garrison

guar'ni|re vt trim; (Culin) garnish. **~zi'one** f trimming; (Culin) garnish; (Mech) gasket

gua'star|e vt spoil; (rovinare) ruin; break (meccanismo). **~si** vr spoil; (andare a male) go bad; (tempo:) change for the worse; (meccanismo:) break down. **gu'asto** adj broken; (ascensore, telefono) out of order; (auto) broken down; (cibo, dente) bad •m breakdown; (danno) damage

guazza'buglio m muddle

guaz'zare vi wallow

gu'ercio adj cross-eyed

gu'err|a f war; (tecnica bellica) warfare. **~ mondiale** world war. **~eggi'are** vi wage war. **guer'resco** adj (di guerra) war; (bellicoso) warlike. **~i'ero** m warrior

guer'rigli|a f guerrilla warfare. **~'ero, -a** mf guerrilla

'gufo m owl

'guglia f spire

gu'id|a f guide; (direzione) guidance; (comando) leadership; (Auto) driving; (tappeto) runner; **~a a destra/ sinistra** right-/left-hand drive. **~a telefonica** telephone directory. **~a turistica** tourist guide. **gui'dare** vt guide; (Auto) drive; steer (nave). **~a'tore, ~a'trice** mf driver

guin'zaglio m leash

guiz'zare vi dart; (luce:) flash. **gu'izzo** m dart; (di luce) flash

'guscio m shell

gu'stare vt taste •vi like. **'gusto** m taste; (piacere) liking; **mangiare di gusto** eat well; **prenderci gusto** develop a taste for. **gu'stoso** adj tasty; fig delightful

guttu'rale adj guttural

g

Hh

habitué mf inv regular
ham'burger m inv hamburger
'handicap m inv handicap
handicap'pa|re vt handicap. **~to, -a** mf disabled person • adj disabled
'hascisc m hashish
henné m henna
hi-fi m inv hi-fi
'hippy adj hippy
hockey m hockey. **~ su ghiaccio** ice hockey. **~ su prato** hockey
hollywoodi'ano adj Hollywood
ho'tel m inv hotel

Ii

i def art mpl the; ▸**il**
iber'na|re vi hibernate. **~zi'one** f hibernation
i'bisco m hibiscus
'ibrido adj & m hybrid
'iceberg m inv iceberg
i'cona f icon
Id'dio m God
i'dea f idea; (opinione) opinion; (ideale) ideal; (indizio) inkling; (piccola quantità) hint; (intenzione) intention; **cambiare ~** change one's mind; **neanche per ~!** not on your life!; **chiarirsi le idee** get one's ideas straight. **~ fissa** obsession
ide'a|le adj & m ideal. **~'lista** mf idealist. **~liz'zare** vt idealize
ide'a|re vt conceive. **~'tore, ~'trice** mf originator
'idem adv the same
i'dentico adj identical
identifi'cabile adj identifiable
identifi'ca|re vt identify. **~zi'one** f identification
identità f inv identity
ideolo'gia f ideology. **ideo'logico** adj ideological
idi'oma m idiom. **idio'matico** adj idiomatic
idi'ota adj idiotic • mf idiot. **idio'zia** f (cosa stupida) idiocy
idola'trare vt worship
idoleggi'are vt idolize. **'idolo** m idol
idoneità f suitability; (Mil) fitness; **esame di ~** qualifying examination. **i'doneo** adj **idoneo a** suitable for; (Mil) fit for
i'drante m hydrant
idra'ta|nte adj (crema, gel) moisturizing. **~zi'one** f moisturizing
i'draulico adj hydraulic • m plumber
'idrico adj water attrib
idrocar'buro m hydrocarbon
idroe'lettrico adj hydroelectric
i'drofilo adj ▸**cotone**
i'drogeno m hydrogen
i'ella f [!] bad luck; **portare ~** be bad luck. **iel'lato** adj [!] jinxed, plagued by bad luck
i'ena f hyena
i'eri adv yesterday; **~ l'altro, l'altro ~** the day before yesterday; **~ pomeriggio** yesterday afternoon; **il giornale di ~** yesterday's paper
ietta|'tore mf jinx. **~ tura** f (sfortuna) bad luck

igi'en|e f hygiene. **~ico** adj hygienic. **igie'nista** mf hygienist

i'gnaro adj unaware

i'gnobile adj base; (non onorevole) dishonourable

igno'ran|te adj ignorant •mf ignoramus. **~za** f ignorance

igno'rare vt (non sapere) be unaware of; (trascurare) ignore

i'gnoto adj unknown

il def art m the

! L'articolo determinativo in inglese non si usa quando si parla in generale: **il latte fa bene** milk is good for you

····> **il signor Magnetti** Mr Magnetti; **il dottor Piazza** Dr Piazza; **ha il naso storto** he has a bent nose; **mettiti il cappello** put your hat on; **il lunedì** on Mondays; **il 2007** 2007; **5 euro il chilo** 5 euros a kilo

'ilar|e adj merry. **~ità** f hilarity

illazi'one f inference

illecita'mente adv illicitly. **il'lecito** adj illicit

ille'gal|e adj illegal. **~ità** f illegality. **~'mente** adv illegally

illeg'gibile adj illegible; (libro) unreadable

illegittimità f illegitimacy. **ille'gittimo** adj illegitimate

il'leso adj unhurt

illette'rato, -a adj & mf illiterate

illimi'tato adj unlimited

illivi'dire vt bruise •vi (per rabbia) become livid

il'logico adj illogical

il'luder|e vt deceive. **~si** vr deceive oneself

illumi'na|re vt light [up]; fig enlighten; **~re a giorno** floodlight. **~rsi** vr light up. **~zi'one** f lighting; fig enlightenment

Illumi'nismo m Enlightenment

illusi'one f illusion; **farsi illusioni** delude oneself

il'luso, -a pp di **illudere** •adj deluded •mf day-dreamer.

illu'stra|re vt illustrate. **~'tivo** adj illustrative. **~'tore, ~'trice** mf illustrator. **~zi'one** f illustration

il'lustre adj distinguished

imbacuc'ca|re vt, **~rsi** vr wrap up. **~to** adj wrapped up

imbal'la|ggio m packing. **~re** vt pack; (Auto) race

imbalsa'ma|re vt embalm; stuff (animale). **~to** adj embalmed; (animale) stuffed

imbambo'lato adj vacant

imbaraz'zante adj embarrassing

imbaraz'za|re vt embarrass; (ostacolare) encumber. **~to** adj embarrassed

imba'razzo m embarrassment; (ostacolo) hindrance; **trarre qcno d'~** help sb out of a difficulty. **~ di stomaco** indigestion

imbarca'dero m landing-stage

imbar'ca|re vt embark; (!: rimorchiare) score. **~rsi** vr embark. **~zi'one** f boat. **~zione di salvataggio** lifeboat. **im'barco** m embarkation; (banchina) landing-stage

imba'sti|re vt tack; fig sketch. **~'tura** f tacking, basting

im'battersi vr **~ in** run into

imbat't|ibile adj unbeatable. **~uto** adj unbeaten

imbavagli'are vt gag

imbe'cille adj stupid •mf imbecile

imbel'lire vt embellish

imbestia'li|re vi, **~rsi** vr fly into a rage. **~to** adj enraged

im'bever|e vt imbue (**di** with). **~si** vr absorb

imbe'v|ibile adj undrinkable. **~uto** adj **~uto di** (acqua) soaked in; (nozioni) imbued with

imbian'c|are vt whiten •vi turn white. **~hino** m house painter

imbizzar'rir|e vi, **~si** vr become restless; (arrabbiarsi) get angry

imboc'ca|re vt feed; (entrare) enter; fig prompt. **~'tura** f opening; (ingresso) entrance; (Mus: di strumento) mouthpiece. **im'bocco** m entrance

imbo'scar|e vt hide. **~si** vr (Mil) shirk military service

imbo'scata f ambush

imbottigli'a|re vt bottle. **~rsi** vr get snarled up in a traffic jam. **~to** adj (vino, acqua) bottled

imbot'ti|re vt stuff; pad (giacca); (Culin) fill. **~rsi** vr **~rsi di** (fig: di pasticche) stuff oneself with. **~ta** f quilt. **~to** adj (spalle) padded; (cuscino) stuffed; (panino) filled. **~'tura** f stuffing; (di giacca) padding; (Culin) filling

imbra'nato adj clumsy

imbrat'tar|e vt mark. **~si** vr dirty oneself

imbroc'car|e vt hit; **~la giusta** hit the nail on the head

imbrogli|'are vt muddle; (raggirare) cheat. **im'broglio** m tangle; (pasticcio) mess; (inganno) trick. **~'one, -a** mf cheat

imbronci'a|re vi, **~rsi** vr sulk. **~to** adj sulky

imbru'nire vi get dark; **all'~** at dusk

imbrut'tire vt make ugly •vi become ugly

imbu'care vt post, mail; (nel biliardo) pot

imbur'rare vt butter

im'buto m funnel

imi'ta|re vt imitate. **~'tore, ~'trice** mf imitator. **~zi'one** f imitation

immaco'lato adj immaculate

immagazzi'nare vt store

immagi'na|re vt imagine; (supporre) suppose; **s'immagini!** imagine that!. **~rio** adj imaginary. **~zi'one** f imagination. **im'magine** f image; (rappresentazione, idea) picture

imman'cabil|e adj unfailing. **~'mente** adv without fail

im'mane adj huge; (orribile) terrible

imma'nente adj immanent

immangi'abile adj inedible

immatrico'la|re vt register. **~rsi** vr (studente:) matriculate. **~zi'one** f registration; (di studente) matriculation

immaturità f immaturity. **imma'turo** adj unripe; (persona) immature; (precoce) premature

immedesi'ma|rsi vr **~rsi in** identify oneself with. **~zi'one** f identification

immedia|ta'mente adv immediately. **~'tezza** f immediacy. **immedi'ato** adj immediate

immemo'rabile adj immemorial

immens|a'mente adv enormously. **~ità** f immensity. **im'menso** adj immense

immensu'rabile adj immeasurable

im'merger|e vt immerse. **~si** vr plunge; (sommergibile:) dive; **~si in** immerse oneself in

immersi'one f immersion; (di sommergibile) dive. **im'merso** pp di **immergere**

immi'gra|nte adj & mf immigrant. **~re** vi immigrate. **~to, -a** mf immigrant. **~zi'one** f immigration

immi'nen|te adj imminent. **~za** f imminence

immischi'ar|e vt involve. **~si** vr **~si in** meddle in

immis'sario m tributary

immissi'one f insertion

im'mobile adj motionless

im'mobili mpl real estate. **~'are** adj **società ~are** building society, savings and loan Am

immobili|tà f immobility. **~z'zare** vt immobilize; (Comm) tie up

immo'lare vt sacrifice

immondez'zaio m rubbish tip. **immon'dizia** f filth; (spazzatura) rubbish. **im'mondo** adj filthy

immo'ral|e adj immoral. **~ità** f immorality

immorta'lare vt immortalize. **immor'tale** adj immortal

immoti'vato adj (gesto) unjustified

im'mun|e adj exempt; (Med) immune. **~ità** f immunity. **~iz'zare** vt immunize. **~izzazi'one** f immunization

immunodefici'enza f immunodeficiency

immuso'ni|rsi vr sulk. **~to** adj sulky

immu'ta|bile adj unchangeable. **~to** adj unchanging

impacchet'tare vt wrap up

impacci'a|re vt hamper; (disturbare) inconvenience; (imbarazzare) embarrass. **~to** adj embarrassed; (goffo) awkward. **im'paccio** m embarrassment; (ostacolo) hindrance; (situazione difficile) awkward situation

im'pacco m compress

impadro'nirsi vr **~ di** take possession of; (fig: imparare) master

impa'gabile adj priceless

impagi'na|re vt paginate. **~zi'one** f pagination

impagli'are vt stuff (animale)

impa'lato adj fig stiff

impalca'tura f scaffolding; fig structure

impalli'dire vi turn pale; (fig: perdere d'importanza) pale into insignificance

impa'nare vt roll in breadcrumbs

impanta'narsi vr get bogged down

impape'rarsi, **impappi'narsi** vr falter, stammer

impa'rare vt learn

impareggi'abile adj incomparable

imparen'ta|rsi vr **~ con** become related to. **~to** adj related

'impari adj unequal; (dispari) odd

impar'tire vt impart

imparzi'al|e adj impartial. **~ità** f impartiality

impas'sibile adj impassive

impa'sta|re vt (Culin) knead; blend (colori). **im'pasto** m (Culin) dough; (miscuglio) mixture

im'patto m impact

impau'rir|e vt frighten. **~si** vr become frightened

im'pavido adj fearless

impazi'en|te adj impatient; **~te di fare qcsa** eager to do sth. **~'tirsi** vr lose patience. **~za** f impatience

impaz'zata f **all'~** full speed

impaz'zire vi go mad; (maionese:) separate; **far ~ qcno** drive sb mad; **~ per** be crazy about; **da ~** (mal di testa) blinding

impec'cabile adj impeccable

impedi'mento m hindrance; (ostacolo) obstacle

impe'dire vt **~ di** prevent from; (impacciare) hinder; (ostruire) obstruct; **~ a qcno di fare qcsa** prevent sb [from] doing sth

impe'gna|re vt (dare in pegno) pawn; (vincolare) bind; (prenotare) reserve; (assorbire) take up. **~rsi** vr apply oneself; **~rsi a fare qcsa** commit oneself to doing sth. **~'tiva** f referral. **~'tivo** adj binding; (lavoro) demanding. **~ato** adj engaged; (Pol) committed. **im'pegno** m engagement; (Comm) commitment; (zelo) care

impel'lente adj pressing

impen'na|rsi vr (cavallo:) rear; fig bristle. **~ta** f sharp rise; (di cavallo) rearing; (di moto) wheelie

impen'sa|bile adj unthinkable. **~to** adj unexpected

impensie'rir|e vt, **~si** vr worry

impe'ra|nte adj prevailing. **~re** vi reign; (tendenza:) prevail

impera'tivo adj & m imperative

impera'tore, -'trice m emperor •f empress

impercet'tibile adj imperceptible

imperdo'nabile adj unforgivable

imper'fe|tto adj & m imperfect. **~zi'one** f imperfection

imperi'a|le adj imperial. **~'lismo** m imperialism

imperi'oso adj imperious; (impellente) urgent

impe'rizia f lack of skill

imperme'abile adj waterproof •m raincoat

imperni'ar|e vt pivot; (fondare) base. **~si** vr **~si su** be based on

im'pero m empire; (potere) rule

imperscru'tabile adj inscrutable

imperso'nale adj impersonal

imperso'nare vt personify; (interpretare) act [the part of]

imper'territo adj undaunted

imperti'nen|te adj impertinent. **~za** f impertinence

imperver'sare vi rage

im'pervio adj inaccessible

'impet|o m impetus; (impulso) impulse; (slancio) transport. **~u'oso** adj impetuous; (vento) blustering

impet'tito adj stiff

impian'tare vt install; set up (azienda)

impi'anto m plant; (sistema) system;

(operazione) installation. ~ **radio** (Auto) car stereo system

impia'strare vt plaster; (sporcare) dirty. **impi'astro** m poultice; (persona noiosa) bore; (pasticcione) cack-handed person

impic'car|e vt hang. **~si** vr hang oneself

impicci|'arsi vr meddle. **im'piccio** m hindrance; (seccatura) bother. **~'one, -a** mf nosey parker

impie'ga|re vt employ; (usare) use; spend (tempo, denaro); Fin invest; **l'autobus ha ~to un'ora** it took the bus an hour. **~rsi** vr get [oneself] a job

impiega'tizio adj clerical

impie'gato, -a mf employee. ~ **di banca** bank clerk. **impi'ego** m employment; (posto) job; Fin investment

impieto'sir|e vt move to pity. **~si** vr be moved to pity

impie'trito adj petrified

impigli'ar|e vt entangle. **~si** vr get entangled

impi'grir|e vt make lazy. **~si** vr get lazy

impli'ca|re vt implicate; (sottintendere) imply. **~rsi** vr become involved. **~zi'one** f implication

implicita'mente adv implicitly. **im'plicito** adj implicit

implo'ra|re vt implore. **~zi'one** f entreaty

impolve'ra|re vt cover with dust. **~rsi** vr get covered with dust. **~to** adj dusty

imponde'rabile adj imponderable; (causa, evento) unpredictable

impo'nen|te adj imposing. **~za** f impressiveness

impo'nibile adj taxable •m taxable income

impopo'lar|e adj unpopular. **~ità** f unpopularity

im'por|re vt impose; (ordinare) order. **~si** vr assert oneself; (aver successo) be successful; **~si di** (prefiggersi di) set oneself the task of

impor'tan|te adj important •m important thing. **~za** f importance

impor'ta|re vt import; (comportare) cause •vi matter; (essere necessario) be necessary. **non importa ~!** it doesn't matter!; **non me ne importa niente!** I couldn't care less!. **~'tore, ~'trice** mf importer. **~zi'one** f importation; (merce importata) import

im'porto m amount

importu'nare vt pester. **impor'tuno** adj troublesome; (inopportuno) untimely

imposizi'one f imposition; (imposta) tax

imposses'sarsi vr ~ **di** seize

impos'sibil|e adj impossible •m **fare l'~e** do absolutely all one can. **~ità** f impossibility

im'posta[1] f tax; ~ **sul reddito** income tax; ~ **sul valore aggiunto** value added tax

im'posta[2] f (di finestra) shutter

impo'sta|re vt (progettare) plan; (basare) base; (Mus) pitch; (imbucare) post, mail; set out (domanda, problema). **~zi'one** f planning; (di voce) pitching

im'posto pp di **imporre**

impo'store, -a mf impostor

impo'ten|te adj powerless; (Med) impotent. **~za** f powerlessness; (Med) impotence

impove'rir|e vt impoverish. **~si** vr become poor

imprati'cabile adj impracticable; (strada) impassable

imprati'chir|e vt train. **~si** vr **~si in** o **a** get practice in

impre'care vi curse

impreci's|abile adj indeterminable. **~ato** adj indeterminate. **~i'one** f inaccuracy. **impre'ciso** adj inaccurate

impre'gnar|e vt impregnate; (imbevere) soak; fig imbue. **~si** vr become impregnated with

imprendi'tor|e, -'trice mf entrepreneur. **~i'ale** adj entrepreneurial

imprepa'rato adj unprepared

im'presa f undertaking; (gesta) exploit; (azienda) firm

impre'sario m impresario; (appaltatore) contractor

imprescin'dibile adj inescapable

impressio'na|bile adj impressionable. **~nte** adj impressive; (spaventoso) frightening

impressi|o'nare vt impress; (spaventare) frighten; expose (foto). **~o'narsi** vr be affected; (spaventarsi) be frightened. **~'one** f impression; (sensazione) sensation; (impronta) mark; **far ~one a qcno** upset sb

impressio'nis|mo m impressionism. **~ta** mf impressionist

im'presso pp di **imprimere** • adj printed

impre'stare vt lend

impreve'dibile adj unforeseeable; (persona) unpredictable

imprevi'dente adj improvident

impre'visto adj unforeseen • m unforeseen event

imprigio|na'mento m imprisonment. **~'nare** vt imprison

im'primere vt impress; (stampare) print; (comunicare) impart

impro'babil|e adj unlikely, improbable. **~ità** f improbability

improdut'tivo adj unproductive

im'pronta f impression; fig mark. **~ digitale** fingerprint. **~ del piede** footprint

impro'perio m insult; **improperi** pl abuse sg

im'proprio adj improper

improvvi'sa|re vt/i improvise. **~rsi** vr turn oneself into a. **~ta** f surprise. **~zi'one** f improvisation

improv'viso adj sudden; **all'~** unexpectedly

impru'den|te adj imprudent. **~za** f imprudence

impu'gna|re vt grasp; (Jur) contest. **~'tura** f grip; (manico) handle

impulsività f impulsiveness. **impul'sivo** adj impulsive

im'pulso m impulse; **agire d'~** act on impulse

impune'mente adv with impunity. **impu'nito** adj unpunished

impun'tura f stitching

impurità f inv impurity. **im'puro** adj impure

impu'tabile adj attributable (**a** to)

impu'ta|re vt attribute; (accusare) charge. **~to, -a** mf accused. **~zi'one** f charge

imputri'dire vi rot

in prep in; (moto a luogo) to; (su) on; (entro) within; (mezzo) by; (con materiale) made of; **essere in casa/ufficio** be at home/at the office; **in mano/tasca** in one's hand/pocket; **andare in Francia/campagna** go to France/the country; **salire in treno** get on the train; **versa la birra nel bicchiere** pour the beer into the glass; **in alto** up there; **in giornata** within the day; **nel 2007** in 2007; **una borsa in pelle** a bag made of leather, a leather bag; **in macchina** (viaggiare, venire) by car; **in contanti** [in] cash; **in vacanza** on holiday; **se fossi in te** if I were you; **siamo in sette** there are seven of us

inabbor'dabile adj unapproachable

i'nabil|e adj incapable; (fisicamente) unfit. **~ità** f incapacity

inabi'tabile adj uninhabitable

inacces'sibile adj inaccessible; (persona) unapproachable

inaccet'tabil|e adj unacceptable. **~ità** f unacceptability

inacer'bi|re vt embitter; exacerbate (rapporto). **~si** vr grow bitter

inaci'dir|e vt turn sour. **~si** vr go sour; (persona:) become bitter

ina'datto adj unsuitable

inadegu'ato adj inadequate

inadempi|'ente mf defaulter. **~'mento** m nonfulfilment

inaffer'rabile adj elusive

ina'la|re vt inhale. **~'tore** m inhaler. **~zi'one** f inhalation

inalbe'rar|e vt hoist. **~si** vr (cavallo:) rear [up]; (adirarsi) lose one's temper

inalte'ra|bile adj unchangeable; (colore) fast. **~to** adj unchanged

inami'da|re vt starch. **~to** adj starched

inammis'sibile adj inadmissible

inamovi'bile adj irremovable

inani'mato adj inanimate; (senza vita) lifeless

inappa'ga|bile adj unsatisfiable. **~to** adj unfulfilled

inappe'tenza f lack of appetite
inappli'cabile adj inapplicable
inappun'tabile adj faultless
inar'car|e vt arch; raise (sopracciglia). **~si** vr (legno:) warp; (ripiano:) sag; (linea:) curve
inari'dir|e vt parch; empty of feelings (persona). **~si** vr dry up; (persona:) become empty of feelings
inartico'lato adj inarticulate
inaspettata'mente adv unexpectedly. **inaspet'tato** adj unexpected
inaspri'mento m embitterment; (di conflitto) worsening
ina'sprir|e vt embitter. **~si** vr become embittered
inattac'cabile adj unassailable; (irreprensibile) irreproachable
inatten'dibile adj unreliable. **inat'teso** adj unexpected
inattività f inactivity. **inat'tivo** adj inactive
inattu'abile adj impracticable
inau'dito adj unheard of
inaugu'rale adj inaugural; **viaggio ~** maiden voyage
inaugu'ra|re vt inaugurate; open (mostra); unveil (statua); christen (lavastoviglie ecc). **~zi'one** f inauguration; (di mostra) opening; (di statua) unveiling
inavver't|enza f inadvertence. **~ita'mente** adv inadvertently
incagli'ar|e vi ground •vt hinder. **~si** vr run aground
incalco'labile adj incalculable
incal'li|rsi vr grow callous; (abituarsi) become hardened. **~to** adj callous; (abituato) hardened
incal'za|nte adj (ritmo) driving; (richiesta) urgent. **~re** vt pursue; fig press
incame'rare vt appropriate
incammi'nar|e vt get going; (fig: guidare) set off. **~si** vr set out
incana'lar|e vt canalize; fig channel. **~si** vr converge on
incande'scen|te adj incandescent; (discussione) burning
incan'ta|re vt enchant. **~rsi** vr stand spellbound; (incepparsi) jam. **~'tore, ~'trice** m enchanter •f enchantress
incan'tesimo m spell
incan'tevole adj enchanting
in'canto m spell; fig delight; (asta) auction; **come per ~** as if by magic
incanu'ti|re vt turn white. **~to** adj white
inca'pac|e adj incapable. **~ità** f incapability
incapo'nirsi vr be set (**a fare** on doing)
incap'pare vi **~ in** run into
incappucci'arsi vr wrap up
incapricci'arsi vr **~ di** take a fancy to
incapsu'lare vt seal; crown (dente)
incarce'ra|re vt imprison. **~zi'one** f imprisonment
incari'ca|re vt charge. **~rsi** vr take upon oneself; **me ne incarico io** I will see to it. **~to, -a** adj in charge •mf representative. **in'carico** m charge; **per incarico di** on behalf of
incar'na|re vt embody. **~rsi** vr become incarnate
incarta'mento m documents pl. **incar'tare** vt wrap [in paper]
incas'sa|re vt pack; (Mech) embed; box in (mobile, frigo); (riscuotere) cash; take (colpo). **~to** adj set; (fiume) deeply embanked. **in'casso** m collection; (introito) takings pl
incasto'na|re vt set. **~'tura** f setting. **~to** adj embedded; (anello) inset (**di** with)
inca'strar|e vt fit in; (ⓘ: in situazione) corner. **~si** vr fit. **in'castro** m joint; **a incastro** (pezzi) interlocking
incate'nare vt chain
incatra'mare vt tar
incatti'vire vt turn nasty
in'cauto adj imprudent
inca'va|re vt hollow out. **~to** adj hollow. **~'tura** f hollow. **in'cavo** m hollow; (scanalatura) groove
incendi'ar|e vt set fire to; fig inflame. **~si** vr catch fire. **~io, -a** adj incendiary; fig: (discorso) inflammatory; fig: (bellezza) sultry •mf arsonist. **in'cendio** m fire. **incendio doloso** arson

incene'ri|re vt burn to ashes; (cremare) cremate. **~rsi** vr be burnt to ashes. **~'tore** m incinerator

in'censo m incense

incensu'rato adj blameless; **essere ~** (Jur) have a clean record

incenti'vare vt motivate. **incen'tivo** m incentive

incen'trarsi vr **~ su** centre on

incep'par|e vt block; fig hamper. **~si** vr jam

ince'rata f oilcloth

incerot'tato adj with a plaster on

incer'tezza f uncertainty. **in'certo** adj uncertain •m uncertainty

inces'sante adj unceasing. **~'mente** adv incessantly

in'cest|o m incest. **~u'oso** adj incestuous

in'cetta f buying up; **fare ~ di** stockpile

inchi'esta f investigation

inchi'nar|e vt, **~si** vr bow. **in'chino** m bow; (di donna) curtsy

inchio'dare vt nail; nail down (coperchio); **~ a letto** (malattia:) confine to bed

inchi'ostro m ink

inciam'pare vi stumble; **~ in** (imbattersi) run into. **inci'ampo** m hindrance

inciden'tale adj incidental

inci'den|te m (episodio) incident; (infortunio) accident. **~za** f incidence

in'cidere vt cut; (arte) engrave; (registrare) record •vi **~ su** (gravare) weigh upon

in'cinta adj pregnant

incipi'ente adj incipient

incipri'ar|e vt powder. **~si** vr powder one's face

in'circa adv **all'~** more or less

incisi'one f incision; (arte) engraving; (acquaforte) etching; (registrazione) recording

inci'sivo adj incisive •m (dente) incisor

in'ciso m **per ~** incidentally

incita'mento m incitement. **inci'tare** vt incite

inci'vil|e adj uncivilized; (maleducato) impolite. **~tà** f barbarism; (maleducazione) rudeness

incle'men|te adj harsh

incli'nabile adj reclining

incli'na|re vt tilt •vi **~re a** be inclined to. **~rsi** vr list. **~to** adj tilted; (terreno) sloping. **~zi'one** f slope, inclination. **in'cline** adj inclined

in'clu|dere vt include; (allegare) enclose. **~si'one** f inclusion. **~'sivo** adj inclusive. **~so** pp di **includere** •adj included; (compreso) inclusive; (allegato) enclosed

incoe'ren|te adj (contraddittorio) inconsistent. **~za** f inconsistency

in'cognit|a f unknown quantity. **~o** adj unknown •m **in ~o** incognito

incol'lar|e vt stick; (con colla liquida) glue. **~si** vr stick to; **~si a qcno** stick close to sb

incolle'ri|rsi vr lose one's temper. **~to** adj enraged

incol'mabile adj (differenza) unbridgeable; (vuoto) unfillable

incolon'nare vt line up

inco'lore adj colourless

incol'pare vt blame

in'colto adj uncultivated; (persona) uneducated

in'colume adj unhurt

incom'ben|te adj impending. **~za** f task

in'combere vi **~ su** hang over; **~ a** (spettare) be incumbent on

incominci'are vt/i begin, start

incomo'dar|e vt inconvenience. **~si** vr trouble. **in'comodo** adj uncomfortable; (inopportuno) inconvenient •m inconvenience

incompa'rabile adj incomparable

incompe'ten|te adj incompetent. **~za** f incompetence

incompi'uto adj unfinished

incom'pleto adj incomplete

incompren'si|bile adj incomprehensible. **~'one** f lack of understanding; (malinteso) misunderstanding. **incom'preso** adj misunderstood

inconce'pibile adj inconceivable

inconclu'dente adj inconclusive;

(persona) ineffectual
incondizio|nata'mente adv unconditionally. **~'nato** adj unconditional
inconfes'sabile adj unmentionable
inconfon'dibile adj unmistakable
incongru'ente adj inconsistent
in'congruo adj inadequate
inconsa'pevol|e adj unaware; (inconscio) unconscious. **~'mente** adv unwittingly
inconscia'mente adv unconsciously. **in'conscio** adj & m (Psych) unconscious
inconsi'sten|te adj insubstantial; (notizia ecc) unfounded. **~za** f (di ragionamento, prove) flimsiness
inconsu'eto adj unusual
incon'sulto adj rash
incontami'nato adj uncontaminated
inconte'nibile adj irrepressible
inconten'tabile adj insatiable; (esigente) hard to please
inconti'nen|te adj incontinent. **~za** f incontinence
incon'trar|e vt meet; encounter, meet with (difficoltà). **~si** vr meet (**con qcno** sb)
incon'trario: **all'~** adv the other way around; (in modo sbagliato) the wrong way around
incontra'sta|bile adj incontrovertible. **~to** adj undisputed
in'contro m meeting; Sport match. **~ al vertice** summit meeting •prep **~ a** towards; **andare ~ a qcno** go to meet sb; fig meet sb half way
inconveni'ente m drawback
incoraggi|a'mento m encouragement. **~'ante** adj encouraging. **~'are** vt encourage
incornici'a|re vt frame. **~'tura** f framing
incoro'na|re vt crown. **~zi'one** f coronation
incorpo'rar|e vt incorporate; (mescolare) blend. **~si** vr blend; (territori:) merge
incorreg'gibile adj incorrigible
in'correre vt **~ in** incur; **~ nel pericolo di...** run the risk of...
incorrut'tibile adj incorruptible
incosci'en|te adj unconscious; (irresponsabile) reckless •mf irresponsible person. **~za** f unconsciousness; recklessness
inco'stan|te adj changeable; (persona) fickle. **~za** f changeableness; (di persona) fickleness
incre'dibile adj unbelievable, incredible
incredulità f incredulity. **in'credulo** adj incredulous
incremen'tare vt increase; (intensificare) step up. **incre'mento** m increase. **incremento demografico** population growth
incresci'oso adj regrettable
incre'spar|e vt ruffle; wrinkle (tessuto); make frizzy (capelli); **~e la fronte** frown. **~si** vr (acqua:) ripple; (tessuto:) wrinkle; (capelli:) go frizzy
incrimi'na|re vt indict; fig incriminate. **~zi'one** f indictment
incri'na|re vt crack; fig affect (amicizia). **~rsi** vr crack; (amicizia:) be affected. **~'tura** f crack
incroci'a|re vt cross •vi (Aeron, Naut) cruise. **~rsi** vr cross. **~'tore** m cruiser
in'crocio m crossing; (di strade) crossroads sg
incrol'labile adj indestructible
incro'sta|re vt encrust. **~zi'one** f encrustation
incuba|'trice f incubator. **~zi'one** f incubation
'incubo m nightmare
in'cudine f anvil
incu'rabile adj incurable
incu'rante adj careless
incurio'sir|e vt make curious. **~si** vr become curious
incursi'one f raid. **~ aerea** air raid
incurva'mento m bending
incur'va|re vt, **~rsi** vr bend. **~'tura** f bending
in'cusso pp di **incutere**
incusto'dito adj unguarded
in'cutere vt arouse
'indaco m indigo

indaffa'rato adj busy

inda'gare vt/i investigate

in'dagine f research; (giudiziaria) investigation. **~ di mercato** market survey

indebi'tar|e vt, **~si** vr get into debt

in'debito adj undue

indeboli'mento m weakening

indebo'lir|e vt, **~si** vr weaken

inde'cen|te adj indecent. **~za** f indecency; (vergogna) disgrace

indeci'frabile adj indecipherable

indecisi'one f indecision. **inde'ciso** adj undecided

inde'fesso adj tireless

indefi'ni|bile adj indefinable. **~to** adj indefinite

indefor'mabile adj crushproof

in'degno adj unworthy

indelica'tezza f indelicacy; (azione) tactless act. **indeli'cato** adj indiscreet; (grossolano) indelicate

in'denn|e adj uninjured; (da malattia) unaffected. **~ità** f inv allowance; (per danni) compensation. **~ità di trasferta** travel allowance. **~iz'zare** vt compensate. **inden'nizzo** m compensation

indero'gabile adj binding

indeside'ra|bile adj undesirable. **~to** adj (figlio, ospite) unwanted

indetermi'na|bile adj indeterminable. **~'tezza** f vagueness. **~to** adj indeterminate

'Indi|a f India. **i~'ano, -a** adj & mf Indian; **in fila i~ana** in single file

indiavo'lato adj possessed; (vivace) wild

indi'ca|re vt show, indicate; (col dito) point at; (far notare) point out; (consigliare) advise. **~'tivo** adj indicative • m (Gram) indicative. **~'tore** m indicator; (Techn) gauge; (prontuario) directory. **~zi'one** f indication; (istruzione) direction

indice m (dito) forefinger; (lancetta) pointer; (di libro, statistica) index; (fig: segno) sign

indietreggi'are vi draw back; (Mil) retreat

indi'etro adv back, behind; **all'~** backwards; **avanti e ~** back and forth; **essere ~** be behind; (mentalmente) be backward; (con pagamenti) be in arrears; (di orologio) be slow; **fare marcia ~** reverse; **rimandare ~** send back; **rimanere ~** be left behind; **torna ~!** come back!

indi'feso adj undefended; (inerme) helpless

indiffe'ren|te adj indifferent; **mi è ~te** it is all the same to me. **~za** f indifference

in'digeno, -a adj indigenous • mf native

indi'gen|te adj needy. **~za** f poverty

indigesti'one f indigestion. **indi'gesto** adj indigestible

indi'gna|re vt make indignant. **~rsi** vr be indignant. **~to** adj indignant. **~zi'one** f indignation

indimenti'cabile adj unforgettable

indipen'den|te adj independent. **~te'mente** adv independently; **~temente dal tempo** regardless of the weather, whatever the weather. **~za** f independence

in'dire vt announce

indiretta'mente adv indirectly. **indi'retto** adj indirect

indiriz'zar|e vt address; (mandare) send; (dirigere) direct. **~si** vr direct one's steps. **indi'rizzo** m address; (direzione) direction

indisci'pli|na f lack of discipline. **~'nato** adj undisciplined

indi'scre|to adj indiscreet. **~zi'one** f indiscretion

indi'scusso adj unquestioned

indiscu'tibil|e adj unquestionable. **~'mente** adv unquestionably

indispen'sabile adj essential, indispensable

indispet'tir|e vt irritate. **~si** vr get irritated

indi'spo|rre vt antagonize. **~sto** pp di **indisporre** • adj indisposed. **~sizi'one** f indisposition

indisso'lubile adj indissoluble

indistin'guibile adj indiscernible

indistinta'mente adv without exception. **indi'stinto** adj indistinct

indistrut'tibile adj indestructible

indistur'bato adj undisturbed

in'divia f endive

individu'a|le adj individual. **~'lista** mf individualist. **~lità** f individuality. **~re** vt individualize; (localizzare) locate; (riconoscere) single out

indi'viduo m individual

indivi'sibile adj indivisible. **indi'viso** adj undivided

indizi'a|re vt throw suspicion on. **~to, -a** adj suspected •mf suspect. **in'dizio** m sign; (Jur) circumstantial evidence

'indole f nature

indolenzi'mento m stiffness

indolen'zi|rsi vr go stiff. **~to** adj stiff

indo'lore adj painless

indo'mani m **l'~** the following day

Indo'nesia f Indonesia

indo'rare vt gild

indos'sa|re vt wear; (mettere addosso) put on. **~'tore, ~'trice** mf model

in'dotto pp di **indurre**

indottri'nare vt indoctrinate

indovi'n|are vt guess; (predire) foretell. **~ato** adj successful; (scelta) well-chosen. **~ello** m riddle. **indo'vino, -a** mf fortune-teller

indubbia'mente adv undoubtedly. **in'dubbio** adj undoubted

indugi'ar|e vi, **~si** vr linger. **in'dugio** m delay

indul'gen|te adj indulgent. **~za** f indulgence

in'dul|gere vi **~gere a** indulge in. **~to** pp di **indulgere** •m (Jur) pardon

indu'mento m garment; **indumenti** pl clothes

induri'mento m hardening

indu'rir|e vt, **~si** vr harden

in'durre vt induce

in'dustri|a f industry. **~'ale** adj industrial •mf industrialist

industrializ'za|re vt industrialize. **~to** adj industrialized. **~zi'one** f industrialization

industri|'arsi vr try one's hardest. **~'oso** adj industrious

induzi'one f induction

inebe'tito adj stunned

inebri'ante adj intoxicating, exciting

i'nedia f starvation

i'nedito adj unpublished

ineffi'cace adj ineffective

inefficì'en|te adj inefficient. **~za** f inefficiency

ineguagli'abile adj incomparable

inegu'ale adj unequal; (superficie) uneven

inelut'tabile adj inescapable

ine'rente adj **~ a** concerning

i'nerme adj unarmed; fig defenceless

inerpi'carsi vr **~ su** clamber up; (pianta:) climb up

i'ner|te adj inactive; (Phys) inert. **~zia** f inactivity; (Phys) inertia

inesat'tezza f inaccuracy. **ine'satto** adj inaccurate; (erroneo) incorrect; (non riscosso) uncollected

inesau'ribile adj inexhaustible

inesi'sten|te adj non-existent. **~za** f non-existence

inesperi'enza f inexperience. **ine'sperto** adj inexperienced

inespli'cabile adj inexplicable

ine'sploso adj unexploded

inesti'mabile adj inestimable

inetti'tudine f ineptitude. **i'netto** adj inept; **inetto a** unsuited to

ine'vaso adj (pratiche) pending; (corrispondenza) unanswered

inevi'tabil|e adj inevitable. **~'mente** adv inevitably

i'nezia f trifle

infagot'tar|e vt wrap up. **~si** vr wrap [oneself] up

infal'libile adj infallible

infa'ma|re vt defame. **~'torio** adj defamatory

in'fam|e adj infamous; (!: orrendo) awful, shocking. **~ia** f infamy

infan'garsi vr get muddy

infan'tile adj children's; (ingenuità) childlike; pej childish

in'fanzia f childhood; (bambini) children pl; **prima ~** infancy

infar'cire vi pepper (discorso) (**di** with)

infari'na|re vt flour; **~re di**

sprinkle with. **~'tura** f fig smattering

in'farto m coronary

infasti'dir|e vt irritate. **~si** vr get irritated

infati'cabile adj untiring

in'fatti conj as a matter of fact; (veramente) indeed

infatu'a|rsi vr become infatuated (**di** with). **~to** adj infatuated. **~zi'one** f infatuation

infe'condo adj infertile

infe'del|e adj unfaithful. **~tà** f unfaithfulness; **~** pl affairs

infe'lic|e adj unhappy; (inappropriato) unfortunate; (cattivo) bad. **~ità** f unhappiness

infel'tri|rsi vr get matted. **~to** adj matted

inferi'or|e adj (più basso) lower; (qualità) inferior •mf inferior. **~ità** f inferiority

inferme'ria f infirmary; (di nave) sick-bay

infermi'er|a f nurse. **~e** m [male] nurse

infermità f sickness. **~ mentale** mental illness. **in'fermo, -a** adj sick •mf invalid

infer'nale adj infernal; (spaventoso) hellish

in'ferno m hell; **va all'~!** go to hell!

infero'cirsi vr become fierce

inferri'ata f grating

infervo'rar|e vt arouse enthusiasm in. **~si** vr get excited

infe'stare vt infest

infet't|are vt infect. **~arsi** vr become infected. **~ivo** adj infectious. **in'fetto** adj infected. **infezi'one** f infection

infiac'chir|e vt/i, **~si** vr weaken

infiam'mabile adj [in]flammable

infiam'ma|re vt set on fire; (Med, fig) inflame. **~rsi** vr catch fire; (Med) become inflamed. **~zi'one** f (Med) inflammation

in'fido adj treacherous

infie'rire vi (imperversare) rage; **~ su** attack furiously

in'figger|e vt drive. **~si** vr **~si in** penetrate

infi'lar|e vt thread; (mettere) insert; (indossare) put on. **~si** vr slip on (vestito); **~si in** (introdursi in) slip into

infil'tra|rsi vr infiltrate. **~zi'one** f infiltration; (d'acqua) seepage; (Med: iniezione) injection

infil'zare vt pierce; (infilare) string; (conficcare) stick

'infimo adj lowest

in'fine adv finally; (insomma) in short

infinità f infinity; **un'~ di** masses of. **infi'nito** adj infinite; (Gram) infinitive •m infinite; (Gram) infinitive; (Math) infinity; **all'infinito** endlessly

infinocchi'are vt [!] hoodwink

infischi'arsi vr **~ di** not care about; **me ne infischio** [!] I couldn't care less

in'fisso pp di **infiggere** •m fixture; (di porta, finestra) frame

infit'tir|e vt/i, **~si** vr thicken

inflazi'one f inflation

infles'sibil|e adj inflexible. **~ità** f inflexibility

inflessi'one f inflexion

in'fli|ggere vt inflict. **~tto** pp di **infliggere**

influ'en|te adj influential. **~za** f influence; (Med) influenza

influen'za|bile adj (mente, opinione) impressionable. **~re** vt influence. **~to** adj (malato) with the flu

influ'ire vi **~ su** influence

in'flusso m influence

info'carsi vr catch fire; (viso:) go red; (discussione:) become heated

infol'tire vt/i thicken

infon'dato adj unfounded

in'fondere vt instil

infor'care vt fork up; get on (bici); put on (occhiali)

infor'male adj informal

infor'ma|re vt inform. **~rsi** vr inquire (**di** about).

infor'matic|a f computing, IT. **~o** adj computer attrib

infor'ma|tivo adj informative. **infor'mato** adj informed; **male informato** ill-informed. **~'tore, ~'trice** mf (di polizia) informer.

~zi'one f information (solo sg); **un'~zione** a piece of information

in'forme adj shapeless

infor'nare vt put into the oven

infortu'narsi vr have an accident.

infor'tu|nio m accident. **~nio sul lavoro** industrial accident

infos'sa|rsi vr sink; (guance, occhi:) become hollow. **~to** adj sunken, hollow

infradici'ar|e vt drench. **~si** vr get drenched; (diventare marcio) rot

infra'dito m pl (scarpe) flip-flops

in'frang|ere vt break; (in mille pezzi) shatter. **~ersi** vr break. **~'gibile** adj unbreakable

in'franto pp di **infrangere** • adj shattered; (cuore) broken

infra'rosso adj infra-red

infrastrut'tura f infrastructure

infrazi'one f offence

infredda'tura f cold

infreddo'li|rsi vr feel cold. **~to** adj cold

infruttu'oso adj fruitless

infuo'ca|re vt make red-hot. **~to** adj burning

infu'ori adv **all'~** outwards; **all'~ di** except

infuri'a|re vi rage. **~rsi** vr fly into a rage. **~to** adj blustering

infusi'one f infusion. **in'fuso** pp di **infondere** •m infusion

Ing. abbr ingegnere

ingabbi'are vt cage; (fig: mettere in prigione) jail

ingaggi'are vt engage; sign up (calciatori ecc); begin (lotta, battaglia). **in'gaggio** m engagement; (di calciatore) signing [up]

ingan'nar|e vt deceive; (essere infedele a) be unfaithful to. **~si** vr deceive oneself; **se non m'inganno** if I am not mistaken

ingan'nevole adj deceptive. **in'ganno** m deceit; (frode) fraud

ingarbugli'a|re vt entangle; (confondere) confuse. **~rsi** vr get entangled; (confondersi) become confused. **~to** adj confused

inge'gnarsi vr do one's best

inge'gnere m engineer. **ingegne'ria** f engineering

in'gegno m brains pl; (genio) genius; (abilità) ingenuity. **~sa'mente** adv ingeniously

ingelo'sir|e vt make jealous. **~si** vr become jealous

in'gente adj huge

ingenu|a'mente adv naïvely. **~ità** f naïvety. **in'genuo** adj ingenuous; (credulone) naïve

inge'renza f interference

inge'rire vt swallow

inges'sa|re vt put in plaster. **~'tura** f plaster

Inghil'terra f England

inghiot'tire vt swallow

in'ghippo m trick

ingial'li|re vi, **~rsi** vr turn yellow. **~to** adj yellowed

ingigan'tir|e vt magnify •vi, **~si** vr grow to enormous proportions

inginocchi'a|rsi vr kneel [down]. **~to** adj kneeling. **~'toio** m prie-dieu

ingiù adv down; **all'~** downwards; **a testa ~** head downwards

ingi'un|gere vt order. **~zi'one** f injunction. **~zione di pagamento** final demand

ingi'uri|a f insult; (torto) wrong; (danno) damage. **~'are** vt insult; (fare un torto a) wrong. **~'oso** adj insulting

ingiu'stizia f injustice. **ingi'usto** adj unjust, unfair

in'glese adj English •m Englishman; (lingua) English •f Englishwoman

ingoi'are vt swallow

ingol'far|e vt flood (motore). **~si** vr fig get involved; (motore:) flood

ingom'bra|nte adj cumbersome. **~re** vt clutter up; fig cram (mente)

in'gombro m encumbrance; **essere d'~** be in the way

ingor'digia f greed. **in'gordo** adj greedy

ingor'gar|e vt block. **~si** vr be blocked [up]. **in'gorgo** m blockage; (del traffico) jam

ingoz'zar|e vt gobble up; (nutrire eccessivamente) stuff; fatten (animali)

ingra'na|ggio m gear; fig

mechanism. **~re** vt engage • vi be in gear

ingrandi'mento m enlargement

ingran'di|re vt enlarge; (esagerare) magnify. **~rsi** vr become larger; (aumentare) increase

ingras'sar|e vt fatten up; (Mech) grease • vi, **~si** vr put on weight

ingrati'tudine f ingratitude. **in'grato** adj ungrateful; (sgradevole) thankless

ingredi'ente m ingredient

in'gresso m entrance; (accesso) admittance; (sala) hall; **~ gratuito/libero** admission free; **vietato l'~** no entry, no admittance

ingros'sar|e vt make big; (gonfiare) swell • vi, **~si** vr grow big; (gonfiare) swell

in'grosso: **all'~** adv wholesale; (pressappoco) roughly

ingua'ribile adj incurable

'inguine m groin

ingurgi'tare vt gulp down

ini'bi|re vt inhibit; (vietare) forbid. **~to** adj inhibited. **~zi'one** f inhibition; (divieto) prohibition

iniet'tar|e vt inject. **~si** vr **~si di sangue** (occhi:) become bloodshot. **iniezi'one** f injection

inimic'arsi vr make an enemy of. **inimi'cizia** f enmity

inimi'tabile adj inimitable

ininter|rotta'mente adv continuously. **~'rotto** adj continuous

iniquità f iniquity. **i'niquo** adj iniquitous

inizi'are vt begin; (avviare) open; **~ qcno a qcsa** initiate sb in sth • vi begin

inizia'tiva f initiative; **prendere l'~** take the initiative

inizi'a|to, -a adj initiated • mf initiate; **gli ~ti** the initiated. **~'tore, ~'trice** mf initiator. **~zi'one** f initiation

i'nizio m beginning, start; **dare ~ a** start; **avere ~** get under way

innaffi'a|re vt water. **~'toio** m watering-can

innal'zar|e vt raise; (erigere) erect. **~si** vr rise

innamo'ra|rsi vr fall in love (**di** with). **~ta** f girl-friend. **~to** adj in love • m boy-friend

in'nanzi adv (stato in luogo) in front; (di tempo) ahead; (avanti) forward; (prima) before; **d'ora ~** from now on • prep (prima) before; **~ a** in front of. **~'tutto** adv first of all; (soprattutto) above all

in'nato adj innate

innatu'rale adj unnatural

inne'gabile adj undeniable

innervo'sir|e vt make nervous. **~si** vr get irritated

inne'scare vt prime. **in'nesco** m primer

inne'stare vt graft; (Mech) engage; (inserire) insert. **in'nesto** m graft; (Mech) clutch; (Electr) connection

inne'vato adj covered in snow

'inno m hymn. **~ nazionale** national anthem

inno'cen|te adj innocent **~te'mente** adv innocently

in'nocuo adj innocuous

inno'va|re vt make changes in. **~'tivo** adj innovative. **~'tore** adj trail-blazing. **~zi'one** f innovation

innume'revole adj innumerable

ino'doro adj odourless

inoffen'sivo adj harmless

inol'trar|e vt forward. **~si** vr advance

inol'trato adj late

i'noltre adv besides

inon'da|re vt flood. **~zi'one** f flood

inope'roso adj idle

inoppor'tuno adj untimely

inorgo'glir|e vt make proud. **~si** vr become proud

inorri'dire vt horrify • vi be horrified

inosser'vato adj unobserved; (non rispettato) disregarded; **passare ~** go unnoticed

inossi'dabile adj stainless

'inox adj inv (acciaio) stainless

inqua'dra|re vt frame; fig put in context (scrittore, problema). **~rsi** vr fit into. **~'tura** f framing

inqualifi'cabile adj unspeakable

inquie'tar|e vt worry. **~si** get worried; (impazientirsi) get cross. **inqui'eto** adj restless; (preoccupato) worried. **inquie'tudine** f anxiety

inqui'lino, -a mf tenant

inquina'mento m pollution

inqui'na|re vt pollute. **~to** adj polluted

inqui'rente adj (Jur) (magistrato) examining; **commissione ~** commission of enquiry

inqui'si|re vt/i investigate. **~to** adj under investigation. **~'tore, ~'trice** adj inquiring • mf inquisitor. **~zi'one** f inquisition

insabbi'are vt shelve

i

insa'lat|a f salad. **~a belga** endive. **~i'era** f salad bowl

insa'lubre adj unhealthy

insa'nabile adj incurable

insangui'na|re vt cover with blood. **~to** adj bloody

insa'po|re adj tasteless. **~'rire** vt flavour

insa'puta f **all'~ di** unknown to

insazi'abile adj insatiable

insce'nare vt stage

inscin'dibile adj inseparable

insedia'mento m installation

insedi'ar|e vt install. **~si** vr install oneself

in'segna f sign; (bandiera) flag; (decorazione) decoration; (emblema) insignia pl; (stemma) symbol. **~ luminosa** neon sign

insegna'mento m teaching. **inse'gnante** adj teaching • mf teacher

inse'gnare vt/i teach; **~ qcsa a qcno** teach sb sth

insegui'mento m pursuit

insegu'i|re vt pursue. **~'tore, ~'trice** mf pursuer

insemi'na|re vt inseminate. **~zi'one** f insemination. **~zione artificiale** artificial insemination

insena'tura f inlet

insen'sato adj senseless; (folle) crazy

insen'sibil|e adj insensitive; (braccio ecc) numb. **~ità** f insensitivity

inseri'mento m insertion

inse'rir|e vt insert; place (annuncio); (Electr) connect. **~si** vr **~si in** get into. **in'serto** m file; (in un film ecc) insert

inservi'ente mf attendant

inserzi'o|ne f insertion; (avviso) advertisement. **~'nista** mf advertiser

insetti'cida m insecticide

in'setto m insect

insicu'rezza f insecurity. **insi'curo** adj insecure

in'sidi|a f trick; (tranello) snare. **~'are** vt/i lay a trap for. **~'oso** adj insidious

insi'eme adv together; (contemporaneamente) at the same time • prep **~ a** [together] with • m whole; (completo) outfit; (Theat) ensemble; (Math) set; **nell'~** as a whole; **tutto ~** all together; (bere) at one go

in'signe adj renowned

insignifi'cante adj insignificant

insi'gnire vt decorate

insinda'cabile adj final

insinu'ante adj insinuating

insinu'a|re vt insinuate. **~rsi** vr penetrate; **~rsi in** fig creep into

in'sipido adj insipid

insi'sten|te adj insistent. **~te'mente** adv repeatedly. **~za** f insistence. **in'sistere** vi insist; (perseverare) persevere

insoddisfa'cente adj unsatisfactory

insoddi'sfa|tto adj unsatisfied; (scontento) dissatisfied. **~zi'one** f dissatisfaction

insoffe'ren|te adj intolerant. **~za** f intolerance

insolazi'one f sunstroke

inso'len|te adj rude, insolent. **~za** f rudeness, insolence; (commento) insolent remark

in'solito adj unusual

inso'lubile adj insoluble

inso'luto adj unsolved; (non pagato) unpaid

insol'v|enza f insolvency

in'somma adv in short; **~!** well really!; (così così) so so

in'sonn|e adj sleepless. **~ia** f insomnia

insonno'lito adj sleepy

insonoriz'zato adj soundproofed

insoppor'tabile adj unbearable

insor'genza f onset

in'sorgere vi revolt, rise up; (sorgere) arise; (difficoltà) crop up

insormon'tabile adj (ostacolo, difficoltà) insurmountable

in'sorto pp di **insorgere•** adj rebellious •m rebel

insospet'tabile adj unsuspected

insospet'tir|e vt make suspicious •vi, **~si** vr become suspicious

insoste'nibile adj untenable; (insopportabile) unbearable

insostitu'ibile adj irreplaceable

inspe'ra|bile adj **una sua vittoria è ~bile** there is no hope of him winning. **~to** adj unhoped-for

inspie'gabile adj inexplicable

inspi'rare vt breathe in

in'stabil|e adj unstable; (tempo) changeable. **~ità** f instability; (di tempo) changeability

instal'la|re vt install. **~rsi** vr settle in. **~zi'one** f installation

instau'ra|re vt found. **~rsi** vr become established. **~zi'one** f foundation

instra'dare vt direct

insù adv **all'~** upwards

insuc'cesso m failure

insudici'ar|e vt dirty. **~si** vr get dirty

insuffici'en|te adj insufficient; (inadeguato) inadequate •m (Sch) fail. **~za** f insufficiency; (inadeguatezza) inadequacy; (Sch) fail. **~za cardiaca** heart failure. **~za di prove** lack of evidence

insu'lare adj insular

insu'lina f insulin

in'sulso adj insipid; (sciocco) silly

insul'tare vt insult. **in'sulto** m insult

insupe'rabile adj insuperable; (eccezionale) incomparable

insussi'stente adj groundless

intac'care vt nick; (corrodere) corrode; draw on (capitale); (danneggiare) damage

intagli'are vt carve. **in'taglio** m carving

intan'gibile adj untouchable

in'tanto adv meanwhile; (per ora) for the moment; (avversativo) but; **~ che** while

intarsi'a|re vt inlay. **~to** adj **~to di** inset with. **in'tarsio** m inlay

inta'sa|re vt clog; block (traffico). **~rsi** vr get blocked. **~to** adj blocked

inta'scare vt pocket

in'tatto adj intact

intavo'lare vt start

inte'gra|le adj whole; **edizione ~le** unabridged edition; **pane ~le** wholemeal bread. **~nte** adj integral. **'integro** adj complete; (retto) upright

inte'gra|re vt integrate; (aggiungere) supplement. **~rsi** vr integrate. **~'tivo** adj (corso) supplementary. **~zi'one** f integration

integrità f integrity

intelaia'tura f framework

intel'letto m intellect

intellettu'al|e adj & mf intellectual. **~'mente** adv intellectually

intelli'gen|te adj intelligent. **~te'mente** adv intelligently. **~za** f intelligence

intelli'gibile adj intelligible

intempe'ranza f intemperance

intem'perie fpl bad weather

inten'den|te m superintendent. **~za** f **~za di finanza** inland revenue office

in'tender|e vt (comprendere) understand; (udire) hear; (avere intenzione) intend; (significare) mean. **~sela con** have an understanding with; **~si** vr (capirsi) understand each other; **~si di** (essere esperto) have a good knowledge of

intendi|'mento m understanding; (intenzione) intention. **~'tore, ~'trice** mf connoisseur

intene'rir|e vt soften; (commuovere) touch. **~si** vr be touched

intensifi'car|e vt, **~si** vr intensify

intensità f intensity. **inten'sivo** adj intensive. **in'tenso** adj intense

inten'tare vt start up; ~ **causa contro qcno** bring o institute proceedings against sb

in'tento adj engrossed (**a** in) •m purpose

intenzio|'nale adj intentional. **intenzi'one** f intention; **senza ~ne** unintentionally; **avere ~ne di fare qcsa** intend to do sth, have the intention of doing sth.

intenzio'nato adj **essere ~ a fare qcsa** have the intention of doing sth

intera'gire vi interact

intera'mente adv completely

intera|t'tivo adj interactive. **~zi'one** f interaction

i

interca'lare[1] m stock phrase

interca'lare[2] vt insert

intercambi'abile adj interchangeable

interca'pedine f cavity

inter'ce|dere vi intercede. **~ssi'one** f intercession

intercet'ta|re vt intercept; tap (telefono). **~zi'one** f interception. **~zione telefonica** telephone tapping

inter'city m inv inter-city

intercontinen'tale adj intercontinental

inter'correre vi (tempo:) elapse; (esistere) exist

inter'detto pp di **interdire** •adj astonished; (proibito) forbidden; **rimanere ~** be taken aback

inter'di|re vt forbid; (Jur) deprive of civil rights. **~zi'one** f prohibition

interessa'mento m interest

interes'sante adj interesting; **essere in stato ~** be pregnant

interes'sa|re vt interest; (riguardare) concern •vi **~re a** matter to. **~rsi** vr **~rsi a** take an interest in. **~rsi di** take care of. **~to, -a** mf interested party •adj interested; **essere ~to** pej have an interest

inte'resse m interest; **fare qcsa per ~** do sth out of self-interest

inter'faccia f (Comput) interface

interfe'renza f interference

interfe'r|ire vi interfere

interiezi'one f interjection

interi'ora fpl entrails

interi'ore adj interior

inter'ludio m interlude

intermedi'ario, -a adj & mf intermediary

inter'medio adj in-between

inter'mezzo m (Mus, Theat) intermezzo

intermit'ten|te adj intermittent; (luce) flashing. **~za** f **luce a ~za** flashing light

interna'mento m internment; (in manicomio) committal

inter'nare vt intern; (in manicomio) commit [to a mental institution]

internazio'nale adj international

C **'Internet** f Internet, internet

in'terno adj internal; (Geog) inland; (interiore) inner; (politica) national; **alunno ~** boarder •m interior; (di condominio) flat; (Teleph) extension; Cinema interior shot; **all'~** inside

in'tero adj whole, entire; (intatto) intact; (completo) complete; **per ~** in full

interpel'lare vt consult

inter'por|re vt place (ostacolo). **~si** vr come between

interpre'ta|re vt interpret; (Mus) perform. **~zi'one** f interpretation; (Mus) performance. **in'terprete** mf interpreter; (Mus) performer

inter'ra|re vt (seppellire) bury; plant (pianta). **~to** m basement

interro'ga|re vt question; (Sch) test; examine (studenti). **~'tivo** adj interrogative; (sguardo) questioning; **punto ~tivo** question mark •m question. **~'torio** adj & m questioning. **~zi'one** f question; (Sch) oral [test]

inter'romper|e vt interrupt; (sospendere) stop; cut off (collegamento). **~si** vr break off

interrut'tore m switch

interruzi'one f interruption; **senza ~** non-stop. **~ di gravidanza** termination of pregnancy

interse|'care vt, **~'carsi** vr intersect. **~zi'one** f intersection

C *see* A-Z of Italian life and culture

interur'ban|a f long-distance call. **~o** adj inter-city; **telefonata ~a** long-distance call

interval'lare vt space out. **inter'vallo** m interval; (spazio) space; (Sch) break. **intervallo pubblicitario** commercial break

interve'nire vi intervene; (Med: operare) operate; **~ a** take part in. **inter'vento** m intervention; (presenza) presence; (chirurgico) operation; **pronto intervento** emergency services

inter'vista f interview

intervi'sta|re vt interview. **~'tore, ~'trice** mf interviewer

in'tes|a f understanding; **cenno d'~a** acknowledgement. **~o** pp di **intendere** • adj **resta ~o che...** needless to say,...; **~i!** agreed!; **~o a** meant to

inte'sta|re vt head; write one's name and address at the top of (lettera); (Comm) register. **~rsi** vr **~rsi a fare qcsa** take it into one's head to do sth. **~'tario, -a** mf holder. **~zi'one** f heading; (su carta da lettere) letterhead

inte'stino adj (lotte) internal • m intestine

intima'mente adv intimately

inti'ma|re vt order; **~re l'alt a qcno** order sb to stop. **~zi'one** f order

intimida|'torio adj threatening. **~zi'one** f intimidation

intimi'dire vt intimidate

intimità f cosiness. **'intimo** adj intimate; (interno) innermost; (amico) close • m (amico) close friend; (dell'animo) heart

intimo'ri|re vt frighten. **~rsi** vr get frightened. **~to** adj frightened

in'tingere vt dip

in'tingolo m sauce; (pietanza) stew

intiriz'zi|re vt numb. **~rsi** vr grow numb. **~to** adj **essere ~to** (dal freddo) be perished

intito'lar|e vt entitle; (dedicare) dedicate. **~si** vr be called

intolle'rabile adj intolerable

intona'care vt plaster. **in'tonaco** m plaster

into'na|re vt start to sing; tune (strumento); (accordare) match. **~rsi** vr match. **~to** adj (persona) able to sing in tune; (colore) matching

intonazi'one f (inflessione) intonation; (ironica) tone

inton'ti|re vt daze; (gas:) make dizzy • vi be dazed. **~to** adj dazed

intop'pare vi **~ in** run into

in'toppo m obstacle

in'torno adv around • prep **~ a** around; (circa) about

intorpi'di|re vt numb. **~rsi** vr become numb. **~to** adj torpid

intossi'ca|re vt poison. **~rsi** vr be poisoned. **~zi'one** f poisoning

intralci'are vt hamper

in'tralcio m hitch; **essere d'~** be a hindrance (**a** to)

intrallaz'zare vi intrigue. **intral'lazzo** m racket

intramon'tabile adj timeless

intransi'gen|te adj uncompromising. **~za** f intransigence

intransi'tivo adj intransitive

intrappo'lato adj **rimanere ~** be trapped

intrapren'den|te adj enterprising. **~za** f initiative

intra'prendere vt undertake

intrat'tabile adj very difficult

intratte'n|ere vt entertain. **~ersi** vr linger. **~i'mento** m entertainment

intrave'dere vt catch a glimpse of; (presagire) foresee

intrecci'ar|e vt interweave; plait (capelli, corda). **~si** vr intertwine; (aggrovigliarsi) become tangled; **~e le mani** clasp one's hands

in'treccio m (trama) plot

intri'cato adj tangled

intri'gante adj scheming; (affascinante) intriguing

intri'ga|re vt entangle; (incuriosire) intrigue • vi intrigue, scheme. **~rsi** vr meddle. **in'trigo** m plot; **intrighi** pl intrigues

in'triso adj **~ di** soaked in

intri'stirsi vr grow sad

intro'du|rre vt introduce; (inserire) insert; **~rre a** (iniziare a) introduce to. **~rsi** vr get in (**in** to). **~t'tivo** adj (pagine, discorso) introductory. **~zi'one** f introduction

in'troito m income, revenue; (incasso) takings pl

intro'metter|e vt introduce. **~si** vr interfere; (interporsi) intervene. **intromissi'one** f intervention

intro'vabile adj that can't be found; (prodotto) unobtainable

intro'verso, -a adj introverted •mf introvert

intrufo'larsi vr sneak in

in'truglio m concoction

intrusi'one f intrusion. **in'truso, -a** mf intruder

intu'i|re vt perceive

intui|'tivo adj intuitive. **in'tuito** m intuition. **~zi'one** f intuition

inuguagli'anza f inequality

inu'mano adj inhuman

inu'mare vt inter

inumi'dir|e vt dampen; moisten (labbra). **~si** vr become damp

i'nutil|e adj useless; (superfluo) unnecessary. **~ità** f uselessness

inutiliz'za|bile adj unusable. **~to** adj unused

inva'dente adj intrusive

in'vadere vt invade; (affollare) overrun

invali'd|are vt invalidate. **~ità** f disability; (Jur) invalidity. **in'valido, -a** adj invalid; (handicappato) disabled •mf disabled person

in'vano adv in vain

invari'abile adj invariable

invari'ato adj unchanged

invasi'one f invasion. **in'vaso** pp di **invadere**. **inva'sore** adj invading •m invader

invecchia'mento m (di vino) maturation

invecchi'are vt/i age

in'vece adv instead; (anzi) but; **~ di** instead of

inve'ire vi **~ contro** inveigh against

inven'd|ibile adj unsaleable. **~uto** adj unsold

inven'tare vt invent

inventari'are vt make an inventory of. **inven'tario** m inventory

inven|'tivo, -a adj inventive •f inventiveness. **~-'tore, ~'trice** mf inventor. **~zi'one** f invention

inver'nale adj wintry. **in'verno** m winter

invero'simile adj improbable

inversi'one f inversion; (Mech) reversal. **in'verso** adj inverse; (opposto) opposite •m opposite

inverte'brato adj & m invertebrate

inver'ti|re vt reverse; (capovolgere) turn upside down.

investi'ga|re vt investigate. **~'tore** m investigator. **~zi'one** f investigation

investi'mento m investment; (incidente) crash

inve'sti|re vt invest; (urtare) collide with; (travolgere) run over; **~re qcno di** invest sb with. **~'tura** f investiture

invi'a|re vt send. **~to, -a** mf envoy; (di giornale) correspondent

invidi|a f envy. **~'are** vt envy. **~'oso** adj envious

invigo'rir|e vt invigorate. **~si** vr become strong

invin'cibile adj invincible

in'vio m dispatch; (Comput) enter

invipe'ri|rsi vr get nasty. **~to** adj furious

invi'sibil|e adj invisible. **~ità** f invisibility

invi'tante adj (piatto, profumo) enticing

invi'ta|re vt invite. **~to, -a** mf guest. **in'vito** m invitation

invo'ca|re vt invoke; (implorare) beg. **~zi'one** f invocation

invogli'ar|e vt tempt; (indurre) induce. **~si** vr **~si di** take a fancy to

involon|taria'mente adv involuntarily. **~'tario** adj involuntary

invol'tino m (Culin) beef olive

in'volto m parcel; (fagotto) bundle

in'volucro m wrapping

invulne'rabile adj invulnerable

inzacche'rare vt splash with mud

inzup'par|e vt soak; (intingere) dip. **~si** vr get soaked

'io pers pron I; **chi è? – [sono] io** who is it? – [it's] me; **l'ho fatto io [stesso]** I did it myself • m **l'~** the ego

i'odio m iodine

I'onio m **lo ~** the Ionian [Sea]

i'osa: **a ~** adv in abundance

iperat'tivo adj hyperactive

ipermer'cato m hypermarket

iper'metrope adj long-sighted

ipertensi'one f high blood pressure

ip'no|si f hypnosis. **~tico** adj hypnotic. **~'tismo** m hypnotism. **~tiz'zare** vt hypnotize

ipoca'lorico adj low-calorie

ipocon'driaco, -a adj & mf hypochondriac

ipocri'sia f hypocrisy. **i'pocrita** adj hypocritical • mf hypocrite

ipo'te|ca f mortgage. **~'care** vt mortgage

i'potesi f inv hypothesis; (caso, eventualità) eventuality. **ipo'tetico** adj hypothetical. **ipotiz'zare** vt hypothesize

'ippico, -a adj horse attrib • f riding

ippoca'stano m horse-chestnut

ip'podromo m racecourse

ippo'potamo m hippopotamus

'ira f anger. **~'scibile** adj irascible

i'rato adj irate

'iride f (Anat) iris; (arcobaleno) rainbow

Ir'lan|da f Ireland. **~da del Nord** Northern Ireland. **i~'dese** adj Irish • m Irishman; (lingua) Irish • f Irishwoman

iro'nia f irony. **i'ronico** adj ironic[al]

irradi'a|re vt/i radiate. **~zi'one** f radiation

irraggiun'gibile adj unattainable

irragio'nevole adj unreasonable; (speranza, timore) irrational; (assurdo) absurd

irrazio'nal|e adj irrational. **~ità** adj irrationality

irre'a|le adj unreal. **~'listico** adj unrealistic. **~liz'zabile** adj unattainable. **~ltà** f unreality

irrecupe'rabile adj irrecoverable

irrego'lar|e adj irregular. **~ità** f inv irregularity

irremo'vibile adj fig adamant

irrepa'rabile adj irreparable

irrepe'ribile adj not to be found; **sarò ~** I won't be contactable

irrepren'sibile adj irreproachable

irrepri'mibile adj irrepressible

irrequi'eto adj restless

irresi'stibile adj irresistible

irrespon'sabil|e adj irresponsible. **~ità** f irresponsibility

i

irrever'sibile adj irreversible

irricono'scibile adj unrecognizable

irri'ga|re vt irrigate; (fiume:) flow through. **~zi'one** f irrigation

irrigidi'mento m stiffening

irrigi'dir|e vt, **~si** vr stiffen

irrile'vante adj unimportant

irrimedi'abile adj irreparable

irripe'tibile adj unrepeatable

irri'sorio adj derisive; (differenza, particolare, somma) insignificant

irri'ta|bile adj irritable. **~nte** adj aggravating

irri'ta|re vt irritate. **~rsi** vr get annoyed. **~to** adj irritated; (gola) sore. **~zi'one** f irritation

irrobu'stir|e vt fortify. **~si** vr get stronger

ir'rompere vi burst (**in** into)

irro'rare vt sprinkle

irru'ente adj impetuous

irruzi'one f **fare ~ in** burst into

i'scritto, -a pp di **iscrivere** • adj registered • mf member; **per ~** in writing

i'scriver|e vt register. **~si** vr **~si a** register at, enrol at (scuola); join (circolo ecc). **iscrizi'one** f registration; (epigrafe) inscription

i'sla|mico adj Islamic. **~'mismo** m Islam

I'slan|da f Iceland. **i~'dese** adj Icelandic • mf Icelander

'isola f island. **le isole britanniche** the British Isles. **~ pedonale** pedestrian precinct. **~ spartitraffico** traffic island

iso'lante adj insulating • m insulator

iso'la|re vt isolate; (Electr, Mech) insulate; (acusticamente) soundproof. **~to** adj isolated • m (di appartamenti) block

ispes'sir|e vt, **~si** vr thicken

ispetto'rato m inspectorate. **ispet'tore** m inspector. **ispezio'nare** vt inspect. **ispezi'one** f inspection

'ispido adj bristly

ispi'ra|re vt inspire; suggest (idea, soluzione). **~rsi** vr **~rsi a** be based on. **~to** adj inspired. **~zi'one** f inspiration; (idea) idea

Isra'el|e m Israel. **i~i'ano, -a** agg & mf Israeli

istan'taneo, -a adj instantaneous • f snapshot

i'stante m instant; **all'~** instantly

i'stanza f petition

i'sterico adj hysterical. **iste'rismo** m hysteria

isti'ga|re vt instigate; **~re qcno al male** incite sb to evil. **~zi'one** f instigation

istin'tivo adj instinctive. **i'stinto** m instinct; **d'istinto** instinctively

istitu'ire vt institute; (fondare) found; initiate (manifestazione)

isti'tu|to m institute; (universitario) department; (Sch) secondary school. **~to di bellezza** beauty salon. **~'tore, ~'trice** mf (insegnante) tutor; (fondatore) founder

istituzio'nale adj institutional. **istituzi'one** f institution

'istrice m porcupine

istru'i|re vt instruct; (addestrare) train; (informare) inform; (Jur) prepare. **~to** adj educated

istrut't|ivo adj instructive. **~ore, ~rice** mf instructor; **giudice ~ore** examining magistrate. **~oria** f (Jur) investigation. **istruzi'one** f education; (indicazione) instruction

I'tali|a f Italy. **i~'ano, -a** adj & mf Italian

itine'rario m route, itinerary

itte'rizia f jaundice

'ittico adj fishing attrib

I.V.A. f abbr (imposta sul valore aggiunto) VAT

Jj

jack m inv jack

jazz m jazz. **jaz'zista** mf jazz player

jeep f inv jeep

'jolly m inv (carta da gioco) joker

ju'niores mfpl Sport juniors

Kk

ka'jal m inv kohl

kara'oke m inv karaoke

kara'te m karate

kg abbr (chilogrammo) kg

km abbr (chilometro) km

Ll

l' def art mf (before vowel) the; ▸**il**

la def art f the; ▸**il** •pron (oggetto, riferito a persona) her; (riferito a cosa, animale) it; (forma di cortesia) you •m inv (Mus) A

là adv there; **di là** (in quel luogo) in there; (da quella parte) that way; **eccolo là!** there he is!; **farsi più in là** (far largo) make way; **là dentro** in there; **là fuori** out there; **[ma] va là!** come off it!; **più in là** (nel tempo) later on; (nello spazio) further on

'labbro m (pl f (Anat) **labbra**) lip

labi'rinto m labyrinth; (di sentieri ecc) maze

labora'torio m laboratory; (di negozio, officina ecc) workshop

labori'oso adj industrious; (faticoso) laborious

labu'rista adj Labour •mf member of the Labour Party

'lacca f lacquer; (per capelli) hairspray. **lac'care** vt lacquer

'laccio m noose; (lazo) lasso; (trappola) snare; (stringa) lace

lace'rante adj (grido) earsplitting

lace'ra|re vt tear; lacerate (carne). **~rsi** vr tear. **~zi'one** f laceration. **'lacero** adj torn; (cencioso) ragged

'lacri|ma f tear; (goccia) drop. **~'mare** vi weep. **~'mevole** adj tear-jerking

lacri'mogeno adj **gas ~** tear gas

la'cuna f gap. **lacu'noso** adj (preparazione, resoconto) incomplete

la'custre adj lake attrib

'ladro, -a mf thief; **al ~!** stop thief!; **~'cinio** m theft. **la'druncolo** m petty thief

'lager m inv concentration camp

laggiù adv down there; (lontano) over there

'lagna f (!: persona) moaning Minnie; (film) bore

la'gna|nza f complaint. **~rsi** vr moan; (protestare) complain (**di** about)

'lago m lake

la'guna f lagoon

'laico, -a adj lay; (vita) secular •m layman •f laywoman

'lama f blade •m inv llama

lambic'carsi vr **~ il cervello** rack one's brains

lam'bire vt lap

lamé m inv lamé

lamen'tar|e vt lament. **~si** vr moan. **~si di** complain about

lamen'te|la f complaint. **~vole** adj mournful; (pietoso) pitiful. **la'mento** m moan

la'metta f **~ [da barba]** razor blade

lami'era f sheet metal

'lamina f foil. **~ d'oro** gold leaf

lami'na|re vt laminate. **~to** adj laminated •m laminate; (tessuto) lamé

'lampa|da f lamp. **~da abbronzante** sunlamp. **~da a pila** torch. **~'dario** m chandelier. **~'dina** f light bulb

lam'pante adj clear

lampeggi'a|re vi flash. **~'tore** m (Auto) indicator

lampi'one m street lamp

'lampo m flash of lightning; (luce) flash; **lampi** pl lightning sg. **~ di genio** stroke of genius. **[cerniera] ~** zip [fastener], zipper Am

lam'pone m raspberry

'lana f wool; **di ~** woollen. **~ d'acciaio** steel wool. **~ vergine** new wool. **~ di vetro** glass wool

lan'cetta f pointer; (di orologio) hand

'lancia f spear; (Naut) launch

lanci'ar|e vt throw; (da un aereo) drop; launch (missile, prodotto); give (grido); **~e uno sguardo a** glance at. **~si** vr fling oneself; (intraprendere) launch out

lanci'nante adj piercing

'lancio m throwing; (da aereo) drop; (di missile, prodotto) launch. ~ **del disco** discus [throwing]. ~ **del giavellotto** javelin [throwing]

'landa f heath

lani'ero adj wool

lani'ficio m woollen mill

lan'terna f lantern; (faro) lighthouse

la'nugine f down

lapi'dare vt stone; fig demolish

lapi'dario adj (conciso) terse

'lapide f tombstone; (commemorativa) memorial tablet

'lapis m inv pencil

'lapsus m inv lapse, error

'lardo m lard

larga'mente adv widely

lar'ghezza f breadth; fig liberality. ~ **di vedute** broadmindedness

'largo adj wide; (ampio) broad; (abito) loose; (liberale) liberal; (abbondante) generous; **stare alla larga** keep away; **di manica larga** fig generous; ~ **di spalle/vedute** broad-shouldered/-minded •m width; **andare al** ~ (Naut) go out to sea; **fare** ~ make room; **farsi** ~ make one's way; **al** ~ **di** off the coast of

'larice m larch

la'ringe f larynx. **larin'gite** f laryngitis

'larva f larva; (persona emaciata) shadow

la'sagne fpl lasagna sg

lasciapas'sare m inv pass

lasci'ar|e vt leave; (rinunciare) give up; (rimetterci) lose; (smettere di tenere) let go [of]; (concedere) let; **~e di fare qcsa** (smettere) stop doing sth; **lascia perdere!** forget it!; **lascialo venire** let him come. **~si** vr (reciproco) leave each other; **~si andare** let oneself go

'lascito m legacy

'laser adj & m inv [**raggio**] ~ laser [beam]

lassa'tivo adj & m laxative

'lasso m ~ **di tempo** period of time

lassù adv up there

'lastra f slab; (di ghiaccio) sheet; (Phot, di metallo) plate; (radiografia) X-ray [plate]

lastri'ca|re vt pave. **~to, 'lastrico** m pavement

la'tente adj latent

late'rale adj side attrib; (Med, Techn ecc) lateral; **via** ~ side street

late'rizi mpl bricks

lati'fondo m large estate

la'tino adj & m Latin

lati'tan|te adj in hiding •mf fugitive [from justice]

lati'tudine f latitude

'lato adj (ampio) broad; **in senso** ~ broadly speaking •m side; (aspetto) aspect; **a** ~ **di** beside; **dal** ~ **mio** (punto di vista) for my part; **d'altro** ~ fig on the other hand

la'tra|re vi bark. **~to** m barking

la'trina f latrine

'latta f tin, can

lat'taio, -a m milkman •f milkwoman

lat'tante adj breast-fed •mf suckling

'latt|e m milk. **~e acido** sour milk. **~e condensato** condensed milk. **~e detergente** cleansing milk. **~e in polvere** powdered milk. **~e scremato** skimmed milk. **~eo** adj milky. **~e'ria** f dairy. **~i'cini** mpl dairy products. **~i'era** f milk jug

lat'tina f can

lat'tuga f lettuce

🅲 **'laure|a** f degree; **prendere la ~a** graduate. **~'ando, -a** mf final-year student

laure'a|rsi vr graduate. **~to, -a** agg & mf graduate

'lauro m laurel

'lauto adj lavish; ~ **guadagno** handsome profit

'lava f lava

la'vabile adj washable

la'vabo m wash-basin

la'vaggio m washing. ~ **automatico** (per auto) carwash. ~ **a secco** dry-cleaning

la'vagna f slate; (Sch) blackboard

la'van|da f wash; (Bot) lavender; **fare una ~da gastrica** have one's

🅲 see A-Z of Italian life and culture

stomach pumped. **~'daia** f washerwoman. **~de'ria** f laundry. **~deria automatica** launderette

lavan'dino m sink; (! persona) bottomless pit

lavapi'atti mf inv dishwasher

la'var|e vt wash; **~e i piatti** wash up. **~si** vr wash, have a wash; **~si i denti** brush one's teeth; **~si le mani** wash one's hands

lava'secco mf inv dry-cleaner's

lavasto'viglie f inv dishwasher

la'vata f wash; **darsi una ~** have a wash; **~ di capo** fig scolding

lava'tivo, -a mf idler

lava'trice f washing-machine

lavo'rante mf worker

lavo'ra|re vi work • vt work; knead (pasta ecc); till (la terra); **~re a maglia** knit. **~'tivo** adj working. **~to** adj (pietra, legno) carved; (cuoio) tooled; (metallo) wrought. **~'tore, ~'trice** mf worker • adj working. **~zi'one** f manufacture; (di terra) working; (artigianale) workmanship; (del terreno) cultivation. **lavo'rio** m intense activity

la'voro m work; (faticoso, sociale) labour; (impiego) job; (Theat) play; **mettersi al ~** set to work (**su** on). **~ a maglia** knitting. **~ nero** moonlighting. **~ straordinario** overtime. **~ a tempo pieno** full-time job. **lavori** pl **di casa** housework. **lavori** pl **in corso** roadworks. **lavori** pl **stradali** roadworks

le def art fpl the; ▸**il** • pers pron (oggetto) them; (a lei) her; (forma di cortesia) you

le'al|e adj loyal. **~'mente** adv loyally. **~tà** f loyalty

lebbra f leprosy

lecca 'lecca m inv lollipop

leccapi'edi mf inv pej bootlicker

lec'ca|re vt lick; fig suck up to. **~rsi** vr lick; (fig: agghindarsi) doll oneself up; **da ~rsi i baffi** mouth-watering. **~ta** f lick

leccor'nia f delicacy

lecito adj lawful; (permesso) permissible

ledere vt damage; (Med) injure

lega f league; (di metalli) alloy; **far ~ con qcno** take up with sb

le'gaccio m string; (delle scarpe) shoelace

le'gal|e adj legal • m lawyer. **~ità** f legality. **~iz'zare** vt authenticate; (rendere legale) legalize. **~'mente** adv legally

le'game m tie; (amoroso) liaison; (connessione) link

lega'mento m (Med) ligament

le'gar|e vt tie; tie up (persona); tie together (due cose); (unire, rilegare) bind; alloy (metalli); (connettere) connect • vi (far lega) get on well. **~si** vr bind oneself; **~si a qcno** become attached to sb

le'gato m legacy; (Relig) legate

lega'tura f tying; (di libro) binding

le'genda f legend

'legge f law; (parlamentare) act; **a norma di ~** by law

leg'genda f legend; (didascalia) caption. **leggen'dario** adj legendary

'leggere vt/i read

legge'r|ezza f lightness; (frivolezza) frivolity; (incostanza) fickleness. **~'mente** adv slightly

leg'gero adj light; (bevanda) weak; (lieve) slight; (frivolo) frivolous; (incostante) fickle

leg'gibile adj (scrittura) legible; (stile) readable

leg'gio m lectern; (Mus) music stand

legife'rare vi legislate

legio'nario m legionary. **legi'one** f legion

legisla|'tivo adj legislative. **~'tore** m legislator. **~'tura** f legislature. **~zi'one** f legislation

legittimità f legitimacy. **le'gittimo** adj legitimate; (giusto) proper; **legittima difesa** self-defence

'legna f firewood

le'gname m timber

'legno m wood; **di ~** wooden. **~ compensato** plywood. **le'gnoso** adj woody

le'gume m pod

'lei pers pron (soggetto) she; (oggetto, con prep) her; (forma di cortesia) you; **lo ha fatto ~ stessa** she did it herself

'lembo m edge; (di terra) strip

'lena f vigour

le'nire vt soothe

lenta'mente adv slowly

'lente f lens. ~ **a contatto** contact lens. ~ **d'ingrandimento** magnifying glass

len'tezza f slowness

len'ticchia f lentil

len'tiggine f freckle

'lento adj slow; (allentato) slack; (abito) loose

'lenza f fishing-line

len'zuolo m (pl f **lenzuola**) m sheet

le'one m lion; (Astr) Leo

leo'pardo m leopard

'lepre f hare

'lercio adj filthy

'lesbica f lesbian

lesi'nare vt grudge • vi be stingy

lesio'nare vt damage. **lesi'one** f lesion

'leso pp di **ledere** • adj injured

les'sare vt boil

'lessico m vocabulary

'lesso adj boiled • m boiled meat

'lesto adj quick; (mente) sharp

le'tale adj lethal

le'targ|ico adj lethargic. **~o** m lethargy; (di animali) hibernation

le'tizia f joy

'lettera f letter; **alla** ~ literally; ~ **maiuscola** capital letter; ~ **minuscola** small letter; **lettere** pl (letteratura) literature sg; (Univ) Arts; **dottore in lettere** BA, Bachelor of Arts

lette'rale adj literal

lette'rario adj literary

lette'rato adj well-read

lettera'tura f literature

let'tiga f stretcher

let'tino m cot; (Med) couch

'letto m bed. ~ **a castello** bunkbed. ~ **a una piazza** single bed. ~ **a due piazze** double bed. ~ **matrimoniale** double bed

letto'rato m (corso) ≈ tutorial

let'tore, -'trice mf reader; (Univ) language assistant • m (Comput) disk drive. ~ **di CD-ROM** CD-Rom drive

let'tura f reading

leuce'mia f leukaemia

'leva f lever; (Mil) call-up; **far** ~ lever. ~ **del cambio** gear lever

le'vante m East; (vento) east wind

le'va|re vt (alzare) raise; (togliere) take away; (rimuovere) take off; (estrarre) pull out; **~re di mezzo qcsa** get sth out of the way. **~rsi** vr rise; (da letto) get up; **~rsi di mezzo, ~rsi dai piedi** get out of the way. **~ta** f rising; (di posta) collection

leva'taccia f **fare una** ~ get up at the crack of dawn

leva'toio adj **ponte** ~ drawbridge

levi'ga|re vt smooth; (con carta vetro) rub down. **~to** adj (superficie) polished

levri'ero m greyhound

lezi'one f lesson; (Univ) lecture; (rimprovero) rebuke

lezi'oso adj (stile, modi) affected

li pers pron mpl them

lì adv there; **fin lì** as far as there; **giù di lì** thereabouts; **lì per lì** there and then

Li'bano m Lebanon

'libbra f (peso) pound

li'beccio m south-west wind

li'bellula f dragon-fly

libe'rale adj liberal; (generoso) generous • mf liberal

libe'ra|re vt free; release (prigioniero); vacate (stanza); (salvare) rescue. **~rsi** vr (stanza:) become vacant; (Teleph) become free; (da impegno) get out of it; **~rsi di** get rid of. **~'tore, ~'trice** adj liberating • mf liberator. **~zi'one** f liberation; ◼**la L~zione** Liberation Day

'liber|o adj free; (strada) clear. **~o docente** qualified university lecturer. **~o professionista** selfemployed person. **~tà** f inv freedom; (di prigioniero) release. **~tà provvisoria** (Jur) bail; **~tà** pl (confidenze) liberties

'liberty m & adj inv Art Nouveau

'Libi|a f Libya. **l~co, -a** adj & mf Libyan

◼ *see* A-Z of Italian life and culture

libra'io m bookseller

libre'ria f (negozio) bookshop; (mobile) bookcase; (biblioteca) library

li'bretto m booklet; (Mus) libretto. ~ **degli assegni** cheque book. ~ **di circolazione** logbook. ~ **d'istruzioni** instruction booklet. ~ **di risparmio** bankbook. ~ **universitario** student record of exam results

'libro m book. ~ **giallo** thriller. ~ **paga** payroll

lice'ale mf secondary-school student •adj secondary-school attrib

li'cenza f licence; (permesso) permission; (Mil) leave; (Sch) school-leaving certificate; **essere in** ~ be on leave

licenzia'mento m dismissal

licenzi'a|re vt dismiss, sack [!]. ~**rsi** vr (da un impiego) resign; (accomiatarsi) take one's leave

li'ceo m secondary school. ~ **classico** secondary school emphasizing humanities. ~ **scientifico** secondary school emphasizing science

'lido m beach

li'eto adj glad; (evento) happy; **molto** ~**!** pleased to meet you!

li'eve adj light; (debole) faint; (trascurabile) slight

lievi'tare vi rise •vt leaven. **li'evito** m yeast. **lievito in polvere** baking powder

lifting m inv face-lift

ligio adj **essere** ~ **al dovere** have a sense of duty

lilla[1] (colore) lilac

lillà[2] m inv (Bot) lilac

lima f file

limacci'oso adj slimy

li'mare vt file

li'metta f nail-file

limi'ta|re m threshold •vt limit. ~**rsi** vr ~**rsi a fare qcsa** restrict oneself to doing sth; ~**rsi in qcsa** cut down on sth. ~**'tivo** adj limiting. ~**zi'one** f limitation

limite m limit; (confine) boundary. ~ **di velocità** speed limit

li'mitrofo adj neighbouring

limo'nata f (bibita) lemonade; (succo) lemon juice

li'mone m lemon; (albero) lemon tree

'limpido adj clear; (occhi) limpid

'lince f lynx

linci'are vt lynch

'lindo adj neat; (pulito) clean

'linea f line; (di autobus, aereo) route; (di metro) line; (di abito) cut; (di auto, mobile) design; (fisico) figure; **è caduta la** ~ I've been cut off; **in** ~ (Comput) on line; **mantenere la** ~ keep one's figure; **mettersi in** ~ line up; **nave di** ~ liner; **volo di** ~ scheduled flight. ~ **d'arrivo** finishing line. ~ **continua** unbroken line

linea'menti mpl features

line'are adj linear; (discorso) to the point; (ragionamento) consistent

line'etta f (tratto lungo) dash; (d'unione) hyphen

lin'gotto m ingot

'lingu|a f tongue; (linguaggio) language. ~**'accia** f (persona) backbiter. ~**'aggio** m language. ~**'etta** f (di scarpa) tongue; (di strumento) reed; (di busta) flap

lingu'ist|a mf linguist. ~**ica** f linguistics sg. ~**ico** adj linguistic

'lino m (Bot) flax; (tessuto) linen

li'noleum m linoleum

liofiliz'za|re vt freeze-dry. ~**to** adj freeze-dried

liposuzi'one f liposuction

lique'far|e vt, ~**si** vr liquefy; (sciogliersi) melt

liqui'da|re vt liquidate; settle (conto); pay off (debiti); clear (merce); ([!]: uccidere) get rid of. ~**zi'one** f liquidation; (di conti) settling; (di merce) clearance sale

'liquido adj & m liquid

liqui'rizia f liquorice

li'quore m liqueur; **liquori** pl (bevande alcooliche) liquors

'lira f lira; (Mus) lyre

'lirico, -a adj lyrical; (poesia) lyric; (cantante, musica) opera attrib •f lyric poetry; (Mus) opera

lisci'are vt smooth; (accarezzare) stroke. **'liscio** adj smooth; (capelli)

[C] *see* A-Z of Italian life and culture

straight; (liquore) neat; (acqua minerale) still; **passarla liscia** get away with it

'liso adj worn [out]

'lista f list; (striscia) strip. **~ di attesa** waiting list; **in ~ di attesa** (Aeron) stand-by. **~ elettorale** electoral register. **~ nera** blacklist. **~ di nozze** wedding list. **li'stare** vt edge; (Comput) list

li'stino m list. **~ prezzi** price list

Lit. abbr (lire italiane) Italian lire

'lite f quarrel; (baruffa) row; (Jur) lawsuit

liti'gare vi quarrel. **li'tigio** m quarrel. **litigi'oso** adj quarrelsome

lito'rale adj coastal •m coast

'litro m litre

li'turgico adj liturgical

li'vella f level. **~ a bolla d'aria** spirit level

livel'lar|e vt level. **~si** vr level out

li'vello m level; **passaggio a ~** level crossing; **sotto/sul ~ del mare** below/above sea level

'livido adj livid; (per il freddo) blue; (per una botta) black and blue •m bruise

Li'vorno f Leghorn

'lizza f lists pl; **essere in ~ per qcsa** be in the running for sth

lo def art m (before s + consonant, gn, ps, z) the; ▹**il** •pron (riferito a persona) him; (riferito a cosa) it; **non lo so** I don't know

'lobo m lobe

lo'cal|e adj local •m (stanza) room; (treno) local train; **~i** pl (edifici) premises. **~e notturno** night-club. **~ità** f inv locality

localiz'zare vt localize; (trovare) locate

localizza'zione f localization

lo'cand|a f inn

locan'dina f bill, poster

loca|'tario, -a mf tenant. **~'tore, ~'trice** m landlord •f landlady. **~zi'one** f tenancy

locomo|'tiva f locomotive. **~zi'one** f locomotion; **mezzi di ~zione** means of transport

'loculo m burial niche

lo'custa f locust

locuzi'one f expression

lo'dare vt praise. **'lode** f praise; **laurea con lode** first-class degree

'loden m inv (cappotto) loden coat

'lodola f lark

'loggia f loggia; (massonica) lodge

loggi'one m gallery, the gods

'logica f logic

logica'mente adv (in modo logico) logically; (ovviamente) of course

'logico adj logical

lo'gistica f logistics sg

logo'ra|re vt wear out; (sciupare) waste. **~rsi** vr wear out; (persona:) wear oneself out. **logo'rio** m wear and tear. **'logoro** adj worn-out

lom'baggine f lumbago

Lombar'dia f Lombardy

lom'bata f loin. **'lombo** m (Anat) loin

lom'brico m earthworm

'Londra f London

lon'gevo adj long-lived

longi'lineo adj tall and slim

longi'tudine f longitude

lontana'mente adv distantly; (vagamente) vaguely; **neanche ~** not for a moment

lonta'nanza f distance; (separazione) separation; **in ~** in the distance

lon'tano adj far; (distante) distant; (nel tempo) far-off, distant; (parente) distant; (vago) vague; (assente) absent; **più ~** further •adv far [away]; **da ~** from a distance

'lontra f otter

lo'quace adj talkative

'lordo adj dirty; (somma, peso) gross

'loro¹ pron pl (soggetto) they; (oggetto) them; (forma di cortesia) you; **sta a ~** it is up to them

'loro² (il ~ m, **la ~** f, **i ~** mpl, **le ~** fpl) poss adj their; (forma di cortesia) your; **un ~ amico** a friend of theirs; (forma di cortesia) a friend of yours •poss pron theirs; (forma di cortesia) yours; **i** ~ (famiglia) their folk

losanga f lozenge; **a losanghe** diamond-shaped

'losco adj suspicious

'lott|a f fight, struggle; (contrasto) conflict; Sport wrestling. **lot'tare** vi fight, struggle; Sport, fig wrestle. **~a'tore** m wrestler

lotte'ria f lottery

'lotto m [national] lottery; (porzione) lot; (di terreno) plot

lozi'one f lotion

lubrifi'ca|nte adj lubricating • m lubricant. **~re** vt lubricate

luc'chetto m padlock

lucci'ca|nte adj sparkling. **~re** vi sparkle. **lucci'chio** m sparkle

'luccio m pike

'lucciola f glow-worm

'luce f light; **far ~ su** shed light on; **dare alla ~** give birth to. **~ della luna** moonlight. **luci** pl **di posizione** sidelights. **~ del sole** sunlight

lu'cen|te adj shining. **~'tezza** f shine

lucer'nario m skylight

lu'certola f lizard

lucida'labbra m inv lip gloss

luci'da|re vt polish. **~'trice** f [floor-]polisher. **'lucido** adj shiny; (pavimento, scarpe) polished; (chiaro) clear; (persona, mente) lucid; (occhi) watery • m shine. **lucido [da scarpe]** [shoe] polish

lucra'tivo adj lucrative

'luglio m July

'lugubre adj gloomy

'lui pron (soggetto) he; (oggetto, con prep) him; **lo ha fatto ~ stesso** he did it himself

lu'maca f (mollusco) snail; fig slowcoach

'lume m lamp; (luce) light; **a ~ di candela** by candlelight

luminosità f brightness. **lumi'noso** adj luminous; (stanza, cielo ecc) bright

'luna f moon; **chiaro di ~** moonlight. **~ di miele** honeymoon

luna park m inv fairground

lu'nario m almanac; **sbarcare il ~** make both ends meet

lu'natico a moody

lunedì m inv Monday

lu'netta f half-moon [shape]

lun'gaggine f slowness

lun'ghezza f length. **~ d'onda** wavelength

'lungi adv **ero [ben] ~ dall'immaginare che...** I never dreamt for a moment that...

lungimi'rante adj far-sighted

'lungo adj long; (diluito) weak; (lento) slow; **saperla lunga** be shrewd • m length; **di gran lunga** by far; **andare per le lunghe** drag on • prep (durante) throughout; (per la lunghezza di) along

lungofi'ume m riverside

lungo'lago m lakeside

lungo'mare m sea front

lungome'traggio m feature film

lu'notto m rear window

lu'ogo m place; (punto preciso) spot; (passo d'autore) passage; **aver ~** take place; **dar ~ a** give rise to; **del ~** (usanze) local. **~ pubblico** public place

luogote'nente m (Mil) lieutenant

lu'petto m Cub [Scout]

'lupo m wolf

'luppolo m hop

'lurido adj filthy. **luri'dume** m filth

lusin'g|are vt flatter. **~arsi** vr flatter oneself; (illudersi) fool oneself. **~hi'ero** a flattering

lus'sa|re vt, **~rsi** vr dislocate. **~zi'one** f dislocation

Lussem'burgo m Luxembourg

'lusso m luxury; **di ~** luxury attrib

lussu'oso adj luxurious

lus'suria f lust

lu'strare vt polish

'lustro adj shiny • m sheen; fig prestige; (quinquennio) five-year period

'lutt|o m mourning; **~o stretto** deep mourning. **~u'oso** a mournful

l

see A-Z of Italian life and culture

Mm

m abbr (metro) m

ma conj but; (eppure) yet; **ma!** (dubbio) I don't know; (indignazione) really!; **ma davvero?** really?; **ma sì!** why not!; (certo che si) of course!

'macabro adj macabre

macché int of course not!

macche'roni mpl macaroni sg

macche'ronico adj (italiano) broken

'macchia[1] f stain; (di diverso colore) spot; (piccola) speck; **senza ~** spotless

'macchia[2] f (boscaglia) scrub

macchi'a|re vt, **~rsi** vr stain. **~to** adj (caffè) with a dash of milk; **~to di** (sporco) stained with

'macchina f machine; (motore) engine; (automobile) car. **~ da cucire** sewing machine. **~ da presa** cine camera. **~ da scrivere** typewriter. **~ fotografica (digitale)** (digital) camera

macchinal'mente adv mechanically

macchi'nare vt plot

macchi'nario m machinery

macchi'netta f (per i denti) brace

macchi'nista m (Rail) engine-driver; (Naut) engineer; (Theat) stagehand

macchi'noso adj complicated

mace'donia f fruit salad

Mace'donia f Macedonia

macel'la|io m butcher. **~re** vt slaughter, butcher. **macelle'ria** f butcher's [shop]. **ma'cello** m (mattatoio) slaughterhouse; fig shambles sg; **andare al macello** fig go to the slaughter

mace'rar|e vt macerate; fig distress. **~si** vr be consumed

ma'cerie fpl rubble sg; (rottami) debris sg

ma'cigno m boulder

'macina f millstone

macinacaffè m inv coffee mill

macina'pepe m inv pepper mill

maci'na|re vt mill. **~to** adj ground •m (carne) mince. **maci'nino** m mill; (hum) old banger

maciul'lare vt (stritolare) crush

macrobiotic|a f **negozio di ~a** health-food shop. **~o** adj macrobiotic

macu'lato adj spotted

'madido adj **~ di** moist with

Ma'donna f Our Lady

mador'nale adj gross

'madre f mother. **~'lingua** adj inv **inglese ~lingua** English native speaker. **~'patria** f native land. **~'perla** f mother-of-pearl

ma'drina f godmother

maestà f majesty

maestosità f majesty. **mae'stoso** adj majestic

mae'strale m northwest wind

mae'stranza f workers pl

mae'stria f mastery

ma'estro, -a mf teacher •m master; (Mus) maestro. **~ di cerimonie** master of ceremonies •adj (principale) chief; (di grande abilità) skilful

C **'mafi|a** f Mafia. **~'oso** adj of the Mafia •m member of the Mafia, Mafioso

ma'gagna f fault

ma'gari adv (forse) maybe •int I wish! •conj (per esprimere desiderio) if only; (anche se) even if

magazzini'ere m storesman, warehouseman. **magaz'zino** m warehouse; (emporio) shop; **grande magazzino** department store

'maggio m May

maggio'lino m May bug

maggio'rana f marjoram

maggio'ranza f majority

C *see* A-Z of Italian life and culture

maggio'rare vt increase

maggior'domo m butler

maggi'ore adj (di dimensioni, numero) bigger, larger; (superlativo) biggest, largest; (di età) older; (superlativo) oldest; (di importanza, musica) major; (superlativo) greatest; **la maggior parte di** most; **la maggior parte del tempo** most of the time •pron (di dimensioni) the bigger, the larger; (superlativo) the biggest, the largest; (di età) the older; (superlativo) the oldest; (di importanza) the major; (superlativo) the greatest •m (Mil) major; (Aeron) squadron leader. **maggio'renne** adj of age •mf adult

maggior|i'tario adj (sistema) first-past-the-post attrib. **~'mente** adv [all] the more; (più di tutto) most

'Magi mpl **i re ~** the Magi

ma'gia f magic; (trucco) magic trick. **magica'mente** adv magically. **'magico** adj magic

magi'stero m (insegnamento) teaching; (maestria) skill; **facoltà di ~** arts faculty

magi'stra|le adj masterly; **istituto ~e** teachers' training college

magi'stra|to m magistrate. **~'tura** f magistrature. **la ~tura** the Bench

'magli|a f stitch; (lavoro ai ferri) knitting; (tessuto) jersey; (di rete) mesh; (di catena) link; (indumento) vest; **fare la ~a** knit. **~a diritta** knit. **~a rosa** (ciclismo) ≈ yellow jersey. **~a rovescia** purl. **~e'ria** f knitwear. **~'etta** f **~etta [a maniche corte]** tee-shirt. **~'ficio** m knitwear factory. **ma'glina** f (tessuto) jersey

magli'one m sweater

'magma m magma

ma'gnanimo adj magnanimous

ma'gnate m magnate

ma'gnesi|a f magnesia. **~o** m magnesium

ma'gne|te m magnet. **~tico** adj magnetic. **~'tismo** m magnetism

magne'tofono m tape recorder

magnifi|ca'mente adv magnificently. **~'cenza** f magnificence; (generosità) munificence. **ma'gnifico** adj magnificent; (generoso) munificent

ma'gnolia f magnolia

ma'gone m **avere il ~** be down; **mi è venuto il ~** I've got a lump in my throat

'magr|a f low water. **ma'grezza** f thinness. **~o** adj thin; (carne) lean; (scarso) meagre

'mai adv never; (inter, talvolta) ever; **caso ~** if anything; **caso ~ tornasse** in case he comes back; **come ~?** why?; **cosa ~?** what on earth?; **~ più** never again; **più che ~** more than ever; **quando ~?** whenever?; **quasi ~** hardly ever

mai'ale m pig; (carne) pork

mai'olica f majolica

maio'nese f mayonnaise

'mais m maize

mai'uscol|a f capital [letter]. **~o** adj capital

mal ▸**male**

'mala f **la ~** ⊠ the underworld

mala'fede f bad faith

malaf'fare m **gente di ~** shady characters pl

mala'lingua f backbiter

mala'mente adv (ridotto) badly

malan'dato adj in bad shape; (di salute) in poor health

ma'lanimo m ill will

ma'lanno m misfortune; (malattia) illness; **prendersi un ~** catch something

mala'pena: **a ~** adv hardly

ma'laria f malaria

mala'ticcio adj sickly

ma'lato, -a adj ill, sick; (pianta) diseased •mf sick person. **~ di mente** mentally ill person. **malat'tia** f disease, illness; **ho preso due giorni di malattia** I had two days off sick. **malattia venerea** venereal disease

malaugu'rato adj ill-omened. **malau'gurio** m bad o ill omen

mala'vita f underworld

mala'voglia f unwillingness; **di ~** unwillingly

malcapi'tato adj wretched

malce'lato adj ill-concealed

mal'concio adj battered

m

malcon'tento m discontent
malco'stume m immorality
mal'destro adj awkward; (inesperto) inexperienced
maldi'cen|te adj slanderous. **~za** f slander
maldi'sposto adj ill-disposed
'male adv badly; **funzionare ~** not work properly; **star ~** be ill; **star ~ a qcno** (vestito ecc:) not suit sb; **rimanerci ~** be hurt; **non c'è ~!** not bad at all! •m evil; (dolore) pain; (malattia) illness; (danno) harm. **distinguere il bene dal ~** know right from wrong; **andare a ~** go off; **aver ~ a** have a pain in; **dove hai ~?** where does it hurt?; **far ~ a qcno** (provocare dolore) hurt sb; (cibo:) be bad for sb; **le cipolle mi fanno ~** onions don't agree with me; **mi fa ~ la schiena** my back is hurting; **mal d'auto** car-sickness. **mal di denti** toothache. **mal di gola** sore throat. **mal di mare** sea-sickness; **avere il mal di mare** be sea-sick. **mal di pancia** stomach ache. **mal di testa** headache
male'detto adj cursed; (orribile) awful
male'di|re vt curse. **~zi'one** f curse; **~zione!** damn!
maledu|'cato adj ill-mannered. **~cazi'one** f rudeness
male'fatta f misdeed
ma'lefico adj (azione) evil; (nocivo) harmful
maleodo'rante adj foul-smelling
ma'lessere m indisposition; fig uneasiness
ma'levolo adj malevolent
malfa'mato adj of ill repute
mal'fat|to adj badly done; (malformato) ill-shaped. **~'tore** m wrongdoer
mal'fermo adj unsteady; (salute) poor
malfor'ma|to adj misshapen. **~zi'one** f malformation
mal'grado prep in spite of •conj although
ma'lia f spell
mali'gn|are vi malign. **~ità** f malice; (Med) malignancy. **ma'ligno** adj malicious; (perfido) evil; (Med) malignant
malinco'ni|a f melancholy. **malin'conico** adj melancholy
malincu'ore: a ~ adv reluctantly
malinfor'mato adj misinformed
malintenzio'nato, -a mf miscreant
malin'teso adj mistaken •m misunderstanding
ma'lizi|a f malice; (astuzia) cunning; (espediente) trick. **~'oso** adj malicious; (birichino) mischievous
malle'abile adj malleable
malme'nare vt ill-treat
mal'messo adj (vestito male) shabbily dressed; (casa) poorly furnished; (fig: senza soldi) hard up
malnu'tri|to adj undernourished. **~zi'one** f malnutrition
'malo adj **in ~ modo** badly
ma'locchio m evil eye
ma'lora f ruin; **della ~** awful; **andare in ~** go to ruin
ma'lore m illness; **essere colto da ~** be suddenly taken ill
malri'dotto adj (persona) in a sorry state
mal'sano adj unhealthy
'malta f mortar
mal'tempo m bad weather
'malto m malt
maltrat|ta'mento m ill-treatment. **~'tare** vt ill-treat
malu'more m bad mood; **di ~** in a bad mood
mal'vagi|o adj wicked. **~tà** f wickedness
malversazi'one f embezzlement
mal'visto adj unpopular (**da** with)
malvi'vente m criminal
malvolenti'eri adv unwillingly
malvo'lere vt **farsi ~** make oneself unpopular
'mamma f mummy, mum; **~ mia!** good gracious!
mam'mella f breast
mam'mifero m mammal
'mammola f violet
ma'nata f handful; (colpo) slap
'manca f ▸**manco**

m

manca'mento m **avere un ~** faint

man'can|te adj missing. **~za** f lack; (assenza) absence; (insufficienza) shortage; (fallo) fault; (imperfezione) defect; **sento la sua ~za** I miss him

man'care vi be lacking; (essere assente) be missing; (venir meno) fail; (morire) pass away; **~ di** be lacking in; **~ a** fail to keep (promessa); **mi manca casa** I miss home; **mi manchi** I miss you; **mi è mancato il tempo** I didn't have [the] time; **mi manca un euro** I'm one euro short; **quanto manca alla partenza?** how long before we leave?; **è mancata la corrente** there was a power failure; **sentirsi ~** feel faint; **sentirsi ~ il respiro** be unable to breathe [properly] •vt miss (bersaglio); **è mancato poco che cadesse** he nearly fell

manche f inv heat

man'chevole adj defective

mancia f tip

manci'ata f handful

man'cino adj left-handed

manco, -a adj left •f left hand •adv (nemmeno) not even

man'dante mf (di delitto) instigator

manda'rancio m clementine

man'dare vt send; (emettere) give off; utter (suono); **~ a chiamare** send for; **~ avanti la casa** run the house; **~ giù** (ingoiare) swallow

manda'rino m (Bot) mandarin

man'data f consignment; (di serratura) turn; **chiudere a doppia ~** double lock

man'dato m (incarico) mandate; (Jur) warrant; (di pagamento) money order. **~ di comparizione [in giudizio]** subpoena. **~ di perquisizione** search warrant

man'dibola f jaw

mando'lino m mandolin

mandor|la f almond; **a ~la** (occhi) almond-shaped. **~'lato** m nut brittle (type of nougat). **~lo** m almond[-tree]

mandria f herd

maneg'gevole adj easy to handle. **maneggi'are** vt handle

ma'neggio m handling; (intrigo) plot; (scuola di equitazione) riding school

ma'netta f hand lever; **manette** pl handcuffs

man'forte m **dare ~ a qcno** support sb

manga'nello m truncheon

manga'nese m manganese

mange'reccio adj edible

mangia'dischi® m inv type of portable record player

mangia'fumo adj inv **candela ~** air-purifier in the form of candle

mangia'nastri m inv cassette player

mangi'a|re vt/i eat; (consumare) eat up; (corrodere) eat away; take (scacchi, carte ecc) •m eating; (cibo) food; (pasto) meal. **~rsi** vr **~rsi le parole** mumble; **~rsi le unghie** bite one's nails

mangi'ata f big meal; **farsi una bella ~ di...** feast on...

man'gime m fodder

mangiucchi'are vt nibble

'mango m mango

ma'nia f mania. **~ di grandezza** delusions of grandeur •mf maniac

'manica f sleeve; (!: gruppo) band; **a maniche lunghe** long-sleeved; **essere in maniche di camicia** be in shirt sleeves

'Manica f **la ~** the [English] Channel

manica'retto m tasty dish

mani'chetta f hose

mani'chino m dummy

'manico m handle; (Mus) neck

mani'comio m mental home; (!: confusione) tip

mani'cotto m muff; (Mech) sleeve

mani'cure f manicure •mf inv (persona) manicurist

mani'e|ra f manner; **in ~ra che** so that. **~'rato** adj affected; (stile) mannered. **~'rismo** m mannerism

manifat'tura f manufacture; (fabbrica) factory

manife'stante mf demonstrator

manife'sta|re vt show; (esprimere) express •vi demonstrate. **~rsi** vr show oneself. **~zi'one** f show; (espressione) expression; (sintomo) manifestation; (dimostrazione pubblica) demonstration

mani'festo adj evident •m poster; (dichiarazione pubblica) manifesto

ma'niglia f handle; (sostegno, in autobus ecc) strap

manipo'la|re vt handle; (massaggiare) massage; (alterare) adulterate; fig manipulate. **~'tore, ~'trice** mf manipulator. **~zi'one** f handling; (massaggio) massage; (alterazione) adulteration; fig manipulation

mani'scalco m smith

man'naia f axe; (da macellaio) cleaver

man'naro adj **lupo** m **~** werewolf

'mano f hand; (strato di vernice ecc) coat; **alla ~** informal; **fuori ~** out of the way; **man ~** little by little; **man ~ che** as; **sotto ~** to hand

mano'dopera f labour

ma'nometro m gauge

mano'mettere vt tamper with; (violare) violate

ma'nopola f knob; (guanto) mitten; (su pullman) handle

m

mano'scritto adj handwritten •m manuscript

mano'vale m labourer

mano'vella f handle; (Techn) crank

ma'no|vra f manoeuvre; (Rail) shunting; **fare le ~vre** (Auto) manoeuvre. **~'vrabile** adj fig easy to manipulate. **~'vrare** vt operate; fig manipulate (persona) •vi manoeuvre

manro'vescio m slap

man'sarda f attic

mansi'one f task; (dovere) duty

mansu'eto adj meek; (animale) docile

man'tell|a f cape. **~o** m cloak; (soprabito, di animale) coat; (di neve) mantle

mante'ner|e vt keep; (in buono stato, sostentare) maintain. **~si** vr **~si in forma** keep fit. **manteni'mento** m maintenance

'mantice m bellows pl; (di automobile) hood

'manto m cloak; (coltre) mantle

manto'vana f (di tende) pelmet

manu'al|e adj & m manual. **~e d'uso** user manual. **~'mente** adv manually

ma'nubrio m handle; (di bicicletta) handlebars pl; (per ginnastica) dumb-bell

manu'fatto adj manufactured

manutenzi'one f maintenance

'manzo m steer; (carne) beef

'mappa f map

mappa'mondo m globe

mar ▸**mare**

ma'rasma m fig decline

mara'to|na f marathon. **~'neta** mf marathon runner

'marca f mark; (Comm) brand; (fabbricazione) make; (scontrino) ticket. **~ da bollo** revenue stamp

mar'ca|re vt mark; Sport score. **~ta'mente** adv markedly. **~to** adj (tratto, accento) strong. **~'tore** m (nel calcio) scorer

mar'chese, -a m marquis •f marchioness

marchi'are vt brand

'marchio m brand; (caratteristica) mark **~ di fabbrica** trademark. **~ registrato** registered trademark

'marcia f march; (Auto) gear; Sport walk; **mettere in ~** put into gear; **mettersi in ~** start off; **fare ~ indietro** reverse; fig back-pedal. **~ funebre** funeral march. **~ nuziale** wedding march

marciapi'ede m pavement; (di stazione) platform

marci'a|re vi march; (funzionare) go, work. **~'tore, ~'trice** mf walker

'marcio adj rotten •m rotten part; fig corruption. **mar'cire** vi go bad, rot

'marco m (moneta) mark

'mare m sea; (luogo di mare) seaside; **sul ~** (casa) at the seaside; (città) on the sea; **in alto ~** on the high seas. **~ Adriatico** Adriatic Sea. **mar Ionio** Ionian Sea. **mar Mediterraneo** Mediterranean. **mar Tirreno** Tyrrhenian Sea

ma'rea f tide; **una ~ di** hundreds of; **alta ~** high tide; **bassa ~** low tide

mareggi'ata f [sea] storm

mare'moto m tidal wave, seaquake

maresci'allo m marshal; (sottufficiale) warrant officer

marga'rina f margarine

marghe'rita f marguerite. **margheri'tina** f daisy

margi'nale adj marginal

'margine m margin; (orlo) brink; (bordo) border. ~ **di errore** margin of error. ~ **di sicurezza** safety margin

ma'rina f navy; (costa) seashore; (quadro) seascape. ~ **mercantile** merchant navy. ~ **militare** navy

mari'naio m sailor

mari'na|re vt marinate. **~ta** f marinade. **~to** adj (Culin) marinated

ma'rino adj sea attrib, marine

mario'netta f puppet

ma'rito m husband

ma'rittimo adj maritime

mar'maglia f rabble

marmel'lata f jam; (di agrumi) marmalade

mar'mitta f pot; (Auto) silencer. ~ **catalitica** catalytic converter

'marmo m marble

mar'mocchio m [!] brat

mar'mor|eo adj marble. **~iz'zato** adj marbled

mar'motta f marmot

Ma'rocco m Morocco

ma'roso m breaker

mar'rone adj brown •m brown; (castagna) chestnut; **marroni** pl **canditi** marrons glacés

mar'sina f tails pl

mar'supio m (borsa) bumbag

marte'dì m inv Tuesday. ~ **grasso** Shrove Tuesday

martel'la|re vt hammer •vi throb. **~ta** f hammer blow

martel'letto m (di giudice) gavel

mar'tello m hammer; (di battente) knocker. ~ **pneumatico** pneumatic drill

marti'netto m (Mech) jack

'martire mf martyr. **mar'tirio** m martyrdom

'martora f marten

martori'are vt torment

mar'xis|mo m Marxism. **~ta** agg & mf Marxist

marza'pane m marzipan

marzi'ale adj martial

marzi'ano, -a mf Martian

'marzo m March

mascal'zone m rascal

ma'scara m inv mascara

mascar'pone m full-fat cream cheese

ma'scella f jaw

'mascher|a f mask; (costume) fancy dress; (Cinema,Theat) usher m, usherette f; (nella commedia dell'arte) stock character. **~a antigas** gas mask. **~a di bellezza** face pack. **~a ad ossigeno** oxygen mask. **~a'mento** m masking; (Mil) camouflage. **masche'rare** vt mask. **~arsi** vr put on a mask; **~arsi da** dress up as. **~ata** f masquerade

maschi'accio m tomboy

ma'schi|le adj masculine; (sesso) male •m masculine [gender]. **~'lista** adj sexist. **'maschio** adj male; (virile) manly •m male; (figlio) son. **masco'lino** adj masculine

ma'scotte f inv mascot

maso'chis|mo m masochism. **~ta** adj & mf masochist

'massa f mass; (Electr) earth, ground Am; **comunicazioni di** ~ mass media

massa'crare vt massacre. **mas'sacro** m massacre; fig mess

massaggi'a|re vt massage. **mas'saggio** m massage. **~'tore, ~'trice** m masseur •f masseuse

mas'saia f housewife

masse'rizie fpl household effects

mas'siccio adj massive; (oro ecc) solid; (corporatura) heavy •m massif

'massim|a f maxim; (temperatura) maximum. **~o** adj greatest; (quantità) maximum, greatest •m **il ~o** the maximum; **al ~o** at [the] most, as a maximum

'masso m rock

mas'sone m [Free]mason. **~'ria** Freemasonry

ma'stello m wooden box for the grape or olive harvest

masteriz'zare vt (Comput) burn

masterizza'tore m (Comput) burner

masti'care vt chew; (borbottare) mumble

'mastice m mastic; (per vetri) putty

ma'stino m mastiff

masto'dontico adj gigantic

'mastro m master; **libro ~** ledger

mastur'ba|rsi vr masturbate. **~zi'one** f masturbation

ma'tassa f skein

mate'matic|a f mathematics, maths. **~o, -a** adj mathematical •mf mathematician

materas'sino m **~ gonfiabile** air bed

mate'rasso m mattress. **~ a molle** spring mattress

ma'teria f matter; (materiale) material; (di studio) subject. **~ prima** raw material

materi'a|le adj material; (grossolano) coarse •m material. **~'lismo** m materialism. **~'lista** adj materialistic •mf materialist. **~liz'zarsi** vr materialize. **~l'mente** adv physically

maternità f motherhood; **ospedale di ~** maternity hospital

ma'terno adj maternal; **lingua materna** mother tongue

ma'tita f pencil

ma'trice f matrix; (origini) roots pl; (Comm) counterfoil

ma'tricola f (registro) register; (Univ) fresher

ma'trigna f stepmother

matrimoni'ale adj matrimonial; **vita ~** married life. ■**matri'monio** m marriage; (cerimonia) wedding

ma'trona f matron

'matta f (nelle carte) joker

matta'toio m slaughterhouse

matte'rello m rolling-pin

mat'ti|na f morning; **la ~na** in the morning. **~'nata** f morning; (Theat) matinée. **~no** m morning

'matto, -a adj mad, crazy; (Med) insane; (falso) false; (opaco) matt; **~ da legare** barking mad; **avere una voglia matta di** be dying for •mf madman; madwoman

mat'tone m brick; (libro) bore

matto'nella f tile

mattu'tino adj morning attrib

matu'rare vt ripen. ■**maturità** f maturity; (Sch) school-leaving certificate. **ma'turo** adj mature; (frutto) ripe

mauso'leo m mausoleum

maxi+ pref maxi+

'mazza f club; (martello) hammer; (da baseball, cricket) bat. **~ da golf** golf-club. **maz'zata** f blow

maz'zetta f (di banconote) bundle

'mazzo m bunch; (carte da gioco) pack

me pers pron me; **me lo ha dato** he gave it to me; **fai come me** do as I do; **è più veloce di me** he is faster than me o faster than I am

me'andro m meander

M.E.C. m abbr (Mercato Comune Europeo) EEC

mec'canica f mechanics sg

meccanica'mente adv mechanically

mec'canico adj mechanical •m mechanic. **mecca'nismo** m mechanism

mèche fpl **[farsi] fare le ~** have one's hair streaked

me'dagli|a f medal. **~'one** m medallion; (gioiello) locket

me'desimo adj same

'medi|a f average; (Sch) average mark; (Math) mean; **essere nella ~a** be in the mid-range. **~'ano** adj middle •m (calcio) half-back

medi'ante prep by

medi'a|re vt act as intermediary in. **~'tore, ~'trice** mf mediator; (Comm) middleman

medica'mento m medicine

medi'ca|re vt treat; dress (ferita). **~zi'one** f medication; (di ferita) dressing

medi'c|ina f medicine. **~ina legale** forensic medicine. **~i'nale** adj medicinal •m medicine

'medico adj medical •m doctor. **~ generico** general practitioner. **~ legale** forensic scientist. **~ di turno** duty doctor

■ see A-Z of Italian life and culture

medie'vale adj medieval

'medio adj average; (punto) middle; (statura) medium • m (dito) middle finger

medi'ocre adj mediocre; (scadente) poor

medio'evo m Middle Ages pl

medi'ta|re vt meditate; (progettare) plan; (considerare attentamente) think over • vi meditate. **~zi'one** f meditation

mediter'raneo adj Mediterranean; **il [mar] M~** the Mediterranean [Sea]

me'dusa f jellyfish

me'gafono m megaphone

mega'lomane mf megalomaniac

me'gera f hag

'meglio adv better; **tanto ~, ~ così** so much the better • adj better; (superlativo) best • mf best • f **avere la ~ su** have the better of; **fare qcsa alla [bell'e] ~** do sth as best one can • m **fare del proprio ~** do one's best; **fare qcsa il ~ possibile** make an excellent job of sth; **al ~** to the best of one's ability

'mela f apple. **~ cotogna** quince

mela'grana f pomegranate

mela'nina f melanin

melan'zana f aubergine, eggplant Am

me'lassa f molasses sg

me'lenso adj (persona, film) dull

mel'lifluo adj (parole) honeyed; (voce) sugary

'melma f slime. **mel'moso** adj slimy

melo m apple[-tree]

melo'di|a f melody. **me'lodico** adj melodic. **~'oso** adj melodious

melo'dram|ma m melodrama. **~'matico** adj melodramatic

melo'grano m pomegranate tree

me'lone m melon

'membro m member; (pl f **membra** (Anat)) limb

memo'rabile adj memorable

'memore adj mindful; (riconoscente) grateful

me'mori|a f memory; (oggetto ricordo) souvenir. **imparare a ~a** learn by heart. **~a tampone** (Comput) buffer. **~a volatile** (Comput) volatile memory; **memorie** pl (biografiche) memoirs. **~'ale** m memorial. **~z'zare** vt memorize; (Comput) save, store

mena'dito: **a ~** adv perfectly

me'nare vt lead; (🅘: picchiare) hit

mendi'ca|nte mf beggar. **~re** vt/i beg

me'ningi fpl **spremersi le ~** rack one's brains

menin'gite f meningitis

'meno adv less; (superlativo) least; (in operazioni, con temperatura) minus; **far qcsa alla ~ peggio** do sth as best one can; **fare a ~ di qcsa** do without sth; **non posso fare a ~ di ridere** I can't help laughing; **~ male!** thank goodness!; **sempre ~** less and less; **venir ~** (svenire) faint; **venir ~ a qcno** (coraggio:) fail sb; **sono le tre ~ un quarto** it's a quarter to three; **che tu venga o ~** whether you're coming or not; **quanto ~** at least • adj inv less; (con nomi plurali) fewer • m least; (Math) minus sign; **il ~ possibile** as little as possible; **per lo ~** at least • prep except [for] • conj **a ~ che** unless

meno'ma|re vt (incidente:) maim. **~to** adj disabled

meno'pausa f menopause

'mensa f table; (Mil) mess; (Sch, Univ) refectory

men'sil|e adj monthly • m (stipendio) [monthly] salary; (rivista) monthly. **~ità** f inv monthly salary. **~'mente** adv monthly

'mensola f bracket; (scaffale) shelf

'menta f mint. **~ peperita** peppermint

men'tal|e adj mental. **~ità** f inv mentality

'mente f mind; **a ~ fredda** in cold blood; **venire in ~ a qcno** occur to sb

men'tina f mint

men'tire vi lie

'mento m chin

'mentre conj (temporale) while; (invece) whereas

menu m inv menu. **~ fisso** set menu.

~ **a tendina** (Comput) pulldown menu

menzio'nare vt mention. **menzi'one** f mention

men'zogna f lie

mera'viglia f wonder; **a ~** marvellously; **che ~!** how wonderful!; **con mia grande ~** much to my amazement; **mi fa ~ che...** I am surprised that...

meravigli'ar|e vt surprise. **~si** vr **~si di** be surprised at

meravigli'oso adj marvellous

mer'can|te m merchant. **~teggi'are** vi trade; (sul prezzo) bargain. **~'zia** f merchandise, goods pl • m merchant ship

mer'cato m market; Fin market[-place]. **a buon ~** (comprare) cheap[ly]; (articolo) cheap. **~ dei cambi** foreign exchange market. **~ coperto** covered market. **~ libero** free market. **~ nero** black market

'merce f goods pl

mercé f **alla ~ di** at the mercy of

merce'nario adj & m mercenary

merce'ria f haberdashery; (negozio) haberdasher's

mercoledì m inv Wednesday. **~ delle Ceneri** Ash Wednesday

mer'curio m mercury

me'renda f afternoon snack; **far ~** have an afternoon snack

meridi'ana f sundial

meridi'ano adj midday • m meridian

meridio'nale adj southern • mf southerner. **meridi'one** m south

me'rin|ga f meringue. **~'gata** f meringue pie

meri'tare vt deserve. **meri'tevole** adj deserving

'meri|to m merit; (valore) worth; **in ~to a** as to; **per ~to di** thanks to. **~'torio** adj meritorious

mer'letto m lace

'merlo m blackbird

mer'luzzo m cod

'mero adj mere

meschine'ria f meanness.

me'schino adj wretched; (gretto) mean • m wretch

mesco|la'mento m mixing. **~'lanza** f mixture

mesco'la|re vt mix; shuffle (carte); (confondere) mix up; blend (tè, tabacco ecc). **~rsi** vr mix; (immischiarsi) meddle. **~ta** f (a carte) shuffle; (Culin) stir

'mese m month

me'setto m **un ~** about a month

'messa[1] f Mass

'messa[2] f (il mettere) putting. **~ in moto** (Auto) starting. **~ in piega** (di capelli) set. **~ a punto** adjustment. **~ in scena** production. **~ a terra** earthing, grounding Am

messag'gero m messenger. **mes'saggio** m message

'messe f harvest

Mes'sia m Messiah

messi'cano, -a adj & mf Mexican

'Messico m Mexico

messin'scena f staging; fig act

'messo pp di **mettere** • m messenger

mesti'ere m trade; (lavoro) job; **essere del ~** be an expert

'mesto adj sad

'mestola f (di cuoco) ladle

mestru'a|le adj menstrual. **~zi'one** f menstruation. **~zi'oni** pl period

'meta f destination; fig aim

metà f inv half; (centro) middle; **a ~ strada** half-way; **fare a ~ con qcno** go halves with sb

metabo'lismo m metabolism

meta'done m methadone

me'tafora f metaphor. **meta'forico** adj metaphorical

me'talli|co adj metallic. **~z'zato** adj (grigio) metallic

me'tall|o m metal. **~ur'gia** f metallurgy

metalmec'canico adj engineering • m engineering worker

me'tano m methane. **~'dotto** m methane pipeline

meta'nolo m methanol

me'teora f meteor. **meteo'rite** m meteorite

see A-Z of Italian life and culture

meteoro|lo'gia f meteorology. **~'logico** adj meteorological

me'ticcio, -a mf half-caste

metico'loso adj meticulous

me'tod|ico adj methodical. **'metodo** m method. **~olo'gia** f methodology

me'traggio m length (in metres)

'metrico, -a adj metric; (in poesia) metrical • f metrics sg

'metro m metre; (nastro) tape measure • f inv (!: metropolitana) tube Br, subway

me'tronomo m metronome

metro'notte mf inv night security guard

me'tropoli f inv metropolis. **~'tana** f subway, underground Br. **~'tano** adj metropolitan

'metter|e vt put; (indossare) put on; (!: installare) put in; **~e al mondo** bring into the world; **~e da parte** set aside; **~e fiducia** inspire trust; **~e qcsa in chiaro** make sth clear; **~e in mostra** display; **~e a posto** tidy up; **~e in vendita** put up for sale; **~e su** set up (casa, azienda); **ci ho messo un'ora** it took me an hour; **mettiamo che...** let's suppose that... **~si** vr (indossare) put on; (diventare) turn out; **~si a** start to; **~si con qcno** (!: formare una coppia) start to go out with sb; **~si a letto** go to bed; **~si a sedere** sit down; **~si in viaggio** set out

'mezza f **è la ~** it's half past twelve; **sono le quattro e ~** it's half past four

mezza'luna f half moon; (simbolo islamico) crescent; (coltello) two-handled chopping knife

mezza'manica f **a ~** (maglia) short-sleeved

mez'zano adj middle

mezza'notte f midnight

mezz'asta: **a ~** adv at half mast

'mezzo adj half; **di mezza età** middle-aged; **~ bicchiere** half a glass; **una mezza idea** a vague idea; **sono le quattro e ~** it's half past four. **mezz'ora** f half an hour. **mezza pensione** f half board. **mezza stagione** f **una giacca da mezza stagione** a spring/autumn jacket • adv (a metà) half • m (metà) half; (centro) middle; (per raggiungere un fine) means sg; **uno e ~** one and a half; **tre anni e ~** three and a half years; **in ~ a** in the middle of; **il giusto ~** the happy medium; **levare di ~** clear away; **per ~ di** by means of; **a ~ posta** by mail; **via di ~** fig halfway house; (soluzione) middle way. **mezzi** pl (denaro) means pl. **mezzi pubblici** public transport. **mezzi di trasporto** [means of] transport

mezzo'busto: **a ~** adj (foto, ritratto) half-length

mezzo'fondo m middle-distance running

mezzogi'orno m midday; (sud) South. 🅲 **il M~** Southern Italy. **~ in punto** high noon

mi[1] pers pron me; (refl) myself; **mi ha dato un libro** he gave me a book; **mi lavo le mani** I wash my hands; **eccomi** here I am

mi[2] m (Mus) E

'mica[1] f mica

'mica[2] adv ! (per caso) by any chance; **hai ~ visto Paolo?** have you seen Paul, by any chance?; **non è ~ bello** it is not at all nice; **~ male** not bad

'miccia f fuse

micidi'ale adj deadly

'micio m pussy-cat

'microbo m microbe

micro'cosmo m microcosm

micro'fiche f inv microfiche

micro'film m inv microfilm

mi'crofono m microphone

microorga'nismo m microorganism

microproces'sore m microprocessor

micro'scopi|o m microscope

micro'solco m (disco) long-playing record

mi'dollo m (pl f **midolla** (Anat)) marrow; **fino al ~** through and through. **~ spinale** spinal cord

mi'ele m honey

'mie, mi'ei ▸**mio**

mi'et|ere vt reap. **~i'trice** f (Mech)

🅲 see A-Z of Italian life and culture

m

harvester. **~i'tura** f harvest
migli'aio m (pl f **migliaia**) thousand. **a migliaia** in thousands
'miglio m (Bot) millet; (misura: pl f **miglia**) mile
migliora'mento m improvement
miglio'rare vt/i improve
migli'ore adj better; (superlativo) the best •mf **il/la ~** the best
'mignolo m little finger; (del piede) little toe
mi'gra|re vi migrate. **~zi'one** f migration
'mila ▹**mille**
Mi'lano f Milan
miliar'dario, -a m millionaire; (plurimiliardario) billionaire •f millionairess; billionairess. **mili'ardo** m billion
mili'are adj **pietra** f **~** milestone
milio'nario, -a m millionaire •f millionairess
mili'one m million
milio'nesimo adj millionth
mili'tante adj & mf militant
mili'tare vi **~ in** be a member of (partito ecc) •adj military •m soldier; **fare il ~** do one's military service. **~ di leva** national serviceman
'milite m soldier. **mil'izia** f militia
'mille adj & m (pl f **mila**) a o one thousand; **due/tremila** two/three thousand; **~ grazie!** thanks a lot!
mille'foglie m inv (Culin) vanilla slice
mil'lennio m millennium
millepi'edi m inv centipede
mil'lesimo adj & m thousandth
milli'grammo m milligram
mil'limetro m millimetre
mi'mare vt mimic (persona) •vi mime
mi'metico adj camouflage attrib
mimetiz'zar|e vt camouflage. **~si** vr camouflage oneself
'mim|ica f mime. **~ico** adj mimic. **~o** m mime
mi'mosa f mimosa
'mina f mine; (di matita) lead
mi'naccia f threat
minacci|'are vt threaten. **~'oso** adj threatening
mi'nare vt mine; fig undermine
mina'tor|e m miner. **~io** adj threatening
mine'ra|le adj & m mineral. **~rio** adj mining attrib
mi'nestra f soup. **mine'strone** m vegetable soup; (!: insieme confuso) hotchpotch
mini+ pref mini+
minia'tura f miniature. **miniaturiz'zato** adj miniaturized
mini'era f mine
mini'golf m miniature golf
mini'gonna f miniskirt
minima'mente adv minimally
mini'market m inv minimarket
minimiz'zare vt minimize
'minimo adj least, slightest; (il più basso) lowest; (salario, quantità ecc) minimum •m minimum
mini'stero m ministry; (governo) government
mi'nistro m minister. **M~ del Tesoro** Finance Minister
mino'ranza f minority attrib
mino'rato, -a adj disabled •mf disabled person
mi'nore adj (gruppo, numero) smaller; (superlativo) smallest; (distanza) shorter; (superlativo) shortest; (prezzo) lower; (superlativo) lowest; (di età) younger; (superlativo) youngest; (di importanza) minor; (superlativo) least important •mf younger; (superlativo) youngest; (Jur) minor; **i minori di 14 anni** children under 14. **mino'renne** adj under age •mf minor
minori'tario adj minority attrib
minu'etto m minuet
mi'nuscolo, -a adj tiny •f small letter
mi'nuta f rough copy
mi'nuto[1] adj minute; (persona) delicate; (ricerca) detailed; (pioggia, neve) fine; **al ~** (Comm) retail
mi'nuto[2] m (di tempo) minute; **spaccare il ~** be dead on time
mi'nuzi|a f trifle. **~'oso** adj detailed; (persona) meticulous
'mio (**il mio** m, **la mia** f, **i miei** mpl, **le mie** fpl) adj poss my; **questa**

macchina è mia this car is mine; **~ padre** my father; **un ~ amico** a friend of mine •poss pron mine; **i miei** (genitori ecc) my folks

'miope adj short-sighted. **mio'pia** f short-sightedness

'mira f aim; (bersaglio) target; **prendere la ~** take aim

mi'racolo m miracle. **~sa'mente** adv miraculously. **miraco'loso** adj miraculous

mi'raggio m mirage

mi'rar|e vi [take] aim. **~si** vr (guardarsi) look at oneself

mi'riade f myriad

mi'rino m sight; (Phot) view-finder

mir'tillo m blueberry

mi'santropo, -a mf misanthropist

mi'scela f mixture; (di caffè, tabacco ecc) blend. **~'tore** m (di acqua) mixer tap

miscel'lanea f miscellany

'mischia f scuffle; (nel rugby) scrum

mischi'ar|e vt mix; shuffle (carte da gioco). **~si** vr mix; (immischiarsi) interfere

misco'noscere vt not appreciate

mi'scuglio m mixture

mise'rabile adj wretched

misera'mente adv (finire) miserably; (vivere) in abject poverty

mi'seria f poverty; (infelicità) misery; **guadagnare una ~** earn a pittance; **porca ~!** hell!

miseri'cordi|a f mercy. **~'oso** adj merciful

misero adj (miserabile) wretched; (povero) poor; (scarso) paltry

mi'sfatto m misdeed

mi'sogino m misogynist

mis'saggio m vision mixer

missile m missile

missio'nario, -a mf missionary. **missi'one** f mission

misteri|'oso adj mysterious. **mi'stero** m mystery

misti|ca f mysticism. **~'cismo** m mysticism. **~co** adj mystic[al] •m mystic

mistifi'ca|re vt distort (verità). **~zi'one** f (della verità) distortion

'misto adj mixed; **scuola mista** mixed or co-educational school •m mixture; **~ lana/cotone** wool/ cotton mix

mi'sura f measure; (dimensione) measurement; (taglia) size; (limite) limit; **su ~** (abiti) made to measure; (mobile) custom-made; **a ~** (andare, calzare) perfectly. **~ di sicurezza** safety measure. **misu'rare** vt measure; try on (indumenti); (limitare) limit. **misu'rarsi** vr **misurarsi con** (gareggiare) compete with. **misu'rato** adj measured. **misu'rino** m measuring spoon

'mite adj mild; (prezzo) moderate

'mitico adj mythical

miti'gar|e vt mitigate. **~si** vr calm down; (clima:) become mild

'mito m myth. **~lo'gia** f mythology. **~'logico** adj mythological

'mitra f (Relig) mitre •m inv (Mil) machine-gun

mitragli'a|re vt machine-gun; **~re di domande** fire questions at. **~'trice** f machine-gun

mit'tente mf sender

mo' m **a ~ di** by way of (esempio, consolazione)

'mobbing m harassment

'mobile[1] adj mobile; (volubile) fickle; (che si può muovere) movable; **beni mobili** personal estate; **squadra ~** flying squad

'mobi|le[2] m piece of furniture; **mobili** pl furniture sg. **mo'bilia** f furniture. **~li'ficio** m furniture factory

mo'bilio m furniture

mobilità f mobility

mobili'ta|re vt mobilize. **~zi'one** f mobilization

mocas'sino m moccasin

'moccolo m candle-end; (moccio) snot

'moda f fashion; **di ~** in fashion; **alla ~** (musica, vestiti) up-to-date; **fuori ~** unfashionable

modalità f inv formality; **~ d'uso** instruction

mo'della f model. **model'lare** vt model

model'li|no m model. **~sta** mf designer

mo'dello m model; (stampo) mould; (di carta) pattern; (modulo) form

'modem m inv modem

mode'ra|re vt moderate; (diminuire) reduce. **~rsi** vr control oneself. **~ta'mente** adv moderately **~to** adj moderate. **~'tore, ~'trice** mf (in tavola rotonda) moderator. **~zi'one** f moderation

modern|a'mente adv (in modo moderno) in a modern style. **~iz'zare** vt modernize. **mo'derno** adj modern

mo'dest|ia f modesty. **~o** adj modest

'modico adj reasonable

mo'difica f modification

modifi'ca|re vt modify. **~zi'one** f modification

mo'dista f milliner

'modo m way; (garbo) manners pl; (occasione) chance; (Gram) mood; **ad ogni ~** anyhow; **di ~ che** so that; **fare in ~ di** try to; **in che ~** (inter) how; **in qualche ~** somehow; **in questo ~** like this; **~ di dire** idiom; **per ~ di dire** so to speak

m

modu'la|re vt modulate. **~zi'one** f modulation. **~zione di frequenza** frequency modulation

'modulo m form; (lunare, di comando) module. **~ continuo** continuous paper

'mogano m mahogany

'mogio adj dejected

'moglie f wife

'mola f millstone; (Mech) grindstone

mo'lare m molar

'mole f mass; (dimensione) size

mo'lecola f molecule

mole'stare vt bother; (più forte) molest. **mo'lestia** f nuisance. **mo'lesto** adj bothersome

'molla f spring; **molle** pl tongs

mol'lare vt let go; ([!]: lasciare) leave; [!] give (ceffone); (Naut) cast off • vi cease; **mollala!** [!] stop that!

'molle adj soft; (bagnato) wet

mol'letta f (per capelli) hair-grip; (per bucato) clothes-peg; **mollette** pl (per ghiaccio ecc) tongs

mol'lezz|a f softness; **~e** pl fig luxury

mol'lica f crumb

'molo m pier; (banchina) dock

mol'teplic|e adj manifold; (numeroso) numerous. **~ità** f multiplicity

moltipli'ca|re vt, **~rsi** vr multiply. **~'tore** m multiplier. **~'trice** f calculating machine. **~zi'one** f multiplication

molti'tudine f multitude

'molto

- adj a lot of; (*con negazione e interrogazione*) much, a lot of; (*con nomi plurali*) many, a lot of; **non ~ tempo** not much time, not a lot of time
- adv very; (*con verbi*) a lot; (*con avverbi*) much; **~ stupido** very stupid; **mangiare ~** eat a lot; **~ più veloce** much faster; **non mangiare ~** not eat much
- pron a lot; (*molto tempo*) a lot of time; (*con negazione e interrogazione*) much, a lot; (*plurale*) many; **non ne ho ~** I don't have much; **non ne ho molti** I don't have many, I don't have a lot; **non ci metterò ~** I won't be long; **fra non ~** before long; **molti** (*persone*) a lot of people; **eravamo in molti** there were a lot of us

momentanea'mente adv momentarily; **è ~ assente** he's not here at the moment. **momen'taneo** adj momentary

mo'mento m moment; **a momenti** (a volte) sometimes; (fra un momento) in a moment; **dal ~ che** since; **per il ~** for the time being; **da un ~ all'altro** (cambiare idea ecc) from one moment to the next; (aspettare qcno ecc) at any moment

'monac|a f nun. **~o** m monk

'Monaco m Monaco • f (di Baviera) Munich

mo'narc|a m monarch. **monar'chia** monarchy

mona'stero m (di monaci) monastery; (di monache) convent. **mo'nastico** adj monastic.

monche'rino m stump

'monco adj maimed; (fig: troncato) truncated; **~ di un braccio** one-armed

mon'dano adj worldly; **vita**

mondana social life

nondi'ale adj world attrib; **di fama ~** world-famous

nondo m world; **il bel ~** fashionable society; **un ~** (molto) a lot

nondovisi'one f **in ~** transmitted worldwide

no'nello, -a mf urchin

no'neta f coin; (denaro) money; (denaro spicciolo) [small] change. **~ estera** foreign currency. **~ legale** legal tender. **~ unica** single currency. **mone'tario** adj monetary

nongolfi'era f hot air balloon

no'nile m jewel

monito m warning

noni'tore m monitor

nonoco'lore adj (Pol) one-party

nono'dose adj inv individually packaged

nonogra'fia f monograph

nono'gramma m monogram

nono'kini m inv monokini

nono'lingue adj monolingual

nonolo'cale m studio apartment

no'nologo m monologue

nono'pattino m [child's] scooter

nono'poli|o m monopoly. **~o di Stato** state monopoly. **~z'zare** vt monopolize

nono'sci m inv monoski

nonosil'labico adj monosyllabic. **mono'sillabo** m monosyllable

nonoto'nia f monotony. **mo'notono** adj monotonous

nono'uso adj disposable

nonsi'gnore m monsignor

non'sone m monsoon

nonta'carichi m inv hoist

non'taggio m (Mech) assembly; Cinema editing; **catena di ~** production line

non'ta|gna f mountain; (zona) mountains pl. **montagne** pl **russe** big dipper. **~'gnoso** adj mountainous. **~'naro, -a** mf highlander. **~no** adj mountain attrib

non'tante m (di finestra, porta) upright

non'ta|re vt/i mount; get on (veicolo); (aumentare) rise; (Mech) assemble; frame (quadro); (Culin) whip; edit (film); (a cavallo) ride; fig blow up; **~rsi la testa** get big-headed. **~to, -a** mf poser. **~'tura** f (Mech) assembling; (di occhiali) frame; (di gioiello) mounting; fig exaggeration

'monte m mountain; **a ~** up-stream; **andare a ~** be ruined; **mandare a ~ qcsa** ruin sth. **~ di pietà** pawnshop

Monte'negro m Montenegro

monte'premi m inv jackpot

mon'tone m ram; **carne di ~** mutton

montu'oso adj mountainous

monumen'tale adj monumental. **monu'mento** m monument

mo'quette f fitted carpet

'mora f (del gelso) mulberry; (del rovo) blackberry

mo'ral|e adj moral • f morals pl; (di storia) moral • m morale. **mora'lista** mf moralist. **~ità** f morality; (condotta) morals pl. **~iz'zare** vt/i moralize. **~'mente** adv morally

m

morbi'dezza f softness

'morbido adj soft

mor'billo m measles sg

'morbo m disease. **~sità** f (qualità) morbidity

mor'boso adj morbid

mor'dente adj biting. **'mordere** vt bite; (corrodere) bite into. **mordicchi'are** vt gnaw

mor'fina f morphine. **morfi'nomane** mf morphine addict

mori'bondo adj dying; (istituzione) moribund

morige'rato adj moderate

mo'rire vi die; fig die out; **fa un freddo da ~** it's freezing cold, it's perishing; **~ di noia** be bored to death

mor'mone mf Mormon

mormo'r|are vt/i murmur; (brontolare) mutter. **~io** m murmuring; (lamentela) grumbling

'moro adj dark • m Moor

mo'roso adj in arrears

'morsa f vice; fig grip

'morse adj **alfabeto ~** Morse code

mor'setto m clamp

morsi'care vt bite. **'morso** m bite; (di cibo, briglia) bit; **i morsi della fame** hunger pangs

morta'della f mortadella (type of salted pork)

mor'taio m mortar

mor'tal|e adj mortal; (simile a morte) deadly; **di una noia ~e** deadly. **~ità** f mortality. **~'mente** adv (ferito) fatally; (offeso) mortally

morta'retto m firecracker

'morte f death

mortifi'ca|re vt mortify. **~rsi** vr be mortified. **~to** adj mortified. **~zi'one** f mortification

'morto, -a pp di **morire** • adj dead; **~ di freddo** frozen to death; **stanco ~** dead tired • m dead man • f dead woman

mor'torio m funeral

mo'saico m mosaic

'mosca f fly. **~ cieca** blindman's buff

'Mosca f Moscow

mo'scato adj muscat; **noce moscata** nutmeg • m muscatel

mosce'rino m midge

mo'schea f mosque

moschi'cida adj fly attrib

'moscio adj limp; **avere l'erre moscia** not be able to say one's r's properly

mo'scone m bluebottle; (barca) pedalo

'moss|a f movement; (passo) move. **~o** pp di **muovere** • adj (mare) rough; (capelli) wavy; (fotografia) blurred

mo'starda f mustard

'mostra f show; (d'arte) exhibition; **far ~ di** pretend; **in ~** on show; **mettersi in ~** make oneself conspicuous

mo'stra|re vt show; (indicare) point out; (spiegare) explain. **~rsi** vr show oneself; (apparire) appear

'mostro m monster; (fig: persona) genius; **~ sacro** fig sacred cow

mostru|osa'mente adv tremendously. **~'oso** adj monstrous; (incredibile) enormous

mo'tel m inv motel

moti'va|re vt cause; (Jur) justify. **~to** adj (persona) motivated. **~zi'one** f motivation; (giustificazione) justification

mo'tivo m reason; (movente) motive; (in musica, letteratura) theme; (disegno) motif

'moto m motion; (esercizio) exercise; (gesto) movement; (sommossa) rising • f inv (motocicletta) motor bike; **mettere in ~** start (motore)

moto'carro m three-wheeler

motoci'cl|etta f motor cycle. **~ismo** m motorcycling. **~ista** mf motor-cyclist

moto'cros|s m motocross. **~'sista** mf scrambler

moto'lancia f motor launch

moto'nave f motor vessel

mo'tore adj motor • m motor, engine. **~ di ricerca** (Comput) search engine. **moto'retta** f motor scooter. **moto'rino** m moped. **motorino d'avviamento** starter

motoriz'za|to adj (Mil) motorized. **~zi'one** f (ufficio) vehicle licensing office

moto'scafo m motorboat

motove'detta f patrol vessel

'motto m motto; (facezia) witticism; (massima) saying

mouse m inv (Comput) mouse

mo'vente m motive

movimen'ta|re vt enliven. **~to** adj lively. **movi'mento** m movement; **essere sempre in movimento** be always on the go

mozi'one f motion

mozzafi'ato adj inv nail-biting

moz'zare vt cut off; dock (coda); **~ il fiato a qcno** take sb's breath away

mozza'rella f mozzarella (mild, white cheese)

mozzi'cone m (di sigaretta) stub

'mozzo m (Mech) hub; (Naut) ship's

boy • adj (coda) truncated; (testa) severed

mucca f cow. **morbo della ~ pazza** mad cow disease

mucchio m heap, pile; **un ~ di** fig lots of

muco m mucus

muffa f mould; **fare la ~** go mouldy. **muf'fire** vi go mouldy

muf'fole fpl mittens

mug'gi|re vi (mucca:) moo, low; (toro:) bellow

mu'ghetto m lily of the valley

mugo'lare vi whine; (persona:) moan. **mugo'lio** m whining

mulatti'era f mule track

mu'latto, -a mf mulatto

muli'nello m (d'acqua) whirl-pool; (di vento) eddy; (giocattolo) windmill

mu'lino m mill. **~ a vento** windmill

mulo m mule

multa f fine. **mul'tare** vt fine

multico'lore adj multicoloured

multi'lingue adj multilingual

multi'media mpl multimedia

multimedi'ale adj multimedia attrib

multimiliar'dario, -a mf multi-millionaire

multinazio'nale f multinational

multiplo adj & m multiple

multiproprietà f inv time-share

multi'uso adj (utensile) all-purpose

mummia f mummy

mungere vt milk

munici'pal|e adj municipal. **~ità** f inv town council. **muni'cipio** m town hall

mu'nifico adj munificent

mu'nire vt fortify; **~ di** (provvedere) supply with

munizi'oni fpl ammunition sg

munto pp di **mungere**

mu'over|e vt move; (suscitare) arouse. **~si** vr move

mura fpl (cinta di città) walls

mu'raglia f wall

mu'rale adj mural; (pittura) wall attrib

mur'a|re vt wall up. **~'tore** m bricklayer; (con pietre) mason; (operaio edile) builder. **~'tura** f (di pietra) masonry, stonework; (di mattoni) brickwork

mu'rena f moray eel

'muro m wall; (di nebbia) bank; **a ~** (armadio) built-in. **~ portante** load-bearing wall. **~ del suono** sound barrier

'muschio m (Bot) moss

musco'la|re adj muscular. **~'tura** f muscles pl. **'muscolo** m muscle

mu'seo m museum

museru'ola f muzzle

'musi|ca f music. **~cal** m inv musical. **~'cale** adj musical. **~'cista** mf musician.

'muso m muzzle; (pej: di persona) mug; (di aeroplano) nose; **fare il ~** sulk. **mu'sone, -a** mf sulker

'mussola f muslin

musul'mano, -a mf Moslem

'muta f (cambio) change; (di penne) moult; (di cani) pack; (per immersione subacquea) wetsuit

muta'mento m change

mu'tan|de fpl pants; (da donna) knickers. **~'doni** mpl (da uomo) long johns; (da donna) bloomers

mu'tare vt change

mu'tevole adj changeable

muti'la|re vt mutilate. **~to, -a** mf disabled person. **~to di guerra** disabled ex-serviceman

mu'tismo m dumbness; fig obstinate silence

'muto adj dumb; (silenzioso) silent; (fonetica) mute

'mutu|a f [**cassa** f] **~** sickness benefit fund. **~'ato, -a** mf ≈ NHS patient

'mutuo¹ adj mutual

'mutuo² m loan; (per la casa) mortgage; **fare un ~** take out a mortgage. **~ ipotecario** mortgage

Nn

n° abbr (numero) No

'nacchera f castanet

'nafta f naphtha; (per motori) diesel oil

'naia f cobra; (☒: servizio militare) national service

'nailon m nylon

'nano, -a adj & mf dwarf

napole'tano, -a adj & mf Neapolitan

'Napoli f Naples

'nappa f tassel; (pelle) soft leather

nar'ciso m narcissus

nar'cotico adj & m narcotic

na'rice f nostril

nar'ra|re vt tell. **~'tivo, -a** adj narrative •f fiction. **~'tore, ~'trice** mf narrator. **~zi'one** f narration; (racconto) story

na'sale adj nasal

'nasc|ere vi (venire al mondo) be born; (germogliare) sprout; (sorgere) rise; **~ere da** fig arise from. **~ita** f birth. **~i'turo** m unborn child

na'sconder|e vt hide. **~si** vr hide

nascon'di|glio m hiding-place. **~no** m hide-and-seek. **na'scosto** pp di **nascondere** •adj hidden; **di nascosto** secretly

na'sello m (pesce) hake

'naso m nose

'nastro m ribbon; (di registratore ecc) tape. **~ adesivo** adhesive tape. **~ isolante** insulating tape. **~ trasportatore** conveyor belt

na'tal|e adj (paese) of one's birth. **N~e** m Christmas; **~i** pl parentage. **~ità** f [number of] births. **nata'lizio** adj (del Natale) Christmas attrib; (di nascita) of one's birth

na'tante adj floating •m craft

'natica f buttock

na'tio adj native

Natività f Nativity. **na'tivo, -a** agg & mf native

'nato pp di **nascere** •adj born; **uno scrittore ~** a born writer; **nata Rossi** née Rossi

NATO f Nato, NATO

na'tura f nature; **pagare in ~** pay in kind. **~ morta** still life

natu'ra|le adj natural; **al ~le** (alimento) plain, natural; **~le!** naturally, of course. **~'lezza** f naturalness. **~liz'zare** vt naturalize **~l'mente** adv naturally

natu'rista mf naturalist

naufra'gare vi be wrecked; (persona: be shipwrecked. **nau'fragio** m shipwreck; fig wreck. **'naufrago, -a** mf survivor

'nause|a f nausea; **avere la ~a** feel sick. **~'ante** adj nauseating. **~'are** v nauseate

'nautic|a f navigation. **~o** adj nautical

na'vale adj naval

na'vata f nave; (laterale) aisle

'nave f ship. **~ cisterna** tanker. **~ da guerra** warship. **~ spaziale** spaceship

na'vetta f shuttle

navicella f **~ spaziale** nose cone

navi'gabile adj navigable

navi'ga|re vi sail; **~re in Internet** surf the Net. **~'tore, ~'trice** mf navigator. **~zi'one** f navigation

na'viglio m fleet; (canale) canal

nazio'na|le adj national •f Sport national team. **~'lismo** m nationalism. **~'lista** mf nationalist **~lità** f inv nationality.

nazionaliz'zare vt nationalize. **nazi'one** f nation

na'zista adj & mf Nazi

N.B. abbr (nota bene) N.B.

n

ne

> **!** Spesso non si traduce: **Ne ho cinque** I've got five (of them)

• pers pron (*di lui*) about him; (*di lei*) about her; (*di loro*) about them; (*di ciò*) about it; (*da ciò*) from that; (*di un insieme*) of it; (*di un gruppo*) of them

····➤ **non ne conosco nessuno** I don't know any of them; **ne ho** I have some; **non ne ho più** I don't have any left

• adv from there; **ne vengo ora** I've just come from there; **me ne vado** I'm off

né conj **né... né...**neither... nor...; **non ne ho il tempo né la voglia** I don't have either the time or the inclination; **né tu né io vogliamo andare** neither you nor I want to go; **né l'uno né l'altro** neither [of them/us]

ne'anche adv (neppure) not even; (senza neppure) without even • conj (e neppure) neither... nor; **non parlo inglese, e lui ~** I don't speak English, neither does he o and he doesn't either

nebbi|a f mist; (in città, su strada) fog. **~'oso** adj misty; foggy

necessaria'mente adv necessarily. **neces'sario** adj necessary

necessità f inv necessity; (bisogno) need

necessi'tare vi **~ di** need; (essere necessario) be necessary

necro'logio m obituary

ne'fando adj wicked

ne'fasto adj ill-omened

ne'ga|re vt deny; (rifiutare) refuse; **essere ~to per qcsa** be no good at sth. **~'tivo, -a** adj negative • f negative. **~zi'one** f negation; (diniego) denial; (Gram) negative

ne'gletto adj neglected

negli = **in + gli**

negli'gen|te adj negligent. **~za** f negligence

negozi'abile adj negotiable

negozi'ante mf dealer; (bottegaio) shopkeeper

negozi'a|re vt negotiate • vi **~re in** trade in. **~ti** mpl negotiations

🅲 **ne'gozio** m shop

'negro, -a adj black • mf black; (scrittore) ghost writer

'nei = **in + i**. **nel** = **in + il**. **'nella** = **in + la**. **'nelle** = **in + le**. **'nello** = **in + lo**

'nembo m nimbus

ne'mico, -a adj hostile • mf enemy

nem'meno conj not even

'nenia f dirge; (per bambini) lullaby; (piagnucolio) wail

'neo+ pref neo+

neofa'scismo m neofascism

neo'litico adj Neolithic

neo'nato, -a adj newborn • mf newborn baby

neozelan'dese adj New Zealand • mf New Zealander

nep'pure conj not even

'nerb|o m (forza) strength; fig backbone. **~o'ruto** adj brawny

ne'retto m (Typ) bold [type]

'nero adj black; (🅸: arrabbiato) fuming • m black; **mettere ~ su bianco** put in writing

nerva'tura f nerves pl; (Bot) veining; (di libro) band

'nervo m nerve; (Bot) vein; **avere i nervi** be bad-tempered; **dare ai nervi a qcno** get on sb's nerves. **~'sismo** m nerviness

ner'voso adj nervous; (irritabile) bad-tempered; **avere il ~** be irritable; **esaurimento** m **~** nervous breakdown

'nespol|a f medlar. **~o** m medlar[-tree]

'nesso m link

nes'suno adj no, not... any; (qualche) any; **non ho nessun problema** I don't have any problems, I have no problems; **non lo trovo da nessuna parte** I can't find it anywhere; **in nessun modo** on no account • pron nobody, no one, not... anybody, not... anyone; (qualcuno) anybody, anyone; **hai delle domande? – nessuna** do you have any questions? – none; **~ di voi** none of you; **~ dei due** (di voi due)

🅲 *see* A-Z of Italian life and culture

n

neither of you; **non ho visto ~ dei tuoi amici** I haven't seen any of your friends; **c'è ~?** is anybody there?

net'tare vt clean

net'tezza f cleanliness. **~ urbana** cleansing department

'netto adj clean; (chiaro) clear; (Comm) net; **di ~** just like that

nettur'bino m dustman

neu'tral|e adj & m neutral. **~ità** f neutrality. **~iz'zare** vt neutralize. **'neutro** adj neutral; (Gram) neuter • m (Gram) neuter

neu'trone m neutron

'neve f snow

nevi|'care vi snow; **~ca** it is snowing. **~'cata** f snowfall. **ne'vischio** m sleet. **ne'voso** adj snowy

nevral'gia f neuralgia

ne'vro|si f inv neurosis. **~tico** adj neurotic

'nibbio m kite

'nicchia f niche

nicchi'are vi shilly-shally

'nichel m nickel

nichi'lista adj & mf nihilist

nico'tina f nicotine

nidi'ata f brood. **'nido** m nest; (giardino d'infanzia) crèche

ni'ente pron nothing, not... anything; (qualcosa) anything; **non ho fatto ~ di male** I didn't do anything wrong, I did nothing wrong; **grazie! – di ~!** thank you! – don't mention it!; **non serve a ~** it is no use; **vuoi ~?** do you want anything?; **da ~** (poco importante) minor; (di poco valore) worthless • adj inv [!] **non ho ~ fame** I'm not the slightest bit hungry • adv **non fa ~** (non importa) it doesn't matter; **per ~** at all; (litigare) over nothing; **~ affatto!** no way! • m **un bel ~** absolutely nothing

nientedi'meno, niente'meno adv **~ che** no less than • int fancy that!

'ninfa f nymph

nin'fea f water-lily

'ninnolo m plaything; (fronzolo) knick-knack

ni'pote m (di zii) nephew; (di nonni) grandson, grandchild • f (di zii) niece; (di nonni) granddaughter, grandchild

'nitido adj neat; (chiaro) clear

ni'trato m nitrate

ni'tri|re vi neigh. **~to** m (di cavallo) neigh

no adv no; (con congiunzione) not; **dire di no** say no; **credo di no** I don't think so; **perché no?** why not?; **io no** not me; **fa freddo, no?** it's cold, isn't it?

'nobil|e adj noble • m noble, nobleman • f noble, noblewoman. **~i'are** adj noble. **~tà** f nobility

'nocca f knuckle

nocci'ol|a f hazelnut. **~o** m (albero) hazel

'nocciolo m stone; fig heart

'noce f walnut • m (albero, legno) walnut. **~ moscata** nutmeg. **~'pesca** f nectarine

no'civo adj harmful

'nodo m knot; fig lump; (Comput) node; **fare il ~ della cravatta** do up one's tie. **no'doso** adj knotty

'noi pers pron (soggetto) we; (oggetto, con prep) us; **chi è? – siamo ~** who is it? – it's us

'noia f boredom; (fastidio) bother; (persona) bore; **dar ~** annoy

noi'altri pers pron we

noi'oso adj boring; (fastidioso) tiresome

noleggi'are vt hire; (dare a noleggio) hire out; charter (nave, aereo). **no'leggio** m hire; (di nave, aereo) charter. **'nolo** m hire; (Naut) freight; **a nolo** for hire

'nomade adj nomadic • mf nomad

'nome m name; (Gram) noun; **a ~ di** in the name of; **di ~** by name. **~ di famiglia** surname. **~ da ragazza** maiden name. **no'mea** f reputation

nomencla'tura f nomenclature

no'mignolo m nickname

'nomina f appointment. **nomi'nale** adj nominal; (Gram) noun attrib

nomi'na|re vt name; (menzionare) mention; (eleggere) appoint. **~'tivo** adj nominative; (Comm) registered • m nominative; (nome) name

non adv not; ~ **ti amo** I do not love you; ~ **c'è di che** not at all

! Per formare il negativo dei verbi regolari si usa l'ausiliare *do*: **non mi piace** I don' like it

nonché conj (tanto meno) let alone; (e anche) as well as

noncu'ran|te adj nonchalant; (negligente) indifferent. **~za** f nonchalance; (negligenza) indifference

nondi'meno conj nevertheless

'nonna f grandmother

'nonno m grandfather; **nonni** pl grandparents

non'nulla m inv trifle

'nono adj & m ninth

nono'stante prep in spite of • conj although

nonvio'lento adj nonviolent

nord m north; **del** ~ northern

nor'd-est m northeast; **a** ~ northeasterly

'nordico adj northern

nordocciden'tale adj northwestern

nordorien'tale adj northeastern

nor'd-ovest m northwest; **a** ~ northwesterly

'norma f rule; (istruzione) instruction; **a ~ di legge** according to law; **è buona** ~ it's advisable

nor'mal|e adj normal. **~ità** f normality. **~iz'zare** vt normalize. **~'mente** adv normally

norve'gese adj & mf Norwegian. **Nor'vegia** f Norway

nossi'gnore adv no way

nostal'gia f (di casa, patria) homesickness; (del passato) nostalgia; **aver** ~ be homesick; **aver ~ di qcno** miss sb. **no'stalgico, -a** adj nostalgic • mf reactionary

no'strano adj local; (fatto in casa) home-made

'nostro (**il nostro** m, **la nostra** f, **i nostri** mpl, **le nostre** fpl) poss adj our; **quella macchina è nostra** that car is ours; ~ **padre** our father; **un ~ amico** a friend of ours • poss pron ours

'nota f (segno) sign; (comunicazione, commento, musica) note; (conto) bill; (lista) list; **degno di** ~ noteworthy; **prendere** ~ take note. **note** pl **caratteristiche** distinguishing marks

no'tabile adj & m notable

no'taio m notary

no'ta|re vt (segnare) mark; (annotare) note down; (osservare) notice; **far ~re qcsa** point sth out. **~zi'one** f marking; (annotazione) notation

'notes m inv notepad

no'tevole adj (degno di nota) remarkable; (grande) considerable

no'tifica f notification. **notifi'care** vt notify; (Comm) advise. **~zi'one** f notification

no'tizi|a f **una ~a** a piece of news; (informazione) a piece of information; **le ~e** the news sg. **~'ario** m news sg

'noto adj [well-]known; **rendere** ~ (far sapere) announce

notorietà f fame; **raggiungere la** ~ become famous. **no'torio** adj well-known; pej notorious

not'tambulo m night-bird

not'tata f night; **far** ~ stay up all night

'notte f night; **di** ~ at night; ~ **bianca** sleepless night. **~'tempo** adv at night

not'turno adj nocturnal; (servizio ecc) night

no'vanta adj & m ninety

novan't|enne adj & mf ninety-year-old. **~esimo** adj ninetieth. **~ina** f about ninety. **'nove** adj & m nine. **nove'cento** adj & m nine hundred. **il Novecento** the twentieth century

no'vella f short story

novel'lino, -a adj inexperienced • mf novice, beginner. **no'vello** adj new

no'vembre m November

novità f inv novelty; (notizie) news sg; **l'ultima** ~ (moda) the latest fashion

novizi'ato m (Relig) novitiate; (tirocinio) apprenticeship

nozi'one f notion; **nozioni** pl rudiments

'nozze fpl marriage sg; (cerimonia)

see A-Z of Italian life and culture

wedding sg. ~ **d'argento** silver wedding [anniversary]. ~ **d'oro** golden wedding [anniversary]

'**nub|e** f cloud. ~**e tossica** toxic cloud. ~**i'fragio** m cloudburst

'**nubile** adj unmarried •f unmarried woman

'**nuca** f nape

nucle'are adj nuclear

'**nucleo** m nucleus; (unità) unit

nu'di|sta mf nudist. ~**tà** f inv nudity

'**nudo** adj naked; (spoglio) bare; **a occhio** ~ to the naked eye

'**nugolo** m large number

'**nulla** pron = **niente**

nulla'osta m inv permit

nullità f inv (persona) nonentity

'**nullo** adj (Jur) null and void

nume'ra|bile adj countable. ~**le** adj & m numeral

nume'ra|re vt number. ~**zi'one** f numbering. **nu'merico** adj numerical

'**numero** m number; (romano, arabo) numeral; (di scarpe ecc) size; **dare i numeri** be off one's head. ~ **cardinale** cardinal [number]. ~ **decimale** decimal. ~ **ordinale** ordinal [number]. ~ **di telefono** phone number. ~ **verde** Freephone®. **nume'roso** adj numerous

'**nunzio** m nuncio

nu'ocere vi ~ **a** harm

nu'ora f daughter-in-law

nuo'ta|re vi swim; fig wallow. **nu'oto** m swimming. ~**'tore,** ~**'trice** mf swimmer

nu'ov|a f (notizia) news sg. ~**a'mente** adv again. ~**o** adj new; **di** ~**o** again; **rimettere a** ~**o** give a new lease of life to

nutri|'ente adj nourishing. ~**'mento** m nourishment

nu'tri|re vt nourish; harbour (sentimenti). ~**rsi** eat; ~**rsi di** fig live on. ~**'tivo** adj nourishing. ~**zi'one** f nutrition

'**nuvola** f cloud. **nuvo'loso** adj cloudy

nuzi'ale adj nuptial; (vestito, anello ecc) wedding attrib

Oo

o conj or; ~ **l'uno** ~ **l'altro** one or the other, either

O abbr (ovest) W

'**oasi** f inv oasis

obbedi'ente ecc = **ubbidiente** ecc

obbli'ga|re vt force, oblige; ~**rsi** vr ~**rsi a** undertake to. ~**to** adj obliged. ~**'torio** adj compulsory. ~**zi'one** f obligation; (Comm) bond. '**obbligo** m obligation; (dovere) duty; **avere obblighi verso** be under an obligation to; **d'obbligo** obligatory

obbligatoria'mente adv **fare qcsa** ~ be obliged to do sth

ob'bro|brio m disgrace. ~**'brioso** adj disgraceful

obe'lisco m obelisk

obe'rare vt overburden

obesità f obesity. **o'beso** adj obese

obiet'tare vt/i object; ~ **su** object to

obiettivi'tà f objectivity. **obiet'tivo** adj objective •m objective; (scopo) object

obie|t'tore m objector. ~**ttore di coscienza** conscientious objector. ~**zi'one** f objection

obi'torio m mortuary

o'blio m oblivion

o'bliquo adj oblique; fig underhand

oblite'rare vt obliterate

oblò m inv porthole

'**oboe** m oboe

obso'leto adj obsolete

'oca f (pl **oche**) goose

occasio'nal|e adj occasional. **~'mente** adv occasionally

occasi'one f occasion; (buon affare) bargain; (motivo) cause; (opportunità) chance; **d'~** secondhand

occhi'aia f eye socket; **occhiaie** pl shadows under the eyes

occhi'ali mpl glasses, spectacles. **~ da sole** sunglasses. **~ da vista** glasses, spectacles

occhi'ata f look; **dare un'~ a** have a look at

occhieggi'are vt ogle •vi peep

occhi'ello m buttonhole; (asola) eyelet

'occhio m eye; **~!** watch out!; **a quattr'occhi** in private; **tenere d'~ qcno** keep an eye on sb; **a ~ [e croce]** roughly; **chiudere un ~** turn a blind eye; **dare nell'~** attract attention; **pagare** o **spendere un ~** pay an arm and a leg. **~ nero** (pesto) black eye. **~ di pernice** (callo) corn. **~'lino** m **fare l'~lino a qcno** wink at sb

occiden'tale adj western •mf westerner. **occi'dente** m west

oc'clu|dere vt obstruct. **~si'one** f occlusion

occor'ren|te adj necessary •m the necessary. **~za** f need; **all'~za** if need be

oc'correre vi be necessary

occulta'mento m **~ di prove** concealment of evidence

occul't|are vt hide. **~ismo** m occult. **oc'culto** adj hidden; (magico) occult

occu'pante mf occupier; (abusivo) squatter

occu'pa|re vt occupy; spend (tempo); take up (spazio); (dar lavoro a) employ. **~rsi** vr occupy oneself; (trovare lavoro) find a job; **~rsi di** (badare) look after. **~to** adj engaged; (persona) busy; (posto) taken. **~zi'one** f occupation

o'ceano m ocean. **~ Atlantico** Atlantic [Ocean]. **~ Pacifico** Pacific [Ocean]

'ocra f ochre

ocu'lare adj ocular; (testimone, bagno) eye attrib

ocula'tezza f care. **ocu'lato** adj (scelta) wise

ocu'lista mf optician; (per malattie) ophthalmologist

od conj or

'ode f ode

odi'are vt hate

odi'erno adj of today; (attuale) present

'odi|o m hatred; **avere in ~o** hate. **~'oso** adj hateful

odo'ra|re vt smell; (profumare) perfume •vi **~re di** smell of. **~to** m sense of smell. **o'dore** m smell; (profumo) scent; **c'è odore di...** there's a smell of...; **sentire odore di** smell; **odori** pl (Culin) herbs. **odo'roso** adj fragrant

of'fender|e vt offend; (ferire) injure. **~si** vr take offence

offen'siv|a f (Mil) offensive. **~o** adj offensive

offe'rente mf offerer; (in aste) bidder

of'fert|a f offer; (donazione) donation; (Comm) supply; (nelle aste) bid; **in ~a speciale** on special offer. **~o** pp di **offrire**

of'fes|a f offence. **~o** pp di **offendere** •adj offended

offi'ciare vt officiate

offi'cina f workshop; **~ [meccanica]** garage

of'frir|e vt offer. **~si** vr offer oneself; (occasione:) present itself; **~si di fare qcsa** offer to do sth

offu'scar|e vt darken; fig dull (memoria, bellezza); blur (vista). **~si** vr darken; fig: (memoria, bellezza:) fade away; (vista:) become blurred

of'talmico adj ophthalmic

oggettività f objectivity. **ogget'tivo** adj objective

og'getto m object; (argomento) subject; **oggetti** pl **smarriti** lost property, lost and found Am

'oggi adv & m today; (al giorno d'oggi) nowadays; **da ~ in poi** from today on; **~ a otto** a week today; **dall'~ al domani** overnight; **al giorno d'~** nowadays. **~gi'orno** adv nowadays

'ogni adj inv every; (qualsiasi) any; **~ tre giorni** every three days; **ad ~**

costo at any cost; **ad ~ modo** anyway; **~ cosa** everything; **~ tanto** now and then; **~ volta che** whenever

o'gnuno pron everyone, everybody; **~ di voi** each of you

'ola f inv Mexican wave

O'lan|da f Holland. **o~'dese** adj Dutch •m Dutchman; (lingua) Dutch •f Dutchwoman

ole'andro m oleander

ole'at|o adj oiled; **carta ~a** grease-proof paper

oleo'dotto m oil pipeline. **ole'oso** adj oily

ol'fatto m sense of smell

oli'are vt oil

oli'era f cruet

olim'piadi fpl Olympic Games. **o'limpico** adj Olympic. **olim'pionico** adj (primato, squadra) Olympic

'olio m oil; **sott'~** in oil; **colori a ~** oils; **quadro a ~** oil painting. **~ di mais** corn oil. **~ d'oliva** olive oil. **~ di semi** vegetable oil. **~ solare** sun-tan oil

o'liv|a f olive. **oli'vastro** adj olive. **oli'veto** m olive grove. **~o** m olive tree

'olmo m elm

oltraggi'are vt offend. **ol'traggio** m offence

ol'tranza f **ad ~** to the bitter end

'oltre adv (di luogo) further; (di tempo) longer •prep (di luogo) over; (di tempo) later than; (più di) more than; (in aggiunta) besides; **~ a** (eccetto) except, apart from; **per ~ due settimane** for more than two weeks. **~'mare** adv overseas. **~'modo** adv extremely

oltrepas'sare vt go beyond; (eccedere) exceed

o'maggio m homage; (dono) gift; **in ~ con** free with; **omaggi** pl (saluti) respects

ombeli'cale adj umbilical. **ombe'lico** m navel

'ombr|a f (zona) shade; (immagine oscura) shadow; **all'~a** in the shade. **~eggi'are** vt shade

om'brello m umbrella. **ombrel'lone** m beach umbrella

om'bretto m eye-shadow

om'broso adj shady

ome'lette f inv omelette

ome'lia f (Relig) sermon

omeopa'tia f homoeopathy. **omeo'patico** adj homoeopathic •m homoeopath

omertà f conspiracy of silence

o'messo pp di **omettere**

o'mettere vt omit

OMG m abbr (organismo modificato geneticamente) GMO

omi'cid|a adj murderous •mf murderer. **~io** m murder. **~io colposo** manslaughter

omissi'one f omission

omogeneiz'zato adj homogenized. **omo'geneo** adj homogeneous

omolo'gare vt approve

o'monimo, -a mf namesake •m (parola) homonym

omosessu'al|e adj & mf homosexual. **~ità** f homosexuality

On. abbr (onorevole) MP

'oncia f ounce

'onda f wave; **andare in ~** Radio go on the air. **onde** pl **corte** short wave. **onde** pl **lunghe** long wave. **onde** pl **medie** medium wave. **on'data** f wave

ondeggi'are vi wave; (barca:) roll

ondula|'torio adj undulating. **~zi'one** f undulation; (di capelli) wave

'oner|e m burden. **~'oso** adj onerous

onestà f honesty; (rettitudine) integrity. **o'nesto** adj honest; (giusto) just

'onice f onyx

onnipo'tente adj omnipotent

onnipre'sente adj ubiquitous; Rel omnipresent

🅲 **ono'mastico** m name-day

ono'ra|bile adj honourable. **~re** vt (fare onore a) be a credit to; honour (promessa). **~rio** adj honorary •m fee. **~rsi** vr **~rsi di** be proud of

o'nore m honour; **in ~ di** (festa, ricevimento) in honour of; **fare ~ a**

🅲 see A-Z of Italian life and culture

do justice to (pranzo); **farsi ~ in** excel in

ono'revole adj honourable •mf Member of Parliament

onorifi'cenza f honour; (decorazione) decoration. **ono'rifico** adj honorary

O.N.U. f abbr (Organizzazione delle Nazioni Unite) UN

o'paco adj opaque; (colori ecc) dull; (fotografia, rossetto) matt

o'pale f opal

'opera f (lavoro) work; (azione) deed; (Mus) opera; (teatro) opera house; (ente) institution; **mettere in ~** put into effect; **mettersi all'~** get to work; **opere** pl **pubbliche** public works. **~ d'arte** work of art. **~ lirica** opera

ope'raio, -a adj working •mf worker; **~ specializzato** skilled worker

ope'ra|re vt (Med) operate on; **farsi ~re** have an operation •vi operate; (agire) work. **~'tivo, ~'torio** adj operating attrib. **~'tore, ~'trice** mf operator; (TV) cameraman. **~tore turistico** tour operator. **~zi'one** f operation; (Comm) transaction

ope'retta f operetta

ope'roso adj industrious

opini'one f opinion. **~ pubblica** public opinion, vox pop

'oppio m opium

oppo'nente adj opposing •mf opponent

op'por|re vt oppose; (obiettare) object; **~re resistenza** offer resistance. **~si** vr **~si a** oppose

opportu'ni|smo m expediency. **~sta** mf opportunist. **~tà** f inv opportunity; (l'essere opportuno) timeliness. **oppor'tuno** adj opportune; (adeguato) appropriate; **il momento opportuno** the right moment

opposi|'tore m opposer. **~zi'one** f opposition; **d'~zione** (giornale, partito) opposition

op'posto pp di **opporre** •adj opposite; (opinioni) opposing •m opposite; **all'~** on the contrary

oppres|si'one f oppression. **~'sivo** adj oppressive. **op'presso** pp di **opprimere** •adj oppressed. **~'sore** m oppressor

oppri'me|nte adj oppressive. **op'primere** vt oppress; (gravare) weigh down

op'pure conj otherwise, or [else]; **lunedì ~ martedì** Monday or Tuesday

op'tare vi **~ per** opt for

opu'lento adj opulent

o'puscolo m booklet; (pubblicitario) brochure

opzio'nale adj optional. **opzi'one** f option

'ora¹ f time; (unità) hour; **di buon'~** early; **che ~ è?, che ore sono?** what time is it?; **mezz'~** half an hour; **a ore** (lavorare, pagare) by the hour; **50 km all'~** 50 km an hour; **a un'~ di macchina** one hour by car. **~ d'arrivo** arrival time. **l'~ esatta** (Teleph) speaking clock. **~ legale** daylight saving time. **~ di punta, ore** pl **di punta** peak time; (per il traffico) rush hour

'ora² adv now; (tra poco) presently; **~ come ~** at the moment; **d'~ in poi** from now on; **per ~** for the time being, for now; **è ~ di finirla!** that's enough now! •conj (dunque) now [then]; **~ che ci penso,...** now that I come to think about it,...

O

'orafo m goldsmith

o'rale adj & m oral; **per via ~** by mouth

ora'mai adv = **ormai**

o'rario adj (tariffa) hourly; (segnale) time attrib; (velocità) per hour •m time; (tabella dell'orario) timetable, schedule Am; **essere in ~** be on time; **in senso ~** clockwise. **~ di chiusura** closing time. **~ flessibile** flexitime. **~ di sportello** banking hours. **~ d'ufficio** business hours. **~ di visita** (Med) consulting hours

o'rata f gilthead

ora'tore, -'trice mf speaker

ora'torio, -a adj oratorical •m (Mus) oratorio •f oratory. **orazi'one** f (Relig) prayer

'orbita f orbit; (Anat) [eye-]socket

see A-Z of Italian life and culture

or'chestra f orchestra; (parte del teatro) pit

orche'stra|le adj orchestral •mf member of an/the orchestra. **~re** vt orchestrate

orchi'dea f orchid

'orco m ogre

'orda f horde

or'digno m device; (arnese) tool. **~ esplosivo** explosive device

ordi'nale adj & m ordinal

ordina'mento m order; (leggi) rules pl.

ordi'nanza f bylaw; **d'~** (soldato) on duty

ordi'nare vt (sistemare) arrange; (comandare) order; (prescrivere) prescribe; (Relig) ordain

ordi'nario adj ordinary; (grossolano) common; (professore) with tenure; **di ordinaria amministrazione** routine •m ordinary; (Univ) professor

ordi'nato adj (in ordine) tidy

ordinazi'one f order; **fare un'~** place an order

'ordine m order; (di avvocati, medici) association; **mettere in ~** put in order; **di prim'~** first-class; **di terz'~** (film, albergo) third- rate; **di ~ pratico/economico** of a practical/ economic nature; **fino a nuovo ~** until further notice; **parola d'~** password. **~ del giorno** agenda. **ordini sacri** pl Holy Orders

or'dire vt (tramare) plot

orec'chino m ear-ring

o'recchi|o m (pl f **orecchie**) ear; **avere ~o** have a good ear; **mi è giunto all'~o che...** I've heard that...; **~'oni** pl (Med) mumps sg

o'refice m jeweller. **~'ria** f (arte) goldsmith's art; (negozio) goldsmith's [shop]

'orfano, -a adj orphan •mf orphan. **~'trofio** m orphanage

orga'netto m barrel-organ; (a bocca) mouth-organ; (fisarmonica) accordion

or'ganico adj organic •m personnel

orga'nismo m organism; (corpo umano) body

orga'nista mf organist

organiz'za|re vt organize. **~rsi** vr get organized. **~'tore, ~'trice** mf organizer. **~zi'one** f organization

'organo m organ

or'gasmo m orgasm

'orgia f orgy

or'gogli|o m pride. **~'oso** adj proud

orien'tale adj eastern; (cinese ecc) oriental

orienta'mento m orientation; **perdere l'~** lose one's bearings; **senso dell'~** sense of direction

orien'ta|re vt orientate. **~rsi** vr find one's bearings; (tendere) tend

ori'ente m east. **l'Estremo O~** the Far East. **il Medio O~** the Middle East

o'rigano m oregano

origi'na|le adj original; (eccentrico) odd •m original. **~lità** f originality. **~re** vt/i originate. **~rio** adj (nativo) native

o'rigine f origin; **in ~** originally; **aver ~ da** originate from; **dare ~ a** give rise to

o'rina f urine. **ori'nale** m chamber-pot. **ori'nare** vi urinate

ori'undo adj native

orizzon'tale adj horizontal

orizzon'tare vt = **orientare**. **oriz'zonte** m horizon

or'la|re vt hem. **~'tura** f hem. **'orlo** m edge; (di vestito ecc) hem

'orma f track; (di piede) footprint; (impronta) mark

or'mai adv by now; (passato) by then; (quasi) almost

ormeg'giare vt moor

ormo'nale adj hormonal. **or'mone** m hormone

ornamen'tale adj ornamental. **orna'mento** m ornament

or'na|re vt decorate. **~rsi** vr deck oneself. **~to** adj (stile) ornate

ornitolo'gia f ornithology

'oro m gold; **d'~** gold; fig golden

orologi'aio, -a mf clockmaker, watchmaker

oro'logio m watch; (da tavolo, muro ecc) clock. **~ a pendolo** grandfather clock. **~ da polso** wrist-watch. **~ a**

sveglia alarm clock

o'roscopo m horoscope

or'rendo adj awful, dreadful

or'ribile adj horrible

orripi'lante adj horrifying

or'rore m horror; **avere qcsa in ~** hate sth

orsacchi'otto m teddy bear

'orso m bear; (persona scontrosa) hermit. **~ bianco** polar bear

or'taggio m vegetable

or'tensia f hydrangea

or'tica f nettle

orticol'tura f horticulture. **'orto** m vegetable plot

orto'dosso adj orthodox

ortogo'nale adj perpendicular

orto|gra'fia f spelling. **~'grafico** adj spelling attrib

orto'lano m market gardener; (negozio) greengrocer's

orto|pe'dia f orthopaedics sg. **~'pedico** adj orthopaedic • m orthopaedist

orzai'olo m sty

or'zata f barley-water

o'sare vt/i dare; (avere audacia) be daring

oscenità f inv obscenity. **o'sceno** adj obscene

oscil'la|re vi swing; (prezzi ecc:) fluctuate; Tech oscillate; (fig: essere indeciso) vacillate. **~zi'one** f swinging; (di prezzi) fluctuation; Tech oscillation

oscura'mento m darkening; (di vista, mente) dimming; (totale) black-out

oscu'r|are vt darken; fig obscure. **~arsi** vr get dark. **~ità** f darkness. **o'scuro** adj dark; (triste) gloomy; (incomprensibile) obscure

ospe'dal|e m hospital. **~i'ero** adj hospital attrib

ospi'ta|le adj hospitable. **~lità** f hospitality. **~re** vt give hospitality to. **'ospite** m (chi ospita) host; (chi viene ospitato) guest • f hostess; guest

o'spizio m [old people's] home

ossa'tura f bone structure; (di romanzo) structure, framework. **'osseo** adj bone attrib

ossequi|'are vt pay one's respects to. **os'sequio** m homage; **ossequi** pl respects. **~'oso** adj obsequious

osser'van|te adj (cattolico) practising. **~za** f observance

osser'va|re vt observe; (notare) notice; keep (ordine, silenzio). **~'tore, ~'trice** mf observer. **~'torio** m (Astr) observatory; (Mil) observation post. **~zi'one** f observation; (rimprovero) reproach

ossessio'na|nte adj haunting; (persona) nagging. **~re** vt obsess; (infastidire) nag. **ossessi'one** f obsession. **osses'sivo** adj obsessive. **os'sesso** adj obsessed

os'sia conj that is

ossi'dabile adj liable to tarnish

ossi'dar|e vt, **~si** vr oxidize

'ossido m oxide. **~ di carbonio** carbon monoxide

os'sidrico adj **fiamma ossidrica** blowlamp

ossige'nar|e vt oxygenate; (decolorare) bleach; fig put back on its feet (azienda). **~si** vr **~si i capelli** dye one's hair blonde. **os'sigeno** m oxygen

'osso m ((Anat): pl f **ossa**) bone; (di frutto) stone

osso'buco m marrowbone

os'suto adj bony

ostaco'lare vt hinder, obstruct. **o'stacolo** m obstacle; Sport hurdle

o'staggio m hostage; **prendere in ~** take hostage

o'stello m **~ della gioventù** youth hostel

osten'ta|re vt show off; **~re indifferenza** pretend to be indifferent. **~zi'one** f ostentation

oste'ria f inn

o'stetrico, -a adj obstetric • mf obstetrician

'ostia f host; (cialda) wafer

'ostico adj tough

o'stil|e adj hostile. **~ità** f inv hostility

osti'na|rsi vr persist (**a** in). **~to** adj obstinate. **~zi'one** f obstinacy

'ostrica f oyster

ostru|'ire vt obstruct. **~zi'one** f obstruction

otorinolaringoi'atra mf ear, nose and throat specialist

ottago'nale adj octagonal. **ot'tagono** m octagon

ot'tan|ta adj & m eighty. **~'tenne** adj & mf eighty-year-old. **~'tesimo** adj eightieth. **~'tina** f about eighty

ot'tav|a f octave. **~o** adj eighth

otte'nere vt obtain; (più comune) get; (conseguire) achieve

'ottico, -a adj optic[al] • mf optician • f (scienza) optics sg; (di lenti ecc) optics pl

otti'ma|le adj optimum. **~'mente** adv very well

otti'mis|mo m optimism. **~ta** mf optimist. **~tico** adj optimistic

'ottimo adj very good • m optimum

'otto adj & m eight

ot'tobre m October

otto'cento adj & m eight hundred; **l'O~** the nineteenth century

ot'tone m brass

ottu'ra|re vt block; fill (dente). **~rsi** vr clog. **~'tore** m (Phot) shutter. **~zi'one** f stopping; (di dente) filling

ot'tuso pp di **ottundere** • adj obtuse

o'vaia f ovary

o'vale adj & m oval

o'vatta f cotton wool

ovazi'one f ovation

over'dose f inv overdose

'ovest m west

o'vi|le m sheep-fold. **~no** adj sheep attrib

ovo'via f two-seater cable car

ovulazi'one f ovulation

o'vunque adv = **dovunque**

ov'vero conj or; (cioè) that is

ovvia'mente adv obviously

ovvi'are vi **~ a qcsa** counter sth. **'ovvio** adj obvious

ozi'are vi laze around. **'ozio** m idleness. **ozi'oso** adj idle; (questione) pointless

o'zono m ozone; **buco nell'~** hole in the ozone layer

Pp

pa'ca|re vt quieten. **~to** adj quiet

pac'chetto m packet; (postale) parcel, package; (di sigarette) pack, packet. **~ software** software package

'pacchia f 🄸 bed of roses

pacchi'ano adj garish

'pacco m parcel; (involto) bundle. **~ regalo** gift-wrapped package

paccot'tiglia f junk, rubbish

'pace f peace; **darsi ~** forget it; **fare ~ con qcno** make it up with sb; **lasciare in ~ qcno** leave sb in peace

pachi'stano, -a mf & adj Pakistani

pacifi'ca|re vt reconcile; (mettere pace) pacify. **~zi'one** f reconciliation

pa'cifico adj pacific; (calmo) peaceful; **il P~** the Pacific

paci'fis|mo m pacifism. **~ta** mf pacifist

pa'dano adj **pianura padana** Po Valley

pa'del|la f frying-pan; (per malati) bedpan

padigli'one m pavilion

'padr|e m father; **~i** pl (antenati) forefathers. **pa'drino** m godfather. **~e'nostro** m **il ~enostro** the Lord's Prayer. **~e'terno** m God Almighty

padro'nanza f mastery. **~ di sé** self-control

pa'drone, -a mf master; mistress; (datore di lavoro) boss; (proprietario) owner. **~ggi'are** vt master

pae'sag|gio m scenery; (pittura)

landscape. ~'**gista** mf landscape architect

pae'sano, -a adj country • mf villager

pa'ese m (nazione) country; (territorio) land; (villaggio) village; **il Bel P~** Italy; **va' a quel ~!** get lost!; **Paesi** pl **Bassi** Netherlands

paf'futo adj plump

'paga f pay, wages pl

pa'gabile adj payable

pa'gaia f paddle

paga'mento m payment; **a ~** (parcheggio) which you have to pay to use. **~ anticipato** (Comm) advance payment. **~ alla consegna** cash on delivery, COD

pa'gano, -a adj & mf pagan

pa'gare vt/i pay; **~ da bere a qcno** buy sb a drink

pa'gella f [school] report

'pagina f page. **Pagine** pl **Gialle®** Yellow Pages. **~ web** (Comput) web page

'paglia f straw

pagliac'cetto m (per bambini) rompers pl

pagliac'ciata f farce

pagli'accio m clown

pagli'aio m haystack

paglie'riccio m straw mattress

pagli'etta f (cappello) boater; (per pentole) steel wool

pagli'uzza f wisp of straw; (di metallo) particle

pa'gnotta f [round] loaf

pail'lette f inv sequin

'paio m (pl f **paia**) pair; **un ~** (circa due) a couple; **un ~ di** (scarpe, forbici) a pair of

'Pakistan m Pakistan

'pala f shovel; (di remo, elica) blade; (di ruota) paddle

pala'fitta f pile-dwelling

pala'sport m inv indoor sports arena

pa'late fpl **a ~** (fare soldi) hand over fist

pa'lato m palate

palaz'zetto m **~ dello sport** indoor sports arena

palaz'zina f villa

pa'lazzo m palace; (edificio) building. **~ delle esposizioni** exhibition centre. **~ di giustizia** law courts pl, courthouse. **~ dello sport** indoor sports arena

'palco m (pedana) platform; (Theat) box. ~[**'scenico**] m stage

pale'sar|e vt disclose. **~si** vr reveal oneself. **pa'lese** adj evident

Pale'sti|na f Palestine. ~'**nese** mf Palestinian

pa'lestra f gymnasium, gym; (ginnastica) gymnastics pl

pa'letta f spade; (per focolare) shovel. **~ [della spazzatura]** dustpan

pa'letto m peg

'palio m (premio) prize. ▣**il P~** horse-race held at Siena

paliz'zata f fence

'palla f ball; (proiettile) bullet; (!: bugia) porkie; **che palle!** ! this is a pain in the arse!. **~ di neve** snowball. **~ al piede** fig millstone round one's neck

pallaca'nestro f basketball

palla'mano f handball

pallanu'oto f water polo

palla'volo f volley-ball

palleggi'are vi (calcio) practise ball control; Tennis knock up

pallia'tivo m palliative

'pallido adj pale

pal'lina f (di vetro) marble

pal'lino m **avere il ~ del calcio** be crazy about football

pallon'cino m balloon; (lanterna) Chinese lantern; (!: etilometro) Breathalyzer®

pal'lone m ball; (calcio) football; (aerostato) balloon

pal'lore m pallor

pal'loso adj ☒ boring

pal'lottola f pellet; (proiettile) bullet

'palm|a f (Bot) palm. **~o** m (Anat) palm; (misura) hand's-breadth; **restare con un ~o di naso** feel disappointed

pal'mare m palmtop

▣ *see* A-Z of Italian life and culture

P

'palo m pole; (di sostegno) stake; (in calcio) goalpost; **fare il ~** (ladro:) keep a lookout. **~ della luce** lamppost

palom'baro m diver

pal'pare vt feel

'palpebra f eyelid

palpi'ta|re vi throb; (fremere) quiver. **~zi'one** f palpitation. **'palpito** m throb; (del cuore) beat

pa'lude f marsh, swamp

palu'doso adj marshy

pa'lustre adj marshy; (piante, uccelli) marsh attrib

'pampino m vine leaf

'panca f bench; (in chiesa) pew

pancarré m sliced bread

pan'cetta f (Culin) bacon; (di una certa età) paunch

pan'chetto m [foot]stool

pan'china f garden seat; (in calcio) bench

'pancia f belly; **mal di ~** stomach-ache; **metter su ~** develop a paunch; **a ~ in giù** lying face down

panci'olle: **stare in ~** adv lounge about

panci'one m (persona) pot belly

panci'otto m waistcoat

P

pande'monio m pandemonium

pan'doro m sponge cake eaten at Christmas

'pane m bread; (pagnotta) loaf; (di burro) block. **~ a cassetta** sliced bread. **pan grattato** breadcrumbs pl. **~ di segale** rye bread. **pan di Spagna** sponge cake. **~ tostato** toast

panett|e'ria f bakery; (negozio) baker's [shop]. **~i'ere, -a** mf baker

panet'tone m kind of Christmas cake

'panfilo m yacht

pan'forte m nougat-like delicacy from Siena

'panico m panic; **lasciarsi prendere dal ~** panic

pani'ere m basket; (cesta) hamper

pani'ficio m bakery; (negozio) baker's [shop]

pa'nino m [bread] roll. **~ imbottito** filled roll. **~ al prosciutto** ham roll. **~'teca** f sandwich bar

'panna f cream. **~ da cucina** [single] cream. **~ montata** whipped cream

'panne f (Mech) **in ~** broken down; **restare in ~** break down

pan'nello m panel. **~ solare** solar panel

'panno m cloth; **panni** pl (abiti) clothes

pan'nocchia f (di granoturco) cob

panno'lino m (per bambini) nappy; (da donna) sanitary towel

pano'ram|a m panorama; fig overview. **~ico** adj panoramic

pantacol'lant mpl leggings

pantalon'cini mpl **~ [corti]** shorts

panta'loni mpl trousers, pants Am

pan'tano m bog

pan'tera f panther; (auto della polizia) high-speed police car

pan'tofo|la f slipper

pan'zana f fib

pao'nazzo adj purple

'papa m Pope

papà m inv dad[dy]

pa'pale adj papal

papa'lina f skull-cap

papa'razzo m paparazzo

pa'pato m papacy

pa'pavero m poppy

'paper|a f (errore) slip of the tongue. **~o** m gosling

papil'lon m inv bow tie

pa'piro m papyrus

'pappa f (per bambini) pap

pappa'gallo m parrot

pappa'molle mf wimp

'para f **suole** fpl **di ~** crêpe soles

pa'rabola f parable; (curva) parabola. **~ satellitare** satellite dish

para'bolico adj parabolic

para'brezza m inv windscreen, windshield Am

paracadu'tar|e vt parachute. **~si** vr parachute

paraca'du|te m inv parachute. **~'tista** mf parachutist

para'carro m roadside post

paradi'siaco adj heavenly

para'diso m paradise. **~ terrestre**

Eden, earthly paradise

parados'sale adj paradoxical. **para'dosso** m paradox

para'fango m mudguard

paraf'fina f paraffin

parafra'sare vt paraphrase

para'fulmine m lightning-conductor

pa'raggi mpl neighbourhood sg

parago'na|bile adj comparable (**a** to). **~re** vt compare. **para'gone** m comparison; **a paragone di** in comparison with

pa'ragrafo m paragraph

pa'ra|lisi f inv paralysis. **~'litico, -a** adj & mf paralytic. **~liz'zare** vt paralyse

paral'lel|a f parallel line. **~a'mente** adv in parallel. **~o** agg & m parallel; **~e** pl parallel bars. **~o'gramma** m parallelogram

para'lume m lampshade

para'medico m paramedic

pa'rametro m parameter

para'noia f paranoia

para'occhi mpl blinkers. **parao'recchie** mpl earmuffs

Paraolim'piadi fpl Paralympic Games

para'petto m parapet

para'piglia m turmoil

para'plegico, -a adj & mf paraplegic

pa'rar|e vt (addobbare) adorn; (riparare) shield; save (tiro, pallone); ward off, parry (schiaffo, pugno) •vi (mirare) lead up to. **~si** vr (abbigliarsi) dress up; (da pioggia, pugni) protect oneself; **~si dinanzi a qcno** appear in front of sb

para'sole m inv parasol

paras'sita adj parasitic •m parasite

parasta'tale adj government-controlled

pa'rata f parade; (in calcio) save; (in scherma, pugilato) parry

para'urti m inv (Auto) bumper, fender Am

para'vento m screen

par'cella f bill

parcheggi'a|re vt park. **par'cheggio** m parking; (posteggio) carpark, parking lot Am. **~'tore, ~'trice** mf parking attendant. **~tore abusivo** person extorting money for guarding cars

par'chimetro m parking-meter

'parco[1] adj sparing; (moderato) moderate

'parco[2] m park. **~ a tema** theme park. **~ di divertimenti** fun-fair. **~ giochi** playground. **~ naturale** wildlife park. 🅲 **~ nazionale** national park. **~ regionale** [regional] wildlife park

pa'recchi adj a good many •pron several

pa'recchio adj quite a lot of •pron quite a lot •adv rather; (parecchio tempo) quite a time

pareggi'are vt level; (eguagliare) equal; (Comm) balance •vi draw

pa'reggio m (Comm) balance; Sport draw

paren'tado m relatives pl; (vincolo di sangue) relationship

pa'rente mf relative. **~ stretto** close relation

paren'tela f relatives pl; (vincolo di sangue) relationship

pa'rentesi f inv parenthesis; (segno grafico) bracket; (fig: pausa) break. **~** pl **graffe** curly brackets. **~ quadre** square brackets. **~ tonde** round brackets

pa'reo m sarong

pa'rere[1] m opinion; **a mio ~** in my opinion

pa'rere[2] vi seem; (pensare) think; **che te ne pare?** what do you think of it?; **pare di sì** it seems so

pa'rete f wall; (in alpinismo) face. **~ divisoria** partition wall

'pari adj inv equal; (numero) even; **andare di ~ passo** keep pace; **arrivare ~** draw; **~ ~** (copiare, ripetere) word for word •mf inv equal; **ragazza alla ~** au pair [girl] •m (titolo nobiliare) peer

Pa'rigi f Paris

pa'riglia f pair

pari|tà f equality; Tennis deuce. **~'tario** adj parity attrib

parlamen'tare adj parliamentary

P

🅲 *see* A-Z of Italian life and culture

•mf Member of Parliament •vi discuss. **Parla'mento** m Parliament. **il Parlamento europeo** the European Parliament

par'la|re vt/i speak, talk; (confessare) talk; ~ **bene/male di qcno** speak well/ill of somebody; **non parliamone più** let's forget about it; **non se ne parla nemmeno!** don't even mention it!. **~to** adj (lingua) spoken. **~'torio** m parlour; (in prigione) visiting room

parlot'tare vi mutter. **parlot'tio** m muttering

parmigi'ano m Parmesan

paro'dia f parody

pa'rola f word; (facoltà) speech; **parole** pl (di canzone) words, lyrics; **rivolgere la ~ a** address; **dare a qcno la propria ~** give sb one's word; **in parole povere** crudely speaking. **parole** pl **crociate** crossword [puzzle] sg. ~ **d'ordine** password. **paro'laccia** f swear-word

par'quet m inv (pavimento) parquet flooring

par'rocchi|a f parish. **~'ale** adj parish attrib. **~'ano, -a** mf parishioner. **'parr'oco** m parish priest

par'rucca f wig

parrucchi'ere, -a mf hairdresser

parruc'chino m toupée, hairpiece

parsi'moni|a f thrift

'parso pp di **parere**

'parte f part; (lato) side; (partito) party; (porzione) share; **a ~** apart from; **in ~** in part; **la maggior ~ di** the majority of; **d'altra ~** on the other hand; **da ~** aside; (in disparte) to one side; **farsi da ~** stand aside; **da ~ di** from; (per conto di) on behalf of; **è gentile da ~ tua** it is kind of you; **fare una brutta ~ a qcno** behave badly towards sb; **da che ~ è...?** whereabouts is...?; **da una ~..., dall'altra...** on the one hand..., on the other hand...; **dall'altra ~ di** on the other side of; **da nessuna ~** nowhere; **da tutte le parti** (essere) everywhere; **da questa ~** (in questa direzione) this way; **da un anno a questa ~** for about a year now; **essere dalla ~ di qcno** be on sb's side; **essere ~ in causa** be involved; **prendere ~ a** take part in. ~ **civile** plaintiff

parteci'pante mf participant

parteci'pa|re vi **~re a** participate in, take part in; (condividere) share in. **~zi'one** f participation; (annuncio) announcement; Fin shareholding; (presenza) presence. **par'tecipe** adj participating

parteggi'are vi ~ **per** side with

par'tenza f departure; Sport start; **in ~ per** leaving for

parti'cella f particle

parti'cipio m participle

partico'lar|e adj particular; (privato) private •m detail, particular; **fin nei minimi ~i** down to the smallest detail. **~eggi'ato** adj detailed. **~ità** f inv particularity; (dettaglio) detail

partigi'ano, -a adj & mf partisan

par'tire vi leave; (aver inizio) start; **a ~ da** [beginning] from

par'tita f game; (incontro) match; (Comm) lot; (contabilità) entry. ~ **di calcio** football match. ~ **a carte** game of cards

par'tito m party; (scelta) choice; (occasione di matrimonio) match

'parto m childbirth; **un ~ facile** an easy birth o labour; **dolori** pl **del ~** labour pains. ~ **cesareo** Caesarian section. **~'rire** vt give birth to

par'venza f appearance

parzi'al|e adj partial. **~ità** f partiality. **~'mente** adv (non completamente) partially; **~mente scremato** semi-skimmed

pasco'lare vt graze. **'pascolo** m pasture

'Pasqua f Easter. **pa'squale** adj Easter attrib

'passa: **e ~** adv (e oltre) plus

pas'sabile adj passable

pas'saggio m passage; (traversata) crossing; Sport pass; (su veicolo) lift; **essere di ~** be passing through. ~ **a livello** level crossing, grade crossing Am. ~ **pedonale** pedestrian crossing

pas'sante mf passer-by •m (di cintura) loop •adj Tennis passing

passa'porto m passport

pas'sa|re vi pass; (attraversare) pass through; (far visita) call; (andare) go; (essere approvato) be passed; **~re alla storia** go down in history; **mi è ~to di mente** it slipped my mind; **~re per un genio/idiota** be taken for a genius/an idiot • vt (far scorrere) pass over; (sopportare) go through; (al telefono) put through; (Culin) strain; **~re di moda** go out of fashion; **le passo il signor Rossi** I'll put you through to Mr Rossi; **~rsela bene** be well off; **come te la passi?** how are you doing?. **~ta** f (di vernice) coat; (spolverata) dusting; (occhiata) look

passa'tempo m pastime

pas'sato adj past; **l'anno ~** last year; **sono le tre passate** it's past o after three o'clock • m past; (Culin) purée; (Gram) past tense. **~ prossimo** (Gram) present perfect. **~ remoto** (Gram) [simple] past. **~ di verdure** cream of vegetable soup

passaver'dure m inv food mill

passeg'gero, -a adj passing • mf passenger

passeggi'a|re vi walk, stroll. 🅲 **~ta** f walk, stroll; (luogo) public walk; (in bicicletta) ride; **fare una ~ta** go for a walk

passeg'gino m pushchair, stroller Am

pas'seggio m walk; (luogo) promenade; **andare a ~** go for a walk; **scarpe da ~** walking shoes

passe-partout m inv master-key

passe'rella f gangway; (Aeron) boarding bridge; (per sfilate) catwalk

'passero m sparrow. **passe'rotto** m (passero) sparrow

pas'sibile adj **~ di** liable to

passio'nale adj passionate. **passi'one** f passion

pas'sivo adj passive • m passive; (Comm) liabilities pl; **in ~** (bilancio) loss-making

pass magnetico m inv swipe card

'passo m step; (orma) footprint; (andatura) pace; (brano) passage; (valico) pass; **a due passi da qui** a stone's throw away; **a ~ d'uomo** at walking pace; **fare due passi** go for a stroll; **di pari ~** fig hand in hand. **~ carrabile, ~ carraio** driveway

🅲 **'past|a** f (impasto per pane ecc) dough; (per dolci, pasticcino) pastry; (pastasciutta) pasta; (massa molle) paste; fig nature. **~a frolla** shortcrust pastry. **pa'stella** f batter

pastasci'utta f pasta

pa'stello m pastel

pa'sticca f pastille; (ⓘ: pastiglia) pill

pasticc|e'ria f cake shop, patisserie; (pasticcini) pastries pl; (arte) confectionery

pasticci'are vi make a mess • vt make a mess of

pasticci'ere, -a mf confectioner

pastic'cino m little cake

pa'sticci|o m (Culin) pie; (lavoro disordinato) mess. **~'one, -a** mf bungler • adj bungling

pasti'ficio m pasta factory

pa'stiglia f (Med) pill, tablet; (di menta) sweet. **~ dei freni** brake pad

'pasto m meal

pasto'rale adj pastoral. **pa'store** m shepherd; (Relig) pastor. **pastore tedesco** German shepherd

pastoriz'za|re vt pasteurize. **~zi'one** f pasteurization

pa'stoso adj doughy; fig mellow

pa'stura f pasture; (per pesci) bait

pa'tacca f (macchia) stain; (fig: oggetto senza valore) piece of junk

pa'tata f potato. **patate** pl **fritte** chips Br, French fries. **pata'tine** fpl [potato] crisps, chips Am

pata'trac m inv (crollo) crash

pâté m inv pâté

pa'tella f limpet

pa'tema m anxiety

pa'tente f licence. **~ di guida** driving licence

pater'na|le f scolding. **~'lista** m paternalist

paternità f paternity. **pa'terno** adj paternal; (affetto ecc) fatherly

pa'tetico adj pathetic. **'pathos** m pathos

pa'tibolo m gallows sg

🅲 see A-Z of Italian life and culture

P

'patina f patina; (sulla lingua) coating

pa'ti|re vt/i suffer. **~to, -a** adj suffering • mf fanatic. **~to della musica** music lover

patolo'gia f pathology. **pato'logico** adj pathological

'patria f native land

patri'arca m patriarch

pa'trigno m stepfather

patrimoni'ale adj property attrib. **patri'monio** m estate

patri'o|ta mf patriot

pa'trizio, -a adj & mf patrician

patro|ci'nare vt support. **~'cinio** m support

patro'nato m patronage. **pa'trono** m (Relig) patron saint; (Jur) counsel

'patta[1] f (di tasca) flap

'patta[2] f (pareggio) draw

patteggi|a'mento m bargaining. **~'are** vt/i negotiate

patti'naggio m skating. **~ su ghiaccio** ice skating. **~ a rotelle** roller skating

patti'na|re vi skate; (auto:) skid. **~'tore, ~'trice** mf skater. **'pattino** m skate; (Aeron) skid. **pattino da ghiaccio** iceskate. **pattino a rotelle** roller skate; **pattini** mpl **in linea** roller blades®.

'patto m deal; (Pol) pact; **a ~ che** on condition that

pat'tuglia f patrol. **~ stradale** patrol car; highway patrol

pattu'ire vt negotiate

pattumi'era f dustbin, trashcan Am

pa'ura f fear; (spavento) fright; **aver ~** be afraid; **mettere ~ a** frighten. **pau'roso** adj (che fa paura) frightening; (che ha paura) fearful; ([!]: enorme) awesome

'pausa f pause; (nel lavoro) break; **fare una ~** pause; (nel lavoro) have a break

pavimen'ta|re vt pave (strada). **~zi'one** f (operazione) paving. **pavi'mento** m floor

pa'vone m peacock

pazien'tare vi be patient

pazi'ente adj & mf patient. **~'mente** adv patiently. **pazi'enza** f patience

'pazza f madwoman. **~'mente** adv madly

paz'z|esco adj foolish; (esagerato) crazy. **~ia** f madness; (azione) [act of] folly. **'pazzo** adj mad; fig crazy • m madman; **essere pazzo di/per** be crazy about; **darsi alla pazza gioia** live it up. **paz'zoide** adj whacky

'pecca f fault; **senza ~** flawless. **peccami'noso** adj sinful

pec'ca|re vi sin; **~re di** be guilty of (ingratitudine). **~to** m sin; **~to che...** it's a pity that...; **[che] ~to!** [what a] pity!. **~'tore, ~'trice** mf sinner

'pece f pitch

'peco|ra f sheep. **~ra nera** black sheep. **~'raio** m shepherd. **~'rella** f **cielo a ~relle** sky full of fluffy white clouds. **~'rino** m (formaggio) sheep's milk cheese

peculi'ar|e adj **~ di** peculiar to. **~ità** f inv peculiarity

pe'daggio m toll

pedago'gia f pedagogy. **peda'gogico** adj pedagogical

peda'lare vi pedal. **pe'dale** m pedal. **pedalò** m inv pedalo

pe'dana f footrest; Sport springboard

pe'dante adj pedantic. **~'ria** f pedantry. **pedan'tesco** adj pedantic

pe'data f (in calcio) kick; (impronta) footprint

pede'rasta m pederast

pe'destre adj pedestrian

pedi'atra mf paediatrician. **pedia'tria** f paediatrics sg

pedi'cure mf inv chiropodist, podiatrist Am • m pedicure

pedi'gree m inv pedigree

pe'dina f (nella dama) piece; fig pawn. **~'mento** m shadowing. **pedi'nare** vt shadow

pe'dofilo, -a mf paedophile

pedo'nale adj pedestrian. **pe'done, -a** mf pedestrian

peeling m inv exfoliation treatment

'peggio adv worse; **~ per te!** too bad!; **la persona ~ vestita** the worst-dressed person • adj worse; **niente di ~** nothing worse • m **il ~ è che...** the worst of it is that...; **pensare al ~** think the worst • f **alla ~** at worst; **avere la ~** get the worst of it; **alla meno ~** as best I can

peggiora'mento m worsening

peggio'ra|re vt make worse, worsen • vi get worse. **~'tivo** adj pejorative

peggi'ore adj worse; (superlativo) worst • mf **il/la ~** the worst

'pegno m pledge; (nei giochi di società) forfeit; fig token

pelan'drone m slob

pe'la|re vt (spennare) pluck; (spellare) skin; (sbucciare) peel; ([!]: spillare denaro) fleece. **~rsi** vr [!] lose one's hair. **~to** adj bald. **~ti** mpl (pomodori) peeled tomatoes

pel'lame m skins pl

'pelle f skin; (cuoio) leather; (buccia) peel; **avere la ~ d'oca** have goose-flesh

pellegri'naggio m pilgrimage. **pelle'grino, -a** mf pilgrim

pelle'rossa mf Red Indian

pellette'ria f leather goods pl

pelli'cano m pelican

pellicc|e'ria f furrier's [shop]. **pel'licc'ia** f fur; (indumento) fur coat. **~i'aio, -a** mf furrier

pel'licola f film. **~ [trasparente]** cling film

'pelo m hair; (di animale) coat; (di lana) pile; **per un ~** by the skin of one's teeth. **pe'loso** adj hairy

'peltro m pewter

pe'luche m: **giocattolo di ~** soft toy

pe'luria f down

'pelvico adj pelvic

'pena f (punizione) punishment; (sofferenza) pain; (dispiacere) sorrow; (disturbo) trouble; **a mala ~** hardly; **mi fa ~** I pity him; **vale la ~ andare** it is worth [while] going. **~ di morte** death sentence

pe'nal|e adj criminal; **diritto** m **~e** criminal law. **~ità** f inv penalty

penaliz'za|re vt penalize. **~zi'one** f (penalità) penalty

pe'nare vi suffer; (faticare) find it difficult

pen'daglio m pendant

pen'dant m inv **fare ~ [con]** match

pen'den|te adj hanging; (Comm) outstanding • m (ciondolo) pendant; **~ti** pl drop earrings. **~za** f slope; (Comm) outstanding account

'pendere vi hang; (superficie:) slope; (essere inclinato) lean

pen'dio m slope; **in ~** sloping

pendo'l|are adj pendulum • mf commuter. **~ino** m (treno) special, first class only, fast train

'pendolo m pendulum

'pene m penis

pene'trante adj penetrating; (freddo) biting

pene'tra|re vt/i penetrate; (trafiggere) pierce • vt (odore:) get into • vi (entrare furtivamente) steal in. **~zi'one** f penetration

penicil'lina f penicillin

pe'nisola f peninsula

peni'ten|te adj & mf penitent. **~za** f penitence; (in gioco) forfeit. **~zi'ario** m penitentiary

'penna f pen; (di uccello) feather. **~ a feltro** felt-tip[ped pen]. **~ a sfera** ball-point [pen]

pen'nacchio m plume

penna'rello m felt-tip[ped pen]

pennel'la|re vt paint. **~ta** f brushstroke. **pen'nello** m brush; **a pennello** (alla perfezione) perfectly

pen'nino m nib

pen'none m flagpole

pen'nuto adj feathered

pe'nombra f half-light

pe'noso adj ([!]: pessimo) painful

pen'sa|re vi think; **penso di sì** I think so; **~re a** think of; remember to (chiudere il gas ecc); **ci penso io** I'll take care of it; **~re di fare qcsa** think of doing sth; **~re tra sé e sé** think to oneself • vt think. **~ta** f idea

pensi'e|ro m thought; (mente) mind; (preoccupazione) worry; **stare in ~ro per** be anxious about. **~'roso** adj pensive

'pensi|le adj hanging; **giardino ~le** roof-garden • m (mobile) wall unit. **~'lina** f bus shelter

pensio'nante mf boarder; (ospite pagante) lodger

pensio'nato, -a mf pensioner • m

(per anziani) [old folks'] home; (per studenti) hostel. **pensi'one** f pension; (albergo) boarding-house; (vitto e alloggio) board and lodging; **andare in pensione** retire; **mezza pensione** half board. **pensione completa** full board

pen'soso adj pensive

pen'tagono m pentagon

Pente'coste f Whitsun

pen'ti|rsi vr **~rsi di** repent of; (rammaricarsi) regret. **~'tismo** m turning informant. **~to** m Mafioso turned informant

'pentola f saucepan; (contenuto) potful. **~ a pressione** pressure cooker

pe'nultimo adj penultimate

pe'nuria f shortage

penzo'l|are vi dangle. **~oni** adv dangling

pe'pa|re vt pepper. **~to** adj peppery

'pepe m pepper; **grano di ~** peppercorn. **~ in grani** whole peppercorns. **~ macinato** ground pepper

pepero'n|ata f peppers cooked in olive oil with onion, tomato and garlic. **~'cino** m chilli pepper. **pepe'rone** m pepper. **peperone verde** green pepper

pe'pita f nugget

per prep for; (attraverso) through; (stato in luogo) in, on; (distributivo) per; (mezzo, entro) by; (causa) with; (in qualità di) as; **~ strada** on the street; **~ la fine del mese** by the end of the month; **in fila ~ due** in double file; **l'ho sentito ~ telefono** I spoke to him on the phone; **~ iscritto** in writing; **~ caso** by chance; **ho aspettato ~ ore** I've been waiting for hours; **~ tempo** in time; **~ sempre** forever; **~ scherzo** as a joke; **gridare ~ il dolore** scream with pain; **vendere ~ 10 milioni** sell for 10 million; **uno ~ volta** one at a time; **uno ~ uno** one by one; **venti ~ cento** twenty per cent; **~ fare qcsa** [in order to] do sth; **stare ~** be about to

'pera f pear; **farsi una ~** (⊠: di eroina) shoot up

per'cento adv per cent. **percentu'ale** f percentage

perce'pibile adj perceivable; (somma) payable

perce'pi|re vt perceive; (riscuotere) cash

perce|t'tibile adj perceptible. **~zi'one** f perception

perché conj (in interrogazioni) why; (per il fatto che) because; (affinché) so that; **~ non vieni?** why don't you come?; **dimmi ~** tell me why; **~ no/sì!** because!; **la ragione ~ l'ho fatto** the reason [that] I did it, the reason why I did it; **è troppo difficile ~ lo possa capire** it's too difficult for me to understand •m inv reason [why]; **senza un ~** without any reason

perciò conj so

per'correre vt cover (distanza); (viaggiare) travel. **per'corso** pp di **percorrere** •m (distanza) distance; (viaggio) journey

per'coss|a f blow. **~o** pp di **percuotere**. **percu'otere** vt strike

percussi'o|ne f percussion; **strumenti** pl **a ~ne** percussion instruments. **~'nista** mf percussionist

per'dente mf loser

'perder|e vt lose; (sprecare) waste; (non prendere) miss; fig: ruin; (vizio:) **~e tempo** waste time •vi lose; (recipiente:) leak; **lascia ~e!** forget it!. **~si** vr get lost; (reciproco) lose touch

perdigi'orno mf inv idler

'perdita f loss; (spreco) waste; (falla) leak; **a ~ d'occhio** as far as the eye can see. **~ di tempo** waste of time. **perdi'tempo** m time-waster

perdo'nare vt forgive; (scusare) excuse. **per'dono** m forgiveness; (Jur) pardon

perdu'rare vi last; (perseverare) persist

perduta'mente adv hopelessly. **per'duto** pp di **perdere** •adj lost; (rovinato) ruined

pe'renne adj everlasting; (Bot) perennial. **~'mente** adv perpetually

peren'torio adj peremptory

per'fetto adj perfect •m (Gram) perfect [tense]

perfezio'nar|e vt perfect; (migliorare) improve. **~si** vr improve oneself; (specializzarsi) specialize

perfezi'o|ne f perfection; **alla ~ne**

to perfection. ∼'**nista** mf perfectionist

per'fidia f wickedness; (atto) wicked act. '**perfido** adj treacherous; (malvagio) perverse

per'fino adv even

perfo'ra|re vt pierce; punch (schede); (Mech) drill. ∼'**tore,** ∼'**trice** mf punch-card operator •m perforator. ∼**zi'one** f perforation; (di schede) punching

per'formance f inv performance

perga'mena f parchment

perico'lante adj precarious; (azienda) shaky

pe'rico|lo m danger; (rischio) risk; **mettere in** ∼**lo** endanger. ∼'**loso** adj dangerous

perife'ria f periphery; (di città) outskirts pl; fig fringes pl

peri'feric|a f peripheral; (strada) ring road. ∼**o** adj (quartiere) outlying

pe'rifrasi f inv circumlocution

pe'rimetro m perimeter

peri'odico m periodical •adj periodical; (vento, mal di testa) (Math) recurring. **pe'riodo** m period; (Gram) sentence. **periodo di prova** trial period

peripe'zie fpl misadventures

pe'rire vi perish

pe'ri|to, -a adj skilled •mf expert

perito'nite f peritonitis

pe'rizia f skill; (valutazione) survey

perla f pearl. **per'lina** f bead

perlo'meno adv at least

perlu'stra|re vt patrol. ∼**zi'one** f patrol; **andare in** ∼**zione** go on patrol

perma'loso adj touchy

perma'ne|nte adj permanent •f perm; **farsi [fare] la** ∼**nte** have a perm. ∼**nza** f permanence; (soggiorno) stay; **in** ∼**nza** permanently. ∼**re** vi remain

perme'are vt permeate

per'messo pp di **permettere** •m permission; (autorizzazione) permit; (Mil) leave; **[è]** ∼**?** (posso entrare?) may I come in?; (posso passare?) excuse me. ∼ **di lavoro** work permit

per'mettere vt allow, permit; **potersi** ∼ **qcsa** (finanziariamente) afford sth; **come si permette?** how dare you?

permutazi'one f exchange; (Math) permutation

per'nic|e f partridge. ∼**i'oso** adj pernicious

'**perno** m pivot

pernot'tare vi stay overnight

'**pero** m pear-tree

però conj but; (tuttavia) however

pero'rare vt plead

perpendico'lare adj & f perpendicular

perpe'trare vt perpetrate

perpetu'are vt perpetuate. **per'petuo** adj perpetual

perplessità f inv perplexity; (dubbio) doubt. **per'plesso** adj perplexed

perqui'si|re vt search. ∼**zi'one** f search. ∼**zione domiciliare** search of the premises

persecu|'tore, -'trice mf persecutor. ∼**zi'one** f persecution

persegu'ire vt pursue

persegui'tare vt persecute

perseve'ra|nza f perseverance. ∼**re** vi persevere

persi'ano, -a adj Persian •f (di finestra) shutter. '**persico** adj Persian

per'sino adv = **perfino**

persi'sten|te adj persistent. ∼**za** f persistence. **per'sistere** vi persist

'**perso** pp di **perdere** •adj lost; **a tempo** ∼ in one's spare time

per'sona f person; (un tale) somebody; **di** ∼**, in** ∼ in person, personally; **per** ∼ per person, a head; **per interposta** ∼ through an intermediary; **persone** pl people

perso'naggio m personality; (Theat) character

perso'nal|e adj personal •m staff. ∼**e di terra** ground crew. ∼**ità** f inv personality. ∼**iz'zare** vt customize (auto ecc); personalize (penna ecc)

personifi'ca|re vt personify. ∼**zi'one** f personification

perspi'cace adj shrewd

P

persua|'dere vt convince; impress (critici); **~dere qcno a fare qcsa** persuade sb to do sth. **~si'one** f persuasion. **~'sivo** adj persuasive. **persu'aso** pp di **persuadere**

per'tanto conj therefore

'pertica f pole

perti'nente adj relevant

per'tosse f whooping cough

pertur'ba|re vt perturb. **~rsi** vr be perturbed. **~zi'one** f disturbance. **~zione atmosferica** atmospheric disturbance

per'va|dere vt pervade. **~so** pp di **pervadere**

perven'ire vi reach; **far ~ qcsa a qcno** send sth to sb

pervers|i'one f perversion. **~ità** f perversity. **per'verso** adj perverse

perver'ti|re vt pervert. **~to** adj perverted • m pervert

per'vinca m (colore) blue with a touch of purple

p.es. abbr (per esempio) e.g.

pesa f weighing; (bilancia) weighing machine; (per veicoli) weighbridge

pe'sante adj heavy; (stomaco) overfull • adv (vestirsi) warmly. **~'mente** adv (cadere) heavily. **pesan'tezza** f heaviness

pe'sar|e vt/i weigh; **~e su** fig lie heavy on; **~e le parole** weigh one's words. **~si** vr weigh oneself

'pesca¹ f (frutto) peach

'pesca² f fishing; **andare a ~** go fishing. **~ subacquea** underwater fishing. **pe'scare** vt fish for; (prendere) catch; (fig: trovare) fish out. **~'tore** m fisherman

'pesce m fish. **~ d'aprile!** April Fool!. **~ grosso** fig big fish. **~ piccolo** fig small fry. **~ rosso** goldfish. **~ spada** swordfish. **Pesci** pl (Astr) Pisces

pesce'cane m shark

pesche'reccio m fishing boat

pesc|he'ria f fishmonger's [shop]. **~hi'era** f fish-pond. **~i'vendolo** m fishmonger

'pesco m peach-tree

'peso m weight; **essere di ~ per qcno** be a burden to sb; **di poco ~** (senza importanza) not very important

pessi'mis|mo m pessimism. **~ta** mf pessimist • adj pessimistic. **'pessimo** adj very bad

pe'staggio m beating-up. **pe'stare** vt tread on; (schiacciare) crush; (picchiare) beat; crush (aglio, prezzemolo)

'peste f plague; (persona) pest

pe'stello m pestle

pesti'cida m pesticide

pesti'len|za f pestilence; (fetore) stench. **~zi'ale** adj noxious

'pesto adj ground; **occhio ~** black eye • m basil and garlic sauce

'petalo m petal

pe'tardo m banger

petizi'one f petition; **fare una ~** draw up a petition

petro|li'era f [oil] tanker. **~'lifero** adj oil-bearing. **pe'trolio** m oil

pettego|'lare vi gossip. **~'lezzo** m piece of gossip; **far ~lezzi** gossip

pet'tegolo, -a adj gossipy • mf gossip

petti'na|re vt comb. **~rsi** vr comb one's hair. **~'tura** f combing; (acconciatura) hair-style. **'pettine** m comb

'petting m petting

petti'nino m (fermaglio) comb

petti'rosso m robin

'petto m chest; (seno) breast; **a doppio ~** double-breasted

petto|'rale m (in gare sportive) number. **~'rina** f (di salopette) bib. **~'ruto** adj (donna) full-breasted; (uomo) broad-chested

petu'lante adj impertinent

'pezza f cloth; (toppa) patch; (rotolo di tessuto) roll

pez'zente mf tramp; (avaro) miser

'pezzo m piece; (parte) part; **un ~** (di tempo) some time; (di spazio) a long way; **al ~** (costare) each; **fare a pezzi** tear to shreds. **~ grosso** bigwig

pia'cente adj attractive

pia'ce|re
• m pleasure; (*favore*) favour; **a ~re** as much as one likes; **per ~re!** please!; **~re [di conoscerla]!** pleased to meet you!; **con ~re** with pleasure
• vi **la Scozia mi piace** I like Scotland; **mi piacciono i dolci** I like sweets; **ti piace?** do you like it?; **faccio come mi pare e piace** I do as I please; **lo spettacolo è piaciuto** the show was a success.

! Nota che il soggetto in italiano corrisponde al complemento oggetto in inglese, mentre il complemento indiretto in italiano corrisponde al soggetto in inglese: **non mi piace** I don't like it

ia'cevole adj pleasant

iaci'mento m **a ~** as much as you like

ia'dina f unleavened bread

i'aga f sore; scourge; (persona noiosa) pain; (fig: ricordo doloroso) wound

iagni'steo m whining

'agnuco'lare vi whimper

i'alla f plane. **pial'lare** vt plane

'ana f plane. **pianeggi'ante** adj level

ane'rottolo m landing

a'neta m planet

'angere vi cry; (disperatamente) weep • vt (lamentare) lament; (per un lutto) mourn

anifi'ca|re vt plan. **~zi'one** f planning

a'nista mf (Mus) pianist

'ano adj flat; (a livello) flush; (regolare) smooth; (facile) easy • adv slowly; (con cautela) gently; **andarci ~** go carefully • m plain; (di edificio) floor; (livello) plane; (progetto) plan; (Mus) piano; **di primo ~** first-rate; **primo ~** (Phot) close-up; **in primo ~** in the foreground. **~ regolatore** town plan. **~ di studi** syllabus

ano'forte m piano. **~ a coda** grand piano

ano'terra m inv ground floor

anta f plant; (del piede) sole; (disegno) plan; **di sana ~** (totalmente) entirely; **in ~ stabile** permanently. **~ stradale** road map. **~gi'one** f plantation

pian'tar|e vt plant; (conficcare) drive; ([!]: abbandonare) dump; **piantala!** [!] stop it!. **~si** vr plant oneself; ([!]: lasciarsi) leave each other

pianter'reno m ground floor

pi'anto pp di **piangere** • m crying; (disperato) weeping; (lacrime) tears pl

pian|to'nare vt guard. **~'tone** m guard

pia'nura f plain

p'iastra f plate; (lastra) slab; (Culin) griddle. **~ elettronica** circuit board. **~ madre** (Comput) motherboard

pia'strella f tile

pia'strina f (Mil) identity disc; (Med) platelet; (Comput) chip

piatta'forma f platform. **~ di lancio** launch pad

piat'tino m saucer

pi'atto adj flat • m plate; (da portata, vivanda) dish; (portata) course; (parte piatta) flat; (di giradischi) turntable; **piatti** pl (Mus) cymbals; **lavare i piatti** do the washing-up. **~ fondo** soup plate. **~ piano** [ordinary] plate

pi'azza f square; (Comm) market; **letto a una ~** single bed; **letto a due piazze** double bed; **far ~ pulita** make a clean sweep. **~'forte** m stronghold. **piaz'zale** m large square. **~'mento** m (in classifica) placing

piaz'za|re vt place. **~rsi** vr Sport be placed; **~rsi secondo** come second. **~to** adj (cavallo) placed; **ben ~to** (robusto) well built

piaz'zista m salesman

piaz'zuola f **~ di sosta** pull-in

pic'cante adj hot; (pungente) sharp; (salace) spicy

pic'carsi vr (risentirsi) take offence; **~ di** (vantarsi di) claim to

'picche fpl (in carte) spades

picchet'tare vt stake; (scioperanti:) picket. **pic'chetto** m picket

picchi'a|re vt beat, hit • vi (bussare) knock; (Aeron) nosedive; **~re in testa** (motore:) knock. **~ta** f beating;

P

(Aeron) nosedive; **scendere in ~ta** nosedive

picchiet'tare vt tap; (punteggiare) spot

'picchio m woodpecker

pic'cino adj tiny; (gretto) mean; (di poca importanza) petty • m little one, child

picci'one m pigeon

'picco m peak; **a ~** vertically; **colare a ~** sink

'piccolo, -a adj small, little; (di età) young; (di statura) short; (gretto) petty • mf child; **da ~** as a child

pic'co|ne m pickaxe. **~zza** f ice axe

pic'nic m inv picnic

pi'docchio m louse

piè m inv **a ~ di pagina** at the foot of the page; **saltare a ~ pari** skip

pi'ede m foot; **a piedi** on foot; **andare a piedi** walk; **a piedi nudi** barefoot; **a ~ libero** free; **in piedi** standing; **alzarsi in piedi** stand up; **ai piedi di** (montagna) at the foot of; **prendere ~** fig gain ground; (moda:) catch on; **mettere in piedi** (allestire) set up

piedi'stallo m pedestal

pi'ega f (piegatura) fold; (di gonna) pleat; (di pantaloni) crease; (grinza) wrinkle; (andamento) turn; **non fare una ~** (ragionamento:) be flawless

pie'ga|re vt fold; (flettere) bend • vi bend. **~rsi** vr bend. **~rsi a** fig yield to. **~'tura** f folding

pieghet'ta|re vt pleat. **~to** adj pleated. **pie'ghevole** adj pliable; (tavolo) folding • m leaflet

piemon'tese adj Piedmontese

pi'en|a f (di fiume) flood; (folla) crowd. **~o** adj full; (massiccio) solid; **in ~a estate** in the middle of summer; **a ~i voti** (diplomarsi) ≈ with A-grades, with first class honours • m (colmo) height; (carico) full load; **in ~o** (completamente) fully; **fare il ~o** (di benzina) fill up

pie'none m **c'era il ~** the place was packed

'piercing m inv body piercing

pietà f pity; (misericordia) mercy; **senza ~** (persona) pitiless; (spietatamente) pitilessly; **avere ~ di qcno** take pity on sb; **far ~** (far pena) be pitiful

pie'tanza f dish

pie'toso adj pitiful, merciful; (pessimo) terrible

pi'etr|a f stone. **~a dura** semi-precious stone. **~a preziosa** precious stone. **~a dello scandalo** cause of the scandal. **pie'trame** m stones pl. **~ifi'care** vt petrify. **pie'trina** f flint. **pie'troso** adj stony

pigi'ama m pyjamas pl

'pigia 'pigia m inv crowd, crush. **pigi'are** vt press

pigi'one f rent; **dare a ~** let, rent out; **prendere a ~** rent

pigli'are vt (!: afferrare) catch. **'piglio** m air

pig'mento m pigment

'pigna f cone

pi'gnolo adj pedantic

pigo'lare vi chirp. **pigo'lio** m chirping

pi'grizia f laziness. **'pigro** adj lazy; (intelletto) slow

'pila f pile; (Electr) battery; (!: lampadina tascabile) torch; (vasca) basin; **a pile** battery powered

pi'lastro m pillar

'pillola f pill; **prendere la ~** be on the pill

pi'lone m pylon; (di ponte) pier

pi'lota mf pilot • m (Auto) driver. **pilo'tare** vt pilot; drive (auto)

pinaco'teca f art gallery

pi'neta f pine-wood

ping-'pong m table tennis, ping-pong

'pingu|e adj fat. **~'edine** f fatness

pingu'ino m penguin; (gelato) choc ice on a stick

'pinna f fin; (per nuotare) flipper

'pino m pine[-tree]; **~ marittimo** cluster pine. **pi'nolo** m pine kernel

'pinta f pint

'pinza f pliers pl; (Med) forceps pl

pin'za|re vt (con pinzatrice) staple. **~'trice** f stapler

pin'zette fpl tweezers pl

pinzi'monio m sauce for crudités

'pio adj pious; (benefico) charitable

pi'oggia f rain; (fig: di pietre, insulti)

hail, shower; **sotto la ~** in the rain. **~ acida** acid rain

pi'olo m (di scala) rung

piom'ba|re vi fall heavily; **~re su** fall upon • vt fill (dente). **~'tura** f (di dente) filling. **piom'bino** m (sigillo) [lead] seal; (da pesca) sinker; (in gonne) weight

pi'ombo m lead; (sigillo) [lead] seal; **a ~** plumb; **senza ~** (benzina) lead-free

pioni'ere, -a mf pioneer

pi'oppo m poplar

pio'vano adj **acqua piovana** rainwater

pi'ov|ere vi rain; **~e** it's raining; **~iggi'nare** vi drizzle. **pio'voso** adj rainy

pipa f pipe

pipì f **fare [la] ~** pee

pipi'strello m bat

pi'ramide f pyramid

pi'ranha m inv piranha

pi'rat|a m pirate. **~a della strada** road-hog • adj inv pirate. **~e'ria** f piracy

pi'rofil|a f (tegame) oven-proof dish. **~o** adj heat-resistant

pi'romane mf pyromaniac

pi'roscafo m steamer. **~ di linea** liner

pi'scina f swimming pool. **~ coperta** indoor swimming pool. **~ scoperta** outdoor swimming pool

pi'sello m pea; (!: pene) willie

piso'lino m nap; **fare un ~** have a nap

pista f track; (Aeron) runway; (orma) footprint; (sci) slope, piste. **~ d'atterraggio** airstrip. **~ da ballo** dance floor. **~ ciclabile** cycle track

pi'stacchio m pistachio

pi'stola f pistol; (per spruzzare) spray-gun. **~ a spruzzo** paint spray

pi'stone m piston

pi'tone m python

pit'to|re, -'trice mf painter. **~'resco** adj picturesque. **pit'torico** adj pictorial

pit'tu|ra f painting. **~'rare** vt paint

più

• adv more; (*superlativo*) most

> **!** Il comparativo e il superlativo di aggettivi di una sillaba o che terminano in *-y* si formano con i suffissi *-er* e *-est*: **più breve** shorter **il più giovane** the youngest

~ importante more important; **il ~ importante** the most important; **~ caro** more expensive; **il ~ caro** the most expensive; **di ~** more; **una coperta in ~** an extra blanket; **non ho ~ soldi** I don't have any more money; **non vive ~ a Milano** he doesn't live in Milan any longer; **~ o meno** more or less; **il ~ lentamente possibile** as slowly as possible; **per di ~** what's more; **mai ~!** never again!; **~ di** more than; **sempre ~** more and more; (Math) plus

• adj more; (*superlativo*) most; **~ tempo** more time; **la classe con ~ alunni** the class with most pupils; **~ volte** several times

• m most; (Math) plus sign; **il ~ è fatto** the worst is over; **parlare del ~ e del meno** make small talk; **i ~** the majority

piuccheper'fetto m pluperfect

pi'uma f feather. **piu'maggio** m plumage. **piu'mino** m (di cigni) down; (copriletto) eiderdown; (per cipria) powder-puff; (per spolverare) feather duster; (giacca) down jacket. **piu'mone®** m duvet

piut'tosto adv rather; (invece) instead

pi'vello m ! greenhorn

'pizza f pizza; Cinema reel.

pizzai'ola f slices of beef in tomato sauce, oregano and anchovies

pizze'ria f pizza restaurant

pizzi'c|are vt pinch; (pungere) sting; (di sapore) taste sharp; (!: sorprendere) catch; (Mus) pluck • vi scratch; (cibo:) be spicy **'pizzico** m, **~otto** m pinch

'pizzo m lace; (di montagna) peak

pla'car|e vt placate; assuage (fame, dolore). **~si** vr calm down

'placca f plate; (commemorativa, dentale)

see A-Z of Italian life and culture

P

plaque; (Med) patch

plac'ca|re vt plate. **~to** adj **~to d'argento** silver-plated. **~to d'oro** gold-plated. **~'tura** f plating

pla'centa f placenta

'placido adj placid

plagi'are vt plagiarize; pressure (persona). **'plagio** m plagiarism

plaid m inv tartan rug

pla'nare vi glide

'plancia f (Naut) bridge; (passerella) gangplank

pla'smare vt mould

'plastic|a f (arte) plastic art; (Med) plastic surgery; (materia) plastic. **~o** adj plastic • m plastic model

'platano m plane[-tree]

pla'tea f stalls pl; (pubblico) audience

'platino m platinum

plau'sibil|e adj plausible. **~ità** f plausibility

ple'baglia f pej mob

pleni'lunio m full moon

'plettro m plectrum

pleu'rite f pleurisy

'plico m packet; **in ~ a parte** under separate cover

P

plissé adj inv plissé; (gonna) accordeon-pleated

plo'tone m platoon; (di ciclisti) group. **~ d'esecuzione** firing-squad

'plumbeo adj leaden

plu'ral|e adj & m plural; **al ~e** in the plural. **~ità** f majority

pluridiscipli'nare adj multidisciplinary

plurien'nale adj **~ esperienza** many years' experience

pluripar'titico adj (Pol) multi-party

plu'tonio m plutonium

pluvi'ale adj rain attrib

pneu'matico adj pneumatic • m tyre

pneu'monia f pneumonia

po' ▸**poco**

po'chette f inv clutch bag

po'chino m **un ~** a little bit

'poco

- adj little; (tempo) short; (*con nomi plurali*) few
- adv (*con verbi*) not much; (*con avverbi*) not very; **parla ~** he doesn't speak much; **lo conosco ~** I don't know him very well

> **!** **poco** + aggettivo spesso si traduce con un aggettivo specifico: **~ probabile** unlikely, **~ profondo** shallow

- pron little; (*poco tempo*) a short time; (*plurale*) few
- m little; **un po'** a little [bit]; **un po' di** a little, some; **a ~ a ~** little by little; **fra ~** soon; **per ~** (*a poco prezzo*) cheap; (*quasi*) nearly; **~ fa** a little while ago; **sono arrivato da ~** I have just arrived; **un bel po'** quite a lot

po'dere m farm

pode'roso adj powerful

'podio m dais; (Mus) podium

po'dis|mo m walking. **~ta** mf walker

po'e|ma m poem. **~'sia** f poetry; (componimento) poem. **~ta** m poet. **~'tessa** f poetess. **~tico** adj poetic

poggiapi'edi m inv footrest

poggi'a|re vt lean; (posare) place • vi **~re su** be based on. **~'testa** m inv head-rest

poggi'olo m balcony

'poi adv (dopo) then; (più tardi) later [on]; (finalmente) finally. **d'ora in ~** from now on; **questa ~!** well!

poiché conj since

pois m inv **a ~** polka-dot

'poker m poker

po'lacco, -a adj Polish • mf Pole • m (lingua) Polish

po'lar|e adj polar. **~iz'zare** vt polarize

'polca f polka

po'lemi|ca f controversy. **~ca'mente** adv controversially. **~co** adj controversial. **~z'zare** vi engage in controversy

po'lenta f cornmeal porridge

poli'clinico m general hospital

poli'estere m polyester

polio[mie'lite] f polio[myelitis]

'**polipo** m polyp
polisti'rolo m polystyrene
poli'tecnico m polytechnic
po'litic|a f politics sg; (linea di condotta) policy; **fare ~a** be in politics. **~iz'zare** vt politicize. **~o, -a** adj political • mf politician
poliva'lente adj catch-all
poli'zi|a f police. **~a giudiziaria** ≈ Criminal Investigation Department. **~a stradale** traffic police. **~'esco** adj police attrib; (romanzo, film) detective attrib. **~'otto** m policeman
'**polizza** f policy
pol'la|io m chicken run; (🅘: luogo chiassoso) mad house. **~me** m poultry. **~'strello** m spring chicken. **~stro** m cockerel
'**pollice** m thumb; (unità di misura) inch
'**polline** m pollen; **allergia al ~** hay fever
polli'vendolo, -a mf poulterer
'**pollo** m chicken; (🅘: semplicione) simpleton
polmo|'nare adj pulmonary. **pol'mone** m lung. **~'nite** f pneumonia
'**polo** m pole; Sport polo; (maglietta) polo top. **~ nord** North Pole. **~ sud** South Pole
Po'lonia f Poland
'**polpa** f pulp
pol'paccio m calf
polpa'strello m fingertip
pol'pet|ta f meatball. **~'tone** m meat loaf
'**polpo** m octopus
pol'sino m cuff
'**polso** m pulse; (Anat) wrist; fig authority; **avere ~** be strict
pol'tiglia f mush
pol'trire vi lie around
pol'tron|a f armchair; (Theat) seat in the stalls. **~e** adj lazy
'**polve|re** f dust; (sostanza polverizzata) powder; **in ~re** powdered; **sapone in ~re** soap powder. **~'rina** f (medicina) powder. **~riz'zare** vt pulverize; (nebulizzare) atomize. **~'rone** m cloud of dust. **~'roso** adj dusty
po'mata f ointment, cream
po'mello m knob; (guancia) cheek
pomeridi'ano adj afternoon attrib; **alle tre pomeridiane** at three in the afternoon. **pome'riggio** m afternoon
'**pomice** f pumice
'**pomo** m (oggetto) knob. **~ d'Adamo** Adam's apple
pomo'doro m tomato
'**pompa** f pump; (sfarzo) pomp. **pompe** pl **funebri** (funzione) funeral. **pom'pare** vt pump; (gonfiare d'aria) pump up; (fig: esagerare) exaggerate; **pompare fuori** pump out
pom'pelmo m grapefruit
pompi'ere m fireman; **i pompieri** the fire brigade
pom'poso adj pompous
ponde'rare vt ponder
po'nente m west
'**ponte** m bridge; (Naut) deck; (impalcatura) scaffolding; **fare il ~** make a long weekend of it
pon'tefice m pontiff
pontifi'ca|re vi pontificate. **~to** m pontificate
ponti'ficio adj papal
pon'tile m jetty
popò f inv 🅘 pooh
popo'lano adj of the people
popo'la|re adj popular; (comune) common • vt populate. **~rsi** vr get crowded. **~rità** f popularity. **~zi'one** f population. '**popolo** m people. **popo'loso** adj populous
'**poppa** f (Naut) stern; (mammella) breast; **a ~** astern
pop'pa|re vt suck. **~ta** f (pasto) feed. **~'toio** m [feeding-]bottle
popu'lista mf populist
por'cata f load of rubbish; **porcate** pl (🅘: cibo) junk food
porcel'lana f porcelain
porcel'lino m piglet. **~ d'India** guinea-pig
porche'ria f dirt; (cosa orrenda) piece of filth; (robaccia) rubbish
por'ci|le m pigsty. **~no** adj pig attrib • m (fungo) edible mushroom. '**porco** m pig; (carne) pork

🅒 *see* A-Z of Italian life and culture

'porgere vt give; (offrire) offer; **porgo distinti saluti** (in lettera) I remain, yours sincerely

porno|gra'fia f pornography. **~'grafico** adj pornographic

'poro m pore. **po'roso** adj porous

'porpora f purple

'por|re vt put; (collocare) place; (supporre) suppose; ask (domanda); present (candidatura); **poniamo il caso che...** let us suppose that...; **~re fine** o **termine a** put an end to. **~si** vr put oneself; **~si a sedere** sit down; **~si in cammino** set out

'porro m (Bot) leek; (verruca) wart

'porta f door; Sport goal; (di città) gate; (Comput) port. **~ a ~** door-to-door; **mettere alla ~** show sb the door. **~ di servizio** tradesmen's entrance

portaba'gagli m inv porter; (di treno ecc) luggage rack; (Auto) boot, trunk Am; (sul tetto di un'auto) roof rack

portabot'tiglie m inv bottle rack, wine rack

porta'cenere m inv ashtray

portachi'avi m inv keyring

porta'cipria m inv compact

portadocu'menti m inv document wallet

porta'erei f inv aircraft carrier

P

portafi'nestra f French window

porta'foglio m wallet; (per documenti) portfolio; (ministero) ministry

portafor'tuna m inv lucky charm •adj inv lucky

portagi'oie m inv jewellery box

por'tale m door

portama'tite m inv pencil case

porta'mento m carriage; (condotta) behaviour

porta'mina m inv propelling pencil

portamo'nete m inv purse

portaom'brelli m inv umbrella stand

porta'pacchi m inv roof rack; (su bicicletta) luggage rack

porta'penne m inv pencil case

por'ta|re vt (verso chi parla) bring; (lontano da chi parla) take; (sorreggere) (Math) carry; (condurre) lead; (indossare) wear; (avere) bear; **~re bene/male gli anni** look young/old for one's age. **~rsi** vr (trasferirsi) move; (comportarsi) behave

portari'viste m inv magazine rack

porta'sci m inv ski rack

portasiga'rette m inv cigarette-case

por'ta|ta f (di pranzo) course; (Auto) carrying capacity; (di arma) range; (fig: abilità) capability; **a ~ta di mano** within reach. **por'tatile** agg & m portable. **~to** adj (indumento) worn; (dotato) gifted; **essere ~to per qcsa** have a gift for sth; **essere ~to a** (tendere a) be inclined to. **~'tore, ~'trice** mf bearer; **al ~tore** to the bearer. **~tore di handicap** disabled person

portatovagli'olo m napkin ring

portau'ovo m inv egg-cup

porta'voce m inv spokesman •f inv spokeswoman

por'tento m marvel; (persona dotata) prodigy

'portico m portico

porti'er|a f door; (tendaggio) door curtain. **~e** m porter, doorman; Sport goalkeeper. **~e di notte** night porter

porti'n|aio, -a mf caretaker. **~e'ria** f concierge's room; (di ospedale) porter's lodge

'porto pp di **porgere** •m harbour; (complesso) port; (vino) port [wine]; (spesa di trasporto) carriage; **andare in ~** succeed. **~ d'armi** gun licence

Porto'g|allo m Portugal. **p~hese** adj & mf Portuguese

por'tone m main door

portu'ale m docker

porzi'one f portion

'posa f laying; (riposo) rest; (Phot) exposure; (atteggiamento) pose; **mettersi in ~** pose

po'sa|re vt put; (giù) put [down] •vi (poggiare) rest; (per un ritratto) pose. **~rsi** vr alight; (sostare) rest; (Aeron) land. **~ta** f piece of cutlery; **~te** pl cutlery sg. **~to** adj sedate

po'scritto m postscript

posi'tivo adj positive

posizio'nare vt position

posizi'one f position; **farsi una ~** get ahead

posolo'gia f dosage

po'spo|rre vt place after; (posticipare) postpone. **~sto** pp di **posporre**

posse'd|ere vt possess, own. **~i'mento** m possession

posses|'sivo adj possessive. **pos'sesso** m ownership; (bene) possession. **~'sore** m owner

pos'sibil|e adj possible; **il più presto ~e** as soon as possible •m **fare [tutto] il ~e** do one's best. **~ità** f inv possibility; (occasione) chance •fpl (mezzi) means

possi'dente mf land-owner

'posta f post, mail; (ufficio postale) post office; (al gioco) stake; **spese di ~** postage; **per ~** by post, by mail; **a bella ~** on purpose; **Poste e Telecomunicazioni** pl [Italian] Post Office. **~ elettronica** e-mail. **~ prioritaria** ≈ first-class mail. **~ vocale** voice-mail

posta'giro m postal giro

po'stale adj postal

postazi'one f position

postda'tare vt postdate (assegno)

posteggi'a|re vt/i park. **~'tore, ~'trice** mf parking attendant. **po'steggio** m car-park, parking lot Am; (di taxi) taxi-rank

'posteri mpl descendants. **~'ore** adj rear; (nel tempo) later **~tà** f posterity

po'sticcio adj artificial; (baffi, barba) false •m hair-piece

postici'pare vt postpone

po'stilla f note; (Jur) rider

po'stino m postman, mailman Am

'posto pp di **porre** •m place; (spazio) room; (impiego) job; (Mil) post; (sedile) seat; **a/fuori ~** in/out of place; **prendere ~** take up room; **sul ~** on-site; **essere a ~** (casa, libri) be tidy; **fare ~ a** make room for; **al ~ di** (invece di) in place of, instead of. **~ di blocco** checkpoint. **~ di guida** driving seat. **~ di lavoro** workstation. **posti** pl **in piedi** standing room. **~ di polizia** police station

post-'partum adj post-natal

'postumo adj posthumous •m after-effect

po'tabile adj drinkable; **acqua ~** drinking water

po'tare vt prune

po'tassio m potassium

po'ten|te adj powerful; (efficace) potent. **~za** f power; (efficacia) potency. **~zi'ale** adj & m potential

po'tere m power; **al ~** in power •vi can, be able to; **posso entrare?** may I come in?; **posso fare qualche cosa?** can I do something?; **che tu possa essere felice!** may you be happy!; **non ne posso più** (sono stanco) I can't go on; (sono stufo) I can't take any more; **può darsi** perhaps; **può darsi che sia vero** perhaps it's true; **potrebbe aver ragione** he could be right, he might be right; **avresti potuto telefonare** you could have phoned, you might have phoned; **spero di poter venire** I hope to be able to come

potestà f inv power

'pover|o, -a adj poor; (semplice) plain •m poor man •f poor woman; **i ~i** the poor. **~tà** f poverty

'pozza f pool. **poz'zanghera** f puddle

'pozzo m well; (minerario) pit. **~ petrolifero** oil-well

PP.TT. abbr (Poste e Telegrafi) [Italian] Post Office

prali'nato adj (mandorla, gelato) praline-coated

pram'matica f **essere di ~** be customary

pran'zare vi dine; (a mezzogiorno) lunch. 🅲 **'pranzo** m dinner; (a mezzogiorno) lunch. **pranzo di nozze** wedding breakfast

'prassi f standard procedure

prate'ria f grassland

'prati|ca f practice; (esperienza) experience; (documentazione) file; **avere ~ca di qcsa** be familiar with sth; **far ~ca** gain experience. **~'cabile** adj practicable; (strada) passable. **~ca'mente** adv practically. **~'cante** mf apprentice; (Relig) [regular] church-goer

prati'ca|re vt practise; (frequentare) associate with; (fare) make

praticità f practicality. **'pratico** adj practical; (esperto) experienced;

🅲 *see* A-Z of Italian life and culture

P

essere pratico di qcsa know about sth

'prato m meadow; (di giardino) lawn

pre'ambolo m preamble

preannunci'are vt give advance notice of

preavvi'sare vt forewarn. **preav'viso** m warning

pre'cario adj precarious

precauzi'one f precaution; (cautela) care

prece'den|te adj previous • m precedent. **~te'mente** adv previously. **~za** f precedence; (di veicoli) right of way; **dare la ~za** give way. **pre'cedere** vt precede

pre'cetto m precept

precipi'ta|re vt **~re le cose** precipitate events • vi fall headlong; (situazione, eventi:) come to a head. **~rsi** vr (gettarsi) throw oneself; (affrettarsi) rush; **~rsi a fare qcsa** rush to do sth. **~zi'one** f (fretta) haste; (atmosferica) precipitation. **precipi'toso** adj hasty; (avventato) reckless; (caduta) headlong

preci'pizio m precipice; **a ~** headlong

precisa'mente adv precisely

preci'sa|re vt specify; (spiegare) clarify. **~zi'one** f clarification

precisi'one f precision. **pre'ciso** adj precise; (ore) sharp; (identico) identical

pre'clu|dere vt preclude. **~so** pp di **precludere**

pre'coc|e adj precocious; (prematuro) premature

precon'cetto adj preconceived • m prejudice

pre'corr|ere vt **~ere i tempi** be ahead of one's time

precur'sore m precursor

'preda f prey; (bottino) booty; **essere in ~ al panico** be panic-stricken; **in ~ alle fiamme** engulfed in flames. **pre'dare** vt plunder. **~'tore** m predator

predeces'sore mf predecessor

pre'del|la f platform. **~'lino** m step

predesti'na|re vt predestine. **~to** adj (Relig) predestined, preordained

predetermi'nato adj predetermined, preordained

pre'detto pp di **predire**

'predica f sermon; fig lecture

predi'care vt preach

predi'le|tto, -a pp di **prediligere** • adj favourite • mf pet. **~zi'one** f predilection. **predi'ligere** vt prefer

pre'dire vt foretell

predi'spo|rre vt arrange. **~rsi** vr **~rsi a** prepare oneself for. **~sizi'one** f predisposition; (al disegno ecc) bent (**a** for). **~sto** pp di **predisporre**

predizi'one f prediction

predomi'na|nte adj predominant. **~re** vi predominate. **predo'minio** m predominance

pre'done m robber

prefabbri'cato adj prefabricated • m prefabricated building

prefazi'one f preface

prefe'renz|a f preference; **di ~a** preferably. **~i'ale** adj preferential; **corsia ~iale** bus and taxi lane

prefe'ribil|e adj preferable. **~'mente** adv preferably

prefe'ri|re vt prefer. **~to, -a** agg & mf favourite

pre'fet|to m prefect. **~'tura** f prefecture

pre'figgersi vr be determined

pre'fisso pp di **prefiggere** • m prefix; (Teleph) [dialling] code

pre'gare vt/i pray; (supplicare) beg; **farsi ~** need persuading

pre'gevole adj valuable

preghi'era f prayer; (richiesta) request

pregi'ato adj esteemed; (prezioso) valuable. **'pregio** m esteem; (valore) value; (di persona) good point; **di pregio** valuable

pregiudi'ca|re vt prejudice; (danneggiare) harm. **~to** adj prejudiced • m (Jur) previous offender

pregiu'dizio m prejudice; (danno) detriment

'prego int (non c'è di che) don't mention it!; (per favore) please; **~?** I beg your pardon?

pregu'stare vt look forward to

pre'lato m prelate

prela'vaggio m prewash

preleva'mento m withdrawal. **prele'vare** vt withdraw (denaro); collect (merci); (Med) take. **preli'evo** m (di soldi) withdrawal. **prelievo di sangue** blood sample

prelimi'nare adj preliminary • m **preliminari** pl preliminaries

pre'ludio m prelude

prema'man m inv maternity dress • adj maternity attrib

prema'turo, -a adj premature • mf premature baby

premedi'ta|re vt premeditate. **~zi'one** f premeditation

'premere vt press; (Comput) hit (tasto) • vi **~ a** (importare) matter to; **mi preme sapere** I need to know; **~ su** press on; push (pulsante)

pre'messa f introduction

pre'me|sso pp di **premettere. ~sso che** bearing in mind that. **~ttere** vt put forward; (mettere prima) put before.

premi'a|re vt give a prize to; (ricompensare) reward. **~zi'one** f prize giving

premi'nente adj pre-eminent

'premio m prize; (ricompensa) reward; (Comm) premium. **~ di consolazione** booby prize

premoni|'tore adj (sogno, segno) premonitory. **~zi'one** f premonition

premu'nir|e vt fortify. **~si** vr take protective measures; **~si di** provide oneself with; **~si contro** protect oneself against

pre'mu|ra f (fretta) hurry; (cura) care. **~'roso** adj thoughtful

prena'tale adj antenatal

'prender|e vt take; (afferrare) seize; catch (treno, malattia, ladro, pesce); have (cibo, bevanda); (far pagare) charge; (assumere) take on; (ottenere) get; (occupare) take up; **~e informazioni** make inquiries; **~e a calci/pugni** kick/punch; **quanto prende?** what do you charge?; **~e una persona per un'altra** mistake a person for someone else • vi (voltare) turn; (attecchire) take root; (rapprendersi) set; **~e a destra/sinistra** turn right/left; **~e a fare qcsa** start doing sth. **~si** vr **~si a pugni** come to blows; **~si cura di** take care of (ammalato)

prendi'sole m inv sundress

preno'ta|re vt book, reserve. **~to** adj booked, reserved **~zi'one** f booking, reservation

preoccu'pante adj alarming

preoccu'pa|re vt worry. **~rsi** vr **~rsi** worry (**di** about); **~rsi di fare qcsa** take the trouble to do sth. **~to** adj (ansioso) worried. **~zi'one** f worry; (apprensione) concern

prepa'gato adj prepaid

prepa'ra|re vt prepare. **~rsi** vr get ready. **~'tivi** mpl preparations. **~to** m (prodotto) preparation. **~'torio** adj preparatory. **~zi'one** f preparation

prepensiona'mento m early retirement

preponde'ran|te adj predominant. **~za** f prevalence

pre'porre vt place before

preposizi'one f preposition

pre'posto pp di **preporre** • adj **~ a** (addetto a) in charge of

prepo'ten|te adj overbearing • mf bully

preroga'tiva f prerogative

'presa f taking; (conquista) capture; (stretta) hold; (di cemento ecc) setting; (Electr) socket; (pizzico) pinch; **essere alle prese con** be struggling with; **a ~ rapida** (cemento, colla) quick-setting; **fare ~ su qcno** influence sb. **~ d'aria** air vent. **~ multipla** adaptor

pre'sagio m omen. **presa'gire** vt foretell

'presbite adj long-sighted

presbi'terio m presbytery

pre'scelto adj selected

pre'scindere vi **~ da** leave aside; **a ~ da** apart from

presco'lare adj **in età ~** pre-school

pre'scri|tto pp di **prescrivere**

pre'scri|vere vt prescribe. **~zi'one** f prescription; (norma) rule

preselezi'one f **chiamare qcno in ~** call sb via the operator

presen'ta|re vt present; (far conoscere)

introduce; show (documento); (inoltrare) submit. **~rsi** vr present oneself; (farsi conoscere) introduce oneself; (a ufficio) attend; (alla polizia ecc) report; (come candidato) stand, run; (occasione:) occur; **~rsi bene/male** (persona:) make a good/bad impression; (situazione:) look good/bad. **~'tore, ~'trice** mf presenter; (di notizie) announcer. **~zi'one** f presentation; (per conoscersi) introduction

pre'sente adj present; (attuale) current; (questo) this; **aver ~** remember •m present; **i presenti** those present •f **allegato alla ~** (in lettera) enclosed

presenti'mento m foreboding

pre'senza f presence; (aspetto) appearance; **in ~ di, alla ~ di** in the presence of; **di bella ~** personable. **~ di spirito** presence of mind

presenzi'are vi **~ a** attend

pre'sepe m, ■**pre'sepio** m crib

preser'va|re vt preserve; (proteggere) protect (**da** from). **~'tivo** m condom. **~zi'one** f preservation

'preside m headmaster; (Univ) dean •f headmistress; (Univ) dean

presi'den|te m chairman; (Pol) president •f chairwoman; (Pol) president. ■**~ del consiglio** [**dei ministri**] Prime Minister. ■**~ della repubblica** President of the Republic. **~za** f presidency; (di assemblea) chairmanship

presidi'are vt garrison. **pre'sidio** m garrison

presi'edere vt preside over

'preso pp di **prendere**

'pressa f (Mech) press

pres'sante adj urgent

pressap'poco adv about

pres'sare vt press

pressi'one f pressure. **~ del sangue** blood pressure

'presso prep near; (a casa di) with; (negli indirizzi) care of, c/o; (lavorare) for •**pressi** mpl: **nei pressi di...** in the neighbourhood o vicinity of...

pressoché adv almost

■ *see A-Z of Italian life and culture*

pressuriz'za|re vt pressurize. **~to** adj pressurized

prestabi'li|re vt arrange in advance. **~to** adj agreed

prestam'pato adj printed •m (modulo) form

pre'stante adj good-looking

pre'star|e vt lend; **~e attenzione** pay attention; **~e aiuto** lend a hand; **farsi ~e** borrow (**da** from). **~si** vr (frase:) lend itself; (persona:) offer

prestazi'one f performance; **prestazioni** pl (servizi) services

prestigia'tore, -'trice mf conjurer

pre'stigi|o m prestige; **gioco di ~o** conjuring trick. **~'oso** m prestigious

'prestito m loan; **dare in ~** lend; **prendere in ~** borrow

'presto adv soon; (di buon'ora) early; (in fretta) quickly; **a ~** see you soon; **al più ~** as soon as possible; **~ o tardi** sooner or later

pre'sumere vt presume; (credere) think

presu'mibile adj **è ~ che...** presumably,...

pre'sunto adj (colpevole) presumed

presun|tu'oso adj presumptuous. **~zi'one** f presumption

presup'po|rre vt suppose; (richiedere) presuppose. **~sizi'one** f presupposition. **~sto** m essential requirement

'prete m priest

preten'dente mf pretender •m (corteggiatore) suitor

pre'ten|dere vt (sostenere) claim; (esigere) demand •vi **~dere a** claim to; **~dere di** (esigere) demand to. **~si'one** f pretension. **~zi'oso** adj pretentious

pre'tes|a f pretension; (esigenza) claim; **senza ~e** unpretentious. **~o** pp di **pretendere**

pre'testo m pretext

pre'tore m magistrate

pre'tura f magistrate's court

preva'le|nte adj prevalent. **~nte'mente** adv primarily. **~nza** f prevalence. **~re** vi prevail

pre'valso pp di **prevalere**

preve'dere vt foresee; forecast (tempo); (legge ecc.) provide for

preve'nire vt precede; (evitare) prevent; (avvertire) forewarn

preven|ti'vare vt estimate; (aspettarsi) budget for. **~'tivo** adj preventive •m (Comm) estimate

preve'n|uto adj forewarned; (mal disposto) prejudiced. **~zi'one** f prevention; (preconcetto) prejudice

previ'den|te adj provident. **~za** f foresight. **~za sociale** social security, welfare Am. **~zi'ale** adj provident

'previo adj **~ pagamento** on payment

previsi'one f forecast; **in ~ di** in anticipation of

pre'visto pp di **prevedere** •adj foreseen •m **più/meno/prima del ~** more/less/earlier than expected

prezi'oso adj precious

prez'zemolo m parsley

'prezzo m price. **~ di fabbrica** factory price. **~ all'ingrosso** wholesale price. [**a**] **metà ~** half price

prigi'on|e f prison; (pena) imprisonment. **prigio'nia** f imprisonment. **~i'ero, -a** adj imprisoned •mf prisoner

'prima adv before; (più presto) earlier; (in primo luogo) first; **~, finiamo questo** let's finish this first; **~ o poi** sooner or later; **quanto ~** as soon as possible •prep **~ di** before; **~ d'ora** before now •conj **~ che** before •f first class; (Theat) first night; (Auto) first [gear]

pri'mario adj primary; (principale) principal

pri'mat|e m primate. **~o** m supremacy; Sport record

prima've|ra f spring. **~'rile** adj spring attrib

primeggi'are vi excel

primi'tivo adj primitive; (originario) original

pri'mizie fpl early produce sg

■ **'primo** adj first; (fondamentale) principal; (precedente di due) former; (iniziale) early; (migliore) best •m first; **primi** pl (i primi giorni) the beginning; **in un ~ tempo** at first. **prima copia** master copy

primordi'ale adj primordial

'primula f primrose

princi'pale adj main •m head, boss [!]

princi|'pato m principality. **'principe** m prince. **~'pessa** f princess

principi'ante mf beginner

prin'cipio m beginning; (concetto) principle; (causa) cause; **per ~** on principle

pri'ore m prior

priori|tà f inv priority. **~'tario** adj having priority

'prisma m prism

pri'va|re vt deprive. **~rsi** vr deprive oneself

privatizzazi'one f privatization. **pri'vato, -a** adj private •mf private citizen

privazi'one f deprivation

privilegi'are vt privilege; (considerare più importante) favour. **privi'legio** m privilege

'privo adj **~ di** devoid of; (mancante) lacking in

pro prep for •m advantage; **a che ~?** what's the point?

pro'babil|e adj probable. **~ità** f inv probability. **~'mente** adv probably

pro'ble|ma m problem. **~'matico** adj problematic

pro'boscide f trunk

procacci'ar|e vt, **~si** vr obtain

pro'cace adj (ragazza) provocative

pro'ced|ere vi proceed; (iniziare) start; **~ere contro** (Jur) start legal proceedings against. **~i'mento** m process; (Jur) proceedings pl. **proce'dura** f procedure

proces'sare vt (Jur) try

processi'one f procession

pro'cesso m process; (Jur) trial

proces'sore m processor

processu'ale adj trial

pro'cinto m **essere in ~ di** be about to

pro'clama m proclamation

■ *see* A-Z of Italian life and culture

P

procla'ma|re vt proclaim. **~zi'one** f proclamation

procreazi'one f procreation

pro'cura f power of attorney; **per ~** by proxy

procu'ra|re vt/i procure; (causare) cause; (cercare) try. **~'tore** m attorney. **~tore generale** Attorney General. **~tore legale** lawyer. **~tore della repubblica** public prosecutor

'prode adj brave. **pro'dezza** f bravery

prodi'gar|e vt lavish. **~si** vr do one's best

pro'digi|o m prodigy. **~'oso** adj prodigious

pro'dotto pp di **produrre** •m product. **prodotti agricoli** farm produce sg. **~ derivato** by-product. **~ interno lordo** gross domestic product. **~ nazionale lordo** gross national product

pro'du|rre vt produce. **~rsi** vr (attore:) play; (accadere) happen. **~ttività** f productivity. **~t'tivo** adj productive. **~t'tore, ~t'trice** mf producer. **~zi'one** f production

Prof. abbr (Professore) Prof.

profa'na|re vt desecrate

profe'rire vt utter

Prof.essa abbr (Professoressa) Prof.

P

profes'sare vt profess; practise (professione)

professio'nale adj professional

professi'o|ne f profession; **libera ~ne** profession. **~'nismo** m professionalism. **~'nista** mf professional

profes'sor|e, -'essa mf (Sch) teacher; (Univ) lecturer; (titolare di cattedra) professor

pro'fe|ta m prophet

pro'ficuo adj profitable

profi'lar|e vt outline; (ornare) border; (Aeron) streamline. **~si** vr stand out

profi'lattico adj prophylactic •m condom

pro'filo m profile; (breve studio) outline; **di ~** in profile

profit'tare vi **~ di** (avvantaggiarsi) profit by; (approfittare) take advantage of. **pro'fitto** m profit; (vantaggio) advantage

profond|a'mente adv deeply, profoundly. **~ità** f inv depth

pro'fondo adj deep; fig profound; (cultura) great

'profugo, -a mf refugee

profu'mar|e vt perfume. **~si** vr put on perfume

profu'mato adj (fiore) fragrant; (fazzoletto ecc) scented

profume'ria f perfumery. **pro'fumo** m perfume, scent

profusi'one f profusion; **a ~** in profusion. **pro'fuso** pp di **profondere** •adj profuse

proget|'tare vt plan. **~'tista** mf designer. **pro'getto** m plan; (di lavoro importante) project. **progetto di legge** bill

prog'nosi f inv prognosis; **in ~ riservata** on the danger list

pro'gramma m programme; (Comput) program. **~ scolastico** syllabus

program'ma|re vt programme; (Comput) program. **~'tore, ~'trice** mf [computer] programmer. **~zi'one** f programming

progre'dire vi [make] progress

progres|'sione f progression. **~'sivo** adj progressive. **pro'gresso** m progress

proi'bi|re vt forbid. **~'tivo** adj prohibitive. **~to** adj forbidden. **~zi'one** f prohibition

proie|t'tare vt project; show (film). **~t'tore** m projector; (Auto) headlight

proi'ettile m bullet

proiezi'one f projection

'prole f offspring. **prole'tario** agg & m proletarian

prolife'rare vi proliferate. **pro'lifico** adj prolific

pro'lisso adj verbose, prolix

'prologo m prologue

pro'lunga f (Electr) extension

prolun'gar|e vt prolong; (allungare) lengthen; extend (contratto, scadenza). **~si** vr continue; **~si su** (dilungarsi) dwell upon

prome'moria m inv memo; (per se stessi) reminder, note; (formale) memorandum

pro'me|ssa f promise. **~sso** pp di **promettere. ~ttere** vt/i promise

promet'tente adj promising

promi'nente adj prominent

promiscuità f promiscuity. **pro'miscuo** adj promiscuous

promon'torio m promontory

pro'mo|sso pp di **promuovere** • adj (Sch) who has gone up a year; (Univ) who has passed an exam. **~'tore, ~'trice** mf promoter

promozio'nale adj promotional. **promozi'one** f promotion

promul'gare vt promulgate

promu'overe vt promote; (Sch) move up a class

proni'pote m (di bisnonno) great-grandson; (di prozio) great-nephew • f (di bisnonno) great-granddaughter; (di prozio) great-niece

pro'nome m pronoun

pronosti'care vt forecast. **pro'nostico** m forecast

pron'tezza f readiness; (rapidità) quickness

'pronto adj ready; (rapido) quick; **~!** (Teleph) hello!; **tenersi ~** be ready (**per** for); **pronti, via!** (in gare) ready! steady! go!. **~ soccorso** first aid; (in ospedale) accident and emergency

prontu'ario m handbook

pro'nuncia f pronunciation

pronunci'a|re vt pronounce; (dire) utter; deliver (discorso). **~rsi** vr (su un argomento) give one's opinion. **~to** adj pronounced; (prominente) prominent

pro'nunzia ecc = **pronuncia** ecc

propa'ganda f propaganda

propa'ga|re vt propagate. **~rsi** vr spread. **~zi'one** f propagation

prope'deutico adj introductory

pro'pen|dere vi **~dere per** be in favour of. **~so** pp di **propendere** • adj **essere ~so a fare qcsa** be inclined to do sth

propi'nare vt administer

pro'pizio adj favourable

proponi'mento m resolution

pro'por|re vt propose; (suggerire) suggest. **~si** vr set oneself (obiettivo, meta); **~si di** intend to

proporzio'na|le adj proportional. **~re** vt proportion. **proporzi'one** f proportion

pro'posito m purpose; **a ~** by the way; **a ~ di** with regard to; **di ~** (apposta) on purpose

proposizi'one f clause; (frase) sentence

pro'post|a f proposal. **~o** pp di **proporre**

proprietà f inv property; (diritto) ownership; (correttezza) propriety. **~ immobiliare** property. **~ privata** private property. **proprie'taria** f owner; (di casa affittata) landlady. **proprie'tario** m owner; (di casa affittata) landlord

'proprio adj one's [own]; (caratteristico) typical; (appropriato) proper • adv just; (veramente) really; **non ~** not really, not exactly; (affatto) not... at all • pron one's own • m one's [own]; **lavorare in ~** be one's own boss; **mettersi in ~** set up on one's own

propul|si'one f propulsion. **~'sore** m propeller

'proroga f extension

proro'ga|bile adj extendable. **~re** vt extend

pro'rompere vi burst out

'prosa f prose. **pro'saico** adj prosaic

pro'scio|gliere vt release; (Jur) acquit. **~lto** pp di **prosciogliere**

prosciu'gar|e vt dry up; (bonificare) reclaim. **~si** vr dry up

prosci'utto m ham. **~ cotto** cooked ham. **~ crudo** Parma ham

pro'scri|tto, -a pp di **proscrivere** • mf exile

prosecuzi'one f continuation

prosegui'mento m continuation; **buon ~!** (viaggio) have a good journey!; (festa) enjoy the rest of the party!

prosegu'ire vt continue • vi go on, continue

prospe'r|are vi prosper. **~ità** f prosperity. **'prospero** adj prosperous; (favorevole) favourable. **~oso** adj flourishing; (ragazza) buxom

prospet'tar|e vt show. **~si** vr seem

prospet'tiva f perspective; (panorama) view; fig prospect. **pro'spetto** m (vista) view; (facciata) façade; (tabella) table

prospici'ente adj facing

prossima'mente adv soon

prossimità f proximity

'prossimo, -a adj near; (seguente) next; (molto vicino) close; **l'anno ~** next year • mf neighbour

prosti'tu|ta f prostitute. **~zi'one** f prostitution

protago'nista mf protagonist

pro'teggere vt protect; (favorire) favour

prote'ina f protein

pro'tender|e vt stretch out. **~si** vr (in avanti) lean out. **pro'teso** pp di **protendere**

pro'te|sta f protest; (dichiarazione) protestation. **~'stante** adj & mf Protestant. **~'stare** vt/i protest

prote|t'tivo adj protective. **~tto** pp di **proteggere**. **~t'tore, ~t'trice** mf protector; (sostenitore) patron • m (di prostituta) pimp. **~zi'one** f protection

protocol'lare adj (visita) protocol • vt register

proto'collo m protocol; (registro) register; **carta ~** official stamped paper

P

pro'totipo m prototype

pro'tra|rre vt protract; (differire) postpone. **~rsi** vr go on, continue. **~tto** pp di **protrarre**

protube'ran|te adj protuberant. **~za** f protuberance

'prova f test; (dimostrazione) proof; (tentativo) try; (di abito) fitting; Sport heat; (Theat) rehearsal; (bozza) proof; **in ~** (assumere) for a trial period; **mettere alla ~** put to the test. **~ generale** dress rehearsal

pro'var|e vt test; (dimostrare) prove; (tentare) try; try on (abiti ecc); (sentire) feel; (Theat) rehearse. **~si** vr try

proveni'enza f origin. **prove'nire** vi **provenire da** come from

pro'vento m proceeds pl

prove'nuto pp di **provenire**

pro'verbio m proverb

pro'vetta f test-tube; **bambino in ~** test-tube baby

pro'vetto adj skilled

'provider m inv ISP, Internet Service Provider

🅲 **pro'vinci|a** f province; (strada) B road, secondary road. **~'ale** adj provincial; **strada ~ale** B road

pro'vino m specimen; Cinema screen test

provo'ca|nte adj provocative. **~re** vt provoke; (causare) cause. **~'tore, ~'trice** mf trouble-maker. **~'torio** adj provocative. **~zi'one** f provocation

provve'd|ere vi **~ere a** provide for. **~i'mento** m measure; (previdenza) precaution

provvi'denz|a f providence. **~i'ale** adj providential

provvigi'one f commission

provvi'sorio adj provisional

prov'vista f supply

pro'zio, -a m great-uncle • f great-aunt

'prua f prow

pru'den|te adj prudent. **~za** f prudence; **per ~za** as a precaution

'prudere vi itch

'prugn|a f plum. **~a secca** prune. **~o** m plum[-tree]

pru'rito m itch.

pseu'donimo m pseudonym

psica'na|lisi f psychoanalysis. **~'lista** mf psychoanalyst. **~liz'zare** vt psychoanalyse

'psiche f psyche

psichi'a|tra mf psychiatrist. **~'tria** f psychiatry. **~trico** adj psychiatric

'psichico adj mental

psico|lo'gia f psychology. **~'lo-gico** adj psychological. **psi'cologo, -a** mf psychologist

psico'patico, -a mf psychopath

PT abbr (Posta e Telecomunicazioni) PO

pubbli'ca|re vt publish. **~zi'one** f publication. **~zioni** pl (di matrimonio) banns

pubbli'cista mf Journ correspondent

pubblicità f inv publicity; (annuncio) advertisement, advert; **fare ~ a**

🅲 *see* A-Z of Italian life and culture

qcsa advertise sth; **piccola ~** small advertisements. **pubblici'tario** adj advertising

'pubblico adj public; **scuola pubblica** state school • m public; (spettatori) audience; **grande ~** general public. **Pubblica Sicurezza** Police. **~ ufficiale** civil servant

'pube m pubis

pubertà f puberty

pu'dico adj modest

pue'rile adj children's; pej childish

pugi'lato m boxing. **'pugile** m boxer

pugna'la|re vt stab. **~ta** f stab. **pu'gnale** m dagger

'pugno m fist; (colpo) punch; (manciata) fistful; (numero limitato) handful; **dare un ~ a** punch

'pulce f flea; (microfono) bug

pul'cino m chick; (nel calcio) junior

pu'ledra f filly

pu'ledro m colt

pu'li|re vt clean. **~re a secco** dry-clean. **~to** adj clean. **~'tura** f cleaning. **~'zia** f (il pulire) cleaning; (l'essere pulito) cleanliness; **~zie** pl housework; **fare le ~zie** do the cleaning

'pullman m inv bus, coach; (urbano) bus

pul'mino m minibus

'pulpito m pulpit

pul'sante m button; (Electr) [push-]button. **~ di accensione** on/off switch

pul'sa|re vi pulsate. **~zi'one** f pulsation

pul'viscolo m dust

'puma m inv puma

pun'gente adj prickly; (insetto) stinging; (odore ecc) sharp

'punger|e vt prick; (insetto:) sting

pungigli'one m sting

pu'ni|re vt punish. **~'tivo** adj punitive. **~zi'one** f punishment; Sport free kick

'punta f point; (estremità) tip; (di monte) peak; (un po') pinch; Sport forward; **doppie punte** (di capelli) split ends

pun'tare vt point; (spingere con forza) push; (scommettere) bet; ([!]: appuntare) fasten • vi **~ su** fig rely on; **~ verso** (dirigersi) head for; **~ a** aspire to

punta'spilli m inv pincushion

pun'tat|a f (di una storia) instalment; (televisiva) episode; (al gioco) stake, bet; (breve visita) flying visit; **a ~e** serialized, in instalments

punteggia'tura f punctuation

pun'teggio m score

puntel'lare vt prop. **pun'tello** m prop

pun'tigli|o m spite; (ostinazione) obstinacy. **~'oso** adj punctilious, pernickety pej

pun'tin|a f (da disegno) drawing pin, thumb tack Am; (di giradischi) stylus. **~o** m dot; **a ~o** perfectly; (cotto) to a T

'punto m point; (Med, in cucito,) stitch; (in punteggiatura) full stop; **in che ~?** where, exactly?; **due punti** colon; **in ~** sharp; **mettere a ~** put right; fig fine tune; tune up (motore); **essere sul ~ di fare qcsa** be about to do sth, be on the point of doing sth. **~ esclamativo** exclamation mark. **~ interrogativo** question mark. **~ nero** (Med) blackhead. **~ di riferimento** landmark; (per la qualità) benchmark. **~ di vendita** point of sale. **~ e virgola** semicolon. **~ di vista** point of view

puntu'al|e adj punctual. **~ità** f punctuality. **~'mente** adv punctually

pun'tura f (di insetto) sting; (di ago ecc) prick; (Med) puncture; (iniezione) injection; (fitta) stabbing pain

punzecchi'are vt prick; fig tease

'pupa f doll. **pu'pazzo** m puppet. **pupazzo di neve** snowman

pup'illa f (Anat) pupil

pu'pillo, -a mf (di professore) favourite

purché conj provided

'pure adv too, also; (concessivo) **fate ~!** please do! • conj (tuttavia) yet; (anche se) even if; **pur di** just to

purè m inv purée. **~ di patate** creamed potatoes

pu'rezza f purity

'purga f purge. **pur'gante** m laxative. **pur'gare** vt purge

P

purga'torio m purgatory
purifi'care vt purify
puri'tano, -a adj & mf Puritan
'puro adj pure; (vino ecc) undiluted; **per ~ caso** purely by chance
puro'sangue adj & m thoroughbred
pur'troppo adv unfortunately
pus m pus. **'pustola** f pimple
puti'ferio m uproar
putre'far|e vi, **~si** vr putrefy
'putrido adj putrid
'puzza f = **puzzo**
puz'zare vi stink; **~ di bruciato** fig smell fishy
'puzzo m stink, bad smell. **~la** f polecat. **~'lente** adj stinking
p.zza abbr (piazza) Sq.

Qq

qua adv here; **da un anno in ~** for the last year; **da quando in ~?** since when?; **di ~** this way; **di ~ di** on this side of; **~ dentro** in here; **~ sotto** under here; **~ vicino** near here; **~ e là** here and there
qua'derno m exercise book; (per appunti) notebook
quadrango'lare adj (forma) quadrangular. **qua'drangolo** m quadrangle
qua'drante m quadrant; (di orologio) dial
qua'dra|re vt square; (contabilità) balance •vi fit in. **~to** adj square; (equilibrato) level-headed •m square; (pugilato) ring; **al ~to** squared

quadret'tato adj squared; (carta) graph attrib. **qua'dretto** m square; (piccolo quadro) small picture; **a quadretti** (tessuto) check
quadrien'nale adj (che dura quattro anni) four-year
quadri'foglio m four-leaf clover
quadri'latero m quadrilateral
quadri'mestre m four-month period
'quadro m picture, painting; (quadrato) square; (fig: scena) sight; (tabella) table; (Theat) scene; (Comm) executive **quadri** pl (carte) diamonds; **a quadri** (tessuto, giacca, motivo) check. **quadri** pl **direttivi** senior management
quaggiù adv down here
'quaglia f quail
'qualche adj (alcuni) a few, some; (un certo) some; (in interrogazioni) any; **ho ~ problema** I have a few problems, I have some problems; **~ tempo fa** some time ago; **hai ~ libro italiano?** have you any Italian books?; **posso prendere ~ libro?** can I take some books?; **in ~ modo** somehow; **in ~ posto** somewhere; **~ volta** sometimes; **~ cosa** = **qualcosa**
qual'cos|a pron something; (in interrogazioni) anything; **~'altro** something else; **vuoi ~'altro?** would you like anything else?; **~a di strano** something strange; **vuoi ~a da mangiare?** would you like something to eat?
qual'cuno pron someone, somebody; (in interrogazioni) anyone, anybody; (alcuni) some; (in interrogazioni) any; **c'è ~?** is anybody in?; **qualcun altro** someone else, somebody else; **c'è qualcun altro che aspetta?** is anybody else waiting?; **ho letto ~ dei suoi libri** I've read some of his books; **conosci ~ dei suoi amici?** do you know any of his friends?
'quale adj which; (indeterminato) what; (come) as, like; **~ macchina è la tua?** which car is yours?; **~ motivo avrà di parlare così?** what reason would he have to speak like that?; **~ onore!** what an honour!; **città quali Venezia** towns like Venice; **~ che sia la tua opinione** whatever you may think •pron inter which [one]; **~**

preferisci? which [one] do you prefer? •pron rel **il/la ~** (persona) who; (animale, cosa) that, which; (oggetto: con prep) whom; (animale, cosa) which; **ho incontrato tua madre, la ~ mi ha detto...** I met your mother, who told me...; **l'ufficio nel ~ lavoro** the office in which I work; **l'uomo con il ~ parlavo** the man to whom I was speaking •adv (come) as

qua'lifica f qualification; (titolo) title

qualifi'ca|re vt qualify; (definire) define. **~rsi** vr be placed. **~'tivo** adj qualifying. **~to** adj (operaio) semiskilled. **~zi'one** f qualification

qualità f inv quality; (specie) kind; **in ~ di** in one's capacity as. **qualita'tivo** adj qualitative

qua'lora conj in case

qual'siasi, qua'lunque adj any; (non importa quale) whatever; (ordinario) ordinary; **dammi una penna ~** give me any pen [whatsoever]; **farei ~ cosa** I would do anything; **~ cosa io faccia** whatever I do; **~ persona** anyone; **in ~ caso** in any case; **uno ~** any one, whichever; **l'uomo qualunque** the man in the street

qualunqu'ismo m lack of political views

'**quando** conj & adv when; **da ~ ti ho visto** since I saw you; **da ~ esci con lui?** how long have you been going out with him?; **da ~ in qua?** since when?; **~... ~...** sometimes..., sometimes...

quantifi'care vt quantify

quantità f inv quantity; **una ~ di** (gran numero) a great deal of. **quantita'tivo** m amount •adj quantitative

'**quanto**

•adj inter how much; (*con nomi plurali*) how many; (*in esclamazione*) what a lot of; **~ tempo?** how long?; **quanti anni hai?** how old are you?

•adj rel as much... as; (*con nomi plurali*) as many... as; **prendi ~ denaro ti serve** take as much money as you need; **prendi quanti libri vuoi** take as many books as you like

•pron inter how much; (*quanto tempo*) how long; (*plurale*) how many; **quanti ne abbiamo oggi?** what date is it today?, what's the date today?

•pron rel as much as; (*quanto tempo*) as long as; (*plurale*) as many as; **prendine ~/quanti ne vuoi** take as much/as many as you like; **stai ~ vuoi** stay as long as you like; **questo è ~** that's it

•adv inter how much; (*quanto tempo*) how long; **~ sei alto?** how tall are you?; **~ hai aspettato?** how long did you wait for?; **~ costa?** how much is it?; **~ mi dispiace!** I'm so sorry!; **~ è bello!** how nice!

•adv rel as much as; **lavoro ~ posso** I work as much as I can; **è tanto intelligente ~ bello** he's as intelligent as he's good-looking; **in ~** (*in qualità di*) as; (*poiché*) since; **in ~ a me** as far as I'm concerned; **per ~** however; **per ~ ne sappia** as far as I know; **per ~ mi riguarda** as far as I'm concerned; **~ a** as for; **~ prima** (*al più presto*) as soon as possible

quan'tunque conj although

qua'ranta adj & m forty

quaran'tena f quarantine

quaran'tenn|e adj forty-year-old. **~io** m period of forty years

quaran't|esimo adj fortieth. **~ina** f **una ~ina** about forty

qua'resima f Lent

quar'tetto m quartet

quarti'ere m district; (Mil) quarters pl. **~ generale** headquarters

quarto adj fourth •m fourth; (quarta parte) quarter; **le sette e un ~** a quarter past seven. **quarti** pl **di finale** quarterfinals. **~ d'ora** quarter of an hour. **quar'tultimo, -a** mf fourth from the end

'**quarzo** m quartz

'**quasi** adv almost, nearly; **~ mai** hardly ever •conj (come se) as if; **~ ~ sto a casa** I'm tempted to stay home

quassù adv up here

'**quatto** adj crouching; (silenzioso) silent

quat'tordici adj & m fourteen

quat'trini mpl money sg

'quattro adj & m four; **dirne ~ a qcno** give sb a piece of one's mind; **farsi in ~ (per qcno/per fare qcsa)** go to a lot of trouble (for sb/to do sth); **in ~ e quattr'otto** in a flash. **~ per ~** m inv (Auto) four-wheel drive [vehicle]

quat'trocchi: **a ~** adv in private

quattro|'cento adj & m four hundred; **il Q~cento** the fifteenth century

quattro'mila adj & m four thousand

'quell|o adj that (pl those); **quell'albero** that tree; **quegli alberi** those trees; **quel cane** that dog; **quei cani** those dogs •pron that [one] (pl those [ones]); **~o lì** that one over there; **~o che** the one that; (ciò che) what; **quelli che** the ones that, those that; **~o a destra** the one on the right

'quercia f oak

que'rela f [legal] action

quere'lare vt bring an action against

que'sito m question

questio'nario m questionnaire

quest'ione f question; (faccenda) matter; (litigio) quarrel; **in ~** in doubt; **è fuori ~** it's out of the question

q

'quest|o adj this (pl these) •pron this [one] (pl these [ones]); **~o qui, ~o qua** this one here; **~o è quello che ha detto** that's what he said; **per ~o** for this or that reason. **quest'oggi** today

que'store m chief of police

que'stura f police headquarters

see A-Z of Italian life and culture

qui adv here; **da ~ in poi** from now on; **fin ~** (di tempo) up till now, until now; **~ dentro** in here; **~ sotto** under here; **~ vicino** near here •m **~ pro quo** misunderstanding

quie'scienza f **trattamento di ~** retirement package

quie'tanza f receipt

quie'tar|e vt calm. **~si** vr quieten down

qui'et|e f quiet; **disturbo della ~e pubblica** breach of the peace. **~o** adj quiet

'quindi adv then •conj therefore

'quindi|ci adj & m fifteen. **~'cina** f **una ~cina** about fifteen; **una ~cina di giorni** two weeks pl

quinquen'nale adj (che dura cinque anni) five-year. **quin'quennio** m [period of] five years

quin'tale m a hundred kilograms

'quinte fpl (Theat) wings

quin'tetto m quintet

'quinto adj fifth

quin'tuplo adj quintuple

'quota f quota; (rata) instalment; (altitudine) height; (Aeron) altitude, height; (ippica) odds pl; **perdere ~** lose altitude; **prendere ~** gain altitude. **~ di iscrizione** entry fee

quo'ta|re vt (Comm) quote. **~to** adj quoted; **essere ~to in Borsa** be quoted on the Stock Exchange. **~zi'one** f quotation

quotidi|ana'mente adv daily. **~'ano** adj daily; (ordinario) everyday •m daily [paper]

quozi'ente m quotient. **~ d'intelligenza** intelligence quotient, IQ

Rr

ra'barbaro m rhubarb

'rabbia f rage; (ira) anger; (Med) rabies sg; **che ~!** what a nuisance!; **mi fa ~** it makes me angry

rab'bino m rabbi

rabbiosa'mente adv furiously. **rabbi'oso** adj hot-tempered; (Med) rabid; (violento) violent

rabbo'nir|e vt pacify. **~si** vr calm down

rabbrivi'dire vi shudder; (di freddo) shiver

rabbui'arsi vr become dark

raccapez'zar|e vt put together. **~si** vr see one's way ahead

raccapricci'ante adj horrifying

raccatta'palle m inv ball boy •f inv ball girl

raccat'tare vt pick up

rac'chetta f racket. **~ da ping pong** table-tennis bat. **~ da sci** ski pole. **~ da tennis** tennis racket

racchi'udere vt contain

rac'cogli|ere vt pick; (da terra) pick up; (mietere) harvest; (collezionare) collect; (radunare) gather; win (voti ecc); (dare asilo a) take in. **~ersi** vr gather; (concentrarsi) collect one's thoughts. **~'mento** m concentration. **~'tore, ~'trice** mf collector •m (cartella) ring-binder

rac'colto, -a pp di **raccogliere** •adj (rannicchiato) hunched; (intimo) cosy; (concentrato) engrossed •m (mietitura) harvest •f collection; (di scritti) compilation; (del grano ecc) harvesting; (adunata) gathering

raccoman'dabile adj recommendable; **poco ~** (persona) shady

raccoman'da|re vt recommend; (affidare) entrust. **~rsi** vr (implorare) beg. **~ta** f registered letter; **~ta con ricevuta di ritorno** recorded delivery. **~ta-espresso** f next-day delivery of recorded items. **~zi'one** f recommendation

raccon'tare vt tell. **rac'conto** m story

raccorci'are vt shorten

raccor'dare vt join. **rac'cordo** m connection; (stradale) feeder. **raccordo anulare** ring road. **raccordo ferroviario** siding

ra'chitico adj rickety; (poco sviluppato) stunted

racimo'lare vt scrape together

'racket m inv racket

'radar m inv radar

raddol'cir|e vt sweeten; fig soften. **~si** vr become milder; (carattere:) mellow

raddoppi'are vt double. **rad'doppio** m doubling

raddriz'zare vt straighten

'rader|e vt shave; graze (muro); **~e al suolo** raze. **~si** vr shave

radi'are vt strike off; **~ dall'albo** strike off

radia|'tore m radiator. **~zi'one** f radiation

'radica f briar

radi'cale adj radical •m (Gram) root; (Pol) radical

ra'dicchio m chicory

ra'dice f root

'radio f inv radio; **via ~** by radio. **~ a transistor** transistor radio •m (Chem) radium.

radioama'tore, -'trice mf [radio] ham

radioascolta'tore, -'trice mf listener

radioat|tività f radioactivity. **~'tivo** adj radioactive

radio'cro|naca f radio commentary; **fare la ~naca di** commentate on. **~'nista** mf radio reporter

radiodiffusi'one f broadcasting

r

radio'fonico adj radio attrib

radiogra|'fare vt X-ray. **~'fia** f X-ray [photograph]; (radiologia) radiography; **fare una ~fia** (paziente:) have an X-ray; (dottore:) take an X-ray

radio'lina f transistor

radi'ologo, -a mf radiologist

radi'oso adj radiant

radio'sveglia f radio alarm

radio'taxi m inv radio taxi

radiote'lefono m radiotelephone; (privato) cordless [phone]

radiotelevi'sivo adj broadcasting attrib

'rado adj sparse; (non frequente) rare; **di ~** seldom

radu'nar|e vt, **~si** vr gather [together]. **ra'duno** m meeting; Sport rally

ra'dura f clearing

'rafano m horseradish

raf'fermo adj stale

'raffica f gust; (di armi da fuoco) burst; (di domande) barrage

raffigu'ra|re vt represent. **~zi'one** f representation

raffi'na|re vt refine. **~ta'mente** adv elegantly. **~to** adj refined. **raffine'ria** f refinery

rafforza|'mento m reinforcement; (di muscolatura) strengthening. **~re** vt reinforce. **~'tivo** m (Gram) intensifier

r

raffredda'mento m (processo) cooling

raffred'd|are vt cool. **~arsi** vr get cold; (prendere un raffreddore) catch a cold. **~ore** m cold. **~ore da fieno** hay fever

raf'fronto m comparison

'rafia f raffia

Rag. abbr **ragioniere**

ra'gaz|za f girl; (fidanzata) girlfriend. **~za alla pari** au pair [girl]. **~'zata** f prank. **~zo** m boy; (fidanzato) boyfriend

ragge'lar|e vt fig freeze. **~si** vr fig turn to ice

raggi'ante adj radiant; **~ di successo** flushed with success

raggi'era f **a ~** with a pattern like spokes radiating from a centre

'raggio m ray; (Math) radius; (di ruota) spoke; **~ d'azione** range. **~ laser** laser beam

raggi'rare vt trick. **rag'giro** m trick

raggi'un|gere vt reach; (conseguire) achieve. **~'gibile** adj (luogo) within reach

raggomito'lar|e vt wind. **~si** vr curl up

raggranel'lare vt scrape together

raggrin'zir|e vt, **~si** vr wrinkle

raggrup|pa'mento m (gruppo) group; (azione) grouping. **~'pare** vt group together

ragguagli'are vt compare; (informare) inform. **raggu'aglio** m comparison; (informazione) information

ragguar'devole adj considerable

'ragia f resin; **acqua ~** turpentine

ragiona'mento m reasoning; (discussione) discussion. **ragio'nare** vi reason; (discutere) discuss

ragi'one f reason; (ciò che è giusto) right; **a ~ o a torto** rightly or wrongly; **aver ~** be right; **perdere la ~** go out of one's mind

ragione'ria f accountancy

ragio'nevol|e adj reasonable. **~'mente** adv reasonably

ragioni'ere, -a mf accountant

ragli'are vi bray

ragna'tela f cobweb. **'ragno** m spider

ragù m inv meat sauce

RAI f abbr (Radio Audizioni Italiane) Italian public broadcasting company

ralle'gra|re vt gladden. **~rsi** vr rejoice; **~rsi con qcno** congratulate sb. **~'menti** mpl congratulations

rallenta'mento m slowing down

rallen'ta|re vt/i slow down; (allentare) slacken. **~rsi** vr slow down. **~'tore** m speed bump; **al ~tore** in slow motion

raman'zina f reprimand

ra'marro m type of lizard

ra'mato adj copper[-coloured]

'rame m copper

ramifi'ca|re vi, **~rsi** vr branch out;

(strada:) branch. **~zi'one** f ramification

rammari'carsi vr **~ di** regret; (lamentarsi) complain (**di** about). **ram'marico** m regret

rammen'dare vt darn. **ram'mendo** m darning

rammen'tar|e vt remember; **~e qcsa a qcno** (richiamare alla memoria) remind sb of sth. **~si** vr remember

rammol'li|re vt soften. **~rsi** vr go soft. **~to, -a** mf wimp

'ramo m branch. **~'scello** m twig

'rampa f (di scale) flight. **~ d'accesso** slip road. **~ di lancio** launch[ing] pad

ram'pante adj **giovane ~** yuppie

rampi'cante adj climbing •m (Bot) creeper

ram'pollo m hum brat; (discendente) descendant

ram'pone m harpoon; (per scarpe) crampon

'rana f frog; (nel nuoto) breaststroke; **uomo ~** frogman

ran'core m resentment

ran'dagio adj stray

'rango m rank

rannicchi'arsi vr huddle up

rannuvo'larsi vr cloud over

ra'nocchio m frog

ranto'lare vi wheeze. **'rantolo** m wheeze; (di moribondo) death rattle

'rapa f turnip

ra'pace adj rapacious; (uccello) predatory

ra'pare vt crop

'rapida f rapids pl. **~'mente** adv rapidly

rapidità f speed

'rapido adj swift •m (treno) express [train]

rapi'mento m kidnapping

ra'pina f robbery; **~ a mano armata** armed robbery. **~ in banca** bank robbery. **rapi'nare** vt rob. **~'tore** m robber

ra'pi|re vt abduct; (a scopo di riscatto) kidnap; (estasiare) ravish. **~'tore, ~'trice** mf kidnapper

rappacifi'ca|re vt pacify. **~rsi** vr be reconciled. **~zi'one** f reconciliation

rappor'tare vt reproduce (disegno); (confrontare) compare

rap'porto m report; (connessione) relation; (legame) relationship; (Math, Techn) ratio; **rapporti** pl relationship; **essere in buoni rapporti** be on good terms. **~ di amicizia** friendship. **~ di lavoro** working relationship. **rapporti** pl **sessuali** sexual intercourse

rap'prendersi vr set; (latte:) curdle

rappre'saglia f reprisal

rappresen'tan|te mf representative. **~te di commercio** sales representative. **~za** f delegation; (Comm) agency; **spese** pl **di ~za** entertainment expenses; **di ~za** (appartamento ecc) company

rappresen'ta|re vt represent; (Theat) perform. **~'tivo** adj representative. **~zi'one** f representation; (spettacolo) performance

rap'preso pp di **rapprendersi**

rapso'dia f rhapsody

'raptus m inv fit of madness

rara'mente adv rarely, seldom

rare'fa|re vt, **~rsi** vr rarefy. **~tto** adj rarefied

rarità f inv rarity. **'raro** adj rare

ra'sar|e vt shave; trim (siepe ecc). **~si** vr shave

raschi'are vt scrape; (togliere) scrape off

rasen'tare vt go close to. **ra'sente** prep very close to

'raso pp di **radere** •adj smooth; (colmo) full to the brim; (barba) close-cropped; **~ terra** close to the ground; **un cucchiaio ~** a level spoonful •m satin

ra'soio m razor

ras'segna f review; (mostra) exhibition; (musicale, cinematografica) festival; **passare in ~** review; (Mil) inspect

rasse'gna|re vt present. **~rsi** vr resign oneself. **~to** adj (persona, aria, tono) resigned. **~zi'one** f resignation

rassere'nar|e vt clear; fig cheer up. **~si** vr become clear; fig cheer up

rasset'tare vt tidy up; (riparare) mend

rassicu'ra|nte adj reassuring. **~re** vt reassure. **~zi'one** f reassurance

rasso'dare vt harden; fig strengthen

rassomigli'a|nza f resemblance. **~re** vi **~re a** resemble

rastrella'mento m (di fieno) raking; (perlustrazione) combing. **rastrel'lare** vt rake; (perlustrare) comb

rastrelli'era f rack; (per biciclette) bicycle rack; (scolapiatti) [plate] rack. **ra'strello** m rake

'rata f instalment; **pagare a rate** pay by instalments. **rate'ale** adj by instalments; **pagamento rateale** payment by instalments

rate'are, rateiz'zare vt divide into instalments

ra'tifica f (Jur) ratification

ratifi'care vt (Jur) ratify

'ratto m abduction; (roditore) rat

rattop'pare vt patch. **rat'toppo** m patch

rattrap'pir|e vt make stiff. **~si** vr become stiff

rattri'star|e vt sadden. **~si** vr become sad

rau'cedine f hoarseness. **'rauco** adj hoarse

rava'nello m radish

ravi'oli mpl ravioli sg

ravve'dersi vr mend one's ways

ravvicina'mento m reconciliation; (Pol) rapprochement

ravvici'nar|e vt bring closer; (riconciliare) reconcile. **~si** vr be reconciled

r

ravvi'sare vt recognize

ravvi'var|e vt revive; fig brighten up. **~si** vr revive

'rayon m rayon

razio'cinio m rational thought; (buon senso) common sense

razio'nal|e adj rational. **~ità** f (raziocinio) rationality; (di ambiente) functional nature. **~iz'zare** vt rationalize (programmi, metodi, spazio). **~'mente** adv rationally

razio'nare vt ration. **razi'one** f ration

'razza f race; (di cani ecc) breed; (genere) kind; **che ~ di idiota!** [!] what an idiot!

raz'zia f raid

razzi'ale adj racial

raz'zis|mo m racism. **~ta** adj & mf racist

'razzo m rocket. **~ da segnalazione** flare

razzo'lare vi (polli:) scratch about

re m inv king; (Mus) D

rea'gire vi react

re'ale adj real; (di re) royal

rea'lis|mo m realism. **~ta** mf realist; (fautore del re) royalist

realistica'mente adv realistically. **rea'listico** adj realistic

'reality tv f reality tv

realiz'zabile adj feasible

realiz'za|re vt (attuare) carry out, realize; (Comm) make; score (gol, canestro); (rendersi conto di) realize. **~rsi** vr come true; (nel lavoro ecc) fulfil oneself. **~zi'one** f realization; (di sogno, persona) fulfilment. **~zione scenica** production

rea'lizzo m (vendita) proceeds pl; (riscossione) yield

real'mente adv really

realtà f inv reality. **~ virtuale** virtual reality

re'ato m crime

reat'tivo adj reactive

reat'tore m reactor; (Aeron) jet [aircraft]

reazio'nario, -a adj & mf reactionary

reazi'one f reaction. **~ a catena** chain reaction

'rebus m inv rebus; (enigma) puzzle

recapi'tare vt deliver. **re'capito** m address; (consegna) delivery. **recapito a domicilio** home delivery. **recapito telefonico** contact telephone number

re'car|e vt bear; (produrre) cause. **~si** vr go

re'cedere vi recede; fig give up

recensi'one f review

recen's|ire vt review. **~ore** m reviewer

re'cente adj recent; **di ~** recently. **~'mente** adv recently

recessi'one f recession

re'cesso m recess

re'cidere vt cut off

reci'divo, -a adj (Med) recurrent • mf repeat offender

recin|'tare vt close off. **re'cinto** m enclosure; (per animali) pen; (per bambini) play-pen. **~zi'one** f (muro) wall; (rete) wire fence; (cancellata) railings pl

recipi'ente m container

re'ciproco adj reciprocal

re'ciso pp di **recidere**

'recita f performance. **reci'tare** vt recite; (Theat) act; play (ruolo). **~zi'one** f recitation; (Theat) acting

recla'mare vi protest • vt claim

ré'clame f inv advertising; (avviso pubblicitario) advertisement

re'clamo m complaint; **ufficio reclami** complaints department

recli'na|bile adj reclining; **sedile ~bile** reclining seat. **~re** vt tilt (sedile); lean (capo)

reclusi'one f imprisonment. **re'cluso, -a** adj secluded • mf prisoner

'recluta f recruit

reclu|ta'mento m recruitment. **~'tare** vt recruit

'record m inv record • adj inv (cifra) record attrib

recrimi'na|re vi recriminate

recupe'rare vt recover. **re'cupero** m recovery; **corso di recupero** additional classes; **minuti di recupero** Sport injury time

redargu'ire vt rebuke

re'datto pp di **redigere**

redat'tore, -'trice mf editor; (di testo) writer

redazi'one f (ufficio) editorial office; (di testi) editing

reddi'tizio adj profitable

'reddito m income. **~ imponibile** taxable income

re'den|to pp di **redimere**. **~'tore** m redeemer. **~zi'one** f redemption

re'digere vt write; draw up (documento)

re'dimer|e vt redeem. **~si** vr redeem oneself

'redini fpl reins

'reduce adj **~ da** back from • mf survivor

refe'rendum m inv referendum

refe'renza f reference

refet'torio m refectory

refrat'tario adj refractory; **essere ~ a** have no aptitude for

refrige'ra|re vt refrigerate. **~zi'one** f refrigeration

refur'tiva f stolen goods pl

rega'lare vt give

re'galo m present, gift

re'gata f regatta

reg'gen|te mf regent. **~za** f regency

'regger|e vt (sorreggere) bear; (tenere in mano) hold; (dirigere) run; (governare) govern; (Gram) take • vi (resistere) hold out; (durare) last; fig stand. **~si** vr stand

'reggia f royal palace

reggi'calze m inv suspender belt

reggi'mento m regiment

reggi'petto, reggi'seno m bra

re'gia f Cinema direction; (Theat) production

re'gime m regime; (dieta) diet; (Mech) speed

re'gina f queen

'regio adj royal

regio'na|le adj regional. **~'lismo** m (parola) regionalism

◘ **regi'one** f region

re'gista mf (Cinema) director; (Theat, TV) producer

regi'stra|re vt register; (Comm) enter; (incidere su nastro) tape, record; (su disco) record. **~'tore** m recorder; (magnetofono) tape-recorder. **~tore di cassa** cash register. **~zi'one** f registration; (Comm) entry; (di programma) recording

re'gistro m register; (ufficio) registry. **~ di cassa** ledger

re'gnare vi reign

'regno m kingdom; (sovranità) reign. **R~ Unito** United Kingdom

'regola f rule; **essere in ~** be in order; (persona:) have one's papers in order. **rego'labile** adj (meccanismo)

◘ *see A-Z of Italian life and culture*

r

adjustable. ~'**mento** m regulation; (Comm) settlement

rego'lar|e adj regular • vt regulate; (ridurre, moderare) limit; (sistemare) settle. **~si** vr (agire) act; (moderarsi) control oneself. **~ità** f regularity. **~iz'zare** vt settle (debito)

rego'la|ta f **darsi una ~ta** pull oneself together. **~'tore, ~'trice** adj **piano ~tore** urban development plan

'regolo m ruler

regres'sivo adj regressive. **re'gresso** m decline

reinseri'mento m (di persona) reintegration

reinser'irsi vr (in ambiente) reintegrate

reinte'grare vt restore

relativa'mente adv relatively; **~ a** as regards. **rela'tivo** adj relative

rela'tore, -'trice mf (in una conferenza) speaker

re'lax m relaxation

relazi'one f relation[ship]; (rapporto amoroso) [love] affair; (resoconto) report; **pubbliche relazioni** pl public relations

rele'gare vt relegate

religi'o|ne f religion. **~so, -a** adj religious • m monk • f nun

re'liqui|a f relic. **~'ario** m reliquary

re'litto m wreck

re'ma|re vi row. **~'tore, ~'trice** mf rower

r

remini'scenza f reminiscence

remissi'one f remission; (sottomissione) submissiveness. **remis'sivo** adj submissive

'remo m oar

'remora f **senza remore** without hesitation

re'moto adj remote

remune'ra|re vt remunerate. **~zi'one** f remuneration

'render|e vt (restituire) return; (esprimere) render; (fruttare) yield; (far diventare) make. **~si** vr become; **~si conto di qcsa** realize sth; **~si utile** make oneself useful

rendi'conto m report

rendi'mento m rendering; (produzione) yield

'rendita f income; (dello Stato) revenue

'rene m kidney. **~ artificiale** kidney machine

'reni fpl (schiena) back

reni'tente adj **essere ~ a** (consigli di qcno) be unwilling to accept

'renna f reindeer (pl inv); (pelle) buckskin

'reo, -a adj guilty • mf offender

re'parto m department; (Mil) unit

repel'lente adj repulsive

repen'taglio m **mettere a ~** risk

repen'tino adj sudden

reper'ibile adj available; **non è ~** (perduto) it's not to be found

repe'rire vt trace (fondi)

re'perto m **~ archeologico** find

reper'torio m repertory; (elenco) index; **immagini** pl **di ~** archive footage

'replica f reply; (obiezione) objection; (copia) replica; (Theat) repeat performance. **repli'care** vt reply; (Theat) repeat

repor'tage m inv report

repres|si'one f repression. **~'si-vo** adj repressive. **re'presso** pp di **reprimere**. **re'primere** vt repress

🅲 **re'pubbli|ca** f republic. **~'cano, -a** adj & mf republican

repu'tare vt consider

reputazi'one f reputation

requi'sito m requirement

requisi'toria f (arringa) closing speech

'resa f surrender; (Comm) rendering. **~ dei conti** rendering of accounts

'residence m inv residential hotel

resi'den|te adj & mf resident. **~za** f residence; (soggiorno) stay. **~zi'ale** adj residential; **zona ~ziale** residential district

re'siduo adj residual • m remainder

'resina f resin

resi'sten|te adj resistant; **~te all'acqua** water-resistant. **~za** f

🅲 *see* A-Z of Italian life and culture

resistance; (fisica) stamina; (Electr) resistor; **la R~za** the Resistance

re'sistere vi ~ [**a**] resist; (a colpi, scosse) stand up to; ~ **alla pioggia/al vento** be rain-/wind-resistant

'reso pp di **rendere**

reso'conto m report

re'spin|gere vt repel; (rifiutare) reject; (bocciare) fail. **~to** pp di **respingere**

respi'ra|re vt/i breathe. **~'tore** m respirator. **~tore** [**a tubo**] snorkel; **~'torio** adj respiratory. **~zi'one** f breathing; (Med) respiration. **~zione bocca a bocca** mouth-to-mouth resuscitation, kiss of life. **re'spiro** m breath; (il respirare) breathing; fig respite

respon'sabil|e adj responsible (**di** for); (Jur) liable •mf person responsible. **~e della produzione** production manager. **~ità** f inv responsibility; (Jur) liability. **~iz'zare** vt give responsibility to

re'sponso m response

'ressa f crowd

re'stante adj remaining •m remainder

re'stare vi = **rimanere**

restau'ra|re vt restore. **~'tore, ~'trice** mf restorer. **~zi'one** f restoration. **re'stauro** m (riparazione) repair

re'stio adj restive; ~ **a** reluctant to

restitu|'ire vt return; (reintegrare) restore. **~zi'one** f return; (Jur) restitution

resto m remainder; (saldo) balance; (denaro) change; **resti** pl (avanzi) remains; **del** ~ besides

re'stringer|e vt contract; take in (vestiti); (limitare) restrict; shrink (stoffa). **~si** vr contract; (farsi più vicini) close up; (stoffa:) shrink. **restringi'mento** m (di tessuto) shrinkage

restri|t'tivo adj restrictive. **~zi'one** f restriction

resurrezi'one f resurrection

resusci'tare vt/i revive

re'tata f round-up

rete f net; (sistema) network; (televisiva) channel; (in calcio) goal; fig trap; (per la spesa) string bag. ~ **locale** (Comput) local [area] network. ~ **stradale** road network. ~ **televisiva** television channel

reti'cen|te adj reticent. **~za** f reticence

retico'lato m grid; (rete metallica) wire netting. **re'ticolo** m network

re'torico, -a adj rhetorical; **domanda retorica** rhetorical question •f rhetoric

retribu|'ire vt remunerate. **~zi'one** f remuneration

'retro adv behind; **vedi** ~ see over •m inv back. ~ **di copertina** outside back cover

retroat'tivo adj retroactive

retro'ce|dere vi retreat •vt (Mil) demote; Sport relegate. **~ssi'one** f Sport relegation

retroda'tare vt backdate

re'trogrado adj retrograde; fig old-fashioned; (Pol) reactionary

retrogu'ardia f (Mil) rearguard

retro'marcia f reverse [gear]

retro'scena m inv (Theat) backstage; fig background details pl

retrospet'tivo adj retrospective

retro'stante adj **il palazzo** ~ the building behind

retrovi'sore m rear-view mirror

'retta[1] f (Math) straight line; (di collegio, pensionato) fee

'retta[2] f **dar** ~ **a qcno** take sb's advice

rettango'lare adj rectangular. **ret'tangolo** m rectangle

ret'tifi|ca f rectification. **~'care** vt rectify

'rettile m reptile

retti'lineo adj rectilinear; (retto) upright •m Sport back straight

'retto pp di **reggere** •adj straight; fig upright; (giusto) correct; **angolo** ~ right angle

ret'tore m (Relig) rector; (Univ) principal, vice-chancellor

reu'matico adj rheumatic

reuma'tismi mpl rheumatism

reve'rendo adj reverend

see A-Z of Italian life and culture

rever'sibile adj reversible

revisio'nare vt revise; (Comm) audit; (Auto) overhaul. **revisi'one** f revision; (Comm) audit; (Auto) overhaul. **revi'sore** m (di conti) auditor; (di bozze) proof-reader; (di traduzioni) revisor

re'vival m inv revival

'revoca f repeal. **revo'care** vt repeal

riabili'ta|re vt rehabilitate. **~zi'one** f rehabilitation

riabitu'ar|e vt reaccustom. **~si** vr reaccustom oneself

riac'cender|e vt rekindle (fuoco). **~si** vr (luce:) come back on

riacqui'stare vt buy back; regain (libertà, prestigio); recover (vista, udito)

riagganci'are vt replace (ricevitore); **~ la cornetta** hang up •vi hang up

riallac'ciare vt refasten; reconnect (corrente); renew (amicizia)

rial'zare vt raise •vi rise. **ri'alzo** m rise

riani'mar|e vt (Med) resuscitate; (ridare forza a) revive; (ridare coraggio a) cheer up. **~si** vr regain consciousness; (riprendere forza) revive; (riprendere coraggio) cheer up

riaper'tura f reopening

ria'prir|e vt, **~si** vr reopen

rias'sumere vt summarize

riassun'tivo adj summarizing. **rias'sunto** pp di **riassumere** •m summary

r

ria'ver|e vt get back; regain (salute, vista). **~si** vr recover

riavvicina'mento m reconciliation

riavvici'nar|e vt reconcile (paesi, persone). **~si** vr (riconciliarsi) be reconciled, make it up

riba'dire vt (confermare) reaffirm

ri'balta f flap; (Theat) footlights pl; fig limelight

ribal'tar|e vt/i, **~si** vr tip over; (Naut) capsize

ribas'sare vt lower •vi fall. **ri'basso** m fall; (sconto) discount

ri'battere vt (a macchina) retype; (controbattere) deny •vi answer back

ribel'l|arsi vr rebel. **ri'belle** adj rebellious •mf rebel. **~'ione** f rebellion

'ribes m inv (rosso) redcurrant; (nero) blackcurrant

ribol'lire vi ferment; fig seethe

ri'brezzo m disgust; **far ~ a** disgust

rica'dere vi fall back; (nel peccato ecc) lapse; (pendere) hang [down]; **~ su** (riversarsi) fall on. **rica'duta** f relapse

rical'care vt trace

rica'ma|re vt embroider. **~to** adj embroidered

ri'cambi mpl spare parts

ricambi'are vt return; reciprocate (sentimento); **~ qcsa a qcno** repay sb for sth. **ri'cambio** m replacement; (Biol) metabolism; **pezzo di ricambio** spare [part]

ri'camo m embroidery

ricapito'la|re vt sum up. **~zi'one** f summary, recap [!]

ri'carica f (di sveglia) rewinding; (Teleph) top-up card

ricari'care vt reload (macchina fotografica, fucile, camion); recharge (batteria); (Comput) reboot

ricat'ta|re vt blackmail. **~'tore, ~'trice** mf blackmailer. **ri'catto** m blackmail

rica'va|re vt get; (ottenere) obtain; (dedurre) draw. **~to** m proceeds pl. **ri'cavo** m proceeds pl

'ricca f rich woman. **~'mente** adv lavishly

ric'chezza f wealth; fig richness

'riccio adj curly •m curl; (animale) hedgehog. **~ di mare** sea-urchin. **~lo** m curl. **~'luto** adj curly. **ricci'uto** adj (barba) curly

'ricco adj rich •m rich man

ri'cerca f search; (indagine) investigation; (scientifica) research; (Sch) project

ricer'ca|re vt search for; (fare ricerche su) research. **~ta** f wanted woman. **~'tezza** f refinement. **~to** adj sought-after; (raffinato) refined; (affettato) affected •m (dalla polizia) wanted man

ricetrasmit'tente f transceiver

ri'cetta f prescription; (Culin) recipe

ricet'tacolo m receptacle

ricet'tario m (di cucina) recipe book

ricetta|'tore, -'trice mf fence,

receiver of stolen goods. **~zi'one** f receiving [stolen goods]

'ice'vente adj (apparecchio, stazione) receiving • mf receiver

'i'cev|ere vt receive; (dare il benvenuto) welcome; (di albergo) accommodate. **~i'mento** m receiving; (accoglienza) welcome; (trattenimento) reception

icevi'tor|e m receiver. **~'ia** f **~ia del lotto** agency authorized to sell lottery tickets

'ice'vuta f receipt

icezi'one f (Radio, TV) reception

'ichia'mare vt (al telefono) call back; (far tornare) recall; (rimproverare) rebuke; (attirare) draw; **~ alla mente** call to mind. **richi'amo** m recall; (attrazione) call

'ichi'edere vt ask for; (di nuovo) ask again for; **~ a qcno di fare qcsa** ask o request sb to do sth. **richi'esta** f request; (Comm) demand

i'chiuder|e vt close again. **~si** vr (ferita:) heal

ici'claggio m recycling

ici'clare vt recycle (carta, vetro); launder (denaro sporco)

ricino m **olio di ~** castor oil

icognizi'one f reconnaissance

'i'colmo adj full

icominci'are vt/i start again

icompa'rire vi reappear

icom'pen|sa f reward. **~'sare** vt reward

icom'por|re vt (riscrivere) rewrite; (ricostruire) reform; (Typ) reset. **~si** vr regain one's composure

iconcili'a|re vt reconcile. **~rsi** vr be reconciled. **~zi'one** f reconciliation

icono'scen|te adj grateful. **~za** f gratitude

ico'nosc|ere vt recognize; (ammettere) acknowledge. **~i'mento** m recognition; (ammissione) acknowledgement; (per la polizia) identification. **~i'uto** adj recognized

iconside'rare vt rethink

ico'prire vt re-cover; (rivestire) coat; (di insulti) shower (**di** with); hold (carica)

icor'dar|e vt remember; (richiamare alla memoria) recall; (far ricordare) remind; (rassomigliare) look like. **~si** vr **~si [di]** remember. **ri'cordo** m memory; (oggetto) memento; (di viaggio) souvenir; **ricordi** pl (memorie) memoirs

ricor'ren|te adj recurrent. **~za** f recurrence; (anniversario) anniversary

ri'correre vi recur; (accadere) occur; (data:) fall; **~ a** have recourse to; (rivolgersi a) turn to. **ri'corso** pp di **ricorrere** • m recourse; (Jur) appeal

ricostitu'ente m tonic

ricostitu'ire vt re-establish

ricostru|'ire vt reconstruct. **~zi'one** f reconstruction

ricove'ra|re vt give shelter to; **~re in ospedale** admit to hospital, hospitalize. **~to, -a** mf hospital patient. **ri'covero** m shelter; (ospizio) home

ricre'a|re vt re-create; (ristorare) restore. **~rsi** vr amuse oneself. **~'tivo** adj recreational. **~zi'one** f recreation; (Sch) break

ri'credersi vr change one's mind

ricupe'rare vt recover; rehabilitate (tossicodipendente); **~ il tempo perduto** make up for lost time. **ri'cupero** m recovery; (di tossicodipendente) rehabilitation; (salvataggio) rescue; **[minuti** mpl **di] ricupero** injury time

ri'curvo adj bent

ri'dare vt give back, return

ri'dente adj (piacevole) pleasant

'ridere vi laugh; **~ di** (deridere) laugh at

ri'detto pp di **ridire**

ridicoliz'zare vt ridicule. **ri'dicolo** adj ridiculous

ridimensio'nare vt reshape; fig see in the right perspective

ri'dire vt repeat; (criticare) find fault with

ridon'dante adj redundant

ri'dotto pp di **ridurre** • m (Theat) foyer • adj reduced

ri'du|rre vt reduce. **~rsi** vr diminish. **~rsi a** be reduced to. **~t'tivo** adj reductive. **~zi'one** f reduction; (per cinema, teatro) adaptation

rieducazi'one f (di malato) rehabilitation

riem'pi|re vt fill [up]; fill in (moduli ecc). **~rsi** vr fill [up]. **~'tivo** adj filling • m filler

rien'tranza f recess

rien'trare vi go/come back in; (tornare) return; (piegare indentro) recede; **~ in** (far parte) fall within. **ri'entro** m return; (di astronave) re-entry

riepilo'gare vt recapitulate. **rie'pilogo** m roundup

riesami'nare vt reappraise

riesu'mare vt exhume

rievo'ca|re vt commemorate. **~zi'one** f commemoration

rifaci'mento m remake

ri'fa|re vt do again; (creare) make again; (riparare) repair; (imitare) imitate; make (letto). **~rsi** vr (rimettersi) recover; (vendicarsi) get even; **~rsi una vita/carriera** make a new life/career for oneself; **~rsi di** make up for. **~tto** pp di **rifare**

riferi'mento m reference

rife'rir|e vt report; **~e a** attribute to • vi make a report. **~si** vr **~si a** refer to

rifi'lare vt (tagliare a filo) trim; (🅵: affibbiare) saddle

rifi'ni|re vt finish off. **~'tura** f finish

rifiu'tare vt refuse. **rifi'uto** m refusal; **rifiuti** pl (immondizie) rubbish sg. **rifiuti** pl **urbani** urban waste sg

riflessi'one f reflection; (osservazione) remark. **rifles'sivo** adj thoughtful; (Gram) reflexive

ri'flesso pp di **riflettere** • m (luce) reflection; (Med) reflex; **per ~** indirectly

ri'fletter|e vt reflect • vi think. **~si** vr be reflected

riflet'tore m reflector; (proiettore) searchlight

ri'flusso m ebb

rifocil'lar|e vt restore. **~si** vr liter, hum take some refreshment

ri'fondere vt refund

ri'forma f reform; (Relig) reformation; (Mil) medical exemption

rifor'ma|re vt re-form; (migliorare) reform; (Mil) declare unfit for military service. **~to** adj (chiesa) Reformed. **~'tore, ~'trice** mf reformer. **~'torio** m reformatory. **rifor'mista** adj reformist

riforni'mento m supply; (scorta) stock; (di combustibile) refuelling; **stazione** f **di ~** petrol station

rifor'nir|e vt **~e di** provide with. **~si** vr restock, stock up (**di** with)

ri'fra|ngere vt refract. **~tto** pp di **rifrangere. ~zi'one** f refraction

rifug'gire vi **~ da** fig shun

rifugi'a|rsi vr take refuge. **~to, -a** mf refugee. **~to economico** economic refugee

ri'fugio m shelter; (nascondiglio) hideaway

'riga f line; (fila) row; (striscia) stripe; (scriminatura) parting; (regolo) rule; **a righe** (stoffa) striped; (quaderno) ruled; **mettersi in ~** line up

ri'gagnolo m rivulet

ri'gare vt rule (foglio) • vi **~ dritto** behave well

rigatti'ere m junk dealer

rigene'rare vt regenerate

riget'tare vt throw back; (respingere) reject; (vomitare) throw up. **ri'getto** m rejection

ri'ghello m ruler

rigid|a'mente adv rigidly. **~ità** f rigidity; (di clima) severity; (severità) strictness. **'rigido** adj rigid; (freddo) severe; (severo) strict

rigi'rar|e vt turn again; (ripercorrere) go round; fig twist (argomentazione) • vi walk about. **~si** vr turn round; (nel letto) turn over. **ri'giro** m (imbroglio) trick

'rigo m line; (Mus) staff

ri'gogli|o m bloom. **~'oso** adj luxuriant

ri'gonfio adj swollen

ri'gore m rigours pl; **a ~** strictly speaking; **calcio di ~** penalty [kick]; **area di ~** penalty area; **essere di ~** be compulsory

rigo'roso adj (severo) strict; (scrupoloso) rigorous

riguada'gnare vt regain (quota, velocità)

riguar'dar|e vt look at again; (considerare) regard; (concernere) concern; **per quanto riguarda**

with regard to. **~si** vr take care of oneself. **rigu'ardo** m care; (considerazione) consideration; **nei riguardi di** towards; **riguardo a** with regard to

ri'gurgito m regurgitation

rilanci'are vt throw back (palla); (di nuovo) throw again; increase (offerta); revive (moda); relaunch (prodotto) •vi (a carte) raise the stakes

rilasci'ar|e vt (concedere) grant; (liberare) release; issue (documento). **~si** vr relax. **ri'lascio** m release; (di documento) issue

rilassa'mento m relaxation

rilas'sa|re vt, **~rsi** vr relax. **~to** adj (ambiente) relaxed

rile'ga|re vt bind (libro). **~to** adj bound. **~'tura** f binding

ri'leggere vt reread

ri'lento: **a ~** adv slowly

rileva'mento m survey; (Comm) buyout

rile'van|te adj considerable

rile'va|re vt (trarre) get; (mettere in evidenza) point out; (notare) notice; (topografia) survey; (Comm) take over; (Mil) relieve. **~zi'one** f (statistica) survey

rili'evo m relief; (Geog) elevation; (topografia) survey; (importanza) importance; (osservazione) remark; **mettere in ~ qcsa** point sth out

rilut'tan|te adj reluctant. **~za** f reluctance

'rima f rhyme

riman'dare vt (posporre) postpone; (mandare indietro) send back; (mandare di nuovo) send again; (far ridare un esame) make resit an examination. **ri'mando** m return; (in un libro) crossreference

rima'nen|te adj remaining •m remainder. **~za** f remainder

rima'ne|re vi stay, remain; (essere d'avanzo) be left; (venirsi a trovare) be; (restare stupito) be astonished; (restare d'accordo) agree

rimar'chevole adj remarkable

ri'mare vt/i rhyme

rimargi'nar|e vt, **~si** vr heal

ri'masto pp di **rimanere**

rimbal'zare vi rebound; (proiettile:) ricochet; **far ~** bounce. **rim'balzo** m rebound; (di proiettile) ricochet

rimbam'bi|re vi be in one's dotage •vt stun. **~to** adj in one's dotage

rimboc'care vt turn up; roll up (maniche); tuck in (coperte)

rimbom'bare vi resound

rimbor'sare vt reimburse, repay. **rim'borso** m reimbursement, repayment. **rimborso spese** reimbursement of expenses

rimedi'are vi **~ a** remedy; make up for (errore); (procurare) scrape up. **ri'medio** m remedy

rimesco'lare vt mix [up]; shuffle (carte); (rivangare) rake up

ri'messa f (locale per veicoli) garage; (per aerei) hangar; (per autobus) depot; (di denaro) remittance; (di merci) consignment

ri'messo pp di **rimettere**

ri'metter|e vt put back; (restituire) return; (affidare) entrust; (perdonare) remit; (rimandare) put off; (vomitare) bring up. **~si** vr (ristabilirsi) recover; (tempo:) clear up; **~si a** start again

'rimmel® m inv mascara

rimoder'nare vt modernize

rimon'tare vt (risalire) go up; (Mech) reassemble •vi remount; **~ a** (risalire) go back to

rimorchi'a|re vt tow; [!] pick up (ragazza). **~'tore** m tug[boat]. **ri'morchio** m tow; (veicolo) trailer

ri'morso m remorse

rimo'stranza f complaint

rimozi'one f removal; (da un incarico) dismissal. **~ forzata** illegally parked vehicles removed at owner's expense

rim'pasto m (Pol) reshuffle

rimpatri'are vt/i repatriate. **rim'patrio** m repatriation

rim'pian|gere vt regret. **~to** pp di **rimpiangere** •m regret

rimpiaz'zare vt replace

rimpiccio'lire vi become smaller

rimpinz'ar|e vt **~e di** stuff with. **~si** vr stuff oneself

rimprove'rare vt reproach; **~ qcsa a qcno** reproach sb for sth. **rim'provero** m reproach

rimune'ra|re vt remunerate. **~'tivo**

adj remunerative. **~zi'one** f remuneration

ri'muovere vt remove

ri'nascere vi be reborn

rinascimen'tale adj Renaissance. **Rinasci'mento** m Renaissance

ri'nascita f rebirth

rincal'zare vt (sostenere) support; (rimboccare) tuck in. **rin'calzo** m support; **rincalzi** pl (Mil) reserves

rincantucci'arsi vr hide oneself away in a corner

rinca'rare vt increase the price of •vi become more expensive. **rin'caro** m price increase

rinca'sare vi return home

rinchi'uder|e vt shut up. **~si** vr shut oneself up

rin'correre vt run after

rin'cors|a f run-up. **~o** pp di **rincorrere**

rin'cresc|ere vi **mi rincresce di non...** I'm sorry o I regret that I can't...; **se non ti ~e** if you don't mind. **~i'mento** m regret. **~i'uto** pp di **rincrescere**

rincreti'nire vi be stupid

rincu'lare vi (arma:) recoil; (cavallo:) shy. **rin'culo** m recoil

rincuo'rar|e vt encourage. **~si** vr take heart

rinfacci'are vt **~ qcsa a qcno** throw sth in sb's face

rinfor'zar|e vt strengthen; (rendere più saldo) reinforce. **~si** vr become stronger. **rin'forzo** m reinforcement; fig support

rinfran'care vt reassure

rinfre'scante adj cooling

rinfre'scar|e vt cool; (rinnovare) freshen up •vi get cooler. **~si** vr freshen [oneself] up. **rin'fresco** m light refreshment; (ricevimento) party

rin'fusa f **alla ~** at random

ringhi'era f railing; (di scala) banisters pl

ringiova'nire vt rejuvenate (pelle, persona); (vestito:) make look younger •vi become young again; (sembrare) look young again

ringrazi|a'mento m thanks pl. **~'are** vt thank

rinne'ga|re vt disown. **~to, -a** mf renegade

rinnova'mento m renewal; (di edifici) renovation

rinno'var|e vt renew; renovate (edifici). **~si** vr be renewed; (ripetersi) recur, happen again. **rin'novo** m renewal

rinoce'ronte m rhinoceros

rino'mato adj renowned

rinsal'dare vt consolidate

rinsa'vire vi come to one's senses

rinsec'chi|re vi shrivel up. **~to** adj shrivelled up

rinta'narsi vr hide oneself away; (animale:) retreat into its den

rintoc'care vi (campana:) toll; (orologio:) strike. **rin'tocco** m toll; (di orologio) stroke

rinton'ti|re vt stun. **~to** adj dazed

rintracci'are vt trace

rintro'nare vt stun •vi boom

ri'nuncia f renunciation

rinunci'a|re vi **~re a** renounce, give up. **~'tario** adj defeatist

ri'nunzia, rinunzi'are = **rinuncia, rinunciare**

rinveni'mento m (di reperti) discovery; (di refurtiva) recovery. **rinve'nire** vt find •vi (riprendere i sensi) come round; (ridiventare fresco) revive

rinvi'are vt put off; (mandare indietro) return; (in libro) refer; **~ a giudizio** indict

rin'vio m Sport goal kick; (in libro) cross-reference; (di appuntamento) postponement; (di merce) return

rio'nale adj local. **ri'one** m district

riordi'nare vt tidy [up]; (ordinare di nuovo) reorder; (riorganizzare) reorganize

riorganiz'zare vt reorganize

ripa'gare vt repay

ripa'ra|re vt protect; (aggiustare) repair; (porre rimedio) remedy •vi **~re a** make up for. **~rsi** vr take shelter. **~to** adj (luogo) sheltered. **~zi'one** f repair; fig reparation. **ri'paro** m shelter; (rimedio) remedy

ripar'ti|re vt (dividere) divide •vi leave again. **~zi'one** f division

ripas'sa|re vt recross; (rivedere) revise

r

•vi pass again. **ri'passo** m (di lezione) revision

ripensa'mento m second thoughts pl

ripen'sare vi change one's mind; ~ **a** think of; **ripensaci!** think again!

riper'correre vt go back over

riper'cosso pp di **ripercuotere**

ripercu'oter|e vt strike again. ~**si** vr (suono:) reverberate; ~**si su** (avere conseguenze) impact on. **ripercussi'one** f repercussion

ripe'scare vt fish out (oggetti)

ripe'tente mf student repeating a year

ri'pet|ere vt repeat. ~**ersi** vr (evento:) recur. ~**izi'one** f repetition; (di lezione) revision; (lezione privata) private lesson. ~**uta'mente** adv repeatedly

ri'piano m (di scaffale) shelf; (terreno pianeggiante) terrace

ri'picc|a f **fare qcsa per** ~**a** do sth out of spite. ~**o** m spite

'ripido adj steep

ripie'gar|e vt refold; (abbassare) lower •vi (indietreggiare) retreat. ~**si** vr bend; (sedile:) fold. **ripi'ego** m expedient; (via d'uscita) way out

ripi'eno adj full; (Culin) stuffed •m filling; (Culin) stuffing

ri'porre vt put back; (mettere da parte) put away; (collocare) place; repeat (domanda)

ripor'tar|e vt (restituire) bring/take back; (riferire) report; (subire) suffer; (Math) carry; win (vittoria); transfer (disegno). ~**si** vr go back; (riferirsi) refer

ripo'sante adj (colore) restful, soothing

ripo'sa|re vi rest •vt put back. ~**rsi** vr rest. ~**to** adj (mente) fresh. **ri'poso** m rest; **andare a riposo** retire; **riposo!** (Mil) at ease!; **giorno di riposo** day off

ripo'stiglio m cupboard

ri'posto pp di **riporre**

ri'prender|e vt take again; (prendere indietro) take back; (riconquistare) recapture; (ricuperare) recover; (ricominciare) resume; (rimproverare) reprimand; take in (cucitura); Cinema shoot. ~**si** vr recover; (correggersi) correct oneself

ri'presa f resumption; (ricupero) recovery; (Theat) revival; Cinema shot; (Auto) acceleration; (Mus) repeat. ~ **aerea** bird's-eye view

ripresen'tar|e vt resubmit (domanda, certificato). ~**si** vr go/come back again; (come candidato) run again; (occasione:) arise again

ri'preso pp di **riprendere**

ripristi'nare vt restore

ripro'dotto pp di **riprodurre**

ripro'du|rre vt, ~**rsi** vr reproduce. ~**t'tivo** adj reproductive. ~**zi'one** f reproduction

ripro'mettersi vr intend

ri'prova f confirmation

ripudi'are vt repudiate

ripu'gnan|te adj repugnant. ~**za** f disgust. **ripu'gnare** vi **ripugnare a** disgust

ripu'li|re vt clean [up]; fig polish

ripuls|i'one f repulsion. ~**'ivo** adj repulsive

ri'quadro m square; (pannello) panel

ri'sacca f undertow

risa'lire vt go back up •vi ~ **a** (nel tempo) go back to; (essere datato a) date back to, go back to

risal'tare vi stand out. **ri'salto** m prominence; (rilievo) relief

risa'nare vt heal; (bonificare) reclaim

risa'puto adj well-known

risarci'mento m compensation. **risar'cire** vt indemnify

ri'sata f laugh

riscalda'mento m heating. ~ **autonomo** central heating (for one flat)

riscal'dar|e vt heat; warm (persona). ~**si** vr warm up

riscat'tar|e vt ransom. ~**si** vr redeem oneself. **ri'scatto** m ransom; (morale) redemption

rischia'rar|e vt light up; brighten (colore). ~**si** vr light up; (cielo:) clear up

rischi|'are vt risk •vi run the risk. **'rischio** m risk. ~**'oso** adj risky

risciac'quare vt rinse

riscon'trare vt (confrontare) compare; (verificare) check; (rilevare) find.

r

ri'**scontro** m comparison; check; (Comm: risposta) reply

ri'**scossa** f revolt; (riconquista) recovery

riscossi'one f collection

ri'**scosso** pp di **riscuotere**

riscu'oter|e vt shake; (percepire) draw; (ottenere) gain; cash (assegno). **~si** vr rouse oneself

risen'ti|re vt hear again; (provare) feel • vi **~re di** feel the effect of. **~rsi** vr (offendersi) take offence. **~to** adj resentful

ri'**serbo** m reserve; **mantenere il ~** remain tight-lipped

ri'**serva** f reserve; (di caccia, pesca) preserve; Sport substitute, reserve. **~ di caccia** game reserve. **~ naturale** wildlife reserve

riser'va|re vt reserve; (prenotare) book; (per occasione) keep. **~rsi** vr (ripromettersi) plan for oneself (cambiamento). **~'tezza** f reserve. **~to** adj reserved

ri'**siedere** vi **~ a** live in/at

'**riso**[1] m (cereale) rice

'**riso**[2] pp di **ridere** • m (pl f **risa**) laughter; (singolo) laugh. **~'lino** m giggle

ri'**solto** pp di **risolvere**

risolu|'tezza f determination. **riso'luto** adj resolute, determined. **~zi'one** f resolution

ri'**solver|e** vt resolve; (Math) solve. **~si** vr (decidersi) decide; **~si in** turn into

riso'na|nza f resonance; **aver ~nza** arouse great interest. **~re** vi resound; (rimbombare) echo

ri'**sorgere** vi rise again

risorgi'mento m revival; (storico) Risorgimento

ri'**sorsa** f resource; (espediente) resort

ri'**sorto** pp di **risorgere**

ri'**sotto** m risotto

ri'**sparmi** mpl (soldi) savings

risparmi'a|re vt save; (salvare) spare. **~'tore, ~'trice** mf saver ri'**sparmio** m saving

rispecchi'are vt reflect

see A-Z of Italian life and culture

rispet'tabil|e adj respectable. **~ità** f respectability

rispet'tare vt respect; **farsi ~** command respect

rispet'tivo adj respective

ri'**spetto** m respect; **~ a** as regards; (in confronto a) compared to

rispet|tosa'mente adv respectfully. **~'toso** adj respectful

risplen'dente adj shining. ri'**splendere** vi shine

rispon'den|te adj **~te a** in keeping with. **~za** f correspondence

ri'**spondere** vi answer; (rimbeccare) answer back; (obbedire) respond; **~ a** reply to; **~ di** (rendersi responsabile) answer for

ri'**spost|a** f answer, reply; (reazione) response. **~o** pp di **rispondere**

'**rissa** f brawl. **ris'soso** adj pugnacious

ristabi'lir|e vt re-establish. **~si** vr (in salute) recover

rista'gnare vi stagnate; (sangue:) coagulate. ri'**stagno** m stagnation

ri'**stampa** f reprint; (azione) reprinting. **ristam'pare** vt reprint

risto'rante m restaurant

risto'ra|re vt refresh. **~rsi** vr liter take some refreshment; (riposarsi) take a rest. **~'tore, ~'trice** mf (proprietario di ristorante) restaurateur; (fornitore) caterer • adj refreshing. ri'**storo** m refreshment; (sollievo) relief

ristret'tezza f narrowness; (povertà) poverty

ri'**stretto** pp di **restringere** • adj narrow; (condensato) condensed; (limitato) restricted; **di idee ristrette** narrow-minded

ristruttu'rare vt restructure (ditta); refurbish (casa)

risucchi'are vt suck in. ri'**succhio** m whirlpool; (di corrente) undertow

risul'ta|re vi result; (riuscire) turn out. **~to** m result

risuo'nare vi echo; (Phys) resonate

risurrezi'one f resurrection

risusci'tare vt resuscitate; fig revive • vi return to life

risvegli'ar|e vt reawaken (interesse).

~si vr wake up; (natura:) awake; (desiderio:) be aroused. **ri'sveglio** m waking up; (dell'interesse) revival; (del desiderio) arousal

i'svolto m lapel; (di pantaloni) turn-up, cuff Am; (di manica) cuff; (di tasca) flap; (di libro) inside flap

itagli'are vt cut out. **ri'taglio** m cutting; (di stoffa) scrap

itar'da|re vi be late; (orologio:) be slow • vt delay; slow down (progresso); (differire) postpone. **~'tario, -a** mf late-comer

i'tardo m delay; **essere in ~** be late; (volo:) be delayed

i'tegno m reserve

ite'n|ere vt retain; deduct (somma); (credere) believe. **~uta** f deduction

iti'ra|re vt throw back (palla); (prelevare) withdraw; (riscuotere) draw; collect (pacco). **~rsi** vr withdraw; (stoffa:) shrink; (da attività) retire; (marea:) recede. **~ta** f retreat; (WC) toilet. **ri'tiro** m withdrawal; (Relig) retreat; (da attività) retirement. **ritiro bagagli** baggage reclaim

ritmo m rhythm

ito m rite; **di ~** customary

itoc'care vt touch up

itor'nare vi return; (andare venire indietro) go/come back; (ricorrere) recur; (ridiventare) become again

itor'nello m refrain

i'torno m return

itorsi'one f retaliation

i'trarre vt withdraw; (distogliere) turn away; (rappresentare) portray

itrat'ta|re vt deal with again; retract (dichiarazione). **~zi'one** f withdrawal, retraction

itrat'tista mf portrait painter. **ri'tratto** pp di **ritrarre** • m portrait

itro'sia f shyness. **ri'troso** adj backward; (timido) shy; **a ritroso** backwards; **ritroso a** reluctant to

itro'va|re vt find [again]; regain (salute). **~rsi** vr meet; (di nuovo) meet again; (capitare) find oneself; (raccapezzarsi) see one's way. **~to** m discovery. **ri'trovo** m meeting-place; (notturno) night-club

itto adj upright; (diritto) straight

tu'ale adj & m ritual

riunifi'ca|re vt reunify. **~rsi** vr be reunited. **~zi'one** f reunification

riuni'one f meeting; (fra amici) reunion

riu'nir|e vt (unire) join together; (radunare) gather. **~si** vr be re-united; (adunarsi) meet

riusc'i|re vi (aver successo) succeed; (in matematica ecc) be good (**in** at); (aver esito) turn out; **le è riuscito simpatico** she found him likeable. **~ta** f result; (successo) success

'riva f shore; (di fiume) bank

ri'val|e mf rival. **~ità** f inv rivalry

rivalutazi'one f revaluation

rive'dere vt see again; revise (lezione); (verificare) check

rive'la|re vt reveal. **~rsi** vr (dimostrarsi) turn out. **~'tore** adj revealing • m (Techn) detector. **~zi'one** f revelation

ri'vendere vt resell

rivendi'ca|re vt claim. **~zi'one** f claim

ri'vendi|ta f (negozio) shop. **~'tore, ~'trice** mf retailer. **~tore autorizzato** authorized dealer

ri'verbero m reverberation; (bagliore) glare

rive'renza f reverence; (inchino) curtsy; (di uomo) bow

rive'rire vt respect; (ossequiare) pay one's respects to

river'sar|e vt pour. **~si** vr (fiume:) flow

rivesti'mento m covering

rive'sti|re vt (rifornire di abiti) clothe; (ricoprire) cover; (internamente) line; hold (carica). **~rsi** vr get dressed again; (per una festa) dress up

C **rivi'era** f coast; **la ~ ligure** the Italian Riviera

ri'vincita f Sport return match; (vendetta) revenge

rivis'suto pp di **rivivere**

ri'vista f review; (pubblicazione) magazine; (Theat) revue; **passare in ~** review

ri'vivere vi come to life again; (riprendere le forze) revive • vt relive

ri'volger|e vt turn; (indirizzare)

C *see A-Z of Italian life and culture*

address; ~**e da** (distogliere) turn away from. ~**si** vr turn round; ~**si a** (indirizzarsi) turn to

ri'volta f revolt

rivol'tante adj disgusting

rivol'tar|e vt turn [over]; (mettendo l'interno verso l'esterno) turn inside out; (sconvolgere) upset. ~**si** vr (ribellarsi) revolt

rivol'tella f revolver

ri'volto pp di **rivolgere**

rivoluzio'nar|e vt revolutionize. ~**io, -a** adj & mf revolutionary. **rivoluzi'one** f revolution; (fig: disordine) chaos

riz'zar|e vt raise; (innalzare) erect; prick up (orecchie). ~**si** vr stand up; (capelli:) stand on end; (orecchie:) prick up

'roaming m inv (Teleph) ~ [**internazionale**] roaming

'roba f stuff; (personale) belongings pl, stuff; (faccenda) thing; (⊠: droga) drugs pl. ~ **da mangiare** things to eat

ro'baccia f rubbish

ro'bot m inv robot. ~ **da cucina** food processor

robu'stezza f sturdiness, robustness; (forza) strength. **ro'busto** adj sturdy, robust; (forte) strong

'rocca f fortress. ~**'forte** f stronghold

roc'chetto m reel

'roccia f rock

ro'da|ggio m running in. ~**re** vt run in

'roder|e vt gnaw; (corrodere) corrode. ~**si** vr ~**si da** be consumed with. **rodi'tore** m rodent

rodo'dendro m rhododendron

ro'gnone m (Culin) kidney

'rogo m (supplizio) stake; (per cadaveri) pyre

'Roma f Rome

Roma'nia f Romania

ro'manico adj Romanesque

ro'mano, -a adj & mf Roman

romanti'cismo m romanticism. **ro'mantico** adj romantic

ro'man|za f romance. ~**'zato** adj romanticized. ~**'zesco** adj fictional; (stravagante) wild, unrealistic. ~**zi'ere** m novelist

ro'manzo adj Romance • m novel. ~ **giallo** thriller

'rombo m rumble; (Math) rhombus; (pesce) turbot

'romper|e vt break; break off (relazione); **non** ~**e [le scatole]!** (!: seccare) don't be a pain [in the neck]!. ~**si** vr break; ~**si una gamba** break one's leg

rompi'capo m nuisance; (indovinello) puzzle

rompi'collo m daredevil; **a** ~ at breakneck speed

rompighi'accio m ice-breaker

rompi'scatole mf inv ! pain

'ronda f rounds pl

ron'della f (Mech) washer

'rondine f swallow

ron'done m swift

ron'fare vi snore

ron'zino m jade

ron'zio m buzz

'rosa f rose. ~ **dei venti** wind rose • adj & m pink. **ro'saio** m rose-bush

ro'sario m rosary

ro'sato adj rosy • m (vino) rosé

'roseo adj pink

ro'seto m rose garden

rosma'rino m rosemary

'roso pp di **rodere**

roso'lare vt brown

roso'lia f German measles

ro'sone m rosette; (apertura) rose-window

'rospo m toad

ros'setto m (per labbra) lipstick

'rosso adj & m red; **passare con il** ~ jump a red light. ~ **d'uovo** [egg] yolk. **ros'sore** m redness; (della pelle) flush

rosticce'ria f shop selling cooked meat and other prepared food

ro'tabile adj **strada** ~ carriageway

ro'taia f rail; (solco) rut

ro'ta|re vt/i rotate. **~zi'one** f rotation

rote'are vt/i roll

ro'tella f small wheel; (di mobile) castor

roto'lar|e vt/i roll. **~si** vr roll [about]. **'rotolo** m roll; **andare a rotoli** go to rack and ruin

rotondità f roundness; ~ pl (curve femminili) curves. **ro'tondo, -a** adj round •f (spiazzo) terrace

ro'tore m rotor

'rotta¹ f (Naut, Aeron) course; **far ~ per** make course for; **fuori ~** off course

'rotta² f **a ~ di collo** at breakneck speed; **essere in ~ con** be on bad terms with

rot'tame m scrap; fig wreck

'rotto pp di **rompere** •adj broken; (stracciato) torn

rot'tura f break

'rotula f kneecap

rou'lette f inv roulette

rou'lotte f inv caravan, trailer Am

rou'tine f inv routine; **di ~** (operazioni, controlli) routine

ro'vente adj scorching

'rovere m (legno) oak

rovesci'ar|e vt knock over; (sottosopra) turn upside down; (rivoltare) turn inside out; spill (liquido); overthrow (governo); reverse (situazione). **~si** vr (capovolgersi) overturn; (riversarsi) pour. **ro'vescio** adj (contrario) reverse; **alla rovescia** (capovolto) upside down; (con l'interno all'esterno) inside out •m reverse; (nella maglia) purl; (di pioggia) downpour; Tennis backhand

ro'vina f ruin; (crollo) collapse

rovi'na|re vt ruin; (guastare) spoil •vi crash. **~rsi** vr be ruined. **~to** adj (oggetto) ruined. **rovi'noso** adj ruinous

rovi'stare vt ransack

'rovo m bramble

'rozzo adj rough

R.R. abbr (ricevuta di ritorno) return receipt for registered mail

'ruba f **andare a ~** sell like hot cakes

ru'bare vt steal

rubi'netto m tap, faucet Am

ru'bino m ruby

ru'brica f column; (in programma televisivo) TV report; (quaderno con indice) address book. **~ telefonica** telephone and address book

'rude adj rough

'rudere m ruin

rudimen'tale adj rudimentary. **rudi'menti** mpl rudiments

ruffi'an|a f procuress. **~o** m pimp; (adulatore) bootlicker

'ruga f wrinkle

'ruggine f rust; **fare la ~** go rusty

rug'gi|re vi roar. **~to** m roar

rugi'ada f dew

ru'goso adj wrinkled

rul'lare vi roll; (Aeron) taxi

rul'lino m film

rul'lio m rolling; (Aeron) taxiing

rum m inv rum

ru'meno, -a adj & mf Romanian

ru'mor|e m noise; fig rumour. **~eggi'are** vi rumble. **rumo'roso** adj noisy; (sonoro) loud

ru'olo m roll; (Theat) role; **di ~** on the staff

ru'ota f wheel; **andare a ~ libera** free-wheel. **~ di scorta** spare wheel

'rupe f cliff

ru'rale adj rural

ru'scello m stream

'ruspa f bulldozer

rus'sare vi snore

'Russ|ia f Russia. **r~o, -a** adj & mf Russian; (lingua) Russian

'rustico adj rural; (carattere) rough

rut'tare vi belch. **'rutto** m belch

'ruvido adj coarse

ruzzo'l|are vi tumble down. **~one** m tumble; **cadere ruzzoloni** tumble down

r

Ss

'sabato m Saturday

'sabbi|a f sand. **~e** pl **mobili** quicksand. **~'oso** a sandy

sabo'ta|ggio m sabotage. **~re** vt sabotage. **~'tore, ~'trice** mf saboteur

'sacca f bag. **~ da viaggio** travelling-bag

sacca'rina f saccharin

sac'cente adj pretentious •mf know-all

saccheggi'a|re vt sack; hum raid (frigo)

sac'chetto m bag

'sacco m sack; (Anat) sac; **mettere nel ~** fig swindle; **un ~** (moltissimo) a lot; **un ~ di** (gran quantità) lots of. **~ a pelo** sleeping-bag

sacer'do|te m priest

sacra'mento m sacrament

sacrifi'ca|re vt sacrifice. **~rsi** vr sacrifice oneself. **~to** adj (non valorizzato) wasted. **sacri'ficio** m sacrifice

sa'crilego adj sacrilegious

'sacro adj sacred •m (Anat) sacrum

sacro'santo adj sacrosanct

'sadico, -a adj sadistic •mf sadist. **sa'dismo** m sadism

sa'etta f arrow

sa'fari m inv safari

'saga f saga

sa'gace adj shrewd

sag'gezza f wisdom

saggi'are vt test

'saggio[1] m (scritto) essay; (prova) proof; (di metallo) assay; (campione) sample; (esempio) example

'saggio[2] adj wise

sag'gistica f non-fiction

Sagit'tario m (Astr) Sagittarius

'sagoma f shape; (profilo) outline. **sago'mato** adj shaped

🅒 **'sagra** f festival

sagre|'stano m sacristan. **~'stia** f sacristy

'sala f hall; (stanza) room; (salotto) living room. **~ d'attesa** waiting room. **~ da ballo** ballroom. **~ d'imbarco** departure lounge. **~ macchine** engine room. **~ operatoria** operating theatre. **~ parto** delivery room. **~ da pranzo** dining room

sa'lame m salami

sala'moia f brine

sa'lare vt salt

sa'lario m wages pl

sa'lasso m **essere un ~** fig cost a fortune

sala'tini mpl savouries (eaten with aperitifs)

sa'lato adj salty; (costoso) dear

sal'ciccia f = **salsiccia**

sal'dar|e vt weld; set (osso); pay off (debito); settle (conto); **~e a stagno** solder. **~si** vr (Med: osso:) knit

salda'trice f welder; (a stagno) soldering iron

salda'tura f weld; (azione) welding; (di osso) knitting

'saldo adj firm; (resistente) strong •m settlement; (svendita) sale; (Comm) balance

'sale m salt. **~ fine** table salt. **~ grosso** cooking salt. **sali** pl **e tabacchi** tobacconist's shop

'salice m willow. **~ piangente** weeping willow

sali'ente adj outstanding; **i punti salienti di un discorso** the main points of a speech

sali'era f salt-cellar

sa'lina f salt-works sg

sa'li|re vi go/come up; (levarsi) rise; (su treno ecc) get on; (in macchina) get in

🅒 see A-Z of Italian life and culture

• vt go/come up (scale). **~ta** f climb; (aumento) rise; **in ~ta** uphill

sa'liva f saliva

salma f corpse

salmo m psalm

sal'mone m & adj inv salmon

sa'lone m hall; (salotto) living room; (di parrucchiere) salon. **~ di bellezza** beauty parlour

salo'pette f inv dungarees pl

salot'tino m bower

sa'lotto m drawing room; (soggiorno) sitting room; (mobili) [three-piece] suite

sal'pare vt/i sail; **~ l'ancora** weigh anchor

salsa f sauce

sal'sedine f saltiness

sal'siccia f sausage

sal'ta|re vi jump; (venir via) come off; (balzare) leap; (esplodere) blow up; **~r fuori** spring from nowhere; (oggetto cercato:) turn up; **è ~to fuori che...** it emerged that...; **~re fuori con...** come out with...; **~re in mente** spring to mind • vt jump [over]; skip (pasti, lezioni); (Culin) sauté. **~to** adj (Culin) sautéed

saltel'lare vi hop; (di gioia) skip

saltim'banco m acrobat

salto m jump; (balzo) leap; (dislivello) drop; (omissione, lacuna) gap; **fare un ~ da** drop in on. **~ in alto** high jump. **~ con l'asta** pole-vault. **~ in lungo** long jump. **~ pagina** (Comput) page down

saltuaria'mente adv occasionally. **saltu'ario** adj desultory; **lavoro saltuario** casual work

sa'lubre adj healthy

salume'ria f delicatessen. **sa'lumi** mpl cold cuts

salu'tare vt greet; (congedandosi) say goodbye to; (portare i saluti a) give one's regards to; (Mil) salute • adj healthy

sa'lute f health; **~!** (dopo uno starnuto) bless you!; (a un brindisi) your health!

sa'luto m greeting; (di addio) goodbye; (Mil) salute; **saluti** pl (ossequi) regards

salva f salvo; **sparare a salve** fire blanks

salvada'naio m money box

salva'gente m lifebelt; (a giubbotto) life-jacket; (ciambella) rubber ring; (spartitraffico) traffic island

salvaguar'dare vt safeguard. **salvagu'ardia** f safeguard

sal'var|e vt save; (proteggere) protect. **~si** vr save oneself

salva'slip m inv panty-liner

salva|'taggio m rescue; (Naut) salvage; (Comput) saving; **battello di ~taggio** lifeboat

sal'vezza f safety; (Relig) salvation

'salvia f sage

salvi'etta f serviette

'salvo adj safe • prep except [for] • conj **~ che** (a meno che) unless; (eccetto che) except that

samari'tano, -a adj & mf Samaritan

sam'buco m elder

san m **S~ Francesco** Saint Francis

sa'nare vt heal

sana'torio m sanatorium

san'cire vt sanction

'sandalo m sandal

'sangu|e m blood; **al ~e** (carne) rare; **farsi cattivo ~e per** worry about. **~e freddo** composure; **a ~e freddo** in cold blood. **~'igno** adj blood

sangui'naccio m (Culin) black pudding

sangui'nante adj bleeding

sangui'nar|e vi bleed. **~io** adj bloodthirsty

sangui'noso adj bloody

sangui'suga f leech

sanità f soundness; (salute) health. **~ mentale** mental health

sani'tario adj sanitary; **Servizio S~** Health Service

'sano adj sound; (salutare) healthy; **~ di mente** sane; **~ come un pesce** as fit as a fiddle

San Sil'vestro m New Year's Eve

santifi'care vt sanctify

'santo adj holy; (con nome proprio) saint • m saint. **san'tone** m guru. **santu'ario** m sanctuary

sanzi'one f sanction

sa'pere vt know; (essere capace di) be able to; (venire a sapere) hear; **saperla lunga** know a thing or two •vi ~ **di** know about; (aver sapore di) taste of; (aver odore di) smell of; **saperci fare** have the know-how •m knowledge

sapi'en|te adj wise; (esperto) expert •m (uomo colto) sage. **~za** f wisdom

sa'pone m soap. ~ **da bucato** washing soap. **sapo'netta** f bar of soap

sa'pore m taste. **saporita'mente** adv soundly. **sapo'rito** adj tasty

sapu'tello, -a adj & m ☒ know-all, know-it-all Am

saraci'nesca f roller shutter

sar'cas|mo m sarcasm. **~tico** adj sarcastic

Sar'degna f Sardinia

sar'dina f sardine

'sardo, -a adj & mf Sardinian

sar'donico adj sardonic

'sarto, -a m tailor •f dressmaker. **~'ria** f tailor's; dressmaker's; (arte) couture

'sasso m stone; (ciottolo) pebble

sassofo'nista mf saxophonist. **sas'sofono** m saxophone

sas'soso adj stony

sa'tellite adj inv & nm satellite

sati'nato adj glossy

'satira f satire. **sa'tirico** adj satirical

satu'ra|re vt saturate. **~zi'one** f saturation. **'saturo** adj saturated; (pieno) full

'sauna f sauna

savoi'ardo m (biscotto) sponge finger

sazi'ar|e vt satiate. **~si** vr **~si di** fig grow tired of

sazietà f **mangiare a** ~ eat one's fill. **'sazio** adj satiated

sbaciucchi'ar|e vt smother with kisses. **~si** vr kiss and cuddle

sbada'ta|ggine f carelessness; **è stata una ~ggine** it was careless. **~'mente** adv carelessly. **sba'dato** adj careless

sbadigli'are vi yawn. **sba'diglio** m yawn

sba'fa|re vt sponge

'sbafo m sponging; **a** ~ without paying

sbagli'ar|e vi make a mistake; (aver torto) be wrong •vt make a mistake in; **~e strada** go the wrong way; **~e numero** get the number wrong; (Teleph) dial a wrong number. **~si** vr make a mistake. **'sbaglio** m mistake; **per sbaglio** by mistake

sbal'l|are vt unpack; ! screw up (conti) •vi ! go crazy. **~ato** adj (squilibrato) unbalanced

sballot'tare vt toss about

sbalor'di|re vt stun •vi be stunned. **~'tivo** adj amazing. **~to** adj stunned

sbal'zare vt throw; (da una carica) dismiss •vi bounce; (saltare) leap. **'sbalzo** m bounce; (sussulto) jolt; (di temperatura) sudden change; **a sbalzi** in spurts; **a sbalzo** (lavoro a rilievo) embossed

sban'care vt bankrupt; ~ **il banco** break the bank

sbanda'mento m (Auto) skid; (Naut) list; fig going off the rails

sban'da|re vi (Auto) skid; (Naut) list. **~rsi** vr (disperdersi) disperse. **~ta** f skid; (Naut) list. **~to, -a** adj mixed-up •mf mixed-up person

sbandie'rare vt wave; fig display

sbarac'care vt/i clear up

sbaragli'are vt rout. **sba'raglio** m rout; **mettere allo sbaraglio** rout

sbaraz'zar|e vt clear. **~si** vr **~si di** get rid of

sbaraz'zino, -a adj mischievous •mf scamp

sbar'bar|e vt, **~si** vr shave

sbar'care vt/i disembark; ~ **il lunario** make ends meet. **'sbarco** m landing; (di merci) unloading

'sbarra f bar; (di passaggio a livello) barrier. **~'mento** m barricade. **sbar'rare** vt bar; (ostruire) block; cross (assegno); (spalancare) open wide

sbatacchi'are vt/i ☒ bang

'sbatter|e vt bang; slam, bang (porta); (urtare) knock; (Culin) beat; flap (ali); shake (tappeto) •vi bang; (porta:) slam, bang. **~si** vr ☒ rush around; **~sene di qcsa** not give a damn about sth. **sbat'tuto** adj tossed; (Culin) beaten; fig run down

S

see A-Z of Italian life and culture

sba'va|re vi dribble; (colore:) smear. **~'tura** f smear; **senza ~ture** fig faultless

sbelli'carsi vr **~ dalle risa** split one's sides [with laughter]

'sberla f slap

sbia'di|re vt/i, **~rsi** vr fade. **~to** adj faded; fig colourless

sbian'car|e vt/i, **~si** vr whiten

sbi'eco adj slanting; **di ~** on the slant; (guardare) sidelong; **guardare qcno di ~** look askance at sb; **tagliare di ~** cut on the bias

sbigot'ti|re vt dismay • vi, **~rsi** vr be dismayed. **~to** adj dismayed

sbilanci'ar|e vt unbalance • vi (perdere l'equilibrio) overbalance. **~si** vr lose one's balance

sbizzar'rirsi vr satisfy one's whims

sbloc'care vt unblock; (Mech) release; decontrol (prezzi)

sboc'care vi **~ in** (fiume:) flow into; (strada:) lead to; (folla:) pour into

sboc'cato adj foul-mouthed

sbocci'are vi blossom

'sbocco m flowing; (foce) mouth; (Comm) outlet

sbolo'gnare vt [!] get rid of

'sbornia f **prendere una ~** get drunk

sbor'sare vt pay out

sbot'tare vi burst out

sbotto'nar|e vt unbutton. **~si** vr ([!]: confidarsi) open up; **~si la camicia** unbutton one's shirt

sbra'carsi vr put on something more comfortable; **~ dalle risate** [!] kill oneself laughing

sbracci'a|rsi vr wave one's arms. **~to** adj bare-armed; (abito) sleeveless

sbrai'tare vi bawl

sbra'nare vt tear to pieces

sbricio'lar|e vt, **~si** vr crumble

sbri'ga|re vt expedite; (occuparsi di) attend to. **~rsi** vr be quick. **~'tivo** adj quick

sbrindel'lare vt tear to shreds. **~to** adj in rags

sbrodo'l|are vt stain

'sbronz|a f **prendersi una ~a** get tight. **sbron'zarsi** vr get tight. **~o** adj (ubriaco) tight

sbruffo'nata f boast. **sbruf'fone, -a** mf boaster

sbu'care vi come out

sbucci'ar|e vt peel; shell (piselli). **~si** vr graze oneself

sbuf'fare vi snort; (per impazienza) fume. **'sbuffo** m puff

'scabbia f scabies sg

sca'broso adj rough; fig difficult; (scena) indecent

scacci'are vt chase away

'scacc|o m check; **~hi** pl (gioco) chess; (pezzi) chessmen; **dare ~o matto a** checkmate; **a ~hi** (tessuto) checked. **~hi'era** f chess-board

sca'dente adj shoddy

sca'de|nza f expiry; (Comm) maturity; (di progetto) deadline; **a breve/lunga ~nza** short-/long-term. **~re** vi expire; (valore:) decline; (debito:) be due. **sca'duto** adj out-of-date

sca'fandro m diving suit; (di astronauta) spacesuit

scaf'fale m shelf; (libreria) bookshelf

sca'fista m motor-boat operator; (pej) refugee smuggler (using motorboat)

'scafo m hull

scagion'are vt exonerate

'scaglia f scale; (di sapone) flake; (scheggia) chip

scagli'ar|e vt fling. **~si** vr fling oneself; **~si contro** fig rail against

scagli|o'nare vt space out. **~'one** m group; **a ~oni** in groups. **~one di reddito** tax bracket

'scala f staircase; (portatile) ladder; (Mus, misura, fig) scale; **scale** pl stairs. **~ mobile** escalator; (dei salari) cost of living index

sca'la|re vt climb; layer (capelli); (detrarre) deduct. **~ta** f climb; (dell'Everest ecc) ascent; **fare delle ~te** go climbing. **~'tore, ~'trice** mf climber

scalca'gnato adj down at heel

scalci'are vi kick

scalci'nato adj shabby

scalda'bagno m water heater

scalda'muscoli m inv leg-warmer
scal'dar|e vt heat. **~si** vr warm up; (eccitarsi) get excited
scal'fi|re vt scratch. **~t'tura** f scratch
scali'nata f flight of steps. **sca'lino** m step; (di scala a pioli) rung
scalma'narsi vr get worked up
'scalo m slipway; (Aeron, Naut) port of call; **fare ~ a** call at; (Aeron) land at
sca'lo|gna f bad luck. **~'gnato** adj unlucky
scalop'pina f escalope
scal'pello m chisel
'scalpo m scalp
scal'pore m noise; **far ~** fig cause a sensation
scal'trezza f shrewdness. **'scaltro** adj shrewd
scal'zare vt bare the roots of (albero); fig undermine; (da una carica) oust
'scalzo adj & adv barefoot
scambi|'are vt exchange; **~are qcno per qualcun altro** mistake sb for somebody else. **~'evole** adj reciprocal
'scambio m exchange; (Comm) trade; **libero ~** free trade
scamosci'ato adj suede
scampa'gnata f trip to the country
scampa'nato adj (gonna) flared
scampanel'lata f [loud] ring
scam'pare vt save; (evitare) escape. **'scampo** m escape
'scampolo m remnant
scanala'tura f groove
scandagli'are vt sound
scanda'listico adj sensational
scandal|iz'zare vt scandalize. **~iz'zarsi** vr be scandalized
'scanda|lo m scandal. **~'loso** adj (somma) ecc scandalous; (fortuna) outrageous
Scandi'navia f Scandinavia. **scandi'navo, -a** adj & mf Scandinavian
scan'dire vt scan (verso); pronounce clearly (parole)
scan'nare vt slaughter
'scanner m inv scanner
scanneriz'zare vt (Comput) scan
scan'sar|e vt shift; (evitare) avoid. **~si** vr get out of the way
scansi'one f (Comput) scanning
'scanso m **a ~ di** in order to avoid; **a ~ di equivoci** to avoid any misunderstanding
scanti'nato m basement
scanto'nare vi turn the corner; (svignarsela) sneak off
scanzo'nato adj easy-going
scapacci'one m smack
scape'strato adj dissolute
'scapito m loss
'scapola f shoulder-blade
'scapolo m bachelor
scappa'mento m (Auto) exhaust
scap'pa|re vi escape; (andarsene) dash [off]; (sfuggire) slip; **mi ~ da ridere!** I want to burst out laughing. **~ta** f short visit. **~'tella** f escapade; (infedeltà) fling. **~'toia** f way out
scappel'lotto m cuff
scarabocchi'are vt scribble
scara'bocchio m scribble
scara'faggio m cockroach
scara'muccia f skirmish
scaraven'tare vt hurl
scarce'rare vt release [from prison]
scardi'nare vt unhinge
'scarica f discharge; (di arma da fuoco) volley; fig shower
scari'ca|re vt discharge; unload (arma, merci); (Comput) download; fig unburden. **~rsi** vr (fiume:) flow; (orologio, batteria:) run down; fig unwind. **~'tore** m loader; (di porto) docker. **'scarico** adj unloaded; (vuoto) empty; (orologio) run-down; (batteria) flat; fig untroubled • m unloading; (di rifiuti) dumping; (di acqua) draining; (di sostanze inquinanti) discharge; (luogo) [rubbish] dump; (Auto) exhaust; (idraulico) drain; (tubo) waste pipe
scarlat'tina f scarlet fever
scar'latto adj scarlet
'scarno adj thin; (stile) bare
sca'ro|gna f [!] bad luck. **~'gnato** adj [!] unlucky
'scarpa f shoe. **scarpe** pl **da ginnastica** trainers, gym shoes

scar'pata f slope; (burrone) escarpment

scarpi'nare vi hike

scar'pone m boot. **scarponi** pl **da sci** ski boot. **scarponi** pl **da trekking** walking boots

scarroz'zare vt/i drive around

scarseggi'are vi be scarce; **~ di** (mancare) be short of

scar'sezza f scarcity, shortage. **scarsità** f shortage. **'scarso** adj scarce; (manchevole) short

scarta'mento m (Rail) gauge. **~ ridotto** narrow gauge

scar'tare vt discard; unwrap (pacco); (respingere) reject •vi (deviare) swerve. **'scarto** m scrap; (in carte) discard; (deviazione) swerve; (distacco) gap

scas'sa|re vt break. **~to** adj [!] clapped out

scassi'nare vt force open

scassina'tore, -'trice mf burglar. **'scasso** m (furto) house-breaking

scate'na|re vt fig stir up. **~rsi** vr break out; fig: (temporale:) break; ([!]: infiammarsi) get excited. **~to** adj crazy

'scatola f box; (di latta) can, tin Br; **in ~** (cibo) canned, tinned Br

scat'tare vi go off; (balzare) spring up; (adirarsi) lose one's temper; take (foto). **'scatto** m (balzo) spring; (d'ira) outburst; (di telefono) unit; (dispositivo) release; **a scatti** jerkily; **di scatto** suddenly

scatu'rire vi spring

scaval'care vt jump over (muretto); climb over (muro); (fig: superare) overtake

sca'vare vt dig (buca); dig up (tesoro); excavate (città sepolta). **'scavo** m excavation

'scegliere vt choose, select

scelle'rato adj wicked

'scelt|a f choice; (di articoli) range; **...a ~a** (in menu) choice of...; **prendine uno a ~a** take your choice o pick; **di prima ~a** top-grade, choice. **~o** pp di **scegliere** •adj select; (merce ecc) choice

sce'mare vt/i diminish

sce'menza f silliness; (azione) silly thing to do/say. **'scemo** adj silly

'scempio m havoc; (fig: di paesaggio) ruination; **fare ~ di** play havoc with

'scena f scene; (palcoscenico) stage; **entrare in ~** go/come on; fig enter the scene; **fare ~** put on an act; **fare una ~** make a scene; **andare in ~** (Theat) be staged, be put on. **sce'nario** m scenery

sce'nata f row, scene

'scendere vi go/come down; (da treno, autobus) get off; (da macchina) get out; (strada:) slope; (notte, prezzi:) fall •vt go/come down (scale)

sceneggi'a|re vt dramatize. **~to** m television serial. **~'tura** f screenplay

'scenico adj scenic

scervel'la|rsi vr rack one's brains. **~to** adj brainless

'sceso pp di **scendere**

scetti'cismo m scepticism. **'scettico, -a** adj sceptical •mf sceptic

'scheda f card. **~ elettorale** ballot-paper. **~ di espansione** (Comput) expansion card. **~ telefonica** phonecard. **sche'dare** vt file. **sche'dario** m file; (mobile) filing cabinet

sche'dina f ≈ pools coupon; **giocare la ~** do the pools

'scheggi|a f fragment; (di legno) splinter. **~'arsi** vr chip; (legno:) splinter

'scheletro m skeleton

'schema m diagram; (abbozzo) outline. **sche'matico** adj schematic

'scherma f fencing

scher'mirsi vr protect oneself

'schermo m screen; **grande ~** big screen

scher'nire vt mock. **'scherno** m mockery

scher'zare vi joke; (giocare) play

'scherzo m joke; (trucco) trick; (effetto) play; (Mus) scherzo; **fare uno ~ a qcno** play a joke on sb. **scher'zoso** adj playful

schiaccia'noci m inv nutcrackers pl

schiacci'ante adj damning

schiacci'are vt crush; Sport smash; press (pulsante); crack (noce)

schiaffeggi'are vt slap. **schi'affo** m

slap; **dare uno schiaffo a** slap

schiamaz'zare vi make a racket; (galline:) cackle

schian'tar|e vt break. •vi **schianto dalla fatica** I'm wiped out. **~si** vr crash **'schianto** m crash; [!] knock-out; (divertente) scream

schia'rir|e vt clear; (sbiadire) fade •vi, **~si** vr brighten up; **~si la gola** clear one's throat

schiavitù f slavery. **schi'avo, -a** mf slave

schi'ena f back; **mal di ~** backache. **schie'nale** m (di sedia) back

schi'er|a f (Mil) rank; (moltitudine) crowd. **~a'mento** m lining up

schie'rar|e vt draw up. **~si** vr draw up; **~si con** (parteggiare) side with

schiet'tezza f frankness. **schi'etto** adj frank; (puro) pure

schi'fezza f **una ~** rubbish. **schifil'toso** adj fussy. **'schifo** m disgust; **mi fa schifo** it makes me sick. **schi'foso** adj disgusting; (di cattiva qualità) rubbishy

schioc'care vt crack; snap (dita). **schi'occo** m (di frusta) crack; (di bacio) smack; (di dita, lingua) click

schi'uder|e vt, **~si** vr open

schi'u|ma f foam; (di sapone) lather; (feccia) scum. **~ma da barba** shaving foam. **~'mare** vt skim •vi foam

schi'uso pp di **schiudere**

schi'vare vt avoid. **'schivo** adj bashful

schizo'frenico adj schizophrenic

schiz'zare vt squirt; (inzaccherare) splash; (abbozzare) sketch •vi spurt; **~ via** scurry away

schizzi'noso adj squeamish

'schizzo m squirt; (di fango) splash; (abbozzo) sketch

sci m inv ski; (sport) skiing. **~ d'acqua** water-skiing

'scia f wake; (di fumo ecc) trail

sci'abola f sabre

scia'callo m jackal; fig profiteer

sciac'quar|e vt rinse. **~si** vr rinse oneself. **sci'acquo** m mouthwash

scia'gu|ra f disaster. **~'rato** adj unfortunate; (scellerato) wicked

scialac'quare vt squander

scia'lare vi squander

sci'albo adj pale; fig dull

sci'alle m shawl

scia'luppa f dinghy. **~ di salvataggio** lifeboat

sci'ame m swarm

sci'ampo m shampoo

scian'cato adj lame

sci'are vi ski

sci'arpa f scarf

sci'atica f (Med) sciatica

scia'tore, -'trice mf skier

sci'atto adj slovenly; (stile) careless. **sciat'tone, -a** mf slovenly person

scienti'fico adj scientific

sci'enz|a f science; (sapere) knowledge. **~i'ato, -a** mf scientist

'scimmi|a f monkey. **~ot'tare** vt ape

scimpanzé m inv chimpanzee, chimp

scimu'nito adj idiotic

'scinder|e vt, **~si** vr split

scin'tilla f spark. **scintil'lante** adj sparkling. **scintil'lare** vi sparkle

scioc'ca|nte adj shocking. **~re** vt shock

scioc'chezza f foolishness; (assurdità) nonsense. **sci'occo** adj foolish

sci'oglier|e vt untie; (liberare) release; (liquefare) melt; dissolve (contratto, qcsa nell'acqua); loosen up (muscoli). **~si** vr release oneself; (liquefarsi) melt; (contratto:) be dissolved; (pastiglia:) dissolve

sciogli'lingua m inv tongue-twister

scio'lina f wax

sciol'tezza f agility; (disinvoltura) ease

sci'olto pp di **sciogliere** •adj loose; (agile) agile; (disinvolto) easy; **versi sciolti** blank verse sg

sciope'ra|nte mf striker. **~re** vi go on strike, strike. **sci'opero** m strike. **sciopero a singhiozzo** on-off strike

sciori'nare vt fig show off

sci'pito adj insipid

scip'pa|re vt [!] snatch. **~'tore, ~'trice** mf bag snatcher. **'scippo** m bag-snatching

sci'rocco m sirocco

scirop'pato adj (frutta) in syrup. **sci'roppo** m syrup

'scisma m schism

scissi'one f division

'scisso pp di **scindere**

sciu'par|e vt spoil; (sperperare) waste. **~si** vr get spoiled; (deperire) wear oneself out. **sciu'pio** m waste

scivo'l|are vi slide; (involontariamente) slip. **'scivolo** m slide; (Techn) chute. **~oso** adj slippery

scoc'care vt shoot • vi (scintilla:) shoot out; (ora:) strike

scocci'a|re vt (dare noia a) bother. **~rsi** vr be bothered. **~to** adj [!] narked. **~'tore, ~'trice** mf bore. **~'tura** f nuisance

sco'della f bowl

scodinzo'lare vi wag its tail

scogli'era f cliff; (a fior d'acqua) reef. **'scoglio** m rock; (fig: ostacolo) stumbling block

scoi'attolo m squirrel

scola|'pasta m inv colander. **~pi'atti** m inv dish drainer

sco'lara f schoolgirl

sco'lare vt drain; strain (pasta, verdura) • vi drip

sco'la|ro m schoolboy. **~'resca** f pupils pl. **~stico** adj school attrib

scol'la|re vt cut away the neck of (abito); (staccare) unstick. **~to** adj low-necked. **~'tura** f neckline

'scolo m drainage

scolo'ri|re vt, **~rsi** vr fade. **~to** adj faded

scol'pire vt carve; (imprimere) engrave

scombi'nare vt upset

scombusso'lare vt muddle up

scom'mess|a f bet. **~o** pp di **scommettere**. **scom'mettere** vt bet

scomo'dar|e vt, **~si** vr trouble. **scomodità** f discomfort. **'scomodo** adj uncomfortable

scompa'rire vi disappear; (morire) pass on. **scom'parsa** f disappearance; (morte) passing, death. **scom'parso, -a** pp di **scomparire** • mf departed

scomparti'mento m compartment. **scom'parto** f compartment

scom'penso m imbalance

scompigli'are vt disarrange. **scom'piglio** m confusion

scom'po|rre vt take to pieces; (fig: turbare) upset. **~rsi** vr get flustered. **~sto** pp di **scomporre** • adj (sguaiato) unseemly; (disordinato) untidy

sco'muni|ca f excommunication. **~'care** vt excommunicate

sconcer'ta|re vt disconcert; (rendere perplesso) bewilder. **~to** adj disconcerted; bewildered

scon'cezza f obscenity. **'sconcio** adj dirty • m **è uno sconcio che...** it's a disgrace that...

sconclusio'nato adj incoherent

scon'dito adj unseasoned; (insalata) with no dressing

sconfes'sare vt disown

scon'figgere vt defeat

sconfi'na|re vi cross the border; (in proprietà privata) trespass. **~to** adj unlimited

scon'fitt|a f defeat. **~o** pp di **sconfiggere**

scon'forto m dejection

sconge'lare vt thaw out (cibo), defrost

scongi|u'rare vt beseech; (evitare) avert. **~'uro** m **fare gli scongiuri** touch wood, knock on wood Am

scon'nesso pp di **sconnettere** • adj fig incoherent. **scon'nettere** vt disconnect

sconosci'uto, -a adj unknown • mf stranger

sconquas'sare vt smash; (sconvolgere) upset

sconside'rato adj inconsiderate

sconsigli'a|bile adj not advisable. **~re** vt advise against

sconso'lato adj disconsolate

scon'ta|re vt discount; (dedurre) deduct; (pagare) pay off; serve (pena). **~to** adj discount; (ovvio) expected; **~to del 10%** with 10% discount

scon'tento adj displeased • m discontent

'sconto m discount; **fare uno ~** give a discount

scon'trarsi vr clash; (urtare) collide

scon'trino m ticket; (di cassa) receipt

S

'scontro m clash; (urto) collision
scon'troso adj unsociable
sconveni'ente adj unprofitable; (scorretto) unseemly
sconvol'gente adj mind-blowing
scon'vol|gere vt upset; (mettere in disordine) disarrange. **~gi'mento** m upheaval. **~to** pp di **sconvolgere** • adj distraught
'scopa f broom. **sco'pare** vt sweep
scoperchi'are vt take the lid off (pentola); take the roof off (casa)
sco'pert|a f discovery. **~o** pp di **scoprire** • adj uncovered; (senza riparo) exposed; (conto) overdrawn; (spoglio) bare
'scopo m aim; **allo ~ di** in order to
scoppi'are vi burst; fig break out. **scoppiet'tare** vi crackle. **'scoppio** m burst; (di guerra) outbreak; (esplosione) explosion
sco'prire vt discover; (togliere la copertura a) uncover
scoraggi'a|re vt discourage. **~rsi** vr lose heart
scor'butico adj peevish
scorcia'toia f short cut
'scorcio m (di epoca) end; (di cielo) patch; (in arte) foreshortening; **di ~** (vedere) from an angle. **~ panoramico** panoramic view
scor'da|re vt, **~rsi** vr forget. **~to** adj (Mus) out of tune
'scorgere vt make out; (notare) notice
'scoria f waste; (di metallo, carbone) slag; **scorie** pl **radioattive** radioactive waste
scor'nato adj fig hangdog. **'scorno** m humiliation
scorpi'one m scorpion; (Astr) **S~** Scorpio
scorraz'zare vi run about
'scorrere vt (dare un'occhiata) glance through • vi run; (scivolare) slide; (fluire) flow; (Comput) scroll. **scor'revole** adj **porta scorrevole** sliding door
scorre'ria f raid
scorret'tezza f (mancanza di educazione) bad manners pl. **scor'retto** adj incorrect; (sconveniente) improper
scorri'banda f raid; fig excursion
'scors|a f glance. **~o** pp di **scorrere** • adj last
scor'soio adj **nodo ~** noose
'scor|ta f escort; (provvista) supply. **~'tare** vt escort
scor'te|se adj discourteous. **~'sia** f discourtesy
scorti'ca|re vt skin. **~'tura** f graze
'scorto pp di **scorgere**
'scorza f peel; (crosta) crust; (corteccia) bark
sco'sceso adj steep
'scossa f shake; (Electr, fig) shock; **prendere la ~** get an electric shock. **~ elettrica** electric shock. **~ sismica** earth tremor
'scosso pp di **scuotere** • adj shaken; (sconvolto) upset
sco'stante adj off-putting
sco'sta|re vt push away. **~rsi** vr stand aside
scostu'mato adj dissolute; (maleducato) ill-mannered
scot'tante adj dangerous
scot'ta|re vt scald • vi burn; (bevanda:) be too hot; (sole, pentola:) be very hot. **~rsi** vr burn oneself; (al sole) get sunburnt; fig get one's fingers burnt. **~'tura** f burn; (da liquido) scald; **~tura solare** sunburn; fig painful experience
'scotto adj overcooked
sco'vare vt (scoprire) discover
'Scoz|ia f Scotland. **~'zese** adj Scottish • mf Scot
scredi'tare vt discredit
scre'mare vt skim
screpo'la|re vt, **~rsi** vr crack. **~to** adj (labbra) chapped. **~'tura** f crack
screzi'ato adj speckled
'screzio m disagreement
scribac|chi'are vt scribble. **~'chino, -a** mf scribbler; (impiegato) penpusher
scricchio'l|are vi creak. **~io** m creaking
'scricciolo m wren
'scrigno m casket
scrimina'tura f parting
'scrit|ta f writing; (su muro) graffiti. **~to** pp di **scrivere** • adj written • m

writing; (lettera) letter. ~'**toio** m writing-desk. ~'**tore,** ~'**trice** mf writer. ~'**tura** f writing; (Relig) scripture

scrittu'rare vt engage

scriva'nia f desk

'**scrivere** vt write; (descrivere) write about; ~ **a macchina** type

scroc'c|are vt ~**are a** sponge off. '**scrocco** m [!] **a scrocco** [!] without paying. ~**one, -a** mf sponger

'**scrofa** f sow

scrol'lar|e vt shake; ~**e le spalle** shrug one's shoulders. ~**si** vr shake oneself; ~**si qcsa di dosso** shake sth off

scrosci'are vi roar; (pioggia:) pelt down. '**scroscio** m roar; (di pioggia) pelting

scro'star|e vt scrape. ~**si** vr peel off

'**scrupo|lo** m scruple; (diligenza) care; **senza scrupoli** unscrupulous, without scruples. ~'**loso** adj scrupulous

scru'ta|re vt scan; (indagare) search. ~'**tore** m (alle elezioni) returning officer

scruti'nare vt scrutinize. **scru'tinio** m (di voti alle elezioni) poll; (Sch) assessment of progress

scu'cire vt unstitch

scude'ria f stable

scu'detto m Sport championship shield

'**scudo** m shield

sculacci|'are vt spank. ~'**ata** f spanking. ~'**one** m spanking

sculet'tare vi wiggle one's hips

scul|'tore, -'trice m sculptor •f sculptress. ~'**tura** f sculpture

scu'ola f school. ~ **elementare** primary school. ~ **guida** driving school. ~ **materna** day nursery. ~ **media** [**inferiore**] secondary school (10-13). ~ [**media**] **superiore** secondary school (13-18)

scu'oter|e vt shake. ~**si** vr (destarsi) rouse oneself; ~**si di dosso** shake off

'**scure** f axe

scu'reggia f [!] fart. **scureggi'are** vi [!] fart

scu'rire vt/i darken

'**scuro** adj dark •m darkness; (imposta) shutter

'**scusa** f excuse; (giustificazione) apology; **chiedere** ~ apologize; **chiedo** ~**!** I'm sorry!

scu'sar|e vt excuse. ~**si** vr ~**si** apologize (**di** for); [**mi**] **scusi!** excuse me!; (chiedendo perdono) [I'm] sorry!

sdebi'tarsi vr repay a kindness

sde'gna|re vt despise. ~**rsi** vr get angry. ~**to** adj indignant. '**sdegno** m disdain. **sde'gnoso** adj disdainful

sdolci'nato adj sentimental

sdoppi'are vt halve

sdrai'arsi vr lie down. '**sdraio** m [**sedia a**] **sdraio** deckchair

sdrammatiz'zare vi provide some comic relief

sdruccio'levole adj slippery

se

•conj if; (*interrogativo*) whether, if; **se mai** (*caso mai*) if need be; **se mai telefonasse,...** should he call,..., if he calls,...; **se no** otherwise, or else; **se non altro** at least, if nothing else; **se pure** (*sebbene*) even though; (*anche se*) even if; **non so se sia vero** I don't know whether it's true, I don't know if it's true; **come se** as if; **se lo avessi saputo prima!** if only I had known before!; **e se andassimo fuori a cena?** how about going out for dinner?

•m inv if

sé pers pron oneself; (lui) himself; (lei) herself; (esso, essa) itself; (loro) themselves; **l'ha fatto da sé** he did it himself; **ha preso i soldi con sé** he took the money with him; **si sono tenuti le notizie per sé** they kept the news to themselves

seb'bene conj although

'**secca** f shallows pl; **in** ~ (nave) aground

sec'cante adj annoying

sec'ca|re vt dry; (importunare) annoy •vi dry up. ~**rsi** vr dry up; (irritarsi) get annoyed; (annoiarsi) get bored.

S

~'**tore,** ~'**trice** mf nuisance. ~'**tura** f bother

secchi'ello m pail

'**secchio** m bucket. ~ **della spazzatura** rubbish bin, trash can Am

'**secco, -a** adj dry; (disseccato) dried; (magro) thin; (brusco) curt; (preciso) sharp •m (siccità) drought; **lavare a** ~ dry-clean

secessi'one f secession

seco'lare adj age-old; (laico) secular. '**secolo** m century; (epoca) age

se'cond|a f (Rail, Sch) second class; (Auto) second [gear]. ~**o** adj second •m second; (secondo piatto) main course •prep according to; ~**o me** in my opinion

secrezi'one f secretion

'**sedano** m celery

seda'tivo adj & m sedative

'**sede** f seat; (centro) centre; (Relig) see; (Comm) head office. ~ **sociale** registered office

seden'tario adj sedentary

se'der|e vi sit. ~**si** vr sit down •m (deretano) bottom

'**sedia** f chair. ~ **a dondolo** rocking chair. ~ **a rotelle** wheelchair

sedi'cente adj self-styled

'**sedici** adj & m sixteen

se'dile m seat

sedizi'o|ne f sedition. ~**so** adj seditious

se'dotto pp di **sedurre**

sedu'cente adj seductive

se'durre vt seduce

se'duta f session; (di posa) sitting. ~ **stante** adv here and now

seduzi'one f seduction

'**sega** f saw

'**segala** f rye

se'gare vt saw

'**seggio** m seat. ~ **elettorale** polling station

seg'gio|la f chair. ~'**lino** m seat; (da bambino) child's seat. ~'**lone** m (per bambini) high chair

seggio'via f chair lift

seghe'ria f sawmill

se'ghetto m hacksaw

seg'mento m segment

segna'lar|e vt signal; (annunciare) announce; (indicare) point out. ~**si** vr distinguish oneself

se'gna|le m signal; (stradale) sign. ~**le acustico** beep. ~**le orario** time signal. ~'**letica** f signals pl. ~**letica stradale** road signs pl

se'gnar|e vt mark; (prendere nota) note; (indicare) indicate; Sport score. ~**si** vr cross oneself. '**segno** m sign; (traccia, limite) mark; (bersaglio) target; **far segno** (col capo) nod; (con la mano) beckon. **segno zodiacale** birth sign

segre'ga|re vt segregate. ~**zi'one** f segregation

segretari'ato m secretariat

segre'tario, -a mf secretary. ~ **comunale** town clerk

segrete'ria f [administrative] office; (segretariato) secretariat. ~ **telefonica** answering machine

segre'tezza f secrecy

se'greto adj & m secret; **in** ~ in secret

segu'ace mf follower

segu'ente adj following, next

se'gugio m bloodhound

segu'ire vt/i follow; (continuare) continue

segui'tare vt/i continue

'**seguito** m retinue; (sequela) series; (continuazione) continuation; **di** ~ in succession; **in** ~ later on; **in** ~ **a** following; **al** ~ owing to; **fare** ~ **a** follow up

'**sei** adj & m six. **sei'cento** adj & m six hundred; **il Seicento** the seventeenth century. **sei'mila** adj & m six thousand

sel'ciato m paving

selet'tivo adj selective. **selezio'nare** vt select. **selezi'one** f selection

'**sella** f saddle. **sel'lare** vt saddle

seltz m soda water

'**selva** f forest

selvag'gina f game

sel'vaggio, -a adj wild; (primitivo) savage •mf savage

sel'vatico adj wild

S

se'maforo m traffic lights pl

se'mantica f semantics sg

sem'brare vi seem; (assomigliare) look like; **che te ne sembra?** what do you think?; **mi sembra che...** I think...

'seme m seed; (di mela) pip; (di carte) suit; (sperma) semen

se'mestre m half-year

semi'cerchio m semicircle

semifi'nale f semifinal

semi'freddo m ice cream and sponge dessert

'semina f sowing

semi'nare vt sow; ! shake off (inseguitori)

semi'nario m seminar; (Relig) seminary

seminter'rato m basement

se'mitico adj Semitic

sem'mai conj in case • adv **è lui, ~, che...** if anyone, it's him who...

'semola f bran. **semo'lino** m semolina

'sempli|ce adj simple; **in parole semplici** in plain words. **~'cemente** adv simply. **~cità** f simplicity. **~fi'care** vt simplify

'sempre adv always; (ancora) still; **per ~** for ever

sempre'verde adj & m evergreen

'senape f mustard

se'nato m senate. **sena'tore** m senator

se'nil|e adj senile. **~ità** f senility

'senno m sense

'seno m breast; (Math) sine

sen'sato adj sensible

sensazi|o'nale adj sensational. **~'one** f sensation

sen'sibil|e adj sensitive; (percepibile) perceptible; (notevole) considerable. **~ità** f sensitivity. **~iz'zare** vt make more aware (**a** of)

sensi'tivo, -a adj sensory • mf sensitive person; (medium) medium

'senso m sense; (significato) meaning; (direzione) direction; **non ha ~** it doesn't make sense; **perdere i sensi** lose consciousness. **~ dell'umorismo** sense of humour. **~ unico** (strada) one-way; **~ vietato** no entry

sensu'al|e adj sensual. **~ità** f sensuality

sen'tenz|a f sentence; (massima) saying. **~i'are** vi pass judgment

senti'ero m path

sentimen'tale adj sentimental. **senti'mento** m feeling

senti'nella f sentry

sen'ti|re vt feel; (udire) hear; (ascoltare) listen to; (gustare) taste; (odorare) smell • vi feel; (udire) hear; **~re caldo/freddo** feel hot/cold. **~rsi** vr feel; **~rsi di fare qcsa** feel like doing sth; **~rsi bene** feel well; **~rsi poco bene** feel unwell. **~to** adj sincere

sen'tore m inkling

'senza prep without; **~ correre** without running; **senz'altro** certainly; **~ ombrello** without an umbrella

senza'tetto m inv **i ~** the homeless

sepa'ra|re vt separate. **~rsi** vr separate; (amici:) part; **~rsi da** be separated from. **~ta'mente** adv separately. **~zi'one** f separation

se'pol|cro m sepulchre. **~to** pp di **seppellire**. **~'tura** f burial

seppel'lire vt bury

'seppia f cuttle fish; **nero di ~** sepia

sep'pure conj even if

se'quenza f sequence

seque'strare vt (rapire) kidnap; (Jur) impound; (confiscare) confiscate. **se'questro** m impounding; (di persona) kidnap[ping]

'sera f evening; **di ~** in the evening. **se'rale** adj evening. **se'rata** f evening; (ricevimento) party

ser'bare vt keep; harbour (odio); cherish (speranza)

serba'toio m tank. **~ d'acqua** water tank; (per una città) reservoir

'Serbia f Serbia

'serbo, -a adj & mf Serbian • m (lingua) Serbian

sere'nata f serenade

serenità f serenity. **se'reno** adj

see A-Z of Italian life and culture

S

serene; (cielo) clear

ser'gente m sergeant

seria'mente adv seriously

'serie f inv series; (complesso) set; Sport division; **fuori ~** custom-built; **produzione in ~** mass production; **di ~ B** second-rate

serietà f seriousness. **'serio** adj serious; (degno di fiducia) reliable; **sul serio** seriously; (davvero) really

ser'mone m sermon

'serpe f liter viper. **~ggi'are** vi meander; (diffondersi) spread

ser'pente m snake

'serra f greenhouse; **effetto ~** greenhouse effect

ser'randa f shutter

ser'ra|re vt shut; (stringere) tighten; (incalzare) press on. **~'tura** f lock

'server m inv (Comput) server

ser'vir|e vt serve; (al ristorante) wait on •vi serve; (essere utile) be of use; **non serve** it's no good. **~si** vr (di cibo) help oneself; **~si da** buy from; **~si di** use

servitù f servitude; (personale di servizio) servants pl

ser'vizio m service; (da caffè ecc) set; (di cronaca, sportivo) report; **servizi** pl bathroom; **essere di ~** be on duty; **fare ~** (autobus ecc:) run; **fuori ~** (bus) not in service; (ascensore) out of order; **~ compreso** service charge included. **~ in camera** room service. **~ civile** civilian duties done instead of national service. **~ militare** military service. **~ pubblico** utility company. **~ al tavolo** waiter service

S

'servo, -a mf servant

servo'sterzo m power steering

ses'san|ta adj & m sixty. **~'tina** f **una ~tina** about sixty

sessi'one f session

'sesso m sex

sessu'al|e adj sexual. **~ità** f sexuality

'sesto[1] adj sixth

'sesto[2] m (ordine) order

'seta f silk

setacci'are vt sieve. **se'taccio** m sieve

'sete f thirst; **avere ~** be thirsty

'setta f sect

set'tan|ta adj & m seventy. **~'tina** f **una ~tina** about seventy

'sette adj & m seven. **~'cento** agg & m seven hundred; **il S~cento** the eighteenth century

set'tembre m September

settentri|o'nale adj northern •mf northerner. **~'one** m north

setti'ma|na f week. **~'nale** agg & m weekly

'settimo adj seventh

set'tore m sector

severità f severity. **se'vero** adj severe; (rigoroso) strict

se'vizi|a f torture; **se'vizie** pl torture sg. **~'are** vt torture

sezio'nare vt divide; (Med) dissect. **sezi'one** f section; (reparto) department; (Med) dissection

sfaccen'dato adj idle

sfacchi'na|re vi toil. **~ta** f drudgery

sfacci|a'taggine f insolence. **~'ato** adj cheeky, fresh Am

sfa'celo m ruin; **in ~** in ruins

sfal'darsi vr flake off

sfa'mar|e vt feed. **~si** vr satisfy one's hunger

sfar'zoso adj sumptuous

sfa'sato adj [!] confused; (motore) which needs tuning

sfasci'a|re vt unbandage; (fracassare) smash. **~rsi** vr fall to pieces. **~to** adj beat-up

sfa'tare vt explode

sfati'cato adj lazy

sfavil'lare vi sparkle

sfavo'revole adj unfavourable

sfavo'rire vt disadvantage

'sfer|a f sphere. **~ico** adj spherical

sfer'rare vt unshoe (cavallo); (scagliare) land

sfer'zare vt whip

sfian'carsi vr wear oneself out

sfi'bra|re vt exhaust. **~to** adj exhausted

'sfida f challenge. **sfi'dare** vt challenge

sfi'duci|a f mistrust. **~'ato** adj discouraged

sfigu'rare vt disfigure • vi (far cattiva figura) look out of place

sfilacci'ar|e vt, **~si** vr fray

sfi'la|re vt unthread; (togliere di dosso) take off • vi (truppe:) march past; (in parata) parade. **~rsi** vr come unthreaded; (collant:) ladder; take off (pantaloni). **~ta** f parade; (sfilza) series. **~ta di moda** fashion show

'sfilza f (di errori) string

'sfinge f sphinx

sfi'nito adj worn out

sfio'rare vt skim; touch on (argomento)

sfio'rire vi wither; (bellezza:) fade

'sfitto adj vacant

'sfizio m whim, fancy; **togliersi uno ~** satisfy a whim

sfo'cato adj out of focus

sfoci'are vi **~ in** flow into

sfode'ra|re vt draw (pistola, spada). **~to** adj unlined

sfo'gar|e vt vent. **~si** vr give vent to one's feelings

sfoggi'are vt/i show off. **'sfoggio** m show, display; **fare sfoggio di** show off

'sfoglia f sheet of pastry; **pasta ~** puff pastry

sfogli'are vt leaf through

'sfogo m outlet; fig outburst; (Med) rash; **dare ~ a** give vent to

sfolgo'rare vi blaze

sfol'lare vt clear • vi (Mil) be evacuated

sfol'tire vt thin [out]

sfon'dare vt break down • vi (aver successo) make a name for oneself

'sfondo m background

sfor'ma|re vt pull out of shape (tasche). **~rsi** vr lose its shape; (persona:) lose one's figure. **~to** m (Culin) flan

sfor'nito adj **~ di** (negozio) out of

sfor'tuna f bad luck. **~ta'mente** adv unfortunately. **sfortu'nato** adj unlucky

sfor'zar|e vt force. **~si** vr try hard. **'sforzo** m effort; (tensione) strain

'sfottere vt ☒ tease

sfracel'larsi vr smash

sfrat'tare vt evict. **'sfratto** m eviction

sfrecci'are vi flash past

sfregi'a|re vt slash. **~to** adj scarred

'sfregio m slash

sfre'na|rsi vr run wild. **~to** adj wild

sfron'tato adj shameless

sfrutta'mento m exploitation. **sfrut'tare** vt exploit

sfug'gente adj elusive; (mento) receding

sfug'gi|re vi escape; **~re a** escape [from]; **mi sfugge** it escapes me; **mi è sfuggito di mano** I lost hold of it • vt avoid. **~ta** f **di ~ta** in passing

sfu'ma|re vi (svanire) vanish; (colore:) shade off • vt soften (colore). **~'tura** f shade

sfuri'ata f outburst [of anger]

sga'bello m stool

sgabuz'zino m cupboard

sgambet'tare vi kick one's legs; (camminare) trot. **sgam'betto** m **fare lo sgambetto a qcno** trip sb up

sganasci'arsi vr **~ dalle risa** roar with laughter

sganci'ar|e vt unhook; (Rail) uncouple; drop (bombe); ! cough up (denaro). **~si** vr become unhooked; fig get away

sganghe'rato adj ramshackle

sgar'bato adj rude. **'sgarbo** m discourtesy

sgargi'ante adj garish

sgar'rare vi be wrong; (da regola) stray from the straight and narrow. **'sgarro** m mistake, slip

sgattaio'lare vi sneak away; **~ via** decamp

sghignaz'zare vi laugh scornfully, sneer

sgoccio'lare vi drip

sgo'larsi vr shout oneself hoarse

sgomb[e]'rare vt clear [out]. **'sgombro** adj clear • m (trasloco) removal; (pesce) mackerel

sgomen'tar|e vt dismay. **~si** vr be dismayed. **sgo'mento** m dismay

sgomi'nare vt defeat

sgom'mata f screech of tyres

sgonfi'ar|e vt deflate. **~si** vr go down. **'sgonfio** adj flat

'sgorbio m scrawl; (fig: vista sgradevole) sight

sgor'gare vi gush [out] • vt flush out, unblock (lavandino)

sgoz'zare vt **~ qcno** cut sb's throat

sgra'd|evole adj disagreeable. **~ito** adj unwelcome

sgrammati'cato adj ungrammatical

sgra'nare vt shell (piselli); open wide (occhi)

sgran'chir|e vt, **~si** vr stretch

sgranocchi'are vt munch

sgras'sare vt remove the grease from

sgrazi'ato adj ungainly

sgreto'lar|e vt, **~si** vr crumble

sgri'da|re vt scold. **~ta** f scolding

sgros'sare vt rough-hew (marmo); fig polish

sguai'ato adj coarse

sgual'cire vt crumple

sgu'ardo m look; (breve) glance

sguaz'zare vi splash; (nel fango) wallow

sguinzagli'are vt unleash

sgusci'are vt shell • vi (sfuggire) slip away; **~ fuori** slip out

shake'rare vt shake

si

• pers pron (*riflessivo*) oneself; (*lui*) himself; (*lei*) herself; (*esso, essa*) itself; (*loro*) themselves; (*reciproco*) each other; (*tra più di due*) one another; (*impersonale*) you, one; **lavarsi** wash [oneself]; **si è lavata** she washed [herself]; **lavarsi le mani** wash one's hands; **si è lavata le mani** she washed her hands; **si è mangiato un pollo intero** he ate an entire chicken by himself; **incontrarsi** meet each other; **la gente si aiuta a vicenda** people help one another; **non si sa mai** you never know, one never knows fml; **queste cose si dimenticano facilmente** these things are easily forgotten

• m (*chiave, nota*) B

sì adv yes

'sia[1] ▹**essere**

'sia[2] conj **~...~...** (entrambi) both...and...; (o l'uno o l'altro) either...or...; **~ che venga, ~ che non venga** whether he comes or not; **scegli ~ questo ~ quello** choose either this one or that one; **voglio ~ questo che quello** I want both this one and that one

sia'mese adj Siamese

sibi'lare vi hiss

si'cario m hired killer

sicché conj (perciò) so [that]; (allora) then

siccità f drought

sic'come conj as

Si'cili|a f Sicily. **s~'ano, -a** adj & mf Sicilian

si'cura f safety catch; (di portiera) child-proof lock. **~'mente** adv definitely

sicu'rezza f certainty; (salvezza) safety; **uscita di ~** emergency exit. **~ delle frontiere** homeland security

si'curo adj safe; (certo) sure; (saldo) steady; (Comm) sound • adv certainly • m safety; **al ~** safe; **andare sul ~** play [it] safe; **di ~** definitely; **di ~, sarà arrivato** he must have arrived

siderur'gia f iron and steel industry

'sidro m cider

si'epe f hedge

si'ero m serum

sieroposi'tivo adj HIV positive

si'esta f afternoon nap

si'fone m siphon

Sig. abbr (signore) Mr

Sig.a abbr (signora) Mrs, Ms

siga'retta f cigarette

'sigaro m cigar

Sigg. abbr (signori) Messrs

sigil'lare vt seal. **si'gillo** m seal

'sigla f initials pl. **~ musicale** signature tune. **si'glare** vt initial

Sig.na abbr (signorina) Miss, Ms

signifi'ca|re vt mean. **~'tivo** adj significant. **~to** m meaning

si'gnora f lady; (davanti a nome proprio) Mrs; (non sposata) Miss; (in lettere ufficiali) Madam; **il signor Vené e ~** Mr and Mrs Vené

si'gnore m gentleman; (Relig) lord; (davanti a nome proprio) Mr; (in lettere ufficiali) Sir. **signo'rile** adj gentlemanly; (di lusso) luxury

signo'rina f young lady; (seguito da nome proprio) Miss

silenzia'tore m silencer

si'lenzi|o m silence. **~'oso** adj silent

silhou'ette f silhouette

si'licio m **piastrina di ~** silicon chip

sili'cone m silicone

'sillaba f syllable

silu'rare vt torpedo. **si'luro** m torpedo

simboleggi'are vt symbolize

sim'bolico adj symbolic[al]

'simbolo m symbol

similarità f inv similarity

'simil|e adj similar; (tale) such; **~e a** like •m (il prossimo) fellow man. **~'mente** adv similarly. **~'pelle** f Leatherette®

simme'tria f symmetry. **sim'metrico** adj symmetric[al]

simpa'ti|a f liking; (compenetrazione) sympathy; **prendere qcno in ~a** take a liking to sb. **sim'patico** adj nice. **~z'zante** mf well-wisher. **~z'zare** vt **~zzare con** take a liking to; **~zzare per qcsa/qcno** lean towards sth/sb

sim'posio m symposium

simu'la|re vt simulate; feign (amicizia, interesse). **~zi'one** f simulation

simul'taneo adj simultaneous

sina'goga f synagogue

sincerità f sincerity. **sin'cero** adj sincere

'sincope f syncopation; (Med) fainting fit

sincron'ia f synchronization

sincroniz'zare vt synchronize

sinda'ca|le adj [trade] union, [labor] union Am. **~'lista** mf trade unionist, labor union member Am. **~re** vt inspect. **~to** m [trade] union, [labor] union Am; (associazione) syndicate

'sindaco m mayor

'sindrome f syndrome

sinfo'nia f symphony. **sin'fonico** adj symphonic

singhi|oz'zare vi (di pianto) sob. **~'ozzo** m hiccup; (di pianto) sob

singo'lar|e adj singular •m singular. **~'mente** adv individually; (stranamente) peculiarly

'singolo adj single •m individual; Tennis singles pl

si'nistra f left; **a ~** on the left; **girare a ~** turn to the left; **con la guida a ~** (auto) with left-hand drive

sini'strato adj injured

si'nistr|o, -a adj left[-hand]; (avverso) sinister •m accident •f left [hand]; (Pol) left [wing]

'sino prep = **fino**[1]

si'nonimo adj synonymous •m synonym

sin'tassi f syntax

'sintesi f inv synthesis; (riassunto) summary

sin'teti|co adj synthetic; (conciso) summary. **~z'zare** vt summarize

sintetizza'tore m synthesizer

sinto'matico adj symptomatic. **'sintomo** m symptom

sinto'nia f tuning; **in ~** on the same wavelength

sinu'oso adj (strada) winding

si'pario m curtain

si'rena f siren

'Siri|a f Syria. **s~'ano, -a** adj & mf Syrian

si'ringa f syringe

'sismico adj seismic

si'stem|a m system. **~a operativo** (Comput) operating system

siste'ma|re vt (mettere) put; tidy up (casa, camera); (risolvere) sort out; (procurare lavoro a) fix up with a job; (trovare alloggio a) find accommodation for; (sposare) marry off; (!: punire) sort out. **~rsi** vr settle down; (trovare un lavoro) find a job; (trovare alloggio) find accommodation; (sposarsi) marry. **~tico** adj systematic. **~zi'one** f arrangement; (di questione) settlement; (lavoro) job; (alloggio)

see A-Z of Italian life and culture

S

accommodation; (matrimonio) marriage

'sito m site. ~ **web** web site

situ'are vt place

situazi'one f situation

ski-'lift m inv ski tow

slacci'are vt unfasten

slanci'a|rsi vr hurl oneself. **~to** adj slender. **'slancio** m impetus; (impulso) impulse

sla'vato adj fair

'slavo adj Slav[onic]

sle'al|e adj disloyal. **~tà** f disloyalty

sle'gare vt untie

'slitta f sledge, sleigh. **~'mento** m (di macchina) skid; (fig: di riunione) postponement

slit'ta|re vi (Auto) skid; (riunione:) be put off. **~ta** f skid

slit'tino m toboggan

'slogan m inv slogan

slo'ga|re vt dislocate. **~rsi** vr **~rsi una caviglia** sprain one's ankle. **~'tura** f dislocation

sloggi'are vi move out

Slo'vacchia f Slovakia

Slo'venia f Slovenia

smacchi'a|re vt clean. **~'tore** m stain remover

'smacco m humiliating defeat

smagli'ante adj dazzling

smagli'a|rsi vr (calza:) run. **~'tura** f run

smalizi'ato adj cunning

smal'ta|re vt enamel; glaze (ceramica); varnish (unghie). **~to** adj enamelled

smalti'mento m disposal; (di merce) selling off. **~ rifiuti** waste disposal; (di grassi) burning off

smal'tire vt burn off; (merce) sell off; fig get through (corrispondenza); **~ la sbornia** sober up

'smalto m enamel; (di ceramica) glaze; (per le unghie) nail varnish

smantel|la'mento m dismantling. **~'lare** vt dismantle

smarri'mento m loss; (psicologico) bewilderment

smar'ri|re vt lose; (temporaneamente) mislay. **~rsi** vr get lost; (turbarsi) be bewildered

smasche'rar|e vt unmask. **~si** vr (tradirsi) give oneself away

smemo'rato, -a adj forgetful • mf scatterbrain

smen'ti|re vt deny. **~ta** f denial

sme'raldo m & adj emerald

smerci'are vt sell off

smerigli'ato adj emery; **vetro ~** frosted glass. **sme'riglio** m emery

'smesso pp di **smettere** • adj (abiti) cast-off

'smett|ere vt stop; stop wearing (abiti); **~ila!** stop it!

smidol'lato adj spineless

sminu'ir|e vt diminish. **~si** vr fig belittle oneself

sminuz'zare vt crumble; (fig: analizzare) analyse in detail

smista'mento m clearing; (postale) sorting. **smi'stare** vt sort; (Mil) post

smisu'rato adj boundless; (esorbitante) excessive

smobili'ta|re vt demobilize. **~zi'one** f demobilization

smo'dato adj immoderate

smog m smog

'smoking m inv dinner jacket, tuxedo Am

smon'tar|e vt take to pieces; (scoraggiare) dishearten • vi (da veicolo) get off; (da cavallo) dismount; (dal servizio) go off duty. **~si** vr lose heart

'smorfi|a f grimace; (moina) simper; **fare ~e** make faces. **~'oso** adj affected

'smorto adj pale; (colore) dull

smor'zare vt dim (luce); tone down (colori); deaden (suoni); quench (sete)

'smosso pp di **smuovere**

smotta'mento m landslide

sms m inv (short message service) text message

'smunto adj emaciated

smu'over|e vt shift; (commuovere) move. **~si** vr move; (commuoversi) be moved

smus'sar|e vt round off; (fig: attenuare) tone down. **~si** vr go blunt

snatu'rato adj inhuman

snel'lir|e vt slim down. **~si** vr slim [down]. **'snello** adj slim

sner'va|re vt enervate. **~rsi** vr get exhausted

sni'dare vt drive out

snif'fare vt snort

snob'bare vt snub. **sno'bismo** m snobbery

snoccio'lare vt stone; fig blurt out

sno'da|re vt untie; (sciogliere) loosen. **~rsi** vr come untied; (strada:) wind. **~to** adj (persona) double-jointed; (dita) flexible

so'ave adj gentle

sobbal'zare vi jerk; (trasalire) start. **sob'balzo** m jerk; (trasalimento) start

sobbar'carsi vr **~ a** undertake

sob'borgo m suburb

sobil'la|re vt stir up

'sobrio adj sober

soc'chiu|dere vt half-close. **~so** pp di **socchiudere** •adj (occhi) half-closed; (porta) ajar

soc'cor|rere vt assist. **~so** pp di **soccorrere** •m assistance; **soccorsi** pl rescuers; (dopo disastro) relief workers. **~so stradale** breakdown service

socialdemo'cra|tico, -a adj Social Democratic •mf Social Democrat. **~'zia** f Social Democracy

soci'ale adj social

socia'li|smo m Socialism. **~sta** agg & mf Socialist. **~z'zare** vi socialize

società f inv society; (Comm) company. **~ per azioni** plc. **~ a responsabilità limitata** limited liability company

soci'evole adj sociable

'socio, -a mf member; (Comm) partner

sociolo'gia f sociology. **socio'logico** adj sociological

'soda f soda

soddisfa'cente adj satisfactory

soddi'sfa|re vt/i satisfy; meet (richiesta); make amends for (offesa). **~tto** pp di **soddisfare** •adj satisfied. **~zi'one** f satisfaction

'sodo adj hard; fig firm; (uovo) hard-boiled •adv hard; **dormire ~** sleep soundly

sofà m inv sofa

soffe'ren|te adj ill

soffer'marsi vr pause; **~ su** dwell on

sof'ferto pp di **soffrire**

soffi'a|re vt blow; reveal (segreto); (rubare) pinch [I] •vi blow. **~ta** f fig [x] tip-off

'soffice adj soft

'soffio m puff; (Med) murmur

sof'fitt|a f attic. **~o** m ceiling

soffo|ca'mento m suffocation

soffo'ca|nte adj suffocating. **~re** vt/i suffocate; (con cibo) choke; fig stifle

sof'friggere vt fry lightly

sof'frire vt/i suffer; (sopportare) bear; **~ di** suffer from

sof'fritto pp di **soffriggere**

sof'fuso adj (luce) soft

sofisti'ca|re vt (adulterare) adulterate •vi (sottilizzare) quibble. **~to** adj sophisticated

sogget'tivo adj subjective

sog'getto m subject •adj subject; **essere ~ a** be subject to

soggezi'one f subjection; (rispetto) awe

sogghi'gnare vi sneer

soggio'gare vt subdue

soggior'nare vi stay. **soggi'orno** m stay; (stanza) living room

soggi'ungere vt add

'soglia f threshold

'sogliola f sole

so'gna|re vt/i dream; **~re a occhi aperti** daydream. **~'tore, ~'trice** mf dreamer. **'sogno** m dream; **fare un sogno** have a dream; **neanche per sogno!** not at all!

'soia f soya

sol m (Mus) G

so'laio m attic

sola'mente adv only

so'lar|e adj (energia, raggi) solar; (crema) sun attrib. **~ium** m inv solarium

sol'care vt plough. **'solco** m furrow; (di ruota) track; (di nave) wake; (di disco) groove

sol'dato m soldier

'soldo m **non ha un ~** he hasn't got a penny; **senza un ~** penniless; **soldi** pl (denaro) money sg

'sole m sun; (luce del sole) sun[light]; **al ~** in the sun; **prendere il ~** sunbathe

soleggi'ato adj sunny

so'lenn|e adj solemn. **~ità** f solemnity

so'lere vi be in the habit of; **come si suol dire** as they say

sol'fato m sulphate

soli'da|le adj in agreement. **~rietà** f solidarity

solidifi'car|e vt/i, **~si** vr solidify

solidità f solidity; (di colori) fastness. **'solido** adj solid; (robusto) sturdy; (colore) fast • m solid

so'lista adj solo • mf soloist

solita'mente adv usually

soli'tario adj solitary; (isolato) lonely • m (brillante) solitaire; (gioco di carte) patience, solitaire

'solito adj usual; **essere ~ fare qcsa** be in the habit of doing sth • m usual; **di ~** usually

soli'tudine f solitude

solleci'ta|re vt speed up; urge (persona). **~zi'one** f (richiesta) request; (preghiera) entreaty

sol'leci|to adj prompt • m reminder. **~'tudine** f promptness; (interessamento) concern

solle'one m noonday sun; (periodo) dog days of summer

solleti'care vt tickle

solleva'mento m **~ pesi** weightlifting

solle'var|e vt lift; (elevare) raise; (confortare) comfort. **~si** vr rise; (riaversi) recover

S

solli'evo m relief

'solo, -a adj alone; (isolato) lonely; (unico) only; (Mus) solo; **da ~** by myself/yourself/himself etc • mf **il ~, la sola** the only one • m (Mus) solo • adv only

sol'stizio m solstice

sol'tanto adv only

so'lubile adj soluble; (caffè) instant

soluzi'one f solution; (Comm) payment

sol'vente adj & m solvent; **~ per unghie** nail polish remover

so'maro m ass; (Sch) dunce

so'matico adj somatic

somigli'an|te adj similar. **~za** f resemblance

somigli'ar|e vi **~e a** resemble. **~si** vr be alike

'somma f sum; (Math) addition

som'mare vt add; (totalizzare) add up

som'mario adj & m summary

som'mato adj **tutto ~** all things considered

sommeli'er m inv wine waiter

som'mer|gere vt submerge. **~'gibile** m submarine. **~so** pp di **sommergere**

som'messo adj soft

sommini'stra|re vt administer. **~zi'one** f administration

sommità f inv summit

'sommo adj highest; fig supreme • m summit

som'mossa f rising

sommozza'tore m frogman

so'naglio m bell

so'nata f sonata; fig ! beating

'sonda f (Mech) drill; (Med, spaziale). **son'daggio** m drilling; (Med, spaziale) probe; (indagine) survey. **sondaggio d'opinioni** opinion poll. **son'dare** vt sound; (investigare) probe

sonnambu'lismo m sleepwalking. **son'nambulo, -a** mf sleepwalker

sonnecchi'are vi doze

son'nifero m sleeping-pill

'sonno m sleep; **aver ~** be sleepy. **~'lenza** f sleepiness

so'noro adj resonant; (rumoroso) loud; (onde, scheda) sound attrib

sontu'oso adj sumptuous

sopo'rifero adj soporific

sop'palco m platform

soppe'rire vi **~ a qcsa** provide for sth

soppe'sare vt weigh up

soppor'ta|re vt support; (tollerare) stand; bear (dolore)

soppressi'one f removal; (di legge) abolition; (di diritti, pubblicazione) suppression; (annullamento) cancellation. **sop'presso** pp di **sopprimere**

sop'primere vt get rid of; abolish (legge); suppress (diritti, pubblicazione); (annullare) cancel

'sopra adv on top; (più in alto) higher [up]; (al piano superiore) upstairs; (in testo) above; **mettilo lì ~** put it up there; **di ~** upstairs; **pensarci ~** think about it; **vedi ~** see above •prep **~ [a]** on; (senza contatto, oltre) over; (riguardo a) about; **è ~ al tavolo, è ~ il tavolo** it's on the table; **il quadro è appeso ~ al camino** the picture is hanging over the fireplace; **il ponte passa ~ all'autostrada** the bridge crosses over the motorway; **è caduto ~ il tetto** it fell on the roof; **l'uno ~ l'altro** one on top of the other; (senza contatto) one above the other; **abita ~ di me** he lives upstairs from me; **i bambini ~ i dieci anni** children over ten; **20° ~ lo zero** 20° above zero; **~ il livello del mare** above sea level; **rifletti ~ quello che è successo** think about what happened •m **il [di] ~** the top

so'prabito m overcoat

soprac'ciglio m (pl f **sopracciglia**) eyebrow

sopracco'per|ta f bedspread; (di libro) [dust-]jacket. **~'tina** f book jacket

soprad'detto adj above-mentioned

sopraele'vata f elevated railway

sopraf'fa|re vt overwhelm. **~tto** pp di **sopraffare**. **~zi'one** f abuse of power

sopraf'fino adj excellent; (gusto, udito) highly refined

sopraggi'ungere vi (persona:) turn up; (accadere) happen

sopralluogo m inspection

sopram'mobile m ornament

soprannatu'rale adj & m supernatural

sopran'nome m nickname

so'prano mf soprano

soprappensi'ero adv lost in thought

sopras'salto m **di ~** with a start

soprasse'dere vi **~ a** postpone

soprat'tutto adv above all

sopravvalu'tare vt overvalue

soprav|ve'nire vi turn up; (accadere) happen. **~'vento** m fig upper hand

sopravvi|s'suto pp di **sopravvivere**. **~'venza** f survival. **soprav'vivere** vi survive; **sopravvivere a** outlive (persona)

soprinten'den|te mf supervisor; (di museo ecc) keeper. **~za** f supervision; (ente) board

so'pruso m abuse of power

soq'quadro m **mettere a ~** turn upside down

sor'betto m sorbet

'sordido adj sordid; (avaro) stingy

sor'dina f mute; **in ~** on the quiet

sordità f deafness. **'sordo, -a** adj deaf; (rumore, dolore) dull •mf deaf person. **sordo'muto, -a** adj deaf-and-dumb

so'rel|la f sister. **~'lastra** f stepsister

sor'gente f spring; (fonte) source

'sorgere vi rise; fig arise

sormon'tare vt surmount

sorni'one adj sly

sorpas'sa|re vt surpass; (eccedere) exceed; overtake (veicolo). **~to** adj old-fashioned. **sor'passo** m overtaking

sorpren'dente adj surprising; (straordinario) remarkable

sor'prendere vt surprise; (cogliere in flagrante) catch

sor'pres|a f surprise; **di ~a** by surprise. **~o** pp di **sorprendere**

sor're|ggere vt support; (tenere) hold up. **~ggersi** vr support oneself. **~tto** pp di **sorreggere**

sor'ri|dere vi smile. **~so** pp di **sorridere** •m smile

sorseggi'are vt sip. **'sorso** m sip; (piccola quantità) drop

'sorta f sort; **di ~** whatever; **ogni ~ di** all sorts of

'sorte f fate; (caso imprevisto) chance; **tirare a ~** draw lots. **sor'teggio** m draw

sorti'legio m witchcraft

sor'ti|re vi come out. **~ta** f (Mil) sortie; (battuta) witticism

'sorto pp di **sorgere**

sorvegli'an|te mf keeper; (controllore)

overseer. ~**za** f watch; (Mil ecc) surveillance

sorvegli'are vt watch over; (controllare) oversee; (polizia:) keep under surveillance

sorvo'lare vt fly over; fig skip

'sosia m inv double

so'spen|dere vt hang; (interrompere) stop; (privare di una carica) suspend. ~**si'one** f suspension

so'speso pp di **sospendere** •adj (impiegato, alunno) suspended; ~ **a** hanging from; ~ **a un filo** fig hanging by a thread •m **in** ~ pending; (emozionato) in suspense

sospet|'tare vt suspect. **so'spetto** adj suspicious; **persona sospetta** suspicious person •m suspicion; (persona) suspect. ~**'toso** adj suspicious

so'spin|gere vt drive. ~**to** pp di **sospingere**

sospi'rare vi sigh •vt long for. **so'spiro** m sigh

'sosta f stop; (pausa) pause; **senza** ~ non-stop; **"divieto di** ~**"** "no parking"

sostan'tivo m noun

so'stanz|a f substance; ~**e** pl (patrimonio) property sg. ~**i'oso** adj substantial; (cibo) nourishing

so'stare vi stop; (fare una pausa) pause

so'stegno m support

soste'ner|e vt support; (sopportare) bear; (resistere) withstand; (affermare) maintain; (nutrire) sustain; sit (esame); ~**e le spese** meet the costs. ~**si** vr support oneself

S

sosteni'tore, -'trice mf supporter

sostenta'mento m maintenance

soste'nuto adj (stile) formal; (prezzi, velocità) high

sostitu'ir|e vt substitute (**a** for), replace (**con** with). ~**si** vr ~**si a** replace

sosti'tu|to, -ta mf replacement, stand-in •m (surrogato) substitute. ~**zi'one** f substitution

sot'tana f petticoat; (di prete) cassock

sotter'raneo adj underground •m cellar

sotter'rare vt bury

sottigli'ezza f slimness; fig subtlety

sot'til|e adj thin; (udito, odorato) keen; (osservazione, distinzione) subtle. ~**iz'zare** vi split hairs

sottin'te|ndere vt imply. ~**so** pp di **sottintendere** •m allusion; **senza** ~**si** openly •adj implied

'sotto adv below; (più in basso) lower [down]; (al di sotto) underneath; (al piano di sotto) downstairs; **è lì** ~ it's underneath; ~ ~ deep down; (di nascosto) on the quiet; **di** ~ downstairs; **mettersi** ~ fig get down to it; **mettere** ~ (!: investire) knock down •prep ~ [**a**] under; (al di sotto di) under[neath]; **abita** ~ **di me** he lives downstairs from me; **i bambini** ~ **i dieci anni** children under ten; **20°** ~ **zero** 20° below zero; ~ **il livello del mare** below sea level; ~ **la pioggia** in the rain; ~ **calmante** under sedation; ~ **condizione che...** on condition that...; ~ **giuramento** under oath; ~ **sorveglianza** under surveillance; ~ **Natale/gli esami** around Christmas/exam time; **al di** ~ **di** under; **andare** ~ **i 50 all'ora** do less than 50km an hour •m **il** [**di**] ~ the bottom

sotto'banco adv under the counter

sottobicchi'ere m coaster

sotto'bosco m undergrowth

sotto'braccio adv arm in arm

sotto'fondo m background

sottoline'are vt underline; fig stress

sot'tolio adv in oil

sotto'mano adv within reach

sottoma'rino adj & m submarine

sotto'messo pp di **sottomettere**

sotto'metter|e vt submit; subdue (popolo). ~**si** vr submit. **sottomissi'one** f submission

sottopas'saggio m underpass; (pedonale) subway

sotto'por|re vt submit; (costringere) subject. ~**si** vr submit oneself; ~**si a** undergo. **sotto'posto** pp di **sottoporre**

sotto'scala m cupboard under the stairs

sotto'scritto pp di **sottoscrivere** •m undersigned

sotto'scri|vere vt sign; (approvare) sanction, subscribe to. ~**zi'one** f (petizione) petition; (approvazione) sanction; (raccolta di denaro) appeal

sotto'sopra adv upside down

sotto'stante adj **la strada ~** the road below

sottosu'olo m subsoil

sottosvilup'pato adj underdeveloped

sotto'terra adv underground

sotto'titolo m subtitle

sottovalu'tare vt underestimate

sotto'veste f slip

sotto'voce adv in a low voice

sottovu'oto adj vacuum-packed

sot'tra|rre vt remove; embezzle (fondi); (Math) subtract. **~rsi** vr **~rsi a** escape from; avoid (responsabilità). **~tto** pp di **sottrarre. ~zi'one** f removal; (di fondi) embezzlement; (Math) subtraction

sottuffici'ale m non-commissioned officer; (Naut) petty officer

sou'brette f inv showgirl

so'vietico, -a adj & mf Soviet

sovraccari'care vt overload. **sovrac'carico** adj overloaded (**di** with) • m overload

sovrannatu'rale adj & m = **soprannaturale**

so'vrano, -a adj sovereign; fig supreme • mf sovereign

sovrap'por|re vt superimpose. **~si** vr overlap

sovra'stare vt dominate; fig: (pericolo:) hang over

sovrinten'den|te, ~za = **soprintendente, soprintendenza**

sovru'mano adj superhuman

sovvenzi'one f subsidy

sovver'sivo adj subversive

'sozzo adj filthy

S.p.A. abbr (società per azioni) plc

spac'ca|re vt split; chop (legna). **~rsi** vr split. **~'tura** f split

spacci'a|re vt deal in, push (droga); **~re qcsa per qcsa** pass sth off as sth. **~rsi** vr **~rsi per** pass oneself off as. **~'tore, ~'trice** mf (di droga) pusher; (di denaro falso) distributor of forged bank notes. **'spaccio** m (di droga) dealing; (negozio) shop

'spacco m split

spac'cone, -a mf boaster

'spada f sword. **~c'cino** m swordsman

spae'sato adj disorientated

spa'ghetti mpl spaghetti sg

spa'ghetto m ([!]: spavento) fright

'Spagna f Spain

spa'gnolo, -a adj Spanish • mf Spaniard • m (lingua) Spanish

'spago m string; **dare ~ a qcno** encourage sb

spai'ato adj odd

spalan'ca|re vt, **~rsi** vr open wide. **~to** adj wide open

spa'lare vt shovel

'spall|a f shoulder; (di comico) straight man; **~e** pl (schiena) back; **alle ~e di qcno** (ridere) behind sb's back. **~eggi'are** vt back up

spal'letta f parapet

spalli'era f back; (di letto) headboard; (ginnastica) wall bars pl

spal'lina f strap; (imbottitura) shoulder pad

spal'mare vt spread

'spander|e vt spread; (versare) spill. **~si** vr spread

spappo'lare vt crush

spa'ra|re vt/i shoot; **~rle grosse** talk big. **~'toria** f shooting

sparecchi'are vt clear

spa'reggio m (Comm) deficit; Sport play-off

'sparg|ere vt scatter; (diffondere) spread; shed (lacrime, sangue). **~ersi** vr spread. **~i'mento** m scattering; **~imento di sangue** bloodshed

spa'ri|re vi disappear; **~sci!** get lost!. **~zi'one** f disappearance

spar'lare vi **~ di** run down

'sparo m shot

sparpagli'ar|e vt, **~si** vr scatter

'sparso pp di **spargere** • adj scattered; (sciolto) loose

spar'tire vt share out; (separare) separate

sparti'traffico m inv traffic island; (di autostrada) central reservation, median strip Am

spartizi'one f division

spa'ruto adj gaunt; (gruppo) small; (peli, capelli) sparse

sparvi'ero m sparrow-hawk

'spasimo m spasm

spa'smodico adj spasmodic

spas'sar|si vr amuse oneself; **~sela** have a good time

spassio'nato adj dispassionate

'spasso m fun; **essere uno ~** be hilarious; **andare a ~** go for a walk. **spas'soso** adj hilarious

'spatola f spatula

spau'racchio m scarecrow; fig bugbear. **spau'rire** vt frighten

spa'valdo adj defiant

spaventa'passeri m inv scarecrow

spaven'tar|e vt frighten. **~si** vr be frightened. **spa'vento** m fright. **spaven'toso** adj frightening; ([!]: enorme) incredible

spazi'ale adj spatial; (cosmico) space attrib

spazi'are vt space out • vi range

spazien'tirsi vr lose patience

'spazi|o m space. **~'oso** adj spacious

spaz'z|are vt sweep; **~are via** sweep away; ([!]: mangiare) devour. **~a'tura** f rubbish. **~ino** m road sweeper; (netturbino) dustman

'spazzo|la f brush; (di tergicristallo) blade. **~'lare** vt brush. **~'lino** m small brush. **~lino da denti** toothbrush. **~'lone** m scrubbing brush

S **specchi'arsi** vr look at oneself in the mirror; (riflettersi) be mirrored; **~ in qcno** model oneself on sb

specchi'etto m **~ retrovisore** driving mirror

'specchio m mirror

speci'a|le adj special • m (TV) special [programme]. **~'lista** mf specialist. **~lità** f inv specialty

specializ'za|re vt, **~rsi** vr specialize. **~to** adj skilled

special'mente adv especially

'specie f inv species; (tipo) kind; **fare ~ a** surprise

specifi'care vt specify. **spe'cifico** adj specific

specu'lare[1] vi speculate; **~ su** (indagare) speculate on; (Fin) speculate in

specu'lare[2] adj mirror attrib

specula|'tore, -'trice mf speculator. **~zi'one** f speculation

spe'di|re vt send. **~to** pp di **spedire** • adj quick; (parlata) fluent. **~zi'one** f dispatch; (Comm) consignment; (scientifica) expedition

'spegner|e vt put out; turn off (gas, luce); switch off (motore); slake (sete). **~si** vr go out; (morire) pass away

spelacchi'ato adj (tappeto) threadbare; (cane) mangy

spe'lar|e vt skin (coniglio). **~si** vr (cane:) moult

speleolo'gia f potholing

spel'lar|e vt skin; fig fleece. **~si** vr peel off

spe'lonca f cave; fig hole

spendacci'one, -a mf spendthrift

'spendere vt spend; **~ fiato** waste one's breath

spen'nare vt pluck; [!] fleece (cliente)

spennel'lare vt brush

spensie|ra'tezza f lightheartedness. **~'rato** adj carefree

'spento pp di **spegnere** • adj off; (gas) out; (smorto) dull

spe'ranza f hope; **pieno di ~** hopeful; **senza ~** hopeless

spe'rare vt hope for; (aspettarsi) expect • vi **~ in** trust in; **spero di sì** I hope so

'sper|dersi vr get lost. **~'duto** adj lost; (isolato) secluded

spergi'uro, -a mf perjurer • m perjury

sperimen'ta|le adj experimental. **~re** vt experiment with; test (resistenza, capacità, teoria). **~zi'one** f experimentation

'sperma m sperm

spe'rone m spur

sperpe'rare vt squander. **'sperpero** m waste

'spes|a f expense; (acquisto) purchase; **andare a far ~e** go shopping; **fare la ~a** do the shopping; **fare le ~e di** pay for. **~e** pl **bancarie** bank charges. **~e a carico del destinatario** carriage forward. **spe'sato** adj all-expenses-paid. **~o** pp di **spendere**

spesso[1] adj thick

spesso[2] adv often

spes'sore m thickness; (fig: consistenza) substance

spet'tabile adj (Comm) abbr (**Spett.**) **S~ ditta Rossi** Messrs Rossi

spettaco|'lare adj spectacular. **spet'tacolo** m spectacle; (rappresentazione) show. **~'loso** adj spectacular

spet'tare vi **~ a** be up to; (diritto:) be due to

spetta'tore, -'trice mf spectator; **spettatori** pl audience sg

spettego'lare vi gossip

spet'trale adj ghostly. **'spettro** m ghost; (Phys) spectrum

spezie fpl spices

spez'zar|e vt, **~si** vr break

spezza'tino m stew

spez'zato m coordinated jacket and trousers

spezzet'tare vt break into small pieces

spia f spy; (della polizia) informer; (di porta) peep-hole; **fare la ~** sneak. **~** [**luminosa**] light. **~ dell'olio** oil [warning] light

spiacci'care vt squash

spia'ce|nte adj sorry. **~vole** adj unpleasant

spi'aggia f beach

spia'nare vt level; (rendere liscio) smooth; roll out (pasta); raze to the ground (edificio)

spian'tato adj fig penniless

spi'are vt spy on; wait for (occasione ecc)

spiattel'lare vt blurt out; shove (oggetto)

spi'azzo m (radura) clearing

spic'ca|re vt **~re un salto** jump; **~re il volo** take flight •vi stand out. **~to** adj marked

spicchio m (di agrumi) segment; (di aglio) clove

spicci'a|rsi vr hurry up. **~'tivo** adj speedy

'spicciolo adj (comune) banal; (denaro, 5 euro) in change. **spiccioli** pl change sg

'spicco m relief; **fare ~** stand out

'spider f inv open-top sports car

spie'dino m kebab. **spi'edo** m spit; **allo spiedo** on a spit, spit-roasted

spie'ga|re vt explain; open out (cartina); unfurl (vele). **~rsi** vr explain oneself; (vele, bandiere:) unfurl. **~zi'one** f explanation

spiegaz'zato adj crumpled

spie'tato adj ruthless

spiffe'rare vt blurt out •vi (vento:) whistle. **'spiffero** m draught

'spiga f spike; (Bot) ear

spigli'ato adj self-possessed

'spigolo m edge; (angolo) corner

'spilla f brooch. **~ da balia** safety pin. **~ di sicurezza** safety pin

spil'lare vt tap

'spillo m pin. **~ di sicurezza** safety pin; (in arma) safety catch

spi'lorcio adj stingy

'spina f thorn; (di pesce) bone; (Electr) plug. **~ dorsale** spine

spi'naci mpl spinach

spi'nale adj spinal

spi'nato adj (filo) barbed; (pianta) thorny

spi'nello m [!] joint

'spinger|e vt push; fig drive. **~si** vr (andare) proceed

spi'noso adj thorny

'spint|a f push; (violenta) thrust; fig spur. **~o** pp di **spingere**

spio'naggio m espionage

spio'vente adj sloping

spi'overe vi liter stop raining; (ricadere) fall; (scorrere) flow down

'spira f coil

spi'raglio m small opening; (soffio d'aria) breath of air; (raggio di luce) gleam of light

spi'rale adj spiral •f spiral; (negli orologi) hairspring; (anticoncezionale) coil

spi'rare vi (soffiare) blow; (morire) pass away

spiri't|ato adj possessed; (espressione)

wild. **'spirito** m spirit; (arguzia) wit; (intelletto) mind; **fare dello spirito** be witty; **sotto spirito** in brandy. **~o'saggine** f witticism. **spiri'toso** adj witty

spiritu'ale adj spiritual

'splen|dere vi shine. **~dido** adj splendid. **~'dore** m splendour

'spoglia f (di animale) skin; **spoglie** pl (salma) mortal remains; (bottino) spoils

spogli'a|re vt strip; (svestire) undress; (fare lo spoglio di) go through. **~'rello** m strip-tease. **~rsi** vr strip, undress. **~'toio** m dressing room; Sport changing room; (guardaroba) cloakroom, checkroom Am. **'spoglio** adj undressed; (albero, muro) bare •m (scrutinio) perusal

'spola f shuttle; **fare la ~** shuttle

spol'pare vt flesh; fig fleece

spolve'rare vt dust; [!] devour (cibo)

'sponda f shore; (di fiume) bank; (bordo) edge

sponsoriz'zare vt sponsor

spon'taneo adj spontaneous

spopo'lar|e vt depopulate •vi (avere successo) draw the crowds. **~si** vr become depopulated

sporadica'mente adv sporadically. **spo'radico** adj sporadic

spor'c|are vt dirty; (macchiare) soil. **~arsi** vr get dirty. **~izia** f dirt. **'sporco** adj dirty; **avere la coscienza sporca** have a guilty conscience •m dirt

spor'gen|te adj jutting. **~za** f projection

S

'sporger|e vt stretch out; **~e querela contro** take legal action against •vi jut out. **~si** vr lean out

sport m inv sport

'sporta f shopping basket

spor'tello m door; (di banca ecc) window. **~ automatico** cash dispenser

spor'tivo, -a adj sports attrib; (persona) sporty •m sportsman •f sportswoman

'sporto pp di **sporgere**

'sposa f bride. **~'lizio** m wedding

spo'sa|re vt marry; fig espouse. **~rsi** vr get married; (vino:) go (**con** with). **~to** adj married. **'sposo** m bridegroom; **sposi** pl [**novelli**] newlyweds

spossa'tezza f exhaustion. **spos'sato** adj exhausted, worn out

spo'sta|re vt move; (differire) postpone; (cambiare) change. **~rsi** vr move. **~to, -a** adj ill-adjusted •mf (disadattato) misfit

'spranga f bar. **spran'gare** vt bar

'sprazzo m (di colore) splash; (di luce) flash; fig glimmer

spre'care vt waste. **'spreco** m waste

spre'g|evole adj despicable. **~ia'tivo** adj pejorative. **'spregio** m contempt

spregiudi'cato adj unscrupulous

'spremer|e vt squeeze. **~si** vr **~si le meningi** rack one's brains

spremia'grumi m lemon squeezer

spre'muta f juice. **~ d'arancia** fresh orange [juice]

sprez'zante adj contemptuous

sprigio'nar|e vt emit. **~si** vr burst out

spriz'zare vt/i spurt; be bursting with (salute, gioia)

sprofon'dar|e vi sink; (crollare) collapse. **~si** vr **~si in** sink into; fig be engrossed in

'sprone m spur; (sartoria) yoke

sproporzi|o'nato adj disproportionate. **~'one** f disproportion

spropositato adj full of blunders; (enorme) huge. **spro'posito** m blunder; (eccesso) excessive amount

sprovve'duto adj unprepared; **~ di** lacking in

sprov'visto adj **~ di** out of; lacking in (fantasia, pazienza); **alla sprovvista** unexpectedly

spruz'za|re vt sprinkle; (vaporizzare) spray; (inzaccherare) spatter. **~'tore** m spray; **'spruzzo** m spray; (di fango) splash

spudo|ra'tezza f shamelessness. **~'rato** adj shameless

'spugna f sponge; (tessuto) towelling. **spu'gnoso** adj spongy '**spuma** f foam; (schiuma) froth; (Culin) mousse. ▣**spu'mante** m sparkling wine. **spumeggi'are** vi foam

spun'ta|re vt break the point of; trim (capelli); **~rla** fig win • vi (pianta:) sprout; (capelli:) begin to grow; (sorgere) rise; (apparire) appear. **~rsi** vr get blunt. **~ta** f trim

spun'tino m snack

spunto m cue; fig starting point; **dare ~ a** give rise to

spur'gar|e vt purge. **~si** vr (Med) expectorate

spu'tare vt/i spit; **~ sentenze** pass judgment. '**sputo** m spit

squadra f team, squad; (di polizia ecc) squad; (da disegno) square. **squa'drare** vt square; (guardare) look up and down

squa'dr|iglia f, **~one** m squadron

squagli'ar|e vt, **~si** vr melt; **~sela** (!: svignarsela) steal out

squa'lifi|ca f disqualification. **~'care** vt disqualify

squallido adj squalid. **squal'lore** m squalor

squalo m shark

squama f scale; (di pelle) flake

squa'm|are vt scale. **~arsi** vr (pelle:) flake off. **~'moso** adj scaly; (pelle) flaky

squarcia'gola: **a ~** adv at the top of one's voice

squarci'are vt rip. '**squarcio** m rip; (di ferita, in nave) gash; (di cielo) patch

squattri'nato adj penniless

squilib'ra|re vt unbalance. **~to, -a** adj unbalanced • mf lunatic. **squi'librio** m imbalance

squil'la|nte adj shrill. **~re** vi (campana:) peal; (tromba:) blare; (telefono:) ring. '**squillo** m blare; (Teleph) ring • f (ragazza) call girl

squi'sito adj exquisite

sradi'care vt uproot; eradicate (vizio, male)

sragio'nare vi rave

srego'lato adj inordinate; (dissoluto) dissolute

s.r.l. abbr (società a responsabilità limitata) Ltd

sroto'lare vt uncoil

SS abbr (strada statale) national road

'**stabile** adj stable; (permanente) lasting; (saldo) steady; **compagnia ~** (Theat) repertory company • m (edificio) building

stabili'mento m factory; (industriale) plant; (edificio) establishment. ▣**~ balneare** lido

stabi'li|re vt establish; (decidere) decide. **~rsi** vr settle. **~tà** f stability

stabiliz'za|re vt stabilize. **~rsi** vr stabilize. **~'tore** m stabilizer

stac'car|e vt detach; pronounce clearly (parole); (separare) separate; turn off (corrente) • vi (!: finire di lavorare) knock off. **~si** vr come off; **~si da** break away from (partito, famiglia)

staccio'nata f fence

'**stacco** m gap

'**stadio** m stadium

'**staffa** f stirrup

staf'fetta f dispatch rider

stagio'nale adj seasonal

stagio'na|re vt season (legno); mature (formaggio). **~to** adj (legno) seasoned; (formaggio) matured

stagi'one f season; **alta/bassa ~** high/low season

stagli'arsi vr stand out

sta'gna|nte adj stagnant. **~re** vt (saldare) solder; (chiudere ermeticamente) seal • vi stagnate. '**stagno** adj watertight • m pond; (metallo) tin

sta'gnola f tinfoil

'**stall|a** f stable; (per buoi) cowshed. **~i'ere** m groom

stal'lone m stallion

sta'mani, stamat'tina adv this morning

stam'becco m ibex

stam'berga f hovel

'**stampa** f (Typ) printing; (giornali, giornalisti) press; (riproduzione) print

stam'pa|nte f printer. **~nte laser** laser printer. **~re** vt print. **~'tello** m block letters pl

stam'pella f crutch

'**stampo** m mould; **di vecchio ~** (persona) of the old school

▣ *see* A-Z of Italian life and culture

sta'nare vt drive out

stan'car|e vt tire; (annoiare) bore. **~si** vr get tired

stan'chezza f tiredness. **'stanco** adj tired; **stanco di** fed up with. **stanco morto** dead tired, exhausted

'standard adj & m inv standard. **~iz'zare** vt standardize

'stan|ga f bar; (persona) beanpole. **~'gata** f fig blow; ([!]: nel calcio) big kick. **stan'ghetta** f (di occhiali) leg

sta'notte adv tonight; (la notte scorsa) last night

'stante prep on account of; **a sé ~** separate

stan'tio adj stale

stan'tuffo m piston

'stanza f room; (metrica) stanza

stanzi'are vt allocate

stap'pare vt uncork

'stare

• vi (*rimanere*) stay; (*abitare*) live; (*con gerundio*) be; **sto solo cinque minuti** I'll stay only five minutes; **sto in piazza Peyron** I live in Peyron Square; **sta dormendo** he's sleeping; **~ a** (*attenersi*) keep to; (*spettare*) be up to; **~ bene** (*economicamente*) be well off; (*di salute*) be well; (*addirsi*) suit; **~ dietro a** (*seguire*) follow; (*sorvegliare*) keep an eye on; (*corteggiare*) run after; **~ in piedi** stand; **~ per** be about to; **come stai/sta?** how are you?; **lasciar ~** leave alone; **starci** (*essere contenuto*) go into; (*essere d'accordo*) agree; **il 3 nel 12 ci sta 4 volte** 3 into 12 goes 4; **non sa ~ agli scherzi** he can't take a joke; **~ sulle proprie** keep oneself to oneself.

• **starsene** vr (*rimanere*) stay

starnu'tire vi sneeze. **star'nuto** m sneeze

sta'sera adv this evening, tonight

sta'tale adj state attrib • mf state employee • f main road

'statico adj static

sta'tista m statesman

sta'tistic|a f statistics sg. **~o** adj statistical

'stato pp di **essere, stare** • m state; (posizione sociale) position; (Jur) status. **~ d'animo** frame of mind. **~ civile** marital status. **S~ Maggiore** (Mil) General Staff. **Stati** pl **Uniti [d'America]** United States [of America]

'statua f statue

statuni'tense adj United States attrib, US attrib • mf citizen of the United States, US citizen

sta'tura f height; **di alta ~** tall; **di bassa ~** short

sta'tuto m statute

stazio'nario adj stationary

stazi'one f station; (città) resort. **~ balneare** seaside resort. **~ ferroviaria** train station. **~ di servizio** service station. **~ termale** spa

'stecca f stick; (di ombrello) rib; (da biliardo) cue; (Med) splint; (di sigarette) carton; (di reggiseno) stiffener

stec'cato m fence

stec'chito adj skinny; (rigido) stiff; (morto) stone cold dead

'stella f star; **salire alle stelle** (prezzi:) rise sky-high. **~ alpina** edelweiss. **~ cadente** shooting star. **~ filante** streamer. **~ di mare** starfish

stel'lare adj stellar

'stelo m stem; **lampada** f **a ~** standard lamp

'stemma m coat of arms

stempi'ato adj bald at the temples

sten'dardo m standard

'stender|e vt spread out; (appendere) hang out; (distendere) stretch [out]; (scrivere) write down. **~si** vr stretch out

stendibianche'ria m inv, **stendi'toio** m clothes horse

stenodatti|logra'fia f shorthand typing

stenogra'f|are vt take down in shorthand. **~ia** f shorthand

sten'ta|re vi **~re a** find it hard to. **~to** adj laboured. **'stento** m effort; **a stento** with difficulty; **stenti** pl hardships, privations

'sterco m dung

'stereo['fonico] adj stereo[phonic]

S

stereoti'pato adj stereotyped; (sorriso) insincere. **stere'otipo** m stereotype

steril|e adj sterile; (terreno) barren. **~ità** f sterility. **~iz'zare** vt sterilize. **~izzazi'one** f sterilization

ster'lina f pound; **lira ~** [pound] sterling

stermi'nare vt exterminate

stermi'nato adj immense

ster'minio m extermination

ste'roide m steroid

ster'zare vi steer. **'sterzo** m steering

steso pp di **stendere**

stesso adj same; **io ~** myself; **tu ~** yourself; **me ~** myself; **se ~** himself; **in quel momento ~** at that very moment; **dalla stessa regina** by the Queen herself; **coi miei stessi occhi** with my own eyes • pron **lo ~** the same one; (la stessa cosa) the same; **fa lo ~** it's all the same; **ci vado lo ~** I'll go just the same

ste'sura f drawing up; (documento) draft

stick m **colla a ~** glue stick; **deodorante a ~** stick deodorant

stigma m stigma. **~te** fpl stigmata

sti'lare vt draw up

stil|e m style. **sti'lista** mf stylist. **~iz'zato** adj stylized

stil'lare vi ooze

stilo'grafic|a f fountain pen. **~o** adj **penna ~a** fountain pen

stima f esteem; (valutazione) estimate. **sti'mare** vt esteem; (valutare) estimate; (ritenere) consider

stimo'la|nte adj stimulating • m stimulant. **~re** vt stimulate; (incitare) incite

stimolo m stimulus; (fitta) pang

stinco m shin

stinger|e vt/i fade. **~si** vr fade. **'stinto** pp di **stingere**

sti'par|e vt cram. **~si** vr crowd together

stipendi'ato adj salaried • m salaried worker. **sti'pendio** m salary

stipite m doorpost

stipu'la|re vt stipulate. **~zi'one** f stipulation; (accordo) agreement

stira'mento m sprain

sti'ra|re vt iron; (distendere) stretch. **~rsi** vr (distendersi) stretch; pull (muscolo). **~'tura** f ironing. **'stiro** m **ferro da stiro** iron

'stirpe f stock

stiti'chezza f constipation. **'stitico** adj constipated

'stiva f (Naut) hold

sti'vale m boot. **stivali** pl **di gomma** Wellington boots

'stizza f anger

stiz'zi|re vt irritate. **~rsi** vr become irritated. **~to** adj irritated. **stiz'zoso** adj peevish

stocca'fisso m stockfish

stoc'cata f stab; (battuta pungente) gibe

'stoffa f material; fig stuff

'stola f stole

'stolto adj foolish

stoma'chevole adj revolting

'stomaco m stomach; **mal di ~** stomach-ache

sto'na|re vt/i sing/play out of tune • vi (non intonarsi) clash. **~to** adj out of tune; (discordante) clashing; (confuso) bewildered. **~'tura** f false note; (discordanza) clash

'stoppia f stubble

stop'pino m wick

stop'poso adj tough

'storcer|e vt, **~si** vr twist

stor'di|re vt stun; (intontire) daze. **~rsi** vr dull one's senses. **~to** adj stunned; (intontito) dazed; (sventato) heedless

'storia f history; (racconto, bugia) story; (pretesto) excuse; **fare [delle] storie** make a fuss

'storico, -a adj historical; (di importanza storica) historic • mf historian

stori'one m sturgeon

'stormo m flock

'storno m starling

storpi'a|re vt cripple; mangle (parole). **~'tura** f deformation. **'storpio, -a** adj crippled • mf cripple

'stort|a f (distorsione) sprain; **prendere una ~a alla caviglia**

sprain one's ankle. **~o** pp di **storcere** • adj crooked; (ritorto) twisted; (gambe) bandy; fig wrong

sto'viglie fpl crockery sg

'strabico adj cross-eyed

strabili'ante adj astonishing

stra'bismo m squint

straboc'care vi overflow

stra'carico adj overloaded

stracci|'are vt tear; ([!]: vincere) thrash. **~'ato** adj torn; (persona) in rags; (prezzi) slashed; **a un prezzo ~ato** dirt cheap. **'straccio** adj torn • m rag; (strofinaccio) cloth. **~'one** m tramp

stra'cotto adj overdone; ([!]: innamorato) head over heels • m stew

'strada f road; (di città) street; **essere fuori ~** be on the wrong track; **fare ~** lead the way; **farsi ~** make one's way. **~ maestra** main road. **~ a senso unico** one-way street. **~ senza uscita** blind alley. **stra'dale** adj road attrib

strafalci'one m blunder

stra'fare vi overdo things

stra'foro: **di ~** adv on the sly

strafot'ten|te adj arrogant. **~za** f arrogance

'strage f slaughter

'stralcio m (parte) extract

stralu'na|re vt **~re gli occhi** open one's eyes wide. **~to** adj (occhi) staring; (persona) distraught

stramaz'zare vi fall heavily

strambe'ria f oddity. **'strambo** adj strange

strampa'lato adj odd

stra'nezza f strangeness

strango'lare vt strangle

strani'ero, -a adj foreign • mf foreigner

'strano adj strange

straordi|naria'mente adv extraordinarily. **~'nario** adj extraordinary; (notevole) remarkable; (edizione) special; **lavoro ~nario** overtime; **treno ~nario** special train

strapaz'zar|e vt ill-treat; scramble (uova). **~si** vr tire oneself out. **stra'pazzo** m strain; **da strapazzo** fig worthless

strapi'eno adj overflowing

strapi'ombo m projection; **a ~** sheer

strap'par|e vt tear; (per distruggere) tear up; pull out (dente, capelli); (sradicare) pull up; (estorcere) wring. **~si** vr get torn; (allontanarsi) tear oneself away. **'strappo** m tear; (strattone) jerk; ([!]: passaggio) lift; **fare uno strappo alla regola** make an exception to the rule. **~ muscolare** muscle strain

strapun'tino m folding seat

strari'pare vi flood

strasci'c|are vt trail; shuffle (piedi); drawl (parole). **'strascico** m train; fig after-effect

strass m inv rhinestone

strata'gemma m stratagem

strate'gia f strategy. **stra'tegico** adj strategic

'strato m layer; (di vernice ecc) coat; (roccioso, sociale) stratum. **~'sfera** f stratosphere. **~'sferico** adj stratospheric

stravac'carsi vr [!] slouch

strava'gan|te adj extravagant; (eccentrico) eccentric. **~za** f extravagance; (eccentricità) eccentricity

stra'vecchio adj ancient

strave'dere vt **~ per** worship

stravizi'are vi indulge oneself. **stra'vizio** m excess

stra'volg|ere vt twist; (turbare) upset. **~i'mento** m twisting. **stra'volto** adj distraught; ([!]: stanco) done in

strazi'a|nte adj heartrending; (dolore) agonizing. **~re** vt grate on (orecchie); break (cuore). **'strazio** m agony; **che strazio!** [!] it's awful!

'strega f witch. **stre'gare** vt bewitch. **stre'gone** m wizard

'stregua f **alla ~ di** like

stre'ma|re vt exhaust. **~to** adj exhausted

'strenuo adj strenuous

strepi|'tare vi make a din. **'strepito** m noise. **~'toso** adj noisy; fig resounding

res'sa|nte adj (lavoro, situazione) stressful. **~to** adj stressed [out]

tretta f grasp; (dolore) pang; **essere alle strette** be in dire straits. **~ di mano** handshake

ret'tezza f narrowness; **stret'tezze** pl (difficoltà finanziarie) financial difficulties

tret|to pp di **stringere** •adj narrow; (serrato) tight; (vicino) close; (dialetto) broad; (rigoroso) strict; **lo ~to necessario** the bare minimum •m (Geog) strait. **~'toia** f bottleneck; (!: difficoltà) tight spot

ri'a|to adj striped. **~'tura** f streak

ri'dente adj strident

tridere vi squeak; fig clash. **stri'dore** m screech

tridulo adj shrill

rigli'a|re vt groom. **~ta** f grooming; fig dressing down

ril'l|are vi t scream. **'strillo** m scream

rimin'zito adj skimpy; (magro) skinny

rimpel'lare vt strum

trin|ga f lace; (Comput) string. **~'gato** adj fig terse

tringer|e vt press; (serrare) squeeze; (tenere stretto) hold tight; take in (abito); (comprimere) be tight; (restringere) tighten; **~e la mano a** shake hands with •vi (premere) press. **~si** vr (accostarsi) draw close (**a** to); (avvicinarsi) squeeze up

triscia f strip; (riga) stripe. **strisce** [**pedonali**] zebra crossing sg

risci'ar|e vi crawl; (sfiorare) graze •vt drag (piedi). **~si** vr **~si a** rub against. **'striscio** m graze; (Med) smear; **colpire di striscio** graze

risci'one m banner

rito'lare vt grind

riz'zare vt squeeze; (torcere) wring [out]; **~ l'occhio** wink

rofa f strophe

rofi'naccio m cloth; (per spolverare) duster

rofi'nare vt rub

rombaz'zare vt boast about •vi hoot

rombaz'zata f hoot

stron'care vt cut off; (reprimere) crush; (criticare) tear to shreds

stropicci'are vt rub; crumple (vestito)

stroz'za|re vt strangle. **~'tura** f strangling; (di strada) narrowing

strozzi'naggio m loan-sharking

stroz'zino m pej usurer; (truffatore) shark

strug'gente adj all-consuming

strumen'tale adj instrumental

strumentaliz'zare vt make use of

stru'mento m instrument; (arnese) tool. **~ a corda** string instrument. **~ musicale** musical instrument

strusci'are vt rub

'strutto m lard

strut'tura f structure. **struttu'rale** adj structural

struttu'rare vt structure

strutturazi'one f structuring

'struzzo m ostrich

stuc'ca|re vt stucco

stuc'chevole adj nauseating

'stucco m stucco

stu'den|te, -t'essa mf student; (di scuola) schoolboy; schoolgirl. **~'tesco** adj student; (di scolaro) school attrib

studi'ar|e vt study. **~si** vr **~si di** try to

'studi|o m studying; (stanza, ricerca) study; (di artista, TV ecc) studio; (di professionista) office. **~'oso, -a** adj studious •mf scholar

'stufa f stove. **~ elettrica** electric fire

stu'fa|re vt (Culin) stew; (dare fastidio) bore. **~rsi** vr get bored. **~to** m stew

'stufo adj bored; **essere ~ di** be fed up with

stu'oia f mat

stupefa'cente adj amazing •m drug

stu'pendo adj stupendous

stupi'd|aggine f (azione) stupid thing; (cosa da poco) nothing. **~ata** f stupid thing. **~ità** f stupidity. **'stupido** adj stupid

stu'pir|e vt astonish •vi, **~si** vr be astonished. **stu'pore** m amazement

stu'pra|re vt rape. **~'tore** m rapist. **'stupro** m rape

S

sturalavan'dini m inv plunger

stu'rare vt uncork; unblock (lavandino)

stuzzi'care vt prod [at]; pick (denti); poke (fuoco); (molestare) tease; whet (appetito)

stuzzi'chino m (Culin) appetizer

su prep on; (senza contatto) over; (riguardo a) about; (circa, intorno a) about, around; **le chiavi sono sul tavolo** the keys are on the table; **il quadro è appeso sul camino** the picture is hanging over the fireplace; **un libro sull'antico Egitto** a book on o about Ancient Egypt; **costa sui 25 euro** it costs about 25 euros; **decidere sul momento** decide at the time; **su commissione** on commission; **su due piedi** on the spot; **uno su dieci** one out of ten •adv (sopra) up; (al piano di sopra) upstairs; (addosso) on; **ho su il cappotto** I've got my coat on; **in su** (guardare) up; **dalla vita in su** from the waist up; **su!** come on!

su'bacqueo adj underwater

subaffit'tare vt sublet. **subaf'fitto** m sublet

subal'terno adj & m subordinate

sub'buglio m turmoil

sub'conscio adj & m subconscious

'subdolo adj devious

suben'trare vi (circostanze:) come up; ~ **a** take the place of

su'bire vt undergo; (patire) suffer

subis'sare vt fig ~ **di** overwhelm with

'subito adv at once; ~ **dopo** straight after

su'blime adj sublime

subodo'rare vt suspect

subordi'nato, -a adj & mf subordinate

subur'bano adj suburban

suc'ceder|e vi (accadere) happen; **~e a** succeed; (venire dopo) follow; **~e al trono** succeed to the throne. **~si** vr happen one after the other

successi'one f succession; **in** ~ in succession

succes|siva'mente adv subsequently. **~'sivo** adj successive

suc'ces|so pp di **succedere** •m success; (esito) outcome; (disco ecc) hit

succes'sore m successor

succhi'are vt suck [up]

suc'cinto adj (conciso) concise; (abito) scanty

'succo m juice; fig essence; ~ **di frutta** fruit juice. **suc'coso** adj juicy

succu'lento adj succulent

succur'sale f branch [office]

sud m south; **del** ~ southern

su'da|re vi sweat; (faticare) sweat blood; **~re freddo** be in a cold sweat. **~ta** f sweat. **~'ticcio** adj sweaty. **~to** adj sweaty

sud'detto adj above-mentioned

'suddito, -a mf subject

suddi'vi|dere vt subdivide. **~si'one** f subdivision

su'd-est m southeast

'sudici|o adj filthy. **~'ume** m filth

su'dore m sweat; fig sweat

su'd-ovest m southwest

suffici'en|te adj sufficient; (presuntuoso) conceited •m bare essentials pl; (Sch) pass mark. **~za** sufficiency; (presunzione) conceit; (Sch) pass; **a ~za** enough

suf'fisso m suffix

suf'fragio m vote. ~ **universale** universal suffrage

suggeri'mento m suggestion

sugge'ri|re vt suggest; (Theat) prompt. **~'tore, ~'trice** mf (Theat) prompter

suggestiona'bile adj suggestible

suggestio'na|re vt influence **suggesti'one** f influence

sugge'stivo adj suggestive; (musica ecc) evocative

'sughero m cork

'sugli = **su + gli**

'sugo m (di frutta) juice; (di carne) gravy; (salsa) sauce; (sostanza) substance

'sui = **su + i**

sui'cid|a adj suicidal •mf suicide. **suici'darsi** vr commit suicide. **~io** m suicide

su'ino adj **carne suina** pork •m swine

sul = **su + il**. '**sullo** = **su + lo**. '**sulla** = **su + la**. '**sulle** = **su + le**

sul'ta|na f sultana. **~'nina** adj **uva ~nina** sultana. **~no** m sultan

sunto m summary

suo, -a poss adj **il ~, i suoi** his; (di cosa, animale) its; (forma di cortesia) your; **la sua, le sue** her; (di cosa, animale) its; (forma di cortesia) your; **questa macchina è sua** this car is his/hers; **~ padre** his/her/your father; **un ~ amico** a friend of his/hers/yours •poss pron **il ~, i suoi** his; (di cosa, animale) its; (forma di cortesia) yours; **la sua, le sue** hers; (di cosa animale) its; (forma di cortesia) yours; **i suoi** his/her folk

su'ocera f mother-in-law

su'ocero m father-in-law

su'ola f sole

su'olo m ground; (terreno) soil

suo'na|re vt/i (Mus) play; ring (campanello); sound (allarme, clacson); (orologio:) strike. **~'tore, ~'trice** mf player. **suone'ria** f alarm. **su'ono** m sound

su'ora f nun; **Suor Maria** Sister Maria

superal'colico m spirit •adj **bevande** pl **superalcoliche** spirits

supera'mento m (di timidezza) overcoming; (di esame) success (**di** in)

supe'rare vt surpass; (eccedere) exceed; (vincere) overcome; overtake (veicolo); pass (esame)

su'perbo adj haughty; (magnifico) superb

superdo'tato adj highly gifted

superfici'al|e adj superficial •mf superficial person. **~ità** f superficiality. **super'ficie** f surface; (area) area

su'perfluo adj superfluous

superi'or|e adj superior; (di grado) senior; (più elevato) higher; (sovrastante) upper; (al di sopra) above •mf superior. **~ità** f superiority

superla'tivo adj & m superlative

supermer'cato m supermarket

super'sonico adj supersonic

su'perstite adj surviving •mf survivor

superstizi'o|ne f superstition. **~so** adj superstitious

super'strada f toll-free motorway

supervi|si'one f supervision. **~'sore** m supervisor

su'pino adj supine

suppel'lettili fpl furnishings

suppergiù adv about

supplemen'tare adj supplementary

supple'mento m supplement; **~ rapido** express train supplement

sup'plen|te adj temporary •mf (Sch) supply teacher. **~za** f temporary post

'**suppli|ca** f plea; (domanda) petition. **~'care** vt beg

sup'plire vt replace •vi **~ a** (compensare) make up for

sup'plizio m torture

sup'porre vt suppose

sup'porto m support

supposizi'one f supposition

sup'posta f suppository

sup'posto pp di **supporre**

suprema'zia f supremacy. **su'premo** adj supreme

sur'fare vi **~ in Internet** surf the Net

surge'la|re vt deep-freeze. **~ti** mpl frozen food sg. **~to** adj frozen

surrea'lis|mo m surrealism. **~ta** mf surrealist

surriscal'dare vt overheat

surro'gato m substitute

suscet'tibil|e adj touchy. **~ità** f touchiness

susci'tare vt stir up; arouse (ammirazione ecc)

su'sin|a f plum. **~o** m plumtree

su'spense f suspense

sussegu|'ente adj subsequent. **~'irsi** vr follow one after the other

sussidi'ar|e vt subsidize. **~io** adj

subsidiary. **sus'sidio** m subsidy; (aiuto) aid. **sussidio di disoccupazione** unemployment benefit

sussi'ego m haughtiness

sussi'stenza f subsistence. **sus'sistere** vi subsist; (essere valido) hold good

sussul'tare vi start. **sus'sulto** m start

sussur'rare vt whisper. **sus'surro** m whisper

sva'gar|e vt amuse. **~si** vr amuse oneself. **'svago** m relaxation; (divertimento) amusement

svaligi'are vt rob; burgle (casa)

svalu'ta|re vt devalue; fig underestimate. **~rsi** vr lose value. **~zi'one** f devaluation

svam'pito adj absent-minded

sva'nire vi vanish

svantaggi|'ato adj at a disadvantage; (bambino, paese) disadvantaged. **svan'taggio** m disadvantage; **essere in svantaggio** Sport be losing; **~'oso** adj disadvantageous

svapo'rare vi evaporate

svari'ato adj varied

sva'sato adj flared

'svastica f swastika

sve'dese adj & m (lingua) Swedish •mf Swede

'sveglia f (orologio) alarm [clock]; **~!** get up!; **mettere la ~** set the alarm [clock]

S

svegli'ar|e vt wake up; fig awaken. **~si** vr wake up. **'sveglio** adj awake; (di mente) quick-witted

sve'lare vt reveal

svel'tezza f speed; fig quick-wittedness

svel'tir|e vt quicken. **~si** vr (persona:) liven up. **'svelto** adj quick; (slanciato) svelte; **alla svelta** quickly

'svend|ere vt undersell. **~ita** f [clearance] sale

sve'nire vi faint

sven'ta|re vt foil. **~to** adj thoughtless •mf thoughtless person

'sventola f slap

svento'lare vt/i wave

sven'trare vt disembowel; fig demolish (edificio)

sven'tura f misfortune. **sventu'rato** adj unfortunate

sve'nuto pp di **svenire**

svergo'gnato adj shameless

sver'nare vi winter

sve'stir|e vt undress

'Svezia f Sweden

svez'zare vt wean

svi'ar|e vt divert; (corrompere) lead astray. **~si** vr fig go astray

svico'lare vi turn down a side street; (dalla questione ecc) evade the issue; (da una persona) dodge out of the way

svi'gnarsela vr slip away

svi'lire vt debase

svilup'par|e vt, **~si** vr develop. **svi'luppo** m development; **paese in via di sviluppo** developing country

svinco'lar|e vt release; clear (merce). **~si** vr free oneself. **'svincolo** m clearance; (di autostrada) exit

svisce'ra|re vt gut; fig dissect. **~to** adj passionate; (ossequioso) obsequious

'svista f oversight

svi'ta|re vt unscrew. **~to** adj (!: matto) cracked, nutty

🇨 **'Svizzer|a** f Switzerland. **s~o, -a** adj & mf Swiss

svogli|a'tezza f half-heartedness. **~'ato** adj lazy

svolaz'za|nte adj (capelli) wind-swept. **~re** vi flutter

'svolger|e vt unwind; unwrap (pacco); (risolvere) solve; (portare a termine) carry out; (sviluppare) develop. **~si** vr (accadere) take place. **svolgi'mento** m course; (sviluppo) development

'svolta f turning; fig turning-point. **svol'tare** vi turn

'svolto pp di **svolgere**

svuo'tare vt empty [out]

Tt

tabac'c|aio, -a mf tobacconist. **~he'ria** f tobacconist's. **ta'bacco** m tobacco

ta'bel|la f table; (lista) list. **~la dei prezzi** price list. **~'lina** f (Math) multiplication table. **~'lone** m wall chart. **~lone del canestro** backboard

taber'nacolo m tabernacle

tabù adj & m inv taboo

tabu'lato m [data] printout

'tacca f notch; **di mezza ~** (attore, giornalista) second-rate

tac'cagno adj [!] stingy

tac'cheggio m shoplifting

tac'chetto m Sport stud

tac'chino m turkey

tacci'are vt **~ qcno di qcsa** accuse sb of sth

'tacco m heel; **alzare i tacchi** take to one's heels; **scarpe senza ~** flat shoes. **tacchi** pl **a spillo** stiletto heels

taccu'ino m notebook

ta'cere vi be silent • vt say nothing about; **mettere a ~ qcsa** (scandalo) hush sth up

ta'chimetro m speedometer

'tacito adj silent; (inespresso) tacit. **taci'turno** adj taciturn

ta'fano m horsefly

taffe'ruglio m scuffle

'taglia f (riscatto) ransom; (ricompensa) reward; (statura) height; (misura) size. **~ unica** one size

taglia'carte m inv paperknife

taglia'erba m inv lawn-mower

tagliafu'oco adj inv **porta ~** fire door; **striscia ~** fire break

tagli'ando m coupon; **fare il ~** ≈ put one's car in for its MOT

tagli'ar|e vt cut; (attraversare) cut across; (interrompere) cut off; (togliere) cut out; carve (carne); mow (erba); **farsi ~e i capelli** have a haircut • vi cut. **~si** vr cut oneself; **~si i capelli** have a haircut

taglia'telle fpl tagliatelle sg, thin, flat strips of egg pasta

taglieggi'are vt extort money from

tagli'e|nte adj sharp • m cutting edge. **~re** m chopping board

'taglio m cut; (il tagliare) cutting; (di stoffa) length; (parte tagliente) edge. **~ cesareo** Caesarean section

tagli'ola f trap

tagliuz'zare vt cut

tail'leur m inv [lady's] suit

'talco m talcum powder

'tale adj such a; (con nomi plurali) such; **c'è un ~ disordine** there is such a mess; **non accetto tali scuse** I won't accept such excuses; **il rumore era ~ che non si sentiva nulla** there was so much noise you couldn't hear yourself think; **il ~ giorno** on such and such a day; **quel tal signore** that gentleman; **~ quale** just like • pron **un ~** someone; **quel ~** that man; **il tal dei tali** such and such a person

ta'lento m talent

tali'smano m talisman

tallo'nare vt be hot on the heels of

tallon'cino m coupon

tal'lone m heel

tal'mente adv so

ta'lora adv = **talvolta**

'talpa f mole

tal'volta adv sometimes

tamburel'lare vi (con le dita) drum; (pioggia:) beat, drum. **tambu'rello** m tambourine. **tambu'rino** m drummer. **tam'buro** m drum

tampona'mento m (Auto) collision; (di ferita) dressing; (di falla) plugging. **~ a catena** pile-up. **tampo'nare** vt

[!] see A-Z of Italian life and culture

t

(urtare) crash into; (otturare) plug. **tam'pone** m swab; (per timbri) pad; (per mestruazioni) tampon; (Comput, per treni) buffer

'tana f den

'tanfo m stench

'tanga m inv tanga

tan'gen|te adj tangent • f tangent; (somma) bribe. ▣ **~'topoli** f widespread corruption in Italy in the early 90s. **~zi'ale** f orbital road

tan'gibile adj tangible

'tango m tango

tan'tino: **un ~** adv a little [bit]

'tanto adj [so] much; (con nomi plurali) [so] many, [such] a lot of; **~ tempo** [such] a long time; **non ha tanta pazienza** he doesn't have much patience; **~ tempo quanto ti serve** as much time as you need; **non è ~ intelligente quanto suo padre** he's not as intelligent as his father; **tanti amici quanti parenti** as many friends as relatives • pron much; (plurale) many; (tanto tempo) a long time; **è un uomo come tanti** he's just an ordinary man; **tanti** (molte persone) many people; **non ci vuole così ~** it doesn't take that long; **~ quanto** as much as; **tanti quanti** as many as • conj (comunque) anyway, in any case • adv (così) so; (con verbi) so much; **~ debole** so weak; **è ~ ingenuo da crederle** he's naive enough to believe her; **di ~ in ~** every now and then; **~ l'uno come l'altro** both; **~ quanto** as much as; **tre volte ~** three times as much; **una volta ~** once in a while; **tant'è** so much so; **~ per cambiare** for a change

'tappa f stop; (parte di viaggio) stage

tappa'buchi m inv stopgap

tap'par|e vt plug; cork (bottiglia); **~e la bocca a qcno** ! shut sb up. **~si** vr **~si gli occhi** cover one's eyes; **~si il naso** hold one's nose

tappa'rella f ! roller blind

tappe'tino m mat; (Comput) mouse mat

tap'peto m carpet; (piccolo) rug; **mandare qcno al ~** knock sb down

▣ *see* A-Z of Italian life and culture

tappez'z|are vt paper (pareti); (rivestire) cover. **~e'ria** f tapestry; (di carta) wallpaper; (arte) upholstery. **~i'ere** m upholsterer; (imbianchino) decorator

'tappo m plug; (di sughero) cork; (di metallo, per penna) top; (!: persona piccola) dwarf. **~ di sughero** cork

'tara f (difetto) flaw; (ereditaria) hereditary defect; (peso) tare

ta'rantola f tarantula

ta'ra|re vt calibrate (strumento). **~to** adj (Comm) discounted; (Techn) calibrated; (Med) with a hereditary defect; ! crazy

tarchi'ato adj stocky

tar'dare vi be late • vt delay

'tard|i adv late; **al più ~i** at the latest; **più ~i** later [on]; **sul ~i** late in the day; **far ~i** (essere in ritardo) be late; (con gli amici) stay up late; **a più ~i** see you later. **tar'divo** adj late; (bambino) retarded. **~o** adj slow; (tempo) late

'targ|a f plate; (Auto) numberplate. **~a di circolazione** numberplate. **tar'gato** adj **un'auto targata...** a car with the registration number.... **~'hetta** f (su porta) nameplate; (sulla valigia) name tag

ta'rif|fa f rate, tariff. **~'fario** m price list

'tarlo m woodworm

'tarma f moth

ta'rocco m tarot; **ta'rocchi** pl tarot

tartagli'are vi stutter

'tartaro adj & m tartar

tarta'ruga f tortoise; (di mare) turtle; (per pettine ecc) tortoiseshell

tartas'sare vt harass

tar'tina f canapé

tar'tufo m truffle

'tasca f pocket; (in borsa) compartment; **da ~** pocket attrib. **~ da pasticciere** icing bag

ta'scabile adj pocket attrib • m paperback

tasca'pane m inv haversack

ta'schino m breast pocket

'tassa f tax; (d'scrizione ecc) fee; (doganale) duty. **~ di circolazione** road tax. **~ d'iscrizione** registration fee

as'sametro m taximeter

as'sare vt tax

:assa|tiva'mente adv without question

assazi'one f taxation

.as'sello m wedge; (di stoffa) gusset

assì m inv taxi. **tas'sista** mf taxi driver

tasso[1] m yew; (animale) badger

tasso[2] m rate. ~ **di cambio** exchange rate. ~ **di interesse** interest rate

:a'stare vt feel; (sondare) sound; ~ **il terreno** fig test the water

asti'e|ra f keyboard. ~**'rista** mf keyboarder

tasto m key; (tatto) touch. ~ **delicato** fig touchy subject. ~ **funzione** (Comput) function key. ~ **tabulatore** tab key

tattica f tactics pl

tattico adj tactical

tatto m (senso) touch; (accortezza) tact; **aver** ~ be tactful

atu'a|ggio m tattoo. ~**re** vt tattoo

tavola f table; (illustrazione) plate; (asse) plank. ~ **calda** snackbar

avo'lato m boarding; (pavimento) wood floor

avo'letta f bar; (medicinale) tablet; **andare a** ~ (Auto) drive flat out

avo'lino m small table

tavolo m table. ~ **operatorio** (Med) operating table

avo'lozza f palette

tazza f cup; (del water) bowl. ~ **da caffè/tè** coffee-cup/teacup

az'zina f ~ **da caffè** espresso coffee cup

.C.I. abbr (Touring Club Italiano) Italian Touring Club

e pers pron you; **te l'ho dato** I gave it to you

è m inv tea

ea'trale adj theatrical

e'atro m theatre. ~ **all'aperto** open-air theatre. ~ **di posa** Cinema set. ~ **tenda** marquee for theatre performances

:ecnico, -a adj technical • mf technician • f technique

tec'nigrafo m drawing board

tecno|lo'gia f technology. ~**'logico** adj technological

te'desco, -a adj & mf German

'tedioso adj tedious

te'game m saucepan

'teglia f baking tin

'tegola f tile; fig blow

tei'era f teapot

tek m teak

'tela f cloth; (per quadri, vele) canvas; (Theat) curtain. ~ **cerata** oilcloth. ~ **di lino** linen

te'laio m (di bicicletta, finestra) frame; (Auto) chassis; (per tessere) loom

tele'camera f television camera

teleco|man'dato adj remote-controlled, remote control attrib. ~**'mando** m remote control

Telecom Italia f Italian State telephone company

telecomunicazi'oni fpl telecommunications

tele'cro|naca f [television] commentary. ~**naca diretta** live [television] coverage. ~**'nista** mf television commentator

tele'ferica f cableway

telefo'na|re vt/i [tele]phone, ring. ~**ta** f call. ~**ta interurbana** long-distance call

telefonica'mente adv by [tele-]phone

tele'fo|nico adj [tele]phone attrib. ~**'nino** m mobile [phone]. ~**'nista** mf operator

te'lefono m [tele]phone. ~ **senza filo** cordless [phone]. ~ **interno** internal telephone. ~ **satellitare** satphone. ~ **a schede** cardphone

telegior'nale m television news sg

tele'grafico adj telegraphic; (risposta) monosyllabic; **sii telegrafico** keep it brief

tele'gramma m telegram

telela'voro m teleworking

tele'matica f data communications, telematics

teleno'vela f soap opera

teleobiet'tivo m telephoto lens

telepa'tia f telepathy

t

telero'manzo m television serial

tele'scopio m telescope

teleselezi'one f subscriber trunk dialling, STD; **chiamare in ~** dial direct

telespetta'tore, -'trice mf viewer

tele'text® m Teletext®

televisi'one f television; **guardare la ~** watch television

televi'sivo adj television attrib; **operatore ~** television cameraman; **apparecchio ~** television set

televi'sore m television [set]

'tema m theme; (Sch) essay. **te'matica** f main theme

teme'rario adj reckless

te'mere vt be afraid of, fear •vi be afraid, fear

temperama'tite m inv pencil-sharpener

tempera'mento m temperament

tempe'ra|re vt temper; sharpen (matita). **~to** adj temperate. **~'tura** f temperature. **~tura ambiente** room temperature

tempe'rino m penknife

tem'pe|sta f storm. **~sta di neve** snowstorm. **~sta di sabbia** sandstorm

tempe|stiva'mente adv quickly. **~'stivo** adj timely. **~'stoso** adj stormy

'tempia f (Anat) temple

'tempio m (Relig) temple

tem'pismo m timing

'tempo m time; (atmosferico) weather; (Mus) tempo; (Gram) tense; (di film) part; (di partita) half; **a suo ~** in due course; **~ fa** some time ago; **un ~** once; **ha fatto il suo ~** it's superannuated. **~ supplementare** Sport extra time, overtime Am. **~'rale** adj temporal •m [thunder]storm. **~ranea'mente** adv temporarily. **~'raneo** adj temporary. **~reggi'are** vi play for time

tem'prare vt temper

te'nac|e adj tenacious. **~ia** f tenacity

te'naglia f pincers pl

'tenda f curtain; (per campeggio) tent; (tendone) awning. **~ a ossigeno** oxygen tent

ten'denz|a f tendency. **~ial'mente** adv by nature

'tendere vt (allargare) stretch [out]; (tirare) tighten; (porgere) hold out; fig lay (trappola) •vi **~ a** aim at; (essere portato a) tend to

'tendine m tendon

ten'do|ne m awning; (di circo) tent. **~poli** f inv tent city

tene'broso adj gloomy

te'nente m lieutenant

tenera'mente adv tenderly

te'ner|e vt hold; (mantenere) keep; (gestire) run; (prendere) take; (seguire) follow; (considerare) consider •vi hold **~ci a, ~e a** be keen on; **~e per** support (squadra). **~si** vr hold on (**a** to); (in una condizione) keep oneself; (seguire) stick to; **~si indietro** stand back

tene'rezza f tenderness. **'tenero** adj tender

'tenia f tapeworm

'tennis m tennis. **~ da tavolo** table tennis. **ten'nista** mf tennis player

te'nore m standard; (Mus) tenor; **a ~ di legge** by law. **~ di vita** standard of living

tensi'one f tension; (Electr) voltage; **alta ~** high voltage

ten'tacolo m tentacle

ten'ta|re vt attempt; (sperimentare) try (indurre in tentazione) tempt. **~'tivo** m attempt. **~zi'one** f temptation

tenten'nare vi waver

'tenue adj fine; (debole) weak; (esiguo) small; (leggero) slight

te'nuta f (capacità) capacity; (Sport: resistenza) stamina; (possedimento) estate; (divisa) uniform; (abbigliamento) clothes pl; **a ~ d'aria** airtight. **~ di strada** road holding

teolo'gia f theology. **teo'logico** adj theological. **te'ologo** m theologian

teo'rema m theorem

teo'ria f theory

teorica'mente adv theoretically. **te'orico** adj theoretical

te'pore m warmth

'teppa f mob. **tep'pismo** m hooliganism. **tep'pista** m hooligan

tera'peutico adj therapeutic. **tera'pia** f therapy

t

tergicri'stallo m windscreen wiper, windshield wiper Am

tergilu'notto m rear windscreen wiper

tergiver'sare vi hesitate

tergo m **a** ~ behind

ter'male adj thermal; **stazione** ~ spa. **'terme** fpl thermal baths

'termico adj thermal

termi'na|le adj & m terminal; **malato** ~**le** terminally ill person. ~**re** vt/i finish, end. **'termine** m (limite) limit; (fine) end; (condizione, espressione) term

terminolo'gia f terminology

'termite f termite

termoco'perta f electric blanket

ter'mometro m thermometer

'termos m inv thermos®

termosi'fone m radiator; (sistema) central heating

ter'mostato m thermostat

'terra f earth; (regione) land; (terreno) ground; (argilla) clay; (cosmetico) dark face powder (for impression of tan); **a** ~ (sulla costa) ashore; (installazioni) onshore; **per** ~ on the ground; **sotto** ~ underground. ~**'cotta** f terracotta; **vasellame di** ~**cotta** earthenware. ~**pi'eno** m embankment

ter'razz|a f, ~**o** m balcony

terremo'tato, -a adj (zona) affected by an earthquake •mf earthquake victim. **terre'moto** m earthquake

ter'reno adj earthly •m ground; (suolo) soil; (proprietà terriera) land; **perdere/guadagnare** ~ lose/gain ground. ~ **di gioco** playing field

ter'restre adj terrestrial; **esercito** ~ land forces pl

ter'ribil|e adj terrible. ~**'mente** adv terribly

ter'riccio m potting compost

terrifi'cante adj terrifying

territori'ale adj territorial. **terri'torio** m territory

ter'rore m terror

terro'ris|mo m terrorism. ~**ta** mf terrorist

terroriz'zare vt terrorize

terso adj clear

ter'zetto m trio

terzi'ario adj tertiary

'terzo adj third; **di terz'ordine** (locale, servizio) third-rate; **la terza età** the third age •m third; **terzi** pl (Jur) third party sg. **ter'zultimo, -a** agg & mf third from last

'tesa f brim

'teschio m skull

'tesi f inv thesis

'teso pp di **tendere** •adj taut; fig tense

tesor|e'ria f treasury. ~**i'ere** m treasurer

te'soro m treasure; (tesoreria) treasury

'tessera f card; (abbonamento all'autobus) season ticket

'tessere vt weave; hatch (complotto)

tesse'rino m travel card

'tessile adj textile. **tessili** mpl textiles; (operai) textile workers

tessi|'tore, -'trice mf weaver

tes'suto m fabric; (Anat) tissue

'testa f head; (cervello) brain; **essere in** ~ **a** be ahead of; **in** ~ Sport in the lead; ~ **o croce?** heads or tails?

'testa-'coda m inv **fare un** ~ spin right round

testa'mento m will; **T**~ (Relig) Testament

testar'daggine f stubbornness. **te'stardo** adj stubborn

te'stata f head; (intestazione) heading; (colpo) butt

'teste mf witness

te'sticolo m testicle

testi'mon|e mf witness. ~**e oculare** eye witness

testi'monial mf inv celebrity promoting brand of cosmetics

testimoni|'anza f testimony. ~**'are** vt testify to •vi give evidence

'testo m text; **far** ~ be an authority

te'stone, -a mf blockhead

testu'ale adj textual

'tetano m tetanus

'tetro adj gloomy

tetta'rella f teat

'tetto m roof. ~ **apribile** sunshine roof. **tet'toia** f roofing. **tet'tuccio** m **tettuccio apribile** sun-roof

t

'Tevere m Tiber

ti pers pron you; (riflessivo) yourself; **ti ha dato un libro** he gave you a book; **lavati le mani** wash your hands; **eccoti!** here you are!; **sbrigati!** hurry up!

ti'ara f tiara

ticchet't|are vi tick. **~io** m ticking

'ticchio m tic; (ghiribizzo) whim

'ticket m inv (per farmaco, esame) amount paid by National Health patients

tiepida'mente adv half-heartedly. **ti'epido** adj lukewarm

ti'fare vi ~ **per** shout for. **'tifo** m (Med) typhus; **fare il tifo per** fig be a fan of

tifoi'dea f typhoid

ti'fone m typhoon

ti'foso, -a mf fan

'tiglio m lime

ti'grato adj **gatto** ~ tabby [cat]

'tigre f tiger

'tilde mf tilde

tim'ballo m (Culin) pie

tim'brare vt stamp; ~ **il cartellino** clock in/out

'timbro m stamp; (di voce) tone

timida'mente adv timidly, shyly. **timi'dezza** f timidity, shyness. **'timido** adj timid, shy

'timo m thyme

ti'mon|e m rudder. **~i'ere** m helmsman

ti'more m fear; (soggezione) awe

'timpano m eardrum; (Mus) kettledrum

ti'nello m dining-room

'tinger|e vt dye; (macchiare) stain. **~si** vi (viso, cielo:) be tinged (**di** with); **~si i capelli** have one's hair dyed; (da solo) dye one's hair

'tino m, **ti'nozza** f tub

'tint|a f dye; (colore) colour; **in ~a unita** plain. **~a'rella** f [!] suntan

tintin'nare vi tinkle

'tinto pp di **tingere**. **~'ria** f (negozio) cleaner's. **tin'tura** f dyeing; (colorante) dye.

'tipico adj typical

'tipo m type; (individuo) guy

tipogra'fia f printery; (arte) typography. **tipo'grafico** adj typographic[al]. **ti'pografo** m printer

tip tap m tap dancing

ti'raggio m draught

tiramisù m inv dessert made of coffee-soaked sponge, eggs, Marsala, cream and cocoa powder

tiran'nia f tyranny. **ti'ranno, -a** adj tyrannical •mf tyrant

ti'rar|e vt pull; (gettare) throw; kick (palla); (sparare) fire; (tracciare) draw; (stampare) print •vi pull; (vento:) blow; (abito:) be tight; (sparare) fire; **~e avanti** get by; **~e su** (crescere) bring up; (da terra) pick up. **~si** vr **~si indietro** fig back out

tiras'segno m target shooting; (alla fiera) rifle range

ti'rata f tug; **in una** ~ in one go

tira'tore m shot. ~ **scelto** marksman

tira'tura f printing; (di giornali) circulation; (di libri) [print] run

'tirchio adj mean

tiri'tera f spiel

'tiro m (traino) draught; (lancio) throw; (sparo) shot; (scherzo) trick. ~ **con l'arco** archery. ~ **alla fune** tug-of-war. ~ **a segno** rifle-range

tiro'cinio m apprenticeship

ti'roide f thyroid

Tir'reno m **il [mar]** ~ the Tyrrhenian Sea

ti'sana f herb[al] tea

tito'lare adj regular •mf principal; (proprietario) owner; (calcio) regular player

'titolo m title; (accademico) qualification; (Comm) security; **a ~ di** as; **a ~ di favore** as a favour. **titoli** pl **di studio** qualifications

titu'ba|nte adj hesitant. **~nza** f hesitation. **~re** vi hesitate

tivù f inv [!] TV, telly

'tizio m fellow

tiz'zone m brand

toc'cante adj touching

toc'ca|re vt touch; touch on (argomento); (tastare) feel; (riguardare) concern •vi **~re a** (capitare) happen to; **mi tocca aspettare** I'll have to wait; **tocca a te** it's your turn; (pagare da bere) it's your round

tocca'sana m inv cure-all

'**tocco** m touch; (di pennello, orologio) stroke; (di pane ecc) chunk • adj [!] crazy, touched

'**toga** f toga; (accademica, di magistrato) gown

'**toglier|e** vt take off (coperta); take away (bambino da scuola, sete) (Math); take out, remove (dente); **~e qcsa di mano a qcno** take sth away from sb; **~e qcno dai guai** get sb out of trouble; **ciò non toglie che...** nevertheless... **~si** vr take off (abito); **~si la vita** take one's [own] life

toilette f inv, **to'letta** f toilet; (mobile) dressing table

tolle'ra|nte adj tolerant. **~nza** f tolerance. **~re** vt tolerate

'**tolto** pp di **togliere**

to'maia f upper

'**tomba** f grave, tomb

tom'bino m manhole cover

'**tombola** f bingo; (caduta) tumble

'**tomo** m tome

'**tonaca** f habit

tonalità f inv (Mus) tonality

'**tondo** adj round • m circle

'**tonico** adj & m tonic

tonifi'care vt brace

tonnel'la|ggio m tonnage. **~ta** f ton

'**tonno** m tuna [fish]

'**tono** m tone

ton'sil|la f tonsil. **~'lite** f tonsillitis

'**tonto** adj [!] thick

top m inv (indumento) sun-top

to'pazio m topaz

'**topless** m inv **in ~** topless

'**topo** m mouse. **~ di biblioteca** fig bookworm

to'ponimo m place name

'**toppa** f patch; (serratura) keyhole

to'race m chest

'**torba** f peat

'**torbido** adj cloudy; fig troubled

'**torcer|e** vt twist; wring [out] (biancheria). **~si** vr twist

'**torchio** m press

'**torcia** f torch

torci'collo m stiff neck

'**tordo** m thrush

to'rero m bullfighter

To'rino f Turin

tor'menta f snowstorm

tormen'tare vt torment. **tor'mento** m torment

torna'conto m benefit

tor'nado m tornado

tor'nante m hairpin bend

tor'nare vi return, go/come back; (ridiventare) become again; (conto:) add up; **~ a sorridere** become happy again

tor'neo m tournament

'**tornio** m lathe

'**torno** m **togliersi di ~** get out of the way

'**toro** m bull; (Astr) **T~**Taurus

tor'pedin|e f torpedo

tor'pore m torpor

'**torre** f tower; (scacchi) castle. **~ di controllo** control tower

torrefazi'one f roasting

tor'ren|te m torrent, mountain stream; (fig: di lacrime) flood. **~zi'ale** adj torrential

tor'retta f turret

'**torrido** adj torrid

torri'one m keep

tor'rone m nougat

'**torso** m torso; (di mela, pera) core; **a ~ nudo** bare-chested

'**torsolo** m core

'**torta** f cake; (crostata) tart

tortel'lini mpl tortellini, small packets of pasta stuffed with pork, ham, Parmesan and nutmeg

torti'era f baking tin

tor'tino m pie

'**torto** pp di **torcere** • adj twisted • m wrong; (colpa) fault; **aver ~** be wrong; **a ~** wrongly

'**tortora** f turtle-dove

tortu'oso adj winding; (ambiguo) tortuous

tor'tu|ra f torture. **~'rare** vt torture
'torvo adj grim
to'sare vt shear
tosa'tura f shearing
To'scana f Tuscany
'tosse f cough
'tossico adj toxic •m poison. **tossi'comane** mf drug addict
tos'sire vi cough
tosta'pane m inv toaster
to'stare vt toast (pane); roast (caffè)
'tosto adv (subito) soon •adj [!] cool
tot adj inv **una cifra ~** such and such a figure •m **un ~** so much
to'tal|e adj & m total. **~ità** f entirety; **la ~ità dei presenti** all those present
totali'tario adj totalitarian
totaliz'zare vt total; score (punti)
total'mente adv totally
'totano m squid
toto'calcio m ≈ [football] pools pl
tournée f inv tour
to'vagli|a f tablecloth. **~'etta** f **~etta [all'americana]** place mat. **~'olo** m napkin
'tozzo adj squat
tra = **fra**
trabal'la|nte adj staggering; (sedia) rickety. **~re** vi stagger; (veicolo:) jolt
tra'biccolo m [!] contraption; (auto) jalopy
traboc'care vi overflow
traboc'chetto m trap
tracan'nare vt gulp down
'tracci|a f track; (orma) footstep; (striscia) trail; (residuo) trace; fig sign. **~'are** vt trace; sketch out (schema); draw (linea). **~'ato** m (schema) layout
tra'chea f windpipe
tra'colla f shoulder-strap; **borsa a ~** shoulder-bag
tra'collo m collapse
tradi'mento m betrayal
tra'di|re vt betray; be unfaithful to (moglie, marito). **~'tore, ~'trice** mf traitor
tradizio'na|le adj traditional. **~'lista** mf traditionalist. **~l'mente** adv traditionally. **tradizi'one** f tradition
tra'dotto pp di **tradurre**
tra'du|rre vt translate. **~t'tore, ~t'trice** mf translator. **~ttore elettronico** electronic phrasebook. **~zi'one** f translation
tra'ente mf (Comm) drawer
trafe'lato adj breathless
traffi'ca|nte mf dealer. **~nte di droga** [drug] pusher. **~re** vi (affaccendarsi) busy oneself; **~re in** pej traffic in. **'traffico** m traffic; (Comm) trade
tra'figgere vt stab; (straziare) pierce
tra'fila f fig rigmarole
trafo'rare vt bore, drill. **tra'foro** m boring; (galleria) tunnel
trafu'gare vt steal
tra'gedia f tragedy
traghet'tare vt ferry. **tra'ghetto** m ferrying; (nave) ferry
tragica'mente adv tragically. **'tragico** adj tragic
tra'gitto m journey; (per mare) crossing
tragu'ardo m finishing post; (meta) goal
traiet'toria f trajectory
trai'nare vt drag; (rimorchiare) tow
tralasci'are vt interrupt; (omettere) leave out
'tralcio m (Bot) shoot
tra'liccio m trellis
tram m inv tram, streetcar Am
'trama f weft; (di film ecc) plot
traman'dare vt hand down
tra'mare vt weave; (macchinare) plot
tram'busto m turmoil
trame'stio m bustle
tramez'zino m sandwich
tra'mezzo m partition
'tramite prep through •m link; **fare da ~** act as go-between
tramon'tana f north wind
tramon'tare vi set; (declinare) decline. **tra'monto** m sunset; (declino) decline
tramor'tire vt stun •vi faint
trampo'lino m springboard; (per lo sci) ski-jump

trampolo m stilt

tramu'tare vt transform

trancia f shears pl; (fetta) slice

tra'nello m trap

trangugi'are vt gulp down

tranne prep except

tranquilla'mente adv peacefully

tranquil'lante m tranquillizer

tranquilli|tà f calm; (di spirito) tranquillity. **~z'zare** vt reassure. **tran'quillo** adj quiet; (pacifico) peaceful; (coscienza) easy

transat'lantico adj transatlantic • m ocean liner

tran'sa|tto pp di **transigere**. **~zi'one** f (Comm) transaction

tran'senna f (barriera) barrier

trans'genico adj genetically modified, transgenic

tran'sigere vi reach an agreement; (cedere) yield

transi'ta|bile adj passable. **~re** vi pass

transi'tivo adj transitive

'transi|to m transit; **diritto di ~to** right of way; **"divieto di ~to"** "no thoroughfare". **~'torio** adj transitory. **~zi'one** f transition

tranvi'ere m tram driver

'trapano m drill

trapas'sare vt go [right] through • vi (morire) pass away

tra'passo m passage

tra'pezio m trapeze; (Math) trapezium

trapi|an'tare vt transplant. **~'anto** m transplant

'trappola f trap

tra'punta f quilt

'trarre vt draw; (ricavare) obtain; **~ in inganno** deceive

trasa'lire vi start

trasan'dato adj shabby

trasbor'dare vt transfer; (Naut) tran[s]ship • vi change. **tra'sbordo** m trans[s]hipment

tra'scendere vt transcend • vi (eccedere) go too far

trasci'nar|e vt drag; (entusiasmo:) carry away. **~si** vr drag oneself

tra'scorrere vt spend • vi pass

tra'scri|tto pp di **trascrivere**. **~vere** vt transcribe. **~zi'one** f transcription

trascu'ra|bile adj negligible. **~re** vt neglect; (non tenere conto di) disregard. **~'tezza** f negligence. **~to** adj negligent; (curato male) neglected; (nel vestire) slovenly

traseco'lato adj amazed

trasferi'mento m transfer; (trasloco) move

trasfe'ri|re vt transfer. **~rsi** vr move

tra'sferta f transfer; (indennità) subsistence allowance; Sport away match; **giocare in ~** play away

trasfigu'rare vt transfigure

trasfor'ma|re vt transform; (in rugby) convert. **~'tore** m transformer. **~zi'one** f transformation; (in rugby) conversion

trasfor'mista mf quick-change artist

trasfusi'one f transfusion

trasgre'dire vt disobey; (Jur) infringe

trasgredi'trice f transgressor

trasgres|si'one f infringement. **~'sore** m transgressor

tra'slato adj metaphorical

traslo'car|e vt move • vi, **~si** vr move house. **tra'sloco** m removal

tra'smesso pp di **trasmettere**

tra'smett|ere vt pass on; (Radio, TV) broadcast; (Med, Techn) transmit. **~i'tore** m transmitter

trasmis'si|bile adj transmissible. **~'one** f transmission; (Radio, TV) programme

trasmit'tente m transmitter • f broadcasting station

traso'gna|re vi day-dream

traspa'ren|te adj transparent. **~za** f transparency; **in ~za** against the light. **traspa'rire** vi show [through]

traspi'ra|re vi perspire; fig transpire. **~zi'one** f perspiration

tra'sporre vt transpose

traspor'tare vt transport; **lasciarsi ~ da** get carried away by. **tra'sporto** m transport; (passione) passion

t

trastul'lar|e vt amuse. **~si** vr amuse oneself

trasu'dare vt ooze with •vi sweat

trasver'sale adj transverse

trasvo'la|re vt fly over •vi **~re su** fig skim over. **~ta** f crossing [by air]

'tratta f illegal trade; (Comm) draft

trat'tabile adj or near offer

tratta'mento m treatment. **~ di riguardo** special treatment

trat'ta|re vt treat; (commerciare in) deal in; (negoziare) negotiate •vi **~re di** deal with. **~rsi** vr **di che si tratta?** what is it about?; **si tratta di...** it's about.... **~'tive** fpl negotiations. **~to** m treaty; (opera scritta) treatise

tratteggi'are vt outline; (descrivere) sketch

tratte'ner|e vt (far restare) keep; hold (respiro, in questura); hold back (lacrime, riso); (frenare) restrain; (da paga) withhold; **sono stato trattenuto** (ritardato) I got held up. **~si** vr restrain oneself; (fermarsi) stay; **~si su** (indugiare) dwell on. **tratteni'mento** m entertainment; (ricevimento) party

tratte'nuta f deduction

trat'tino m dash; (in parole composte) hyphen

'tratto pp di **trarre** •m (di spazio, tempo) stretch; (di penna) stroke; (linea) line; (brano) passage; **tratti** pl features; **a tratti** at intervals; **ad un ~** suddenly

trat'tore m tractor

tratto'ria f restaurant

'trauma m trauma. **trau'matico** adj traumatic

tra'vaglio m labour; (angoscia) anguish

trava'sare vt decant

'trave f beam

tra'versa f crossbar; **è una ~ di Via Roma** it's off Via Roma

traver'sa|re vt cross. **~ta** f crossing

traver'sie fpl misfortunes

traver'sina f (Rail) sleeper

tra'vers|o adj crosswise •adv **di ~o** crossways; **andare di ~o** (cibo:) go down the wrong way; **camminare di ~o** not walk in a straight line. **~one** m (in calcio) cross

travesti'mento m disguise

trave'sti|re vt disguise. **~rsi** vr disguise oneself. **~to** adj disguised •m transvestite

travi'are vt lead astray

travi'sare vt distort

tra'vol|gere vt sweep away; (sopraffare) overwhelm. **~to** pp di **travolgere**

trazi'one f traction. **~ anteriore/posteriore** front-/rear-wheel drive

tre adj & m three

trebbi'a|re vt thresh

'treccia f plait, braid

tre'cento adj & m three hundred; **il T~** the fourteenth century

tredi'cesima f Christmas bonus of one month's pay

'tredici adj & m thirteen

'tregua f truce; fig respite

tre'mare vi tremble; (di freddo) shiver

tremenda'mente adv terribly. **tre'mendo** adj terrible; **ho una fame tremenda** I'm very hungry

tremen'tina f turpentine

tre'mila adj & m three thousand

'tremito m tremble

tremo'lare vi shake; (luce:) flicker. **tre'more** m trembling

tre'nino m miniature railway

'treno m train

'tren|ta adj & m thirty; **~ta e lode** top marks. **~tatré giri** m inv LP. **~'tenne** adj & mf thirty-year-old. **~'tesimo** adj & m thirtieth. **~'tina** f **una ~tina di** about thirty

trepi'dare vi be anxious. **'trepido** adj anxious

treppi'ede m tripod

'tresca f intrigue; (amorosa) affair

tri'angolo m triangle

tri'bale adj tribal

tribo'la|re vi suffer; (fare fatica) go through trials and tribulations. **~zi'one** f tribulation

tribù f inv tribe

tri'buna f tribune; (per uditori) gallery;

see A-Z of Italian life and culture

Sport stand. ~ **coperta** stand

tribu'nale m court

tribu'tare vt bestow

tribu'tario adj tax attrib. **tri'buto** m tribute; (tassa) tax

tri'checo m walrus

tri'ciclo m tricycle

▣ **trico'lore** adj three-coloured • m (bandiera) tricolour

tri'dente m trident

trien'nale adj (ogni tre anni) three-yearly; (lungo tre anni) three-year. **tri'ennio** m three-year period

tri'foglio m clover

trifo'lato adj sliced and cooked with olive oil, parsley and garlic

'triglia f mullet

trigonome'tria f trigonometry

tri'mestre m quarter; (Sch) term

'trina f lace

trin'ce|a f trench

trincia'pollo m inv poultry shears pl

trinci'are vt cut up

Trinità f Trinity

'trio m trio

trion'fa|le adj triumphal. **~nte** adj triumphant. **~re** vi triumph; **~re su** triumph over. **tri'onfo** m triumph

tripli'care vt triple. **'triplice** adj triple; **in triplice copia** in triplicate. **'triplo** adj treble • m **il triplo (di)** three times as much (as)

'trippa f tripe; (!: pancia) belly

'trist|e adj sad; (luogo) gloomy. **tri'stezza** f sadness. **~o** adj wicked; (meschino) miserable

trita'carne m inv mincer

tri'ta|re vt mince. **'trito** adj **trito e ritrito** well-worn, trite

'trittico m triptych

tritu'rare vt chop finely

triumvi'rato m triumvirate

tri'vella f drill. **trivel'lare** vt drill

trivi'ale adj vulgar

tro'feo m trophy

'trogolo m (per maiali) trough

'troia f sow; (vulg: donna) whore

'tromba f trumpet; (Auto) horn; (delle scale) well. ~ **d'aria** whirlwind

trom'b|etta m toy trumpet. **~one** m trombone

trom'bosi f thrombosis

tron'care vt sever; truncate (parola)

'tronco adj truncated; **licenziare in ~** fire on the spot • m trunk; (di strada) section. **tron'cone** m stump

troneggi'are vi ~ **su** tower over

'trono m throne

tropi'cale adj tropical. **'tropico** m tropic

'troppo adj too much; (con nomi plurali) too many • pron too much; (plurale) too many; (troppo tempo) too long; **troppi** (troppa gente) too many people • adv too; (con verbi) too much; **~ stanco** too tired; **ho mangiato ~** I ate too much; **hai fame? – non ~** are you hungry? – not very

'trota f trout

trot'tare vi trot. **trotterel'lare** vi trot along; (bimbo:) toddle

'trotto m trot; **andare al ~** trot

'trottola f [spinning] top; (movimento) spin

troupe f inv ~ **televisiva** camera crew

tro'va|re vt find; (scoprire) find out; (incontrare) meet; (ritenere) think; **andare a ~re** go and see. **~rsi** vr find oneself; (luogo:) be; (sentirsi) feel. **~ta** f bright idea. **~ta pubblicitaria** advertising gimmick

truc'ca|re vt make up; (falsificare) fix ⊠. **~rsi** vr make up

'trucco m (cosmetico) make-up; (imbroglio) trick

'truce adj fierce; (delitto) appalling

truci'dare vt slay

'truciolo m shaving

trucu'lento adj truculent

'truffa f fraud. **truf'fare** vt swindle. **~'tore, ~trice** mf swindler

'truppa f troops pl; (gruppo) group

tu pers pron you; **sei tu?** is that you?; **l'hai fatto tu?** did you do it yourself?; **a tu per tu** in private; **darsi del tu** use the familiar tu

'tuba f tuba; (cappello) top hat

▣ *see* A-Z of Italian life and culture

t

tuba'tura f piping
tubazi'oni fpl piping sg, pipes
tuberco'losi f tuberculosis
tu'betto m tube
tu'bino m (vestito) shift
'tubo m pipe; (Anat) canal; **non ho capito un ~** ! I understood zilch. **~ di scappamento** exhaust [pipe]
tuf'fa|re vt plunge. **~rsi** vr dive. **~'tore, ~'trice** mf diver
'tuffo m dive; (bagno) dip; **ho avuto un ~ al cuore** my heart missed a beat. **~ di testa** dive
'tufo m tufa
tu'gurio m hovel
tuli'pano m tulip
'tulle m tulle
tume'fa|tto adj swollen. **~zi'one** f swelling. **'tumido** adj swollen
tu'more m tumour
tumulazi'one f burial
tu'mult|o m turmoil; (sommossa) riot. **~u'oso** adj uproarious
'tunica f tunic
Tuni'sia f Tunisia
'tunnel m inv tunnel
'tuo (**il ~** m, **la tua** f, **i ~i** mpl, **le tue** fpl) poss adj your; **è tua questa macchina?** is this car yours?; **un ~ amico** a friend of yours; **~ padre** your father •poss pron yours; **i tuoi** your folks
tuo'nare vi thunder. **tu'ono** m thunder
tu'orlo m yolk
tu'racciolo m stopper; (di sughero) cork
tu'rar|e vt stop; cork (bottiglia). **~si** vr become blocked; **~si il naso** hold one's nose
turba'mento m disturbance; (sconvolgimento) upsetting. **~ della quiete pubblica** breach of the peace
tur'bante m turban
tur'ba|re vt upset. **~rsi** vr get upset. **~to** adj upset
tur'bina f turbine
turbi'nare vi whirl. **'turbine** m whirl. **turbine di vento** whirlwind
turbo'lenza f turbulence
turboreat'tore m turbo-jet
tur'chese adj & mf turquoise
Tur'chia f Turkey
tur'chino adj & m deep blue
'turco, -a adj Turkish •mf Turk •m (lingua) Turkish; fig double Dutch; **fumare come un ~** smoke like a chimney
tu'ris|mo m tourism. **~ culturale** heritage tourism. **~ta** mf tourist. **~tico** adj tourist attrib
'turno m turn; **a ~** in turn; **di ~** on duty; **fare a ~** take turns. **~ di notte** night shift
'turp|e adj base
'tuta f overalls pl; Sport tracksuit. **~ da lavoro** overalls pl. **~ mimetica** camouflage. **~ spaziale** spacesuit. **~ subacquea** wetsuit
tu'tela f (Jur) guardianship; (protezione) protection. **tute'lare** vt protect
tu'tina f sleepsuit; (da danza) leotard
tu'tore, -'trice mf guardian
'tutta f **mettercela ~ per fare qcsa** go flat out for sth
tutta'via conj nevertheless
'tutto adj whole; (con nomi plurali) all; (ogni) every; **tutta la classe** the whole class, all the class; **tutti gli alunni** all the pupils; **a tutta velocità** at full speed; **ho aspettato ~ il giorno** I waited all day [long]; **in ~ il mondo** all over the world; **noi tutti** all of us; **era tutta contenta** she was delighted; **tutti e due** both; **tutti e tre** all three •pron all; (tutta la gente) everybody; (tutte le cose) everything; (qualunque cosa) anything; **l'ho mangiato ~** I ate it all; **le ho lavate tutte** I washed them all; **raccontami ~** tell me everything; **lo sanno tutti** everybody knows; **è capace di ~** he's capable of anything; **~ compreso** all in; **del ~** quite; **in ~** altogether •adv completely; **tutt'a un tratto** all at once; **tutt'altro** not at all; **tutt'altro che** anything but •m whole. **~'fare** adj inv & nmf **[impiegato] ~** general handyman; **donna ~** general maid
tut'tora adv still
tutù m inv tutu, ballet dress
tv f inv TV

Uu

ubbidi'en|te adj obedient. **~za** f obedience. **ubbi'dire** vi **~ (a)** obey

ubi'ca|to adj located. **~zi'one** f location

ubria'car|e vt get drunk. **~si** vr get drunk; **~si di** fig become intoxicated with

ubria'chezza f drunkenness; **in stato di ~** inebriated

ubri'aco, -a adj drunk • mf drunk

ubria'cone m drunkard

uccelli'era f aviary. **uc'cello** m bird; (vulg: pene) cock

uc'cider|e vt kill. **~si** vr kill oneself

ucci|si'one f killing. **uc'ciso** pp di **uccidere**. **~'sore** m killer

u'dente adj **i non udenti** the hearing-impaired

u'dibile adj audible

udi'enza f audience; (colloquio) interview; (Jur) hearing

u'di|re vt hear. **~'tivo** adj auditory. **~to** m hearing. **~'tore, ~'trice** mf listener; (Sch) unregistered student (allowed to attend lectures). **~'torio** m audience

uffici'al|e adj official • m officer; (funzionario) official; **pubblico ~e** public official. **~iz'zare** vt make official

uf'ficio m office; (dovere) duty. **~ di collocamento** employment office. **~ informazioni** information office. **~ del personale** personnel department. **~sa'mente** adv unofficially

uffici'oso adj unofficial

'ufo[1] m inv ufo

'ufo[2]: **a ~** adv without paying

uggi'oso adj boring

uguagli'a|nza f equality. **~re** vt make equal; (essere uguale) equal; (livellare) level. **~rsi** vr **~rsi a** compare oneself to

ugu'al|e adj equal; (lo stesso) the same; (simile) like. **~'mente** adv equally; (malgrado tutto) all the same

'ulcera f ulcer

uli'veto m olive grove

ulteri'or|e adj further. **~'mente** adv further

ultima'mente adv lately

ulti'ma|re vt complete. **~tum** m inv ultimatum

ulti'missime fpl stop press sg

'ultimo adj last; (notizie ecc) latest; (più lontano) farthest; fig ultimate • m last; **fino all'~** to the last; **per ~** at the end; **l'~ piano** the top floor

ultrà mf inv Sport fanatical supporter

ultramo'derno adj ultramodern

ultra'rapido adj extra-fast

ultrasen'sibile adj ultrasensitive

ultra's|onico adj ultrasonic. **~u'ono** m ultrasound

ultravio'letto adj ultraviolet

ulu'la|re vi howl. **~to** m howling

umana'mente adv (trattare) humanely; **~ impossibile** not humanly possible

uma'nesimo m humanism

umanità f humanity. **umani'tario** adj humanitarian. **u'mano** adj human; (benevolo) humane

umidifica'tore m humidifier

umidità f dampness; (di clima) humidity. **'umido** adj damp; (clima) humid; (mani, occhi) moist • m dampness; **in umido** (Culin) stewed

'umile adj humble

umili'a|nte adj humiliating. **~re** vt humiliate. **~rsi** vr humble oneself. **~zi'one** f humiliation. **umil'mente** adv humbly. **umilità** f humility

u'more m humour; (stato d'animo) mood; **di cattivo/buon ~** in a bad/ good mood

umo'ris|mo m humour. **~ta** mf humorist. **~tico** adj humorous

un *indef* art

! **Un**/**una** si traduce con *one* quando si tratta di un numero

a;

····➤ (*davanti a vocale o h muta*) an; ▷**uno**

una indef art f a; ▷**un**

u'nanim|e adj unanimous. **~e'mente** adv unanimously. **~ità** f unanimity; **all'~ità** unanimously

unci'nato adj hooked; (parentesi) angle

un'cino m hook

'undici adj & m eleven

'unger|e vt grease; (sporcare) get greasy; (Relig) anoint; (blandire) flatter. **~si** vr (con olio solare) oil oneself; **~si le mani** get one's hands greasy

unghe'rese adj & mf Hungarian. **Unghe'ria** f Hungary

'unghi|a f nail; (di animale) claw. **~'ata** f (graffio) scratch

ungu'ento m ointment

unica'mente adv only. **'unico** adj only; (singolo) single; (incomparabile) unique

unifi'ca|re vt unify. **~zi'one** f unification

unifor'mar|e vt level. **~si** vr conform (**a** to)

uni'form|e adj & f uniform. **~ità** f uniformity

unilate'rale adj unilateral

uni'one f union; (armonia) unity. **U~ Europea** European Union. **U~ Monetaria Europea** European Monetary Union. **~ sindacale** trade union

U

u'ni|re vt unite; (collegare) join; blend (colori ecc). **~rsi** vr unite; (collegarsi) join

'unisex adj inv unisex

unità f inv unity; (Math, Mil) unit; (Comput) drive. **~rio** adj unitary

u'nito adj united; (tinta) plain

univer'sal|e adj universal. **~'mente** adv universally

C università f inv university. **~rio, -a** adj university attrib ●mf (insegnante) university lecturer; (studente) undergraduate

uni'verso m universe

uno, -a *indef* art (*before s + consonant, gn, ps, z*) a

● pron one; **a ~ a ~** one by one; **l'~ e l'altro** both [of them]; **né l'~ né l'altro** neither [of them]; **~ di noi** one of us; **~ fa quello che può** you do what you can

● adj a, one

● m (*numerale*) one; (*un tale*) some man;

● f some woman

'unt|o pp di **ungere** ● adj greasy ● m grease. **~u'oso** adj greasy. **unzi'one** f **l'Estrema Unzione** Extreme Unction

u'omo m (pl **uomini**) man. **~ d'affari** business man. **~ di fiducia** right-hand man. **~ di Stato** statesman

u'ovo m (pl f **uova**) egg. **~ in camicia** poached egg. **~ alla coque** boiled egg. **~ di Pasqua** Easter egg. **~ sodo** hard-boiled egg. **~ strapazzato** scrambled egg

ura'gano m hurricane

u'ranio m uranium

urba'n|esimo m urbanization. **~ista** mf town planner. **~istica** f town planning. **~istico** adj urban. **urbanizzazi'one** f urbanization. **ur'bano** adj urban; (cortese) urbane

ur'gen|te adj urgent. **~te'mente** adv urgently. **~za** f urgency; **in caso d'~za** in an emergency; **d'~za** (misura, chiamata) emergency

'urgere vi be urgent

u'rina f urine. **uri'nare** vi urinate

ur'lare vi yell; (cane, vento:) howl. **'urlo** m (pl m **urli,** f **urla**) shout; (di cane, vento) howling

'urna f urn; (elettorale) ballot box; **andare alle urne** go to the polls

urrà int hurrah!

ur'tar|e vt knock against; (scontrarsi) bump into; fig irritate. **~si** vr collide; fig clash

'urto m knock; (scontro) crash; (contrasto) conflict; fig clash; **d'~** (misure, terapia) shock

C *see* A-Z of Italian life and culture

usa e getta adj inv (rasoio, siringa) disposable

u'sanza f custom; (moda) fashion

u'sa|re vt use; (impiegare) employ; (esercitare) exercise; **~re fare qcsa** be in the habit of doing sth • vi (essere di moda) be fashionable; **non si usa più** it is out of fashion; it's not used any more. **~to** adj used; (non nuovo) second-hand

u'scente adj (presidente) outgoing

usci'ere m usher. '**uscio** m door

u'sci|re vi come out; (andare fuori) go out; (sfuggire) get out; (essere sorteggiato) come up; (giornale:) come out; **~re da** (Comput) exit from, quit; **~re di strada** leave the road. **~ta** f exit, way out; (spesa) outlay; (di autostrada) junction; (battuta) witty remark; **essere in libera ~ta** be off duty. **~ta di servizio** back door. **~ta di sicurezza** emergency exit

usi'gnolo m nightingale

uso m use; (abitudine) custom; (usanza) usage; **fuori ~** out of use; **per ~ esterno** for external use only

U.S.S.L. f abbr (Unità Socio-Sanitaria Locale) local health centre

ustio'na|rsi vr burn oneself • **~to** adj burnt. **usti'one** f burn

usu'ale adj usual

usufru'ire vi **~ di** take advantage of

u'sura f usury

usur'pare vt usurp

u'tensile m tool; (Culin) utensil; **cassetta degli utensili** tool box

u'tente mf user. **~ finale** end user

u'tenza f use; (utenti) users pl. **~ finale** end users

ute'rino adj uterine. '**utero** m womb

'**util|e** adj useful • m (Comm) profit. **~ità** f usefulness; (Comput) utility. **~i'taria** f (Auto) small car. **~i'tario** adj utilitarian

utiliz'za|re vt utilize. **~zi'one** f utilization. **uti'lizzo** m use

uto'pistico adj Utopian

'**uva** f grapes pl; **chicco d'~** grape. **~ passa** raisins pl. **~ sultanina** currants pl

Vv

va'cante adj vacant

va'canza f holiday; (posto vacante) vacancy. **essere in ~** be on holiday

vacca f cow. **~ da latte** dairy cow

vacc|i'nare vt vaccinate. **~inazi'one** f vaccination. **vac'cino** m vaccine

vacil'la|nte adj tottering; (oggetto) wobbly; (luce) flickering; fig wavering. **~re** vi totter; (oggetto:) wobble; (luce:) flicker; fig waver

vacuo adj (vano) vain; fig empty • m vacuum

vagabon'dare vi wander. **vaga'bondo, -a** adj (cane) stray; **gente vagabonda** tramps pl • mf tramp

va'gare vi wander

vagheggi'are vt long for

va'gi|na f vagina. **~'nale** adj vaginal

va'gi|re vi whimper

'**vaglia** m inv money order. **~ bancario** bank draft. **~ postale** postal order

vagli'are vt sift; fig weigh

'**vago** adj vague

vagon'cino m (di funivia) car

va'gone m (per passeggeri) carriage; (per merci) wagon. **~ letto** sleeper. **~ ristorante** restaurant car

vai'olo m smallpox

va'langa f avalanche

va'lente adj skilful

va'ler|e vi be worth; (contare) count; (regola:) apply (**per** to); (essere valido) be valid; **far ~e i propri diritti** assert one's rights; **farsi ~e** assert

oneself; **non vale!** that's not fair! • vt **~re qcsa a qcno** (procurare) earn sb sth; **~ne la pena** be worth it; **vale la pena di vederlo** it's worth seeing; **~si di** avail oneself of

valeri'ana f valerian

va'levole adj valid

vali'care vt cross. **'valico** m pass

validità f validity; **con ~ illimitata** valid indefinitely

'valido adj valid; (efficace) efficient; (contributo) valuable

valige'ria f (fabbrica) leather factory; (negozio) leather goods shop

va'ligia f suitcase; **fare le valigie** pack one's bags. **~ diplomatica** diplomatic bag

val'lata f valley. **'valle** f valley; **a valle** downstream

val'lett|a f (TV) assistant. **~o** m valet; (TV) assistant

val'lone m (valle) deep valley

va'lor|e m value; (merito) merit; (coraggio) valour; **~i** pl (Comm) securities; **di ~e** (oggetto) valuable; **oggetti** pl **di ~e** valuables; **senza ~e** worthless. **~iz'zare** vt (mettere in valore) use to advantage; (aumentare di valore) increase the value of; (migliorare l'aspetto di) enhance

valo'roso adj courageous

'valso pp di **valere**

va'luta f currency. **~ estera** foreign currency

valu'ta|re vt value; weigh up (situazione). **~rio** adj (mercato, norme) currency. **~zi'one** f valuation

'valva f valve. **'valvola** f valve; (Electr) fuse

vam'pata f blaze; (di calore) blast; (al viso) flush

vam'piro m vampire

vana'mente adv in vain

van'da|lico adj **atto ~lico** act of vandalism. **~'lismo** m vandalism. **'vandalo** m vandal

vaneggi'are vi rave

'vanga f spade. **van'gare** vt dig

van'gelo m Gospel; ([!]: verità) gospel [truth]

vanifi'care vt nullify

va'nigli|a f vanilla. **~'ato** adj (zucchero) vanilla attrib

vanità f vanity. **vani'toso** adj vain

'vano adj vain • m (stanza) room; (spazio vuoto) hollow

van'taggi|o m advantage; Sport lead; Tennis advantage; **trarre ~o da qcsa** derive benefit from sth. **~'oso** adj advantageous

van't|are vt praise; (possedere) boast. **~arsi** vr boast. **~e'ria** f boasting. **'vanto** m boast

'vanvera f **a ~** at random; **parlare a ~** talk nonsense

va'por|e m steam; (di benzina, cascata) vapour; **a ~e** steam attrib; **al ~e** (Culin) steamed. **~e acqueo** steam, water vapour; **battello a ~e** steamboat. **vapo'retto** m ferry. **~i'era** f steam engine

vaporiz'za|re vt vaporize. **~'tore** m spray

vapo'roso adj (vestito) filmy; **capelli vaporosi** big hair sg

va'rare vt launch

var'care vt cross. **'varco** m passage; **aspettare al varco** lie in wait

vari'abil|e adj variable • f variable. **~ità** f variability

vari'a|nte f variant. **~re** vt/i vary; **~re di umore** change one's mood. **~zi'one** f variation

va'rice f varicose vein

vari'cella f chickenpox

vari'coso adj varicose

varie'gato adj variegated

varietà f inv variety • m inv variety show

'vario adj varied; (al pl, parecchi) various; **vari** pl (molti) several; **varie ed eventuali** any other business

vario'pinto adj multicoloured

'varo m launch

va'saio m potter

'vasca f tub; (piscina) pool; (lunghezza) length. **~ da bagno** bath

va'scello m vessel

va'schetta f tub

vase'lina f Vaseline®

vasel'lame m china. **~ d'oro/d'argento** gold/silver plate

'vaso m pot; (da fiori) vase; (Anat)

vessel; (per cibi) jar. ~ **da notte** chamber pot

vas'soio m tray

vastità f vastness. '**vasto** adj vast; **di vaste vedute** broad-minded

Vati'cano m Vatican

ve pers pron you; **ve l'ho dato** I gave it to you

'**vecchia** f old woman. **vecchi'aia** f old age. '**vecchio** adj old •mf old man; **i vecchi** old people

vece f **in ~ di** in place of; **fare le veci di qcno** take sb's place

ve'dente adj **i non vedenti** the visually handicapped

ve'der|e vt/i see; **far ~e** show; **farsi ~e** show one's face; **non vedo l'ora di...** I can't wait to.... **~si** vr see oneself; (reciproco) see each other

ve'detta f lookout; (Naut) patrol vessel

vedovo, -a m widower •f widow

ve'duta f view

vee'mente adj vehement

vege'ta|le adj & m vegetable. **~li'ano** adj & mf vegan. **~re** vi vegetate. **~ri'ano, -a** adj & mf vegetarian. **~zi'one** f vegetation

vegeto adj ▸**vivo**

veg'gente mf clairvoyant

veglia f watch; **fare la ~** keep watch. ~ **funebre** vigil

vegli|'are vi be awake; **~are su** watch over. **~'one** m **~one di Capodanno** New Year's Eve celebration

ve'icolo m vehicle

vela f sail; (Sport) sailing; **far ~** set sail

ve'la|re vt veil; (fig: nascondere) hide. **~rsi** vr (vista:) mist over; (voce:) go husky. **~ta'mente** adv indirectly. **~to** adj veiled; (occhi) misty; (collant) sheer

velcro® m velcro®

veleggi'are vi sail

ve'leno m poison. **vele'noso** adj poisonous

veli'ero m sailing ship

ve'lina f **(carta) ~** tissue paper; (copia) carbon copy

ve'lista m yachtsman •f yachtswoman

ve'livolo m aircraft

vellei'tario adj unrealistic

'**vello** m fleece

vellu'tato adj velvety. **vel'luto** m velvet. **velluto a coste** corduroy

'**velo** m veil; (di zucchero, cipria) dusting; (tessuto) voile

ve'loc|e adj fast. **~e'mente** adv quickly. **velo'cista** mf (Sport) sprinter. **~ità** f inv speed; (Auto: marcia) gear. **~iz'zare** vt speed up

ve'lodromo m cycle track

'**vena** f vein; **essere in ~ di** be in the mood for

ve'nale adj venal; (persona) mercenary, venal

ve'nato adj grainy

vena'torio adj hunting attrib

vena'tura f (di legno) grain; (di foglia, marmo) vein

ven'demmi|a f grape harvest. **~'are** vt harvest

'**vender|e** vt sell. **~si** vr sell oneself; "**vendesi**" "for sale"

ven'detta f revenge

vendi'ca|re vt avenge. **~rsi** vr get one's revenge. **~'tivo** adj vindictive

'**vendi|ta** f sale; **in ~ta** on sale. **~ta all'asta** sale by auction. **~ta al dettaglio** retailing. **~ta all'ingrosso** wholesaling. **~ta al minuto** retailing. **~'tore, ~'trice** mf seller. **~tore ambulante** hawker, pedlar

vene'ra|bile, ~ndo adj venerable

vene'ra|re vt revere

venerdì m inv Friday. **V~ Santo** Good Friday

'**Venere** f Venus. **ve'nereo** adj venereal

Ve'nezi|a f Venice. **v~'ano, -a** agg & mf Venetian •f (persiana) Venetian blind; (Culin) sweet bun

veni'ale adj venial

ve'nire vi come; (riuscire) turn out; (costare) cost; (in passivi) be; **~ a sapere** learn; **~ in mente** occur; **~ meno** (svenire) faint; **~ meno a un**

see A-Z of Italian life and culture

contratto go back on a contract; ~ **via** come away; (staccarsi) come off; **vieni a prendermi** come and pick me up

ven'taglio m fan

ven'tata f gust [of wind]; fig breath

ven'te|nne adj & mf twenty-year-old. ~**simo** adj & m twentieth. '**venti** adj & m twenty

venti'la|re vt air. ~'**tore** m fan. ~**zi'one** f ventilation

ven'tina f **una** ~ (circa venti) about twenty

ventiquat'trore f inv (valigia) overnight case

'**vento** m wind; **farsi** ~ fan oneself

ven'tosa f sucker

ven'toso adj windy

'**ventre** m stomach. **ven'triloquo** m ventriloquist

ven'tura f fortune

ven'turo adj next

ve'nuta f coming

vera'mente adv really

ve'randa f veranda

ver'bal|e adj verbal •m (di riunione) minutes pl. ~'**mente** adv verbally

'**verbo** m verb. ~ **ausiliare** auxiliary [verb]

'**verde** adj green •m green; (vegetazione) greenery; (semaforo) green light. ~ **oliva** olive green. ~'**rame** m verdigris

ver'detto m verdict

ver'dura f vegetables pl; **una** ~ a vegetable

'**verga** f rod

vergi'n|ale adj virginal. '**vergine** f virgin; (Astr) **V**~ Virgo •adj virgin; (cassetta) blank. ~**ità** f virginity

ver'gogna f shame; (timidezza) shyness

vergo'gn|arsi vr feel ashamed; (essere timido) feel shy. ~**oso** adj ashamed; (timido) shy; (disonorevole) shameful

ve'rifica f check. **verifi'cabile** adj verifiable

verifi'car|e vt check. ~**si** vr come true

ve'rismo m realism

verit|à f truth. ~**i'ero** adj truthful

'**verme** m worm. ~ **solitario** tapeworm

ver'miglio adj & m vermilion

'**vermut** m inv vermouth

ver'nacolo m vernacular

ver'nic|e f paint; (trasparente) varnish; (pelle) patent leather; fig veneer; **"vernice fresca"** "wet paint". ~**i'are** vt paint; (con vernice trasparente) varnish. ~**ia'tura** f painting; (strato) paintwork; fig veneer

'**vero** adj true; (autentico) real; (perfetto) perfect; **è** ~**?** is that so?; **sei stanca,** ~**?** you're tired, aren't you •m truth; (realtà) life

verosimigli'anza f probability. **vero'simile** adj probable

ver'ruca f wart; (sotto la pianta del piede) verruca

versa'mento m payment; (in banca) deposit

ver'sante m slope

ver'sa|re vt pour; (spargere) shed; (rovesciare) spill; pay (denaro). ~**rsi** vr spill; (sfociare) flow

ver'satil|e adj versatile. ~**ità** f versatility

ver'setto m verse

versi'one f version; (traduzione) translation; **"**~ **integrale"** "unabridged version"

'**verso**[1] m verse; (grido) cry; (gesto) gesture; (senso) direction; (modo) manner; **non c'è** ~ **di** there is no way of

'**verso**[2] prep towards; (nei pressi di) round about; ~ **dove?** which way?

'**vertebra** f vertebra

'**vertere** vi ~ **su** focus on

verti'cal|e adj vertical; (in parole crociate) down •m vertical •f handstand. ~'**mente** adv vertically

'**vertice** m summit; (Math) vertex; **conferenza al** ~ summit conference

ver'tigine f dizziness; (Med) vertigo. **vertigini** pl giddy spells

vertigi|nosa'mente adv dizzily. ~'**noso** adj dizzy; (velocità) breakneck; (prezzi) sky-high; (scollatura) plunging

ve'scica f bladder; (sulla pelle) blister

'vescovo m bishop

'vespa f wasp

vespasi'ano m urinal

'vespro m vespers pl

ves'sillo m standard

ve'staglia f dressing gown

'vest|e f dress; (rivestimento) covering; **in ~e di** in the capacity of. **~i'ario** m clothing

ve'stibolo m hall

ve'stigio m (pl m **vestigi**, pl f **vestigia**) trace

ve'sti|re vt dress. **~rsi** vr get dressed. **~ti** pl clothes. **~to** adj dressed • m (da uomo) suit; (da donna) dress

vete'rano, -a adj & mf veteran

veteri'naria f veterinary science

veteri'nario adj veterinary • m veterinary surgeon

'veto m inv veto

ve'tra|io m glazier. **~ta** f big window; (in chiesa) stained-glass window; (porta) glass door. **~to** adj glazed. **vetre'ria** f glass works

ve'tri|na f [shop-]window; (mobile) display cabinet. **~'nista** mf window dresser

vetri'olo m vitriol

'vetro m glass; (di finestra, porta) pane. **~'resina** f fibreglass

'vetta f peak

vet'tore m vector

vetto'vaglie fpl provisions

vet'tura f coach; (ferroviaria) carriage; (Auto) car. **vettu'rino** m coachman

vezzeggi'a|re vt fondle. **~'tivo** m pet name. **'vezzo** m habit; (attrattiva) charm; **vezzi** pl (moine) affectation sg. **vez'zoso** adj charming; pej affected

vi pers pron you; (riflessivo) yourselves; (reciproco) each other; (tra più persone) one another; **vi ho dato un libro** I gave you a book; **lavatevi le mani** wash your hands; **eccovi!** here you are! • adv = **ci**

'via[1] f street, road; fig way; (Anat) tract; **in ~ di** in the course of; **per ~ di** on account of; **~ ~ che** as; **per ~ aerea** by airmail

'via[2] adv away; (fuori) out; **andar ~** go away; **e così ~** and so on; **e ~ dicendo** and whatnot • int **~!** go away!; Sport go!; (andiamo) come on! • m starting signal

viabilità f road conditions pl; (rete) road network; (norme) road and traffic laws pl

via'card f inv motorway card

viaggi'a|re vi travel. **~'tore, ~'trice** mf traveller

vi'aggio m journey; (breve) trip; **buon ~!** safe journey!, have a good trip!; **fare un ~** go on a journey. **~ di nozze** honeymoon

vi'ale m avenue; (privato) drive

vi'bra|nte adj vibrant. **~re** vi vibrate; (fremere) quiver. **~zi'one** f vibration

vi'cario m vicar

'vice mf deputy. **~diret'tore** m assistant manager

vi'cenda f event; **a ~** (fra due) each other; (a turno) in turn[s]

vice'versa adv vice versa

vici'na|nza f nearness; **~nze** pl (paraggi) neighbourhood. **~to** m neighbourhood; (vicini) neighbours pl

vi'cino, -a adj near; (accanto) next • adv near, close. **~ a** prep near [to] • mf neighbour. **~ di casa** nextdoor neighbour

'vicolo m alley

'video m video. **~'camera** f camcorder. **~cas'setta** f video cassette

videoci'tofono m video entry phone

video'clip m inv video clip

videogi'oco m video game

videoregistra'tore m video-recorder

video'teca f video library

video'tel® m ≈ Videotex®

videote'lefono m videophone

videotermi'nale m visual display unit, VDU

vidi'mare vt authenticate

vie'ta|re vt forbid; **sosta ~ta** no parking; **~to fumare** no smoking

vi'gente adj in force. **'vigere** vi be in force

vigi'la|nte adj vigilant. **~nza** f

V

vigilance. **~re** vt keep an eye on • vi keep watch

'**vigile** adj watchful • m 🅲 **~ [urbano]** policeman. **~ del fuoco** fireman

vi'gilia f eve

vigliacche'ria f cowardice. **vigli'acco, -a** adj cowardly • mf coward

'**vigna** f, **vi'gneto** m vineyard

vi'gnetta f cartoon

vi'gore m vigour; **entrare in ~** come into force. **vigo'roso** adj vigorous

'**vile** adj cowardly; (abietto) vile

'**villa** f villa

vil'laggio m village. **~ turistico** holiday village

vil'lano adj rude • m boor; (contadino) peasant

villeggi'a|nte mf holiday-maker. **~re** vi spend one's holidays. **~'tura** f holiday[s] [pl]

vil'l|etta f small detached house. **~ino** m detached house

viltà f cowardice

'**vimine** m wicker

'**vinc|ere** vt win; (sconfiggere) beat; (superare) overcome. **~ita** f win; (somma vinta) winnings pl. **~i'tore, ~i'trice** mf winner

vinco'la|nte adj binding. **~re** vt bind; (Comm) tie up. '**vincolo** m bond

vi'nicolo adj wine attrib

vinil'pelle® f Leatherette®

🅲'**vino** m wine. **~ spumante** sparkling wine. **~ da taglio** blending wine. **~ da tavola** table wine

'**vinto** pp di **vincere**

vi'ola f (Bot) violet; (Mus) viola. **viola** adj & m inv purple

vio'la|re vt violate. **~zi'one** f violation. **~zione di domicilio** breaking and entering

violen'tare vt rape

vio'len|to adj violent. **~za** f violence. **~za carnale** rape

vio'letta f violet

vio'letto adj & m (colore) violet

🅲 *see* A-Z of Italian life and culture

violi'nista mf violinist. **vio'lino** m violin. **violon'cello** m cello

vi'ottolo m path

'**vipera** f viper

vi'ra|ggio m (Phot) toning; (Aeron, Naut) turn. **~re** vi turn

'**virgol|a** f comma. **~ette** fpl inverted commas

vi'ril|e adj virile; (da uomo) manly. **~ità** f virility; manliness

virtù f inv virtue; **in ~ di** (legge) under. **virtu'ale** adj virtual. **virtu'oso** adj virtuous • m virtuoso

viru'lento adj virulent

'**virus** m inv virus

visa'gista mf beautician

visce'rale adj visceral; (odio) deep-seated; (reazione) gut

'**viscere** m internal organ • fpl guts

'**vischi|o** m mistletoe. **~'oso** adj viscous; (appiccicoso) sticky

vi'scont|e m viscount. **~'essa** f viscountess

vi'scoso adj viscous

vi'sibile adj visible

visi'bilio m profusion; **andare in ~** go into ecstasies

visibilità f visibility

visi'era f (di elmo) visor; (di berretto) peak

visio'nare vt examine; Cinema screen. **visi'one** f vision; **prima visione** Cinema first showing

'**visit|a** f visit; (breve) call; (Med) examination. **~a di controllo** (Med) checkup. **visi'tare** vt visit; (brevemente) call on; (Med) examine; **~a'tore, ~a'trice** mf visitor

vi'sivo adj visual

'**viso** m face

vi'sone m mink

'**vispo** adj lively

vis'suto pp di **vivere** • adj experienced

'**vist|a** f sight; (veduta) view; **a ~a d'occhio** (crescere) visibly; (estendersi) as far as the eye can see; **in ~a di** in view of. **~o** pp di **vedere** • m visa. **vi'stoso** adj showy; (notevole) considerable

visu'al|e adj visual. **~izza'tore** m

(Comput) display, VDU. **~izzazi'one** f (Comput) display

'vita f life; (durata della vita) lifetime; (Anat) waist; **a ~** for life; **essere in ~** be alive

vi'tal|e adj vital. **~ità** f vitality

vita'lizio adj life attrib •m [life] annuity

vita'min|a f vitamin. **~iz'zato** adj vitamin-enriched

'vite f (Mech) screw; (Bot) vine

vi'tello m calf; (Culin) veal; (pelle) calfskin

vi'ticcio m tendril

viticol't|ore m wine grower. **~ura** f wine growing

'vitreo adj vitreous; (sguardo) glassy

'vittima f victim

'vitto m food; (pasti) board. **~ e alloggio** board and lodging

vit'toria f victory

vittori'oso adj victorious

vi'uzza f narrow lane

'viva int hurrah!; **~ la Regina!** long live the Queen!

vi'vac|e adj vivacious; (mente) lively; (colore) bright. **~ità** f vivacity; (di mente) liveliness; (di colore) brightness. **~iz'zare** vt liven up

vi'vaio m nursery; (per pesci) pond; fig breeding ground

viva'mente adv (ringraziare) warmly

vi'vanda f food; (piatto) dish

vi'vente adj living •mpl **i viventi** the living

'vivere vi live; **~ di** live on •vt (passare) go through •m life

'viveri mpl provisions

'vivido adj vivid

vivisezi'one f vivisection

'vivo adj alive; (vivente) living; (vivace) lively; (colore) bright; **~ e vegeto** alive and kicking; **farsi ~** keep in touch; (arrivare) turn up •m **dal ~** (trasmissione) live; (disegnare) from life; **i vivi** the living

vizi|'are vt spoil (bambino ecc); (guastare) vitiate. **~'ato** adj spoilt; (aria) stale. **'vizio** m vice; (cattiva abitudine) bad habit; (difetto) flaw. **~'oso** adj dissolute; (difettoso) faulty; **circolo ~oso** vicious circle

vocabo'lario m dictionary; (lessico) vocabulary. **vo'cabolo** m word

vo'cale adj vocal •f vowel. **vo'calico** adj (corde) vocal; (suono) vowel attrib

vocazi'one f vocation

'voce f voice; (diceria) rumour; (di bilancio, dizionario) entry

voci'are vi (spettegolare) gossip •m buzz of conversation

vocife'rare vi shout

'vog|a f rowing; (lena) enthusiasm; (moda) vogue; **essere in ~a** be in fashion. **vo'gare** vi row. **~a'tore** m oarsman; (attrezzo) rowing machine

'vogli|a f desire; (volontà) will; (della pelle) birthmark; **aver ~a di fare qcsa** feel like doing sth

'voi pers pron you; **siete ~?** is that you?; **l'avete fatto ~?** did you do it yourself?. **~a'ltri** pers pron you

vo'lano m shuttlecock; (Mech) flywheel

vo'lante adj flying; (foglio) loose •m steering-wheel

volan'tino m leaflet

vo'la|re vi fly. **~ta** f Sport final sprint; **di ~ta** in a rush

vo'latile adj (liquido) volatile •m bird

volée f inv Tennis volley

vo'lente adj **~ o nolente** whether you like it or not

volenti'eri adv willingly; **~!** with pleasure!

vo'lere vt want; (chiedere di) ask for; (aver bisogno di) need; **vuole che lo faccia io** he wants me to do it; **fai come vuoi** do as you like; **se tuo padre vuole, ti porto al cinema** if your father agrees, I'll take you to the cinema; **vorrei un caffè** I'd like a coffee; **la vuoi smettere?** will you stop that!; **senza ~** without meaning to; **voler bene/male a qcno** love/have something against sb; **voler dire** mean; **ci vuole il latte** we need milk; **ci vuole tempo/pazienza** it takes time/patience; **volerne a** have a grudge against; **vuoi... vuoi...** either... or... •m will; **voleri** pl wishes

vol'gar|e adj vulgar; (popolare)

common. **~ità** f inv vulgarity. **~iz'zare** vt popularize. **~'mente** adv (grossolanamente) vulgarly, coarsely; (comunemente) commonly

'volger|e vt/i turn. **~si** vr turn [round]; **~si a** (dedicarsi) take up

voli'era f aviary

voli'tivo adj strong-minded

'volo m flight; **al ~** (fare qcsa) quickly; (prendere qcsa) in mid-air; **alzarsi in ~** (uccello:) take off; **in ~** airborne. **~ di linea** scheduled flight. **~ nazionale** domestic flight. **~ a vela** gliding.

volontà f inv will; (desiderio) wish; **a ~** (mangiare) as much as you like. **volontaria'mente** adv voluntarily. **volon'tario** adj voluntary • m volunteer

volonte'roso adj willing

'volpe f fox

volt m inv volt

'volta f time; (turno) turn; (curva) bend; (Archit) vault; **4 volte 4** 4 times 4; **a volte** sometimes; **c'era una ~...** once upon a time, there was...; **una ~** once; **due volte** twice; **tre/quattro volte** three/four times; **una ~ per tutte** once and for all; **uno per ~** one at a time; **uno alla ~** one at a time; **alla ~ di** in the direction of

volta'faccia m inv volte-face

vol'taggio m voltage

vol'ta|re vt/i turn; (rigirare) turn round; (rivoltare) turn over. **~rsi** vr turn [round]

volta'stomaco m nausea

volteggi'are vi circle; (ginnastica) vault

'volto pp di **volgere** • m face; **mi ha mostrato il suo vero ~** he revealed his true colours

vo'lubile adj fickle

vo'lum|e m volume. **~i'noso** adj voluminous

voluta'mente adv deliberately

voluttu|osità f voluptuousness. **~'oso** adj voluptuous

vomi'tare vt vomit, be sick. **'vomito** m vomit

'vongola f clam

vo'race adj voracious

vo'ragine f abyss

'vortice m whirl; (gorgo) whirlpool; (di vento) whirlwind

'vostro (**il ~** m, **la vostra** f, **i vostri** mpl, **le vostre** fpl) poss adj your; **è vostra questa macchina?** is this car yours?; **un ~ amico** a friend of yours; **~ padre** your father • poss pron yours; **i vostri** your folks

vo'ta|nte mf voter. **~re** vi vote. **~zi'one** f voting; (Sch) marks pl. **'voto** m vote; (Sch) mark; (Relig) vow

vs. abbr (Comm: vostro) yours

vul'canico adj volcanic. **vul'cano** m volcano

vulne'rabil|e adj vulnerable. **~ità** f vulnerability

vuo'tare vt, **vuo'tarsi** vr empty

vu'oto adj empty; (non occupato) vacant; **~ di** (sprovvisto) devoid of • m empty space; (Phys) vacuum; fig void; **assegno a ~** dud cheque; **sotto ~** (prodotto) vacuum-packed; **~ a perdere** no deposit. **~ d'aria** air pocket

Ww

W abbr (viva) long live

'wafer m inv (biscotto) wafer

walkie-'talkie m inv walkie-talkie

watt m inv watt

WC m WC

'Web m inv Web

'webmaster m webmaster

'western adj inv cowboy attrib • m Cinema western

Xx

X, x adj **raggi** pl **X** X-rays; **il giorno X** D-day

xenofo'bia f xenophobia. **xe'nofobo, -a** adj xenophobic •mf xenophobe

xi'lofono m xylophone

Yy

yacht m inv yacht

yen m inv Fin yen

'yoga m yoga; (praticante) yogi

'yogurt m inv yoghurt. **~i'era** f yoghurt-maker

Zz

zaba[gl]i'one m zabaglione (dessert made from eggs, wine or marsala and sugar)

zaf'fata f whiff; (di fumo) cloud

zaffe'rano m saffron

zaf'firo m sapphire

'zaino m rucksack

'zampa f leg; **a quattro zampe** (animale) four-legged; (carponi) on all fours

zampil'la|nte adj spurting. **~re** vi spurt. **zam'pillo** m spurt

zam'pogna f bagpipe

zam'pone fpl stuffed pig's trotter with lentils

'zanna f fang; (di elefante) tusk

zan'zar|a f mosquito. **~i'era** f (velo) mosquito net; (su finestra) insect screen

'zappa f hoe. **zap'pare** vt hoe

'zattera f raft

zatte'roni mpl (scarpe) wedge shoes

za'vorra f ballast; fig dead wood

'zazzera f mop of hair

'zebra f zebra; **zebre** pl (passaggio pedonale) zebra crossing

'zecca[1] f mint; **nuovo di ~** brand-new

'zecca[2] f (parassita) tick

zec'chino m sequin; **oro ~** pure gold

ze'lante adj zealous. **'zelo** m zeal

'zenit m zenith

'zenzero m ginger
'zeppa f wedge
'zeppo adj packed full; **pieno ~ di** crammed o packed with
zer'bino m doormat
'zero m zero, nought; (in calcio) nil; Tennis love; **due a ~** (in partite) two nil
'zeta f zed, zee Am
'zia f aunt
zibel'lino m sable
'zigomo m cheek-bone
zig'zag m inv zigzag; **andare a ~** zigzag
zim'bello m decoy; (oggetto di scherno) laughing-stock
'zinco m zinc
'zingaro, -a mf gypsy
'zio m uncle
zi'tel|la f spinster; pej old maid. **~'lona** f pej old maid
zit'tire vi fall silent •vt silence. **'zitto** adj silent; **sta' zitto!** keep quiet!
ziz'zania f (discordia) discord
'zoccolo m clog; (di cavallo) hoof; (di terra) clump; (di parete) skirting board, baseboard Am; (di colonna) base
zodia'cale adj of the zodiac. **zo'diaco** m zodiac
'zolfo m sulphur
'zolla f clod; (di zucchero) lump
zol'letta f sugar lump
'zombi mf inv fig zombie
'zona f zone; (area) area. **~ di depressione** area of low pressure. **~ disco** area for parking discs only. **~ pedonale** pedestrian precinct. **~ verde** green belt
'zonzo adv **andare a ~** stroll about
zoo m inv zoo
zoolo'gia f zoology. **zoo'logico** adj zoological. **zo'ologo, -a** mf zoologist
zoo sa'fari m inv safari park
zoppi'ca|nte adj limping; fig shaky. **~re** vi limp; (essere debole) be shaky. **'zoppo, -a** adj lame •mf cripple
zoti'cone m boor
'zucca f marrow; ([!]: testa) head; ([!]: persona) thickie
zucche'r|are vt sugar. **~i'era** f sugar bowl. **~i'ficio** m sugar refinery. **zucche'rino** adj sugary •m sugar lump
'zucchero m sugar. **~ di canna** cane sugar. **~ vanigliato** vanilla sugar. **~ a velo** icing sugar. **zucche'roso** adj honeyed
zuc'chin|a f, **~o** m courgette, zucchini Am
'zuffa f scuffle
zufo'lare vt/i whistle
zu'mare vi zoom
'zuppa f soup. **~ inglese** trifle
zup'petta f **fare ~ [con]** dunk
zuppi'era f soup tureen
'zuppo adj soaked

Games, Culture, Letter-Writing

Test yourself with word games

This section contains a number of word games which will help you to use your dictionary more effectively and to build up your knowledge of Italian vocabulary and usage in a fun and entertaining way. You will find answers to all puzzles and games at the end of the section.

1 X files

A freak power cut in the office has caused all the computers to go down. When they are re-booted, all the words on the screen have become mysteriously jumbled. Use the English to Italian side of the dictionary to help you decipher these Italian names of everyday office and computer equipment.

ATTAIM

TECHISOTD

DANEGA

TALARCEL

PUMETROC

NANEP

RIBICOF

ATTERISA

2 Crowded suitcase

You are at the airport on your way to visit your Welsh cousins in Patagonia when you are told that your suitcase is overweight. Luckily, you had packed a number of things that you did not need because you had forgotten that it was wintertime in the southern hemisphere. Decide which 5 items to jettison from your luggage.

occhiali da sole calzettoni sandali

pigiama guanti spazzolino da denti maglietta

crema solare maglione cintura

costume da bagno cappotto riviste

pantaloncini sciarpa

: What are they like?

'ere are two lists of adjectives you can use to describe people's haracteristics. Each word in the second column is the opposite of one f the adjectives in the first column. Can you link them?

1.	**grande**	**A.**	**intelligente**
2.	**biondo**	**B.**	**cattivo**
3.	**stupido**	**C.**	**grasso**
4.	**nervoso**	**D.**	**piccolo**
5.	**buono**	**E.**	**simpatico**
6.	**alto**	**F.**	**bruno**
7.	**paziente**	**G.**	**calmo**
8.	**antipatico**	**H.**	**basso**
9.	**educato**	**I.**	**impaziente**
10.	**magro**	**J.**	**maleducato**

xample: 1.D. **grande** è il contrario di **piccolo**.

4 Link-up

The Italian nouns on the left-hand side are all made up of two separate words but they have been split apart. Try to link up the two halves of each compound, then do the same for the English compounds in the right-hand columns. Now you can match up the Italian compounds with their English translations.

spaventa	**capelli**	**nut**	**sport**
macina	**noci**	**pencil**	**gloss**
taglia	**labbra**	**pepper**	**screw**
dopo	**erba**	**hair**	**shave**
guasta	**matite**	**key**	**crackers**
schiaccia	**barba**	**spoil**	**crow**
porta	**tappi**	**lawn**	**sharpener**
lucida	**feste**	**after**	**ring**
tempera	**pepe**	**lip**	**mill**
asciuga	**chiavi**	**scare**	**dryer**
cava	**passeri**	**cork**	**mower**

5 Body parts

Can you put the right number in the boxes next to the Italian words in the list?

- [ ] l'alluce
- [ ] la bocca
- [ ] il braccio
- [ ] la caviglia
- [ ] il collo
- [ ] la coscia
- [ ] il dito
- [ ] il fianco
- [ ] la fronte
- [ ] la gamba
- [ ] il ginocchio
- [ ] il gomito
- [ ] la mano
- [ ] il mento
- [ ] il naso
- [ ] l'occhio
- [ ] l'ombelico
- [ ] l'orecchio
- [ ] il piede
- [ ] il polpaccio
- [ ] il polso
- [ ] la spalla
- [ ] la testa
- [ ] lo zigomo

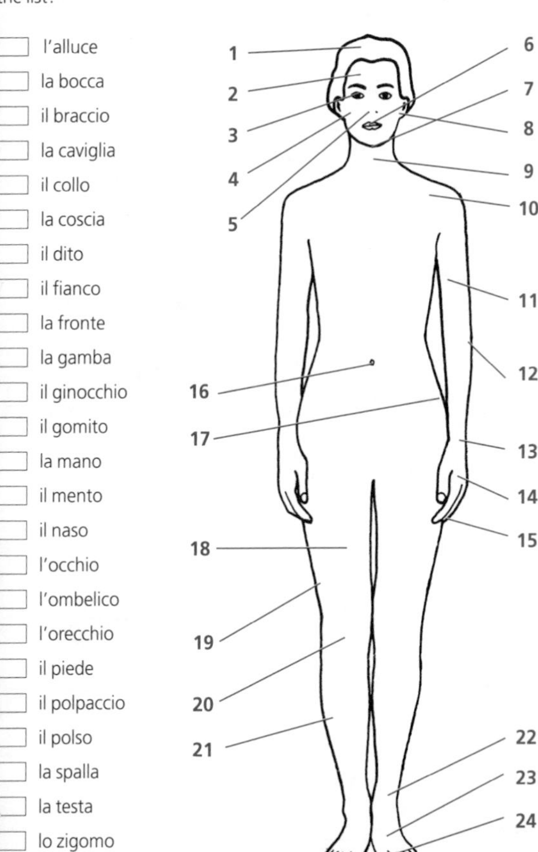

6 Mystery word

To fill in the grid, find the Italian words for all the musical instruments illustrated below. Once you have completed the grid, you'll discover the name of a famous Italian opera singer.

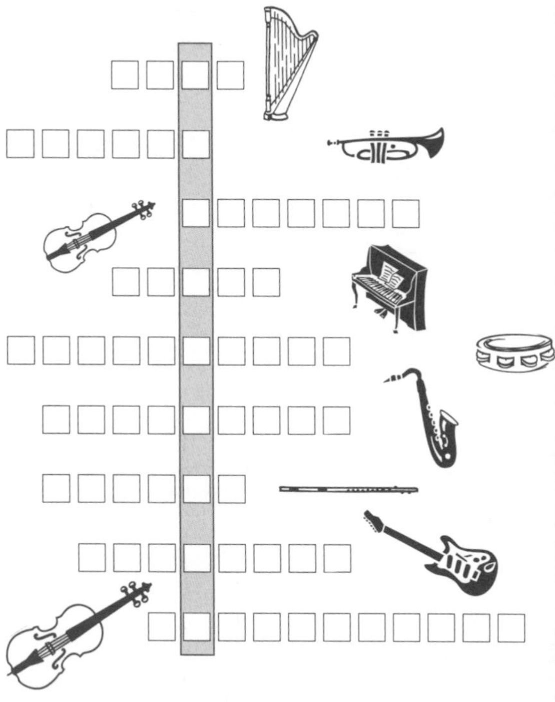

The opera singer is _ _ _ _ _ _ _ _ _

7 The odd one out

In each of the following series, all the words but one are related. Find the odd one out and explain why. If there are words you don't know, use your dictionary to find out what they mean.

example:

- ❑ **penna**
- ❑ **diario**
- ❑ **libro**
- ❑ **quaderno**
- ☑ **spazzola**

The odd one out is '**spazzola**', because you wouldn't find it in a school-bag.

- ❑ **auto**
- ❑ **aereo**
- ❑ **motore**
- ❑ **treno**
- ❑ **camion**

- ❑ **nuoto**
- ❑ **calcio**
- ❑ **pugilato**
- ❑ **equitazione**
- ❑ **ciclismo**

- ❑ **pentola**
- ❑ **padella**
- ❑ **caffettiera**
- ❑ **portacenere**
- ❑ **friggitrice**

- ❑ **correre**
- ❑ **saltare**
- ❑ **ballare**
- ❑ **sognare**
- ❑ **salire**

- ❑ **televisore**
- ❑ **registratore**
- ❑ **stereo**
- ❑ **videocassetta**
- ❑ **giradischi**

- ❑ **batteria**
- ❑ **chitarra**
- ❑ **violino**
- ❑ **arpa**
- ❑ **contrabbasso**

8 Hidden words — false friends

Hidden in the grid are nine Italian words. First look at the list of false friends below – look up the translation of the Italian words listed, then using your own knowledge and the dictionary, find the translations of the English to search for in the grid.

O	S	E	P	O	G	D	I	C	B
I	S	O	G	L	I	O	L	A	Q
S	U	P	T	C	U	S	T	R	O
C	R	M	S	R	M	A	E	I	V
I	O	U	L	G	E	S	N	N	E
M	F	L	V	A	N	C	U	O	N
M	V	T	O	I	T	Q	T	L	D
I	I	A	T	M	A	R	A	F	I
A	P	S	V	U	B	O	C	H	T
F	D	A	T	I	Z	A	X	E	A

English	Italian		
fine[1]	fine	....	....
sale	sale	....	....
mare	mare	....	....
sole[2]	sole	....	....
estate	estate	....	....
dove	dove	....	....
data	data	....	....
ape	ape	....	....
cute	cute	....	....

9 Curly words

One word is missing in each of the curly lists. Which day, month, capital city and number are missing?

Can you write out the four lists in the right order?

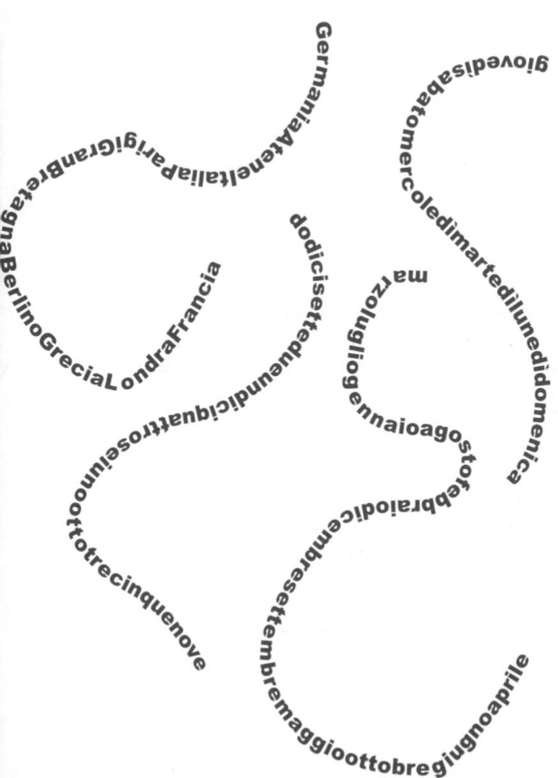

10 Amelia's shooting stars

Amelia is very good at predicting the future, but she is not very good at conjugating Italian verbs in the future tense. Help her to replace all the verbs in brackets with the correct future form.

Leone

23 luglio–22 agosto

(Essere) una settimana fortunata per i Leoni. Lavoro: Un superiore vi (affidare) un compito di grande responsabilità e ciò (potere) creare gelosie tra i colleghi, ma con un po' di diplomazia (risolvere) la situazione. Un viaggio (portare) spese impreviste. Amore: (Fare) incontri piacevoli e interessanti e con Venere che vi protegge nessuno (sapere) resistere al vostro fascino! Gli amici (avere) bisogno del vostro aiuto. Salute: Attenzione allo stress: fate dello sport o prendete una vacanza, (essere) più rilassati e anche l'umore (migliorare).

11 Recipe of the week

The printers have left out some important words in this recipe. Can you supply the missing words from the jumble below?

Ricetta della settimana

Soffriggete una .... piccola e uno spicchio d' .... in 5 cucchiai di ....

Dopo un paio di minuti aggiungete 2 .... sottolio e spappolatele con una ....

Poi, sempre a .... basso, aggiungete il .... sottolio spezzettato e una scatola di ...., ... e ....

Cuocete per una ventina di minuti, poi aggiungete il ....

Nel frattempo lessate 350 grammi di .... in abbondante acqua salata, scolatela al dente e servitela con la .... preparata e, se volete, con ....

prezzemolo pasta **acciughe**

cipolla salsa parmigiano **pelati**

sale **tonno** **olio d'oliva** **pepe**

aglio **forchetta** fuoco

12 My life's a mess

Sabrina has a busy schedule but she is a creature of habit and likes to stick to her daily routine. The order of her normal workday has been muddled up in the sentences below. Link up the matching halves of each sentence in the two columns and then try to put the complete sentences in sequence. Be careful, some can link up with more than one from the other column, so you'll have to do them all before you can be sure which go together best.

legge il giornale	**per pranzo**
torna a casa	**come prima cosa**
non beve mai caffè	**prima delle nove**
di solito porta fuori il cane	**stanchissima**
le piace fare un giro	**durante il viaggio di ritorno**
legge la corrispondenza	**dopo cena**
esce a mezzogiorno	**durante una riunione**
preferisce fare la doccia	**di mattina**
entra al lavoro	**prima di tornare in ufficio**
insiste a tenere le riunioni	**prima di cena**

13 Crossword

Across

1 chicken
4 dog
7 indefinite article (masculine)
8 veil
9 bag
12 ship
13 future of the verb meaning 'to burn' (1st person singular)
15 to tie up
16 one
18 art
19 interrogative pronoun
20 beautiful (feminine)
21 you and me, us
22 beginning of the word meaning 'den'
23 three
24 heart
26 definite article (feminine)
27 age

Down

1 advertising
2 honour
3 fishbone
4 past historic of the verb meaning 'to have dinner' (3rd person singular)
5 wing
6 ninety
10 rust
11 aerobics
14 king
16 to yell
17 first and last letter of the word meaning 'smell'
18 high
25 beginning of the word meaning 'label'

Answers

1

matita, dischetto, agenda, cartella
computer, penna, forbici, tastiera

2

sandali, maglietta, crema solare
costume da bagno, pantaloncini

3

1.D. *grande* è il contrario di *piccolo*.
2.F. *biondo* è il contrario di *bruno*.
3.A. *stupido* è il contrario di *intelligente*.
4.G. *nervoso* è il contrario di *calmo*.
5.B. *buono* è il contrario di *cattivo*.
6.H. *alto* è il contrario di *basso*.
7.I. *paziente* è il contrario di *impaziente*.
8.E. *antipatico* è il contrario di *simpatico*.
9.J. *educato* è il contrario di *maleducato*.
10.C. *magro* è il contrario di *grasso*.

4

spaventapasseri = scarecrow
macinapepe = peppermill
tagliaerba = lawn-mower
dopobarba = aftershave
guastafeste = spoilsport
schiaccianoci = nutcrackers
portachiavi = keyring
lucidalabbra = lipgloss
temperamatite = pencil sharpener
asciugacapelli = hairdryer
cavatappi = corkscrew

5

1 la testa
2 la fronte
3 l'occhio
4 lo zigomo
5 il naso
6 la bocca
7 il mento
8 l'orecchio
9 il collo
10 la spalla
11 il braccio
12 il gomito
13 il polso
14 la mano
15 il dito
16 l'ombelico
17 il fianco
18 la coscia
19 la gamba
20 il ginocchio
21 il polpaccio
22 la caviglia
23 il piede
24 l'alluce

6

AR**P**A
TROMB**A**
VIOLINO
PI**A**NO
TAMBU**R**ELLO
SASS**O**FONO
FLAU**T**O
CHI**T**ARRA
V**I**OLONCELLO

The opera singer's name is **PAVAROTTI**

7

motore – because it isn't a vehicle
portacenere – because it isn't used for cooking
videocassetta – because it isn't an electrical device
calcio – because it's the only team game in the list
sognare – because it's the only verb in the list which doesn't describe a movement
batteria – because it isn't a stringed instrument

8

end	summer	skin	giumenta	dati
salt	where		sogliola	scimmia
sea	date	multa	tenuta	carino
sun	bee	vendita	colomba	

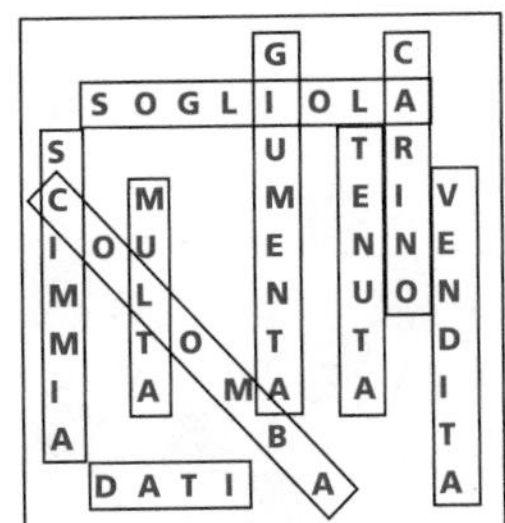

9

venerdì; domenica, lunedì, martedì, mercoledì, giovedì, venerdì, sabato
novembre; gennaio, febbraio, marzo, aprile, maggio, giugno, luglio, agosto, settembre, ottobre, novembre, dicembre
Roma; Germania/Berlino, Francia/Parigi, Grecia/Atene, Gran Bretagna/Londra, Italia/Roma
dieci; uno, due, tre, quattro, cinque, sei, sette, otto, nove, dieci, undici, dodici

10

sarà
porterà
sarete
affiderà
farete
migliorerà
potrà
saprà
risolverete
avranno

11

Soffriggete una **CIPOLLA** piccola e uno spicchio **d'AGLIO** in 5 cucchiai di **OLIO D'OLIVA**.
Dopo un paio di minuti aggiungete 2 **ACCIUGHE** sottolio e spappolatele con una **FORCHETTA**.
Poi, sempre a **FUOCO** basso, aggiungete il **TONNO** sottolio spezzettato e una scatola di **PELATI, SALE** e **PEPE**.
Cuocete per una ventina di minuti, poi aggiungete il **PREZZEMOLO**.
Nel frattempo lessate 350 grammi di **PASTA** in abbondante acqua salata, scolatela al dente e servitela con la **SALSA** preparata e, se volete, con **PARMIGIANO**.

12

entra al lavoro prima delle nove
legge la corrispondenza come prima cosa
insiste a tenere le riunioni di mattina
non beve mai caffè durante una riunione
esce a mezzogiorno per pranzo
le piace fare un giro prima di tornare in ufficio
legge il giornale durante il viaggio di ritorno
torna a casa stanchissima
preferisce fare la doccia prima di cena
di solito porta fuori il cane dopo cena

13

Calendar of Italian traditions, festivals, and holidays

January

1	8	15	22	29
2	9	16	23	30
3	10	17	24	31
4	11	18	25	
5	12	19	26	
6	13	20	27	
7	14	21	28	

February

1	8	15	22
2	9	16	23
3	10	17	24
4	11	18	25
5	12	19	26
6	13	20	27
7	**14**	21	28

March

1	**8**	15	22	29
2	9	16	23	30
3	10	17	24	31
4	11	18	25	
5	12	**19**	26	
6	13	20	27	
7	14	21	28	

April

1	8	15	22	29
2	9	16	23	30
3	10	17	24	31
4	11	18	**25**	
5	12	19	26	
6	13	20	27	
7	14	21	28	

May

1	8	15	22	29
2	9	16	23	30
3	10	17	24	31
4	11	18	25	
5	12	19	26	
6	13	20	27	
7	14	21	28	

June

1	8	15	22	29
2	9	16	23	30
3	10	17	24	
4	11	18	25	
5	12	19	26	
6	13	20	27	
7	14	21	28	

July

1	8	15	22	29
2	9	16	23	30
3	10	17	24	31
4	11	18	25	
5	12	19	26	
6	13	20	27	
7	14	21	28	

August

1	8	**15**	22	29
2	9	16	23	30
3	10	17	24	31
4	11	18	25	
5	12	19	26	
6	13	20	27	
7	14	21	28	

September

1	8	15	22	29
2	9	16	23	30
3	10	17	24	
4	11	18	25	
5	12	19	26	
6	13	20	27	
7	14	21	28	

October

1	8	15	22	29
2	9	16	23	30
3	10	17	24	31
4	11	18	25	
5	12	19	26	
6	13	20	27	
7	14	21	28	

November

1	8	15	22	29
2	9	16	23	30
3	10	17	24	
4	11	18	25	
5	12	19	26	
6	13	20	27	
7	14	21	28	

December

1	**8**	15	22	29
2	9	16	23	30
3	10	17	**24**	**31**
4	11	18	**25**	
5	12	19	**26**	
6	13	20	27	
7	14	21	28	

1st January

Capodanno New Year's Day – a public holiday often spent getting over the excesses of New Year's Eve.

6th January

Epifania Twelfth Night – a public holiday and religious festival celebrating the adoration of Jesus by the three kings. By popular tradition it is also the day when 'la Befana', an old woman on a broomstick, brings children gifts: they hang up their stockings the night before and in the morning find them full of sweets, cakes, and little presents or, if they have been naughty, coal (nowadays usually made of sugar).

14th February

San Valentino As in other countries, a day for lovers, marked by flowers, chocolates, and candlelit dinners.

8th March

Festa delle donne Since the 1970s Women's Day has been celebrated with sprays of mimosa and discussions on women's issues.

19th March

Festa del papà St. Joseph's day is the day on which Italian fathers are celebrated.

1st April

Pesce d'aprile April Fool's Day, when it is traditional to play jokes and tricks on people. Children have fun trying to stick paper fish onto people's backs without their noticing.

25th April

Anniversario della Liberazione
A public holiday, this is a day of official ceremonies to commemorate the liberation of Italy from Nazi occupation on 25th April 1945.

1st May

Festa del lavoro Public holiday – a civil festival celebrating the workers of the world.

2nd June

Festa della Repubblica Public holiday – a civil festival to commemorate the referendum of 2nd June 1946 which led to the proclamation of the Italian Republic.

15th August

l'Assunzione Public holiday – a religious festival that also marks the peak of the summer holidays. Just before and after this date, also known as 'Ferragosto', people set off on or return from their holidays. The factories in the north are closed, as are many shops except for those in tourist areas.

1st November

I Santi/Ognissanti Public holiday and religious festival celebrating all the saints. Typically, cakes made with nuts and raisins, which vary from region to region, are eaten during this festival. People go to the cemetery to take flowers for their dead loved ones, although the Festival of the Dead ('I Morti') is the following day, 2nd November, which is not a holiday.

8th December

L'immacolata Concezione Public holiday and religious festival that celebrates the purity of the Virgin Mary.

24th December

La vigilia di Natale Christmas Eve is not a public holiday although the schools are usually closed. Families get together, and often a large dinner is prepared. Afterwards people open their Christmas presents from under the tree. The faithful go to midnight Mass.

25th December

Natale Christmas Day is a public holiday and one of the most important religious festivals. Families who did not open their presents the night before do so on Christmas morning. Children who believe in Father Christmas think that he has come down the chimney to bring their presents during the night. Families get together to eat a big dinner, typically including a capon and ending with panettone and a glass of spumante.

26th December

Santo Stefano A public holiday during which Christmas celebrations continue.

31st December

San Silvestro New Year's Eve – the celebration of the end of the old year and beginning of the new. It is a working day for many people, although students are on holiday, but in the evening there is usually a big meal and a party, either at home or in a restaurant. Typical dishes are lentils (which are said to bring wealth) and cotechino (a large pork sausage), and a great deal of champagne and spumante is drunk. On the stroke of midnight fireworks are set off. In days gone by it was traditional to throw crockery out of the window but this no longer happens, to avoid damage to parked cars and injury to people passing by.

Movable feasts and holidays

Giovedì grasso (the Thursday before Lent). Fancy dress parties are held and people traditionally eat pancakes and fried pastries.

Martedì grasso (Shrove Tuesday). In some regions schools are closed.

Mercoledì delle Ceneri (Ash Wednesday). A religious occasion that marks the beginning of Lent. Some people fast on this day.

Venerdì santo (Good Friday). A religious occasion that is not a public holiday although some schools are closed.

Pasqua (Easter). The most important Catholic festival, celebrating the resurrection of Christ. A popular saying goes: *'Natale con i tuoi, Pasqua con chi vuoi'* (Christmas with your family, Easter with whoever you want), and in fact Italians often take the opportunity of the holiday period to go away on holiday. Those who stay at home cook a big meal, usually of lamb because of its symbolic meaning. A **colomba** (dove-shaped cake) is the traditional Easter cake.

Pasquetta (Easter Monday). A public holiday when people often go out for the day, to the sea, the mountains, or the countryside.

L'Ascensione (Ascension). A religious festival celebrating the ascension of Christ to heaven. It falls on the Thursday 40 days after Easter.

Pentecoste (Whitsun). A religious festival celebrating the descent of the holy spirit to the apostles. It falls 50 days after Easter.

Festa della mamma (Mothers' Day). This celebration is held on the second Sunday in May. Cards are sent and sometimes a present: perfume, chocolates, or flowers, especially roses.

A–Z of Italian life and culture

Accademia della Crusca

An academy for the study of the Italian language, founded in Florence in 1583, with the original aim of establishing the supremacy of the literary dialect in Florence – or of separating the 'flour' of pure language from the 'bran' (*crusca* – hence its name) of vulgarity. From 1612 it published the *Vocabolario degli accademici della Crusca* (Dictionary of the Members of the Accademia della Crusca), which became a model for similar works on the major European languages, and was printed in various editions until 1923. With only one interruption, from 1783 to 1811, the Academy has continued its work down to the present day. Currently based in the Villa di Castello near Florence, it is a centre for linguistic, philological, and lexicographical research. Unlike the French Académie Française or the Spanish Real Academia, however, it does not have the last word on what is correct or incorrect in Italian.

acqua alta

An exceptionally high tide that sometimes affects the lagoon of Venice during the winter months. It is caused by particular wind conditions, but exacerbated by human interference with the environment. When the level of the lagoon rises, peaking sometimes at 1.4 metres (4.6 feet) and over, many of the streets and piazzas of Venice disappear under centimetres of water. Sirens are sounded three or four hours before the *acqua alta* reaches full height, and footbridges are put up to allow pedestrians to continue to use the busiest routes.

agriturismo

A holiday based on a farm. It was originally intended that the holiday-makers would help with work on the farm in some capacity, but nowadays this virtually never happens. The word *agriturismo* is also used for the venue – the farmhouse, often renovated and refurbished specially for tourists. This type of holiday offers activities such as walking, horse-riding, etc. Good food and the open-air lifestyle are the main attractions. It is becoming much more popular and more expensive than it was at first.

Alimentari

Alimentari are food shops offering a range of products, from groceries, fruit and vegetables to prepared foods like cheeses, cured hams and salamis. Some even bake their own bread. An *alimentari* will also usually prepare *panini* (filled rolls) using their own ingedients. Small villages which have no other shops usually have an *alimentari*.

Alto Adige

The northern part of the Trentino-Alto Adige region, consisting of the province of Bolzano (called Südtirol [South Tirol] in German), ceded to Italy after the First World War. The majority of the population are German-speaking and of German descent. Since 1948 it has had a degree of autonomy, reinforced in 1972; place names are shown in Italian and German and holders of public offices have to pass an exam to show they are bilingual. Teaching in schools, however, is in German only for those of German descent, or Italian only for those of Italian descent. In future, this system is to be replaced by genuine bilingualism.

anno scolastico

The Italian school year usually begins in mid-September and ends at the beginning of June (except for students who are taking exams). As well as a few days' holiday for the various civil and religious festivals, there are about ten days' holiday over Christmas, New Year, and Twelfth Night, plus a few days at Easter. *See also* **SCUOLA**.

aperitivo

It is an Italian tradition to have an aperitif, which may or may not be alcoholic and is served with a few peanuts, olives, or other appetizers, before lunch or dinner. Many bars have their own, homemade *aperitivo*, based on liqueurs and fruit juices. Taking time for a pre-meal drink also provides a chance to catch up with friends.

ASL – Azienda Sanitaria Locale

The Servizio Nazionale di Assistenza Sanitaria (or National Health Service) provides care for citizens through these local health authorities.

autostrade

Italy has a network of motorways – toll roads with two or more lanes on each carriageway. The tolls paid for using motorways finance their construction, management, and maintenance. The tariff depends on the vehicle in which you are travelling and the stretch of motorway concerned, the relative costs of construction and maintenance being taken into account (e.g. mountain stretches can be more expensive). Usually you take a ticket from the booth when joining the motorway and hand it in for payment at the other end. The maximum speed limit for cars is 130 km/h (80 mph), or up to 150 km/h (94 mph) on some stretches.

Azzurri

A popular name for the Italian national team in sports such as football, rugby, and hockey, from the blue shirts worn by the players.

Banca d'Italia

The Italian central bank, founded in 1893. Since 1926 it has had a monopoly on the issue of currency, and supervisory jurisdiction over the Italian banking system. It also acts as the state treasury. Its central offices are located in the Via Nazionale in Rome. In the media, Via Nazionale is often used to mean the Bank of Italy.

Bancomat

This is the name of the system of automatic cash withdrawal, of the actual cash machine, and of the card itself. The same card is often used as both a credit card and a bancomat card, so when you pay with the card in a shop you can use it as a credit card, or – by keying in your PIN on a special keypad – as a debit card.

bandiera arancione

The orange flag is the mark of environmental quality awarded by the Italian Touring Club in inland areas. The criteria for the awarding of the orange flag are the development of cultural heritage, protection of the environment, standards of hospitality, and quality both of restoration and of local products.

bandiera blu

The blue flag is an award given to beaches and ports in the member countries of the FEE (Federation for Environmental Education). The criteria that have to be met are, for beaches, the quality of the water and the coast, safety measures and services, and the promotion of environmental education. For ports, it is the quality of the water in the harbour, safety and disposal services, and environmental information.

bar

A real institution of Italian life and culture, the bar is the place where you can have snacks, sandwiches, coffees, soft and alcoholic drinks, etc. Usually drinks are taken standing at the bar. In many bars there are also tables where you can sit and read the newspapers. Bars also play an important role in the lives of sports fans, as they meet there to watch football matches or other events on the television.

Befana

La Befana, whose name is derived from *Epifania* (Epiphany), is an old woman who is said to visit children on 6 January, bringing presents and sweets. *Befana* is also the name for the Epiphany holiday and usually signals the end of the Christmas celebrations and the return to school.

bel canto

A style of singing, still practised today, that combines a light, bright quality of voice with the ability to sustain a beautifully clear and even tone through complicated passages. It emerged in Italy in the 15th and 16th centuries and was at its height in the early 19th century, when the composers Rossini, Bellini, and Donizetti exploited it to the full in their operas.

Biennale di Venezia

An international show for the visual arts, cinema, architecture, dance, music, and theatre. The visual arts section still takes place every two years and often welcomes avant-garde artists. *See also* **MOSTRA INTERNAZIONALE D'ARTE CINEMATOGRAFICA**.

Bocconi

With its headquarters in Milan, the Bocconi commercial university is an extremely prestigious private university, with only one faculty – economics.

caffè

Coffee is a favourite Italian drink. Outside the home it can be drunk quickly standing at a bar counter, or in a more leisurely fashion while chatting at a table. In bars or restaurants you can order *un caffè* (normal), *ristretto* or *lungo* (stronger or weaker), *macchiato* (hot or cold, with a drop of milk), or *corretto* (with a drop of spirits). Also on offer are decaff (decaffeinato) and hot malt drinks (*caffè d'orzo*).

calcio

Football is the sport that Italians love most, and of course it is a sport in which Italian teams have always excelled. The national league is divided into Serie A, Serie B, and Serie C. Some of the most famous Italian teams are Juventus, Milan, Inter (also in Milan), Roma, and Lazio. *See also* **AZZURRI**.

Camera dei Deputati

The legislative assembly that, along with the **SENATO**, makes up the Italian Parliament. It is composed of 630 deputies, elected by universal direct suffrage by citizens over 18 years of age.

Camicie rosse ▶ I MILLE

Camorra

An organized-crime network operating in Naples and the Campania. The Camorra is not a single organization but made up of groups (families) who often fight for control of criminal activities. Emerging in the 1500s, it has for centuries practised blackmail and extortion on small businesses in Naples. After the Second World War, and particularly from the 1980s, it began to control drugs and arms trafficking, prostitution, and the allocation of public contracts, developing political links and assuming ever greater control of the Naples area.

Canton Ticino

This is the only canton of the Swiss Confederation which has Italian as its official language. It is also the only Swiss region located south of the Alps. The history, culture, and language of this area are intermingled with those of the neighbouring Italian regions.

Canzone

Italians are very proud of their tradition of popular song and it is celebrated at the Festival of Sanremo (*Festival della Canzone Italiana*). The festival has been held since 1951 and is watched by millions on Italian TV every year. The festival includes a competition for the best new song and the winner is guaranteed chart success.

Capitoline

One of the **SEVEN HILLS OF ROME**, the Capitoline was the acropolis and religious centre of the ancient city, and is now the headquarters of the City of Rome. The Piazza del Campidoglio at its top was designed by Michelangelo; the square is flanked by three palazzi now housing the Capitoline Museums. In the centre of the piazza stands a statue of Roman emperor, Marcus Aurelius, on horseback.

Caporetto

A First World War battle in which Italian troops were heavily defeated. On 24 October 1917, Austrian and German troops launched a major offensive on the Italian front, breaking through near the small town of

Caporetto (now Kobarid in Slovenia). The Italians retreated in disorder with very heavy losses. The name Caporetto entered the language as a byword for a total defeat or failure.

Capri

An island close to the southern entrance to the Bay of Naples, and favourite tourist destination. Capri is chiefly famous for its romantic setting, for the Blue Grotto – a sea cave with a low entrance, which gets its name from the colour of the light filtered through the water, and for the remains of Roman villas built by the Emperor Tiberius, who made Capri his headquarters from AD 27–37.

Carabinieri

The *Carabinieri* are a national Italian police force which is part of the army. They deal with issues of public order and serious crimes, but there is a certain amount of overlap with the duties of the **POLIZIA DI STATO**, which is not part of the army and is controlled by the Interior Ministry. *Carabinieri* wear a distinctive dark uniform with a red stripe.

Carnevale

This is the period before Lent running from Twelfth Night to Ash Wednesday. It is celebrated with fancy dress parties, confetti, and streamers, especially during the weekend running from '*giovedì grasso*' (the last Thursday) to '*martedì grasso*' (Shrove Tuesday), which is the final day. The Venice Carnival is one of the most famous, with its open-air thowsand fancy-dress balls, and the Viareggio Carnival is also well known.

carta d'identità

An identity document issued to all citizens aged 15 and over. It is valid for foreign travel within the countries of the European Union, and for trips to some other countries with which there is an agreement. It is renewed every five years at the town hall. An electronic card, the same size as a credit card, can be requested.

Cassa integrazione or Cassa integrazione guadagni

The benefit system for employees who are temporarily laid off because of a crisis in the company they work for. It is run by the **INPS**, which undertakes to pay 80 per cent of normal salary for a period of one or two years.

Cattolica

The 'Catholic university' is a prestigious private institute with humanities and science faculties, spread over five different campuses throughout Italy.

Cavaliere

– short for *Cavaliere al merito del lavoro* (Knight for services to industry) – is an official title, conferred since 1901 on those who make a major contribution to economic development. However, it is not uncommon for successful entrepreneurs to give their surnames the prefix *cavaliere* unofficially. Another frequently encountered title is that of *commendatore*, in common use over the past few decades as an honorific for any wealthy person.

Cavallino rampante

The 'prancing horse' symbol of Ferrari. Enzo Ferrari adopted the symbol from a coat of arms belonging to a First World War flying ace. He first used it on the Alfa Romeo cars in his racing stable, then on the cars he began to produce himself in 1947 in Maranello (near Modena). Today it is synonymous with Ferrari both as a car-maker and as a Formula 1 team.

Cena

Cena is the evening meal, traditionally a lighter meal than **PRANZO**, although it too may start with a **PRIMO** (often small pasta shapes in broth). A *cena* can also be a dinner party or a dinner at a restaurant, two of the principal ways in which Italians socialize.

Centro storico

The layout and much of the fabric of most Italian town and city centres derive from medieval or even Roman times, with the result that the *centro storico* is a place of narrow streets. Some (like Lucca) are surrounded by city walls. This makes life difficult for the motorist, and cars have been banned from many city centres.

Cinecittà

A complex of all of the different cinematographic studios set up on the outskirts of Rome in 1937. It includes a large number of film studios as well as studios for soundtracking.

CNR

The Consiglio Nazionale delle Ricerche (National Research Council) is a national public body which carries out and promotes research activities for the scientific, technological, economic, and social development of the country.

codice civile e penale

The civil and penal codes. The Italian codes, like those of other continental European countries, were modelled on the Code Napoléon, the French civil code first introduced in 1804. These superseded the common law, restructuring it on the enlightened principles of the French Revolution. The unified Italian state, founded in 1861, brought together the codes of the various states that made it up to constitute the civil code, the code of civil procedure, and the code of criminal procedure (on the French model) in 1865, and the criminal code in 1889. The new codes drawn up in the 20th century followed the same lines, with some modifications.

codice fiscale

A combination of letters and numbers, based on the holder's particulars, which identifies every citizen or resident of Italy for tax purposes and other dealings with the authorities. It is indispensable if a person wishes to work, open a bank account, use the health service, etc. In current usage the term *codice fiscale* (tax code) also refers to the plastic card, similar in size to a credit card, issued to everybody by the Ministry of the Economy and Finance and bearing the holder's code and personal details.

Colosseo

The name given in the Middle Ages to the 'colossal' Flavian Amphitheatre, the most famous monument of Ancient Rome, which was begun by Vespasian in about 75 AD and inaugurated by Titus in 80 AD. It is oval in shape and up to 50,000 spectators could attend the bloody battles between gladiators and beasts that were staged there.

comuni

Each province is subdivided into municipalities (*comuni*), each of which is run by a council and municipal committee headed by a **SINDACO** (mayor). The functions of the *comuni* are mainly administrative.

Confederazioni sindacali

The three large Italian trade union organizations that represent workers in all categories and sectors: the formerly Communist-oriented CGIL (Confederazione generale italiana del lavoro); the Christian-oriented CISL (Confederazione italiana sindacati lavoratori) and the social-democrat-oriented UIL (Unione italiana del lavoro). During the 1970s and 1980s they formed an alliance and collaborated to play a central role in politics and in the Italian economy. However, recent transformations in the economy and the labour market have reduced their unity of action, and their role has been partly reshaped by the rise of autonomous sectoral unions.

consiglio dei ministri

A body composed of ministers and headed by the **PRESIDENTE DEL CONSIGLIO**: it forms the government.

consultorio familiare

Social-health service set up in the mid-1970s. It provides health education (including preventive medicine) in the fields of gynaecology and paediatrics, as well as advice and support for people with mental health or legal problems.

Corte Costituzionale

The constitutional court, in operation since 1955, which has the duty of ensuring that laws passed by parliament do not conflict with the **COSTITUZIONE** and of ruling on conflicts between the powers of the state and those of the regions. It is made up partly of magistrates and partly of jurists chosen by the parliament and the **PRESIDENTE DELLA REPUBBLICA**. It is based in Rome, in the Palazzo della Consulta (the Consulta being a former papal institution) next door to the **QUIRINALE**, and is often referred to as La Consulta.

costituzione

The constitution of the Italian Republic, which came into force on 1 January 1948. It was drawn up by a constituent assembly, elected by the people, and based on the principles of liberty, equality, and democracy. A constitutional court (**CORTE COSTITUZIONALE**) ensures that any individual laws passed by parliament conform to the constitution.

denominazione di origine controllata (*DOC*)

The state-certified mark of quality awarded to Italian wines that possess certain verified characteristics, such as origin within a defined zone of production, derivation from particular types of vines and soils, ratio between the quantity of grapes used and quantity of wine obtained, and methods used in production. *DOC* wines that have become particularly famous for their special qualities are now certified as *DOCG* (*denominazione di origine controllata e garantita*), a mark based on even stricter standards of verification. *See also* **VINO**.

Dialetto

As Italy was not unified until 1861, standard Italian was slow to become widely used except by the cultural elite. As a result dialects are used by many Italians, with 60% using their dialect regularly. Ranging from Neapolitan and Sicilian to Milanese and Venetian, they vary considerably from each other. Tuscan dialects are the closest to standard Italian.

Divina Commedia

The most celebrated and important work in Italian literature, written by Dante Alighieri between 1306 and 1321. *The Divine Comedy* is divided into three parts, *Inferno* (Hell), *Purgatorio* (Purgatory), and *Paradiso* (Heaven), each containing thirty-three cantos (plus one introductory canto to make 100). It describes a journey through the Christian afterlife and is probably best known and loved for its retelling of the stories of the characters Dante discovers in the three realms. Part of Dante's purpose was to prove that the Italian language could be used for serious works of literature. In his writing, he blended the language of court with the most expressive elements of his native Tuscan and other dialects, helping to lay the foundations of modern Italian.

Dolce Vita, La

A film, whose title literally means 'The Sweet Life', made by the director Federico Fellini and released in 1960. It depicted the emptiness and squalor of high society in Rome. Its title very quickly became a cliché for a worldly Italian lifestyle that perhaps never even existed, and it ended up as banal slogan for mass tourism.

dottore

The legally recognized title in Italy for a person who receives a degree after completing a university course lasting at least four years (recent reforms in higher education have reduced this to three years). It is widely used both in writing (on letters or on business cards) or as a form of address to refer formally to all graduates, not simply graduates in medicine. There is a saying in Italy that 'no one ever denies being doctor', meaning that anyone – with or without a degree – is happy to accept *dottore* as a term of deference from waiters, parking attendants, and so on. *See also* **LAUREA**.

enoteca

A place where good local wines are offered for sale and often for tasting. In many *enoteche* you can also eat while tasting the wines.

Extracomunitari

The Italian term used to refer to immigrants from Third World countries (black Africa, the Arab countries of North Africa, the Philippines, Sri Lanka, and China) or European countries that are not yet members of the European Union (Albania). Though the term may seem purely bureaucratic, *extracomunitario* (literally, 'outside the community') is a discriminatory word in common speech reflecting deep-seated prejudices; it is used with mistrust or fear, sometimes with scorn or hostility as a label for poor immigrants, exploited as underpaid labour, often staying illegally without a residence permit, and involved in illegal trafficking or criminal activities.

Extravergine

Olive oil which is obtained from the first pressing of the olives is called *extravergine* (extra virgin). It has a distinctive peppery flavour and is often a cloudy greenish colour. A less refined grade, suitable for cooking, is obtained by using chemical methods. This is called simply *olio d'oliva*.

FAI

The Fondo per l'Ambiente Italiano (Fund for the Italian Environment), set up in 1975 with the aim of contributing to the protection, conservation, and use of Italy's artistic and environmental heritage. It has acquired, mostly through donations, many important buildings and sites (villas, palaces, castles, parks, and gardens) that it has subsequently restored and opened to the public.

Farmacia

A *farmacia* in Italy sells medicines and health-related products, whereas a *profumeria* sells not only perfume, but also beauty and personal hygiene products. For film and developing services it is necessary to go to a shop specializing in photographic equipment.

Farnesina

A term used in the media to refer to the Italian Ministry of Foreign Affairs which, since 1959, has been housed in the Palazzo della Farnesina, a vast building constructed in a functional style between 1938 and the 1950s outside the historic centre of Rome.

Fascism

A movement, based on an ultra-conservative, anti-socialist, nationalist, racist, and authoritarian ideology, which controlled Italy from 1922 to 1943. The name comes from the *fasces*, an axe with its handle encased in a bundle of rods, which was a symbol of power and unity in Roman times. The Fascists, led by Benito Mussolini (known as *il duce*, the leader), were both a political party and a paramilitary organization. They ruled dictatorially, intimidating, imprisoning, and sometimes murdering, their political opponents. Under the Fascist regime Italian armies conquered Abyssinia and Albania, but military failures during World War II, in which Italy was initially allied with Germany and Japan, led to the Fascists' downfall.

Fiamme Gialle

The nickname (literally meaning 'Yellow Flames') for the *guardia di finanza*, an Italian police force organized along military lines, which specializes in combating economic, financial, and fiscal crime (fraud, tax evasion, and money laundering) and guarding Italy's land and sea borders (against smuggling, drug trafficking, and illegal immigration). It was set up in 1881 and its members wear uniforms with yellow insignia, hence the nickname.

Figlio di papà

With the rapid rise in living standards which took place in Italy after 1945, many more children grow up in affluent families than was previously the case, and *figli unici* (only children) are often the norm. Children, both young and grown-up, are often given considerable financial help by their parents, and are sometimes termed *figli di papà*, implying that they are also spoilt.

foglio rosa
This is the provisional driving licence, which can be applied for at the minimum age (18 years old for driving cars) and is valid for six months.

Fratelli d'Italia
The name by which Italy's national anthem is commonly known. Its official name is the *Inno di Mameli* (Mameli's hymn), after its author, the poet and patriot Goffredo Mameli, who died in 1849, aged 22, fighting with Garibaldi for the defence of the Roman Republic (*see* **I MILLE**). It was adopted as the national anthem in 1946. The common name comes from the opening lines of the first verse: *Fratelli d'Italia, l'Italia s'è desta, / dell'elmo di Scipio s'è cinta la testa* (Brothers of Italy, Italy has awoken / It has circled its head with the helmet of Scipio). All Italians know the tune (composed by Mameli's friend, the choirmaster Michele Novaro), but very few know the rest of the words (it has five verses) by heart.

Funghi
Wild mushrooms are an Italian passion, and the most prized is the *porcino* (cep), which can be bought fresh or dried. However, many Italians are also avid mushroom-pickers and are expert at differentiating edible mushrooms (*funghi commestibili*) from poisonous ones. Local authorities often have a department controlling the picking and selling of mushrooms.

Gazzetta dello Sport
This is the sports daily, printed on its characteristic pink paper. It was founded in Milan in 1896 and is the most widely read sports newspaper in Italy. It organizes the **GIRO D'ITALIA**.

Gazzetta Ufficiale
The official newspaper of the Italian state, which publishes approved laws, decrees, and various official announcements.

gelato
Made with milk, sugar, eggs, and various other ingredients, this is an Italian speciality. The hand-made variety, bought in *gelaterie*, can be served in a dish or in a cone. There are dozens of flavours to choose from.

giornali
Among the main Italian dailies are *Repubblica* and *Corriere della Sera*. The daily financial paper is *il Sole 24 ore*. The weekly magazines *L'Espresso* and *Panorama* deal with current affairs, politics, and culture. As well as Italian versions of international titles, the weekly magazines *Grazia*, *Anna*, and *Donna Moderna* cater for women. *Famiglia Cristiana* is the Catholic weekly. Of the gossip magazines, *Novella 2000* is the most popular.

giro d'Italia
Like the Tour de France, one of the most famous cycling races in the world. It takes place from mid-May to the beginning of June. The route changes every year, but the last stage always ends in Milan. The winner is awarded the pink jersey. *See also* **GAZZETTA DELLO SPORT**.

gondola
A low narrow boat with a raised curved prow, used on the canals of Venice. The gondola is propelled by a *gondoliere* (gondolier) using a single oar that pivots on a small post

attached to the starboard side. The gondoliers usually dress in traditional striped tops and a straw hat. A 17th-century *doge* (*see* **VENETIAN REPUBLIC**) ordered that all gondolas should be painted black, so as not to glorify worldly wealth. They remain black, but are now used almost exclusively for tourists.

Herculaneum ▶ VESUVIUS

Informagiovani

As the name suggests, this is a service of information and guidance for young people. Promoted by local bodies, the various centres (and their web sites) provide information about all areas of interest to young people: courses and training, jobs, culture, politics, voluntary work, travel, etc. The first centres opened in Turin and Milan in the early 1980s; now there are about 600 centres throughout Italy. In addition to supplying information, they carry out a role of 'listening' to young people and also promote projects created by young people for young people.

INPS – Istituto Nazionale per la Previdenza Sociale

(National Institute of Social Security). This is the major public body in Italy that pays workers' old-age pensions after receiving contributions from them during their working lives. It also manages the various kinds of assistance provided by the welfare state, such as the **CASSA INTEGRAZIONE**, sickness, maternity, unemployment, and invalidity benefit.

Internet

The World Wide Web is much used in Italy, as elsewhere. All major Italian newspapers and television stations have their own websites, as do councils, museums, etc. The suffix for Italian sites is '.it'.

Italo-

Descendants of those who emigrated from Italy are often referred to as *italo-americani*, *italo-brasiliani*, etc. Massive emigration started in the 1870s, mainly from the North of Italy to South America. Buenos Aires and Sao Paolo have the highest concentrations of Italians outside Italy. Subsequently more and more southern Italians emigrated to the United States.

Ladino

Ladin (*ladino* in Italian) is a direct descendant of the Latin spoken in the valleys of north-eastern Italy. Western Ladin is spoken in Alto Adige, alongside German, and Eastern Ladin (also called Friulian) in Friuli-Venezia Giulia. Numbers of speakers are shrinking as gradually German or Italian predominate.

laghi

The north of Italy is the area with the highest concentration of lakes, which includes the three largest and most famous: Lake Garda (the largest of all), Lake Maggiore, and Lake Como. The area's mild climate and abundant greenery have always held a great attraction for both Italians and foreigners. Some lakes are equipped for water sports; others offer luxurious hotels and health farms.

laurea

The title, meaning 'degree', that is traditionally awarded in Italy to people who complete a course of study at a university, usually lasting four years. Recently a *laurea triennale* (or *breve*) was introduced; this 'three-year' or 'short degree' gives immediate access to the labour market. In contrast the *laurea specialistica*, 'specialist degree', requires a further two years of study and entitles the holder to be known as **DOTTORE**.

Leaning Tower of Pisa

The eight-storey bell tower of the cathedral of Pisa. Building work began in 1183, but the tower started to lean noticeably to the north, as the ground beneath it was unstable. Work continued on and off on the tower for the next 200 years, and by 1360 it was complete – it was now leaning to the south, however. Over the centuries, the problem worsened. Finally, in the late 1990s, engineers removed rock and soil from under the north side of the tower and succeeded in reducing the angle of tilt from 10 per cent to 5 per cent. The tower is now said to be safe for the next 300 years.

Liberazione, La

The effective end of the Second World War in Italy in late April 1945, when a general uprising staged by the **RESISTENZA** in the northern cities (Turin, Milan, and Genoa) led to the surrender or retreat of German troops before the arrival in Northern Italy of the victorious Anglo-American forces. It is celebrated by the Festa della Liberazione (Liberation Day holiday) on 25 April each year.

liceo

A type of secondary school, similar to a grammar school, which aims to form students' characters, pass on theoretical rather than applied knowledge, and develop the capacity for independent judgement and criticism. These aims are fully embodied in the more traditional type of *liceo*, the *liceo classico*, focused on the study of ancient languages (Latin and Greek). In the *liceo scientifico*, a more recent type, mathematics and the sciences are strongly represented in the curriculum along with Latin and philosophy, the latter being trademark subjects of *liceo* teaching whatever the school's specialism, whether science, modern languages, or art, etc. The evolution of the Italian school system is leading to the term *liceo* also being applied to schools that specialize in technical or business subjects.

Lotto

The lottery game first appeared in Italy in Genoa during the 16th century, and during the following century spread to the other Italian states. From the 19th century it has been run directly by the state, and since 1871 there have been weekly Saturday draws in ten cities (known as *ruote*). Over the centuries a popular myth has grown up that the interpretation of dreams can help in the selection of winning numbers. The principles, a mixture of esotericism and cabbalism, are set out in the book of *Smorfia* (a corruption of Morpheus, the name of the Greek and Roman god of sleep and dreams). This ancient game still has great potential, as the development of recent variants such as the hugely popular Superenalotto has shown.

Mafia

Since the Second World War, the Sicilian Mafia (also called Cosa Nostra) has expanded and developed substantially, creating an alternative power that is partly complementary to that of the state. Starting from illegal activities such as extortion and usury, it then assumed control of the building trade and the award of public contracts, and finally took over the traffic in illegal drugs, which brought in enormous profits. The Mafia has a vertical structure (a strict hierarchy of 'families'), but it is distinguished from other criminal organizations above all by its close relationships and complicity with political authorities.

Mani pulite

The name (meaning 'clean hands') given to the landmark judicial inquiry, which, beginning in 1992 in Milan, brought to light the system of *tangenti* (payments on the side) and corruption in which the governing parties were involved. It resulted in their dissolution and the end of the so-called 'first republic' (**PRIMA REPUBBLICA**).

manifesti funebri

Small posters printed by the family of someone who has died, announcing the death, saying a few words about the deceased, and giving the date and time of the funeral. These are put up on special boards – or indeed on any available surface – to inform local people of what has happened and to ensure a large attendance at the funeral.

matrimoni

Traditionally, marriages in Italy were arranged by the couple's families, and it is still not uncommon for a male relative of the groom to visit the bride's father or uncle to ask formally for the girl's hand on the groom's behalf. Traditionally, too, the bride would be given a dowry – nowadays her family and friends will usually arrange bridal showers before the wedding to provide her with household goods, and she carries a satin bag at the reception into which guests put money. Weddings in Italy do not usually take place during the solemn church seasons of Advent and Lent, or during the months of May and August. Other customs include the throwing of *confetti* (not scraps of paper, but small bags of sugared almonds) and the breaking of a glass or vase at the end of the wedding feast, which is usually sumptuous. The number of pieces into which the object breaks is supposed to represent the number of years the couple will live together.

maturità

This is the exam that students take at the end of the five years of secondary school, between the ages of 18 and 19. It consists of two written tests (one of which is Italian language) and two orals. Marks (the maximum is 60 out of 60) depend on both the result of the tests and the average marks achieved over the previous three years. The diploma is a requirement for university entrance and, depending on the type of secondary school attended, it can be in science, classics, arts, or technology, etc.

mercati

Every Italian town and city has its own market, either open-air or covered, where fruit, vegetables, cheeses, cooked meats, and a range of other produce is sold. There is also a weekly market where it is possible to buy clothes, bags, household goods, and other items. The prices are cheaper than in the shops, and people often haggle over the goods displayed on the stalls.

Mezzogiorno

A term referring to southern Italy, including Sicily and Sardinia, which is less economically developed than the north. The name literally means 'midday', i.e. siesta time, indicating that – though it has a wealth of artistic treasures and beautiful countryside – the pace of life here is markedly less frenetic than in northern Italy.

I Mille

In 1860, soldier Giuseppe Garibaldi (1807–82) set sail from Genoa with two ships and just over 1,000 volunteers (*i Mille*), known as the *Camicie rosse* (Red Shirts). Garibaldi and his followers managed to wrest Sicily and Naples from Bourbon hands, territory which he then handedover to King Victor Emmanuel II of Sardinia. In the following year, Victor Emmanuel was declared king of the newly unified Italy. The original 1,000 volunteers remained a symbol of the most notable event of the Italian **RISORGIMENTO**, and are commemorated in street names in many Italian cities.

Minoranza linguistica

Minoranze linguistiche (linguistic minorities) are protected by the Italian constitution. As well as dialects of Italian, and the related languages Sardinian and Ladin, other languages are spoken. They include German in Alto Adige; French in Valdaosta; Greek, Albanian, and Serbo-Croat in the rural south; Slovenian in the north-east and Catalan in Alghero.

Mole Antonelliana

The Mole Antonelliana, an extremely unusual monument (167 m – 548 ft – high), is the symbol of Turin. Destined to be a synagogue, the building was begun in 1863 but, following financial problems and arguments about its stability, it was not finished until 1889. Subsequently acquired by the city, it is now the home of the New Museum of the Cinema. A glass lift provides access to the steeple.

Montecitorio

A palace, built between 1650 and 1697, to house papal courts. It is situated in a piazza of the same name in the centre of Rome. Since 1871 it has been home to the lower house of the Italian parliament, the **CAMERA DEI DEPUTATI** (Chamber of Deputies). The term Montecitorio is used in the media to refer to the Chamber itself.

Monza

A small city north of Milan, best known as the site of Autodromo nazionale, the motor-racing circuit where the Italian Grand Prix is held.

Mostra Internazionale d'Arte Cinematografica

Also known as the Venice Film Festival, this is the film section of the **BIENNALE DI VENEZIA**. It was started in the 1930s and takes place every year at the end of August at the Palazzo del Cinema on the Venice Lido. One of the largest film festivals in Europe (and indeed the world), it attracts films, actors, directors, and ther technicians from around the 'orld. The festival winners are warded the Golden Lion.

egozi

ne hours of opening for shops vary ccording to the type of shop and 'here it is located. In general, food nops open at about 8 a.m. and close t 7.30 p.m. with a lunch break from 2.30 to 3.30 p.m. Clothes shops, ookshops, etc. open from 9 a.m. ntil 12.30 or 1 p.m. and then again 'om 3.30 to 7.30 p.m. In summer the ınch break is longer and shops stay pen until 8.00 p.m. Some ıpermarkets and department stores the big cities are open all day. Veekly closing also varies according the type of shop. Some shops close r two to three weeks in August, fter the summer sales, then reopen vith the new autumn-season stock.

lordest

he northeast, the area comprising ne regions Veneto, Trentino, and riuli, where a highly successful model f industrial development was applied luring the 1990s. This led to the apid emergence of many small and nedium-sized companies, producing nainly textiles, footwear, and nechanical goods, and to strong xport growth. Since then, however, ne 'northeastern model' has been iscussed mainly in terms of its downsides (damage to the environment, absence of general social development, lack of professional training for workers). Today it is in difficulties because of globalized competition; it no longer appears to be a more successful alternative to the traditional industrial area of the northwest, the **TRIANGOLO INDUSTRIALE**.

Normale

The Scuola Normale Superiore di Pisa was set up in the early 1800s as a branch of the Paris Ecole Normale. Today, it is an extremely prestigious institute offering first degree courses and research doctorates in science and the humanities.

onomastico

This is the feast day of the saint whose name a person bears. Although less important than his or her birthday, a saint's day is always celebrated with cards and sometimes with a small gift.

oratorio

In Italy there are thousand of *oratorios* (usually buildings with courtyards and playing fields attached to Catholic parishes), which are used by pupils – on afternoons when they are not in school – as meeting places and for recreation (typically for ball games, but also for many other sporting or theatrical activities, etc.) and educational purposes. They are supervised by priests or their lay assistants. Created in the 19th century to rescue poor boys from immorality and crime, they have become a typical feature of young people's lives at all social levels in Italy.

Padania

A term used by the political party Lega

Nord (the Northern League) to refer to the whole of northern Italy, roughly the area falling within the basin of the River Po and the Venetian regions, supposed to be inhabited by a population of Celtic rather than Latin origin. According to its more extreme proponents, Padania should aim to secede from the rest of Italy (dominated by a 'corrupt' Rome), and especially from the uncivilized and backward south. But, for critics and opponents of the League, Padania is a meaningless term, because it does not correspond to a unified area that can be defined geographically, historically, or linguistically – and because the idea that the Padanians are direct descendants of the ancient Celts is mythical nonsense.

Palazzo Chigi

The seat of the Italian government since 1961. The Palazzo Chigi, built in the 16th and 17th centuries, is situated in Piazza Colonna in the heart of Rome near the **MONTECITORIO** palace. In the media, the term Palazzo Chigi means the Italian government or **PRESIDENTE DEL CONSIGLIO**.

Palio di Siena

A popular event that takes place every year in Siena on 2 July and 16 August. The *contrade*, or districts of the city, fight for the *palio*, a banner, in a frantic race on horseback around the medieval Piazza del Campo. It has deep historical roots but is still passionately followed by the Sienese and is a huge attraction for tourists from all over the world. Thereis a spectacular historical procession in brightly coloured Renaissance costumes before the race.

Papal States

Areas of central Italy owned and governed by the Pope from the early Middle Ages until the 19th century, including Latium, Umbria, Marche, and the city of Rome itself. The process of transferring these areas to secular government began with the conquest of Italy by Napoleon Bonaparte, but was not completed until 1870, when the Pope was force to relinquish control of Rome, enabling it to become the capital of a united Italy.

parchi nazionali

In Italy there are about twenty national parks covering 5 per cent of the territory. Controlled by the Ministry of the Environment, their objective is the protection and development of large areas that are c particular importance in terms of environment and landscape. The best-known are 'Gran Paradiso', the national parks in Abruzzi, Lazio, and Molise, and the National Park of the Maddalena Archipelago. The marine parks, which aim to protect stretches of sea, coast, and sometimes whole islands and archipelagos, are becoming increasingly important.

partiti politici

Even today Italy has problems in reuniting various political tendencies in a small number of major political parties. So there are still many political parties, which can still be roughly classified as belonging to the left, right, or centre. Under the so-called **PRIMA REPUBBLICA**, the centre ruled supreme, but it is now divided. Of the minor Catholic parties (La Margherita, UDC, Udeur), some are aligned with the left (in an alliance alled L'Ulivo [the Olive Tree], then 'Unione), others with the right (in an alliance called Casa delle Libertà House of Freedoms]). On the left here are the Democratici di Sinistra DS) or Democrats of the Left, former Communists who have abandoned Marxism, the more radical Partito della Rifondazione Comunista (PRC) Party of Communist Refoundation) and the Verdi (Greens). On the right here are the Alleanza Nazionale (AN) National Alliance), an ex-neofascist group, and the Lega Nord (Northern eague), which has separatist and enophobic tendencies. Forza Italia FI) (literally 'Go on, Italy'), the large entre-right party, which first came to power under Silvio Berlusconi in 1994 and returned to power in 2001, draws ts support from former Christian Democrats, Socialists, and Liberals.

passeggiata

This typical Italian custom involves walking with family or friends in the square or main street, or along the promenade. It usually takes place before eating, on Saturday afternoon or Sunday morning, and in the summer it can also take place in the evening after dinner. Depending on the time and the weather, people might have an aperitif or an ice cream. The purpose is to stretch one's legs, chat, see who is around, and be seen.

pasta

The basic ingredient of many Italian dishes, which is made by mixing flour from durum (hard) wheat with water, and sometimes adding other ingredients such as beaten egg or cooked spinach. Fresh pasta is soft and can be moulded into a variety of different forms, such as flat sheets (lasagne), long thin sticks (spaghetti), tubes (macaroni, cannelloni), or small square pillow shapes (ravioli). Commercially made pasta is dried after shaping until hard. In this form it will keep for a long time. Pasta is also a healthy food as it contains very little fat.

patente a punti

Following reform of the Italian highway code, each driving licence is now given an initial value of twenty points, which are reduced if traffic offences are committed. For example, for the more serious offences (overtaking on a bend, drink driving, or driving while under the effect of drugs), ten points are deducted; passing a red light costs you six points, while parking in an area reserved for public transport costs two points. Once the number of infringements committed has reduced the initial number of points to zero, the licence is withdrawn and the driving test has to be retaken. Drivers with the worst records are required to undergo courses of 're-education'. The points system is also applied to foreign citizens who are passing though Italy: the penalties are totted up and filed in a special register.

permesso di soggiorno

Foreigners who enter Italy with a passport and visa, especially for work or study, have to apply for this residence permit from the state police – that is from a **QUESTURA** or a *commissariato* (police headquarters or local police station) – within eight days of arrival. The permit is valid for between three months and two years, depending on the circumstances, and is renewable. It entitles the holder to be issued with an identity card (**CARTA D'IDENTITÀ**) and a tax code (**CODICE FISCALE**). *See also* **POLIZIA DI STATO**.

Piazza Affari

A term commonly used in the media to refer to the Milan stock exchange, the most important in Italy. The stock exchange came into existence in 1808 and is now housed in the Palazzo della Borsa (built between 1928 and 1931), situated in the centre of the city in the Piazza degli Affari.

Pinocchio

The hero of the children's book, *Le Avventure di Pinocchio* (The Adventures of Pinocchio) by Carlo Collodi (1826–90), Pinocchio is a wooden puppet whose nose grows whenever he tells a lie. After various tribulations, accompanied by such famous characters as Geppetto (the puppetmaker), the Blue Fairy, the Fire-Eater, Lucignolo, and the whale, etc., Pinocchio is turned into a real boy. Adapted for television and as a cartoon, the story has also been reinterpreted from a sociological and psychoanalytical point of view.

pizza

Now a 'global food', pizza was for centuries a speciality of the city of Naples, and many people still think that it cannot be properly appreciated elsewhere. Pizze (flattened pieces of bread dough) were eaten in Naples in the late Middle Ages with garlic and lard, cheese and basil, or small fish. The modern pizza, with tomato, appeared in the late 1700s. The first pizzeria was opened in Naples in 1830 (before that, pizza was sold and eaten in the street). In 1889 the *pizzaiolo* (pizza-maker) Raffaele Esposito made a pizza topped with tomato, ricotta, and some leaves of basil (thus red, white, and green, the colours of the Italian flag) for Queen Margherita, the wife of Umberto I. Since then, this, the most widespread type of pizza, has been known as pizza margherita.

politecnico

A scientific and technological university that includes faculties of engineering and architecture among its specializations. There are three in Italy. The oldest and most famous are those of Turin (1859) and Milan (1863); the latest is in Bari.

polizia di stato

The name, meaning 'state police', of the Italian civil police force. The force was organized along military lines from 1919 to 1981 and called the Corpo delle Guardie di Pubblica Sicurezza (PS), Guards of Public Safety. It had headquarters (**QUESTURE**) in the capital city of each province, and police stations (*commissariati*) in city districts and minor centres. The reform of 1981 demilitarized and democratized it, and many of its officers and staff are now women. It continues to assist the **CARABINIERI** (who cover a wider area) in the task of maintaining law and order.

Pompeii ▶ VESUVIUS

Ponte Vecchio

The ancient bridge in Florence that spans the River Arno. It carries a roadway lined with goldsmiths' and jewellers' shops.

popular music

In Italy the popular and classical traditions of vocal music tend to merge. The repertoires of star singers such as Luciano Pavarotti and Andrea Bocelli include popular Italian, especially Neapolitan songs, alongside operatic arias. Italian pop singers are less well known abroad. Singers such as Mina, Lucio Battisti, and Eros Ramazzotti tend to specialize in romantic ballads or songs exploiting Mediterranean folk rhythms. Italy does, however, have its share of rock, hip-hop, etc, artists and groups, of whom the most famous is perhaps the singer Zucchero.

Pranzo

Pranzo is traditionally the day's main meal and school timetables and hours of business are geared to a break between one and four o'clock. It starts with a **PRIMO** (usually pasta), followed by a secondo (main course). Gradually Italians, especially city-dwellers, are adopting a more northern-European timetable and making less of *pranzo*.

Premio Strega

The most famous literary prize in Italy, instituted in 1947 and sponsored by a wealthy liquor manufacturer (producer of the Strega liqueur). Previous winners have included Edoardo De Filippo, Pierpaolo Pasolini, and Umberto Eco. The prize is awarded annually, in July, in the 16th-century Ninfeo (a garden with monumental fountain) of the Villa Giulia in Rome.

presepio (or *presepe*)

A 'crib', a representation of the Nativity and the Adoration of the Magi in the form of wood or terracotta statues against a painted landscape. Cribs first appeared in Tuscany in the 13th and 14th centuries, but it was in Naples in the 17th and 18th centuries, during the baroque and rococo periods, that churches began to display magnificent examples. Scenes of everyday life were reproduced down to the smallest detail. During the 19th century, families began to build their own cribs for the Christmas season, with terracotta, plaster, or papier-mâché figurines. In recent years this custom has become a little less common with the introduction of the Christmas tree from northern Europe.

presidente del consiglio

This is the title of the Italian prime minister, the head of the government and of the **CONSIGLIO DEI MINISTRI**. Nominated by the **PRESIDENTE DELLA REPUBBLICA**, he proposes the ministers. He controls and is responsible for government policy.

presidente della repubblica

The head of state who represents the nation. He/she is elected by parliament and remains in office for seven years. As Italy is a parliamentary republic, the duties of the president are: to enact laws, to dissolve parliament and call new elections when necessary, to nominate the prime minister and ratify his choice of the ministers, and to grant pardons. He/she also chairs the body which oversees the appointment of judges.

Prima repubblica

The name (meaning 'first republic') given to the political system that collapsed in 1992–93 in the wake of scandals revealed by the **MANI PULITE** (Clean Hands) inquiry and the weakening of the opposing ideological positions associated with the Cold War. The big governing parties of those days – especially the Christian Democrats and the Socialist Party – disbanded, and new parties emerged; these are still active today (*see also* **PARTITI POLITICI**).

Primo

In Italy, lunch invariably includes a *primo*, or first course, before the main course. The most common *primi* are pasta (traditional in the Centre and South) and risotto (traditional in the North), but a *primo* may also consist of soup (often containing small pasta shapes) or *gnocchi* (potato dumplings).

provincia

In Italy's system of local government, each province is made up of neighbouring municipalities, the most important of which acts as the provincial capital. Each province is served by a provincial council, a committee, and a president.

quadrilatero della moda

The 'fashion quadrilateral' is an area in the centre of Milan defined by the Via Montenapoleone, Via della Spiga, Via Manzoni, and Via Sant'Andrea, where the biggest names in Italian fashion, such as Armani, Trussardi, Valentino, Versace, Prada, Missoni, and Dolce & Gabbana, have their boutiques and showrooms.

questure

Provincial headquarters of the police force. Thefts are reported to the *questura* and passports renewed there.

Quirinale

A 16th-century building on the hill of the same name in Rome, now the residence of the **PRESIDENTE DELLA REPUBBLICA**. It was formerly the summer residence of the popes and then of the kings of Italy.

RAI

The state radio and television company. There are three television channels, RAI 1, RAI 2, and RAI 3, and three radio stations, Radio 1, Radio 2, and Radio 3, which tend to be supportive of the government.

Reality TV

Reality television has become as popular in Italy as in other countries. Most Italian shows follow the same formats used elsewhere. Italy has its own version of 'Big Brother' (*Grande fratello*), of 'Survivor' (*Isola dei Famosi*) and various 'life-swap' programmes, such as *Una giornata particolare*, in which Italian sports and media stars spend a day doing a very ordinary job, like being a cleaner or mechanic. Italy has, however, contributed at least one reality show of its own. The popular Sunday programme, *Domenica In*, features *A Spasso con Mamma*, which is similar to 'Blind Date', except that it sends single young men out on dates with the mothers of single girls, and only if the mother gives a favourable report does the young man get to meet the girl.

regione

Italy is subdivided into twenty regions, five of which have a certain amount of political autonomy. Each region is subdivided in its turn into provinces (*see* **PROVINCIA**) and municipalities.

he regions can issue legislative :andards. They also have dministrative duties which can be elegated to the provinces and the 1unicipalities. Each region is served y a council, a committee, and a egional president.

epubblica

he Italian republic was founded after e Second World War, based on the esults of the referendum of 2 June 946, which abolished the monarchy 1 favour of a republican form of overnment. The **COSTITUZIONE** ublished in 1948 established its arliamentary character.

esistenza

n 8 September 1943, Italy, which ad been allied to Hitler's Germany, urrendered to British and US forces. he Germans reacted immediately by 1vading the greater part of the eninsula, which was not yet ccupied by allied forces, and by nposing a harshly oppressive regime n their former ally. Soldiers from the isbanded army and antifascist ivilians organized themselves into roups of partisans to fight the iermans and their Fascist ollaborators behind the lines, leading o the Liberation in 1945. The ideals f liberty and democracy that inspired ne partisans and their unity of action 1 spite of differing political views were he foundation of the new post-war alian republic. For this reason, the esistance still carries considerable olitical weight in present-day Italy.

isorgimento

he name, meaning 'the Resurgence', iven to the historical period marked y the struggles for Italian independence and unification. After its beginnings in 1820–21 and 1831 and the uprisings of1848–49, its principal events were the three wars of independence against Austria-Hungary (1848–49, 1859, and 1866) and the expedition of Garibaldi and **I MILLE** (the 1,000) in 1860. The moderate monarchical movement prevailed against the republican and revolutionary tendency of Giuseppe Mazzini, so that the House of Savoy (under Victor Emmanuel II) obtained the Italian crown in 1861. Rome became the capital city in 1871 (*see also* **PAPAL STATES**).

riviera

The Italian word *riviera* means a 'coastal region'. It has been borrowed by many other languages and come to mean an area with a warm climate, fashionable resorts, and beaches for holidaymakers. The Italian, or Ligurian, Riviera is the stretch of coastline that begins at the French border and extends as far as Tuscany. The main city and port in the region is Genoa – popular holiday towns include Portofino, San Remo, and Rapallo.

rugby

Both rugby union and rugby league are played in Italy, mainly in northern regions. There has been a national championship in rugby union since 1929, and in 2000 Italy joined

England, Wales, Scotland, Ireland, and France to make up the Six Nations competition.

sagra

A popular festival with a fair and market, which takes place in many villages once a year, sometimes more frequently. *Sagre* usually have a theme such as wine, sausages, fish, or truffles – depending on what the local speciality is.

St Peter's

The largest Christian church in the world, situated in the **VATICANO** in Rome. The Basilica of St Peter's is not a cathedral; its importance lies in its closeness to the papal residence and its use for most papal ceremonies, as well as in its size and architectural magnificence. The present building was designed by Bramante – various other famous artists participated, including Michelangelo, who designed the dome – and it was constructed between 1506 and 1615.

San Marino

The republic of San Marino forms an enclave within Italian territory, but is an independent sovereign state completely surrounded by Italian soil, lying between Emilia-Romagna and the Marche, not far from the Adriatic coast. At just over 60 sq. km (23 sq. miles) in area, it is one of the smallest states in the world.

santo patrono

In Italy the worship of saints is widespread. The patron saint of a town or community is considered to be its protector. His or her saint's day is a religious holiday on which schools, offices, and most shops are closed. It is celebrated with a special mass and processions. In towns and cities, illuminations are put up and there are stalls and sometimes a fair, in a mixture of the sacred and the secular.

Sardo

Sardo is Sardinia's traditional language. It is considered to be an independent language because of its many differences from Italian and its long independent history. Sardinian preserves many features derived from Latin which were lost in Italian, e.g. the k-sound in words like *chelu* (Italian *cielo*).

Scala, La

The Teatro alla Scala, the Milan opera house, is one of the most famous opera houses in the world. Built in 1776–78, it has recently undergone a programme of restoration, during which the Teatro degli Arcimboldi, outside the city, staged its productions.

scuola

The Italian system provides for primary schools, middle schools, and secondary schools. Primary school lasts for five years from the age of six, middle school lasts for three years, and secondary school for five. Primary and middle schools all follow the same curriculum but there are a number of different types of secondary schools: scientific, classical, linguistic, and artistic grammar schools, various technical and commercial institutes, and schools for training nursery school teachers (*see also* **LICEO**).

Senato The upper house of the Italian Parliament. Three hundred and fifteen senators are elected by universal suffrage by citizens over 25 years of age. Senators must be at least 40 years old. These 315 seats are elected on a regional basis, i.e. they are split between the regions in proportion to population. The elected senators are joined by ex-heads of state and life senators. These are nominated by the **PRESIDENTE DELLA REPUBBLICA** from people who have given exceptional service to the country in the scientific, social, artistic, or literary fields.

settimana bianca
A winter holiday spent with family or schoolfriends in a ski resort.

Seven Hills of Rome
A group of seven small hills lying east of the River Tiber. According to tradition, the ancient city of Rome was founded by Romulus on the Palatine hill. The city gradually spread to cover the other six, the **CAPITOLINE**, Quirinal (**QUIRINALE**), Viminal (**VIMINALE**), Esquiline, Caelian, and Aventine hills. The hills are no longer a prominent geographical feature in modern Rome, but some are still associated with districts that have a distinctive character. The Capitoline hill, for instance, remains a seat of government, just as it was in Roman times.

sindaco
The mayor is the head of local government and holds power for four years. He chairs and represents the council and municipal committee.

Sistine Chapel
A chapel in the Vatican, built by Pope Sixtus IV. In 1505, Pope Julius II commissioned Michelangelo to decorate the ceiling with a series of scenes from the book of Genesis. Michelangelo also painted his vision of the *Last Judgement* on the east wall.

spaghetti western
A low-budget western made in Europe by an Italian director or production company, often in English and with an American star, usually featuring lots of explicit violence. The best and most famous of these films are *A Fistful of Dollars*, *For a Few Dollars More*, and *The Good, the Bad and the Ugly*, directed by Sergio Leone.

spumante
A sparkling white wine, sometimes seen as the poor relation of French champagne but also often greatly prized. It can be dry or sweet and always features on Italian Christmas, New Year, and party menus.

stabilimento balneare
A stretch of beach equipped with parasols, loungers, showers, huts, perhaps a swimming-pool, and a bar. There is a charge for using it. These beach clubs vary from large and crowded to very chic and exclusive, and from fairly basic to luxurious. Many of them organize sports tournaments, card games, beauty contests, and dances.

stellone
A big star, *stellone d'Italia* or *stellone italico* (star of Italy) which, since the **RISORGIMENTO**, has been associated with the personification of Italy (a woman with a star on her forehead or in her crown). Representing a beacon of hope in times of difficulty, it became part of the coat of arms of the unified kingdom and was then incorporated into the emblem of the

Republic. Today it is mainly used ironically or polemically to criticize the tendency of Italians – a sign both of their vitality and of their happy-go-lucky attitude and fatalism – to trust to good luck rather than to hard work to get them through times of national crisis.

Svizzera

Italian is one of the four national languages of Switzerland, but is spoken widely only in the canton of Ticino in the south of the country, and to a lesser extent in Grisons. Around half a million people in Switzerland have Italian as their first language. Their language rights are protected by the Swiss constitution.

tabaccaio

The tobacconist sells cigarettes and tobacco and is also the only shop apart from the post office where you can buy revenue stamps and postage stamps. It also sells bus tickets and other products. Sometimes there is also a bar. Its sign features a white 'T' on a black background.

Tangentopoli

A name ('kick-back city') widely used in the Italian media to refer first to Milan, where the judiciary investigated a series of episodes of corruption, and then extended to mean the whole system of illicit financing used by the governing parties, unmasked by the famous **MANI PULITE** inquiry in 1992–93.

Telecom Italia

One of the largest telephone companies supplying both land lines and mobile phones.

terrone

A pejorative, racist term typically applied by northern Italians to southern Italians, and usually accompanied by equally disparaging adjectives such as 'ignorant', 'filthy', and 'uncivilized'. The word derives from *terra* (earth, land), depicting the typical southerner as an argicultural labourer. It became widespread in the 1960s and 1970s when large-scale immigration from the south to the industrial northwest took place. In present-day Italy, racist insults are mainly reserved for despised foreign immigrants (**EXTRACOMUNITARI**), while the term *terrone* is less widely used and has even acquired a jocular tone (the more so since it is used by southerners themselves). The pejorative sense has, however, been given a new lease of life in the anti-southern polemics of the Northern League (*see* **PARTITI POLITICI**).

trattoria

A trattoria used to be distinguishable from a restaurant because it was simpler, often family-run, and less expensive. Nowadays it is merely a 'typical' local restaurant, serving traditional local dishes in a country-style setting. It can also be very sophisticated, and sometimes quite expensive.

triangolo industriale

A name for the industrial zone of northwestern Italy, a triangle with the cities of Milan, Turin, and Genoa at its corners, where modern industry began to develop at the end of the 19th century. It has been the major productive centre in Italy, attracting large-scale internal immigration from the south, especially between the

1950s and 1970s. The subsequent decline of heavy industry has transformed the industrial triangle into an area where small and medium-sized enterprises and the tertiary sector now predominate. Other models of strong development have emerged elsewhere, particularly in the areas around Venice (*see* **NORDEST**).

Tricolore

The Italian national flag: green, white, and red in vertical bands of equal width. It was designed at the end of 1700s and adopted as the flag of the republic after the Second World War.

Uffizi

A vast art gallery in Florence, famous for its collection of works by Italian Renaissance painters such as Botticelli, Piero della Francesca, Leonardo, and Raphael. The building containing the gallery was built in the late 15th century to house government administration – hence its name, which means 'offices'.

Ultima cena

The Last Supper, one of Leonardo da Vinci's most famous works, painted on the wall of the refectory of the monastery of St Maria delle Grazie in Milan. Leonardo was experimenting with a new technique for fresco (painting directly onto fresh plaster), which was not altogether successful. As a result, the painting has deteriorated badly over the centuries and been restored several times.

Università

Italy's first university was founded in Bologna in 1088, and they are still run on traditional lines. Oral exams are the norm. Students study for a number of exams, which can be taken in a flexible order. For this reason Italian students often combine study with a job. The drop-out rate is high.

Valle dei Templi

An archaeological zone in the province of Agrigento that provides the most glorious evidence of Ancient Greek civilization in Sicily. The remains of many temples are to be found on a ridge (not a valley as the name suggests), among the almond trees. Built in the Doric style in the 5th century BC, the temples were burnt down by the Carthaginians, restored by the Romans in the 1st century AD, then half-destroyed by earthquakes and plundered over the following centuries, so that the only one that now remains intact is the magnificent Tempio della Concordia.

Vaticano

The Vatican (also called Vatican City) has been an independent state within the city of Rome and the seat of the Pope since 1929. The Vatican Palace, which surrounds **ST PETER'S**, is the Pope's residence and houses artistic treasures such as the **SISTINE CHAPEL** and Raphael's frescos, as well as museums.

Venetian Republic

For over a thousand years, from 697 to 1797, the island city of Venice and the mainland territory surrounding it formed an independent republic ruled by an elected chief magistrate (the *doge*) and a council of ten (the *dieci*). From the time of the Crusades to the late 15th century, Venice was the major power in the eastern Mediterranean and became enormously wealthy thanks to its trade with the Muslim world and Asia. From the 16th century, however, its power began to wane. It lost its independence when conquered by Napoleon, and eventually became part of Italy in 1866.

Vespa

A motor scooter designed by aeronautical engineer, Corradino D'Ascanio, for the Piaggio company just after World War II. D'Ascanio's brief was to design a vehicle that would be affordable, easy to drive, carry a passenger, and not get the driver's clothes dirty – hence the trademark upswept mudguard behind the handlebars. The Vespa is particularly associated with the 1950s and 1960s in Italy, but it remains a popular means of transport to this day.

Vesuvius

An active volcano, near Naples, that has erupted many times, most notably in AD 79, when it overwhelmed the ancient Roman cities of Pompeii and Herculaneum. The explosion buried the area under volcanic ash, preserving many of the buildings, as well as the bodies of those who did not flee, virtually intact. The towns were only rediscovered in the 18th century; excavations have revealed a stunning record of daily life in Roman times.

vigile urbano

This policeman is responsible for controlling traffic and levying fines for traffic offences, for environmental protection, and for ensuring that municipal regulations and town laws are observed. He also deals with social problems, such as abandoned children, and the monitoring of refugees' and travellers' camps.

Viminale

A media name for the Italian Ministry of Internal Affairs (or Home Office), which since 1961 has been housed in the Palazzo del Viminale, a vast Renaissance-style building erected in the early 20th century on the Viminal hill in Rome (*see* **SEVEN HILLS OF ROME**).

vino

Wine is produced in every region of Italy, and the Italian wine-making tradition dates back 4,000 years to prehistoric times. Italy produces some white wine, but is mainly renowned for its red wines. The most internationally famous of these is Chianti, produced in Tuscany. Other famous varieties include Valpolicella, Barolo, Marsala, and Soave. High-quality Italian wines are labelled *DOC* (**DENOMINAZIONE DI ORIGINE CONTROLLATA**) or *DOCG* (*denominazione di origine controllata e garantita*).

-etter-writing

Christmas and New Year wishes (informal)

Natale 2007

Cari Teresa e Federico,

Buon Natale e Felice Anno Nuovo

Vi auguro con tutto il cuore un anno pieno di belle sorprese e spero che ci sia al più presto l'occasione di rivederci.

Un abbraccio a tutti e due,

Paola

- You write the date like this on greetings cards. For Easter you write Pasqua and the year. For other occasions (birthdays, etc.) you can write the date in full: *6 febbraio 2007* with the number, the month without a capital letter, then the year, or as a number: *6/2/07*.
- Standard greeting for Christmas and New Year cards.

Christmas and New Year wishes (formal)

On the envelope:

Gentile Dott. Bossi e famiglia

- In Italy fewer people send Christmas cards than in Great Britain. Young people don't send them; it's considered slightly formal. If you send a present to someone you might attach a card, but if you exchange presents in person you don't normally give them a card, just wish them *Buon Natale*. The same goes for birthdays.

Monza, Natale 2007

BUON NATALE E FELICE ANNO NUOVO

I miei più sentiti auguri a Lei **1** e alla famiglia

Fausto Mameli

- Inside greetings cards you can write the place you are writing from in front of the date.

1 *Lei* is written with a capital letter in more formal letters.

Invitation to a wedding and wedding reception

Filippo Bartolini *Cristiana Tedeschi*

Annunciano il loro matrimonio

Chiesa di S. Jacopo – Siena
Sabato 22 maggio 2007 – ore 16.30

Siena –
Via della Salute, 50

Volterra –
Via A. Diaz, 6

- Invitations to weddings are called 'partecipazioni' and are written or printed.
- Very formal invitations are sent out by the parents who are announcing their son's or daughter's wedding.

Filippo e Cristiana

dopo la cerimonia saranno lieti di salutare
parenti ed amici presso la
Villa 'Il Poggio'
Via Marradi 45 – Siena

R.S.V.P.

Invitation to a christening

Invitations to parties are usually by word of mouth, while for christenings announcements are usually sent out.

Fabrizio Castelli e Katherine Ferguson
partecipano la nascita di Luigi

Vi invitano al suo battesimo nel Duomo di Barga
il 15 febbraio 2007 alle ore 12.00
e al rinfresco che seguirà alla Locanda da Gabriele
in località la Mocchia di Barga

RSVP tel. 0583 – 861042

- When a phone number is given after RSVP you reply to the invitation by phone.

Accepting an invitation (formal)

CARLO E BEATRICE BUOZZI

ringraziano calorosamente per il gentile invito
e sono lieti di poter partecipare.

Invitation (informal)

Cara Claudia

È un po' che non ci sentiamo ma spero che tutto vada bene, sia con Andrea che con l'università. Il 7 agosto è il mio compleanno e pensavo di fare una festa. Che ne dici **1** *di venire qui a Napoli? Naturalmente sei invitata a casa mia per qualche giorno e ne approfitteremo per fare un po' di chiacchiere e un po' di mare. Fammi sapere al più presto! Spero tanto che tu venga, da sola o accompagnata, se tu e Andrea state ancora insieme. Il mio indirizzo email è grazia@hotmail.com.*

Un bacione **2** *e a prestissimo,*
Grazia

- Invitations to parties are usually made in person or on the phone, unless it's a really formal occasion.

1 For a letter to a friend you use the 'tu' form.

2 This affectionate ending is used with close friends or relatives. Other informal endings are *Baci* or *Un abbraccio*.

Accepting an invitation (informal)

24 aprile 2007

Cara Grazia

Quanto tempo! Scusa se non mi sono fatta più viva ma tra gli esami e altre storie il tempo è volato. Certo che vengo giù a Napoli. L'ultimo esame lo dovrei avere a fine luglio e non ho ancora programmato niente per le vacanze, tanto più che adesso sono sola (mollata da Andrea due mesi fa, ma senza troppi drammi). Ora che ci siamo rimesse in contatto prometto di non sparire e non vedo l'ora di rivederti di persona. Torno a studiare.

Un abbraccio,
Claudia

- In informal letters you write the date at the top but not your address.
- In replies to informal invitations you also use only the Christian name, the 'tu' form and an affectionate ending.

Inquiry to a tourist office

9 febbraio 2007

Azienda di promozione turistica
Piazza Duomo 2
07100 Sassari

Gentili Signori

Sto programmando di trascorrere le vacanze in Sardegna con la famiglia e sarei grato se volessero inviarmi un elenco delle case vacanza e dei campeggi nella zona di San Teodoro.

Grazie per l'attenzione.

Distinti saluti

Brian McGregor

Brian McGregor
16 Victoria Road
London
SW2 5HU
Regno Unito

■ Standard formula for closing a formal letter.

Booking a hotel room

18 giugno 2007

Hotel La rosa
Corso del Partigiano, 56
22100 Como

Gentile Signora Pacini **1**
In seguito alla conversazione telefonica di stamattina, le scrivo per confermare la prenotazione di una camera doppia con bagno **2** dall'8 al 12 luglio. Mia moglie ed io arriveremo nel tardo pomeriggio di giovedì 8. Per ogni comunicazione urgente il mio numero di telefono è +44 031 5790 3352.

Cordiali saluti

P. Bromfield
Cardross Gardens
Edinburgh
EH2 5EG
Gran Bretagna

1 Alternatively you can write *Gentili Signori* if you don't know the name of the person you are writing to.

2 Or: *una camera singola/con doccia*

Booking a place in a campsite

Campeggio 'Il Gabbiano'
Via del Parco
14100 Asti

5 maggio 2007

Egregi signori,

il Vostro campeggio mi è stato segnalato dall'Ufficio del turismo di Asti. Vorrei prenotare una piazzola per la nostra tenda dal 5 al 15 agosto. Preferirei un posto tranquillo, possibilmente non troppo vicino al mini-market.

Resto in attesa di una Vostra conferma.

Cordiali saluti,

Mary J Stevens
55 Old Road
Wallingford OX10 5DH
Gran Bretagna

Cancelling a reservation

16 maggio 2007

Pensione La Torre
via Don Bosco 61
Chiusdino
Grosseto

Gentili Signori,

la settimana scorsa ho prenotato telefonicamente una camera singola dal 6 al 12 giugno. Sono molto spiacente ma, per motivi familiari, mi trovo costretta a rimandare il soggiorno in Toscana e perciò a disdire la prenotazione.

Sperando di non aver arrecato troppo disturbo, porgo distinti saluti.

Sally Lewis
56 Nelson Rd
Farnborough
GU14 9RK
Hants
UK

Sending an e-mail

The illustration shows a typical interface for sending e-mail.

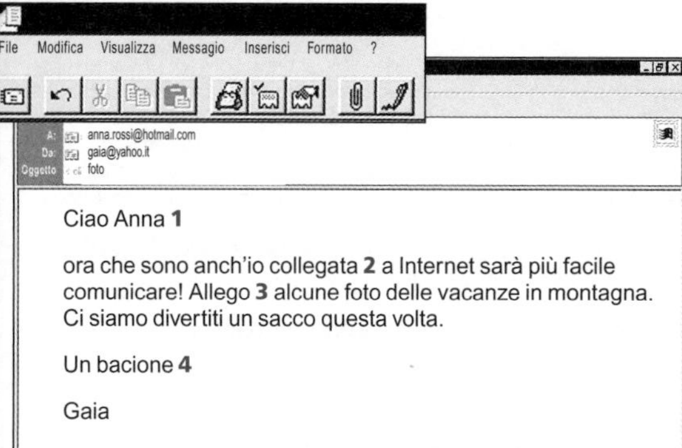

1 The beginning changes according to how formal it is. You can use *caro/cara* or leave it out.

2 *Collegata* if the person writing is a girl or woman.

3 *Allegare* means to enclose and also to attach in e-mails.

4 In more formal e-mails you can end with '*Distinti saluti*' like in letters.

Texting

The basic principles governing Italian SMS abbreviations are similar to those governing English SMS. Certain words or syllables can be represented by letters or numbers that sound the same but take up less space. The word 'sei', for example, can be replaced by '6', and the word 'che' shortened to 'ke'. Another way of shortening words and phrases is simply to omit certain letters, especially vowels. For example, 'comunque' becomes 'cmq' and 'ci vediamo dopo' becomes 'cvd'.

As in English, 'faccine' (emoticons) are very popular, and some of the more established ones are included in the table below.

Glossary of Italian SMS abbreviations

Abbreviation	Full word
"xxx"	tanti baci
+o-	più o meno
6 la +	sei la migliore
6 sxme	sei speciale per me
amò	amore
ap	a presto
axitivo	aperitivo
ba	bacio
cel	cellulare
cmq	comunque
cvd	ci vediamo dopo
dom	domani
dx	destra
ke	che
-male	meno male
midi	mi dispiace
MMT+	mi manchi tantissimo
msg	messaggio
Nm	numero
Nn	non

Abbreviation	Full word
qlc	qualcuno
qls	qualcosa
risp	rispondimi
sx	sinistra
t tel + trd	ti telefono + tardi
tat	ti amo tanto
tel	telefono
tipe	ti penso
to	ti odio
ttp	torno tra un pò
tu6	tu sei
tvb	ti voglio bene
tvtb	ti voglio tanto bene
vng dp	vengo dopo
x	per
x fv	per favore
x me	per me
xdere	perdere
xh	per ora
xké	perché

Emoticons*	
:-)	sorriso
:-(	tristezza
:-D	risata
;-)	strizzare l'occhio
:-*	baciare
!(	occhio nero
:-/	scettico
:'(	piangere
#:-o	traumatizzato
:-i	penso
:-o	sorpreso
:-q	nauseato
:-P	linguaccia
$)	felice di aver vinto la lotteria
:*)	pagliaccio
*<:-)	Babbo Natale

*NB: the '-' which depicts the nose is often omitted or replaced by an '**o**' e.g. :) or **:o)**

The Italian words you must know

A

bbastanza
abbigliamento (*m*)
bitare
abito (*m*)
ccadere
ccanto a
ccendere
ccettare
ccomodarsi
ccompagnare
aceto (*m*)
acqua (*f*)
desso
adolescente (*m/f*)
adulto (*m*)
aereo (*m*)
aeroporto (*m*)
ffittare
affitto (*m*)
agnello (*m*)
gosto
iutare
aiuto (*m*)
albergo (*m*)
albero (*m*)
lcolico
limentari (m)
llegro
llora
lto
ltro
lzarsi
mare
ambiente (*m*)
ambulanza (*f*)
michevole
amico/a (*m/f*)
mmalato
nche
ncora
andare (a)
l'angolo (*m*)
l'animale (*m*)
l'anno (*m*)
annoiarsi
antico
l'antipasto (*m*)
antipatico
anziano
aperto
a piedi
l'appartamento (*m*)
appena
l'appuntamento (*m*)
aprile
aprire
l'arancia (*f*)
arancione
l'argento (*m*)
l'aria (*f*)
l'armadio (*m*)
arrabbiato
arrivare
arrivederci
l'arrivo (*m*)
l'arte (*f*)
l'articolo (*m*)
l'artista (*m/f*)
l'ascensore (*m*)
l'asciugamano (*m*)
asciutto
ascoltare
aspettare
l'aspirina (*f*)
l'assegno (*m*)
assente
attraversare
augurare
l'aula (*f*)
l'autista (*m/f*)
l'autobus (m *inv*)
l'autonoleggio (*m*)
l'autostrada (*f*)
l'autunno (*m*)
avanti
avere
avvenire
l'avventura (*f*)
l'azienda (*f*)
azzurro

B

il babbo
baciare
il bacio
il bagaglio
bagnato
il bagno
ballare
il ballo
il/la bambino/a
la banca
il banco
la barba
basso
bello
bene
benvenuto/a
la benzina
bere
bianco
la bibita
la biblioteca
il bicchiere
il biglietto
biondo
la birra
il biscotto
la bistecca
blu (*inv*)
la bocca
la borsa
il bosco
la bottiglia
il braccio
bravo
bruno
brutto
la buca delle lettere
buon anno!
buon compleanno!
buonasera!
buongiorno
buono
il burro
la busta
buttare

C

il caffè (*inv*)
il calcio
caldo
le calze
cambiare
il cambio
la camera
il/la cameriere/a
la camicia/camicetta
la campagna
il campeggio
il canale
il cane
cantare
i capelli
capire
il cappello
il cappotto
la carne
il carnevale
caro/carino
la carriera
la carta di credito
il cartello

la cartolina
i cartoni animati
la casa
la casalinga
il casco
la cassa
il cassetto
castano
il castello
la cattedrale
cattivo
il cavallo
il cellulare
la cena
il centimetro
il centro
cercare
il cerotto
certamente
che (cosa)
chi
chiacchierare
chiamare/si
chiaro
la chiave
la chiesa
il chilogrammo/
chilo
il chilometro
chiudere
chiuso
ciao
il cibo
il cielo
cin cin
il cinema
la cintura
il cioccolato/tino
la cipolla
circa
la città
il clima
la coda
il cognome
la colazione
i collant
la collezione
la collina
il colore
il coltello
come
cominciare
comodo
il/la compagno/a
il compleanno
completare
completo
comprare
compreso
con
il concerto
il congelatore
congratulazioni!
conoscere
il consiglio
contanti
contento
continuare
il conto
il contorno
contro
controllare
la coperta
il corpo
correre
corretto
il corso
corto
la costa
costare
costoso
cotto
credere
crudo
il cucchiaio
la cucina
cucinare
il/la cugino/a
cui
il cuore
il cuscino

D

da
d'accordo
dappertutto
dare
la data
davanti a
davvero
decidere
delizioso
il denaro
il dentifricio
il/la dentista
dentro
desiderare
destra
di
dicembre
di solito
dietro
differente
la differenza
difficile
dimenticare
dire
diretto
il direttore/la
direttrice
il/la dirigente
diritto/dritto
disoccupato
dispiacere
disponibile
la distanza
il dito
la ditta
il divano
diventare
diverso
divertente
il divertimento
divertirsi
divieto
divorziato
la doccia
il documentario
il documento
la dogana
il dolce
dolce
il dolore
la domanda
domandare
domani
(la) domenica
la donna
dopo
doppio
dormire
il/la dottore/ssa
dove, dov'è
dovere
la droga
dunque
il duomo
durante
durare
duro

E

e/ed
eccellente
ecco
l'economia (*f*)
economico
l'edicola (*f*)
elegante
elettrico
entrare
l'entrata (*f*)
entro
l'erba (*f*)
l'errore (*m*)
esatto
l'esempio (*m*)
l'espresso (*m*)
essere
l'est (*m*)
l'estate (*f*)
l'estero (*m*)
l'età (*f inv*)
l'etto (*m*)
l'euro (*m*)
europeo

F

la fabbrica
la faccia
facile
falso

fame
la famiglia
famoso
fantastico
fare
la farmacia
febbraio
la febbre
felice
feriale
le ferie
Ferragosto
la festa
festivo
una fetta
fidanzato/a
la fiera
il/la figlio/a
il film
finalmente
la fine
il fine settimana (*inv*)
la finestra
finire
fino a
il fiore
la firma
firmare
il fiume
la foglia
la fontana
la forchetta
la foresta
il formaggio
il fornaio
forse
forte
la fotografia/foto
fra
la fragola
il francobollo
la frase
il fratello
freddo
fresco
il frigorifero
la frittata
fritto
la frutta
fumare
il fungo
funzionare
fuori .... (di)
il futuro

G

il gabinetto
il Galles
gallese
la gamba
il gatto
gelare
la gelateria
il gelato
il gelo
il/la gemello/a
il genitore
gennaio
la gente
gentile
gettare
il ghiaccio
già
la giacca
giallo
il giardino
il ginocchio
giocare
il gioco
la gioielleria
il giornale
il giorno
giovane
(il) giovedì
il giro
la gita
giù
giugno
giusto
la gola
la gonna
il grado
il grammo
la Gran Bretagna
grande
il grande magazzino
grasso
gratis
grazie
grigio
grosso
il gruppo
guadagnare
il guanto
guardare
guasto
la guida
guidare
gusto

I

l'idea
ieri
imparare
importante
impossibile
improvvisamente
in
in bocca al lupo!
in orario
in ritardo
incluso
l'incontro (*m*)
l'incrocio (*m*)
indietro
l'indirizzo (*m*)
l'industria (*f*)
inferiore
l'infermiere/a (*m/f*)
l'influenza (*f*)
l'informazione (*f*)
l'ingegnere (*m*)
l'Inghilterra (*f*)
inglese
l'inizio (*m*)
l'inquinamento (*m*)
l'insalata (*f*)
l'insegnante (*m/f*)
insieme
intelligente
interessante
l'intervista (*f*)
intorno (a)
l'inverno (*m*)
l'Irlanda (*f*)
irlandese
l'Italia (*f*)
italiano

L

là, lì
il lago
la lampada/ina
il lampone
largo
lasciare
il lato
il latte
la lattina
la laurea
il lavandino
la lavatrice
lavorare
il lavoro
la legge
leggere
leggero
il legno
lento
la lettera
il letto
la lettura
libero
la libreria
il libro
il liceo
lieto
la linea
la lingua
liscio
il litro
locale
lontano (da)
la luce
luglio
(il) lunedì
lungo
il luogo

M
ma
la macchina
la macchina fotografica
la macelleria
la madre
il/la maestro/a
maggio
maggiore
la maglia
magro
mai
il maiale
malato
male
la mamma
mandare
mangiare
la mano
la mappa
il mare
il marito
la marmellata
marrone
(il) martedì
marzo
massimo
il matrimonio
la mattina
la maturità
la medicina
il medico
medio
meglio
la mela
meno
mentre
il mercato
(il) mercoledì
la merenda
meridionale
il mese
il messaggio
la metà
la metropolitana
mettere
mezzanotte
mezzo/a
mezzogiorno
migliore
la minestra
minimo
minore
il minuto
misto
la moda
moderno
la moglie
molto
il momento
il mondo
la moneta
la montagna
morto
il muro
il museo
le mutande

N
il naso
Natale
nato
la natura
la nazionalità
neanche
la nebbia
necessario
negativo
il negozio
nero
nervoso
nessuno
la neve
niente
il/la nipote
no
la noce
noioso
noleggiare
il nome
non
non ancora
non vedo l'ora di
il/la nonno/a
nonostante
il nord
normale
la notizia
la notte
novembre
nulla
il numero
nuotare
nuovo
la nuvola

O
o (...o)
gli occhiali
l'occhio (*m*)
occidentale
occupato
l'odore (*m*)
oggi
ogni
l'olio (*m*)
l'oliva (*f*)
l'ombra (*f*)
l'ombrello (*m*)
l'opera (*f*)
ora
l'ora (*f*)
l'orario (*m*)
ordinare
l'orecchio (*m*)
orientale
l'oro (*m*)
l'orologio (*m*)
l'ospedale (*m*)
ottimo
ottobre
l'ovest (*m*)

P
il pacco
il padre
il padrone
il paesaggio
il paese
la paga
pagare
la pagina
un paio
la palestra
la palla
il pane
la panetteria
il panino
i pantaloni
il papà
il paragrafo
il parcheggio
il parco
il/la parente
la parete
parlare
la parola
il/la parrucchiere/a
la parte
la partenza
partire
la partita
Pasqua
il passaporto
passare (un esame)
il passato
il passeggero
passeggiare
la pasta
il pasto
la patata
le patate fritte
la patente
peggiore
la pelle
la penna
pensare
il/la pensionato/a
la pensione (completa)
il pepe
per
per caso
per favore
per piacere
la pera
perché
perdere
pericoloso
la periferia

permesso
però
la persona
pesante
il pesce
pessimo
il pettine
il pezzo
piangere
il piano
il pianterreno
il piatto
la piazza
piccante
piccolo
il piede
pieno di
pigro
la pioggia
la piscina
la pista
più
plastica
poco/po'
poi
la polizia
il pollo
il pomeriggio
il pomodoro
il pompiere
il ponte
la porta
il portafoglio
portare
positivo
possibile
la posta
il posto
il pranzo
preferire
prego
prendere
prenotare
la prenotazione
presentare
presente
presto
le previsioni del tempo
il prezzo
prima di
la primavera
privato
il problema
il/la professore/ssa
il profumo
il progetto
il programma
pronto
proprio
il prosciutto
prossimo
provare
la pubblicità
pulire
pulito
il punto
purtroppo

Q

qua, qui
quadrato
il quadro
qualche
il/la quale
quale
la qualità (*inv*)
quando
quanto
il quartiere
quasi
quello
questo
quindi

R

raccontare
il racconto
la radio (*inv*)
il raffreddore
il/la ragazzo/a
rallentare
rapido
il regalo
il registratore
il Regno Unito
la regola
restare
il resto
ricco
ricevere
riciclare
ricordare
ridere
riempire
i rifiuti
la riga
rimanere
ripetere
riposarsi
il riso
risparmiare
rispondere
il ristorante
la rivista
rosa (*inv*)
rosso
il rumore
rumoroso

S

(il) sabato
la sala da pranzo
salato
il saldo
il sale
salire
il salotto
salutare
la salute
il sangue
sano
sapere
il sapone
il sapore
la Sardegna
sardo
sbagliato
lo sbaglio
gli scacchi
le scale
lo scambio
la scarpa
la scatola
scegliere
la scelta
la scena
scendere
la schiena
sciare
la sciarpa
la scienza
lo sciopero
lo sconto
lo scontrino
scorso
la Scozia
scozzese
scrivere
la scuola
se
secco
il secolo
secondo
un secondo
sedersi
la sedia
il segnale
il/la segretario/a
seguente
il semaforo
sembrare
sempre
senso unico
sentire
sentirsi
senza
la sera
serio
il servizio
la sete
settembre
settentrionale
la settimana
sì
la Sicilia
siciliano
la sigaretta
significare
la signora
il signore

la signorina
il silenzio
simpatico
sinistra
il soggiorno
il sogno
i soldi
il sole
solo
soltanto
sopra
la sorella
il sorriso
sottile
sotto
i sottotitoli
la spalla
spazioso
lo specchio
speciale
la specialità (*inv*)
spedire
spegnere
spendere
sperare
la spesa
spesso
lo spettacolo
la spiaggia
gli spiccioli
spiegare
spingere
sporco
lo sport
sposarsi
sposato
lo spuntino
la squadra
la stagione
stamattina
stanco
stanotte

la stanza
stare
stasera
la stazione
la stella
stesso
lo stipendio
lo stivale
lo stomaco
la storia
la strada
straniero
stretto
lo/la studente/ssa
studiare
lo studio
stupido
su
subito
succedere
il sud
suonare
il suono
superiore
il supermercato
il supplemento
lo svantaggio
svegliarsi

T

la tabaccheria
tacere
la taglia
tardi
la tavola
il tavolo
la tazza
il tè (*inv*)
il teatro
telefonare
il telefonino
il telefono

la televisione
la temperatura
il tempo
il tempo libero
il temporale
la terra
la tessera
la testa
il tetto
tirare
toccare
il tonno
tornare
la torta
il/la tossicodipendente
la tovaglia
tra
il traffico
il traghetto
tranquillo
trascorrere
il trasporto
il treno
triste
troppo
trovare
trovarsi
il/la turista
turistico
tutto

U

l'uccello (*m*)
l'ufficio (*m*)
ultimo
l'università (*inv*)
l'uomo (*m*)
l'uovo (*m*)
uscire
l'uscita (*f*)
utile

V

il vantaggio
vecchio
vedere
veloce
(il) venerdì
venire
il vento
veramente
verde
la verdura
la verità
vero
verso
vestirsi
il vestito
il vetro
la via
viaggiare
il viaggio
vicino (a)
vincere
il vino
viola (*inv*)
visitare
la vista
la vita
il vitello
vivace
vivere
la voce
volentieri
volere
la volta
il voto
vuoto

Z

lo zaino
lo/la zio/a
lo zucchero
la zuppa

Aa

a /ə/, *accentato* /eɪ/ indef art; *davanti a una vocale* **an**

····➤ un m, una f; (*before s + consonant, gn, ps and z*) uno; (*before feminine noun starting with a vowel*) un'; **a tiger is a feline** la tigre è un felino; **a knife and fork** un coltello e una forchetta; **a Mr Smith is looking for you** un certo signor Smith ti sta cercando

····➤ (*each*) a; **£2 a kilo/a head** due sterline al chilo/a testa

! when *a* refers to professions, it is not translated: **I am a lawyer** sono avvocato

A /eɪ/ n (Mus) la m inv

aback /ə'bæk/ adv **be taken ~** essere preso in contropiede

abandon /ə'bændən/ vt abbandonare; (give up) rinunciare a •n abbandono m. **~ed** adj abbandonato

abashed /ə'bæʃt/ adj imbarazzato

abate /ə'beɪt/ vi calmarsi

abattoir /'æbətwɑ:(r)/ n mattatoio m

abbey /'æbɪ/ n abbazia f

abbreviat|e /ə'bri:vɪeɪt/ vt abbreviare. **~ion** n abbreviazione f

abdicat|e /'æbdɪkeɪt/ vi abdicare •vt rinunciare a. **~ion** n abdicazione f

abdom|en /'æbdəmən/ n addome m. **~inal** adj addominale

abduct /əb'dʌkt/ vt rapire. **~ion** n rapimento m

abhor /əb'hɔ:(r)/ vt (pt/pp **abhorred**) aborrire. **~rence** n orrore m

abid|e /ə'baɪd/ vt (pt/pp **abided**) (tolerate) sopportare •**abide by** vi rispettare. **~ing** adj perpetuo

ability /ə'bɪlətɪ/ n capacità f inv

abject /'æbdʒekt/ adj (poverty) degradante; (apology) umile; (coward) abietto

ablaze /ə'bleɪz/ adj in fiamme; **be ~ with light** risplendere di luci

able /'eɪbl/ adj capace, abile; **be ~ to do sth** poter fare qcsa; **were you ~ to...?** sei riuscito a...? **~-'bodied** adj robusto; (Mil) abile

ably /'eɪblɪ/ adv abilmente

abnormal /æb'nɔ:ml/ adj anormale. **~ity** n anormalità f inv. **~ly** adv in modo anormale

aboard /ə'bɔ:d/ adv & prep a bordo

abol|ish /ə'bɒlɪʃ/ vt abolire. **~ition** n abolizione f

abomina|ble /ə'bɒmɪnəbl/ adj abominevole

abort /ə'bɔ:t/ vt fare abortire; fig annullare. **~ion** n aborto m; **have an ~ion** abortire. **~ive** adj (attempt) infruttuoso

abound /ə'baʊnd/ vi abbondare; **~ in** abbondare di

about /ə'baʊt/ adv (here and there) [di] qua e [di] là; (approximately) circa; **be ~** (illness, tourists:) essere in giro; **be up and ~** essere alzato; **leave sth lying ~** lasciare in giro qcsa •prep (concerning) su; (in the region of) intorno a; (here and there in) per; **what is the book/the film ~?** di cosa parla il libro/il film?; **he wants to see you – what ~?** ti vuole vedere – a che proposito?; **talk/know ~** parlare/sapere di; **I know nothing ~ it** non ne so niente; **~ 5 o'clock** intorno alle 5; **travel ~ the world** viaggiare per il mondo; **be ~ to do sth** stare per fare qcsa; **how ~ going to the cinema?** e se andassimo al cinema?

about: ~-'face n, **~-'turn** n dietro front m inv

above /ə'bʌv/ adv & prep sopra; **~ all** soprattutto

above: ~-'board adj onesto. **~-'mentioned** adj suddetto

abrasive /ə'breɪsɪv/ adj abrasivo; (remark) caustico •n abrasivo m

abreast /ə'brest/ adv fianco a fianco; **come ~ of** allinearsi con; **keep ~ of** tenersi al corrente di

abroad /ə'brɔ:d/ adv all'estero

a

abrupt /ə'brʌpt/ adj brusco

abscess /'æbsɪs/ n ascesso m

abscond /əb'skɒnd/ vi fuggire

absence /'æbsəns/ n assenza f; (lack) mancanza f

absent¹ /'æbsənt/ adj assente

absent² /æb'sent/ vt ~ **oneself** essere assente

absentee /æbsən'ti:/ n assente mf

absent-minded /æbsənt'maɪndɪd/ adj distratto

absolute /'æbsəlu:t/ adj assoluto; **an ~ idiot** un perfetto idiota. **~ly** adv assolutamente; (!: indicating agreement) esattamente

absolve /əb'zɒlv/ vt assolvere

absorb /əb'sɔ:b/ vt assorbire; **~ed in** assorto in. **~ent** adj assorbente

absorption /əb'sɔ:pʃn/ n assorbimento m; (in activity) concentrazione f

abstain /əb'steɪn/ vi astenersi (**from** da)

abstemious /əb'sti:mɪəs/ adj moderato

abstention /əb'stenʃn/ n (Pol) astensione f

abstract /'æbstrækt/ adj astratto •n astratto m; (summary) estratto m

absurd /əb'sɜ:d/ adj assurdo. **~ity** n assurdità f inv

abundan|ce /ə'bʌndəns/ n abbondanza f. **~t** adj abbondante

abuse¹ /ə'bju:z/ vt (misuse) abusare di; (insult) insultare; (ill-treat) maltrattare

abus|e² /ə'bju:s/ n abuso m; (verbal) insulti mpl; (ill-treatment) maltrattamento m. **~ive** adj offensivo

abysmal /ə'bɪzml/ adj ! pessimo; (ignorance) abissale

abyss /ə'bɪs/ n abisso m

academic /ækə'demɪk/ adj teorico; (qualifications, system) scolastico; **be ~** (person:) avere predisposizione allo studio •n docente mf universitario, -a

academy /ə'kædəmɪ/ n accademia f; (of music) conservatorio m

accelerat|e /ək'seləreɪt/ vt/i accelerare. **~ion** n accelerazione f. **~or** n (Auto) acceleratore m

accent /'æksənt/ n accento m

accept /ək'sept/ vt accettare. **~able** adj accettabile. **~ance** n accettazione f

access /'ækses/ n accesso m. **~ible** adj accessibile

accession /ək'seʃn/ n (to throne) ascesa f al trono

accessory /ək'sesərɪ/ n accessorio m; (Jur) complice mf

accident /'æksɪdənt/ n incidente m; (chance) caso m; **by ~** per caso; (unintentionally) senza volere; **I'm sorry, it was an ~** mi dispiace, non l'ho fatto apposta. **~al** adj (meeting) casuale; (death) incidentale; (unintentional) involontario. **~ally** adv per caso; (unintentionally) inavvertitamente

acclaim /ə'kleɪm/ n acclamazione f •vt acclamare (**as** come)

accolade /'ækəleɪd/ n riconoscimento m

accommodat|e /ə'kɒmədeɪt/ vt ospitare; (oblige) favorire. **~ing** adj accomodante. **~ion** n (place to stay) sistemazione f

accompan|iment /ə'kʌmpənɪmənt/ n accompagnamento m. **~ist** n (Mus) accompagnatore, -trice mf

accompany /ə'kʌmpənɪ/ vt (pt/pp **-ied**) accompagnare

accomplice /ə'kʌmplɪs/ n complice mf

accomplish /ə'kʌmplɪʃ/ vt (achieve) concludere; realizzare (aim). **~ed** ad[j] dotato; (fact) compiuto. **~ment** n realizzazione f; (achievement) risultat[o] m; (talent) talento m

accord /ə'kɔ:d/ n (treaty) accordo m; **with one ~** tutti d'accordo; **of his own ~** di sua spontanea volontà. **~ance** n **in ~ance with** in conformità di o a

according /ə'kɔ:dɪŋ/ adv **~ to** secondo. **~ly** adv di conseguenza

accordion /ə'kɔ:dɪən/ n fisarmonica

accost /ə'kɒst/ vt abbordare

account /ə'kaʊnt/ n conto m; (report) descrizione f; (of eye-witness) resoconto m; **~s** pl (Comm) conti mpl; **on ~ of** a causa di; **on no ~** per nessun motivo; **on this ~** per questo motivo; **on my ~** per causa mia; **of no** ~ di nessuna importanza; **take into** ~ tener conto di •**account for** vi (explain) spiegare; (person:) render conto di; (constitute) costituire. ~**ability** n responsabilità f inv. ~**able** adj responsabile (**for** di)

accountant /ə'kaʊntənt/ n (bookkeeper) contabile mf; (consultant) commercialista mf

accumulat|e /ə'kju:mjʊleɪt/ vt accumulare •vi accumularsi. ~**ion** n accumulazione f

accura|cy /'ækʊrəsɪ/ n precisione f. ~**te** adj preciso. ~**tely** adv con precisione

accusation /ækjʊ'zeɪʃn/ n accusa f

accuse /ə'kju:z/ vt accusare; ~ **sb of doing sth** accusare qcno di fare qcsa. ~**d** n **the** ~**d** l'accusato m, l'accusata f

accustom /ə'kʌstəm/ vt abituare (**to** a); **grow** or **get** ~**ed to** abituarsi a. ~**ed** adj abituato

ace /eɪs/ n (Cards) asso m; (tennis) ace m inv

ache /eɪk/ n dolore m •vi dolere, far male; ~ **all over** essere tutto indolenzito

achieve /ə'tʃi:v/ vt ottenere (success); realizzare (goal, ambition). ~**ment** n (feat) successo m

acid /'æsɪd/ adj acido •n acido m. ~**ity** n acidità f. ~ '**rain** n pioggia f acida

acknowledge /ək'nɒlɪdʒ/ vt riconoscere; rispondere a (greeting); far cenno di aver notato (sb's presence); ~ **receipt of** accusare ricevuta di. ~**ment** n riconoscimento m; **send an** ~**ment of a letter** confermare il ricevimento di una lettera

acne /'æknɪ/ n acne f

acorn /'eɪkɔ:n/ n ghianda f

acoustic /ə'ku:stɪk/ adj acustico. ~**s** npl acustica fsg

acquaint /ə'kweɪnt/ vt ~ **sb with** metter qcno al corrente di; **be** ~**ed with** conoscere (person); essere a conoscenza di (fact). ~**ance** n (person) conoscente mf; **make sb's** ~**ance** fare la conoscenza di qcno

acquiesce /ækwɪ'es/ vi acconsentire (**to, in** a). ~**nce** n acquiescenza f

acquire /ə'kwaɪə(r)/ vt acquisire

acquisit|ion /ækwɪ'zɪʃn/ n acquisizione f. ~**ive** adj avido

acquit /ə'kwɪt/ vt (pt/pp **acquitted**) assolvere; ~ **oneself well** cavarsela bene. ~**tal** n assoluzione f

acre /'eɪkə(r)/ n acro m (= 4 047 m²)

acrid /'ækrɪd/ adj acre

acrimon|ious /ækrɪ'məʊnɪəs/ adj aspro. ~**y** n asprezza f

acrobat /'ækrəbæt/ n acrobata mf. ~**ic** adj acrobatico

across /ə'krɒs/ adv dall'altra parte; (wide) in larghezza; (not lengthwise) attraverso; (in crossword) orizzontale; **come** ~ **sth** imbattersi in qcsa; **go** ~ attraversare •prep (crosswise) di traverso su; (on the other side of) dall'altra parte di

act /ækt/ n atto m; (in variety show) numero m; **put on an** ~ [!] fare scena •vi agire; (behave) comportarsi; (Theat) recitare; (pretend) fingere; ~ **as** fare da •vt recitare (role). ~**ing** adj (deputy) provvisorio •n (Theat) recitazione f; (profession) teatro m. ~**ing profession** n professione f dell'attore

action /'ækʃn/ n azione f; (Mil) combattimento m; (Jur) azione f legale; **out of** ~ (machine:) fuori uso; **take** ~ agire. ~ '**replay** n replay m inv

activ|e /'æktɪv/ adj attivo. ~**ely** adv attivamente. ~**ity** n attività f inv

act|or /'æktə(r)/ n attore m. ~**ress** n attrice f

actual /'æktʃʊəl/ adj (real) reale. ~**ly** adv in realtà

acute /ə'kju:t/ adj acuto; (shortage, hardship) estremo

ad /æd/ n [!] pubblicità f inv

AD abbr (Anno Domini) d.C.

adapt /ə'dæpt/ vt adattare (play) •vi adattarsi. ~**ability** n adattabilità f. ~**able** adj adattabile

adaptation /ædæp'teɪʃn/ n (Theat) adattamento m

adapter, adaptor /ə'dæptə(r)/ n adattatore m; (two-way) presa f multipla

add /æd/ vt aggiungere; (Math) addizionare •vi addizionare; ~ **to** (fig: increase) aggravare. □ ~ **up** vt addizionare (figures) •vi addizionare; ~ **up to** ammontare a; **it doesn't ~ up** fig non quadra

adder /'ædə(r)/ n vipera f

addict /'ædɪkt/ n tossicodipendente mf; fig fanatico, -a mf

addict|ed /ə'dɪktɪd/ adj assuefatto (**to** a); **~ed to drugs** tossicodipendente; **he's ~ed to television** è videodipendente. **~ion** n dipendenza f; (to drugs) tossicodipendenza f. **~ive** adj **be ~ive** dare assuefazione

addition /ə'dɪʃn/ n (Math) addizione f; (thing added) aggiunta f; **in ~** in aggiunta. **~al** adj supplementare. **~ally** adv in più

additive /'ædɪtɪv/ n additivo m

address /ə'dres/ n indirizzo m; (speech) discorso m; **form of ~** formula f di cortesia •vt indirizzare; (speak to) rivolgersi a (person); tenere un discorso a (meeting). **~ee** n destinatario, -a mf

adept /'ædept/ adj & n esperto, -a mf (**at** in)

adequate /'ædɪkwət/ adj adeguato. **~ly** adv adeguatamente

adhere /əd'hɪə(r)/ vi aderire; **~ to** attenersi a (principles, rules)

adhesive /əd'hi:sɪv/ adj adesivo • n adesivo m

adjacent /ə'dʒeɪsənt/ adj adiacente

adjective /'ædʒɪktɪv/ n aggettivo m

adjourn /ə'dʒɜ:n/ vt/i aggiornare (**until** a). **~ment** n aggiornamento m

adjust /ə'dʒʌst/ vt modificare; regolare (focus, sound etc) •vi adattarsi. **~able** adj regolabile. **~ment** n adattamento m; (Techn) regolamento m

administer /əd'mɪnɪstə(r)/ vt amministrare; somministrare (medicine)

administrat|ion /ədmɪnɪ'streɪʃn/ n amministrazione f; (Pol) governo m. **~or** n amministratore, -trice mf

admirable /'ædmərəbl/ adj ammirevole

admiral /'ædmərəl/ n ammiraglio m

admiration /ædmə'reɪʃn/ n ammirazione f

admire /əd'maɪə(r)/ vt ammirare. **~r** n ammiratore, -trice mf

admission /əd'mɪʃn/ n ammissione f; (to hospital) ricovero m; (entry) ingresso m

admit /əd'mɪt/ vt (pt/pp **admitted**) (let in) far entrare; (to hospital) ricoverare; (acknowledge) ammettere •vi **~ to sth** ammettere qcsa. **~tance** n ammissione f; **'no ~tance'** 'vietato l'ingresso'. **~tedly** adv bisogna riconoscerlo

admonish /əd'mɒnɪʃ/ vt ammonire

ado /ə'du:/ n **without more ~** senza ulteriori indugi

adolescen|ce /ædə'lesns/ n adolescenza f. **~t** adj & n adolescente mf

adopt /ə'dɒpt/ vt adottare; (Pol) scegliere (candidate). **~ion** n adozione f. **~ive** adj adottivo

ador|able /ə'dɔ:rəbl/ adj adorabile. **~ation** n adorazione f

adore /ə'dɔ:(r)/ vt adorare

adrenalin /ə'drenəlɪn/ n adrenalina f

Adriatic /eɪdrɪ'ætɪk/ adj & n **the ~ [Sea]** il mare Adriatico, l'Adriatico m

adrift /ə'drɪft/ adj alla deriva; **be ~** andare alla deriva; **come ~** staccarsi

adult /'ædʌlt/ n adulto, -a mf

adultery /ə'dʌltərɪ/ n adulterio m

advance /əd'vɑ:ns/ n avanzamento m; (Mil) avanzata f; (payment) anticipo m; **in ~** in anticipo •vi avanzare; (make progress) fare progressi •vt avanzare (theory); promuovere (cause); anticipare (money). **~ booking** n prenotazione f [in anticipo]. **~d** adj avanzato. **~ment** n promozione f

advantage /əd'vɑ:ntɪdʒ/ n vantaggio m; **take ~ of** approfittare di. **~ous** adj vantaggioso

advent /'ædvent/ n avvento m

adventur|e /əd'ventʃə(r)/ n avventura f. **~ous** adj avventuroso

adverb /'ædvɜ:b/ n avverbio m

adversary /'ædvəsərɪ/ n avversario, -a mf

advers|e /'ædvɜ:s/ adj avverso. **~ity** n avversità f

dvert /'ædvɜ:t/ n [!] = **advertisement**

dvertise /'ædvətaɪz/ vt reclamizzare; mettere un annuncio per (job, flat) • vi fare pubblicità; (for job, flat) mettere un annuncio

dvertisement /əd'vɜ:tɪsmənt/ n pubblicità f inv; (in paper) inserzione f, annuncio m

dvertis|er /'ædvətaɪzə(r)/ n (in newspaper) inserzionista mf. **~ing** n pubblicità f • attrib pubblicitario

dvice /əd'vaɪs/ n consigli mpl; **piece of ~** consiglio m

dvisable /əd'vaɪzəbl/ adj consigliabile

dvis|e /əd'vaɪz/ vt consigliare; (inform) avvisare; **~e sb to do sth** consigliare a qcno di fare qcsa; **~e sb against sth** sconsigliare qcsa a qcno. **~er** n consulente mf. **~ory** adj consultivo

dvocate[1] /'ædvəkət/ n (supporter) fautore, -trice mf

dvocate[2] /'ædvəkeɪt/ vt propugnare

erial /'eərɪəl/ adj aereo • n antenna f

erobics /eə'rəʊbɪks/ n aerobica fsg

ero|drome /'eərədrəʊm/ n aerodromo m. **~plane** n aeroplano m

erosol /'eərəsɒl/ n bomboletta f spray

esthetic /i:s'θetɪk/ adj estetico

far /ə'fɑ:(r)/ adv **from ~** da lontano

ffable /'æfəbl/ adj affabile

ffair /ə'feə(r)/ n affare m; (scandal) caso m; (sexual) relazione f

ffect /ə'fekt/ vt influire su; (emotionally) colpire; (concern) riguardare. **~ation** n affettazione f. **~ed** adj affettato

ffection /ə'fekʃn/ n affetto m. **~ate** adj affettuoso

ffirm /ə'fɜ:m/ vt affermare; (Jur) dichiarare solennemente

ffirmative /ə'fɜ:mətɪv/ adj affermativo • n **in the ~** affermativamente

fflict /ə'flɪkt/ vt affliggere. **~ion** n afflizione f

ffluen|ce /'æflʊəns/ n agiatezza f. **~t** adj agiato

fford /ə'fɔ:d/ vt **be able to ~ sth** potersi permettere qcsa. **~able** adj abbordabile

affront /ə'frʌnt/ n affronto m

afield /ə'fi:ld/ adv **further ~** più lontano

afloat /ə'fləʊt/ adj a galla

afraid /ə'freɪd/ adj **be ~** aver paura; **I'm ~ not** purtroppo no; **I'm ~ so** temo di sì; **I'm ~ I can't help you** mi dispiace, ma non posso esserle d'aiuto

afresh /ə'freʃ/ adv da capo

Africa /'æfrɪkə/ n Africa f. **~n** adj & n africano, -a mf

after /'ɑ:ftə(r)/ adv dopo; **the day ~** il giorno dopo; **be ~** cercare • prep dopo; **~ all** dopotutto; **the day ~ tomorrow** dopodomani • conj dopo che

after: ~-effect n conseguenza f. **~math** /-mɑ:θ/ n conseguenze fpl; **the ~math of war** il dopoguerra; **in the ~math of** nel periodo successivo a. **~'noon** n pomeriggio m; **good ~noon!** buon giorno!. **~shave** n [lozione f] dopobarba m inv. **~thought** n **added as an ~thought** aggiunto in un secondo momento; **~wards** adv in seguito

again /ə'geɪn/ adv di nuovo; [**then**] **~** (besides) inoltre; (on the other hand) d'altra parte; **~ and ~** continuamente

against /ə'geɪnst/ prep contro

age /eɪdʒ/ n età f inv; (era) era f; **~s** [!] secoli; **what ~ are you?** quanti anni hai?; **be under ~** non avere l'età richiesta; **he's two years of ~** ha due anni • vt/i (pres p **ageing**) invecchiare

aged[1] /eɪdʒd/ adj **~ two** di due anni

aged[2] /'eɪdʒɪd/ adj anziano • n **the ~** pl gli anziani

agency /'eɪdʒənsɪ/ n agenzia f; **have the ~ for** essere un concessionario di

agenda /ə'dʒendə/ n ordine m del giorno; **on the ~** all'ordine del giorno; fig in programma

agent /'eɪdʒənt/ n agente mf

aggravat|e /'ægrəveɪt/ vt aggravare; (annoy) esasperare. **~ion** n aggravamento m; (annoyance) esasperazione f

a

aggress|ion /ə'greʃn/ n aggressione f. **~ive** adj aggressivo. **~iveness** n aggressività f. **~or** n aggressore m

aghast /ə'gɑ:st/ adj inorridito

agil|e /'ædʒaɪl/ adj agile. **~ity** n agilità f

agitat|e /'ædʒɪteɪt/ vt mettere in agitazione; (shake) agitare •vi fig **~e for** creare delle agitazioni per. **~ed** adj agitato. **~ion** n agitazione f. **~or** n agitatore, -trice mf

ago /ə'gəʊ/ adv fa; **a long time/a month ~** molto tempo/un mese fa

agoniz|e /'ægənaɪz/ vi angosciarsi (**over** per). **~ing** adj angosciante

agony /'ægənɪ/ n agonia f; (mental) angoscia f; **be in ~** avere dei dolori atroci

agree /ə'gri:/ vt accordarsi su; **~ to do sth** accettare di fare qcsa; **~ that** essere d'accordo [sul fatto] che •vi essere d'accordo; (figures:) concordare; (reach agreement) mettersi d'accordo; (get on) andare d'accordo; (consent) acconsentire (**to** a); **it doesn't ~ with me** mi fa male; **~ with sth** (approve of) approvare qcsa

agreeable /ə'gri:əbl/ adj gradevole; (willing) d'accordo

agreed /ə'gri:d/ adj convenuto

agreement /ə'gri:mənt/ n accordo m; **in ~** d'accordo

agricultur|al /ægrɪ'kʌltʃərəl/ adj agricolo. **~e** n agricoltura f

aground /ə'graʊnd/ adv **run ~** (ship:) arenarsi

ahead /ə'hed/ adv avanti; **be ~ of** essere davanti a; fig essere avanti rispetto a; **draw ~** passare davanti (**of** a); **get ~** (in life) riuscire; **go ~!** fai pure!; **look ~** pensare all'avvenire; **plan ~** fare progetti per l'avvenire

aid /eɪd/ n aiuto m; **in ~ of** a favore di •vt aiutare

Aids /eɪdz/ n AIDS m

aim /eɪm/ n mira f; fig scopo m; **take ~** prendere la mira •vt puntare (gun) (**at** contro) •vi mirare; **~ to do sth** aspirare a fare qcsa. **~less** adj, **~lessly** adv senza scopo

air /eə(r)/ n aria f; **be on the ~** (programme:) essere in onda; **put on ~s** darsi delle arie; **by ~** in aereo; (airmail) per via aerea •vt arieggiare; far conoscere (views)

air: ~-conditioned adj con aria condizionata. **~-conditioning** n aria f condizionata. **~craft** n aereo m. **~craft carrier** n portaerei f inv. **~field** n campo m d'aviazione. **~ force** n aviazione f. **~ freshener** n deodorante m per l'ambiente. **~gun** n fucile m pneumatico. **~ hostess** n hostess f inv. **~line** n compagnia f aerea. **~mail** n posta f aerea. **~plane** n Am aereo m. **~port** n aeroporto m. **~tight** adj ermetico. **~-traffic controller** n controllore m di volo

airy /'eərɪ/ adj (**-ier, -iest**) arieggiato; (manner) noncurante

aisle /aɪl/ n corridoio m; (in supermarket) corsia f; (in church) navata f

ajar /ə'dʒɑ:(r)/ adj socchiuso

alarm /ə'lɑ:m/ n allarme m; **set the ~** (of alarm clock) mettere la sveglia •vt allarmare. **~ clock** n sveglia f

Albania /æl'beɪnɪə/ n Albania f

album /'ælbəm/ n album m inv

alcohol /'ælkəhɒl/ n alcol m. **~ic** adj alcolico •n alcolizzato, -a mf. **~ism** alcolismo m

alcove /'ælkəʊv/ n alcova f

alert /ə'lɜ:t/ adj sveglio; (watchful) vigile •n segnale m d'allarme; **be on the ~** stare allerta •vt allertare

algebra /'ældʒɪbrə/ n algebra f

Algeria /æl'dʒɪərɪə/ n Algeria f. **~n** adj & n algerino, -a mf

alias /'eɪlɪəs/ n pseudonimo m •adv alias

alibi /'ælɪbaɪ/ n alibi m inv

alien /'eɪlɪən/ adj straniero; fig estraneo •n straniero, -a mf; (from space) alieno, -a mf

alienat|e /'eɪlɪəneɪt/ vt alienare. **~ion** n alienazione f

alight[1] /ə'laɪt/ vi scendere; (bird:) posarsi

alight[2] adj **be ~** essere in fiamme; **set ~** dar fuoco a

align /ə'laɪn/ vt allineare. **~ment** n allineamento m; **out of ~ment** non allineato

alike /ə'laɪk/ adj simile; **be ~** rassomigliarsi •adv in modo simile;

look ~ rassomigliarsi; **summer and winter** ~ sia d'estate che d'inverno

imony /'ælɪmənɪ/ n alimenti mpl

ive /ə'laɪv/ adj vivo; ~ **with** brulicante di; ~ **to** sensibile a; ~ **and kicking** vivo e vegeto

kali /'ælkəlaɪ/ n alcali m

ll /ɔːl/

• adj tutto; ~ **the children,** ~ **children** tutti i bambini; ~ **day** tutto il giorno; **he refused** ~ **help** ha rifiutato qualsiasi aiuto; **for** ~ **that** (*nevertheless*) ciononostante; **in** ~ **sincerity** in tutta sincerità; **be** ~ **for** essere favorevole a

• pron tutto; ~ **of you/them** tutti voi/loro; ~ **of it** tutto; ~ **of the town** tutta la città; **in** ~ in tutto; ~ **in** ~ tutto sommato; **most of** ~ più di ogni altra cosa; **once and for** ~ una volta per tutte

• adv completamente; ~ **but** quasi; ~ **at once** (*at the same time*) tutto in una volta; ~ **at once,** ~ **of a sudden** all'improvviso; ~ **too soon** troppo presto; ~ **the same** (*nevertheless*) ciononostante; ~ **the better** meglio ancora; **she's not** ~ **that good an actress** non è poi così brava come attrice; ~ **in** in tutto; [!] esausto; **thirty/three** ~ (*in sport*) trenta/tre pari; ~ **over** (*finished*) tutto finito; (*everywhere*) dappertutto; **it's** ~ **right** (*I don't mind*) non fa niente; **I'm** ~ **right** (*not hurt*) non ho niente; ~ **right!** va bene!

lay /ə'leɪ/ vt placare (suspicions, anger)

llegation /ælɪ'geɪʃn/ n accusa f

llege /ə'ledʒ/ vt dichiarare. ~**d** adj presunto. ~**dly** adv a quanto si dice

llegiance /ə'liːdʒəns/ n fedeltà f

llerg|ic /ə'lɜːdʒɪk/ adj allergico. ~**y** n allergia f

lleviate /ə'liːvɪeɪt/ vt alleviare

lley /'ælɪ/ n vicolo m; (for bowling) corsia f

lliance /ə'laɪəns/ n alleanza f

lligator /'ælɪgeɪtə(r)/ n alligatore m

llocat|e /'æləkeɪt/ vt assegnare; distribuire (resources). ~**ion** n assegnazione f; (of resources) distribuzione f

allot /ə'lɒt/ vt (pt/pp **allotted**) distribuire. ~**ment** n distribuzione f; (share) parte f; (land) piccolo lotto m di terreno

allow /ə'laʊ/ vt permettere; (grant) accordare; (reckon on) contare; (agree) ammettere; ~ **for** tener conto di; ~ **sb to do sth** permettere a qcno di fare qcsa; **you are not** ~**ed to...** è vietato...

allowance /ə'laʊəns/ n sussidio m; (Am: pocket money) paghetta f; (for petrol etc) indennità f inv; (of luggage, duty free) limite m; **make** ~**s for** essere indulgente verso (sb); tener conto di (sth)

alloy /'ælɔɪ/ n lega f

allusion /ə'luːʒn/ n allusione f

ally[1] /'ælaɪ/ n alleato, -a mf

ally[2] /ə'laɪ/ vt (pt/pp **-ied**) alleare; ~ **oneself with** allearsi con

almighty /ɔːl'maɪtɪ/ adj ([!]: big) mega inv • n **the A**~ l'Onnipotente m

almond /'ɑːmənd/ n mandorla f; (tree) mandorlo m

almost /'ɔːlməʊst/ adv quasi

alone /ə'ləʊn/ adj solo; **leave me** ~**!** lasciami in pace!; **let** ~ (not to mention) figurarsi • adv da solo

along /ə'lɒŋ/ prep lungo • adv ~ **with** assieme a; **all** ~ tutto il tempo; **come** ~**!** (hurry up) vieni qui!; **I'll be** ~ **in a minute** arrivo tra un attimo; **move** ~ spostarsi; **move** ~**!** circolare!

along'side adv lungo bordo • prep lungo; **work** ~ **sb** lavorare fianco a fianco con qcno

aloof /ə'luːf/ adj distante

aloud /ə'laʊd/ adv ad alta voce

alphabet /'ælfəbet/ n alfabeto m. ~**ical** adj alfabetico

Alps /ælps/ npl Alpi fpl

already /ɔːl'redɪ/ adv già

Alsatian /æl'seɪʃn/ n (dog) pastore m tedesco

also /'ɔːlsəʊ/ adv anche; ~**, I need...** [e] inoltre, ho bisogno di...

altar /'ɔːltə(r)/ n altare m

alter /'ɔːltə(r)/ vt cambiare; aggiustare (clothes) • vi cambiare.

a

a

~ation n modifica f

alternate¹ /'ɔ:ltəneɪt/ vi alternarsi •vt alternare

alternate² /ɔ:l'tɜ:nət/ adj alterno; **on ~ days** a giorni alterni

alternative /ɔ:l'tɜ:nətɪv/ adj alternativo •n alternativa f. **~ly** adv alternativamente

although /ɔ:l'ðəʊ/ conj benché, sebbene

altitude /'æltɪtju:d/ n altitudine f

altogether /ɔ:ltə'geðə(r)/ adv (in all) in tutto; (completely) completamente; **I'm not ~ sure** non sono del tutto sicuro

aluminium /ælju'mɪnɪəm/ n, Am **aluminum** /ə'lu:mɪnəm/ n alluminio m

always /'ɔ:lweɪz/ adv sempre

am /æm/ ▸**be**

a.m. abbr (ante meridiem) del mattino

amalgamate /ə'mælgəmeɪt/ vt fondere •vi fondersi

amass /ə'mæs/ vt accumulare

amateur /'æmətə(r)/ n non professionista mf; pej dilettante mf •attrib dilettante; **~ dramatics** filodrammatica f. **~ish** adj dilettantesco

amaze /ə'meɪz/ vt stupire. **~d** adj stupito. **~ment** n stupore m

amazing /ə'meɪzɪŋ/ adj incredibile

ambassador /æm'bæsədə(r)/ n ambasciatore, -trice mf

ambigu|ity /æmbɪ'gju:ətɪ/ n ambiguità f inv. **~ous** adj ambiguo

ambiti|on /æm'bɪʃn/ n ambizione f; (aim) aspirazione f. **~ous** adj ambizioso

ambivalent /æm'bɪvələnt/ adj ambivalente

amble /'æmbl/ vi camminare senza fretta

ambulance /'æmbjʊləns/ n ambulanza f

ambush /'æmbʊʃ/ n imboscata f •vt tendere un'imboscata a

amend /ə'mend/ vt modificare. **~ment** n modifica f. **~s** npl **make ~s** fare ammenda (**for** di, per)

amenities /ə'mi:nətɪz/ npl comodità fpl

America /ə'merɪkə/ n America f. **~n** adj & n americano, -a mf

amiable /'eɪmɪəbl/ adj amabile

amicable /'æmɪkəbl/ adj amichevole

ammonia /ə'məʊnɪə/ n ammoniaca

ammunition /æmjʊ'nɪʃn/ n munizioni fpl

amnesty /'æmnəstɪ/ n amnistia f

among[st] /ə'mʌŋ[st]/ prep tra, fra

amount /ə'maʊnt/ n quantità f inv; (sum of money) importo m •vi **~ to** ammontare a; fig equivalere a

amphibi|an /æm'fɪbɪən/ n anfibio m **~ous** adj anfibio

amphitheatre /'æmfɪ-/ n anfiteatro m

ampl|e /'æmpl/ adj (large) grande; (proportions) ampio; (enough) largamente sufficiente

amplif|ier /'æmplɪfaɪə(r)/ n amplificatore m. **~y** vt (pt/pp **-ied**) amplificare (sound)

amputat|e /'æmpjʊteɪt/ vt amputare **~ion** n amputazione f

amuse /ə'mju:z/ vt divertire. **~ment** n divertimento m. **~ment arcade** n sala f giochi

amusing /ə'mju:zɪŋ/ adj divertente

an /ən/, accentato /æn/ ▸**a**

anaem|ia /ə'ni:mɪə/ n anemia f. **~ic** adj anemico

anaesthetic /ænəs'θetɪk/ n anestesia f

anaesthet|ist /ə'ni:sθətɪst/ n anestesista mf

analogy /ə'nælədʒɪ/ n analogia f

analyse /'ænəlaɪz/ vt analizzare

analysis /ə'næləsɪs/ n analisi f inv

analyst /'ænəlɪst/ n analista mf

analytical /ænə'lɪtɪkl/ adj analitico

anarch|ist /'ænəkɪst/ n anarchico, -a mf. **~y** n anarchia f

anatom|ical /ænə'tɒmɪkl/ adj anatomico. **~ically** adv anatomicamente. **~y** n anatomia f

ancest|or /'ænsestə(r)/ n antenato, -a mf. **~ry** n antenati mpl

anchor /'æŋkə(r)/ n ancora f •vi gettar l'ancora •vt ancorare

anchovy /'æntʃəvɪ/ n acciuga f

a

ncient /'emʃənt/ adj antico; [!] vecchio

ncillary /æn'sɪlərɪ/ adj ausiliario

nd /ənd/, accentato /ænd/ conj e; **two ~ two** due più due; **six hundred ~ two** seicentodue; **more ~ more** sempre più; **nice ~ warm** bello caldo; **try ~ come** cerca di venire; **go ~ get** vai a prendere

necdote /'ænɪkdəʊt/ n aneddoto m

new /ə'nju:/ adv di nuovo

ngel /'eɪndʒl/ n angelo m. **~ic** adj angelico

nger /'æŋgə(r)/ n rabbia f • vt far arrabbiare

ngle¹ /'æŋgl/ n angolo m; fig angolazione f; **at an ~** storto

ngle² vi pescare con la lenza; **~ for** fig cercare di ottenere. **~r** n pescatore, -trice mf

nglican /'æŋglɪkən/ adj & n anglicano, -a mf

ngr|y /'æŋgrɪ/ adj (**-ier, -iest**) arrabbiato; **get ~y** arrabbiarsi; **~y with** or **at sb** arrabbiato con qcno; **~y at** or **about sth** arrabbiato per qcsa. **~ily** adv rabbiosamente

nguish /'æŋgwɪʃ/ n angoscia f

nimal /'ænɪml/ adj & n animale m

nimate¹ /'ænɪmət/ adj animato

nimat|e² /'ænɪmeɪt/ vt animare. **~ed** adj animato; (person) vivace. **~ion** n animazione f

nimosity /ænɪ'mɒsətɪ/ n animosità f inv

nkle /'æŋkl/ n caviglia f

nnihilat|e /ə'naɪəleɪt/ vt annientare. **~ion** n annientamento m

nniversary /ænɪ'vɜ:sərɪ/ n anniversario m

nnounce /ə'naʊns/ vt annunciare. **~ment** n annuncio m. **~r** n annunciatore, -trice mf

nnoy /ə'nɔɪ/ vt dare fastidio a; **get ~ed** essere infastidito. **~ance** n seccatura f; (anger) irritazione f. **~ing** adj fastidioso

nnual /'ænjʊəl/ adj annuale; (income) annuo • n (Bot) pianta f annua; (children's book) almanacco m

nnul /ə'nʌl/ vt (pt/pp **annulled**) annullare

anonymous /ə'nɒnɪməs/ adj anonimo

anorak /'ænəræk/ n giacca f a vento

another /ə'nʌðə(r)/ adj & pron; **~ [one]** un altro, un'altra; **in ~ way** diversamente; **one ~** l'un l'altro

answer /'ɑ:nsə(r)/ n risposta f; (solution) soluzione f • vt rispondere a (person, question, letter); esaudire (prayer); **~ the door** aprire la porta; **~ the telephone** rispondere al telefono • vi rispondere; **~ back** ribattere; **~ for** rispondere di. **~able** adj responsabile; **be ~able to sb** rispondere a qcno. **~ing machine** n (Teleph) segreteria f telefonica

ant /ænt/ n formica f

antagonis|m /æn'tægənɪzm/ n antagonismo m. **~tic** adj antagonistico

antagonize /æn'tægənaɪz/ vt provocare l'ostilità di

Antarctic /æn'tɑ:ktɪk/ n Antartico m • adj antartico

antenatal /æntɪ'neɪtl/ adj prenatale

antenna /æn'tenə/ n antenna f

anthem /'ænθəm/ n inno m

anthology /æn'θɒlədʒɪ/ n antologia f

anthropology /ænθrə'pɒlədʒɪ/ n antropologia f

anti-'aircraft /æntɪ-/ adj antiaereo

antibiotic /æntɪbaɪ'ɒtɪk/ n antibiotico m

anticipat|e /æn'tɪsɪpeɪt/ vt prevedere; (forestall) anticipare. **~ion** n anticipo m; (excitement) attesa f

anti'climax n delusione f

anti'clockwise adj & adv in senso antiorario

antidote /'æntɪdəʊt/ n antidoto m

'antifreeze n antigelo m

antiquated /'æntɪkweɪtɪd/ adj antiquato

antique /æn'ti:k/ adj antico • n antichità f inv. **~ dealer** n antiquario, -a mf

antiquity /æn'tɪkwətɪ/ n antichità f

anti'septic adj & n antisettico m

anti'social adj (behaviour) antisociale; (person) asociale

a

antlers /'æntləz/ npl corna fpl

anus /'eɪnəs/ n ano m

anxiety /æŋ'zaɪətɪ/ n ansia f

anxious /'æŋkʃəs/ adj ansioso. **~ly** adv con ansia

any /'enɪ/
- adj (*no matter which*) qualsiasi, qualunque; **~ colour/number you like** qualsiasi colore/numero ti piaccia; **we don't have ~ wine/biscuits** non abbiamo vino/biscotti; **for ~ reason** per qualsiasi ragione

! **any** is often not translated: **have we ~ wine/biscuits?** abbiamo del vino/dei biscotti?

- pron (*some*) ne; (*no matter which*) uno qualsiasi; **I don't want ~ *[*of it*]*** non ne voglio [nessuno]; **there aren't ~** non ce ne sono; **have we ~?** ne abbiamo?; **have you read ~ of her books?** hai letto qualcuno dei suoi libri?
- adv **I can't go ~ quicker** non posso andare più in fretta; **is it ~ better?** va un po' meglio?; **would you like ~ more?** ne vuoi ancora?; **I can't eat ~ more** non posso mangiare più niente

'**anybody** pron chiunque; (after negative) nessuno; **I haven't seen ~** non ho visto nessuno

'**anyhow** adv ad ogni modo, comunque; (badly) non importa come

'**anyone** pron = **anybody**

'**anything** pron qualche cosa, qualcosa; (no matter what) qualsiasi cosa; (after negative) niente; **take/buy ~ you like** prendi/compra quello che vuoi; **I don't remember ~** non mi ricordo niente; **he's ~ but stupid** è tutto, ma non stupido; **I'll do ~ but that** farò qualsiasi cosa, tranne quello

'**anyway** adv ad ogni modo, comunque

'**anywhere** adv dovunque; (after negative) da nessuna parte; **put it ~** mettilo dove vuoi; **I can't find it ~** non lo trovo da nessuna parte; **~ else** da qualch'altra parte; (after negative) da nessun'altra parte; **I don't want to go ~ else** non voglio andare da nessun'altra parte

apart /ə'pɑ:t/ adv lontano; **live ~** vivere separati; **100 miles ~** lontani 100 miglia; **~ from** a parte **you can't tell them ~** non si possono distinguere; **joking ~** scherzi a parte

apartment /ə'pɑ:tmənt/ n (Am: flat) appartamento m; **in my ~** a casa mia

apathy /'æpəθɪ/ n apatia f

ape /eɪp/ n scimmia f • vt scimmiottare

aperitif /ə'perəti:f/ n aperitivo m

aperture /'æpətʃə(r)/ n apertura f

apex /'eɪpeks/ n vertice m

apologetic /əpɒlə'dʒetɪk/ adj (air, remark) di scusa; **be ~** essere spiacente

apologize /ə'pɒlədʒaɪz/ vi scusarsi (**for** per)

apology /ə'pɒlədʒɪ/ n scusa f; fig **an ~ for a dinner** una sottospecie di cena

apostle /ə'pɒsl/ n apostolo m

apostrophe /ə'pɒstrəfɪ/ n apostrofo m

appal /ə'pɔ:l/ vt (pt/pp **appalled**) sconvolgere. **~ling** adj sconvolgent

apparatus /æpə'reɪtəs/ n apparato n

apparent /ə'pærənt/ adj evidente; (seeming) apparente. **~ly** adv apparentemente

apparition /æpə'rɪʃn/ n apparizione f

appeal /ə'pi:l/ n appello m; (attraction) attrattiva f • vi fare appello; **~ to** (b attractive to) attrarre. **~ing** adj attraente

appear /ə'pɪə(r)/ vi apparire; (seem) sembrare; (publication:) uscire; (Theat) esibirsi. **~ance** n apparizione f; (look) aspetto m; **to all ~ances** a giudicare dalle apparenze; **keep up ~ances** salvare le apparenze

appease /ə'pi:z/ vt placare

appendicitis /əpendɪ'saɪtɪs/ n appendicite f

appendix /ə'pendɪks/ n (pl **-ices** /-ɪsi:z/) (of book) appendice f; (pl **-es**) (Anat) appendice f

appetite /'æpɪtaɪt/ n appetito m

pplau|d /ə'plɔ:d/ vt/i applaudire. **~se** n applauso m

pple /'æpl/ n mela f. **~-tree** n melo m

ppliance /ə'plaɪəns/ n attrezzo m; [**electrical**] ~ elettrodomestico m

pplicable /'æplɪkəbl/ adj **be ~ to** essere valido per; **not ~** (on form) non applicabile

pplicant /'æplɪkənt/ n candidato, -a mf

pplication /æplɪ'keɪʃn/ n applicazione f; (request) domanda f; (for job) candidatura f. **~ form** n modulo m di domanda

pplied /ə'plaɪd/ adj applicato

pply /ə'plaɪ/ vt (pt/pp **-ied**) applicare; **~ oneself** applicarsi •vi applicarsi; (law:) essere applicabile; **~ to** (ask) rivolgersi a; **~ for** fare domanda per (job etc)

ppoint /ə'pɔɪnt/ vt nominare; fissare (time). **~ment** n appuntamento m; (to job) nomina f; (job) posto m

ppraisal /ə'preɪz(ə)l/ n valutazione f

ppreciable /ə'pri:ʃəbl/ adj sensibile

ppreciat|e /ə'pri:ʃɪeɪt/ vt apprezzare; (understand) comprendere •vi (increase in value) aumentare di valore. **~ion** n (gratitude) riconoscenza f; (enjoyment) apprezzamento m; (understanding) comprensione f; (in value) aumento m. **~ive** adj riconoscente

pprehens|ion /æprɪ'henʃn/ n arresto m; (fear) apprensione f. **~ive** adj apprensivo

pprentice /ə'prentɪs/ n apprendista mf. **~ship** n apprendistato m

pproach /ə'prəʊtʃ/ n avvicinamento m; (to problem) approccio m; (access) accesso m; **make ~es to** fare degli approcci con •vi avvicinarsi •vt avvicinarsi a; (with request) rivolgersi a; affrontare (problem). **~able** adj accessibile

ppropriate[1] /ə'prəʊprɪət/ adj appropriato

ppropriate[2] /ə'prəʊprɪeɪt/ vt appropriarsi di

pproval /ə'pru:vl/ n approvazione f; **on ~** in prova

approv|e /ə'pru:v/ vt approvare •vi **~e of** approvare (sth); avere una buona opinione di (sb). **~ing** adj (smile, nod) d'approvazione

approximate /ə'prɒksɪmət/ adj approssimativo. **~ly** adv approssimativamente

approximation /əprɒksɪ'meɪʃn/ n approssimazione f

apricot /'eɪprɪkɒt/ n albicocca f

April /'eɪprəl/ n aprile m; **~ Fool's Day** il primo d'aprile

apron /'eɪprən/ n grembiule m

apt /æpt/ adj appropriato; **be ~ to do sth** avere tendenza a fare qcsa

aptitude /'æptɪtju:d/ n disposizione f. **~ test** n test m inv attitudinale

aquarium /ə'kweərɪəm/ n acquario m

Aquarius /ə'kweərɪəs/ n (Astr) Acquario m

aquatic /ə'kwætɪk/ adj acquatico

Arab /'ærəb/ adj & n arabo, -a mf. **~ian** adj arabo

Arabic /'ærəbɪk/ adj arabo; **~ numerals** numeri mpl arabi •n arabo m

arable /'ærəbl/ adj coltivabile

arbitrary /'ɑ:bɪtrərɪ/ adj arbitrario

arbitrat|e /'ɑ:bɪtreɪt/ vi arbitrare. **~ion** n arbitraggio m

arc /ɑ:k/ n arco m

arcade /ɑ:'keɪd/ n portico m; (shops) galleria f

arch /ɑ:tʃ/ n arco m; (of foot) dorso m del piede

archaeological /ɑ:kɪə'lɒdʒɪkl/ adj archeologico

archaeolog|ist /ɑ:kɪ'ɒlədʒɪst/ n archeologo, -a mf. **~y** n archeologia f

archaic /ɑ:'keɪɪk/ adj arcaico

arch'bishop /ɑ:tʃ-/ n arcivescovo m

architect /'ɑ:kɪtekt/ n architetto m. **~ural** adj architettonico

architecture /'ɑ:kɪtektʃə(r)/ n architettura f

archives /'ɑ:kaɪvz/ npl archivi mpl

archway /'ɑ:tʃweɪ/ n arco m

Arctic /'ɑ:ktɪk/ adj artico •n **the ~** l'Artico

ardent /'ɑ:dənt/ adj ardente

arduous /'ɑ:djʊəs/ adj arduo

a

are /ɑ:(r)/ ▸**be**

area /'eərɪə/ n area f; (region) zona f; (fig: field) campo m. ~ **code** n prefisso m [telefonico]

arena /ə'ri:nə/ n arena f

Argentina /ɑ:dʒən'ti:nə/ n Argentina f

Argentinian /-'tɪnɪən/ adj & n argentino, -a mf

argue /'ɑ:gju:/ vi litigare (**about** su); (debate) dibattere; **don't ~!** non discutere! •vt (debate) dibattere; (reason) ~ **that** sostenere che

argument /'ɑ:gjʊmənt/ n argomento m; (reasoning) ragionamento m; **have an ~** litigare. **~ative** adj polemico

arid /'ærɪd/ adj arido

Aries /'eəri:z/ n (Astr) Ariete m

arise /ə'raɪz/ vi (pt **arose**, pp **arisen**) (opportunity, need, problem:) presentarsi; (result) derivare

aristocracy /ærɪ'stɒkrəsɪ/ n aristocrazia f

aristocrat /'ærɪstəkræt/ n aristocratico, -a mf. **~ic** adj aristocratico

arithmetic /ə'rɪθmətɪk/ n aritmetica f

arm /ɑ:m/ n braccio m; (of chair) bracciolo m; **~s** pl (weapons) armi fpl; ~ **in** ~ a braccetto; **up in ~s** [!] furioso (**about** per) •vt armare

'**armchair** n poltrona f

armed /ɑ:md/ adj armato; ~ **forces** forze fpl armate; ~ **robbery** rapina f a mano armata

armour /'ɑ:mə(r)/ n armatura f. **~ed** adj (vehicle) blindato

'**armpit** n ascella f

army /'ɑ:mɪ/ n esercito m; **join the ~** arruolarsi

aroma /ə'rəʊmə/ n aroma f. **~tic** adj aromatico

arose /ə'rəʊz/ ▸**arise**

around /ə'raʊnd/ adv intorno; **all ~** tutt'intorno; **I'm not from ~ here** non sono di qui; **he's not ~** non c'è •prep intorno a; in giro per (room, shops, world)

arouse /ə'raʊz/ vt svegliare; (sexually) eccitare

arrange /ə'reɪndʒ/ vt sistemare (furniture, books); organizzare (meeting); fissare (date, time); ~ **to do sth** combinare di fare qcsa. **~ment** n (of furniture) sistemazione f; (Mus) arrangiamento m; (agreement) accordo; (of flowers) composizione f; **make ~ments** prendere disposizioni

arrears /ə'rɪəz/ npl arretrati mpl; **be in ~** essere in arretrato; **paid in ~** pagato a lavoro eseguito

arrest /ə'rest/ n arresto m; **under ~** in stato d'arresto •vt arrestare

arrival /ə'raɪvl/ n arrivo m; **new ~s** pl nuovi arrivati mpl

arrive /ə'raɪv/ vi arrivare; ~ **at** fig raggiungere

arrogan|ce /'ærəgəns/ n arroganza f. **~t** adj arrogante

arrow /'ærəʊ/ n freccia f

arse /ɑ:s/ n [!] culo m

arsenic /'ɑ:sənɪk/ n arsenico m

arson /'ɑ:sn/ n incendio m doloso. **~ist** n incendiario, -a mf

art /ɑ:t/ n arte f; **~s and crafts** pl artigianato m; **the A~s** pl l'arte f; **A~s degree** (Univ) laurea f in Lettere

artery /'ɑ:tərɪ/ n arteria f

'**art gallery** n galleria f d'arte

arthritis /ɑ:'θraɪtɪs/ n artrite f

artichoke /'ɑ:tɪtʃəʊk/ n carciofo m

article /'ɑ:tɪkl/ n articolo m; ~ **of clothing** capo m d'abbigliamento

articulate[1] /ɑ:'tɪkjʊlət/ adj (speech) chiaro; **be ~** esprimersi bene

articulate[2] /ɑ:'tɪkjʊleɪt/ vt scandire (words). **~d lorry** n autotreno m

artificial /ɑ:tɪ'fɪʃl/ adj artificiale. **~ly** adv artificialmente; (smile) artificiosamente

artillery /ɑ:'tɪlərɪ/ n artiglieria f

artist /'ɑ:tɪst/ n artista mf

as /æz/ conj come; (since) siccome; (while) mentre; **as he grew older** diventando vecchio; **as you get to know her** conoscendola meglio; **young as she is** per quanto sia giovane •prep come; **as a friend** come amico; **as a child** da bambino; **as a foreigner** in quanto straniero; **disguised as** travestito da •adv **as well** (also) anche; **as**

soon as I get home [non] appena arrivo a casa; **as quick as you** veloce quanto te; **as quick as you can** più veloce che puoi; **as far as** (distance) fino a; **as far as I'm concerned** per quanto mi riguarda; **as long as** finché; (provided that) purché

sbestos /æz'bestɒs/ n amianto m

scend /ə'send/ vi salire • vt salire a (throne)

scension /ə'senʃn/ n (Relig) Ascensione f

scent /ə'sent/ n ascesa f

scertain /æsə'teɪn/ vt accertare

sh¹ /æʃ/ n (tree) frassino m

sh² n cenere f

shamed /ə'ʃeɪmd/ adj **be/feel ~** vergognarsi

shore /ə'ʃɔ:(r)/ adv a terra; **go ~** sbarcare

sh: ~tray n portacenere m. **A~ 'Wednesday** n mercoledì m inv delle Ceneri

sia /'eɪʒə/ n Asia f. **~n** adj & n asiatico, -a mf. **~tic** adj asiatico

side /ə'saɪd/ adv **take sb ~** prendere qcno a parte; **put sth ~** mettere qcsa da parte; **~ from you** Am a parte te

sk /ɑ:sk/ vt fare (question); (invite) invitare; **~ sb sth** domandare or chiedere qcsa a qcno; **~ sb to do sth** domandare or chiedere a qcno di fare qcsa • vi **~ about sth** informarsi su qcsa; **~ after** chiedere [notizie] di; **~ for** chiedere (sth); chiedere di (sb); **~ for trouble** [!] andare in cerca di guai. □ **~ in** vt **~ sb in** invitare qcno ad entrare. □ **~ out** vt **~ sb out** chiedere a qcno di uscire

skew /ə'skju:/ adj & adv di traverso

sleep /ə'sli:p/ adj **be ~** dormire; **fall ~** addormentarsi

sparagus /ə'spærəgəs/ n asparagi mpl

spect /'æspekt/ n aspetto m

sphalt /'æsfælt/ n asfalto m

spire /ə'spaɪə(r)/ vi **~ to** aspirare a

ss /æs/ n asino m

ssassin /ə'sæsɪn/ n assassino, -a mf. **~ate** vt assassinare. **~ation** n assassinio m

assault /ə'sɔ:lt/ n (Mil) assalto m; (Jur) aggressione f • vt aggredire

assemble /ə'sembl/ vi radunarsi • vt radunare; (Techn) montare

assembly /ə'semblɪ/ n assemblea f; (Sch) assemblea f giornaliera di alunni e professori di una scuola; (Techn) montaggio m. **~ line** n catena f di montaggio

assent /ə'sent/ n assenso m • vi acconsentire

assert /ə'sɜ:t/ vt asserire; far valere (one's rights); **~ oneself** farsi valere. **~ion** n asserzione f. **~ive** adj **be ~ive** farsi valere

assess /ə'ses/ vt valutare; (for tax purposes) stabilire l'imponibile di. **~ment** n valutazione f; (of tax) accertamento m

asset /'æset/ n (advantage) vantaggio m; (person) elemento m prezioso. **~s** pl beni mpl; (on balance sheet) attivo msg

assign /ə'saɪn/ vt assegnare. **~ment** n (task) incarico m

assimilate /ə'sɪmɪleɪt/ vt assimilare; integrare (person)

assist /ə'sɪst/ vt/i assistere; **~ sb to do sth** assistere qcno nel fare qcsa. **~ance** n assistenza f. **~ant** adj **~ant manager** vicedirettore, -trice mf • n assistente mf; (in shop) commesso, -a mf

associat|e¹ /ə'səʊʃɪeɪt/ vt associare (**with** a); **be ~ed with sth** (involved in) essere coinvolto in qcsa • vi **~e with** frequentare. **~ion** n associazione f. **A~ion 'Football** n [gioco m del] calcio m

associate² /ə'səʊʃɪət/ adj associato • n collega mf; (member) socio, -a mf

assort|ed /ə'sɔ:tɪd/ adj assortito. **~ment** n assortimento m

assum|e /ə'sju:m/ vt presumere; assumere (control); **~e office** entrare in carica; **~ing that you're right,...** ammettendo che tu abbia ragione,...

assumption /ə'sʌmpʃn/ n supposizione f; **on the ~ that** partendo dal presupposto che; **the A~** (Relig) l'Assunzione f

assurance /ə'ʃʊərəns/ n

assicurazione f; (confidence) sicurezza f

assure /ə'ʃʊə(r)/ vt assicurare. **~d** adj sicuro

asterisk /'æstərɪsk/ n asterisco m

asthma /'æsmə/ n asma f. **~tic** adj asmatico

astonish /ə'stɒnɪʃ/ vt stupire. **~ing** adj stupefacente. **~ment** n stupore m

astound /ə'staʊnd/ vt stupire

astray /ə'streɪ/ adv **go ~** smarrirsi; (morally) uscire dalla retta via; **lead ~** traviare

astronaut /'æstrənɔ:t/ n astronauta mf

astronom|er /ə'strɒnəmə(r)/ n astronomo, -a mf. **~ical** adj astronomico. **~y** n astronomia f

astute /ə'stju:t/ adj astuto

asylum /ə'saɪləm/ n [**political**] **~** asilo m politico; [**lunatic**] **~** manicomio m

at /ət/, accentato /æt/ prep a; **at the station/the market** alla stazione/al mercato; **at the office/the bank** in ufficio/banca; **at the beginning** all'inizio; **at John's** da John; **at the hairdresser's** dal parrucchiere; **at home** a casa; **at work** al lavoro; **at school** a scuola; **at a party/wedding** a una festa/un matrimonio; **at 1 o'clock** all'una; **at 50 km an hour** ai 50 all'ora; **at Christmas/Easter** a Natale/Pasqua; **at times** talvolta; **two at a time** due alla volta; **good at languages** bravo nelle lingue; **at sb's request** su richiesta di qcno; **are you at all worried?** sei preoccupato?

ate /et/ ▸**eat**

atheist /'eɪθɪɪst/ n ateo, -a mf

athlet|e /'æθli:t/ n atleta mf. **~ic** adj atletico. **~ics** n atletica fsg

Atlantic /ət'læntɪk/ adj & n **the ~** [**Ocean**] l'[Oceano m] Atlantico m

atlas /'ætləs/ n atlante m

atmospher|e /'ætməsfɪə(r)/ n atmosfera f. **~ic** adj atmosferico

atom /'ætəm/ n atomo m. **~ bomb** n bomba f atomica

atomic /ə'tɒmɪk/ adj atomico

atrocious /ə'trəʊʃəs/ adj atroce; (meal, weather) abominevole

atrocity /ə'trɒsətɪ/ n atrocità f inv

attach /ə'tætʃ/ vt attaccare; attribuire (importance); **be ~ed to** fig essere attaccato a

attachment /ə'tætʃmənt/ n (affection) attaccamento m; (accessory) accessorio m

attack /ə'tæk/ n attacco m; (physical) aggressione f • vt attaccare; (physically) aggredire. **~er** n assalitore, -trice mf; (critic) detrattore, -trice mf

attain /ə'teɪn/ vt realizzare (ambition); raggiungere (success, age, goal)

attempt /ə'tempt/ n tentativo m • vt tentare

attend /ə'tend/ vt essere presente a; (go regularly to) frequentare; (doctor:) avere in cura • vi essere presente; (pay attention) prestare attenzione. □ **~ to** vt occuparsi di; (in shop) servire. **~ance** n presenza f. **~ant** guardiano, -a mf

attention /ə'tenʃn/ n attenzione f; **~!** (Mil) attenti!; **pay ~** prestare attenzione; **need ~** aver bisogno di attenzioni; (skin, hair, plant:) dover essere curato; (car, tyres:) dover essere riparato; **for the ~ of** all'attenzione di

attentive /ə'tentɪv/ adj (pupil, audience) attento

attic /'ætɪk/ n soffitta f

attitude /'ætɪtju:d/ n atteggiamento m

attorney /ə'tɜ:nɪ/ n (Am: lawyer) avvocato m; **power of ~** delega f

attract /ə'trækt/ vt attirare. **~ion** n attrazione f; (feature) attrattiva f. **~ive** adj (person) attraente; (proposal, price) allettante

attribute[1] /'ætrɪbju:t/ n attributo m

attribute[2] /ə'trɪbju:t/ vt attribuire

aubergine /'əʊbəʒi:n/ n melanzana

auction /'ɔ:kʃn/ n asta f • vt vendere all'asta. **~eer** n banditore m

audaci|ous /ɔ:'deɪʃəs/ adj sfacciato; (daring) audace. **~ty** n sfacciataggine f; (daring) audacia f

audible /'ɔ:dəbl/ adj udibile

audience /'ɔ:dɪəns/ n (Theat) pubblico m; (TV) telespettatori mpl; (Radio) ascoltatori mpl; (meeting) udienza f

a

audit /ˈɔ:dɪt/ n verifica f del bilancio •vt verificare

audition /ɔ:ˈdɪʃn/ n audizione f •vi fare un'audizione

auditor /ˈɔ:dɪtə(r)/ n revisore m di conti

auditorium /ɔ:dɪˈtɔ:rɪəm/ n sala f

augment /ɔ:gˈment/ vt aumentare

augur /ˈɔ:gə(r)/ vi ~ **well/ill** essere di buon/cattivo augurio

August /ˈɔ:gəst/ n agosto m

aunt /ɑ:nt/ n zia f

au pair /əʊˈpeə(r)/ n ~ **[girl]** ragazza f alla pari

aura /ˈɔ:rə/ n aura f

auster|e /ɒˈstɪə(r)/ adj austero. **~ity** n austerità f

Australia /ɒˈstreɪlɪə/ n Australia f. **~n** adj & n australiano, -a mf

Austria /ˈɒstrɪə/ n Austria f. **~n** adj & n austriaco, -a mf

authentic /ɔ:ˈθentɪk/ adj autentico. **~ate** vt autenticare. **~ity** n autenticità f

author /ˈɔ:θə(r)/ n autore m

authoritative /ɔ:ˈθɒrɪtətɪv/ adj autorevole; (manner) autoritario

authority /ɔ:ˈθɒrətɪ/ n autorità f; (permission) autorizzazione f; **be in ~ over** avere autorità su

authorization /ɔ:θəraɪˈzeɪʃn/ n autorizzazione f

authorize /ˈɔ:θəraɪz/ vt autorizzare

autobiˈography /ɔ:tə-/ n autobiografia f

autograph /ˈɔ:tə-/ n autografo m

automate /ˈɔ:təmeɪt/ vt automatizzare

automatic /ɔ:təˈmætɪk/ adj automatico •n (car) macchina f col cambio automatico; (washing machine) lavatrice f automatica. **~ally** adv automaticamente

automation /ɔ:təˈmeɪʃn/ n automazione f

automobile /ˈɔ:təməbi:l/ n automobile f

autonom|ous /ɔ:ˈtɒnəməs/ adj autonomo. **~y** n autonomia f

autopsy /ˈɔtɒpsɪ/ n autopsia f

autumn /ˈɔ:təm/ n autunno m. **~al** adj autunnale

auxiliary /ɔ:gˈzɪlɪərɪ/ adj ausiliario •n ausiliare m

avail /əˈveɪl/ n **to no ~** invano •vi **~ oneself of** approfittare di

available /əˈveɪləbl/ adj disponibile; (book, record etc) in vendita

avalanche /ˈævəlɑ:nʃ/ n valanga f

avarice /ˈævərɪs/ n avidità f

avenue /ˈævənju:/ n viale m; fig strada f

average /ˈævərɪdʒ/ adj medio; (mediocre) mediocre •n media f; **on ~** in media •vt (sales, attendance) etc: raggiungere una media di. □ **~ out at** vt risultare in media

avers|e /əˈvɜ:s/ adj **not be ~e to sth** non essere contro qcsa. **~ion** n avversione f (**to** per)

avert /əˈvɜ:t/ vt evitare (crisis); distogliere (eyes)

aviation /eɪvɪˈeɪʃn/ n aviazione f

avid /ˈævɪd/ adj avido (**for** di); (reader) appassionato

avocado /ævəˈkɑ:dəʊ/ n avocado m

avoid /əˈvɔɪd/ vt evitare. **~able** adj evitabile

await /əˈweɪt/ vt attendere

awake /əˈweɪk/ adj sveglio; **wide ~** completamente sveglio •vi (pt **awoke**, pp **awoken**) svegliarsi

awaken /əˈweɪkn/ vt svegliare. **~ing** n risveglio m

award /əˈwɔ:d/ n premio m; (medal) riconoscimento m; (of prize) assegnazione f •vt assegnare; (hand over) consegnare

aware /əˈweə(r)/ adj **be ~ of** (sense) percepire; (know) essere conscio di; **become ~ of** accorgersi di; (learn) venire a sapere di; **be ~ that** rendersi conto che. **~ness** n percezione f; (knowledge) consapevolezza f

awash /əˈwɒʃ/ adj inondato (**with** di)

away /əˈweɪ/ adv via; **go/stay ~** andare/stare via; **he's ~ from his desk/the office** non è alla sua scrivania/in ufficio; **far ~** lontano; **four kilometres ~** a quattro chilometri; **play ~** (Sport) giocare fuori casa. **~ game** n partita f fuori casa a b

awe /ɔ:/ n soggezione f

awful /'ɔ:fl/ adj terribile. **~ly** adv terribilmente; (pretty) estremamente

awkward /'ɔ:kwəd/ adj (movement) goffo; (moment, situation) imbarazzante; (time) scomodo. **~ly** adv (move) goffamente; (say) con imbarazzo

awning /'ɔ:nɪŋ/ n tendone m

awoke(n) /ə'wəʊk (ən)/ ▸**awake**

axe /æks/ n scure f • vt (pres p **axing**) fare dei tagli a (budget); sopprimere (jobs); annullare (project)

axis /'æksɪs/ n (pl **axes** /-si:z/) asse m

axle /'æksl/ n (Techn) asse m

Bb

BA n abbr Bachelor of Arts

babble /'bæbl/ vi farfugliare; (stream:) gorgogliare

baby /'beɪbɪ/ n bambino, -a mf; (!: darling) tesoro m

baby: ~ carriage n Am carrozzina f. **~ish** adj bambinesco. **~-sit** vi fare da baby-sitter. **~-sitter** n baby-sitter mf

bachelor /'bætʃələ(r)/ n scapolo m; **B~ of Arts/Science** laureato, -a mf in lettere/in scienze

back /bæk/ n schiena f; (of horse, hand) dorso m; (of chair) schienale m; (of house, cheque, page) retro m; (in football) difesa f; **at the ~** in fondo; **in the ~** (Auto) dietro; **~ to front** (sweater) il davanti di dietro; **at the ~ of beyond** in un posto sperduto • adj posteriore; (taxes, payments) arretrato • adv indietro; (returned) di ritorno; **turn/move ~** tornare/spostarsi indietro; **put it ~ here/there** rimettilo qui/là; **~ at home** di ritorno a casa; **I'll be ~ in five minutes** torno fra cinque minuti; **I'm just ~** sono appena tornato; **when do you want the book ~?** quando rivuoi il libro?; **pay ~** ripagare (sb); restituire (money); **~ in power** di nuovo al potere • vt (support) sostenere; (with money) finanziare; puntare su (horse); (cover the back of) rivestire il retro di • vi (Auto) fare retromarcia. □ **~ down** vi battere in ritirata. □ **~ in** vi (Auto) entrare in retromarcia; (person:) entrare camminando all'indietro. □ **~ out** vi (Auto) uscire in retromarcia; (person:) uscire camminando all'indietro; fig tirarsi indietro (**of** da). □ **~ up** vt sostenere; confermare (person's alibi); (Comput) fare una copia di salvataggio di; **be ~ed up** (traffic:) essere congestionato • vi (Auto) fare retromarcia

back: ~ache n mal m di schiena. **~bone** n spina f dorsale. **~date** vt retrodatare (cheque). **~ 'door** n porta f di servizio

backer /'bækə(r)/ n sostenitore, -trice mf; (with money) finanziatore, -trice mf

back: ~'fire vi (Auto) avere un ritorno di fiamma; (fig: plan) fallire. **~ground** n sfondo m; (environment) ambiente m. **~hand** n (tennis) rovescio m

backing /'bækɪŋ/ n (support) supporto m; (material) riserva f; (Mus) accompagnamento m; **~ group** gruppo m d'accompagnamento

back: ~lash n fig reazione f opposta. **~log** n **~log of work** lavoro m arretrato. **~side** n ! fondoschiena m inv. **~slash** n (Typ) barra f retroversa. **~stage** adj & adv dietro le quinte. **~stroke** n dorso m. **~-up** n rinforzi mpl; (Comput) riserva f

backward /'bækwəd/ adj (step) indietro; (child) lento nell'apprendimento; (country) arretrato • adv **~s** (also Am: **~**) indietro; (fall, walk) all'indietro; **~s and forwards** avanti e indietro

back: ~water n fig luogo m allo

scarto. ~ '**yard** n cortile m

acon /'beɪkn/ n ≈ pancetta f

acteria /bæk'tɪərɪə/ npl batteri mpl

ad /bæd/ adj (**worse, worst**) cattivo; (weather, habit, news, accident) brutto; (apple etc) marcio; **the light is ~** non c'è una buona luce; **use ~ language** dire delle parolacce; **feel ~** sentirsi male; (feel guilty) sentirsi in colpa; **have a ~ back** avere dei problemi alla schiena; **smoking is ~ for you** fumare fa male; **go ~** andare a male; **that's just too ~!** pazienza!; **not ~** niente male

ade /bæd/ ▹**bid**

adge /bædʒ/ n distintivo m

adger /'bædʒə(r)/ n tasso m •vt tormentare

adly /'bædlɪ/ adv male; (hurt) gravemente; **~ off** povero; **~ behaved** maleducato; **need ~** aver estremamente bisogno di

ad-'mannered adj maleducato

adminton /'bædmɪntən/ n badminton m

ad-'tempered adj irascibile

affle /'bæfl/ vt confondere

ag /bæg/ n borsa f; (of paper) sacchetto m; **old ~** ☒ megera f; **~s under the eyes** occhiaie fpl; **~s of** ! un sacco di

aggage /'bægɪdʒ/ n bagagli mpl

aggy /'bægɪ/ adj (clothes) ampio

bagpipes npl cornamusa fsg

ail /beɪl/ n cauzione f; **on ~** su cauzione •**bail out** vt (Naut) aggottare; **~ sb out** (Jur) pagare la cauzione per qcno •vi (Aeron) paracadutarsi

ait /beɪt/ n esca f •vt innescare; (fig: torment) tormentare

ake /beɪk/ vt cuocere al forno; (make) fare •vi cuocersi al forno

aker /'beɪkə(r)/ n fornaio, -a mf, panettiere, -a mf; **~'s [shop]** panetteria f. **~y** n panificio m, forno m

balance /'bæləns/ n equilibrio m; (Comm) bilancio m; (outstanding sum) saldo m; [**bank**] **~** saldo m; **be** or **hang in the ~** fig essere in sospeso •vt bilanciare; equilibrare (budget); (Comm) fare il bilancio di (books) •vi bilanciarsi; (Comm) essere in pareggio. **~d** adj equilibrato. **~ sheet** n bilancio m [d'esercizio]

balcony /'bælkənɪ/ n balcone m

bald /bɔːld/ adj (person) calvo; (tyre) liscio; (statement) nudo e crudo; **go ~** perdere i capelli

bale /beɪl/ n balla f

ball[1] /bɔːl/ n palla f; (football) pallone m; (of yarn) gomitolo m; **on the ~** ! sveglio

ball[2] n (dance) ballo m

ballad /'bæləd/ n ballata f

ballast /'bæləst/ n zavorra f

ball-'bearing n cuscinetto m a sfera

ballerina /bælə'riːnə/ n ballerina f [classica]

ballet /'bæleɪ/ n balletto m; (art form) danza f; **~ dancer** n ballerino, -a mf [classico, -a]

balloon /bə'luːn/ n pallone m; (Aeron) mongolfiera f

ballot /'bælət/ n votazione f. **~-box** n urna f. **~-paper** n scheda f di votazione

ball: ~-point ['**pen**] n penna f a sfera. **~room** n sala f da ballo

Baltic /'bɔːltɪk/ adj & n **the ~** [**Sea**] il [mar] Baltico

bamboo /bæm'buː/ n bambù m inv

ban /bæn/ n proibizione f •vt (pt/pp **banned**) proibire; **~ from** espellere da (club); **she was ~ned from driving** le hanno ritirato la patente

banal /bə'nɑːl/ adj banale. **~ity** n banalità f inv

banana /bə'nɑːnə/ n banana f

band /bænd/ n banda f; (stripe) nastro m; (Mus: pop group) complesso m; (Mus: brass ~) banda f; (Mil) fanfara f •**band together** vi riunirsi

bandage /'bændɪdʒ/ n benda f•vt fasciare (limb)

b. & b. abbr bed and breakfast

bandit /'bændɪt/ n bandito m

band: ~stand n palco m coperto [dell'orchestra]. **~wagon** n **jump on the ~wagon** fig seguire la corrente

bandy[1] /'bændɪ/ vt (pt/pp **-ied**) scambiarsi (words). □ **~ about** vt far circolare

bandy[2] adj (**-ier, -iest**) **be ~** avere le gambe storte

bang /bæŋ/ n (noise) fragore m; (of gun, firework) scoppio m; (blow) colpo m • adv **~ in the middle of** [!] proprio nel mezzo di; **go ~** (gun:) sparare; (balloon:) esplodere • int bum! • vt battere (fist); battere su (table); sbattere (door, head) • vi scoppiare; (door:) sbattere

banger /ˈbæŋə(r)/ n (firework) petardo m; ([!]: sausage) salsiccia f; **old ~** ([!]: car) macinino m

bangle /ˈbæŋgl/ n braccialetto m

banish /ˈbænɪʃ/ vt bandire

banisters /ˈbænɪstəz/ npl ringhiera fsg

bank[1] /bæŋk/ n (of river) sponda f; (slope) scarpata f • vi (Aeron) inclinarsi in virata

bank[2] n banca f • vt depositare in banca • vi **~ with** avere un conto [bancario] presso. □ **~ on** vt contare su

ˈbank card n carta f assegno.

banker /ˈbæŋkə(r)/ n banchiere m

bank: ~ ˈholiday n giorno m festivo. **~ing** n bancario m. **~note** n banconota f

bankrupt /ˈbæŋkrʌpt/ adj fallito; **go ~** fallire • n persona f che ha fatto fallimento • vt far fallire. **~cy** n bancarotta f

banner /ˈbænə(r)/ n stendardo m; (of demonstrators) striscione m

banquet /ˈbæŋkwɪt/ n banchetto m

banter /ˈbæntə(r)/ n battute fpl di spirito

baptism /ˈbæptɪzm/ n battesimo m

Baptist /ˈbæptɪst/ adj & n battista mf

baptize /bæpˈtaɪz/ vt battezzare

bar /bɑː(r)/ n sbarra f; (Jur) ordine m degli avvocati; (of chocolate) tavoletta f; (café) bar m inv; (counter) banco m; (Mus) battuta f; (fig: obstacle) ostacolo m; **~ of soap/gold** saponetta f/lingotto m; **behind ~s** [!] dietro le sbarre • vt (pt/pp **barred**) sbarrare (way); sprangare (door); escludere (person) • prep tranne; **~ none** in assoluto

barbarian /bɑːˈbeərɪən/ n barbaro, -a mf

barbar|ic /bɑːˈbærɪk/ adj barbarico. **~ity** n barbarie f inv. **~ous** adj barbaro

barbecue /ˈbɑːbɪkjuː/ n barbecue m inv; (party) grigliata f, barbecue m inv • vt arrostire sul barbecue

barber /ˈbɑːbə(r)/ n barbiere m

bare /beə(r)/ adj nudo; (tree, room) spoglio; (floor) senza moquette • vt scoprire; mostrare (teeth)

bare: ~back adv senza sella. **~faced** adj sfacciato. **~foot** adv scalzo. **~ˈheaded** adj a capo scoperto

barely /ˈbeəlɪ/ adv appena

bargain /ˈbɑːgɪn/ n (agreement) patto m; (good buy) affare m; **into the ~** per di più • vi contrattare; (haggle) trattare. □ **~ for** vt (expect) aspettarsi

barge /bɑːdʒ/ n barcone m • **barge in** vi [!] (to room) piombare dentro; (into conversation) interrompere bruscamente. **~ into** vt piombare dentro a (room); venire addosso a (person)

baritone /ˈbærɪtəʊn/ n baritono m

bark[1] /bɑːk/ n (of tree) corteccia f

bark[2] n abbaiamento m • vi abbaiare

barley /ˈbɑːlɪ/ n orzo m

bar: ~maid n barista f. **~man** n barista m

barmy /ˈbɑːmɪ/ adj [!] strampalato

barn /bɑːn/ n granaio m

barometer /bəˈrɒmɪtə(r)/ n barometro m

baron /ˈbærn/ n barone m. **~ess** n baronessa f

baroque /bəˈrɒk/ adj & n barocco m

barracks /ˈbærəks/ npl caserma fsg

barrage /ˈbærɑːʒ/ n (Mil) sbarramento m; (fig: of criticism) sfilza f

barrel /ˈbærl/ n barile m, botte f; (of gun) canna f. **~-organ** n organetto m [a cilindro]

barren /ˈbærən/ adj sterile; (land-scape) brullo

barricade /bærɪˈkeɪd/ n barricata f • vt barricare

barrier /ˈbærɪə(r)/ n barriera f; (Rail) cancello m; fig ostacolo m

barrister /ˈbærɪstə(r)/ n avvocato m

barter /'bɑːtə(r)/ vi barattare (**for** con)

base /beɪs/ n base f •adj vile •vt basare; **be ~d on** basarsi su

base: ~ball n baseball m. **~ment** n seminterrato m

bash /bæʃ/ n colpo m [violento] •vt colpire [violentemente]; (dent) ammaccare; **~ed in** ammaccato

bashful /'bæʃfl/ adj timido

basic /'beɪsɪk/ adj di base; (condition, requirement) basilare; (living conditions) povero; **my Italian is pretty ~** il mio italiano è abbastanza rudimentale; **the ~s** (of language, science) i rudimenti; (essentials) l'essenziale m. **~ally** adv fondamentalmente

basil /'bæzɪl/ n basilico m

basin /'beɪsn/ n bacinella f; (wash-hand ~) lavabo m; (for food) recipiente m; (Geog) bacino m

basis /'beɪsɪs/ n (pl **-ses** /-siːz/) base f

bask /bɑːsk/ vi crogiolarsi

basket /'bɑːskɪt/ n cestino m. **~ball** n pallacanestro f

bass /beɪs/ adj basso; **~ voice** voce f di basso •n basso m

bastard /'bɑːstəd/ n (illegitimate child) bastardo, -a mf; ☒ figlio m di puttana

bat¹ /bæt/ n mazza f; (for table tennis) racchetta f; **off one's own ~** [!] tutto da solo •vt (pt/pp **batted**) battere; **she didn't ~ an eyelid** fig non ha battuto ciglio

bat² n (Zool) pipistrello m

batch /bætʃ/ n gruppo m; (of goods) partita f; (of bread) infornata f

bated /'beɪtɪd/ adj **with ~ breath** col fiato sospeso

bath /bɑːθ/ n (pl **~s** /bɑːðz/) bagno m; (tub) vasca f da bagno; **~s** pl piscina f; **have a ~** fare un bagno •vt fare il bagno a

bathe /beɪð/ n bagno m •vi fare il bagno •vt lavare (wound). **~r** n bagnante mf

bathing /'beɪðɪŋ/ n bagni mpl. **~-cap** n cuffia f. **~-costume** n costume m da bagno

bathroom n bagno m

battalion /bə'tælɪən/ n battaglione m

batter /'bætə(r)/ n (Culin) pastella f; **~ed** adj (car) malandato; (wife, baby) maltrattato

battery /'bætərɪ/ n batteria f; (of torch, radio) pila f

battle /'bætl/ n battaglia f; fig lotta f •vi fig lottare

battle: ~field n campo m di battaglia. **~ship** n corazzata f

bawl /bɔːl/ vt/i urlare

bay¹ /beɪ/ n (Geog) baia f

bay² n **keep at ~** tenere a bada

bay³ n (Bot) alloro m. **~-leaf** n foglia f d'alloro

bayonet /'beɪənɪt/ n baionetta f

bay 'window n bay window f inv (grande finestra sporgente)

bazaar /bə'zɑː(r)/ n bazar m inv

BC abbr (before Christ) a.C.

be /biː/

•vi (pres **am, are, is, are**; pt **was, were**; pp **been**) essere; **he is a teacher** è insegnante, fa l'insegnante; **what do you want to be?** cosa vuoi fare?; **be quiet!** sta' zitto!; **I am cold/hot** ho freddo/caldo; **it's cold/hot, isn't it?** fa freddo/caldo, vero?; **how are you?** come stai?; **I am well** sto bene; **there is** c'è; **there are** ci sono; **I have been to Venice** sono stato a Venezia; **has the postman been?** è passato il postino?; **you're coming too, aren't you?** vieni anche tu, no?; **it's yours, is it?** è tuo, vero?; **was John there? – yes, he was** c'era John? – sì; **John wasn't there – yes he was!** John non c'era – sì che c'era!; **three and three are six** tre più tre fanno sei; **he is five** ha cinque anni; **that will be £10, please** fanno 10 sterline, per favore; **how much is it?** quanto costa?; **that's £5 you owe me** mi devi 5 sterline

•v aux **I am coming/reading** sto venendo/leggendo; **I'm staying** (*not leaving*) resto; **I am being lazy** sono pigro; **I was thinking of you** stavo pensando a te; **you are not to tell him** non devi

b

dirglielo; **you are to do that immediately** devi farlo subito •passive essere; **I have been robbed** sono stato derubato

beach /biːtʃ/ n spiaggia f. **~wear** n abbigliamento m da spiaggia
bead /biːd/ n perlina f
beak /biːk/ n becco m
beaker /ˈbiːkə(r)/ n coppa f
beam /biːm/ n trave f; (of light) raggio m •vi irradiare; (person:) essere raggiante. **~ing** adj raggiante
bean /biːn/ n fagiolo m; (of coffee) chicco m
bear[1] /beə(r)/ n orso m
bear[2] v (pt **bore**, pp **borne**) •vt (endure) sopportare; mettere al mondo (child); (carry) portare; **~ in mind** tenere presente •vi **~ left/right** andare a sinistra/a destra. ▫ **~ with** vt aver pazienza con. **~able** adj sopportabile
beard /bɪəd/ n barba f. **~ed** adj barbuto
bearer /ˈbeərə(r)/ n portatore, -trice mf; (of passport) titolare mf
bearing /ˈbeərɪŋ/ n portamento m; (Techn) cuscinetto m [a sfera]; **have a ~ on** avere attinenza con; **get one's ~s** orientarsi
beast /biːst/ n bestia f; (!: person) animale m
beat /biːt/ n battito m; (rhythm) battuta f; (of policeman) giro m d'ispezione •v (pt **beat**, pp **beaten**) •vt battere; picchiare (person); **~ it!** ! diamocela a gambe!; **it ~s me why...** ! non capisco proprio perché... **beat up** vt picchiare
beating /ˈbiːtɪŋ/ n bastonata f; **get a ~ing** (with fists) essere preso a pugni; (team, player:) prendere una batosta
beautician /bjuːˈtɪʃn/ n estetista mf
beauti|ful /ˈbjuːtɪfl/ adj bello. **~fully** adv splendidamente
beauty /ˈbjuːtɪ/ n bellezza f. **~ parlour** n istituto m di bellezza. **~ spot** n neo m; (place) luogo m pittoresco
beaver /ˈbiːvə(r)/ n castoro m
became /bɪˈkeɪm/ ▹**become**
because /bɪˈkɒz/ conj perché; **~ you didn't tell me, I...** poiché non me lo hai detto,... •adv **~ of** a causa di
beckon /ˈbekn/ vt/i **~ [to]** chiamare con un cenno
becom|e /bɪˈkʌm/ v (pt **became**, pp **become**) •vt diventare •vi diventare; **what has ~e of her?** che ne è di lei? **~ing** adj (clothes) bello
bed /bed/ n letto m; (of sea, lake) fondo m; (layer) strato m; (of flowers) aiuola f; **in ~** a letto; **go to ~** andare a letto; **~ and breakfast** pensione f familiare in cui il prezzo della camera comprende la prima colazione. **~clothes** npl lenzuola fpl e coperte fpl. **~ding** n biancheria f per il letto, materasso e guanciali
bed: ~room n camera f da letto. **~'sitter** n ≈ camera f ammobiliata fornita di cucina. **~spread** n copriletto m. **~time** n l'ora f di andare a letto
bee /biː/ n ape f
beech /biːtʃ/ n faggio m
beef /biːf/ n manzo m. **~burger** n hamburger m inv
bee: ~hive n alveare m. **~-line** n **make a ~line for** ! precipitarsi verso
been /biːn/ ▹**be**
beer /bɪə(r)/ n birra f
beetle /ˈbiːtl/ n scarafaggio m
beetroot /ˈbiːtruːt/ n barbabietola f
before /bɪˈfɔː(r)/ prep prima di; **the day ~ yesterday** ieri l'altro; **~ long** fra poco •adv prima; **never ~ have I seen...** non ho mai visto prima...; **~ that** prima; **~ going** prima di andare •conj (time) prima che; **~ you go** prima che tu vada. **~hand** adv in anticipo
befriend /bɪˈfrend/ vt trattare da amico
beg /beg/ v (pt/pp **begged**) •vi mendicare •vt pregare; chiedere (favour, forgiveness)
began /bɪˈgæn/ ▹**begin**
beggar /ˈbegə(r)/ n mendicante mf; **poor ~!** povero cristo!
begin /bɪˈgɪn/ vt/i (pt **began**, pp **begun**, pres p **beginning**) cominciare. **~ner** n principiante mf. **~ning** n principio m

begrudge /bɪ'grʌdʒ/ vt (envy) essere invidioso di; dare malvolentieri (money)

begun /bɪ'gʌn/ ▹**begin**

behalf /bɪ'hɑːf/ n **on ~ of** a nome di; **on my ~** a nome mio

behave /bɪ'heɪv/ vi comportarsi; **~ [oneself]** comportarsi bene

behaviour /bɪ'heɪvjə(r)/ n comportamento m; (of prisoner, soldier) condotta f

behead /bɪ'hed/ vt decapitare

behind /bɪ'haɪnd/ prep dietro; **be ~ sth** fig stare dietro qcsa • adv dietro, indietro; (late) in ritardo; **a long way ~** molto indietro • n [!] didietro m. **~hand** adv indietro

beige /beɪʒ/ adj & n beige m inv

being /'biːɪŋ/ n essere m; **come into ~** nascere

belated /bɪ'leɪtɪd/ adj tardivo

belch /beltʃ/ vi ruttare • vt **~ [out]** eruttare (smoke)

belfry /'belfrɪ/ n campanile m

Belgian /'beldʒən/ adj & n belga mf

Belgium /'beldʒəm/ n Belgio m

belief /bɪ'liːf/ n fede f; (opinion) convinzione f

believe /bɪ'liːv/ vt/i credere. **~r** n (Relig) credente mf; **be a great ~r in** credere fermamente in

belittle /bɪ'lɪtl/ vt sminuire (person, achievements)

bell /bel/ n campana f; (on door) campanello m

belligerent /bɪ'lɪdʒərənt/ adj belligerante; (aggressive) bellicoso

bellow /'beləʊ/ vi gridare a squarciagola; (animal:) muggire

bellows /'beləʊz/ npl (for fire) soffietto msg

belly /'belɪ/ n pancia f

belong /bɪ'lɒŋ/ vi appartenere (**to** a); (be member) essere socio (**to** di). **~ings** npl cose fpl

beloved /bɪ'lʌvɪd/ adj & n amato, -a mf

below /bɪ'ləʊ/ prep sotto; (with numbers) al di sotto di • adv sotto, di sotto; (Naut) sotto coperta; **see ~** guardare qui di seguito

belt /belt/ n cintura f; (area) zona f; (Techn) cinghia f • vi **~ along** ([!]: rush) filare velocemente • vt ([!]: hit) picchiare

bench /bentʃ/ n panchina f; (work~) piano m da lavoro; **the B~** (Jur) la magistratura

bend /bend/ n curva f; (of river) ansa f • v (pt/pp **bent**) • vt piegare • vi piegarsi; (road:) curvare; **~ [down]** chinarsi. ▫ **~ over** vi inchinarsi

beneath /bɪ'niːθ/ prep sotto, al di sotto di; **he thinks it's ~ him** fig pensa che sia sotto al suo livello • adv giù

beneficial /benɪ'fɪʃl/ adj benefico

beneficiary /benɪ'fɪʃərɪ/ n beneficiario, -a mf

benefit /'benɪfɪt/ n vantaggio m; (allowance) indennità f inv • v (pt/pp **-fited**, pres p **-fiting**) • vt giovare a • vi trarre vantaggio (**from** da)

benign /bɪ'naɪn/ adj benevolo; (Med) benigno

bent /bent/ ▹**bend** • adj (person) ricurvo; (distorted) curvato; ([!]: dishonest) corrotto; **be ~ on doing sth** essere ben deciso a fare qcsa • n predisposizione f

bereave|d /bɪ'riːvd/ n **the ~d** pl i familiari del defunto. **~ment** n lutto m

beret /'bereɪ/ n berretto m

berry /'berɪ/ n bacca f

berserk /bə'sɜːk/ adj **go ~** diventare una belva

berth /bɜːθ/ n (bed) cuccetta f; (anchorage) ormeggio m • vi ormeggiare

beside /bɪ'saɪd/ prep accanto a; **~ oneself** fuori di sé

besides /bɪ'saɪdz/ prep oltre a • adv inoltre

besiege /bɪ'siːdʒ/ vt assediare

best /best/ adj migliore; **the ~ part of a year** la maggior parte dell'anno; **~ before** (Comm) preferibilmente prima di • n **the ~** il meglio; (person) il/la migliore; **at ~** tutt'al più; **all the ~!** tanti auguri!; **do one's ~** fare del proprio meglio; **to the ~ of my knowledge** per quel che ne so; **make the ~ of it** cogliere il lato buono della cosa • adv meglio, nel modo migliore; **as ~ I could**

meglio che potevo. ~ '**man** n testimone m

bestow /bɪ'stəʊ/ vt conferire (**on** a)

best'seller n bestseller m inv

bet /bet/ n scommessa f •vt/i (pt/pp **bet** or **betted**) scommettere

betray /bɪ'treɪ/ vt tradire. **~al** n tradimento m

better /'betə(r)/ adj migliore, meglio; **get ~** migliorare; (after illness) rimettersi •adv meglio; **~ off** meglio; (wealthier) più ricco; **all the ~** tanto meglio; **the sooner the ~** prima è, meglio è; **I've thought ~ of it** ci ho ripensato; **you'd ~ stay** faresti meglio a restare; **I'd ~ not** è meglio che non lo faccia •vt migliorare; **~ oneself** migliorare le proprie condizioni

between /bɪ'twi:n/ prep fra, tra; **~ you and me** detto fra di noi; **~ us** (together) tra me e te •adv **[in] ~** in mezzo; (time) frattempo

beverage /'bevərɪdʒ/ n bevanda f

beware /bɪ'weə(r)/ vi guardarsi (**of** da); **~ of the dog!** attenti al cane!

bewilder /bɪ'wɪldə(r)/ vt disorientare; **~ed** perplesso. **~ment** n perplessità f

beyond /bɪ'jɒnd/ prep oltre; **~ reach** irraggiungibile; **~ doubt** senza alcun dubbio; **~ belief** da non credere; **it's ~ me** [!] non riesco proprio a capire •adv più in là

bias /'baɪəs/ n (preference) preferenza f; pej pregiudizio m •vt (pt/pp **biased**) (influence) influenzare. **~ed** adj parziale

bib /bɪb/ n bavaglino m

Bible /'baɪbl/ n Bibbia f

biblical /'bɪblɪkl/ adj biblico

biceps /'baɪseps/ n bicipite m

bicker /'bɪkə(r)/ vi litigare

bicycle /'baɪsɪkl/ n bicicletta f •vi andare in bicicletta

bid[1] /bɪd/ n offerta f; (attempt) tentativo m •vt/i (pt/pp **bid**, pres p **bidding**) offrire; (in cards) dichiarare

bid[2] vt (pt **bade** or **bid**, pp **bidden** or **bid**, pres p **bidding**) liter (command) comandare; **~ sb welcome** dare il benvenuto a qcno

bidder /'bɪdə(r)/ n offerente mf

bide /baɪd/ vt **~ one's time** aspettare il momento buono

bifocals /baɪ'fəʊklz/ npl occhiali mpl bifocali

big /bɪg/ adj (**bigger, biggest**) grande; (brother, sister) più grande; ([!]: generous) generoso •adv **talk ~** [!] spararle grosse

bigam|ist /'bɪgəmɪst/ n bigamo, -a mf **~y** n bigamia f

big-'headed adj [!] gasato

bigot /'bɪgət/ n fanatico, -a mf. **~ed** adj di mentalità ristretta

bike /baɪk/ n [!] bici f inv

bikini /bɪ'ki:nɪ/ n bikini m inv

bile /baɪl/ n bile f

bilingual /baɪ'lɪŋgwəl/ adj bilingue

bill[1] /bɪl/ n fattura f; (in restaurant etc) conto m; (poster) manifesto m; (Pol) progetto m di legge; (Am: note) biglietto m di banca •vt fatturare

bill[2] n (beak) becco m

'**billfold** n Am portafoglio m

billiards /'bɪljədz/ n biliardo m

billion /'bɪljən/ n (thousand million) miliardo m; (old-fashioned Br: million million) mille miliardi mpl

bin /bɪn/ n bidone m

bind /baɪnd/ vt (pt/pp **bound**) legare (**to** a); (bandage) fasciare; (Jur) obbligare. **~ing** adj (promise, contract) vincolante •n (of book) rilegatura f; (on ski) attacco m [di sicurezza]

binge /bɪndʒ/ n [!] **have a ~** fare baldoria; (eat a lot) abbuffarsi •vi abbuffarsi (**on** di)

binoculars /bɪ'nɒkjʊləz/ npl **[pair of] ~** binocolo msg

biograph|er /baɪ'ɒgrəfə(r)/ n biografo, -a mf. **~y** n biografia f

biological /baɪə'lɒdʒɪkl/ adj biologico

biolog|ist /baɪ'ɒlədʒɪst/ n biologo, -a mf. **~y** n biologia f

birch /bɜ:tʃ/ n (tree) betulla f

bird /bɜ:d/ n uccello m; ([!]: girl) ragazza f

Biro® /'baɪrəʊ/ n biro® f inv

birth /bɜ:θ/ n nascita f

birth: ~ certificate n certificato m di nascita. **~-control** n controllo m delle nascite. ~**day** n compleanno m. ~**mark** n voglia f. ~**-rate** n natalità f

biscuit /ˈbɪskɪt/ n biscotto m

bisect /baɪˈsekt/ vt dividere in due [parti]

bishop /ˈbɪʃəp/ n vescovo m; (in chess) alfiere m

bit[1] /bɪt/ n pezzo m; (smaller) pezzetto m; (for horse) morso m; (Comput) bit m inv; **a ~ of** un pezzo di (cheese, paper); un po' di (time, rain, silence); **~ by ~** poco a poco; **do one's ~** fare la propria parte

bit[2] ▹**bite**

bitch /bɪtʃ/ n cagna f; ☒ stronza f. ~**y** adj velenoso

bit|e /baɪt/ n morso m; (insect ~) puntura f; (mouthful) boccone m •vt (pt **bit**, pp **bitten**) mordere; (insect:) pungere; ~**e one's nails** mangiarsi le unghie •vi mordere; (insect:) pungere. ~**ing** adj (wind, criticism) pungente; (remark) mordace

bitter /ˈbɪtə(r)/ adj amaro •n Br birra f amara. ~**ly** adv amaramente; **it's ~ly cold** c'è un freddo pungente. ~**ness** n amarezza f

bizarre /bɪˈzɑː(r)/ adj bizzarro

black /blæk/ adj nero; **be ~ and blue** essere pieno di lividi •n negro, -a mf •vt boicottare (goods). ▫ **~ out** vt cancellare •vi (lose consciousness) perdere coscienza

black: ~**berry** n mora f. ~**bird** n merlo m. ~**board** n (Sch) lavagna f. ~ˈ**currant** n ribes m inv nero; ~ˈ**eye** n occhio m nero. ~ ˈ**ice** n ghiaccio m (sulla strada). ~**leg** n Br crumiro m. ~**list** vt mettere sulla lista nera. ~**mail** n ricatto m •vt ricattare. ~**mailer** n ricattatore, -trice mf. ~**-out** n blackout m inv; **have a ~-out** (Med) perdere coscienza. ~**smith** n fabbro m

bladder /ˈblædə(r)/ n (Anat) vescica f

blade /bleɪd/ n lama f; (of grass) filo m

blame /bleɪm/ n colpa f •vt dare la colpa a; **~ sb for doing sth** dare la colpa a qcno per aver fatto qcsa; **no one is to ~** non è colpa di nessuno. ~**less** adj innocente

bland /blænd/ adj (food) insipido; (person) insulso

blank /blæŋk/ adj bianco; (look) vuoto •n spazio m vuoto; (cartridge) a salve. ~ ˈ**cheque** n assegno m in bianco

blanket /ˈblæŋkɪt/ n coperta f

blare /bleə(r)/ vi suonare a tutto volume. ▫ **~ out** vt far risuonare •vi (music, radio:) strillare

blaspheme /blæsˈfiːm/ vi bestemmiare

blasphem|ous /ˈblæsfəməs/ adj blasfemo. ~**y** n bestemmia f

blast /blɑːst/ n (gust) raffica f; (sound) scoppio m •vt (with explosive) far saltare •int ☒ maledizione!. ~**ed** adj ☒ maledetto

blast-off n (of missile) lancio m

blatant /ˈbleɪtənt/ adj sfacciato

blaze /bleɪz/ n incendio m; **a ~ of colour** un'esplosione f di colori •vi ardere

blazer /ˈbleɪzə(r)/ n blazer m inv

bleach /bliːtʃ/ n decolorante m; (for cleaning) candeggina f •vt sbiancare; ossigenare (hair)

bleak /bliːk/ adj desolato; (fig: prospects, future) tetro

bleat /bliːt/ vi belare •n belato m

bleed /bliːd/ v (pt/pp **bled**) •vi sanguinare •vt spurgare (brakes, radiator)

bleep /bliːp/ n bip m •vi suonare •vt chiamare (col cercapersone) (doctor). ~**er** n cercapersone m inv

blemish /ˈblemɪʃ/ n macchia f

blend /blend/ n (of tea, coffee, whisky) miscela f; (of colours) insieme m •vt mescolare •vi (colours, sounds:) fondersi (**with** con). ~**er** n (Culin) frullatore m

bless /bles/ vt benedire. ~**ed** adj also ☒ benedetto. ~**ing** n benedizione f

blew /bluː/ ▹**blow**[2]

blight /blaɪt/ n (Bot) ruggine f •vt far avvizzire (plants)

blind[1] /blaɪnd/ adj cieco; **the ~** npl i ciechi mpl; **~ man/woman** cieco/cieca •vt accecare

blind[2] n **[roller] ~** avvolgibile m; **[Venetian] ~** veneziana f

blind: ~ ˈ**alley** n vicolo m cieco. ~**fold** adj **be ~fold** avere gli occhi bendati •n benda f •vt bendare gli occhi a. ~**ly** adv ciecamente. ~**ness** n cecità f

blink /blɪŋk/ vi sbattere le palpebre; (light:) tremolare

blinkers /'blɪŋkəz/ npl paraocchi mpl

bliss /blɪs/ n (Rel) beatitudine f; (happiness) felicità f. **~ful** adj beato; (happy) meraviglioso

blister /'blɪstə(r)/ n (Med) vescica f; (in paint) bolla f •vi (paint:) formare una bolla/delle bolle

blizzard /'blɪzəd/ n tormenta f

bloated /'bləʊtɪd/ adj gonfio

blob /blɒb/ n goccia f

bloc /blɒk/ n (Pol) blocco m

block /blɒk/ n blocco m; (building) isolato m; (building ~) cubo m (per giochi di costruzione); **~ of flats** palazzo m •vt bloccare. □ **~ up** vt bloccare

blockade /blɒ'keɪd/ n blocco m •vt bloccare

blockage /'blɒkɪdʒ/ n ostruzione f

block: ~head n [!] testone, -a mf. **~ 'letters** npl stampatello m

bloke /bləʊk/ n [!] tizio m

blonde /blɒnd/ adj biondo •n bionda f

blood /blʌd/ n sangue m

blood: ~ bath n bagno m di sangue. **~ group** n gruppo m sanguigno. **~hound** n segugio m. **~ pressure** n pressione f del sangue. **~shed** n spargimento m di sangue. **~shot** adj iniettato di sangue. **~stream** n sangue m. **~thirsty** adj assetato di sangue

bloody /'blʌdɪ/ adj (**-ier, -iest**) insanguinato; [✖] maledetto •adv [✖] **~ easy/difficult** facile/difficile da matti. **~-'minded** adj scorbutico

bloom /blu:m/ n fiore m; **in ~** (flower:) sbocciato; (tree:) in fiore •vi fiorire; fig essere in forma smagliante

blossom /'blɒsəm/ n fiori mpl (d'albero); (single one) fiore m •vi sbocciare

blot /blɒt/ n also fig macchia f •**blot out** vt (pt/pp **blotted**) fig cancellare

blotch /blɒtʃ/ n macchia f. **~y** adj chiazzato

'blotting-paper n carta f assorbente

blouse /blaʊz/ n camicetta f

blow[1] /bləʊ/ n colpo m

blow[2] v (pt **blew**, pp **blown**) •vi (wind:) soffiare; (fuse:) saltare •vt ([!]: squander) sperperare; **~ one's nose** soffiarsi il naso. □ **~ away** vt far volar via (papers) •vi (papers:) volare via. □ **~ down** vt abbattere •vi abbattersi al suolo. □ **~ out** vt (extinguish) spegnere. □ **~ over** vi (storm:) passare; (fuss, trouble:) dissiparsi. □ **~ up** vt (inflate) gonfiare; (enlarge) ingrandire (photograph); (by explosion) far esplodere •vi esplodere

blow: ~-dry vt asciugare col fon. **~lamp** n fiamma f ossidrica

'blowtorch n fiamma f ossidrica

blue /blu:/ adj (pale) celeste; (navy) blu inv; (royal) azzurro; **~ with cold** livido per il freddo •n blu m inv; **have the ~s** essere giù [di tono]; **out of the ~** inaspettatamente

blue: ~bell n giacinto m di bosco. **~berry** n mirtillo m. **~bottle** n moscone m. **~ film** n film m inv a luci rosse. **~print** n fig riferimento m

bluff /blʌf/ n bluff m inv •vi bluffare

blunder /'blʌndə(r)/ n gaffe f inv •vi fare una/delle gaffe

blunt /blʌnt/ adj spuntato; (person) reciso. **~ly** adv schiettamente

blur /blɜ:(r)/ n **it's all a ~** fig è tutto un insieme confuso •vt (pt/pp **blurred**) rendere confuso. **~red** adj (vision, photo) sfocato

blurb /blɜ:b/ n soffietto m editoriale

blurt /blɜ:t/ vt **~ out** spifferare

blush /blʌʃ/ n rossore m •vi arrossire

boar /bɔ:(r)/ n cinghiale m

board /bɔ:d/ n tavola f; (for notices) tabellone m; (committee) assemblea f; (of directors) consiglio m; **full ~** Br pensione f completa; **half ~** Br mezza pensione f; **~ and lodging** vitto e alloggio m; **go by the ~** [!] andare a monte •vt (Naut, Aeron) salire a bordo di •vi (passengers:) salire a bordo. □ **~ up** vt sbarrare con delle assi. □ **~ with** vt stare a pensione da.

boarder /'bɔ:də(r)/ n pensionante mf; (Sch) convittore, -trice mf

board: ~ing-house n pensione f. **~ing-school** n collegio m

boast /bəʊst/ vi vantarsi (**about** di). **~ful** adj vanaglorioso

boat /bəʊt/ n barca f; (ship) nave f. **~er** n (hat) paglietta f

bob /bɒb/ n (hairstyle) caschetto m •vi (pt/pp **bobbed**) (also **~ up and down**) andare su e giù

'**bob-sleigh** n bob m inv

bode /bəʊd/ vi **~ well/ill** essere di buono/cattivo augurio

bodily /'bɒdɪlɪ/ adj fisico •adv (forcibly) fisicamente

body /'bɒdɪ/ n corpo m; (organization) ente m; (amount: of poems etc) quantità f. **~guard** n guardia f del corpo. **~ part** n pezzo m del corpo. **~work** n (Auto) carrozzeria f

bog /bɒg/ n palude f •vt (pt/pp **bogged**) **get ~ged down** impantanarsi

boggle /'bɒgl/ vi **the mind ~s** non posso neanche immaginarlo

bogus /'bəʊgəs/ adj falso

boil[1] /bɔɪl/ n (Med) foruncolo m

boil[2] n **bring/come to the ~** portare/arrivare ad ebollizione •vt [far] bollire •vi bollire; (fig: with anger) ribollire; **the water** or **kettle's ~ing** l'acqua bolle. **boil down to** vt fig ridursi a. □ **~ over** vi straboccare (bollendo). □ **~ up** vt far bollire

boiler /'bɔɪlə(r)/ n caldaia f. **~suit** n tuta f

boisterous /'bɔɪstərəs/ adj chiassoso

bold /bəʊld/ adj audace •n (Typ) neretto m. **~ness** n audacia f

bolster /'bəʊlstə(r)/ n cuscino m (lungo e rotondo) •vt **~ [up]** sostenere

bolt /bəʊlt/ n (for door) catenaccio m; (for fixing) bullone m •vt fissare (con i bulloni) (**to** a); chiudere col chiavistello (door); ingurgitare (food) •vi svignarsela; (horse:) scappar via •adv **~ upright** diritto come un fuso

bomb /bɒm/ n bomba f •vt bombardare

bombard /bɒm'bɑːd/ vt also fig bombardare

bomb|er /'bɒmə(r)/ n (Aeron) bombardiere m; (person) dinamitardo m. **~er jacket** giubbotto m, bomber m inv. **~shell** n (fig: news) bomba f

bond /bɒnd/ n fig legame m; (Comm) obbligazione f •vt (glue:) attaccare

bondage /'bɒndɪdʒ/ n schiavitù f

bone /bəʊn/ n osso m; (of fish) spina f •vt disossare (meat); togliere le spine da (fish). **~-'dry** adj secco

bonfire /'bɒn-/ n falò m inv. **~ night** festa celebrata la notte del 5 novembre con fuochi d'artificio e falò

bonnet /'bɒnɪt/ n cuffia f; (of car) cofano m

bonus /'bəʊnəs/ n (individual) gratifica f; (production **~**) premio m; (life insurance) dividendo m; **a ~** fig qualcosa in più

bony /'bəʊnɪ/ adj (**-ier, -iest**) ossuto; (fish) pieno di spine

boo /buː/ interj (to surprise or frighten) bu! •vt/i fischiare

boob /buːb/ n ! (mistake) gaffe f inv; (breast) tetta f •vi ! fare una gaffe

book /bʊk/ n libro m; (of tickets) blocchetto m; **keep the ~s** (Comm) tenere la contabilità; **be in sb's bad/good ~s** essere nel libro nero/nelle grazie di qcno •vt (reserve) prenotare; (for offence) multare •vi (reserve) prenotare

book: ~case n libreria f. **~ing-office** n biglietteria f. **~keeping** n contabilità f. **~let** n opuscolo m. **~maker** n allibratore m. **~mark** n segnalibro m. **~seller** n libraio, -a mf. **~shop** n libreria f. **~worm** n topo m di biblioteca

boom /buːm/ n (Comm) boom m inv; (upturn) impennata f; (of thunder, gun) rimbombo m •vi (thunder, gun:) rimbombare; fig prosperare

boost /buːst/ n spinta f •vt stimolare (sales); sollevare (morale); far crescere (hopes). **~er** n (Med) dose f supplementare

boot /buːt/ n stivale m; (up to ankle) stivaletto m; (football) scarpetta f; (climbing) scarpone m; (Auto) portabagagli m inv •vt (Comput) inizializzare

booth /buːð/ n (telephone, voting) cabina f; (at market) bancarella f

booze /buːz/ ! n alcolici mpl. **~-up** n bella bevuta f

border /'bɔːdə(r)/ n bordo m; (frontier) frontiera f; (in garden) bordura f •vi **~ on** confinare con; fig essere ai

b

confini di (madness). **~line** n linea f di demarcazione; **~line case** caso m dubbio

bore¹ /bɔ:(r)/ ▹**bear²**

bore² vt (Techn) forare

bor|e³ n (of gun) calibro m; (person) seccatore, -trice mf; (thing) seccatura f • vt annoiare. **~edom** n noia f. **be ~ed (to tears** or **to death)** annoiarsi (da morire). **~ing** adj noioso

born /bɔ:n/ pp **be ~** nascere; **I was ~ in 1966** sono nato nel 1966 • adj nato; **a ~ liar/actor** un bugiardo/attore nato

borne /bɔ:n/ ▹**bear²**

borough /'bʌrə/ n municipalità f inv

borrow /'bɒrəʊ/ vt prendere a prestito (**from** da); **can I ~ your pen?** mi presti la tua penna?

boss /bɒs/ n direttore, -trice mf • vt (also **~ about**) comandare a bacchetta. **~y** adj autoritario

botanical /bə'tænɪkl/ adj botanico

botan|ist /'bɒtənɪst/ n botanico, -a mf. **~y** n botanica f

both /bəʊθ/ adj & pron tutti e due, entrambi • adv **~ men and women** entrambi uomini e donne; **~ [of] the children** tutti e due i bambini; **they are ~ dead** sono morti entrambi; **~ of them** tutti e due

bother /'bɒðə(r)/ n preoccupazione f; (minor trouble) fastidio m; **it's no ~** non c'è problema • int [!] che seccatura! • vt (annoy) dare fastidio a; (disturb) disturbare • vi preoccuparsi (**about** di); **don't ~** lascia perdere

bottle /'bɒtl/ n bottiglia f; (baby's) biberon m inv • vt imbottigliare. □ **~ up** vt fig reprimere

bottle: ~-neck n fig ingorgo m. **~-opener** n apribottiglie m inv

bottom /'bɒtm/ adj ultimo; **the ~ shelf** l'ultimo scaffale in basso • n (of container) fondo m; (of river) fondale m; (of hill) piedi mpl; (buttocks) sedere m; **at the ~ of the page** in fondo alla pagina; **get to the ~ of** fig vedere cosa c'è sotto. **~less** adj senza fondo

bough /baʊ/ n ramoscello m

bought /bɔ:t/ ▹**buy**

boulder /'bəʊldə(r)/ n masso m

bounce /baʊns/ vi rimbalzare; ([!]: cheque:) essere respinto • vt far rimbalzare (ball)

bound¹ /baʊnd/ n balzo m • vi balzare

bound² ▹**bind** • adj **~ for** (ship) diretto a; **be ~ to do** (likely) dovere fare per forza; (obliged) essere costretto a fare

boundary /'baʊndərɪ/ n limite m

bouquet /bʊ'keɪ/ n mazzo m di fiori; (of wine) bouquet m

bout /baʊt/ n (Med) attacco m; (Sport) incontro m

bow¹ /bəʊ/ n (weapon) arco m; (Mus) archetto m; (knot) nodo m

bow² /baʊ/ n inchino m • vi inchinars[i] • vt piegare (head)

bow³ /baʊ/ n (Naut) prua f

bowl¹ /bəʊl/ n (for soup, cereal) scodell[a] f; (of pipe) fornello m

bowl² n (ball) boccia f • vt lanciare • v[i] (Cricket) servire; (in bowls) lanciare. □ **~ over** vt buttar giù; (fig: leave speechless) lasciar senza parole

bowler¹ /'bəʊlə(r)/ n (Cricket) lanciatore m; (Bowls) giocatore m di bocce

bowler² n **~ [hat]** bombetta f

bowling /'bəʊlɪŋ/ n gioco m delle bocce. **~-alley** n pista f da bowling

bow-'tie /bəʊ-/ n cravatta f a farfalla

box¹ /bɒks/ n scatola f; (Theat) palco m

box² vi (Sport) fare il pugile • vt **~ sb's ears** dare uno scappaccione a qcno

box|er /'bɒksə(r)/ n pugile m. **~ing** n pugilato m. **B~ing Day** n [giorno m di] Santo Stefano m

box: ~-office n (Theat) botteghino m. **~-room** n Br sgabuzzino m

boy /bɔɪ/ n ragazzo m; (younger) bambino m

'boy band n boy band f inv

boycott /'bɔɪkɒt/ n boicottaggio m • vt boicottare

boy: ~friend n ragazzo m. **~ish** adj da ragazzino

bra /brɑ:/ n reggiseno m

brace /breɪs/ n sostegno m; (dental) apparecchio m; **~s** npl bretelle fpl • vt **~ oneself** fig farsi forza (**for** per affrontare)

bracelet /'breɪslɪt/ n braccialetto m

bracken /'brækn/ n felce f

bracket /'brækɪt/ n mensola f; (group) categoria f; (Typ) parentesi f inv •vt mettere fra parentesi

brag /bræg/ vi (pt/pp **bragged**) vantarsi (**about** di)

braid /breɪd/ n (edging) passamano m

brain /breɪn/ n cervello m; **~s** pl fig testa fsg

brain: ~child n invenzione f personale. **~wash** vt fare il lavaggio del cervello a. **~wave** n lampo m di genio

brainy /'breɪnɪ/ adj (**-ier, -iest**) intelligente

brake /breɪk/ n freno m •vi frenare. **~-light** n stop m inv

bramble /'bræmbl/ n rovo m; (fruit) mora f

bran /bræn/ n crusca f

branch /brɑːntʃ/ n also fig ramo m; (Comm) succursale f •vi (road:) biforcarsi. □ **~ off** vi biforcarsi. □ **~ out** vi **~ out into** allargare le proprie attività nel ramo di

brand /brænd/ n marca f; (on animal) marchio m •vt marcare (animal); fig tacciare (**as** di)

brandish /'brændɪʃ/ vt brandire

brandy /'brændɪ/ n brandy m inv

brash /bræʃ/ adj sfrontato

brass /brɑːs/ n ottone m; **the ~** (Mus) gli ottoni mpl; **top ~** [!] pezzi mpl grossi. **~ band** n banda f (di soli ottoni)

brassiere /'bræzɪə(r)/ n fml, Am reggipetto m

brat /bræt/ n pej marmocchio, -a mf

bravado /brə'vɑːdəʊ/ n bravata f

brave /breɪv/ adj coraggioso •vt affrontare. **~ry** n coraggio m

brawl /brɔːl/ n rissa f •vi azzuffarsi

brazen /'breɪzn/ adj sfrontato

Brazil /brə'zɪl/ n Brasile m. **~ian** adj & n brasiliano, -a mf. **~ nut** n noce f del Brasile

breach /briːtʃ/ n (of law) violazione f; (gap) breccia f; (fig: in party) frattura f; **~ of contract** inadempienza f di contratto; **~ of the peace** violazione f della quiete pubblica •vt recedere (contract)

bread /bred/ n pane m; **a slice of ~ and butter** una fetta di pane imburrato

breadcrumbs npl briciole fpl; (Culin) pangrattato m

breadth /bredθ/ n larghezza f

'**bread-winner** n quello, -a mf che porta i soldi a casa

break /breɪk/ n rottura f; (interval) intervallo m; (interruption) interruzione f; ([!]: chance) opportunità f inv •v (pt **broke**, pp **broken**) •vt rompere; (interrupt) interrompere; **~ one's arm** rompersi un braccio •vi rompersi; (day:) spuntare; (storm:) scoppiare; (news:) diffondersi; (boy's voice:) cambiare. □ **~ away** vi scappare; fig chiudere (**from** con). □ **~ down** vi (machine, car:) guastarsi; (emotionally) cedere (psicologicamente) •vt sfondare (door); ripartire (figures). □ **~ into** vt introdursi (con la forza) in; forzare (car). □ **~ off** vt rompere (engagement) •vi (part of whole:) rompersi. □ **~ out** vi (fight, war:) scoppiare. □ **~ up** vt far cessare (fight); disperdere (crowd) •vi (crowd:) disperdersi; (couple:) separarsi; (Sch) iniziare le vacanze

'**break|able** /'breɪkəbl/ adj fragile. **~age** n rottura f. **~down** n (of car, machine) guasto m; (Med) esaurimento m nervoso; (of figures) analisi f inv. **~er** n (wave) frangente m

breakfast /'brekfəst/ n [prima] colazione f

break: ~through n scoperta f. **~water** n frangiflutti m inv

breast /brest/ n seno m. **~-feed** vt allattare [al seno]. **~-stroke** n nuoto m a rana

breath /'breθ/: **~less** adj senza fiato. **~-taking** adj mozzafiato. **~ test** n prova [etilica] f del palloncino

breathalyse /'breθəlaɪz/ vt sottoporre alla prova [etilica] del palloncino. **~r®** n Br alcoltest m inv

breathe /briːð/ vt/i respirare. □ **~ in** vi inspirare •vt respirare (scent, air). □ **~ out** vt/i espirare

breath|er /'briːðə(r)/ n pausa f. **~ing** n respirazione f

bred /bred/ ▸**breed**

breed /briːd/ n razza f •v (pt/pp **bred**)

• vt allevare; (give rise to) generare • vi riprodursi. **~er** n allevatore, -trice mf. **~ing** n allevamento m; fig educazione f

breez|e /bri:z/ n brezza f. **~y** adj ventoso

brew /bru:/ n infuso m • vt mettere in infusione (tea); produrre (beer) • vi fig (trouble:) essere nell'aria. **~er** n birraio m. **~ery** n fabbrica f di birra

bribe /braɪb/ n (money) bustarella f; (large sum of money) tangente f • vt corrompere. **~ry** n corruzione f

brick /brɪk/ n mattone m. '**~layer** n muratore m • **brick up** vt murare

bridal /'braɪdl/ adj nuziale

bride /braɪd/ n sposa f. **~groom** n sposo m. **~smaid** n damigella f d'onore

bridge[1] /brɪdʒ/ n ponte m; (of nose) dorso m; (of spectacles) ponticello m • vt fig colmare (gap)

bridge[2] n (Cards) bridge m

bridle /'braɪdl/ n briglia f

brief[1] /bri:f/ adj breve

brief[2] n istruzioni fpl; (Jur: case) causa f • vt dare istruzioni a; (Jur) affidare la causa a. **~case** n cartella f

briefs /bri:fs/ npl slip m inv

brigad|e /brɪ'geɪd/ n brigata f. **~ier** n generale m di brigata

bright /braɪt/ adj (metal, idea) brillante; (day, room, future) luminoso; (clever) intelligente; **~ red** rosso m acceso

bright|en /'braɪtn/ v **~en [up]** • vt ravvivare; rallegrare (person) • vi (weather:) schiarirsi; (face:) illuminarsi; (person:) rallegrarsi. **~ly** adv (shine) intensamente; (smile) allegramente. **~ness** n luminosità f; (intelligence) intelligenza f

brilliance /'brɪljəns/ n luminosità f; (of person) genialità f

brilliant /'brɪljənt/ adj (very good) eccezionale; (very intelligent) brillante; (sunshine) splendente

brim /brɪm/ n bordo m; (of hat) tesa f • **brim over** vi (pt/pp **brimmed**) traboccare

brine /braɪn/ n salamoia f

bring /brɪŋ/ vt (pt/pp **brought**) portare (person, object). □ **~ about** vt causare. □ **~ along** vt portare [con sé]. □ **~ back** vt restituire (sth borrowed); reintrodurre (hanging); fare ritornare in mente (memories). □ **~ down** vt portare giù; fare cadere (government); fare abbassare (price). □ **~ off** vt **~ sth off** riuscire a fare qcsa. □ **~ on** vt (cause) provocare. □ **~ out** vt (emphasize) mettere in evidenza; pubblicare (book). □ **~ round** vt portare; (persuade) convincere; far rinvenire (unconscious person). □ **~ up** vt (vomit) rimettere; allevare (children); tirare fuori (question, subject)

brink /brɪŋk/ n orlo m

brisk /brɪsk/ adj svelto; (person) sbrigativo; (trade, business) redditizio; (walk) a passo spedito

brist|le /'brɪsl/ n setola f • vi **~ling with** pieno di. **~ly** adj (chin) ispido

Brit|ain /'brɪtn/ n Gran Bretagna f. **~ish** adj britannico; (ambassador) della Gran Bretagna • npl **the ~ish** il popolo britannico. **~on** n cittadino, -a britannico, -a mf

brittle /'brɪtl/ adj fragile

broach /brəʊtʃ/ vt toccare (subject)

broad /brɔ:d/ adj ampio; (hint) chiaro; (accent) marcato. **two metres ~** largo due metri; **in ~ daylight** in pieno giorno. **~ band** n banda f larga. **~ beans** npl fave fpl

'**broadcast** n trasmissione f • vt/i (pt/pp **-cast**) trasmettere. **~er** n giornalista mf radiotelevisivo, -a. **~ing** n diffusione f radiotelevisiva; **be in ~ing** lavorare per la televisione/radio

broaden /'brɔ:dn/ vt allargare • vi allargarsi

broadly /'brɔ:dlɪ/ adv largamente; **~ [speaking]** generalmente

broad'minded adj di larghe vedute

broccoli /'brɒkəlɪ/ n inv broccoli mpl

brochure /'brəʊʃə(r)/ n opuscolo m; (travel **~**) dépliant m inv

broke /brəʊk/ ▸**break** • adj [!] al verde

broken /'brəʊkn/ ▸**break** • adj rotto; (fig: marriage) fallito. **~ English** inglese m stentato. **~-hearted** adj affranto

broker /'brəʊkə(r)/ n broker m inv

brolly /ˈbrɒlɪ/ n [!] ombrello m

bronchitis /brɒŋˈkaɪtɪs/ n bronchite f

bronze /brɒnz/ n bronzo m •attrib di bronzo

brooch /brəʊtʃ/ n spilla f

brood /bruːd/ n covata f; (hum: children) prole f •vi fig rimuginare

brook /brʊk/ n ruscello m

broom /bruːm/ n scopa f. **~stick** n manico m di scopa

broth /brɒθ/ n brodo m

brothel /ˈbrɒθl/ n bordello m

brother /ˈbrʌðə(r)/ n fratello m

brother: ~-in-law n (pl **~s-in-law**) cognato m. **~ly** adj fraterno

brought /brɔːt/ ▸**bring**

brow /braʊ/ n fronte f; (of hill) cima f

ˈ**browbeat** vt (pt **-beat**, pp **-beaten**) intimidire

brown /braʊn/ adj marrone; castano (hair) •n marrone m •vt rosolare (meat) •vi (meat:) rosolarsi. **~ ˈpaper** n carta f da pacchi

browse /braʊz/ vi (read) leggicchiare; (in shop) curiosare

bruise /bruːz/ n livido m; (on fruit) ammaccatura f •vt ammaccare (fruit); **~ one's arm** farsi un livido sul braccio. **~d** adj contuso

brunette /bruːˈnet/ n bruna f

brunt /brʌnt/ n **bear the ~ of sth** subire maggiormente qcsa

brush /brʌʃ/ n spazzola f; (with long handle) spazzolone m; (for paint) pennello m; (bushes) boscaglia f; (fig: conflict) breve scontro m •vt spazzolare (hair); lavarsi (teeth); scopare (stairs, floor). □ **~ against** vt sfiorare. □ **~ aside** vt fig ignorare. □ **~ off** vt spazzolare; (with hands) togliere; ignorare (criticism). □ **~ up** vt/i fig **~ up [on]** rinfrescare

brusque /brʊsk/ adj brusco

Brussels /ˈbrʌslz/ n Bruxelles f. **~ sprouts** npl cavoletti mpl di Bruxelles

brutal /ˈbruːtl/ adj brutale. **~ity** n brutalità f inv

brute /bruːt/ n bruto m. **~ force** n forza f bruta

BSc n abbr Bachelor of Science

BSE n abbr (bovine spongiform encephalitis) encefalite f bovina spongiforme

bubble /ˈbʌbl/ n bolla f; (in drink) bollicina f

buck[1] /bʌk/ n maschio m del cervo; (rabbit) maschio m del coniglio •vi (horse:) saltare a quattro zampe. □ **~ up** vi [!] tirarsi su; (hurry) sbrigarsi

buck[2] n Am [!] dollaro m

buck[3] n **pass the ~** scaricare la responsabilità

bucket /ˈbʌkɪt/ n secchio m

buckle /ˈbʌkl/ n fibbia f •vt allacciare •vi (shelf:) piegarsi; (wheel:) storcersi

bud /bʌd/ n bocciolo m

Buddhis|m /ˈbʊdɪzm/ n buddismo m. **~t** adj & n buddista mf

buddy /ˈbʌdɪ/ n [!] amico, -a mf

budge /bʌdʒ/ vt spostare •vi spostarsi

budgerigar /ˈbʌdʒərɪgɑː(r)/ n cocorita f

budget /ˈbʌdʒɪt/ n bilancio m; (allotted to specific activity) budget m inv •vi (pt/pp **budgeted**) prevedere le spese; **~ for sth** includere qcsa nelle spese previste

buffalo /ˈbʌfələʊ/ n (inv or pl **-es**) bufalo m

buffer /ˈbʌfə(r)/ n (Rail) respingente m; **old ~** [!] vecchio bacucco m; **~ zone** n zona f cuscinetto

buffet[1] /ˈbʊfeɪ/ n buffet m inv

buffet[2] /ˈbʌfɪt/ vt (pt/pp **buffeted**) sferzare

bug /bʌg/ n (insect) insetto m; (Comput) bug m inv; ([!]: device) cimice f •vt (pt/pp **bugged**) [!] installare delle microspie in (room); mettere sotto controllo (telephone); ([!]: annoy) scocciare

buggy /ˈbʌgɪ/ n **[baby] ~** passeggino m

bugle /ˈbjuːgl/ n tromba f

build /bɪld/ n (of person) corporatura f •vt/i (pt/pp **built**) costruire. □ **~ on** vt aggiungere (extra storey); sviluppare (previous work). □ **~ up** vt **~ up one's strength** rimettersi in forza •vi (pressure, traffic:) aumentare; (excitement, tension:) crescere

b

builder /'bɪldə(r)/ n (company) costruttore m; (worker) muratore m

building /'bɪldɪŋ/ n edificio m. **~ site** n cantiere m [di costruzione]. **~ society** n istituto m di credito immobiliare

'**build-up** n (of gas etc) accumulo m; fig battage m inv pubblicitario

built /bɪlt/ ▹**build**. **~-in** adj (unit) a muro; (fig: feature) incorporato. **~-up area** n (Auto) centro m abitato

bulb /bʌlb/ n bulbo m; (Electr) lampadina f

Bulgaria /bʌl'geərɪə/ n Bulgaria f

bulg|e /bʌldʒ/ n rigonfiamento m •vi esser gonfio (**with** di); (stomach, wall:) sporgere; (eyes, with surprise:) uscire dalle orbite. **~ing** adj gonfio; (eyes) sporgente

bulk /bʌlk/ n volume m; (greater part) grosso m; **in ~** in grande quantità; (loose) sfuso. **~y** adj voluminoso

bull /bʊl/ n toro m

'**bulldog** n bulldog m inv

bulldozer /'bʊldəʊzə(r)/ n bulldozer m inv

bullet /'bʊlɪt/ n pallottola f

bulletin /'bʊlɪtɪn/ n bollettino m. **~ board** n (Comput) bacheca f elettronica

'**bullet-proof** adj antiproiettile inv; (vehicle) blindato

'**bullfight** n corrida f. **~er** n torero m

bull: ~ring n arena f. **~'s-eye** n centro m del bersaglio; **score a ~'s-eye** fare centro

bully /'bʊlɪ/ n prepotente mf •vt fare il/la prepotente con. **~ing** n prepotenze fpl

bum[1] /bʌm/ n ☒ sedere m

bum[2] n Am ! vagabondo, -a mf •**bum around** vi ! vagabondare

bumble-bee /'bʌmbl-/ n calabrone m

bump /bʌmp/ n botta f; (swelling) bozzo m, gonfiore m; (in road) protuberanza f •vt sbattere. □ **~ into** vt sbattere contro; (meet) imbattersi in. □ **~ off** vt ! far fuori

bumper /'bʌmpə(r)/ n (Auto) paraurti m inv •adj abbondante

bun /bʌn/ n focaccina f (dolce); (hair) chignon m inv

bunch /bʌntʃ/ n (of flowers, keys) mazzo m; (of bananas) casco m; (of people) gruppo m; **~ of grapes** grappolo m d'uva

bundle /'bʌndl/ n fascio m; (of money) mazzetta f; **a ~ of nerves** ! un fascio di nervi •vt **~ [up]** affastellare

bungalow /'bʌŋgələʊ/ n bungalow m inv

bungle /'bʌŋgl/ vt fare un pasticcio di

bunk /bʌŋk/ n cuccetta f. **~-beds** npl letti mpl a castello

bunny /'bʌnɪ/ n ! coniglietto m

buoy /bɔɪ/ n boa f

burden /'bɜːdn/ n carico m •vt caricare. **~some** adj gravoso

bureau /'bjʊərəʊ/ n (pl **-x** /-əʊz/ or **~s**) (desk) scrivania f; (office) ufficio m

bureaucracy /bjʊə'rɒkrəsɪ/ n burocrazia f

bureaucrat /'bjʊərəkræt/ n burocrate mf. **~ic** adj burocratico

burger /'bɜːgə(r)/ n hamburger m inv

burglar /'bɜːglə(r)/ n svaligiatore, -trice mf. **~ alarm** n antifurto m inv

burgle /'bɜːgl/ vt svaligiare

burial /'berɪəl/ n sepoltura f. **~ ground** cimitero m

burly /'bɜːlɪ/ adj (**-ier, -iest**) corpulento

burn /bɜːn/ n bruciatura f •v (pt/pp **burnt** or **burned**) •vt bruciare•vi bruciare. □ **~ down** vt/i bruciare. □ **~ out** vi fig esaurirsi. **~er** n •(on stove) bruciatore m •(Comput) masterizzatore m

burnt /bɜːnt/ ▹**burn**

burp /bɜːp/ n ! rutto m •vi ! ruttare

burrow /'bʌrəʊ/ n tana f •vt scavare (hole)

bursar /'bɜːsə(r)/ n economo, -a mf. **~y** n borsa f di studio

burst /bɜːst/ n (of gunfire, energy, laughter) scoppio m; (of speed) scatto m •v (pt/pp **burst**) •vt far scoppiare •vi scoppiare; ~ **into tears** scoppiare in lacrime; **she ~ into the room** ha fatto irruzione nella stanza. □ ~ **out** vi ~ **out laughing/crying** scoppiare a ridere/piangere

bury /'berɪ/ vt (pt/pp **-ied**) seppellire; (hide) nascondere

bus /bʌs/ n autobus m inv, pullman m inv; (long distance) pullman m inv, corriera f

bush /bʊʃ/ n cespuglio m; (land) boscaglia f. ~**y** adj (**-ier, -iest**) folto

business /'bɪznɪs/ n affare m; (Comm) affari mpl; (establishment) attività f di commercio; **on** ~ per affari; **he has no ~ to** non ha alcun diritto di; **mind one's own** ~ farsi gli affari propri; **that's none of your** ~ non sono affari tuoi. ~**-like** adj efficiente. ~**man** n uomo m d'affari. ~**woman** n donna f d'affari

busker /'bʌskə(r)/ n suonatore, -trice mf ambulante

bus station n stazione f degli autobus

bus-stop n fermata f d'autobus

bust[1] /bʌst/ n busto m; (chest) petto m

bust[2] adj [!] rotto; **go** ~ fallire • v (pt/pp **busted** or **bust**) [!] • vt far scoppiare • vi scoppiare

bust-up n [!] lite f

busy /'bɪzɪ/ adj (**-ier, -iest**) occupato; (day, time) intenso; (street) affollato; (with traffic) pieno di traffico; **be ~ doing** essere occupato a fare • vt ~ **oneself** darsi da fare

busybody n ficcanaso mf inv

but /bʌt/, atono /bət/ conj ma • prep eccetto, tranne; **nobody ~ you** nessuno tranne te; ~ **for** (without) se non fosse stato per; **the last ~ one** il penultimo; **the next ~ one** il secondo • adv (only) soltanto; **there were ~ two** ce n'erano soltanto due

butcher /'bʊtʃə(r)/ n macellaio m; ~**'s [shop]** macelleria f • vt macellare; fig massacrare

butler /'bʌtlə(r)/ n maggiordomo m

butt /bʌt/ n (of gun) calcio m; (of cigarette) mozzicone m; (for water) barile m; (fig: target) bersaglio m • vt dare una testata a; (goat:) dare una cornata a. □ ~ **in** vi interrompere

butter /'bʌtə(r)/ n burro m • vt imburrare. □ ~ **up** vt [!] arruffianarsi

butter: ~**cup** n ranuncolo m. ~**fingers** nsg [!] **be a ~fingers** avere le mani di pasta frolla. ~**fly** n farfalla f

button /'bʌtn/ n bottone m • vt ~ **[up]** abbottonare • vi abbottonarsi. ~**hole** n occhiello m, asola f

buy /baɪ/ n **good/bad** ~ buon/cattivo acquisto m • vt (pt/pp **bought**) comprare; ~ **sb a drink** pagare da bere a qcno; **I'll ~ this one** (drink) questo, lo offro io. ~**er** n compratore, -trice mf

buzz /bʌz/ n ronzio m; **give sb a** ~ [!] (on phone) dare un colpo di telefono a qcno; (excite) mettere in fermento qcno • vi ronzare • vt ~ **sb** chiamare qcno col cicalino. □ ~ **off** vi [!] levarsi di torno

buzzer /'bʌzə(r)/ n cicalino m

by /baɪ/

• prep (*near, next to*) vicino a; (*at the latest*) per; **by Mozart** di Mozart; **he was run over by a bus** è stato investito da un autobus; **by oneself** da solo; **by the sea** al mare; **by sea** via mare; **by car/bus** in macchina/autobus; **by day/night** di giorno/notte; **by the hour/metre** a ore/metri; **six metres by four** sei metri per quattro; **he won by six metres** ha vinto di sei metri; **I missed the train by a minute** ho perso il treno per un minuto; **I'll be home by six** sarò a casa per le sei; **by this time next week** a quest'ora tra una settimana; **he rushed by me** mi è passato accanto di corsa

• adv **she'll be here by and by** sarà qui fra poco; **by and large** in complesso

bye[-bye] /baɪ['baɪ]/ int [!] ciao

by: ~**-election** n elezione f straordinaria indetta per coprire una carica rimasta vacante in Parlamento. ~**-law** n legge f locale. ~**pass** n circonvallazione f; (Med) by-pass m inv • vt evitare. ~**-product** n sottoprodotto m. ~**stander** n spettatore, -trice mf

Cc

C

cab /kæb/ n taxi m inv; (of lorry, train) cabina f

cabaret /ˈkæbəreɪ/ n cabaret m inv

cabbage /ˈkæbɪdʒ/ n cavolo m

cabin /ˈkæbɪn/ n (of plane, ship) cabina f; (hut) capanna f

cabinet /ˈkæbɪnɪt/ n armadietto m; [**display**] ~ vetrina f; **C~** (Pol) consiglio m dei ministri. **~-maker** n ebanista mf

cable /ˈkeɪbl/ n cavo m. ~ **ˈrailway** n funicolare f. ~ **ˈtelevision** n televisione f via cavo

cackle /ˈkækl/ vi ridacchiare

cactus /ˈkæktəs/ n (pl **-ti** /-taɪ/ or **-tuses**) cactus m inv

caddie /ˈkædɪ/ n portabastoni m inv

caddy /ˈkædɪ/ n [**tea-**]~ barattolo m del tè

cadet /kəˈdet/ n cadetto m

cadge /kædʒ/ vt/i ! scroccare

café /ˈkæfeɪ/ n caffè m inv

cafeteria /kæfəˈtɪərɪə/ n tavola f calda

caffeine /ˈkæfiːn/ n caffeina f

cage /keɪdʒ/ n gabbia f

cake /keɪk/ n torta f; (small) pasticcino m. **~d** adj incrostato (**with** di)

calamity /kəˈlæmətɪ/ n calamità f inv

calcium /ˈkælsɪəm/ n calcio m

calculat|e /ˈkælkjʊleɪt/ vt calcolare. **~ing** adj fig calcolatore. **~ion** n calcolo m. **~or** n calcolatrice f

calendar /ˈkælɪndə(r)/ n calendario m

calf[1] /kɑːf/ n (pl **calves**) vitello m

calf[2] n (pl **calves**) (Anat) polpaccio m

calibre /ˈkælɪbə(r)/ n calibro m

call /kɔːl/ n grido m; (Teleph) telefonata f; (visit) visita f; **be on** ~ (doctor:) essere di guardia •vt chiamare; indire (strike); **be ~ed** chiamarsi •vi chiamare; ~ [**in** or **round**] passare. □ ~ **back** vt/i richiamare. □ ~ **for** vt (ask for) chiedere; (require) richiedere; (fetch) passare a prendere. □ ~ **off** vt richiamare (dog); disdire (meeting); revocare (strike). □ ~ **on** vt chiamare; (appeal to) fare un appello a; (visit) visitare. □ ~ **out** vt chiamare ad alta voce (names) •vi chiamare ad alta voce. □ ~ **together** vt riunire. □ ~ **up** vt (Mil) chiamare alle armi; (Teleph) chiamare

call: ~-box n cabina f telefonica. ~ **centre** n call centre m inv. **~er** n visitatore, -trice mf; (Teleph) persona f che telefona. **~ing** n vocazione f

callous /ˈkæləs/ adj insensibile

calm /kɑːm/ adj calmo •n calma f. □ ~ **down** vt calmare •vi calmarsi. **~ly** adv con calma

calorie /ˈkælərɪ/ n caloria f

calves /kɑːvz/ npl ▸**calf**

camcorder /ˈkæmkɔːdə(r)/ n videocamera f

came /keɪm/ ▸**come**

camel /ˈkæml/ n cammello m

camera /ˈkæmərə/ n macchina f fotografica; (TV) telecamera f. **~man** n operatore m [televisivo], cameraman m inv

camouflage /ˈkæməflɑːʒ/ n mimetizzazione f •vt mimetizzare

camp /kæmp/ n campeggio f; (Mil) campo m •vi campeggiare; (Mil) accamparsi

campaign /kæmˈpeɪn/ n campagna f •vi fare una campagna

camp: ~-bed n letto m da campo. **~er** n campeggiatore, -trice mf; (Auto) camper m inv. **~ing** n campeggio m. **~site** n campeggio m

campus /ˈkæmpəs/ n (pl **-puses**) (Univ) città f universitaria, campus m inv

can[1] /kæn/ n (for petrol) latta f; (tin) scatola f; ~ **of beer** lattina f di birra •vt mettere in scatola

can² /kæn/, *atono* /kən/ v aux (pres **can**, pt **could**) (*be able to*) potere; (*know how to*) sapere; **I cannot** *or* **can't go** non posso andare; **he could not** *or* **couldn't go** non poteva andare; **she can't swim** non sa nuotare; **I ~ smell something burning** sento odor di bruciato

Canad|a /'kænədə/ n Canada m. **~ian** adj & n canadese mf

canal /kə'næl/ n canale m

Canaries /kə'neərɪz/ npl Canarie fpl

canary /kə'neərɪ/ n canarino m

cancel /'kænsl/ v (pt/pp **cancelled**) • vt disdire (meeting, newspaper); revocare (contract, order); annullare (reservation, appointment, stamp). **~lation** n (of meeting, contract) revoca f; (in hotel, restaurant, for flight) cancellazione f

cancer /'kænsə(r)/ n cancro m; **C~** (Astr) Cancro m. **~ous** adj canceroso

candid /'kændɪd/ adj franco

candidate /'kændɪdət/ n candidato, -a mf

candle /'kændl/ n candela f. **~stick** n portacandele m inv

candour /'kændə(r)/ n franchezza f

candy /'kændɪ/ n Am caramella f; **a [piece of]** ~ una caramella. **~floss** n zucchero m filato

cane /keɪn/ n (stick) bastone m; (Sch) bacchetta f • vt prendere a bacchettate (pupil)

canister /'kænɪstə(r)/ n barattolo m (di metallo)

cannabis /'kænəbɪs/ n cannabis f

cannibal /'kænɪbl/ n cannibale mf. **~ism** n cannibalismo m

cannon /'kænən/ n inv cannone m. **~-ball** n palla f di cannone

cannot /'kænɒt/ ▸**can²**

canoe /kə'nu:/ n canoa f • vi andare in canoa

can-opener n apriscatole m inv

canopy /'kænəpɪ/ n baldacchino f; (of parachute) calotta f

cantankerous /kæn'tæŋkərəs/ adj stizzoso

canteen /kæn'ti:n/ n mensa f; **~ of cutlery** servizio m di posate

canter /'kæntə(r)/ vi andare a piccolo galoppo

canvas /'kænvəs/ n tela f; (painting) dipinto m su tela

canvass /'kænvəs/ vi (Pol) fare propaganda elettorale. **~ing** n sollecitazione f di voti

canyon /'kænjən/ n canyon m inv

cap /kæp/ n berretto m; (nurse's) cuffia f; (top, lid) tappo m • vt (pt/pp **capped**) (fig: do better than) superare

capability /keɪpə'bɪlətɪ/ n capacità f

capabl|e /'keɪpəbl/ adj capace; (skilful) abile; **be ~e of doing sth** essere capace di fare qcsa. **~y** adv con abilità

capacity /kə'pæsətɪ/ n capacità f; (function) qualità f; **in my ~ as** in qualità di

cape¹ /keɪp/ n (cloak) cappa f

cape² n (Geog) capo m

capital /'kæpɪtl/ n (town) capitale f; (money) capitale m; (letter) lettera f maiuscola. **~ city** n capitale f

capital|ism /'kæpɪtəlɪzm/ n capitalismo m. **~ist** adj & n capitalista mf. **~ize** vi **~ize on** fig trarre vantaggio da. **~ 'letter** n lettera f maiuscola. **~ 'punishment** n pena f capitale

capitulat|e /kə'pɪtjʊleɪt/ vi capitolare. **~ion** n capitolazione f

Capricorn /'kæprɪkɔ:n/ n (Astr) Capricorno m

capsize /kæp'saɪz/ vi capovolgersi • vt capovolgere

capsule /'kæpsjʊl/ n capsula f

captain /'kæptɪn/ n capitano m • vt comandare (team)

caption /'kæpʃn/ n intestazione f; (of illustration) didascalia f

captivate /'kæptɪveɪt/ vt incantare

captiv|e /'kæptɪv/ adj prigionero; **hold/take ~e** tenere/fare prigioniero • n prigioniero, -a mf. **~ity** n prigionia f; (animals) cattività f

capture /'kæptʃə(r)/ n cattura f • vt catturare; attirare (attention)

car /kɑ:(r)/ n macchina f; **by ~** in macchina

carafe /kə'ræf/ n caraffa f

caramel /'kærəmel/ n (sweet)

C

caramella f al mou; (Culin) caramello m

caravan /'kærəvæn/ n roulotte f inv; (horse-drawn) carovana f

carbohydrate /kɑ:bə'haɪdreɪt/ n carboidrato m

carbon /'kɑ:bən/ n carbonio m

carbon di'oxide n anidride f carbonica

carburettor /kɑ:bjʊ'retə(r)/ n carburatore m

carcass /'kɑ:kəs/ n carcassa f

card /kɑ:d/ n (for birthday, Christmas etc) biglietto m di auguri; (playing ~) carta f [da gioco]; (membership ~) tessera f; (business ~) biglietto m da visita; (credit ~) carta f di credito; (Comput) scheda f

'cardboard n cartone m. ~ **'box** n scatola f di cartone; (large) scatolone m

cardigan /'kɑ:dɪgən/ n cardigan m inv

cardinal /'kɑ:dɪnl/ adj cardinale; ~ **number** numero m cardinale •n (Relig) cardinale m

care /keə(r)/ n cura f; (caution) attenzione f; (worry) preoccupazione f; ~ **of** (on letter abbr **c/o**) presso; **take** ~ (be cautious) fare attenzione; **bye, take** ~ ciao, stammi bene; **take** ~ **of** occuparsi di; **be taken into** ~ essere preso in custodia da un ente assistenziale •vi ~ **about** interessarsi di; ~ **for** (feel affection for) volere bene a; (look after) aver cura di; **I don't** ~ **for chocolate** non mi piace il cioccolato; **I don't** ~ non me ne importa; **who** ~**s?** chi se ne frega?

career /kə'rɪə(r)/ n carriera f; (profession) professione f •vi andare a tutta velocità

care: ~**free** adj spensierato. ~**ful** adj attento; (driver) prudente. ~**fully** adv con attenzione. ~**less** adj irresponsabile; (in work) trascurato; (work) fatto con poca cura; (driver) distratto. ~**lessly** adv negligentemente. ~**lessness** n trascuratezza f. ~**r** n persona f che accudisce a un anziano o a un malato

caress /kə'res/ n carezza f •vt accarezzare

'caretaker n custode mf; (in school) bidello m

'car ferry n traghetto m (per il trasporto di auto)

cargo /'kɑ:gəʊ/ n (pl **-es**) carico m

Caribbean /kærɪ'bi:ən/ n **the** ~ (sea) il Mar dei Caraibi •adj caraibico

caricature /'kærɪkətjʊə(r)/ n caricatura f

carnage /'kɑ:nɪdʒ/ n carneficina f

carnation /kɑ:'neɪʃn/ n garofano m

carnival /'kɑ:nɪvl/ n carnevale m

carol /'kærəl/ n [**Christmas**] ~ canzone f natalizia

carp[1] /kɑ:p/ n inv carpa f

carp[2] vi ~ **at** trovare da ridire su

'car park n parcheggio m

carpent|er /'kɑ:pɪntə(r)/ n falegname m. ~**ry** n falegnameria f

carpet /'kɑ:pɪt/ n tappeto m; (wall-to-wall) moquette f inv •vt mettere la moquette in (room)

carriage /'kærɪdʒ/ n carrozza f; (of goods) trasporto m; (cost) spese fpl di trasporto; (bearing) portamento m; ~**way** n strada f carrozzabile; **north-bound** ~**way** carreggiata f nord

carrier /'kærɪə(r)/ n (company) impresa f di trasporti; (Aeron) compagnia f di trasporto aereo; (of disease) portatore m. ~ **bag** n borsa f [per la spesa]

carrot /'kærət/ n carota f

carry /'kærɪ/ v (pt/pp **-ied**) •vt portare (transport) trasportare; **get carried away** [!] lasciarsi prender la mano •vi (sound:) trasmettersi. □ ~ **off** vt portare via; vincere (prize). □ ~ **on** vi continuare; ([!]: make scene) fare delle storie; ~ **on with sth** continuare qcsa; ~ **on with sb** [!] intendersela con qcno •vt mantenere (business). □ ~ **out** vt portare fuori; eseguire (instructions, task); mettere in atto (threat); effettuare (experiment, survey)

'carry-cot n porte-enfant m inv

cart /kɑ:t/ n carretto m •vt ([!]: carry) portare

carton /'kɑ:tn/ n scatola f di cartone; (for drink) cartone m; (of cream, yoghurt) vasetto m; (of cigarettes) stecca f

cartoon /kɑ:'tu:n/ n vignetta f; (strip) vignette fpl; (film) cartone m animato; (in art) bozzetto m. **~ist** n vignettista mf; (for films) disegnatore, -trice mf di cartoni animati

cartridge /ˈkɑːtrɪdʒ/ n cartuccia f; (for film) bobina f; (of record player) testina f

carve /kɑːv/ vt scolpire; tagliare (meat)

case[1] /keɪs/ n caso m; **in any ~** in ogni caso; **in that ~** in questo caso; **just in ~** per sicurezza; **in ~ he comes** nel caso in cui venisse

case[2] n (container) scatola f; (crate) cassa f; (for spectacles) astuccio m; (suitcase) valigia f; (for display) vetrina f

cash /kæʃ/ n denaro m contante; (!: money) contanti mpl; **pay [in] ~** pagare in contanti; **~ on delivery** pagamento alla consegna • vt incassare (cheque). **~ desk** n cassa f

cashier /kæˈʃɪə(r)/ n cassiere, -a mf

casino /kəˈsiːnəʊ/ n casinò m inv

casket /ˈkɑːskɪt/ n scrigno m; (Am: coffin) bara f

casserole /ˈkæsərəʊl/ n casseruola f; (stew) stufato m

cassette /kəˈset/ n cassetta f. **~ recorder** n registratore m (a cassette)

cast /kɑːst/ n (mould) forma f; (Theat) cast m inv; **[plaster] ~** (Med) ingessatura f • vt (pt/pp **cast**) dare (vote); (Theat) assegnare le parti di (play); fondere (metal); (throw) gettare; **~ an actor as** dare ad un attore il ruolo di; **~ a glance at** lanciare uno sguardo a. □ **~ off** vi (Naut) sganciare gli ormeggi • vt (in knitting) diminuire. □ **~ on** vt (in knitting) avviare

castaway /ˈkɑːstəweɪ/ n naufrago, -a mf

caster /ˈkɑːstə(r)/ n (wheel) rotella f. **~ sugar** n zucchero m raffinato

cast 'iron n ghisa f

cast-'iron adj di ghisa; fig solido

castle /ˈkɑːsl/ n castello m; (in chess) torre f

cast-offs npl abiti mpl smessi

castrat|e /kæˈstreɪt/ vt castrare. **~ion** n castrazione f

casual /ˈkæʒʊəl/ adj (chance) casuale; (remark) senza importanza; (glance) di sfuggita; (attitude, approach) disinvolto; (chat) informale; (clothes) casual inv; (work) saltuario; **~ wear** abbigliamento m casual. **~ly** adv (dress) casual; (meet) casualmente

casualty /ˈkæʒʊəltɪ/ n (injured person) ferito m; (killed) vittima f. **~ [department]** n pronto soccorso m

cat /kæt/ n gatto m; pej arpia f

catalogue /ˈkætəlɒg/ n catalogo m • vt catalogare

catalyst /ˈkætəlɪst/ n (Chem) & fig catalizzatore m

catapult /ˈkætəpʌlt/ n catapulta f; (child's) fionda f • vt fig catapultare

catarrh /kəˈtɑː(r)/ n catarro m

catastroph|e /kəˈtæstrəfɪ/ n catastrofe f. **~ic** adj catastrofico

catch /kætʃ/ n (of fish) pesca f; (fastener) fermaglio m; (on door) fermo m; (on window) gancio m; (!: snag) tranello m • v (pt/pp **caught**) • vt acchiappare (ball); (grab) afferrare; prendere (illness, fugitive, train); **~ a cold** prendersi un raffreddore; **~ sight of** scorgere; **I caught him stealing** l'ho sorpreso mentre rubava; **~ one's finger in the door** chiudersi il dito nella porta; **~ sb's eye** or **attention** attirare l'attenzione di qcno • vi (fire:) prendere; (get stuck) impigliarsi. □ **~ on** vi ! (understand) afferrare; (become popular) diventare popolare. □ **~ up** vt raggiungere • vi recuperare; (runner:) riguadagnare terreno; **~ up with** raggiungere (sb); mettersi in pari con (work)

catching /ˈkætʃɪŋ/ adj contagioso

catchphrase n tormentone m

catchy /ˈkætʃɪ/ adj (**-ier, -iest**) orecchiabile

categor|ical /kætɪˈgɒrɪkl/ adj categorico. **~y** n categoria f

cater /ˈkeɪtə(r)/ vi **~ for** provvedere a (needs); fig venire incontro alle esigenze di. **~ing** n (trade) ristorazione f; (food) rinfresco m

caterpillar /ˈkætəpɪlə(r)/ n bruco m

cathedral /kəˈθiːdrl/ n cattedrale f

Catholic /ˈkæθəlɪk/ adj & n cattolico, -a mf. **~ism** n cattolicesimo m

cat's eyes npl catarifrangente msg (inserito nell'asfalto)

cattle /ˈkætl/ npl bestiame msg

catwalk /ˈkætwɔːk/ n passerella f

caught /kɔ:t/ ▸**catch**

cauliflower /'kɒlɪ-/ n cavolfiore m

cause /kɔ:z/ n causa f •vt causare; ~ **sb to do sth** far fare qcsa a qcno

caution /'kɔ:ʃn/ n cautela f; (warning) ammonizione f •vt mettere in guardia; (Jur) ammonire

cautious /'kɔ:ʃəs/ adj cauto

cavalry /'kævəlrɪ/ n cavalleria f

cave /keɪv/ n caverna f •**cave in** vi (roof:) crollare; (fig: give in) capitolare

cavern /'kævən/ n caverna f

caviare /'kævɪɑ:(r)/ n caviale m

cavity /'kævətɪ/ n cavità f inv; (in tooth) carie f inv

CD n CD m inv. ~ **player** n lettore m [di] compact

CD-Rom /si:di:'rɒm/ n CD-Rom m inv. ~ **drive** n lettore m [di] CD-Rom

cease /si:s/ n **without** ~ incessantemente •vt/i cessare. ~**-fire** n cessate il fuoco m inv. ~**less** adj incessante

cedar /'si:də(r)/ n cedro m

ceiling /'si:lɪŋ/ n soffitto m; fig tetto m [massimo]

celebrat|e /'selɪbreɪt/ vt festeggiare (birthday, victory) •vi far festa. ~**ed** adj celebre (**for** per). ~**ion** n celebrazione f

celebrity /sɪ'lebrətɪ/ n celebrità f inv

celery /'selərɪ/ n sedano m

cell /sel/ n cella f; (Biol) cellula f

cellar /'selə(r)/ n scantinato m; (for wine) cantina f

cello /'tʃeləʊ/ n violoncello m

Cellophane® /'seləfeɪn/ n cellofan m inv

cellphone /'selfəʊn/ n cellulare m

cellular phone /seljʊlə'fəʊn/ n [telefono m] cellulare m

celluloid /'seljʊlɔɪd/ n celluloide f

Celsius /'selsɪəs/ adj Celsius

cement /sɪ'ment/ n cemento m; (adhesive) mastice m •vt cementare; fig consolidare

cemetery /'semətrɪ/ n cimitero m

censor /'sensə(r)/ n censore m •vt censurare. ~**ship** n censura f

censure /'senʃə(r)/ vt biasimare

census /'sensəs/ n censimento m

cent /sent/ n (of dollar) centesimo m; (of euro) cent m inv, centesimo m

centenary /sen'ti:nərɪ/ n, Am **centennial** /sen'tenɪəl/ n centenario m

center /'sentə(r)/ n Am = **centre**

centi|grade /'sentɪ-/ adj centigrado. ~**metre** n centimetro m. ~**pede** n centopiedi m inv

central /'sentrəl/ adj centrale. ~ '**heating** n riscaldamento m autonomo. ~**ize** vt centralizzare. ~**ly** adv al centro; ~**ly heated** con riscaldamento autonomo. ~ **reser'vation** n (Auto) banchina f spartitraffico

centre /'sentə(r)/ n centro m •v (pt/pp **centred**) •vt centrare •vi ~ **on** fig incentrarsi su. ~**-'forward** n centravanti m inv

century /'sentʃərɪ/ n secolo m

cereal /'sɪərɪəl/ n cereale m

ceremon|ial /serɪ'məʊnɪəl/ adj da cerimonia •n cerimoniale m. ~**ious** adj cerimonioso

ceremony /'serɪmənɪ/ n cerimonia f

certain /'sɜ:tn/ adj certo; **for** ~ di sicuro; **make** ~ accertarsi ; **he is** ~ **to win** è certo di vincere; **it's not** ~ **whether he'll come** non è sicuro che venga. ~**ly** adv certamente; ~**ly not!** no di certo! ~**ty** n certezza f; **it's a** ~**ty** è una cosa certa

certificate /sə'tɪfɪkət/ n certificato m

certify /'sɜ:tɪfaɪ/ vt (pt/pp **-ied**) certificare; (declare insane) dichiarare malato di mente

chafe /tʃeɪf/ vt irritare

chain /tʃeɪn/ n catena f •vt incatenare (prisoner); attaccare con la catena (dog) (**to** a). □ ~ **up** vt legare alla catena (dog)

chain: ~ **re'action** n reazione f a catena. ~**-smoker** n fumatore, -trice mf accanito, -a. ~ **store** n negozio m appartenente a una catena

chair /tʃeə(r)/ n sedia f; (Univ) cattedra f •vt presiedere. ~**-lift** n seggiovia f. ~**man** n presidente m

chalet /'ʃæleɪ/ n chalet m inv; (in holiday camp) bungalow m inv

chalk /tʃɔːk/ n gesso m. **~y** adj gessoso

challeng|e /ˈtʃælɪndʒ/ n sfida f; (Mil) intimazione f •vt sfidare; (Mil) intimare il chi va là a; fig mettere in dubbio (statement). **~er** n sfidante mf. **~ing** adj (job) impegnativo

chamber /ˈtʃeɪmbə(r)/ n **C~ of Commerce** camera f di commercio

chambermaid n cameriera f [d'albergo]

champagne /ʃæmˈpeɪn/ n champagne m inv

champion /ˈtʃæmpɪən/ n (Sport) campione m; (of cause) difensore, difenditrice mf •vt (defend) difendere; (fight for) lottare per. **~ship** n (Sport) campionato m

chance /tʃɑːns/ n caso m; (possibility) possibilità f inv; (opportunity) occasione f; **by ~** per caso; **take a ~** provarci; **give sb a second ~** dare un'altra possibilità a qcno •attrib fortuito •vt **I'll ~ it** [!] corro il rischio

chancellor /ˈtʃɑːnsələ(r)/ n cancelliere m; (Univ) rettore m; **C~ of the Exchequer** ≈ ministro m del tesoro

chandelier /ʃændəˈlɪə(r)/ n lampadario m

change /tʃeɪndʒ/ n cambiamento m; (money) resto m; (small coins) spiccioli mpl; **for a ~** tanto per cambiare; **a ~ of clothes** un cambio di vestiti; **the ~ [of life]** la menopausa •vt cambiare; (substitute) scambiare (**for** con); **~ one's clothes** cambiarsi [i vestiti]; **~ trains** cambiare treno •vi cambiare; (~ clothes) cambiarsi; **all ~!** stazione terminale!

changeable /ˈtʃeɪndʒəbl/ adj mutevole; (weather) variabile

changing-room n camerino m; (for sports) spogliatoio m

channel /ˈtʃænl/ n canale m; **the [English] C~** la Manica; **the C~ Islands** le Isole del Canale •vt (pt/pp **channelled**) **~ one's energies into sth** convogliare le proprie energie in qcsa

chant /tʃɑːnt/ n cantilena f; (of demonstrators) slogan m inv di protesta •vt cantare; (demonstrators:) gridare

chao|s /ˈkeɪɒs/ n caos m. **~tic** adj caotico

chap /tʃæp/ n [!] tipo m

chapel /ˈtʃæpl/ n cappella f

chaperon /ˈʃæpərəʊn/ n chaperon f inv •vt fare da chaperon a (sb)

chapter /ˈtʃæptə(r)/ n capitolo m

char¹ /tʃɑː(r)/ n [!] donna f delle pulizie

char² vt (pt/pp **charred**) (burn) carbonizzare

character /ˈkærɪktə(r)/ n carattere m; (in novel, play) personaggio m; **quite a ~** [!] un tipo particolare

characteristic /kærɪktəˈrɪstɪk/ adj caratteristico •n caratteristica f. **~ally** adv tipicamente

characterize /ˈkærɪktəraɪz/ vt caratterizzare

charade /ʃəˈrɑːd/ n farsa f

charcoal /ˈtʃɑː-/ n carbonella f

charge /tʃɑːdʒ/ n (cost) prezzo m; (Electr, Mil) carica f; (Jur) accusa f; **free of ~** gratuito; **be in ~** essere responsabile (**of** di); **take ~** assumersi la responsabilità; **take ~ of** occuparsi di •vt far pagare (fee); far pagare a (person); (Electr, Mil) caricare; (Jur) accusare (**with** di); **~ sb for sth** far pagare qcsa a qcno; **~ it to my account** lo addebiti sul mio conto •vi (attack) caricare

charitable /ˈtʃærɪtəbl/ adj caritatevole; (kind) indulgente

charity /ˈtʃærətɪ/ n carità f; (organization) associazione f di beneficenza; **concert given for ~** concerto m di beneficenza; **live on ~** vivere di elemosina

charm /tʃɑːm/ n fascino m; (object) ciondolo m •vt affascinare. **~ing** adj affascinante

chart /tʃɑːt/ n carta f nautica; (table) tabella f

charter /ˈtʃɑːtə(r)/ n **~ [flight]** [volo m] charter m inv •vt noleggiare. **~ed accountant** n commercialista mf

chase /tʃeɪs/ n inseguimento m •vt inseguire. **chase away** or **off** vt cacciare via

chassis /ˈʃæsɪ/ n (pl **chassis** /-sɪz/) telaio m

chastity /ˈtʃæstətɪ/ n castità f

C

C

chat /tʃæt/ n chiacchierata f; **have a ~ with** fare quattro chiacchere con •vi (pt/pp **chatted**) chiacchierare; (Comput) chattare. **~ show** n talk show m inv

chatter /ˈtʃætə(r)/ n chiacchiere fpl •vi chiacchierare; (teeth:) battere. **~box** n [!] chiacchierone, -a mf

chauffeur /ˈʃəʊfə(r)/ n autista mf

chauvin|ism /ˈʃəʊvɪnɪzm/ n sciovinismo m. **~ist** n sciovinista mf. **male ~ist** n [!] maschilista m

cheap /tʃi:p/ adj a buon mercato; (rate) economico; (vulgar) grossolano; (of poor quality) scadente •adv a buon mercato. **~ly** adv a buon mercato

cheat /tʃi:t/ n imbroglione, -a mf; (at cards) baro m •vt imbrogliare; **~ sb out of sth** sottrarre qcsa a qcno con l'inganno •vi imbrogliare; (at cards) barare. □**~ on** vt [!] tradire (wife)

check¹ /tʃek/ adj (pattern) a quadri •n disegno m a quadri

check² n verifica f; (of tickets) controllo m; (in chess) scacco m; (Am: bill) conto m; (Am: cheque) assegno m; (Am: tick) segnetto m; **keep a ~ on** controllare; **keep in ~** tenere sotto controllo •vt verificare; controllare (tickets); (restrain) contenere; (stop) bloccare •vi controllare; **~ on sth** controllare qcsa. □**~ in** vi registrarsi all'arrivo (in albergo); (Aeron) fare il check-in •vt registrare all'arrivo (in albergo). □**~ out** vi (of hotel) saldare il conto •vt ([!]: investigate) controllare. □**~ up** vi accertarsi; **~ up on** prendere informazioni su

check: ~-in n (in airport: place) banco m accettazione, check-in m inv; **~mate** int scacco matto! **~-out** n (in supermarket) cassa f. **~-up** n (Med) visita f di controllo, check-up m inv

cheek /tʃi:k/ n guancia f; (impudence) sfacciataggine f. **~y** adj sfacciato

cheep /tʃi:p/ vi pigolare

cheer /tʃɪə(r)/ n evviva m inv; **three ~s** tre urrà; **~s!** salute!; (goodbye) arrivederci!; (thanks) grazie! •vt/i acclamare. □**~ up** vt tirare su [di morale] •vi tirarsi su [di morale]; **~ up!** su con la vita!. **~ful** adj allegro. **~fulness** n allegria f. **~ing** n acclamazione f

cheerio /tʃɪərɪˈəʊ/ int [!] arrivederci

ˈcheerless adj triste, tetro

cheese /tʃi:z/ n formaggio m. **~cake** n dolce m al formaggio

chef /ʃef/ n cuoco, -a mf, chef mf inv

chemical /ˈkemɪkl/ adj chimico •n prodotto m chimico

chemist /ˈkemɪst/ n (pharmacist) farmacista mf; (scientist) chimico, -a mf; **~'s [shop]** farmacia f. **~ry** n chimica f

cheque /tʃek/ n assegno m. **~-book** n libretto m degli assegni. **~ card** n carta f assegni

cherish /ˈtʃerɪʃ/ vt curare teneramente; (love) avere caro; nutrire (hope)

cherry /ˈtʃerɪ/ n ciliegia f; (tree) ciliegio m

chess /tʃes/ n scacchi mpl

chessboard n scacchiera f

chest /tʃest/ n petto m; (box) cassapanca f

chestnut /ˈtʃesnʌt/ n castagna f; (tree) castagno m

chest of ˈdrawers n cassettone m

chew /tʃu:/ vt masticare. **~inggum** n gomma f da masticare

chic /ʃi:k/ adj chic inv

chick /tʃɪk/ n pulcino m; ([!]: girl) ragazza f

chicken /ˈtʃɪkn/ n pollo m •adj attrib (soup) di pollo •**chicken out** vi [!] **he ~ed out** gli è venuta fifa. **~pox** n varicella f

chicory /ˈtʃɪkərɪ/ n cicoria f

chief /tʃi:f/ adj principale •n capo m. **~ly** adv principalmente

chilblain /ˈtʃɪlbleɪn/ n gelone m

child /tʃaɪld/ n (pl **~ren**) bambino, -a mf; (son/daughter) figlio, -a mf

child: ~birth n parto m. **~hood** n infanzia f. **~ish** adj infantile. **~less** adj senza figli. **~like** adj ingenuo

Chile /ˈtʃɪlɪ/ n Cile m. **~an** adj & n cileno, -a mf

chill /tʃɪl/ n freddo m; (illness) infreddatura f •vt raffreddare

chilli /ˈtʃɪlɪ/ n (pl **-es**) **~ [pepper]** peperoncino m

chilly /ˈtʃɪlɪ/ adj freddo

hime /tʃaɪm/ vi suonare

himney /'tʃɪmnɪ/ n camino m. **~-pot** n comignolo m. **~-sweep** n spazzacamino m

himpanzee /tʃɪmpæn'ziː/ n scimpanzé m inv

hin /tʃɪn/ n mento m

hina /'tʃaɪnə/ n porcellana f

hin|a n Cina f. **~ese** adj & n cinese mf; (language) cinese m; **the ~ese** pl i cinesi

hink¹ /tʃɪŋk/ n (slit) fessura f

hink² n (noise) tintinnio m

hip /tʃɪp/ n (fragment) scheggia f; (in china, paintwork) scheggiatura f; (Comput) chip m inv; (in gambling) fiche f inv; **~s** pl Br (Culin) patatine fpl fritte; Am (Culin) patatine fpl • vt (pt/pp **chipped**) (damage) scheggiare. □ **~ in** vi 🗈 intromettersi; (with money) contribuire. **~ped** adj (damaged) scheggiato

hiropod|ist /kɪ'rɒpədɪst/ n podiatra mf inv. **~y** n podiatria f

hirp /tʃɜːp/ vi cinguettare; (cricket:) fare cri cri. **~y** adj 🗈 pimpante

hisel /'tʃɪzl/ n scalpello m

hival|rous /'ʃɪvlrəs/ adj cavalleresco. **~ry** n cavalleria f

hives /tʃaɪvz/ npl erba f cipollina

hlorine /'klɔːriːn/ n cloro m

hock-a-block /tʃɒkə'blɒk/, **chock-full** /tʃɒk'fʊl/ adj pieno zeppo

hocolate /'tʃɒkələt/ n cioccolato m; (drink) cioccolata f; **a ~** un cioccolatino

hoice /tʃɔɪs/ n scelta f • adj scelto

hoir /'kwaɪə(r)/ n coro m. **~boy** n corista m

hoke /tʃəʊk/ n (Auto) aria f • vt/i soffocare

holera /'kɒlərə/ n colera m

holesterol /kə'lestərɒl/ n colesterolo m

hoose /tʃuːz/ vt/i (pt **chose**, pp **chosen**) scegliere; **as you ~** come vuoi

hop /tʃɒp/ n (blow) colpo m (d'ascia); (Culin) costata f • vt (pt/pp **chopped**) tagliare. □ **~ down** vt abbattere (tree). □ **~ off** vt spaccare

hop|per /'tʃɒpə(r)/ n accetta f; 🗈 elicottero m. **~py** adj increspato

chord /kɔːd/ n (Mus) corda f

chore /tʃɔː(r)/ n corvé f inv; [**household**] **~s** faccende fpl domestiche

C

chorus /'kɔːrəs/ n coro m; (of song) ritornello m

chose, chosen /tʃəʊz/, /'tʃəʊzn/ ▸**choose**

Christ /kraɪst/ n Cristo m

christen /'krɪsn/ vt battezzare. **~ing** n battesimo m

Christian /'krɪstʃən/ adj & n cristiano, -a mf. **~ity** n cristianesimo m. **~ name** n nome m di battesimo

Christmas /'krɪsməs/ n Natale m • attrib di Natale. '**~ card** n biglietto m d'auguri di Natale. **~ 'Day** n il giorno di Natale. **~ 'Eve** n la vigilia di Natale. '**~ present** n regalo m di Natale. **~ 'pudding** dolce m natalizio a base di frutta candita e liquore. '**~ tree** n albero m di Natale

chrome /krəʊm/ n, **chromium** /'krəʊmɪəm/ n cromo m

chromosome /'krəʊməsəʊm/ n cromosoma m

chronic /'krɒnɪk/ adj cronico

chronicle /'krɒnɪkl/ n cronaca f

chronological /krɒnə'lɒdʒɪkl/ adj cronologico. **~ly** adv (ordered) in ordine cronologico

chubby /'tʃʌbɪ/ adj (**-ier, -iest**) paffuto

chuck /tʃʌk/ vt 🗈 buttare. □ **~ out** vt 🗈 buttare via (object); buttare fuori (person)

chuckle /'tʃʌkl/ vi ridacchiare

chug /tʃʌg/ vi (pt/pp **chugged**) **the train ~ged out of the station** il treno è uscito dalla stazione sbuffando

chum /tʃʌm/ n amico, -a mf. **~my** adj 🗈 **be ~my with** essere amico di

chunk /tʃʌŋk/ n grosso pezzo m

church /tʃɜːtʃ/ n chiesa f. **~yard** n cimitero m

churn /tʃɜːn/ vt **churn out** sfornare

chute /ʃuːt/ n scivolo m; (for rubbish) canale m di scarico

cider /'saɪdə(r)/ n sidro m

cigar /sɪ'gɑː(r)/ n sigaro m

C

cigarette /sɪgəˈret/ n sigaretta f

cine-camera /ˈsɪnɪ-/ n cinepresa f

cinema /ˈsɪnɪmə/ n cinema m inv

cinnamon /ˈsɪnəmən/ n cannella f

circle /ˈsɜːkl/ n cerchio m; (Theat) galleria f; **in a ~** in cerchio • vt girare intorno a; cerchiare (mistake) • vi descrivere dei cerchi

circuit /ˈsɜːkɪt/ n circuito m; (lap) giro m; **~ board** n circuito m stampato. **~ous** adj **~ous route** percorso m lungo e indiretto

circular /ˈsɜːkjʊlə(r)/ adj circolare • n circolare f

circulat|e /ˈsɜːkjʊleɪt/ vt far circolare • vi circolare. **~ion** n circolazione f; (of newspaper) tiratura f

circumcis|e /ˈsɜːkəmsaɪz/ vt circoncidere. **~ion** n circoncisione f

circumference /ʃəˈkʌmfərəns/ n conconferenza f

circumstance /ˈsɜːkəmstəns/ n circostanza f; **~s** pl (financial) condizioni fpl finanziarie

circus /ˈsɜːkəs/ n circo m

cistern /ˈsɪstən/ n (tank) cisterna f; (of WC) serbatoio m

cite /saɪt/ vt citare

citizen /ˈsɪtɪzn/ n cittadino, -a mf; (of town) abitante mf. **~ship** n cittadinanza f

citrus /ˈsɪtrəs/ n **~ [fruit]** agrume m

city /ˈsɪtɪ/ n città f inv; **the C~** la City (di Londra)

civic /ˈsɪvɪk/ adj civico

civil /ˈʃɪvl/ adj civile

civilian /sɪˈvɪljən/ adj civile; **in ~ clothes** in borghese • n civile mf

civiliz|ation /sɪvɪlaɪˈzeɪʃn/ n civiltà f inv. **~e** vt civilizzare

civil: ~ ˈservant n impiegato, -a mf statale. **C~ ˈService** n pubblica amministrazione f

clad /klæd/ adj vestito (**in** di)

claim /kleɪm/ n richiesta f; (right) diritto m; (assertion) dichiarazione f; **lay ~ to sth** rivendicare qcsa • vt richiedere; reclamare (lost property); rivendicare (ownership); **~ that** sostenere che. **~ant** n richiedente mf

clairvoyant /kleəˈvɔɪənt/ n chiaroveggente mf

clam /klæm/ n (Culin) vongola f • **clam up** vi (pt/pp **clammed**) zittirs

clamber /ˈklæmbə(r)/ vi arrampicar

clammy /ˈklæmɪ/ adj (**-ier, -iest**) appiccicaticcio

clamour /ˈklæmə(r)/ n (protest) rimostranza f • vi **~ for** chiedere a gran voce

clamp /klæmp/ n morsa f • vt ammorsare; (Auto) mettere i ceppi bloccaruote a. □ **~ down** vi ! essere duro; **~ down on** reprimer

clan /klæn/ n clan m inv

clang /klæŋ/ n suono m metallico. **~er** n ! gaffe f inv

clap /klæp/ n **give sb a ~** applaudire qcno; **~ of thunder** tuono m • vt/i (pt/pp **clapped**) applaudire; **~ one's hands** applaudire. **~ping** n applausi mpl

clari|fication /klærɪfɪˈkeɪʃn/ n chiarimento m. **~fy** vt/i (pt/pp **-ied**) chiarire

clarinet /klærɪˈnet/ n clarinetto m

clarity /ˈklærətɪ/ n chiarezza f

clash /klæʃ/ n scontro m; (noise) fragore m • vi scontrarsi; (colours:) stonare; (events:) coincidere

clasp /klɑːsp/ n chiusura f • vt agganciare; (hold) stringere

class /klɑːs/ n classe f; (lesson) corso • vt classificare

classic /ˈklæsɪk/ adj classico • n classico m; **~s** pl (Univ) lettere fpl classiche. **~al** adj classico

classi|fication /klæsɪfɪˈkeɪʃn/ n classificazione f. **~fy** vt (pt/pp **-ied**) classificare

classroom n aula f

classy /ˈklɑːsɪ/ adj (**-ier, -iest**) ! d'alta classe

clatter /ˈklætə(r)/ n fracasso m • vi fa fracasso

clause /klɔːz/ n clausola f; (Gram) proposizione f

claustrophob|ia /klɔːstrəˈfəʊbɪə/ n claustrofobia f

claw /klɔː/ n artiglio m; (of crab, lobster & (Techn)) tenaglia f • vt (cat:) graffiare

clay /kleɪ/ n argilla f

clean /kliːn/ adj pulito, lindo • adv

completamente • vt pulire (shoes, windows); ~ **one's teeth** lavarsi i denti; **have a coat ~ed** portare un cappotto in lavanderia. **clean up** vt pulire • vi far pulizia

cleaner /'kli:nə(r)/ n uomo m/donna f delle pulizie; (substance) detersivo m; [**dry**] **~'s** lavanderia f, tintoria f

cleanliness /'klenlɪnɪs/ n pulizia f

cleanse /klenz/ vt pulire. **~r** n detergente m

cleansing cream /'klenz-/ n latte m detergente

clear /klɪə(r)/ adj chiaro; (conscience) pulito; (road) libero; (profit, advantage, majority) netto; (sky) sereno; (water) limpido; (glass) trasparente; **make sth ~** mettere qcsa in chiaro; **have I made myself ~?** mi sono fatto capire?; **five ~ days** cinque giorni buoni • adv **stand ~ of** allontanarsi da; **keep ~ of** tenersi alla larga da • vt sgombrare (room, street); sparecchiare (table); (acquit) scagionare; (authorize) autorizzare; scavalcare senza toccare (fence, wall); guadagnare (sum of money); passare (Customs); **~ one's throat** schiarirsi la gola • vi (face, sky:) rasserenarsi; (fog:) dissiparsi. □ **~ away** vt metter via. □ **~ off** vi ⓘ filar via. □ **~ out** vt sgombrare • vi ⓘ filar via. □ **~ up** vt (tidy) mettere a posto; chiarire (mystery) • vi (weather:) schiarirsi

clearance /'klɪərəns/ n (space) spazio m libero; (authorization) autorizzazione f; (Customs) sdoganamento m. **~ sale** n liquidazione f

clear|ing /'klɪərɪŋ/ n radura f. **~ly** adv chiaramente. **~way** n (Auto) strada f con divieto di sosta

cleavage /'kli:vɪdʒ/ n (woman's) décolleté m inv

clench /klentʃ/ vt serrare

clergy /'klɜ:dʒɪ/ npl clero m. **~man** n ecclesiastico m

cleric /'klerɪk/ n ecclesiastico m. **~al** adj impiegatizio; (Relig) clericale

clerk /klɑ:k/, Am /klɜ:k/ n impiegato, -a mf; (Am: shop assistant) commesso, -a mf

clever /'klevə(r)/ adj intelligente; (skilful) abile

cliché /'kli:ʃeɪ/ n cliché m inv

click /klɪk/ vi scattare; (Comput) cliccare • n (Comput) click m. **click on** vt (Comput) cliccare su

client /'klaɪənt/ n cliente mf

cliff /klɪf/ n scogliera f

climat|e /'klaɪmət/ n clima f. **~ic** adj climatico

climax /'klaɪmæks/ n punto m culminante

climb /klaɪm/ n salita f • vt scalare (mountain); arrampicarsi su (ladder, tree) • vi arrampicarsi; (rise) salire; (road:) salire. □ **~ down** vi scendere; (from ladder, tree) scendere; fig tornare sui propri passi

climber /'klaɪmə(r)/ n alpinista mf; (plant) rampicante m

clinch /klɪntʃ/ vt ⓘ concludere (deal) • n (in boxing) clinch m inv

cling /klɪŋ/ vi (pt/pp **clung**) aggrapparsi; (stick) aderire. **~ film** n pellicola f trasparente

clinic /'klɪnɪk/ n ambulatorio m. **~al** adj clinico

clink /klɪŋk/ n tintinnio m; (ⓘ: prison) galera f • vi tintinnare

clip¹ /klɪp/ n fermaglio m; (jewellery) spilla f • vt (pt/pp **clipped**) attaccare

clip² n (extract) taglio m • vt obliterare (ticket). **~board** n fermabloc m inv. **~pers** npl (for hair) rasoio m; (for hedge) tosasiepi m inv; (for nails) tronchesina f. **~ping** n (from newspaper) ritaglio m

cloak /kləʊk/ n mantello m. **~room** n guardaroba m inv; (toilet) bagno m

clock /klɒk/ n orologio m; (ⓘ: speedometer) tachimetro m □ **~ in** vi attaccare. □ **~ out** vi staccare

clock: ~wise adj & adv in senso orario. **~work** n meccanismo m

clog /klɒg/ n zoccolo m • vt (pt/pp **clogged**) ~ [**up**] intasare (drain); inceppare (mechanism) • vi (drain:) intasarsi

cloister /'klɔɪstə(r)/ n chiostro m

clone /kləʊn/ n clone m

close¹ /kləʊs/ adj vicino; (friend) intimo; (weather) afoso; **have a ~ shave** ⓘ scamparla bella; **be ~ to sb** essere unito a qcno • adv vicino; **~ by** vicino; **~ on five o'clock** quasi le cinque

close² /kləʊz/ n fine f • vt chiudere • vi

chiudersi; (shop:) chiudere. □ ~ **down** vt chiudere •vi (TV station:) interrompere la trasmissione; (factory:) chiudere

C

closely /'kləʊslɪ/ adv da vicino; (watch, listen) attentamente

closet /'klɒzɪt/ n Am armadio m

close-up /'kləʊs-/ n primo piano m

closure /'kləʊʒə(r)/ n chiusura f

clot /klɒt/ n grumo m; ([!]: idiot) tonto, -a mf •vi (pt/pp **clotted**) (blood:) coagularsi

cloth /klɒθ/ n (fabric) tessuto m; (duster etc) straccio m

clothe /kləʊð/ vt vestire

clothes /kləʊðz/ npl vestiti mpl, abiti mpl. **~-brush** n spazzola f per abiti. **~-line** n corda f stendibiancheria

clothing /'kləʊðɪŋ/ n abbigliamento m

cloud /klaʊd/ n nuvola f •**cloud over** vi rannuvolarsi. **~burst** n acquazzone m

cloudy /'klaʊdɪ/ adj (**-ier, -iest**) nuvoloso; (liquid) torbido

clout /klaʊt/ n [!] colpo m; (influence) impatto m (**with** su) •vt [!] colpire

clove /kləʊv/ n chiodo m di garofano; **~ of garlic** spicchio m d'aglio

clover /'kləʊvə(r)/ n trifoglio m

clown /klaʊn/ n pagliaccio m •vi **~ [about]** fare il pagliaccio

club /klʌb/ n club m inv; (weapon) clava f; (Sport) mazza f; **~s** pl (Cards) fiori mpl •v (pt/pp **clubbed**) •vt bastonare. □ **~ together** vi unirsi

cluck /klʌk/ vi chiocciare

clue /klu:/ n indizio m; (in crossword) definizione f; **I haven't a ~** [!] non ne ho idea

clump /klʌmp/ n gruppo m

clumsiness /'klʌmzɪnɪs/ n goffaggine f

clumsy /'klʌmzɪ/ adj (**-ier, -iest**) maldestro; (tool) scomodo; (remark) senza tatto

clung /klʌŋ/ ▸**cling**

cluster /'klʌstə(r)/ n gruppo m •vi raggrupparsi (**round** intorno a)

clutch /klʌtʃ/ n stretta f; (Auto) frizione f; **be in sb's ~es** essere in balia di qcno •vt stringere; (grab) afferrare •vi **~ at** afferrare

clutter /'klʌtə(r)/ n caos m •vt **~ [up]** ingombrare

coach /kəʊtʃ/ n pullman m inv; (Rail) vagone m; (horse-drawn) carrozza f; (Sport) allenatore, -trice mf •vt fare esercitare; (Sport) allenare

coal /kəʊl/ n carbone m

coalition /kəʊə'lɪʃn/ n coalizione f

coarse /kɔ:s/ adj grossolano; (joke) spinto

coast /kəʊst/ n costa f •vi (freewheel) scendere a ruota libera **~al** adj costiero. **~er** n (mat) sottobicchiere m inv

coast: ~guard n guardia f costiera. **~line** n litorale m

coat /kəʊt/ n cappotto m; (of animal) manto m; (of paint) mano f; **~ of arms** stemma f •vt coprire; (with paint) ricoprire. **~-hanger** n gruccia f. **~-hook** n gancio m [appendiabiti]

coating /'kəʊtɪŋ/ n rivestimento m; (of paint) stato m

coax /kəʊks/ vt convincere con le moine

cobweb /'kɒb-/ n ragnatela f

cocaine /kə'keɪn/ n cocaina f

cock /kɒk/ n gallo m; (any male bird) maschio m •vt sollevare il grilletto di (gun); **~ its ears** (animal:) drizzare le orecchie

cockerel /'kɒkərəl/ n galletto m

cock-'eyed adj [!] storto; (absurd) assurdo

cockney /'kɒknɪ/ n (dialect) dialetto m londinese; (person) abitante mf dell'est di Londra

cock: ~pit n (Aeron) cabina f. **~roach** /-rəʊtʃ/ n scarafaggio m. **~tail** n cocktail m inv. **~-up** n [x] **make a ~-up** fare un casino (**of** con)

cocky /'kɒkɪ/ adj (**-ier, -iest**) [!] presuntuoso

cocoa /'kəʊkəʊ/ n cacao m

coconut /'kəʊkənʌt/ n noce f di cocco

cocoon /kə'ku:n/ n bozzolo m

cod /kɒd/ n inv merluzzo m

COD abbr (cash on delivery) pagamento m alla consegna

code /kəʊd/ n codice m. **~d** adj codificato

coedu'cational /kəʊ-/ adj misto

coerc|e /kəʊ'ɜːs/ vt costringere. **~ion** n coercizione f

coffee /'kɒfɪ/ n caffè m inv

coffeepot n caffettiera f

coffin /'kɒfɪn/ n bara f

cog /kɒg/ n (Techn) dente m (di ruota)

coherent /kəʊ'hɪərənt/ adj coerente; (when speaking) logico

coil /kɔɪl/ n rotolo m; (Electr) bobina f; **~s** pl spire fpl • vt ~ [**up**] avvolgere

coin /kɔɪn/ n moneta f • vt coniare (word)

coincide /kəʊɪn'saɪd/ vi coincidere

coinciden|ce /kəʊ'ɪnsɪdəns/ n coincidenza f. **~tal** adj casuale. **~tally** adv casualmente

coke /kəʊk/ n [carbone m] coke m

Coke® n Coca[-cola]® f

cold /kəʊld/ adj freddo; **I'm ~** ho freddo • n freddo m; (Med) raffreddore m

cold-'blooded adj spietato

coleslaw /'kəʊlslɔː/ n insalata f di cavolo crudo, cipolle e carote in maionese

collaborat|e /kə'læbəreɪt/ vi collaborare; **~e on sth** collaborare in qcsa. **~ion** n collaborazione f; (with enemy) collaborazionismo m. **~or** n collaboratore, -trice mf; (with enemy) collaborazionista mf

collaps|e /kə'læps/ n crollo m • vi (person:) svenire; (roof, building:) crollare. **~ible** adj pieghevole

collar /'kɒlə(r)/ n colletto m; (for animal) collare m. **~-bone** n clavicola f

colleague /'kɒliːg/ n collega mf

collect /kə'lekt/ vt andare a prendere (person); ritirare (parcel, tickets); riscuotere (taxes); raccogliere (rubbish); (as hobby) collezionare • vi riunirsi • adv **call ~** Am telefonare a carico del destinatario. **~ed** adj controllato

collection /kə'lekʃn/ n collezione f; (in church) questua f; (of rubbish) raccolta f; (of post) levata f

collector /kə'lektə(r)/ n (of stamps etc) collezionista mf

college /'kɒlɪdʒ/ n istituto m parauniversitario; **C~ of...** Scuola f di...

collide /kə'laɪd/ vi scontrarsi

collision /kə'lɪʒn/ n scontro m

colloquial /kə'ləʊkwɪəl/ adj colloquiale. **~ism** n espressione f colloquiale

colon /'kəʊlən/ n due punti mpl; (Anat) colon m inv

colonel /'kɜːnl/ n colonnello m

colonial /kə'ləʊnɪəl/ adj coloniale

colon|ize /'kɒlənaɪz/ vt colonizzare. **~y** n colonia f

colossal /kə'lɒsl/ adj colossale

colour /'kʌlə(r)/ n colore m; (complexion) colorito m; **~s** pl (flag) bandiera fsg; **off ~** 🅸 giù di tono • vt colorare; ~ [**in**] colorare • vi (blush) arrossire

colour: ~-blind adj daltonico. **~ed** adj colorato; (person) di colore • n (person) persona f di colore. **~ful** adj pieno di colore. **~less** adj incolore

column /'kɒləm/ n colonna f. **~ist** n giornalista mf che cura una rubrica

coma /'kəʊmə/ n coma m inv

comb /kəʊm/ n pettine m; (for wearing) pettinino m • vt pettinare; (fig: search) setacciare; **~ one's hair** pettinarsi i capelli

combat /'kɒmbæt/ n combattimento m • vt (pt/pp **combated**) combattere

combination /kɒmbɪ'neɪʃn/ n combinazione f

combine[1] /kəm'baɪn/ vt unire; **~ a job with being a mother** conciliare il lavoro con il ruolo di madre • vi (chemical elements:) combinarsi

combine[2] /'kɒmbaɪn/ n (Comm) associazione f. **~ harvester** n mietitrebbia f

combustion /kəm'bʌstʃn/ n combustione f

come /kʌm/ vi (pt **came**, pp **come**) venire; **where do you ~ from?** da dove vieni?; **~ to** (reach) arrivare a; **that ~s to £10** fanno 10 sterline; **~ into money** ricevere dei soldi; **~ true/open** verificarsi/aprirsi; **~ first** arrivare primo; fig venire prima di tutto; **~ in two sizes** esistere in due misure; **the years**

C

to ~ gli anni a venire; **how** ~**?** [!] come mai? **come about** vi succedere. □ ~ **across** vi ~ **across as being** [!] dare l'impressione di essere • vt (find) imbattersi in. □ ~ **along** vi venire; (job, opportunity:) presentarsi; (progress) andare bene. □ ~ **apart** vi smontarsi; (break) rompersi. □ ~ **away** vi venir via; (button, fastener:) staccarsi. □ ~ **back** vi ritornare. □ ~ **by** vi passare • vt (obtain) avere. □ ~ **down** vi scendere; ~ **down to** (reach) arrivare a. **come in** vi entrare; (in race) arrivare; (tide:) salire. □ ~ **in for** vt ~ **in for criticism** essere criticato. □ ~ **off** vi staccarsi; (take place) esserci; (succeed) riuscire. □ ~ **on** vi (make progress) migliorare; ~ **on!** (hurry) dai!; (indicating disbelief) ma va là!. □ ~ **out** vi venir fuori; (book, sun:) uscire; (stain:) andar via. □ ~ **over** vi venire. □ ~ **round** vi venire; (after fainting) riaversi; (change one's mind) farsi convincere. □ ~ **to** vi (after fainting) riaversi. □ ~ **up** vi salire; (sun:) sorgere; (plant:) crescere; **something came up** (I was prevented) ho avuto un imprevisto. □ ~ **up with** vt tirar fuori

'**come-back** n ritorno m

comedian /kə'mi:dɪən/ n comico m

comedy /'kɒmədɪ/ n commedia f

comet /'kɒmɪt/ n cometa f

comfort /'kʌmfət/ n benessere m; (consolation) conforto m • vt confortare

comfortabl|e /'kʌmfətəbl/ adj comodo; **be** ~**e** (person:) stare comodo; (fig: in situation) essere a proprio agio; (financially) star bene. ~**y** adv comodamente

'**comfort station** n Am bagno m pubblico

comic /'kɒmɪk/ adj comico • n comico, -a mf; (periodical) fumetto m. ~**al** adj comico. ~ **strip** n striscia f di fumetti

coming /'kʌmɪŋ/ n venuta f; ~**s and goings** viavai m

comma /'kɒmə/ n virgola f

command /kə'mɑ:nd/ n comando m; (order) ordine m; (mastery) padronanza f • vt ordinare; comandare (army)

commandeer /kɒmən'dɪə(r)/ vt requisire

command|er /kə'mɑ:ndə(r)/ n comandante m. ~**ing** adj (view) imponente; (lead) dominante. ~**ing officer** n comandante m. ~**ment** n comandamento m

commemorat|e /kə'meməreɪt/ vt commemorare. ~**ion** n commemorazione f. ~**ive** adj commemorativo

commence /kə'mens/ vt/i cominciare. ~**ment** n inizio m

commend /kə'mend/ vt complimentarsi con (**on** per); (recommend) raccomandare (**to** a). ~**able** adj lodevole

comment /'kɒment/ n commento m • vi fare commenti (**on** su)

commentary /'kɒməntrɪ/ n commento m; [**running**] ~ (on radio, TV) cronaca f diretta

commentat|e /'kɒmənteɪt/ vt ~**e on** (TV, Radio) fare la cronaca di. ~**or** n cronista mf

commerce /'kɒmɜ:s/ n commercio m

commercial /kə'mɜ:ʃl/ adj commerciale • n (TV) pubblicità f inv. ~**ize** vt commercializzare

commiserate /kə'mɪzəreɪt/ vi esprimere il proprio rincrescimento (**with** a)

commission /kə'mɪʃn/ n commissione f; **receive one's** ~ (Mil) essere promosso ufficiale; **out of** ~ fuori uso • vt commissionare

commissionaire /kəmɪʃə'neə(r)/ n portiere m

commit /kə'mɪt/ vt (pt/pp **committed**) commettere; (to prison, hospital) affidare (**to** a); impegnare (funds); ~ **oneself** impegnarsi. ~**ment** n impegno m; (involvement) compromissione f. ~**ted** adj impegnato

committee /kə'mɪtɪ/ n comitato m

commodity /kə'mɒdətɪ/ n prodotto m

common /'kɒmən/ adj comune; (vulgar) volgare • n prato m pubblico; **have in** ~ avere in comune; **House of C**~**s** Camera f dei Comuni. ~**er** n persona f non nobile

common: ~'**law** n diritto m consuetudinario. ~**ly** adv comunemente. **C**~ '**Market** n Mercato m Comune. ~**place** adj banale. ~-**room** n sala f dei professori/degli studenti. ~ '**sense** n buon senso m

commotion /kə'məʊʃn/ n confusione f

communicate /kə'mju:nɪkeɪt/ vt/i comunicare

communication /kəmju:nɪ'keɪʃn/ n comunicazione f; (of disease) trasmissione f; **be in ~ with sb** essere in contatto con qcno; **~s** pl (technology) telecomunicazioni fpl. ~ **cord** n fermata f d'emergenza

communicative /kə'mju:nɪkətɪv/ adj comunicativo

communion /kə'mju:nɪən/ n [**Holy**] ~ comunione f

communis|m /'kɒmjʊnɪzm/ n comunismo m. **~t** adj & n comunista mf

community /kə'mju:nətɪ/ n comunità f. ~ **centre** n centro m sociale

commute /kə'mju:t/ vi fare il pendolare •vt (Jur) commutare. **~r** n pendolare mf

compact[1] /kəm'pækt/ adj compatto

compact[2] /'kɒmpækt/ n portacipria m inv. ~ **disc** n compact disc m inv

companion /kəm'pænjən/ n compagno, -a mf. **~ship** n compagnia f

company /'kʌmpənɪ/ n compagnia f; (guests) ospiti mpl. ~ **car** n macchina f della ditta

comparable /'kɒmpərəbl/ adj paragonabile

comparative /kəm'pærətɪv/ adj comparativo; (relative) relativo •n (Gram) comparativo m. **~ly** adv relativamente

compare /kəm'peə(r)/ vt paragonare (**with**/**to** a) •vi essere paragonato

comparison /kəm'pærɪsn/ n paragone m

compartment /kəm'pɑ:tmənt/ n compartimento m; (Rail) scompartimento m

compass /'kʌmpəs/ n bussola f. **~es** npl, **pair of ~es** compasso msg

compassion /kəm'pæʃn/ n compassione f. **~ate** adj compassionevole

compatible /kəm'pætəbl/ adj compatibile

compel /kəm'pel/ vt (pt/pp **compelled**) costringere. **~ling** adj (reason) inconfutabile

compensat|e /'kɒmpənseɪt/ vt risarcire •vi **~e for** fig compensare di. **~ion** n risarcimento m; (fig: comfort) consolazione f

compère /'kɒmpeə(r)/ n presentatore, -trice mf

compete /kəm'pi:t/ vi competere; (take part) gareggiare

competen|ce /'kɒmpɪtəns/ n competenza f. **~t** adj competente

competition /kɒmpə'tɪʃn/ n concorrenza f; (contest) gara f

competitive /kəm'petɪtɪv/ adj competitivo; ~ **prices** prezzi mpl concorrenziali

competitor /kəm'petɪtə(r)/ n concorrente mf

complacen|cy /kəm'pleɪsənsɪ/ n compiacimento m. **~t** adj compiaciuto

complain /kəm'pleɪn/ vi lamentarsi (**about** di); (formally) reclamare; ~ **of** (Med) accusare. **~t** n lamentela f; (formal) reclamo m; (Med) disturbo m

complement[1] /'kɒmplɪmənt/ n complemento m

complement[2] /'kɒmplɪment/ vt complementare; ~ **each other** complementarsi a vicenda. **~ary** adj complementare

complete /kəm'pli:t/ adj completo; (utter) finito •vt completare; compilare (form). **~ly** adv completamente

completion /kəm'pli:ʃn/ n fine f

complex /'kɒmpleks/ adj complesso •n complesso m

complexion /kəm'plekʃn/ n carnagione f

complexity /kəm'pleksətɪ/ n complessità f inv

complicat|e /'kɒmplɪkeɪt/ vt complicare. **~ed** adj complicato. **~ion** n complicazione f

compliment /'kɒmplɪmənt/ n complimento m; **~s** pl omaggi mpl •vt complimentare. **~ary** adj complimentoso; (given free) in omaggio

comply /kəm'plaɪ/ vi (pt/pp **-ied**) ~ **with** conformarsi a

component /kəm'pəʊnənt/ adj & n ~ [**part**] componente m

compose /kəm'pəʊz/ vt comporre; ~ **oneself** ricomporsi; **be ~d of** essere composto da. **~d** adj (calm) composto. **~r** n compositore, -trice mf

composition /kɒmpə'zɪʃn/ n composizione f; (essay) tema m

compost /'kɒmpɒst/ n composta f

composure /kəm'pəʊʒə(r)/ n calma f

compound /'kɒmpaʊnd/ adj composto. ~ **fracture** n frattura f esposta. ~ **'interest** n interesse m composto • n (Chem) composto m; (Gram) parola f composta; (enclosure) recinto m

comprehen|d /kɒmprɪ'hend/ vt comprendere. **~sible** adj comprensibile. **~sion** n comprensione f

comprehensive /kɒmprɪ'hensɪv/ adj & n comprensivo; ~ [**school**] scuola f media in cui gli allievi hanno capacità d'apprendimento diverse. ~ **insurance** n (Auto) polizza f casco

compress¹ /'kɒmpres/ n compressa f

compress² /kəm'pres/ vt comprimere; **~ed air** aria f compressa

comprise /kəm'praɪz/ vt comprendere; (form) costituire

compromise /'kɒmprəmaɪz/ n compromesso m • vt compromettere • vi fare un compromesso

compuls|ion /kəm'pʌlʃn/ n desiderio m irresistibile. **~ive** adj (Psych) patologico. **~ive eating** voglia f ossessiva di mangiare. **~ory** adj obbligatorio

compute /kəm'pju:t/ vt calcolare

comput|er /kəm'pju:tə(r)/ n computer m inv. **~erize** vt computerizzare. **~ing** n informatica f

comrade /'kɒmreɪd/ n camerata m; (Pol) compagno, -a mf. **~ship** n cameratismo m

con¹ /kɒn/ ▸**pro**

con² n [!] fregatura f • vt (pt/pp **conned**) [!] fregare

concave /'kɒnkeɪv/ adj concavo

conceal /kən'si:l/ vt nascondere

concede /kən'si:d/ vt (admit) ammettere; (give up) rinunciare a; lasciar fare (goal)

conceit /kən'si:t/ n presunzione f. **~ed** adj presuntuoso

conceivable /kən'si:vəbl/ adj concepibile

conceive /kən'si:v/ vt (Biol) concepire • vi aver figli. □ ~ **of** vt fig concepire

concentrat|e /'kɒnsəntreɪt/ vt concentrare • vi concentrarsi. **~ion** n concentrazione f. **~ion camp** n campo m di concentramento

concept /'kɒnsept/ n concetto m. **~ion** n concezione f; (idea) idea f

concern /kən'sɜ:n/ n preoccupazione f; (Comm) attività f inv • vt (be about, affect) riguardare; (worry) preoccupare; **be ~ed about** essere preoccupato per; ~ **oneself with** preoccuparsi di; **as far as I am ~ed** per quanto mi riguarda. **~ing** prep riguardo a

concert /'kɒnsət/ n concerto m. **~ed** adj collettivo

concertina /kɒnsə'ti:nə/ n piccola fisarmonica f

concerto /kən'tʃeətəʊ/ n concerto m

concession /kən'seʃn/ n concessione f; (reduction) sconto m. **~ary** adj (reduced) scontato

concise /kən'saɪs/ adj conciso

conclu|de /kən'klu:d/ vt concludere • vi concludersi. **~ding** adj finale

conclusion /kən'klu:ʒn/ n conclusione f; **in** ~ per concludere

conclusive /kən'klu:sɪv/ adj definitivo. **~ly** adv in modo definitivo

concoct /kən'kɒkt/ vt confezionare; fig inventare. **~ion** n mistura f; (drink) intruglio m

concrete /'kɒŋkri:t/ adj concreto • n calcestruzzo m

concussion /kən'kʌʃn/ n commozione f cerebrale

condemn /kən'dem/ vt condannare; dichiarare inagibile (building). **~ation** n condanna f

condensation /kɒnden'seɪʃn/ n condensazione f

condense /kən'dens/ vt condensare

(Phys) condensare •vi condensarsi. **~d milk** n latte m condensato

ɔndescend /kɒndɪ'send/ vi degnarsi. **~ing** adj condiscendente

ɔndition /kən'dɪʃn/ n condizione f; **on ~ that** a condizione che •vt (Psych) condizionare. **~al** adj (acceptance) condizionato; (Gram) condizionale •n (Gram) condizionale m. **~er** n balsamo m; (for fabrics) ammorbidente m

ɔndolences /kən'dəʊlənsɪz/ npl condoglianze fpl

ɔndom /'kɒndəm/ n preservativo m

ɔndo[minium] /'kɒndə ('mɪnɪəm)/ n Am condominio m

ɔndone /kən'dəʊn/ vt passare sopra a

onduct¹ /'kɒndʌkt/ n condotta f

ɔnduct² /kən'dʌkt/ vt condurre; dirigere (orchestra). **~or** n direttore m d'orchestra; (of bus) bigliettaio m; (Phys) conduttore m. **~ress** n bigliettaia f

one /kəʊn/ n cono m; (Bot) pigna f; (Auto) birillo m **•cone off** vt **be ~d off** (Auto) essere chiuso da birilli

ɔnfederation /kənfedə'reɪʃn/ n confederazione f

onference /'kɒnfərəns/ n conferenza f

ɔnfess /kən'fes/ vt confessare •vi confessare; (Relig) confessarsi. **~ion** n confessione f. **~ional** n confessionale m. **~or** n confessore m

ɔnfetti /kən'fetɪ/ n coriandoli mpl

onfide /kən'faɪd/ vt confidare. □ **~ in** vt **~ in sb** fidarsi di qcno

onfidence /'kɒnfɪdəns/ n (trust) fiducia f; (self-assurance) sicurezza f di sé; (secret) confidenza f; **in ~** in confidenza. **~ trick** n truffa f

onfident /'kɒnfɪdənt/ adj fiducioso; (self-assured) sicuro di sé. **~ly** adv con aria fiduciosa

onfidential /kɒnfɪ'denʃl/ adj confidenziale

onfigur|ation /kənfɪgə'reɪʃn/ n configurazione f. **~e** vt configurare

onfine /kən'faɪn/ vt rinchiudere; (limit) limitare; **be ~d to bed** essere confinato a letto. **~d** adj (space) limitato. **~ment** n detenzione f; (Med) parto m

confirm /kən'fɜːm/ vt confermare; (Relig) cresimare. **~ation** n conferma f; (Relig) cresima f. **~ed** adj incallito; **~ed bachelor** scapolo m impenitente

confiscat|e /'kɒnfɪskeɪt/ vt confiscare. **~ion** n confisca f

conflict¹ /'kɒnflɪkt/ n conflitto m

conflict² /kən'flɪkt/ vi essere in contraddizione. **~ing** adj contraddittorio

conform /kən'fɔːm/ vi (person:) conformarsi; (thing:) essere conforme (**to** a). **~ist** n conformista mf

confounded /kən'faʊndɪd/ adj [!] maledetto

confront /kən'frʌnt/ vt affrontare; **the problems ~ing us** i problemi che dobbiamo affrontare. **~ation** n confronto m

confus|e /kən'fjuːz/ vt confondere. **~ing** adj che confonde. **~ion** n confusione f

congeal /kən'dʒiːl/ vi (blood:) coagularsi

congest|ed /kən'dʒestɪd/ adj congestionato. **~ion** n congestione f

congratulat|e /kən'grætjʊleɪt/ vt congratularsi con (**on** per). **~ions** npl radunarsi.

congregat|e /'kɒŋgrɪgeɪt/ vi radunarsi. **~ion** n (Relig) assemblea f

congress /'kɒŋgres/ n congresso m. **~man** n Am (Pol) membro m del congresso

conifer /'kɒnɪfə(r)/ n conifera f

conjugat|e /'kɒndʒʊgeɪt/ vt coniugare. **~ion** n coniugazione f

conjunction /kən'dʒʌŋkʃn/ n congiunzione f; **in ~ with** insieme a

conjur|e /'kʌndʒə(r)/ vi **~ing tricks** npl giochi mpl di prestigio. **~or** n prestigiatore, -trice mf. □ **~ up** vt evocare (image); tirar fuori dal nulla (meal)

conk /kɒŋk/ vi **~ out** [!] (machine:) guastarsi; (person:) crollare

'con-man n [!] truffatore m

connect /kə'nekt/ vt collegare; **be ~ed with** avere legami con; (be related to) essere imparentato con; **be well ~ed** aver conoscenze

C

C

influenti •vi essere collegato (**with** a); (train:) fare coincidenza

connection /kə'nekʃn/ n (between ideas) nesso m; (in travel) coincidenza f; (Electr) collegamento m; **in ~ with** con riferimento a. **~s** pl (people) conoscenze fpl

connoisseur /kɒnə'sɜ:(r)/ n intenditore, -trice mf

conquer /'kɒŋkə(r)/ vt conquistare; fig superare (fear). **~or** n conquistatore m

conquest /'kɒŋkwest/ n conquista f

conscience /'kɒnʃəns/ n coscienza f

conscientious /kɒnʃɪ'enʃəs/ adj coscienzioso. **~ ob'jector** n obiettore m di coscienza

conscious /'kɒnʃəs/ adj conscio; (decision) meditato; [**fully**] **~** cosciente; **be/become ~ of sth** rendersi conto di qcsa. **~ly** adv consapevolmente. **~ness** n consapevolezza f; (Med) conoscenza f

conscript¹ /'kɒnskrɪpt/ n coscritto m

conscript² /kən'skrɪpt/ vt (Mil) chiamare alle armi. **~ion** n coscrizione f, leva f

consecrat|e /'kɒnsɪkreɪt/ vt consacrare. **~ion** n consacrazione f

consecutive /kən'sekjʊtɪv/ adj consecutivo

consensus /kən'sensəs/ n consenso m

consent /kən'sent/ n consenso m •vi acconsentire

consequen|ce /'kɒnsɪkwəns/ n conseguenza f; (importance) importanza f. **~t** adj conseguente. **~tly** adv di conseguenza

conservation /kɒnsə'veɪʃn/ n conservazione f. **~ist** n fautore, -trice mf della tutela ambientale

conservative /kən'sɜ:vətɪv/ adj conservativo; (estimate) ottimistico. **C~** (Pol) adj conservatore •n conservatore, -trice mf

conservatory /kən'sɜ:vətrɪ/ n spazio m chiuso da vetrate adiacente alla casa

conserve /kən'sɜ:v/ vt conservare

consider /kən'sɪdə(r)/ vt considerare; **~ doing sth** considerare la possibilità di fare qcsa. **~able** adj considerevole. **~ably** adv considerevolmente

consider|ate /kən'sɪdərət/ adj pieno di riguardo. **~ately** adv con riguardo. **~ation** n considerazione f; (thoughtfulness) attenzione f; (respect) riguardo m; (payment) compenso m; **take sth into ~ation** prendere qcsa in considerazione. **~ing** prep considerando

consign /kən'saɪn/ vt affidare. **~ment** n consegna f

consist /kən'sɪst/ vi **~ of** consistere di

consisten|cy /kən'sɪstənsɪ/ n coerenza f; (density) consistenza f. **~t** adj coerente; (loyalty) costante. **~tly** adv coerentemente; (late, loyal) costantemente

consolation /kɒnsə'leɪʃn/ n consolazione f. **~ prize** n premio m di consolazione

console /kən'səʊl/ vt consolare

consolidate /kən'sɒlɪdeɪt/ vt consolidare

consonant /'kɒnsənənt/ n consonante f

conspicuous /kən'spɪkjʊəs/ adj facilmente distinguibile

conspiracy /kən'spɪrəsɪ/ n cospirazione f

conspire /kən'spaɪə(r)/ vi cospirare

constable /'kʌnstəbl/ n agente m [di polizia]

constant /'kɒnstənt/ adj costante. **~ly** adv costantemente

constellation /kɒnstə'leɪʃn/ n costellazione f

consternation /kɒnstə'neɪʃn/ n costernazione f

constipat|ed /'kɒnstɪpeɪtɪd/ adj stitico. **~ion** n stitichezza f

constituency /kən'stɪtjʊənsɪ/ n area elettorale di un deputato nel Regno Unito

constituent /kən'stɪtjʊənt/ n costituente m; (Pol) elettore, -trice mf

constitut|e /'kɒnstɪtju:t/ vt costituire. **~ion** n costituzione f. **~ional** adj costituzionale

construct /kən'strʌkt/ vt costruire. **~ion** n costruzione f; **under ~ion** in costruzione. **~ive** adj costruttivo

consul /'kɒnsl/ n console m. **~ar** adj consolare. **~ate** n consolato m

onsult /kən'sʌlt/ vt consultare. **~ant** n consulente mf; (Med) specialista mf. **~ation** n consultazione f; (Med) consulto m

onsume /kən'sju:m/ vt consumare. **~r** n consumatore, -trice mf. **~r goods** npl beni mpl di consumo. **~er organization** n organizzazione f per la tutela dei consumatori

onsummate /'kɒnsəmeɪt/ vt consumare

onsumption /kən'sʌmpʃn/ n consumo m

ontact /'kɒntækt/ n contatto m; (person) conoscenza f •vt mettersi in contatto con. **~ 'lenses** npl lenti fpl a contatto

ontagious /kən'teɪdʒəs/ adj contagioso

ontain /kən'teɪn/ vt contenere; **~ oneself** controllarsi. **~er** n recipiente m; (for transport) container m inv

ontaminat|e /kən'tæmɪneɪt/ vt contaminare. **~ion** n contaminazione f

ontemplat|e /'kɒntəmpleɪt/ vt contemplare; (consider) considerare; **~e doing sth** considerare di fare qcsa. **~ion** n contemplazione f

ontemporary /kən'tempərərɪ/ adj & n contemporaneo, -a mf

ontempt /kən'tempt/ n disprezzo m; **beneath ~** più che vergognoso; **~ of court** oltraggio m alla Corte. **~ible** adj spregevole. **~uous** adj sprezzante

contend /kən'tend/ vi **~ with** occuparsi di •vt (assert) sostenere. **~er** n concorrente mf

content¹ /'kɒntent/ n contenuto m

content² /kən'tent/ adj soddisfatto •vt **~ oneself** accontentarsi (**with** di). **~ed** adj soddisfatto. **~edly** adv con aria soddisfatta

contentment /kən'tentmənt/ n soddisfazione f

contents /'kɒntents/ npl contenuto m

contest¹ /'kɒntest/ n gara f

contest² /kən'test/ vt contestare (statement); impugnare (will); (Pol) (candidates:) contendersi; (one candidate:) aspirare a. **~ant** n concorrente mf

context /'kɒntekst/ n contesto m

continent /'kɒntɪnənt/ n continente m; **the C~** l'Europa f continentale

continental /kɒntɪ'nentl/ adj continentale. **~ breakfast** n prima colazione f a base di pane, burro, marmellata, croissant, ecc. **~ quilt** n piumone m

C

contingency /kən'tɪndʒənsɪ/ n eventualità f inv

continual /kən'tɪnjʊəl/ adj continuo

continuation /kəntɪnjʊ'eɪʃn/ n continuazione f

continue /kən'tɪnju:/ vt continuare; **~ doing** or **to do sth** continuare a fare qcsa; **to be ~d** continua •vi continuare. **~d** adj continuo

continuity /kɒntɪ'nju:ətɪ/ n continuità f

continuous /kən'tɪnjʊəs/ adj continuo

contort /kən'tɔ:t/ vt contorcere. **~ion** n contorsione f. **~ionist** n contorsionista mf

contour /'kɒntʊə(r)/ n contorno m; (line) curva f di livello

contraband /'kɒntrəbænd/ n contrabbando m

contracep|tion /kɒntrə'sepʃn/ n contraccezione f. **~tive** n contraccettivo m

contract¹ /'kɒntrækt/ n contratto m

contract² /kən'trækt/ vi (get smaller) contrarsi •vt contrarre (illness). **~ion** n contrazione f. **~or** n imprenditore, -trice mf

contradict /kɒntrə'dɪkt/ vt contraddire. **~ion** n contraddizione f. **~ory** adj contradditorio

contraption /kən'træpʃn/ n [!] aggeggio m

contrary¹ /'kɒntrərɪ/ adj contrario •adv **~ to** contrariamente a •n contrario m; **on the ~** al contrario

contrary² /kən'treərɪ/ adj disobbediente

contrast¹ /'kɒntrɑ:st/ n contrasto m

contrast² /kən'trɑ:st/ vt confrontare •vi contrastare. **~ing** adj contrastante

contraven|e /kɒntrə'vi:n/ vt trasgredire. **~tion** n trasgressione f

contribut|e /kən'trɪbju:t/ vt/i contribuire. **~ion** n contribuzione f;

C

(what is contributed) contributo m. **~or** n contributore, -trice mf

contrive /kən'traɪv/ vt escogitare; **~ to do sth** riuscire a fare qcsa

control /kən'trəʊl/ n controllo m; **~s** pl (of car, plane) comandi mpl; **get out of ~** sfuggire al controllo •vt (pt/pp **controlled**) controllare; **~ oneself** controllarsi

controvers|ial /kɒntrə'vɜːʃl/ adj controverso. **~y** n controversia f

convalesce /kɒnvə'les/ vi essere in convalescenza

convector /kən'vektə(r)/ n **~ [heater]** convettore m

convene /kən'viːn/ vt convocare •vi riunirsi

convenience /kən'viːnɪəns/ n convenienza f; **[public] ~** gabinetti mpl pubblici; **with all modern ~s** con tutti i comfort

convenient /kən'viːnɪənt/ adj comodo; **be ~ for sb** andar bene per qcno; **if it is ~ [for you]** se ti va bene. **~ly** adv comodamente; **~ly located** in una posizione comoda

convent /'kɒnvənt/ n convento m

convention /kən'venʃn/ n convenzione f; (assembly) convegno m. **~al** adj convenzionale

converge /kən'vɜːdʒ/ vi convergere

conversation /kɒnvə'seɪʃn/ n conversazione f. **~al** adj di conversazione. **~alist** n conversatore, -trice mf

converse[1] /kən'vɜːs/ vi conversare

converse[2] /'kɒnvɜːs/ n inverso m. **~ly** adv viceversa

conversion /kən'vɜːʃn/ n conversione f

convert[1] /'kɒnvɜːt/ n convertito, -a mf

convert[2] /kən'vɜːt/ vt convertire (**into** in); sconsacrare (church). **~ible** adj convertibile •n (Auto) macchina f decappottabile

convex /'kɒnveks/ adj convesso

convey /kən'veɪ/ vt portare; trasmettere (idea, message). **~or belt** n nastro m trasportatore

convict[1] /'kɒnvɪkt/ n condannato, -a mf

convict[2] /kən'vɪkt/ vt giudicare colpevole. **~ion** n condanna f; (belief) convinzione f; **previous ~ion** precedente m penale

convinc|e /kən'vɪns/ vt convincere. **~ing** adj convincente

convoluted /'kɒnvəluːtɪd/ adj contorto

convoy /'kɒnvɔɪ/ n convoglio m

convuls|e /kən'vʌls/ vt sconvolgere; **be ~ed with laughter** contorcersi dalle risa. **~ion** n convulsione f

coo /kuː/ vi tubare

cook /kʊk/ n cuoco, -a mf •vt cucinare; **is it ~ed?** è cotto?; **~ the books** [!] truccare i libri contabili •vi (food:) cuocere; (person:) cucinare. **~book** n libro m di cucina

cooker /'kʊkə(r)/ n cucina f; (apple) mela f da cuocere. **~y** n cucina f. **~y book** n libro m di cucina

cookie /'kʊkɪ/ n Am biscotto m

cool /kuːl/ adj fresco; (calm) calmo; (unfriendly) freddo •n fresco m •vt rinfrescare •vi rinfrescarsi. **~-box** borsa f termica. **~ness** n freddezza

coop /kuːp/ n stia f •vt **~ up** rinchiudere

co-operat|e /kəʊ'ɒpəreɪt/ vi cooperare. **~ion** n cooperazione f

co-operative /kəʊ'ɒpərətɪv/ adj cooperativo •n cooperativa f

co-opt /kəʊ'ɒpt/ vt eleggere

co-ordinat|e /kəʊ'ɔːdɪneɪt/ vt coordinare. **~ion** n coordinazione f

cop /kɒp/ n [!] poliziotto m

cope /kəʊp/ vi [!] farcela; **can she ~ by herself?** ce la fa da sola?; **~ with** farcela con

copious /'kəʊpɪəs/ adj abbondante

copper[1] /'kɒpə(r)/ n rame m; **~s** pl monete fpl da uno o due pence •attrib di rame

copper[2] n [!] poliziotto m

copy /'kɒpɪ/ n copia f •vt (pt/pp **-ied**) copiare

copyright n diritti mpl d'autore

coral /'kɒrəl/ n corallo m

cord /kɔːd/ n corda f; (thinner) cordoncino m; (fabric) velluto m a coste; **~s** pl pantaloni mpl di velluto a coste

cordial /'kɔːdɪəl/ adj cordiale •n analcolico m

ordon /'kɔ:dn/ n cordone m (di persone) •**cordon off** vt mettere un cordone (di persone) intorno a

ore /kɔ:(r)/ n (of apple, pear) torsolo m; (fig: of organization) cuore m; (of problem, theory) nocciolo m

ork /kɔ:k/ n sughero m; (for bottle) turacciolo m. **~screw** n cavatappi m inv

orn¹ /kɔ:n/ n grano m; (Am: maize) granturco m

orn² n (Med) callo m

orned beef /kɔ:nd'bi:f/ n manzo m sotto sale

orner /'kɔ:nə(r)/ n angolo m; (football) calcio m d'angolo, corner m inv •vt fig bloccare; (Comm) accaparrarsi (market)

ornet /'kɔ:nɪt/ n (Mus) cornetta f; (for ice-cream) cono m

orn: ~flour n, Am **~starch** n farina f di granturco

orny /'kɔ:nɪ// adj (-ier, -iest) (!: joke, film) scontato; (person) banale; (sentimental) sdolcinato

oronary /'kɒrənərɪ/ adj coronario •n ~ [**thrombosis**] trombosi f coronarica

oronation /kɒrə'neɪʃn/ n incoronazione f

oroner /'kɒrənə(r)/ n coroner m inv (nel diritto britannico, ufficiale incaricato delle indagini su morti sospette)

orporal¹ /'kɔ:pərəl/ n (Mil) caporale m

orporal² adj corporale; ~ **punishment** punizione f corporale

corporate /'kɔ:pərət/ adj (decision, policy, image) aziendale; ~ **life** la vita in un'azienda

corporation /kɔ:pə'reɪʃn/ n ente m; (of town) consiglio m comunale

corps /kɔ:(r)/ n (pl **corps** /kɔ:z/) corpo m

corpse /kɔ:ps/ n cadavere m

corpulent /'kɔ:pjʊlənt/ adj corpulento

correct /kə'rekt/ adj corretto; **be ~** (person:) aver ragione; **~!** esatto! •vt correggere. **~ion** n correzione f. **~ly** adv correttamente

correspond /kɒrɪ'spɒnd/ vi corrispondere (**to** a); (two things:) corrispondere; (write) scriversi. **~ence** n corrispondenza f. **~ent** n corrispondente mf. **~ing** adj corrispondente. **~ingly** adv in modo corrispondente

corridor /'kɒrɪdɔ:(r)/ n corridoio m

corro|de /kə'rəʊd/ vt corrodere •vi corrodersi. **~sion** n corrosione f

corrugated /'kɒrəgeɪtɪd/ adj ondulato. ~ **iron** n lamiera f ondulata

corrupt /kə'rʌpt/ adj corrotto •vt corrompere. **~ion** n corruzione f

corset /'kɔ:sɪt/ n & **-s** pl busto m

Corsica /'kɔ:sɪkə/ n Corsica f. **~n** adj & n corso, -a mf

cosmetic /kɒz'metɪk/ adj cosmetico •n **~s** pl cosmetici mpl

cosmic /'kɒzmɪk/ adj cosmico

cosmopolitan /kɒzmə'pɒlɪtən/ adj cosmopolita

cosmos /'kɒzmɒs/ n cosmo m

cosset /'kɒsɪt/ vt coccolare

cost /kɒst/ n costo m; **~s** pl (Jur) spese fpl processuali; **at all ~s** a tutti i costi; **I learnt to my ~** ho imparato a mie spese •vt (pt/pp **cost**) costare; **it ~ me £20** mi è costato 20 sterline •vt (pt/pp **costed**) ~ [**out**] stabilire il prezzo di

costly /'kɒstlɪ/ adj (**-ier, -iest**) costoso

costume /'kɒstju:m/ n costume m. ~ **jewellery** n bigiotteria f

cosy /'kəʊzɪ/ adj (**-ier, -iest**) (pub, chat) intimo; **it's nice and ~ in here** si sta bene qui

cot /kɒt/ n lettino m; (Am: camp-bed) branda f

cottage /'kɒtɪdʒ/ n casetta f. ~ **'cheese** n fiocchi mpl di latte

cotton /'kɒtn/ n cotone m •attrib di cotone •**cotton on** vi ! capire

cotton 'wool n cotone m idrofilo

couch /kaʊtʃ/ n divano m. ~ **potato** n pantofolaio, -a mf

cough /kɒf/ n tosse f •vi tossire. □ ~ **up** vt/i sputare; (!: pay) sborsare

'cough mixture n sciroppo m per la tosse

C

C

could /kʊd/, *atono* /kəd/ v aux (*see also* **can²**) **~ I have a glass of water?** potrei avere un bicchier d'acqua?; **I ~n't do it even if I wanted to** non potrei farlo nemmeno se lo volessi; **I ~n't care less** non potrebbe importarmene di meno; **he ~n't have done it without help** non avrebbe potuto farlo senza aiuto; **you ~ have phoned** avresti potuto telefonare

council /ˈkaʊnsl/ n consiglio m. **~ house** n casa f popolare

councillor /ˈkaʊnsələ(r)/ n consigliere, -a mf

counsel /ˈkaʊnsl/ n consigli mpl; (Jur) avvocato m •vt (pt/pp **counselled**) consigliare a (person). **~lor** n consigliere, -a mf

count¹ /kaʊnt/ n (nobleman) conte m

count² n conto m; **keep ~** tenere il conto •vt/i contare. □ **~ on** vt contare su

countdown /ˈkaʊntdaʊn/ n conto m alla rovescia

counter¹ /ˈkaʊntə(r)/ n banco m; (in games) gettone m

counter² adv **~ to** contro, in contrasto a; **go ~ to sth** andare contro qcsa •vt/i opporre (measure, effect); parare (blow)

counterˈact vt neutralizzare

ˈcounter-attack n contrattacco m

ˈcounterfeit /-fɪt/ adj contraffatto •n contraffazione f •vt contraffare

ˈcounterfoil n matrice f

counter-proˈductive adj controproduttivo

countess /ˈkaʊntɪs/ n contessa f

countless /ˈkaʊntlɪs/ adj innumerevole

country /ˈkʌntrɪ/ n nazione f, paese m; (native land) patria f; (countryside) campagna f; **in the ~** in campagna; **go to the ~** andare in campagna; (Pol) indire le elezioni politiche. **~man** n uomo m di campagna; (fellow ~man) compatriota m. **~side** n campagna f

county /ˈkaʊntɪ/ n contea f (unità amministrativa britannica)

coup /ku:/ n (Pol) colpo m di stato

couple /ˈkʌpl/ n coppia f; **a ~ of** un paio di

coupon /ˈku:pɒn/ n tagliando m; (for discount) buono m sconto

courage /ˈkʌrɪdʒ/ n coraggio m. **~ous** adj coraggioso

courgette /kʊəˈʒet/ n zucchino m

courier /ˈkʊrɪə(r)/ n corriere m; (for tourists) guida f

course /kɔ:s/ n (Sch) corso m; (Naut) rotta f; (Culin) portata f; (for golf) campo m; **~ of treatment** (Med) serie f inv di cure; **of ~** naturalmente; **in the ~ of** durante **in due ~** a tempo debito

court /kɔ:t/ n tribunale m; (Sport) campo m; **take sb to ~** citare qcno in giudizio •vt fare la corte a (woman); sfidare (danger); **~ing couples** coppiette fpl

courteous /ˈkɜ:tɪəs/ adj cortese

courtesy /ˈkɜ:təsɪ/ n cortesia f

court: ~ ˈmartial n (pl **~s martial**) corte f marziale **~-martial** vt (pt **~-martialled**) portare davanti alla corte marziale; **~yard** n cortile m

cousin /ˈkʌzn/ n cugino, -a mf

cove /kəʊv/ n insenatura f

cover /ˈkʌvə(r)/ n copertura f; (of cushion, to protect sth) fodera f; (of book, magazine) copertina f; **take ~** mettersi al riparo; **under separate ~** a parte •vt coprire; foderare (cushion); (Journ) fare un servizio su. □ **~ up** vt coprire; fig soffocare (scandal)

coverage /ˈkʌvərɪdʒ/ n (Journ) **it got a lot of ~** i media gli hanno dedicato molto spazio

cover: ~ charge n coperto m. **~ing** n copertura f; (for floor) rivestimento m; **~ing letter** lettera f d'accompagnamento

covet /ˈkʌvɪt/ vt bramare

cow /kaʊ/ n vacca f, mucca f

coward /ˈkaʊəd/ n vigliacco, -a mf. **~ice** n vigliaccheria f. **~ly** adj da vigliacco

ˈcowboy n cowboy m inv; [!] buffone m

cower /ˈkaʊə(r)/ vi acquattarsi

coy /kɔɪ/ adj falsamente timido;

(flirtatiously) civettuolo; **be ~ about sth** essere evasivo su qcsa

crab /kræb/ n granchio m

crack /kræk/ n (in wall) crepa f; (in china, glass, bone) incrinatura f; (noise) scoppio m; (!: joke) battuta f; **have a ~** (try) fare un tentativo • adj (!: best) di prim'ordine • vt incrinare (china, glass); schiacciare (nut); decifrare (code); ! risolvere (problem); **~ a joke** ! fare una battuta • vi (china, glass:) incrinarsi; (whip:) schioccare. □ **~ down** vi ! prendere seri provvedimenti. □ **~ down on** vt ! prendere seri provvedimenti contro

cracker /'krækə(r)/ n (biscuit) cracker m inv; (firework) petardo m; [**Christmas**] ~ tubo m di cartone colorato contenente una sorpresa

crackle /'krækl/ vi crepitare

cradle /'kreɪdl/ n culla f

craft[1] /krɑ:ft/ n inv (boat) imbarcazione f

craft[2] n mestiere m; (technique) arte f. **~sman** n artigiano m

crafty /'krɑ:ftɪ/ adj (**-ier, -iest**) astuto

cram /kræm/ v (pt/pp **crammed**) • vt stipare (**into** in) • vi (for exams) sgobbare

cramp /kræmp/ n crampo m. **~ed** adj (room) stretto; (handwriting) appiccicato

cranberry /'krænbərɪ/ n (Culin) mirtillo m rosso

crane /kreɪn/ n (at docks, bird) gru f inv • vt **~ one's neck** allungare il collo

crank[1] /kræŋk/ n tipo, -a mf strampalato, -a

crank[2] n (Techn) manovella f. **~shaft** n albero m a gomiti

cranky /'kræŋkɪ/ adj strampalato; (Am: irritable) irritabile

cranny /'krænɪ/ n fessura f

crash /kræʃ/ n (noise) fragore m; (Aeron, Auto) incidente m; (Comm) crollo m • vi schiantarsi (**into** contro); (plane:) precipitare • vt schiantare (car)

crash: ~ course n corso m intensivo. **~-helmet** n casco m

crate /kreɪt/ n (for packing) cassa f

crater /'kreɪtə(r)/ n cratere m

crav|e /kreɪv/ vt morire dalla voglia di. **~ing** n voglia f smodata

crawl /krɔ:l/ n (swimming) stile m libero; **do the ~** nuotare a stile libero; **at a ~** a passo di lumaca • vi andare carponi; **~ with** brulicare di. **~er lane** n (Auto) corsia f riservata al traffico lento

crayon /'kreɪən/ n pastello m a cera; (pencil) matita f colorata

craze /kreɪz/ n mania f

crazy /'kreɪzɪ/ adj (**-ier, -iest**) matto; **be ~ about** andar matto per

creak /kri:k/ n scricchiolio m • vi scricchiolare

cream /kri:m/ n crema f; (fresh) panna f • adj (colour) [bianco] panna inv • vt (Culin) sbattere. **~ 'cheese** n formaggio m cremoso. **~y** adj cremoso

crease /kri:s/ n piega f • vt stropicciare • vi stropicciarsi. **~-resistant** adj che non si stropiccia

creat|e /kri:'eɪt/ vt creare. **~ion** n creazione f. **~ive** adj creativo. **~or** n creatore, -trice mf

creature /'kri:tʃə(r)/ n creatura f

crèche /kreʃ/ n asilo m nido

credibility /kredə'bɪlətɪ/ n credibilità f

credible /'kredəbl/ adj credibile

credit /'kredɪt/ n credito m; (honour) merito m; **take the ~ for** prendersi il merito di • vt (pt/pp **credited**) accreditare; **~ sb with sth** (Comm) accreditare qcsa a qcno; fig attribuire qcsa a qcno. **~able** adj lodevole

credit: ~ card n carta f di credito. **~or** n creditore, -trice mf

creed /kri:d/ n credo m inv

creek /kri:k/ n insenatura f; (Am: stream) torrente m

creep /kri:p/ vi (pt/pp **crept**) muoversi furtivamente • n ! tipo m viscido. **~er** n pianta f rampicante. **~y** adj che fa venire i brividi

cremat|e /krɪ'meɪt/ vt cremare. **~ion** n cremazione f

crematorium /kremə'tɔ:rɪəm/ n crematorio m

crept /krept/ ▸**creep**

C

crescent /ˈkresənt/ n mezzaluna f
crest /krest/ n cresta f; (coat of arms) cimiero m
Crete /kriːt/ n Creta f
crevice /ˈkrevɪs/ n crepa f
crew /kruː/ n equipaggio m; (gang) équipe f inv. ~ **cut** n capelli mpl a spazzola. ~ **neck** n girocollo m
crib[1] /krɪb/ n (for baby) culla f
crib[2] vt/i (pt/pp **cribbed**) [!] copiare
crick /krɪk/ n ~ **in the neck** torcicollo m
cricket[1] /ˈkrɪkɪt/ n (insect) grillo m
cricket[2] n cricket m. ~**er** n giocatore m di cricket
crime /kraɪm/ n crimine m; (criminality) criminalità f
criminal /ˈkrɪmɪnl/ adj criminale; (law, court) penale •n criminale mf
crimson /ˈkrɪmzn/ adj cremisi inv
cringe /krɪndʒ/ vi (cower) acquattarsi; (at bad joke etc) fare una smorfia
crinkle /ˈkrɪŋkl/ vt spiegazzare •vi spiegazzarsi
cripple /ˈkrɪpl/ n storpio, -a mf •vt storpiare; fig danneggiare. ~**d** adj (person) storpio; (ship) danneggiato
crisis /ˈkraɪsɪs/ n (pl **-ses** /-siːz/) crisi f inv
crisp /krɪsp/ adj croccante; (air) frizzante; (style) incisivo. ~**bread** n crostini mpl di pane. ~**s** npl patatine fpl
criterion /kraɪˈtɪərɪən/ n (pl **-ria** /-rɪə/) criterio m
critic /ˈkrɪtɪk/ n critico, -a mf. ~**al** adj critico. ~**ally** adv in modo critico; ~**ally ill** gravemente malato
criticism /ˈkrɪtɪsɪzm/ n critica f; **he doesn't like** ~ non ama le critiche
criticize /ˈkrɪtɪsaɪz/ vt criticare
croak /krəʊk/ vi gracchiare; (frog:) gracidare
Croatia /krəʊˈeɪʃə/ n Croazia f
crochet /ˈkrəʊʃeɪ/ n lavoro m all'uncinetto •vt fare all'uncinetto. ~**-hook** n uncinetto m
crockery /ˈkrɒkərɪ/ n terrecotte fpl
crocodile /ˈkrɒkədaɪl/ n coccodrillo m. ~ **tears** lacrime fpl di coccodrillo
crocus /ˈkrəʊkəs/ n (pl **-es**) croco m
crook /krʊk/ n ([!]: criminal) truffatore, -trice mf
crooked /ˈkrʊkɪd/ adj storto; (limb) storpiato; ([!]: dishonest) disonesto
crop /krɒp/ n raccolto m; fig quantità f inv •v (pt/pp **cropped**) •vt coltivare. □ ~ **up** vi [!] presentarsi
croquet /ˈkrəʊkeɪ/ n croquet m
croquette /krəʊˈket/ n crocchetta f
cross /krɒs/ adj (annoyed) arrabbiato; **talk at** ~ **purposes** fraintendersi •n croce f; (Bot, Zool) incrocio m •vt sbarrare (cheque); incrociare (road, animals); ~ **oneself** farsi il segno della croce; ~ **one's arms** incrociare le braccia; ~ **one's legs** accavallare le gambe; **keep one's fingers** ~**ed for sb** tenere le dita incrociate per qcno; **it** ~**ed my mind** mi è venuto in mente •vi (go across) attraversare; (lines:) incrociarsi. □ ~ **out** vt depennare
cross: ~**bar** n (of goal) traversa f; (on bicycle) canna f. ~**exˈamine** vt sottoporre a controinterrogatorio. ~**-ˈeyed** adj strabico. ~**fire** n fuoco m incrociato. ~**ing** n (for pedestrians) passaggio m pedonale; (sea journey) traversata f. ~**-ˈreference** n rimando m. ~**roads** n incrocio m. ~**-ˈsection** n sezione f; (of community) campione m. ~**word** n ~**word [puzzle]** parole fpl crociate
crouch /kraʊtʃ/ vi accovacciarsi
crow /krəʊ/ n corvo m; **as the** ~ **flies** in linea d'aria •vi cantare. ~**bar** n piede m di porco
crowd /kraʊd/ n folla f •vt affollare •vi affollarsi. ~**ed** adj affollato
crown /kraʊn/ n corona f •vt incoronare; incapsulare (tooth)
crucial /ˈkruːʃl/ adj cruciale
crucifix /ˈkruːsɪfɪks/ n crocifisso m
crucif|ixion /kruːsɪˈfɪkʃn/ n crocifissione f. ~**y** vt (pt/pp **-ied**) crocifiggere
crude /kruːd/ adj (oil) greggio; (language) crudo; (person) rozzo
cruel /kruːəl/ adj (**crueller, cruellest**) crudele (**to** verso). ~**ly** adv con crudeltà. ~**ty** n crudeltà f
cruis|e /kruːz/ n crociera f •vi fare una crociera; (car:) andare a velocità di crociera. ~**er** n (Mil) incrociatore m; (motor boat) motoscafo m. ~**ing**

speed n velocità m inv di crociera

crumb /krʌm/ n briciola f

crumb|le /ˈkrʌmbl/ vt sbriciolare •vi sbriciolarsi; (building, society:) sgretolarsi. **~ly** adj friabile

crumple /ˈkrʌmpl/ vt spiegazzare •vi spiegazzarsi

crunch /krʌntʃ/ n ! **when it comes to the ~** quando si viene al dunque •vt sgranocchiare •vi (snow:) scricchiolare

crusade /kruːˈseɪd/ n crociata f. **~r** n crociato m

crush /krʌʃ/ n (crowd) calca f; **have a ~ on sb** essersi preso una cotta per qcno •vt schiacciare; sgualcire (clothes)

crust /krʌst/ n crosta f

crutch /krʌtʃ/ n gruccia f; (Anat) inforcatura f

crux /krʌks/ n fig punto m cruciale

cry /kraɪ/ n grido m; **have a ~** farsi un pianto; **a far ~ from** fig tutta un'altra cosa rispetto a •vi (pt/pp **cried**) (weep) piangere; (call) gridare

crypt /krɪpt/ n cripta f. **~ic** adj criptico

crystal /ˈkrɪstl/ n cristallo m; (glassware) cristalli mpl. **~lize** vi (become clear) concretizzarsi

cub /kʌb/ n (animal) cucciolo m; **C~ [Scout]** lupetto m

Cuba /ˈkjuːbə/ n Cuba f

cubby-hole /ˈkʌbɪ-/ n (compartment) scomparto m; (room) ripostiglio m

cub|e /kjuːb/ n cubo m. **~ic** adj cubico

cubicle /ˈkjuːbɪkl/ n cabina f

cuckoo /ˈkʊkuː/ n cuculo m. **~ clock** n orologio m a cucù

cucumber /ˈkjuːkʌmbə(r)/ n cetriolo m

cuddl|e /ˈkʌdl/ vt coccolare •vi **~e up to** starsene accoccolato insieme a •n **have a ~e** (child:) farsi coccolare; (lovers:) abbracciarsi. **~y** adj tenerone; (wanting cuddles) coccolone. **~y ˈtoy** n peluche m inv

cue[1] /kjuː/ n segnale m; (Theat) battuta f d'entrata

cue[2] n (in billiards) stecca f. **~ ball** n pallino m

cuff /kʌf/ n polsino m; (Am: turn-up) orlo m; (blow) scapaccione m; **off the ~** improvvisando •vt dare una pacca a. **~-link** n gemello m

cul-de-sac /ˈkʌldəsæk/ n vicolo m cieco

culinary /ˈkʌlɪnərɪ/ adj culinario

cull /kʌl/ vt scegliere (flowers); (kill) selezionare e uccidere

culminat|e /ˈkʌlmɪneɪt/ vi culminare. **~ion** n culmine m

culprit /ˈkʌlprɪt/ n colpevole mf

cult /kʌlt/ n culto m

cultivate /ˈkʌltɪveɪt/ vt coltivare; fig coltivarsi (person)

cultural /ˈkʌltʃərəl/ adj culturale

culture /ˈkʌltʃə(r)/ n cultura f. **~d** adj colto

cumbersome /ˈkʌmbəsəm/ adj ingombrante

cunning /ˈkʌnɪŋ/ adj astuto •n astuzia f

cup /kʌp/ n tazza f; (prize, of bra) coppa f

cupboard /ˈkʌbəd/ n armadio m. **~love** ! amore m interessato

curator /kjʊəˈreɪtə(r)/ n direttore, -trice mf (di museo)

curb /kɜːb/ vt tenere a freno

curdle /ˈkɜːdl/ vi coagularsi

cure /kjʊə(r)/ n cura f •vt curare; (salt) mettere sotto sale; (smoke) affumicare

curfew /ˈkɜːfjuː/ n coprifuoco m

curiosity /kjʊərɪˈɒsətɪ/ n curiosità f

curious /ˈkjʊərɪəs/ adj curioso. **~ly** adv (strangely) curiosamente

curl /kɜːl/ n ricciolo m •vt arricciare •vi arricciarsi. □ **~ up** vi raggomitolarsi

curler /ˈkɜːlə(r)/ n bigodino m

curly /ˈkɜːlɪ/ adj (**-ier, -iest**) riccio

currant /ˈkʌrənt/ n (dried) uvetta f

currency /ˈkʌrənsɪ/ n valuta f; (of word) ricorrenza f; **foreign ~** valuta f estera

current /ˈkʌrənt/ adj corrente •n corrente f. **~ affairs** or **events** npl attualità fsg. **~ly** adv attualmente

curriculum /kəˈrɪkjʊləm/ n programma m di studi. **~ vitae** n curriculum vitae m inv

curry /'kʌrɪ/ n curry m inv; (meal) piatto m cucinato nel curry •vt (pt/pp -ied) ~ **favour with sb** cercare d'ingraziarsi qcno

curse /kɜːs/ n maledizione f; (oath) imprecazione f •vt maledire •vi imprecare

cursory /'kɜːsərɪ/ adj sbrigativo

curt /kɜːt/ adj brusco

curtain /'kɜːtn/ n tenda f; (Theat) sipario m

curtsy /'kɜːtsɪ/ n inchino m •vi (pt/pp -ied) fare l'inchino

curve /kɜːv/ n curva f •vi curvare; ~ **to the right**/**left** curvare a destra/sinistra. ~**d** adj curvo

cushion /'kʊʃn/ n cuscino m •vt attutire; (protect) proteggere

cushy /'kʊʃɪ/ adj (-ier, -iest) [!] facile

custard /'kʌstəd/ n (liquid) crema f pasticciera

custody /'kʌstədɪ/ n (of child) custodia f; (imprisonment) detenzione f preventiva

custom /'kʌstəm/ n usanza f; (Jur) consuetudine f; (Comm) clientela f. ~**ary** adj (habitual) abituale; **it's** ~**ary to...** è consuetudine.... ~**er** n cliente mf

customs /'kʌstəmz/ npl dogana f. ~ **officer** n doganiere m

cut /kʌt/ n (with knife etc, of clothes) taglio m; (reduction) riduzione f; (in public spending) taglio m •vt/i (pt/pp **cut**, pres p **cutting**) tagliare; (reduce) ridurre; ~ **one's finger** tagliarsi il dito; ~ **sb's hair** tagliare i capelli a qcno •vi (with cards) alzare. □ ~ **back** vt tagliare (hair); potare (hedge); (reduce) ridurre. □ ~ **down** vt abbattere (tree); (reduce) ridurre. □ ~ **off** vt tagliar via; (disconnect) interrompere; fig isolare; **I was** ~ **off** (Teleph) la linea è caduta. □ ~ **out** vt ritagliare; (delete) eliminare; **be** ~ **out for** [!] essere tagliato per; ~ **it out!** [!] dacci un taglio!. □ ~ **up** vt (slice) tagliare a pezzi

cute /kjuːt/ adj [!] (in appearance) carino; (clever) acuto

cutlery /'kʌtlərɪ/ n posate fpl

cutlet /'kʌtlɪt/ n cotoletta f

'**cut-price** adj a prezzo ridotto; (shop) che fa prezzi ridotti

'**cut-throat** adj spietato

cutting /'kʌtɪŋ/ adj (remark) tagliente •n (from newspaper) ritaglio m; (of plant) talea f

CV n abbr curriculum vitae

cycl|e /'saɪkl/ n ciclo m; (bicycle) bicicletta f, bici f inv [!] •vi andare in bicicletta. ~**ing** n ciclismo m. ~**ist** n ciclista mf

cylind|er /'sɪlɪndə(r)/ n cilindro m. ~**rical** adj cilindrico

cynic /'sɪnɪk/ n cinico, -a mf. ~**al** adj cinico. ~**ism** n cinismo m

Cyprus /'saɪprəs/ n Cipro m

Czech /tʃek/ adj ceco; ~ **Republic** Repubblica f Ceca •n ceco, -a mf

Dd

dab /dæb/ n colpetto m; **a** ~ **of** un pochino di •vt (pt/pp **dabbed**) toccare leggermente (eyes). □ ~ **on** vt mettere un po' di (paint etc)

dad[dy] /'dæd[ɪ]/ n [!] papà m inv, babbo m

daddy-'long-legs n zanzarone m [dei boschi]; (Am: spider) ragno m

daffodil /'dæfədɪl/ n giunchiglia f

daft /dɑːft/ adj sciocco

dagger /'dægə(r)/ n stiletto m

daily /'deɪlɪ/ adj giornaliero •adv giornalmente •n (newspaper) quotidiano m; ([!]: cleaner) donna f delle pulizie

dainty /'deɪntɪ/ adj (-ier, -iest) grazioso; (movement) delicato

dairy /'deərɪ/ n caseificio m; (shop) latteria f. ~ **cow** n mucca f da latte. ~ **products** npl latticini mpl

aisy /ˈdeɪzɪ/ n margheritina f; (larger) margherita f

am /dæm/ n diga f •vt (pt/pp **dammed**) costruire una diga su

amag|e /ˈdæmɪdʒ/ n danno m (**to** a); **~es** pl (Jur) risarcimento msg •vt danneggiare; fig nuocere a. **~ing** adj dannoso

ame /deɪm/ n liter dama f; Am ☒ donna f

amn /dæm/ adj ⓘ maledetto •adv (lucky, late) maledettamente •n **I don't give a ~** ⓘ non me ne frega un accidente •vt dannare. **~ation** n dannazione f •int ⓘ accidenti!

amp /dæmp/ adj umido •n umidità f •vt inumidire

ance /dɑːns/ n ballo m •vt/i ballare. **~-hall** n sala f da ballo. **~ music** n musica f da ballo

ancer /ˈdɑːnsə(r)/ n ballerino, -a mf

andelion /ˈdændɪlaɪən/ n dente m di leone

andruff /ˈdændrʌf/ n forfora f

ane /deɪn/ n danese mf; **Great ~** danese m

anger /ˈdeɪndʒə(r)/ n pericolo m; **in/out of ~** in/fuori pericolo. **~ous** adj pericoloso. **~ously** adv pericolosamente; **~ously ill** in pericolo di vita

angle /ˈdæŋgl/ vi penzolare •vt far penzolare

anish /ˈdeɪnɪʃ/ adj & n danese m. **~ 'pastry** n dolce m a base di pasta sfoglia contenente pasta di mandorle, mele ecc

are /deə(r)/ vt/i osare; (challenge) sfidare (**to** a); **~ [to] do sth** osare fare qcsa; **I ~ say!** molto probabilmente! •n sfida f. **~devil** n spericolato, -a mf

aring /ˈdeərɪŋ/ adj audace •n audacia f

ark /dɑːk/ adj buio; **~ blue/brown** blu/marrone scuro; **it's getting ~** sta cominciando a fare buio; **~ horse** fig (in race, contest) vincitore m imprevisto; (not much known about) misterioso m; **keep sth ~** fig tenere qcsa nascosto •n **after ~** col buio; **in the ~** al buio; **keep sb in the ~** fig tenere qcno all'oscuro

ark|en /ˈdɑːkn/ vt oscurare •vi oscurarsi. **~ness** n buio m

'dark-room n camera f oscura

darling /ˈdɑːlɪŋ/ adj adorabile; **my ~ Joan** carissima Joan •n tesoro m

darn /dɑːn/ vt rammendare. **~ing-needle** n ago m da rammendo

dart /dɑːt/ n dardo m; (in sewing) pince f inv; **~s** sg (game) freccette fpl •vi lanciarsi

dartboard /ˈdɑːtbɔːd/ n bersaglio m [per freccette]

dash /dæʃ/ n (Typ) trattino m; (in Morse) linea f; **a ~ of milk** un goccio di latte; **make a ~ for** lanciarsi verso •vi **I must ~** devo scappare •vt far svanire (hopes). □ **~ off** vi scappar via •vt (write quickly) buttare giù. □ **~ out** vi uscire di corsa

'dashboard n cruscotto m

data /ˈdeɪtə/ npl & sg dati mpl. **~base** n base [di] dati f, database m inv. **~comms** n telematica f. **~ processing** n elaborazione f [di] dati

date¹ /deɪt/ n (fruit) dattero m

date² n data f; (meeting) appuntamento m; **to ~** fino ad oggi; **out of ~** (not fashionable) fuori moda; (expired) scaduto; (information) non aggiornato; **make a ~ with sb** dare un appuntamento a qcno; **be up to ~** essere aggiornato •vt/i datare; (go out with) uscire con. □ **~ back to** vi risalire a

dated /ˈdeɪtɪd/ adj fuori moda; (language) antiquato

daub /dɔːb/ vt imbrattare (walls)

daughter /ˈdɔːtə(r)/ n figlia f. **~-in-law** n (pl **~s-in-law**) nuora f

dawdle /ˈdɔːdl/ vi bighellonare; (over work) cincischiarsi

dawn /dɔːn/ n alba f; **at ~** all'alba •vi albeggiare; **it ~ed on me** fig mi è apparso chiaro

day /deɪ/ n giorno m; (whole day) giornata f; (period) epoca f; **these ~s** oggigiorno; **in those ~s** a quei tempi; **it's had its ~** ⓘ ha fatto il suo tempo

day: ~break n **at ~break** allo spuntar del giorno. **~-dream** n sogno m ad occhi aperti •vi sognare ad occhi aperti. **~light** n luce f del giorno. **~time** n giorno m; **in the ~time** di giorno

d

daze /deɪz/ n **in a ~** stordito; fig sbalordito. **~d** adj stordito; fig sbalordito

dazzle /'dæzl/ vt abbagliare

dead /ded/ adj morto; (numb) intorpidito; **~ body** morto m; **~ centre** pieno centro m • adv **~ tired** stanco morto; **~ slow/easy** lentissimo/facilissimo; **you're ~ right** hai perfettamente ragione; **stop ~** fermarsi di colpo; **be ~ on time** essere in perfetto orario • n **the ~** pl i morti; **in the ~ of night** nel cuore della notte

deaden /'dedn/ vt attutire (sound); calmare (pain)

dead: ~ 'end n vicolo m cieco. **~line** n scadenza f. **~lock** n **reach ~lock** fig giungere a un punto morto

deadly /'dedlɪ/ adj (**-ier, -iest**) mortale; (🄸: dreary) barboso; **~ sins** peccati mpl capitali

deaf /def/ adj sordo; **~ and dumb** sordomuto. **~-aid** n apparecchio m acustico

deaf|en /'defn/ vt assordare; (permanently) render sordo. **~ening** adj assordante. **~ness** n sordità f

deal /di:l/ n (agreement) patto m; (in business) accordo m; **whose ~?** (in cards) a chi tocca dare le carte?; **a good** or **great ~** molto; **get a raw ~** 🄸 ricevere un trattamento ingiusto • vt (pt/pp **dealt** /delt/) (in cards) dare; **~ sb a blow** dare un colpo a qcno. □ **~ in** vt trattare in. □ **~ out** vt (hand out) distribuire. □ **~ with** vt (handle) occuparsi di; trattare con (company); (be about) trattare di; **that's been ~t with** è stato risolto

deal|er /'di:lə(r)/ n commerciante mf; (in drugs) spacciatore, -trice mf. **~ings** npl **have ~ings with** avere a che fare con

dean /di:n/ n decano m; (Univ) ≈ preside mf di facoltà

dear /dɪə(r)/ adj caro; (in letter) Caro; (formal) Gentile • n caro, -a mf • int **oh ~!** Dio mio!. **~ly** adv (love) profondamente; (pay) profumatamente

death /deθ/ n morte f. **~ certificate** n certificato m di morte. **~ duty** n tassa f di successione

death trap n trappola f mortale

debatable /dɪ'beɪtəbl/ adj discutibile

debate /dɪ'beɪt/ n dibattito m • vt discutere; (in formal debate) dibattere • vi **~ whether to...** considerare se...

debauchery /dɪ'bɔ:tʃərɪ/ n dissolutezza f

debit /'debɪt/ n debito m • vt (pt/pp **debited**) (Comm) addebitare (sum)

debris /'debri:/ n macerie fpl

debt /det/ n debito m; **be in ~** avere dei debiti. **~or** n debitore, -trice mf

decade /'dekeɪd/ n decennio m

decaden|ce /'dekədəns/ n decadenza f. **~t** adj decadente

decay /dɪ'keɪ/ n (also fig) decadenza f (rot) decomposizione f; (of tooth) carie f inv • vi imputridire; (rot) decomporsi; (tooth:) cariarsi

deceased /dɪ'si:st/ adj defunto • n **the ~** il defunto; la defunta

deceit /dɪ'si:t/ n inganno m. **~ful** adj falso

deceive /dɪ'si:v/ vt ingannare

December /dɪ'sembə(r)/ n dicembre m

decency /'di:sənsɪ/ n decenza f

decent /'di:sənt/ adj decente; (respectable) rispettabile; **very ~ of you** molto gentile da parte tua. **~ly** adv decentemente; (kindly) gentilmente

decept|ion /dɪ'sepʃn/ n inganno m. **~ive** adj ingannevole. **~ively** adv ingannevolmente; **it looks ~ively easy** sembra facile, ma non lo è

decibel /'desɪbel/ n decibel m inv

decide /dɪ'saɪd/ vt decidere • vi decidere (**on** di)

decided /dɪ'saɪdɪd/ adj risoluto. **~ly** adv risolutamente; (without doubt) senza dubbio

decimal /'desɪml/ adj decimale • n numero m decimale. **~ 'point** n virgola f

decipher /dɪ'saɪfə(r)/ vt decifrare

decision /dɪ'sɪʒn/ n decisione f

decisive /dɪ'saɪsɪv/ adj decisivo

deck¹ /dek/ vt abbigliare

deck² n (Naut) ponte m; **on ~** in coperta; **top ~** (of bus) piano m di sopra; **~ of cards** mazzo m. **~-chair** n [sedia f a] sdraio f inv

eclaration /deklə'reɪʃn/ n dichiarazione f

eclare /dɪ'kleə(r)/ vt dichiarare; **anything to ~?** niente da dichiarare?

ecline /dɪ'klaɪn/ n declino m •vt also (Gram) declinare •vi (decrease) diminuire; (health:) deperire; (say no) rifiutare

ecode /di:'kəʊd/ vt decifrare; (Comput) decodificare

ecompose /di:kəm'pəʊz/ vi decomporsi

écor /'deɪkɔ:(r)/ n decorazione f; (including furniture) arredamento m

ecorat|e /'dekəreɪt/ vt decorare; (paint) pitturare; (wallpaper) tappezzare. **~ion** n decorazione f. **~ive** adj decorativo. **~or** n **painter and ~or** imbianchino m

ecoy¹ /'di:kɔɪ/ n esca f

ecoy² /dɪ'kɔɪ/ vt adescare

ecrease¹ /'di:kri:s/ n diminuzione f

ecrease² /dɪ'kri:s/ vt/i diminuire

ecree /dɪ'kri:/ n decreto m •vt (pt/pp **decreed**) decretare

ecrepit /dɪ'krepɪt/ adj decrepito

edicat|e /'dedɪkeɪt/ vt dedicare. **~ed** adj (person) scrupoloso. **~ion** n dedizione f; (in book) dedica f

educe /dɪ'dju:s/ vt dedurre (**from** da)

educt /dɪ'dʌkt/ vt dedurre

eduction /dɪ'dʌkʃn/ n deduzione f

eed /di:d/ n azione f; (Jur) atto m di proprietà

eem /di:m/ vt ritenere

eep /di:p/ adj profondo; **go off the ~ end** [!] arrabbiarsi

eepen /'di:pn/ vt approfondire; scavare più profondamente (trench) •vi approfondirsi; (fig: mystery:) infittirsi

eep-'freeze n congelatore m

eeply /'di:plɪ /adv profondamente

eer /dɪə(r)/ n inv cervo m

eface /dɪ'feɪs/ vt sfigurare (picture); deturpare (monument)

efault /dɪ'fɔ:lt/ n (non-payment) morosità f; (failure to appear) contumacia f; **win by ~** (Sport) vincere per abbandono dell'avversario; **in ~ of** per mancanza di •adj **~ drive** (Comput) lettore m di default •vi (not pay) venir meno a un pagamento

defeat /dɪ'fi:t/ n sconfitta f •vt sconfiggere; (frustrate) vanificare (attempts); **that ~s the object** questo fa fallire l'obiettivo

defect¹ /dɪ'fekt/ vi (Pol) fare defezione

defect² /'di:fekt/ n difetto m. **~ive** adj difettoso

defence /dɪ'fens/ n difesa f. **~less** adj indifeso

defend /dɪ'fend/ vt difendere; (justify) giustificare. **~ant** n (Jur) imputato, -a mf

defensive /dɪ'fensɪv/ adj difensivo •n difensiva f; **on the ~** sulla difensiva

defer /dɪ'fɜ:(r)/ v (pt/pp **deferred**) •vt (postpone) rinviare •vi **~ to sb** rimettersi a qcno

deferen|ce /'defərəns/ n deferenza f. **~tial** adj deferente

defian|ce /dɪ'faɪəns/ n sfida f; **in ~ce of** sfidando. **~t** adj (person) ribelle; (gesture, attitude) di sfida. **~tly** adv con aria di sfida

deficien|cy /dɪ'fɪʃənsɪ/ n insufficienza f. **~t** adj insufficiente; **be ~t in** mancare di

deficit /'defɪsɪt/ n deficit m inv

define /dɪ'faɪn/ vt definire

definite /'defɪnɪt/ adj definito; (certain) (answer, yes) definitivo; (improvement, difference) netto; **he was ~ about it** è stato chiaro in proposito. **~ly** adv sicuramente

definition /defɪ'nɪʃn/ n definizione f

definitive /dɪ'fɪnətɪv/ adj definitivo

deflat|e /dɪ'fleɪt/ vt sgonfiare. **~ion** n (Comm) deflazione f

deflect /dɪ'flekt/ vt deflettere

deform|ed /dɪ'fɔ:md/ adj deforme. **~ity** n deformità f inv

defrost /di:'frɒst/ vt sbrinare (fridge); scongelare (food)

deft /deft/ adj abile

d

defuse /di:'fju:z/ vt disinnescare; calmare (situation)

defy /dɪ'faɪ/ vt (pt/pp **-ied**) (challenge) sfidare; resistere a (attempt); (not obey) disobbedire a

degenerate[1] /dɪ'dʒenəreɪt/ vi degenerare; ~ **into** fig degenerare in

degenerate[2] /dɪ'dʒenərət/ adj degenerato

degree /dɪ'gri:/ n grado m; (Univ) laurea f; **20 ~s** 20 gradi; **not to the same ~** non allo stesso livello

deign /deɪn/ vi ~ **to do sth** degnarsi di fare qcsa

deity /'di:ɪtɪ/ n divinità f inv

dejected /dɪ'dʒektɪd/ adj demoralizzato

delay /dɪ'leɪ/ n ritardo m; **without ~** senza indugio •vt ritardare; **be ~ed** (person:) essere trattenuto; (train, aircraft:) essere in ritardo •vi indugiare

delegate[1] /'delɪgət/ n delegato, -a mf

delegat|e[2] /'delɪgeɪt/ vt delegare. **~ion** n delegazione f

delet|e /dɪ'li:t/ vt cancellare. **~ion** n cancellatura f

deliberate[1] /dɪ'lɪbərət/ adj deliberato; (slow) posato. **~ly** adv deliberatamente; (slowly) in modo posato

deliberat|e[2] /dɪ'lɪbəreɪt/ vt/i deliberare. **~ion** n deliberazione f

delicacy /'delɪkəsɪ/ n delicatezza f; (food) prelibatezza f

delicate /'delɪkət/ adj delicato

delicatessen /delɪkə'tesn/ n negozio m di specialità gastronomiche

delicious /dɪ'lɪʃəs/ adj delizioso

delight /dɪ'laɪt/ n piacere m •vt deliziare •vi ~ **in** dilettarsi con. **~ed** adj lieto. **~ful** adj delizioso

deli|rious /dɪ'lɪrɪəs/ adj **be ~rious** delirare; (fig: very happy) essere pazzo di gioia. **~rium** n delirio m

deliver /dɪ'lɪvə(r)/ vt consegnare; recapitare (post, newspaper); tenere (speech); dare (message); tirare (blow); (set free) liberare; ~ **a baby** far nascere un bambino. **~ance** n liberazione f. **~y** n consegna f; (of post) distribuzione f; (Med) parto m; **cash on ~y** pagamento m alla consegna

delude /dɪ'lu:d/ vt ingannare; ~ **oneself** illudersi

deluge /'delju:dʒ/ n diluvio m •vt (fi with requests etc) inondare

delusion /dɪ'lu:ʒn/ n illusione f

de luxe /də'lʌks/ adj di lusso

delve /delv/ vi ~ **into** (into pocket etc) frugare in; (into notes, the past) fare ricerche in

demand /dɪ'mɑ:nd/ n richiesta f; (Comm) domanda f; **in ~** richiesto; **on ~** a richiesta •vt esigere (**of/ from** da). **~ing** adj esigente

demented /dɪ'mentɪd/ adj demente

demister /di:'mɪstə(r)/ n (Auto) sbrinatore m

demo /'deməʊ/ n (pl **~s**) [!] manifestazione f; ~ **disk** (Comput) demodisk m inv

democracy /dɪ'mɒkrəsɪ/ n democrazia f

democrat /'deməkræt/ n democratico, -a mf. **~ic** adj democratico

demo|lish /dɪ'mɒlɪʃ/ vt demolire. **~lition** n demolizione f

demon /'di:mən/ n demonio m

demonstrat|e /'demənstreɪt/ vt dimostrare; fare una dimostrazion sull'uso di (appliance) •vi (Pol) manifestare. **~ion** n dimostrazion f; (Pol) manifestazione f

demonstrator /'demənstreɪtə(r)/ n (Pol) manifestante mf; (for product) dimostratore, -trice mf

demoralize /dɪ'mɒrəlaɪz/ vt demoralizzare

demote /dɪ'məʊt/ vt retrocedere di grado; (Mil) degradare

demure /dɪ'mjʊə(r)/ adj schivo

den /den/ n tana f; (room) rifugio m

denial /dɪ'naɪəl/ n smentita f

denim /'denɪm/ n [tessuto m] jeans r **~s** pl [blue]jeans mpl

Denmark /'denmɑ:k/ n Danimarca

denounce /dɪ'naʊns/ vt denunciare

dens|e /dens/ adj denso; (crowd, forest fitto; (stupid) ottuso. **~ely** adv (populated) densamente; **~ely wooded** fittamente ricoperto di alberi. **~ity** n densità f inv; (of forest) fittezza f

dent /dent/ n ammaccatura f • vt ammaccare; **~ed** adj ammaccato

dental /'dentl/ adj dei denti; (treatment) dentistico; (hygiene) dentale. **~ surgeon** n odontoiatra mf, medico m dentista

dentist /'dentɪst/ n dentista mf. **~ry** n odontoiatria f

dentures /'dentʃəz/ npl dentiera fsg

deny /dɪ'naɪ/ vt (pt/pp **-ied**) negare; (officially) smentire; **~ sb sth** negare qcsa a qcno

deodorant /di:'əʊdərənt/ n deodorante m

depart /dɪ'pɑ:t/ vi (plane, train:) partire; (liter: person) andare via; (deviate) allontanarsi (**from** da)

department /dɪ'pɑ:tmənt/ n reparto m; (Pol) ministero m; (of company) sezione f; (Univ) dipartimento m. **~ store** n grande magazzino m

departure /dɪ'pɑ:tʃə(r)/ n partenza f; (from rule) allontanamento m; **new ~** svolta f

depend /dɪ'pend/ vi dipendere (**on** da); (rely) contare (**on** su); **it all ~s** dipende; **~ing on what he says** a seconda di quello che dice. **~able** adj fidato. **~ant** n persona f a carico. **~ence** n dipendenza f. **~ent** adj dipendente (**on** da)

depict /dɪ'pɪkt/ vt (in writing) dipingere; (with picture) rappresentare

deplete /dɪ'pli:t/ vt ridurre; **totally ~d** completamente esaurito

deplor|able /dɪ'plɔ:rəbl/ adj deplorevole. **~e** vt deplorare

deploy /dɪ'plɔɪ/ vt (Mil) spiegare • vi schierarsi

deport /dɪ'pɔ:t/ vt deportare. **~ation** n deportazione f

depose /dɪ'pəʊz/ vt deporre

deposit /dɪ'pɒzɪt/ n deposito m; (against damage) cauzione f; (first instalment) acconto m • vt (pt/pp **deposited**) depositare. **~ account** n libretto m di risparmio; (without instant access) conto m vincolato

depot /'depəʊ/ n deposito m; Am (Rail) stazione f ferroviaria

depress /dɪ'pres/ vt deprimere; (press down) premere. **~ed** adj depresso; **~ed area** zona f depressa. **~ing** adj deprimente. **~ion** n depressione f

deprivation /deprɪ'veɪʃn/ n privazione f

deprive /dɪ'praɪv/ vt **~ sb of sth** privare qcno di qcsa. **~d** adj (area, childhood) disagiato

depth /depθ/ n profondità f inv; **in ~** (study, analyse) in modo approfondito; **in the ~s of winter** in pieno inverno; **be out of one's ~** (in water) non toccare il fondo; fig sentirsi in alto mare

deputize /'depjʊtaɪz/ vi **~ for** fare le veci di

deputy /'depjʊtɪ/ n vice mf; (temporary) sostituto, -a mf • attrib **~ leader** ≈ vicesegretario, -a mf; **~ chairman** vicepresidente mf

derail /dɪ'reɪl/ vt **be ~ed** (train:) essere deragliato. **~ment** n deragliamento m

derelict /'derəlɪkt/ adj abbandonato

deri|de /dɪ'raɪd/ vt deridere. **~sion** n derisione f

derisory /dɪ'raɪsərɪ/ adj (laughter) derisorio; (offer) irrisorio

derivation /derɪ'veɪʃn/ n derivazione f

derivative /dɪ'rɪvətɪv/ adj derivato • n derivato m

derive /dɪ'raɪv/ vt (obtain) derivare; **be ~d from** (word:) derivare da

derogatory /dɪ'rɒgətrɪ/ adj (comments) peggiorativo

descend /dɪ'send/ vi scendere • vt scendere da; **be ~ed from** discendere da. **~ant** n discendente mf

descent /dɪ'sent/ n discesa f; (lineage) origine f

describe /dɪ'skraɪb/ vt descrivere

descrip|tion /dɪ'skrɪpʃn/ n descrizione f; **they had no help of any ~tion** non hanno avuto proprio nessun aiuto. **~tive** adj descrittivo; (vivid) vivido

desecrat|e /'desɪkreɪt/ vt profanare. **~ion** n profanazione f

desert[1] /'dezət/ n deserto m • adj deserto; **~ island** isola f deserta

desert[2] /dɪ'zɜ:t/ vt abbandonare • vi disertare. **~ed** adj deserto. **~er** n

(Mil) disertore m. **~ion** n (Mil) diserzione f; (of family) abbandono m

deserts /dɪ'zɜ:ts/ npl **get one's just ~** ottenere ciò che ci si merita

deserv|e /dɪ'zɜ:v/ vt meritare. **~ing** adj meritevole; **~ing cause** opera f meritoria

design /dɪ'zaɪn/ n progettazione f; (fashion ~, appearance) design m inv; (pattern) modello m; (aim) proposito m • vt progettare; disegnare (clothes, furniture, model); **be ~ed for** essere fatto per

designat|e /'dezɪgneɪt/ vt designare. **~ion** n designazione f

designer /dɪ'zaɪnə(r)/ n progettista mf; (of clothes) stilista mf; (Theat: of set) scenografo, -a mf

desirable /dɪ'zaɪərəbl/ adj desiderabile

desire /dɪ'zaɪə(r)/ n desiderio m • vt desiderare

desk /desk/ n scrivania f; (in school) banco m; (in hotel) reception f inv; (cash ~) cassa f. **~top 'publishing** n desktop publishing m, editoria f da tavolo

desolat|e /'desələt/ adj desolato. **~ion** n desolazione f

despair /dɪ'speə(r)/ n disperazione f; **in ~** disperato; (say) per disperazione • vi **I ~ of that boy** quel ragazzo mi fa disperare

desperat|e /'despərət/ adj disperato; **be ~e** (criminal:) essere un disperato; **be ~e for sth** morire dalla voglia di. **~ely** adv disperatamente; **he said ~ely** ha detto, disperato. **~ion** n disperazione f; **in ~ion** per disperazione

despicable /dɪ'spɪkəbl/ adj disprezzevole

despise /dɪ'spaɪz/ vt disprezzare

despite /dɪ'spaɪt/ prep malgrado

despondent /dɪ'spɒndənt/ adj abbattuto

despot /'despɒt/ n despota m

dessert /dɪ'zɜ:t/ n dolce m. **~ spoon** n cucchiaio m da dolce

destination /destɪ'neɪʃn/ n destinazione f

destiny /'destɪnɪ/ n destino m

destitute /'destɪtju:t/ adj bisognoso

destroy /dɪ'strɔɪ/ vt distruggere. **~er** n (Naut) cacciatorpediniere m

destruc|tion /dɪ'strʌkʃn/ n distruzione f. **~tive** adj distruttivo; (fig: criticism) negativo

detach /dɪ'tætʃ/ vt staccare. **~able** adj separabile. **~ed** adj fig distaccato; **~ed house** villetta f

detachment /dɪ'tætʃmənt/ n distacco m; (Mil) distaccamento m

detail /'di:teɪl/ n particolare m, dettaglio m; **in ~** particolareggiatamente • vt esporre con tutti i particolari; (Mil) assegnare. **~ed** adj particolareggiato, dettagliato

detain /dɪ'teɪn/ vt (police:) trattenere; (delay) far ritardare. **~ee** n detenuto, -a mf

detect /dɪ'tekt/ vt individuare; (perceive) percepire. **~ion** n scoperta f

detective /dɪ'tektɪv/ n investigatore, -trice mf. **~ story** n racconto m poliziesco

detector /dɪ'tektə(r)/ n (for metal) metal detector m inv

detention /dɪ'tenʃn/ n detenzione f; (Sch) punizione f

deter /dɪ'tɜ:(r)/ vt (pt/pp **deterred**) impedire; **~ sb from doing sth** impedire a qcno di fare qcsa

detergent /dɪ'tɜ:dʒənt/ n detersivo m

deteriorat|e /dɪ'tɪərɪəreɪt/ vi deteriorarsi. **~ion** n deterioramento m

determination /dɪtɜ:mɪ'neɪʃn/ n determinazione f

determine /dɪ'tɜ:mɪn/ vt (ascertain) determinare; **~ to** (resolve) decidere di. **~d** adj deciso

deterrent /dɪ'terənt/ n deterrente m

detest /dɪ'test/ vt detestare. **~able** adj detestabile

detonat|e /'detəneɪt/ vt far detonare • vi detonare. **~or** n detonatore m

detour /'di:tʊə(r)/ n deviazione f

detract /dɪ'trækt/ vi **~ from** sminuire (merit); rovinare (pleasure, beauty)

detriment /'detrɪmənt/ n **to the ~ of** a danno di. **~al** adj dannoso

de'value vt svalutare (currency)

devastat|e /'devəsteɪt/ vt devastare. **~ed** adj [!] sconvolto. **~ing** adj devastante; (news) sconvolgente. **~ion** n devastazione f

develop /dɪ'veləp/ vt sviluppare; contrarre (illness); (add to value of) valorizzare (area) •vi svilupparsi; **~ into** divenire. **~er** n [**property**] **~er** imprenditore, -trice mf edile

development /dɪ'veləpmənt/ n sviluppo m; (of vaccine etc) messa f a punto

deviant /'di:vɪənt/ adj deviato

deviat|e /'di:vɪeɪt/ vi deviare. **~ion** n deviazione f

device /dɪ'vaɪs/ n dispositivo m

devil /'devl/ n diavolo m

devious /'di:vɪəs/ adj (person) subdolo; (route) tortuoso

devise /dɪ'vaɪz/ vt escogitare

devoid /dɪ'vɔɪd/ adj **~ of** privo di

devolution /di:və'lu:ʃn/ n (of power) decentramento m

devot|e /dɪ'vəʊt/ vt dedicare. **~ed** adj (daughter etc) affezionato; **be ~ed to sth** consacrarsi a qcsa. **~ee** n appassionato, -a mf

devotion /dɪ'vəʊʃn/ n dedizione f; **~s** pl (Relig) devozione fsg

devour /dɪ'vaʊə(r)/ vt divorare

devout /dɪ'vaʊt/ adj devoto

dew /dju:/ n rugiada f

dexterity /dek'sterətɪ/ n destrezza f

diabet|es /daɪə'bi:ti:z/ n diabete m. **~ic** adj diabetico •n diabetico, -a mf

diabolical /daɪə'bɒlɪkl/ adj diabolico

diagnose /daɪəg'nəʊz/ vt diagnosticare

diagnosis /daɪəg'nəʊsɪs/ n (pl **-oses** /-si:z/) diagnosi f inv

diagonal /daɪ'ægənl/ adj diagonale •n diagonale f

diagram /'daɪəgræm/ n diagramma m

dial /'daɪəl/ n (of clock, machine) quadrante m; (Teleph) disco m combinatore •v (pt/pp **dialled**) •vi (Teleph) fare il numero; **~ direct** chiamare in teleselezione •vt fare (number)

dialect /'daɪəlekt/ n dialetto m

dialling: ~ code n prefisso m. **~ tone** n segnale m di linea libera

dialogue /'daɪəlɒg/ n dialogo m

'dial tone n Am (Teleph) segnale m di linea libera

diameter /daɪ'æmɪtə(r)/ n diametro m

diamond /'daɪəmənd/ n diamante m, brillante m; (shape) losanga f; **~s** pl (in cards) quadri mpl

diaper /'daɪəpə(r)/ n Am pannolino m

diaphragm /'daɪəfræm/ n diaframma m

diarrhoea /daɪə'ri:ə/ n diarrea f

diary /'daɪərɪ/ n (for appointments) agenda f; (for writing in) diario m

dice /daɪs/ n inv dadi mpl •vt (Culin) tagliare a dadini

dictat|e /dɪk'teɪt/ vt/i dettare. **~ion** n dettato m

dictator /dɪk'teɪtə(r)/ n dittatore m. **~ial** adj dittatoriale. **~ship** n dittatura f

dictionary /'dɪkʃənrɪ/ n dizionario m

did /dɪd/ ▸**do**

didn't /'dɪdnt/ = **did not**

die /daɪ/ vi (pres p **dying**) morire (**of** di); **be dying to do sth** [!] morire dalla voglia di fare qcsa. □ **~ down** vi calmarsi; (fire, flames:) spegnersi. □ **~ out** vi estinguersi; (custom:) morire

diesel /'di:zl/ n diesel m

diet /'daɪət/ n regime m alimentare; (restricted) dieta f; **be on a ~** essere a dieta •vi essere a dieta

differ /'dɪfə(r)/ vi differire; (disagree) non essere d'accordo

difference /'dɪfrəns/ n differenza f; (disagreement) divergenza f

different /'dɪfrənt/ adj diverso, differente; (various) diversi; **be ~ from** essere diverso da

differently /'dɪfrəntlɪ/ adv in modo diverso; **~ from** diversamente da

difficult /'dɪfɪkəlt/ adj difficile. **~y** n difficoltà f inv

diffuse[1] /dɪ'fju:s/ adj diffuso; (wordy) prolisso

diffuse[2] /dɪ'fju:z/ vt (Phys) diffondere

dig /dɪg/ n (poke) spinta f; (remark) frecciata f; (Archaeol) scavo m; **~s** pl [!] camera fsg ammobiliata •vt/i (pt/pp **dug**, pres p **digging**) scavare (hole);

vangare (garden); (thrust) conficcare; ~ **sb in the ribs** dare una gomitata a qcno. □ ~ **out** vt fig tirar fuori. □ ~ **up** vt scavare (garden, street, object); sradicare (plant); (fig: find) scovare

digest[1] /ˈdaɪdʒest/ n compendio m

digest[2] /daɪˈdʒest/ vt digerire. **~ible** adj digeribile. **~ion** n digestione f

digger /ˈdɪɡə(r)/ n (Techn) scavatrice f

digit /ˈdɪdʒɪt/ n cifra f; (finger) dito m

digital /ˈdɪdʒɪtl/ adj digitale; ~ **camera** fotocamera f digitale. ~ **clock** orologio m digitale

digitize /ˈdɪdʒɪtaɪz/ vt digitalizzare

dignified /ˈdɪɡnɪfaɪd/ adj dignitoso

dignitary /ˈdɪɡnɪtərɪ/ n dignitario m

dignity /ˈdɪɡnɪtɪ/ n dignità f

digress /daɪˈɡres/ vi divagare. **~ion** n digressione f

dike /daɪk/ n diga f

dilapidated /dɪˈlæpɪdeɪtɪd/ adj cadente

dilate /daɪˈleɪt/ vi dilatarsi

dilemma /dɪˈlemə/ n dilemma m

dilute /daɪˈluːt/ vt diluire

dim /dɪm/ adj (**dimmer, dimmest**) debole (light); (dark) scuro; (prospect, chance) scarso; (indistinct) impreciso; (!: stupid) tonto •vt/i (pt/pp **dimmed**) affievolire. **~ly** adv (see, remember) indistintamente; (shine) debolmente

dime /daɪm/ n Am moneta f da dieci centesimi

dimension /daɪˈmenʃn/ n dimensione f

diminish /dɪˈmɪnɪʃ/ vt/i diminuire

dimple /ˈdɪmpl/ n fossetta f

din /dɪn/ n baccano m

dine /daɪn/ vi pranzare. **~r** n (Am: restaurant) tavola f calda; **the last ~r in the restaurant** l'ultimo cliente nel ristorante

dinghy /ˈdɪŋɡɪ/ n dinghy m; (inflatable) canotto m pneumatico

dingy /ˈdɪndʒɪ/ adj (**-ier, -iest**) squallido e tetro

dinner /ˈdɪnə(r)/ n cena f; (at midday) pranzo m. **~-jacket** n smoking m inv

dinosaur /ˈdaɪnəsɔː(r)/ n dinosauro m

dint /dɪnt/ n **by ~ of** a forza di

dip /dɪp/ n (in ground) inclinazione f; (Culin) salsina f; **go for a ~** andare a fare una nuotata •v (pt/pp **dipped**) •vt (in liquid) immergere; abbassare (head, headlights) •vi (land:) formare un avvallamento. □ ~ **into** vt scorrere (book)

diphthong /ˈdɪfθɒŋ/ n dittongo m

diploma /dɪˈpləʊmə/ n diploma m

diplomacy /dɪˈpləʊməsɪ/ n diplomazia f

diplomat /ˈdɪpləmæt/ n diplomatico, -a mf. **~ic** adj diplomatico. **~ically** adv con diplomazia

ˈ**dip-stick** n (Auto) astina f dell'olio

dire /ˈdaɪə(r)/ adj (situation, conse-quences) terribile

direct /dɪˈrekt/ adj diretto •adv direttamente •vt (aim) rivolgere (attention, criticism); (control) dirigere; fare la regia di (film, play); ~ **sb** (show the way) indicare la strada a qcno; ~ **sb to do sth** ordinare a qcno di fare qcsa. ~ ˈ**current** n corrente m continua

direction /dɪˈrekʃn/ n direzione f; (of play, film) regia f; **~s** pl indicazioni fpl

directly /dɪˈrektlɪ/ adv direttamente; (at once) immediatamente •conj [non] appena

director /dɪˈrektə(r)/ n (Comm) direttore, -trice mf; (of play, film) regista mf

directory /dɪˈrektərɪ/ n elenco m; (Teleph) elenco m [telefonico]; (of streets) stradario m

dirt /dɜːt/ n sporco m; ~ **cheap** ! a [un] prezzo stracciato

dirty /ˈdɜːtɪ/ adj (**-ier, -iest**) sporco; ~ **trick** brutto scherzo m; ~ **word** parolaccia f •vt (pt/pp **-ied**) sporcare

dis|aˈbility /dɪs-/ n infermità f inv. **~abled** adj invalido

disadˈvan|tage n svantaggio m; **at a ~tage** in una posizione di svantaggio. **~taged** adj svantaggiato. **~ˈtageous** adj svantaggioso

disaˈgree vi non essere d'accordo; ~ **with** (food:) far male a

disaˈgreeable adj sgradevole

disaˈgreement n disaccordo m; (quarrel) dissidio m

disap'pear vi scomparire. **~ance** n scomparsa f

disap'point vt deludere; **I'm ~ed** sono deluso. **~ing** adj deludente. **~ment** n delusione f

disap'proval n disapprovazione f

disap'prove vi disapprovare; **~ of sb/sth** disapprovare qcno/qcsa

dis'arm vt disarmare •vi (Mil) disarmarsi. **~ament** n disarmo m. **~ing** adj (frankness etc) disarmante

disar'ray n **in ~** in disordine

disast|er /dɪ'zɑ:stə(r)/ n disastro m. **~rous** adj disastroso

dis'band vt scogliere; smobilitare (troops) •vi scogliersi; (regiment:) essere smobilitato

disbe'lief n incredulità f; **in ~** con incredulità

disc /dɪsk/ n disco m; (CD) compact disc m inv

discard /dɪ'skɑ:d/ vt scartare; (throw away) eliminare; scaricare (boyfriend)

discern /dɪ'sɜ:n/ vt discernere. **~ible** adj discernibile. **~ing** adj perspicace

discharge¹ n (Electr) scarica f; (dismissal) licenziamento m; (Mil) congedo m; (Med: of blood) emissione f; (of cargo) scarico m

dis'charge² vt scaricare (battery, cargo); (dismiss) licenziare; (Mil) congedare; (Jur) assolvere (accused); dimettere (patient) •vi (Electr) scaricarsi

disciple /dɪ'saɪpl/ n discepolo m

disciplinary /'dɪsɪplɪnərɪ/ adj disciplinare

discipline /'dɪsɪplɪn/ n disciplina f •vt disciplinare; (punish) punire

disc jockey n disc jockey m inv

dis'claim vt disconoscere. **~er** n rifiuto m

dis'clos|e vt svelare. **~ure** n rivelazione f

disco /'dɪskəʊ/ n discoteca f

dis'colour vt scolorire •vi scolorirsi

dis'comfort n scomodità f; fig disagio m

disconcert /dɪskən'sɜ:t/ vt sconcertare

discon'nect vt disconnettere

disconsolate /dɪs'kɒnsələt/ adj sconsolato

discon'tent n scontentezza f. **~ed** adj scontento

discon'tinue vt cessare, smettere; (Comm) sospendere la produzione di; **~d line** fine f serie

'discord n discordia f; (Mus) dissonanza f. **~ant** adj **~ant note** nota f discordante

'discount¹ n sconto m

dis'count² vt (not believe) non credere a; (leave out of consideration) non tener conto di

dis'courage vt scoraggiare; (dissuade) dissuadere

dis'courteous adj scortese

discover /dɪ'skʌvə(r)/ vt scoprire. **~y** n scoperta f

dis'credit n discredito m •vt (pt/pp **discredited**) screditare

discreet /dɪ'skri:t/ adj discreto

discrepancy /dɪ'skrepənsɪ/ n discrepanza f

discretion /dɪ'skreʃn/ n discrezione f

discriminat|e /dɪ'skrɪmɪneɪt/ vi discriminare (**against** contro); **~e between** distinguere tra. **~ing** adj esigente. **~ion** n discriminazione f; (quality) discernimento m

discus /'dɪskəs/ n disco m

discuss /dɪ'skʌs/ vt discutere; (examine critically) esaminare. **~ion** n discussione f

disdain /dɪs'deɪn/ n sdegno f •vt sdegnare. **~ful** adj sdegnoso

disease /dɪ'zi:z/ n malattia f. **~d** adj malato

disem'bark vi sbarcare

disen'tangle vt districare

dis'figure vt deformare

dis'grace n vergogna f; **I am in ~** sono caduto in disgrazia; **it's a ~** è una vergogna •vt disonorare. **~ful** adj vergognoso

disgruntled /dɪs'grʌntld/ adj malcontento

disguise /dɪs'gaɪz/ n travestimento m; **in ~** travestito •vt contraffare (voice); dissimulare (emotions); **~d as** travestito da

disgust /dɪs'gʌst/ n disgusto m; **in ~**

d

con aria disgustata •vt disgustare. ~ing adj disgustoso

dish /dɪʃ/ n piatto m; **do the ~es** lavare i piatti •**dish out** vt (serve) servire; (distribute) distribuire. □ ~ **up** vt servire

'**dishcloth** n strofinaccio m

d

dis'honest adj disonesto. ~**y** n disonestà f

dis'honour n disonore m •vt disonorare (family); non onorare (cheque). ~**able** adj disonorevole. ~**ably** adv in modo disonorevole

'**dishwasher** n lavapiatti f inv

disil'lusion vt disilludere. ~**ment** n disillusione f

disin'fect vt disinfettare. ~**ant** n disinfettante m

dis'integrate vi disintegrarsi

dis'interested adj disinteressato

dis'jointed adj sconnesso

disk /dɪsk/ n (Comput) disco m; (diskette) dischetto m

dis'like n avversione f; **your likes and ~s** i tuoi gusti •vt **I ~ him/it** non mi piace; **I don't ~ him/it** non mi dispiace

dislocate /'dɪsləkeɪt/ vt slogare; ~ **one's shoulder** slogarsi una spalla

dis'lodge vt sloggiare

dis'loyal adj sleale. ~**ty** n slealtà f

dismal /'dɪzməl/ adj (person) abbacchiato; (news, weather) deprimente; (performance) mediocre

dismantle /dɪs'mæntl/ vt smontare (tent, machine); fig smantellare

dis'may n sgomento m. ~**ed** adj sgomento

dis'miss vt licenziare (employee); (reject) scartare (idea, suggestion). ~**al** n licenziamento m

dis'mount vi smontare

diso'bedien|ce n disubbidienza f. ~**t** adj disubbidiente

diso'bey vt disubbidire a (rule) •vi disubbidire

dis'order n disordine m; (Med) disturbo m. ~**ly** adj disordinato; (crowd) turbolento; ~**ly conduct** turbamento m della quiete pubblica

dis'organized adj disorganizzato

dis'orientate vt disorientare

dis'own vt disconoscere

disparaging /dɪ'spærɪdʒɪŋ/ adj sprezzante

dispatch /dɪ'spætʃ/ n (Comm) spedizione f; (Mil, report) dispaccio m; **with** ~ con prontezza •vt spedire; (kill) spedire al creatore

dispel /dɪ'spel/ vt (pt/pp **dispelled**) dissipare

dispensable /dɪ'spensəbl/ adj dispensabile

dispense /dɪ'spens/ vt distribuire; ~ **with** fare a meno di; **dispensing chemist** farmacista mf; (shop) farmacia f. ~**r** n (device) distributore m

dispers|al /dɪ'spɜ:sl/ n disperzione f. ~**e** vt disperdere •vi disperdersi

dispirited /dɪ'spɪrɪtɪd/ adj scoraggiato

display /dɪ'spleɪ/ n mostra f; (Comm) esposizione f; (of feelings) manifestazione f; pej ostentazione f; (Comput) display m inv •vt mostrare; esporre (goods); manifestare (feeling); (Comput) visualizzare

dis'please vt non piacere a; **be ~d with** essere scontento di

dis'pleasure n malcontento m

disposable /dɪ'spəʊzəbl/ adj (throwaway) usa e getta; (income) disponibile

disposal /dɪ'spəʊzl/ n (getting rid of) eliminazione f; **be at sb's** ~ essere a disposizione di qcno

disproportionate /dɪsprə'pɔ:ʃə-nət/ adj sproporzionato

dis'prove vt confutare

dispute /dɪ'spju:t/ n disputa f; (industrial) contestazione f •vt contestare (statement)

disqualifi'cation n squalifica f; (from driving) ritiro m della patente

dis'qualify vt (pt/pp **-ied**) escludere; (Sport) squalificare; ~ **sb from driving** ritirare la patente a qcno

disre'gard n mancanza f di considerazione •vt ignorare

dis'reputable adj malfamato

disre'spect n mancanza f di rispetto. ~**ful** adj irrispettoso

disrupt /dɪs'rʌpt/ vt creare scompiglio in; sconvolgere (plans).

~ion n scompiglio m; (of plans) sconvolgimento m. **~ive** adj (person, behaviour) indisciplinato

dissatis'faction n malcontento m

dis'satisfied adj scontento

dissect /dɪ'sekt/ vt sezionare. **~ion** n dissezione f

dissent /dɪ'sent/ n dissenso m •vi dissentire

dissertation /dɪsə'teɪʃn/ n tesi f inv

dissident /'dɪsɪdənt/ n dissidente mf

dis'similar adj dissimile (**to** da)

dissolute /'dɪsəlu:t/ adj dissoluto

dissolve /dɪ'zɒlv/ vt dissolvere •vi dissolversi

dissuade /dɪ'sweɪd/ vt dissuadere

distance /'dɪstəns/ n distanza f; **it's a short ~ from here to the station** la stazione non è lontana da qui; **in the ~** in lontananza; **from a ~** da lontano

distant /'dɪstənt/ adj distante; (relative) lontano

dis'taste n avversione f. **~ful** adj spiacevole

distil /dɪ'stɪl/ vt (pt/pp **distilled**) distillare. **~lation** n distillazione f. **~lery** n distilleria f

distinct /dɪ'stɪŋkt/ adj chiaro; (different) distinto. **~ion** n distinzione f; (Sch) massimo m dei voti. **~ive** adj caratteristico. **~ly** adv chiaramente

distinguish /dɪ'stɪŋgwɪʃ/ vt/i distinguere; **~ oneself** distinguersi. **~ed** adj rinomato; (appearance) distinto; (career) brillante

distort /dɪ'stɔ:t/ vt distorcere. **~ion** n distorsione f

distract /dɪ'strækt/ vt distrarre. **~ed** adj assente; (!: worried) preoccupato. **~ing** adj che distoglie. **~ion** n distrazione f; (despair) disperazione f; **drive sb to ~** portare qcno alla disperazione

distraught /dɪ'strɔ:t/ adj sconvolto

distress /dɪ'stres/ n angoscia f; (pain) sofferenza f; (danger) difficoltà f •vt sconvolgere; (sadden) affliggere. **~ing** adj penoso; (shocking) sconvolgente. **~ signal** n segnale m di richiesta di soccorso

distribut|e /dɪ'strɪbju:t/ vt distribuire. **~ion** n distribuzione f. **~or** n distributore m

district /'dɪstrɪkt/ n regione f; (Admin) distretto m. **~ nurse** n infermiere, -a mf che fa visite a domicilio

dis'trust n sfiducia f •vt non fidarsi di. **~ful** adj diffidente

disturb /dɪ'stɜ:b/ vt disturbare; (emotionally) turbare; spostare (papers). **~ance** n disturbo m; **~ances** (pl: rioting etc) disordini mpl. **~ed** adj turbato; [**mentally**] **~ed** malato di mente. **~ing** adj inquietante

dis'used adj non utilizzato

ditch /dɪtʃ/ n fosso m •vt (!: abandon) abbandonare (plan, car); piantare (lover)

dither /'dɪðə(r)/ vi titubare

divan /dɪ'væn/ n divano m

dive /daɪv/ n tuffo m; (Aeron) picchiata f; (!: place) bettola f •vi tuffarsi; (when in water) immergersi; (Aeron) scendere in picchiata; (!: rush) precipitarsi

diver /'daɪvə(r)/ n (from board) tuffatore, -trice mf; (scuba) sommozzatore, -trice mf; (deep sea) palombaro m

diver|ge /daɪ'vɜ:dʒ/ vi divergere. **~gent** adj divergente

diverse /daɪ'vɜ:s/ adj vario

diversify /daɪ'vɜ:sɪfaɪ/ vt/i (pt/pp **-ied**) diversificare

diversion /daɪ'vɜ:ʃn/ n deviazione f; (distraction) diversivo m

diversity /daɪ'vɜ:sətɪ/ n varietà f

divert /daɪ'vɜ:t/ vt deviare (traffic); distogliere (attention)

divide /dɪ'vaɪd/ vt dividere (**by** per); **six ~d by two** sei diviso due •vi dividersi

dividend /'dɪvɪdend/ n dividendo m; **pay ~s** fig ripagare

divine /dɪ'vaɪn/ adj divino

diving /'daɪvɪŋ/ n (from board) tuffi mpl; (scuba) immersione f. **~-board** n trampolino m. **~ mask** n maschera f [subacquea]. **~-suit** n muta f; (deep sea) scafandro m

division /dɪ'vɪʒn/ n divisione f; (in sports league) serie f

divorce /dɪ'vɔ:s/ n divorzio m •vt divorziare da. **~d** adj divorziato;

d

get ~d divorziare

divorcee /dɪvɔːˈsiː/ n divorziato, -a mf

divulge /daɪˈvʌldʒ/ vt rendere pubblico

DIY n abbr do-it-yourself

dizziness /ˈdɪzɪnɪs/ n giramenti mpl di testa

dizzy /ˈdɪzɪ/ adj (**-ier, -iest**) vertiginoso; **I feel ~** mi gira la testa

do¹ /duː/

! *3* sing pres tense **does**; past tense **did**; past participle **done**

- vt fare; (🅸: *cheat*) fregare; **be done** (Culin) essere cotto; **well done** bravo; (Culin) ben cotto; **do the flowers** sistemare i fiori; **do the washing up** lavare i piatti; **do one's hair** farsi i capelli
- vi (*be suitable*) andare; (*be enough*) bastare; **this will do** questo va bene; **that will do!** basta così!; **do well/badly** cavarsela bene/male; **how is he doing?** come sta?
- v aux (*used to form questions and negatives; often not translated*) **do you speak Italian?** parli italiano?; **you don't like him, do you?** non ti piace, vero?; (*expressing astonishment*) non dirmi che ti piace!; **yes, I do** sì; (*emphatic*) invece sì; **no, I don't** no; **I don't smoke** non fumo; **don't you/doesn't he?** vero?; **so do I** anch'io; **do come in, John** entra, John; **how do you do?** piacere. □ **~ away with** vt abolire (rule). □ **~ for** vt **done for** 🅸 rovinato. □ **~ in** vt (🅸: *kill*) uccidere; farsi male a (back); **done in** 🅸 esausto. □ **~ up** vt (*fasten*) abbottonare; (*renovate*) rimettere a nuovo; (*wrap*) avvolgere. □ **~ with** vt **I could do with a spanner** mi ci vorrebbe una chiave inglese. □ **~ without** vt fare a meno di

do² /duː/ n (pl **dos** or **do's**) 🅸 festa f

docile /ˈdəʊsaɪl/ adj docile

dock¹ /dɒk/ n (Jur) banco m degli imputati

dock² n (Naut) bacino m • vi entrare in porto; (spaceship:) congiungersi. **~er** n portuale m. **~s** npl porto m. **~yard** n cantiere m navale

doctor /ˈdɒktə(r)/ n dottore m, dottoressa f • vt alterare (drink); castrare (cat). **~ate** n dottorato m

doctrine /ˈdɒktrɪn/ n dottrina f

document /ˈdɒkjʊmənt/ n documento m. **~ary** adj documentario • n documentario m

dodge /dɒdʒ/ n 🅸 trucco m • vt schivare (blow); evitare (person) • vi scansarsi; **~ out of the way** scansarsi

dodgems /ˈdɒdʒəmz/ npl autoscontro msg

dodgy /ˈdɒdʒɪ/ adj (**-ier, -iest**) (🅸: dubious) sospetto

doe /dəʊ/ n femmina f (di daino, renna, lepre); (rabbit) coniglia f

does /dʌz/ ▸**do**

doesn't /ˈdʌznt/ = **does not**

dog /dɒg/ n cane m • vt (pt/pp **dogged**) (illness, bad luck:) perseguitare

dogged /ˈdɒgɪd/ adj ostinato

ˈdog house n **in the ~** 🅸 in disgrazia

dogma /ˈdɒgmə/ n dogma m. **~tic** adj dogmatico

do-it-yourself /duːɪtjəˈself/ n fai da te m, bricolage m. **~ shop** n negozio m di bricolage

dole /dəʊl/ n sussidio m di disoccupazione; **be on the ~** essere disoccupato • **dole out** vt distribuire

doleful /ˈdəʊlfl/ adj triste

doll /dɒl/ n bambola f • **doll oneself up** vt 🅸 mettersi in ghingheri

dollar /ˈdɒlə(r)/ n dollaro m

dollop /ˈdɒləp/ n 🅸 cucchiaiata f

dolphin /ˈdɒlfɪn/ n delfino m

dome /dəʊm/ n cupola f

domestic /dəˈmestɪk/ adj domestico; (Pol) interno; (Comm) nazionale

domesticated /dəˈmestɪkeɪtɪd/ adj (animal) addomesticato

domestic flight n volo m nazionale

dominant /ˈdɒmɪnənt/ adj dominante

dominat|e /ˈdɒmɪneɪt/ vt/i dominare. **~ion** n dominio m

ɔmineering /dɒmɪ'nɪərɪŋ/ adj ɪutoritario

ɔminion /də'mɪnjən/ n Br (Pol) lominion m inv

ɔnat|e /dəʊ'neɪt/ vt donare. **~ion** n lonazione f

ɔne /dʌn/ ▸**do**

ɔnkey /'dɒŋkɪ/ n asino m; **~'s years** [!] secoli mpl. **~-work** n sgobbata f

ɔnor /'dəʊnə(r)/ n donatore, trice mf

ɔodle /'du:dl/ vi scarabocchiare

ɔom /du:m/ n fato m; (ruin) rovina f • vt **be ~ed [to failure]** essere lestinato al fallimento; **~ed** (ship) lestinato ad affondare

ɔor /dɔ:(r)/ n porta f; (of car) ɔortiera f; **out of ~s** all'aperto

ɔor: ~mat n zerbino m. **~step** n gradino m della porta. **~way** n vano m della porta

ɔpe /dəʊp/ n [!] (drug) droga f leggera; (information) indiscrezioni fpl; (idiot) idiota mf • vt drogare; (Sport) lopare

ɔrmant /'dɔ:mənt/ adj latente; (volcano) inattivo

ɔrmitory /'dɔ:mɪtərɪ/ n lormitorio m

ɔrmouse /'dɔ:-/ n ghiro m

ɔsage /'dəʊsɪdʒ/ n dosaggio m

ɔse /dəʊs/ n dose f

ɔt /dɒt/ n punto m; **at 8 o'clock on the ~** alle 8 in punto

ɔt-com /dɒt'kɒm/ n azienda f legata a Internet

ɔte /dəʊt/ vi **~ on** stravedere per

ɔtty /'dɒtɪ/ adj (**-ier, -iest**) [!] tocco; (idea) folle

ɔuble /'dʌbl/ adj doppio • adv **cost ~** costare il doppio; **see ~** vedere loppio; **~ the amount** la quantità loppia • n doppio m; (person) sosia m nv; **~s** pl (Tennis) doppio m; **at the ~** li corsa • vt raddoppiare; (fold) piegare in due • vi raddoppiare. □ **~ back** vi (go back) fare dietro front. □ **~ up** vi (bend) piegarsi in due (**with** per); (share) dividere una stanza

ɔuble: ~-'bass n contrabbasso m. **~ 'bed** n letto m matrimoniale. **~ 'chin** n doppio mento m. **~-'click** vt/i cliccare due volte, fare doppio clic (**on** su). **~-'cross** vt ingannare. **~-'decker** n autobus m inv a due piani. **~ 'Dutch** n [!] ostrogoto m. **~ 'glazing** n doppiovetro m

doubly /'dʌblɪ/ adv doppiamente

doubt /daʊt/ n dubbio m • vt dubitare di. **~ful** adj dubbio; (having doubts) in dubbio. **~fully** adv con aria dubbiosa. **~less** adv indubbiamente

dough /dəʊ/ n pasta f; (for bread) impasto m; ([!]: money) quattrini mpl. **~nut** n bombolone m, krapfen m inv

dove /dʌv/ n colomba f. **~tail** n (Techn) incastro m a coda di rondine

down[1] /daʊn/ n (feathers) piumino m

down[2] adv giù; **go/come ~** scendere; **~ there** laggiù; **sales are ~** le vendite sono diminuite; **£50 ~** 50 sterline d'acconto; **~ 10%** ridotto del 10%; **~ with...!** abbasso...! • prep **walk ~ the road** camminare per strada; **~ the stairs** giù per le scale; **fall ~ the stairs** cadere giù dalle scale; **get that ~ you!** [!] butta giù!; **be ~ the pub** [!] essere al pub • vt bere tutto d'un fiato (drink)

down: ~-and-'out n spiantato, -a mf. **~cast** adj abbattuto. **~fall** n caduta f; (of person) rovina f. **~-'hearted** adj scoraggiato. **~'hill** adv in discesa; **go ~hill** essere in declino. **~'load** vt scaricare. **~ payment** n deposito m. **~pour** n acquazzone m. **~right** adj (absolute) totale; (lie) bell'e buono; (idiot) perfetto • adv (completely) completamente. **~'stairs** adv al piano di sotto • adj del piano di sotto. **~'stream** adv a valle. **~-to-'earth** adj (person) con i piedi per terra. **~town** adv Am in centro. **~ward[s]** adj verso il basso; (slope) in discesa • adv verso il basso

dowry /'daʊrɪ/ n dote f

doze /dəʊz/ n sonnellino m • vi sonnecchiare. □ **~ off** vi assopirsi

dozen /'dʌzn/ n dozzina f; **~s of books** libri a dozzine

Dr abbr doctor

drab /dræb/ adj spento

draft[1] /drɑ:ft/ n abbozzo m; (Comm) cambiale f; Am (Mil) leva f • vt

d

abbozzare; Am (Mil) arruolare

draft² n Am = **draught**

drag /dræg/ n [!] scocciatura f; **in ~** [!] (man) travestito da donna • vt (pt/pp **dragged**) trascinare; dragare (river). □ **~ on** vi (time, meeting:) trascinarsi

dragon /ˈdrægən/ n drago m. **~-fly** n libellula f

drain /dreɪn/ n tubo m di scarico; (grid) tombino m; **the ~s** pl le fognature; **be a ~ on sb's finances** prosciugare le finanze di qcno • vt drenare (land, wound); scolare (liquid, vegetables); svuotare (tank, glass, person) • vi **~** [**away**] andar via

drama /ˈdrɑːmə/ n arte f drammatica; (play) opera f teatrale; (event) dramma m

dramatic /drəˈmætɪk/ adj drammatico

dramat|ist /ˈdræmətɪst/ n drammaturgo, -a mf. **~ize** vt adattare per il teatro; fig drammatizzare

drank /dræŋk/ ▹**drink**

drape /dreɪp/ n Am tenda f • vt appoggiare (**over** su)

drastic /ˈdræstɪk/ adj drastico; **~ally** adv drasticamente

draught /drɑːft/ n corrente f [d'aria]; **~s** sg (game) [gioco m della] dama fsg

draught beer n birra f alla spina

draughty /ˈdrɑːftɪ/ adj pieno di correnti d'aria; **it's ~** c'è corrente

draw /drɔː/ n (attraction) attrazione f; (Sport) pareggio m; (in lottery) sorteggio m • v (pt **drew**, pp **drawn**) • vt tirare; (attract) attirare; disegnare (picture); tracciare (line); ritirare (money); **~ lots** tirare a sorte • vi (tea:) essere in infusione; (Sport) pareggiare; **~ near** avvicinarsi. □ **~ back** vt tirare indietro; ritirare (hand); tirare (curtains) • vi (recoil) tirarsi indietro. □ **~ in** vt ritrarre (claws etc) • vi (train:) arrivare; (days:) accorciarsi. □ **~ out** vt (pull out) tirar fuori; ritirare (money) • vi (train:) partire; (days:) allungarsi. □ **~ up** vt redigere (document); accostare (chair); **~ oneself up to one's full height** farsi grande • vi (stop) fermarsi

draw: ~back n inconveniente m. **~bridge** n ponte m levatoio

drawer /drɔː(r)/ n cassetto m

drawing /ˈdrɔːɪŋ/ n disegno m

drawing: ~ pin n puntina f. **~ room** n salotto m

drawl /drɔːl/ n pronuncia f strascicata

drawn /drɔːn/ ▹**draw**

dread /dred/ n terrore m • vt aver il terrore di

dreadful /ˈdredfʊl/ adj terribile. **~ly** adv terribilmente

dream /driːm/ n sogno m • attrib di sogno • vt/i (pt/pp **dreamt** /dremt/ or **dreamed**) sognare (**about**/**of** di)

dreary /ˈdrɪərɪ/ adj (**-ier, -iest**) tetro; (boring) monotono

dredge /dredʒ/ vt/i dragare

dregs /dregz/ npl feccia fsg

drench /drentʃ/ vt **get ~ed** inzupparsi; **~ed** zuppo

dress /dres/ n (woman's) vestito m; (clothing) abbigliamento m • vt vestire; (decorate) adornare; (Culin) condire; (Med) fasciare; **~ oneself**, **get ~ed** vestirsi • vi vestirsi. □ **~ up** vi mettersi elegante; (in disguise) travestirsi (**as** da)

dress circle n (Theat) prima galleria

dressing /ˈdresɪŋ/ n (Culin) condimento m; (Med) fasciatura f

dressing: ~-gown n vestaglia f. **~-room** n (in gym) spogliatoio m; (Theat) camerino m. **~-table** n toilette f inv

dress: ~maker n sarta f. **~ rehearsal** n prova f generale

drew /druː/ ▹**draw**

dribble /ˈdrɪbl/ vi gocciolare; (baby:) sbavare; (Sport) dribblare

dried /draɪd/ adj (food) essiccato

drier /ˈdraɪə(r)/ n asciugabiancheria m inv

drift /drɪft/ n movimento m lento; (of snow) cumulo m; (meaning) senso m • vi (off course) andare alla deriva; (snow:) accumularsi; (fig: person:) procedere enza meta. □ ~ **apart** vi (people:) llontanarsi l'uno dall'altro

ill /drɪl/ n trapano m; (Mil) sercitazione f •vt trapanare; (Mil) are esercitare •vi (Mil) esercitarsi; ~ **for oil** trivellare in cerca di etrolio

ink /drɪŋk/ n bevanda f; (alcoholic) icchierino m; **have a ~** bere ualcosa; **a ~ of water** un po' 'acqua •vt/i (pt **drank**, pp **drunk**) ere. □ ~ **up** vt finire •vi finire il icchiere

ink|able /'drɪŋkəbl/ adj potabile. **~er** n bevitore, -trice mf

rinking-water n acqua f potabile

ip /drɪp/ n gocciolamento m; (drop) occia f; (Med) flebo f inv; (🅸: person) nollaccione, -a mf •vi (pt/pp **dripped**) occiolare. **~-'dry** adj che non si tira. **~ping** n (from meat) grasso m l'arrosto •adj **~ping [wet]** fradicio

ive /draɪv/ n (in car) giro m; entrance) viale m; (energy) grinta f; Psych) pulsione f; (organized effort) operazione f; (Techn) motore m; Comput) lettore m •v (pt **drove**, pp **driven**) •vt portare (person by car); uidare (car); (Sport: hit) mandare; Techn) far funzionare; **~ sb mad** ar diventare matto qcno •vi uidare. □ ~ **at** vt **what are you driving at?** dove vuoi arrivare? **drive away** vt portare via in macchina; (chase) cacciare •vi andare ia in macchina. □ ~ **in** vt piantare nail) •vi arrivare [in macchina]. □ ~ **off** vt portare via in macchina; chase) cacciare •vi andare via in macchina. □ ~ **on** vi proseguire (in macchina). □ ~ **up** vi arrivare (in macchina)

ivel /'drɪvl/ n 🅸 sciocchezze fpl

iver /'draɪvə(r)/ n guidatore, -trice mf; (of train) conducente mf

iving /'draɪvɪŋ/ adj (rain) violento; force) motore •n guida f

iving: ~ licence n patente f di guida. **~ test** n esame m di guida

izzle /'drɪzl/ n pioggerella f •vi piovigginare

one /drəʊn/ n (bee) fuco m; (sound) ronzio m

droop /druːp/ vi abbassarsi; (flowers:) afflosciarsi

drop /drɒp/ n (of liquid) goccia f; (fall) caduta f; (in price, temperature) calo m •v (pt/pp **dropped**) •vt far cadere; sganciare (bomb); (omit) omettere; (give up) abbandonare •vi cadere; (price, temperature, wind:) calare; (ground:) essere in pendenza. □ ~ **in** vi passare. □ ~ **off** vt depositare (person) •vi cadere; (fall asleep) assopirsi. □ ~ **out** vi cadere; (of race, society) ritirarsi; **~ out of school** lasciare la scuola

'drop-out n persona f contro il sistema sociale

drought /draʊt/ n siccità f

drove /drəʊv/ ▹**drive**

drown /draʊn/ vi annegare •vt annegare; coprire (noise); **he was ~ed** è annegato

drowsy /'draʊzɪ/ adj sonnolento

drudgery /'drʌdʒərɪ/ n lavoro m pesante e noioso

drug /drʌg/ n droga f; (Med) farmaco m; **take ~s** drogarsi •vt (pt/pp **drugged**) drogare

drug: ~ addict n tossicomane, -a mf. **~ dealer** n spacciatore, -trice mf [di droga]. **~gist** n Am farmacista mf. **~store** n Am negozio m di generi vari, inclusi medicinali, che funge anche da bar; (dispensing) farmacia f

drum /drʌm/ n tamburo m; (for oil) bidone m; **~s** (pl: in pop-group) batteria f •v (pt/pp **drummed**) •vi suonare il tamburo; (in pop-group) suonare la batteria •vt **~ sth into sb** ripetere qcsa a qcno cento volte. **~mer** n percussionista mf; (in pop-group) batterista mf. **~stick** n bacchetta f; (of chicken, turkey) coscia f

drunk /drʌŋk/ ▹**drink** •adj ubriaco; **get ~** ubriacarsi •n ubriaco, -a mf

drunk|ard /'drʌŋkəd/ n ubriacone, -a mf. **~en** adj ubriaco; **~en driving** guida f in stato di ebbrezza

dry /draɪ/ adj (**drier, driest**) asciutto; (climate, country) secco •vt/i (pt/pp **dried**) asciugare; **~ one's eyes** asciugarsi le lacrime. □ ~ **up** vi seccarsi; (fig: source:) prosciugarsi; (🅸: be quiet) stare zitto; (do dishes) asciugare i piatti

dry: ~-'**clean** vt pulire a secco. ~-'**cleaner's** n (shop) tintoria f. ~**ness** n secchezza f

DTD n abbr (digital type definition) DTD f

dual /'dju:əl/ adj doppio

dual 'carriageway n strada f a due carreggiate

dub /dʌb/ vt (pt/pp **dubbed**) doppiare (film); (name) soprannominare

dubious /'dju:bɪəs/ adj dubbio; **be ~ about** avere dei dubbi riguardo

duchess /'dʌtʃɪs/ n duchessa f

duck /dʌk/ n anatra f • vt (in water) immergere; **~ one's head** abbassare la testa • vi abbassarsi. ~**ling** n anatroccolo m

duct /dʌkt/ n condotto m; (Anat) dotto m

dud /dʌd/ [!] adj (Mil) disattivato; (coin) falso; (cheque) a vuoto • n (banknote) banconota f falsa

due /dju:/ adj dovuto; **be ~** (train:) essere previsto; **the baby is ~ next week** il bambino dovrebbe nascere la settimana prossima; **~ to** (owing to) a causa di; **be ~ to** (causally) essere dovuto a; **I'm ~ to...** dovrei...; **in ~ course** a tempo debito • adv **~ north** direttamente a nord

duel /'dju:əl/ n duello m

dues /dju:z/ npl quota f [di iscrizione]

duet /dju:'et/ n duetto m

dug /dʌg/ ▸**dig**

duke /dju:k/ n duca m

dull /dʌl/ adj (overcast, not bright) cupo; (not shiny) opaco; (sound) soffocato; (boring) monotono; (stupid) ottuso • vt intorpidire (mind); attenuare (pain)

dumb /dʌm/ adj muto; ([!]: stupid) ottuso. ~**founded** adj sbigottito. ▫ **~ down** vt semplificare il livello di

dummy /'dʌmɪ/ n (tailor's) manichino m; (for baby) succhiotto m; (model) riproduzione f

dump /dʌmp/ n (for refuse) scarico m; ([!]: town) mortorio m; **be down in the ~s** [!] essere depresso • vt scaricare; ([!]: put down) lasciare; ([!]: get rid of) liberarsi di

dumpling /'dʌmplɪŋ/ n gnocco m

dunce /dʌns/ n zuccone, -a mf

dung /dʌŋ/ n sterco m

dungarees /dʌŋgə'ri:z/ npl tuta fsg

dungeon /'dʌndʒən/ n prigione f sotterranea

duplicate[1] /'dju:plɪkət/ adj doppio duplicato m; (document) copia f; **in ~** in duplicato

duplicat|e[2] /'dju:plɪkeɪt/ vt fare un duplicato di; (research:) essere una ripetizione di (work)

durable /'djʊərəbl/ adj resistente; durevole (basis, institution)

duration /djʊə'reɪʃn/ n durata f

duress /djʊə'res/ n costrizione f; **under ~** sotto minaccia

during /'djʊərɪŋ/ prep durante

dusk /dʌsk/ n crepuscolo m

dust /dʌst/ n polvere f • vt spolverar (sprinkle) cospargere (cake) (**with** di • vi spolverare

dust: ~**bin** n pattumiera f. ~**er** n strofinaccio m. ~**-jacket** n sopraccoperta f. ~**man** n spazzinc m. ~**pan** n paletta f per la spazzatura

dusty /'dʌstɪ/ adj (**-ier, -iest**) polveroso

Dutch /dʌtʃ/ adj olandese; **go ~** [!] fare alla romana • n (language) olandese m; **the ~** pl gli olandesi. ~**man** n olandese m

duty /'dju:tɪ/ n dovere m; (task) compito m; (tax) dogana f; **be on ~** essere di servizio. ~**-free** adj esen da dogana

duvet /'du:veɪ/ n piumone m

dwarf /dwɔ:f/ n (pl **-s** or **dwarves**) nano, -a mf • vt rimpicciolire

dwell /dwel/ vi (pt/pp **dwelt**) liter dimorare. ▫ **~ on** vt fig soffermarsi su. ~**ing** n abitazione f

dwindle /'dwɪndl/ vi diminuire

dye /daɪ/ n tintura f • vt (pres p **dyeing**) tingere

dying /'daɪɪŋ/ ▸**die**[2]

dynamic /daɪ'næmɪk/ adj dinamico

dynamite /'daɪnəmaɪt/ n dinamite

dynamo /'daɪnəməʊ/ n dinamo f inv

dynasty /'dɪnəstɪ/ n dinastia f

Ee

ach /iːtʃ/ adj ogni • pron ognuno; **£1 ~** una sterlina ciascuno; **they love/hate ~ other** si amano/odiano; **we lend ~ other money** ci prestiamo i soldi

ager /ˈiːgə(r)/ adj ansioso (**to do** di fare); (pupil) avido di sapere. **~ly** adv (wait) ansiosamente; (offer) premurosamente. **~ness** n premura f

agle /ˈiːgl/ n aquila f

ar¹ /ɪə(r)/ n (of corn) spiga f

ar² n orecchio m. **~ache** n mal m d'orecchi. **~-drum** n timpano m

arl /ɜːl/ n conte m

arly /ˈɜːlɪ/ adj (**-ier, -iest**) (before expected time) in anticipo; (spring) prematuro; (reply) pronto; (works, writings) primo; **be here ~!** sii puntuale!; **you're ~!** sei in anticipo!; **~ morning walk** passeggiata f mattutina; **in the ~ morning** la mattina presto; **in the ~ spring** all'inizio della primavera; **~ retirement** prepensionamento m • adv presto; (ahead of time) in anticipo; **~ in the morning** la mattina presto

arn /ɜːn/ vt guadagnare; (deserve) meritare

arnest /ˈɜːnɪst/ adj serio • n **in ~** sul serio. **~ly** adv con aria seria

arnings /ˈɜːnɪŋz/ npl guadagni mpl; (salary) stipendio m

ar: ~phones npl cuffia fsg. **~-ring** n orecchino m. **~shot** n **within ~shot** a portata d'orecchio; **he is out of ~shot** non può sentire

arth /ɜːθ/ n terra f; **where/what on ~?** dove/che diavolo? • vt (Electr) mettere a terra

earthquake n terremoto m

arwig /ˈɪəwɪg/ n forbicina f

ase /iːz/ n **at ~** a proprio agio; **at ~!** (Mil) riposo!; **ill at ~** a disagio; **with ~** con facilità • vt calmare (pain); alleviare (tension, shortage); (slow down) rallentare; (loosen) allentare • vi (pain, situation, wind:) calmarsi

easel /ˈiːzl/ n cavalletto m

easily /ˈiːzɪlɪ/ adv con facilità; **~ the best** certamente il meglio

east /iːst/ n est m; **to the ~ of** a est di • adj dell'est • adv verso est

Easter /ˈiːstə(r)/ n Pasqua f. **~ egg** n uovo m di Pasqua

east|erly /ˈiːstəlɪ/ adj da levante. **~ern** adj orientale. **~ward[s]** /-wəd[z]/ adv verso est

easy /ˈiːzɪ/ adj (**-ier, -iest**) facile; **take it** or **things ~** prendersela con calma; **take it ~!** (don't get excited) calma!; **go ~ with** andarci piano con

easy: ~ chair n poltrona f. **~ˈgoing** adj conciliante; **too ~going** troppo accomodante

eat /iːt/ vt/i (pt **ate**, pp **eaten**) mangiare. □**~ into** vt intaccare. □**~ up** vt mangiare tutto (food); fig inghiottire (profits)

eaves /iːvz/ npl cornicione msg. **~drop** vi (pt/pp **~dropped**) origliare; **~drop on** ascoltare di nascosto

ebb /eb/ n (tide) riflusso m; **at a low ~** fig a terra • vi rifluire; fig declinare

ebony /ˈebənɪ/ n ebano m

eccentric /ɪkˈsentrɪk/ adj & n eccentrico, -a mf

echo /ˈekəʊ/ n (pl **-es**) eco f or m • v (pt/pp **echoed**, pres p **echoing**) • vt echeggiare; ripetere (words) • vi risuonare (**with** di)

eclipse /ɪˈklɪps/ n (Astr) eclissi f inv • vt fig eclissare

ecolog|ical /iːkəˈlɒdʒɪkl/ adj ecologico. **~y** n ecologia f

e-commerce /ˈiːˈkɒmɜːs/ n e-commerce m inv, commercio m elettronico

economic /iːkəˈnɒmɪk/ adj economico; **~ refugee** rifugiato, -a mf economico, -a. **~al** adj economico. **~ally** adv economicamente; (thriftily) in economia. **~s** n economia f

economist /ɪ'kɒnəmɪst/ n economista mf

economize /ɪ'kɒnəmaɪz/ vi economizzare (**on** su)

economy /ɪ'kɒnəmɪ/ n economia f

e

ecstasy /'ekstəsɪ/ n estasi f inv; (drug) ecstasy f

eczema /'eksɪmə/ n eczema m

edge /edʒ/ n bordo m; (of knife) filo m; (of road) ciglio m; **on ~** con i nervi tesi; **have the ~ on** 🅘 avere un vantaggio su • vt bordare. □ **~ forward** vi avanzare lentamente

edgeways /'edʒweɪz/ adv di fianco; **I couldn't get a word in ~** non ho potuto infilare neanche mezza parola nel discorso

edgy /'edʒɪ/ adj nervoso

edible /'edɪbl/ adj commestibile; **this pizza's not ~** questa pizza è immangiabile

edit /'edɪt/ vt (pt/pp **edited**) far la revisione di (text); curare l'edizione di (anthology, dictionary); dirigere (newspaper); montare (film); editare (tape); **~ed by** (book) a cura di

edition /ɪ'dɪʃn/ n edizione f

editor /'edɪtə(r)/ n (of anthology, dictionary) curatore, -trice mf; (of newspaper) redattore, -trice mf; (of film) responsabile mf del montaggio

editorial /edɪ'tɔ:rɪəl/ adj redazionale • n (Journ) editoriale m

educate /'edjʊkeɪt/ vt istruire; educare (public, mind); **be ~d at Eton** essere educato a Eton. **~d** adj istruito

education /edjʊ'keɪʃn/ n istruzione f; (culture) cultura f, educazione f. **~al** adj istruttivo; (visit) educativo; (publishing) didattico

eel /i:l/ n anguilla f

eerie /'ɪərɪ/ adj (**-ier, -iest**) inquietante

effect /ɪ'fekt/ n effetto m; **in ~** in effetti; **take ~** (law:) entrare in vigore; (medicine:) fare effetto • vt effettuare

effective /ɪ'fektɪv/ adj efficace; (striking) che colpisce; (actual) di fatto; **~ from** in vigore a partire da. **~ly** adv efficacemente; (actually) di fatto. **~ness** n efficacia f

effeminate /ɪ'femɪnət/ adj effeminato

efficiency /ɪ'fɪʃənsɪ/ n efficienza f; (of machine) rendimento m

efficient /ɪ'fɪʃənt/ adj efficiente. **~ly** adv efficientemente

effort /'efət/ n sforzo m; **make an ~** sforzarsi. **~less** adj facile. **~lessly** adv con facilità

e.g. abbr (exempli gratia) per es.

egg[1] /eg/ vt **~ on** 🅘 incitare

egg[2] n uovo m. **~-cup** n portauovo m inv. **~head** n 🅘 intellettuale mf. **~shell** n guscio m d'uovo. **~timer** clessidra f per misurare il tempo di cottura delle uova

ego /'i:gəʊ/ n ego m. **~centric** adj egocentrico. **~ism** n egoismo m. **~ist** n egoista mf. **~tism** n egotismo m. **~tist** n egotista mf

Egypt /'i:dʒɪpt/ n Egitto m. **~ian** adj & n egiziano, -a mf

eiderdown /'aɪdə-/ n (quilt) piumino m

eigh|t /eɪt/ adj otto • n otto m. **~'teen** adj diciotto. **~'teenth** adj diciottesimo

eighth /eɪtθ/ adj ottavo • n ottavo m

eightieth /'eɪtɪɪθ/ adj ottantesimo

eighty /'eɪtɪ/ adj ottanta

either /'aɪðə(r)/ adj & pron **~ [of them]** l'uno o l'altro; **I don't like ~ [of them]** non mi piace né l'uno né l'altro; **on ~ side** da tutte e due le parti • adv **I don't ~** nemmeno io; **I don't like John or his brother ~** non mi piace John e nemmeno suo fratello • conj **~ John or his brother will be there** ci saranno o John o suo fratello; **I don't like ~ John or his brother** non mi piacciono né John né suo fratello; **~ you go to bed or else...** o vai a letto o altrimenti ...

eject /ɪ'dʒekt/ vt eiettare (pilot); espellere (tape, drunk)

eke /i:k/ vt **~ out** far bastare; (increase) arrotondare; **~ out a living** arrangiarsi

elaborate[1] /ɪ'læbərət/ adj elaborato

elaborate[2] /ɪ'læbəreɪt/ vi entrare nei particolari (**on** di)

elapse /ɪ'læps/ vi trascorrere

elastic /ɪ'læstɪk/ adj elastico •n elastico m. ~ '**band** n elastico m

elated /ɪ'leɪtɪd/ adj esultante

elbow /'elbəʊ/ n gomito m

elder[1] /'eldə(r)/ n (tree) sambuco m

eld|er[2] adj maggiore •n **the** ~ il/la maggiore. ~**erly** adj anziano. ~**est** adj maggiore •n **the** ~**est** il/la maggiore

elect /ɪ'lekt/ adj **the president** ~ il futuro presidente •vt eleggere; ~ **to do sth** decidere di fare qcsa. ~**ion** n elezione f

elector /ɪ'lektə(r)/ n elettore, -trice mf. ~**al** adj elettorale; ~**al roll** liste fpl elettorali. ~**ate** n elettorato m

electric /ɪ'lektrɪk/ adj elettrico

electrical /ɪ'lektrɪkl/ adj elettrico; ~ **engineering** elettrotecnica f

electric 'blanket n termocoperta f

electrician /ɪlek'trɪʃn/ n elettricista m

electricity /ɪlek'trɪsətɪ/ n elettricità f

electrify /ɪ'lektrɪfaɪ/ vt (pt/pp **-ied**) elettrificare; fig elettrizzare. ~**ing** adj fig elettrizzante

electrocute /ɪ'lektrəkju:t/ vt fulminare; (execute) giustiziare sulla sedia elettrica

electrode /ɪ'lektrəʊd/ n elettrodo m

electron /ɪ'lektrɒn/ n elettrone m

electronic /ɪlek'trɒnɪk/ adj elettronico. ~ **mail** n posta f elettronica. ~**s** n elettronica f

elegance /'elɪgəns/ n eleganza f

elegant /'elɪgənt/ adj elegante

element /'elɪmənt/ n elemento m. ~**ary** adj elementare

elephant /'elɪfənt/ n elefante m

elevat|e /'elɪveɪt/ vt elevare. ~**ion** n elevazione f; (height) altitudine f; (angle) alzo m

elevator /'elɪveɪtə(r)/ n Am ascensore m

eleven /ɪ'levn/ adj undici •n undici m. ~**th** adj undicesimo; **at the** ~**th hour** [!] all'ultimo momento

elf /elf/ n (pl **elves**) elfo m

eligible /'elɪdʒəbl/ adj eleggibile; **be** ~ **for** aver diritto a

eliminate /ɪ'lɪmɪneɪt/ vt eliminare

élite /eɪ'li:t/ n fior fiore m

ellip|se /ɪ'lɪps/ n ellisse f. ~**tical** adj ellittico

elm /elm/ n olmo m

elope /ɪ'ləʊp/ vi fuggire [per sposarsi]

eloquen|ce /'eləkwəns/ n eloquenza f. ~**t** adj eloquente. ~**tly** adv con eloquenza

else /els/ adv altro; **who** ~**?** e chi altro?; **he did of course, who** ~**?** l'ha fatto lui e chi, se no?; **nothing** ~ nient'altro; **or** ~ altrimenti; **someone** ~ qualcun altro; **somewhere** ~ da qualche altra parte; **anyone** ~ chiunque altro; (as question) nessun'altro?; **anything** ~ qualunque altra cosa; (as question) altro?. ~**where** adv altrove

elude /ɪ'lu:d/ vt eludere; (avoid) evitare; **the name** ~**s me** il nome mi sfugge

elusive /ɪ'lu:sɪv/ adj elusivo

emaciated /ɪ'meɪsɪeɪtɪd/ adj emaciato

e-mail /'i:meɪl/ n posta f elettronica •vt spedire via posta elettronica. ~ **address** n indirizzo m e-mail

embankment /ɪm'bæŋkmənt/ n argine m; (Rail) massicciata f

embargo /em'bɑ:gəʊ/ n (pl **-es**) embargo m

embark /ɪm'bɑ:k/ vi imbarcarsi; ~ **on** intraprendere. ~**ation** n imbarco m

embarrass /em'bærəs/ vt imbarazzare. ~**ed** adj imbarazzato. ~**ing** adj imbarazzante. ~**ment** n imbarazzo m

embassy /'embəsɪ/ n ambasciata f

embedded /ɪm'bedɪd/ adj (in concrete) cementato; (traditions, feelings) radicato

embellish /ɪm'belɪʃ/ vt abbellire

embers /'embəz/ npl braci fpl

embezzle /ɪm'bezl/ vt appropriarsi indebitamente di. ~**ment** n appropriazione f indebita

emblem /'embləm/ n emblema m

embrace /ɪm'breɪs/ n abbraccio m •vt abbracciare •vi abbracciarsi

embroider /ɪm'brɔɪdə(r)/ vt ricamare (design); fig abbellire. ~**y** n ricamo m

embryo /'embrɪəʊ/ n embrione m

emerald /'emərəld/ n smeraldo m

emer|ge /ɪ'mɜːdʒ/ vi emergere; (come into being: nation) nascere; (sun, flowers) spuntare fuori. **~gence** n emergere m; (of new country) nascita f

emergency /ɪ'mɜːdʒənsɪ/ n emergenza f; **in an ~** in caso di emergenza. **~ exit** n uscita f di sicurezza

e

emigrant /'emɪgrənt/ n emigrante mf

emigrat|e /'emɪgreɪt/ vi emigrare. **~ion** n emigrazione f

eminent /'emɪnənt/ adj eminente. **~ly** adv eminentemente

emission /ɪ'mɪʃn/ n emissione f; (of fumes) esalazione f

emit /ɪ'mɪt/ vt (pt/pp **emitted**) emettere; esalare (fumes)

emotion /ɪ'məʊʃn/ n emozione f. **~al** adj denso di emozione; (person, reaction) emotivo; **become ~al** avere una reazione emotiva

emotive /ɪ'məʊtɪv/ adj emotivo

emperor /'empərə(r)/ n imperatore m

emphasis /'emfəsɪs/ n enfasi f; **put the ~ on sth** accentuare qcsa

emphasize /'emfəsaɪz/ vt accentuare (word, syllable); sottolineare (need)

emphatic /ɪm'fætɪk/ adj categorico

empire /'empaɪə(r)/ n impero m

empirical /em'pɪrɪkl/ adj empirico

employ /em'plɔɪ/ vt impiegare; fig usare (tact). **~ee** n impiegato, -a mf. **~er** n datore m di lavoro. **~ment** n occupazione f; (work) lavoro m. **~ment agency** n ufficio m di collocamento

empower /ɪm'paʊə(r)/ vt autorizzare; (enable) mettere in grado

empress /'emprɪs/ n imperatrice f

empty /'emptɪ/ adj vuoto; (promise, threat) vano •v (pt/pp **-ied**) •vt vuotare (container) •vi vuotarsi

emulate /'emjʊleɪt/ vt emulare

emulsion /ɪ'mʌlʃn/ n emulsione f

enable /ɪ'neɪbl/ vt **~ sb to** mettere qcno in grado di

enact /ɪ'nækt/ vt (Theat) rappresentare; decretare (law)

enamel /ɪ'næml/ n smalto m •vt (pt/pp **enamelled**) smaltare

enchant /ɪn'tʃɑːnt/ vt incantare. **~ing** adj incantevole. **~ment** n incanto m

encircle /ɪn'sɜːkl/ vt circondare

enclave /'enkleɪv/ n enclave f inv; fig territorio m

enclos|e /ɪn'kləʊz/ vt circondare (land); (in letter) allegare (**with** a). **~ed** adj (space) chiuso; (in letter) allegato. **~ure** n (at zoo) recinto m; (in letter) allegato m

encore /'ɒŋkɔː(r)/ n & int bis m inv

encounter /ɪn'kaʊntə(r)/ n incontro m; (battle) scontro m •vt incontrare

encourag|e /ɪn'kʌrɪdʒ/ vt incoraggiare; promuovere (the arts, independence). **~ement** n incoraggiamento m; (of the arts) promozione f. **~ing** adj incoraggiante; (smile) di incoraggiamento

encroach /ɪn'krəʊtʃ/ vt **~ on** invadere (land, privacy); abusare di (time); interferire con (rights)

encyclop[a]ed|ia /ɪnsaɪklə'piːdɪə/ n enciclopedia f. **~ic** adj enciclopedico

end /end/ n fine f; (of box, table, piece of string) estremità f; (of town, room) parte f; (purpose) fine m; **in the ~** alla fine; **at the ~ of May** alla fine di maggio; **at the ~ of the street/garden** in fondo alla strada/al giardino; **on ~** (upright) in piedi; **for days on ~** per giorni e giorni; **for six days on ~** per sei giorni di fila, **put an ~ to sth** mettere fine a qcsa; **make ~s meet** 🄸 sbarcare il lunario; **no ~ of** 🄸 un sacco di •vt/i finire. □ **~ up** vi finire; **~ up doing sth** finire col fare qcsa

endanger /ɪn'deɪndʒə(r)/ vt rischiare (one's life); mettere a repentaglio (sb else, success of sth)

endear|ing /ɪn'dɪərɪŋ/ adj accattivante. **~ment** n **term of ~ment** vezzeggiativo m

endeavour /ɪn'devə(r)/ n tentativo m •vi sforzarsi (**to** di)

ending /'endɪŋ/ n fine f; (Gram) desinenza f

endless /'endlɪs/ adj interminabile; (patience) infinito. **~ly** adv continuamente; (patient) infinitamente

ndorse /en'dɔ:s/ vt girare (cheque); (sports personality:) fare pubblicità a (product); approvare (plan). **~ment** n (of cheque) girata f; (of plan) conferma f; (on driving licence) registrazione f su patente di un'infrazione

ndur|e /ɪn'djʊə(r)/ vt sopportare •vi durare. **~ing** adj duraturo

nemy /'enəmɪ/ n nemico, -a mf •attrib nemico

nergetic /enə'dʒetɪk/ adj energico

nergy /'enədʒɪ/ n energia f

nforce /ɪn'fɔ:s/ vt far rispettare (law). **~d** adj forzato

ngage /ɪn'geɪdʒ/ vt assumere (staff); (Theat) ingaggiare; (Auto) ingranare (gear) •vi (Techn) ingranare; **~ in** impegnarsi in. **~d** adj (in use, busy) occupato; (person) impegnato; (to be married) fidanzato; **get ~d** fidanzarsi (**to** con); **~d tone** (Teleph) segnale m di occupato. **~ment** n fidanzamento m; (appointment) appuntamento m; (Mil) combattimento m; **~ment ring** anello m di fidanzamento

ngine /'endʒɪn/ n motore m; (Rail) locomotrice f. **~-driver** n macchinista m

ngineer /endʒɪ'nɪə(r)/ n ingegnere m; (service, installation) tecnico m; (Naut), Am (Rail) macchinista m •vt fig architettare. **~ing** n ingegneria f

ngland /'ɪŋglənd/ n Inghilterra f

nglish /'ɪŋglɪʃ/ adj inglese; **the ~ Channel** la Manica •n (language) inglese m; **the ~** pl gli inglesi. **~man** n inglese m. **~woman** n inglese f

ngrav|e /ɪn'greɪv/ vt incidere. **~ing** n incisione f

ngulf /ɪn'gʌlf/ vt (fire, waves:) inghiottire

nhance /ɪn'hɑ:ns/ vt accrescere (beauty, reputation); migliorare (performance)

nigma /ɪ'nɪgmə/ n enigma m. **~tic** adj enigmatico

njoy /ɪn'dʒɔɪ/ vt godere di (good health); **~ oneself** divertirsi; **I ~ cooking/painting** mi piace cucinare/dipingere; **~ your meal** buon appetito. **~able** adj piacevole. **~ment** n piacere m

enlarge /ɪn'lɑ:dʒ/ vt ingrandire •vi **~ upon** dilungarsi su. **~ment** n ingrandimento m

enlighten /ɪn'laɪtn/ vt illuminare. **~ed** adj progressista. **~ment** n **the E~ment** l'Illuminismo m

enlist /ɪn'lɪst/ vt (Mil) reclutare; **~ sb's help** farsi aiutare da qcno •vi (Mil) arruolarsi

enliven /ɪn'laɪvn/ vt animare

enormity /ɪ'nɔ:mətɪ/ n enormità f

enormous /ɪ'nɔ:məs/ adj enorme. **~ly** adv estremamente; (grateful) infinitamente

enough /ɪ'nʌf/ adj & n abbastanza; **I didn't bring ~ clothes** non ho portato abbastanza vestiti; **have you had ~?** (to eat/drink) hai mangiato/bevuto abbastanza?; **I've had ~!** [!] ne ho abbastanza!; **is that ~?** basta?; **that's ~!** basta così!; **£50 isn't ~** 50 sterline non sono sufficienti •adv abbastanza; **you're not working fast ~** non lavori abbastanza in fretta; **funnily ~** stranamente

enquir|e /ɪn'kwaɪə(r)/ vi domandare; **~e about** chiedere informazioni su. **~y** n domanda f; (investigation) inchiesta f

enrage /ɪn'reɪdʒ/ vt fare arrabbiare

enrol /ɪn'rəʊl/ vi (pt/pp **-rolled**) (for exam, in club) iscriversi (**for, in** a). **~ment** n iscrizione f

ensu|e /ɪn'sju:/ vi seguire; **the ~ing discussion** la discussione che ne è seguita

ensure /ɪn'ʃʊə(r)/ vt assicurare; **~ that** (person:) assicurarsi che; (measure:) garantire che

entail /ɪn'teɪl/ vt comportare; **what does it ~?** in che cosa consiste?

entangle /ɪn'tæŋgl/ vt **get ~d in** rimanere impigliato in; fig rimanere coinvolto in

enter /'entə(r)/ vt entrare in; iscrivere (horse, runner in race); cominciare (university); partecipare a (competition); (Comput) immettere (data); (write down) scrivere •vi entrare; (Theat) entrare in scena; (register as competitor) iscriversi; (take part) partecipare (**in** a)

enterpris|e /'entəpraɪz/ n impresa f;

e

(quality) iniziativa f. **~ing** adj intraprendente

entertain /entəˈteɪn/ vt intrattenere; (invite) ricevere; nutrire (ideas, hopes); prendere in considerazione (possibility) •vi intrattenersi; (have guests) ricevere. **~er** n artista mf. **~ing** adj (person) di gradevole compagnia; (evening, film, play) divertente. **~ment** n (amusement) intrattenimento m

e

enthral /ɪnˈθrɔːl/ vt (pt/pp **enthralled**) **be ~led** essere affascinato (**by** da)

enthusias|m /ɪnˈθjuːzɪæzm/ n entusiasmo m. **~t** n entusiasta mf. **~tic** adj entusiastico

entice /ɪnˈtaɪs/ vt attirare. **~ment** n (incentive) incentivo m

entire /ɪnˈtaɪə(r)/ adj intero. **~ly** adv del tutto; **I'm not ~ly satisfied** non sono completamente soddisfatto. **~ty** n **in its ~ty** nell'insieme

entitlement /ɪnˈtaɪtlmənt/ n diritto m

entity /ˈentətɪ/ n entità f

entrance¹ /ˈentrəns/ n entrata f; (Theat) entrata f in scena; (right to enter) ammissione f; **'no ~'** 'ingresso vietato'. **~ examination** n esame m di ammissione. **~ fee** n **how much is the ~ fee?** quanto costa il biglietto di ingresso?

entrance² /ɪnˈtrɑːns/ vt estasiare

entrant /ˈentrənt/ n concorrente mf

entreat /ɪnˈtriːt/ vt supplicare

entrenched /ɪnˈtrentʃt/ adj (ideas, views) radicato

entrust /ɪnˈtrʌst/ vt **~ sb with sth, ~ sth to sb** affidare qcsa a qcno

entry /ˈentrɪ/ n ingresso m; (way in) entrata f; (in directory etc) voce f; (in appointment diary) appuntamento m; **no ~** ingresso vietato; (Auto) accesso vietato. **~ form** n modulo m di ammissione. **~ visa** n visto m di ingresso

enumerate /ɪˈnjuːməreɪt/ vt enumerare

envelop /ɪnˈveləp/ vt (pt/pp **enveloped**) avviluppare

envelope /ˈenvələʊp/ n busta f

enviable /ˈenvɪəbl/ adj invidiabile

envious /ˈenvɪəs/ adj invidioso. **~ly** adv con invidia

environment /ɪnˈvaɪrənmənt/ n ambiente m

environmental /ɪnvaɪrənˈmentl/ adj ambientale. **~ist** n ambientalista mf. **~ly** adv **~ly friendly** che rispetta l'ambiente

envisage /ɪnˈvɪzɪdʒ/ vt prevedere

envoy /ˈenvɔɪ/ n inviato, -a mf

envy /ˈenvɪ/ n invidia f •vt (pt/pp **-ied**) **~ sb sth** invidiare qcno per qcsa

enzyme /ˈenzaɪm/ n enzima m

epic /ˈepɪk/ adj epico •n epopea f

epidemic /epɪˈdemɪk/ n epidemia f

epilep|sy /ˈepɪlepsɪ/ n epilessia f. **~tic** adj & n epilettico, -a mf

epilogue /ˈepɪlɒg/ n epilogo m

episode /ˈepɪsəʊd/ n episodio m

epitaph /ˈepɪtɑːf/ n epitaffio m

epitom|e /ɪˈpɪtəmɪ/ n epitome f. **~ize** vt essere il classico esempio d

epoch /ˈiːpɒk/ n epoca f

equal /ˈiːkwl/ adj (parts, amounts) uguale; **of ~ height** della stessa altezza; **be ~ to the task** essere a l'altezza del compito •n pari m inv •vt (pt/pp **equalled**) (be same in quantity as) essere pari a; (rival) uguagliare; **5 plus 5 ~s 10** 5 più 5 [è] uguale a 10. **~ity** n uguaglianza f

equalize /ˈiːkwəlaɪz/ vi (Sport) pareggiare. **~r** n (Sport) pareggio m

equally /ˈiːkwəlɪ/ adv (divide) in parti uguali; **~ intelligent** della stessa intelligenza; **~,...** allo stesso tempo...

equator /ɪˈkweɪtə(r)/ n equatore m

equilibrium /iːkwɪˈlɪbrɪəm/ n equilibrio m

equinox /ˈiːkwɪnɒks/ n equinozio m

equip /ɪˈkwɪp/ vt (pt/pp **equipped**) equipaggiare; attrezzare (kitchen, office). **~ment** n attrezzatura f

equivalent /ɪˈkwɪvələnt/ adj equivalente; **be ~ to** equivalere a •n equivalente m

equivocal /ɪˈkwɪvəkl/ adj equivoco

era /ˈɪərə/ n età f; (geological) era f

eradicate /ɪˈrædɪkeɪt/ vt eradicare

erase /ɪˈreɪz/ vt cancellare. **~r** n

gomma f [da cancellare]; (for blackboard) cancellino m

erect /ɪ'rekt/ adj eretto • vt erigere. **~ion** n erezione f

ero|de /ɪ'rəʊd/ vt (water:) erodere; (acid:) corrodere. **~sion** n erosione f; (by acid) corrosione f

erotic /ɪ'rɒtɪk/ adj erotico.

err /ɜ:(r)/ vi errare; (sin) peccare

errand /'erənd/ n commissione f

erratic /ɪ'rætɪk/ adj irregolare; (person, moods) imprevedibile; (exchange rate) incostante

erroneous /ɪ'rəʊnɪəs/ adj erroneo

error /'erə(r)/ n errore m; **in ~** per errore

erudit|e /'erʊdaɪt/ adj erudito. **~ion** n erudizione f

erupt /ɪ'rʌpt/ vi eruttare; (spots:) spuntare; (fig: in anger) dare in escandescenze. **~ion** n eruzione f; fig scoppio m

escalat|e /'eskəleɪt/ vi intensificarsi • vt intensificare. **~ion** n escalation f. **~or** n scala f mobile

escapade /'eskəpeɪd/ n scappatella f

escape /ɪ'skeɪp/ n fuga f; (from prison) evasione f; **have a narrow ~** cavarsela per un pelo • vi (prisoner:) evadere (**from** da); sfuggire (**from sb** alla sorveglianza di qcno); (animal:) scappare; (gas:) fuoriuscire • vt **~ notice** passare inosservato; **the name ~s me** mi sfugge il nome

escapism /ɪ'skeɪpɪzm/ n evasione f [dalla realtà]

escort¹ /'eskɔ:t/ n accompagnatore, -trice mf; (Mil etc) scorta f

escort² /ɪ'skɔ:t/ vt accompagnare; (Mil etc) scortare

Eskimo /'eskɪməʊ/ n esquimese mf

especial /ɪ'speʃl/ adj speciale. **~ly** adv specialmente; (kind) particolarmente

espionage /'espɪənɑ:ʒ/ n spionaggio m

essay /'eseɪ/ n saggio m; (Sch) tema f

essence /'esns/ n essenza f; **in ~** in sostanza

essential /ɪ'senʃl/ adj essenziale • npl **the ~s** l'essenziale m. **~ly** adv essenzialmente

establish /ɪ'stæblɪʃ/ vt stabilire (contact, lead); fondare (firm); (prove) accertare; **~ oneself as** affermarsi come. **~ment** n (firm) azienda f; **the E~ment** l'ordine m costituito

estate /ɪ'steɪt/ n tenuta f; (possessions) patrimonio m; (housing) quartiere m residenziale. **~ agent** n agente m immobiliare. **~ car** n giardiniera f

esteem /ɪ'sti:m/ n stima f • vt stimare; (consider) giudicare

estimate¹ /'estɪmət/ n valutazione f; (Comm) preventivo m; **at a rough ~** a occhio e croce

estimat|e² /'estɪmeɪt/ vt stimare. **~ion** n (esteem) stima f; **in my ~ion** (judgement) a mio giudizio

estuary /'estjʊərɪ/ n estuario m

etc /et'setərə/ abbr (et cetera) ecc

etching /'etʃɪŋ/ n acquaforte f

eternal /ɪ'tɜ:nl/ adj eterno

eternity /ɪ'θɜ:nətɪ/ n eternità f

ethic /'eθɪk/ n etica f. **~al** adj etico. **~s** n etica f

ethnic /'eθnɪk/ adj etnico

etiquette /'etɪket/ n etichetta f

EU n abbr (European Union) UE f

euphemis|m /'ju:fəmɪzm/ n eufemismo m. **~tic** adj eufemistico

euphoria /ju:'fɔ:rɪə/ n euforia f

euro /'jʊərəʊ/ n euro m inv

Euro- /'jʊərəʊ-/ pref **~cheque** n eurochèque m inv. **~dollar** n eurodollaro m

Europe /'jʊərəp/ n Europa f

European /jʊərə'pɪən/ adj europeo; **~ Union** Unione f Europea • n europeo, -a mf

Euro-sceptic /jʊərəʊ'skeptɪk/ adj euroscettico • n euroscettico, -a mf

evacuat|e /ɪ'vækjʊeɪt/ vt evacuare (building, area). **~ion** n evacuazione f

evade /ɪ'veɪd/ vt evadere (taxes); evitare (the enemy, authorities); **~ the issue** evitare l'argomento

evaluat|e /ɪ'væljʊeɪt/ vt valutare. **~ion** /-'eɪʃn/ n valutazione f

evange|lical /i:væn'dʒelɪkl/ adj evangelico. **~list** n evangelista m

evaporat|e /ɪ'væpəreɪt/ vi evaporare; fig svanire. **~ion** n evaporazione f

evasion /ɪ'veɪʒn/ n evasione f

e

evasive /ɪ'veɪsɪv/ adj evasivo

eve /iːv/ n liter vigilia f

even /'iːvn/ adj (level) piatto; (same, equal) uguale; (regular) regolare; (number) pari; **get ~ with** vendicarsi di; **now we're ~** adesso siamo pari • adv anche, ancora; **~ if** anche se; **~ so** con tutto ciò; **not ~** nemmeno; **~ bigger/hotter** ancora più grande/caldo • vt **~ the score** (Sport) pareggiare. □**~ out** vi livellarsi. □**~ up** vt livellare

evening /'iːvnɪŋ/ n sera f; (whole evening) serata f; **this ~** stasera; **in the ~** la sera. **~ class** n corso m serale. **~ dress** n abito m scuro; (woman's) abito m da sera

event /ɪ'vent/ n avvenimento m; (function) manifestazione f; (Sport) gara f; **in the ~ of** nell'eventualità di; **in the ~** alla fine. **~ful** adj movimentato

eventual /ɪ'ventjʊəl/ adj **the ~ winner was...** alla fine il vincitore è stato.... **~ity** n eventualità f. **~ly** adv alla fine; **~ly!** finalmente!

ever /'evə(r)/ adv mai; **I haven't ~...** non ho mai...; **for ~** per sempre; **hardly ~** quasi mai; **~ since** da quando; (since that time) da allora; **~ so** [!] veramente

'evergreen n sempreverde m

ever'lasting adj eterno

every /'evrɪ/ adj ogni; **~ one** ciascuno; **~ other day** un giorno si un giorno no

every: ~body pron tutti pl. **~day** adj quotidiano, di ogni giorno. **~one** pron tutti pl; **~thing** pron tutto; **~where** adv dappertutto; (wherever) dovunque

evict /ɪ'vɪkt/ vt sfrattare. **~ion** n sfratto m

eviden|ce /'evɪdəns/ n evidenza f; (Jur) testimonianza f; **give ~ce** testimoniare. **~t** adj evidente. **~tly** adv evidentemente

evil /'iːvl/ adj cattivo • n male m

evocative /ɪ'vɒkətɪv/ adj evocativo; **be ~ of** evocare

evoke /ɪ'vəʊk/ vt evocare

evolution /iːvə'luːʃn/ n evoluzione f

evolve /ɪ'vɒlv/ vt evolvere • vi evolversi

ewe /juː/ n pecora f

exact /ɪg'zækt/ adj esatto • vt esigere. **~ing** adj esigente. **~itude** n esattezza f. **~ly** adv esattamente; **not ~ly** non proprio. **~ness** n precisione f

exaggerat|e /ɪg'zædʒəreɪt/ vt/i esagerare. **~ion** n esagerazione f

exam /ɪg'zæm/ n esame m

examination /ɪgzæmɪ'neɪʃn/ n esame m; (of patient) visita f

examine /ɪg'zæmɪn/ vt esaminare; visitare (patient). **~r** n (Sch) esaminatore, -trice mf

example /ɪg'zɑːmpl/ n esempio m; **for ~** per esempio; **make an ~ of sb** punire qcno per dare un esempio; **be an ~ to sb** dare il buon esempio a qcno

exasperat|e /ɪg'zæspəreɪt/ vt esasperare. **~ion** n esasperazione f

excavat|e /'ekskəveɪt/ vt scavare; (Archaeol) fare gli scavi di. **~ion** n scavo m

exceed /ɪk'siːd/ vt eccedere. **~ingly** adv estremamente

excel /ɪk'sel/ v (pt/pp **excelled**) • vi eccellere • vt **~ oneself** superare se stessi

excellen|ce /'eksələns/ n eccellenza f. **E~cy** n (title) Eccellenza f. **~t** adj eccellente

except /ɪk'sept/ prep eccetto, tranne; **~ for** eccetto, tranne; **~ that...** eccetto che... • vt eccettuare. **~ing** prep eccetto, tranne

exception /ɪk'sepʃn/ n eccezione f; **take ~ to** fare obiezioni a. **~al** adj eccezionale. **~ally** adv eccezionalmente

excerpt /'eksɜːpt/ n estratto m

excess /ɪk'ses/ n eccesso m; **in ~ of** oltre. **~ baggage** n bagaglio m in eccedenza. **~ 'fare** n supplemento m

excessive /ɪk'sesɪv/ adj eccessivo. **~ly** adv eccessivamente

exchange /ɪks'tʃeɪndʒ/ n scambio m; (Teleph) centrale f; (Comm) cambio m; **in ~** in cambio (**for** di) • vt scambiare (**for** con); cambiare (money). **~ rate** n tasso m di cambio

excise[1] /'eksaɪz/ n dazio m; **~ duty** dazio m

excise[2] /ek'saɪz/ vt recidere

excitable /ɪk'saɪtəbl/ adj eccitabile

excit|e /ɪk'saɪt/ vt eccitare. **~ed** adj eccitato; **get ~ed** eccitarsi. **~edly** adv tutto eccitato. **~ement** n eccitazione f. **~ing** adj eccitante; (story, film) appassionante; (holiday) entusiasmante

exclaim /ɪk'skleɪm/ vt/i esclamare

exclamation /ekskləˈmeɪʃn/ n esclamazione f. **~ mark** n, Am **~ point** n punto m esclamativo

exclu|de /ɪk'sklu:d/ vt escludere. **~ding** pron escluso. **~sion** n esclusione f

exclusive /ɪk'sklu:sɪv/ adj (rights, club) esclusivo; (interview) in esclusiva; **~ of...** ...escluso. **~ly** adv esclusivamente

excruciating /ɪk'skru:ʃɪeɪtɪŋ/ adj atroce (pain); (🄸: very bad) spaventoso

excursion /ɪk'skɜ:ʃn/ n escursione f

excusable /ɪk'skju:zəbl/ adj perdonabile

excuse[1] /ɪk'skju:s/ n scusa f

excuse[2] /ɪk'skju:z/ vt scusare; **~ from** esonerare da; **~ me!** (to get attention) scusi!; (to get past) permesso!, scusi!; (indignant) come ha detto?

ex-di'rectory adj **be ~** non figurare sull'elenco telefonico

execute /'eksɪkju:t/ vt eseguire; (put to death) giustiziare; attuare (plan)

execution /eksɪ'kju:ʃn/ n esecuzione f; (of plan) attuazione f. **~er** n boia m inv

executive /ɪg'zekjʊtɪv/ adj esecutivo •n dirigente mf; (Pol) esecutivo m

executor /ɪg'zekjʊtə(r)/ n (Jur) esecutore, -trice mf

exempt /ɪg'zempt/ adj esente •vt esentare (**from** da). **~ion** n esenzione f

exercise /'eksəsaɪz/ n esercizio m; (Mil) esercitazione f; **physical ~s** ginnastica f; **take ~** fare del moto •vt esercitare (muscles, horse); portare a spasso (dog); mettere in pratica (skills) •vi esercitarsi. **~ book** n quaderno m

exert /ɪg'zɜ:t/ vt esercitare; **~ oneself** sforzarsi. **~ion** n sforzo m

exhale /eks'heɪl/ vt/i esalare

exhaust /ɪg'zɔ:st/ n (Auto) scappamento m; (pipe) tubo m di scappamento; **~ fumes** fumi mpl di scarico m •vt esaurire. **~ed** adj esausto. **~ing** adj estenuante; (climate, person) sfibrante. **~ion** n esaurimento m. **~ive** adj fig esauriente

exhibit /ɪg'zɪbɪt/ n oggetto m esposto; (Jur) reperto m •vt esporre; fig dimostrare

e

exhibition /eksɪ'bɪʃn/ n mostra f; (of strength, skill) dimostrazione f. **~ist** n esibizionista mf

exhibitor /ɪg'zɪbɪtə(r)/ n espositore, -trice mf

exhort /ɪg'zɔ:t/ vt esortare

exile /'eksaɪl/ n esilio m; (person) esule mf •vt esiliare

exist /ɪg'zɪst/ vi esistere. **~ence** n esistenza f; **in ~** esistente; **be in ~ence** esistere. **~ing** adj attuale

exit /'eksɪt/ n uscita f; (Theat) uscita f di scena •vi (Theat) uscire di scena; (Comput) uscire

exorbitant /ɪg'zɔ:bɪtənt/ adj esorbitante

exotic /ɪg'zɒtɪk/ adj esotico

expand /ɪk'spænd/ vt espandere •vi espandersi; (Comm) svilupparsi; (metal:) dilatarsi; **~ on** (fig: explain better) approfondire

expans|e /ɪk'spæns/ n estensione f. **~ion** n espansione f; (Comm) sviluppo m; (of metal) dilatazione f. **~ive** adj espansivo

expatriate /eks'pætrɪət/ n espatriato, -a mf

expect /ɪk'spekt/ vt aspettare (letter, baby); (suppose) pensare; (demand) esigere; **I ~ so** penso di sì; **be ~ing** essere in stato interessante

expectan|cy /ɪk'spektənsɪ/ n aspettativa f. **~t** adj in attesa; **~t mother** donna f incinta. **~tly** adv con impazienza

expectation /ekspek'teɪʃn/ n aspettativa f, speranza f

expedient /ɪk'spi:dɪənt/ adj conveniente •n espediente m

expedition /ekspɪ'dɪʃn/ n spedizione f. **~ary** adj (Mil) di spedizione

expel /ɪk'spel/ vt (pt/pp **expelled**) espellere

e

expend /ɪk'spend/ vt consumare. **~able** adj sacrificabile

expenditure /ɪk'spendɪtʃə(r)/ n spesa f

expense /ɪk'spens/ n spesa f; **business ~s** pl spese fpl; **at my ~** a mie spese; **at the ~ of** fig a spese di

expensive /ɪk'spensɪv/ adj caro, costoso. **~ly** adv costosamente

experience /ɪk'spɪərɪəns/ n esperienza f •vt provare (sensation); avere (problem). **~d** adj esperto

experiment /ɪk'sperɪmənt/ n esperimento •vi sperimentare. **~al** adj sperimentale

expert /'ekspɜ:t/ adj & n esperto, -a mf. **~ly** adv abilmente

expertise /ekspɜ:'ti:z/ n competenza f

expire /ɪk'spaɪə(r)/ vi scadere

expiry /ɪk'spaɪərɪ/ n scadenza f. **~ date** n data f di scadenza

explain /ɪk'spleɪn/ vt spiegare

explana|tion /eksplə'neɪʃn/ n spiegazione f. **~tory** adj esplicativo

explicit /ɪk'splɪsɪt/ adj esplicito. **~ly** adv esplicitamente

explode /ɪk'spləʊd/ vi esplodere •vt fare esplodere

exploit[1] /'eksplɔɪt/ n impresa f

exploit[2] /ɪk'splɔɪt/ vt sfruttare. **~ation** n sfruttamento m

explora|tion /eksplə'reɪʃn/ n esplorazione f. **~tory** adj esplorativo

explore /ɪk'splɔ:(r)/ vt esplorare; fig studiare (implications). **~r** n esploratore, -trice mf

explos|ion /ɪk'spləʊʒn/ n esplosione f. **~ive** adj & n esplosivo m

export /'ekspɔ:t/ n esportazione f •vt /-'spɔ:t/ esportare. **~er** n esportatore, -trice mf

expos|e /ɪk'spəʊz/ vt esporre; (reveal) svelare; smascherare (traitor etc). **~ure** n esposizione f; (Med) esposizione f prolungata al freddo/caldo; (of crimes) smascheramento m; **24 ~ures** (Phot) 24 pose

express /ɪk'spres/ adj espresso •adv (send) per espresso •n (train) espresso m •vt esprimere; **~ oneself** esprimersi. **~ion** n espressione f. **~ive** adj espressivo. **~ly** adv espressamente

expulsion /ɪk'spʌlʃn/ n espulsione f

exquisite /ek'skwɪzɪt/ adj squisito

extend /ɪk'stend/ vt prolungare (visit, road); prorogare (visa, contract); ampliare (building, knowledge); (stretch out) allungare; tendere (hand) •vi (garden, knowledge:) estendersi

extension /ɪk'stenʃn/ n prolungamento m; (of visa, contract) proroga f; (of treaty) ampliamento m; (part of building) annesso m; (length of cable) prolunga f; (Teleph) interno m; **~ 226** interno 226

extensive /ɪk'stensɪv/ adj ampio, vasto. **~ly** adv ampiamente

extent /ɪk'stent/ n (scope) portata f; **to a certain ~** fino a un certo punto; **to such an ~ that...** fino al punto che...

exterior /ɪk'stɪərɪə(r)/ adj & n esterno m

exterminat|e /ɪk'stɜ:mɪneɪt/ vt sterminare. **~ion** n sterminio m

external /ɪk'stɜ:nl/ adj esterno; **for ~ use only** (Med) per uso esterno. **~ly** adv esternamente

extinct /ɪk'stɪŋkt/ adj estinto. **~ion** n estinzione f

extinguish /ɪk'stɪŋgwɪʃ/ vt estinguere. **~er** n estintore m

extort /ɪk'stɔ:t/ vt estorcere. **~ion** n estorsione f

extortionate /ɪk'stɔ:ʃənət/ adj esorbitante

extra /'ekstrə/ adj in più; (train) straordinario; **an ~ £10** 10 sterline extra, 10 sterline in più •adv in più; (especially) più; **pay ~** pagare in più, pagare extra; **~ strong/busy** fortissimo/occupatissimo •n (Theat) comparsa f; **~s** pl extra mpl

extract[1] /'ekstrækt/ n estratto m

extract[2] /ɪk'strækt/ vt estrarre (tooth, oil); strappare (secret); ricavare (truth). **~or [fan]** n aspiratore m

extradit|e /'ekstrədaɪt/ vt (Jur) estradare. **~ion** n estradizione f

extraordinar|y /ɪk'strɔ:dɪnərɪ/ adj straordinario. **~ily** adv straordinariamente

extravagan|ce /ɪk'strævəgəns/ n

(with money) prodigalità f; (of behaviour) stravaganza f. ~t adj spendaccione; (bizarre) stravagante; (claim) esagerato

extrem|e /ɪk'striːm/ adj estremo • n estremo m; **in the ~e** al massimo. **~ely** adv estremamente. **~ist** n estremista mf

extricate /'ekstrɪkeɪt/ vt districare

extrovert /'ekstrəvɜːt/ n estroverso, -a mf

exuberant /ɪg'zjuːbərənt/ adj esuberante

exude /ɪg'zjuːd/ vt also fig trasudare

exult /ɪg'zʌlt/ vi esultare

eye /aɪ/ n occhio m; (of needle) cruna f; **keep an ~ on** tener d'occhio; **see ~ to ~** aver le stesse idee • vt (pt/pp **eyed**, pres p **ey[e]ing**) guardare

eye: ~ball n bulbo m oculare. **~brow** n sopracciglio m (pl sopracciglia f). **~lash** n ciglio m (pl ciglia f). **~lid** n palpebra f. **~-opener** n rivelazione f. **~-shadow** n ombretto m. **~sight** n vista f. **~sore** n [!] pugno m nell'occhio. **~witness** n testimone mf oculare

Ff

fable /'feɪbl/ n favola f

fabric /'fæbrɪk/ n also fig tessuto m

fabulous /'fæbjʊləs/ adj [!] favoloso

façade /fə'sɑːd/ n (of building, person) facciata f

face /feɪs/ n faccia f, viso m; (grimace) smorfia f; (surface) faccia f; (of clock) quadrante m; **pull ~s** far boccacce; **in the ~ of** di fronte a; **on the ~ of it** in apparenza • vt essere di fronte a; (confront) affrontare; **~ north** (house:) dare a nord; **~ the fact that** arrendersi al fatto che. □ **~ up to** vt accettare (facts); affrontare (person)

face: ~-flannel n ≈ guanto m di spugna. **~less** adj anonimo. **~-lift** n plastica f facciale

facetious /fə'siːʃəs/ adj spiritoso. **~ remarks** spiritosaggini mpl

facial /'feɪʃl/ adj facciale • n trattamento m di bellezza al viso

facile /'fæsaɪl/ adj semplicistico

facilitate /fə'sɪlɪteɪt/ vt rendere possibile; (make easier) facilitare

facilit|y /fə'sɪlətɪ/ n facilità f; **~ies** pl (of area, in hotel etc) attrezzature fpl

fact /fækt/ n fatto m; **in ~** infatti

faction /'fækʃn/ n fazione f

factor /'fæktə(r)/ n fattore m

factory /'fæktərɪ/ n fabbrica f

factual /'fæktʃʊəl/ adj **be ~** attenersi ai fatti. **~ly** adv (inaccurate) dal punto di vista dei fatti

faculty /'fækəltɪ/ n facoltà f inv

fad /fæd/ n capriccio m

fade /feɪd/ vi sbiadire; (sound, light:) affievolirsi; (flower:) appassire. □ **~ in** vt cominciare in dissolvenza (picture). □ **~ out** vt finire in dissolvenza (picture)

fag /fæg/ n (chore) fatica f; ([!]: cigarette) sigaretta f; (Am [x]: homosexual) frocio m. **~ end** n [!] cicca f

Fahrenheit /'færənhaɪt/ adj Fahrenheit

fail /feɪl/ n **without ~** senz'altro • vi (attempt:) fallire; (eyesight, memory:) indebolirsi; (engine, machine:) guastarsi; (marriage:) andare a rotoli; (in exam) essere bocciato; **~ to do sth** non fare qcsa; **I tried but I ~ed** ho provato ma non ci sono riuscito • vt non superare (exam); bocciare (candidate); (disappoint) deludere; **words ~ me** mi mancano le parole

failing /'feɪlɪŋ/ n difetto m • prep **~ that** altrimenti

failure /'feɪljə(r)/ n fallimento m; (mechanical) guasto m; (person) incapace mf

faint /feɪnt/ adj leggero; (memory) vago; **feel ~** sentirsi mancare • n svenimento m • vi svenire

faint: ~-'hearted adj timido. **~ly** adv (slightly) leggermente

fair[1] /feə(r)/ n fiera f

fair[2] adj (hair, person) biondo; (skin) chiaro; (weather) bello; (just) giusto; (quite good) discreto; (Sch) abbastanza bene; **a ~ amount** abbastanza • adv **play ~** fare un gioco pulito. **~ly** adv con giustizia; (rather) discretamente, abbastanza. **~ness** n giustizia f. **~ play** n fair play m inv

f

fairy /'feərɪ/ n fata f; **~ story, ~-tale** n fiaba f

faith /feɪθ/ n fede f; (trust) fiducia f; **in good/bad ~** in buona/mala fede

faithful /'feɪθfl/ adj fedele. **~ly** adv fedelmente; **yours ~ly** distinti saluti. **~ness** n fedeltà f

fake /feɪk/ adj falso • n falsificazione f; (person) impostore m • vt falsificare; (pretend) fingere

falcon /'fɔːlkən/ n falcone m

fall /fɔːl/ n caduta f; (in prices) ribasso m; (Am: autumn) autunno m; **have a ~** fare una caduta • vi (pt **fell**, pp **fallen**) cadere; (night:) scendere; **~ in love** innamorarsi. □ **~ about** vi (with laughter) morire dal ridere. □ **~ back on** vt ritornare su. □ **~ for** vt [!] innamorarsi di (person); cascarci (sth, trick). □ **~ down** vi cadere; (building:) crollare. □ **~ in** vi caderci dentro; (collapse) crollare; (Mil) mettersi in riga; **~ in with** concordare con (suggestion, plan). □ **~ off** vi cadere; (diminish) diminuire. □ **~ out** vi (quarrel) litigare; **his hair is ~ing out** perde i capelli. □ **~ over** vi cadere. □ **~ through** vi (plan:) andare a monte

fallacy /'fæləsɪ/ n errore m

fallible /'fæləbl/ adj fallibile

'fall-out n pioggia f radioattiva

false /fɔːls/ adj falso; **~ bottom** doppio fondo m; **~ start** (Sport) falsa partenza f. **~hood** n menzogna f. **~ness** n falsità f

false 'teeth npl dentiera f

falsify /'fɔːlsɪfaɪ/ vt (pt/pp **-ied**) falsificare

falter /'fɔːltə(r)/ vi vacillare; (making speech) esitare

fame /feɪm/ n fama f

familiar /fə'mɪljə(r)/ adj familiare; **be ~ with** (know) conoscere. **~ity** n familiarità f. **~ize** vt familiarizzare; **~ize oneself with** familiarizzarsi con

family /'fæməlɪ/ n famiglia f

family: ~ 'planning n pianificazione f familiare. **~ 'tree** n albero m genealogico

famine /'fæmɪn/ n carestia f

famished /'fæmɪʃt/ adj **be ~** [!] avere una fame da lupo

famous /'feɪməs/ adj famoso

fan[1] /fæn/ n ventilatore m; (handheld) ventaglio m • vt (pt/pp **fanned**) far vento a; **~ oneself** sventagliarsi; fig **~ the flames** soffiare sul fuoco. □ **~ out** vi spiegarsi a ventaglio

fan[2] n (admirer) ammiratore, -trice mf; (Sport) tifoso m; (of Verdi etc) appassionato, -a mf

fanatic /fə'nætɪk/ n fanatico, -a mf. **~al** adj fanatico. **~ism** n fanatismo m

'fan belt n cinghia f per ventilatore

fanciful /'fænsɪfl/ adj fantasioso

fancy /'fænsɪ/ n fantasia f; **I've taken a real ~ to him** mi è molto simpatico; **as the ~ takes you** come ti pare • adj [a] fantasia • vt (pt/pp **-ied**) (believe) credere; ([!]: want) aver voglia di; **he fancies you** [!] gli piaci; **~ that!** ma guarda un po'! **~ 'dress** n costume m (per maschera)

fanfare /'fænfeə(r)/ n fanfara f

fang /fæŋ/ n zanna f; (of snake) dente m

fantas|ize /'fæntəsaɪz/ vi fantasticare. **~tic** adj fantastico. **~y** n fantasia f

far /fɑː(r)/ adv lontano; (much) molto; **by ~** di gran lunga; **~ away** lontano; **as ~ as the church** fino alla chiesa; **how ~ is it from here?** quanto dista da qui?; **as ~ as I know** per quanto io sappia • adj (end, side) altro; **the F~ East** l'Estremo Oriente m

farc|e /fɑːs/ n farsa f. **~ical** adj ridicolo

fare /feə(r)/ n tariffa f; (food) vitto m.

~-dodger n passeggero, -a mf senza biglietto

farewell /feə'wel/ int liter addio! • n addio m

far-'fetched adj improbabile

farm /fɑ:m/ n fattoria f • vi fare l'agricoltore • vt coltivare (land). **~er** n agricoltore m

farm: ~house n casa f colonica. **~ing** n agricoltura f. **~yard** n aia f

far: ~-'reaching adj di larga portata. **~-'sighted** adj fig prudente; (Am: long-sighted) presbite

farther /'fɑ:ðə(r)/ adv più lontano • adj **at the ~ end of** all'altra estremità di

fascinat|e /'fæsɪneɪt/ vt affascinare. **~ing** adj affascinante. **~ion** n fascino m

fascis|m /'fæʃɪzm/ n fascismo m. **~t** n fascista mf • adj fascista

fashion /'fæʃn/ n moda f; (manner) maniera f • vt modellare. **~able** adj di moda; **be ~able** essere alla moda. **~ably** adv alla moda

fast[1] /fɑ:st/ adj veloce; (colour) indelebile; **be ~** (clock:) andare avanti • adv velocemente; (firmly) saldamente; **~er!** più in fretta!; **be ~ asleep** dormire profondamente

fast[2] n digiuno m • vi digiunare

fasten /'fɑ:sn/ vt allacciare; chiudere (window); (stop flapping) mettere un fermo a • vi allacciarsi. **~er** n, **~ing** n chiusura f

fat /fæt/ adj (**fatter, fattest**) (person, cheque) grasso • n grasso m

fatal /'feɪtl/ adj mortale; (error) fatale. **~ism** n fatalismo m. **~ist** n fatalista mf. **~ity** n morte f. **~ly** adv mortalmente

fate /feɪt/ n destino m. **~ful** adj fatidico

father /'fɑ:ðə(r)/ n padre m; **F~ Christmas** Babbo m Natale • vt generare (child)

father: ~hood n paternità f. **~-in-law** n (pl **~s-in-law**) suocero m. **~ly** adj paterno

fathom /'fæð(ə)m/ n (Naut) braccio m • vt **~ [out]** comprendere

fatigue /fə'ti:g/ n fatica f

fatten /'fætn/ vt ingrassare (animal). **~ing** adj **cream is ~ing** la panna fa ingrassare

fatty /'fætɪ/ adj grasso • n [!] ciccione, -a mf

fatuous /'fætjʊəs/ adj fatuo

faucet /'fɔ:sɪt/ n Am rubinetto m

fault /fɔ:lt/ n difetto m; (Geol) faglia f; (Tennis) fallo m; **be at ~** avere torto; **find ~ with** trovare da ridire su; **it's your ~** è colpa tua • vt criticare. **~less** adj impeccabile

faulty /'fɔ:ltɪ/ adj difettoso

favour /'feɪvə(r)/ n favore m; **be in ~ of sth** essere a favore di qcsa; **do sb a ~** fare un piacere a qcno • vt (prefer) preferire. **~able** adj favorevole

favourit|e /'feɪv(ə)rɪt/ adj preferito • n preferito, -a mf; (Sport) favorito, -a mf. **~ism** n favoritismo m

fawn /fɔ:n/ adj fulvo • n (animal) cerbiatto m

fax /fæks/ n (document, machine) fax m inv; **by ~** per fax • vt faxare. **~ machine** n fax m inv. **~-modem** n modem-fax m inv, fax-modem m inv

fear /fɪə(r)/ n paura f; **no ~!** [!] vai tranquillo! • vt temere • vi **~ for sth** temere per qcsa

fear|ful /'fɪəfl/ adj pauroso; (awful) terribile. **~less** adj impavido. **~some** adj spaventoso

feas|ibility /fi:zɪ'bɪlɪtɪ/ n praticabilità f. **~ible** adj fattibile; (possible) probabile

feast /fi:st/ n festa f; (banquet) banchetto m • vi banchettare; **~ on** godersi

feat /fi:t/ n impresa f

feather /'feðə(r)/ n piuma f

feature /'fi:tʃə(r)/ n (quality) caratteristica f; (Journ) articolo m; **~s** (pl: of face) lineamenti mpl • vt (film:) avere come protagonista • vi (on a list etc) comparire. **~ film** n lungometraggio m

February /'febrʊərɪ/ n febbraio m

fed /fed/ ▸**feed** • adj **be ~ up** [!] essere stufo (**with** di)

federal /'fed(ə)rəl/ adj federale

federation /fedə'reɪʃn/ n federazione f

fee /fi:/ n tariffa f; (lawyer's, doctor's)

f

onorario m; (for membership, school) quota f

feeble /'fi:bl/ adj debole; (excuse) fiacco

feed /fi:d/ n mangiare m; (for baby) pappa f • v (pt/pp **fed**) • vt dar da mangiare a (animal); (support) nutrire; **~ sth into sth** inserire qcsa in qcsa • vi mangiare

'feedback n controreazione f; (of information) reazione f, feedback m

feel /fi:l/ v (pt/pp **felt**) • vt sentire; (experience) provare; (think) pensare; (touch: searching) tastare; (touch: for texture) toccare • vi **~ soft/hard** essere duro/morbido al tatto; **~ hot/hungry** aver caldo/fame; **~ ill** sentirsi male; **I don't ~ like it** non ne ho voglia; **how do you ~ about it?** (opinion) che te ne pare?; **it doesn't ~ right** non mi sembra giusto. **~er** n (of animal) antenna f; **put out ~ers** fig tastare il terreno. **~ing** n sentimento m; (awareness) sensazione f

feet /fi:t/ ▸**foot**

feign /feɪn/ vt simulare

fell[1] /fel/ vt (knock down) abbattere

fell[2] ▸**fall**

fellow /'feləʊ/ n (of society) socio m; (❗: man) tipo m

fellow 'countryman n compatriota m

felony /'felənɪ/ n delitto m

felt[1] /felt/ ▸**feel**

felt[2] n feltro m. **~[-tipped] 'pen** /[-tɪpt]/ n pennarello m

female /'fi:meɪl/ adj femminile; **the ~ antelope** l'antilope femmina • n femmina f

femin|ine /'femɪnɪn/ adj femminile • n (Gram) femminile m. **~inity** n femminilità f. **~ist** adj & n femminista mf

fenc|e /fens/ n recinto m; (❗: person) ricettatore m • vi (Sport) tirar di scherma. □ **~ in** vt chiudere in un recinto. **~er** n schermidore m. **~ing** n steccato m; (Sport) scherma f

fend /fend/ vi **~ for oneself** badare a se stesso. □ **~ off** vt parare; difendersi da (criticisms)

fender /'fendə(r)/ n parafuoco m inv; (Am: on car) parafango m

fennel /'fenl/ n finocchio m

ferment[1] /'fɜ:ment/ n fermento m

ferment[2] /fə'ment/ vi fermentare • vt far fermentare. **~ation** n fermentazione f

fern /fɜ:n/ n felce f

feroc|ious /fə'rəʊʃəs/ adj feroce. **~ity** n ferocia f

ferret /'ferɪt/ n furetto m • **ferret out** vt scovare

ferry /'ferɪ/ n traghetto m • vt traghettare

fertil|e /'fɜ:taɪl/ adj fertile. **~ity** n fertilità f

fertilize /'fɜ:tɪlaɪz/ vt fertilizzare (land, ovum). **~r** n fertilizzante m

fervent /'fɜ:vənt/ adj fervente

fervour /'fɜ:və(r)/ n fervore m

fester /'festə(r)/ vi suppurare

festival /'festɪvl/ n (Mus, Theat) festival m; (Relig) festa f

festiv|e /'festɪv/ adj festivo; **~e season** periodo m delle feste natalizie. **~ities** npl festeggiamenti m

fetch /fetʃ/ vt andare/venire a prendere; (be sold for) raggiungere [il prezzo di]

fetching /'fetʃɪŋ/ adj attraente

fête /feɪt/ n festa f • vt festeggiare

fetish /'fetɪʃ/ n feticcio m

fetter /'fetə(r)/ vt incatenare

feud /fju:d/ n faida f

feudal /'fju:dl/ adj feudale

fever /'fi:və(r)/ n febbre f. **~ish** adj febbricitante; fig febbrile

few /fju:/ adj pochi; **every ~ days** ogni due o tre giorni; **a ~ people** alcuni; **~er reservations** meno prenotazioni; **the ~est number** il numero più basso • pron pochi; **~ of us** pochi di noi; **a ~** alcuni; **quite a ~** parecchi; **~er than last year** meno dell'anno scorso

fiancé /fɪ'ɒnseɪ/ n fidanzato m. **~e** n fidanzata f

fiasco /fɪ'æskəʊ/ n fiasco m

fib /fɪb/ n storia f; **tell a ~** raccontare una storia

fibre /'faɪbə(r)/ n fibra f. **~glass** n fibra f di vetro

fickle /'fɪkl/ adj incostante

fiction /'fɪkʃn/ n [**works of**] ~ narrativa f; (fabrication) finzione f. **~al** adj immaginario

fictitious /fɪk'tɪʃəs/ adj fittizio

fiddle /'fɪdl/ n ! violino m; (cheating) imbroglio m •vi gingillarsi (**with** con) •vt ! truccare (accounts)

fidget /'fɪdʒɪt/ vi agitarsi. **~y** adj agitato

field /fi:ld/ n campo m

field: ~-glasses npl binocolo msg. **F~ 'Marshal** n feldmaresciallo m. **~work** n ricerche fpl sul terreno

fiend /fi:nd/ n demonio m

fierce /fɪəs/ adj feroce. **~ness** n ferocia f

fiery /'faɪərɪ/ adj (**-ier, -iest**) focoso

fifteen /fɪf'ti:n/ adj & n quindici m. **~th** adj quindicesimo

fifth /fɪfθ/ adj quinto

fiftieth /'fɪftɪɪθ/ adj cinquantesimo

fifty /'fɪftɪ/ adj cinquanta

fig /fɪg/ n fico m

fight /faɪt/ n lotta f; (brawl) zuffa f; (argument) litigio m; (boxing) incontro m •v (pt/pp **fought**) •vt also fig combattere •vi combattere; (brawl) azzuffarsi; (argue) litigare. **~er** n combattente mf; (Aeron) caccia m inv. **~ing** n combattimento m

figment /'fɪgmənt/ n **it's a ~ of your imagination** questo è tutta una tua invenzione

figurative /'fɪgjərətɪv/ adj (sense) figurato; (art) figurativo

figure /'fɪgə(r)/ n (digit) cifra f; (carving, sculpture, illustration, form) figura f; (body shape) linea f; **~ of speech** modo m di dire •vi (appear) figurare •vt (Am: think) pensare. □ **~ out** vt dedurre; capire (person)

figurehead n figura f simbolica

file[1] /faɪl/ n scheda f; (set of documents) incartamento m; (folder) cartellina f; (Comput) file m inv •vt archiviare (documents)

file[2] n (line) fila f; **in single ~** in fila

file[3] n (Techn) lima f •vt limare

filing cabinet /'faɪlɪŋkæbɪnət/ n schedario m, classificatore m

fill /fɪl/ n **eat one's ~** mangiare a sazietà •vt riempire; otturare (tooth) •vi riempirsi. □ **~ in** vt compilare (form). □ **~ out** vt compilare (form). □ **~ up** vi (room, tank:) riempirsi; (Auto) far il pieno •vt riempire

fillet /'fɪlɪt/ n filetto m •vt (pt/pp **filleted**) disossare

filling /'fɪlɪŋ/ n (Culin) ripieno m; (of tooth) piombatura f. **~ station** n stazione f di rifornimento

film /fɪlm/ n (Cinema) film m inv; (Phot) pellicola f; [**cling**] ~ pellicola f per alimenti •vt/i filmare. **~ star** n star f inv, divo, -a mf

filter /'fɪltə(r)/ n filtro m •vt filtrare. □ **~ through** vi (news:) trapelare. **~ tip** n filtro m; (cigarette) sigaretta f col filtro

filth /fɪlθ/ n sudiciume m. **~y** adj (**-ier, -iest**) sudicio; (word) sconcio

fin /fɪn/ n pinna f

final /'faɪnl/ adj finale; (conclusive) decisivo •n (Sport) finale f; **~s** pl (Univ) esami mpl finali

finale /fɪ'nɑ:lɪ/ n finale m

final|ist /'faɪnəlɪst/ n finalista mf. **~ity** n finalità f

final|ize /'faɪnəlaɪz/ vt mettere a punto (text); definire (agreement). **~ly** adv (at last) finalmente; (at the end) alla fine; (to conclude) per finire

finance /'faɪnæns/ n finanza f •vt finanziare

financial /faɪ'nænʃl/ adj finanziario

find /faɪnd/ n scoperta f •vt (pt/pp **found**) trovare; (establish) scoprire; **~ sb guilty** (Jur) dichiarare qcno colpevole. □ **~ out** vt scoprire •vi (enquire) informarsi

findings /'faɪndɪŋz/ npl conclusioni fpl

fine[1] /faɪn/ n (penalty) multa f •vt multare

fine[2] adj bello; (slender) fine; **he's ~** (in health) sta bene. **~ arts** npl belle arti fpl. •adv bene; **that's cutting it ~** non ci lascia molto tempo •int [va] bene. **~ly** adv (cut) finemente

finger /'fɪŋgə(r)/ n dito m (pl dita f) •vt tastare

finger: ~nail n unghia f. **~print** n impronta f digitale. **~tip** n punta f del dito; **have sth at one's ~tips** sapere qcsa a menadito; (close at

f

hand) avere qcsa a portata di mano

finish /ˈfɪnɪʃ/ n fine f; (finishing line) traguardo m; (of product) finitura f; **have a good ~** (runner:) avere un buon finale •vt finire; **~ reading** finire di leggere •vi finire

finite /ˈfaɪnaɪt/ adj limitato

Finland /ˈfɪnlənd/ n Finlandia f

Finn /fɪn/ n finlandese mf. **~ish** adj finlandese •n (language) finnico m

f

fiord /fjɔːd/ n fiordo m

fir /fɜː(r)/ n abete m

fire /ˈfaɪə(r)/ n fuoco m; (forest, house) incendio m; **be on ~** bruciare; **catch ~** prendere fuoco; **set ~ to** dar fuoco a; **under ~** sotto il fuoco •vt cuocere (pottery); sparare (shot); tirare (gun); (ⓘ: dismiss) buttar fuori •vi sparare (**at** a)

fire: ~ alarm n allarme m antincendio. **~arm** n arma f da fuoco. **~ brigade** n vigili mpl del fuoco. **~-engine** n autopompa f. **~-escape** n uscita f di sicurezza. **~ extinguisher** n estintore m. **~man** n pompiere m, vigile m del fuoco. **~place** n caminetto m. **~side** n **by** or **at the ~side** accanto al fuoco. **~wood** n legna f (da ardere). **~work** n fuoco m d'artificio

firm¹ /fɜːm/ n ditta f, azienda f

firm² adj fermo; (soil) compatto; (stable, properly fixed) solido; (resolute) risoluto. **~ly** adv (hold) stretto; (say) con fermezza

first /fɜːst/ adj & n primo, -a mf; **at ~** all'inizio; **who's ~?** chi è il primo?; **from the ~** [fin] dall'inizio •adv (arrive, leave) per primo; (beforehand) prima; (in listing) prima di tutto, innanzitutto

first: ~ 'aid n pronto soccorso m. **~-'aid kit** n cassetta f di pronto soccorso. **~-class** adj di prim'ordine; (Rail) di prima classe •adv (travel) in prima classe. **~ 'floor** n primo piano m; (Am: ground floor) pianterreno m. **~ly** adv in primo luogo. **~ name** n nome m di battesimo. **~-rate** adj ottimo

fish /fɪʃ/ n pesce m •vt/i pescare. ▫ **~ out** vt tirar fuori

fish: ~erman n pescatore m. **~ 'finger** n bastoncino m di pesce

fishing /ˈfɪʃɪŋ/ n pesca f. **~ boat** n peschereccio m. **~-rod** n canna f da pesca

fish: ~monger /-mʌŋgə(r)/ n pescivendolo m. **~y** adj (ⓘ: suspicious) sospetto

fission /ˈfɪʃn/ n (Phys) fissione f

fist /fɪst/ n pugno m

fit¹ /fɪt/ n (attack) attacco m; (of rage) accesso m; (of generosity) slancio m

fit² adj (**fitter, fittest**) (suitable) adatto; (healthy) in buona salute; (Sport) in forma; **be ~ to do sth** essere in grado di fare qcsa; **~ to eat** buono da mangiare; **keep ~** tenersi in forma

fit³ n (of clothes) taglio m; **it's a good ~** (coat) etc: ti/le sta bene •v (pt/pp **fitted**) •vi (be the right size) andare bene; **it won't ~** (no room) non ci sta •vt (fix) applicare (**to** a); (install) installare; **it doesn't ~ me** (coat etc:) non mi va bene; **~ with** fornire di. ▫ **~ in** vi (person:) adattarsi; **it won't ~ in** (no room) non ci sta •vt (in schedule, vehicle) trovare un buco per

fit|ful /ˈfɪtfl/ adj irregolare. **~fully** adv (sleep) a sprazzi. **~ments** npl (in house) impianti mpl fissi. **~ness** n (suitability) capacità f; [**physical**] **~ness** forma f, fitness m

fitting /ˈfɪtɪŋ/ adj appropriato •n (of clothes) prova f; (Techn) montaggio m; **~s** pl accessori mpl. **~ room** n camerino m

five /faɪv/ adj & n cinque m. **~r** n ⓘ biglietto m da cinque sterline

fix /fɪks/ n (ⓧ: drugs) pera f; **be in a ~** ⓘ essere nei guai •vt fissare; (repair) aggiustare; preparare (meal). ▫ **~ up** vt fissare (meeting)

fixed /fɪkst/ adj fisso

fixture /ˈfɪkstʃə(r)/ n (Sport) incontro m; **~s and fittings** impianti mpl fissi

fizz /fɪz/ vi frizzare

fizzle /ˈfɪzl/ vi **~ out** finire in nulla

fizzy /ˈfɪzɪ/ adj gassoso. **~ drink** n bibita f gassata

flabbergasted /ˈflæbəgɑːstɪd/ adj **be ~** rimanere a bocca aperta

flabby /ˈflæbɪ/ adj floscio

flag¹ /flæg/ n bandiera f •**flag down**

vt (pt/pp **flagged**) far segno di fermarsi a (taxi)

lag² vi (pt/pp **flagged**) cedere

lag-pole n asta f della bandiera

lagrant /ˈfleɪgrənt/ adj flagrante

lair /fleə(r)/ n (skill) talento m; (style) stile m

lake /fleɪk/ n fiocco m •vi ~ [**off**] cadere in fiocchi

laky /ˈfleɪkɪ/ adj a scaglie. ~ **pastry** n pasta f sfoglia

lamboyant /flæmˈbɔɪənt/ adj (personality) brillante; (tie) sgargiante

lame /fleɪm/ n fiamma f

lammable /ˈflæməbl/ adj infiammabile

lan /flæn/ n [**fruit**] ~ crostata f

lank /flæŋk/ n fianco m •vt fiancheggiare

lannel /ˈflæn(ə)l/ n flanella f; (for washing) ≈ guanto m di spugna; ~**s** (trousers) pantaloni mpl di flanella

lap /flæp/ n (of pocket, envelope) risvolto m; (of table) ribalta f; **in a** ~ [!] in grande agitazione •v (pt/pp **flapped**) •vi sbattere; [!] agitarsi •vt ~ **its wings** battere le ali

lare /fleə(r)/ n fiammata f; (device) razzo m •**flare up** vi (rash:) venire fuori; (fire:) fare una fiammata; (person, situation:) esplodere. ~**d** adj (garment) svasato

lash /flæʃ/ n lampo m; **in a** ~ [!] in un attimo •vi lampeggiare; ~ **past** passare come un bolide •vt lanciare (smile); ~ **one's head-lights** lampeggiare; ~ **a torch at** puntare una torcia su

lash: ~**back** n scena f retrospettiva. ~**light** n (Phot) flash m inv; (Am: torch) torcia f [elettrica]. ~**y** adj vistoso

lask /flɑːsk/ n fiasco m; (vacuum ~) termos m inv

lat /flæt/ adj (**flatter, flattest**) piatto; (refusal) reciso; (beer) sgassato; (battery) scarico; (tyre) a terra; **A** ~ (Mus) la bemolle •n appartamento m; (Mus) bemolle m; (puncture) gomma f a terra

lat: ~**ly** adv (refuse) categoricamente. ~ **rate** n tariffa f unica

latten /ˈflætn/ vt appiattire

flatter /ˈflætə(r)/ vt adulare. ~**ing** adj (comments) lusinghiero; (colour, dress) che fa sembrare più bello. ~**y** n adulazione f

flaunt /flɔːnt/ vt ostentare

flavour /ˈfleɪvə(r)/ n sapore m •vt condire; **chocolate** ~**ed** al sapore di cioccolato. ~**ing** n condimento m

flaw /flɔː/ n difetto m. ~**less** adj perfetto

flea /fliː/ n pulce m. ~ **market** n mercato m delle pulci

fleck /flek/ n macchiolina f

fled /fled/ ▹**flee**

flee /fliː/ vt/i (pt/pp **fled**) fuggire (**from** da)

fleec|e /fliːs/ n pelliccia f •vt [!] spennare. ~**y** adj (lining) felpato

fleet /fliːt/ n flotta f; (of cars) parco m

fleeting /ˈfliːtɪŋ/ adj **catch a** ~ **glance of sth** intravedere qcsa; **for a** ~ **moment** per un attimo

flesh /fleʃ/ n carne f; **in the** ~ in persona. ~**y** adj carnoso

flew /fluː/ ▹**fly²**

flex¹ /fleks/ vt flettere (muscle)

flex² n (Electr) filo m

flexib|ility /fleksɪˈbɪlətɪ/ n flessibilità f. ~**le** adj flessibile

ˈ**flexitime** /ˈfleksɪ-/ n orario m flessibile

flick /flɪk/ vt dare un buffetto a; ~ **sth off sth** togliere qcsa da qcsa con un colpetto. □ ~ **through** vt sfogliare

flicker /ˈflɪkə(r)/ vi tremolare

flight¹ /flaɪt/ n (fleeing) fuga f; **take** ~ darsi alla fuga

flight² n (flying) volo m; ~ **of stairs** rampa f

flight recorder n registratore m di volo

flimsy /ˈflɪmzɪ/ adj (**-ier, -iest**) (material) leggero; (shelves) poco robusto; (excuse) debole

flinch /flɪntʃ/ vi (wince) sussultare; (draw back) ritirarsi; ~ **from a task** fig sottrarsi a un compito

fling /flɪŋ/ n **have a** ~ ([!]: affair) aver un'avventura •vt (pt/pp **flung**) gettare

flint /flɪnt/ n pietra f focaia; (for lighter) pietrina f

flip /flɪp/ v (pt/pp **flipped**) •vt dare un colpetto a; buttare in aria (coin) •vi [!] uscire dai gangheri; (go mad) impazzire. □ ~ **through** vt sfogliare

flippant /ˈflɪpənt/ adj irriverente

flipper /ˈflɪpə(r)/ n pinna f

flirt /flɜːt/ n civetta f •vi flirtare

flit /flɪt/ vi (pt/pp **flitted**) volteggiare

f

float /fləʊt/ n galleggiante m; (in procession) carro m; (money) riserva f di cassa •vi galleggiare; (Fin) fluttuare

flock /flɒk/ n gregge m; (of birds) stormo m •vi affollarsi

flog /flɒg/ vt (pt/pp **flogged**) bastonare; ([!]: sell) vendere

flood /flʌd/ n alluvione f; (of river) straripamento m; (fig: of replies, letters, tears) diluvio m; **be in** ~ (river:) essere straripato •vt allagare •vi (river:) straripare

ˈ**floodlight** n riflettore m •vt (pt/pp **floodlit**) illuminare con riflettori

floor /flɔː(r)/ n pavimento m; (storey) piano m; (for dancing) pista f •vt (baffle) confondere; (knock down) stendere (person)

floor polish n cera f per il pavimento

flop /flɒp/ n [!] (failure) tonfo m; (Theat) fiasco m •vi (pt/pp **flopped**) ([!]: fail) far fiasco. □ ~ **down** vi accasciarsi

floppy /ˈflɒpɪ/ adj floscio. ~ ˈ**disk** n floppy disk m inv. ~ [**disk**] **drive** n lettore di floppy m

floral /ˈflɔːrəl/ adj floreale

florid /ˈflɒrɪd/ adj (complexion) florido; (style) troppo ricercato

florist /ˈflɒrɪst/ n fioraio, -a mf

flounder[1] /ˈflaʊndə(r)/ vi dibattersi; (speaker:) impappinarsi

flounder[2] n (fish) passera f di mare

flour /ˈflaʊə(r)/ n farina f

flourish /ˈflʌrɪʃ/ n gesto m drammatico; (scroll) ghirigoro m •vi prosperare •vt brandire

flout /flaʊt/ vt fregarsene di (rules)

flow /fləʊ/ n flusso m •vi scorrere; (hang loosely) ricadere

flower /ˈflaʊə(r)/ n fiore m •vi fiorire

flower: ~-**bed** n aiuola f. ~**y** adj fiorito

flown /fləʊn/ ▸**fly**[2]

flu /fluː/ n influenza f

fluctuat|e /ˈflʌktjʊeɪt/ vi fluttuare. ~**ion** n fluttuazione f

fluent /ˈfluːənt/ adj spedito; **speak** ~ **Italian** parlare correntemente l'italiano. ~**ly** adv speditamente

fluff /flʌf/ n peluria f. ~**y** adj (**-ier, -iest**) vaporoso; (toy) di peluche

fluid /ˈfluːɪd/ adj fluido•n fluido m

flung /flʌŋ/ ▸**fling**

fluorescent /flʊəˈresnt/ adj fluorescente

flush /flʌʃ/ n (blush) [vampata f di] rossore m •vi arrossire •vt lavare con un getto d'acqua; ~ **the toilet** tirare l'acqua •adj a livello (**with** di); ([!]: affluent) a soldi

flute /fluːt/ n flauto m

flutter /ˈflʌtə(r)/ n battito m •vi svolazzare

flux /flʌks/ n **in a state of** ~ in uno stato di flusso

fly[1] /flaɪ/ n (pl **flies**) mosca f

fly[2] v (pt **flew**, pp **flown**) •vi volare; (go by plane) andare in aereo; (flag:) sventolare; (rush) precipitarsi; ~ **open** spalancarsi •vt pilotare (plane); trasportare [in aereo] (troops, supplies); volare con (Alitalia etc)

fly[3] n (pl **flies**, on trousers) patta f

flying /ˈflaɪɪŋ/: ~ ˈ**buttress** n arco m rampante. ~ ˈ**colours: with** ~ **colours** a pieni voti. ~ ˈ**saucer** n disco m volante. ~ ˈ**start** n **get off to a** ~ **start** fare un'ottima partenza. ~ ˈ**visit** n visita f lampo

fly: ~ **leaf** n risguardo m. ~**over** n cavalcavia m inv

foal /fəʊl/ n puledro m

foam /fəʊm/ n schiuma f; (synthetic) gommapiuma® f •vi spumare; ~ **at the mouth** far la bava alla bocca. ~ ˈ**rubber** n gommapiuma® f

fob /fɒb/ vt (pt/pp **fobbed**) ~ **sth off** affibbiare qcsa (**on sb** a qcno); ~ **sb off** liquidare qcno

focal /ˈfəʊkl/ adj focale

focus /ˈfəʊkəs/ n fuoco m; **in** ~ a fuoco; **out of** ~ sfocato •v (pt/pp **focused** or **focussed**) •vt fig concentrare (**on** su) • vi (Phot) ~ **on** mettere a fuoco; fig concentrarsi (**on** su)

odder /'fɒdə(r)/ n foraggio m

oe /fəʊ/ n nemico, -a mf

oetus /'fi:təs/ n (pl **-tuses**) feto m

og /fɒg/ n nebbia f

oggy /'fɒgɪ/ adj (**foggier, foggiest**) nebbioso; **it's** ~ c'è nebbia

'og-horn n sirena f da nebbia

oil[1] /fɔɪl/ n lamina f di metallo

oil[2] vt (thwart) frustrare

oil[3] n (sword) fioretto m

oist /fɔɪst/ vt appioppare (**on sb** a qcno)

old[1] /fəʊld/ n (for sheep) ovile m

old[2] n piega f• vt piegare; ~ **one's arms** incrociare le braccia • vi piegarsi; (fail) crollare. □~ **up** vt ripiegare (chair) • vi essere pieghevole; (business:) collassare

old|er /'fəʊldə(r)/ n cartella f. ~**ing** adj pieghevole

olk /fəʊk/ npl gente f; **my** ~**s** (family) i miei; **hello there** ~**s** ciao a tutti

olklore n folclore m

ollow /'fɒləʊ/ vt/i seguire; **it doesn't** ~ non è necessariamente così; ~ **suit** fig fare lo stesso; **as** ~**s** come segue. □~ **up** vt fare seguito a (letter)

ollow|er /'fɒləʊə(r)/ n seguace mf. ~**ing** adj seguente •n seguito m; (supporters) seguaci mpl • prep in seguito a

olly /'fɒlɪ/ n follia f

ond /fɒnd/ adj affezionato; (hope) vivo; **be** ~ **of** essere appassionato di (music); **I'm** ~ **of...** (food, person) mi piace moltissimo...

ondle /'fɒndl/ vt coccolare

ondness /'fɒndnɪs/ n affetto m; (for things) amore m

ont /fɒnt/ n fonte f battesimale; (Typ) carattere m di stampa

ood /fu:d/ n cibo m; (for animals, groceries) mangiare m; **let's buy some** ~ compriamo qualcosa da mangiare

ood processor n tritatutto m inv elettrico

ool[1] /fu:l/ n sciocco, -a mf; **she's no** ~ non è una stupida; **make a** ~ **of oneself** rendersi ridicolo • vt prendere in giro • vi ~ **around** giocare; (husband, wife:) avere l'amante

fool[2] n (Culin) crema f

'fool|hardy adj temerario. ~**ish** adj stolto. ~**ishly** adv scioccamente. ~**ishness** n sciocchezza f. ~**proof** adj facilissimo

foot /fʊt/ n (pl **feet**) piede m; (of animal) zampa f; (measure) piede m (= 30,48 cm); **on** ~ a piedi; **on one's feet** in piedi; **put one's** ~ **in it** [!] fare una gaffe

foot: ~**-and-'mouth disease** n afta f epizootica. ~**ball** n calcio m; (ball) pallone m. ~**baller** n giocatore m di calcio. ~**-bridge** n passerella f. ~**hills** npl colline fpl pedemontane. ~**hold** n punto m d'appoggio. ~**ing** n **lose one's** ~**ing** perdere l'appiglio; **on an equal** ~**ing** in condizioni di parità. ~**man** n valletto m. ~**note** n nota f a piè di pagina. ~**path** n sentiero m. ~**print** n orma f. ~**step** n passo m; **follow in sb's** ~**steps** fig seguire l'esempio di qcno. ~**wear** n calzature fpl

for /fə(r)/, *accentato* /fɔ:(r)/

• prep per; ~ **this reason** per questa ragione; **I have lived here** ~ **ten years** vivo qui da dieci anni; ~ **supper** per cena; ~ **all that** nonostante questo; **what** ~**?** a che scopo?; **send** ~ **a doctor** chiamare un dottore; **fight** ~ **a cause** lottare per una causa; **go** ~ **a walk** andare a fare una passeggiata; **there's no need** ~ **you to go** non c'è bisogno che tu vada; **it's not** ~ **me to say** non sta a me dirlo; **now you're** ~ **it** ora sei nei pasticci

• conj poiché, perché

forage /'fɒrɪdʒ/ n foraggio m • vi ~ **for** cercare

forbade /fə'bæd/ ▸**forbid**

forbear|ance /fɔ:'beərəns/ n pazienza f. ~**ing** adj tollerante

forbid /fə'bɪd/ vt (pt **forbade**, pp **forbidden**) proibire. ~**ding** adj (prospect) che spaventa; (stern) severo

force /fɔ:s/ n forza f; **in** ~ in vigore;

f

(in large numbers) in massa; **come into ~** entrare in vigore; **the** [**armed**] **~s** pl le forze armate • vt forzare; **~ sth on sb** (decision) imporre qcsa a qcno; (drink) costringere qcno a fare qcsa

forced /fɔ:st/ adj forzato

force: ~-'feed vt (pt/pp **-fed**) nutrire a forza. **~ful** adj energico

forceps /'fɔ:seps/ npl forcipe m

forcible /'fɔ:sɪbl/ adj forzato

ford /fɔ:d/ n guado m • vt guadare

fore /fɔ:(r)/ n **to the ~** in vista; **come to the ~** salire alla ribalta

fore: ~arm n avambraccio m. **~boding** /-'bəʊdɪŋ/ n presentimento m. **~cast** n previsione f • vt (pt/pp **~cast**) prevedere. **~court** n cortile m anteriore. **~finger** n [dito m] indice m. **~front** n **be in the ~front** essere all'avanguardia. **~gone** adj **be a ~gone conclusion** essere una cosa scontata. **~ground** n primo piano m. **~head** /'fɔ:hed/, /'fɒrɪd/ n fronte f

foreign /'fɒrən/ adj straniero; (trade) estero; (not belonging) estraneo; **he is ~** è uno straniero. **~ currency** n valuta f estera. **~er** n straniero, -a mf. **~ language** n lingua f straniera

fore: ~man n caporeparto m. **~most** adj principale • adv **first and ~most** in primo luogo

'forerunner n precursore m

fore'see vt (pt **-saw**, pp **-seen**) prevedere. **~able** adj **in the ~able future** in futuro per quanto si possa prevedere

'foresight n previdenza f

forest /'fɒrɪst/ n foresta f. **~er** n guardia f forestale

fore'stall vt prevenire

forestry /'fɒrɪstrɪ/ n silvicoltura f

'foretaste n pregustazione f

fore'tell vt (pt/pp **-told**) predire

forever /fə'revə(r)/ adv per sempre; **he's ~ complaining** si lamenta sempre

fore'warn vt avvertire

foreword /'fɔ:wɜ:d/ n prefazione f

forfeit /'fɔ:fɪt/ n (in game) pegno m; (Jur) penalità f • vt perdere

forgave /fə'geɪv/ ▸**forgive**

forge[1] /fɔ:dʒ/ vi **~ ahead** (runner:) lasciarsi indietro gli altri; fig farsi strada

forge[2] n fucina f • vt fucinare; (counterfeit) contraffare. **~r** n contraffattore m. **~ry** n contraffazione f

forget /fə'get/ vt/i (pt **-got**, pp **-gotten**, pres p **-getting**) dimenticare; dimenticarsi di (language, skill). **~ful** adj smemorato. **~fulness** n smemoratezza f. **~-me-not** n non-ti-scordar-dimé m inv. **~table** adj (day, film) da dimenticare

forgive /fə'gɪv/ vt (pt **-gave**, pp **-given**) **~ sb for sth** perdonare qcno per qcsa. **~ness** n perdono m

forgo /fɔ:'gəʊ/ vt (pt **-went**, pp **-gone**) rinunciare a

forgot(ten) /fə'gɒt(n)/ ▸**forget**

fork /fɔ:k/ n forchetta f; (for digging) forca f; (in road) bivio m • vi (road:) biforcarsi; **~ right** prendere a destra. ▫**~ out** vt [!] sborsare

fork-lift 'truck n elevatore m

forlorn /fə'lɔ:n/ adj (look) perduto; (place) derelitto; **~ hope** speranza f vana

form /fɔ:m/ n forma f; (document) modulo m; (Sch) classe f • vt formare formulare (opinion) • vi formarsi

formal /'fɔ:ml/ adj formale. **~ity** n formalità f inv. **~ly** adv in modo formale; (officially) ufficialmente

format /'fɔ:mæt/ n formato m • vt formattare (disk, page)

formation /fɔ:'meɪʃn/ n formazione f

former /'fɔ:mə(r)/ adj precedente; (PM, colleague) ex; **the ~, the latter** il primo, l'ultimo. **~ly** adv precedentemente; (in olden times) in altri tempi

formidable /'fɔ:mɪdəbl/ adj formidabile

formula /'fɔ:mjʊlə/ n (pl **-ae** /-li:/ or **-s**) formula f

formulate /'fɔ:mjʊleɪt/ vt formulare

forsake /fə'seɪk/ vt (pt **-sook** /-sʊk/, pp **-saken**) abbandonare

fort /fɔ:t/ n (Mil) forte m

forth /fɔ:θ/ adv **back and ~** avanti e indietro; **and so ~** e così via

forth: ~'coming adj prossimo; (communicative) communicativo; **no response was ~** non arrivava nessuna risposta. **~right** adj schietto. **~'with** adv immediatamente

fortieth /'fɔ:tɪɪθ/ adj quarantesimo

fortnight /'fɔ:t-/ Br n quindicina f. **~ly** adj bimensile • adv ogni due settimane

fortress /'fɔ:trɪs/ n fortezza f

fortunate /'fɔ:tʃənət/ adj fortunato; **that's ~!** meno male!. **~ly** adv fortunatamente

fortune /'fɔ:tʃu:n/ n fortuna f. **~-teller** n indovino, -a mf

forty /'fɔ:tɪ/ adj & n quaranta m

forum /'fɔ:rəm/ n foro m

forward /'fɔ:wəd/ adv avanti; (towards the front) in avanti • adj in avanti; (presumptuous) sfacciato • n (Sport) attaccante m • vt inoltrare (letter); spedire (goods). **~s** adv avanti

fossil /'fɒsl/ n fossile m. **~ized** adj fossile; (ideas) fossilizzato

foster /'fɒstə(r)/ vt allevare (child). **~-child** n figlio, -a mf in affidamento. **~-mother** n madre f affidataria

fought /fɔ:t/ ▸**fight**

foul /faʊl/ adj (smell, taste) cattivo; (air) viziato; (language) osceno; (mood, weather) orrendo; **~ play** (Jur) delitto m • n (Sport) fallo m • vt inquinare (water); (Sport) commettere un fallo contro; (nets, rope:) impigliarsi in. **~-smelling** adj puzzo

found[1] /faʊnd/ ▸**find**

found[2] vt fondare

foundation /faʊn'deɪʃn/ n (basis) fondamento m; (charitable) fondazione f; **~s** pl (of building) fondamenta fpl; **lay the ~-stone** porre la prima pietra

founder[1] /'faʊndə(r)/ n fondatore, -trice mf

founder[2] vi (ship:) affondare

fountain /'faʊntɪn/ n fontana f. **~-pen** n penna f stilografica

four /fɔ:(r)/ adj & n quattro m

four: ~some /'fɔ:səm/ n quartetto m. **~'teen** adj & n quattordici m. **~'teenth** adj quattordicesimo

fourth /fɔ:θ/ adj quarto

fowl /faʊl/ n pollame m

fox /fɒks/ n volpe f • vt (puzzle) ingannare

foyer /'fɔɪeɪ/ n (Theat) ridotto m; (in hotel) salone m d'ingresso

fraction /'frækʃn/ n frazione f

fracture /'fræktʃə(r)/ n frattura f • vt fratturare • vi fratturarsi

fragile /'frædʒaɪl/ adj fragile

fragment /'frægmənt/ n frammento m. **~ary** adj frammentario

fragran|ce /'freɪgrəns/ n fragranza f. **~t** adj fragrante

frail /freɪl/ adj gracile

frame /freɪm/ n (of picture, door, window) cornice f; (of spectacles) montatura f; (Anat) ossatura f; (structure, of bike) telaio m; **~ of mind** stato m d'animo • vt incorniciare (picture); fig formulare; (☒: incriminate) montare. **~work** n struttura f

France /frɑ:ns/ n Francia f

frank[1] /fræŋk/ vt affrancare (letter)

frank[2] adj franco. **~ly** adv francamente

frantic /'fræntɪk/ adj frenetico; **be ~ with worry** essere agitatissimo. **~ally** adv freneticamente

fraternal /frə'tɜ:nl/ adj fraterno

fraud /frɔ:d/ n frode f; (person) impostore m. **~ulent** adj fraudolento

fraught /frɔ:t/ adj **~ with** pieno di

fray[1] /freɪ/ n mischia f

fray[2] vi sfilacciarsi

freak /fri:k/ n fenomeno m; (person) scherzo m di natura; (!: weird person) tipo m strambo • adj anormale. **~ish** adj strambo

freckle /'frekl/ n lentiggine f. **~d** adj lentigginoso

free /fri:/ adj (**freer, freest**) libero; (ticket, copy) gratuito; (lavish) generoso; **~ of charge** gratuito; **set ~** liberare • vt (pt/pp **freed**) liberare

free: ~dom n libertà f. **~hold** n proprietà f [fondiaria] assoluta. **~'kick** n calcio m di punizione.

~lance adj & adv indipendente. **~ly** adv liberamente; (generously) generosamente; **I ~ly admit that...** devo ammettere che.... **f~mason** n massone m. **~-range** adj **~-range egg** uovo m di gallina ruspante. **~style** n stile m libero. **~way** n Am autostrada f

freez|e /fri:z/ vt (pt **froze**, pp **frozen**) gelare; bloccare (wages) • vi (water:) gelare; **it's ~ing** si gela; **my hands are ~ing** ho le mani congelate

freez|er /'fri:zə(r)/ n freezer m inv, congelatore m. **~ing** adj gelido • n **below ~ing** sotto zero

freight /freɪt/ n carico m. **~er** n nave f da carico. **~ train** n Am treno m merci

French /frentʃ/ adj francese • n (language) francese m; **the ~** pl i francesi mpl

French: ~ 'fries npl patate fpl fritte. **~man** n francese m. **~ 'window** n porta-finestra f. **~woman** n francese f

frenzied /'frenzɪd/ adj frenetico

frenzy /'frenzɪ/ n frenesia f

frequency /'fri:kwənsɪ/ n frequenza f

frequent[1] /'fri:kwənt/ adj frequente. **~ly** adv frequentemente

frequent[2] /frɪ'kwent/ vt frequentare

fresh /freʃ/ adj fresco; (new) nuovo; (Am: cheeky) sfacciato. **~ly** adv di recente

freshen /'freʃn/ vi (wind:) rinfrescare. □ **~ up** vt dare una rinfrescata a • vi rinfrescarsi

freshness /'freʃnɪs/ n freschezza f

fret /fret/ vi (pt/pp **fretted**) inquietarsi. **~ful** adj irritabile

friction /'frɪkʃn/ n frizione f

Friday /'fraɪdeɪ/ n venerdì m inv

fridge /frɪdʒ/ n frigo m

fried /fraɪd/ ▸**fry** • adj fritto; **~ egg** uovo m fritto

friend /frend/ n amico, -a mf. **~ly** adj (**-ier, -iest**) (relations, meeting, match) amichevole; (neighbourhood, smile) piacevole; (software) di facile uso; **be ~ly with** essere amico di. **~ship** n amicizia f

frieze /fri:z/ n fregio m

fright /fraɪt/ n paura f; **take ~** spaventarsi

frighten /'fraɪtn/ vt spaventare. **~ed** adj spaventato; **be ~ed** aver paura (**of** di). **~ing** adj spaventoso

frightful /'fraɪtfl/ adj terribile

frigid /'frɪdʒɪd/ adj frigido. **~ity** n freddezza f; (Psych) frigidità f

frill /frɪl/ n volant m inv. **~y** adj (dress) con tanti volant

fringe /frɪndʒ/ n frangia f; (of hair) frangetta f; (fig: edge) margine m. **~ benefits** npl benefici mpl supplementari

fritter /'frɪtə(r)/ n frittella f • **fritter away** vt sprecare

frivol|ity /frɪ'vɒlətɪ/ n frivolezza f. **~ous** adj frivolo

fro /frəʊ/ ▸**to**

frock /frɒk/ n abito m

frog /frɒg/ n rana f. **~man** n uomo m rana

frolic /'frɒlɪk/ vi (pt/pp **frolicked**) (lambs:) sgambettare; (people:) folleggiare

from /frɒm/ prep da; **~ Monday** da lunedì; **~ that day** da quel giorno; **he's ~ London** è di Londra; **this is a letter ~ my brother** questa è una lettera di mio fratello; **documents ~ the 16th century** documenti del XVI secolo; **made ~** fatto con; **she felt ill ~ fatigue** si sentiva male dalla stanchezza; **~ now on** d'ora in poi

front /frʌnt/ n parte f anteriore; (fig: organization etc) facciata f; (of garment) davanti m; (sea~) lungomare m; (Mil, Pol, Meteorol) fronte m; **in ~ of** davanti a; **in** or **at the ~** davanti; **to the ~** avanti • adj davanti; (page, row, wheel) anteriore

frontal /'frʌntl/ adj frontale

front 'door n porta f d'entrata

frontier /'frʌntɪə(r)/ n frontiera f

frost /frɒst/ n gelo m; (hoar~) brina f. **~bite** n congelamento m. **~bitten** adj congelato

frost|ed /'frɒstɪd/ adj **~ed glass** vetro m smerigliato. **~ily** adv gelidamente. **~ing** n Am (Culin) glassa f. **~y** adj also fig gelido

froth /frɒθ/ n schiuma f • vi far schiuma. **~y** adj schiumoso

rown /fraʊn/ n cipiglio m •vi aggrottare le sopraciglia. □ ~ **on** vt disapprovare

roze /frəʊz/ ▸**freeze**

rozen /'frəʊzn/ ▸**freeze** •adj (corpse, hand) congelato; (wastes) gelido; (Culin) surgelato; **I'm** ~ sono gelato. ~ **food** n surgelati mpl

rugal /'fru:gl/ adj frugale

ruit /fru:t/ n frutto m; (collectively) frutta f; **eat more** ~ mangia più frutta. ~ **cake** n dolce m con frutta candita

ruition /fru:'ɪʃn/ n **come to** ~ dare dei frutti

ruit: ~**less** adj infruttuoso. ~ '**salad** n macedonia f [di frutta]

rustrat|e /frʌ'streɪt/ vt frustrare; rovinare (plans). ~**ing** adj frustrante. ~**ion** n frustrazione f

ry[1] vt/i (pt/pp **fried**) friggere

ry[2] /fraɪ/ n inv **small** ~ fig pesce m piccolo

rying pan n padella f

udge /fʌdʒ/ n caramella f a base di zucchero, burro e latte

uel /'fju:əl/ n carburante m; fig nutrimento m •vt fig alimentare

ugitive /'fju:dʒɪtɪv/ n fuggiasco, -a mf

ulfil /fʊl'fɪl/ vt (pt/pp **-filled**) soddisfare (conditions, need); realizzare (dream, desire); ~ **oneself** realizzarsi. ~**ling** adj soddisfacente. ~**ment** n **sense of** ~**ment** senso m di appagamento

ull /fʊl/ adj pieno (**of** di); (detailed) esauriente; (bus, hotel) completo; (skirt) ampio; **at** ~ **speed** a tutta velocità; **in** ~ **swing** in pieno fervore •n **in** ~ per intero

ull: ~ '**moon** n luna f piena. ~**-scale** adj (model) in scala reale; (alert) di massima gravità. ~ '**stop** n punto m. ~**-time** adj & adv a tempo pieno

ully /'fʊlɪ/ adv completamente; (in detail) dettagliatamente; ~ **booked** (hotel, restaurant) tutto prenotato

umble /'fʌmbl/ vi ~ **in** rovistare in; ~ **with** armeggiare con; ~ **for one's keys** rovistare alla ricerca delle chiavi

fume /fju:m/ vi (be angry) essere furioso

fumes /fju:mz/ npl fumi mpl; (from car) gas mpl di scarico

fumigate /'fju:mɪgeɪt/ vt suffumicare

fun /fʌn/ n divertimento m; **for** ~ per ridere; **make** ~ **of** prendere in giro; **have** ~ divertirsi

function /'fʌŋkʃn/ n funzione f; (event) cerimonia f •vi funzionare; ~ **as** (serve as) funzionare da. ~**al** adj funzionale

fund /fʌnd/ n fondo m; fig pozzo m; ~**s** pl fondi mpl •vt finanziare

fundamental /fʌndə'mentl/ adj fondamentale

funeral /'fju:nərəl/ n funerale m

funeral directors n impresa f di pompe funebri

'**funfair** n luna park m inv

fungus /'fʌŋgəs/ n (pl **-gi** /-gaɪ/) fungo m

funnel /'fʌnl/ n imbuto m; (on ship) ciminiera f

funnily /'fʌnɪlɪ/ adv comicamente; (oddly) stranamente; ~ **enough** strano a dirsi

funny /'fʌnɪ/ adj (**-ier, -iest**) buffo; (odd) strano. ~ **business** n affare m losco

fur /fɜ:(r)/ n pelo m; (for clothing) pelliccia f; (in kettle) deposito m. ~ '**coat** n pelliccia f

furious /'fjʊərɪəs/ adj furioso

furnace /'fɜ:nɪs/ n fornace f

furnish /'fɜnɪʃ/ vt ammobiliare (flat); fornire (supplies). ~**ed** adj ~**ed room** stanza f ammobiliata. ~**ings** npl mobili mpl

furniture /'fɜ:nɪtʃə(r)/ n mobili mpl

furrow /'fʌrəʊ/ n solco m

furry /'fɜ:rɪ/ adj (animal) peloso; (toy) di peluche

further /'fɜ:ðə(r)/ adj (additional) ulteriore; **at the** ~ **end** all'altra estremità; **until** ~ **notice** fino a nuovo avviso •adv più lontano; ~**,...** inoltre,...; ~ **off** più lontano •vt promuovere

further'more adv per di più

furthest /'fɜ:ðɪst/ adj più lontano •adv più lontano

furtive /ˈfɜːtɪv/ adj furtivo
fury /ˈfjʊərɪ/ n furore m
fuse[1] /fjuːz/ n (of bomb) detonatore m; (cord) miccia f
fuse[2] n (Electr) fusibile m •vt fondere; (Electr) far saltare •vi fondersi; (Electr) saltare; **the lights have ~d** sono saltate le luci. **~-box** n scatola f dei fusibili
fuselage /ˈfjuːzəlɑːʒ/ n (Aeron) fusoliera f
fusion /ˈfjuːʒn/ n fusione f
fuss /fʌs/ n storie fpl; **make a ~** fare storie; **make a ~ of** colmare di attenzioni •vi fare storie
fussy /ˈfʌsɪ/ adj (**-ier, -iest**) (person) difficile da accontentare; (clothes etc) pieno di fronzoli
futil|e /ˈfjuːtaɪl/ adj inutile. **~ity** n futilità f
future /ˈfjuːtʃə(r)/ adj & n futuro; **in ~** in futuro. **~ perfect** futuro m anteriore
futuristic /fjuːtʃəˈrɪstɪk/ adj futuristico
fuzz /fʌz/ n **the ~** (☒: police) la pula
fuzzy /ˈfʌzɪ/ adj (**-ier, -iest**) (hair) crespo; (photo) sfuocato

Gg

gab /gæb/ n ! **have the gift of the ~** avere la parlantina
gabble /ˈgæb(ə)l/ vi parlare troppo in fretta
gad /gæd/ vi (pt/pp **gadded**) **~ about** andarsene in giro
gadget /ˈgædʒɪt/ n aggeggio m
Gaelic /ˈgeɪlɪk/ adj & n gaelico m
gaffe /gæf/ n gaffe f inv
gag /gæg/ n bavaglio m; (joke) battuta f •vt (pt/pp **gagged**) imbavagliare
gaily /ˈgeɪlɪ/ adv allegramente
gain /geɪn/ n guadagno m; (increase) aumento m •vt acquisire; **~ weight** aumentare di peso; **~ access** accedere •vi (clock:) andare avanti. **~ful** adj **~ful employment** lavoro m remunerativo
gait /geɪt/ n andatura f
gala /ˈgɑːlə/ n gala f; **swimming ~** manifestazione f di nuoto •attrib di gala
galaxy /ˈgæləksɪ/ n galassia f
gale /geɪl/ n bufera f
gall /gɔːl/ n (impudence) impudenza f
gallant /ˈgælənt/ adj coraggioso; (chivalrous) galante. **~ry** n coraggio m
ˈgall-bladder n cistifellea f
gallery /ˈgælərɪ/ n galleria f
galley /ˈgælɪ/ n (ship's kitchen) cambusa f; **~ [proof]** bozza f in colonna
gallivant /ˈgælɪvænt/ vi ! andare in giro
gallon /ˈgælən/ n gallone m (= 4,5 l; Am = 3,7 l)
gallop /ˈgæləp/ n galoppo m •vi galoppare
gallows /ˈgæləʊz/ n forca f
galore /gəˈlɔː(r)/ adv a bizzeffe
galvanize /ˈgælvənaɪz/ vt (Techn) galvanizzare; fig stimolare (**into** a)
gambl|e /ˈgæmbl/ n (risk) azzardo m •vi giocare; (on Stock Exchange) speculare; **~e on** (rely) contare su. **~er** n giocatore, -trice mf [d'azzardo]. **~ing** n gioco m [d'azzardo]
game /geɪm/ n gioco m; (match) partita f; (animals, birds) selvaggina f; **~s** (Sch) ≈ ginnastica f •adj (brave) coraggioso; **are you ~?** ti va?; **be ~ for** essere pronto per. **~keeper** n guardacaccia m inv
gammon /ˈgæmən/ n coscia f di maiale
gamut /ˈgæmət/ n fig gamma f
gander /ˈgændə(r)/ n oca f maschio
gang /gæŋ/ n banda f; (of workmen) squadra f •**gang up** vi far comunella (**on** contro)

angling /ˈgæŋglɪŋ/ adj spilungone

angmaster /ˈgæŋmɑːstə(r)/ n caporale m (di manodopera abusiva)

angrene /ˈgæŋgriːn/ n cancrena f

angster /ˈgæŋstə(r)/ n gangster m inv

angway /ˈgæŋweɪ/ n passaggio m; (Aeron, Naut) passerella f

aol /dʒeɪl/ n carcere m • vt incarcerare. **~er** n carceriere m

ap /gæp/ n spazio m; (in ages, between teeth) scarto m; (in memory) vuoto m; (in story) punto m oscuro

ap|e /geɪp/ vi stare a bocca aperta; (be wide open) spalancarsi; **~e at** guardare a bocca aperta. **~ing** adj aperto

arage /ˈgærɑːʒ/ n garage m inv; (for repairs) meccanico m; (for petrol) stazione f di servizio

arbage /ˈgɑːbɪdʒ/ n immondizia f; (nonsense) idiozie fpl. **~ can** n Am bidone m dell'immondizia

arden /ˈgɑːdn/ n giardino m; [**public**] **~s** pl giardini mpl pubblici • vi fare giardinaggio. **~ centre** n negozio m di piante e articoli da giardinaggio. **~er** n giardiniere, -a mf. **~ing** n giardinaggio m

argle /ˈgɑːgl/ n gargarismo m • vi fare gargarismi

argoyle /ˈgɑːgɔɪl/ n gargouille f inv

arish /ˈgeərɪʃ/ adj sgargiante

arland /ˈgɑːlənd/ n ghirlanda f

arlic /ˈgɑːlɪk/ n aglio m. **~ bread** n pane m condito con aglio

arment /ˈgɑːmənt/ n indumento m

arnish /ˈgɑːnɪʃ/ n guarnizione f • vt guarnire

arrison /ˈgærɪsn/ n guarnigione f

arter /ˈgɑːtə(r)/ n giarrettiera f; (for socks) reggicalze m inv da uomo

as /gæs/ n gas m inv; (Am [!]: petrol) benzina f • v (pt/pp **gassed**) • vt asfissiare • vi [!] blaterare. **~ cooker** n cucina f a gas. **~ ˈfire** n stufa f a gas

ash /gæʃ/ n taglio m • vt tagliare

asket /ˈgæskɪt/ n (Techn) guarnizione f

as: ~ mask n maschera f antigas. **~-meter** n contatore m del gas

gasoline /ˈgæsəliːn/ n Am benzina f

gasp /gɑːsp/ vi avere il fiato mozzato

ˈgas station n Am distributore m di benzina

gastric /ˈgæstrɪk/ adj gastrico. **~ ˈflu** n influenza f gastro-intestinale. **~ ˈulcer** n ulcera f gastrica

gate /geɪt/ n cancello m; (at airport) uscita f

gate: ~crash vt entrare senza invito a. **~crasher** n intruso, -a mf. **~way** n ingresso m

gather /ˈgæðə(r)/ vt raccogliere; (conclude) dedurre; (in sewing) arricciare; **~ speed** acquistare velocità; **~ together** radunare (people, belongings); (obtain gradually) acquistare • vi (people:) radunarsi. **~ing** n **family ~ing** ritrovo m di famiglia

gaudy /ˈgɔːdɪ/ adj (**-ier, -iest**) pacchiano

gauge /geɪdʒ/ n calibro m; (Rail) scartamento m; (device) indicatore m • vt misurare; fig stimare

gaunt /gɔːnt/ adj (thin) smunto

gauze /gɔːz/ n garza f

gave /geɪv/ ▸**give**

gawky /ˈgɔːkɪ/ adj (**-ier, -iest**) sgraziato

gawp /gɔːp/ vi **~** [**at**] [!] guardare con aria da ebete

gay /geɪ/ adj gaio; (homosexual) omosessuale; (bar, club) gay

gaze /geɪz/ n sguardo m fisso • vi guardare; **~ at** fissare

GB abbr (Great Britain) GB

gear /gɪə(r)/ n equipaggiamento m; (Techn) ingranaggio m; (Auto) marcia f; **in ~** con la marcia innestata; **change ~** cambiare marcia • vt finalizzare (**to** a)

gearbox n (Auto) scatola f del cambio

geese /giːs/ ▸**goose**

gel /dʒel/ n gel m inv

gelatine /ˈdʒelətɪn/ n gelatina f

gelignite /ˈdʒelɪgnaɪt/ n gelatina esplosiva f

gem /dʒem/ n gemma f

Gemini /ˈdʒemɪnaɪ/ n (Astr) Gemelli mpl

gender /'dʒendə(r)/ n (Gram) genere m

gene /dʒi:n/ n gene m

genealogy /dʒi:nɪ'ælədʒɪ/ n genealogia f

general /'dʒenrəl/ adj generale • n generale m; **in ~** in generale. **~ e'lection** n elezioni fpl politiche

generaliz|ation /dʒenrəlaɪ'zeɪʃn/ n generalizzazione f. **~e** vi generalizzare

generally /'dʒenrəlɪ/ adv generalmente

general prac'titioner n medico m generico

generate /'dʒenəreɪt/ vt generare

generation /dʒenə'reɪʃn/ n generazione f

generator /'dʒenəreɪtə(r)/ n generatore m

generosity /dʒenə'rɒsɪtɪ/ n generosità f

generous /'dʒenərəs/ adj generoso. **~ly** adv generosamente

genetic /dʒɪ'netɪk/ adj genetico. **~ engineering** n ingegneria f genetica. **~s** n genetica f

Geneva /dʒɪ'ni:və/ n Ginevra f

genial /'dʒi:nɪəl/ adj gioviale

genitals /'dʒenɪtlz/ npl genitali mpl

genitive /'dʒenɪtɪv/ adj & n **~ [case]** genitivo m

genius /'dʒi:nɪəs/ n (pl **-uses**) genio m

genocide /'dʒenəsaɪd/ n genocidio m

genre /'ʒæig.rə/ n genere m [letterario]

gent /dʒent/ n [!] signore m; **the ~s** sg il bagno per uomini

genteel /dʒen'ti:l/ adj raffinato

gentle /'dʒentl/ adj delicato; (breeze, tap, slope) leggero

gentleman /'dʒentlmən/ n signore m; (well-mannered) gentiluomo m

gent|leness /'dʒentlnɪs/ n delicatezza f. **~ly** adv delicatamente

genuine /'dʒenjʊɪn/ adj genuino. **~ly** adv (sorry) sinceramente

geograph|ical /dʒɪə'græfɪkl/ adj geografico. **~y** n geografia f

geological /dʒɪə'lɒdʒɪkl/ adj geologico

geolog|ist /dʒɪ'ɒlədʒɪst/ n geologo, -a mf. **~y** n geologia f

geranium /dʒə'reɪnɪəm/ n geranio m

geriatric /dʒerɪ'ætrɪk/ adj geriatrico **~ ward** n reparto m geriatria. **~s** n geriatria f

germ /dʒɜ:m/ n germe m; **~s** pl microbi mpl

German /'dʒɜ:mən/ n & adj tedesco, -a mf; (language) tedesco m

Germanic /dʒə'mænɪk/ adj germanico

German 'measles n rosolia f

Germany /'dʒɜ:mənɪ/ n Germania f

germinate /'dʒɜ:mɪneɪt/ vi germogliare

gesticulate /dʒe'stɪkjʊleɪt/ vi gesticolare

gesture /'dʒestʃə(r)/ n gesto m

get /get/ *verb*

! past tense/past participle **got**, past participle Am **gotten**, pres participle **getting**)

• vt (*receive*) ricevere; (*obtain*) ottenere trovare (job); (*buy, catch, fetch*) prendere; (*transport, deliver to airport* etc) portare; (*reach on telephone*) trovare; ([!]*: understand*) comprendere; preparare (meal); **~ sb to do sth** far fare qcsa a qcno

• vi (*become*) **~ tired/bored/angry** stancarsi/annoiarsi/arrabbiarsi; **I'm ~ting hungry** mi sta venendo fame; **~ dressed/married** vestirsi/sposarsi; **~ sth ready** preparare qcsa; **~ nowhere** non concludere nulla; **this is ~ting us nowhere** questo non ci è di nessun aiuto; **~ to** (*reach*) arrivare a. □ **~ at** vi (*criticize*) criticare; **I see what you're ~ting at** ho capito cosa vuoi dire; **what are you ~ting at?** dove vuoi andare a parare?. □ **~ away** vi (*leave*) andarsene; (*escape*) scappare. □ **~ back** vi tornare • vt (*recover*) riavere; **~ one's own back** rifarsi. □ **~ by** vi passare; (*manage*) cavarsela. □ **~ down** vi scendere; **~ down to work** mettersi al lavoro • vt (*depress*) buttare giù. □ **~ in** vi entrare • vt mettere dentro (washing); far venire (plumber). □ **~ off** vi scendere; (*from* work) andarsene; (*Jur*) essere assolto; **~ off the bus/one's bike** scendere dal pullman/dalla bici •vt (*remove*) togliere. ▫ **~ on** vi salire; (*be on good terms*) andare d'accordo; (*make progress*) andare avanti; (*in life*) riuscire; **~ on the bus/one's bike** salire sul pullman/sulla bici; **how are you ~ting on?** come va?. ▫ **~ out** vi uscire; (*of car*) scendere; **~ out!** fuori!; **~ out of** (*avoid doing*) evitare •vt togliere (cork, stain). ▫ **~ over** vi andare al di là •vt fig riprendersi da (illness). ▫ **~ round** vt aggirare (rule); rigirare (person) •vi **I never ~ round to it** non mi sono mai deciso a farlo. ▫ **~ through** vi (*on telephone*) prendere la linea. ▫ **~ up** vi alzarsi; (*climb*) salire; **~ up a hill** salire su una collina

eyser /ˈgiːzə(r)/ n scaldabagno m; (Geol) geyser m inv

hastly /ˈgɑːstlɪ/ adj (**-ier, -iest**) terribile; **feel ~** sentirsi da cani

herkin /ˈgɜːkɪn/ n cetriolino m

hetto /ˈgetəʊ/ n ghetto m

host /gəʊst/ n fantasma m. **~ly** adj spettrale

iant /ˈdʒaɪənt/ n gigante m •adj gigante

ibberish /ˈdʒɪbərɪʃ/ n stupidaggini fpl

ibe /dʒaɪb/ n malignità f inv

iblets /ˈdʒɪblɪts/ npl frattaglie fpl

iddiness /ˈgɪdɪnɪs/ n vertigini fpl

iddy /ˈgɪdɪ/ adj (**-ier, -iest**) vertiginoso; **feel ~** avere le vertigini

ift /gɪft/ n dono m; (to charity) donazione f. **~ed** adj dotato. **~-wrap** vt impacchettare in carta da regalo

ig /gɪg/ n (Mus) [!] concerto m

igantic /dʒaɪˈgæntɪk/ adj gigantesco

iggle /ˈgɪgl/ n risatina f •vi ridacchiare

ild /gɪld/ vt dorare

ills /gɪlz/ npl branchia fsg

ilt /gɪlt/ adj dorato •n doratura f. **~-edged stock** n investimento m sicuro

gimmick /ˈgɪmɪk/ n trovata f

gin /dʒɪn/ n gin m inv

ginger /ˈdʒɪndʒə(r)/ adj rosso fuoco inv; (cat) rosso •n zenzero m. **~ ale** n, **~ beer** n bibita f allo zenzero. **~bread** n panpepato m

gipsy /ˈdʒɪpsɪ/ n = **gypsy**

giraffe /dʒɪˈrɑːf/ n giraffa f

girder /ˈgɜːdə(r)/ n (Techn) trave f

girl /gɜːl/ n ragazza f; (female child) femmina f. **~ band** n girl band f inv. **~friend** n amica f; (of boy) ragazza f. **~ish** adj da ragazza

giro /ˈdʒaɪərəʊ/ n bancogiro m; (cheque) sussidio m di disoccupazione

girth /gɜːθ/ n circonferenza f

gist /dʒɪst/ n **the ~** la sostanza

give /gɪv/ n elasticità f •v (pt **gave**, pp **given**) •vt dare; (as present) regalare (**to** a); fare (lecture, present, shriek); donare (blood); **~ birth** partorire •vi (to charity) fare delle donazioni; (yield) cedere. ▫ **~ away** vt dar via; (betray) tradire; (distribute) assegnare; **~ away the bride** portare la sposa all'altare. ▫ **~ back** vt restituire. ▫ **~ in** vt consegnare •vi (yield) arrendersi. ▫ **~ off** vt emanare. ▫ **~ over** vi **~ over!** piantala!. ▫ **~ up** vt rinunciare a; **~ oneself up** arrendersi •vi rinunciare. ▫ **~ way** vi cedere; (Auto) dare la precedenza; (collapse) crollare

given /ˈgɪvn/ ▸**give** •adj **~ name** nome m di battesimo

glacier /ˈglæsɪə(r)/ n ghiacciaio m

glad /glæd/ adj contento (**of** di). **~den** vt rallegrare

gladly /ˈglædlɪ/ adv volentieri

glamour /ˈglæmə(r)/ n fascino m

glance /glɑːns/ n sguardo m •vi **~ at** dare un'occhiata a. ▫ **~ up** vi alzare gli occhi

gland /glænd/ n glandola f

glare /gleə(r)/ n bagliore m; (look) occhiataccia f •vi **~ at** dare un'occhiataccia a

glaring /ˈgleərɪŋ/ adj sfolgorante; (mistake) madornale

glass /glɑːs/ n vetro m; (for drinking) bicchiere m; **~es** (pl: spectacles) occhiali mpl. **~y** adj vitreo

g

g

glaze /gleɪz/ n smalto m •vt mettere i vetri a (door, window); smaltare (pottery); (Culin) spennellare. **~d** adj (eyes) vitreo

gleam /gliːm/ n luccichio m •vi luccicare

glean /gliːn/ vt racimolare (information)

glee /gliː/ n gioia f. **~ful** adj gioioso

glib /glɪb/ adj pej insincero

glid|e /glaɪd/ vi scorrere; (through the air) planare. **~er** n aliante m

glimmer /ˈglɪmə(r)/ n barlume m •vi emettere un barlume

glimpse /glɪmps/ n **catch a ~ of** intravedere •vt intravedere

glint /glɪnt/ vi luccicare

glisten /ˈglɪsn/ vi luccicare

glitter /ˈglɪtə(r)/ vi brillare

gloat /gləʊt/ vi gongolare (**over** su)

global /ˈgləʊbl/ adj mondiale. **~ization** n globalizzazione f

globe /gləʊb/ n globo m; (map) mappamondo m

gloom /gluːm/ n oscurità f; (sadness) tristezza f. **~ily** adv (sadly) con aria cupa

gloomy /ˈgluːmɪ/ adj (**-ier, -iest**) cupo

glorif|y /ˈglɔːrɪfaɪ/ vt (pt/pp **-ied**) glorificare; **a ~ied waitress** niente più che una cameriera

glorious /ˈglɔːrɪəs/ adj splendido; (deed, hero) glorioso

glory /ˈglɔːrɪ/ n gloria f; (splendour) splendore m; (cause for pride) vanto m •vi (pt/pp **-ied**) **~ in** vantarsi di

gloss /glɒs/ n lucentezza f. **~ paint** n vernice f lucida •**gloss over** vt sorvolare su

glossary /ˈglɒsərɪ/ n glossario m

glossy /ˈglɒsɪ/ adj (**-ier, -iest**) lucido; **~ [magazine]** rivista f femminile

glove /glʌv/ n guanto m. **~ compartment** n (Auto) cruscotto m

glow /gləʊ/ n splendore m; (in cheeks) rossore m; (of candle) luce f soffusa •vi risplendere; (candle:) brillare; (person:) avvampare. **~ing** adj ardente; (account) entusiastico. **~-worm** n lucciola f

glucose /ˈgluːkəʊs/ n glucosio m

glue /gluː/ n colla f •vt (pres p **gluing**) incollare

glum /glʌm/ adj (**glummer, glummest**) tetro

glutton /ˈglʌtən/ n ghiottone, -a mf. **~ous** adj ghiotto. **~y** n ghiottoneria f

gnarled /nɑːld/ adj nodoso

gnash /næʃ/ vt **~ one's teeth** digrignare i denti

gnaw /nɔː/ vt rosicchiare

go¹ /gəʊ/ n (pl **goes**) energia f; (attempt) tentativo m; **on the go** in movimento; **at one go** in una sola volta; **it's your go** tocca a te; **make a go of it** riuscire

go² /gəʊ/

! 3 sing pres tense **goes**, past tense **went**, past participle **gone**

• vi andare; (*leave*) andar via; (*vanish*) sparire; (*become*) diventare; (*be sold*) vendersi; **go and see** andare a vedere; **go swimming/shopping** andare a nuotare/fare spese; **where's the time gone?** come ha fatto il tempo a volare così?; **it's all gone** è finito; **be going to do** stare per fare; **I'm not going to** non ne ho nessuna intenzione; **to go** (! hamburgers etc) da asporto; **a coffee to go** un caffè da portar via. ◻ **~ about** vi andare in giro. ◻ **~ away** vi andarsene. ◻ **~ back** vi ritornare. ◻ **~ by** vi passare. ◻ **~ down** vi scendere; (sun:) tramontare; (ship:) affondare; (swelling:) diminuire. ◻ **~ for** vt andare a prendere; andare a cercare (doctor); (*choose*) optare per; (!: *attack*) aggredire; **he's not the kind I go for** non è il genere che mi attira. ◻ **~ in** vi entrare. ◻ **~ in for** vt partecipare a (competition); darsi a (tennis). ◻ **~ off** vi andarsene; (alarm:) scattare; (gun, bomb:) esplodere; (food, milk:) andare a male; **go off well** riuscire. ◻ **~ on** vi andare avanti; **what's going on?** cosa succede? **go on at** vt ! scocciare. ◻ **~ out** vi uscire; (light, fire:) spegnersi. ◻ **~ over** vi andare •vt (*check*) controllare. ◻ **~ round** vi andare in giro; (*visit*) andare; (*turn*) girare; **is there enough to go round?** ce n'è abbastanza per tutti? **go through** vi (bill, proposal:) passare •vt (*suffer*) subire; (*check*) controllare; (*read*) leggere. □ ~ **under** vi passare sotto; (ship, swimmer:) andare sott'acqua; (*fail*) fallire. □ ~ **up** vi salire; (Theat: curtain:) aprirsi. □ ~ **with** vt accompagnare. □ ~ **without** vt fare a meno di (supper, sleep) •vi fare senza

oad /gəʊd/ vt spingere (**into** a); (taunt) spronare

o-ahead adj (person, company) ntraprendente •n okay m

oal /gəʊl/ n porta f; (point scored) gol n inv; (in life) obiettivo m; **score a ~** segnare. **~ie** ▣, **~keeper** n portiere m. **~-post** n palo m

oat /gəʊt/ n capra f

obble /'gɒbl/ vt ~ [**down, up**] rangugiare

od, **god** /gɒd/ n Dio m, dio m

od: ~child n figlioccio, -a mf. **~-daughter** n figlioccia f. **~dess** n dea f. **~father** n padrino m. **~-forsaken** adj dimenticato da Dio. **~mother** n madrina f. **~send** n manna f. **~son** n figlioccio m

oing /'gəʊɪŋ/ adj (price, rate) corrente; **~ concern** azienda f florida •n **it's hard ~** è una faticaccia; **while the ~ is good** finché si può. **~s-'on** npl avvenimenti mpl

old /gəʊld/ n oro m •adj d'oro

olden /'gəʊldn/ adj dorato. **~ handshake** n buonuscita f (al termine di un rapporto di lavoro). **~ mean** n giusto mezzo m. **~ 'wedding** n nozze fpl d'oro

old: ~fish n inv pesce m rosso. **~-mine** n miniera f d'oro. **~-plated** adj placcato d'oro. **~smith** n orefice m

olf /gɒlf/ n golf m

olf: ~-club n circolo m di golf; (implement) mazza f da golf. **~-course** n campo m di golf. **~er** n giocatore, -trice mf di golf

ondo|la /'gɒndələ/ n gondola f. **~lier** n gondoliere m

one /gɒn/ ▸**go**

ong /gɒŋ/ n gong m inv

ood /gʊd/ adj (**better, best**) buono; (child, footballer, singer) bravo; (holiday, film) bello; **~ at** bravo in; **a ~ deal of anger** molta rabbia; **as ~ as** (almost) quasi; **~ morning, ~ afternoon** buon giorno; **~ evening** buona sera; **~ night** buonanotte; **have a ~ time** divertirsi •n bene m; **for ~** per sempre; **do ~** far del bene; **do sb ~** far bene a qcno; **it's no ~** è inutile; **be up to no ~** combinare qualcosa

goodbye /gʊd'baɪ/ int arrivederci

good: ~-for-nothing n buono, -a mf a nulla. **G~ 'Friday** n Venerdì m Santo

good-'looking adj bello

goodness /'gʊdnɪs/ n bontà f; **my ~!** santo cielo!; **thank ~!** grazie al cielo!

goods /gʊdz/ npl prodotti mpl. **~ train** n treno m merci

good'will n buona volontà f; (Comm) avviamento m

goody /'gʊdɪ/ n (▣: person) buono m. **~-goody** n santarellino, -a mf

gooey /'gu:ɪ/ adj ▣ appiccicaticcio; fig sdolcinato

google /'gu:gl/ vt/i googlare

goose /gu:s/ (pl **geese**) n oca f. **~-flesh** n, **~-pimples** npl pelle fsg d'oca

gooseberry /'gʊzbərɪ/ n uva f spina

gore[1] /gɔ:(r)/ n sangue m

gore[2] vt incornare

gorge /gɔ:dʒ/ n (Geog) gola f •vt **~ oneself** ingozzarsi

gorgeous /'gɔ:dʒəs/ adj stupendo

gorilla /gə'rɪlə/ n gorilla m inv

gorse /gɔ:s/ n ginestrone m

gory /'gɔ:rɪ/ adj (**-ier, -iest**) cruento

gosh /gɒʃ/ int ▣ caspita

gospel /'gɒspl/ n vangelo m. **~ truth** n sacrosanta verità f

gossip /'gɒsɪp/ n pettegolezzi mpl; (person) pettegolo, -a mf •vi pettegolare. **~y** adj pettegolo

got /gɒt/ ▸**get**; **have ~** avere; **have ~ to do sth** dover fare qcsa

gotten /'gɒtn/ Am see **get**

gouge /gaʊdʒ/ vt **~ out** cavare

gourmet /'gʊəmeɪ/ n buongustaio, -a mf

govern /'gʌv(ə)n/ vt/i governare;

g

(determine) determinare

government /ˈɡʌvnmənt/ n governo m. **~al** adj governativo

governor /ˈɡʌvənə(r)/ n governatore m; (of school) membro m del consiglio di istituto; (of prison) direttore, -trice mf; ([!]: boss) capo m

gown /ɡaʊn/ n vestito m; (Jur, Univ) toga f

GP n abbr general practitioner

GPS abbr (Global Positioning System) GPS m

grab /ɡræb/ vt (pt/pp **grabbed**) **~ [hold of]** afferrare

grace /ɡreɪs/ n grazia f; (before meal) benedicite m inv; **with good ~** volentieri; **three days' ~** tre giorni di proroga. **~ful** adj aggraziato. **~fully** adv con grazia

gracious /ˈɡreɪʃəs/ adj cortese; (elegant) lussuoso

grade /ɡreɪd/ n livello m; (Comm) qualità f; (Sch) voto m; (Am Sch: class) classe f; Am = **gradient** •vt (Comm) classificare; (Sch) dare il voto a. **~ crossing** n Am passaggio m a livello

gradient /ˈɡreɪdɪənt/ n pendenza f

gradual /ˈɡrædʒʊəl/ adj graduale. **~ly** adv gradualmente

graduate¹ /ˈɡrædʒʊət/ n laureato, -a mf

graduate² /ˈɡrædʒʊeɪt/ vi (Univ) laurearsi

graduation /ɡrædʒʊˈeɪʃn/ n laurea f

graffiti /ɡrəˈfiːtɪ/ npl graffiti mpl

graft /ɡrɑːft/ n (Bot, Med) innesto m; (Med: organ) trapianto m; ([!]: hard work) duro lavoro m; ([!]: corruption) corruzione f •vt innestare; trapiantare (organ)

grain /ɡreɪn/ n (of sand, salt) granello m; (of rice) chicco m; (cereals) cereali mpl; (in wood) venatura f; **it goes against the ~** fig è contro la mia/sua natura

gram /ɡræm/ n grammo m

grammar /ˈɡræmə(r)/ n grammatica f. **~ school** n ≈ liceo m

grammatical /ɡrəˈmætɪkl/ adj grammaticale

grand /ɡrænd/ adj grandioso; [!] eccellente

ˈgrandchild n nipote mf

ˈgranddaughter n nipote f

grandeur /ˈɡrændʒə(r)/ n grandiosità f

ˈgrandfather n nonno m. **~ clock** pendolo m (che poggia a terra)

grandiose /ˈɡrændɪəʊs/ adj grandioso

grand: ~mother n nonna f. **~parents** npl nonni mpl. **~ piˈan** n pianoforte m a coda. **~son** n nipote m. **~stand** n tribuna f

granite /ˈɡrænɪt/ n granito m

granny /ˈɡrænɪ/ n [!] nonna f

grant /ɡrɑːnt/ n (money) sussidio m; (Univ) borsa f di studio •vt accordare; (admit) ammettere; **take sth for ~ed** dare per scontato qc

granule /ˈɡrænjuːl/ n granello m

grape /ɡreɪp/ n acino m; **~s** pl uva f

grapefruit /ˈɡreɪp-/ n inv pompelmo m

graph /ɡrɑːf/ n grafico m

graphic /ˈɡræfɪk/ adj grafico; (vivid) vivido. **~s** n grafica f

grapple /ˈɡræpl/ vi **~ with** also fig essere alle prese con

grasp /ɡrɑːsp/ n stretta f; (understanding) comprensione f •vt afferrare. **~ing** adj avido

grass /ɡrɑːs/ n erba f; **at the ~ roots** alla base. **~hopper** n cavalletta f. **~land** n prateria f

grassy /ˈɡrɑːsɪ/ adj erboso

grate¹ /ɡreɪt/ n grata f

grate² vt (Culin) grattugiare •vi stridere

grateful /ˈɡreɪtfl/ adj grato. **~ly** adv con gratitudine

grater /ˈɡreɪtə(r)/ n (Culin) grattugia

gratif|y /ˈɡrætɪfaɪ/ vt (pt/pp **-ied**) appagare. **~ied** adj appagato. **~yir** adj appagante

grating /ˈɡreɪtɪŋ/ n grata f

gratitude /ˈɡrætɪtjuːd/ n gratitudine f

gratuitous /ɡrəˈtjuːɪtəs/ adj gratuit

gratuity /ɡrəˈtjuːɪtɪ/ n gratifica f

grave¹ /ɡreɪv/ adj grave

grave² n tomba f

gravel /ˈɡrævl/ n ghiaia f

grave: ~stone n lapide f. **~yard** cimitero m

avitate /'grævɪteɪt/ vi gravitare

'avity /'grævɪtɪ/ n gravità f

avy /'greɪvɪ/ n sugo m della carne

ay /greɪ/ adj Am = **grey**

aze¹ /greɪz/ vi (animal:) pascolare

aze² n escoriazione f • vt (touch ghtly) sfiorare; (scrape) escoriare; bucciarsi (knee)

'ease /gri:s/ n grasso m • vt ungere. **~-proof 'paper** n carta f oleata

easy /'gri:sɪ/ adj (**-ier, -iest**) ɪntuoso; (hair, skin) grasso

'eat /greɪt/ adj grande; (🅘: marvellous) eccezionale

'eat: G~ 'Britain n Gran Bretagna f. **~-'grandfather** n bisnonno m. **~-'grandmother** n bisnonna f

eat|ly /'greɪtlɪ/ adv enormemente. **~ness** n grandezza f

reece /gri:s/ n Grecia f

'eed /gri:d/ n avidità f; (for food) ingordigia f

'eedy /'gri:dɪ/ adj (**-ier, -iest**) avido; (for food) ingordo

'eek /gri:k/ adj & n greco, -a mf; (language) greco m

'een /gri:n/ adj verde; (fig: nexperienced) immaturo • n verde m; **~s** pl verdura f; **the G~s** pl (Pol) i verdi. **~ belt** n zona f verde intorno a una città. **~ card** n (Auto) carta f verde

eenery /'gri:nərɪ/ n verde m

'een: ~grocer n fruttivendolo, -a mf. **~house** n serra f. **~house effect** n effetto m serra. **~ light** n 🅘 verde m

reet /gri:t/ vt salutare; (welcome) accogliere. **~ing** n saluto m; (welcome) accoglienza f. **~ings card** n biglietto m d'auguri

regarious /grɪ'geərɪəs/ adj gregario; (person) socievole

renade /grɪ'neɪd/ n granata f

'ew /gru:/ ▸**grow**

rey /greɪ/ adj grigio; (hair) bianco • n grigio m. **~hound** n levriero m

'id /grɪd/ n griglia f; (on map) reticolato m; (Electr) rete f

'ief /gri:f/ n dolore m; **come to ~** (plans:) naufragare

rievance /'gri:vəns/ n lamentela f

grieve /gri:v/ vt addolorare • vi essere addolorato

grill /grɪl/ n graticola f; (for grilling) griglia f; **mixed ~** grigliata f mista • vt/i cuocere alla griglia; (interrogate) sottoporre al terzo grado

grille /grɪl/ n grata f

grim /grɪm/ adj (**grimmer, grimmest**) arcigno; (determination) accanito

grimace /grɪ'meɪs/ n smorfia f • vi fare una smorfia

grime /graɪm/ n sudiciume m

grimy /'graɪmɪ/ adj (**-ier, -iest**) sudicio

grin /grɪn/ n sorriso m • vi (pt/pp **grinned**) fare un gran sorriso

grind /graɪnd/ n (🅘: hard work) sfacchinata f • vt (pt/pp **ground**) macinare; affilare (knife); (Am: mince) tritare; **~ one's teeth** digrignare i denti

grip /grɪp/ n presa f; fig controllo m; (bag) borsone m; **get a ~ on oneself** controllarsi • vt (pt/pp **gripped**) afferrare; (tyres:) far presa su; tenere avvinto (attention)

grisly /'grɪzlɪ/ adj (**-ier, -iest**) raccapricciante

gristle /'grɪsl/ n cartilagine f

grit /grɪt/ n graniglia f; (for roads) sabbia f; (courage) coraggio m • vt (pt/pp **gritted**) spargere sabbia su (road); **~ one's teeth** serrare i denti

groan /grəʊn/ n gemito m • vi gemere

grocer /'grəʊsə(r)/ n droghiere, -a mf; **~'s [shop]** drogheria f. **~ies** npl generi mpl alimentari

groggy /'grɒgɪ/ adj (-ier, -iest) stordito; (unsteady) barcollante

groin /grɔɪn/ n (Anat) inguine m

groom /gru:m/ n sposo m; (for horse) stalliere m • vt strigliare (horse); fig preparare; **well-~ed** ben curato

groove /gru:v/ n scanalatura f

grope /grəʊp/ vi brancolare; **~ for** cercare a tastoni

gross /grəʊs/ adj obeso; (coarse) volgare; (glaring) grossolano; (salary, weight) lordo • n inv grossa f. **~ly** adv (very) enormemente

grotesque /grəʊ'tesk/ adj grottesco

ground¹ /graʊnd/ ▸**grind**

ground² n terra f; (Sport) terreno m;

(reason) ragione f; **~s** pl (park) giardini mpl; (of coffee) fondi mpl • vi (ship:) arenarsi • vt bloccare a terra (aircraft); Am (Electr) mettere a terra

ground: ~ floor n pianterreno m. **~ing** n base f. **~less** adj infondato. **~sheet** n telone m impermeabile. **~work** n lavoro m di preparazione

group /gru:p/ n gruppo m • vt raggruppare • vi raggrupparsi

grouse[1] /graʊs/ n inv gallo m cedrone

grouse[2] vi [!] brontolare

g

grovel /ˈgrɒvl/ vi (pt/pp **grovelled**) strisciare. **~ling** adj leccapiedi inv

grow /grəʊ/ v (pt **grew**, pp **grown**) • vi crescere; (become) diventare; (unemployment, fear:) aumentare; (town:) ingrandirsi • vt coltivare; **~ one's hair** farsi crescere i capelli. □**~ up** vi crescere; (town:) svilupparsi

growl /graʊl/ n grugnito m • vi ringhiare

grown /grəʊn/ ▸**grow** • adj adulto. **~-up** adj & n adulto, -a mf

growth /grəʊθ/ n crescita f; (increase) aumento m; (Med) tumore m

grub /grʌb/ n larva f; ([!]: food) mangiare m

grubby /ˈgrʌbɪ/ adj (**-ier, -iest**) sporco

grudg|e /grʌdʒ/ n rancore m; **bear sb a ~e** portare rancore a qcno • vt dare a malincuore. **~ing** adj riluttante. **~ingly** adv a malincuore

gruelling /ˈgru:əlɪŋ/ adj estenuante

gruesome /ˈgru:səm/ adj macabro

gruff /grʌf/ adj burbero

grumble /ˈgrʌmbl/ vi brontolare (**at** contro)

grumpy /ˈgrʌmpɪ/ adj (**-ier, -iest**) scorbutico

grunt /grʌnt/ n grugnito m • vi fare un grugnito

guarant|ee /gærənˈti:/ n garanzia f • vt garantire. **~or** n garante mf

guard /gɑ:d/ n guardia f; (security) guardiano m; (on train) capotreno m; (Techn) schermo m protettivo; **be on ~** essere di guardia • vt sorvegliare; (protect) proteggere. □**~ against** vt guardarsi da. **~-dog** n cane m da guardia

guarded /ˈgɑ:dɪd/ adj guardingo

guardian /ˈgɑ:dɪən/ n (of minor) tutore, -trice mf

guerrilla /gəˈrɪlə/ n guerrigliero, -a mf. **~ warfare** n guerriglia f

guess /ges/ n supposizione f • vt indovinare • vi indovinare; (Am: suppose) supporre. **~work** n supposizione f

guest /gest/ n ospite mf; (in hotel) cliente mf. **~-house** n pensione f

guffaw /gʌˈfɔ:/ n sghignazzata f • vi sghignazzare

guidance /ˈgaɪdəns/ n guida f; (advice) consigli mpl

guide /gaɪd/ n guida f; [**Girl**] **G~** giovane esploratrice f • vt guidare. **~book** n guida f turistica

guide: ~-dog n cane m per ciechi. **~lines** npl direttive fpl

guild /gɪld/ n corporazione f

guile /gaɪl/ n astuzia f

guillotine /ˈgɪləti:n/ n ghigliottina (for paper) taglierina f

guilt /gɪlt/ n colpa f. **~ily** adv con ar colpevole

guilty /ˈgɪltɪ/ adj (**-ier, -iest**) colpevole; **have a ~ conscience** avere la coscienza sporca

guinea-pig /ˈgɪnɪ-/ n porcellino m d'India; (fig: used for experiments) cavia

guitar /gɪˈtɑ:(r)/ n chitarra f. **~ist** n chitarrista mf

gulf /gʌlf/ n (Geog) golfo m; fig abisso m

gull /gʌl/ n gabbiano m

gullet /ˈgʌlɪt/ n esofago m; (throat) gola f

gullible /ˈgʌlɪbl/ adj credulone

gully /ˈgʌlɪ/ n burrone m; (drain) canale m di scolo

gulp /gʌlp/ n azione f di deglutire; (food) boccone m; (of liquid) sorso m • deglutire. □**~ down** vt trangugiar (food); scolarsi (liquid)

gum[1] /gʌm/ n (Anat) gengiva f

gum[2] n gomma f; (chewing gum) gomma f da masticare, chewing gum m inv • vt (pt/pp **gummed**) ingommare (**to** a)

gun /gʌn/ n pistola f; (rifle) fucile m; (cannon) cannone m • **gun down** vt (pt/pp **gunned**) freddare

gun: ~fire n spari mpl; (of cannon)

colpi mpl [di cannone]. **~man** uomo m armato

un: ~powder n polvere f da sparo. **~shot** n colpo m [di pistola]

urgle /'gɜːgl/ vi gorgogliare; (baby:) fare degli urletti

ush /gʌʃ/ vi sgorgare; (enthuse) parlare con troppo entusiasmo (**over** di). □**~ out** vi sgorgare. **~ing** adj eccessivamente entusiastico

ust /gʌst/ n (of wind) raffica f

usto /'gʌstəʊ/ n **with ~** con trasporto

usty /'gʌstɪ/ adj ventoso

ut /gʌt/ n intestino m; **~s** pl pancia f; (!: courage) fegato m • vt (pt/pp **gutted**) (Culin) svuotare delle interiora; **~ted by fire** sventrato da un incendio

gutter /'gʌtə(r)/ n canale m di scolo; (on roof) grondaia f; fig bassifondi mpl

guttural /'gʌtərəl/ adj gutturale

guy /gaɪ/ n ! tipo m, tizio m

guzzle /'gʌzl/ vt ingozzarsi con (food); **he's ~d the lot** si è sbafato tutto

gym /dʒɪm/ n ! palestra f; (gymnastics) ginnastica f

gymnasium /dʒɪm'neɪzɪəm/ n palestra f

gymnast /'dʒɪmnæst/ n ginnasta mf. **~ics** n ginnastica f

gymslip n (Sch) ≈ grembiule m (da bambina)

gynaecolog|ist /gaɪnɪ'kɒlədʒɪst/ n ginecologo, -a mf. **~y** n ginecologia f

gypsy /'dʒɪpsɪ/ n zingaro, -a mf

gyrate /dʒaɪ'reɪt/ vi roteare

g

h

Hh

aberdashery /hæbə'dæʃərɪ/ n merceria f; Am negozio m d'abbigliamento da uomo

abit /'hæbɪt/ n abitudine f; (Relig: costume) tonaca f; **be in the ~ of doing sth** avere l'abitudine di fare qcsa

abitable /'hæbɪtəbl/ adj abitabile

abitat /'hæbɪtæt/ n habitat m inv

abitation /hæbɪ'teɪʃn/ n **unfit for human ~** inagibile

abitual /hə'bɪtjʊəl/ adj abituale; (smoker, liar) inveterato. **~ly** adv regolarmente

ack[1] /hæk/ n (writer) scribacchino, -a mf

ack[2] vt tagliare; **~ to pieces** tagliare a pezzi

ackneyed /'hæknɪd/ adj trito [e ritrito]

ad /hæd/ ▸**have**

addock /'hædək/ n inv eglefino m

aemorrhage /'hemərɪdʒ/ n emorragia f

haemorrhoids /'hemərɔɪdz/ npl emorroidi fpl

hag /hæg/ n **old ~** vecchia befana f

haggard /'hægəd/ adj sfatto

hail[1] /heɪl/ vt salutare; far segno a (taxi) • vi **~ from** provenire da

hail[2] n grandine f • vi grandinare. **~stone** n chicco m di grandine. **~storm** n grandinata f

hair /heə(r)/ n capelli mpl; (on body, of animal) pelo m

hair: ~brush n spazzola f per capelli. **~cut** n taglio m di capelli; **have a ~cut** farsi tagliare i capelli. **~-do** n ! pettinatura f. **~dresser** n parrucchiere, -a mf. **~-dryer** n fon m inv; (with hood) casco m [asciugacapelli]. **~-grip** n molletta f. **~pin** n forcina f. **~pin 'bend** n tornante m, curva f a gomito. **~-raising** adj terrificante. **~-style** n acconciatura f

hairy /'heərɪ/ adj (**-ier, -iest**) peloso; (!: frightening) spaventoso

half /hɑːf/ n (pl **halves**) metà f inv;

cut in ~ tagliare a metà; **one and a ~** uno e mezzo; **~ a dozen** mezza dozzina; **~ an hour** mezz'ora • adj mezzo; [**at**] **~ price** [a] metà prezzo • adv a metà; **~ past two** le due e mezza

half: ~-'hearted adj esitante. **~ 'mast** n **at ~ mast** a mezz'asta. **~-'term** n vacanza f di metà trimestre. **~-'time** n (Sport) intervallo m. **~'way** adj **the ~way mark/stage** il livello intermedio • adv a metà strada; **get ~way** fig arrivare a metà

hall /hɔːl/ n (entrance) ingresso m; (room) sala f; (mansion) residenza f di campagna; **~ of residence** (Univ) casa f dello studente

'hallmark n marchio m di garanzia; fig marchio m

hallo /hə'ləʊ/ int ciao!; (on telephone) pronto!; **say ~ to** salutare

Hallowe'en /hæləʊ'iːn/ n vigilia f d'Ognissanti e notte delle streghe, celebrata soprattutto dai bambini

hallucination /həluːsɪ'neɪʃn/ n allucinazione f

halo /'heɪləʊ/ n (pl **-es**) aureola f; (Astr) alone m

halt /hɔːlt/ n alt m inv; **come to a ~** fermarsi; (traffic:) bloccarsi • vi fermarsi; **~!** alt! • vt fermare. **~ing** adj esitante

halve /hɑːv/ vt dividere a metà; (reduce) dimezzare

ham /hæm/ n prosciutto m; (Theat) attore, -trice mf da strapazzo

hamburger /'hæmbɜːgə(r)/ n hamburger m inv

hammer /'hæmə(r)/ n martello m • vt martellare • vi **~ at/on** picchiare a

hammock /'hæmək/ n amaca f

hamper¹ /'hæmpə(r)/ n cesto m; [**gift**] **~** cestino m

hamper² vt ostacolare

hamster /'hæmstə(r)/ n criceto m

hand /hænd/ n mano f; (of clock) lancetta f; (writing) scrittura f; (worker) manovale m; **at ~, to ~** a portata di mano; **on the one ~** da un lato; **on the other ~** d'altra parte; **out of ~** incontrollabile; (summarily) su due piedi; **give sb a ~** dare una mano a qcno • vt porgere. □**~ down** vt tramandare. □**~ in** vt consegnare. □**~ out** vt distribuire. □**~ over** vt passare; (to police) consegnare

hand: ~bag n borsa f (da signora). **~brake** n freno m a mano. **~cuffs** npl manette fpl. **~ful** n manciata f; **be [quite] a ~ful** [!] essere difficile da tenere a freno

handicap /'hændɪkæp/ n handicap m inv. **~ped** adj **mentally/physically ~ped** mentalmente/fisicamente handicappato

handi|craft /'hændɪkrɑːft/ n artigianato m. **~work** n opera f

handkerchief /'hæŋkətʃɪf/ n (pl **~s** & **-chieves**) fazzoletto m

handle /'hændl/ n manico m; (of door) maniglia f; **fly off the ~** [!] perdere le staffe • vt maneggiare; occuparsi di (problem, customer); prendere (difficult person); trattare (subject). **~bars** npl manubrio m

hand: ~-out n (at lecture) foglio m informativo; ([!]: money) elemosina f. **~shake** n stretta f di mano

handsome /'hænsəm/ adj bello; (fig: generous) generoso

handwriting n calligrafia f

handy /'hændɪ/ adj (**-ier, -iest**) utile; (person) abile; **have/keep ~** avere/tenere a portata di mano. **~man** n tuttofare m inv

hang /hæŋ/ vt (pt/pp **hung**) appendere (picture); (pt/pp **hanged**) impiccare (criminal); **~ oneself** impiccarsi • vi (pt/pp **hung**) pendere (hair:) scendere • n **get the ~ of it** [!] afferrare. □**~ about** vi gironzolare. □**~ on** vi tenersi stretto; ([!]: wait) aspettare; (Teleph) restare in linea. □**~ on to** vt tenersi stretto a; (keep) tenere. □**~ out** vi spuntare; **where does he usually ~ out?** [!] dove bazzica di solito? • vt stendere (washing). □**~ up** vt appendere; (Teleph) riattaccare • vi essere appeso; (Teleph) riattaccare

hangar /'hæŋə(r)/ n (Aeron) hangar m inv

hanger /'hæŋə(r)/ n gruccia f. **~-on** leccapiedi mf

hang: ~-glider n deltaplano m. **~over** n [!] postumi mpl da sbornia. **~-up** n [!] complesso m

anky /'hæŋkɪ/ n [!] fazzoletto m

aphazard /hæp'hæzəd/ adj a casaccio

appen /'hæpn/ vi capitare, succedere; **as it ~s** per caso; **I ~ed to meet him** mi è capitato di incontrarlo; **what has ~ed to him?** cosa gli è capitato?; (become of) che fine ha fatto? **~ing** n avvenimento m

appi|ly /'hæpɪlɪ/ adv felicemente; (fortunately) fortunatamente. **~ness** n felicità f

appy /'hæpɪ/ adj (**-ier, -iest**) contento, felice. **~-go-'lucky** adj spensierato

arass /'hærəs/ vt perseguitare. **~ed** adj stressato. **~ment** n persecuzione f; **sexual ~ment** molestie fpl sessuali

arbour /'hɑ:bə(r)/ n porto m •vt dare asilo a; nutrire (grudge)

ard /hɑ:d/ adj duro; (question, problem) difficile; **~ of hearing** duro d'orecchi; **be ~ on sb** (person:) essere duro con qcno •adv (work) duramente; (pull, hit, rain, snow) forte; **~ hit by unemployment** duramente colpito dalla disoccupazione; **take sth ~** non accettare qcsa; **think ~!** pensaci bene!; **try ~** mettercela tutta; **try ~er** metterci più impegno; **~ done by** [!] trattato ingiustamente

ard: hard-boiled adj (egg) sodo. **~ disk** n hard disk m inv, disco m rigido

arden /'hɑ:dn/ vi indurirsi

ard: ~-'headed adj (businessman) dal sangue freddo. **~line** adj duro

ard|ly /'hɑ:dlɪ/ adv appena; **~ly ever** quasi mai. **~ness** n durezza f. **~ship** n avversità f inv

ard: ~ 'shoulder n (Auto) corsia f d'emergenza. **~ware** n ferramenta fpl; (Comput) hardware m inv. **~-'working** adj **be ~-working** essere un gran lavoratore

ardy /'hɑ:dɪ/ adj (**-ier, -iest**) dal fisico resistente; (plant) che sopporta il gelo

are /heə(r)/ n lepre f. **~-brained** adj [!] (scheme) da scervellati

hark /hɑ:k/ vi **~ back to** fig ritornare su

harm /hɑ:m/ n male m; (damage) danni mpl; **out of ~'s way** in un posto sicuro; **it won't do any ~** non farà certo male •vt far male a; (damage) danneggiare. **~ful** adj dannoso. **~less** adj innocuo

harmonica /hɑ:'mɒnɪkə/ n armonica f [a bocca]

harmonious /hɑ:'məʊnɪəs/ adj armonioso. **~ly** adv in armonia

harness /'hɑ:nɪs/ n finimenti mpl; (of parachute) imbracatura f •vt bardare (horse); sfruttare (resources)

harp /hɑ:p/ n arpa f •**harp on** vi [!] insistere (**about** su). **~ist** n arpista mf

harpoon /hɑ:'pu:n/ n arpione m

harpsichord /'hɑ:psɪkɔ:d/ n clavicembalo m

harrowing /'hærəʊɪŋ/ adj straziante

harsh /hɑ:ʃ/ adj duro; (light) abbagliante. **~ness** n durezza f

harvest /'hɑ:vɪst/ n raccolta f; (of grapes) vendemmia f; (crop) raccolto m •vt raccogliere

has /hæz/ ▸**have**

hassle /'hæsl/ [!] n rottura f •vt rompere le scatole a

haste /heɪst/ n fretta f

hast|y /'heɪstɪ/ adj (**-ier, -iest**) frettoloso; (decision) affrettato. **~ily** adv frettolosamente

hat /hæt/ n cappello m

hatch¹ /hætʃ/ n (for food) sportello m passavivande; (Naut) boccaporto m

hatch² vi **~[out]** rompere il guscio; (egg:) schiudersi •vt covare; tramare (plot)

'hatchback n tre/cinque porte m inv; (door) porta f del bagagliaio

hatchet /'hætʃɪt/ n ascia f

hate /heɪt/ n odio m •vt odiare. **~ful** adj odioso

hatred /'heɪtrɪd/ n odio m

haught|y /'hɔ:tɪ/ adj (**-ier, -iest**) altezzoso. **~ily** adv altezzosamente

haul /hɔ:l/ n (fish) pescata f; (loot) bottino m; (pull) tirata f •vt tirare; trasportare (goods) •vi **~ on** tirare. **~age** n trasporto m. **~ier** n autotrasportatore m

haunt /hɔ:nt/ n ritrovo m •vt

h

frequentare; (linger in the mind) perseguitare; **this house is ~ed** questa casa è abitata da fantasmi

have /hæv/

- vt (*3 sg pres tense* **has**; pt/pp **had**) avere; fare (breakfast, bath, walk etc); **~ a drink** bere qualcosa; **~ lunch/dinner** pranzare/cenare; **~ a rest** riposarsi; **I had my hair cut** mi sono tagliata i capelli; **we had the house painted** abbiamo fatto tinteggiare la casa; **I had it made** l'ho fatto fare; **~ to do sth** dover fare qcsa; **~ him telephone me tomorrow** digli di telefonarmi domani; **he has** *or* **he's got two houses** ha due case; **you've got the money, ~n't you?** hai i soldi, no?
- v aux avere; (*with verbs of motion & some others*) essere; **I ~ seen him** l'ho visto; **he has never been there** non ci è mai stato. □ **~ on** vt (*be wearing*) portare; (*dupe*) prendere in giro; **I've got something on tonight** ho un impegno stasera. □ **~ out** vt **~ it out with sb** chiarire le cose con qcno
- npl **the ~s and the ~-nots** i ricchi e i poveri

haven /'heɪvn/ n fig rifugio m

haversack /'hævə-/ n zaino m

havoc /'hævək/ n strage f; **play ~ with** fig scombussolare

hawk /hɔːk/ n falco m

hay /heɪ/ n fieno m. **~ fever** n raffreddore m da fieno. **~stack** n pagliaio m

'haywire adj [!] **go ~** dare i numeri; (plans:) andare all'aria

hazard /'hæzəd/ n (risk) rischio m • vt rischiare; **~ a guess** azzardare un'ipotesi. **~ous** adj rischioso. **~ [warning] lights** npl (Auto) luci fpl d'emergenza

haze /heɪz/ n foschia f

hazel /'heɪz(ə)l/ n nocciolo m; (colour) [color m] nocciola m. **~-nut** n nocciola f

hazy /'heɪzɪ/ adj (**-ier, -iest**) nebbioso; (fig: person) confuso; (memories) vago

he /hiː/ pron lui; **he's tired** è stanco; **I'm going but he's not** io vengo, ma lui no

head /hed/ n testa f; (of firm) capo m; (of primary school) direttore, -trice mf; (of secondary school) preside mf; (on beer) schiuma f; **be off one's ~** essere fuori di testa; **have a good ~ for business** avere il senso degl affari; **have a good ~ for height** non soffrire di vertigini; **10 pounds a ~** 10 sterline a testa; **20 ~ of cattle** 20 capi di bestiame; **~ first** a capofitto; **~ over heels in love** innamorato pazzo; **~s or tails?** testa o croce? • vt essere a capo di; essere in testa a (list); colpire di testa (ball) • vi **~ for** dirigersi verso.

head: ~ache n mal m di testa. **~er** /'hedə(r)/ n rinvio m di testa; (dive) tuffo m di testa. **~ing** n (in list etc) titolo m. **~lamp** n (Auto) fanale m. **~land** n promontorio m. **~line** n titolo m. **~long** adj & adv a capofitto **~'master** n (of primary school) direttore m; (of secondary school) preside m. **~'mistress** n (of primary school) direttrice f; (of secondary school) preside f. **~-on** adj (collision) frontale • adv frontalmente. **~phones** npl cuffie fpl. **~quarters** npl sede fsg; (Mil) quartier m generale msg. **~strong** adj testardo

heady /'hedɪ/ adj che dà alla testa

heal /hiːl/ vt/i guarire

health /helθ/ n salute f

health|y /'helθɪ/ adj (**-ier, -iest**) sano. **~ily** adv in modo sano

heap /hiːp/ n mucchio m; **~s of** [!] un sacco di • vt **~ [up]** ammucchiare; **~ed teaspoon** un cucchiaino abbondante

hear /hɪə(r)/ vt/i (pt/pp **heard**) sentire; **~, ~!** bravo! **~ from** vi aver notizie di. □ **~ of** vi sentir parlare di; **he would not ~ of it** non ne ha voluto sentir parlare

hearing /'hɪərɪŋ/ n udito m; (Jur) udienza f. **~-aid** n apparecchio m acustico

'hearsay n **from ~** per sentito dire

hearse /hɜːs/ n carro m funebre

heart /hɑːt/ n cuore m; **~s** pl (in cards) cuori mpl; **by ~** a memoria

heart: ~ache n pena f. **~ attack** n

ıfarto m. **~-break** n afflizione f. **~-breaking** adj straziante. **~burn** n mal m di stomaco. **~felt** dj di cuore

earth /hɑ:θ/ n focolare m

eart|ily /'hɑ:tılı/ adv di cuore; (eat) on appetito; **be ~ily sick of sth** ıon poterne più di qcsa. **~less** adj pietato. **~-searching** n esame m di oscienza. **~-to-~** n conversazione f cuore aperto •adj a cuore aperto. **~y** adj caloroso; (meal) copioso; person) gioviale

eat /hi:t/ n calore m; (Sport) prova f liminatoria •vt scaldare •vi caldarsi. **~ed** adj (swimming pool) iscaldato; (discussion) animato. **~er** n for room) stufa f; (for water) boiler m ıv; (Auto) riscaldamento m

eath /hi:θ/ n brughiera f

eathen /'hi:ðn/ adj & n pagano, -a mf

eather /'heðə(r)/ n erica f

eating /'hi:tıŋ/ n riscaldamento m

eat: ~-stroke n colpo m di sole. **~wave** n ondata f di calore

eave /hi:v/ vt tirare; (lift) tirare su; (!: throw) gettare; emettere (sigh) •vi irare

eaven /'hev(ə)n/ n paradiso m; **~ help you if...** Dio ti scampi se...; **H~s!** santo cielo!. **~ly** adj celeste; ! delizioso

eav|y /'hevı/ adj (**-ier, -iest**) pesante; traffic) intenso; (rain, cold) forte; **be a ~y smoker/drinker** essere un gran fumatore/bevitore. **~ily** adv pesantemente; (smoke, drink etc) molto. **~yweight** n peso m massimo

ebrew /'hi:bru:/ adj ebreo

eckle /'hekl/ vt interrompere di continuo. **~r** n disturbatore, trice mf

ectic /'hektık/ adj frenetico

edge /hedʒ/ n siepe f •vi fig essere evasivo. **~hog** n riccio m

eed /hi:d/ n **pay ~ to** prestare ascolto a •vt prestare ascolto a. **~less** adj noncurante

eel¹ /hi:l/ n tallone m; (of shoe) tacco m; **take to one's ~s** ! darsela a gambe

eel² vi **~ over** (Naut) inclinarsi

efty /'heftı/ adj (**-ier, -iest**) massiccio

heifer /'hefə(r)/ n giovenca f

height /haıt/ n altezza f; (of plane) altitudine f; (of season, fame) culmine m. **~en** vt fig accrescere

heir /eə(r)/ n erede mf. **~ess** n ereditiera f. **~loom** n cimelio m di famiglia

held /held/ ▸**hold²**

helicopter /'helıkɒptə(r)/ n elicottero m

hell /hel/ n inferno m; **go to ~!** ⊠ va' al diavolo! •int porca miseria!

hello /hə'ləʊ/ int & n = **hallo**

helm /helm/ n timone m; **at the ~** fig al timone

h

helmet /'helmıt/ n casco m

help /help/ n aiuto m; (employee) aiuto m domestico; **that's no ~** non è d'aiuto •vt aiutare; **~ oneself to sth** servirsi di qcsa; **~ yourself** (at table) serviti pure; **I could not ~ laughing** non ho potuto trattenermi dal ridere; **it cannot be ~ed** non c'è niente da fare; **I can't ~ it** non ci posso far niente •vi aiutare

help|er /'helpə(r)/ n aiutante mf. **~ful** adj (person) di aiuto; (advice) utile. **~ing** n porzione f. **~less** adj (unable to manage) incapace; (powerless) impotente

hem /hem/ n orlo m •vt (pt/pp **hemmed**) orlare. □ **~ in** vt intrappolare

hemisphere /'hemı-/ n emisfero m

hen /hen/ n gallina f; (any female bird) femmina f

hence /hens/ adv (for this reason) quindi. **~'forth** adv d'ora innanzi

henpecked adj tiranneggiato dalla moglie

her /hɜ:(r)/ poss adj il suo m, la sua f, i suoi mpl, le sue fpl; **~ mother/father** sua madre/suo padre • pers pron (direct object) la; (indirect object) le; (after prep) lei; **I know ~** la conosco; **give ~ the money** dalle i soldi; **give it to ~** daglielo; **I came with ~** sono venuto con lei; **it's ~** è lei; **I've seen ~** l'ho vista; **I've seen ~, but not him** ho visto lei, ma non lui

herb /hɜ:b/ n erba f

herbal /'hɜ:b(ə)l/ adj alle erbe; ~ **tea** tisana f

herd /hɜ:d/ n gregge m •vt (tend) sorvegliare; (drive) far muovere; fig ammassare

here /hɪə(r)/ adv qui, qua; **in** ~ qui dentro; **come**/**bring** ~ vieni/porta qui; ~ **is...**, ~ **are...** ecco...; ~ **you are!** ecco qua!. ~'**after** adv in futuro. ~'**by** adv con la presente

heredit|ary /hə'redɪtərɪ/ adj ereditario. ~**y** n eredità f

here|sy /'herəsɪ/ n eresia f. ~**tic** n eretico, -a mf

here'with adv (Comm) con la presente

h

heritage /'herɪtɪdʒ/ n eredità f. ~ '**tourism** n turismo m culturale

hernia /'hɜ:nɪə/ n ernia f

hero /'hɪərəʊ/ n (pl **-es**) eroe m

heroic /hɪ'rəʊɪk/ adj eroico

heroin /'herəʊɪn/ n eroina f (droga)

hero|ine /'herəʊɪn/ n eroina f. ~**ism** n eroismo m

heron /'herən/ n airone m

herring /'herɪŋ/ n aringa f

hers /hɜ:z/ poss pron il suo m, la sua f, i suoi mpl, le sue fpl; **a friend of** ~ un suo amico; **friends of** ~ dei suoi amici; **that is** ~ quello è suo; (as opposed to mine) quello è il suo

her'self pers pron (reflexive) si; (emphatic) lei stessa; (after prep) sé, se stessa; **she poured** ~ **a drink** si è versata da bere; **she told me so** ~ me lo ha detto lei stessa; **she's proud of** ~ è fiera di sé; **by** ~ da sola

hesitant /'hezɪtənt/ adj esitante. ~**ly** adv con esitazione

hesitat|e /'hezɪteɪt/ vi esitare. ~**ion** n esitazione f

hetero'sexual /hetərəʊ-/ adj eterosessuale

hexagon /'heksəgən/ n esagono m. ~**al** adj esagonale

hey /heɪ/ int ehi

heyday /'heɪ-/ n tempi mpl d'oro

hi /haɪ/ int ciao!

hibernat|e /'haɪbəneɪt/ vi andare in letargo. ~**ion** n letargo m

hiccup /'hɪkʌp/ n singhiozzo m; (!: hitch) intoppo m •vi fare un singhiozzo

hide[1] /haɪd/ n (leather) pelle f (di animale)

hide[2] vt (pt **hid**, pp **hidden**) nascondere •vi nascondersi. ~**-and-'seek** n **play** ~**-and-seek** giocare a nascondino

hideous /'hɪdɪəs/ adj orribile

'hide-out n nascondiglio m

hiding[1] /'haɪdɪŋ/ n (!: beating) bastonata f; (defeat) batosta f

hiding[2] n **go into** ~ sparire dalla circolazione

hierarchy /'haɪərɑ:kɪ/ n gerarchia f

hieroglyphics /haɪərə'glɪfɪks/ npl geroglifici mpl

hi-fi /'haɪfaɪ/ n ! stereo m, hi-fi m in •adj ! ad alta fedeltà

high /haɪ/ adj alto; (meat) che comincia ad andare a male; (wind) forte; (on drugs) fatto; **it's** ~ **time we did something about it** è or di fare qualcosa in proposito •adv alto; ~ **and low** in lungo e in larg •n massimo m; (temperature) massim f; **be on a** ~ ! essere fatto

high: ~**er education** n formazione f universitaria. ~'**-handed** adj dispotico. ~ **heel** npl tacchi mpl alti

highlight /'haɪlaɪt/ n fig momento m clou; ~**s** pl (in hair) mèche fpl •vt (emphasize) evidenziare. ~**er** n (marker) evidenziatore m

highly /'haɪlɪ/ adv molto; **speak** ~ lodare; **think** ~ **of** avere un'alta opinione di. ~**-'strung** adj nervoso

high: ~**-rise** adj (building) molto alto •n edificio m molto alto. ~ **school** n ≈ scuola f superiore. ~ **street** n strada f principale. ~**way code** n codice m stradale

hijack /'haɪdʒæk/ vt dirottare •n dirottamento m. ~**er** n dirottatore, -trice mf

hike /haɪk/ n escursione f a piedi •vi fare un'escursione a piedi. ~**r** n escursionista mf

hilarious /hɪ'leərɪəs/ adj esilarante

hill /hɪl/ n collina f; (mound) collinett f; (slope) altura f

hill: ~**side** n pendio m. ~**y** adj collinoso

hilt /hɪlt/ n impugnatura f; **to the** ~

(support) fino in fondo; (mortgaged) fino al collo

'm /hɪm/ pers pron (direct object) lo; (indirect object) gli; (with prep) lui; **I know ~** lo conosco; **give ~ the money** dagli i soldi; **give it to ~** daglielo; **I spoke to ~** gli ho parlato; **it's ~** è lui; **she loves ~** lo ama; **she loves ~, not you** ama lui, non te. **~'self** pers pron (reflexive) si; (emphatic) lui stesso; (after prep) sé, se stesso; **he poured ~ a drink** si è versato da bere; **he told me so ~self** me lo ha detto lui stesso; **he's proud of ~self** è fiero di sé; **by ~self** da solo

ind|er /'hɪndə(r)/ vt intralciare. **~rance** n intralcio m

indsight /'haɪnd-/ n **with ~** con il senno del poi

indu /'hɪndu:/ n indù mf inv • adj indù. **~ism** n induismo m

inge /hɪndʒ/ n cardine m • vi **~ on** fig dipendere da

int /hɪnt/ n (clue) accenno m; (advice) suggerimento m; (indirect suggestion) allusione f; (trace) tocco m • vt **~ that...** far capire che... • vi **~ at** alludere a

ip /hɪp/ n fianco m

ippie /'hɪpɪ/ n hippy mf inv

ippopotamus /hɪpə'pɒtəməs/ n (pl **-muses** or **-mi** /-maɪ/) ippopotamo m

ire /'haɪə(r)/ vt affittare; assumere (person); **~ [out]** affittare • n noleggio m; **'for ~'** 'affittasi'. **~ car** n macchina f a noleggio. **~ purchase** n acquisto m rateale

is /hɪz/ poss adj il suo m, la sua f, i suoi mpl, le sue fpl; **~ mother/father** sua madre/suo padre • poss pron il suo m, la sua f, i suoi mpl, le sue fpl; **a friend of ~** un suo amico; **friends of ~** dei suoi amici; **that is ~** questo è suo; (as opposed to mine) questo è il suo

iss /hɪs/ n sibilo m; (of disapproval) fischio m • vt fischiare • vi sibilare; (in disapproval) fischiare

istorian /hɪ'stɔ:rɪən/ n storico, -a mf

istory /'hɪstərɪ/ n storia f; **make ~** passare alla storia

it /hɪt/ n (blow) colpo m; (!: success) successo m; **score a direct ~** (missile:) colpire in pieno • vt/i (pt/pp **hit**, pres p **hitting**) colpire; **~ one's head on the table** battere la testa contro il tavolo; **the car ~ the wall** la macchina ha sbattuto contro il muro; **~ the roof** ! perdere le staffe. □ **~ off** vt **~ it off** andare d'accordo. □ **~ on** vt fig trovare

hitch /hɪtʃ/ n intoppo m; **technical ~** problema m tecnico • vt attaccare; **~ a lift** chiedere un passaggio. □ **~ up** vt tirarsi su (trousers). **~-hike** vi fare l'autostop. **~-hiker** n autostoppista mf

hither /'hɪðə(r)/ adv **~ and thither** di qua e di là. **~'to** adv finora

hit-or-'miss adj **on a very ~ basis** all'improvvisata

hive /haɪv/ n alveare m; **~ of industry** fucina f di lavoro • **hive off** vt (Comm) separare

hoard /hɔ:d/ n provvista f; (of money) gruzzolo m • vt accumulare

hoarding /'hɔ:dɪŋ/ n palizzata f; (with advertisements) tabellone m per manifesti pubblicitari

hoarse /hɔ:s/ adj rauco. **~ly** adv con voce rauca. **~ness** n raucedine f

hoax /həʊks/ n scherzo m; (false alarm) falso allarme m. **~er** n burlone, -a mf

hob /hɒb/ n piano m di cottura

hobble /'hɒbl/ vi zoppicare

hobby /'hɒbɪ/ n hobby m inv. **~-horse** n fig fissazione f

hockey /'hɒkɪ/ n hockey m

hoe /həʊ/ n zappa f

hog /hɒg/ n maiale m • vt (pt/pp **hogged**) ! monopolizzare

hoist /hɔɪst/ n montacarichi m inv; (!: push) spinta f in su • vt sollevare; innalzare (flag); levare (anchor)

hold[1] /həʊld/ n (Aeron, Naut) stiva f

hold[2] n presa f; (fig: influence) ascendente m; **get ~ of** trovare; procurarsi (information) • v (pt/pp **held**) • vt tenere; (container:) contenere; essere titolare di (licence, passport); trattenere (breath, suspect); mantenere vivo (interest); (civil servant etc:) occupare (position); (retain) mantenere; **~ sb's hand** tenere qcno per mano; **~ one's tongue** tenere la bocca chiusa; **~ sb responsible** considerare qcno

h

responsabile; ~ **that** (believe) ritenere che • vi tenere; (weather, luck:) durare; (offer:) essere valido; (Teleph) restare in linea; **I don't ~ with the idea that...** [!] non sono d'accordo sul fatto che... □~ **back** vt rallentare • vi esitare. □~ **down** vt tenere a bada (sb). □~ **on** vi (wait) attendere; (Teleph) restare in linea. □~ **on to** vt aggrapparsi a; (keep) tenersi. □~ **out** vt porgere (hand); fig offrire (possibility) • vi (resist) resistere. □~ **up** vt tenere su; (delay) rallentare; (rob) assalire; ~ **one's head up** fig tenere la testa alta

'**hold:** ~**all** n borsone m. ~**er** n titolare mf; (of record) detentore, -trice mf; (container) astuccio m. ~**-up** n ritardo m; (attack) rapina f a mano armata

h

hole /həʊl/ n buco m

holiday /'hɒlɪdeɪ/ n vacanza f; (public) giorno m festivo; (day off) giorno m di ferie; **go on** ~ andare in vacanza • vi andare in vacanza. ~**-maker** n vacanziere mf

holiness /'həʊlɪnɪs/ n santità f; **Your H~** Sua Santità

Holland /'hɒlənd/ n Olanda f

hollow /'hɒləʊ/ adj cavo; (promise) a vuoto; (voice) assente; (cheeks) infossato • n cavità f inv; (in ground) affossamento m

holly /'hɒlɪ/ n agrifoglio m

holocaust /'hɒləkɔ:st/ n olocausto m

holster /'həʊlstə(r)/ n fondina f

holy /'həʊlɪ/ adj (**-ier, -est**) santo; (water) benedetto. **H~ Ghost** or **Spirit** n Spirito m Santo. **H~ Scriptures** npl sacre scritture fpl. **H~ Week** n settimana f santa

homage /'hɒmɪdʒ/ n omaggio m; **pay ~ to** rendere omaggio a

home /həʊm/ n casa f; (for children) istituto m; (for old people) casa f di riposo; (native land) patria f • adv **at ~** a casa; (football) in casa; **feel at ~** sentirsi a casa propria; **come/go ~** venire/andare a casa; **drive a nail ~** piantare un chiodo a fondo • adj domestico; (movie, video) casalingo; (team) ospitante; (Pol) nazionale

home: ~ **ad'dress** n indirizzo m di casa. ~**land** n patria f; ~**land se'curity** n sicurezza f delle frontiere. ~**less** adj senza tetto

homely /'həʊmlɪ/ adj (**-ier, -iest**) semplice; (atmosphere) familiare; (Am ugly) bruttino

home: ~**-'made** adj fatto in casa. **H~ Office** n Br ministero m degli interni. ~**sick** adj **be ~sick** avere nostalgia (**for** di). ~ **'town** n città f inv natia. ~**work** n (Sch) compiti mpl

homicide /'hɒmɪsaɪd/ n (crime) omicidio m

homoeopath|ic /həʊmɪə'pæθɪk/ adj omeopatico. ~**y** n omeopatia f

homogeneous /hɒmə'dʒi:nɪəs/ adj omogeneo

homo'sexual adj & n omosessuale mf

honest /'ɒnɪst/ adj onesto; (frank) sincero. ~**ly** adv onestamente; (frankly) sinceramente; ~**ly!** ma insomma!. ~**y** n onestà f; (frankness) sincerità f

honey /'hʌnɪ/ n miele m; ([!]: darling) tesoro m

honey: ~**comb** n favo m. ~**moon** n luna f di miele. ~**suckle** n caprifoglio m

honorary /'ɒnərərɪ/ adj onorario

honour /'ɒnə(r)/ n onore m • vt onorare. ~**able** adj onorevole. ~**ably** adv con onore. ~**s degree** n ≈ diploma m di laurea

hood /hʊd/ n cappuccio m; (of pram) tettuccio m; (over cooker) cappa f; Am (Auto) cofano m

hoodlum /'hu:dləm/ n teppista m

'**hoodwink** vt [!] infinocchiare

hoof /hu:f/ n (pl ~**s** or **hooves**) zoccolo m

hook /hʊk/ n gancio m; (for fishing) amo m; **off the ~** (Teleph) staccato; fig fuori pericolo • vt agganciare • vi agganciarsi

hook|ed /hʊkt/ adj (nose) adunco ~**ed on** ([!]: drugs) dedito a; **be ~ed on skiing** essere un fanatico dello sci. ~**er** n Am [✖] battona f

hookey /'hʊkɪ/ n **play ~** Am [!] marinare la scuola

hooligan /'hu:lɪgən/ n teppista mf. ~**ism** n teppismo m

hoop /hu:p/ n cerchio m

hooray /hʊ'reɪ/ int & n = **hurrah**

oot /hu:t/ n colpo m di clacson; (of siren) ululato m; (of owl) grido m •vi (owl:) gridare; (car:) clacsonare; (siren:) ululare; (jeer) fischiare. **~er** n (of factory) sirena f; (Auto) clacson m inv

oover® /'hu:və(r)/ n aspirapolvere m inv •vt passare l'aspirapolvere su (carpet); passare l'aspirapolvere in (room)

op /hɒp/ n saltello m •vi (pt/pp **hopped**) saltellare; **~ it!** [!] tela!. □ **~ in** vi [!] saltar su

ope /həʊp/ n speranza f •vi sperare (**for** in); **I ~ so/not** spero di sì/no •vt **~ that** sperare che

ope|ful /'həʊpfl/ adj pieno di speranza; (promising) promettente; **be ~ful that** avere buone speranze che. **~fully** adv con speranza; (it is hoped) se tutto va bene. **~less** adj senza speranze; (useless) impossibile; (incompetent) incapace. **~lessly** adv disperatamente; (inefficient, lost) completamente. **~lessness** n disperazione f

orde /hɔ:d/ n orda f

orizon /hə'raɪzn/ n orizzonte m

orizontal /hɒrɪ'zɒntl/ adj orizzontale

ormone /'hɔ:məʊn/ n ormone m

orn /hɔ:n/ n corno m; (Auto) clacson m inv

oroscope /'hɒrəskəʊp/ n oroscopo m

orribl|e /'hɒrɪbl/ adj orribile. **~y** adv spaventosamente

orrid /'hɒrɪd/ adj orrendo

orrific /hə'rɪfɪk/ adj raccapricciante; (accident, prices, story) terrificante

horrify /'hɒrɪfaɪ/ vt (pt/pp **-ied**) far inorridire; **I was horrified** ero sconvolto. **~ing** adj terrificante

horror /'hɒrə(r)/ n orrore m. **~ film** n film m dell'orrore

horse /hɔ:s/ n cavallo m

horse: ~back n **on ~back** a cavallo. **~power** n cavallo m [vapore]. **~-racing** n corse fpl di cavalli. **~shoe** n ferro m di cavallo

horti'cultural /hɔ:tɪ-/ adj di orticoltura

'horticulture n orticoltura f

hose /həʊz/ n (pipe) manichetta f

•hose down vt lavare con la manichetta

hospice /'hɒspɪs/ n (for the terminally ill) ospedale m per i malati in fase terminale

hospitabl|e /hɒ'spɪtəbl/ adj ospitale. **~y** adv con ospitalità

hospital /'hɒspɪtl/ n ospedale m

hospitality /hɒspɪ'tælətɪ/ n ospitalità f

host[1] /həʊst/ n **a ~ of** una moltitudine di

host[2] n ospite m

host[3] n (Relig) ostia f

hostage /'hɒstɪdʒ/ n ostaggio m; **hold sb ~** tenere qcno in ostaggio

hostel /'hɒstl/ n ostello m

hostess /'həʊstɪs/ n padrona f di casa; (Aeron) hostess f inv

hostile /'hɒstaɪl/ adj ostile

hostilit|y /hɒ'stɪlətɪ/ n ostilità f; **~ies** pl ostilità fpl

hot /hɒt/ adj (**hotter, hottest**) caldo; (spicy) piccante; **I am** or **feel ~** ho caldo; **it is ~** fa caldo

'hotbed n fig focolaio m

hotchpotch /'hɒtʃpɒtʃ/ n miscuglio m

'hot-dog n hot dog m inv

hotel /həʊ'tel/ n albergo m. **~ier** n albergatore, -trice mf

hot: ~house n serra f. **~plate** n piastra f riscaldante **~-'water bottle** n borsa f dell'acqua calda

hound /haʊnd/ n cane m da caccia •vt fig perseguire

hour /'aʊə(r)/ n ora f. **~ly** adj ad ogni ora; (pay, rate) a ora •adv ogni ora

house /haʊs/: **~boat** n casa f galleggiante. **~breaking** n furto m con scasso. **~hold** n casa f, famiglia f. **~holder** n capo m di famiglia. **~keeper** n governante f di casa. **~keeping** n governo m della casa; (money) soldi mpl per le spese di casa. **~-plant** n pianta f da appartamento. **~-trained** adj che non sporca in casa. **~-warming party** n festa f di inaugurazione della nuova casa. **~wife** n casalinga f. **~work** n lavoro m domestico

house[1] /haʊs/ n casa f; (Pol) camera f;

(Theat) sala f; **at my ~** a casa mia, da me

house² /haʊz/ vt alloggiare (person)

housing /ˈhaʊzɪŋ/ n alloggio m. **~ estate** n zona f residenziale

hovel /ˈhɒvl/ n tugurio m

hover /ˈhɒvə(r)/ vi librarsi; (linger) indugiare. **~craft** n hovercraft m inv

how /haʊ/ adv come; **~ are you?** come stai?; **~ about a coffee/going on holiday?** che ne diresti di un caffè/di andare in vacanza?; **~ do you do?** molto lieto!; **~ old are you?** quanti anni hai?; **~ long** quanto tempo; **~ many** quanti; **~ much** quanto; **~ often** ogni quanto; **and ~!** eccome!; **~ odd!** che strano!

h

howˈever adv (nevertheless) comunque; **~ small** per quanto piccolo

howl /haʊl/ n ululato m •vi ululare; (cry, with laughter) singhiozzare. **~er** n [!] strafalcione m

HP n abbr hire purchase; n abbr (horse power) C.V.

hub /hʌb/ n mozzo m; fig centro m

ˈhub-cap n coprimozzo m

huddle /ˈhʌdl/ vi **~ together** rannicchiarsi

hue¹ /hju:/ n colore m

hue² n **~ and cry** clamore m

huff /hʌf/ n **be in/go into a ~** fare il broncio

hug /hʌg/ n abbraccio m •vt (pt/pp **hugged**) abbracciare; (keep close to) tenersi vicino a

huge /hju:dʒ/ adj enorme

hull /hʌl/ n (Naut) scafo m

hullo /həˈləʊ/ int = **hallo**

hum /hʌm/ n ronzio m •v (pt/pp **hummed**) •vt canticchiare •vi (motor:) ronzare; fig fervere (di attività); **~ and haw** esitare

human /ˈhju:mən/ adj umano •n essere m umano. **~ ˈbeing** n essere m umano

humane /hju:ˈmeɪn/ adj umano

humanitarian /hju:mænɪˈteərɪən/ adj & n umanitario, -a mf

humanit|y /hju:ˈmænətɪ/ n umanità f; **~ies** pl (Univ) dottrine fpl umanistiche

humbl|e /ˈhʌmbl/ adj umile •vt umiliare

ˈhumdrum adj noioso

humid /ˈhju:mɪd/ adj umido. **~ifier** umidificatore m. **~ity** /-ˈmɪdətɪ/ n umidità f

humiliat|e /hju:ˈmɪlɪeɪt/ vt umiliare **~ion** n umiliazione f

humility /hju:ˈmɪlətɪ/ n umiltà f

humorous /ˈhju:mərəs/ adj umoristico. **~ly** adv con spirito

humour /ˈhju:mə(r)/ n umorismo m; (mood) umore m; **have a sense of ~** avere il senso dell'umorismo •vt compiacere

hump /hʌmp/ n protuberanza f; (of camel, hunchback) gobba f

hunch /hʌntʃ/ n (idea) intuizione f

ˈhunch|back n gobbo, -a mf. **~ed** adj **~ed up** incurvato

hundred /ˈhʌndrəd/ adj **one/a ~** cento •n cento m; **~s of** centinaia di. **~th** adj centesimo •n centesimo m. **~weight** n cinquanta chili m

hung /hʌŋ/ ▸**hang**

Hungarian /hʌŋˈgeərɪən/ n & adj ungherese mf; (language) ungherese m

Hungary /ˈhʌŋgərɪ/ n Ungheria f

hunger /ˈhʌŋgə(r)/ n fame f. **~-strike** n sciopero m della fame m

hungr|y /ˈhʌŋgrɪ/ adj (**-ier, -iest**) affamato; **be ~y** aver fame. **~ily** adv con appetito

hunk /hʌŋk/ n [grosso] pezzo m

hunt /hʌnt/ n caccia f•vt andare a caccia di (animal); dare la caccia a (criminal) •vi andare a caccia; **~ for** cercare. **~er** n cacciatore m. **~ing** n caccia f

hurl /hɜ:l/ vt scagliare

hurrah /hʊˈrɑ:/, **hurray** /hʊˈreɪ/ int urrà! •n urrà m

hurricane /ˈhʌrɪkən/ n uragano m

hurried /ˈhʌrɪd/ adj affrettato; (job) fatto in fretta. **~ly** adv in fretta

hurry /ˈhʌrɪ/ n fretta f; **be in a ~** aver fretta •vi (pt/pp **-ied**) affrettarsi. □ **~ up** vi sbrigarsi •vt fare sbrigare (person); accelerare (things)

hurt /hɜ:t/ v (pt/pp **hurt**) •vt far male a; (offend) ferire •vi far male; **my**

leg ~s mi fa male la gamba. **~ful** adj fig offensivo

urtle /'hɜ:tl/ vi **~ along** andare a tutta velocità

usband /'hʌzbənd/ n marito m

ush /hʌʃ/ n silenzio m • **hush up** vt mettere a tacere. **~ed** adj (voice) sommesso. **~-'hush** adj [!] segretissimo

usky /'hʌskɪ/ adj (**-ier, -iest**) (voice) rauco

ustle /'hʌsl/ vt affrettare • n attività f incessante; **~ and bustle** trambusto m

ut /hʌt/ n capanna f

ybrid /'haɪbrɪd/ adj ibrido • n ibrido m

ydrant /'haɪdrənt/ n [**fire**] **~** idrante m

ydraulic /haɪ'drɔ:lɪk/ adj idraulico

ydroe'lectric /haɪdrəʊ-/ adj idroelettrico

ydrofoil /'haɪdrə-/ n aliscafo m

ydrogen /'haɪdrədʒən/ n idrogeno m

yena /haɪ'i:nə/ n iena f

hygien|e /'haɪdʒi:n/ n igiene f. **~ic** adj igienico

hymn /hɪm/ n inno m. **~-book** n libro m dei canti

hypermarket /'haɪpəmɑ:kɪt/ n ipermercato m

hyphen /'haɪfn/ n lineetta f. **~ate** vt unire con lineetta

hypno|sis /hɪp'nəʊsɪs/ n ipnosi f. **~tic** adj ipnotico

hypno|tism /'hɪpnətɪzm/ n ipnotismo m. **~tist** n ipnotizzatore, -trice mf. **~tize** vt ipnotizzare

hypochondriac /haɪpə'kɒndrɪæk/ adj ipocondriaco • n ipocondriaco, -a mf

hypocrisy /hɪ'pɒkrəsɪ/ n ipocrisia f

hypocrit|e /'hɪpəkrɪt/ n ipocrita mf. **~ical** adj ipocrita

hypodermic /haɪpə'dɜ:mɪk/ adj & n **~** [**syringe**] siringa f ipodermica

hypothe|sis /haɪ'pɒθəsɪs/ n ipotesi f inv. **~tical** adj ipotetico. **~tically** adv in teoria; (speak) per ipotesi

hyster|ia /hɪ'stɪərɪə/ n isterismo m. **~ical** adj isterico. **~ically** adv istericamente; **~ically funny** da morir dal ridere. **~ics** npl attacco m isterico

Ii

/aɪ/ pron io; **I'm tired** sono stanco; **he's going, but I'm not** lui va, ma io no

ice /aɪs/ n ghiaccio m • vt glassare (cake). ▫ **~ over/up** vi ghiacciarsi

ice: ~-axe n piccozza f per il ghiaccio. **~berg** /-bɜ:g/ n iceberg m inv. **~box** n Am frigorifero m. **~-'cream** n gelato m. **~-cube** n cubetto m di ghiaccio

Iceland /'aɪslənd/ n Islanda f. **~er** n islandese mf; **~ic** /-'lændɪk/ adj & n islandese m

ice: ~'lolly n ghiacciolo m. **~ rink** n pista f di pattinaggio. **~ skater** pattinatore, -trice mf sul ghiaccio. **~ skating** pattinaggio m su ghiaccio

icicle /'aɪsɪkl/ n ghiacciolo m

icing /'aɪsɪŋ/ n glassa f. **~ sugar** n zucchero m a velo

icon /'aɪkɒn/ n icona f

ic|y /'aɪsɪ/ adj (**-ier, -iest**) ghiacciato; fig gelido. **~ily** adv gelidamente

idea /aɪ'dɪə/ n idea f; **I've no ~!** non ne ho idea!

ideal /aɪ'dɪəl/ adj ideale • n ideale m. **~ism** n idealismo m. **~ist** n idealista mf. **~istic** adj idealistico. **~ize** vt idealizzare. **~ly** adv idealmente

identical /aɪ'dentɪkl/ adj identico

identi|fication /aɪdentɪfɪ'keɪʃn/ n identificazione f; (proof of identity) documento m di riconoscimento. **~fy** vt (pt/pp **-ied**) identificare

identity /aɪ'dentətɪ/ n identità f inv. **~ card** n carta f d'identità. **~ theft** n furto m d'identità

ideolog|ical /aɪdɪə'lɒdʒɪkl/ adj ideologico. **~y** n ideologia f

idiom /'ɪdɪəm/ n idioma f. **~atic** adj idiomatico

idiot /'ɪdɪət/ n idiota mf. **~ic** adj idiota

idl|e /'aɪd(ə)l/ adj (lazy) pigro, ozioso; (empty) vano; (machine) fermo • vi oziare; (engine:) girare a vuoto. **~eness** n ozio m. **~y** adv oziosamente

i

idol /'aɪdl/ n idolo m. **~ize** vt idolatrare

idyllic /ɪ'dɪlɪk/ adj idillico

i.e. abbr (id est) cioè

if /ɪf/ conj se; **as if** come se

ignite /ɪg'naɪt/ vt dar fuoco a • vi prender fuoco

ignition /ɪg'nɪʃn/ n (Auto) accensione f. **~ key** n chiave f d'accensione

ignoramus /ɪgnə'reɪməs/ n ignorante mf

ignoran|ce /'ɪgnərəns/ n ignoranza f. **~t** adj (lacking knowledge) ignaro; (rude) ignorante

ignore /ɪg'nɔ:(r)/ vt ignorare

ill /ɪl/ adj ammalato; **feel ~ at ease** sentirsi a disagio • adv male • n male m. **~-advised** adj avventato. **~-bred** adj maleducato

illegal /ɪ'li:gl/ adj illegale

illegibl|e /ɪ'ledʒɪbl/ adj illeggibile

illegitima|cy /ɪlɪ'dʒɪtɪməsɪ/ n illegittimità f. **~te** adj illegittimo

illitera|cy /ɪ'lɪtərəsɪ/ n analfabetismo m. **~te** adj & n analfabeta mf

illness /'ɪlnɪs/ n malattia f

illogical /ɪ'lɒdʒɪkl/ adj illogico

illuminat|e /ɪ'lu:mɪneɪt/ vt illuminare. **~ing** adj chiarificatore. **~ion** n illuminazione f

illusion /ɪ'lu:ʒn/ n illusione f; **be under the ~ that** avere l'illusione che

illustrat|e /'ɪləstreɪt/ vt illustrare. **~ion** n illustrazione f. **~or** n illustratore, -trice mf

illustrious /ɪ'lʌstrɪəs/ adj illustre

ill 'will n malanimo m

image /'ɪmɪdʒ/ n immagine f; (exact likeness) ritratto m

imagin|able /ɪ'mædʒɪnəbl/ adj immaginabile. **~ary** adj immaginario

imaginat|ion /ɪmædʒɪ'neɪʃn/ n immaginazione f, fantasia f; **it's your ~ion** è solo una tua idea. **~ive** adj fantasioso. **~ively** adv con fantasia or immaginazione

imagine /ɪ'mædʒɪn/ vt immaginare; (wrongly) inventare

im'balance n squilibrio m

imbecile /'ɪmbəsi:l/ n imbecille mf

imitat|e /'ɪmɪteɪt/ vt imitare. **~ion** n imitazione f. **~or** n imitatore, -trice mf

immaculate /ɪ'mækjʊlət/ adj immacolato. **~ly** adv immacolatamente

imma'ture adj immaturo

immediate /ɪ'mi:dɪət/ adj immediato; (relative) stretto; **in the ~ vicinity** nelle immediate vicinanze. **~ly** adv immediatamente **~ly next to** subito accanto a • conj [non] appena

immense /ɪ'mens/ adj immenso

immers|e /ɪ'mɜ:s/ vt immergere; **be ~ed in** fig essere immerso in. **~ion** n immersione f. **~ion heater** n scaldabagno m elettrico

immigrant /'ɪmɪgrənt/ n immigrante mf

imminent /'ɪmɪnənt/ adj imminente

immobil|e /ɪ'məʊbaɪl/ adj immobile. **~ize** vt immobilizzare

immoderate /ɪ'mɒdərət/ adj smodato

immoral /ɪ'mɒrəl/ adj immorale. **~ity** n immoralità f

immortal /ɪ'mɔ:tl/ adj immortale. **~ity** n immortalità f. **~ize** vt immortalare

immune /ɪ'mju:n/ adj immune (**to/from** da). **~ system** n sistema m immunitario

immunity /ɪ'mju:nətɪ/ n immunità f

immuniz|e /'ɪmjʊnaɪz/ vt immunizzare

imp /ɪmp/ n diavoletto m

impact /ˈɪmpækt/ n impatto m

impair /ɪmˈpeə(r)/ vt danneggiare

impale /ɪmˈpeɪl/ vt impalare

impart /ɪmˈpɑːt/ vt impartire

imˈparti|al adj imparziale. **~ˈality** n imparzialità f

imˈpassable adj impraticabile

imˈpassive adj impassibile

imˈpatien|ce n impazienza f. **~t** adj impaziente. **~tly** adv impazientemente

impeccabl|e /ɪmˈpekəbl/ adj impeccabile. **~y** adv in modo impeccabile

impede /ɪmˈpiːd/ vt impedire

impediment /ɪmˈpedɪmənt/ n impedimento m; (in speech) difetto m

impending /ɪmˈpendɪŋ/ adj imminente

impenetrable /ɪmˈpenɪtrəbl/ adj impenetrabile

imperative /ɪmˈperətɪv/ adj imperativo • n (Gram) imperativo m

imperˈceptible adj impercettibile

imˈperfect adj imperfetto; (faulty) difettoso • n (Gram) imperfetto m. **~ion** n imperfezione f

imperial /ɪmˈpɪərɪəl/ adj imperiale. **~ism** n imperialismo m. **~ist** n imperialista mf

imˈpersonal adj impersonale

impersonat|e /ɪmˈpɜːsəneɪt/ vt impersonare. **~or** n imitatore, -trice mf

impertinen|ce /ɪmˈpɜːtɪnəns/ n impertinenza f. **~t** adj impertinente

impervious /ɪmˈpɜːvɪəs/ adj **~ to** fig indifferente a

impetuous /ɪmˈpetjʊəs/ adj impetuoso. **~ly** adv impetuosamente

impetus /ˈɪmpɪtəs/ n impeto m

implacable /ɪmˈplækəbl/ adj implacabile

imˈplant¹ vt trapiantare; fig inculcare

ˈimplant² n trapianto m

implement¹ /ˈɪmplɪmənt/ n attrezzo m

implement² /ˈɪmplɪment/ vt mettere in atto. **~ation** /-ˈeɪʃn/ n attuazione f

implicat|e /ˈɪmplɪkeɪt/ vt implicare. **~ion** n implicazione f; **by ~ion** implicitamente

implicit /ɪmˈplɪsɪt/ adj implicito; (absolute) assoluto

implore /ɪmˈplɔː(r)/ vt implorare

imply /ɪmˈplaɪ/ vt (pt/pp **-ied**) implicare; **what are you ~ing?** che cosa vorresti insinuare?

impoˈlite adj sgarbato

import¹ /ˈɪmpɔːt/ n (Comm) importazione f

import² /ɪmˈpɔːt/ vt importare

importan|ce /ɪmˈpɔːtəns/ n importanza f. **~t** adj importante

importer /ɪmˈpɔːtə(r)/ n importatore, -trice mf

impos|e /ɪmˈpəʊz/ vt imporre (**on** a) • vi imporsi; **~e on** abusare di. **~ing** adj imponente. **~ition** n imposizione f

impossiˈbility n impossibilità f

imˈpossibl|e adj impossibile

impostor /ɪmˈpɒstə(r)/ n impostore, -trice mf

impoten|ce /ˈɪmpətəns/ n impotenza f. **~t** adj impotente

impound /ɪmˈpaʊnd/ vt confiscare

impoverished /ɪmˈpɒvərɪʃt/ adj impoverito

imˈpractical adj non pratico

impregnable /ɪmˈpregnəbl/ adj imprendibile

impregnate /ˈɪmpregneɪt/ vt impregnare (**with** di); (Biol) fecondare

imˈpress vt imprimere; fig colpire (positivamente); **~ sth on sb** fare capire qcsa a qcno

impression /ɪmˈpreʃn/ n impressione f; (imitation) imitazione f. **~able** adj (child, mind) influenzabile. **~ism** n impressionismo m. **~ist** n imitatore, -trice mf; (artist) impressionista mf

impressive /ɪmˈpresɪv/ adj imponente

ˈimprint¹ n impressione f

imˈprint² vt imprimere; **~ed on my mind** impresso nella mia memoria

imˈprison vt incarcerare. **~ment** n reclusione f

im'probable adj improbabile

impromptu /ɪm'prɒmptju:/ adj improvvisato

im'proper adj (use) improprio; (behaviour) scorretto. **~ly** adv scorrettamente

improve /ɪm'pru:v/ vt/i migliorare. **improve on** vt perfezionare. **~ment** n miglioramento m

improvis|e /'ɪmprəvaɪz/ vt/i improvvisare

impuden|ce /'ɪmpjʊdəns/ n sfrontatezza f. **~t** adj sfrontato

impuls|e /'ɪmpʌls/ n impulso m; **on [an] ~e** impulsivamente. **~ive** adj impulsivo

im'pur|e adj impuro. **~ity** n impurità f inv; **~ities** pl impurità fpl

in /ɪn/ prep in; (with names of towns) a; **in the garden** in giardino; **in the street** in or per strada; **in bed/hospital** a letto/all'ospedale; **in the world** nel mondo; **in the rain** sotto la pioggia; **in the sun** al sole; **in this heat** con questo caldo; **in summer/winter** in estate/inverno; **in 1995** nel 1995; **in the evening** la sera; **he's arriving in two hours time** arriva fra due ore; **deaf in one ear** sordo da un orecchio; **in the army** nell'esercito; **in English/Italian** in inglese/italiano; **in ink/pencil** a penna/matita; **in red** (dressed, circled) di rosso; **the man in the raincoat** l'uomo con l'impermeabile; **in a soft/loud voice** a voce bassa/alta; **one in ten people** una persona su dieci; **in doing this, he...** nel far questo,...; **in itself** in sé; **in that** in quanto • adv (at home) a casa; (indoors) dentro; **he's not in yet** non è ancora arrivato; **in there/here** lì/qui dentro; **ten in all** dieci in tutto; **day in, day out** giorno dopo giorno; **have it in for sb** [!] avercela con qcno; **send him in** fallo entrare; **come in** entrare; **bring in the washing** portare dentro i panni • adj ([!]: in fashion) di moda • n **the ins and outs** i dettagli

ina'bility n incapacità f

inac'cessible adj inaccessibile

in'accura|cy n inesattezza f. **~te** adj inesatto

in'ac|tive adj inattivo. **~'tivity** n inattività f

in'adequate adj inadeguato. **~ly** adv inadeguatamente

inadvertently /ɪnəd'vɜ:təntlɪ/ adv inavvertitamente

inad'visable adj sconsigliabile

inane /ɪ'neɪn/ adj stupido

in'animate adj esanime

inap'propriate adj inadatto

inar'ticulate adj inarticolato

inat'tentive adj disattento

in'audibl|e adj impercettibile

inaugurat|e /ɪ'nɔ:gjʊreɪt/ vt inaugurare. **~ion** n inaugurazione f

inborn /'ɪnbɔ:n/ adj innato

inbred /ɪn'bred/ adj congenito

incalculable /ɪn'kælkjʊləbl/ adj incalcolabile

in'capable adj incapace

incapacitate /ɪnkə'pæsɪteɪt/ vt rendere incapace

incarnat|e /ɪn'kɑ:nət/ adj **the devil ~e** il diavolo in carne e ossa

incendiary /ɪn'sendɪərɪ/ adj incendiario

incense[1] /'ɪnsens/ n incenso m

incense[2] /ɪn'sens/ vt esasperare

incentive /ɪn'sentɪv/ n incentivo m

incessant /ɪn'sesənt/ adj incessante

incest /'ɪnsest/ n incesto m

inch /ɪntʃ/ n pollice m (= 2.54 cm) • vi **~ forward** avanzare gradatamente

inciden|ce /'ɪnsɪdəns/ n incidenza f. **~t** n incidente m

incidental /ɪnsɪ'dentl/ adj incidentale; **~ expenses** spese fpl accessorie. **~ly** adv incidentalmente; (by the way) a proposito

incinerat|e /ɪn'sɪnəreɪt/ vt incenerire. **~or** n inceneritore m

incision /ɪn'sɪʒn/ n incisione f

incite /ɪn'saɪt/ vt incitare. **~ment** n incitamento m

inclination /ɪnklɪ'neɪʃn/ n inclinazione f

incline[1] /ɪn'klaɪn/ vt inclinare; **be ~d to do sth** essere propenso a fare qcsa

incline[2] /'ɪnklaɪn/ n pendio m

inclu|de /ɪn'klu:d/ vt includere. **~ding** prep incluso. **~sion** n inclusione f

inclusive /ɪn'klu:sɪv/ adj incluso; **~ of** comprendente; **be ~ of** comprendere •adv incluso

incognito /ɪnkɒg'ni:təʊ/ adv incognito

inco'herent adj incoerente; (because drunk etc) incomprensibile

income /'ɪnkʌm/ n reddito m. **~ tax** n imposta f sul reddito

'incoming adj in arrivo. **~ tide** n marea f montante

in'comparable adj incomparabile

incom'patible adj incompatibile

in'competen|ce n incompetenza f. **~t** adj incompetente

incom'plete adj incompleto

incompre'hensible adj incomprensibile

incon'ceivable adj inconcepibile

incon'clusive adj inconcludente

incongruous /ɪn'kɒŋgrʊəs/ adj contrastante

incon'siderate adj trascurabile

incon'sistency n incoerenza f

incon'sistent adj incoerente; **be ~ with** non essere coerente con. **~ly** adv in modo incoerente

incon'spicuous adj non appariscente. **~ly** adv modestamente

incon'venien|ce n scomodità f; (drawback) inconveniente m; **put sb to ~ce** dare disturbo a qcno. **~t** adj scomodo; (time, place) inopportuno. **~tly** adv in modo inopportuno

incorporate /ɪn'kɔ:pəreɪt/ vt incorporare; (contain) comprendere

incor'rect adj incorretto. **~ly** adv scorrettamente

increase¹ /'ɪnkri:s/ n aumento m; **on the ~** in aumento

increas|e² /ɪn'kri:s/ vt/i aumentare. **~ing** adj (impatience etc) crescente; (numbers) in aumento. **~ingly** adv sempre più

in'credible adj incredibile

incredulous /ɪn'kredjʊləs/ adj incredulo

incriminate /ɪn'krɪmɪneɪt/ vt (Jur) incriminare

incubat|e /'ɪŋkjʊbeɪt/ vt incubare. **~ion** n incubazione f. **~ion period** n (Med) periodo m di incubazione. **~or** n (for baby) incubatrice f

incur /ɪn'kɜ:(r)/ vt (pt/pp **incurred**) incorrere; contrarre (debts)

in'curable adj incurabile

indebted /ɪn'detɪd/ adj obbligato (**to** verso)

in'decent adj indecente

inde'cision n indecisione f

inde'cisive adj indeciso. **~ness** n indecisione f

indeed /ɪn'di:d/ adv (in fact) difatti; **yes ~!** sì, certamente!; **~ I am/do** veramente!; **very much ~** moltissimo; **thank you very much ~** grazie infinite; **~?** davvero?

inde'finable adj indefinible

in'definite adj indefinito. **~ly** adv indefinitamente; (postpone) a tempo indeterminato

indelible /ɪn'delɪbl/ adj indelebile

indemnity /ɪn'demnɪtɪ/ n indennità f inv

indent¹ /'ɪndent/ n (Typ) rientranza f dal margine

indent² /ɪn'dent/ vt (Typ) fare rientrare dal margine. **~ation** n (notch) intaccatura f

inde'penden|ce n indipendenza f. **~t** adj indipendente. **~tly** adv indipendentemente

indescribable /ɪndɪ'skraɪbəbl/ adj indescrivibile

indestructible /ɪndɪ'strʌktəbl/ adj indistruttibile

indeterminate /ɪndɪ'tɜ:mɪnət/ adj indeterminato

index /'ɪndeks/ n indice m

index: ~ finger n dito m indice. **~-'linked** adj (pension) legato al costo della vita

India /'ɪndɪə/ n India f. **~n** adj indiano; (American) indiano [d'America] •n indiano, -a mf; (American) indiano, -a mf [d'America]

indicat|e /'ɪndɪkeɪt/ vt indicare; (register) segnare •vi (Auto) mettere la freccia. **~ion** n indicazione f

indicative /ɪn'dɪkətɪv/ adj **be ~ of**

essere indicativo di •n (Gram) indicativo m

indicator /'ɪndɪkeɪtə(r)/ n (Auto) freccia f

indict /ɪn'daɪt/ vt accusare. **~ment** n accusa f

in'differen|ce n indifferenza f. **~t** adj indifferente; (not good) mediocre

indi'gest|ible adj indigesto. **~ion** n indigestione f

indigna|nt /ɪn'dɪgnənt/ adj indignato. **~ntly** adv con indignazione. **~tion** n indignazione f

indi'rect adj indiretto. **~ly** adv indirettamente

indi'screet adj indiscreto

indis'cretion n indiscrezione f

indiscriminate /ɪndɪ'skrɪmɪnət/ adj indiscriminato. **~ly** adv senza distinzione

indi'spensable adj indispensabile

indisposed /ɪndɪ'spəʊzd/ adj indisposto

indisputable /ɪndɪ'spju:təbl/ adj indisputabile

indistinguishable /ɪndɪ'stɪŋgwɪʃəbl/ adj indistinguibile

individual /ɪndɪ'vɪdjʊəl/ adj individuale •n individuo m. **~ity** n individualità f

indoctrinate /ɪn'dɒktrɪneɪt/ vt indottrinare

indomitable /ɪn'dɒmɪtəbl/ adj indomito

indoor /'ɪndɔ:(r)/ adj interno; (shoes) per casa; (plant) da appartamento; (swimming pool etc) coperto. **~s** adv dentro

induce /ɪn'dju:s/ vt indurre (**to** a); (produce) causare. **~ment** n (incentive) incentivo m

indulge /ɪn'dʌldʒ/ vt soddisfare; viziare (child) •vi **~ in** concedersi. **~nce** n lusso m; (leniency) indulgenza f. **~nt** adj indulgente

industrial /ɪn'dʌstrɪəl/ adj industriale; **take ~ action** scioperare. **~ist** n industriale mf. **~ized** adj industrializzato

industr|ious /ɪn'dʌstrɪəs/ adj industrioso. **~y** n industria f; (zeal) operosità f

inebriated /ɪ'ni:brɪeɪtɪd/ adj ebbro

in'edible adj immangiabile

inef'fective adj inefficace

ineffectual /ɪnɪ'fektʃʊəl/ adj inutile; (person) inconcludente

inef'ficien|cy n inefficienza f. **~t** adj inefficiente

in'eligible adj inadatto

inept /ɪ'nept/ adj inetto

ine'quality n ineguaglianza f

inert /ɪ'nɜ:t/ adj inerte. **~ia** n inerzia f

inescapable /ɪnɪ'skeɪpəbl/ adj inevitabile

inevitabl|e /ɪn'evɪtəbl/ adj inevitabile. **~y** adv inevitabilmente

ine'xact adj inesatto

inex'cusable adj imperdonabile

inex'pensive adj poco costoso

inex'perience n inesperienza f. **~d** adj inesperto

inexplicable /ɪnɪk'splɪkəbl/ adj inesplicabile

in'fallible adj infallibile

infam|ous /'ɪnfəməs/ adj infame; (person) famigerato. **~y** n infamia f

infan|cy /'ɪnfənsɪ/ n infanzia f; **in its ~cy** fig agli inizi. **~t** n bambino, -a mf piccolo, -a. **~tile** adj infantile

infantry /'ɪnfəntrɪ/ n fanteria f

infatuat|ed /ɪn'fætʃʊeɪtɪd/ adj infatuato (**with** di). **~ion** n infatuazione f

infect /ɪn'fekt/ vt infettare; **become ~ed** (wound:) infettarsi. **~ion** adj infettivo

infer /ɪn'fɜ:(r)/ vt (pt/pp **inferred**) dedurre (**from** da); (imply) implicare. **~ence** n deduzione f

inferior /ɪn'fɪərɪə(r)/ adj inferiore; (goods) scadente; (in rank) subalterno •n inferiore mf; (in rank) subalterno, -a mf

inferiority /ɪnfɪərɪ'ɒrətɪ/ n inferiorità f. **~ complex** n complesso m di inferiorità

in'fer|tile adj sterile. **~'tility** n sterilità f

infest /ɪn'fest/ vt **be ~ed with** essere infestato di

infi'delity n infedeltà f

infiltrate /'ɪnfɪltreɪt/ vt infiltrare; (Pol) infiltrarsi in

infinite /ˈɪnfɪnət/ adj infinito

infinitive /ɪnˈfɪnətɪv/ n (Gram) infinito m

infinity /ɪnˈfɪnətɪ/ n infinità f

infirm /ɪnˈfɜːm/ adj debole. **~ary** n infermeria f. **~ity** n debolezza f

inflame /ɪnˈfleɪm/ vt infiammare. **~d** adj infiammato; **become ~d** infiammarsi

inˈflammable adj infiammabile

inflammation /ɪnfləˈmeɪʃn/ n infiammazione f

inflat|e /ɪnˈfleɪt/ vt gonfiare. **~ion** n inflazione f. **~ionary** adj inflazionario

inˈflexible adj inflessibile

inflict /ɪnˈflɪkt/ vt infliggere (**on** a)

influen|ce /ˈɪnflʊəns/ n influenza f •vt influenzare. **~tial** adj influente

influenza /ɪnflʊˈenzə/ n influenza f

influx /ˈɪnflʌks/ n affluenza f

inform /ɪnˈfɔːm/ vt informare; **keep sb ~ed** tenere qcno al corrente •vi **~ against** denunziare

inˈfor|mal adj informale; (agreement) ufficioso. **~mally** adv in modo informale. **~ˈmality** n informalità f inv

informat|ion /ɪnfəˈmeɪʃn/ n informazioni fpl; **a piece of ~ion** un'informazione. **~ion highway** n autostrada f telematica. **~ion technology** n informatica f. **~ive** adj informativo; (film, book) istruttivo

informer /ɪnˈfɔːmə(r)/ n informatore, -trice mf; (Pol) delatore, -trice mf

infra-ˈred /ɪnfrə-/ adj infrarosso

infringe /ɪnˈfrɪndʒ/ vt **~ on** usurpare. **~ment** n violazione f

infuriat|e /ɪnˈfjʊərɪeɪt/ vt infuriare. **~ing** adj esasperante

ingenious /ɪnˈdʒiːnɪəs/ adj ingegnoso

ingenuity /ɪndʒɪˈnjuːətɪ/ n ingegnosità f

ingot /ˈɪŋgət/ n lingotto m

ingrained /ɪnˈgreɪnd/ adj (in person) radicato; (dirt) incrostato

ingratiate /ɪnˈgreɪʃɪeɪt/ vt **~ oneself with sb** ingraziarsi qcno

inˈgratitude n ingratitudine f

ingredient /ɪnˈgriːdɪənt/ n ingrediente m

ingrowing /ˈɪngrəʊɪŋ/ adj (nail) incarnito

inhabit /ɪnˈhæbɪt/ vt abitare. **~ant** n abitante mf

inhale /ɪnˈheɪl/ vt aspirare; (Med) inalare •vi inspirare; (when smoking) aspirare. **~r** n (device) inalatore m

inherent /ɪnˈhɪərənt/ adj inerente

inherit /ɪnˈherɪt/ vt ereditare. **~ance** n eredità f inv

inhibit /ɪnˈhɪbɪt/ vt inibire. **~ed** adj inibito. **~ion** n inibizione f

inhoˈspitable adj inospitale

initial /ɪˈnɪʃl/ adj iniziale •n iniziale f •vt (pt/pp **initialled**) siglare. **~ly** adv all'inizio

initiat|e /ɪˈnɪʃɪeɪt/ vt iniziare. **~ion** n iniziazione f

initiative /ɪˈnɪʃətɪv/ n iniziativa f

inject /ɪnˈdʒekt/ vt iniettare. **~ion** n iniezione f

injur|e /ˈɪndʒə(r)/ vt ferire; (wrong) nuocere. **~y** n ferita f; (wrong) torto m

inˈjustice n ingiustizia f; **do sb an ~** giudicare qcno in modo sbagliato

ink /ɪŋk/ n inchiostro m

inland /ˈɪnlənd/ adj interno •adv all'interno. **I~ Revenue** n fisco m

in-laws /ˈɪnlɔːz/ npl [!] parenti mpl acquisiti

inlay /ˈɪnleɪ/ n intarsio m

inlet /ˈɪnlet/ n insenatura f; (Techn) entrata f

inmate /ˈɪnmeɪt/ n (of hospital) degente mf; (of prison) carcerato, -a mf

inn /ɪn/ n locanda f

innate /ɪˈneɪt/ adj innato

inner /ˈɪnə(r)/ adj interno. **~most** adj il più profondo. **~ tube** camera f d'aria

innocen|ce /ˈɪnəsəns/ n innocenza f. **~t** adj innocente

innocuous /ɪˈnɒkjʊəs/ adj innocuo

innovat|e /ˈɪnəveɪt/ vi innovare. **~ion** n innovazione f. **~ive** adj innovativo. **~or** n innovatore, -trice mf

innuendo /ɪnjʊˈendəʊ/ n (pl **-es**) insinuazione f

i

innumerable /ɪ'nju:mərəbl/ adj innumerevole

inoculat|e /ɪ'nɒkjʊleɪt/ vt vaccinare. **~ion** n vaccinazione f

inof'fensive adj inoffensivo

in'opportune adj inopportuno

input /'ɪnpʊt/ n input m inv, ingresso m

inquest /'ɪnkwest/ n inchiesta f

inquir|e /ɪn'kwaɪə(r)/ vi informarsi (**about** su); **~e into** far indagini su •vt domandare. **~y** n domanda f; (investigation) inchiesta f

inquisitive /ɪn'kwɪzətɪv/ adj curioso

in'sane adj pazzo; fig insensato

in'sanity n pazzia f

insatiable /ɪn'seɪʃəbl/ adj insaziabile

inscri|be /ɪn'skraɪb/ vt iscrivere. **~ption** n iscrizione f

inscrutable /ɪn'skru:təbl/ adj impenetrabile

insect /'ɪnsekt/ n insetto m. **~icide** n insetticida m

inse'cur|e adj malsicuro; (fig: person) insicuro. **~ity** n mancanza f di sicurezza

in'sensitive adj insensibile

in'separable adj inseparabile

insert[1] /'ɪnsɜ:t/ n inserto m

insert[2] /ɪn'sɜ:t/ vt inserire. **~ion** n inserzione f

inside /ɪn'saɪd/ n interno m. **~s** npl [!] pancia f •attrib (Auto) **~ lane** n corsia f interna •adv dentro; **~ out** a rovescio; (thoroughly) a fondo •prep dentro; (of time) entro

insight /'ɪnsaɪt/ n intuito m (**into** per); **an ~ into** un quadro di

insig'nificant adj insignificante

insin'cer|e adj poco sincero. **~ity** n mancanza f di sincerità

insinuat|e /ɪn'sɪnjʊeɪt/ vt insinuare. **~ion** n insinuazione f

insipid /ɪn'sɪpɪd/ adj insipido

insist /ɪn'sɪst/ vi insistere (**on** per) •vt **~ that** insistere che. **~ence** n insistenza f. **~ent** adj insistente

insolen|ce /'ɪnsələns/ n insolenza f. **~t** adj insolente

in'soluble adj insolubile

insomnia /ɪn'sɒmnɪə/ n insonnia f

inspect /ɪn'spekt/ vt ispezionare; controllare (ticket). **~ion** n ispezion f; (of ticket) controllo m. **~or** n ispettore, -trice mf; (of tickets) controllore m

inspiration /ɪnspə'reɪʃn/ n ispirazione f

inspire /ɪn'spaɪə(r)/ vt ispirare

insta'bility n instabilità f

install /ɪn'stɔ:l/ vt installare. **~atio** n installazione f

instalment /ɪn'stɔ:lmənt/ n (Comm) rata f; (of serial) puntata f; (of publication) fascicolo m

instance /'ɪnstəns/ n (case) caso m; (example) esempio m; **in the first ~** in primo luogo; **for ~** per esempi

instant /'ɪnstənt/ adj immediato; (Culin) espresso •n istante m. **~aneous** adj istantaneo

instead /ɪn'sted/ adv invece; **~ of doing** anziché fare; **~ of me** al mio posto; **~ of going** invece di andare

instigat|e /'ɪnstɪgeɪt/ vt istigare. **~ion** n istigazione f; **at his ~ion** dietro suo suggerimento. **~or** n istigatore, -trice mf

instinct /'ɪnstɪŋkt/ n istinto m. **~ive** adj istintivo

institut|e /'ɪnstɪtju:t/ n istituto m • istituire (scheme); iniziare (search); intentare (legal action). **~ion** n istituzione f; (home for elderly) istitut m per anziani; (for mentally ill) istitut m per malati di mente

instruct /ɪn'strʌkt/ vt istruire; (order ordinare. **~ion** n istruzione f; **~s** (orders) ordini mpl. **~ive** adj istruttivo. **~or** n istruttore, -trice

instrument /'ɪnstrʊmənt/ n strumento m. **~al** adj strumentale; **be ~al in** contribuire a. **~alist** n strumentista mf

insu'bordi|nate adj insubordinato. **~nation** n insubordinazione f

in'sufferable adj insopportabile

insuf'ficient adj insufficiente

insular /'ɪnsjʊlə(r)/ adj fig gretto

insulat|e /'ɪnsjʊleɪt/ vt isolare. **~in tape** n nastro m isolante. **~ion** n isolamento m

insulin /'ɪnsjʊlɪn/ n insulina f

insult[1] /'ɪnsʌlt/ n insulto m

ɪsult² /ɪn'sʌlt/ vt insultare

ɪsur|ance /ɪn'ʃʊərəns/ n assicurazione f. **~e** vt assicurare

ɪtact /ɪn'tækt/ adj intatto

ɪtegral /'ɪntɪgrəl/ adj integrale

ɪtegrat|e /'ɪntɪgreɪt/ vt integrare • vi integrarsi. **~ion** n integrazione f

ɪtegrity /ɪn'tegrətɪ/ n integrità f

ɪtellect /'ɪntəlekt/ n intelletto m. **~ual** adj & n intellettuale mf

ɪtelligen|ce /ɪn'telɪdʒəns/ n intelligenza f; (Mil) informazioni fpl. **~t** adj intelligente

ɪtelligible /ɪn'telɪdʒəbl/ adj intelligibile

ɪtend /ɪn'tend/ vt destinare; (have in mind) aver intenzione di; **be ~ed for** essere destinato a. **~ed** adj (effect) voluto • n **my ~ed** [!] il mio/la mia fidanzato, -a

ɪtense /ɪn'tens/ adj intenso; (person) dai sentimenti intensi. **~ly** adv intensamente; (very) estremamente

ɪtensity /ɪn'tensətɪ/ n intensità f

ɪtensive /ɪn'tensɪv/ adj intensivo. **~ care** (for people in coma) rianimazione f; **~ care [unit]** terapia f intensiva

ɪtent /ɪn'tent/ adj intento; **~ on** (absorbed in) preso da; **be ~ on doing sth** essere intento a fare qcsa • n intenzione f; **to all ~s and purposes** a tutti gli effetti. **~ly** adv attentamente

ɪtention /ɪn'tenʃn/ n intenzione f. **~al** adj intenzionale. **~ally** adv intenzionalmente

ɪter'acti|on n cooperazione f. **~ve** adj interattivo

ɪtercept /ɪntə'sept/ vt intercettare

ɪnterchange n scambio m; (Auto) raccordo m [autostradale]

ɪter'changeable adj interscambiabile

ɪntercourse n (sexual) rapporti mpl [sessuali]

ɪterest /'ɪntrəst/ n interesse m; **have an ~ in** (Comm) essere cointeressato in; **be of ~** essere interessante; **~ rate** n tasso m di interesse • vt interessare. **~ed** adj interessato. **~ing** adj interessante

ɪterface /'ɪntəfeɪs/ n interfaccia f • vt interfacciare • vi interfacciarsi

interfere /ɪntə'fɪə(r)/ vi interferire; **~ with** interferire con. **~nce** n interferenza f

interior /ɪn'tɪərɪə(r)/ adj interiore • n interno m. **~ designer** n arredatore, -trice mf

interlude /'ɪntəlu:d/ n intervallo m

intermediary /ɪntə'mi:dɪərɪ/ n intermediario, -a mf

interminable /ɪn'tɜ:mɪnəbl/ adj interminabile

intermittent /ɪntə'mɪtənt/ adj intermittente

intern /ɪn'tɜ:n/ vt internare

internal /ɪn'tɜ:nl/ adj interno. **I~ 'Revenue** (Am) n fisco m. **~ly** adv internamente; (deal with) all'interno

i

inter'national adj internazionale • n (game) incontro m internazionale; (player) competitore, -trice mf in gare internazionali. **~ly** adv internazionalmente

Internet /'ɪntənet/ n Internet m

interpret /ɪn'tɜ:prɪt/ vt interpretare • vi fare l'interprete. **~ation** n interpretazione f. **~er** n interprete mf

interrogat|e /ɪn'terəgeɪt/ vt interrogare. **~ion** n interrogazione f; (by police) interrogatorio m

interrogative /ɪntə'rɒgətɪv/ adj & n **~ [pronoun]** interrogativo m

interrupt /ɪntə'rʌpt/ vt/i interrompere. **~ion** n interruzione f

intersect /ɪntə'sekt/ vi intersecarsi • vt intersecare. **~ion** n intersezione f; (of street) incrocio m

inter'twine vi attorcigliarsi

interval /'ɪntəvl/ n intervallo m; **bright ~s** pl schiarite fpl

interven|e /ɪntə'vi:n/ vi intervenire. **~tion** n intervento m

interview /'ɪntəvju:/ n (Journ) intervista f; (for job) colloquio m [di lavoro] • vt intervistare. **~er** n intervistatore, -trice mf

intestin|e /ɪn'testɪn/ n intestino m. **~al** adj intestinale

intimacy /'ɪntɪməsɪ/ n intimità f

intimate¹ /'ɪntɪmət/ adj intimo. **~ly** adv intimamente

intimate² /'ɪntɪmeɪt/ vt far capire; (imply) suggerire

intimidat|e /ɪn'tɪmɪdeɪt/ vt intimidire. **~ion** n intimidazione f

into /'ɪntə/, di fronte a una vocale /'ɪntʊ/ prep dentro, in; **go ~ the house** andare dentro [casa] o in casa; **be ~** ([!]: like) essere appassionato di; **I'm not ~ that** questo non mi piace; **7 ~ 21 goes 3** il 7 nel 21 ci sta 3 volte; **translate ~ French** tradurre in francese; **get ~ trouble** mettersi nei guai

in'tolerable adj intollerabile

in'toleran|ce n intolleranza f. **~t** adj intollerante

intoxicat|ed /ɪn'tɒksɪkeɪtɪd/ adj inebriato. **~ion** n ebbrezza f

in'transitive adj intransitivo

intravenous /ɪntrə'vi:nəs/ adj endovenoso. **~ly** adv per via endovenosa

intrepid /ɪn'trepɪd/ adj intrepido

intricate /'ɪntrɪkət/ adj complesso

intrigu|e /ɪn'tri:g/ n intrigo m • vt intrigare • vi tramare. **~ing** adj intrigante

intrinsic /ɪn'trɪnsɪk/ adj intrinseco

introduce /ɪntrə'dju:s/ vt presentare; (bring in, insert) introdurre

introduct|ion /ɪntrə'dʌkʃn/ n introduzione f; (to person) presentazione f; (to book) prefazione f. **~ory** adj introduttivo

introvert /'ɪntrəvɜ:t/ n introverso, -a mf

intru|de /ɪn'tru:d/ vi intromettersi. **~der** n intruso, -a mf. **~sion** n intrusione f

intuit|ion /ɪntjʊ'ɪʃn/ n intuito m. **~ive** adj intuitivo

inundate /'ɪnəndeɪt/ vt (flood) inondare (**with** di)

invade /ɪn'veɪd/ vt invadere. **~r** n invasore m

invalid¹ /'ɪnvəlɪd/ n invalido, -a mf

invalid² /ɪn'vælɪd/ adj non valido. **~ate** vt invalidare

in'valuable adj prezioso; (priceless) inestimabile

in'variabl|e adj invariabile. **~y** adv invariabilmente

invasion /ɪn'veɪʒn/ n invasione f

invent /ɪn'vent/ vt inventare. **~ion** invenzione f. **~ive** adj inventivo. **~or** n inventore, -trice mf

inventory /'ɪnvəntrɪ/ n inventario m

invest /ɪn'vest/ vt investire • vi fare investimenti; **~ in** ([!]: buy) comprarsi

investigat|e /ɪn'vestɪgeɪt/ vt investigare. **~ion** n investigazione

invest|ment /ɪn'vestmənt/ n investimento m. **~or** n investitore, -trice mf

inveterate /ɪn'vetərət/ adj inveterato

invidious /ɪn'vɪdɪəs/ adj ingiusto; (position) antipatico

invincible /ɪn'vɪnsəbl/ adj invincibile

in'visible adj invisibile

invitation /ɪnvɪ'teɪʃn/ n invito m

invit|e /ɪn'vaɪt/ vt invitare; (attract) attirare. **~ing** adj invitante

invoice /'ɪnvɔɪs/ n fattura f • vt **~ sb** emettere una fattura a qcno

in'voluntar|y adj involontario

involve /ɪn'vɒlv/ vt comportare; (affect, include) coinvolgere; (entail) implicare; **get ~d with sb** legarsi a qcno; (romantically) legarsi sentimentalmente a qcno. **~d** adj complesso. **~ment** n coinvolgimento m

inward /'ɪnwəd/ adj interno; (thoughts etc) interiore; **~ investment** (Comm) investimento m straniero. **~ly** adv interiormente. **~[s]** adv verso l'interno

iodine /'aɪədi:n/ n iodio m

iota /aɪ'əʊtə/ n briciolo m

IOU n abbr (I owe you) pagherò m inv

IQ n abbr (intelligence quotient) Q.I.

Iran /ɪ'rɑ:n/ n Iran m. **~ian** adj & n iraniano, -a mf

Iraq /ɪ'rɑ:k/ n Iraq m. **~i** adj & n iracheno, -a mf

irate /aɪ'reɪt/ adj adirato

Ireland /'aɪələnd/ n Irlanda f

iris /'aɪrɪs/ n (Anat) iride f; (Bot) iris f inv

Irish /'aɪrɪʃ/ adj irlandese • n **the ~** pl gli irlandesi mpl. **~man** n irlandese m. **~woman** n irlandese f

iron /'aɪən/ adj di ferro. **I~ Curtain** n cortina f di ferro • n ferro m; (appliance) ferro m [da stiro] • vt/i stirare. □**~ out** vt eliminare stirando; fig appianare

ironmonger /-mʌŋgə(r)/ n **~'s [shop]** negozio m di ferramenta

irony /'aɪrənɪ/ n ironia f

irrational /ɪ'ræʃənl/ adj irrazionale

irrefutable /ɪrɪ'fju:təbl/ adj irrefutabile

irregular /ɪ'regjʊlə(r)/ adj irregolare. **~ity** n irregolarità f inv

irrelevant /ɪ'reləvənt/ adj non pertinente

irreparabl|e /ɪ'repərəbl/ adj irreparabile. **~y** adv irreparabilmente

irreplaceable /ɪrɪ'pleɪsəbl/ adj insostituibile

irresistible /ɪrɪ'zɪstəbl/ adj irresistibile

irrespective /ɪrɪ'spektɪv/ adj **~ of** senza riguardo per

irresponsible /ɪrɪ'spɒnsɪbl/ adj irresponsabile

irreverent /ɪ'revərənt/ adj irreverente

irrevocabl|e /ɪ'revəkəbl/ adj irrevocabile. **~y** adv irrevocabilmente

irrigat|e /'ɪrɪgeɪt/ vt irrigare. **~ion** n irrigazione f

irritable /'ɪrɪtəbl/ adj irritabile

irritat|e /'ɪrɪteɪt/ vt irritare. **~ing** adj irritante. **~ion** n irritazione f

is /ɪz/ ▷**be**

Islam /'ɪzlɑ:m/ n Islam m. **~ic** adj islamico

island /'aɪlənd/ n isola f; (in road) isola f spartitraffico. **~er** n isolano, -a mf

isolat|e /'aɪsəleɪt/ vt isolare. **~ed** adj isolato. **~ion** n isolamento m

Israel /'ɪzreɪl/ n Israele m. **~i** adj & n israeliano, -a mf

issue /'ɪʃu:/ n (outcome) risultato m; (of magazine) numero m; (of stamps etc) emissione f; (offspring) figli mpl; (matter, question) questione f; **at ~** in questione; **take ~ with sb** prendere posizione contro qcno • vt distribuire (supplies); rilasciare (passport); emettere (stamps, order); pubblicare (book); **be ~d with sth** ricevere qcsa • vi **~ from** uscire da

it /ɪt/ pron (direct object) lo m, la f; (indirect object) gli m, le f; **it's broken** è rotto/rotta; **will it be enough?** basterà?; **it's hot** fa caldo; **it's raining** piove; **it's me** sono io; **who is it?** chi è?; **it's two o'clock** sono le due; **I doubt it** ne dubito; **take it with you** prendilo con te; **give it a wipe** dagli una pulita

Italian /ɪ'tæljən/ adj & n italiano, -a mf; (language) italiano m

Italy /'ɪtəlɪ/ n Italia f

itch /ɪtʃ/ n prurito m • vi avere prurito, prudere; **be ~ing to** [!] avere una voglia matta di. **~y** adj che prude; **my foot is ~y** ho prurito al piede

item /'aɪtəm/ n articolo m; (on agenda, programme) punto m; (on invoice) voce f; **~ [of news]** notizia f. **~ize** vt dettagliare (bill)

itinerary /aɪ'tɪnərərɪ/ n itinerario m

itself /ɪt'self/ pron (reflexive) si; (emphatic) esso, -a stesso, -a; **the baby looked at ~ in the mirror** il bambino si è guardato nello specchio; **by ~** da solo; **the machine in ~ is simple** la macchina di per sé è semplice

ITV n abbr (Independent Television) stazione f televisiva privata britannica

ivory /'aɪvərɪ/ n avorio m

ivy /'aɪvɪ/ n edera f

Jj

jab /dʒæb/ n colpo m secco; (⚠: injection) puntura f • vt (pt/pp **jabbed**) punzecchiare

jack /dʒæk/ n (Auto) cric m inv; (in cards) fante m, jack m inv • **jack up** vt (Auto) sollevare [con il cric]

jackdaw /ˈdʒækdɔ:/ n taccola f

jacket /ˈdʒækɪt/ n giacca f; (of book) sopraccoperta f. ~ **poˈtato** n patata f cotta al forno con la buccia

ˈjackpot n premio m (di una lotteria); **win the** ~ vincere alla lotteria; **hit the** ~ fig fare un colpo grosso

jade /dʒeɪd/ n giada f • attrib di giada

jagged /ˈdʒægɪd/ adj dentellato

jail /dʒeɪl/ = **gaol**

jam¹ /dʒæm/ n marmellata f

jam² n (Auto) ingorgo m; (⚠: difficulty) guaio m • v (pt/pp **jammed**) • vt (cram) pigiare; disturbare (broadcast); inceppare (mechanism, drawer etc); **be ~med** (roads:) essere congestionato • vi (mechanism:) incepparsi; (window, drawer:) incastrarsi

Jamaica /dʒəˈmeɪkə/ n Giamaica f. **~n** adj & n giamaicano, -a mf

jangle /ˈdʒæŋgl/ vt far squillare • vi squillare

janitor /ˈdʒænɪtə(r)/ n (caretaker) custode m; (in school) bidello, -a mf

January /ˈdʒænjʊərɪ/ n gennaio m

Japan /dʒəˈpæn/ n Giappone m. **~ese** adj & n giapponese mf; (language) giapponese m

jar¹ /dʒɑ:(r)/ n (glass) barattolo m

jar² vi (pt/pp **jarred**) (sound:) stridere

jargon /ˈdʒɑ:gən/ n gergo m

jaundice /ˈdʒɔ:ndɪs/ n itterizia f. **~d** adj fig inacidito

jaunt /dʒɔ:nt/ n gita f

jaunty /ˈdʒɔ:ntɪ/ adj (**-ier, -iest**) sbarazzino

jaw /dʒɔ:/ n mascella f; (bone) mandibola f

jay-walker /ˈdʒeɪwɔ:kə(r)/ n pedone m distratto

jazz /dʒæz/ n jazz m • **jazz up** vt ravvivare. **~y** adj vistoso

jealous /ˈdʒeləs/ adj geloso. **~y** n gelosia f

jeans /dʒi:nz/ npl [blue] jeans mpl

jeep /dʒi:p/ n jeep f inv

jeer /dʒɪə(r)/ n scherno m • vi schernire; ~ **at** prendersi gioco di • vt (boo) fischiare

jelly /ˈdʒelɪ/ n gelatina f. **~fish** n medusa f

jeopar|dize /ˈdʒepədaɪz/ vt mettere in pericolo. **~dy** n **in ~dy** in pericolo

jerk /dʒɜ:k/ n scatto m, scossa f • vt scattare • vi sobbalzare; (limb, muscle:) muoversi a scatti. **~ily** adv a scatti. **~y** adj traballante

jersey /ˈdʒɜ:zɪ/ n maglia f; (Sport) maglietta f; (fabric) jersey m

jest /dʒest/ n scherzo m; **in** ~ per scherzo • vi scherzare

Jesus /ˈdʒi:zəs/ n Gesù m

jet¹ /dʒet/ n (stone) giaietto m

jet² n (of water) getto m; (nozzle) becco m; (plane) aviogetto m, jet m inv

jet: **~-ˈblack** adj nero ebano. **~lag** scombussolamento m da fuso orario. **~-proˈpelled** adj a reazione

jettison /ˈdʒetɪsn/ vt gettare a mare; fig abbandonare

jetty /ˈdʒetɪ/ n molo m

Jew /dʒu:/ n ebreo m

jewel /ˈdʒu:əl/ n gioiello m. **~ler** n gioielliere m; **~ler's [shop]** gioielleria f. **~lery** n gioielli mpl

jiffy /ˈdʒɪfɪ/ n ⚠ **in a** ~ in un batter d'occhio

jigsaw /ˈdʒɪgsɔ:/ n ~ **[puzzle]** puzzle m inv

jilt /dʒɪlt/ vt piantare

jingle /ˈdʒɪŋgl/ n (rhyme) canzoncina f

pubblicitaria •vi tintinnare

job /dʒɒb/ n lavoro m; **this is going to be quite a ~** [!] [questa] non sarà un'impresa facile; **it's a good ~ that...** meno male che.... **~ centre** n ufficio m statale di collocamento. **~less** adj senza lavoro

jockey /'dʒɒkɪ/ n fantino m

jocular /'dʒɒkjʊlə(r)/ adj scherzoso

jog /dʒɒg/ n colpetto m; **at a ~** in un balzo; (Sport) **go for a ~** andare a fare jogging •v (pt/pp **jogged**) •vt (hit) urtare; **~ sb's memory** farlo ritornare in mente a qcno •vi (Sport) fare jogging. **~ging** n jogging m

join /dʒɔɪn/ n giuntura f •vt raggiungere, unire; raggiungere (person); (become member of) iscriversi a; entrare in (firm) •vi (roads:) congiungersi. □ **~ in** vi partecipare. □ **~ up** vi (Mil) arruolarsi •vt unire

joiner /'dʒɔɪnə(r)/ n falegname m

joint /dʒɔɪnt/ adj comune •n articolazione f; (in wood, brickwork) giuntura f; (Culin) arrosto m; ([!]: bar) bettola f; ([x]:drug) spinello m. **~ly** adv unitamente

joist /dʒɔɪst/ n travetto m

jok|e /dʒəʊk/ n (trick) scherzo m; (funny story) barzelletta f •vi scherzare. **~er** n burlone, -a mf; (in cards) jolly m inv. **~ing** n **~ing apart** scherzi a parte. **~ingly** adv per scherzo

jolly /'dʒɒlɪ/ adj (**-ier, -iest**) allegro •adv [!] molto

jolt /dʒəʊlt/ n scossa f, sobbalzo m •vt far sobbalzare •vi sobbalzare

jostle /'dʒɒsl/ vt spingere

jot /dʒɒt/ n nulla f •**jot down** vt (pt/pp **jotted**) annotare. **~ter** n taccuino m

journal /'dʒɜ:nl/ n giornale m; (diary) diario m. **~ese** n gergo m giornalistico. **~ism** n giornalismo m. **~ist** n giornalista mf

journey /'dʒɜ:nɪ/ n viaggio m

jovial /'dʒəʊvɪəl/ adj gioviale

joy /dʒɔɪ/ n gioia f. **~ful** adj gioioso. **~ride** n [!] giro m con una macchina rubata. **~stick** n (Comput) joystick m inv

jubil|ant /'dʒu:bɪlənt/ adj giubilante. **~ation** n giubilo m

jubilee /'dʒu:bɪli:/ n giubileo m

judge /dʒʌdʒ/ n giudice m •vt giudicare; (estimate) valutare; (consider) ritenere •vi giudicare (**by** da). **~ment** n giudizio m; (Jur) sentenza f

judic|ial /dʒu:'dɪʃl/ adj giudiziario. **~iary** n magistratura f. **~ious** adj giudizioso

judo /'dʒu:dəʊ/ n judo m

jug /dʒʌg/ n brocca f; (small) bricco m

juggernaut /'dʒʌgənɔ:t/ n [!] grosso autotreno m

juggle /'dʒʌgl/ vi fare giochi di destrezza. **~r** n giocoliere, -a mf

juice /dʒu:s/ n succo m

juicy /'dʒu:sɪ/ adj (**-ier, -iest**) succoso; ([!]: story) piccante

juke-box /'dʒu:k-/ n juke-box m inv

July /dʒʊ'laɪ/ n luglio m

jumble /'dʒʌmbl/ n accozzaglia f •vt **~ [up]** mischiare. **~ sale** n vendita f di beneficenza

jumbo /'dʒʌmbəʊ/ n **~ [jet]** jumbo jet m inv

jump /dʒʌmp/ n salto m; (in prices) balzo m; (in horse racing) ostacolo m •vi saltare; (with fright) sussultare; (prices:) salire rapidamente; **~ to conclusions** saltare alle conclusioni •vt saltare; **~ the gun** fig precipitarsi; **~ the queue** non rispettare la fila. □ **~ at** vt fig accettare con entusiasmo (offer). □ **~ up** vi rizzarsi in piedi

jumper /'dʒʌmpə(r)/ n (sweater) golf m inv

jumpy /'dʒʌmpɪ/ adj nervoso

junction /'dʒʌŋkʃn/ n (of roads) incrocio m; (of motorway) uscita f; (Rail) nodo m ferroviario

June /dʒu:n/ n giugno m

jungle /'dʒʌŋgl/ n giungla f

junior /'dʒu:nɪə(r)/ adj giovane; (in rank) subalterno; (Sport) junior inv •n **the ~s** (Sch) i più giovani. **~ school** n scuola f elementare

junk /dʒʌŋk/ n cianfrusaglie fpl. **~ food** n [!] cibo m poco sano, porcherie fpl. **~ mail** posta f spazzatura

junkie /'dʒʌŋkɪ/ n [x] tossico, -a mf

'**junk-shop** n negozio m di rigattiere

jurisdiction /dʒʊərɪs'dɪkʃn/ n giurisdizione f

juror /'dʒʊərə(r)/ n giurato, -a mf

jury /'dʒʊərɪ/ n giuria f

just /dʒʌst/ adj giusto •adv (barely) appena; (simply) solo; (exactly) esattamente; ~ **as tall** altrettanto alto; ~ **as I was leaving** proprio quando stavo andando via; **I've** ~ **seen her** l'ho appena vista; **it's** ~ **as well** meno male; ~ **at that moment** proprio in quel momento; ~ **listen!** ascolta!; **I'm** ~ **going** sto andando proprio ora

justice /'dʒʌstɪs/ n giustizia f; **do** ~ **to** rendere giustizia a; **J~ of the Peace** giudice m conciliatore

justifiabl|e /'dʒʌstɪfaɪəbl/ adj giustificabile

justi|fication /dʒʌstɪfɪ'keɪʃn/ n giustificazione f. **~fy** vt (pt/pp **-ied**) giustificare

jut /dʒʌt/ vi (pt/pp **jutted**) ~ **out** sporgere

juvenile /'dʒu:vənaɪl/ adj giovanile; (childish) infantile; (for the young) per i giovani •n giovane mf. ~ **delinquency** n delinquenza f giovanile

Kk

kangaroo /kæŋgə'ru:/ n canguro m

karate /kə'rɑ:tɪ/ n karate m

keel /ki:l/ n chiglia f •**keel over** vi capovolgersi

keen /ki:n/ adj (intense) acuto; (interest) vivo; (eager) entusiastico; (competition) feroce; (wind, knife) tagliente; ~ **on** entusiasta di; **she's** ~ **on him** le piace molto; **be** ~ **to do sth** avere voglia di fare qcsa. **~ness** n entusiasmo m

keep /ki:p/ n (maintenance) mantenimento m; (of castle) maschio m; **for ~s** per sempre •v (pt/pp **kept**) •vt tenere; (not throw away) conservare; (detain) trattenere; mantenere (family, promise); avere (shop); allevare (animals); rispettare (law, rules); ~ **sth hot** tenere qcsa in caldo; ~ **sb from doing sth** impedire a qcno di fare qcsa; ~ **sb waiting** far aspettare qcno; ~ **sth to oneself** tenere qcsa per sè; ~ **sth from sb** tenere nascosto qcsa a qcno •vi (remain) rimanere; (food:) conservarsi; ~ **calm** rimanere calmo; ~ **left/right** tenere la destra/la sinistra; ~ [**on**] **doing sth** continuare a fare qcsa. □ ~ **back** vt trattenere (person); ~ **sth back from sb** tenere nascosto qcsa a qcno •vi tenersi indietro. □ ~ **in with** vt mantenersi in buoni rapporti con. □ ~ **on** vi [!] assillare (**at sb** qcno). □ ~ **up** vi stare al passo •vt (continue) continuare

kennel /'kenl/ n canile m; **~s** pl (boarding) canile m; (breeding) allevamento m di cani

Kenya /'kenjə/ n Kenia m. **~n** adj & n keniota mf

kept /kept/ ▸**keep**

kerb /kɜ:b/ n bordo m del marciapiede

kerosene /'kerəsi:n/ n Am cherosene m

ketchup /'ketʃʌp/ n ketchup m

kettle /'ket(ə)l/ n bollitore m; **put the** ~ **on** mettere l'acqua a bollire

key /ki:/ n also (Mus) chiave f; (of piano, typewriter) tasto m •vt ~ [**in**] digitare (character); **could you** ~ **this?** puoi battere questo?

key: ~board n (Comput, Mus) tastiera f. **~hole** n buco m della serratura. **~-ring** n portachiavi m inv

khaki /'kɑ:kɪ/ adj cachi inv •n cachi m

kick /kɪk/ n calcio m; ([!]: thrill) piacere m; **for ~s** [!] per spasso •vt dar calci a; ~ **the bucket** [!] crepare •vi (animal:) scalciare; (person:) dare calci □ ~ **off** vi (Sport) dare il calcio d'inizio; [!] iniziare. □~ **up** vt ~ **up a row** fare une scenata

kick-off n (Sport) calcio m d'inizio

kid /kɪd/ n capretto m; ([!]: child) ragazzino, -a mf • v (pt/pp **kidded**) • vt [!] prendere in giro • vi [!] scherzare

kidnap /'kɪdnæp/ vt (pt/pp **-napped**) rapire, sequestrare. ~**per** n sequestratore, -trice mf, rapitore, -trice mf. ~**ping** n rapimento m, sequestro m [di persona]

kidney /'kɪdnɪ/ n rene m; (Culin) rognone m. ~ **machine** n rene m artificiale

kill /kɪl/ vt uccidere; fig metter fine a; ammazzare (time). ~**er** n assassino, -a mf. ~**ing** n uccisione f; (murder) omicidio m; **make a** ~**ing** fig fare un colpo grosso

kiln /kɪln/ n fornace f

kilo /'kɪlə/: ~**byte** n kilobyte m inv. ~**gram** n chilogrammo m. ~**metre** n chilometro m. ~**watt** n chilowatt m inv

kilt /kɪlt/ n kilt m inv (gonnellino degli scozzesi)

kin /kɪn/ n congiunti mpl; **next of** ~ parente m stretto; parenti mpl stretti

kind[1] /kaɪnd/ n genere m, specie f; (brand, type) tipo m; ~ **of** [!] alquanto; **two of a** ~ due della stessa specie

kind[2] adj gentile, buono; ~ **to animals** amante degli animali; ~ **regards** cordiali saluti

kindergarten /'kɪndəgɑ:tn/ n asilo m infantile

kindle /'kɪndl/ vt accendere

kind|ly /'kaɪndlɪ/ adj (**-ier, -iest**) benevolo • adv gentilmente; (if you please) per favore. ~**ness** n gentilezza f

king /kɪŋ/ n re m inv. ~**dom** n regno m

king: ~**fisher** n martin m inv pescatore. ~**-sized** adj (cigarette) king-size inv, lungo; (bed) matrimoniale grande

kink /kɪŋk/ n nodo m. ~**y** adj [!] bizzarro

kiosk /'ki:ɒsk/ n chiosco m; (Teleph) cabina f telefonica

kipper /'kɪpə(r)/ n aringa f affumicata

kiss /kɪs/ n bacio m; ~ **of life** respirazione f bocca a bocca • vt baciare • vi baciarsi

kit /kɪt/ n equipaggiamento m, kit m inv; (tools) attrezzi mpl; (construction ~) pezzi mpl da montare, kit m inv • **kit out** vt (pt/pp **kitted**) equipaggiare. ~**bag** n sacco m a spalla

kitchen /'kɪtʃɪn/ n cucina f • attrib di cucina. ~**ette** n cucinino m

kitchen towel Scottex® m inv

kite /kaɪt/ n aquilone m

kitten /'kɪtn/ n gattino m

knack /næk/ n tecnica f; **have the** ~ **for doing sth** avere la capacità di fare qcsa

knead /ni:d/ vt impastare

knee /ni:/ n ginocchio m. ~**cap** n rotula f

kneel /ni:l/ vi (pt/pp **knelt**) ~ [**down**] inginocchiarsi; **be** ~**ing** essere inginocchiato

knelt /nelt/ ▸**kneel**

knew /nju:/ ▸**know**

knickers /'nɪkəz/ npl mutandine fpl

knife /naɪf/ n (pl **knives**) coltello m • vt [!] accoltellare

knight /naɪt/ n cavaliere m; (in chess) cavallo m • vt nominare cavaliere

knit /nɪt/ vt/i (pt/pp **knitted**) lavorare a maglia; ~ **one, purl one** un diritto, un rovescio. ~**ting** n lavorare m a maglia; (work) lavoro m a maglia. ~**ting-needle** n ferro m da calza. ~**wear** n maglieria f

knives /naɪvz/ ▸**knife**

knob /nɒb/ n pomello m; (of stick) pomo m; (of butter) noce f. ~**bly** adj nodoso; (bony) spigoloso

knock /nɒk/ n colpo m; **there was a** ~ **at the door** hanno bussato alla porta • vt bussare a (door); ([!]: criticize) denigrare; ~ **a hole in sth** fare un buco in qcsa; ~ **one's head** battere la testa (**on** contro) • vi (at door) bussare. □~ **about** vt malmenare • vi [!] girovagare. □~ **down** vt far cadere; (with fist) stendere con un pugno; (in car) investire; (demolish) abbattere; ([!]: reduce) ribassare (price). □~ **off** vt ([!]: steal) fregare; ([!]: complete quickly) fare alla bell'e meglio • vi ([!]: cease work) staccare. □~ **out** vt eliminare; (make unconscious) mettere K.O.; ([!]:

anaesthetize) addormentare. □~ **over** vt rovesciare; (in car) investire

knock: ~**er** n battente m. ~**-kneed** /-'ni:d/ adj con gambe storte. ~**-out** n (in boxing) knock-out m inv

knot /nɒt/ n nodo m • vt (pt/pp **knotted**) annodare

know /nəʊ/ v (pt **knew**, pp **known**) • vt sapere; conoscere (person, place); (recognize) riconoscere; **get to ~ sb** conoscere qcno; **~ how to swim** sapere nuotare • vi sapere; **did you ~ about this?** lo sapevi? • n **in the ~** [!] al corrente

know: ~**-all** n [!] sapientone, -a mf. ~**-how** n abilità f. ~**ingly** adv (intentionally) consapevolmente; (smile etc) con un'aria d'intesa

knowledge /'nɒlɪdʒ/ n conoscenza f ~**able** adj ben informato

known /nəʊn/ ▸**know** • adj noto

knuckle /'nʌkl/ n nocca f • **knuckle down** vi darci sotto (**to** con). □~ **under** vi sottomettersi

Koran /kə'rɑ:n/ n Corano m

Korea /kə'rɪə/ n Corea f. ~**n** adj & n coreano, -a mf

kosher /'kəʊʃə(r)/ adj kasher inv

kudos /'kju:dɒs/ n [!] gloria f

Ll

lab /læb/ n laboratorio m

label /'leɪbl/ n etichetta f • vt (pt/pp **labelled**) mettere un'etichetta a; fig etichettare (person)

laboratory /lə'bɒrətrɪ/ n laboratorio m

laborious /lə'bɔ:rɪəs/ adj laborioso

labour /'leɪbə(r)/ n lavoro m; (workers) manodopera f; (Med) doglie fpl; **be in ~** avere le doglie; **L~** (Pol) partito m laburista • attrib (Pol) laburista • vi lavorare • vt **~ the point** fig ribadire il concetto. ~**er** n manovale m

lace /leɪs/ n pizzo m; (of shoe) laccio m • attrib di pizzo • vt allacciare (shoes); correggere (drink)

lacerate /'læsəreɪt/ vt lacerare

lack /læk/ n mancanza f • vt mancare di; **I ~ the time** mi manca il tempo • vi **be ~ing** mancare; **be ~ing in sth** mancare di qcsa

lad /læd/ n ragazzo m

ladder /'lædə(r)/ n scala f; (in tights) sfilatura f

laden /'leɪdn/ adj carico (**with** di)

ladle /'leɪdl/ n mestolo m • vt **~ [out]** versare (col mestolo)

lady /'leɪdɪ/ n signora f; (title) Lady; **ladies [room]** bagno m per donne

lady: ~**bird** n, Am ~**bug** n coccinella f. ~**like** adj signorile

lag[1] /læg/ vi (pt/pp **lagged**) **~ behind** restare indietro

lag[2] vt (pt/pp **lagged**) isolare (pipes)

lager /'lɑ:gə(r)/ n birra f chiara

lagoon /lə'gu:n/ n laguna f

laid /leɪd/ ▸**lay**[3]

lain /leɪn/ ▸**lie**[2]

lair /leə(r)/ n tana f

lake /leɪk/ n lago m

lamb /læm/ n agnello m

lame /leɪm/ adj zoppo; fig (argument) zoppicante; (excuse) traballante

lament /lə'ment/ n lamento m • vt lamentare • vi lamentarsi

lamentable /'læməntəbl/ adj deplorevole

lamp /læmp/ n lampada f; (in street) lampione m. ~**post** n lampione m. ~**shade** n paralume m

lance /lɑ:ns/ n fiocina f • vt (Med) incidere. ~**-'corporal** n appuntato m

land /lænd/ n terreno m; (country) paese m; (as opposed to sea) terra f; **plot of ~** pezzo m di terreno • vt (Naut) sbarcare; (fam: obtain) assicurarsi; **be ~ed with sth** [!]

ritrovarsi fra capo e collo qcsa •vi (Aeron) atterrare; (fall) cadere. □ ~ **up** vi [!] finire

landing /'lændɪŋ/ n (Naut) sbarco m; (Aeron) atterraggio m; (top of stairs) pianerottolo m. **~-stage** n pontile m da sbarco. ~ **strip** n pista f d'atterraggio di fortuna

land: ~lady n proprietaria f; (of flat) padrona f di casa. **~lord** n proprietario m; (of flat) padrone m di casa. **~mark** n punto m di riferimento; fig pietra f miliare. **~scape** /-skeɪp/ n paesaggio m. **~slide** n frana f; (Pol) valanga f di voti

lane /leɪn/ n sentiero m; (Auto, Sport) corsia f

language /'læŋgwɪdʒ/ n lingua f; (speech, style) linguaggio m. ~ **laboratory** n laboratorio m linguistico

lank /læŋk/ adj (hair) diritto

lanky /'læŋkɪ/ adj (**-ier, -iest**) allampanato

lantern /'læntən/ n lanterna f

lap¹ /læp/ n grembo m

lap² n (of journey) tappa f; (Sport) giro m •v (pt/pp **lapped**) •vi (water:) ~ **against** lambire •vt (Sport) doppiare

lap³ vt (pt/pp **lapped**) ~ **up** bere avidamente; bersi completamente (lies); credere ciecamente a (praise)

lapel /lə'pel/ n bavero m

lapse /læps/ n sbaglio m; (moral) sbandamento m [morale]; (of time) intervallo m •vi (expire) scadere; (morally) scivolare; ~ **into** cadere in

laptop /'læptɒp/ n ~ [**computer**] computer m inv portabile, laptop m inv

lard /lɑ:d/ n strutto m

larder /'lɑ:də(r)/ n dispensa f

large /lɑ:dʒ/ adj grande; (number, amount) grande, grosso; **by and** ~ in complesso; **at** ~ in libertà; (in general) ampiamente. **~ly** adv ampiamente; **~ly because of** in gran parte a causa di

lark¹ /lɑ:k/ n (bird) allodola f

lark² n (joke) burla f •**lark about** vi giocherellare

larva /'lɑ:və/ n (pl **-vae** /-vi:/) larva f

laser /'leɪzə(r)/ n laser m inv. ~ **printer** n stampante f laser

lash /læʃ/ n frustata f; (eyelash) ciglio m •vt (whip) frustare; (tie) legare fermamente. □ ~ **out** vi attaccare; (spend) sperperare (**on** in)

lashings /'læʃɪŋz/ npl ~ **of** [!] una marea di

lass /læs/ n ragazzina f

lasso /lə'su:/ n lazo m

last /lɑ:st/ adj (final) ultimo; (recent) scorso; ~ **year** l'anno scorso; ~ **night** ieri sera; **at** ~ alla fine; **at** **~!** finalmente!; **that's the ~ straw** [!] questa è l'ultima goccia •n ultimo, -a mf; **the ~ but one** il penultimo •adv per ultimo; (last time) l'ultima volta •vi durare. **~ing** adj durevole. **~ly** adv infine

late /leɪt/ adj (delayed) in ritardo; (at a late hour) tardo; (deceased) defunto; **it's** ~ (at night) è tardi; **in ~ November** alla fine di Novembre •adv tardi; **stay up** ~ stare alzati fino a tardi. **~comer** n ritardatario, -a mf; (to political party etc) nuovo, -a arrivato, -a mf. **~ly** adv recentemente. **~ness** n ora f tarda; (delay) ritardo m

latent /'leɪtnt/ adj latente

later /'leɪtə(r)/ adj (train) che parte più tardi; (edition) più recente •adv più tardi; ~ **on** più tardi, dopo

lateral /'lætərəl/ adj laterale

latest /'leɪtɪst/ adj ultimo; (most recent) più recente; **the** ~ [**news**] le ultime notizie •n **six o'clock at the** ~ alle sei al più tardi

lathe /leɪð/ n tornio m

lather /'lɑ:ðə(r)/ n schiuma f •vt insaponare •vi far schiuma

Latin /'lætɪn/ adj latino •n latino m. ~ **A'merica** n America f Latina. ~ **A'merican** adj & n latino-americano, -a mf

latitude /'lætɪtju:d/ n (Geog) latitudine f; fig libertà f d'azione

latter /'lætə(r)/ adj ultimo •n **the** ~ quest'ultimo. **~ly** adv ultimamente

Latvia /'lætvɪə/ n Lettonia f. **~n** adj & n lettone mf

laugh /lɑ:f/ n risata f •vi ridere (**at/about** di); ~ **at sb** (mock) prendere in giro qcno. **~able** adj ridicolo. **~ing-stock** n zimbello m

laughter /ˈlɑːftə(r)/ n risata f

launch¹ /lɔːntʃ/ n (boat) varo m

launch² n lancio m; (of ship) varo m •vt lanciare (rocket, product); varare (ship); sferrare (attack)

launder /ˈlɔːndə(r)/ vt lavare e stirare; ~ **money** fig riciclare denaro sporco. ~**ette** n lavanderia f automatica

laundry /ˈlɔːndrɪ/ n lavanderia f; (clothes) bucato m

lava /ˈlɑːvə/ n lava f

lavatory /ˈlævətrɪ/ n gabinetto m

lavish /ˈlævɪʃ/ adj copioso; (wasteful) prodigo; **on a** ~ **scale** su vasta scala •vt ~ **sth on sb** ricoprire qcno di qcsa. ~**ly** adv copiosamente

law /lɔː/ n legge f; **study** ~ studiare giurisprudenza, studiare legge; ~ **and order** ordine m pubblico

lawcourt n tribunale m

lawn /lɔːn/ n prato m [all'inglese]. ~**-mower** n tosaerbe m inv

ˈ**law suit** n causa f

lawyer /ˈlɔːjə(r)/ n avvocato m

lax /læks/ adj negligente; (morals etc) lassista

laxative /ˈlæksətɪv/ n lassativo m

lay¹ /leɪ/ adj laico; fig profano

lay² ▸**lie²**

lay³ vt (pt/pp **laid**) porre, mettere; apparecchiare (table) •vi (hen:) fare le uova. ▫ ~ **down** vt posare; stabilire (rules, conditions). ▫ ~ **off** vt licenziare (workers) •vi (!: stop) ~ **off!** smettila! **lay out** vt (display, set forth) esporre; (plan) pianificare (garden); (spend) sborsare; (Typ) impaginare

lay: ~**about** n fannullone, -a mf. ~**-by** n corsia f di sosta

layer /ˈleɪə(r)/ n strato m

lay: ~**man** n profano m. ~**out** n disposizione f; (Typ) impaginazione f, layout m inv

laze /leɪz/ vi ~ [**about**] oziare

laziness /ˈleɪzɪnɪs/ n pigrizia f

lazy /ˈleɪzɪ/ adj (**-ier, -iest**) pigro. ~**-bones** n poltrone, -a mf

lead¹ /led/ n piombo m; (of pencil) mina f

lead² /liːd/ n guida f; (leash) giunzaglio m; (flex) filo m; (clue) indizio m; (Theat) parte f principale; (distance ahead) distanza f (**over** su); **in the** ~ in testa •v (pt/pp **led**) •vt condurre; dirigere (expedition, party etc); (induce) indurre; ~ **the way** mettersi in testa •vi (be in front) condurre; (in race, competition) essere in testa; (at cards) giocare (per primo). ▫ ~ **away** vt portar via. ▫ ~ **to** vt portare a. ▫ ~ **up to** vt preludere; **what's this** ~**ing up to?** dove porta questo?

leader /ˈliːdə(r)/ n capo m; (of orchestra primo violino m; (in newspaper) articolo m di fondo. ~**ship** n direzione f, leadership f inv; **show** ~**ship** mostrare capacità di comando

leading /ˈliːdɪŋ/ adj principale; ~ **lady**/**man** attrice f/attore m principale; ~ **question** domanda f tendenziosa

leaf /liːf/ n (pl **leaves**) foglia f; (of table) asse f •**leaf through** vt sfogliare. ~**let** n dépliant m inv; (advertising) dépliant m inv pubblicitario; (political) manifestino m

league /liːɡ/ n lega f; (Sport) campionato m; **be in** ~ **with** essere in combutta con

leak /liːk/ n (hole) fessura f; (Naut) falla f; (of gas & fig) fuga f •vi colare; (ship:) fare acqua; (liquid, gas:) fuoriuscire •vt ~ **sth to sb** fig far trapelare qcsa a qcno. ~**y** adj che perde; (Naut) che fa acqua

lean¹ /liːn/ adj magro

lean² v (pt/pp **leaned** or **leant** /lent/) •vt appoggiare (**against**/**on** contro/su) •vi appoggiarsi (**against**/**on** contro/su); (not be straight) pendere; **be** ~**ing against** essere appoggiato contro; ~ **on sb** (depend on) appoggiarsi a qcno; (!: exert pressure on) stare alle calcagne di qcno. ▫ ~ **back** vi sporgersi indietro. ▫ ~ **forward** vi piegarsi in avanti. ▫ ~ **out** vi sporgersi. ▫ ~ **over** vi piegarsi

leaning /ˈliːnɪŋ/ adj pendente; **the L**~ **Tower of Pisa** la torre di Pisa, la torre pendente •n tendenza f

leap /liːp/ n salto m •vi (pt/pp **leapt** /lept/ or **leaped**) saltare; **he leapt at it** ! l'ha preso al volo. ~**-frog** n cavallina f. ~ **year** n anno m bisestile

arn /lɜ:n/ v (pt/pp **learnt** or **learned**) •vt imparare; ~ **to swim** imparare a nuotare; **I have ~ed that...** (heard) sono venuto a sapere che... •vi imparare

arn|ed /'lɜ:nɪd/ adj colto. ~**er** n also (Auto) principiante mf. ~**ing** n cultura f. ~**ing curve** n curva f d'apprendimiento

ase /li:s/ n contratto m d'affitto; (rental) affitto m •vt affittare

ash /li:ʃ/ n guinzaglio m

ast /li:st/ adj più piccolo; (amount) minore; **you've got ~ luggage** hai meno bagagli di tutti •n **the ~** il meno; **at ~** almeno; **not in the ~** niente affatto •adv meno; **the ~ expensive wine** il vino meno caro

ather /'leðə(r)/ n pelle f; (of soles) cuoio m •attrib di pelle/cuoio. ~**y** adj (meat, skin) duro

ave /li:v/ n (holiday) congedo m; (Mil) licenza f; **on ~** in congedo/licenza •v (pt/pp **left**) •vt lasciare; uscire da (house, office); (forget) dimenticare; **there is nothing left** non è rimasto niente •vi andare via; (train, bus:) partire. □ ~ **behind** vt lasciare; (forget) dimenticare. □ ~ **out** vt omettere; (not put away) lasciare fuori

aves /li:vz/ ▹**leaf**

eban|on /'lebənən/ n Libano m ~**ese** /-'ni:z/ adj & n libanese mf

cture /'lektʃə(r)/ n conferenza f; (Univ) lezione f; (reproof) ramanzina f •vi fare una conferenza (**on** su); (Univ) insegnare (**on sth** qcsa) •vt ~ **sb** rimproverare qcno. ~**r** n conferenziere, -a mf; (Univ) docente mf universitario, -a

d /led/ ▹**lead**²

dge /ledʒ/ n cornice f; (of window) davanzale m

ek /li:k/ n porro m

er /lɪə(r)/ n sguardo m libidinoso •vi ~ [**at**] guardare in modo libidinoso

ft¹ /left/ ▹**leave**

ft² adj sinistro •adv a sinistra •n also (Pol) sinistra f; **on the ~** a sinistra;

ft: ~-'**handed** adj mancino. ~-'**luggage office** n deposito m bagagli. ~**overs** npl rimasugli mpl. ~-'**wing** adj (Pol) di sinistra

leg /leg/ n gamba f; (of animal) zampa f; (of journey) tappa f; (Culin: of chicken) coscia f; (: of lamb) cosciotto m

legacy /'legəsɪ/ n lascito m

legal /'li:gl/ adj legale; **take ~ action** intentare un'azione legale. ~**ly** adv legalmente

legality /lɪ'gælətɪ/ n legalità f

legalize /'li:gəlaɪz/ vt legalizzare

legend /'ledʒənd/ n leggenda f. ~**ary** adj leggendario

legib|le /'ledʒəbl/ adj leggibile. ~**ly** adv in modo leggibile

legislat|e /'ledʒɪsleɪt/ vi legiferare. ~**ion** n legislazione f

legitima|te /lɪ'dʒɪtɪmət/ adj legittimo; (excuse) valido

leisure /'leʒə(r)/ n tempo m libero; **at your ~** con comodo. ~**ly** adj senza fretta

lemon /'lemən/ n limone m. ~**ade** n limonata f

lend /lend/ vt (pt/pp **lent**) prestare; ~ **a hand** fig dare una mano. ~**ing library** n biblioteca f per il prestito

length /leŋθ/ n lunghezza f; (piece) pezzo m; (of wallpaper) parte f; (of visit) durata f; **at ~** a lungo; (at last) alla fine

length|en /'leŋθən/ vt allungare •vi allungarsi. ~**ways** adv per lungo

lengthy /'leŋθɪ/ adj (**-ier, -iest**) lungo

lens /lenz/ n lente f; (Phot) obiettivo m; (of eye) cristallino m

lent /lent/ ▹**lend**

Lent n Quaresima f

Leo /'li:əʊ/ n (Astr) Leone m

leopard /'lepəd/ n leopardo m

leotard /'li:ətɑ:d/ n body m inv

lesbian /'lezbɪən/ adj lesbico •n lesbica f

less /les/ adj meno di; ~ **and** ~ sempre meno •adv & prep meno •n meno m

lessen /'lesn/ vt/i diminuire

lesson /'lesn/ n lezione f

lest /lest/ conj liter per timore che

let /let/ vt (pt/pp **let**, pres p **letting**) lasciare, permettere; (rent) affittare; ~ **alone** (not to mention) tanto meno;

l

'to ~' 'affittasi'; **~ us go** andiamo; **~ sb do sth** lasciare fare qcsa a qcno, permettere a qcno di fare qcsa; **~ me know** fammi sapere; **just ~ him try!** che ci provi solamente!; **~ oneself in for sth** [!] impelagarsi in qcsa. □ **~ down** vt sciogliersi (hair); abbassare (blinds); (lengthen) allungare; (disappoint) deludere; **don't ~ me down** conto su di te. □ **~ in** vt far entrare. □ **~ off** vt far partire; (not punish) perdonare; **~ sb off doing sth** abbonare qcsa a qcno. □ **~ out** vt far uscire; (make larger) allargare; emettere (scream, groan). □ **~ through** vt far passare. □ **~ up** vi [!] diminuire

'let-down n delusione f

lethal /'li:θl/ adj letale

letharg|ic /lɪ'θɑ:dʒɪk/ adj apatico. **~y** n apatia f

letter /'letə(r)/ n lettera f. **~-box** n buca f per le lettere. **~-head** n carta f intestata. **~ing** n caratteri mpl

lettuce /'letɪs/ n lattuga f

'let-up n [!] pausa f

leukaemia /lu:'ki:mɪə/ n leucemia f

level /'levl/ adj piano; (in height, competition) allo stesso livello; (spoonful) raso; **draw ~ with sb** affiancare qcno •n livello m; **on the ~** [!] giusto •vt (pt/pp **levelled**) livellare; (aim) puntare (**at** su)

level 'crossing n passaggio m a livello

lever /'li:və(r)/ n leva f •**lever up** vt sollevare (con una leva). **~age** n azione f di una leva; fig influenza f

levy /'levɪ/ vt (pt/pp **levied**) imporre (tax)

lewd /lju:d/ adj osceno

liabilit|y /laɪə'bɪlətɪ/ n responsabilità f; ([!]: burden) peso m; **~ies** pl debiti mpl

liable /'laɪəbl/ adj responsabile (**for** di); **be ~ to** (rain, break etc) rischiare di; (tend to) tendere a

liaise /lɪ'eɪz/ vi [!] essere in contatto

liaison /lɪ'eɪzɒn/ n contatti mpl; (Mil) collegamento m; (affair) relazione f

liar /'laɪə(r)/ n bugiardo, -a mf

libel /'laɪbl/ n diffamazione f •vt (pt/pp **libelled**) diffamare. **~lous** adj diffamatorio

liberal /'lɪb(ə)rəl/ adj (tolerant) di larghe vedute; (generous) generoso. **L~** adj (Pol) liberale •n liberale mf

liberat|e /'lɪbəreɪt/ vt liberare. **~ed** adj (woman) emancipata. **~ion** n liberazione f; (of women) emancipazione f. **~or** n liberatore, -trice mf

liberty /'lɪbətɪ/ n libertà f; **take the ~ of doing sth** prendersi la liber di fare qcsa; **be at ~ to do sth** essere libero di fare qcsa

Libra /'li:brə/ n (Astr) Bilancia f

librarian /laɪ'breərɪən/ n bibliotecario, -a mf

library /'laɪbrərɪ/ n biblioteca f

Libya /'lɪbɪə/ n Libia f. **~n** adj & n libico, -a mf

lice /laɪs/ ▸**louse**

licence /'laɪsns/ n licenza f; (for (TV) canone m televisivo; (for driving) patente f; (freedom) sregolatezza f. **~-plate** n targa f

license /'laɪsns/ vt autorizzare; **be ~d** (car:) avere il bollo; (restaurant:) essere autorizzato alla vendita di alcolici

lick /lɪk/ n leccata f; **a ~ of paint** una passata leggera di pittura •vt leccare; ([!]: defeat) battere; leccarsi (lips)

lid /lɪd/ n coperchio m; (of eye) palpebra f

lie¹ /laɪ/ n bugia f; **tell a ~** mentire •vi (pt/pp **lied**, pres p **lying**) mentire

lie² vi (pt **lay**, pp **lain**, pres p **lying**) (person:) sdraiarsi; (object:) stare; (remain) rimanere; **leave sth lying about** or **around** lasciare qcsa in giro. □ **~ down** vi sdraiarsi

lie-in n [!] **have a ~** restare a letto fino a tardi

lieutenant /lef'tenənt/ n tenente m

life /laɪf/ n (pl **lives**) vita f

life: ~belt n salvagente m. **~-boa** n lancia f di salvataggio; (on ship) scialuppa f di salvataggio. **~buoy** salvagente m. **~ coach** n life coac m/f inv. **~-guard** n bagnino m. **~-jacket** n giubbotto m di salvataggio. **~less** adj inanimato. **~like** adj realistico. **~long** adj di

:utta la vita. **~-size[d]** adj in ȝrandezza naturale. **~time** n vita f; **the chance of a ~time** ın'occasione unica

't /lıft/ n ascensore m; (Auto) ɔassaggio m • vt sollevare; revocare (restrictions); (**!**: steal) rubare • vi (fog:) ılzarsi. ▫**~ up** vt sollevare

ft-off n decollo m (di razzo)

ȝht¹ /laıt/ adj (not dark) luminoso; **~ green** verde chiaro • n luce f; (lamp) ampada f; **in the ~ of** fig alla luce di; **have you got a ~?** ha da ıccendere?; **come to ~** essere rivelato • vt (pt/pp **lit** or **lighted**) ıccendere; (illuminate) illuminare. ▫**~ up** vi (face:) illuminarsi

ȝht² adj (not heavy) leggero • adv **travel ~** viaggiare con poco bagaglio

ght-bulb n lampadina f

ȝhten¹ /'laıtn/ vt illuminare

ȝhten² vt alleggerire (load)

ȝhter /'laıtə(r)/ n accendino m

ȝht: ~-'hearted adj spensierato. **~house** n faro m. **~ly** adv leggermente; (accuse) con leggerezza; (without concern) senza dare importanza alla cosa; **get off ~ly** cavarsela a buon mercato

ȝhtning /'laıtnıŋ/ n lampo m, fulmine m. **~-conductor** n parafulmine m

ȝhtweight adj leggero • n (in boxing) peso m leggero

ke¹ /laık/ adj simile • prep come; **~ this/that** così; **what's he ~?** com'è? • conj (**!**: as) come; (Am: as if) come se

ke² vt piacere, gradire; **I should/would ~** vorrei, gradirei; **I ~ him** mi piace; **I ~ this car** mi piace questa macchina; **I ~ dancing** mi piace ballare; **I ~ that!** **!** questa mi è piaciuta! • n **~s and dislikes** pl gusti mpl

ke|able /'laıkəbl/ adj simpatico. **~lihood** n probabilità f. **~ly** adj (-**ier, -iest**) probabile • adv probabilmente; **not ~ly!** **!** neanche per sogno!

ken /'laıkən/ vt paragonare (**to** a)

ke|ness /'laıknıs/ n somiglianza f. **~wise** adv lo stesso

liking /'laıkıŋ/ n gusto m; **is it to your ~?** è di suo gusto?; **take a ~ to sb** prendere qcno in simpatia

lilac /'laılək/ n lillà m • adj color lillà

lily /'lılı/ n giglio m. **~ of the valley** n mughetto m

limb /lım/ n arto m

lime¹ /laım/ n (fruit) cedro m; (tree) tiglio m

lime² n calce f. **'~light** n **be in the ~light** essere molto in vista. **'~stone** n calcare m

limit /'lımıt/ n limite m; **that's the ~!** **!** questo è troppo! • vt limitare (**to** a). **~ation** n limite m. **~ed** adj ristretto; **~ed company** società f anonima

limousine /'lıməzi:n/ n limousine f inv

limp¹ /lımp/ n andatura f zoppicante; **have a ~** zoppicare • vi zoppicare

limp² adj floscio

line¹ /laın/ n linea f; (length of rope, cord) filo m; (of writing) riga f; (of poem) verso m; (row) fila f; (wrinkle) ruga f; (of business) settore m; (Am: queue) coda f; **in ~ with** in conformità con • vt segnare; fiancheggiare (street). ▫**~ up** vi allinearsi • vt allineare

line² vt foderare (garment)

lined¹ /laınd/ adj (face) rugoso; (paper) a righe

lined² adj (garment) foderato

linen /'lının/ n lino m; (articles) biancheria f • attrib di lino

liner /'laınə(r)/ n nave f di linea

linger /'lıŋgə(r)/ vi indugiare

lingerie /'læia.ʒərı/ n biancheria f intima (da donna)

linguist /'lıŋgwıst/ n linguista mf

linguistic /lıŋ'gwıstık/ adj linguistico. **~s** n linguistica fsg

lining /'laınıŋ/ n (of garment) fodera f; (of brakes) guarnizione f

link /lıŋk/ n (of chain) anello m; fig legame m • vt collegare. ▫**~ up** vi unirsi (**with** a); (TV) collegarsi

lino /'laınəʊ/ n, **linoleum** /lı'nəʊlıəm/ n linoleum m

lint /lınt/ n garza f

lion /'laıən/ n leone m. **~ess** n leonessa f

lip /lɪp/ n labbro m (pl labbra f); (edge) bordo m

lip: ~-read vi leggere le labbra; **~-service** n **pay ~-service to** approvare soltanto a parole. **~salve** n burro m [di] cacao. **~stick** n rossetto m

liqueur /lɪ'kjʊə(r)/ n liquore m

liquid /'lɪkwɪd/ n liquido m • adj liquido

liquidat|e /'lɪkwɪdeɪt/ vt liquidare. **~ion** n liquidazione f; (Comm) **go into ~ion** andare in liquidazione

liquidize /'lɪkwɪdaɪz/ vt rendere liquido. **~r** n (Culin) frullatore m

liquor /'lɪkə(r)/ n bevanda f alcoolica

liquorice /'lɪkərɪs/ n liquirizia f

liquor store n Am negozio m di alcolici

lisp /lɪsp/ n pronuncia f con la lisca • vi parlare con la lisca

list[1] /lɪst/ n lista f • vt elencare

list[2] vi (ship:) inclinarsi

listen /'lɪsn/ vi ascoltare; **~ to** ascoltare. **~er** n ascoltatore, -trice mf

listless /'lɪstlɪs/ adj svogliato

lit /lɪt/ ▹**light**[1]

literacy /'lɪtərəsɪ/ n alfabetizzazione f

literal /'lɪtərəl/ adj letterale. **~ly** adv letteralmente

literary /'lɪtərərɪ/ adj letterario

literate /'lɪtərət/ adj **be ~** saper leggere e scrivere

literature /'lɪtrətʃə(r)/ n letteratura f

Lithuania /lɪθju'eɪnɪə/ n Lituania f. **~n** adj & n lituano, -a mf

litre /'li:tə(r)/ n litro m

litter /'lɪtə(r)/ n immondizie fpl; (Zool) figliata f • vt **be ~ed with** essere ingombrato di. **~-bin** n bidone m della spazzatura

little /'lɪtl/ adj piccolo; (not much) poco • adv & n poco m; **a ~** un po'; **a ~ water** un po' d'acqua; **a ~ better** un po' meglio; **~ by ~** a poco a poco

live[1] /laɪv/ adj vivo; (ammunition) carico; **~ broadcast** trasmissione f in diretta; **be ~** (Electr) essere sotto tensione; **~ wire** n fig persona f dinamica • adv (broadcast) in diretta

live[2] /lɪv/ vi vivere; (reside) abitare; **~ with** convivere con. □**~ down** vt far dimenticare. □**~ off** vt vivere alle spalle di. □**~ on** vt vivere di • sopravvivere. □**~ up** vt **~ it up** fa[re] la bella vita. □**~ up to** vt essere all'altezza di

liveli|hood /'laɪvlɪhʊd/ n mezzi mpl di sostentamento. **~ness** n vivacità f

lively /'laɪvlɪ/ adj (**-ier, -iest**) vivace

liver /'lɪvə(r)/ n fegato m

lives /laɪvz/ ▹**life**

livestock /'laɪv-/ n bestiame m

livid /'lɪvɪd/ adj [!] livido

living /'lɪvɪŋ/ adj vivo • n **earn one's ~** guadagnarsi da vivere; **the ~** pl vivi. **~-room** n soggiorno m

lizard /'lɪzəd/ n lucertola f

load /ləʊd/ n carico m; **~s of** [!] un sacco di • vt caricare. **~ed** adj caric[o] ([!]: rich) ricchissimo

loaf[1] /ləʊf/ n (pl **loaves**) pagnotta f

loaf[2] vi oziare

loan /ləʊn/ n prestito m; **on ~** in prestito • vt prestare

loath|e /ləʊð/ vt detestare. **~ing** n disgusto m. **~some** adj disgustoso

lobby /'lɒbɪ/ n atrio m; (Pol) gruppo di pressione, lobby m inv

lobster /'lɒbstə(r)/ n aragosta f

local /'ləʊkl/ adj locale; **I'm not ~** non sono del posto • n abitante mf del luogo; ([!]: public house) pub m locale. **~ au'thority** n autorità f locale. **~ call** n (Teleph) telefonata f urbana. **~ government** n autorità inv locale

locality /ləʊ'kælətɪ/ n zona f

local|ization /ləʊklaɪ'zeɪʃn/ n localizzazione f. **~ized** adj localizzato

locally /'ləʊkəlɪ/ adv localmente; (liv[e,] work) nei paraggi

locat|e /ləʊ'keɪt/ vt situare; trovare (person); **be ~ed** essere situato. **~ion** n posizione f; **filmed on ~ion** girato in esterni

lock[1] /lɒk/ n (hair) ciocca f

lock[2] n (on door) serratura f; (on canal) chiusa f • vt chiudere a chiave;

bloccare (wheels) • vi chiudersi. □ ~ **in** vt chiudere dentro. □ ~ **out** vt chiudere fuori. □ ~ **up** vt (in prison) mettere dentro • vi chiudere

ocker /ˈlɒkə(r)/ n armadietto m

ocket /ˈlɒkɪt/ n medaglione m

ock: ~-out n serrata f. **~smith** n fabbro m

ocomotive /ləʊkəˈməʊtɪv/ n locomotiva f

odge /lɒdʒ/ n (porter's) portineria f; (masonic) loggia f • vt presentare (claim, complaint); (with bank, solicitor) depositare; **be ~d** essersi conficcato • vi essere a pensione (**with** da); (become fixed) conficcarsi. **~r** n inquilino, -a mf

odgings /ˈlɒdʒɪŋz/ npl camere fpl in affitto

oft /lɒft/ n soffitta f

ofty /ˈlɒftɪ/ adj (**-ier, -iest**) alto; (haughty) altezzoso

og /lɒg/ n ceppo m; (Auto) libretto m di circolazione; (Naut) giornale m di bordo • vt (pt **logged**) registrare. □ ~ **on to** vt (Comput) connettersi a

ogarithm /ˈlɒgərɪðm/ n logaritmo m

og-book n (Naut) giornale m di bordo; (Auto) libretto m di circolazione

oggerheads /ˈlɒgə-/ npl **be at ~** [!] essere in totale disaccordo

ogic /ˈlɒdʒɪk/ n logica f. **~al** adj logico. **~ally** adv logicamente

ogistics /ləˈdʒɪstɪks/ npl logistica f

ogo /ˈləʊgəʊ/ n logo m inv

oin /lɔɪn/ n (Culin) lombata f

oiter /ˈlɔɪtə(r)/ vi gironzolare

oll|ipop /ˈlɒlɪpɒp/ n lecca-lecca m inv. **~y** n lecca-lecca m; ([!]: money) quattrini mpl

ondon /ˈlʌndən/ n Londra f • attrib londinese, di Londra. **~er** n londinese mf

one /ləʊn/ adj solitario. **~liness** n solitudine f

onely /ˈləʊnlɪ/ adj (**-ier, -iest**) solitario; (person) solo

one|r /ˈləʊnə(r)/ n persona f solitaria. **~some** adj solo

ong¹ /lɒŋ/ adj lungo; **a ~ time** molto tempo; **a ~ way** distante; **in the ~ run** a lungo andare; (in the end) alla fin fine • adv a lungo, lungamente; **how ~ is?** quanto è lungo?; (in time) quanto dura?; **all day ~** tutto il giorno; **not ~ ago** non molto tempo fa; **before ~** fra breve; **he's no ~er here** non è più qui; **as** or **so ~as** finché; (provided that) purché; **so ~!** [!] ciao!; **will you be ~?** [ti] ci vuole molto?

long² vi **~ for** desiderare ardentemente

long-ˈdistance adj a grande distanza; (Sport) di fondo; (call) interurbano

longing /ˈlɒŋɪŋ/ adj desideroso • n brama f. **~ly** adv con desiderio

longitude /ˈlɒŋgɪtjuːd/ n (Geog) longitudine f

long: ~ jump n salto m in lungo. **~-range** adj (Aeron, Mil) a lunga portata; (forecast) a lungo termine. **~-sighted** adj presbite. **~-term** adj a lunga scadenza. **~-winded** /-ˈwɪndɪd/ adj prolisso

loo /luː/ n [!] gabinetto m

look /lʊk/ n occhiata f; (appearance) aspetto m; [**good**] **~s** pl bellezza f; **have a ~ at** dare un'occhiata a • vi guardare; (seem) sembrare; **~ here!** mi ascolti bene!; **~ at** guardare; **~ for** cercare; **~ like** (resemble) assomigliare a. □ ~ **after** vt badare a. □ ~ **down** vi guardare in basso; **~ down on sb** fig guardare dall'alto in basso qcno. □ ~ **forward to** vt essere impaziente di. □ ~ **in on** vt passare da. □ ~ **into** vt (examine) esaminare. □ ~ **on to** vt (room:) dare su. □ ~ **out** vi guardare fuori; (take care) fare attenzione; **~ out for** cercare; **~ out!** attento! **look round** vi girarsi; (in shop, town etc) dare un'occhiata. □ ~ **through** vt dare un'occhiata a (script, notes). □ ~ **up** vi guardare in alto; **~ up to sb** fig rispettare qcno • vt cercare [nel dizionario] (word); (visit) andare a trovare

ˈlook-out n guardia f; (prospect) prospettiva f; **be on the ~ for** tenere gli occhi aperti per

loom /luːm/ vi apparire; fig profilarsi

loony /ˈluːnɪ/ adj & n [!] matto, -a mf. **~ bin** n manicomio m

loop /luːp/ n cappio m; (on garment)

passante m. **~hole** n (in the law) scappatoia f

loose /lu:s/ adj libero; (knot) allentato; (page) staccato; (clothes) largo; (morals) dissoluto; (inexact) vago; **be at a ~ end** non sapere cosa fare; **come ~** (knot:) sciogliersi; **set ~** liberare. **~'change** n spiccioli mpl. **~ly** adv scorrevolmente; (defined) vagamente

loosen /'lu:sn/ vt sciogliere

loot /lu:t/ n bottino m •vt/i depredare. **~er** n predatore, -trice mf. **~ing** n saccheggio m

lop /lɒp/ **~ off** vt (pt/pp **lopped**) potare

lop'sided adj sbilenco

lord /lɔ:d/ n signore m; (title) Lord m; **House of L~s** Camera f dei Lords; **the L~'s Prayer** il Padrenostro; **good L~!** Dio mio!

lorry /'lɒrɪ/ n camion m inv; **~ driver** camionista mf

lose /lu:z/ v (pt/pp **lost**) •vt perdere •vi perdere; (clock:) essere indietro; **get lost** perdersi; **get lost!** [!] va a quel paese! **~r** n perdente mf

loss /lɒs/ n perdita f; (Comm) **~es** perdite fpl; **be at a ~** essere perplesso; **be at a ~ for words** non trovare le parole

lost /lɒst/ ▹**lose** •adj perduto. **~ 'property office** n ufficio m oggetti smarriti

lot¹ /lɒt/ (at auction) lotto m; **draw ~s** tirare a sorte

lot² n **the ~** il tutto; **a ~ of, ~s of** molto/i; **the ~ of you** tutti voi; **it has changed a ~** è cambiato molto

lotion /'ləʊʃn/ n lozione f

lottery /'lɒtərɪ/ n lotteria f. **~ ticket** n biglietto m della lotteria

loud /laʊd/ adj sonoro, alto; (colours) sgargiante •adv forte; **out ~** ad alta voce. **~ 'hailer** n megafono m. **~ly** adv forte. **~ 'speaker** n altoparlante m

lounge /laʊndʒ/ n salotto m; (in hotel) salone m •vi poltrire. **~ suit** n vestito m da uomo, completo m da uomo

louse /laʊs/ n (pl **lice**) pidocchio m

lousy /'laʊzɪ/ adj (**-ier, -iest**) [!] schifoso

lout /laʊt/ n zoticone m. **~ish** adj rozzo

lovable /'lʌvəbl/ adj adorabile

love /lʌv/ n amore m; (Tennis) zero m; **in ~** innamorato (**with** di) •vt amare (person, country); **I ~ watching tennis** mi piace molto guardare il tennis. **~-affair** n relazione f [sentimentale]. **~ letter** n lettera f d'amore

lovely /'lʌvlɪ/ adj (**-ier, -iest**) bello; (looks) bello, attraente; (in character) piacevole; (meal) delizioso; **have a ~ time** divertirsi molto

lover /'lʌvə(r)/ n amante mf

loving /'lʌvɪŋ/ adj affettuoso

low /ləʊ/ adj basso; (depressed) giù inv •adv basso; **feel ~** sentirsi giù •n minimo m; (Meteorol) depressione f; **at an all-time ~** (prices etc) al livello minimo

lower /'ləʊə(r)/ adj & adv ▹**low** •vt abbassare; **~ oneself** abbassarsi

loyal /'lɔɪəl/ adj leale. **~ty** n lealtà f; **~ card** carta f fedeltà

lozenge /'lɒzɪndʒ/ n losanga f; (tablet) pastiglia f

LP n abbr long-playing record

Ltd abbr (Limited) s.r.l.

lubricat|e /'lu:brɪkeɪt/ vt lubrificare. **~ion** n lubrificazione f

lucid /'lu:sɪd/ adj (explanation) chiaro; (sane) lucido. **~ity** n lucidità f; (of explanation) chiarezza f

luck /lʌk/ n fortuna f; **bad ~** sfortuna f; **good ~!** buona fortuna! **~ily** adv fortunatamente

lucky /'lʌkɪ/ adj (**-ier, -iest**) fortunato; **be ~** essere fortunato; (thing:) portare fortuna. **~ 'charm** n portafortuna m inv

lucrative /'lu:krətɪv/ adj lucrativo

ludicrous /'lu:dɪkrəs/ adj ridicolo. **~ly** adv (expensive, complex) eccessivamente

lug /lʌg/ vt (pt/pp **lugged**) [!] trascinare

luggage /'lʌgɪdʒ/ n bagaglio m; **~-rack** n portabagagli m inv. **~ trolley** n carrello m portabagagli. **~-van** n bagagliaio m

ukewarm /ˈlu:k-/ adj tiepido; fig poco entusiasta

ull /lʌl/ n pausa f • vt ~ **to sleep** cullare

ullaby /ˈlʌləbaɪ/ n ninna nanna f

umber /ˈlʌmbə(r)/ n cianfrusaglie fpl; (Am: timber) legname m • vt [!] ~ **sb with sth** affibbiare qcsa a qcno. ~ **jack** n tagliaboschi m inv

uminous /ˈlu:mɪnəs/ adj luminoso

ump[1] /lʌmp/ n (of sugar) zolletta f; (swelling) gonfiore m; (in breast) nodulo m; (in sauce) grumo m • vt ~ **together** ammucchiare

ump[2] vt ~ **it** [!] **you'll just have to** ~ **it** che ti piaccia o no è così

ump sum n somma f globale

umpy /ˈlʌmpɪ/ adj (**-ier, -iest**) grumoso

unacy /ˈlu:nəsɪ/ n follia f

unar /ˈlu:nə(r)/ adj lunare

unatic /ˈlu:nətɪk/ n pazzo, -a mf

unch /lʌntʃ/ n pranzo m • vi pranzare

uncheon /ˈlʌntʃn/ n (formal) pranzo m. ~ **meat** n carne f in scatola. ~ **voucher** n buono m pasto

ung /lʌŋ/ n polmone m. ~ **cancer** n cancro m al polmone

lunge /lʌndʒ/ vi lanciarsi (**at** su)

lurch[1] /lɜ:tʃ/ n **leave in the** ~ [!] lasciare nei guai

lurch[2] vi barcollare

lure /lʊə(r)/ n esca f; fig lusinga f • vt adescare

lurid /ˈlʊərɪd/ adj (gaudy) sgargiante; (sensational) sensazionalistico

lurk /lɜ:k/ vi appostarsi

luscious /ˈlʌʃəs/ adj saporito; fig sexy inv

lush /lʌʃ/ adj lussureggiante

lust /lʌst/ n lussuria f • vi ~ **after** desiderare [fortemente]. ~**ful** adj lussurioso

lute /lu:t/ n liuto m

luxuriant /lʌgˈʒʊərɪənt/ adj lussureggiante

luxurious /lʌgˈʒʊərɪəs/ adj lussuoso

luxury /ˈlʌkʃərɪ/ n lusso m • attrib di lusso

lying /ˈlaɪɪŋ/ ▸**lie**[1] & [2] • n mentire m

lynch /lɪntʃ/ vt linciare

lyric /ˈlɪrɪk/ adj lirico. ~**al** adj lirico; ([!]: enthusiastic) entusiasta. ~**s** npl parole fpl

Mm

nac /mæk/ n [!] impermeabile m

nacaroni /mækəˈrəʊnɪ/ n maccheroni mpl

nace[1] /meɪs/ n (staff) mazza f

nace[2] n (spice) macis m o f

nachine /məˈʃi:n/ n macchina f • vt (sew) cucire a macchina; (Techn) lavorare a macchina. ~**-gun** n mitragliatrice f

nachinery /məˈʃi:nərɪ/ n macchinario m

nackerel /ˈmækr(ə)l/ n inv sgombro m

nackintosh /ˈmækɪntɒʃ/ n impermeabile m

nad /mæd/ adj (**madder, maddest**) pazzo, matto; ([!]: angry) furioso (**at** con); **like** ~ [!] come un pazzo; **be** ~ **about sb/sth** ([!]: keen on) andare matto per qcno/qcsa

madam /ˈmædəm/ n signora f

mad cow disease n morbo m della mucca pazza

madden /ˈmædən/ vt (make angry) far diventare matto

made /meɪd/ ▸**make**; ~ **to measure** [fatto] su misura

mad|ly /ˈmædlɪ/ adv [!] follemente; ~**ly in love** innamorato follemente. ~**man** n pazzo m. ~**ness** n pazzia f

madonna /məˈdɒnə/ n madonna f

magazine /mægə'zi:n/ n rivista f; (Mil, Phot) magazzino m

maggot /'mægət/ n verme m

magic /'mædʒɪk/ n magia f; (tricks) giochi mpl di prestigio • adj magico; (trick) di prestigio. **~al** adj magico

magician /mə'dʒɪʃn/ n mago, -a mf; (entertainer) prestigiatore, -trice mf

magistrate /'mædʒɪstreɪt/ n magistrato m

magnet /'mægnɪt/ n magnete m, calamita f. **~ic** adj magnetico. **~ism** n magnetismo m

magnification /mægnɪfɪ'keɪʃn/ n ingrandimento m

magnificen|ce /mæg'nɪfɪsəns/ n magnificenza f. **~t** adj magnifico

magnify /'mægnɪfaɪ/ vt (pt/pp **-ied**) ingrandire; (exaggerate) ingigantire. **~ing glass** n lente f d'ingrandimento

magnitude /'mægnɪtju:d/ n grandezza f; (importance) importanza f

magpie /'mægpaɪ/ n gazza f

mahogany /mə'hɒgənɪ/ n mogano m • attrib di mogano

maid /meɪd/ n cameriera f; **old ~** pej zitella f

maiden /'meɪdn/ n (liter) fanciulla f • adj (speech, voyage) inaugurale. **~ 'aunt** n zia f zitella. **~ name** n nome m da ragazza

mail /meɪl/ n posta f • vt impostare. **~-bag** n sacco m postale. **~box** n Am cassetta f delle lettere; (e-mail) casella f di posta elettronica. **~ing list** n elenco m d'indirizzi per un mailing. **~man** n Am postino m. **~ order** n vendita f per corrispondenza. **~-order firm** n ditta f di vendita per corrispondenza. **~shot** n mailing m inv

maim /meɪm/ vt menomare

main[1] /meɪn/ n (water, gas, electricity) conduttura f principale

main[2] adj principale; **the ~ thing is to...** la cosa essenziale è di... • n **in the ~** in complesso

main: ~land /-lənd/ n continente m. **~ly** adv principalmente. **~ street** n via f principale

maintain /meɪn'teɪn/ vt mantenere; (keep in repair) curare la manutenzione di; (claim) sostenere

maintenance /'meɪntənəns/ n mantenimento m; (care) manutenzione f; (allowance) alimenti mpl

maisonette /meɪzə'net/ n appartamento m a due piani

majestic /mə'dʒestɪk/ adj maestoso

majesty /'mædʒəstɪ/ n maestà f; **His Her M~** Sua Maestà

major /'meɪdʒə(r)/ adj maggiore; **~ road** strada f con diritto di precedenza • n (Mil, Mus) maggiore m • vi Am **~ in** specializzarsi in

Majorca /mə'jɔ:kə/ n Maiorca f

majority /mə'dʒɒrətɪ/ n maggioranza f; **be in the ~** avere la maggioranza

make /meɪk/ n (brand) marca f • v (pt/pp **made**) • vt fare; (earn) guadagnare; rendere (happy, clear); prendere (decision); **~ sb laugh** far ridere qcno; **~ sb do sth** far fare qcsa a qcno; **~ it** (to party, top of hill etc) farcela; **what time do you ~ it?** che ore fai? • vi **~ as if to** fare per. □ **~ do** vi arrangiarsi. □ **~ for** dirigersi verso. □ **~ off** vi fuggire. □ **~ out** vt (distinguish) distinguere; (write out) rilasciare (cheque); compilare (list); (claim) far credere. □ **~ over** vt cedere. □ **~ up** vt (constitute) comporre; (complete) completare; (invent) inventare; (apply cosmetics to) truccare; fare (parcel); **~ up one's mind** decidersi; **~ it up** (after quarrel) riconciliarsi • vi (after quarrel) fare la pace; **~ up for** compensare; **~ up for lost time** recuperare il tempo perso

'make-believe n finzione f

maker /'meɪkə(r)/ n fabbricante mf; **M~** Creatore m

make: ~shift adj di fortuna • n espediente m. **~-up** n trucco m; (character) natura f

making /'meɪkɪŋ/ n **have the ~s of** aver la stoffa di

maladjust|ed /mælə'dʒʌstɪd/ adj disadattato

malaria /mə'leərɪə/ n malaria f

Malaysia /mə'leɪzɪə/ n Malesia f

male /meɪl/ adj maschile • n maschio m. **~ nurse** n infermiere m

nalfunction /mæl'fʌŋkʃn/ n funzionamento m imperfetto •vi funzionare male

nalice /'mælɪs/ n malignità f; **bear sb ~** voler del male a qcno

nalicious /mə'lɪʃəs/ adj maligno

nallet /'mælɪt/ n martello m di legno

nalnu'trition /mæl-/ n malnutrizione f

nal'practice n negligenza f

nalt /mɔ:lt/ n malto m

Malta /'mɔ:ltə/ n Malta f. **~ese** adj & n maltese mf

nammal /'mæml/ n mammifero m

nammoth /'mæməθ/ adj mastodontico •n mammut m inv

nan /mæn/ n (pl **men**) uomo m; (chess, draughts) pedina f •vt (pt/pp **manned**) equipaggiare; essere di servizio a (counter, telephones)

nanage /'mænɪdʒ/ vt dirigere; gestire (shop, affairs); (cope with) farcela; **~ to do sth** riuscire a fare qcsa •vi riuscire; (cope) farcela (**on** con). **~able** adj (hair) docile; (size) maneggevole. **~ment** n gestione f; **the ~ment** la direzione

nanager /'mænɪdʒə(r)/ n direttore m; (of shop, bar) gestore m; (Sport) manager m inv. **~ess** n direttrice f. **~ial** adj **~ial staff** personale m direttivo

nandat|e /'mændeɪt/ n mandato m. **~ory** adj obbligatorio

nane /meɪn/ n criniera f

nangle /'mæŋgl/ vt (damage) maciullare

nan: ~'handle vt malmenare. **~hole** n botola f. **~hood** n età f adulta; (quality) virilità f. **~-hour** n ora f lavorativa. **~-hunt** n caccia f all'uomo

nan|ia /'meɪnɪə/ n mania f. **~iac** n maniaco, -a mf

nanicure /'mænɪkjʊə(r)/ n manicure f •vt fare la manicure a

nanifest /'mænɪfest/ adj manifesto •vt **~ itself** manifestarsi. **~ly** adv palesemente

nanifesto /mænɪ'festəʊ/ n manifesto m

nanipulat|e /mə'nɪpjuleɪt/ vt manipolare. **~ion** n manipolazione f

man'kind n genere m umano

manly /'mænlɪ/ adj virile

'man-made adj artificiale. **~ fibre** n fibra f sintetica

manner /'mænə(r)/ n maniera f; **in this ~** in questo modo; **have no ~s** avere dei pessimi modi; **good/bad ~s** buone/cattive maniere fpl. **~ism** n affettazione f

manor /'mænə(r)/ n maniero m

'manpower n manodopera f

mansion /'mænʃn/ n palazzo m

'manslaughter n omicidio m colposo

mantelpiece /'mæntl-/ n mensola f di caminetto

manual /'mænjʊəl/ adj manuale •n manuale m

manufacture /mænjʊ'fæktʃə(r)/ vt fabbricare •n manifattura f. **~r** n fabbricante m

manure /mə'njʊə(r)/ n concime m

manuscript /'mænjʊskrɪpt/ n manoscritto m

many /'menɪ/ adj & pron molti; **there are as ~ boys as girls** ci sono tanti ragazzi quante ragazze; **as ~ as 500** ben 500; **as ~ as that** così tanti; **as ~** altrettanti; **very ~, a good/great ~** moltissimi; **~ a time** molte volte

map /mæp/ n carta f geografica; (of town) mappa f •**map out** vt (pt/pp **mapped**) fig programmare

mar /mɑ:(r)/ vt (pt/pp **marred**) rovinare

marathon /'mærəθən/ n maratona f

marble /'mɑ:bl/ n marmo m; (for game) pallina f •attrib di marmo

march n marcia f; (protest) dimostrazione f •vi marciare •vt far marciare; **~ sb off** scortare qcno fuori

March /mɑ:tʃ/ n marzo m

mare /meə(r)/ n giumenta f

margarine /mɑ:dʒə'ri:n/ n margarina f

margin /'mɑ:dʒɪn/ n margine m. **~al** adj marginale. **~ally** adv marginalmente

marijuana /mærʊ'wɑ:nə/ n marijuana f

m

marina /mə'ri:nə/ n porticciolo m

marine /mə'ri:n/ adj marino • n (sailor) soldato m di fanteria marina

marionette /mærɪə'net/ n marionetta f

mark[1] /mɑ:k/ n (currency) marco m

mark[2] n (stain) macchia f; (sign, indication) segno m; (Sch) voto m • vt segnare; (stain) macchiare; (Sch) correggere; (Sport) marcare; ~ **time** (Mil) segnare il passo; fig non far progressi; ~ **my words** ricordati quello che dico. □ ~ **out** vt delimitare; fig designare

marked /mɑ:kt/ adj marcato. ~**ly** adv notevolmente

marker /'mɑ:kə(r)/ n (for highlighting) evidenziatore m; (Sport) marcatore m; (of exam) esaminatore, -trice mf

market /'mɑ:kɪt/ n mercato m • vt vendere al mercato; (launch) commercializzare; **on the** ~ sul mercato. ~**ing** n marketing m. ~ **research** n ricerca f di mercato

marksman /'mɑ:ksmən/ n tiratore m scelto

marmalade /'mɑ:məleɪd/ n marmellata f d'arance

maroon /mə'ru:n/ adj marrone rossastro

marquee /mɑ:'ki:/ n tendone m

marriage /'mærɪdʒ/ n matrimonio m

married /'mærɪd/ adj sposato; (life) coniugale

marrow /'mærəʊ/ n (Anat) midollo m; (vegetable) zucca f

marr|y /'mærɪ/ vt (pt/pp **married**) sposare; **get** ~**ied** sposarsi • vi sposarsi

marsh /mɑ:ʃ/ n palude f

marshal /'mɑ:ʃl/ n (steward) cerimoniere m • vt (pt/pp **marshalled**) fig organizzare (arguments)

marshy /'mɑ:ʃɪ/ adj paludoso

martial /'mɑ:ʃl/ adj marziale

martyr /'mɑ:tə(r)/ n martire mf • vt martoriare. ~**dom** n martirio m. ~**ed** adj [!] da martire

marvel /'mɑ:vl/ n meraviglia f • vi (pt/pp **marvelled**) meravigliarsi (**at** di). ~**lous** adj meraviglioso

Marxis|m /'mɑ:ksɪzm/ n marxismo m. ~**t** adj & n marxista mf

m

marzipan /'mɑ:zɪpæn/ n marzapane m

mascara /mæ'skɑ:rə/ n mascara m inv

mascot /'mæskət/ n mascotte f inv

masculin|e /'mæskjʊlɪn/ adj maschile • n (Gram) maschile m. ~**ity** n mascolinità f

mash /mæʃ/ vt impastare. ~**ed potatoes** npl purè m inv di patate

mask /mɑ:sk/ n maschera f • vt mascherare

masochis|m /'mæsəkɪzm/ n masochismo m. ~**t** n masochista mf

mason /'meɪsn/ n muratore m

Mason n massone m. ~**ic** adj massonico

masonry /'meɪsnrɪ/ n massoneria f

masquerade /mæskə'reɪd/ n fig mascherata f • vi ~ **as** (pose) farsi passare per

mass[1] /mæs/ n (Relig) messa f

mass[2] n massa f; ~**es of** [!] un sacco di • vi ammassarsi

massacre /'mæsəkə(r)/ n massacro m • vt massacrare

massage /'mæsɑ:ʒ/ n massaggio m • vt massaggiare; fig manipolare (statistics)

masseu|r /mæ'sɜ:(r)/ n massaggiatore m. ~**se** n massaggiatrice f

massive /'mæsɪv/ adj enorme

mass: ~ **media** npl mezzi mpl di comunicazione di massa, mass media mpl. ~**-pro'duce** vt produrre in serie

mast /mɑ:st/ n (Naut) albero m; (for radio) antenna f

master /'mɑ:stə(r)/ n maestro m, padrone m; (teacher) professore m; (of ship) capitano m; **M**~ (boy) signorino m

master: ~**-key** n passe-partout m inv. ~**-mind** n cervello m • vt ideare e dirigere. ~**piece** n capolavoro m. ~**-stroke** n colpo m da maestro. ~**y** n (of subject) padronanza f

masturbat|e /'mæstəbeɪt/ vi masturbarsi. ~**ion** n masturbazione f

mat /mæt/ n stuoia f; (on table) sottopiatto m

match[1] /mætʃ/ n (Sport) partita f;

(equal) uguale mf; (marriage) matrimonio m; (person to marry) partito m; **be a good ~** (colours:) intonarsi bene; **be no ~ for** non essere dello stesso livello di •vt (equal) uguagliare; (be like) andare bene con •vi intonarsi

match² n fiammifero m. **~box** n scatola f di fiammiferi

matching /'mætʃɪŋ/ adj intonato

mate¹ /meɪt/ n compagno, -a mf; (assistant) aiuto m; (Naut) secondo m; (ℹ: friend) amico, -a mf •vi accoppiarsi •vt accoppiare

mate² n (in chess) scacco m matto

material /mə'tɪərɪəl/ n materiale m; (fabric) stoffa f; **raw ~s** materie fpl prime •adj materiale

maternal /mə'tɜːnl/ adj materno

maternity /mə'tɜːnətɪ/ n maternità f. **~ clothes** npl abiti mpl premaman. **~ ward** n maternità f inv

mathematic|al /mæθə'mætɪkl/ adj matematico. **~ian** n matematico, -a mf

mathematics /mæθ'mætɪks/ n matematica fsg

maths /mæθs/ n ℹ matematica fsg

matinée /'mætɪneɪ/ n (Theat) matinée m

matriculat|e /mə'trɪkjʊleɪt/ vi immatricolarsi. **~ion** n immatricolazione f

matrix /'meɪtrɪks/ n (pl **matrices** /-siːz/) n matrice f

matted /'mætɪd/ adj **~ hair** capelli mpl tutti appiccicati tra loro

matter /'mætə(r)/ n (affair) faccenda f; (question) questione f; (pus) pus m; (phys: substance) materia f; **as a ~ of fact** a dire la verità; **what is the ~?** che cosa c'è? •vi importare; **~ to sb** essere importante per qcno; **it doesn't ~** non importa. **~-of-fact** adj pratico

mattress /'mætrɪs/ n materasso m

matur|e /mə'tʃʊə(r)/ adj maturo; (Comm) in scadenza •vi maturare •vt far maturare. **~ity** n maturità f; (Fin) maturazione f

maul /mɔːl/ vt malmenare

mauve /məʊv/ adj malva

maxim /'mæksɪm/ n massima f

maximum /'mæksɪməm/ adj massimo; **ten minutes ~** dieci minuti al massimo •n (pl **-ima**) massimo m

may /meɪ/ v aux (solo al presente) potere; **~ I come in?** posso entrare?; **if I ~ say so** se mi posso permettere; **~ you both be very happy** siate felici; **I ~ as well stay** potrei anche rimanere; **it ~ be true** potrebbe esser vero; **she ~ be old, but...** sarà anche vecchia, ma...

May /meɪ/ n maggio m

maybe /'meɪbiː/ adv forse, può darsi

'May Day n il primo maggio

mayonnaise /meɪə'neɪz/ n maionese f

mayor /'meə(r)/ n sindaco m. **~ess** n sindaco m; (wife of mayor) moglie f del sindaco

maze /meɪz/ n labirinto m

me /miː/ pron (object) mi; (with preposition) me; **she called me** mi ha chiamato; **she called me, not you** ha chiamato me, non te; **give me the money** dammi i soldi; **give it to me** dammelo; **he gave it to me** me lo ha dato; **it's ~** sono io

meadow /'medəʊ/ n prato m

meagre /'miːgə(r)/ adj scarso

meal¹ /miːl/ n pasto m

meal² n (grain) farina f

mean¹ /miːn/ adj avaro; (unkind) meschino

mean² adj medio •n (average) media f; **Greenwich ~ time** ora f media di Greenwich

mean³ vt (pt/pp **meant**) voler dire; (signify) significare; (intend) intendere; **I ~ it** lo dico seriamente; **~ well** avere buone intenzioni; **be meant for** (present:) essere destinato a; (remark:) essere riferito a

meander /mɪ'ændə(r)/ vi vagare

meaning /'miːnɪŋ/ n significato m. **~ful** adj significativo. **~less** adj senza senso

means /miːnz/ n mezzo m; **~ of transport** mezzo m di trasporto; **by ~ of** per mezzo di; **by all ~!** certamente!; **by no ~** niente affatto •npl (resources) mezzi mpl

meant /ment/ ▸**mean³**

'meantime n **in the** ~ nel frattempo • adv intanto

'meanwhile adv intanto

measles /'mi:zlz/ n morbillo m

measly /'mi:zlɪ/ adj [!] misero

measure /'meʒə(r)/ n misura f • vt/i misurare. □ ~ **up to** vt fig essere all'altezza di. ~**d** adj misurato. ~**ment** n misura f

meat /mi:t/ n carne f. ~ **ball** n (Culin) polpetta f di carne. ~ **loaf** n polpettone m

mechan|ic /mɪ'kænɪk/ n meccanico m. ~**ical** adj meccanico; ~**ical engineering** ingegneria f meccanica. ~**ically** adv meccanicamente. ~**ics** n meccanica f • npl meccanismo msg

mechan|ism /'mekənɪzm/ n meccanismo m. ~**ize** vt meccanizzare

medal /'medl/ n medaglia f

medallist /'medəlɪst/ n vincitore, -trice mf di una medaglia

m

meddle /'medl/ vi immischiarsi (**in** di); (tinker) armeggiare (**with** con)

media /'mi:dɪə/ ▸**medium** • npl **the** ~ i mass media

mediat|e /'mi:dɪeɪt/ vi fare da mediatore. ~**ion** n mediazione f. ~**or** n mediatore, -trice mf

medical /'medɪkl/ adj medico • n visita f medica. ~ **insurance** n assicurazione f sanitaria. ~ **student** n studente, -essa mf di medicina

medicat|ed /'medɪkeɪtɪd/ adj medicato. ~**ion** n (drugs) medicinali mpl

medicinal /mɪ'dɪsɪnl/ adj medicinale

medicine /'medsən/ n medicina f

medieval /medɪ'i:vl/ adj medievale

mediocr|e /mi:dɪ'əʊkə(r)/ adj mediocre. ~**ity** n mediocrità f

meditat|e /'medɪteɪt/ vi meditare (**on** su). ~**ion** n meditazione f

Mediterranean /medɪtə'reɪnɪən/ n **the** ~ **[Sea]** il [mar m] Mediterraneo m • adj mediterraneo

medium /'mi:dɪəm/ adj medio; (Culin) di media cottura • n (pl **media**) mezzo m; (pl **-s**) (person) medium mf inv

medium-sized adj di taglia media

medley /'medlɪ/ n miscuglio m; (Mus) miscellanea f

meek /mi:k/ adj mite, mansueto. ~**ly** adv docilmente

meet /mi:t/ v (pt/pp **met**) • vt incontrare; (at station, airport) andare incontro a; (for first time) far la conoscenza di; pagare (bill); soddisfare (requirements) • vi incontrarsi; (committee:) riunirsi; ~ **with** incontrare (problem); incontrarsi con (person) • n raduno m [sportivo]

meeting /'mi:tɪŋ/ n riunione f, meeting m inv; (large) assemblea f; (by chance) incontro m

megabyte /'megəbaɪt/ n megabyte m

megaphone /'megəfəʊn/ n megafono m

melancholy /'melənkəlɪ/ adj malinconico • n malinconia f

mellow /'meləʊ/ adj (wine) generoso; (sound, colour) caldo; (person) dolce • vi (person:) addolcirsi

melodrama /'melə-/ n melodramma m. ~**tic** adj melodrammatico

melody /'melədɪ/ n melodia f

melon /'melən/ n melone m

melt /melt/ vt sciogliere • vi sciogliersi. □ ~ **down** vt fondere. ~**ing-pot** n fig crogiuolo m

member /'membə(r)/ n membro m; ~ **countries** paesi mpl membri; **M**~ **of Parliament** deputato, -a mf; **M**~ **of the European Parliament** eurodeputato, -a mf. ~**ship** n iscrizione f; (members) soci mpl

membrane /'membreɪn/ n membrana f

memo /'meməʊ/ n promemoria m inv

memorable /'memərəbl/ adj memorabile

memorandum /memə'rændəm/ n promemoria m inv

memorial /mɪ'mɔ:rɪəl/ n monumento m. ~ **service** n funzione f commemorativa

memorize /'meməraɪz/ vt memorizzare

memory /'memərɪ/ n also (Comput) memoria f; (thing remembered) ricordo m; **from** ~ a memoria; **in** ~ **of** in ricordo di

men /men/ ▸**man**

menac|e /'menəs/ n minaccia f; (nuisance) piaga f •vt minacciare. **~ing** adj minaccioso

mend /mend/ vt riparare; (darn) rammendare •n **on the ~** in via di guarigione

menfolk n uomini mpl

menial /'mi:nɪəl/ adj umile

meningitis /menɪn'dʒaɪtɪs/ n meningite f

menopause /'menə-/ n menopausa f

menstruat|e /'menstrʊeɪt/ vi mestruare. **~ion** n mestruazione f

mental /'mentl/ adj mentale; (🄸: mad) pazzo. **~ a'rithmetic** n calcolo m mentale. **~ 'illness** n malattia f mentale

mental|ity /men'tælətɪ/ n mentalità f inv. **~ly** adv mentalmente; **~ly ill** malato di mente

mention /'menʃn/ n menzione f •vt menzionare; **don't ~ it** non c'è di che

menu /'menju:/ n menu m inv

MEP n abbr Member of the European Parliament

mercenary /'mɜ:sɪnərɪ/ adj mercenario •n mercenario m

merchandise /'mɜ:tʃəndaɪz/ n merce f

merchant /'mɜ:tʃənt/ n commerciante mf. **~ bank** n banca f d'affari. **~ 'navy** n marina f mercantile

merci|ful /'mɜ:sɪfl/ adj misericordioso. **~fully** adv 🄸 grazie a Dio. **~less** adj spietato

mercury /'mɜ:kjʊrɪ/ n mercurio m

mercy /'mɜ:sɪ/ n misericordia f; **be at sb's ~** essere alla mercè di qcno, essere in balia di qcno

mere /mɪə(r)/ adj solo. **~ly** adv solamente

merge /mɜ:dʒ/ vi fondersi

merger /'mɜ:dʒə(r)/ n fusione f

meringue /mə'ræŋ/ n meringa f

merit /'merɪt/ n merito m; (advantage) qualità f inv •vt meritare

mermaid /'mɜ:meɪd/ n sirena f

merri|ly /'merɪlɪ/ adv allegramente. **~ment** n baldoria f

merry /'merɪ/ adj (**-ier, -iest**) allegro; **M~ Christmas!** Buon Natale!

merry: ~-go-round n giostra f. **~-making** n festa f

mesh /meʃ/ n maglia f

mesmerize /'mezməraɪz/ vt ipnotizzare. **~d** adj fig ipnotizzato

mess /mes/ n disordine m, casino m 🄸; (trouble) guaio m; (something spilt) sporco m; (Mil) mensa f; **make a ~ of** (botch) fare un pasticcio di •**mess about** vi perder tempo; **~ about with** armeggiare con •vt prendere in giro (person). ▫ **~ up** vt mettere in disordine, incasinare 🄸; (botch) mandare all'aria

message /'mesɪdʒ/ n messaggio m

messenger /'mesɪndʒə(r)/ n messaggero m

Messiah /mɪ'saɪə/ n Messia m

Messrs /'mesəz/ npl (on letter) **~ Smith** Spett. ditta Smith

messy /'mesɪ/ adj (**-ier, -iest**) disordinato; (in dress) sciatto

met /met/ ▸**meet**

metal /'metl/ n metallo m •adj di metallo. **~lic** adj metallico

metaphor /'metəfə(r)/ n metafora f. **~ical** adj metaforico

meteor /'mi:tɪə(r)/ n meteora f. **~ic** adj fig fulmineo

meteorological /mi:tɪərə'lɒdʒɪkl/ adj meteorologico

meteo|rologist /mi:tɪə'rɒlədʒɪst/ n meteorologo, -a mf. **~rology** n meteorologia f

meter[1] /'mi:tə(r)/ n contatore m

meter[2] n Am = **metre**

method /'meθəd/ n metodo m

methodical /mɪ'θɒdɪkl/ adj metodico. **~ly** adv metodicamente

methylated /'meθɪleɪtɪd/ adj **~ spirit[s]** alcol m denaturato

meticulous /mɪ'tɪkjʊləs/ adj meticoloso. **~ly** adv meticolosamente

metre /'mi:tə(r)/ n metro m

metric /'metrɪk/ adj metrico

metropolis /mɪ'trɒpəlɪs/ n metropoli f inv

mew /mju:/ n miao m •vi miagolare

Mexican /'meksɪkən/ adj & n

messicano, -a mf. '**Mexico** n Messico m

miaow /mɪ'aʊ/ n miao m • vi miagolare

mice /maɪs/ ▸**mouse**

mickey /'mɪkɪ/ n **take the ~ out of** prendere in giro

micro /'maɪkrəʊ/: **~chip** n microchip m. **~computer** n microcomputer m. **~film** n microfilm m. **~phone** microfono m. **~processor** n microprocessore m. **~scope** n microscopio m. **~scopic** adj microscopico. **~wave** n microonda f; (oven) forno m a microonde

microbe /'maɪkrəʊb/ n microbo m

mid /mɪd/ adj **~ May** metà maggio; **in ~ air** a mezz'aria

midday /mɪd'deɪ/ n mezzogiorno m

middle /'mɪdl/ adj di centro; **the M~ Ages** il medioevo; **the ~ class[es]** la classe media; **the M~ East** il Medio Oriente • n mezzo m; **in the ~ of** (room, floor etc) in mezzo a; **in the ~ of the night** nel pieno della notte, a notte piena

middle: ~-aged adj di mezza età. **~-class** adj borghese. **~man** n (Comm) intermediario m

middling /'mɪdlɪŋ/ adj discreto

midge /mɪdʒ/ n moscerino m

midget /'mɪdʒɪt/ n nano, -a mf

Midlands /'mɪdləndz/ npl **the ~** l'Inghilterra fsg centrale

'**midnight** n mezzanotte f

midriff /'mɪdrɪf/ n diaframma m

midst /mɪdst/ n **in the ~ of** in mezzo a; **in our ~** fra di noi, in mezzo a noi

mid: ~summer n mezza estate f **~way** adv a metà strada. **~wife** n ostetrica f. **~'winter** n pieno inverno m

might[1] /maɪt/ v aux **I ~** potrei; **will you come? – I ~** vieni? – può darsi; **it ~ be true** potrebbe essere vero; **I ~ as well stay** potrei anche restare; **you ~ have drowned** avresti potuto affogare; **you ~ have said so!** avresti potuto dirlo!

might[2] n potere m

mighty /'maɪtɪ/ adj (**-ier, -iest**) potente • adv ! molto

migraine /'mi:greɪn/ n emicrania f

migrant /'maɪgrənt/ adj migratore • n (bird) migratore, -trice mf; (person: for work) emigrante mf

migrat|e /maɪ'greɪt/ vi migrare. **~ion** n migrazione f

Milan /mɪ'læn/ n Milano f

mild /maɪld/ adj (weather) mite; (person) dolce; (flavour) delicato; (illness) leggero

mildew /'mɪldju:/ n muffa f

mild|ly /'maɪldlɪ/ adv moderatamente; (say) dolcemente; **to put it ~ly** a dir poco, senza esagerazione. **~ness** n (of person, words) dolcezza f; (of weather) mitezza f

mile /maɪl/ n miglio m (= 1,6 km); **~s nicer** ! molto più bello

mile|age /-ɪdʒ/ n chilometraggio m. **~stone** n pietra f miliare

militant /'mɪlɪtənt/ adj & n militante mf

military /'mɪlɪtrɪ/ adj militare. **~ service** n servizio m militare

militia /mɪ'lɪʃə/ n milizia f

milk /mɪlk/ n latte m • vt mungere

milk: ~man n lattaio m. **~ shake** n frappé m inv

milky /'mɪlkɪ/ adj (**-ier, -iest**) latteo; (tea etc) con molto latte. **M~ Way** n (Astr) Via f Lattea

mill /mɪl/ n mulino m; (factory) fabbrica f; (for coffee etc) macinino m • vt macinare (grain). **mill about, mill around** vi brulicare

millennium /mɪ'lenɪəm/ n millennio m

miller /'mɪlə(r)/ n mugnaio m

million /'mɪljən/ n milione m; **a ~ pounds** un milione di sterline. **~aire** n miliardario, -a mf

'**millstone** n fig peso m

mime /maɪm/ n mimo m • vt mimare

mimic /'mɪmɪk/ n imitatore, -trice mf • vt (pt/pp **mimicked**) imitare. **~ry** n mimetismo m

mince /mɪns/ n carne f tritata • vt (Culin) tritare; **not ~ one's words** parlare senza mezzi termini

mince 'pie n pasticcino m a base di frutta secca

mincer /'mɪnsə(r)/ n tritacarne m inv

mind /maɪnd/ n mente f; (sanity) ragione f; **to my ~** a mio parere; **give sb a piece of one's ~** dire chiaro e tondo a qcno quello che si pensa; **make up one's ~** decidersi; **have sth in ~** avere qcsa in mente; **bear sth in ~** tenere presente qcsa; **have something on one's ~** essere preoccupato; **have a good ~ to** avere una grande voglia di; **I have changed my ~** ho cambiato idea; **in two ~s** indeciso; **are you out of your ~?** sei diventato matto? •vt (look after) occuparsi di; **I don't ~ the noise** il rumore non mi dà fastidio; **I don't ~ what we do** non mi importa quello che facciamo; **~ the step!** attenzione al gradino! •vi **I don't ~** non mi importa; **never ~!** non importa!; **do you ~ if...?** ti dispiace se...? **mind out** vi **~ out!** [fai] attenzione!

mind|ful adj **~ful of** attento a. **~less** adj noncurante

mine[1] /maɪn/ poss pron il mio m, la mia f, i miei mpl, le mie fpl; **a friend of ~** un mio amico; **friends of ~** dei miei amici; **that is ~** questo è mio; (as opposed to yours) questo è il mio

mine[2] n miniera f; (explosive) mina f •vt estrarre; (Mil) minare. **~ detector** n rivelatore m di mine. **~field** n campo m minato

mineral /'mɪnərəl/ n minerale m •adj minerale. **~ water** n acqua f minerale

mingle /'mɪŋgl/ vi **~ with** mescolarsi a

mini /'mɪnɪ/ n (skirt) mini f

miniature /'mɪnɪtʃə(r)/ adj in miniatura •n miniatura f

mini|bus /'mɪnɪ-/ n minibus m, pulmino m. **~cab** n taxi m inv

minim|al /'mɪnɪməl/ adj minimo. **~ize** vt minimizzare. **~um** n (pl **-ima**) minimo m •adj minimo; **ten minutes ~um** minimo dieci minuti

mining /'maɪnɪŋ/ n estrazione f •adj estrattivo

miniskirt /'mɪnɪ-/ n minigonna f

minist|er /'mɪnɪstə(r)/ n ministro m; (Relig) pastore m. **~erial** adj ministeriale

ministry /'mɪnɪstrɪ/ n (Pol) ministero m; **the ~** (Relig) il ministero sacerdotale

mink /mɪŋk/ n visone m

minor /'maɪnə(r)/ adj minore •n minorenne mf

minority /maɪ'nɒrətɪ/ n minoranza f; (age) minore età f

mint[1] /mɪnt/ n [!] patrimonio m •adj **in ~ condition** in condizione perfetta

mint[2] n (herb) menta f

minus /'maɪnəs/ prep meno; ([!]: without) senza •n **~ [sign]** meno m

minute[1] /'mɪnɪt/ n minuto m; **in a ~** (shortly) in un minuto; **~s** pl (of meeting) verbale msg

minute[2] /maɪ'nju:t/ adj minuto; (precise) minuzioso

mirac|le /'mɪrəkl/ n miracolo m. **~ulous** adj miracoloso

mirage /'mɪrɑ:ʒ/ n miraggio m

mirror /'mɪrə(r)/ n specchio m •vt rispecchiare

mirth /mɜ:θ/ n ilarità f

misappre'hension n malinteso m; **be under a ~** avere frainteso

misbe'have vi comportarsi male

mis'calcu|late vt/i calcolare male. **~'lation** n calcolo m sbagliato

'miscarriage n aborto m spontaneo; **~ of justice** errore m giudiziario. **mis'carry** vi abortire

miscellaneous /mɪsə'leɪnɪəs/ adj assortito

mischief /'mɪstʃɪf/ n malefatta f; (harm) danno m

mischievous /'mɪstʃɪvəs/ adj (naughty) birichino; (malicious) dannoso

miscon'ception n concetto m erroneo

mis'conduct n cattiva condotta f

misde'meanour n reato m

miser /'maɪzə(r)/ n avaro m

miserabl|e /'mɪzrəbl/ adj (unhappy) infelice; (wretched) miserabile; (fig: weather) deprimente. **~y** adv (live, fail) miseramente; (say) tristemente

m

miserly /ˈmaɪzəlɪ/ adj avaro; (amount) ridicolo

misery /ˈmɪzərɪ/ n miseria f; (!: person) piagnone, -a mf

misˈfire vi (gun:) far cilecca; (plan etc:) non riuscire

ˈmisfit n disadattato, -a mf

misˈfortune n sfortuna f

misˈguided adj fuorviato

mishap /ˈmɪshæp/ n disavventura f

misinˈterpret vt fraintendere

misˈjudge vt giudicar male; (estimate wrongly) valutare male

misˈlay vt (pt/pp **-laid**) smarrire

misˈlead vt (pt/pp **-led**) fuorviare. **~ing** adj fuorviante

misˈmanage vt amministrare male. **~ment** n cattiva amministrazione f

ˈmisprint n errore m di stampa

miss /mɪs/ n colpo m mancato •vt (fail to hit or find) mancare; perdere (train, bus, class); (feel the loss of) sentire la mancanza di; **I ~ed that part** (failed to notice) mi è sfuggita quella parte •vi **but he ~ed** (failed to hit) ma l'ha mancato. □ **~ out** vt saltare, omettere

m

Miss n (pl **-es**) signorina f

misshapen /mɪsˈʃeɪpən/ adj malformato

missile /ˈmɪsaɪl/ n missile m

missing /ˈmɪsɪŋ/ adj mancante; (person) scomparso; (Mil) disperso; **be ~** essere introvabile

mission /ˈmɪʃn/ n missione f

missionary /ˈmɪʃənrɪ/ n missionario, -a mf

mist /mɪst/ n (fog) foschia f •**mist up** vi appannarsi, annebbiarsi

mistake /mɪˈsteɪk/ n sbaglio m; **by ~** per sbaglio •vt (pt **mistook**, pp **mistaken**) sbagliare (road, house); fraintendere (meaning, words); **~ for** prendere per

mistaken /mɪˈsteɪkən/ adj sbagliato; **be ~** sbagliarsi; **~ identity** errore m di persona. **~ly** adv erroneamente

mistletoe /ˈmɪsltəʊ/ n vischio m

mistress /ˈmɪstrɪs/ n padrona f; (teacher) maestra f; (lover) amante f

misˈtrust n sfiducia f •vt non aver fiducia in

misty /ˈmɪstɪ/ adj (**-ier, -iest**) nebbioso

misunderˈstand vt (pt/pp **-stood**) fraintendere. **~ing** n malinteso m

misuse¹ /mɪsˈjuːz/ vt usare male

misuse² /mɪsˈjuːs/ n cattivo uso m

mite /maɪt/ n (child) piccino, -a mf

mitten /ˈmɪtn/ n manopola f, muffola m

mix /mɪks/ n (combination) mescolanza f; (Culin) miscuglio m; (ready-made) preparato m •vt mischiare •vi mischiarsi; (person:) inserirsi; **~ with** (associate with) frequentare. □ **~ up** vt mescolare (papers); (confuse, mistake for) confondere

mixed /mɪkst/ adj misto; **~ up** (person) confuso

mixer /ˈmɪksə(r)/ n (Culin) frullatore m, mixer m inv; **he's a good ~** è un tipo socievole

mixture /ˈmɪkstʃə(r)/ n mescolanza f; (medicine) sciroppo m; (Culin) miscela f

ˈmix-up n (confusion) confusione f; (mistake) pasticcio m

moan /məʊn/ n lamento m •vi lamentarsi; (complain) lagnarsi

moat /məʊt/ n fossato m

mob /mɒb/ n folla f; (rabble) gentaglia f; (!: gang) banda f •vt (pt/pp **mobbed**) assalire

mobile /ˈməʊbaɪl/ adj mobile •n composizione f mobile. **~ ˈhome** n casa f roulotte. **~ [phone]** n [telefono m] cellulare m, telefonino m

mock /mɒk/ adj finto •vt canzonare. **~ery** n derisione f

model /ˈmɒdl/ n modello m; [**fashion**] **~** indossatore, -trice mf, modello, -a mf •adj (yacht, plane) in miniatura; (pupil, husband) esemplare, modello •v (pt/pp **modelled**) •vt indossare (clothes) •vi fare l'indossatore, -trice mf; (for artist) posare

modem /ˈməʊdem/ n modem m inv

moderate¹ /ˈmɒdəreɪt/ vt moderare •vi moderarsi

moderate² /ˈmɒdərət/ adj moderato •n (Pol) moderato, -a mf. **~ly** adv (drink, speak etc) moderatamente; (good, bad etc) relativamente

moderation /mɒdəˈreɪʃn/ n

moderazione f; **in ~** con moderazione

modern /'mɒdn/ adj moderno. **~ize** vt modernizzare

modest /'mɒdɪst/ adj modesto. **~y** n modestia f

modif|ication /mɒdɪfɪ'keɪʃn/ n modificazione f. **~y** vt (pt/pp **-fied**) modificare

module /'mɒdju:l/ n modulo m

moist /mɔɪst/ adj umido

moisten /'mɔɪsn/ vt inumidire

moistur|e /'mɔɪstʃə(r)/ n umidità f. **~izer** n [crema f] idratante m

mole[1] /məʊl/ n (on face etc) neo m

mole[2] n (Zool) talpa f

molecule /'mɒlɪkju:l/ n molecola f

molest /mə'lest/ vt molestare

mollycoddle /'mɒlɪkɒdl/ vt tenere nella bambagia

molten /'məʊltən/ adj fuso

mom /mɒm/ n Am [!] mamma f

moment /'məʊmənt/ n momento m; **at the ~** in questo momento. **~arily** adv momentaneamente. **~ary** adj momentaneo

momentous /mə'mentəs/ adj molto importante

momentum /mə'mentəm/ n impeto m

monarch /'mɒnək/ n monarca m. **~y** n monarchia f

monast|ery /'mɒnəstrɪ/ n monastero m. **~ic** adj monastico

Monday /'mʌndeɪ/ n lunedì m inv

money /'mʌnɪ/ n denaro m

money-box n salvadanaio m

mongrel /'mʌŋgrəl/ n bastardo m

monitor /'mɒnɪtə(r)/ n (Techn) monitor m inv • vt controllare

monk /mʌŋk/ n monaco m

monkey /'mʌŋkɪ/ n scimmia f. **~-nut** n nocciolina f americana. **~-wrench** n chiave f inglese a rullino

mono /'mɒnəʊ/ n mono m

monologue /'mɒnəlɒg/ n monologo m

monopol|ize /mə'nɒpəlaɪz/ vt monopolizzare. **~y** n monopolio m

monotone /'mɒnətəʊn/ n **speak in a ~** parlare con tono monotono

monoton|ous /mə'nɒtənəs/ adj monotono. **~y** n monotonia f

monsoon /mɒn'su:n/ n monsone m

monster /'mɒnstə(r)/ n mostro m

monstrous /'mɒnstrəs/ adj mostruoso

Montenegro /'mɒntɪ'ni:grəʊ/ n Montenegro m

month /mʌnθ/ n mese m. **~ly** adj mensile • adv mensilmente • n (periodical) mensile m

monument /'mɒnjʊmənt/ n monumento m. **~al** adj fig monumentale

moo /mu:/ n muggito m • vi (pt/pp **mooed**) muggire

mood /mu:d/ n umore m; **be in a good/bad ~** essere di buon/cattivo umore; **be in the ~ for** essere in vena di

moody /'mu:dɪ/ adj (**-ier, -iest**) (variable) lunatico; (bad-tempered) di malumore

moon /mu:n/ n luna f; **over the ~** [!] al settimo cielo

moon: ~light n chiaro m di luna • vi [!] lavorare in nero. **~lit** adj illuminato dalla luna

moor[1] /mʊə(r)/ n brughiera f

moor[2] vt (Naut) ormeggiare

mop /mɒp/ n straccio m (per i pavimenti); **~ of hair** zazzera f • vt (pt/pp **mopped**) lavare con lo straccio. □ **~ up** vt (dry) asciugare con lo straccio; (clean) pulire con lo straccio

mope /məʊp/ vi essere depresso

moped /'məʊped/ n ciclomotore m

moral /'mɒrəl/ adj morale • n morale f. **~ly** adv moralmente. **~s** pl moralità f

morale /mə'rɑ:l/ n morale m

morality /mə'rælətɪ/ n moralità f

more /mɔ:(r)/ adj più; **a few ~ books** un po' più di libri; **some ~ tea?** ancora un po' di tè?; **there's no ~ bread** non c'è più pane; **there are no ~ apples** non ci sono più mele; **one ~ word and...** ancora una parola e... • pron di più; **would you like some ~?** ne vuoi ancora?; **no ~, thank you** non ne voglio più, grazie •adv più; ~ **interesting** più interessante; ~ **and ~ quickly** sempre più veloce; ~ **than** più di; **I don't love him any ~** non lo amo più; **once ~** ancora una volta; ~ **or less** più o meno; **the ~ I see him, the ~ I like him** più lo vedo, più mi piace

moreover /mɔːr'əʊvə(r)/ adv inoltre

morgue /mɔːg/ n obitorio m

morning /'mɔːnɪŋ/ n mattino m, mattina f; **in the ~** del mattino; (tomorrow) domani mattina

Morocc|o /mə'rɒkəʊ/ n Marocco m ~**an** adj & n marocchino, -a mf

moron /'mɔːrɒn/ n [!] deficiente mf

morose /mə'rəʊs/ adj scontroso

Morse /mɔːs/ n ~ [**code**] [codice m] Morse m

morsel /'mɔːsl/ n (food) boccone m

mortal /'mɔːtl/ adj & n mortale mf. ~**ity** n mortalità f. ~**ly** adv (wounded, offended) a morte; (afraid) da morire

mortar /'mɔːtə(r)/ n mortaio m

mortgage /'mɔːgɪdʒ/ n mutuo m; (on property) ipoteca f •vt ipotecare

mortuary /'mɔːtjʊərɪ/ n camera f mortuaria

mosaic /məʊ'zeɪɪk/ n mosaico m

Moslem /'mʊzlɪm/ adj & n musulmano, -a mf

mosque /mɒsk/ n moschea f

mosquito /mɒs'kiːtəʊ/ n (pl **-es**) zanzara f

moss /mɒs/ n muschio m. ~**y** adj muschioso

most /məʊst/ adj (majority) la maggior parte di; **for the ~ part** per lo più •adv più, maggiormente; (very) estremamente, molto; **the ~ interesting day** la giornata più interessante; **a ~ interesting day** una giornata estremamente interessante; **the ~ beautiful woman in the world** la donna più bella del mondo; ~ **unlikely** veramente improbabile •pron ~ **of them** la maggior parte di loro; **at [the] ~** al massimo; **make the ~ of** sfruttare al massimo; ~ **of the time** la maggior parte del tempo. ~**ly** adv per lo più

MOT n revisione f obbligatoria di autoveicoli

motel /məʊ'tel/ n motel m inv

moth /mɒθ/ n falena f; [**clothes-**] ~ tarma f

mother /'mʌðə(r)/ n madre f; **M~'s Day** la festa della mamma •vt fare da madre a

mother: ~-in-law n (pl **~s-in-law**) suocera f. ~**ly** adj materno. ~**-of-pearl** n madreperla f. ~**-to-be** n futura mamma f. ~ **tongue** n madrelingua f

motif /məʊ'tiːf/ n motivo m

motion /'məʊʃn/ n moto m; (proposal) mozione f; (gesture) gesto m •vt/i ~ [**to**] **sb to come in** fare segno a qcno di entrare. ~**less** adj immobile. ~**lessly** adv senza alcun movimento

motivat|e /'məʊtɪveɪt/ vt motivare. ~**ion** n motivazione f

motive /'məʊtɪv/ n motivo m

motley /'mɒtlɪ/ adj disparato

motor /'məʊtə(r)/ n motore m; (car) macchina f •adj a motore; (Anat) motore •vi andare in macchina

motor: ~ bike n [!] moto f inv. ~ **boat** n motoscafo m. ~ **car** n automobile f. ~ **cycle** n motocicletta f. ~**-cyclist** n motociclista mf. ~**ing** n automobilismo m. ~**ist** n automobilista mf. ~**way** n autostrada f

motto /'mɒtəʊ/ n (pl **-es**) motto m

mould[1] /məʊld/ n (fungus) muffa f

mould[2] n stampo m •vt foggiare; fig formare. ~**ing** n (Archit) cornice f

mouldy /'məʊldɪ/ adj ammuffito; ([!]: worthless) ridicolo

moult /məʊlt/ vi (bird:) fare la muta; (animal:) perdere il pelo

mound /maʊnd/ n mucchio m; (hill) collinetta f

mount /maʊnt/ n (horse) cavalcatura f; (of jewel, photo, picture) montatura f •vt montare a (horse); salire su (bicycle); incastonare (jewel); incorniciare (photo, picture) •vi aumentare. □ ~ **up** vi aumentare

mountain /'maʊntɪn/ n montagna f; ~ **bike** n mountain bike f inv

mountaineer /maʊntɪ'nɪə(r)/ n

m

alpinista mf. **~ing** n alpinismo m

mountainous /'maʊntɪnəs/ adj montagnoso

mourn /mɔːn/ vt lamentare • vi **~ for** piangere la morte di. **~er** n persona f che partecipa a un funerale. **~ful** adj triste. **~ing** n **in ~ing** in lutto

mouse /maʊs/ n (pl **mice**) topo m; (Comput) mouse m inv. **~trap** n trappola f [per topi]

mousse /muːs/ n (Culin) mousse f inv

moustache /mə'stɑːʃ/ n baffi mpl

mouth[1] /maʊð/ vt **~ sth** dire qcsa silenziosamente muovendo solamente le labbra

mouth[2] /maʊθ/ n bocca f; (of river) foce f

mouth: ~ful n boccone m. **~-organ** n armonica f [a bocca]. **~wash** n acqua f dentifricia

move /muːv/ n mossa f; (moving house) trasloco m; **on the ~** in movimento; **get a ~ on** [!] darsi una mossa • vt muovere; (emotionally) commuovere; spostare (car, furniture); (transfer) trasferire; (propose) proporre; **~ house** traslocare • vi muoversi; (move house) traslocare. □ **~ along** vi andare avanti • vt muovere in avanti. □ **~ away** vi allontanarsi; (move house) trasferirsi • vt allontanare. □ **~ forward** vi avanzare • vt spostare avanti. □ **~ in** vi (to a house) trasferirsi. □ **~ off** vi (vehicle:) muoversi. □ **~ out** vi (of house) andare via. □ **~ over** vi spostarsi • vt spostare. □ **~ up** vi muoversi; (advance, increase) avanzare

movement /'muːvmənt/ n movimento m

movie /'muːvɪ/ n film m inv; **go to the ~s** andare al cinema

moving /'muːvɪŋ/ adj mobile; (touching) commovente

mow /məʊ/ vt (pt **mowed**, pp **mown** or **mowed**) tagliare (lawn). □ **~ down** vt (destroy) sterminare

mower /'məʊə(r)/ n tosaerbe m inv

MP n abbr Member of Parliament

Mr /'mɪstə(r)/ n (pl **Messrs**) Signor m

Mrs /'mɪsɪz/ n Signora f

Ms /mɪz/ n Signora f (modo m formale di rivolgersi ad una donna quando non si vuole connotarla come sposata o nubile)

much /mʌtʃ/ adj, adv & pron molto; **~ as** per quanto; **I love you just as ~ as before/him** ti amo quanto prima/lui; **as ~ as £5 million** ben cinque milioni di sterline; **as ~ as that** così tanto; **very ~** tantissimo, moltissimo; **~ the same** quasi uguale

muck /mʌk/ n (dirt) sporcizia f; (farming) letame m; ([!]: filth) porcheria f. □ **~ about** vi [!] perder tempo; **~ about with** trafficare con. □ **~ up** vt [!] rovinare; (make dirty) sporcare

mud /mʌd/ n fango m

muddle /'mʌdl/ n disordine m; (mix-up) confusione f • vt **~ [up]** confondere (dates)

muddy /'mʌdɪ/ adj (**-ier, -iest**) (path) fangoso; (shoes) infangato

muesli /'muːzlɪ/ n muesli m inv

muffle /'mʌfl/ vt smorzare (sound). **muffle up** vt (for warmth) imbacuccare

muffler /'mʌflə(r)/ n sciarpa f; Am (Auto) marmitta f

mug[1] /mʌg/ n tazza f; (for beer) boccale m; ([!]: face) muso m; ([!]: simpleton) pollo m

mug[2] vt (pt/pp **mugged**) aggredire e derubare. **~ger** n assalitore, -trice mf. **~ging** n aggressione f per furto

muggy /'mʌgɪ/ adj (**-ier, -iest**) afoso

mule /mjuːl/ n mulo m

mull /mʌl/ vt **~ over** rimuginare su

multiple /'mʌltɪpl/ adj multiplo

multiplication /mʌltɪplɪ'keɪʃn/ n moltiplicazione f

multiply /'mʌltɪplaɪ/ v (pt/pp **-ied**) • vt moltiplicare (**by** per) • vi moltiplicarsi

mum[1] /mʌm/ adj **keep ~** [!] non aprire bocca

mum[2] n [!] mamma f

mumble /'mʌmbl/ vt/i borbottare

mummy[1] /'mʌmɪ/ n [!] mamma f

mummy[2] n (Archaeol) mummia f

mumps /mʌmps/ n orecchioni mpl

munch /mʌntʃ/ vt/i sgranocchiare

mundane /mʌn'deɪn/ adj (everyday) banale

municipal /mjʊ'nɪsɪpl/ adj municipale

m

mural /'mjʊərəl/ n dipinto m murale

murder /'mɜːdə(r)/ n assassinio m •vt assassinare; ([!]: ruin) massacrare. **~er** n assassino, -a mf. **~ous** adj omicida

murky /'mɜːkɪ/ adj (**-ier, -iest**) oscuro

murmur /'mɜːmə(r)/ n mormorio m •vt/i mormorare

muscle /'mʌsl/ n muscolo m **•muscle in** vi [x] intromettersi (**on** in)

muscular /'mʌskjʊlə(r)/ adj muscolare; (strong) muscoloso

muse /mjuːz/ vi meditare (**on** su)

museum /mjuː'zɪəm/ n museo m

mushroom /'mʌʃrʊm/ n fungo m •vi fig spuntare come funghi

music /'mjuːzɪk/ n musica f; (written) spartito m.

musical /'mjuːzɪkl/ adj musicale; (person) dotato di senso musicale •n commedia f musicale. **~ box** n carillon m inv. **~ instrument** n strumento m musicale

musician /mjuː'zɪʃn/ n musicista mf

Muslim /'mʊzlɪm/ adj & n musulmano, -a mf

mussel /'mʌsl/ n cozza f

must /mʌst/ v aux (solo al presente) dovere; **you ~ not be late** non devi essere in ritardo; **she ~ have finished by now** (probability) deve aver finito ormai •n **a ~** [!] una cosa da non perdere

mustard /'mʌstəd/ n senape f

musty /'mʌstɪ/ adj (**-ier, -iest**) stantio

mutation /mjuː'teɪʃn/ n (Biol) mutazione f

mute /mjuːt/ adj muto

mutilat|e /'mjuːtɪleɪt/ vt mutilare. **~ion** n mutilazione f

mutter /'mʌtə(r)/ vt/i borbottare

mutton /'mʌtn/ n carne f di montone

mutual /'mjuːtjʊəl/ adj reciproco; ([!]: common) comune. **~ly** adv reciprocamente

muzzle /'mʌzl/ n (of animal) muso m; (of firearm) bocca f; (for dog) museruola f •vt fig mettere il bavaglio a

my /maɪ/ adj il mio m, la mia f, i miei mpl, le mie fpl; **my mother/father** mia madre/mio padre

myself /maɪ'self/ pron (reflexive) mi; (emphatic) me stesso; (after prep) me; **I've seen it ~** l'ho visto io stesso; **by ~** da solo; **I thought to ~** ho pensato tra me e me; **I'm proud of ~** sono fiero di me

mysterious /mɪ'stɪərɪəs/ adj misterioso. **~ly** adv misteriosamente

mystery /'mɪstərɪ/ n mistero m; **~ [story]** racconto m del mistero

mysti|c[al] /'mɪstɪk[l]/ adj mistico. **~cism** n misticismo m

mystify /'mɪstɪfaɪ/ vt (pt/pp **-ied**) disorientare

mystique /mɪ'stiːk/ n mistica f

myth /mɪθ/ n mito m. **~ical** adj mitico

mythology /mɪ'θɒlədʒɪ/ n mitologia f

Nn

nab /næb/ vt (pt/pp **nabbed**) [!] beccare

nag[1] /næg/ n (horse) ronzino m

nag[2] (pt/pp **nagged**) vt assillare •vi essere insistente •n (person) brontolone, -a mf. **~ging** adj (pain) persistente

nail /neɪl/ n chiodo m; (of finger, toe) unghia f **•nail down** vt inchiodare; **~ sb down to a time/price** far fissare a qcno un'ora/un prezzo

nail polish n smalto m [per unghie]

naked /'neɪkɪd/ adj nudo; **with the ~ eye** a occhio nudo

name /neɪm/ n nome m; **what's your ~?** come ti chiami?; **my ~ is Matthew** mi chiamo Matthew; **I know her by ~** la conosco di nome; **by the ~ of Bates** di nome Bates; **call sb ~s** ! insultare qcno •vt (to position) nominare; chiamare (baby); (identify) citare; **be ~d after** essere chiamato col nome di. **~less** adj senza nome. **~ly** adv cioè

namesake n omonimo, -a mf

nanny /'nænɪ/ n bambinaia f. **~-goat** n capra f

nap /næp/ n pisolino m; **have a ~** fare un pisolino •vi (pt/pp **napped**) **catch sb ~ping** cogliere qcno alla sprovvista

napkin /'næpkɪn/ n tovagliolo m

Naples /'neɪplz/ n Napoli f

nappy /'næpɪ/ n pannolino m

narcotic /nɑ:'kɒtɪk/ adj & n narcotico m

narrat|e /nə'reɪt/ vt narrare. **~ion** n narrazione f

narrative /'nærətɪv/ adj narrativo •n narrazione f

narrator /nə'reɪtə(r)/ n narratore, -trice mf

narrow /'nærəʊ/ adj stretto; (fig: views) ristretto; (margin, majority) scarso •vi restringersi. **~ly** adv **~ly escape death** evitare la morte per un pelo. **~-'minded** adj di idee ristrette

nasal /'neɪzl/ adj nasale

nasty /'nɑ:stɪ/ adj (**-ier, -iest**) (smell, person, remark) cattivo; (injury, situation, weather) brutto; **turn ~** (person:) diventare cattivo

nation /'neɪʃn/ n nazione f

national /'næʃənl/ adj nazionale •n cittadino, -a mf

national 'anthem n inno m nazionale

nationalism /'næʃənəlɪzm/ n nazionalismo m

nationality /næʃə'nælətɪ/ n nazionalità f inv

nation-wide adj su scala nazionale

native /'neɪtɪv/ adj nativo; (innate) innato •n nativo, -a mf; (local inhabitant) abitante mf del posto; (outside Europe) indigeno, -a mf; **she's a ~ of Venice** è originaria di Venezia

native: ~ 'land n paese m nativo. **~ 'language** n lingua f madre

Nativity /nə'tɪvətɪ/ n **the ~** la Natività f. **~ play** n rappresentazione f sulla nascita di Gesù

natter /'nætə(r)/ vi ! chiacchierare

natural /'nætʃrəl/ adj naturale

natural 'history n storia f naturale

naturalist /'nætʃ(ə)rəlɪst/ n naturalista mf

naturally /'nætʃ(ə)rəlɪ/ adv (of course) naturalmente; (by nature) per natura

nature /'neɪtʃə(r)/ n natura f; **by ~** per natura. **~ reserve** n riserva f naturale

naughty /'nɔ:tɪ/ adj (**-ier, -iest**) monello; (slightly indecent) spinto

nausea /'nɔ:zɪə/ n nausea f

nautical /'nɔ:tɪkl/ adj nautico. **~ mile** n miglio m marino

naval /'neɪvl/ adj navale

nave /neɪv/ n navata f centrale

navel /'neɪvl/ n ombelico m

navigable /'nævɪgəbl/ adj navigabile

navigat|e /'nævɪgeɪt/ vi navigare; (Auto) fare da navigatore •vt navigare su (river). **~ion** n navigazione f. **~or** n navigatore m

navy /'neɪvɪ/ n marina f •**~ [blue]** adj blu marine inv •n blu m inv marine

Neapolitan /nɪə'pɒlɪtən/ adj & n napoletano, -a mf

near /nɪə(r)/ adj vicino; (future) prossimo; **the ~est bank** la banca più vicina •adv vicino; **draw ~** avvicinarsi; **~ at hand** a portata di mano •prep vicino a; **he was ~ to tears** aveva le lacrime agli occhi •vt avvicinarsi a

near: ~'by adj & adv vicino. **~ly** adv quasi; **it's not ~ly enough** non è per niente sufficiente. **~-sighted** adj Am miope

neat /ni:t/ adj (tidy) ordinato; (clever) efficace; (undiluted) liscio. **~ly** adv ordinatamente; (cleverly) efficacemente. **~ness** n (tidiness) ordine m

necessarily /nesə'serɪlɪ/ adv necessariamente

necessary /'nesəsərɪ/ adj necessario

necessit|ate /nɪ'sesɪteɪt/ vt rendere

n

necessario. **~y** n necessità f inv

neck /nek/ n collo m; (of dress) colletto m; **~ and ~** testa a testa

necklace /'neklɪs/ n collana f

neckline n scollatura f

need /ni:d/ n bisogno m; **be in ~ of** avere bisogno di; **if ~ be** se ce ne fosse bisogno; **there is a ~ for** c'è bisogno di; **there is no ~ for that** non ce n'è bisogno; **there is no ~ for you to go** non c'è bisogno che tu vada •vt aver bisogno di; **I ~ to know** devo saperlo; **it ~s to be done** bisogna farlo •v aux **you ~ not go** non c'è bisogno che tu vada; **~ I come?** devo [proprio] venire?

needle /'ni:dl/ n ago m; (for knitting) ferro m (da maglia); (of record player) puntina f •vt (fam: annoy) punzecchiare

needless /'ni:dlɪs/ adj inutile

'needlework n cucito m

needy /'ni:dɪ/ adj (**-ier, -iest**) bisognoso

negative /'negətɪv/ adj negativo •n negazione f; (Phot) negativo m; **in the ~** (Gram) alla forma negativa

neglect /nɪ'glekt/ n trascuratezza f; **state of ~** stato m di abbandono •vt trascurare; **he ~ed to write** non si è curato di scrivere. **~ed** adj trascurato. **~ful** adj negligente; **be ~ful of** trascurare

negligen|ce /'neglɪdʒəns/ n negligenza f. **~t** adj negligente

negligible /'neglɪdʒəbl/ adj trascurabile

negotiable /nɪ'gəʊʃəbl/ adj (road) transitabile; (Comm) negoziabile; **not ~** (cheque) non trasferibile

negotiat|e /nɪ'gəʊʃɪeɪt/ vt negoziare; (Auto) prendere (bend) •vi negoziare. **~ion** n negoziato m. **~or** n negoziatore, -trice mf

neigh /neɪ/ vi nitrire

neighbour /'neɪbə(r)/ n vicino, -a mf. **~hood** n vicinato m; **in the ~hood of** nei dintorni di; fig circa. **~ing** adj vicino. **~ly** adj amichevole

neither /'naɪðə(r)/ adj & pron nessuno dei due, né l'uno né l'altro •adv **~... nor** né... né •conj nemmeno, neanche; **~ do/did I** nemmeno io

neon /'ni:ɒn/ n neon m. **~ light** n luce f al neon

nephew /'nevju:/ n nipote m

nerve /nɜ:v/ n nervo m; (fam: courage) coraggio m; (fam: impudence) faccia f tosta; **lose one's ~** perdersi d'animo. **~-racking** adj logorante

nervous /'nɜ:vəs/ adj nervoso; **he makes me ~** mi mette in agitazione; **be a ~ wreck** avere i nervi a pezzi. **~ 'breakdown** n esaurimento m nervoso. **~ly** adv nervosamente. **~ness** n nervosismo m; (before important event) tensione f

nervy /'nɜ:vɪ/ adj (**-ier, -iest**) nervoso (Am: impudent) sfacciato

nest /nest/ n nido m •vi fare il nido. **~-egg** n gruzzolo m

nestle /'nesl/ vi accoccolarsi

net¹ /net/ n rete f •vt (pt/pp **netted**) (catch) prendere (con la rete)

net² adj netto •vt (pt/pp **netted**) incassare un utile netto di

'netball n sport m inv femminile, simile a pallacanestro

Netherlands /'neðələndz/ npl **the ~** i Paesi mpl Bassi

netting /'netɪŋ/ n [**wire**] **~** reticolato m

nettle /'netl/ n ortica f

'network n rete f

neur|osis /njʊə'rəʊsɪs/ n (pl **-oses** /-si:z/) nevrosi f inv. **~otic** adj nevrotico

neuter /'nju:tə(r)/ adj (Gram) neutro •n (Gram) neutro m •vt sterilizzare

neutral /'nju:trəl/ adj neutro; (country, person) neutrale •n **in ~** (Auto) in folle. **~ity** n neutralità f. **~ize** vt neutralizzare

never /'nevə(r)/ adv [non...] mai; (fam: expressing disbelief) ma va; **~ again** mai più; **well I ~!** chi l'avrebbe detto!. **~-ending** adj interminabile

nevertheless /nevəðə'les/ adv tuttavia

new /nju:/ adj nuovo

new: ~born adj neonato. **~comer** n nuovo, -a arrivato, -a mf. **~fangled** /-'fæŋgld/ adj pej modernizzante

'newly adv (recently) di recente; **~-built** costruito di recente.

~-weds npl sposini mpl

ews /nju:z/ n notizie fpl; (TV) telegiornale m; (Radio) giornale m radio; **piece of ~** notizia f

ews: ~agent n giornalaio, -a mf. **~caster** n giornalista mf televisivo, -a/radiofonico, -a. **~flash** n notizia f flash. **~letter** n bollettino m d'informazione. **~paper** n giornale m; (material) carta f di giornale. **~reader** n giornalista mf televisivo, -a/radiofonico, -a

ew: ~ year n (next year) anno m nuovo; **N~ Year's Day** n Capodanno m. **N~ Year's 'Eve** n vigilia f di Capodanno. **N~ Zealand** /'zi:lənd/ n Nuova Zelanda f

ext /nekst/ adj prossimo; (adjoining) vicino; **who's ~?** a chi tocca?; **~ door** accanto; **~ to nothing** quasi niente; **the ~ day** il giorno dopo; **~ week** la settimana prossima; **the week after ~** fra due settimane • adv dopo; **when will you see him ~?** quando lo rivedi la prossima volta?; **~ to** accanto a • n seguente mf; **~ of kin** parente m prossimo

ib /nɪb/ n pennino m

ibble /'nɪbl/ vt/i mordicchiare

ice /naɪs/ adj (day, weather, holiday) bello; (person) gentile, simpatico; (food) buono; **it was ~ meeting you** è stato un piacere conoscerla. **~ly** adv gentilmente; (well) bene. **~ties** n pl sottigliezze f pl

iche /ni:ʃ/ n nicchia f

ick /nɪk/ n tacca f; (on chin etc) taglietto m; ([!]: prison) galera f; ([!]: police station) centrale f [di polizia]; **in the ~ of time** [!] appena in tempo • vt intaccare; ([!]: steal) fregare; ([!]: arrest) beccare; **~ one's chin** farsi un taglietto nel mento

ickel /'nɪkl/ n nichel m; Am moneta f da cinque centesimi

ickname n soprannome m • vt soprannominare

icotine /'nɪkəti:n/ n nicotina f

iece /ni:s/ n nipote f

iggling /'nɪglɪŋ/ adj (detail) insignificante; (pain) fastidioso; (doubt) persistente

ight /naɪt/ n notte f; (evening) sera f; **at ~** la notte, di notte; (in the evening) la sera, di sera; **Monday ~** lunedì notte/sera • adj di notte

night: ~cap n papalina f; (drink) bicchierino m bevuto prima di andare a letto. **~-club** n locale m notturno, night[-club] m inv. **~-dress** n camicia f da notte. **~fall** n crepuscolo m. **~-gown**, [!] **~ie** /'naɪtɪ/ n camicia f da notte

night: ~-life n vita f notturna. **~ly** adj di notte, di sera • adv ogni notte, ogni sera. **~mare** n incubo m. **~-school** scuola f serale. **~-time** n **at ~-time** di notte, la notte. **~-'watchman** n guardiano m notturno

nil /nɪl/ n nulla m; (Sport) zero m

nimbl|e /'nɪmbl/ adj agile. **~y** adv agilmente

nine /naɪn/ adj nove inv • n nove m. **~'teen** adj diciannove inv • n diciannove. **~'teenth** adj & n diciannovesimo, -a mf

ninetieth /'naɪntɪɪθ/ adj & n novantesimo, -a mf

ninety /'naɪntɪ/ adj novanta inv • n novanta m

ninth /naɪnθ/ adj & n nono, -a mf

nip /nɪp/ n pizzicotto m; (bite) morso m • vt pizzicare; (bite) mordere; **~ in the bud** fig stroncare sul nascere • vi ([!]: run) fare un salto

nipple /'nɪpl/ n capezzolo m; (Am: on bottle) tettarella f

nippy /'nɪpɪ/ adj (**-ier, -iest**) [!] (cold) pungente; (quick) svelto

nitrogen /'naɪtrədʒn/ n azoto m

no /nəʊ/ adv no • n (pl **noes**) no m inv • adj nessuno; **I have no time** non ho tempo; **in no time** in un baleno; **'no parking'** 'sosta vietata'; **'no smoking'** 'vietato fumare'; **no one** nessuno = **nobody**

noble /'nəʊbl/ adj nobile. **~man** n nobile m

nobody /'nəʊbədɪ/ pron nessuno; **he knows ~** non conosce nessuno • n **he's a ~** non è nessuno

nocturnal /nɒk'tɜ:nl/ adj notturno

nod /nɒd/ n cenno m del capo • vi (pt/pp **nodded**) fare un cenno col capo; (in agreement) fare di sì col capo • vt **~ one's head** fare di sì col capo. □ **~ off** vi assopirsi

noise /nɔɪz/ n rumore m; (loud) rumore m, chiasso m. **~less** adj silenzioso. **~lessly** adv silenziosamente

noisy /'nɔɪzɪ/ adj (**-ier, -iest**) rumoroso

nomad /'nəʊmæd/ n nomade mf. **~ic** adj nomade

nominat|e /'nɒmɪneɪt/ vt proporre come candidato; (appoint) designare. **~ion** n nomina f; (person nominated) candidato, -a mf

nonchalant /'nɒnʃələnt/ adj disinvolto

non-com'mittal adj che non si sbilancia

nondescript /'nɒndɪskrɪpt/ adj qualunque

none /nʌn/ pron (person) nessuno; (thing) niente; **~ of us** nessuno di noi; **~ of this** niente di questo; **there's ~ left** non ce n'è più • adv **she's ~ too pleased** non è per niente soddisfatta; **I'm ~ the wiser** non ne so più di prima

nonentity /nɒ'nentətɪ/ n nullità f

non-ex'istent adj inesistente

nonplussed /nɒn'plʌst/ adj perplesso

nonsens|e /'nɒnsəns/ n sciocchezze fpl. **~ical** adj assurdo

non-'smoker n non fumatore, -trice mf; (compartment) scompartimento m non fumatori

non-'stop adj **~ 'flight** volo m diretto • adv senza sosta; (fly) senza scalo

noodles /'nu:dlz/ npl taglierini mpl

nook /nʊk/ n cantuccio m

noon /nu:n/ n mezzogiorno m; **at ~** a mezzogiorno

noose /nu:s/ n nodo m scorsoio

nor /nɔ:(r)/ adv & conj né; **~ do I** neppure io

norm /nɔ:m/ n norma f

normal /'nɔ:ml/ adj normale. **~ity** n normalità f. **~ly** adv (usually) normalmente

north /nɔ:θ/ n nord m; **to the ~ of** a nord di • adj del nord, settentrionale • adv a nord

north: N~ America n America f del Nord. **~-east** adj di nord-est, nordorientale • n nord-est m • adv a nord-est; (travel) verso nord-est

norther|ly /'nɔ:ðəlɪ/ adj (direction) nord; (wind) del nord. **~n** adj del nord, settentrionale. **N~n Ireland** n Irlanda f del Nord

north: N~ 'Sea n Mare m del Nord **~ward[s]** /-wəd[z]/ adv verso nord **~-west** adj di nord-ovest, nordoccidentale • n nord-ovest m • adv a nord-ovest; (travel) verso nord-ovest

Nor|way /'nɔ:weɪ/ n Norvegia f. **~wegian** adj & n norvegese mf

nose /nəʊz/ n naso m

nose: ~bleed n emorragia f nasale **~dive** n (Aeron) picchiata f

nostalg|ia /nɒ'stældʒɪə/ n nostalgia f. **~ic** adj nostalgico

nostril /'nɒstrəl/ n narice f

nosy /'nəʊzɪ/ adj (**-ier, -iest**) [!] ficcanaso inv

not /nɒt/ adv non; **he is ~ Italian** non è italiano; **I hope ~** spero di no; **~ all of us have been invited** non siamo stati tutti invitati; **if ~** se no; **~ at all** niente affatto; **~ a bit** per niente; **~ even** neanche; **~ yet** non ancora; **~ only... but also...** non solo... ma anche...

notabl|e /'nəʊtəbl/ adj (remarkable) notevole. **~y** adv (in particular) in particolare

notary /'nəʊtərɪ/ n notaio m; **~ 'public** notaio m

notch /nɒtʃ/ n tacca f • **notch up** vt (score) segnare

note /nəʊt/ n nota f; (short letter, banknote) biglietto m; (memo, written comment etc) appunto m; **of ~** (person) di spicco; (comments, event) degno di nota; **make a ~ of** prendere nota di; **take ~ of** (notice) prendere nota di • vt (notice) notare; (write) annotare. □ **~ down** vt annotare

'notebook n taccuino m; (Comput) notebook m inv

noted /'nəʊtɪd/ adj noto, celebre (**for** per)

notepaper n carta f da lettere

nothing /'nʌθɪŋ/ pron niente, nulla • adv niente affatto. **for ~** (free, in vain) per niente; (with no reason) senza motivo; **~ but** nient'altro che; **~**

much poco o nulla; ~ **interesting** niente di interessante; **it's ~ to do with you** non ti riguarda

otice /'nəʊtɪs/ n (on board) avviso m; (review) recensione f; (termination of employment) licenziamento m; [**advance**] ~ preavviso m; **two months** ~ due mesi di preavviso; **at short** ~ con breve preavviso; **until further** ~ fino nuovo avviso; **hand in one's** ~ (employee:) dare le dimissioni; **give an employee** ~ dare il preavviso a un impiegato; **take no** ~ **of** non fare caso a; **take no** ~**!** non farci caso! •vt notare. ~**able** adj evidente. ~**ably** adv sensibilmente. ~**-board** n bacheca f

oti|fication /nəʊtɪfɪ'keɪʃn/ n notifica f. ~**fy** vt (pt/pp **-ied**) notificare

otion /'nəʊʃn/ n idea f, nozione f; ~**s** pl (Am: haberdashery) merceria f

otorious /nəʊ'tɔ:rɪəs/ adj famigerato; **be** ~ **for** essere tristemente famoso per

otwith'standing prep malgrado •adv ciononostante

ougat /'nu:gɑ:/ n torrone m

ought /nɔ:t/ n zero m

oun /naʊn/ n nome m, sostantivo m

ourish /'nʌrɪʃ/ vt nutrire. ~**ing** adj nutriente. ~**ment** n nutrimento m

ovel /'nɒvl/ adj insolito •n romanzo m. ~**ist** n romanziere, -a mf. ~**ty** n novità f; ~**ties** pl (objects) oggettini mpl

ovember /nəʊ'vembə(r)/ n novembre m

ovice /'nɒvɪs/ n novizio, -a mf

ow /naʊ/ adv ora, adesso; **by** ~ ormai; **just** ~ proprio ora; **right** ~ subito; ~ **and again,** ~ **and then** ogni tanto; ~**,** ~**!** su! •conj ~ [**that**] ora che, adesso che

owadays adv oggigiorno

owhere /'nəʊ-/ adv in nessun posto, da nessuna parte

ozzle /'nɒzl/ n bocchetta f

nuance /'nju:æia.s/ n sfumatura f

nuclear /'nju:klɪə(r)/ adj nucleare

nucleus /'nju:klɪəs/ n (pl **-lei** /-lɪaɪ/) nucleo m

nude /nju:d/ adj nudo •n nudo m; **in the** ~ nudo

nudge /nʌdʒ/ n colpetto m di gomito •vt dare un colpetto col gomito a

nudism /'nju:dɪzm/ n nudismo m

nud|ist /'nju:dɪst/ n nudista mf. ~**ity** n nudità f

nuisance /'nju:sns/ n seccatura f; (person) piaga f; **what a** ~**!** che seccatura!

null /nʌl/ adj ~ **and void** nullo

numb /nʌm/ adj intorpidito; ~ **with cold** intirizzito dal freddo

number /'nʌmbə(r)/ n numero m; **a** ~ **of people** un certo numero di persone •vt numerare; (include) annoverare. ~**-plate** n targa f

numeral /'nju:mərəl/ n numero m, cifra f

numerical /nju:'merɪkl/ adj numerico; **in** ~ **order** in ordine numerico

numerous /'nju:mərəs/ adj numeroso

nun /nʌn/ n suora f

nurse /nɜ:s/ n infermiere, -a mf; **children's** ~ bambinaia f •vt curare

nursery /'nɜ:sərɪ/ n stanza f dei bambini; (for plants) vivaio m; [**day**] ~ asilo m. ~ **rhyme** n filastrocca f. ~ **school** n scuola f materna

nut /nʌt/ n noce f; (Techn) dado m; (!: head) zucca f; ~**s** npl frutta f secca; **be** ~**s** ! essere svitato. ~**crackers** npl schiaccianoci m inv. ~**meg** n noce f moscata

nutrit|ion /nju:'trɪʃn/ n nutrizione f. ~**ious** adj nutriente

'**nutshell** n **in a** ~ fig in parole povere

nylon /'naɪlɒn/ n nailon m; ~**s** pl calze fpl di nailon •attrib di nailon

Oo

oaf /əʊf/ n (pl **oafs**) zoticone, -a mf

oak /əʊk/ n quercia f •attrib di quercia

OAP n abbr (old-age pensioner) pensionato, -a mf

oar /ɔ:(r)/ n remo m. **~sman** n vogatore m

oasis /əʊ'eɪsɪs/ n (pl **oases** /-si:z/) oasi f inv

oath /əʊθ/ n giuramento m; (swear-word) bestemmia f

oatmeal /'əʊt-/ n farina f d'avena

oats /əʊts/ npl avena fsg; (Culin) [**rolled**] ~ fiocchi mpl di avena

obedien|ce /ə'bi:dɪəns/ n ubbidienza f. **~t** adj ubbidiente

obes|e /ə'bi:s/ adj obeso. **~ity** n obesità f

obey /ə'beɪ/ vt ubbidire a; osservare (instructions, rules) •vi ubbidire

obituary /ə'bɪtjʊərɪ/ n necrologio m

O

object[1] /'ɒbdʒɪkt/ n oggetto m; (Gram) complemento m oggetto; **money is no ~** i soldi non sono un problema

object[2] /əb'dʒekt/ vi (be against) opporsi (**to** a); **~ that...** obiettare che...

objection /əb'dʒekʃn/ n obiezione f; **have no ~** non avere niente in contrario. **~able** adj discutibile; (person) sgradevole

objectiv|e /əb'dʒektɪv/ adj oggettivo •n obiettivo m. **~ely** adv obiettivamente. **~ity** n oggettività f

obligation /ɒblɪ'geɪʃn/ n obbligo m; **be under an ~** avere un obbligo; **without ~** senza impegno

obligatory /ə'blɪgətrɪ/ adj obbligatorio

oblig|e /ə'blaɪdʒ/ vt (compel) obbligare; **much ~ed** grazie mille. **~ing** adj disponibile

oblique /ə'bli:k/ adj obliquo; fig indiretto •n **~** [**stroke**] barra f

obliterate /ə'blɪtəreɪt/ vt obliterare

oblivion /ə'blɪvɪən/ n oblio m

oblivious /ə'blɪvɪəs/ adj **be ~** esser dimentico (**of, to** di)

oblong /'ɒblɒŋ/ adj oblungo •n rettangolo m

obnoxious /əb'nɒkʃəs/ adj detestabile

oboe /'əʊbəʊ/ n oboe m inv

obscen|e /əb'si:n/ adj osceno; (profits wealth) vergognoso. **~ity** n oscenità inv

obscur|e /əb'skjʊə(r)/ adj oscuro •vt oscurare; (confuse) mettere in ombr **~ity** n oscurità f

obsequious /əb'si:kwɪəs/ adj ossequioso

observatory /əb'zɜ:vətrɪ/ n osservatorio m

observe /əb'zɜ:v/ vt osservare; (notic notare; (keep, celebrate) celebrare. **~r** n osservatore, -trice mf

obsess /əb'ses/ vt **be ~ed by** esser fissato con. **~ion** n fissazione f. **~ive** adj ossessivo

obsolete /'ɒbsəli:t/ adj obsoleto; (word) desueto

obstacle /'ɒbstəkl/ n ostacolo m

obstina|cy /'ɒbstɪnəsɪ/ n ostinazion f. **~te** adj ostinato

obstruct /əb'strʌkt/ vt ostruire; (hinder) ostacolare. **~ion** n ostruzione f; (obstacle) ostacolo m. **~ive** adj **be ~ive** (person:) creare d problemi

obtain /əb'teɪn/ vt ottenere. **~able** adj ottenibile

obtrusive /əb'tru:sɪv/ adj (object) stonato

obtuse /əb'tju:s/ adj ottuso

obvious /'ɒbvɪəs/ adj ovvio. **~ly** adv ovviamente

occasion /ə'keɪʒn/ n occasione f; (event) evento m; **on ~** talvolta; **on the ~ of** in occasione di

occasional /ə'keɪʒənl/ adj saltuario; **he has the ~ glass of wine** ogni tanto beve un bicchiere di vino. **~ly** adv ogni tanto

ccult /ɒ'kʌlt/ adj occulto

ccupant /'ɒkjʊpənt/ n occupante mf; (of vehicle) persona f a bordo

ccupation /ɒkjʊ'peɪʃn/ n occupazione f; (job) professione f **~al** adj professionale

ccupier /'ɒkjʊpaɪə(r)/ n residente mf

ccupy /'ɒkjʊpaɪ/ vt (pt/pp **occupied**) occupare; (keep busy) tenere occupato

ccur /ə'kɜ:(r)/ vi (pt/pp **occurred**) accadere; (exist) trovarsi; **it ~red to me that** mi è venuto in mente che. **~rence** n (event) fatto m

cean /'əʊʃn/ n oceano m

ctave /'ɒktɪv/ n (Mus) ottava f

ctober /ɒk'təʊbə(r)/ n ottobre m

ctopus /'ɒktəpəs/ n (pl **-puses**) polpo m

dd /ɒd/ adj (number) dispari; (not of set) scompagnato; (strange) strano; **forty ~** quaranta e rotti; **~ jobs** lavoretti mpl; **the ~ one out** l'eccezione; **at ~ moments** a tempo perso; **have the ~ glass of wine** avere un bicchiere di vino ogni tanto

dd|ity /'ɒdɪtɪ/ n stranezza f. **~ly** adv stranamente; **~ly enough** stranamente. **~ment** n (of fabric) scampolo m

dds /ɒdz/ npl (chances) probabilità fpl; **at ~** in disaccordo; **~ and ends** cianfrusaglie fpl; **it makes no ~** non fa alcuna differenza

dour /'əʊdə(r)/ n odore m. **~less** adj inodore

f /ɒv/, /əv/ prep di; **a cup of tea/coffee** una tazza di tè/caffè; **the hem of my skirt** l'orlo della mia gonna; **the summer of 1989** l'estate del 1989; **the two of us** noi due; **made of** di; **that's very kind of you** è molto gentile da parte tua; **a friend of mine** un mio amico; **a child of three** un bambino di tre anni; **the fourth of January** il quattro gennaio; **within a year of their divorce** a circa un anno dal loro divorzio; **half of it** la metà; **the whole of the room** tutta la stanza

ff /ɒf/ prep da; (distant from) lontano da; **take £10 ~ the price** ridurre il prezzo di 10 sterline; **~ the coast** presso la costa; **a street ~ the main road** una traversa della via principale; (near) una strada vicino alla via principale; **get ~ the ladder** scendere dalla scala; **get off the bus** uscire dall'autobus; **leave the lid ~ the saucepan** lasciare la pentola senza il coperchio • adv (button, handle) staccato; (light, machine) spento; (brake) tolto; (tap) chiuso; **'off'** (on appliance) 'off'; **2 kilometres ~** a due chilometri di distanza; **a long way ~** molto distante; (time) lontano; **~ and on** di tanto in tanto; **with his hat/coat ~** senza il cappello/cappotto; **with the light ~** a luce spenta; **20% ~** 20% di sconto; **be ~** (leave) andar via; (Sport) essere partito; (food:) essere andato a male; (all gone) essere finito; (wedding, engagement:) essere cancellato; **I'm ~ alcohol** ho smesso di bere; **be ~ one's food** non avere appetito; **she's ~ today** (on holiday) è in ferie oggi; (ill) è malata oggi; **I'm ~ home** vado a casa; **you'd be better ~ doing...** faresti meglio a fare...; **have a day ~** avere un giorno di vacanza; **drive/sail ~** andare via

'off-beat adj insolito

'off-chance n possibilità f remota

offence /ə'fens/ n (illegal act) reato m; **give ~** offendere; **take ~** offendersi (**at** per)

offend /ə'fend/ vt offendere. **~er** n (Jur) colpevole mf

offensive /ə'fensɪv/ adj offensivo • n offensiva f

offer /'ɒfə(r)/ n offerta f • vt offrire; opporre (resistance); **~ sb sth** offrire qcsa a qcno; **~ to do sth** offrirsi di fare qcsa. **~ing** n offerta f

off'hand adj (casual) spiccio • adv su due piedi

office /'ɒfɪs/ n ufficio m; (post, job) carica f. **~ hours** pl orario m d'ufficio

officer /'ɒfɪsə(r)/ n ufficiale m; (police) agente m [di polizia]

official /ə'fɪʃl/ adj ufficiale • n funzionario, -a mf; (Sport) dirigente m. **~ly** adv ufficialmente

'offing n **in the ~** in vista

'off-licence n negozio m per la vendita di alcolici

'offset vt (pt/pp **-set**, pres p **-setting**) controbilanciare

'offshore •adj (wind) di terra; (company, investment) offshore. •adv (sail) al largo; (relocate) all'estero (in paesi dove la manodopera costa meno); **~ rig** n piattaforma f petrolifera, offshore m inv

off'side adj (Sport) [in] fuori gioco; (wheel etc) (left) sinistro; (right) destro

'offspring n prole m

off'stage adv dietro le quinte

often /'ɒfn/ adv spesso; **how ~** ogni quanto; **every so ~** una volta ogni tanto

oh /əʊ/ int oh!; **~ dear** oh Dio!

oil /ɔɪl/ n olio m; (petroleum) petrolio m; (for heating) nafta f •vt oliare

oil: ~field n giacimento m di petrolio. **~-painting** n pittura f a olio. **~ refinery** n raffineria f di petrolio. **~ rig** piattaforma f per trivellazione subacquea

oily /'ɔɪlɪ/ adj (**-ier, -iest**) unto; fig untuoso

ointment /'ɔɪntmənt/ n pomata f

O

OK /əʊ'keɪ/ int va bene, o.k. •adj **if that's OK with you** se ti va bene; **she's OK** (well) sta bene; **is the milk still OK?** il latte è ancora buono? •adv (well) bene •vt (anche **okay**) (pt/pp **okayed**) dare l'o.k.

old /əʊld/ adj vecchio; (girlfriend) ex; **how ~ is she?** quanti anni ha?; **she is ten years ~** ha dieci anni

old: ~ 'age n vecchiaia f. **~'fashioned** adj antiquato

olive /'ɒlɪv/ n (fruit, colour) oliva f; (tree) olivo m •adj d'oliva; (colour) olivastro. **~ branch** n fig ramoscello m d'olivo. **~ 'oil** n olio m di oliva

Olympic /ə'lɪmpɪk/ adj olimpico; **~s, ~ Games** Olimpiadi fpl

omelette /'ɒmlɪt/ n omelette f inv

omission /ə'mɪʃn/ n omissione f

omit /ə'mɪt/ vt (pt/pp **omitted**) omettere

on /ɒn/ prep su; (on horizontal surface) su, sopra; **~ Monday** lunedì; **~ Mondays** di lunedì; **~ the first of May** il primo maggio; **~ arriving** all'arrivo; **~ foot** a piedi; **~ the right/left** a destra/sinistra; **~ the radio/television** alla radio/televisione; **~ the bus/train** in autobus/treno •adv (further on) dopo; (swtiched on) acceso; (in operation) in funzione; **he had his hat/coat ~** portava il cappello/cappotto; **be ~** (event) esserci; **~ and ~** senza sosta; **go ~** continuare

once /wʌns/ adv una volta; (formerly) un tempo; **~ upon a time there was** c'era una volta; **at ~** subito; (at the same time) contemporaneamente; **~ and for all** una volta per tutte •conj [non] appena. **~-over** n ▣ **give sb/sth the ~-over** (look, check) dare un'occhiata veloce a qcno/qcsa

one /wʌn/
- adj uno, una; **not ~ person** nemmeno una persona
- n uno m
- pron uno; (*impersonal*) si; **~ another** l'un l'altro; **~ by ~** [a] uno a uno; **~ never knows** non si sa mai

one: ~self pron (reflexive) si; (emphatic) sé, se stesso; **by ~self** da solo; **be proud of ~self** essere fieri di sé. **~-way** adj (street) a senso unico; (ticket) di sola andata

onion /'ʌnjən/ n cipolla f

on-'line adj/adv su Internet

'onlooker n spettatore, -trice mf

only /'əʊnlɪ/ adj solo; **~ child** figlio, -a mf unico, -a •adv & conj solo, solamente; **~ just** appena

'onset n (beginning) inizio m

onslaught /'ɒnslɔːt/ n attacco m

opaque /əʊ'peɪk/ adj opaco

open /'əʊpən/ adj aperto; (free to all) pubblico; (job) vacante; **in the ~ air** all'aperto •n **in the ~** all'aperto; fig alla luce del sole •vt aprire •vi aprirsi; (shop:) aprire; (flower:) sbocciare. □ **~ up** vt aprire •vi aprirsi

opening /'əʊpənɪŋ/ n apertura f; (beginning) inizio m; (job) posto m libero; **~ hours** npl orario m d'apertura

openly /'əʊpənlɪ/ adv apertamente

en: ~-'minded adj aperto; (broad-minded) di vedute larghe. **~-plan** adj a pianta aperta

era /'ɒpərə/ n opera f

era-house n teatro m lirico

erate /'ɒpəreɪt/ vt far funzionare (machine, lift); azionare (lever, brake); mandare avanti (business) • vi (Techn) funzionare; (be in action) essere in funzione; (Mil, fig) operare; **~ on** (Med) operare

eratic /ɒpə'rætɪk/ adj lirico, operistico

eration /ɒpə'reɪʃn/ n operazione f; (Techn) funzionamento m; **in ~** (Techn) in funzione; **come into ~** fig entrare in funzione; (law:) entrare in vigore; **have an ~** (Med) subire un'operazione. **~al** adj operativo; (law etc) in vigore

erative /'ɒpərətɪv/ adj operativo

erator /'ɒpəreɪtə(r)/ n (user) operatore, -trice mf; (Teleph) centralinista mf

inion /ə'pɪnjən/ n opinione f; **in my ~** secondo me. **~ated** adj dogmatico

ponent /ə'pəʊnənt/ n avversario, -a mf

portun|e /'ɒpətju:n/ adj opportuno. **~ist** n opportunista mf. **~istic** adj opportunistico

portunity /ɒpə'tju:nətɪ/ n opportunità f inv

pos|e /ə'pəʊz/ vt opporsi a; **be ~ed to sth** esssere contrario a qcsa; **as ~ed to** al contrario di. **~ing** adj avversario; (opposite) opposto

posite /'ɒpəzɪt/ adj opposto; (house) di fronte; **~ number** fig controparte f; **the ~ sex** l'altro sesso • n contrario m • adv di fronte • prep di fronte a

position /ɒpə'zɪʃn/ n opposizione f

press /ə'pres/ vt opprimere. **~ion** n oppressione f. **~ive** adj oppressivo; (heat) opprimente. **~or** n oppressore m

t /ɒpt/ vi **~ for** optare per; **~ out** dissociarsi (**of** da)

tical /'ɒptɪkl/ adj ottico; **~ illusion** illusione f ottica

optician /ɒp'tɪʃn/ n ottico, -a mf

optimis|m /'ɒptɪmɪzm/ n ottimismo m. **~t** n ottimista mf. **~tic** adj ottimistico

option /'ɒpʃn/ n scelta f; (Comm) opzione f. **~al** adj facoltativo; **~al extras** pl optional m inv

or /ɔ:(r)/ conj o, oppure; (after negative) né; **or [else]** se no; **in a year or two** fra un anno o due

oral /'ɔ:rəl/ adj orale • n [!] esame m orale. **~ly** adv oralmente

orange /'ɒrɪndʒ/ n arancia f; (colour) arancione m • adj arancione. **~ade** n aranciata f. **~ juice** n succo m d'arancia

orbit /'ɔ:bɪt/ n orbita f • vt orbitare. **~al** adj **~al road** tangenziale f

orchard /'ɔ:tʃəd/ n frutteto m

orches|tra /'ɔ:kɪstrə/ n orchestra f. **~tral** adj orchestrale. **~trate** vt orchestrare

orchid /'ɔ:kɪd/ n orchidea f

ordain /ɔ:'deɪn/ vt decretare; (Relig) ordinare

ordeal /ɔ:'di:l/ n fig terribile esperienza f

order /'ɔ:də(r)/ n ordine m; (Comm) ordinazione f; **out of ~** (machine) fuori servizio; **in ~ that** affinché; **in ~ to** per • vt ordinare

orderly /'ɔ:dəlɪ/ adj ordinato • n (Mil) attendente m; (Med) inserviente m

ordinary /'ɔ:dɪnərɪ/ adj ordinario

ore /ɔ:(r)/ n minerale m grezzo

organ /'ɔ:gən/ n (Anat, Mus) organo m

organic /ɔ:'gænɪk/ adj organico; (without chemicals) biologico. **~ally** adv organicamente; **~ally grown** coltivato biologicamente

organism /'ɔ:gənɪzm/ n organismo m

organist /'ɔ:gənɪst/ n organista mf

organization /ɔ:gənaɪ'zeɪʃn/ n organizzazione f

organize /'ɔ:gənaɪz/ vt organizzare. **~r** n organizzatore, -trice mf

orgasm /'ɔ:gæzm/ n orgasmo m

orgy /'ɔ:dʒɪ/ n orgia f

Orient /'ɔ:rɪənt/ n Oriente m. **o~al** adj orientale • n orientale mf

orient|ate /'ɔ:rɪenteɪt/ vt **~ate**

O

oneself orientarsi. **~ation** n orientamento m

origin /'ɒrɪdʒɪn/ n origine f

original /ə'rɪdʒɪn(ə)l/ adj originario; (not copied, new) originale •n originale m; **in the ~** in versione originale. **~ity** n originalità f. **~ly** adv originariamente

originat|e /ə'rɪdʒɪneɪt/ vi **~e in** avere origine in. **~or** n ideatore, -trice mf

ornament /'ɔ:nəmənt/ n ornamento m; (on mantelpiece etc) soprammobile m. **~al** adj ornamentale. **~ation** n decorazione f

ornate /ɔ:'neɪt/ adj ornato

orphan /'ɔ:fn/ n orfano, -a mf •vt rendere orfano; **be ~ed** rimanere orfano. **~age** n orfanotrofio m

orthodox /'ɔ:θədɒks/ adj ortodosso

oscillate /'ɒsɪleɪt/ vi oscillare

osteopath /'ɒstɪəpæθ/ n osteopata mf

ostracize /'ɒstrəsaɪz/ vt bandire

ostrich /'ɒstrɪtʃ/ n struzzo m

other /'ʌðə(r)/ adj, pron & n altro, -a mf; **the ~ [one]** l'altro, -a mf; **the ~ two** gli altri due; **two ~s** altri due; **~ people** gli altri; **any ~ questions?** altre domande?; **every ~ day** (alternate days) a giorni alterni; **the ~ day** l'altro giorno; **the ~ evening** l'altra sera; **someone/something or ~** qualcuno/qualcosa •adv **~ than him** tranne lui; **somehow or ~** in qualche modo; **somewhere or ~** da qualche parte

'**otherwise** adv altrimenti; (differently) diversamente

otter /'ɒtə(r)/ n lontra f

ouch /aʊtʃ/ int ahi!

ought /ɔ:t/ v aux **I/we ~ to stay** dovrei/dovremmo rimanere; **he ~ not to have done it** non avrebbe dovuto farlo; **that ~ to be enough** questo dovrebbe bastare

ounce /aʊns/ n oncia f (= 28,35 g)

our /'aʊə(r)/ adj il nostro m, la nostra f, i nostri mpl, le nostre fpl; **~ mother/father** nostra madre/nostro padre

ours /'aʊəz/ poss pron il nostro m, la nostra f, i nostri mpl, le nostre fpl; **a friend of ~** un nostro amico; **friends of ~** dei nostri amici; **that is ~** quello è nostro; (as opposed to yours) quello è il nostro

ourselves /aʊə'selvz/ pron (reflexive) ci; (emphatic) noi, noi stessi; **we poured ~ a drink** ci siamo versati da bere; **we heard it ~** l'abbiamo sentito noi stessi; **we are proud of ~** siamo fieri di noi; **by ~** da soli

out /aʊt/ adv fuori; (not alight) spento; **be ~** (flower:) essere sbocciato; (workers:) essere in sciopero; (calculation:) essere sbagliato; (Sport) essere fuori; (unconscious) aver perso i sensi; (fig: not feasible) fuori questione; **the sun is ~** è uscito il sole; **~ and about** in piedi; **get ~** [!] fuori!; **you should get ~ more** dovresti uscire più spesso; **~ with it!** [!] sputa il rospo!; •prep **~ of** fuori da; **~ of date** non aggiornato; (passport) scaduto; **~ of order** guasto; **~ of print/stock** esaurito; **~ of bed/the room** fuori dal letto/dalla stanza; **~ of breath** senza fiato; **~ of danger** fuori pericolo; **~ of work** disoccupato; **nine ~ of ten** nove su dieci; **be ~ of sugar/bread** rimanere senza zucchero/pane; **go ~ of the room** uscire dalla stanza

'**outbreak** n (of war) scoppio m; (of disease) insorgenza f

'**outburst** n esplosione f

'**outcome** n risultato m

'**outcry** n protesta f

out'dated adj sorpassato

out'do vt (pt **-did**, pp **-done**) superare

'**outdoor** adj (life, sports) all'aperto; **~ clothes** pl vestiti per uscire; **~ swimming pool** piscina f scoperta

out'doors adv all'aria aperta; **go ~** uscire [all'aria aperta]

'**outer** adj esterno

'**outfit** n equipaggiamento m; (clothes) completo m; ([!]: organization) organizzazione. **~ter** n **men's ~ter's** negozio m di abbigliamento maschile

'**outgoing** adj (president) uscente; (mail) in partenza; (sociable) estroverso. **~s** npl uscite fpl

ut'grow vi (pt **-grew**, pp **-grown**) diventare troppo grande per

uting /'aʊtɪŋ/ n gita f

utlandish /aʊt'lændɪʃ/ adj stravagante

utlaw n fuorilegge mf inv • vt dichiarare illegale

utlay n spesa f

utlet n sbocco m; fig sfogo m; (Comm) punto m [di] vendita

utline n contorno m; (summary) sommario m • vt tracciare il contorno di; (describe) descrivere

ut'live vt sopravvivere a

utlook n vista f; (future prospect) prospettiva f; (attitude) visione f

utlying adj **~ areas** pl zone fpl periferiche

ut'number vt superare in numero

ut-patient n paziente mf esterno, -a; **~s' department** ambulatorio m

utput n produzione f

utright[1] adj completo; (refusal) netto

ut'right[2] adv completamente; (at once) immediatamente; (frankly) francamente

utset n inizio m; **from the ~** fin dall'inizio

utside[1] adj esterno • n esterno m; **from the ~** dall'esterno; **at the ~** al massimo

ut'side[2] adv all'esterno, fuori; (out of doors) fuori; **go ~** andare fuori • prep fuori da; (in front of) davanti a

utskirts npl sobborghi mpl

ut'spoken adj schietto

ut'standing adj eccezionale; (landmark) prominente; (not settled) in sospeso

ut'stretched adj allungato

ut'strip vt (pt/pp **-stripped**) superare

utward /-wəd/ adj esterno; (journey) di andata • adv verso l'esterno. **~ly** adv esternamente. **~s** adv verso l'esterno

ut'weigh vt aver maggior peso di

out'wit vt (pt/pp **-witted**) battere in astuzia

oval /'əʊvl/ adj ovale • n ovale m

ovary /'əʊvərɪ/ n (Anat) ovaia f

ovation /əʊ'veɪʃn/ n ovazione f

oven /'ʌvn/ n forno m. **~-ready** adj pronto da mettere in forno

over /'əʊvə(r)/ prep sopra; (across) al di là di; (during) durante; (more than) più di; **~ the phone** al telefono; **~ the page** alla pagina seguente; **all ~ Italy** in tutta [l']Italia; (travel) per l'Italia • adv (Math) col resto di; (ended) finito; **~ again** un'altra volta; **~ and ~** più volte; **~ and above** oltre a; **~ here/there** qui/là; **all ~** (everywhere) dappertutto; **it's all ~** è tutto finito; **I ache all ~** ho male dappertutto; **come/bring ~** venire/portare; **turn ~** girare

over- pref (too) troppo

overall[1] /'əʊvərɔːl/ n grembiule m; **~s** pl tuta fsg [da lavoro]

overall[2] /əʊvər'ɔːl/ adj complessivo; (general) generale • adv complessivamente

over'balance vi perdere l'equilibrio

over'bearing adj prepotente

'overboard adv (Naut) in mare

'overcast adj coperto

over'charge vt **~ sb** far pagare più del dovuto a qcno • vi far pagare più del dovuto

'overcoat n cappotto m

over'come vt (pt **-came**, pp **-come**) vincere; **be ~ by** essere sopraffatto da

over'crowded adj sovraffollato

over'do vt (pt **-did**, pp **-done**) esagerare; (cook too long) stracuocere; **~ it** ([!]: do too much) strafare

'overdose n overdose f inv

'overdraft n scoperto m; **have an ~** avere il conto scoperto

over'draw vt (pt **-drew**, pp **-drawn**) **~ one's account** andare allo scoperto; **be ~n by** (account:) essere [allo] scoperto di

over'due adj in ritardo

over'estimate vt sopravvalutare

O

'overflow[1] n (water) acqua f che deborda; (people) pubblico m in eccesso; (outlet) scarico m; ~ **car park** parcheggio m supplementare

over'flow[2] vi debordare

over'grown adj (garden) coperto di erbacce

'overhaul[1] n revisione f

over'haul[2] vt (Techn) revisionare

over'head[1] adv in alto

'overhead[2] adj aereo; (railway) sopraelevato; (lights) da soffitto. **~s** npl spese fpl generali

over'hear vt (pt/pp **-heard**) sentire per caso (conversation)

over'joyed adj felicissimo

'overland adj & adv via terra; ~ **route** via f terrestre

over'lap v (pt/pp **-lapped**) • vi sovrapporsi • vt sovrapporre

over'leaf adv sul retro

over'load vt sovraccaricare

over'look vt dominare; (fail to see, ignore) lasciarsi sfuggire

over'night[1] adv per la notte; **stay** ~ fermarsi a dormire

'overnight[2] adj notturno; ~ **bag** piccola borsa f da viaggio; ~ **stay** sosta f per la notte

'overpass n cavalcavia m inv

over'pay vt (pt/pp **-paid**) strapagare

over'power vt sopraffare. **~ing** adj insostenibile

over'priced adj troppo caro

overre'act vi avere una reazione eccessiva. **~ion** n reazione f eccessiva

over'rid|e vt (pt **-rode**, pp **-ridden**) passare sopra a. **~ing** adj prevalente

over'rule vt annullare (decision)

over'run vt (pt **-ran**, pp **-run**, pres p **-running**) invadere; oltrepassare (time); **be ~ with** essere invaso da

over'seas[1] adv oltremare

'overseas[2] adj d'oltremare

over'see vt (pt **-saw**, pp **-seen**) sorvegliare

over'shadow vt adombrare

over'shoot vt (pt/pp **-shot**) oltrepassare

'oversight n disattenzione f; **an ~** una svista

over'sleep vi (pt/pp **-slept**) svegliars troppo tardi

over'step vt (pt/pp **-stepped**) ~ **the mark** oltrepassare ogni limite

overt /əʊ'vɜːt/ adj palese

over'tak|e vt/i (pt **-took**, pp **-taken**) sorpassare. **~ing** n sorpasso m; **no ~ing** divieto di sorpasso

'overthrow[1] n (Pol) rovesciamento m

over'throw[2] vt (pt **-threw**, pp **-thrown**) (Pol) rovesciare

'overtime n lavoro m straordinario • adv **work ~** fare lo straordinario

overture /'əʊvətjʊə(r)/ n (Mus) preludio m; **~s** pl fig approccio msg

over'turn vt ribaltare • vi ribaltarsi

over'weight adj sovrappeso

overwhelm /-'welm/ vt sommergere (**with** di); (with emotion) confondere. **~ing** adj travolgente; (victory, majority) schiacciante

over'work n lavoro m eccessivo • vt far lavorare eccessivamente • vi lavorare eccessivamente

ow|e /əʊ/ vt also fig dovere ([**to**] **sb** a qcno); **~e sb sth** dovere qcsa a qcno. **~ing** adj **be ~ing** (money:) essere da pagare • prep **~ing to** a causa di

owl /aʊl/ n gufo m

own[1] /əʊn/ adj proprio • pron **a car of my ~** una macchina per conto mio; **on one's ~** da solo; **hold one's ~ with** tener testa a; **get one's ~ back** [!] prendersi una rivincita

own[2] vt possedere; (confess) ammettere; **I don't ~ it** non mi appartiene. □ **~ up** vi confessare (**to sth** qcsa)

owner /'əʊnə(r)/ n proprietario, -a mf. **~ship** n proprietà f

oxygen /'ɒksɪdʒən/ n ossigeno m; **~ mask** maschera f a ossigeno

oyster /'ɔɪstə(r)/ n ostrica f

ozone /'əʊzəʊn/ n ozono m. **~-'friendly** adj che non danneggia l'ozono. **~ layer** n fascia f d'ozono

Pp

ace /peɪs/ n passo m; (speed) ritmo m; **keep ~ with** camminare di pari passo con •vi **~ up and down** camminare avanti e indietro. **~-maker** n (Med) pacemaker m; (runner) battistrada m

acific /pə'sɪfɪk/ adj & n **the ~ [Ocean]** l'oceano m Pacifico, il Pacifico

acifist /'pæsɪfɪst/ n pacifista mf

acify /'pæsɪfaɪ/ vt (pt/pp **-ied**) placare (person); pacificare (country)

ack /pæk/ n (of cards) mazzo m; (of hounds) muta f; (of wolves, thieves) branco m; (of cigarettes etc) pacchetto m; **a ~ of lies** un mucchio di bugie •vt impacchettare (article); fare (suitcase); mettere in valigia (swimsuit etc); (press down) comprimere; **~ed [out]** (crowded) pieno zeppo •vi fare i bagagli; **send sb ~ing** [!] mandare qcno a stendere. ▫**~ up** vt impacchettare •vi [!] (machine:) piantare in asso

ackage /'pækɪdʒ/ n pacco m •vt impacchettare. **~ deal** offerta f tutto compreso. **~ holiday** n vacanza f organizzata. **~ tour** viaggio m organizzato

acket /'pækɪt/ n pacchetto m; **cost a ~** [!] costare un sacco

act /pækt/ n patto m

ad[1] /pæd/ n imbottitura f; (for writing) bloc-notes m, taccuino m; ([!]: home) [piccolo] appartamento m •vt (pt/pp **padded**) imbottire. ▫**~ out** vt gonfiare

ad[2] vi (pt/pp **padded**) camminare con passo felpato

addle[1] /'pæd(ə)l/ n pagaia f •vt (row) spingere remando

addle[2] vi (wade) sguazzare

addock /'pædək/ n recinto m

adlock /'pædlɒk/ n lucchetto m •vt chiudere con lucchetto

aediatrician /pi:dɪə'trɪʃn/ n pediatra mf

page[1] /peɪdʒ/ n pagina f

page[2] n (boy) paggetto m; (in hotel) fattorino m •vt far chiamare (person)

pager /'peɪdʒə(r)/ n cercapersone m inv

paid /peɪd/ ▹**pay** •adj **~ employment** lavoro m remunerato; **put ~ to** mettere un termine a

pail /peɪl/ n secchio m

pain /peɪn/ n dolore m; **be in ~** soffrire; **take ~s** darsi un gran d'affare; **~ in the neck** [!] spina f nel fianco

pain: ~ful adj doloroso; (laborious) penoso. **~-killer** n calmante m. **~less** adj indolore

painstaking /'peɪnzteɪkɪŋ/ adj minuzioso

paint /peɪnt/ n pittura f; **~s** colori mpl •vt/i pitturare; (artist:) dipingere. **~brush** n pennello m. **~er** n pittore, -trice mf; (decorator) imbianchino m. **~ing** n pittura f; (picture) dipinto m. **~work** n pittura f

pair /peə(r)/ n paio m; (of people) coppia f; **~ of trousers** paio m di pantaloni; **~ of scissors** paio m di forbici

pajamas /pə'dʒɑ:məz/ npl Am pigiama msg

Pakistan /pɑ:kɪ'stɑ:n/ n Pakistan m. **~i** adj pakistano •n pakistano, -a mf

pal /pæl/ n [!] amico, -a mf

palace /'pælɪs/ n palazzo m

palatable /'pælətəbl/ adj gradevole (al gusto)

palate /'pælət/ n palato m

pale /peɪl/ adj pallido

Palestin|e /'pælɪstaɪn/ n Palestina f. **~ian** adj palestinese •n palestinese mf

palette /'pælɪt/ n tavolozza f

palm /pɑ:m/ n palmo m; (tree) palma f; **P~ 'Sunday** n Domenica f delle Palme •**palm off** vt **~ sth off on**

sb rifilare qcsa a qcno

palpable /'pælpəbl/ adj palpabile; (perceptible) tangibile

palpitat|e /'pælpɪteɪt/ vi palpitare. **~ions** npl palpitazioni fpl

pamper /'pæmpə(r)/ vt viziare

pamphlet /'pæmflɪt/ n opuscolo m

pan /pæn/ n tegame m, pentola f; (for frying) padella f; (of scales) piatto m •vt (pt/pp **panned**) ([!]: criticize) stroncare

'pancake n crêpe f inv, frittella f

panda /'pændə/ n panda m inv. **~ car** n macchina f della polizia

pandemonium /pændɪ'məʊnɪəm/ n pandemonio m

pander /'pændə(r)/ vi **~ to sb** compiacere qcno

pane /peɪn/ n **~ [of glass]** vetro m

panel /'pænl/ n pannello m; (group of people) giuria f; **~ of experts** gruppo m di esperti. **~ling** n pannelli mpl

pang /pæŋ/ n **~s of hunger** morsi mpl della fame; **~s of conscience** rimorsi mpl di coscienza

panic /'pænɪk/ n panico m •vi (pt/pp **panicked**) lasciarsi prendere dal panico. **~-stricken** adj in preda al panico

panoram|a /pænə'rɑ:mə/ n panorama m. **~ic** adj panoramico

pansy /'pænzɪ/ n viola f del pensiero; ([!]: effeminate man) finocchio m

pant /pænt/ vi ansimare

panther /'pænθə(r)/ n pantera f

panties /'pæntɪz/ npl mutandine fpl

pantomime /'pæntəmaɪm/ n pantomima f

pantry /'pæntrɪ/ n dispensa f

pants /pænts/ npl (underwear) mutande fpl; (woman's) mutandine fpl; (trousers) pantaloni mpl

'pantyhose n Am collant m inv

paper /'peɪpə(r)/ n carta f; (wallpaper) carta f da parati; (newspaper) giornale m; (exam) esame m; (treatise) saggio m; **~s** pl (documents) documenti mpl; (for identification) documento m [d'identità]; **on ~** in teoria; **put down on ~** mettere per iscritto •attrib di carta •vt tappezzare

paper: ~back n edizione f economica. **~-clip** n graffetta f. **~weight** n fermacarte m inv. **~work** n lavoro m d'ufficio

parable /'pærəbl/ n parabola f

parachut|e /'pærəʃu:t/ n paracadut[e] m •vi lanciarsi col paracadute. **~is[t]** n paracadutista mf

parade /pə'reɪd/ n (military) parata f militare •vi sfilare •vt (show off) far sfoggio di

paradise /'pærədaɪs/ n paradiso m

paraffin /'pærəfɪn/ n paraffina f

paragraph /'pærəgrɑ:f/ n paragrafo m

parallel /'pærəlel/ adj & adv parallel[o] **~ bars** npl parallele fpl. **~ port** n (Comput) porta f parallela •n (Geog), fig parallelo m; (line) parallela f •vt essere paragonabile a

Paralympics /pærə'lɪmpɪks/ npl **the P~** le Paraolimpiadi fpl

paralyse /'pærəlaɪz/ vt also fig paralizzare

paralysis /pə'ræləsɪs/ n (pl **-ses**) /-si:z/ paralisi f inv

paramedic /pærə'medɪk/ n paramedico, -a mf

parameter /pə'ræmɪtə(r)/ n parametro m

paranoia /pærə'nɔɪə/ n paranoia f

paraphernalia /pærəfə'neɪlɪə/ n armamentario m

paraplegic /pærə'pli:dʒɪk/ adj paraplegico •n paraplegico, -a mf

parasite /'pærəsaɪt/ n parassita mf

paratrooper /'pærətru:pə(r)/ n paracadutista m

parcel /'pɑ:sl/ n pacco m

parch /pɑ:tʃ/ vt disseccare; **be ~ed** (person:) morire dalla sete

pardon /'pɑ:dn/ n perdono m; (Jur) grazia f; **~?** prego?; **I beg your ~?** fml chiedo scusa?; **I do beg your ~** (sorry) chiedo scusa! •vt perdonare; (Jur) graziare

parent /'peərənt/ n genitore, -trice mf; **~s** pl genitori mpl. **~al** adj dei genitori

parenthesis /pə'renθəsɪs/ n (pl **-ses** /-si:z/) parentesi m inv

Paris /'pærɪs/ n Parigi f

parish /'pærɪʃ/ n parrocchia f.

ioner n parrocchiano, -a mf

rk /pɑ:k/ n parco m •vt/i (Auto) osteggiare, parcheggiare; **~ oneself** [!] installarsi

rk-and-'ride n park and ride m inv

rking /'pɑ:kɪŋ/ n parcheggio m, osteggio m; **'no ~'** 'divieto di osta'. **~-lot** n Am posteggio m, archeggio m. **~-meter** n archimetro m. **~ space** n osteggio m, parcheggio m

rliament /'pɑ:ləmənt/ n arlamento m. **~ary** adj arlamentare

rlour /'pɑ:lə(r)/ n salotto m

rochial /pə'rəʊkɪəl/ adj parrocchiale; fig ristretto

rody /'pærədɪ/ n parodia f •vt (pt/ p **-ied**) parodiare

role /pə'rəʊl/ n **on ~** in libertà condizionale•vt mettere in libertà condizionale

arrot /'pærət/ n pappagallo m

arsley /'pɑ:slɪ/ n prezzemolo m

arsnip /'pɑ:snɪp/ n pastinaca f

art /pɑ:t/ n parte f; (of machine) pezzo m; **for my ~** per quanto mi riguarda; **on the ~ of** da parte di; **take sb's ~** prendere le parti di qcno; **take ~ in** prendere parte a •adv in parte •vt **~ one's hair** farsi la riga •vi (people:) separare; **~ with** separarsi da

artial /'pɑ:ʃl/ adj parziale; **be ~ to** aver un debole per. **~ly** adv parzialmente

articip|ant /pɑ:'tɪsɪpənt/ n partecipante mf. **~ate** vi partecipare (**in** a). **~ation** n partecipazione f

article /'pɑ:tɪkl/ n (Gram, Phys) particella f

articular /pə'tɪkjʊlə(r)/ adj particolare; (precise) meticoloso; pej noioso; **in ~** in particolare. **~ly** adv particolarmente. **~s** npl particolari mpl

arting /'pɑ:tɪŋ/ n separazione f; (in hair) scriminatura f •attrib di commiato

artisan /pɑ:tɪ'zæn/ n partigiano, -a mf

artition /pɑ:'tɪʃn/ n (wall) parete f divisoria; (Pol) divisione f •vt dividere (in parti). **□ ~ off** vt separare

partly /'pɑ:tlɪ/ adv in parte

partner /'pɑ:tnə(r)/ n (Comm) socio, -a mf; (sport, in relationship) compagno, -a mf. **~ship** n (Comm) società f

partridge /'pɑ:trɪdʒ/ n pernice f

part-'time adj & adv part time; **be** or **work ~** lavorare part time

party /'pɑ:tɪ/ n ricevimento m, festa f; (group) gruppo m; (Pol) partito m; (Jur) parte f [in causa]; **be ~ to** essere parte attiva in

pass /pɑ:s/ n lasciapassare m inv; (in mountains) passo m; (Sport) passaggio m; (Sch: mark) [voto m] sufficiente m; **make a ~ at** [!] fare delle avances a •vt passare; (overtake) sorpassare; (approve) far passare; fare (remark); (Jur) pronunciare (sentence); **~ the time** passare il tempo •vi passare; (in exam) essere promosso. **□ ~ away** vi mancare. **□ ~ down** vt passare; fig trasmettere. **□ ~ out** vi [!] svenire. **□ ~ round** vt far passare. **□ ~ through** vt attraversare. **□ ~ up** vt passare; ([!]: miss) lasciarsi scappare

passable /'pɑ:səbl/ adj (road) praticabile; (satisfactory) passabile

passage /'pæsɪdʒ/ n passaggio m; (corridor) corridoio m; (voyage) traversata f

passenger /'pæsɪndʒə(r)/ n passeggero, -a mf. **~ seat** n posto m accanto al guidatore

passer-by /pɑ:sə'baɪ/ n (pl **~sby**) passante mf

passion /'pæʃn/ n passione f. **~ate** adj appassionato

passive /'pæsɪv/ adj passivo •n passivo m. **~ness** n passività f

Passover /'pɑ:səʊvə(r)/ n Pasqua f ebraica

pass: ~port n passaporto m. **~word** n parola f d'ordine

past /pɑ:st/ adj passato; (former) ex; **in the ~ few days** nei giorni scorsi; **that's all ~** tutto questo è passato; **the ~ week** la settimana scorsa •n passato m •prep oltre; **at ten ~ two** alle due e dieci •adv oltre; **go/come ~** passare

pasta /'pæstə/ n pasta[sciutta] f

paste /peɪst/ n pasta f; (dough) impasto m; (adhesive) colla f • vt incollare

pastel /'pæstl/ n pastello m • attrib pastello

pasteurize /'pɑ:stʃəraɪz/ vt pastorizzare

pastime /'pɑ:staɪm/ n passatempo m

pastr|y /'peɪstrɪ/ n pasta f; **~ies** pasticcini mpl

pasture /'pɑ:stʃə(r)/ n pascolo m

pasty¹ /'pæstɪ/ n ≈ pasticcio m

pasty² /'peɪstɪ/ adj smorto

pat /pæt/ n buffetto m; (of butter) pezzetto m • adv **have sth off ~** conoscere qcsa a menadito • vt (pt/pp **patted**) dare un buffetto a; **~ sb on the back** fig congratularsi con qcno

patch /pætʃ/ n toppa f; (spot) chiazza f; (period) periodo m; **not a ~ on** [!] molto inferiore a • vt mettere una toppa su. □ **~ up** vt riparare alla bell'e meglio; appianare (quarrel)

pâté /'pæteɪ/ n pâté m inv

patent /'peɪtnt/ adj palese • n brevetto m • vt brevettare. **~ leather shoes** npl scarpe fpl di vernice. **~ly** adv in modo palese

patern|al /pə'tɜ:nl/ adj paterno. **~ity** n paternità f inv

P

path /pɑ:θ/ n (pl **~s** /pɑ:ðz/) sentiero m; (orbit) traiettoria m; fig strada f

pathetic /pə'θetɪk/ adj patetico; ([!]: very bad) penoso

patience /'peɪʃns/ n pazienza f; (game) solitario m

patient /'peɪʃnt/ adj paziente • n paziente mf. **~ly** adv pazientemente

patio /'pætɪəʊ/ n terrazza f

patriot /'pætrɪət/ n patriota mf. **~ic** adj patriottico. **~ism** n patriottismo m

patrol /pə'trəʊl/ n pattuglia f • vt/i pattugliare. **~ car** n autopattuglia f

patron /'peɪtrən/ n patrono m; (of charity) benefattore, -trice mf; (of the arts) mecenate mf; (customer) cliente mf

patroniz|e /'pætrənaɪz/ vt frequentare abitualmente; fig trattare con condiscendenza. **~ing** adj condiscendente. **~ingly** adv co condiscendenza

pattern /'pætn/ n disegno m (stampato); (for knitting, sewing) modello m

paunch /pɔ:ntʃ/ n pancia f

pause /pɔ:z/ n pausa f • vi fare una pausa

pave /peɪv/ vt pavimentare; **~ the way** preparare la strada (**for** a). **~ment** n marciapiede m

paw /pɔ:/ n zampa f • vt [!] mettere zampe addosso a

pawn¹ /pɔ:n/ n (in chess) pedone m; pedina f

pawn² vt impegnare • n **in ~** in pegno. **~broker** n prestatore, -tri mf su pegno. **~shop** n monte m di pietà

pay /peɪ/ n paga f; **in the ~ of** al soldo di • v (pt/pp **paid**) • vt pagare; prestare (attention); fare (compliment, visit); **~ cash** pagare in contanti • v pagare; (be profitable) rendere; **it doesn't ~ to...** fig è fatica sprecata...; **~ for sth** pagare per qcsa. □ **~ back** vt ripagare. □ **~ in** versare. □ **~ off** vt saldare (debt) • fig dare dei frutti. □ **~ up** vi pagare

payable /'peɪəbl/ adj pagabile; **mak ~ to** intestare a

payment /'peɪmənt/ n pagamento m

PC n abbr (personal computer) PC m inv

pea /pi:/ n pisello m

peace /pi:s/ n pace f; **~ of mind** tranquillità f

peach /pi:tʃ/ n pesca f; (tree) pesco m

peacock /'pi:kɒk/ n pavone m

peak /pi:k/ n picco m; fig culmine m. **~ed 'cap** n berretto m a punta. **~ hours** npl ore fpl di punta

peal /pi:l/ n (of bells) scampanio m; **~ of laughter** fragore m di risate

'peanut n nocciolina f [americana]; **~s** [!] miseria f

pear /peə(r)/ n pera f; (tree) pero m

pearl /pɜ:l/ n perla f

peasant /'peznt/ n contadino, -a mf

pebble /'pebl/ n ciottolo m

peck /pek/ n beccata f; (kiss) bacetto m • vt beccare; (kiss) dare un bacetto a. **~ing order** n gerarchia f. □ **~ at** vt beccare

eculiar /pɪ'kju:lɪə(r)/ adj strano; (special) particolare; ~ **to** tipico di. ~**ity** n stranezza f; (feature) particolarità f inv

edal /'pedl/ n pedale m •vi pedalare. ~ **bin** n pattumiera f a pedale

edantic /pɪ'dæntɪk/ adj pedante

edestal /'pedɪstl/ n piedistallo m

edestrian /pɪ'destrɪən/ n pedone m •adj fig scadente. ~ **'crossing** n passaggio m pedonale. ~ **'precinct** n zona f pedonale

edigree /'pedɪgri:/ n pedigree m inv; (of person) lignaggio m •attrib (animal) di razza, con pedigree

eek /pi:k/ vi 🅘 sbirciare

eel /pi:l/ n buccia f •vt sbucciare •vi (nose) etc: spellarsi; (paint:) staccarsi

eep /pi:p/ n sbirciata f •vi sbirciare

eer¹ /pɪə(r)/ vi ~ **at** scrutare

eer² n nobile m; **his** ~**s** pl (in rank) i suoi pari mpl; (in age) i suoi coetanei mpl. ~**age** n nobiltà f

eg /peg/ n (hook) piolo m; (for tent) picchetto m; (for clothes) molletta f; **off the** ~ 🅘 prêt-à-porter

ejorative /pɪ'dʒɒrətɪv/ adj peggiorativo

elican /'pelɪkən/ n pellicano m

ellet /'pelɪt/ n pallottola f

elt /pelt/ vt bombardare •vi (🅘: run fast) catapultarsi; ~ **down** (rain:) venir giù a fiotti

elvis /'pelvɪs/ n (Anat) bacino m

en¹ /pen/ n (for animals) recinto m

en² n penna f; (ball-point) penna f a sfera

enal /'pi:nl/ adj penale. ~**ize** vt penalizzare

enalty /'penltɪ/ n sanzione f; (fine) multa f; (in football) ~ [**kick**] [calcio m di] rigore m; ~ **area** or **box** area f di rigore

enance /'penəns/ n penitenza f

ence /pens/ ▸**penny**

encil /'pensl/ n matita f. ~**-sharpener** n temperamatite m inv

endulum /'pendjʊləm/ n pendolo m

enetrat|e /'penɪtreɪt/ vt/i penetrare. ~**ing** adj acuto; (sound, stare) penetrante. ~**ion** n penetrazione f

enguin /'peŋgwɪn/ n pinguino m

penicillin /penɪ'sɪlɪn/ n penicillina f

peninsula /pɪ'nɪnsjʊlə/ n penisola f

penis /'pi:nɪs/ n pene m

pen: ~**knife** n temperino m. ~**-name** n pseudonimo m

penniless /'penɪlɪs/ adj senza un soldo

penny /'penɪ/ n (pl **pence**; single coins **pennies**) penny m; Am centesimo m; **spend a** ~ 🅘 andare in bagno

pension /'penʃn/ n pensione f. ~**er** n pensionato, -a mf

pensive /'pensɪv/ adj pensoso

Pentecost /'pentɪkɒst/ n Pentecoste f

pent-up /'pentʌp/ adj represso

penultimate /pɪ'nʌltɪmət/ adj penultimo

people /'pi:pl/ npl persone fpl, gente fsg; (citizens) popolo msg; **a lot of** ~ una marea di gente; **the** ~ la gente; **English** ~ gli inglesi; ~ **say** si dice; **for four** ~ per quattro •vt popolare

pepper /'pepə(r)/ n pepe m; (vegetable) peperone m •vt (season) pepare

pepper: ~**corn** n grano m di pepe. ~ **mill** macinapepe m inv. ~**mint** n menta f peperita; (sweet) caramella f alla menta. ~**pot** n pepiera f

per /pɜ:(r)/ prep per; ~ **annum** all'anno; ~ **cent** percento

perceive /pə'si:v/ vt percepire; (interpret) interpretare

percentage /pə'sentɪdʒ/ n percentuale f

perceptible /pə'septəbl/ adj percettibile; (difference) sensibile

percept|ion /pə'sepʃn/ n percezione f. ~**ive** adj perspicace

perch /pɜ:tʃ/ n pertica f •vi (bird:) appollaiarsi

percolator /'pɜ:kəleɪtə(r)/ n caffettiera f a filtro

percussion /pə'kʌʃn/ n percussione f. ~ **instrument** n strumento m a percussione

perfect¹ /'pɜ:fɪkt/ adj perfetto •n (Gram) passato m prossimo

perfect² /pə'fekt/ vt perfezionare. ~**ion** n perfezione f; **to** ~**ion** alla perfezione. ~**ionist** n perfezionista mf

P

perfectly /ˈpɜːfɪktlɪ/ adv perfettamente

perform /pəˈfɔːm/ vt compiere, fare; eseguire (operation, sonata); recitare (role); mettere in scena (play) •vi (Theat) recitare; (Techn) funzionare. **~ance** n esecuzione f; (at theatre, cinema) rappresentazione f; (Techn) rendimento m. **~er** n artista mf

perfume /ˈpɜːfjuːm/ n profumo m

perhaps /pəˈhæps/ adv forse

peril /ˈperɪl/ n pericolo m. **~ous** adj pericoloso

perimeter /pəˈrɪmɪtə(r)/ n perimetro m

period /ˈpɪərɪəd/ n periodo m; (menstruation) mestruazioni fpl; (Sch) ora f di lezione; (full stop) punto m fermo •attrib (costume) d'epoca; (furniture) in stile. **~ic** adj periodico. **~ical** n periodico m, rivista f

peripher|al /pəˈrɪfərəl/ adj periferico. **~y** n periferia f

perish /ˈperɪʃ/ vi (rot) deteriorarsi; (die) perire. **~able** adj deteriorabile

perjur|e /ˈpɜːdʒə(r)/ vt **~e oneself** spergiurare. **~y** n spergiuro m

perk /pɜːk/ n [!] vantaggio m

perm /pɜːm/ n permanente f •vt **~ sb's hair** fare la permanente a qno

permanent /ˈpɜːmənənt/ adj permanente; (job, address) stabile. **~ly** adv stabilmente

permissible /pəˈmɪsəbl/ adj ammissibile

permission /pəˈmɪʃn/ n permesso m

permit[1] /pəˈmɪt/ vt (pt/pp **-mitted**) permettere; **~ sb to do sth** permettere a qcno di fare qcsa

permit[2] /ˈpɜːmɪt/ n autorizzazione f

perpendicular /pɜːpənˈdɪkjʊlə(r)/ adj perpendicolare •n perpendicolare f

perpetual /pəˈpetjʊəl/ adj perenne. **~ly** adv perennemente

perpetuate /pəˈpetjʊeɪt/ vt perpetuare

perplex /pəˈpleks/ vt lasciare perplesso. **~ed** adj perplesso. **~ity** n perplessità f inv

persecut|e /ˈpɜːsɪkjuːt/ vt perseguitare. **~ion** n persecuzione f

perseverance /pɜːsɪˈvɪərəns/ n perseveranza f

persever|e /pɜːsɪˈvɪə(r)/ vi perseverare. **~ing** adj assiduo

Persian /ˈpɜːʃn/ adj persiano

persist /pəˈsɪst/ vi persistere; **~ in doing sth** persistere nel fare qcsa **~ence** n persistenza f. **~ent** adj persistente. **~ently** adv persistentemente

person /ˈpɜːsn/ n persona f; **in ~** di persona

personal /ˈpɜːsənl/ adj personale. **~ 'hygiene** n igiene f personale. **~ organizer** n (Comput) agenda f elettronica. **~ly** adv personalmente

personality /pɜːsəˈnælətɪ/ n personalità f inv; (on (TV)) personaggio m

personnel /pɜːsəˈnel/ n personale m

perspective /pəˈspektɪv/ n prospettiva f

persp|iration /pɜːspɪˈreɪʃn/ n sudore m. **~ire** vi sudare

persua|de /pəˈsweɪd/ vt persuadere. **~sion** n persuasione f; (belief) convinzione f

persuasive /pəˈsweɪsɪv/ adj persuasivo. **~ly** adv in modo persuasivo

pertinent /ˈpɜːtɪnənt/ adj pertinente (**to** a)

perturb /pəˈtɜːb/ vt perturbare

peruse /pəˈruːz/ vt leggere

pervers|e /pəˈvɜːs/ adj irragionevole **~ion** n perversione f

pervert /ˈpɜːvɜːt/ n pervertito, -a mf

pessimis|m /ˈpesɪmɪzm/ n pessimismo m. **~t** n pessimista mf. **~tic** adj pessimistico. **~tically** adv in modo pessimistico

pest /pest/ n piaga f; ([!]: person) peste f

pester /ˈpestə(r)/ vt molestare

pesticide /ˈpestɪsaɪd/ n pesticida m

pet /pet/ n animale m domestico; (favourite) cocco, -a mf •adj prediletto •v (pt/pp **petted**) •vt coccolare •vi (couple:) praticare il petting

petal /ˈpetl/ n petalo m

petition /pəˈtɪʃn/ n petizione f

pet 'name n vezzeggiativo m

etrol /'petrəl/ n benzina f
etroleum /pɪ'trəʊlɪəm/ n petrolio m
etrol: ~-pump n pompa f di benzina. **~ station** n stazione f di servizio. **~ tank** n serbatoio m della benzina
etticoat /'petɪkəʊt/ n sottoveste f
etty /'petɪ/ adj (**-ier, -iest**) insignificante; (mean) meschino. **~ cash** n cassa f per piccole spese
etulant /'petjʊlənt/ adj petulante
ew /pju:/ n banco m (di chiesa)
hantom /'fæntəm/ n fantasma m
harmaceutical /fɑ:mə'sju:tɪkl/ adj farmaceutico
harmac|ist /'fɑ:məsɪst/ n farmacista mf. **~y** n farmacia f
hase /feɪz/ n fase f • vt **phase in/out** introdurre/eliminare gradualmente
heasant /'feznt/ n fagiano m
henomen|al /fɪ'nɒmɪnl/ adj fenomenale; (incredible) incredibile. **~ally** adv incredibilmente. **~on** n (pl **-na**) fenomeno m
hilistine /'fɪlɪstaɪn/ n filisteo, -a mf
hilosoph|er /fɪ'lɒsəfə(r)/ n filosofo, -a mf. **~ical** adj filosofico. **~ically** adv con filosofia. **~y** n filosofia f
hlegm /flem/ n (Med) flemma f
hlegmatic /fleg'mætɪk/ adj flemmatico
hobia /'fəʊbɪə/ n fobia f
hone /fəʊn/ n telefono m; **be on the ~** avere il telefono; (be phoning) essere al telefono • vt telefonare a • vi telefonare. □ **~ back** vt/i richiamare. **~ book** n guida f del telefono. **~ box** n cabina f telefonica. **~ call** telefonata f. **~ card** n scheda f telefonica. **~-in** n trasmissione f con chiamate in diretta. **~ number** n numero m telefonico
honetic /fə'netɪk/ adj fonetico. **~s** n fonetica f
honey /'fəʊnɪ/ adj (**-ier, -iest**) fasullo
hosphorus /'fɒsfərəs/ n fosforo m
hoto /'fəʊtəʊ/ n foto f; **~ album** album m inv di fotografie. **~copier** n fotocopiatrice f. **~copy** n fotocopia f • vt fotocopiare

photogenic /fəʊtəʊ'dʒenɪk/ adj fotogenico
photograph /'fəʊtəgrɑ:f/ n fotografia f • vt fotografare
photograph|er /fə'tɒgrəfə(r)/ n fotografo, -a mf. **~ic** adj fotografico. **~y** n fotografia f
phrase /freɪz/ n espressione f • vt esprimere. **~-book** n libro m di fraseologia
physical /'fɪzɪkl/ adj fisico. **~ edu'cation** n educazione f fisica. **~ly** adv fisicamente
physician /fɪ'zɪʃn/ n medico m
physic|ist /'fɪzɪsɪst/ n fisico, -a mf. **~s** n fisica f
physiology /fɪzɪ'ɒlədʒɪ/ n fisiologia f
physio'therap|ist /fɪzɪəʊ-/ n fisioterapista mf. **~y** n fisioterapia f
physique /fɪ'zi:k/ n fisico m
pianist /'pɪənɪst/ n pianista mf
piano /pɪ'ænəʊ/ n piano m
pick[1] /pɪk/ n (tool) piccone m
pick[2] n scelta f; **take your ~** prendi quello che vuoi • vt (select) scegliere; cogliere (flowers); scassinare (lock); borseggiare (pockets); **~ and choose** fare il difficile; **~ one's nose** mettersi le dita nel naso; **~ a quarrel** attaccar briga; **~ holes in** [!] criticare; **~ at one's food** spilluzzicare. □ **~ on** vt ([!]: nag) assillare; **he always ~s on me** ce l'ha con me. □ **~ out** vt (identify) individuare. □ **~ up** vt sollevare; (off the ground, information) raccogliere; prendere in braccio (baby); (learn) imparare; prendersi (illness); (buy) comprare; captare (signal); (collect) andare/venire a prendere; prendere (passengers, habit); (police:) arrestare (criminal); [!] rimorchiare (girl); **~ oneself up** riprendersi • vi (improve) recuperare; (weather:) rimettersi
'pickaxe n piccone m
picket /'pɪkɪt/ n picchettista mf • vt picchettare. **~ line** n picchetto m
pickle /'pɪkl/ n **~s** pl sottaceti mpl; **in a ~** fig nei pasticci • vt mettere sottaceto
pick: ~pocket n borsaiolo m. **~-up** n (truck) furgone m; (on record-player) pickup m inv
picnic /'pɪknɪk/ n picnic m • vi (pt/pp

P

-nicked) fare un picnic

picture /ˈpɪktʃə(r)/ n (painting) quadro m; (photo) fotografia f; (drawing) disegno m; (film) film m inv; **put sb in the ~** fig mettere qcno al corrente; **the ~s** il cinema • vt (imagine) immaginare. **~sque** adj pittoresco

pie /paɪ/ n torta f

piece /piːs/ n pezzo m; (in game) pedina f; **a ~ of bread/paper** un pezzo di pane/carta; **a ~ of news/advice** una notizia/un consiglio; **take to ~s** smontare. **~meal** adv un po' alla volta. **~-work** n lavoro m a cottimo • **piece together** vt montare; fig ricostruire

pier /pɪə(r)/ n molo m; (pillar) pilastro m

pierc|e /pɪəs/ vt perforare; **~e a hole in sth** fare un buco in qcsa. **~ing** n [**body**] **~** piercing m inv • adj penetrante

pig /pɪg/ n maiale m

pigeon /ˈpɪdʒɪn/ n piccione m. **~-hole** n casella f

piggy /ˈpɪgɪ/ **~back** n **give sb a ~back** portare qcno sulle spalle. **~ bank** n salvadanaio m

pig'headed adj ▣ cocciuto

pigtail n (plait) treccina f

pile n (heap) pila f • vt **~ sth on to sth** appilare qcsa su qcsa. ▫ **~ up** vt accatastare • vi ammucchiarsi

piles /paɪlz/ npl emorroidi fpl

'pile-up n tamponamento m a catena

pilgrim /ˈpɪlgrɪm/ n pellegrino, -a mf. **~age** n pellegrinaggio m

pill /pɪl/ n pillola f

pillar /ˈpɪlə(r)/ n pilastro m. **~-box** n buca f delle lettere

pillow /ˈpɪləʊ/ n guanciale m. **~case** n federa f

pilot /ˈpaɪlət/ n pilota mf • vt pilotare. **~-light** n fiamma f di sicurezza

pimple /ˈpɪmpl/ n foruncolo m

pin /pɪn/ n spillo m; (Electr) spinotto m; (Med) chiodo m; **I have ~s and needles in my leg** ▣ mi formicola una gamba • vt (pt/pp **pinned**) appuntare (**to**/**on** su); (sewing) fissare con gli spilli; (hold down) immobilizzare; **~ sb down to a date** ottenere un appuntamento da qcno; **~ sth on sb** ▣ addossare a qcno la colpa di qcsa. ▫ **~ up** vt appuntare; (on wall) affiggere

pinafore /ˈpɪnəfɔː(r)/ n grembiule m. **~ dress** n scamiciato m

pincers /ˈpɪnsəz/ npl tenaglie fpl

pinch /pɪntʃ/ n pizzicotto m; (of salt) presa f; **at a ~** ▣ in caso di bisogno • vt pizzicare; (▣: steal) fregare • vi (shoe:) stringere

pine¹ /paɪn/ n (tree) pino m

pine² vi **she is pining for you** le manchi molto. ▫ **~ away** vi deperire

pineapple /ˈpaɪn-/ n ananas m inv

'ping-pong n ping-pong m

pink /pɪŋk/ adj rosa m

pinnacle /ˈpɪnəkl/ n guglia f

PIN number n codice m segreto

pin: ~point vt definire con precisione. **~stripe** adj gessato

pint /paɪnt/ n pinta f (= 0,571, Am: 0,47 l); **a ~** ▣ una birra media

pioneer /paɪəˈnɪə(r)/ n pioniere, -a mf • vt essere un pioniere di

pious /ˈpaɪəs/ adj pio

pip /pɪp/ n (seed) seme m

pipe /paɪp/ n tubo m; (for smoking) pipa f; **the ~s** (Mus) la cornamusa • vt far arrivare con tubature (water, gas etc) ▫ **~ down** vi ▣ abbassare la voce

pipe: ~-dream n illusione f. **~line** n conduttura f; **in the ~line** ▣ in cantiere

piping /ˈpaɪpɪŋ/ adj **~ hot** bollente

pirate /ˈpaɪrət/ n pirata m

Pisces /ˈpaɪsiːz/ n (Astr) Pesci mpl

piss /pɪs/ vi ▣ pisciare

pistol /ˈpɪstl/ n pistola f

piston /ˈpɪstn/ n (Techn) pistone m

pit /pɪt/ n fossa f; (mine) miniera f; (for orchestra) orchestra f • vt (pt/pp **pitted**) fig opporre (**against** a)

pitch¹ /pɪtʃ/ n (tone) tono m; (level) altezza f; (in sport) campo m; (fig: degree) grado m • vt montare (tent). ▫ **~ in** vi ▣ mettersi sotto

pitch² n **~-'black** adj nero come la pece. **~-'dark** adj buio pesto

'pitfall n fig trabocchetto m

pith /pɪθ/ n (of lemon, orange) interno m della buccia

ti|ful /'pɪtɪfl/ adj pietoso. **~less** adj spietato

ttance /'pɪtns/ n miseria f

'ty /'pɪtɪ/ n pietà f; **what a ~!** che peccato!; **take ~ on** avere compassione di • vt aver pietà di

ivot /'pɪvət/ n perno m; fig fulcro m • vi imperniarsi (**on** su)

izza /'pi:tsə/ n pizza f

lacard /'plækɑ:d/ n cartellone m

'acate /plə'keɪt/ vt placare

lace /pleɪs/ n posto m; ([!]: house) casa f; (in book) segno m; **feel out of ~** sentirsi fuori posto; **take ~** aver luogo; **all over the ~** dappertutto • vt collocare; (remember) identificare; **~ an order** fare un'ordinazione; **be ~d** (in race) piazzarsi. **~-mat** n sottopiatto m

lacid /'plæsɪd/ adj placido

lague /pleɪg/ n peste f

laice /pleɪs/ n inv platessa f

lain /pleɪn/ adj chiaro; (simple) semplice; (not pretty) scialbo; (not patterned) normale; (chocolate) fondente; **in ~ clothes** in borghese • adv (simply) semplicemente • n pianura f. **~ly** adv francamente; (simply) semplicemente; (obviously) chiaramente

laintiff /'pleɪntɪf/ n (Jur) parte f lesa

lait /plæt/ n treccia f • vt intrecciare

lan /plæn/ n progetto m, piano m • vt (pt/pp **planned**) progettare; (intend) prevedere

lane[1] /pleɪn/ n (tree) platano m

lane[2] n aeroplano m

lane[3] n (tool) pialla f • vt piallare

lanet /'plænɪt/ n pianeta m

lank /plæŋk/ n asse f

lanning /'plænɪŋ/ n pianificazione f. **~ permission** n licenza f edilizia

lant /plɑ:nt/ n pianta f; (machinery) impianto m; (factory) stabilimento m • vt piantare. **~ation** n piantagione f

laque /plɑ:k/ n placca f

lasma /'plæzmə/ n plasma m

laster /'plɑ:stə(r)/ n intonaco m; (Med) gesso m; (sticking ~) cerotto m; **~ of Paris** gesso m • vt intonacare (wall); (cover) ricoprire. **~ed** adj ⊠ sbronzo. **~er** n intonacatore m

plastic /'plæstɪk/ n plastica f • adj plastico

plastic surgery n chirurgia f plastica

plate /pleɪt/ n piatto m; (flat sheet) placca f; (gold and silverware) argenteria f; (in book) tavola f [fuori testo] • vt (cover with metal) placcare

platform /'plætfɔ:m/ n (stage) palco m; (Rail) marciapiede m; (Pol) piattaforma f; **~ 5** binario 5

platinum /'plætɪnəm/ n platino m • attrib di platino

platitude /'plætɪtju:d/ n luogo m comune

platonic /plə'tɒnɪk/ adj platonico

plausible /'plɔ:zəbl/ adj plausibile

play /pleɪ/ n gioco m; (Theat), (TV) rappresentazione f; (Radio) sceneggiato m radiofonico; **~ on words** gioco m di parole • vt giocare a; (act) recitare; suonare (instrument); giocare (card) • vi giocare; (Mus) suonare; **~ safe** non prendere rischi. □ **~ down** vt minimizzare. □ **~ up** vi [!] fare i capricci

play: ~er n giocatore, -trice mf. **~ful** adj scherzoso. **~ground** n (Sch) cortile m (per la ricreazione). **~group** n asilo m

playing: ~-card n carta f da gioco. **~-field** n campo m da gioco

play: ~-pen n box m inv. **~wright** /-raɪt/ n drammaturgo, -a mf

plc n abbr (public limited company) s.r.l.

plea /pli:/ n richiesta f; **make a ~ for** fare un appello a

plead /pli:d/ vi fare appello (**for** a); **~ guilty** dichiararsi colpevole; **~ with sb** implorare qcno

pleasant /'plez(ə)nt/ adj piacevole. **~ly** adv piacevolmente; (say, smile) cordialmente

pleas|e /pli:z/ adv per favore; **~e do** prego • vt far contento; **~e oneself** fare il proprio comodo; **~e yourself!** come vuoi!; pej fai come ti pare!. **~ed** adj lieto; **~ed with/about** contento di. **~ing** adj gradevole

pleasure /'pleʒə(r)/ n piacere m; **with ~** con piacere, volentieri

pleat /pli:t/ n piega f • vt pieghettare. **~ed 'skirt** n gonna f a pieghe

pledge /pledʒ/ n pegno m; (promise) promessa f •vt impegnarsi a; (pawn) impegnare

plentiful /'plentɪfl/ adj abbondante

plenty /'plentɪ/ n abbondanza f; ~ **of money** molti soldi; ~ **of people** molta gente; **I've got** ~ ne ho in abbondanza

pliable /'plaɪəbl/ adj flessibile

pliers /'plaɪəz/ npl pinze fpl

plight /plaɪt/ n condizione f

plimsolls /'plɪmsəlz/ npl scarpe fpl da ginnastica

plod /plɒd/ vi (pt/pp **plodded**) trascinarsi; (work hard) sgobbare

plot /plɒt/ n complotto m; (of novel) trama f; ~ **of land** appezzamento m [di terreno] •vt/i complottare

plough /plaʊ/ n aratro m; ~**man's lunch** piatto m di formaggi e sottaceti, servito con pane. •vt/i arare. □ ~ **back** vt (Comm) reinvestire

ploy /plɔɪ/ n 🅘 manovra f

pluck /plʌk/ n fegato m •vt strappare; depilare (eyebrows); spennare (bird); cogliere (flower). □ ~ **up** vt ~ **up courage** farsi coraggio

plucky /'plʌkɪ/ adj (**-ier, -iest**) coraggioso

plug /plʌg/ n tappo m; (Electr) spina f; (Auto) candela f; (🅘: advertisement) pubblicità f inv •vt (pt/pp **plugged**) tappare; (🅘: advertise) pubblicizzare con insistenza. □ ~ **in** vt (Electr) inserire la spina di

plum /plʌm/ n prugna f; (tree) prugno m

plumage /'plu:mɪdʒ/ n piumaggio m

plumb|er /'plʌmə(r)/ n idraulico m. ~**ing** n impianto m idraulico

plume /plu:m/ n piuma f

plump /plʌmp/ adj paffuto •**plump for** vt scegliere

plunge /plʌndʒ/ n tuffo m; **take the** ~ 🅘 buttarsi •vt tuffare; fig sprofondare •vi tuffarsi

plural /'plʊərəl/ adj plurale •n plurale m

plus /plʌs/ prep più •adj in più; **500** ~ più di 500 •n più m; (advantage) extra m inv

plush /'plʌʃ[ɪ]/ adj lussuoso

plutonium /plʊ'təʊnɪəm/ n plutonio m

ply /plaɪ/ vt (pt/pp **plied**) ~ **sb with drink** continuare a offrire da bere qcno. ~**wood** n compensato m

p.m. abbr (post meridiem) del pomeriggio

PM n abbr Prime Minister

pneumonia /nju:'məʊnɪə/ n polmonite f

P.O. abbr Post Office

poach /pəʊtʃ/ vt (Culin) bollire; cacciare di frodo (deer); pescare di frodo (salmon); ~**ed egg** uovo m in camicia. ~**er** n bracconiere m

pocket /'pɒkɪt/ n tasca f; **be out of** ~ rimetterci •vt intascare. ~**-book** n taccuino m; (wallet) portafoglio m. ~**-money** n denaro m per le piccole spese

pod /pɒd/ n baccello m

poem /'pəʊɪm/ n poesia f

poet /'pəʊɪt/ n poeta m. ~**ic** adj poetico

poetry /'pəʊɪtrɪ/ n poesia f

poignant /'pɔɪnjənt/ adj emozionante

point /pɔɪnt/ n punto m; (sharp end) punta f; (meaning, purpose) senso m; (Electr) presa f [di corrente]; ~**s** pl (Rail) scambio m; ~ **of view** punto m di vista; **good/bad** ~**s** aspetti m positivi/negativi; **what is the** ~**?** che scopo?; **the** ~ **is** il fatto è; **I don't see the** ~ non vedo il senso; **up to a** ~ fino a un certo punto; **be on the** ~ **of doing sth** essere sul punto di fare qcsa •vt puntare (**at** verso) •vi (with finger) puntare il dito; ~ **at/to** (person:) mostrare col dito; (indicator:) indicare. □ ~ **out** vt far notare (fact); ~ **sth out to sb** far notare qcsa a qcno

point-'blank adj a bruciapelo

point|ed /'pɔɪntɪd/ adj appuntito; (question) diretto. ~**ers** npl (advice) consigli mpl. ~**less** adj inutile

poise /pɔɪz/ n padronanza f. ~**d** adj in equilibrio; ~**d to** sul punto di

poison /'pɔɪzn/ n veleno m •vt avvelenare. ~**ous** adj velenoso

poke /pəʊk/ n [piccola] spinta f •vt spingere; (fire) attizzare; (put) ficcare; ~ **fun at** prendere in giro.

□ ~ **about** vi frugare

oker¹ /'pəʊkə(r)/ n attizzatoio m

oker² n (Cards) poker m

oky /'pəʊkɪ/ adj (**-ier, -iest**) angusto

oland /'pəʊlənd/ n Polonia f

olar /'pəʊlə(r)/ adj polare. ~ **'bear** n orso m bianco. ~**ize** vt polarizzare

ole¹ n palo m

ole² n (Geog, Electr) polo m

ole /pəʊl/ n polacco, -a mf

olice /pə'li:s/ npl polizia f • vt pattugliare (area)

olice: ~**man** n poliziotto m. ~ **station** n commissariato m. ~**woman** n donna f poliziotto

olicy¹ /'pɒlɪsɪ/ n politica f

olicy² n (insurance) polizza f

olio /'pəʊlɪəʊ/ n polio f

olish /'pɒlɪʃ/ n (shine) lucentezza f; (substance) lucido m; (for nails) smalto m; fig raffinatezza f • vt lucidare; fig smussare. □ ~ **off** vt [!] finire in fretta; spazzolare (food)

'olish /'pəʊlɪʃ/ adj polacco • n (language) polacco m

olished /'pɒlɪʃt/ adj (manner) raffinato; (performance) senza sbavature

olite /pə'laɪt/ adj cortese. ~**ly** adv cortesemente. ~**ness** n cortesia f

olitic|al /pə'lɪtɪkl/ adj politico. ~**ally** adv dal punto di vista politico. ~**ian** n politico m

olitics /'pɒlɪtɪks/ n politica f

oll /pəʊl/ n votazione f; (election) elezioni fpl; **opinion** ~ sondaggio m d'opinione; **go to the** ~**s** andare alle urne • vt ottenere (votes)

ollen /'pɒlən/ n polline m

ollut|e /pə'lu:t/ vt inquinare. ~**ion** n inquinamento m

polo /'pəʊləʊ/ n polo m. ~**-neck** n collo m alto. ~ **shirt** n dolcevita f

polythene /'pɒlɪθi:n/ n politene m. ~ **bag** n sacchetto m di plastica

polyun'saturated adj polinsaturo

pomp /pɒmp/ n pompa f

pompous /'pɒmpəs/ adj pomposo

pond /pɒnd/ n stagno m

ponder /'pɒndə(r)/ vt/i ponderare

pony /'pəʊnɪ/ n pony m. ~**-tail** n coda f di cavallo. ~**-trekking** n escursioni fpl col pony

poodle /'pu:dl/ n barboncino m

pool¹ /pu:l/ n (of water, blood) pozza f; [**swimming**] ~ piscina f

pool² n (common fund) cassa f comune; (in cards) piatto m; (game) biliardo m a buca. ~**s** npl ≈ totocalcio msg • vt mettere insieme

poor /pʊə(r)/ adj povero; (not good) scadente; **in** ~ **health** in cattiva salute • npl **the** ~ i poveri. ~**ly** adj **be** ~**ly** non stare bene • adv male

pop¹ /pɒp/ n botto m; (drink) bibita f gasata • v (pt/pp **popped**) • vt ([!]: put) mettere; (burst) far scoppiare • vi (burst) scoppiare. □ ~ **in/out** vi [!] fare un salto/un salto fuori

pop² n [!] musica f pop • attrib pop

'popcorn n popcorn m inv

pope /pəʊp/ n papa m

poplar /'pɒplə(r)/ n pioppo m

poppy /'pɒpɪ/ n papavero m

popular /'pɒpjʊlə(r)/ adj popolare; (belief) diffuso. ~**ity** n popolarità f inv

populat|e /'pɒpjʊleɪt/ vt popolare. ~**ion** n popolazione f

'pop-up n popup m inv

porcelain /'pɔ:səlɪn/ n porcellana f

porch /pɔ:tʃ/ n portico m; Am veranda f

porcupine /'pɔ:kjʊpaɪn/ n porcospino m

pore¹ /pɔ:(r)/ n poro m

pore² vi ~ **over** immergersi in

pork /pɔ:k/ n carne f di maiale

porn /pɔ:n/ n [!] porno m. ~**o** adj [!] porno inv

pornograph|ic /pɔ:nə'græfɪk/ adj pornografico. ~**y** n pornografia f

porpoise /'pɔ:pəs/ n focena f

porridge /'pɒrɪdʒ/ n farinata f di fiocchi d'avena

port¹ /pɔ:t/ n porto m

port² n (Naut: side) babordo m

port³ n (wine) porto m

portable /'pɔ:təbl/ adj portatile

porter /'pɔ:tə(r)/ n portiere m; (for luggage) facchino m

P

'porthole n oblò m inv

portion /'pɔ:ʃn/ n parte f; (of food) porzione f

portrait /'pɔ:trɪt/ n ritratto m

portray /pɔ:'treɪ/ vt ritrarre; (represent) descrivere; (actor:) impersonare. **~al** n ritratto m

Portug|al /'pɔ:tjʊgl/ n Portogallo m. **~uese** adj portoghese •n portoghese mf

pose /pəʊz/ n posa f •vt porre (problem, question) •vi (for painter) posare; **~ as** atteggiarsi a

posh /pɒʃ/ adj [!] lussuoso; (people) danaroso

position /pə'zɪʃn/ n posizione f; (job) posto m; (status) ceto m [sociale] •vt posizionare

positive /'pɒzɪtɪv/ adj positivo; (certain) sicuro; (progress) concreto •n positivo m. **~ly** adv positivamente; (decidedly) decisamente

possess /pə'zes/ vt possedere. **~ion** n possesso m; **~ions** pl beni mpl

possess|ive /pə'zesɪv/ adj possessivo. **~iveness** n carattere m possessivo. **~or** n possessore, -ditrice mf

possibility /pɒsə'bɪlətɪ/ n possibilità f inv

possib|le /'pɒsɪbl/ adj possibile. **~ly** adv possibilmente; **I couldn't ~ly accept** non mi è possibile accettare; **he can't ~ly be right** non è possibile che abbia ragione; **could you ~ly...?** potrebbe per favore...?

P

post¹ /pəʊst/ n (pole) palo m •vt affiggere (notice)

post² n (place of duty) posto m •vt appostare; (transfer) assegnare

post³ n (mail) posta f; **by ~** per posta •vt spedire; (put in letter-box) imbucare; (as opposed to fax) mandare per posta; **keep sb ~ed** tenere qcno al corrente

post- pref dopo

postage /'pəʊstɪdʒ/ n affrancatura f. **~ stamp** n francobollo m

postal /'pəʊstl/ adj postale. **~ order** n vaglia m postale

post: ~-box n cassetta f delle lettere. **~card** n cartolina f. **~code** n codice m postale

poster /'pəʊstə(r)/ n poster m inv; (advertising, election) cartellone m

posterity /pɒ'sterətɪ/ n posterità f

posthumous /'pɒstjʊməs/ adj postumo. **~ly** adv dopo la morte

post: ~man n postino m. **~mark** n timbro m postale

post-mortem /-'mɔ:təm/ n autopsia f

'post office n ufficio m postale

postpone /pəʊst'pəʊn/ vt rimandare. **~ment** n rinvio m

posture /'pɒstʃə(r)/ n posizione f

pot /pɒt/ n vaso m; (for tea) teiera f; (for coffee) caffettiera f; (for cooking) pentola f; **~s of money** [!] un sacco di soldi; **go to ~** [!] andare in malora

potato /pə'teɪtəʊ/ n (pl **-es**) patata f

poten|t /'pəʊtənt/ adj potente. **~tate** n potentato m

potential /pə'tenʃl/ adj potenziale •n potenziale m. **~ly** adv potenzialmente

pot: ~-hole n cavità f inv; (in road) buca f. **~-shot** n **take a ~-shot at** sparare a casaccio a

potter¹ /'pɒtə(r)/ vi **~ about** gingillarsi

potter² n vasaio, -a mf. **~y** n lavorazione f della ceramica; (articles) ceramiche fpl; (place) laboratorio m di ceramiche

potty /'pɒtɪ/ adj (**-ier, -iest**) [!] matto •n vasino m

pouch /paʊtʃ/ n marsupio m

poultry /'pəʊltrɪ/ n pollame m

pounce /paʊns/ vi balzare; **~ on** saltare su

pound¹ /paʊnd/ n libbra f (= 0,454 kg); (money) sterlina f

pound² vt battere •vi (heart:) battere forte; (run heavily) correre pesantemente

pour /pɔ:(r)/ vt versare •vi riversarsi; (with rain) piovere a dirotto. □ **~ out** vi riversarsi fuori •vt versare (drink); sfogare (troubles)

pout /paʊt/ vi fare il broncio •n broncio m

poverty /'pɒvətɪ/ n povertà f

powder /'paʊdə(r)/ n polvere f; (cosmetic) cipria f •vt polverizzare;

(face) incipriare. **~y** adj polveroso

ower /ˈpaʊə(r)/ n potere m; (Electr) corrente f [elettrica]; (Math) potenza f. **~ cut** n interruzione f di corrente. **~ed** adj **~ed by electricity** dotato di corrente [elettrica]. **~ful** adj potente. **~less** adj impotente. **~-station** n centrale f elettrica

R n abbr public relations

racticable /ˈpræktɪkəbl/ adj praticabile

ractical /ˈpræktɪkl/ adj pratico. **~ ˈjoke** n burla f. **~ly** adv praticamente

ractice /ˈpræktɪs/ n pratica f; (custom) usanza f; (habit) abitudine f; (exercise) esercizio m; (Sport) allenamento m; **in ~** (in reality) in pratica; **out of ~** fuori esercizio; **put into ~** mettere in pratica

ractise /ˈpræktɪs/ vt fare pratica in; (carry out) mettere in pratica; esercitare (profession) •vi esercitarsi; (doctor:) praticare. **~d** adj esperto

raise /preɪz/ n lode f •vt lodare. **~worthy** adj lodevole

ram /præm/ n carrozzella f

rank /præŋk/ n tiro m

rawn /prɔːn/ n gambero m. **~ ˈcocktail** n cocktail m inv di gamberetti

ray /preɪ/ vi pregare. **~er** n preghiera f

reach /priːtʃ/ vt/i predicare. **~er** n predicatore, -trice mf

re-arˈrange /priː-/ vt predisporre

recarious /prɪˈkeərɪəs/ adj precario. **~ly** adv in modo precario

recaution /prɪˈkɔːʃn/ n precauzione f; **as a ~** per precauzione. **~ary** adj preventivo

recede /prɪˈsiːd/ vt precedere

receden|ce /ˈpresɪdəns/ n precedenza f. **~t** n precedente m

receding /prɪˈsiːdɪŋ/ adj precedente

recinct /ˈpriːsɪŋkt/ n (traffic-free) zona f pedonale; (Am: district) circoscrizione f

precious /ˈpreʃəs/ adj prezioso; (style) ricercato •adv [!] **~ little** ben poco

precipice /ˈpresɪpɪs/ n precipizio m

precipitate /prɪˈsɪpɪteɪt/ vt precipitare

precis|e /prɪˈsaɪs/ adj preciso. **~ely** adv precisamente. **~ion** n precisione f

precursor /priːˈkɜːsə(r)/ n precursore m

predator /ˈpredətə(r)/ n predatore, -trice mf. **~y** adj rapace

predecessor /ˈpriːdɪsesə(r)/ n predecessore m

predicament /prɪˈdɪkəmənt/ n situazione f difficile

predict /prɪˈdɪkt/ vt predire. **~able** adj prevedibile. **~ion** n previsione f

preen /priːn/ vt lisciarsi; **~ oneself** fig farsi bello

pre|fab /ˈpriːfæb/ n [!] casa f prefabbricata. **~ˈfabricated** adj prefabbricato

preface /ˈprefɪs/ n prefazione f

prefect /ˈpriːfekt/ n (Sch) studente, -tessa mf della scuola superiore con responsabilità disciplinari, ecc

prefer /prɪˈfɜː(r)/ vt (pt/pp **preferred**) preferire

prefera|ble /ˈprefərəbl/ adj preferibile (**to** a). **~bly** adv preferibilmente

preferen|ce /ˈprefərəns/ n preferenza f. **~tial** adj preferenziale

pregnan|cy /ˈpregnənsɪ/ n gravidanza f. **~t** adj incinta

prehiˈstoric /priː-/ adj preistorico

prejudice /ˈpredʒʊdɪs/ n pregiudizio m •vt influenzare (**against** contro); (harm) danneggiare. **~d** adj prevenuto

preliminary /prɪˈlɪmɪnərɪ/ adj preliminare

prelude /ˈpreljuːd/ n preludio m

premature /ˈprematjʊə(r)/ adj prematuro

preˈmeditated /priː-/ adj premeditato

premier /ˈpremɪə(r)/ adj primario •n (Pol) primo ministro m, premier m inv

première /ˈpremɪeə(r)/ n prima f

premises /ˈpremɪsɪz/ npl locali mpl; **on the ~** sul posto

premium /ˈpriːmɪəm/ n premio m; **be at a ~** essere una cosa rara

premonition /preməˈnɪʃn/ n presentimento m

preoccupied /pri:'ɒkjʊpaɪd/ adj preoccupato

preparation /prepə'reɪʃn/ n preparazione f. **~s** preparativi mpl

preparatory /prɪ'pærətrɪ/ adj preparatorio •adv **~ to** per

prepare /prɪ'peə(r)/ vt preparare •vi prepararsi (**for** per); **~d to** disposto a

preposition /prepə'zɪʃn/ n preposizione f

preposterous /prɪ'pɒstərəs/ adj assurdo

prerequisite /pri:'rekwɪzɪt/ n condizione f sine qua non

prescribe /prɪ'skraɪb/ vt prescrivere

prescription /prɪ'skrɪpʃn/ n (Med) ricetta f

presence /'prezns/ n presenza f; **~ of mind** presenza f di spirito

present[1] /'preznt/ adj presente •n presente m; **at ~** attualmente

present[2] n (gift) regalo m; **give sb sth as a ~** regalare qcsa a qcno

present[3] /prɪ'zent/ vt presentare; **~ sb with an award** consegnare un premio a qcno. **~able** adj **be ~able** essere presentabile

presentation /prezn'teɪʃn/ n presentazione f

P

presently /'prezntlɪ/ adv fra poco; (Am: now) attualmente

preservation /prezə'veɪʃn/ n conservazione f

preservative /prɪ'zɜ:vətɪv/ n conservante m

preserve /prɪ'zɜ:v/ vt preservare; (maintain, (Culin) conservare •n (in hunting & fig) riserva f; (jam) marmellata f

preside /prɪ'zaɪd/ vi presiedere (**over** a)

presidency /'prezɪdənsɪ/ n presidenza f

president /'prezɪdənt/ n presidente m. **~ial** adj presidenziale

press /pres/ n (machine) pressa f; (newspapers) stampa f •vt premere; pressare (flower); (iron) stirare; (squeeze) stringere •vi (urge) incalzare. □ **~ for** vi fare pressione per; **be ~ed for** essere a corto di. □ **~ on** vi andare avanti

press: ~ conference n conferenza f stampa. **~ cutting** n ritaglio m di giornale. **~ing** adj urgente. **~-up** n flessione f

pressure /'preʃə(r)/ n pressione f •vt = **pressurize. ~-cooker** n pentola a pressione. **~ group** n gruppo m di pressione

pressurize /'preʃəraɪz/ vt far pressione su. **~d** adj pressurizzato

prestig|e /pre'sti:ʒ/ n prestigio m. **~ious** adj prestigioso

presumably /prɪ'zju:məblɪ/ adv presumibilmente

presume /prɪ'zju:m/ vt presumere; **~ to do sth** permettersi di fare qcsa

presup'pose /pri:-/ vt presupporre

pretence /prɪ'tens/ n finzione f; (pretext) pretesto m; **it's all ~** è tutta una scena

pretend /prɪ'tend/ vt fingere; (claim) pretendere •vi fare finta

pretentious /prɪ'tenʃəs/ adj pretenzioso

pretext /'pri:tekst/ n pretesto m

pretty /'prɪtɪ/ adj (**-ier, -iest**) carino •adv (🅸: fairly) abbastanza

prevail /prɪ'veɪl/ vi prevalere; **~ on sb to do sth** convincere qcno a fare qcsa. **~ing** adj prevalente

prevalen|ce /'prevələns/ n diffusione f. **~t** adj diffuso

prevent /prɪ'vent/ vt impedire; **~ sb [from] doing sth** impedire a qcno di fare qcsa. **~ion** n prevenzione f. **~ive** adj preventivo

preview /'pri:vju:/ n anteprima f

previous /'pri:vɪəs/ adj precedente. **~ly** adv precedentemente

prey /preɪ/ n preda f; **bird of ~** uccello m rapace •vi **~ on** far preda di; **~ on sb's mind** attanagliare qcno

price /praɪs/ n prezzo m •vt (Comm) fissare il prezzo di. **~less** adj inestimabile; (🅸: amusing) spassosissimo. **~y** adj 🅸 caro

prick /prɪk/ n puntura f •vt pungere. □ **~ up** vt **~ up one's ears** rizzare le orecchie

prickl|e /'prɪkl/ n spina f; (sensation) formicolio m. **~y** adj pungente; (person) irritabile

pride /praɪd/ n orgoglio m • vt **~ oneself on** vantarsi di

priest /pri:st/ n prete m

prim /prɪm/ adj (**primmer, primmest**) perbenino

primarily /'praɪmərɪlɪ/ adv in primo luogo

primary /'praɪmərɪ/ adj primario; (chief) principale. **~ school** n scuola f elementare

prime[1] /praɪm/ adj principale, primo; (first-rate) eccellente • n **be in one's ~** essere nel fiore degli anni

prime[2] vt preparare (surface, person)

Prime Minister n Primo m Ministro

primeval /praɪ'mi:vl/ adj primitivo

primitive /'prɪmɪtɪv/ adj primitivo

primrose /'prɪmrəʊz/ n primula f

prince /prɪns/ n principe m

princess /prɪn'ses/ n principessa f

principal /'prɪnsəpl/ adj principale • n (Sch) preside m

principally /'prɪnsəplɪ/ adv principalmente

principle /'prɪnsəpl/ n principio m; **in ~** in teoria; **on ~** per principio

print /prɪnt/ n (mark, trace) impronta f; (Phot) copia f; (picture) stampa f; **in ~** (printed out) stampato; (book) in commercio; **out of ~** esaurito • vt stampare; (write in capitals) scrivere in stampatello. **~ed matter** n stampe fpl

print|er /'prɪntə(r)/ n stampante f; (Typ) tipografo, -a mf. **~er port** n (Comput) porta f per la stampante. **~ing** n tipografia f

printout n (Comput) stampa f

prior /'praɪə(r)/ adj precedente. **~ to** prep prima di

priority /praɪ'ɒrətɪ/ n precedenza f; (matter) priorità f inv

prise /praɪz/ vt **~ open/up** forzare

prison /'prɪz(ə)n/ n prigione f. **~er** n prigioniero, -a mf

privacy /'prɪvəsɪ/ n privacy f inv

private /'praɪvət/ adj privato; (car, secretary, letter) personale • n (Mil) soldato m semplice; **in ~** in privato. **~ly** adv (funded, educated etc) privatamente; (in secret) in segreto; (confidentially) in privato; (inwardly) interiormente

privation /praɪ'veɪʃn/ n privazione f; **~s** npl stenti mpl

privilege /'prɪvəlɪdʒ/ n privilegio m. **~d** adj privilegiato

prize /praɪz/ n premio m • adj (idiot etc) perfetto • vt apprezzare. **~-giving** n premiazione f. **~-winner** n vincitore, -trice mf. **~-winning** adj vincente

pro /prəʊ/ n (!: professional) professionista mf; **the ~s and cons** il pro e il contro

probability /prɒbə'bɪlətɪ/ n probabilità f inv

probabl|e /'prɒbəbl/ adj probabile. **~y** adv probabilmente

probation /prə'beɪʃn/ n prova f; (Jur) libertà f vigilata. **~ary** adj in prova; **~ary period** periodo m di prova

probe /prəʊb/ n sonda f; (fig: investigation) indagine f • vt sondare; (investigate) esaminare a fondo

problem /'prɒbləm/ n problema m • adj difficile. **~atic** adj problematico

procedure /prə'si:dʒə(r)/ n procedimento m

proceed /prə'si:d/ vi procedere • vt **~ to do sth** proseguire facendo qcsa

proceedings /prə'si:dɪŋz/ npl (report) atti mpl; (Jur) azione fsg legale

proceeds /'prəʊsi:dz/ npl ricavato msg

process /'prəʊses/ n processo m; (procedure) procedimento m; **in the ~** nel far ciò • vt trattare; (Admin) occuparsi di; (Phot) sviluppare

procession /prə'seʃn/ n processione f

processor /'prəʊsesə(r)/ n (Comput) processore m; (for food) robot m inv da cucina

proclaim /prə'kleɪm/ vt proclamare

procure /prə'kjʊə(r)/ vt ottenere

prod /prɒd/ n colpetto m • vt (pt/pp **prodded**) punzecchiare; fig incitare

produce[1] /'prɒdju:s/ n prodotti mpl; **~ of Italy** prodotto in Italia

produce[2] /prə'dju:s/ vt produrre; (bring out) tirar fuori; (cause) causare; (!: give birth to) fare. **~r** n produttore m

product /'prɒdʌkt/ n prodotto m.

~ion n produzione f; (Theat) spettacolo m

productiv|e /prəˈdʌktɪv/ adj produttivo. **~ity** n produttività f

profession /prəˈfeʃn/ n professione f. **~al** adj professionale; (not amateur) professionista; (piece of work) da professionista; (man) di professione •n professionista mf. **~ally** adv professionalmente

professor /prəˈfesə(r)/ n professore m [universitario]

proficien|cy /prəˈfɪʃnsɪ/ n competenza f. **~t** adj **be ~t in** essere competente in

profile /ˈprəʊfaɪl/ n profilo m

profit /ˈprɒfɪt/ n profitto m •vi **~ from** trarre profitto da. **~able** adj proficuo. **~ably** adv in modo proficuo

profound /prəˈfaʊnd/ adj profondo. **~ly** adv profondamente

profus|e /prəˈfju:s/ adj **~e apologies/flowers** una profusione di scuse/fiori. **~ion** n profusione f; **in ~ion** in abbondanza

prognosis /prɒgˈnəʊsɪs/ n (pl **-oses**) prognosi f inv

program /ˈprəʊgræm/ n programma m •vt (pt/pp **programmed**) programmare

programme /ˈprəʊgræm/ n Br programma m. **~r** n (Comput) programmatore, -trice mf

progress[1] /ˈprəʊgres/ n progresso m; **in ~** in corso; **make ~** fig fare progressi

progress[2] /prəˈgres/ vi progredire; fig fare progressi

progressive /prəˈgresɪv/ adj progressivo; (reforming) progressista. **~ly** adv progressivamente

prohibit /prəˈhɪbɪt/ vt proibire. **~ive** adj proibitivo

project[1] /ˈprɒdʒekt/ n progetto m; (Sch) ricerca f

project[2] /prəˈdʒekt/ vt proiettare (film, image) •vi (jut out) sporgere

projector /prəˈdʒektə(r)/ n proiettore m

prolific /prəˈlɪfɪk/ adj prolifico

prologue /ˈprəʊlɒg/ n prologo m

prolong /prəˈlɒŋ/ vt prolungare

promenade /prɒməˈnɑ:d/ n lungomare m inv

prominent /ˈprɒmɪnənt/ adj prominente; (conspicuous) di rilievo

promiscu|ity /prɒmɪˈskju:ətɪ/ n promiscuità f. **~ous** adj promiscuo

promis|e /ˈprɒmɪs/ n promessa f •vt promettere; **~e sb that** prometter a qcno che; **I ~ed to** l'ho promesso **~ing** adj promettente

promot|e /prəˈməʊt/ vt promuovere **be ~ed** (Sport) essere promosso. **~ion** n promozione f

prompt /prɒmpt/ adj immediato; (punctual) puntuale •adv in punto •vt incitare (**to** a); (Theat) suggerire a •vi suggerire. **~er** n suggeritore, -trice mf. **~ly** adv puntualmente

Proms /prɒmz/ npl rassegna f di concerti estivi di musica classica presso l'Albert Hall a Londra

prone /prəʊn/ adj **be ~ to do sth** essere incline a fare qcsa

pronoun /ˈprəʊnaʊn/ n pronome m

pronounce /prəˈnaʊns/ vt pronunciare; (declare) dichiarare. **~d** adj (noticeable) pronunciato

pronunciation /prənʌnsɪˈeɪʃn/ n pronuncia f

proof /pru:f/ n prova f; (Typ) bozza f, prova f •adj **~ against** a prova di

propaganda /prɒpəˈgændə/ n propaganda f

propel /prəˈpel/ vt (pt/pp **propelled**) spingere. **~ler** n elica f

proper /ˈprɒpə(r)/ adj corretto; (suitable) adatto; (!: real) vero [e proprio]. **~ly** adv correttamente. **~ 'name, ~ 'noun** n nome m proprio

property /ˈprɒpətɪ/ n proprietà f inv. **~ developer** n agente m immobiliare. **~ market** n mercato m immobiliare

prophecy /ˈprɒfəsɪ/ n profezia f

prophesy /ˈprɒfɪsaɪ/ vt (pt/pp **-ied**) profetizzare

prophet /ˈprɒfɪt/ n profeta m. **~ic** adj profetico

proportion /prəˈpɔ:ʃn/ n proporzione f; (share) parte f; **~s** pl (dimensions) proporzioni fpl. **~al** adj proporzionale. **~ally** adv in proporzione

proposal /prəˈpəʊzl/ n proposta f; (of

marriage) proposta f di matrimonio

propose /prəˈpəʊz/ vt proporre; (intend) proporsi •vi fare una proposta di matrimonio

proposition /prɒpəˈzɪʃn/ n proposta f; (!: task) impresa f

proprietor /prəˈpraɪətə(r)/ n proprietario, -a mf

prose /prəʊz/ n prosa f

prosecut|e /ˈprɒsɪkjuːt/ vt intentare azione contro. **~ion** n azione f giudiziaria; **the ~ion** l'accusa f. **~or** n **[Public] P~or** il Pubblico Ministero m

prospect¹ /ˈprɒspekt/ n (expectation) prospettiva f

prospect² /prəˈspekt/ vi **~ for** cercare

prospect|ive /prəˈspektɪv/ adj (future) futuro; (possible) potenziale. **~or** n cercatore m

prospectus /prəˈspektəs/ n prospetto m

prosper /ˈprɒspə(r)/ vi prosperare; (person:) stare bene finanziariamente. **~ity** n prosperità f

prosperous /ˈprɒspərəs/ adj prospero

prostitut|e /ˈprɒstɪtjuːt/ n prostituta f. **~ion** n prostituzione f

prostrate /ˈprɒstreɪt/ adj prostrato; **~ with grief** fig prostrato dal dolore

protagonist /prəʊˈtægənɪst/ n protagonista mf

protect /prəˈtekt/ vt proteggere (**from** da). **~ion** n protezione f. **~ive** adj protettivo. **~or** n protettore, -trice mf

protein /ˈprəʊtiːn/ n proteina f

protest¹ /ˈprəʊtest/ n protesta f

protest² /prəˈtest/ vt/i protestare

Protestant /ˈprɒtɪstənt/ adj protestante •n protestante mf

protester /prəˈtestə(r)/ n contestatore, -trice mf

protocol /ˈprəʊtəkɒl/ n protocollo m

protrude /prəˈtruːd/ vi sporgere

proud /praʊd/ adj fiero (**of** di). **~ly** adv fieramente

prove /pruːv/ vt provare •vi **~ to be a lie** rivelarsi una bugia. **~n** adj dimostrato

proverb /ˈprɒvɜːb/ n proverbio m. **~ial** adj proverbiale

provide /prəˈvaɪd/ vt fornire; **~ sb with sth** fornire qcsa a qcno •vi **~ for** (law:) prevedere

provided /prəˈvaɪdɪd/ conj **~ [that]** purché

providen|ce /ˈprɒvɪdəns/ n provvidenza f. **~tial** adj provvidenziale

providing /prəˈvaɪdɪŋ/ conj = **provided**

provinc|e /ˈprɒvɪns/ n provincia f; fig campo m. **~ial** adj provinciale

provision /prəˈvɪʒn/ n (of food, water) approvvigionamento m (**of** di); (of law) disposizione f; **~s** pl provviste fpl. **~al** adj provvisorio

provocat|ion /prɒvəˈkeɪʃn/ n provocazione f. **~ive** adj provocatorio; (sexually) provocante. **~ively** adv in modo provocatorio

provoke /prəˈvəʊk/ vt provocare

prow /praʊ/ n prua f

prowess /ˈpraʊɪs/ n abilità f inv

prowl /praʊl/ vi aggirarsi •n **on the ~** in cerca di preda. **~er** n tipo m sospetto

proximity /prɒkˈsɪmətɪ/ n prossimità f

proxy /ˈprɒksɪ/ n procura f; (person) persona f che agisce per procura

prude /pruːd/ n **be a ~** essere eccessivamente pudico

pruden|ce /ˈpruːdəns/ n prudenza f. **~t** adj prudente; (wise) oculatezza f

prudish /ˈpruːdɪʃ/ adj eccessivamente pudico

prune¹ /pruːn/ n prugna f secca

prune² vt potare

pry /praɪ/ vi (pt/pp **pried**) ficcare il naso

psalm /sɑːm/ n salmo m

psychiatric /saɪkɪˈætrɪk/ adj psichiatrico

psychiatr|ist /saɪˈkaɪətrɪst/ n psichiatra mf. **~y** n psichiatria f

psychic /ˈsaɪkɪk/ adj psichico; **I'm not ~** non sono un indovino

psychological /saɪkə'lɒdʒɪkl/ adj psicologico

psycholog|ist /saɪ'kɒlədʒɪst/ n psicologo, -a mf. **~y** n psicologia f

pub /pʌb/ n [!] pub m inv

puberty /'pju:bətɪ/ n pubertà f

public /'pʌblɪk/ adj pubblico • n **the ~** il pubblico; **in ~** in pubblico. **~ly** adv pubblicamente

publican /'pʌblɪkən/ n gestore, -trice mf/proprietario, -a mf di un pub

publication /pʌblɪ'keɪʃn/ n pubblicazione f

public: ~ 'holiday n festa f nazionale. **~ 'house** n pub m

publicity /pʌb'lɪsətɪ/ n pubblicità f

publicize /'pʌblɪsaɪz/ vt pubblicizzare

public: ~ relations pubbliche relazioni fpl. **~ 'school** n scuola f privata; Am scuola f pubblica

publish /'pʌblɪʃ/ vt pubblicare. **~er** n editore m; (firm) editore m, casa f editrice. **~ing** n editoria f

pudding /'pʊdɪŋ/ n dolce m cotto al vapore; (course) dolce m

puddle /'pʌdl/ n pozzanghera f

puff /pʌf/ n (of wind) soffio m; (of smoke) tirata f; (for powder) piumino m • vt sbuffare. **puff at** vt tirare boccate da (pipe). □ **~ out** vt lasciare senza fiato (person); spegnere (candle). **~ed** adj (out of breath) senza fiato. **~ pastry** n pasta f sfoglia

puffy /'pʌfɪ/ adj gonfio

pull /pʊl/ n trazione f; (fig: attraction) attrazione f; ([!]: influence) influenza f • vt tirare; estrarre (tooth); stirarsi (muscle); **~ faces** far boccace; **~ oneself together** cercare di controllarsi; **~ one's weight** mettercela tutta; **~ sb's leg** [!] prendere in giro qcno. □ **~ down** vt (demolish) demolire. □ **~ in** vi (Auto) accostare. □ **~ off** vt togliere; [!] azzeccare. □ **~ out** vt tirar fuori • vi (Auto) spostarsi; (of competition) ritirarsi. □ **~ through** vi (recover) farcela. □ **~ up** vt sradicare (plant); (reprimand) rimproverare • vi (Auto) fermarsi

pullover /'pʊləʊvə(r)/ n pullover m

pulp /pʌlp/ n poltiglia f; (of fruit) polpa f; (for paper) pasta f

pulpit /'pʊlpɪt/ n pulpito m

pulse /pʌls/ n polso m

pummel /'pʌml/ vt (pt/pp **pummelled**) prendere a pugni

pump /pʌmp/ n pompa f • vt pompare; [!] cercare di estrorcere da. □ **~ up** vt (inflate) gonfiare

pumpkin /'pʌmpkɪn/ n zucca f

pun /pʌn/ n gioco m di parole

punch¹ /pʌntʃ/ n pugno m; (device) pinza f per forare • vt dare un pugno a; forare (ticket); perforare (hole)

punch² n (drink) ponce m inv

punctual /'pʌŋktjʊəl/ adj puntuale. **~ity** n puntualità f. **~ly** adv puntualmente

punctuat|e /'pʌŋktjʊeɪt/ vt punteggiare. **~ion** n punteggiatura f. **~ion mark** n segno m di interpunzione

puncture /'pʌŋktʃə(r)/ n foro m; (tyre) foratura f • vt forare

punish /'pʌnɪʃ/ vt punire. **~able** adj punibile. **~ment** n punizione f

punk /pʌŋk/ n punk m inv

punt /pʌnt/ n (boat) barchino m

punter /'pʌntə(r)/ n (gambler) scommettitore, -trice mf; (client) consumatore, -trice mf

puny /'pju:nɪ/ adj (**-ier, -iest**) striminzito

pup /pʌp/ n = **puppy**

pupil /'pju:pl/ n alluno, -a mf; (of eye) pupilla f

puppet /'pʌpɪt/ n marionetta f; (glove ~, fig) burattino m

puppy /'pʌpɪ/ n cucciolo m

purchase /'pɜ:tʃəs/ n acquisto m; (leverage) presa f • vt acquistare. **~r** n acquirente mf

pure /pjʊə(r)/ adj puro. **~ly** adv puramente

purgatory /'pɜ:gətrɪ/ n purgatorio m

purge /pɜ:dʒ/ (Pol) n epurazione f • vt epurare

puri|fication /pjʊərɪfɪ'keɪʃn/ n purificazione f. **~fy** vt (pt/pp **-ied**) purificare

puritan /'pjʊərɪtən/ n puritano, -a mf. **~ical** adj puritano

p

purity /'pjʊərɪtɪ/ n purità f
purple /'pɜ:pl/ adj viola
purpose /'pɜ:pəs/ n scopo m; (determination) fermezza f; **on ~** apposta. **~-built** adj costruito ad hoc. **~ful** adj deciso. **~fully** adv con decisione. **~ly** adv apposta
purr /pɜ:(r)/ vi (cat:) fare le fusa
purse /pɜ:s/ n borsellino m; (Am: handbag) borsa f •vt increspare (lips)
pursue /pə'sju:/ vt inseguire; fig proseguire. **~r** n inseguitore, -trice mf
pursuit /pə'sju:t/ n inseguimento m; (fig: of happiness) ricerca f; (pastime) attività f inv; **in ~** all'inseguimento
pus /pʌs/ n pus m
push /pʊʃ/ n spinta f; (fig: effort) sforzo m; (drive) iniziativa f; **at a ~** in caso di bisogno; **get the ~** [!] essere licenziato •vt spingere; premere (button); (pressurize) far pressione su; **be ~ed for time** [!] non avere tempo •vi spingere. □ **~ aside** vt scostare. □ **~ back** vt respingere. □ **~ off** vt togliere •vi ([!]: leave) levarsi dai piedi. □ **~ on** vi (continue) continuare. □ **~ up** vt alzare (price)
push: ~-chair n passeggino m. **~-up** n flessione f
pushy /'pʊʃɪ/ adj [!] troppo intraprendente
put /pʊt/ vt (pt/pp **put**, pres p **putting**) mettere; **~ the cost of sth at** valutare il costo di qcsa •vi **~ to sea** salpare. □ **~ aside** vt mettere da parte. □ **~ away** vt mettere via. □ **~ back** vt rimettere; mettere indietro (clock). □ **~ by** mettere da parte. □ **~ down** vt mettere giù; (suppress) reprimere; (kill) sopprimere; (write) annotare; **~ one's foot down** [!] essere fermo; (Auto) dare un'accelerata; **~ down to** (attribute) attribuire. □ **~ forward** vt avanzare; mettere avanti (clock). □ **~ in** vt (insert) introdurre; (submit) presentare •vi **~ in for** far domanda di. □ **~ off** vt spegnere (light); (postpone) rimandare; **~ sb off** tenere a bada qcno; (deter) smontare qcno; (disconcert) distrarre qcno; **~ sb off sth** (disgust) disgustare qcno di qcsa. □ **~ on** vt mettersi (clothes); mettere (brake); (Culin) mettere su; accendere (light); mettere in scena (play); prendere (accent); **~ on weight** mettere su qualche chilo. □ **~ out** vt spegnere (fire, light); tendere (hand); (inconvenience) creare degli inconvenienti a. □ **~ through** vt far passare; (Teleph) **I'll ~ you through to him** glielo passo. □ **~ up** vt alzare; erigere (building); montare (tent); aprire (umbrella); affiggere (notice); aumentare (price); ospitare (guest); **~ sb up to sth** mettere qcsa in testa a qcno •vi (at hotel) stare; **~ up with** sopportare •adj **stay ~!** rimani lì!
puzzl|e /'pʌzl/ n enigma m; (jigsaw) puzzle m inv •vt lasciare perplesso •vi **~e over** scervellarsi su. **~ing** adj inspiegabile
pygmy /'pɪgmɪ/ n pigmeo, -a mf
pyjamas /pə'dʒɑ:məz/ npl pigiama msg
pylon /'paɪlən/ n pilone m
pyramid /'pɪrəmɪd/ n piramide f
python /'paɪθn/ n pitone m

p q

Qq

quack¹ /kwæk/ n qua qua m inv •vi fare qua qua
quack² n (doctor) ciarlatano m
quadrangle /'kwɒdræŋgl/ n quadrangolo m; (court) cortile m quadrangolare
quadruped /'kwɒdrʊped/ n quadrupede m
quadruple /'kwɒdrʊpl/ adj quadruplo •vt quadruplicare •vi quadruplicarsi. **~ts** npl quattro gemelli mpl

quagmire /'kwɒgmaɪə(r)/ n pantano m

quaint /kweɪnt/ adj pittoresco; (odd) bizzarro

quake /kweɪk/ n [!] terremoto m •vi tremare

qualif|ication /kwɒlɪfɪ'keɪʃn/ n qualifica f. **~ied** adj qualificato; (limited) con riserva

qualify /'kwɒlɪfaɪ/ v (pt/pp **-ied**) •vt (course:) dare la qualifica a (**as** di); (entitle) dare diritto a; (limit) precisare •vi ottenere la qualifica; (Sport) qualificarsi

quality /'kwɒlətɪ/ n qualità f inv

qualm /kwɑ:m/ n scrupolo m

quandary /'kwɒndərɪ/ n dilemma m

quantity /'kwɒntətɪ/ n quantità f inv; **in ~** in grande quantità

quarantine /'kwɒrənti:n/ n quarantena f

quarrel /'kwɒrəl/ n lite f •vi (pt/pp **quarrelled**) litigare. **~-some** adj litigioso

quarry[1] /'kwɒrɪ/ n (prey) preda f

quarry[2] n cava f

quart /kwɔ:t/ n 1.14 litro

quarter /'kwɔ:tə(r)/ n quarto m; (of year) trimestre m; Am 25 centesimi mpl; **~s** pl (Mil) quartiere msg; **at [a] ~ to six** alle sei meno un quarto •vt dividere in quattro. **~-'final** n quarto m di finale

quarterly /'kwɔ:təlɪ/ adj trimestrale •adv trimestralmente

quartz /kwɔ:ts/ n quarzo m. **~ watch** n orologio m al quarzo

quay /ki:/ n banchina f

queasy /'kwi:zɪ/ adj **I feel ~** ho la nausea

queen /kwi:n/ n regina f. **~ mother** n regina f madre

queer /kwɪə(r)/ adj strano; (dubious) sospetto; ([!]: homosexual) finocchio •n [!] finocchio m

quench /kwentʃ/ vt **~ one's thirst** dissetarsi

query /'kwɪərɪ/ n domanda f; (question mark) punto m interrogativo •vt (pt/pp **-ied**) interrogare; (doubt) mettere in dubbio

quest /kwest/ n ricerca f (**for** di)

question /'kwestʃn/ n domanda f; (for discussion) questione f; **out of the ~** fuori discussione; **without ~** senza dubbio; **in ~** in questione •vt interrogare; (doubt) mettere in dubbio. **~able** adj discutibile. **~ mark** n punto m interrogativo

questionnaire /kwestʃə'neə(r)/ n questionario m

queue /kju:/ n coda f, fila f •vi **~ [up** mettersi in coda (**for** per)

quick /kwɪk/ adj veloce; **be ~** sbrigati!; **have a ~ meal** fare uno spuntino •adv in fretta •n **be cut to the ~** fig essere punto sul vivo. **~ly** adv in fretta. **~-tempered** adj collerico

quid /kwɪd/ n inv [!] sterlina f

quiet /'kwaɪət/ adj (calm) tranquillo; (silent) silenzioso; (voice, music) basso; **keep ~ about** [!] non raccontare a nessuno •n quiete f; **on the ~** di nascosto. **~ly** adv (peacefully) tranquillamente; (say) a bassa voce

quiet|en /'kwaɪətn/ vt calmare. □ **~ down** vi calmarsi. **~ness** n quiete f

quilt /kwɪlt/ n piumino m. **~ed** adj trapuntato

quintet /kwɪn'tet/ n quintetto m

quirk /kwɜ:k/ n stranezza f

quit /kwɪt/ v (pt/pp **quitted, quit**) •vt lasciare; (give up) smettere (**doing** di fare) •vi ([!]: resign) andarsene; (Comput) uscire; **give sb notice to ~** (landlord:) dare a qcno il preavviso di sfratto

quite /kwaɪt/ adv (fairly) abbastanza; (completely) completamente; (really) veramente; **~ [so]!** proprio così!; **~ a few** parecchi

quits /kwɪts/ adj pari

quiver /'kwɪvə(r)/ vi tremare

quiz /kwɪz/ n (game) quiz m inv •vt (pt/pp **quizzed**) interrogare

quota /'kwəʊtə/ n quota f

quotation /kwəʊ'teɪʃn/ n citazione f; (price) preventivo m; (of shares) quota f. **~ marks** npl virgolette fpl

quote /kwəʊt/ n [!] = **quotation; in ~s** tra virgolette •vt citare; quotare (price)

Rr

abbi /'ræbaɪ/ n rabbino m; (title) rabbi

'abbit /'ræbɪt/ n coniglio m

abies /'reɪbi:z/ n rabbia f

'ace¹ /reɪs/ n (people) razza f

ace² n corsa f •vi correre •vt gareggiare con; fare correre (horse)

'ace: ~course n ippodromo m. **~horse** n cavallo m da corsa. **~-track** n pista m

acial /'reɪʃl/ adj razziale. **~ism** n razzismo m

'acing /'reɪsɪŋ/ n corse fpl; (horse-) corse fpl dei cavalli. **~ car** n macchina f da corsa. **~ driver** n corridore m automobilistico

acis|m /'reɪsɪzm/ n razzismo m. **~t** adj razzista •n razzista mf

'ack¹ /ræk/ n (for bikes) rastrelliera f; (for luggage) portabagagli m inv; (for plates) scolapiatti m inv •vt **~ one's brains** scervellarsi

'ack² n **go to ~ and ruin** andare in rovina

'acket¹ /'rækɪt/ n (Sport) racchetta f

'acket² n (din) chiasso m; (swindle) truffa f; (crime) racket m inv, giro m

'adar /'reɪdɑ:(r)/ n radar m inv

'adian|ce /'reɪdɪəns/ n radiosità f inv. **~t** adj raggiante

'adiat|e /'reɪdɪeɪt/ vt irradiare •vi (heat:) irradiarsi. **~ion** n radiazione f

adiator /'reɪdɪeɪtə(r)/ n radiatore m

'adical /'rædɪkl/ adj radicale •n radicale mf. **~ly** adv radicalmente

adio /'reɪdɪəʊ/ n radio f inv

'adio|'active adj radioattivo. **~ac'tivity** n radioattività f

'adish /'rædɪʃ/ n ravanello m

'adius /'reɪdɪəs/ n (pl **-dii** /-dɪaɪ/) raggio m

'affle /'ræfl/ n lotteria f

'aft /rɑ:ft/ n zattera f

'after /'rɑ:ftə(r)/ n trave f

rag /ræg/ n straccio m; (pej: newspaper) giornalaccio m; **in ~s** stracciato

rage /reɪdʒ/ n rabbia f; **all the ~** [!] all'ultima moda •vi infuriarsi; (storm:) infuriare; (epidemic:) imperversare

ragged /'rægɪd/ adj logoro; (edge) frastagliato

raid /reɪd/ n (by thieves) rapina f; (Mil) incursione f, raid m inv; (police) irruzione f •vt (Mil) fare un'incursione in; (police, burglars:) fare irruzione in. **~er** n (of bank) rapinatore, -trice mf

rail /reɪl/ n ringhiera f; (hand~) ringhiera f; (Naut) parapetto m; **by ~** per ferrovia

'railroad n Am = **railway**

'railway n ferrovia f. **~man** n ferroviere m. **~ station** n stazione f ferroviaria

rain /reɪn/ n pioggia f •vi piovere

rain: ~bow n arcobaleno m. **~coat** n impermeabile m. **~fall** n precipitazione f [atmosferica]

rainy /'reɪnɪ/ adj (**-ier, -iest**) piovoso

raise /reɪz/ n Am aumento m •vt alzare; levarsi (hat); allevare (children, animals); sollevare (question); ottenere (money)

raisin /'reɪzn/ n uva f passa

rake /reɪk/ n rastrello m •vt rastrellare. □ **~ up** vt raccogliere col rastrello; [!] rivangare

rally /'rælɪ/ n raduno m; (Auto) rally m inv; (Tennis) scambio m •vt (pt/pp **-ied**) radunare •vi radunarsi; (recover strength) riprendersi

ram /ræm/ n montone m; (Astr) Ariete m •vt (pt/pp **rammed**) cozzare contro

RAM /ræm/ n [memoria f] RAM f

rambl|e /'ræmbl/ n escursione f •vi gironzolare; (in speech) divagare. **~er** n escursionista mf; (rose) rosa f rampicante. **~ing** adj (in speech) sconnesso; (club) escursionistico

ramp /ræmp/ n rampa f; (Aeron) scaletta f mobile (di aerei)

rampage /'ræmpeɪdʒ/ n **be/go on the ~** scatenarsi •vi **~ through the streets** scatenarsi per le strade

ramshackle /'ræmʃækl/ adj sgangherato

ran /ræn/ ▸**run**

ranch /rɑːntʃ/ n ranch m

random /'rændəm/ adj casuale; **~ sample** campione m a caso •n **at ~** a casaccio

rang /ræŋ/ ▸**ring**[2]

range /reɪndʒ/ n serie f; (Comm, Mus) gamma f; (of mountains) catena f; (distance) raggio m; (for shooting) portata f; (stove) cucina f economica; **at a ~ of** a una distanza di •vi estendersi; **~ from... to...** andare da... a.... **~r** n guardia f forestale

rank /ræŋk/ n (row) riga f; (Mil) grado m; (social position) rango m; **the ~ and file** la base f; **the ~s** (Mil) i soldati mpl semplici •vt (place) annoverare (**among** tra) •vi (be placed) collocarsi

ransack /'rænsæk/ vt rovistare; (pillage) saccheggiare

ransom /'rænsəm/ n riscatto m; **hold sb to ~** tenere qcno in ostaggio (per il riscatto)

rant /rænt/ vi **~** [**and rave**] inveire; **what's he ~ing on about?** cosa sta blaterando?

rap /ræp/ n colpo m [secco]; (Mus) rap m •v (pt/pp **rapped**) •vt dare colpetti a •vi **~ at** bussare a

r

rape /reɪp/ n (sexual) stupro m •vt violentare, stuprare

rapid /'ræpɪd/ adj rapido. **~ity** n rapidità f. **~ly** adv rapidamente

rapids /'ræpɪdz/ npl rapida fsg

rapist /'reɪpɪst/ n violentatore m

raptur|e /'ræptʃə(r)/ n estasi f. **~ous** adj entusiastico

rare[1] /reə(r)/ adj raro. **~ly** adv raramente

rare[2] adj (Culin) al sangue

rarefied /'reərɪfaɪd/ adj rarefatto

rarity /'reərətɪ/ n rarità f inv

rascal /'rɑːskl/ n mascalzone m

rash[1] /ræʃ/ n (Med) eruzione f

rash[2] adj avventato. **~ly** adv avventatamente

rasher /'ræʃə(r)/ n fetta f di pancetta

rasp /rɑːsp/ n (noise) stridio m. **~ing** adj stridente

raspberry /'rɑːzbərɪ/ n lampone m

rat /ræt/ n topo m; (!: person) carogna f; **smell a ~** ! sentire puzzo di bruciato

rate /reɪt/ n (speed) velocità f; (of payment) tariffa f; (of exchange) tasso m **~s** pl (taxes) imposte fpl comunali su beni immobili; **at any ~** in ogni caso; **at this ~** di questo passo •vt stimare; **~ among** annoverare tra •vi **~ as** essere considerato

rather /'rɑːðə(r)/ adv piuttosto; **~!** eccome!; **~ too...** un po' troppo...

rating /'reɪtɪŋ/ n **~s** pl (Radio, TV) indice m d'ascolto, audience f inv

ratio /'reɪʃɪəʊ/ n rapporto m

ration /'ræʃn/ n razione f •vt razionare

rational /'ræʃənl/ adj razionale. **~ize** vt/i razionalizzare

rattle /'rætl/ n tintinnio m; (toy) sonaglio m •vi tintinnare •vt (shake) scuotere; ! innervosire. □ **~ off** vt ! sciorinare

raucous /'rɔːkəs/ adj rauco

rave /reɪv/ vi vaneggiare; **~ about** andare in estasi per

raven /'reɪvn/ n corvo m imperiale

ravenous /'rævənəs/ adj (person) affamato

ravine /rə'viːn/ n gola f

raving /'reɪvɪŋ/ adj **~ mad** ! matto da legare

ravishing /'rævɪʃɪŋ/ adj incantevole

raw /rɔː/ adj crudo; (not processed) grezzo; (weather) gelido; (inexperienced) inesperto; **get a ~ deal** ! farsi fregare. **~ ma'terials** npl materie fpl prime

ray /reɪ/ n raggio m; **~ of hope** barlume m di speranza

raze /reɪz/ vt **~ to the ground** radere al suolo

razor /'reɪzə(r)/ n rasoio m. **~ blade** n lametta f da barba

re /riː/ prep con riferimento a

reach /riːtʃ/ n portata f; **within ~** a portata di mano; **out of ~ of** fuori dalla portata di; **within easy ~**

facilmente raggiungibile •vt arrivare a (place, decision); (contact) contattare; (pass) passare; **I can't ~ it** non ci arrivo •vi arrivare (**to** a); **~ for** allungare la mano per prendere

e'act /rɪ-/ vi reagire

e'action /rɪ-/ n reazione f. **~ary** adj reazionario, -a mf

eactor /rɪ'æktə(r)/ n reattore m

ead /ri:d/ vt (pt/pp **read** /red/) leggere; (Univ) studiare • vi leggere; (instrument:) indicare. □ **~ out** vt leggere ad alta voce

eadable /'ri:dəbl/ adj piacevole a leggersi; (legible) leggibile

eader /'ri:də(r)/ n lettore, -trice mf; (book) antologia f

eadi|ly /'redɪlɪ/ adv volentieri; (easily) facilmente. **~ness** n disponibilità f inv; **in ~ness** pronto

eading /'ri:dɪŋ/ n lettura f

ea'djust /ri:-/ vt regolare di nuovo •vi riabituarsi (**to** a)

eady /'redɪ/ adj (**-ier, -iest**) pronto; (quick) veloce; **get ~** prepararsi

eady-'made adj confezionato

eal /ri:l/ adj vero; (increase) reale •adv Am [!] veramente. **~ estate** n beni mpl immobili

ealis|m /'rɪəlɪzm/ n realismo m. **~t** n realista mf. **~tic** adj realistico

eality /rɪ'ælətɪ/ n realtà f inv; **~ TV** n reality TV f

ealization /rɪəlaɪ'zeɪʃn/ n realizzazione f

ealize /'rɪəlaɪz/ vt realizzare

eally /'rɪəlɪ/ adv davvero

ealm /relm/ n regno m

ealtor /'rɪəltə(r)/ n Am agente mf immobiliare

eap /ri:p/ vt mietere

eap'pear /ri:-/ vi riapparire

ear[1] /rɪə(r)/ adj posteriore; (Auto) di dietro; **~ end** [!] didietro m •n **the ~** (of building) il retro m; (of bus, plane) la parte f posteriore; **from the ~** da dietro

ear[2] vt allevare •vi **~ [up]** (horse:) impennarsi

ear'range /ri:-/ vt cambiare la disposizione di

reason /'ri:zn/ n ragione f; **within ~** nei limiti del ragionevole •vi ragionare; **~ with** cercare di far ragionare. **~able** adj ragionevole. **~ably** adv (in reasonable way, fairly) ragionevolmente

reas'sur|ance /ri:-/ n rassicurazione f. **~e** vt rassicurare; **~e sb of sth** rassicurare qcno su qcsa. **~ing** adj rassicurante

rebate /'ri:beɪt/ n rimborso m; (discount) deduzione f

rebel[1] /'rebl/ n ribelle mf

rebel[2] /rɪ'bel/ vi (pt/pp **rebelled**) ribellarsi. **~lion** n ribellione f. **~lious** adj ribelle

re'bound[1] /rɪ-/ vi rimbalzare; fig ricadere

'rebound[2] /ri:-/ n rimbalzo m

rebuff /rɪ'bʌf/ n rifiuto m

re'build /ri:-/ vt (pt/pp **-built**) ricostruire

rebuke /rɪ'bju:k/ vt rimproverare

re'call /rɪ-/ n richiamo m; **beyond ~** irrevocabile •vt richiamare; riconvocare (diplomat, parliament); (remember) rievocare

recap /'ri:kæp/ vt/i [!] = **recapitulate** •n ricapitolazione f

recapitulate /ri:kə'pɪtjʊleɪt/ vt/i ricapitolare

re'capture /ri:-/ vt riconquistare; ricatturare (person, animal)

reced|e /rɪ'si:d/ vi allontanarsi. **~ing** adj (forehead, chin) sfuggente; **have ~ing hair** essere stempiato

receipt /rɪ'si:t/ n ricevuta f; (receiving) ricezione f; **~s** pl (Comm) entrate fpl

receive /rɪ'si:v/ vt ricevere. **~r** n (Teleph) ricevitore m; (Radio, TV) apparecchio m ricevente; (of stolen goods) ricettatore, -trice mf

recent /'ri:snt/ adj recente. **~ly** adv recentemente

reception /rɪ'sepʃn/ n ricevimento m; (welcome) accoglienza f; (Radio) ricezione f; **~ [desk]** (in hotel) reception f inv. **~ist** n persona f alla reception

receptive /rɪ'septɪv/ adj ricettivo

recess /rɪ'ses/ n rientranza f; (holiday) vacanza f; Am (Sch) intervallo m

recession /rɪ'seʃn/ n recessione f

re'charge /riː-/ vt ricaricare

recipe /'resəpɪ/ n ricetta f

recipient /rɪ'sɪpɪənt/ n (of letter) destinatario, -a mf; (of money) beneficiario, -a mf

recital /rɪ'saɪtl/ n recital m inv

recite /rɪ'saɪt/ vt recitare; (list) elencare

reckless /'reklɪs/ adj (action, decision) sconsiderato; **be a ~ driver** guidare in modo spericolato. **~ly** adv in modo sconsiderato. **~ness** n sconsideratezza f

reckon /'rekən/ vt calcolare; (consider) pensare. □ **~ on/with** vt fare i conti con

re'claim /rɪ-/ vt reclamare; bonificare (land)

reclin|e /rɪ'klaɪn/ vi sdraiarsi. **~ing** adj (seat) reclinabile

recluse /rɪ'kluːs/ n recluso, -a mf

recognition /rekəg'nɪʃn/ n riconoscimento m; **beyond ~** irriconoscibile

recognize /'rekəgnaɪz/ vt riconoscere

re'coil /rɪ-/ vi (in fear) indietreggiare

recollect /rekə'lekt/ vt ricordare. **~ion** n ricordo m

recommend /rekə'mend/ vt raccomandare. **~ation** n raccomandazione f

recon|cile /'rekənsaɪl/ vt riconciliare; conciliare (facts); **~cile oneself to** rassegnarsi a. **~ciliation** n riconciliazione f

r

reconnaissance /rɪ'kɒnɪsns/ n (Mil) ricognizione f

reconnoitre /rekə'nɔɪtə(r)/ vi (pres p **-tring**) fare una recognizione

recon'sider /riː-/ vt riconsiderare

recon'struct /riː-/ vt ricostruire. **~ion** n ricostruzione f

record¹ /rɪ'kɔːd/ vt registrare; (make a note of) annotare

record² /'rekɔːd/ n (file) documentazione f; (Mus) disco m; (Sport) record m inv; **~s** pl (files) schedario msg; **keep a ~ of** tener nota di; **off the ~** in via ufficiosa; **have a [criminal] ~** avere la fedina penale sporca

recorder /rɪ'kɔːdə(r)/ n (Mus) flauto m dolce

recording /rɪ'kɔːdɪŋ/ n registrazione f

'record-player n giradischi m inv

recount /rɪ'kaʊnt/ vt raccontare

re-'count¹ /riː-/ vt ricontare

're-count² /'riː-/ n (Pol) nuovo conteggio m

recover /rɪ'kʌvə(r)/ vt/i recuperare. **~y** n recupero m; (of health) guarigione m

re-'cover /riː-/ vt rifoderare

recreation /rekrɪ'eɪʃn/ n ricreazione f. **~al** adj ricreativo

recruit /rɪ'kruːt/ n (Mil) recluta f; **new ~** (member) nuovo, -a adepto, -a mf; (worker) neoassunto, -a mf •vt assumere (staff). **~ment** n assunzione f

rectang|le /'rektæŋgl/ n rettangolo m. **~ular** adj rettangolare

rectify /'rektɪfaɪ/ vt (pt/pp **-ied**) rettificare

recuperate /rɪ'kuːpəreɪt/ vi ristabilirsi

recur /rɪ'kɜː(r)/ vi (pt/pp **recurred**) ricorrere; (illness:) ripresentarsi

recurren|ce /rɪ'kʌrəns/ n ricorrenza f; (of illness) ricomparsa f. **~t** adj ricorrente

recycle /riː'saɪkl/ vt riciclare

red /red/ adj (**redder, reddest**) rosso •n rosso m; **in the ~** (account) scoperto. **R~ Cross** n Croce f rossa

redd|en /'redn/ vt arrossare •vi arrossire. **~ish** adj rossastro

re'decorate /riː-/ vt (paint) ridipingere; (wallpaper) ritappezzare

redeem /rɪ'diːm/ vt **~ing quality** unico aspetto m positivo

redemption /rɪ'dempʃn/ n riscatto m

red: ~-haired adj con i capelli rossi. **~-'handed** adj **catch sb ~-handed** cogliere qcno con le mani nel sacco. **~ 'herring** n diversione f. **~-hot** adj rovente

red: ~ 'light n (Auto) semaforo m rosso

re'double /riː-/ vt raddoppiare

red 'tape n ⊡ burocrazia f

reduc|e /rɪ'djuːs/ vt ridurre; (Culin) far consumare. **~tion** n riduzione f

'edundan|cy /rɪ'dʌndənsɪ/ n licenziamento m; (payment) cassa f integrazione. **~t** adj superfluo; **make ~t** licenziare; **be made ~t** essere licenziato

'eed /ri:d/ n (Bot) canna f

'eef /ri:f/ n scogliera f

'eek /ri:k/ vi puzzare (**of** di)

'eel /ri:l/ n bobina f • vi (stagger) vacillare. □ **~ off** vt fig snocciolare

efectory /rɪ'fektərɪ/ n refettorio m; (Univ) mensa f universitaria

efer /rɪ'fɜ:(r)/ v (pt/pp **referred**) • vt rinviare (matter) (**to** a); indirizzare (person) • vi **~ to** fare allusione a; (consult) rivolgersi a (book)

eferee /refə'ri:/ n arbitro m; (for job) garante mf • vt/i (pt/pp **refereed**) arbitrare

eference /'refərəns/ n riferimento m; (in book) nota f bibliografica; (for job) referenza f; (Comm) **'your ~'** 'riferimento'; **with ~ to** con riferimento a; **make [a] ~ to** fare riferimento a. **~ book** n libro m di consultazione. **~ number** n numero m di riferimento

eferendum /refə'rendəm/ n referendum m inv

e'fill¹ /ri:-/ vt riempire di nuovo; ricaricare (pen, lighter)

refill² /'ri:-/ n (for pen) ricambio m

efine /rɪ'faɪn/ vt raffinare. **~d** adj raffinato. **~ment** n raffinatezza f; (Techn) raffinazione f. **~ry** n raffineria f

eflect /rɪ'flekt/ vt riflettere; **be ~ed in** essere riflesso in • vi (think) riflettere (**on** su); **~ badly on sb** fig mettere in cattiva luce qcno. **~ion** n riflessione f; (image) riflesso m; **on ~ion** dopo riflessione. **~ive** adj riflessivo. **~or** n riflettore m

eflex /'ri:fleks/ n riflesso m • attrib di riflesso

eflexive /rɪ'fleksɪv/ adj riflessivo

eform /rɪ'fɔ:m/ n riforma f • vt riformare • vi correggersi. **R~ation** n (Relig) riforma f. **~er** n riformatore, -trice mf

efrain¹ /rɪ'freɪn/ n ritornello m

efrain² vi astenersi (**from** da)

efresh /rɪ'freʃ/ vt rinfrescare. **~ing** adj rinfrescante. **~ments** npl rinfreschi mpl

refrigerat|e /rɪ'frɪdʒəreɪt/ vt conservare in frigo. **~or** n frigorifero m

re'fuel /ri:-/ v (pt/pp **-fuelled**) • vt rifornire (di carburante) • vi fare rifornimento

refuge /'refju:dʒ/ n rifugio m; **take ~** rifugiarsi

refugee /refjʊ'dʒi:/ n rifugiato, -a mf

'refund¹ /'ri:-/ n rimborso m

re'fund² /rɪ-/ vt rimborsare

refusal /rɪ'fju:zl/ n rifiuto m

refuse¹ /rɪ'fju:z/ vt/i rifiutare; **~ to do sth** rifiutare di fare qcsa

refuse² /'refju:s/ n rifiuti mpl. **~ collection** n raccolta f dei rifiuti

refute /rɪ'fju:t/ vt confutare

re'gain /rɪ-/ vt riconquistare

regal /'ri:gl/ adj regale

regard /rɪ'gɑ:d/ n (heed) riguardo m; (respect) considerazione f; **~s** pl saluti mpl; **send/give my ~s to your brother** salutami tuo fratello • vt (consider) considerare (**as** come); **as ~s** riguardo a. **~ing** prep riguardo a. **~less** adv lo stesso; **~less of** senza badare a

regatta /rɪ'gætə/ n regata f

regime /reɪ'ʒi:m/ n regime m

regiment /'redʒɪmənt/ n reggimento m. **~al** adj reggimentale. **~ation** n irreggimentazione f

region /'ri:dʒən/ n regione f; **in the ~ of** fig approssimativamente. **~al** adj regionale

register /'redʒɪstə(r)/ n registro m • vt registrare; mandare per raccomandata (letter); assicurare (luggage); immatricolare (vehicle); mostrare (feeling) • vi (instrument:) funzionare; (student:) iscriversi (**for** a); **~ with** iscriversi nella lista di (doctor)

registrar /redʒɪ'strɑ:(r)/ n ufficiale m di stato civile

registration /redʒɪ'streɪʃn/ n (of vehicle) immatricolazione f; (of letter) raccomandazione f; (of luggage) assicurazione f; (for course) iscrizione f. **~ number** n (Auto) targa f

registry office /'redʒɪstrɪ-/ n anagrafe f

regret /rɪ'gret/ n rammarico m • vt (pt/pp **regretted**) rimpiangere; **I ~ that** mi rincresce che. **~fully** adv con rammarico

regrettab|le /rɪ'gretəbl/ adj spiacevole. **~ly** adv spiacevolmente; (before adjective) deplorevolmente

regular /'regjʊlə(r)/ adj regolare; (usual) abituale • n cliente mf abituale. **~ity** n regolarità f. **~ly** adv regolarmente

regulat|e /'regʊleɪt/ vt regolare. **~ion** n (rule) regolamento m

rehears|al /rɪ'hɜ:sl/ n (Theat) prova f. **~e** vt/i provare

reign /reɪn/ n regno m • vi regnare

reinforce /ri:ɪn'fɔ:s/ vt rinforzare. **~d 'concrete** n cemento m armato. **~ment** n rinforzo m

reiterate /ri:'ɪtəreɪt/ vt reiterare

reject /rɪ'dʒekt/ vt rifiutare. **~ion** n rifiuto m; (Med) rigetto m

rejoic|e /rɪ'dʒɔɪs/ vi liter rallegrarsi. **~ing** n gioia f

rejuvenate /rɪ'dʒu:vəneɪt/ vt ringiovanire

relapse /rɪ'læps/ n ricaduta f • vi ricadere

relate /rɪ'leɪt/ vt (tell) riportare; (connect) collegare • vi **~ to** riferirsi a; identificarsi con (person). **~d** adj imparentato (**to** a); (ideas etc) affine

relation /rɪ'leɪʃn/ n rapporto m; (person) parente mf. **~ship** n rapporto m (blood tie) parentela f; (affair) relazione f

relative /'relətɪv/ n parente mf • adj relativo. **~ly** adv relativamente

relax /rɪ'læks/ vt rilassare; allentare (pace, grip) • vi rilassarsi. **~ation** n rilassamento m, relax m inv; (recreation) svago m. **~ing** adj rilassante

relay¹ /ri:'leɪ/ vt ritrasmettere; (Radio, TV) trasmettere

relay² /'ri:leɪ/ n (Electr) relais m inv; **work in ~s** fare i turni. **~ [race]** n [corsa f a] staffetta f

release /rɪ'li:s/ n rilascio m; (of film) distribuzione f • vt liberare; lasciare (hand); togliere (brake); distribuire (film); rilasciare (information etc)

relegate /'relɪgeɪt/ vt relegare; **be ~d** (Sport) essere retrocesso

relent /rɪ'lent/ vi cedere. **~less** adj inflessibile; (unceasing) incessante. **~lessly** adv incessantemente

relevan|ce /'reləvəns/ n pertinenza f. **~t** adj pertinente (**to** a)

reliab|ility /rɪlaɪə'bɪlətɪ/ n affidabilità f. **~le** adj affidabile a. **~ly** adv in modo affidabile; **be ~ly informed** sapere da fonte certa

relian|ce /rɪ'laɪəns/ n fiducia f (**on** in). **~t** adj fiducioso (**on** in)

relic /'relɪk/ n (Relig) reliquia f; **~s** npl resti mpl

relief /rɪ'li:f/ n sollievo m; (assistance) soccorso m; (distraction) diversivo m; (replacement) cambio m; (in art) rilievo m; **in ~** in rilievo. **~ map** n carta f in rilievo. **~ train** n treno m supplementare

relieve /rɪ'li:v/ vt alleviare; (take over from) dare il cambio a; **~ of** liberare da (burden)

religion /rɪ'lɪdʒən/ n religione f

religious /rɪ'lɪdʒəs/ adj religioso. **~ly** adv (conscientiously) scrupolosamente

relinquish /rɪ'lɪŋkwɪʃ/ vt abbandonare; **~ sth to sb** rinunciare a qcsa in favore di qcno

relish /'relɪʃ/ n gusto m; (Culin) salsa f • vt fig apprezzare

reluctan|ce /rɪ'lʌktəns/ n riluttanza f. **~t** adj riluttante. **~tly** adv a malincuore

rely /rɪ'laɪ/ vi (pt/pp **-ied**) **~ on** dipendere da; (trust) contare su

remain /rɪ'meɪn/ vi restare. **~der** n resto m. **~ing** adj restante. **~s** npl resti mpl; (dead body) spoglie fpl

remand /rɪ'mɑ:nd/ n **on ~** in custodia cautelare • vt **~ in custody** rinviare con detenzione provvisoria

remark /rɪ'mɑ:k/ n osservazione f • vt osservare. **~able** adj notevole. **~ably** adv notevolmente

remarry /ri:-/ vi risposarsi

remedy /'remədɪ/ n rimedio m (**for** contro) • vt (pt/pp **-ied**) rimediare a

remember /rɪ'membə(r)/ vt ricordare, ricordarsi; **~ to do sth** ricordarsi di fare qcsa; **~ me to him** salutamelo • vi ricordarsi

emind /rɪ'maɪnd/ vt ~ **sb of sth** ricordare qcsa a qcno. **~er** n ricordo m; (memo) promemoria m; (letter) lettera f di sollecito

eminisce /remɪ'nɪs/ vi rievocare il passato. **~nces** npl reminiscenze fpl. **~nt** adj **be ~ of** richiamare alla memoria

emnant /'remnənt/ n resto m; (of material) scampolo m; (trace) traccia f

emorse /rɪ'mɔ:s/ n rimorso m. **~ful** adj pieno di rimorso. **~less** adj spietato. **~lessly** adv senza pietà

emote /rɪ'məʊt/ adj remoto; (slight) minimo. ~ **access** n (Comput) accesso m remoto. ~ **con'trol** n telecomando m. **~-con'trolled** adj telecomandato. **~ly** adv lontanamente; **be not ~ly...** non essere lontanamente...

e'movable /rɪ-/ adj rimovibile

emoval /rɪ'mu:vl/ n rimozione f; (from house) trasloco m. ~ **van** n camion m inv da trasloco

emove /rɪ'mu:v/ vt togliere; togliersi (clothes); eliminare (stain, doubts)

ender /'rendə(r)/ vt rendere (service)

enegade /'renɪgeɪd/ n rinnegato, -a mf

enew /rɪ'nju:/ vt rinnovare (contract). **~al** n rinnovo m

enounce /rɪ'naʊns/ vt rinunciare a

enovat|e /'renəveɪt/ vt rinnovare. **~ion** n rinnovo m

enown /rɪ'naʊn/ n fama f. **~ed** adj rinomato

ent /rent/ n affitto m •vt affittare; ~ [**out**] dare in affitto. **~al** n affitto m

enunciation /rɪnʌnsɪ'eɪʃn/ n rinuncia f

e'open /ri:-/ vt/i riaprire

e'organize /ri:-/ vt riorganizzare

ep /rep/ n (Comm) ! rappresentante mf; (Theat) ≈ teatro m stabile

epair /rɪ'peə(r)/ n riparazione f; **in good/bad ~** in buone/cattive condizioni •vt riparare

epatriat|e /ri:'pætrɪeɪt/ vt rimpatriare. **~ion** n rimpatrio m

e'pay /ri:-/ vt (pt/pp **-paid**) ripagare. **~ment** n rimborso m

repeal /rɪ'pi:l/ n abrogazione f •vt abrogare

repeat /rɪ'pi:t/ n (TV) replica f •vt/i ripetere; ~ **oneself** ripetersi. **~ed** adj ripetuto. **~edly** adv ripetutamente

repel /rɪ'pel/ vt (pt/pp **repelled**) respingere; fig ripugnare. **~lent** adj ripulsivo

repent /rɪ'pent/ vi pentirsi. **~ance** n pentimento m. **~ant** adj pentito

repertoire /'repətwɑ:(r)/ n repertorio m

repetit|ion /repɪ'tɪʃn/ n ripetizione f. **~ive** adj ripetitivo

re'place /rɪ-/ vt (put back) rimettere a posto; (take the place of) sostituire; ~ **sth with sth** sostituire qcsa con qcsa. **~ment** n sostituzione m; (person) sostituto, -a mf. **~ment part** n pezzo m di ricambio

'replay /'ri:-/ n (Sport) partita f ripetuta; [**action**] ~ replay m inv

replenish /rɪ'plenɪʃ/ vt rifornire (stocks); (refill) riempire di nuovo

replica /'replɪkə/ n copia f

reply /rɪ'plaɪ/ n risposta f (**to** a) •vt/i (pt/pp **replied**) rispondere

report /rɪ'pɔ:t/ n rapporto m; (TV, Radio) servizio m; (Journ) cronaca f; (Sch) pagella f; (rumour) diceria f •vt riportare; ~ **sb to the police** denunciare qcno alla polizia •vi riportare; (present oneself) presentarsi (**to** a). **~edly** adv secondo quanto si dice. **~er** n cronista mf, reporter mf inv

reprehensible /reprɪ'hensəbl/ adj riprovevole

represent /reprɪ'zent/ vt rappresentare

representative /reprɪ'zentətɪv/ adj rappresentativo •n rappresentante mf

repress /rɪ'pres/ vt reprimere. **~ion** n repressione f. **~ive** adj repressivo

reprieve /rɪ'pri:v/ n commutazione f della pena capitale; (postponement) sospensione f della pena capitale; fig tregua f •vt sospendere la sentenza a; fig risparmiare

reprimand /'reprɪmɑ:nd/ n rimprovero m •vt rimproverare

reprisal /rɪ'praɪzl/ n rappresaglia f;

in ∼ for per rappresaglia contro

reproach /rɪ'prəʊtʃ/ n ammonimento m •vt ammonire. **∼ful** adj riprovevole. **∼fully** adv con aria di rimprovero

repro'duc|e /riː-/ vt riprodurre •vi riprodursi. **∼tion** n riproduzione f. **∼tive** adj riproduttivo

reprove /rɪ'pruːv/ vt rimproverare

reptile /'reptaɪl/ n rettile m

republic /rɪ'pʌblɪk/ n repubblica f. **∼an** adj repubblicano •n repubblicano, -a mf

repugnan|ce /rɪ'pʌgnəns/ n ripugnanza f. **∼t** adj ripugnante

repuls|ion /rɪ'pʌlʃn/ n repulsione f. **∼ive** adj ripugnante

reputable /'repjʊtəbl/ adj affidabile

reputation /repjʊ'teɪʃn/ n reputazione f

request /rɪ'kwest/ n richiesta f •vt richiedere. **∼ stop** n fermata f a richiesta

require /rɪ'kwaɪə(r)/ vt (need) necessitare di; (demand) esigere. **∼d** adj richiesto; **I am ∼d to do** si esige che io faccia. **∼ment** n esigenza f; (condition) requisito m

rescue /'reskjuː/ n salvataggio m •vt salvare. **∼r** n salvatore, -trice mf

research /rɪ'sɜːtʃ/ n ricerca f •vt fare ricerche su; (Journ) fare un'inchiesta su •vi **∼ into** fare ricerche su. **∼er** n ricercatore, -trice mf

resem|blance /rɪ'zembləns/ n rassomiglianza f. **∼ble** vt rassomigliare a

resent /rɪ'zent/ vt risentirsi per. **∼ful** adj pieno di risentimento. **∼fully** adv con risentimento. **∼ment** n risentimento m

reservation /rezə'veɪʃn/ n (booking) prenotazione f; (doubt, enclosure) riserva f

reserve /rɪ'zɜːv/ n riserva f; (shyness) riserbo m •vt riservare; riservarsi (right). **∼d** adj riservato

reservoir /'rezəvwɑː(r)/ n bacino m idrico

re'shuffle /riː-/ n (Pol) rimpasto m •vt (Pol) rimpastare

residence /'rezɪdəns/ n residenza f; (stay) soggiorno m. **∼ permit** n permesso m di soggiorno

resident /'rezɪdənt/ adj residente •n residente mf. **∼ial** adj residenziale

residue /'rezɪdjuː/ n residuo m

resign /rɪ'zaɪn/ vt dimettersi da; **∼ oneself to** rassegnarsi a •vi dare le dimissioni. **∼ation** n rassegnazione f; (from job) dimissioni fpl. **∼ed** adj rassegnato

resilient /rɪ'zɪlɪənt/ adj elastico; fig con buone capacità di ripresa

resin /'rezɪn/ n resina f

resist /rɪ'zɪst/ vt resistere a •vi resistere. **∼ance** n resistenza f. **∼ant** adj resistente

resolut|e /'rezəluːt/ adj risoluto. **∼ely** adv con risolutezza. **∼ion** n risolutezza f

resolve /rɪ'zɒlv/ vt **∼ to do** decidere di fare

resort /rɪ'zɔːt/ n (place) luogo m di villeggiatura; **as a last ∼** come ultima risorsa •vi **∼ to** ricorrere a

resource /rɪ'sɔːs/ n **∼s** pl risorse fpl. **∼ful** adj pieno di risorse; (solution) ingegnoso. **∼fulness** n ingegnosità f inv

respect /rɪ'spekt/ n rispetto m; (aspect) aspetto m; **with ∼ to** per quanto riguarda •vt rispettare

respect|able /rɪ'spektəbl/ adj rispettabile. **∼ably** adv rispettabilmente. **∼ful** adj rispettoso

respective /rɪ'spektɪv/ adj rispettivo. **∼ly** adv rispettivamente

respiration /respɪ'reɪʃn/ n respirazione f

respite /'respaɪt/ n respiro m

respond /rɪ'spɒnd/ vi rispondere; (react) reagire (**to** a); (patient:) rispondere (**to** a)

response /rɪ'spɒns/ n risposta f; (reaction) reazione f

responsibility /rɪspɒnsɪ'bɪlətɪ/ n responsabilità f inv

responsib|le /rɪ'spɒnsəbl/ adj responsabile; (job) impegnativo

responsive /rɪ'spɒnsɪv/ adj **be ∼** (audience etc:) reagire; (brakes:) essere sensibile

rest[1] /rest/ n riposo m; (Mus) pausa f; **have a ∼** riposarsi •vt riposare;

(lean) appoggiare (**on** su); (place) appoggiare • vi riposarsi; (elbows:) appoggiarsi; (hopes:) riposare

est[2] n **the ~** il resto m; (people) gli altri mpl • vi **it ~s with you** sta a te

estaurant /'restərɒnt/ n ristorante m. **~ car** n vagone m ristorante

estful /'restfl/ adj riposante

estive /'restɪv/ adj irrequieto

estless /'restlɪs/ adj nervoso

estoration /restə'reɪʃn/ n (of building) restauro m

estore /rɪ'stɔ:(r)/ vt ristabilire; restaurare (building); (give back) restituire

estrain /rɪ'streɪn/ vt trattenere; **~ oneself** controllarsi. **~ed** adj controllato. **~t** n restrizione f; (moderation) ritegno m

estrict /rɪ'strɪkt/ vt limitare; **~ to** limitarsi a. **~ion** n limite m; (restraint) restrizione f. **~ive** adj limitativo

est room n Am toilette f inv

esult /rɪ'zʌlt/ n risultato m; **as a ~** a causa (**of** di) • vi **~ from** risultare da; **~ in** portare a

esume /rɪ'zju:m/ vt/i riprendere

ésumé /'rezjʊmeɪ/ n riassunto m; Am curriculum vitae m inv

esurrect /rezə'rekt/ vt fig risuscitare. **~ion** n **the R~ion** (Relig) la Risurrezione

esuscitat|e /rɪ'sʌsɪteɪt/ vt rianimare. **~ion** n rianimazione f

etail /'ri:teɪl/ n vendita f al minuto o al dettaglio • adj & adv al minuto • vt vendere al minuto • vi **~ at** essere venduto al pubblico al prezzo di. **~er** n dettagliante mf

etain /rɪ'teɪn/ vt conservare; (hold back) trattenere

etaliat|e /rɪ'tælɪeɪt/ vi vendicarsi. **~ion** n rappresaglia f; **in ~ion for** per rappresaglia contro

etarded /rɪ'tɑ:dɪd/ adj ritardato

ethink /ri:'θɪŋk/ vt (pt/pp **rethought**) ripensare

eticen|ce /'retɪsəns/ n reticenza f. **~t** adj reticente

etina /'retɪnə/ n retina f

etinue /'retɪnju:/ n seguito m

retire /rɪ'taɪə(r)/ vi andare in pensione; (withdraw) ritirarsi • vt mandare in pensione (employee). **~d** adj in pensione. **~ment** n pensione f; **since my ~ment** da quando sono andato in pensione

retiring /rɪ'taɪərɪŋ/ adj riservato

retort /rɪ'tɔ:t/ n replica f • vt ribattere

re'trace /rɪ-/ vt ripercorrere; **~ one's steps** ritornare sui propri passi

retract /rɪ'trækt/ vt ritirare; ritrattare (statement, evidence) • vi ritrarsi

re'train /ri:-/ vt riqualificare • vi riqualificarsi

retreat /rɪ'tri:t/ n ritirata f; (place) ritiro m • vi ritirarsi; (Mil) battere in ritirata

re'trial /ri:-/ n nuovo processo m

retrieval /rɪ'tri:vəl/ n recupero m

retrieve /rɪ'tri:v/ vt recuperare

retrograde /'retrəgreɪd/ adj retrogrado

retrospect /'retrəspekt/ n **in ~** guardando indietro. **~ive** adj retrospettivo; (legislation) retroattivo • n retrospettiva f

return /rɪ'tɜ:n/ n ritorno m; (giving back) restituzione f; (Comm) profitto m; (ticket) biglietto m di andata e ritorno; **by ~** [**of post**] a stretto giro di posta; **in ~** in cambio (**for** di); **many happy ~s!** cento di questi giorni! • vi ritornare • vt (give back) restituire; ricambiare (affection, invitation); (put back) rimettere; (send back) mandare indietro; (elect) eleggere

return: ~ match n rivincita f. **~ ticket** n biglietto m di andata e ritorno

reunion /ri:'ju:njən/ n riunione f

reunite /ri:jʊ'naɪt/ vt riunire

rev /rev/ n (Auto), ! giro m (di motore) • v (pt/pp **revved**) • vt **~** [**up**] far andare su di giri • vi andare su di giri

reveal /rɪ'vi:l/ vt rivelare; (dress:) scoprire. **~ing** adj rivelatore; (dress) osé

revel /'revl/ vi (pt/pp **revelled**) **~ in sth** godere di qcsa

r

revelation /revə'leɪʃn/ n rivelazione f

revelry /'revlrɪ/ n baldoria f

revenge /rɪ'vendʒ/ n vendetta f; (Sport) rivincita f; **take ~** vendicarsi •vt vendicare

revenue /'revənju:/ n reddito m

revere /rɪ'vɪə(r)/ vt riverire. **~nce** n riverenza f

Reverend /'revərənd/ adj reverendo

reverent /'revərənt/ adj riverente

reverse /rɪ'vɜ:s/ adj opposto; **in ~ order** in ordine inverso •n contrario m; (back) rovescio m; (Auto) marcia m indietro •vt invertire; **~ the car into the garage** entrare in garage a marcia indietro; **~ the charges** (Teleph) fare una telefonata a carico •vi (Auto) fare marcia indietro

revert /rɪ'vɜ:t/ vi **~ to** tornare a

review /rɪ'vju:/ n (survey) rassegna f; (re-examination) riconsiderazione f; (Mil) rivista f; (of book, play) recensione f •vt riesaminare (situation); (Mil) passare in rivista; recensire (book, play). **~er** n critico, -a mf

revis|e /rɪ'vaɪz/ vt rivedere; (for exam) ripassare. **~ion** n revisione f; (for exam) ripasso m

revive /rɪ'vaɪv/ vt resuscitare; rianimare (person) •vi riprendersi; (person:) rianimarsi

revolt /rɪ'vəʊlt/ n rivolta f •vi ribellarsi •vt rivoltare. **~ing** adj rivoltante

revolution /revə'lu:ʃn/ n rivoluzione f; (Auto) **~s per minute** giri mpl al minuto. **~ary** adj & n rivoluzionario, -a mf. **~ize** vt rivoluzionare

revolve /rɪ'vɒlv/ vi ruotare; **~ around** girare intorno

revolv|er /rɪ'vɒlvə(r)/ n rivoltella f, revolver m inv. **~ing** adj ruotante

revue /rɪ'vju:/ n rivista f

revulsion /rɪ'vʌlʃn/ n ripulsione f

reward /rɪ'wɔ:d/ n ricompensa f •vt ricompensare. **~ing** adj gratificante

re'write /ri:-/ vt (pt **rewrote**, pp **rewritten**) riscrivere

rhetoric /'retərɪk/ n retorica f. **~al** adj retorico

rhinoceros /raɪ'nɒsərəs/ n rinoceronte m

rhubarb /'ru:bɑ:b/ n rabarbaro m

rhyme /raɪm/ n rima f; (poem) filastrocca f •vi rimare

rhythm /'rɪðm/ n ritmo m. **~ic[al]** adj ritmico. **~ically** adv con ritmo

rib /rɪb/ n costola f

ribbon /'rɪbən/ n nastro m; **in ~s** a brandelli

rice /raɪs/ n riso m

rich /rɪtʃ/ adj ricco; (food) pesante •n **the ~** pl i ricchi mpl; **~es** pl ricchezze fpl. **~ly** adv riccamente; (deserve) largamente

ricochet /'rɪkəʃeɪ/ vi rimbalzare •n rimbalzo m

rid /rɪd/ vt (pt/pp **rid**, pres p **ridding**) sbarazzare (**of** di); **get ~ of** sbarazzarsi di

riddance /'rɪdns/ n **good ~!** che liberazione!

ridden /'rɪdn/ ▸**ride**

riddle /'rɪdl/ n enigma m

ride /raɪd/ n (on horse) cavalcata f; (in vehicle) giro m; (journey) viaggio m; **take sb for a ~** [!] prendere qcno in giro •v (pt **rode**, pp **ridden**) •vt montare (horse); andare su (bicycle) •vi andare a cavallo; (jockey, showjumper:) cavalcare; (cyclist:) andare in bicicletta; (in vehicle) viaggiare. **~r** n cavallerizzo, -a mf; (in race) fantino m; (on bicycle) ciclista mf; (in document) postilla f

ridge /rɪdʒ/ n spigolo m; (on roof) punta f; (of mountain) cresta f

ridicule /'rɪdɪkju:l/ n ridicolo m •vt mettere in ridicolo

ridiculous /rɪ'dɪkjʊləs/ adj ridicolo

rife /raɪf/ adj **be ~** essere diffuso; **~ with** pieno di

rifle /'raɪfl/ n fucile m; **~-range** tiro m al bersaglio •vt **~ [through]** mettere a soqquadro

rift /rɪft/ n fessura f; fig frattura f

rig[1] /rɪg/ n equipaggiamento m; (at sea) piattaforma f per trivellazioni subacquee •**rig out** vt (pt/pp **rigged**) equipaggiare. □ **~ up** vt allestire

rig[2] vt (pt/pp **rigged**) manovrare (election)

right /raɪt/ adj giusto; (not left) destro

be ~ (person:) aver ragione; (clock:) essere giusto; **put ~** mettere all'ora (clock); correggere (person); rimediare a (situation); **that's ~!** proprio così! • adv (correctly) bene; (not left) a destra; (directly) proprio; (completely) completamente; **~ away** immediatamente • n giusto m; (not left) destra f; (what is due) diritto m; **on/to the ~** a destra; **be in the ~** essere nel giusto; **know ~ from wrong** distinguere il bene dal male; **by ~s** secondo giustizia; **the R~** (Pol) la destra f • vt raddrizzare; **~ a wrong** fig riparare a un torto. **~ angle** n angolo m retto

ightful /'raɪtfl/ adj legittimo

ight: ~-'handed adj che usa la mano destra. **~-hand 'man** n fig braccio m destro

ightly /'raɪtlɪ/ adv giustamente

ight: ~ of way n diritto m di transito; (path) passaggio m; (Auto) precedenza f. **~-'wing** adj (Pol) di destra • n (Sport) ala f destra

igid /'rɪdʒɪd/ adj rigido. **~ity** n rigidità f inv

igorous /'rɪgərəs/ adj rigoroso

im /rɪm/ n bordo m; (of wheel) cerchione m

ind /raɪnd/ n (on fruit) scorza f; (on cheese) crosta f; (on bacon) cotenna f

ing[1] /rɪŋ/ n (circle) cerchio m; (on finger) anello m; (boxing) ring m inv; (for circus) pista f; **stand in a ~** essere in cerchio

ing[2] n suono m; **give sb a ~** (Teleph) dare un colpo di telefono a qcno • v (pt **rang**, pp **rung**) • vt suonare; **~ [up]** (Teleph) telefonare a • vi suonare; (Teleph) **~ [up]** telefonare. □ **~ back** vt/i (Teleph) richiamare. □ **~ off** vi (Teleph) riattaccare

ing: ~leader n capobanda m. **~ road** n circonvallazione f

ink /rɪŋk/ n pista f di pattinaggio

inse /rɪns/ n risciacquo m; (hair colour) cachet m inv • vt sciacquare

iot /'raɪət/ n rissa f; (of colour) accozzaglia f; **~s** pl disordini mpl; **run ~** impazzare • vi creare disordini. **~er** n dimostrante mf. **~ous** adj sfrenato

ip /rɪp/ n strappo m • vt (pt/pp **ripped**) strappare; **~ open** aprire con uno strappo. □ **~ off** vt [!] fregare

ripe /raɪp/ adj maturo; (cheese) stagionato

ripen /'raɪpn/ vi maturare; (cheese:) stagionarsi • vt far maturare; stagionare (cheese)

'rip-off n [!] frode f

ripple /'rɪpl/ n increspatura f; (sound) mormorio m •

rise /raɪz/ n (of sun) levata f; (fig: to fame, power) ascesa f; (increase) aumento m; **give ~ to** dare adito a • vi (pt **rose**, pp **risen**) alzarsi; (sun:) sorgere; (dough:) lievitare; (prices, water level:) aumentare; (to power, position) arrivare (**to** a). **~r** n **early ~r** persona f mattiniera

rising /'raɪzɪŋ/ adj (sun) levante; **~ generation** nuova generazione f • n (revolt) sollevazione f

risk /rɪsk/ n rischio m; **at one's own ~** a proprio rischio e pericolo • vt rischiare

risky /'rɪskɪ/ adj (**-ier, -iest**) rischioso

rite /raɪt/ n rito m; **last ~s** estrema unzione f

ritual /'rɪtjʊəl/ adj rituale • n rituale m

rival /'raɪvl/ adj rivale • n rivale mf; **~s** pl (Comm) concorrenti mpl • vt (pt/pp **rivalled**) rivaleggiare con. **~ry** n rivalità f inv; (Comm) concorrenza f

river /'rɪvə(r)/ n fiume m. **~-bed** n letto m del fiume

rivet /'rɪvɪt/ n rivetto m • vt rivettare; **~ed by** fig inchiodato da

road /rəʊd/ n strada f, via f; **be on the ~** viaggiare

road: ~-map n carta f stradale. **~side** n bordo m della strada. **~-works** npl lavori mpl stradali. **~worthy** adj sicuro

roam /rəʊm/ vi girovagare

roar /rɔː(r)/ n ruggito m; **~s of laughter** scroscio msg di risa • vi ruggire; (lorry, thunder:) rombare; **~ with laughter** ridere fragorosamente. **~ing** adj **do a ~ing trade** [!] fare affari d'oro

roast /rəʊst/ adj arrosto; **~ pork** arrosto m di maiale • n arrosto m • vt arrostire (meat) • vi arrostirsi

rob /rɒb/ vt (pt/pp **robbed**) derubare (**of** di); svaligiare (bank). **~ber** n rapinatore m. **~bery** n rapina f

robe /rəʊb/ n tunica f; (Am: bathrobe) accappatoio m

robin /'rɒbɪn/ n pettirosso m

robot /'rəʊbɒt/ n robot m inv

robust /rəʊ'bʌst/ adj robusto

rock[1] /rɒk/ n roccia f; (in sea) scoglio m; (sweet) zucchero m candito. **on the ~s** (ship) incagliato; (marriage) finito; (drink) con ghiaccio

rock[2] vt cullare (baby); (shake) far traballare; (shock) scuotere •vi dondolarsi

rock[3] n (Mus) rock m inv

rock-'bottom adj bassissimo •n livello m più basso

rocket /'rɒkɪt/ n razzo m •vi salire alle stelle

rocky /'rɒkɪ/ adj (**-ier, -iest**) roccioso; fig traballante

rod /rɒd/ n bacchetta f; (for fishing) canna f

rode /rəʊd/ ▹**ride**

rodent /'rəʊdnt/ n roditore m

rogue /rəʊg/ n farabutto m

role /rəʊl/ n ruolo m

roll /rəʊl/ n rotolo m; (bread) panino m; (list) lista f; (of ship, drum) rullio m •vi rotolare; **be ~ing in money** [!] nuotare nell'oro •vt spianare (lawn, pastry). ▫ **~ over** vi rigirarsi. ▫ **~ up** vt arrotolare; rimboccarsi (sleeves) •vi [!] arrivare

r

'roll-call n appello m

roller /'rəʊlə(r)/ n rullo m; (for hair) bigodino m. **~ blades** npl pattini npl in linea. **~ blind** n tapparella f. **~-coaster** n montagne fpl russe. **~-skate** n pattino m a rotelle

'rolling-pin n mattarello m

Roman /'rəʊmən/ adj romano •n romano, -a mf. **~ Catholic** adj cattolico •n cattolico, -a mf

romance /rəʊ'mæns/ n (love affair) storia f d'amore; (book) romanzo m rosa

Romania /rəʊ'meɪnɪə/ n Romania f. **~n** adj rumeno •n rumeno, -a mf

romantic /rəʊ'mæntɪk/ adj romantico. **~ally** adv romanticamente. **~ism** n romanticismo m

Rome /rəʊm/ n Roma f

romp /rɒmp/ n gioco m rumoroso •vi giocare rumorosamente. **~ers** npl pagliaccetto msg

roof /ru:f/ n tetto m; (of mouth) palato m •vt mettere un tetto su. **~-rack** n portabagagli m inv. **~-top** n tetto m

rook /rʊk/ n corvo m; (in chess) torre f

room /ru:m/ n stanza f; (bedroom) camera f; (for functions) sala f; (space) spazio m. **~y** adj spazioso; (clothes) ampio

roost /ru:st/ vi appollaiarsi

root[1] /ru:t/ n radice f; **take ~** mettere radici •**root out** vt fig scovare

root[2] vi **~ about** grufolare; **~ for sb** Am [!] fare il tifo per qcno

rope /rəʊp/ n corda f; **know the ~s** [!] conoscere i trucchi del mestiere •**rope in** vt [!] coinvolgere

rose[1] /rəʊz/ n rosa f; (of watering-can) bocchetta f

rose[2] ▹**rise**

rosé /'rəʊzeɪ/ n [vino m] rosé m inv

rot /rɒt/ n marciume m; ([!]: nonsense) sciocchezze fpl •vi (pt/pp **rotted**) marcire

rota /'rəʊtə/ n tabella f dei turni

rotary /'rəʊtərɪ/ adj rotante

rotat|e /rəʊ'teɪt/ vt far ruotare; avvicendare (crops) •vi ruotare. **~ion** n rotazione f; **in ~ion** a turno

rote /rəʊt/ n **by ~** meccanicamente

rotten /'rɒtn/ adj marcio; [!] schifoso; (person) penoso

rough /rʌf/ adj (not smooth) ruvido; (ground) accidentato; (behaviour) rozzo; (sport) violento; (area) malfamato; (crossing, time) brutto; (estimate) approssimativo •adv (play) grossolanamente; **sleep ~** dormire sotto i ponti •vt **~ it** vivere senza confort. ▫ **~ out** vt abbozzare

roughage /'rʌfɪdʒ/ n fibre fpl

rough|ly /'rʌflɪ/ adv rozzamente; (more or less) pressappoco. **~ness** n ruvidità f; (of behaviour) rozzezza f

roulette /ru:'let/ n roulette f inv

round /raʊnd/ adj rotondo •n tondo m; (slice) fetta f; (of visits, drinks) giro m (of competition) partita f; (boxing) ripresa f, round m inv; **do one's ~s**

(doctor:) fare il giro delle visite • prep intorno a; **open ~ the clock** aperto ventiquattr'ore • adv **all ~** tutt'intorno; **ask sb ~** invitare qcno; **go/come ~ to** (a friend etc) andare da; **turn/look ~** girarsi; **~ about** (approximately) intorno a • vt arrotondare; girare (corner). □ **~ down** vt arrotondare (per difetto). □ **~ off** vt (end) terminare. □ **~ on** vt aggredire. □ **~ up** vt radunare; arrotondare (prices)

undabout /'raʊndəbaʊt/ adj indiretto • n giostra f; (for traffic) rotonda f

und: ~ 'trip n viaggio m di andata e ritorno

us|e /raʊz/ vt svegliare; risvegliare (suspicion, interest). **~ing** adj di incoraggiamento

ute /ru:t/ n itinerario m; (Aeron, Naut) rotta f; (of bus) percorso m

utine /ru:'ti:n/ adj di routine • n routine f inv; (Theat) numero m

w¹ /rəʊ/ n (line) fila f; **three years in a ~** tre anni di fila

w² vi (in boat) remare

w³ /raʊ/ n 🅸 (quarrel) litigata f; (noise) baccano m • vi 🅸 litigare

wdy /'raʊdɪ/ adj (**-ier, -iest**) chiassoso

wing boat /'rəʊɪŋ-/ n barca f a remi

yal /rɔɪəl/ adj reale

yalt|y /'rɔɪəltɪ/ n appartenenza f alla famiglia reale; (persons) i membri mpl della famiglia reale. **~ies** npl (payments) diritti mpl d'autore

b /rʌb/ n **give sth a ~** dare una sfregata a qcsa • vt (pt/pp **rubbed**) sfregare. □ **~ in** vt **don't ~ it in** 🅸 non rigirare il coltello nella piaga. □ **~ off** vt mandar via sfregando (stain); (from blackboard) cancellare • vi andar via; **~ off on** essere trasmesso a. □ **~ out** vt cancellare

bber /'rʌbə(r)/ n gomma f; (eraser) gomma f [da cancellare]. **~ band** n elastico m. **~y** adj gommoso

bbish /'rʌbɪʃ/ n immondizie fpl; (🅸: nonsense) idiozie fpl; (🅸: junk) robaccia f • vt 🅸 fare a pezzi. **~ bin** n pattumiera f. **~ dump** n discarica f; (official) discarica f comunale

rubble /'rʌbl/ n macerie fpl

ruby /'ru:bɪ/ n rubino m • attrib di rubini; (lips) scarlatta

rucksack /'rʌksæk/ n zaino m

rudder /'rʌdə(r)/ n timone m

rude /ru:d/ adj scortese; (improper) spinto. **~ly** adv scortesemente. **~ness** n scortesia f

ruffian /'rʌfɪən/ n farabutto m

ruffle /'rʌfl/ n gala f • vt scompigliare (hair)

rug /rʌg/ n tappeto m; (blanket) coperta f

rugby /'rʌgbɪ/ n **~ [football]** rugby m

rugged /'rʌgɪd/ adj (coastline) roccioso

ruin /'ru:ɪn/ n rovina f; **in ~s** in rovina • vt rovinare. **~ous** adj estremamente costoso

rule /ru:l/ n regola f; (control) ordinamento m; (for measuring) metro m; **~s** regolamento msg; **as a ~** generalmente • vt governare; dominare (colony, behaviour); **~ that** stabilire che • vi governare. □ **~ out** vt escludere

ruler /'ru:lə(r)/ n capo m di Stato; (sovereign) sovrano, -a mf; (measure) righello m, regolo m

ruling /'ru:lɪŋ/ adj (class) dirigente; (party) di governo • n decisione f

rum /rʌm/ n rum m inv

rumble /'rʌmbl/ n rombo m; (of stomach) brontolio m • vi rombare; (stomach:) brontolare

rummage /'rʌmɪdʒ/ vi rovistare (**in/through** in)

rumour /'ru:mə(r)/ n diceria f • vt **it is ~ed that** si dice che

run /rʌn/ n (on foot) corsa f; (distance to be covered) tragitto m; (outing) giro m; (Theat) rappresentazioni fpl; (in skiing) pista f; (Am: ladder) smagliatura f (in calze); **at a ~** di corsa; **~ of bad luck** periodo m sfortunato; **on the ~** in fuga; **have the ~ of** avere a disposizione; **in the long ~** a lungo termine • v (pt **ran**, pp **run**, pres p **running**) • vi correre; (river:) scorrere; (nose, make-up:) colare; (bus:) fare servizio; (play:) essere in cartellone; (colours:) sbiadire; (in election) presentarsi [come candidato] • vt (manage) dirigere; tenere (house); (drive) dare un passaggio a; correre (risk); (Comput) lanciare; (Journ) pubblicare (article); (pass) far scorrere (eyes, hand); ~ **a bath** far scorrere l'acqua per il bagno. □ ~ **across** vt (meet, find) imbattersi in. □ ~ **away** vi scappare [via]. □ ~ **down** vi scaricarsi; (clock:) scaricarsi; (stocks:) esaurirsi • vt (Auto) investire; (reduce) esaurire; (!: criticize) denigrare. □ ~ **in** vi entrare di corsa. □ ~ **into** vi (meet) imbattersi in; (knock against) urtare. □ ~ **off** vi andare via di corsa • vt stampare (copies). □ ~ **out** vi uscire di corsa; (supplies, money:) esaurirsi; ~ **out of** rimanere senza. □ ~ **over** vi correre; (overflow) traboccare • vt (Auto) investire. □ ~ **through** vi scorrere. □ ~ **up** vi salire di corsa; (towards) arrivare di corsa • vt accumulare (debts, bill); (sew) cucire

'runaway n fuggitivo, -a mf

run-'down adj (area) in abbandono; (person) esaurito • n analisi f

rung[1] /rʌŋ/ n (of ladder) piolo m

rung[2] ▹**ring**[2]

runner /'rʌnə(r)/ n podista mf; (in race) corridore, -trice mf; (on sledge) pattino m. ~ **bean** n fagiolino m. **~-up** n secondo, -a mf classificato, -a

running /'rʌnɪŋ/ adj in corsa; (water) corrente; **four times** ~ quattro volte di seguito • n corsa f; (management) direzione f; **be in the** ~ essere in lizza. ~ **'commentar[y]** n cronaca f

runny /'rʌnɪ/ adj semiliquido; ~ **nose** naso che cola

runway n pista f

rupture /'rʌptʃə(r)/ n rottura f; (Me[d]) ernia f • vt rompere; ~ **oneself** fa[rsi] venire l'ernia • vi rompersi

rural /'rʊərəl/ adj rurale

ruse /ru:z/ n astuzia f

rush[1] /rʌʃ/ n (Bot) giunco m

rush[2] n fretta f; **in a** ~ di fretta • v[i] precipitarsi • vt far premura a; ~ **s[b]** **to hospital** trasportare qcno di corsa all'ospedale. **~-hour** n ora f punta

Russia /'rʌʃə/ n Russia f. **~n** adj & n russo, -a mf; (language) russo m

rust /rʌst/ n ruggine f • vi arruggini[re]

rustle /'rʌsl/ vi frusciare • vt far frusciare; Am rubare (cattle). □ ~ **u[p]** vt ! rimediare

'rustproof adj a prova di ruggine

rusty /'rʌstɪ/ adj (**-ier, -iest**) arrugginito

rut /rʌt/ n solco m; **in a** ~ ! nella routine

ruthless /'ru:θlɪs/ adj spietato. **~ness** n spietatezza f

rye /raɪ/ n segale f

r s

Ss

sabot|age /'sæbətɑ:ʒ/ n sabotaggio m • vt sabotare. **~eur** n sabotatore, -trice mf

saccharin /'sæʃeɪ/ n saccarina f

sachet /'sæʃeɪ/ n bustina f; (scented) sacchetto m profumato

sack[1] /sæk/ vt (plunder) saccheggiare

sack[2] n sacco m; **get the** ~ ! essere licenziato • vt ! licenziare. **~ing** n tela f per sacchi; (!: dismissal) licenziamento m

sacrament /'sækrəmənt/ n sacramento m

sacred /'seɪkrɪd/ adj sacro

sacrifice /'sækrɪfaɪs/ n sacrificio m • vt sacrificare

sacrilege /'sækrɪlɪdʒ/ n sacrilegio [m]

sad /sæd/ adj (**sadder, saddest**) trist[e]. **~den** vt rattristare

saddle /'sædl/ n sella f • vt sellare; **I've been ~d with...** fig mi hann[o] affibbiato...

ad|ly /'sædlɪ/ adv tristemente; (unfortunately) sfortunatamente. **~ness** n tristezza f

afe /seɪf/ adj sicuro; (out of danger) salvo; (object) al sicuro; **~ and sound** sano e salvo •n cassaforte f. **~guard** n protezione f •vt proteggere. **~ly** adv in modo sicuro; (arrive) senza incidenti; (assume) con certezza

afety /'seɪftɪ/ n sicurezza f. **~-belt** n cintura f di sicurezza. **~-deposit box** n cassetta f di sicurezza. **~-pin** n spilla f di sicurezza o da balia. **~-valve** n valvola f di sicurezza

ag /sæg/ vi (pt/pp **sagged**) abbassarsi

aga /'sɑ:gə/ n saga f

age /seɪdʒ/ n (herb) salvia f

agittarius /sædʒɪ'teərɪəs/ n Sagittario m

aid /sed/ ▸**say**

ail /seɪl/ n vela f; (trip) giro m in barca a vela •vi navigare; (Sport) praticare la vela; (leave) salpare •vt pilotare

ailing /'seɪlɪŋ/ n vela f. **~-boat** n barca f a vela. **~-ship** n veliero m

ailor /'seɪlə(r)/ n marinaio m

aint /seɪnt/ n santo, -a mf. **~ly** adj da santo

ake /seɪk/ n **for the ~ of** (person) per il bene di; (peace) per amor di; **for the ~ of it** per il gusto di farlo

alad /'sæləd/ n insalata f. **~ bowl** n insalatiera f. **~ cream** n salsa f per condire l'insalata. **~-dressing** n condimento m per insalata

alary /'sælərɪ/ n stipendio m

ale /seɪl/ n vendita f (at reduced prices) svendita f; **for/on ~** in vendita

ales|man /'seɪlzmən/ n venditore m; (traveller) rappresentante m. **~woman** n venditrice f

aliva /sə'laɪvə/ n saliva f

almon /'sæmən/ n salmone m

aloon /sə'lu:n/ n (Auto) berlina f; (Am: bar) bar m

alt /sɔ:lt/ n sale m •adj salato; (fish, meat) sotto sale •vt salare; (cure) mettere sotto sale. **~-cellar** n saliera f. **~ 'water** n acqua f di mare. **~y** adj salato

alute /sə'lu:t/ (Mil) n saluto m •vt salutare •vi fare il saluto

salvage /'sælvɪdʒ/ n (Naut) recupero m •vt recuperare

salvation /sæl'veɪʃn/ n salvezza f. **S~ 'Army** n Esercito m della Salvezza

same /seɪm/ adj stesso (**as** di) •pron **the ~** lo stesso; **be all the ~** essere tutti uguali •adv **the ~** nello stesso modo; **all the ~** (however) lo stesso; **the ~ to you** altrettanto

sample /'sɑ:mpl/ n campione m •vt testare

sanction /'sæŋkʃn/ n (approval) autorizzazione f; (penalty) sanzione f •vt autorizzare

sanctuary /'sæŋktjʊərɪ/ n (Relig) santuario m; (refuge) asilo m; (for wildlife) riserva f

sand /sænd/ n sabbia f •vt ~ [**down**] carteggiare

sandal /'sændl/ n sandalo m

sandpaper n carta f vetrata •vt cartavetrare

sandwich /'sænwɪdʒ/ n tramezzino m •vt **~ed between** schiacciato tra

sandy /'sændɪ/ adj (**-ier, -iest**) (beach, soil) sabbioso; (hair) biondiccio

sane /seɪn/ adj (not mad) sano di mente; (sensible) sensato

sang /sæŋ/ ▸**sing**

sanitary /'sænɪtərɪ/ adj igienico; (system) sanitario. **~ napkin** n Am, **~ towel** n assorbente m igienico

sanitation /sænɪ'teɪʃn/ n impianti mpl igienici

sanity /'sænətɪ/ n sanità f inv di mente; (common sense) buon senso m

sank /sæŋk/ ▸**sink**

sapphire /'sæfaɪə(r)/ n zaffiro m •adj blu zaffiro

sarcas|m /'sɑ:kæzm/ n sarcasmo m. **~tic** adj sarcastico

sardine /sɑ:'di:n/ n sardina f

sash /sæʃ/ n fascia f; (for dress) fusciacca f

sat /sæt/ ▸**sit**

satchel /'sætʃl/ n cartella f

satellite /'sætəlaɪt/ n satellite m. **~ dish** n antenna f parabolica. **~ television** n televisione f via satellite

satin /'sætɪn/ n raso m • attrib di raso

satire /'sætaɪə(r)/ n satira f

satirical /sə'tɪrɪkl/ adj satirico

satisfaction /sætɪs'fækʃn/ n soddisfazione f; **be to sb's ~** soddisfare qcno

satisfactor|y /sætɪs'fæktərɪ/ adj soddisfacente. **~ily** adv in modo soddisfacente

satisf|y /'sætɪsfaɪ/ vt (pp/pp **-fied**) soddisfare; (convince) convincere; **be ~ied** essere soddisfatto. **~ying** adj soddisfacente

satphone /'sætfəʊn/ n telefono m satellitare

saturat|e /'sætʃəreɪt/ vt inzuppare (**with** di); (Chem), fig saturare (**with** di). **~ed** adj saturo

Saturday /'sætədeɪ/ n sabato m

sauce /sɔ:s/ n salsa f; (cheek) impertinenza f. **~pan** n pentola f

saucer /'sɔ:sə(r)/ n piattino m

saucy /'sɔ:sɪ/ adj (**-ier, -iest**) impertinente

Saudi Arabia /saʊdɪə'reɪbɪə/ n Arabia f Saudita

sauna /'sɔ:nə/ n sauna f

saunter /'sɔ:ntə(r)/ vi andare a spasso

sausage /'sɒsɪdʒ/ n salsiccia f; (dried) salame m

savage /'sævɪdʒ/ adj feroce; (tribe, custom) selvaggio • n selvaggio, -a mf • vt fare a pezzi. **~ry** n ferocia f

save /seɪv/ n (Sport) parata f • vt salvare (**from** da); (keep, collect) tenere; risparmiare (time, money); (avoid) evitare; (Sport) parare (goal); (Comput) salvare, memorizzare • vi **~** [**up**] risparmiare • prep salvo

saver /'seɪvə(r)/ n risparmiatore, -trice mf

savings /'seɪvɪŋz/ npl (money) risparmi mpl. **~ account** n libretto m di risparmio. **~ bank** n cassa f di risparmio

saviour /'seɪvjə(r)/ n salvatore m

savour /'seɪvə(r)/ n sapore m • vt assaporare. **~y** adj salato; fig rispettabile

saw¹ /sɔ:/ ▸**see**

saw² n sega f • vt/i (pt **sawed**, pp **sawn** or **sawed**) segare. **~dust** n segatura f

saxophone /'sæksəfəʊn/ n sassofono m

say /seɪ/ n **have one's ~** dire la propria; **have a ~** avere voce in capitolo • vt/i (pt/pp **said**) dire; **that is to ~** cioè; **that goes without ~ing** questo è ovvio; **when all is said and done** alla fine dei conti. **~ing** n proverbio m

scab /skæb/ n crosta f; pej crumiro m

scald /skɔ:ld/ vt scottare; (milk) scaldare • n scottatura f

scale¹ /skeɪl/ n (of fish) scaglia f

scale² n scala f; **on a grand ~** su vasta scala • vt (climb) scalare. □ **~ down** vt diminuire

scales /skeɪlz/ npl (for weighing) bilancia fsg

scalp /skælp/ n cuoio m capelluto

scamper /'skæmpə(r)/ vi **~ away** sgattaiolare via

scan /skæn/ n (Med) scanning m inv, scansioscintigrafia f • vt (pt/pp **scanned**) scrutare; (quickly) dare un scorsa a; (Med) fare uno scanning d

scandal /'skændl/ n scandalo m; (gossip) pettegolezzi mpl. **~ize** vt scandalizzare. **~ous** adj scandaloso

Scandinavia /skændɪ'neɪvɪə/ n Scandinavia f. **~n** adj & n scandinavo, -a mf

scanner /'skænə(r)/ n (Comput) scanner m inv

scant /skænt/ adj scarso

scant|y /'skæntɪ/ adj (**-ier, -iest**) scarso; (clothing) succinto. **~ily** adv scarsamente; (clothed) succintament

scapegoat /'skeɪp-/ n capro m espiatorio

scar /skɑ:(r)/ n cicatrice f • vt (pt/pp **scarred**) lasciare una cicatrice a

scarc|e /skeəs/ adj scarso; fig raro; **make oneself ~e** [!] svignarsela. **~ely** adv appena; **~ely anything** quasi niente. **~ity** n scarsezza f

scare /skeə(r)/ n spavento m; (panic) panico m • vt spaventare; **be ~d** aver paura (**of** di)

'scarecrow n spaventapasseri m inv

scarf /skɑ:f/ n (pl **scarves**) sciarpa f; (square) foulard m inv

carlet /'skɑ:lət/ adj scarlatto. ~ '**fever** n scarlattina f

cary /'skeərɪ/ adj **be** ~ far paura

cathing /'skeɪðɪŋ/ adj mordace

catter /'skætə(r)/ vt spargere; (disperse) disperdere • vi disperdersi. ~**-brained** adj [!] scervellato. ~**ed** adj sparso

cavenge /'skævɪndʒ/ vi frugare nella spazzatura. ~**r** n persona f che fruga nella spazzatura

cenario /sɪ'nɑ:rɪəʊ/ n scenario m

cene /si:n/ n scena f; (quarrel) scenata f; **behind the** ~**s** dietro le quinte

cenery /'si:nərɪ/ n scenario m

cenic /'si:nɪk/ adj panoramico

cent /sent/ n odore m; (trail) scia f; (perfume) profumo m. ~**ed** adj profumato (**with** di)

ceptic|al /'skeptɪkl/ adj scettico. ~**ism** n scetticismo m

chedule /'ʃedju:l/ n piano m, programma m; (of work) programma m; (timetable) orario m; **behind** ~ indietro; **on** ~ nei tempi previsti; **according to** ~ secondo i tempi previsti • vt prevedere. ~**d flight** n volo m di linea

cheme /ski:m/ n (plan) piano m; (plot) macchinazione f • vi pej macchinare

cholar /'skɒlə(r)/ n studioso, -a mf. ~**ly** adj erudito. ~**ship** n erudizione f; (grant) borsa f di studio

school /sku:l/ n scuola f; (in university) facoltà f; (of fish) branco m

school: ~**boy** n scolaro m. ~**girl** n scolara f. ~**ing** n istruzione f. ~**-teacher** n insegnante mf

sciatica /saɪ'ætɪkə/ n sciatica f

scien|ce /'saɪəns/ n scienza f; ~**ce fiction** fantascienza f. ~**tific** adj scientifico. ~**tist** n scienziato, -a mf

scissors /'sɪzəz/ npl forbici fpl

scoff[1] /skɒf/ vi ~ **at** schernire

scoff[2] vt [!] divorare

scold /skəʊld/ vt sgridare. ~**ing** n sgridata f

scoop /sku:p/ n paletta f; (Journ) scoop m inv • **scoop out** vt svuotare. □~ **up** vt tirar su

scope /skəʊp/ n portata f; (opportunity) opportunità f inv

scorch /skɔ:tʃ/ vt bruciare. ~**er** n [!] giornata f torrida. ~**ing** adj caldissimo

score /skɔ:(r)/ n punteggio m; (individual) punteggio m; (Mus) partitura f; (for film, play) musica f; **a** ~ [**of**] (twenty) una ventina [di]; **keep** [**the**] ~ tenere il punteggio; **on that** ~ a questo proposito • vt segnare (goal); (cut) incidere • vi far punti; (in football etc) segnare; (keep score) tenere il punteggio. ~**r** n segnapunti m inv; (of goals) giocatore, -trice mf che segna

scorn /skɔ:n/ n disprezzo m • vt disprezzare. ~**ful** adj sprezzante

Scorpio /'skɔ:pɪəʊ/ n Scorpione m

scorpion /'skɔ:pɪən/ n scorpione m

Scot /skɒt/ n scozzese mf

scotch vt far cessare

Scotch /skɒtʃ/ adj scozzese • n (whisky) whisky m [scozzese]

Scot|land /'skɒtlənd/ n Scozia f. ~**s**, ~**tish** adj scozzese

scoundrel /'skaʊndrəl/ n mascalzone m

scour[1] /'skaʊə(r)/ vt (search) perlustrare

scour[2] vt (clean) strofinare

scourge /skɜ:dʒ/ n flagello m

scout /skaʊt/ n (Mil) esploratore m • vi ~ **for** andare in cerca di

Scout n [**Boy**] ~ [boy]scout m inv

scowl /skaʊl/ n sguardo m torvo • vi guardare [di] storto

scram /skræm/ vi [!] levarsi dai piedi

scramble /'skræmbl/ n (climb) arrampicata f • vi (clamber) arrampicarsi; ~ **for** azzuffarsi per • vt (Teleph) creare delle interferenze in; (eggs) strapazzare

scrap[1] /skræp/ n ([!]: fight) litigio m

scrap[2] n pezzetto m; (metal) ferraglia f; ~**s** pl (of food) avanzi mpl • vt (pt/pp **scrapped**) buttare via

'**scrap-book** n album m inv

scrape /skreɪp/ vt raschiare; (damage) graffiare. □~ **through** vi passare per un pelo. □~ **together** vt racimolare

scraper /'skreɪpə(r)/ n raschietto m

S

'scrap-yard n deposito m di ferraglia; (for cars) cimitero m delle macchine

scratch /skrætʃ/ n graffio m; (to relieve itch) grattata f; **start from ~** partire da zero; **up to ~** (work) all'altezza •vt graffiare; (to relieve itch) grattare •vi grattarsi. **~ card** n gratta e vinci m inv

scrawl /skrɔ:l/ n scarabocchio m •vt/i scarabocchiare

scream /skri:m/ n strillo m •vt/i strillare

screech /skri:tʃ/ n stridore m •vi stridere •vt strillare

screen /skri:n/ n paravento m; (Cinema, TV) schermo m •vt proteggere; (conceal) riparare; proiettare (film); (candidates) passare al setaccio; (Med) sottoporre a visita medica. **~ing** n (Med) visita f medica; (of film) proiezione f. **~play** n sceneggiatura f

screw /skru:/ n vite f •vt avvitare. □ **~ up** vt (crumple) accartocciare; strizzare (eyes); storcere (face); (☒: bungle) mandare all'aria. **~driver** cacciavite m

scribble /'skrɪbl/ n scarabocchio m •vt/i scarabocchiare

script /skrɪpt/ n scrittura f (a mano); (of film) sceneggiatura f

scroll /skrəʊl/ n rotolo m (di pergamena); (decoration) voluta f. □ **~ down** vi scorrere in giù

scrounge /skraʊndʒ/ vt/i scroccare. **~r** n scroccone, -a mf

scrub¹ /skrʌb/ n (land) boscaglia f

S

scrub² vt/i (pt/pp **scrubbed**) strofinare; (☐: cancel) cancellare (plan)

scruff /skrʌf/ n **by the ~ of the neck** per la collottola

scruffy /'skrʌfɪ/ adj (**-ier, -iest**) trasandato

scruple /'skru:pl/ n scrupolo m

scrupulous /'skru:pjʊləs/ adj scrupoloso

scrutin|ize /'skru:tɪnaɪz/ vt scrutinare. **~y** n (look) esame m minuzioso

scuffle /'skʌfl/ n tafferuglio m

sculpt /skʌlpt/ vt/i scolpire. **~or** n scultore m. **~ure** n scultura f

scum /skʌm/ n schiuma f; (people) feccia f

scurry /'skʌrɪ/ vi (pt/pp **-ied**) affrettare il passo

scuttle /'skʌtl/ vi (hurry) **~ away** correre via

sea /si:/ n mare m; **at ~** in mare; fig confuso; **by ~** via mare. **~board** n costiera f. **~food** n frutti mpl di mare. **~gull** n gabbiano m

seal¹ /si:l/ n (Zool) foca f

seal² n sigillo m; (Techn) chiusura f ermetica •vt sigillare; (Techn) chiudere ermeticamente. □ **~ off** vt bloccare (area)

'sea-level n livello m del mare

seam /si:m/ n cucitura f; (of coal) strato m

'seaman n marinaio m

seamy /'si:mɪ/ adj sordido; (area) malfamato

seance /'seɪɑ:ns/ n seduta f spiritica

search /sɜ:tʃ/ n ricerca f; (official) perquisizione f; **in ~ of** alla ricerca di •vt frugare (**for** alla ricerca di); perlustrare (area); (officially) perquisire •vi **~ for** cercare. **~ing** adj penetrante

search: ~light n riflettore m. **~-party** n squadra f di ricerca

sea: ~sick adj **be/get ~** avere il mal di mare. **~side** n **at/to the ~side** al mare

season /'si:zn/ n stagione f •vt (flavour) condire. **~able** adj, **~al** adj stagionale. **~ing** n condimento m

'season ticket n abbonamento m

seat /si:t/ n (chair) sedia f; (in car) sedile m; (place to sit) posto m [a sedere]; (bottom) didietro m; (of government) sede f; **take a ~** sedersi •vt mettere a sedere; (have seats for) aver posti [a sedere] per; **remain ~ed** mantenere il proprio posto. **~-belt** n cintura f di sicurezza

sea: ~weed n alga f marina. **~worthy** adj in stato di navigare

seclu|ded /sɪ'klu:dɪd/ adj appartato. **~sion** n isolamento m

second¹ /sɪ'kɒnd/ vt (transfer) distaccare

second² /'sekənd/ adj secondo; **on ~ thoughts** ripensandoci meglio •n secondo m; **~s** pl (goods) merce fsg di seconda scelta; **have ~s** (at meal) fare il bis; **John the S~** Giovanni Secondo • adv (in race) al secondo posto • vt assistere; appoggiare (proposal)

secondary /'sekəndrɪ/ adj secondario. **~ school** n ≈ scuola f media (inferiore e superiore)

second: ~ 'class adv (travel, send) in seconda classe. **~-class** adj di seconda classe

second hand n (on clock) lancetta f dei secondi

second-'hand adj & adv di seconda mano

secondly /'sekəndlɪ/ adv in secondo luogo

second-'rate adj di second'ordine

secrecy /'si:krəsɪ/ n segretezza f; **in ~** in segreto

secret /'si:krɪt/ adj segreto • n segreto m

secretarial /sekrə'teərɪəl/ adj (work, staff) di segreteria

secretary /'sekrətərɪ/ n segretario, -a mf

secretive /'si:krətɪv/ adj riservato. **~ness** n riserbo m

sect /sekt/ n setta f. **~arian** adj settario

section /'sekʃn/ n sezione f

sector /'sektə(r)/ n settore m

secular /'sekjʊlə(r)/ adj secolare; (education) laico

secure /sɪ'kjʊə(r)/ adj sicuro • vt proteggere; chiudere bene (door); rendere stabile (ladder); (obtain) assicurarsi. **~ly** adv saldamente

securit|y /sɪ'kjʊərətɪ/ n sicurezza f; (for loan) garanzia f. **~ies** npl titoli mpl

sedate[1] /sɪ'deɪt/ adj posato

sedate[2] vt somministrare sedativi a

sedation /sɪ'deɪʃn/ n somministrazione f di sedativi; **be under ~** essere sotto l'effetto di sedativi

sedative /'sedətɪv/ adj sedativo • n sedativo m

sediment /'sedɪmənt/ n sedimento m

seduce /sɪ'dju:s/ vt sedurre

seduct|ion /sɪ'dʌkʃn/ n seduzione f. **~ive** adj seducente

see /si:/ v (pt **saw**, pp **seen**) • vt vedere; (understand) capire; (escort) accompagnare; **go and ~** andare a vedere; (visit) andare a trovare; **~ you!** ci vediamo!; **~ you later!** a più tardi!; **~ing that** visto che • vi vedere; (understand) capire; **~ that** (make sure) assicurarsi che; **~ about** occuparsi di. □ **~ off** vt veder partire; (chase away) mandar via. □ **~ through** vi vedere attraverso; fig non farsi ingannare da • vt portare a buon fine. □ **~ to** vi occuparsi di

seed /si:d/ n seme m; (Tennis) testa f di serie; **go to ~** fare seme; fig lasciarsi andare. **~ed player** n (Tennis) testa f di serie. **~ling** n pianticella f

seedy /'si:dɪ/ adj (**-ier, -iest**) squallido

seek /si:k/ vt (pt/pp **sought**) cercare

seem /si:m/ vi sembrare. **~ingly** adv apparentemente

seen /si:n/ ▸**see**

seep /si:p/ vi filtrare

see-saw /'si:sɔ:/ n altalena f

seethe /si:ð/ vi **~ with anger** ribollire di rabbia

'see-through adj trasparente

segment /'segmənt/ n segmento m; (of orange) spicchio m

segregat|e /'segrɪgeɪt/ vt segregare. **~ion** n segregazione f

seize /si:z/ vt afferrare; (Jur) confiscare. □ **~ up** vi (Techn) bloccarsi

seizure /'si:ʒə(r)/ n (Jur) confisca f; (Med) colpo m [apoplettico]

seldom /'seldəm/ adv raramente

select /sɪ'lekt/ adj scelto; (exclusive) esclusivo • vt scegliere; selezionare (team). **~ion** n selezione f. **~ive** adj selettivo. **~or** n (Sport) selezionatore, -trice mf

self /self/ n io m

self: ~-ad'dressed adj con il proprio indirizzo. **~-'catering** adj in appartamento attrezzato di cucina. **~-'centred** adj egocentrico. **~-'confidence** n fiducia f in se stesso. **~-'confident** adj sicuro di sé. **~-'conscious** adj impacciato. **~-con'tained** adj (flat) con ingresso indipendente. **~-con'trol**

S

n autocontrollo m. **~-de'fence** n autodifesa f; (Jur) legittima difesa f. **~-em'ployed** adj che lavora in proprio. **~-'evident** adj ovvio. **~-in'dulgent** adj indulgente con se stesso. **~-'interest** n interesse m personale

self|ish /'selfɪʃ/ adj egoista. **~ishness** n egoismo m. **~less** adj disinteressato

self: ~-pity n autocommiserazione f. **~-'portrait** n autoritratto m. **~-re'spect** n amor m proprio. **~-'righteous** adj presuntuoso. **~-'sacrifice** n abnegazione f. **~-'satisfied** adj compiaciuto di sé. **~-'service** n self-service m inv •attrib self-service. **~-suf'ficient** adj autosufficiente

sell /sel/ v (pt/pp **sold**) •vt vendere; **be sold out** essere esaurito •vi vendersi. □ **~ off** vt liquidare

seller /'selə(r)/ n venditore, -trice mf

Sellotape® /'seləʊ-/ n nastro m adesivo, scotch® m

'sell-out n (!: betrayal) tradimento m; **be a ~** (concert:) fare il tutto esaurito

semblance /'sembləns/ n parvenza f

semester /sɪ'mestə(r)/ n Am semestre m

semi /'semɪ/: **~breve** /'semɪbriːv/ n semibreve f. **~circle** n semicerchio m. **~'circular** adj semicircolare. **~'colon** n punto e virgola m. **~-de'tached** adj gemella •n casa f gemella. **~-'final** n semifinale f

seminar /'semɪnɑː(r)/ n seminario m. **~y** n seminario m

senat|e /'senət/ n senato m. **~or** n senatore m

send /send/ vt/i (pt/pp **sent**) mandare; **~ for** mandare a chiamare (person); far venire (thing). **~er** n mittente mf. **~-off** n commiato m

senil|e /'siːnaɪl/ adj arteriosclerotico; (Med) senile. **~ity** n senilismo m

senior /'siːnɪə(r)/ adj più vecchio; (in rank) superiore •n (in rank) superiore mf; (in sport) senior mf; **she's two years my ~** è più vecchia di me di due anni. **~ 'citizen** n anziano, -a mf

seniority /siːnɪ'ɒrətɪ/ n anzianità f inv di servizio

sensation /sen'seɪʃn/ n sensazione f. **~al** adj sensazionale. **~ally** adv in modo sensazionale

sense /sens/ n senso m; (common ~) buon senso m; **in a ~** in un certo senso; **make ~** aver senso •vt sentire. **~less** adj insensato; (unconscious) privo di sensi

sensibl|e /'sensəbl/ adj sensato; (suitable) appropriato. **~y** adv in modo appropriato

sensitiv|e /'sensətɪv/ adj sensibile; (touchy) suscettibile. **~ely** adv con sensibilità. **~ity** n sensibilità f inv

sensual /'sensjʊəl/ adj sensuale. **~ity** n sensualità f inv

sensuous /'sensjʊəs/ adj voluttuoso

sent /sent/ ▸**send**

sentence /'sentəns/ n frase f; (Jur) sentenza f; (punishment) condanna f •vt **~ to** condannare a

sentiment /'sentɪmənt/ n sentimento m; (opinion) opinione f; (sentimentality) sentimentalismo m. **~al** adj sentimentale; pej sentimentalista. **~ality** n sentimentalità f inv

sentry /'sentrɪ/ n sentinella f

separable /'sepərəbl/ adj separabile

separate¹ /'sepərət/ adj separato. **~ly** adv separatamente

separat|e² /'sepəreɪt/ vt separare •vi separarsi. **~ion** n separazione f

September /sep'tembə(r)/ n settembre m

septic /'septɪk/ adj settico; **go ~** infettarsi. **~ tank** n fossa f biologica

sequel /'siːkwəl/ n seguito m

sequence /'siːkwəns/ n sequenza f

Serbia /'sɜːbɪə/ n Serbia f

serenade /serə'neɪd/ n serenata f •vt fare una serenata a

seren|e /sɪ'riːn/ adj sereno. **~ity** n serenità f inv

sergeant /'sɑːdʒənt/ n sergente m

serial /'sɪərɪəl/ n racconto m a puntate; (TV) sceneggiato m a puntate; (Radio) commedia f radiofonica. **~ize** vt pubblicare a puntate; (Radio, TV) trasmettere a puntate. **~ killer** n serial killer mf inv. **~ number** n numero m di serie. **~ port** n (Comput) porta f seriale

S

ries /ˈsɪəriːz/ n serie f inv

rious /ˈsɪərɪəs/ adj serio; (illness, rror) grave. **~ly** adv seriamente; (ill) ravemente; **take ~ly** prendere sul erio. **~ness** n serietà f inv; (of ıtuation) gravità f inv

rmon /ˈsɜːmən/ n predica f

rum /ˈsɪərəm/ n siero m

rvant /ˈsɜːvənt/ n domestico, -a mf

rve /sɜːv/ n (Tennis) servizio m •vt ervire; scontare (sentence); **~ its urpose** servire al proprio scopo; **it ~s you right!** ben ti sta!; **~s two** ıer due persone •vi prestare ervizio; (Tennis) servire; **~ as** servire da. **~r** n (Comput) server m inv

rvice /ˈsɜːvɪs/ n servizio m; (Relig) unzione f; (maintenance) revisione f; **~s** pl forze fpl armate; (on motorway) rea f di servizio; **in the ~s** sotto le rmi; **of ~ to** utile a; **out of ~** machine:) guasto •vt (Techn) evisionare. **~able** adj utilizzabile; hard-wearing) resistente; (practical) ratico

rvice: ~ charge n servizio m. **~ station** n stazione f di servizio

rviette /sɜːvɪˈet/ n tovagliolo m

rvile /ˈsɜːvaɪl/ adj servile

ssion /ˈseʃn/ n seduta f; (Jur) sessione f; (Univ) anno m accademico

et /set/ n serie f, set m inv; (of crockery, cutlery) servizio m; (Radio, TV) apparecchio m; (Math) insieme m; (Theat) scenario m; (Cinema, Tennis) set m inv; (of people) circolo m; (of hair) messa f in piega •adj (ready) pronto; (rigid) fisso; (book) in programma; **be ~ on doing sth** essere risoluto a fare qcsa; **be ~ in one's ways** essere abitudinario •v (pt/pp **set**, pres p **setting**) •vt mettere, porre; mettere (alarm clock); assegnare (task, homework); fissare (date, limit); chiedere (questions); montare (gem); assestare (bone); apparecchiare (table); **~ fire to** dare fuoco a; **~ free** liberare •vi (sun:) tramontare; (jelly, concrete:) solidificare; **~ about doing sth** mettersi a fare qcsa. □ **~ back** vt mettere indietro; (hold up) ritardare; (!: cost) costare a. □ **~ off** vi partire •vt avviare; mettere (alarm); fare esplodere (bomb). □ **~ out** vi partire; **~ out to do sth** proporsi di fare qcsa •vt disporre; (state) esporre. □ **~ to** vi mettersi all'opera. □ **~ up** vt fondare (company); istituire (committee)

ˈset-back n passo m indietro

settee /seˈtiː/ n divano m

setting /ˈsetɪŋ/ n scenario m; (position) posizione f; (of sun) tramonto m; (of jewel) montatura f

settle /ˈsetl/ vt (decide) definire; risolvere (argument); fissare (date); calmare (nerves); saldare (bill) •vi (to live) stabilirsi; (snow, dust, bird:) posarsi; (subside) assestarsi; (sediment:) depositarsi. □ **~ down** vi sistemarsi; (stop making noise) calmarsi. □ **~ for** vt accontentarsi di. □ **~ up** vi regolare i conti

settlement /ˈsetlmənt/ n (agreement) accordo m; (of bill) saldo m; (colony) insediamento m

settler /ˈsetlə(r)/ n colonizzatore, -trice mf

ˈset-to n ! zuffa f; (verbal) battibecco m

ˈset-up n situazione f

seven /ˈsevn/ adj sette. **~ˈteen** adj diciassette. **~ˈteenth** adj diciasettesimo

seventh /ˈsevnθ/ adj settimo

seventieth /ˈsevntɪɪθ/ adj settantesimo

seventy /ˈsevntɪ/ adj settanta

sever /ˈsevə(r)/ vt troncare (relations)

several /ˈsevrəl/ adj & pron parecchi

sever|e /sɪˈvɪə(r)/ adj severo; (pain) violento; (illness) grave; (winter) rigido. **~ely** adv severamente; (ill) gravemente. **~ity** n severità f inv; (of pain) violenza f; (of illness) gravità f; (of winter) rigore m

sew /səʊ/ vt/i (pt **sewed**, pp **sewn** or **sewed**) cucire. □ **~ up** vt ricucire

sewage /ˈsuːɪdʒ/ n acque fpl di scolo

sewer /ˈsuːə(r)/ n fogna f

sewing /ˈsəʊɪŋ/ n cucito m; (work) lavoro m di cucito. **~ machine** n macchina f da cucire

sewn /səʊn/ ▸**sew**

sex /seks/ n sesso m; **have ~** avere rapporti sessuali. **~ist** adj sessista. **~ offender** n colpevole mf di reati a sfondo sessuale

sexual /ˈseksjʊəl/ adj sessuale. ~

S

'**intercourse** n rapporti mpl sessuali. **~ity** n sessualità f inv. **~ly** adv sessualmente

sexy /'seksɪ/ adj (**-ier, -iest**) sexy

shabb|y /'ʃæbɪ/ adj (**-ier, -iest**) scialbo; (treatment) meschino. **~iness** n trasandatezza f; (of treatment) meschinità f inv

shack /ʃæk/ n catapecchia f • **shack up with** vt [!] vivere con

shade /ʃeɪd/ n ombra f; (of colour) sfumatura f; (for lamp) paralume m; (Am: for window) tapparella f; **a ~ better** un tantino meglio • vt riparare dalla luce; (draw lines on) ombreggiare. **~s** npl [!] occhiali mpl da sole

shadow /'ʃædəʊ/ n ombra f; **S~ Cabinet** governo m ombra • vt (follow) pedinare. **~y** adj ombroso

shady /'ʃeɪdɪ/ adj (**-ier, -iest**) ombroso; ([!]: disreputable) losco

shaft /ʃɑ:ft/ n (Techn) albero m; (of light) raggio m; (of lift, mine) pozzo m; **~s** pl (of cart) stanghe fpl

shaggy /'ʃægɪ/ adj (**-ier, -iest**) irsuto; (animal) dal pelo arruffato

shake /ʃeɪk/ n scrollata f • v (pt **shook**, pp **shaken**) • vt scuotere; agitare (bottle); far tremare (building); **~ hands with** stringere la mano a • vi tremare. □ **~ off** vt scrollarsi di dosso. **~-up** n (Pol) rimpasto m; (Comm) ristrutturazione f

shaky /'ʃeɪkɪ/ adj (**-ier, -iest**) tremante; (table etc) traballante; (unreliable) vacillante

shall /ʃæl/ v aux **I ~ go** andrò; **we ~ see** vedremo; **what ~ I do?** cosa faccio?; **I'll come too, ~ I?** vengo anch'io, no?; **thou shalt not kill** liter non uccidere

shallow /'ʃæləʊ/ adj basso, poco profondo; (dish) poco profondo; fig superficiale

sham /ʃæm/ adj falso • n finzione f; (person) spaccone, -a mf • vt (pt/pp **shammed**) simulare

shambles /'ʃæmblz/ n baraonda fsg

shame /ʃeɪm/ n vergogna f; **it's a ~ that** è un peccato che; **what a ~!** che peccato! **~-faced** adj vergognoso

shame|ful /'ʃeɪmfl/ adj vergognoso. **~less** adj spudorato

shampoo /ʃæm'pu:/ n shampoo m • vt fare uno shampoo a

shape /ʃeɪp/ n forma f; (figure) omb f; **take ~** prendere forma; **get back in ~** ritornare in forma • vt dare forma a (**into** di) • vi **~ [up]** mettere la testa a posto; **~ up nicely** mettersi bene. **~less** adj informe

share /ʃeə(r)/ n porzione f; (Comm) azione f • vt dividere; condividere (views) • vi dividere. **~holder** n azionista mf

shark /ʃɑ:k/ n squalo m, pescecane fig truffatore, -trice mf

sharp /ʃɑ:p/ adj (knife etc) tagliente; (pencil) appuntito; (drop) a picco; (reprimand) severo; (outline) marcato; (alert) acuto; (unscrupulous) senza scrupoli; **~ pain** fitta f • adv in punto; (Mus) fuori tono; **look ~!** sbrigati! • n (Mus) diesis m inv. **~en** affilare (knife); appuntire (pencil)

shatter /'ʃætə(r)/ vt frantumare; fig mandare in frantumi; **~ed** ([!]: exhausted) a pezzi • vi frantumarsi

shav|e /ʃeɪv/ n rasatura f; **have a ~e** farsi la barba • vt radere • vi radersi. **~er** n rasoio m elettrico. **~ing-brush** n pennello m da barba **~ing foam** n schiuma f da barba; **~ing soap** n sapone m da barba

shawl /ʃɔ:l/ n scialle m

she /ʃi:/ pron lei

sheaf /ʃi:f/ n (pl **sheaves**) fascio m

shear /ʃɪə(r)/ vt (pt **sheared**, pp **shorn** or **sheared**) tosare

shears /ʃɪəz/ npl (for hedge) cesoie fpl

shed[1] /ʃed/ n baracca f; (for cattle) stalla f

shed[2] vt (pt/pp **shed**, pres p **shedding**) perdere; versare (blood, tears); **~ light on** far luce su

sheep /ʃi:p/ n inv pecora f. **~-dog** n cane m da pastore

sheepish /'ʃi:pɪʃ/ adj imbarazzato. **~ly** adv con aria imbarazzata

sheer /ʃɪə(r)/ adj puro; (steep) a picco (transparent) trasparente • adv a picco

sheet /ʃi:t/ n lenzuolo m; (of paper) foglio m; (of glass, metal) lastra f

shelf /ʃelf/ n (pl **shelves**) ripiano m; (set of shelves) scaffale m

shell /ʃel/ n conchiglia f; (of egg, snail,

ortoise) guscio m; (of crab) corazza f; (of unfinished building) ossatura f; (Mil) granata f •vt sgusciare (peas); (Mil) bombardare. ▫ ~ **out** vi [!] sborsare

hellfish n inv mollusco m; (Culin) frutti mpl di mare

helter /'ʃeltə(r)/ n rifugio m; (air raid ~) rifugio m antiaereo •vt riparare (**from** da); fig mettere al riparo; (give lodging to) dare asilo a •vi rifugiarsi. **~ed** adj (spot) riparato; (life) ritirato

helve /ʃelv/ vt accantonare (project)

helving /'ʃelvɪŋ/ n (shelves) ripiani mpl

hepherd /'ʃepəd/ n pastore m •vt guidare. **~'s pie** n pasticcio m di carne tritata e patate

herry /'ʃerɪ/ n sherry m

hield /ʃi:ld/ n scudo m; (for eyes) maschera f; (Techn) schermo m •vt proteggere (**from** da)

hift /ʃɪft/ n cambiamento m; (in position) spostamento m; (at work) turno m •vt spostare; (take away) togliere; riversare (blame) •vi spostarsi; (wind:) cambiare; ([!]: move quickly) darsi una mossa

hifty /'ʃɪftɪ/ adj (**-ier, -iest**) pej losco; (eyes) sfuggente

himmer /'ʃɪmə(r)/ n luccichio m •vi luccicare

hin /ʃɪn/ n stinco m

hine /ʃaɪn/ n lucentezza f; **give sth a ~** dare una lucidata a qcsa •v (pt/pp **shone**) •vi splendere; (reflect light) brillare; (hair, shoes:) essere lucido •vt **~ a light on** puntare una luce su

hingle /'ʃɪŋgl/ n (pebbles) ghiaia f

hiny /'ʃaɪnɪ/ adj (**-ier, -iest**) lucido

hip /ʃɪp/ n nave f •vt (pt/pp **shipped**) spedire; (by sea) spedire via mare

hip: ~ment n spedizione f; (consignment) carico m. **~ping** n trasporto m; (traffic) imbarcazioni fpl. **~shape** adj & adv in perfetto ordine. **~wreck** n naufragio m. **~wrecked** adj naufragato. **~yard** n cantiere m navale

shirk /ʃɜ:k/ vt scansare. **~er** n scansafatiche mf inv

shirt /ʃɜ:t/ n camicia f; **in ~-sleeves** in maniche di camicia

shit /ʃɪt/ [!] n & int merda f •vi (pt/pp **shit**) cagare

shiver /'ʃɪvə(r)/ n brivido m •vi rabbrividire

shoal /ʃəʊl/ n (of fish) banco m

shock /ʃɒk/ n (impact) urto m; (Electr) scossa f [elettrica]; fig colpo m, shock m inv; (Med) shock m inv; **get a ~** (Electr) prendere la scossa •vt scioccare. **~ing** adj scioccante; ([!]: weather, handwriting etc) tremendo

shod /ʃɒd/ ▸**shoe**

shoddy /'ʃɒdɪ/ adj (**-ier, -iest**) scadente

shoe /ʃu:/ n scarpa f; (of horse) ferro m •vt (pt/pp **shod**, pres p **shoeing**) ferrare (horse)

shoe: ~horn n calzante m. **~-lace** n laccio m da scarpa

shone /ʃɒn/ ▸**shine**

shoo /ʃu:/ vt **~ away** cacciar via •int sciò

shook /ʃʊk/ ▸**shake**

shoot /ʃu:t/ n (Bot) germoglio m; (hunt) battuta f di caccia •v (pt/pp **shot**) •vt sparare; girare (film) •vi (hunt) andare a caccia. ▫ **~ down** vt abbattere. ▫ **~ out** vi (rush) precipitarsi fuori. ▫ **~ up** vi (grow) crescere in fretta; (prices:) salire di colpo

shop /ʃɒp/ n negozio m; (workshop) officina f; **talk ~** [!] parlare di lavoro •vi (pt/pp **shopped**) far compere; **go ~ping** andare a fare compere. ▫ **~ around** vi confrontare i prezzi

shop: ~ assistant n commesso, -a mf. **~keeper** n negoziante mf. **~-lifter** n taccheggiatore, -trice mf. **~-lifting** n taccheggio m; **~per** n compratore, -trice mf

shopping /'ʃɒpɪŋ/ n compere fpl; (articles) acquisti mpl; **do the ~** fare la spesa. **~ bag** n borsa f per la spesa. **~ centre** n centro m commerciale. **~ trolley** n carrello m

shop: ~-steward n rappresentante mf sindacale. **~-'window** n vetrina f

shore /ʃɔ:(r)/ n riva f

shorn /ʃɔ:n/ ▸**shear**

short /ʃɔ:t/ adj corto; (not lasting) breve; (person) basso; (curt) brusco; **a**

S

~ **time ago** poco tempo fa; **be ~ of** essere a corto di; **be in ~ supply** essere scarso; fig essere raro; **Mick is ~ for Michael** Mick è il diminutivo di Michael • adv bruscamente; **in ~** in breve; **~ of doing** a meno di fare; **go ~** essere privato (**of** di); **stop ~ of doing sth** non arrivare fino a fare qcsa; **cut ~** interrompere (meeting, holiday); **to cut a long story ~** per farla breve

shortage /ˈʃɔːtɪdʒ/ n scarsità f inv

short: ~bread n biscotto m di pasta frolla. **~ ˈcircuit** n corto m circuito. **~coming** n difetto m. **~ ˈcut** n scorciatoia f

shorten /ˈʃɔːtn/ vt abbreviare; accorciare (garment)

shorthand n stenografia f

short|ly /ˈʃɔːtlɪ/ adv presto; **~ly before/after** poco prima/dopo. **~ness** n brevità f inv; (of person) bassa statura f

shorts /ʃɔːts/ npl calzoncini mpl corti

short-ˈsighted adj miope

shot /ʃɒt/ ▸**shoot** • n colpo m; (person) tiratore m; (Phot) foto f; (injection) puntura f; ([!]: attempt) prova f; **like a ~** [!] come un razzo. **~gun** n fucile m da caccia

should /ʃʊd/ v aux **I ~ go** dovrei andare; **I ~ have seen him** avrei dovuto vederlo; **I ~ like** mi piacerebbe; **this ~ be enough** questo dovrebbe bastare; **if he ~ come** se dovesse venire

shoulder /ˈʃəʊldə(r)/ n spalla f • vt mettersi in spalla; fig accollarsi. **~-bag** n borsa f a tracolla. **~-blade** n scapola f. **~-strap** n spallina f; (of bag) tracolla f

shout /ʃaʊt/ n grido m • vt/i gridare. □ **~ at** vi alzar la voce con. □ **~ down** vt azzittire gridando

shove /ʃʌv/ n spintone m • vt spingere; ([!]: put) ficcare • vi spingere. □ **~ off** vi [!] togliersi di torno

shovel /ˈʃʌvl/ n pala f • vt (pt/pp **shovelled**) spalare

show /ʃəʊ/ n (display) manifestazione f; (exhibition) mostra f; (ostentation) ostentazione f; (Theat), (TV) spettacolo m; (programme) programma m; **on ~** esposto • v (pt **showed**, pp **shown**) • vt mostrare; (put on display) esporre; proiettare (film) • vi (film:) essere proiettato; **your slip is ~ing** ti si vede la sottoveste. □ **~ in** vt fare accomodare. □ **~ off** vi [!] mettersi in mostra • vt mettere in mostra. □ **~ up** vi risaltare; ([!]: arrive) farsi vedere • vt ([!]: embarrass) far fare una brutta figura a

ˈshow-down n regolamento m dei conti

shower /ˈʃaʊə(r)/ n doccia f; (of rain) acquazzone m; **have a ~** fare la doccia • vt **~ with** coprire di • vi fare la doccia. **~proof** adj impermeabile. **~y** adj da acquazzo

ˈshow-jumping n concorso m ippico

shown /ʃəʊn/ ▸**show**

ˈshow-off n esibizionista mf

showy /ˈʃəʊɪ/ adj appariscente

shrank /ʃræŋk/ ▸**shrink**

shred /ʃred/ n brandello m; fig briciolo m • vt (pt/pp **shredded**) fare brandelli; (Culin) tagliuzzare. **~der** distruttore m di documenti

shrewd /ʃruːd/ adj accorto. **~ness** accortezza f

shriek /ʃriːk/ n strillo m • vt/i strillar

shrift /ʃrɪft/ n **give sb short ~** liquidare qcno rapidamente

shrill /ʃrɪl/ adj penetrante

shrimp /ʃrɪmp/ n gamberetto m

shrine /ʃraɪn/ n (place) santuario m

shrink /ʃrɪŋk/ vi (pt **shrank**, pp **shrunk**) restringersi; (draw back) ritrarsi (**from** da)

shrivel /ˈʃrɪvl/ vi (pt/pp **shrivelled**) raggrinzare

shroud /ʃraʊd/ n sudario m; fig manto m

Shrove /ʃrəʊv/ n **~ ˈTuesday** martedì m grasso

shrub /ʃrʌb/ n arbusto m

shrug /ʃrʌg/ n scrollata f di spalle • vt/i (pt/pp **shrugged**) **~ [one's shoulders]** scrollare le spalle

shrunk /ʃrʌŋk/ ▸**shrink. ~en** adj rimpicciolito

shudder /ˈʃʌdə(r)/ n fremito m • vi fremere

shuffle /ˈʃʌfl/ vi strascicare i piedi

•vt mescolare (cards)

hun /ʃʌn/ vt (pt/pp **shunned**) rifuggire

hunt /ʃʌnt/ vt smistare

hush /ʃʊʃ/ int zitto!

hut /ʃʌt/ v (pt/pp **shut**, pres p **shutting**) •vt chiudere •vi chiudersi; (shop:) chiudere. □ ~ **down** vt/i chiudere. □ ~ **up** vt chiudere; 🅸 far tacere •vi 🅸 stare zitto; ~ **up!** stai zitto!

hutter /'ʃʌtə(r)/ n serranda f; (Phot) otturatore m

huttle /'ʃʌtl/ n navetta f •vi far la spola

huttle: ~**cock** n volano m. ~ **service** n servizio m pendolare

hy /ʃaɪ/ adj (timid) timido. ~**ness** n timidezza f

icil|y /'sɪsɪlɪ/ n Sicilia f. ~**ian** adj & n siciliano, -a mf

ick /sɪk/ adj ammalato; (humour) macabro; **be** ~ (vomit) vomitare; **be** ~ **of sth** 🅸 essere stufo di qcsa; **feel** ~ aver la nausea

ick|ly /'sɪklɪ/ adj (**-ier, -iest**) malaticcio. ~**ness** n malattia f; (vomiting) nausea f. ~**ness benefit** n indennità f di malattia

ide /saɪd/ n lato m; (of person, mountain) fianco m; (of road) bordo m; **on the** ~ (as sideline) come attività secondaria; ~ **by** ~ fianco a fianco; **take** ~**s** immischiarsi; **take sb's** ~ prendere le parti di qcno; **be on the safe** ~ andare sul sicuro •attrib laterale •vi ~ **with** parteggiare per

ide: ~**board** n credenza f. ~**-effect** n effetto m collaterale. ~**lights** npl luci fpl di posizione. ~**line** n attività f inv complementare. ~**-show** n attrazione f. ~**-step** vt schivare. ~**-track** vt sviare. ~**walk** n Am marciapiede m. ~**ways** adv obliquamente

siding /'saɪdɪŋ/ n binario m di raccordo

sidle /'saɪdl/ vi camminare furtivamente (**up to** verso)

siege /si:dʒ/ n assedio m

sieve /sɪv/ n setaccio m •vt setacciare

sift /sɪft/ vt setacciare; ~ [**through**] fig passare al setaccio

sigh /saɪ/ n sospiro m •vi sospirare

sight /saɪt/ n vista f; (on gun) mirino m; **the** ~**s** pl le cose da vedere; **at first** ~ a prima vista; **be within/out of** ~ essere/non essere in vista; **lose** ~ **of** perdere di vista; **know by** ~ conoscere di vista. **have bad** ~ vederci male •vt avvistare

'sightseeing n **go** ~ andare a visitare posti

sign /saɪn/ n segno m; (notice) insegna f •vt/i firmare. □ ~ **on** vi (as unemployed) presentarsi all'ufficio di collocamento; (Mil) arruolarsi

signal /'sɪgnl/ n segnale m •v (pt/pp **signalled**) •vt segnalare •vi fare segnali; ~ **to sb** far segno a qcno (**to** di). ~**-box** n cabina f di segnalazione

signature /'sɪgnətʃə(r)/ n firma f. ~ **tune** n sigla f [musicale]

significan|ce /sɪg'nɪfɪkəns/ n significato m. ~**t** adj significativo

signify /'sɪgnɪfaɪ/ vt (pt/pp **-ied**) indicare

signpost /'saɪn-/ n segnalazione f stradale

silence /'saɪləns/ n silenzio m•vt far tacere. ~**r** n (on gun) silenziatore m; (Auto) marmitta f

silent /'saɪlənt/ adj silenzioso; (film) muto; **remain** ~ rimanere in silenzio. ~**ly** adv silenziosamente

silhouette /sɪlʊ'et/ n sagoma f, silhouette f inv •vt **be** ~**d** profilarsi

silicon /'sɪlɪkən/ n silicio m. ~ **chip** piastrina f di silicio

silk /sɪlk/ n seta f •attrib di seta. ~**worm** n baco m da seta

silky /'sɪlkɪ/ adj (**-ier, -iest**) come la seta

silly /'sɪlɪ/ adj (**-ier, -iest**) sciocco

silt /sɪlt/ n melma f

silver /'sɪlvə(r)/ adj d'argento; (paper) argentato •n argento m; (silverware) argenteria f

silver: ~**-plated** adj placcato d'argento. ~**ware** n argenteria f

similar /'sɪmɪlə(r)/ adj simile. ~**ity** n somiglianza f. ~**ly** adv in modo simile

simile /'sɪmɪlɪ/ n similitudine f

S

simmer /'sɪmə(r)/ vi bollire lentamente •vt far bollire lentamente. □ **~ down** vi calmarsi

simple /'sɪmpl/ adj semplice; (person) sempliciotto. **~-'minded** adj sempliciotto

simplicity /sɪm'plɪsətɪ/ n semplicità f inv

simply /'sɪmplɪ/ adv semplicemente

simulat|e /'sɪmjʊleɪt/ vt simulare. **~ion** n simulazione f

simultaneous /sɪml'teɪnɪəs/ adj simultaneo

sin /sɪn/ n peccato m •vi (pt/pp **sinned**) peccare

since /sɪns/
- prep da **I've been waiting ~ Monday** aspetto da lunedì
- adv da allora
- conj da quando; (*because*) siccome

sincere /sɪn'sɪə(r)/ adj sincero. **~ly** adv sinceramente; **Yours ~ly** distinti saluti

sincerity /sɪn'serətɪ/ n sincerità f inv

sinful /'sɪnfl/ adj peccaminoso

sing /sɪŋ/ vt/i (pt **sang**, pp **sung**) cantare

singe /sɪndʒ/ vt (pres p **singeing**) bruciacchiare

singer /'sɪŋə(r)/ n cantante mf

single /'sɪŋgl/ adj solo; (not double) semplice; (unmarried) celibe; (woman) nubile; (room) singolo; (bed) a una piazza •n (ticket) biglietto m di sola andata; (record) singolo m; **~s** pl (Tennis) singolo m •**single out** vt scegliere; (distinguish) distinguere

single-handed adj & adv da solo

singular /'sɪŋgjʊlə(r)/ adj (Gram) singolare •n singolare m. **~ly** adv singolarmente

sinister /'sɪnɪstə(r)/ adj sinistro

sink /sɪŋk/ n lavandino m •v (pt **sank**, pp **sunk**) •vi affondare •vt affondare (ship); scavare (shaft); investire (money). □ **~ in** vi penetrare; **it took a while to ~ in** (!: be understood) c'è voluto un po' a capirlo

sinner /'sɪnə(r)/ n peccatore, -trice mf

sip /sɪp/ n sorso m •vt (pt/pp **sipped**) sorseggiare

siphon /'saɪfn/ n (bottle) sifone m •**siphon off** vt travasare (con sifone)

sir /sɜː(r)/ n signore m; **S~** (title) Sir; **Dear S~s** Spettabile ditta

siren /'saɪrən/ n sirena f

sister /'sɪstə(r)/ n sorella f; (nurse) [infermiera f] caposala f. **~-in-law** (pl **~s-in-law**) cognata f. **~ly** adj da sorella

sit /sɪt/ v (pt/pp **sat**, pres p **sitting**) •vi essere seduto; (sit down) sedersi; (committee:) riunirsi •vt sostenere (exam). □ **~ back** vi fig starsene con le mani in mano. □ **~ down** vi mettersi a sedere. □ **~ up** vi mettersi seduto; (not slouch) star seduto diritto; (stay up) stare alzato

site /saɪt/ n posto m; (Archaeol) sito m; (building ~) cantiere m •vt collocare

sit-in /'sɪtɪn/ n occupazione f (di fabbrica, ecc.)

sitting /'sɪtɪŋ/ n seduta f; (for meals) turno m. **~-room** n salotto m

situat|e /'sɪtjʊeɪt/ vt situare. **~ed** adj situato. **~ion** n situazione f; (location) posizione f; (job) posto m

six /sɪks/ adj sei. **~teen** adj sedici. **~teenth** adj sedicesimo

sixth /sɪksθ/ adj sesto

sixtieth /'sɪkstɪɪθ/ adj sessantesimo

sixty /'sɪkstɪ/ adj sessanta

size /saɪz/ n dimensioni fpl; (of clothes) taglia f, misura f; (of shoes) numero m; **what ~ is the room?** che dimensioni ha la stanza? •**size up** vt ! valutare

sizzle /'sɪzl/ vi sfrigolare

skate[1] /skeɪt/ n inv (fish) razza f

skate[2] n pattino m •vi pattinare

skateboard /'skeɪtbɔːd/ n skateboard m inv

skater /'skeɪtə(r)/ n pattinatore, -trice mf

skating /'skeɪtɪŋ/ n pattinaggio m. **~-rink** n pista f di pattinaggio

skeleton /'skelɪtn/ n scheletro m. **~ 'key** n passe-partout m inv. **~ 'staff** n personale m ridotto

sketch /sketʃ/ n schizzo m; (Theat) sketch m inv •vt fare uno schizzo di

sketch|y /'sketʃɪ/ adj (**-ier, -iest**) abbozzato. **~ily** adv in modo abbozzato

ski /skiː/ n sci m inv •vi (pt/pp **skied**,

S

ores p **skiing**) sciare; **go ~ing** andare a sciare

kid /skɪd/ n slittata f •vi (pt/pp **skidded**) slittare

kier /'ski:ə(r)/ n sciatore, -trice mf

kiing /'ski:ɪŋ/ n sci m

kilful /'skɪlfl/ adj abile

ki-lift n impianto m di risalita

kill /skɪl/ n abilità f inv. **~ed** adj dotato; (worker) specializzato

kim /skɪm/ vt (pt/pp **skimmed**) schiumare; scremare (milk). ▫ **~ off** vt togliere. ▫ **~ through** vt scorrere

kimp /skɪmp/ vi **~ on** lesinare su

kimpy /'skɪmpɪ/ adj (**-ier, -iest**) succinto

kin /skɪn/ n pelle f; (on fruit) buccia f •vt (pt/pp **skinned**) spellare

kin: ~-deep adj superficiale. **~-diving** n nuoto m subacqueo

kinny /'skɪnɪ/ adj (**-ier, -iest**) molto magro

kip[1] /skɪp/ n (container) benna f

kip[2] n salto m •v (pt/pp **skipped**) •vi saltellare; (with rope) saltare la corda •vt omettere.

kipper /'skɪpə(r)/ n skipper m inv

kipping-rope /'skɪpɪŋrəʊp/n corda f per saltare

kirmish /'skɜ:mɪʃ/ n scaramuccia f

kirt /skɜ:t/ n gonna f •vt costeggiare

kittle /'skɪtl/ n birillo m

kulk /skʌlk/ vi aggirarsi furtivamente

kull /skʌl/ n cranio m

sky /skaɪ/ n cielo m. **~light** n lucernario m. **~ marshal** n guardia f armata a bordo di un aereo. **~scraper** n grattacielo m

slab /slæb/ n lastra f; (slice) fetta f; (of chocolate) tavoletta f

slack /slæk/ adj lento; (person) fiacco •vi fare lo scansafatiche. ▫ **~ off** vi rilassarsi

slacken /'slækn/ vi allentare; **~ [off]** (trade:) rallentare; (speed, rain:) diminuire •vt allentare; diminuire (speed)

slain /sleɪn/ ▸**slay**

slam /slæm/ v (pt/pp **slammed**) •vt sbattere; ([!]: criticize) stroncare •vi sbattere

slander /'slɑ:ndə(r)/ n diffamazione f •vt diffamare. **~ous** adj diffamatorio

slang /slæŋ/ n gergo m. **~y** adj gergale

slant /slɑ:nt/ n pendenza f; (point of view) angolazione f; **on the ~** in pendenza •vt pendere; fig distorcere (report) •vi pendere

slap /slæp/ n schiaffo m •vt (pt/pp **slapped**) schiaffeggiare; (put) schiaffare •adv in pieno

slap: ~dash adj [!] frettoloso

slash /slæʃ/ n taglio m •vt tagliare; ridurre drasticamente (prices)

slat /slæt/ n stecca f

slate /sleɪt/ n ardesia f •vt [!] fare a pezzi

slaughter /'slɔ:tə(r)/ n macello m; (of people) massacro m •vt macellare; massacrare (people). **~house** n macello m

slave /sleɪv/ n schiavo, -a mf •vi **~ [away]** lavorare come un negro. **~-driver** n schiavista mf

slav|ery /'sleɪvərɪ/ n schiavitù f inv. **~ish** adj servile

slay /sleɪ/ vt (pt **slew**, pp **slain**) ammazzare

sleazy /'sli:zɪ/ adj (**-ier, -iest**) sordido

sledge /sledʒ/ n slitta f. **~-hammer** n martello m

sleek /sli:k/ adj liscio, lucente; (well-fed) pasciuto

sleep /sli:p/ n sonno m; **go to ~** addormentarsi; **put to ~** far addormentare •v (pt/pp **slept**) •vi dormire •vt **~s six** ha sei posti letto. **~er** n (Rail) treno m con vagoni letto; (compartment) vagone m letto; **be a light/heavy ~er** avere il sonno leggero/pesante

sleeping: ~-bag n sacco m a pelo. **~-car** n vagone m letto. **~-pill** n sonnifero m

sleepless adj insonne

sleepy /'sli:pɪ/ adj (**-ier, -iest**) assonnato; **be ~** aver sonno

sleet /sli:t/ n nevischio m •vi **it is ~ing** nevischia

sleeve /sli:v/ n manica f; (for record) copertina f. **~less** adj senza maniche

sleigh /sleɪ/ n slitta f

S

slender /'slendə(r)/ adj snello; (fingers, stem) affusolato; fig scarso; (chance) magro

slept /slept/ ▹**sleep**

slew[1] /slu:/ vi girare

slew[2] ▹**slay**

slice /slaɪs/ n fetta f • vt affettare; **~d bread** pane m a cassetta

slick /slɪk/ adj liscio; (cunning) astuto • n (of oil) chiazza f di petrolio

slid|e /slaɪd/ n scivolata f; (in playground) scivolo m; (for hair) fermaglio m (per capelli); (Phot) diapositiva f • v (pt/pp **slid**) • vi scivolare • vt far scivolare. **~-rule** n regolo m calcolatore. **~ing** adj scorrevole; (door, seat) scorrevole; **~ing scale** scala f mobile

slight /slaɪt/ adj leggero; (importance) poco; (slender) esile. **~est** adj minimo; **not in the ~est** niente affatto • vt offendere • n offesa f. **~ly** adv leggermente

slim /slɪm/ adj (**slimmer, slimmest**) snello; fig scarso; (chance) magro • vi dimagrire

slim|e /slaɪm/ n melma f. **~y** adj melmoso; fig viscido

sling /slɪŋ/ n (Med) benda f al collo • vt (pt/pp **slung**) ! lanciare

slip /slɪp/ n scivolata f; (mistake) lieve errore m; (petticoat) sottoveste f; (for pillow) federa f; (paper) scontrino m; **give sb the ~** ! sbarazzarsi di qcno; **~ of the tongue** lapsus m inv • v (pt/pp **slipped**) • vi scivolare; (go quickly) sgattaiolare; (decline) retrocedere • vt **he ~ped it into his pocket** se l'è infilato in tasca; **~ sb's mind** sfuggire di mente a qcno. □ **~ away** vi sgusciar via; (time:) sfuggire. □ **~ into** vi infilarsi (clothes). □ **~ up** vi ! sbagliare

slipper /'slɪpə(r)/ n pantofola f

slippery /'slɪpərɪ/ adj scivoloso

slip-road n bretella f

slipshod /'slɪpʃɒd/ adj trascurato

'**slip-up** n ! sbaglio m

slit /slɪt/ n spacco m; (tear) strappo m; (hole) fessura f • vt (pt/pp **slit**) tagliare

slither /'slɪðə(r)/ vi scivolare

slobber /'slɒbə(r)/ vi sbavare

slog /slɒg/ n [**hard**] **~** sgobbata f • vi (pt/pp **slogged**) (work) sgobbare

slogan /'sləʊgən/ n slogan m inv

slop /slɒp/ v (pt/pp **slopped**) • vt versare. □ **~ over** vi versarsi

slop|e /sləʊp/ n pendenza f; (ski **~**) pista f • vi essere inclinato, inclinarsi. **~ing** adj in pendenza

sloppy /'slɒpɪ/ adj (**-ier, -iest**) (work) trascurato; (worker) negligente; (in dress) sciatto; (sentimental) sdolcinato

slosh /slɒʃ/ vi ! (person, feet:) sguazzare; (water:) scrosciare • vt (! hit) colpire

slot /slɒt/ n fessura f; (time-**~**) spazio m • v (pt/pp **slotted**) • vt infilare. □ **~ in** vi incastrarsi

'**slot-machine** n distributore m automatico; (for gambling) slot-machine f inv

slouch /slaʊtʃ/ vi (in chair) stare scomposto

Slovakia /slə'vækɪə/ n Slovacchia f

Slovenia /slə'vi:nɪə/ n Slovenia f

slovenl|y /'slʌvnlɪ/ adj sciatto. **~iness** n sciatteria f

slow /sləʊ/ adj lento; **be ~** (clock:) essere indietro; **in ~ motion** al rallentatore • adv lentamente • **~ down/up** vt/i rallentare

slowly adv lentamente

sludge /slʌdʒ/ n fanghiglia f

slug /slʌg/ n lumacone m; (bullet) pallottoia f. **~gish** adj lento

slum /slʌm/ n (house) tugurio m; **~s** pl bassifondi mpl

slumber /'slʌmbə(r)/ vi dormire

slump /slʌmp/ n crollo m; (economic) depressione f • vi crollare

slung /slʌŋ/ ▹**sling**

slur /slɜ:(r)/ n (discredit) calunnia f • vt (pt/pp **slurred**) biascicare

slush /slʌʃ/ n pantano m nevoso; fig sdolcinatezza f. **~ fund** n fondi mpl neri. **~y** adj fangoso; (sentimental) sdolcinato

sly /slaɪ/ adj (**-er, -est**) scaltro • n **on the ~** di nascosto

smack[1] /smæk/ n (on face) schiaffo m; (on bottom) sculaccione m • vt (on face) schiaffeggiare; (on bottom) sculacciare; **~ one's lips** far schioccare le labbra • adv ! in pieno

smack² vi ~ **of** fig sapere di

small /smɔ:l/ adj piccolo; **be out/ work** etc **until the ~ hours** fare le ore piccole • adv **chop up ~** fare a pezzettini • n **the ~ of the back** le reni fpl

small: ~ ads npl annunci mpl [commerciali]. ~ **'change** n spiccioli mpl. ~**pox** n vaiolo m. ~ **talk** n chiacchiere fpl

smart /smɑ:t/ adj elegante; (clever) intelligente; (brisk) svelto; **be ~** (⚠: cheeky) fare il furbo • vi (hurt) bruciare

smash /smæʃ/ n fragore m; (collision) scontro m; (Tennis) schiacciata f • vt spaccare; (Tennis) schiacciare • vi spaccarsi; (crash) schiantarsi (**into** contro). ~ **[hit]** n successo m. ~**ing** adj ⚠ fantastico

smattering /'smætərɪŋ/ n infarinatura f

smear /smɪə(r)/ n macchia f; (Med) striscio m • vt imbrattare; (coat) spalmare (**with** di); fig calunniare

smell /smel/ n odore m; (sense) odorato m • v (pt/pp **smelt** or **smelled**) • vt odorare; (sniff) annusare • vi odorare (**of** di)

smelly /'smelɪ/ adj (**-ier, -iest**) puzzolente

smelt¹ /smelt/ ▸**smell**

smelt² vt fondere

smile /smaɪl/ n sorriso m • vi sorridere; ~ **at** sorridere a (sb); sorridere di (sth)

smirk /smɜ:k/ n sorriso m compiaciuto

smithereens /smɪðə'ri:nz/ npl **to/in** ~ in mille pezzi

smock /smɒk/ n grembiule m

smog /smɒg/ n smog m inv

smoke /sməʊk/ n fumo m • vt/i fumare. ~**less** adj senza fumo; (fuel) che non fa fumo

smoker /'sməʊkə(r)/ n fumatore, -trice mf; (Rail) vagone m fumatori

smoky /'sməʊkɪ/ adj (**-ier, -iest**) fumoso; (taste) di fumo

smooth /smu:ð/ adj liscio; (movement) scorrevole; (sea) calmo; (manners) mellifluo • vt lisciare. □ ~ **out** vt lisciare. ~**ly** adv in modo scorrevole

smother /'smʌðə(r)/ vt soffocare

smoulder /'sməʊldə(r)/ vi fumare; (with rage) consumarsi

smudge /smʌdʒ/ n macchia f • vt/i imbrattare

smug /smʌg/ adj (**smugger, smuggest**) compiaciuto. ~**ly** adv con aria compiaciuta

smuggl|e /'smʌgl/ vt contrabbandare. ~**er** n contrabbandiere, a mf. ~**ing** n contrabbando m

snack /snæk/ n spuntino m. ~**-bar** n snack bar m inv

snag /snæg/ n (problem) intoppo m

snail /sneɪl/ n lumaca f; **at a ~'s pace** a passo di lumaca

snake /sneɪk/ n serpente m

snap /snæp/ n colpo m secco; (photo) istantanea f • attrib (decision) istantaneo • v (pt/pp **snapped**) • vi (break) spezzarsi; ~ **at** (dog:) cercare di azzannare; (person:) parlare seccamente a • vt (break) spezzare; (say) dire seccamente; (Phot) fare un'istantanea di. □ ~ **up** vt afferrare

snappy /'snæpɪ/ adj (**-ier, -iest**) scorbutico; (smart) elegante; **make it ~!** sbrigati!

'snapshot n istantanea f

snare /sneə(r)/ n trappola f

snarl /snɑ:l/ n ringhio m • vi ringhiare

snatch /snætʃ/ n strappo m; (fragment) brano m; (theft) scippo m; **make a ~ at** cercare di afferrare qcsa • vt strappare [di mano] (**from** a); (steal) scippare; rapire (child)

sneak /sni:k/ n ⚠ spia mf • vi (⚠: tell tales) fare la spia • vt (take) rubare; ~ **a look at** dare una sbirciata a. □ ~ **in/out** vi sgattaiolare dentro/fuori

sneakers /'sni:kəz/ npl Am scarpe fpl da ginnastica

sneaky /'sni:kɪ/ adj sornione

sneer /snɪə(r)/ n ghigno m • vi sogghignare; (mock) ridere di

sneeze /sni:z/ n starnuto m • vi starnutire

snide /snaɪd/ adj ⚠ insinuante

sniff /snɪf/ n (of dog) annusata f • vi tirare su col naso • vt odorare (flower); sniffare (glue, cocaine); (dog:) annusare

S

snigger /ˈsnɪgə(r)/ n risatina f soffocata •vi ridacchiare

snip /snɪp/ n taglio m; ([!]: bargain) affare m •vt/i (pt/pp **snipped**) ~ [**at**] tagliare

snippet /ˈsnɪpɪt/ n **a ~ of information/news** una breve notizia/informazione

snivel /ˈsnɪvl/ vi (pt/pp **snivelled**) piagnucolare. **~ling** adj piagnucoloso

snob /snɒb/ n snob mf. **~bery** n snobismo m. **~bish** adj da snob

snooker /ˈsnu:kə(r)/ n snooker m

snoop /snu:p/ n spia f •vi [!] curiosare

snooze /snu:z/ n sonnellino m •vi fare un sonnellino

snore /snɔ:(r)/ vi russare

snorkel /ˈsnɔ:kl/ n respiratore m

snort /snɔ:t/ n sbuffo n •vi sbuffare

snout /snaʊt/ n grugno m

snow /snəʊ/ n neve f •vi nevicare; **~ed under with** fig sommerso di

snow: ~ball n palla f di neve •vi fare a palle di neve. **~board** n snowboard m. **~-drift** n cumulo m di neve. **~fall** n nevicata f. **~flake** n fiocco m di neve. **~man** n pupazzo m di neve. **~-plough** n spazzaneve m. **~storm** n tormenta f. **~y** adj nevoso

snub /snʌb/ n sgarbo m •vt (pt/pp **snubbed**) snobbare

ˈ**snub-nosed** adj dal naso all'insù

snug /snʌg/ adj (**snugger, snuggest**) comodo; (tight) aderente

so /səʊ/
- adv così; **so far** finora; **so am I** anch'io; **so I see** così pare; **that is so** è così; **so much** così tanto; **so much the better** tanto meglio; **so it is** proprio così; **if so** se è così; **so as to** in modo da; **so long!** [!] a presto!
- pron **I hope/think/am afraid so** spero/penso/temo di sì; **I told you so** te l'ho detto; **because I say so** perché lo dico io; **I did so!** è vero!; **so saying/doing,...** così dicendo/facendo,...; **or so** circa; **very much so** sì, molto; **and so forth** *or* **on** e così via
- conj (*therefore*) perciò; (*in order that*) così; **so that** affinché; **so there** ecco!; **so what!** e allora?; **so where have you been?** allora, dove sei stato?

soak /səʊk/ vt mettere a bagno•vi stare a bagno; **~ into** (liquid:) penetrare. □ **~ up** vt assorbire

soaking /ˈsəʊkɪŋ/ n ammollo m •adj & adv **~ [wet]** [!] inzuppato

so-and-so /ˈsəʊənsəʊ/ n Tal dei Tali mf; (euphemism) specie f di imbecille

soap /səʊp/ n sapone m. **~ opera** n telenovela f, soap opera f inv. **~ powder** n detersivo m in polvere

soapy /ˈsəʊpɪ/ adj (**-ier, -iest**) insaponato

soar /sɔ:(r)/ vi elevarsi; (prices:) salire alle stelle

sob /sɒb/ n singhiozzo m •vi (pt/pp **sobbed**) singhiozzare

sober /ˈsəʊbə(r)/ adj sobrio; (serious) serio •**sober up** vi ritornare sobrio

ˈ**so-called** adj cosiddetto

soccer /ˈsɒkə(r)/ n calcio m

sociable /ˈsəʊʃəbl/ adj socievole

social /ˈsəʊʃl/ adj sociale; (sociable) socievole

socialis|m /ˈsəʊʃəlɪzm/ n socialismo m. **~t** adj socialista •n socialista mf

socialize /ˈsəʊʃəlaɪz/ vi socializzare

social: ~ seˈcurity n previdenza f sociale. **~ worker** n assistente mf sociale

society /səˈsaɪətɪ/ n società f inv

sociolog|ist /səʊsɪˈɒlədʒɪst/ n sociologo, -a mf. **~y** n sociologia f

sock¹ /sɒk/ n calzino m; (kneelength) calza f

sock² n [!] pugno m •vt [!] dare un pugno a

socket /ˈsɒkɪt/ n (wall plug) presa f [di corrente]; (for bulb) portalampada m inv

soda /ˈsəʊdə/ n soda f; Am gazzosa f. **~ water** n seltz m inv

sodium /ˈsəʊdɪəm/ n sodio m

sofa /ˈsəʊfə/ n divano m. **~ bed** n divano m letto

soft /sɒft/ adj morbido, soffice; (voice)

sommesso; (light, colour) tenue; (not strict) indulgente; (!: silly) stupido; **have a ~ spot for sb** avere un debole per qcno. ~ **drink** n bibita f analcolica

soften /'sɒfn/ vt ammorbidire; fig attenuare • vi ammorbidirsi

softly /'sɒftlɪ/ adv (say) sottovoce; (treat) con indulgenza; (play music) in sottofondo

software n software m

soggy /'sɒgɪ/ adj (**-ier, -iest**) zuppo

soil[1] /sɔɪl/ n suolo m

soil[2] vt sporcare

solar /'səʊlə(r)/ adj solare

sold /səʊld/ ▹**sell**

solder /'səʊldə(r)/ n lega f da saldatura • vt saldare

soldier /'səʊldʒə(r)/ n soldato m • **soldier on** vi perseverare

sole[1] /səʊl/ n (of foot) pianta f; (of shoe) suola f

sole[2] n (fish) sogliola f

sole[3] adj unico, solo. ~**ly** adv unicamente

solemn /'sɒləm/ adj solenne. ~**ity** n solennità f inv

solicitor /sə'lɪsɪtə(r)/ n avvocato m

solid /'sɒlɪd/ adj solido; (oak, gold) massiccio • n (figure) solido m; ~**s** pl (food) cibi mpl solidi

solidarity /sɒlɪ'dærətɪ/ n solidarietà f inv

solidify /sə'lɪdɪfaɪ/ vi (pt/pp **-ied**) solidificarsi

solitary /'sɒlɪtərɪ/ adj solitario; (sole) solo. ~ **con'finement** n cella f di isolamento

solitude /'sɒlɪtju:d/ n solitudine f

solo /'səʊləʊ/ n (Mus) assolo m • adj (flight) in solitario • adv in solitario. ~**ist** n solista mf

solstice /'sɒlstɪs/ n solstizio m

soluble /'sɒljʊbl/ adj solubile

solution /sə'lu:ʃn/ n soluzione f

solve /sɒlv/ vt risolvere

solvent /'sɒlvənt/ adj solvente • n solvente m

sombre /'sɒmbə(r)/ adj tetro; (clothes) scuro

some /sʌm/ adj (a certain amount of) del; (a certain number of) qualche, alcuni; ~ **day** un giorno o l'altro; **I need ~ money/books** ho bisogno di soldi/ libri; **do ~ shopping** fare qualche acquisto • pron (a certain amount) un po'; (a certain number) alcuni; **I want ~** ne voglio

some: ~**body** /-bədɪ/ pron & n qualcuno m. ~**how** adv in qualche modo; ~**how or other** in un modo o nell'altro. ~**one** pron & n = **somebody**

somersault /'sʌməsɔ:lt/ n capriola f; **turn a ~** fare una capriola

'**something** pron qualche cosa, qualcosa; ~ **different** qualcosa di diverso; ~ **like** un po' come; (approximately) qualcosa come; **see ~ of sb** vedere qcno un po'

some: ~**time** adv un giorno o l'altro; ~**times** adv qualche volta. ~**what** adv piuttosto. ~**where** adv da qualche parte • pron ~**where to eat** un posto in cui mangiare

son /sʌn/ n figlio m

sonata /sə'nɑ:tə/ n sonata f

song /sɒŋ/ n canzone f

sonic /'sɒnɪk/ adj sonico. ~ '**boom** n bang m inv sonico

'**son-in-law** n (pl ~**s-in-law**) genero m

sonnet /'sɒnɪt/ n sonetto m

soon /su:n/ adv presto; (in a short time) tra poco; **as ~ as** [non] appena; **as ~ as possible** il più presto possibile; ~**er or later** prima o poi; **the ~er the better** prima è, meglio è; **no ~er had I arrived than...** ero appena arrivato quando...; **I would ~er go** preferirei andare; ~ **after** subito dopo

soot /sʊt/ n fuliggine f

sooth|e /su:ð/ vt calmare

sooty /'sʊtɪ/ adj fuligginoso

sophisticated /sə'fɪstɪkeɪtɪd/ adj sofisticato

sopping /'sɒpɪŋ/ adj & adv **be ~ [wet]** essere bagnato fradicio

soppy /'sɒpɪ/ adj (**-ier, -iest**) ! svenevole

soprano /sə'prɑ:nəʊ/ n soprano m

sordid /'sɔ:dɪd/ adj sordido

sore /sɔ:(r)/ adj dolorante; (Am: vexed)

S

arrabbiato; **it's ~** fa male; **have a ~ throat** avere mal di gola •n piaga f. **~ly** adv (tempted) seriamente

sorrow /'sɒrəʊ/ n tristezza f. **~ful** adj triste

sorry /'sɒrɪ/ adj (**-ier, -iest**) (sad) spiacente; (wretched) pietoso; **you'll be ~!** te ne pentirai!; **I am ~** mi dispiace; **be** or **feel ~ for** provare compassione per; **~!** scusa!; (more polite) scusi!

sort /sɔ:t/ n specie f; ([!]: person) tipo m; **it's a ~ of fish** è un tipo di pesce; **be out of ~s** ([!]: unwell) stare poco bene •vt classificare. □ **~ out** vt selezionare (papers); fig risolvere (problem); occuparsi di (person)

'so-so adj & adv così così

sought /sɔ:t/ ▸**seek**

soul /səʊl/ n anima f

sound¹ /saʊnd/ adj sano; (sensible) saggio; (secure) solido; (thrashing) clamoroso •adv **~ asleep** profondamente addormentato

sound² n suono m; (noise) rumore m; **I don't like the ~ of it** [!] non mi suona bene •vi suonare; (seem) aver l'aria •vt (pronounce) pronunciare; (Med) auscoltare (chest). **~ barrier** n muro m del suono. **~ card** n (Comput) scheda f sonora. **~less** adj silenzioso. □ **~ out** vt fig sondare

soundly /'saʊndlɪ/ adv (sleep) profondamente; (defeat) clamorosamente

'sound: ~proof adj impenetrabile al suono. **~-track** n colonna f sonora

soup /su:p/ n minestra f. **~ed-up** adj [!] (engine) truccato

sour /'saʊə(r)/ adj agro; (not fresh & fig) acido

source /sɔ:s/ n fonte f

south /saʊθ/ n sud m; **to the ~ of** a sud di •adj del sud, meridionale •adv verso il sud

south: S~ 'Africa n Sudafrica m. **S~ A'merica** n America f del Sud. **S~ American** adj & n sud-americano, -a mf. **~-'east** n sud-est m

southerly /'sʌðəlɪ/ adj del sud

southern /'sʌðən/ adj del sud, meridionale; **~ Italy** il Mezzogiorno m. **~er** n meridionale mf

'southward[s] /-wəd[z]/ adv verso sud

souvenir /su:və'nɪə(r)/ n ricordo m, souvenir m inv

sovereign /'sɒvrɪn/ adj sovrano •n sovrano, -a mf. **~ty** n sovranità f inv

Soviet /'səʊvɪət/ adj sovietico; **~ Union** Unione f Sovietica

sow¹ /saʊ/ n scrofa f

sow² /səʊ/ vt (pt **sowed**, pp **sown** or **sowed**) seminare

soya /'sɔɪə/ n **~ bean** soia f

spa /spɑ:/ n stazione f termale

space /speɪs/ n spazio m •adj (research etc) spaziale •vt **~ [out]** distanziare

space: ~ship n astronave f. **~ shuttle** n navetta f spaziale

spade /speɪd/ n vanga f; (for child) paletta f; **~s** pl (in cards) picche fpl. **~work** n lavoro m preparatorio

Spain /speɪn/ n Spagna f

spam /spæm/ spam m

span¹ /spæn/ n spanna f; (of arch) luce f; (of time) arco m; (of wings) apertura f •vt (pt/pp **spanned**) estendersi su

span² ▸**spick**

Span|iard /'spænjəd/ n spagnolo, -a mf. **~ish** adj spagnolo •n (language) spagnolo m; **the ~ish** pl gli spagnoli

spank /spæŋk/ vt sculacciare. **~ing** n sculacciata f

spanner /'spænə(r)/ n chiave f inglese

spare /speə(r)/ adj (surplus) in più; (additional) di riserva •n (part) ricambio m •vt risparmiare; (do without) fare a meno di; **can you ~ five minutes?** avresti cinque minuti?; **to ~** (surplus) in eccedenza. **~ part** n pezzo m di ricambio. **~ time** n tempo m libero. **~ 'wheel** n ruota f di scorta

spark /spɑ:k/ n scintilla f. **~ing-plug** n (Auto) candela f

sparkl|e /'spɑ:kl/ n scintillio m •vi scintillare. **~ing** adj frizzante; (wine) spumante

sparrow /'spærəʊ/ n passero m

sparse /spɑ:s/ adj rado. **~ly** adv

scarsamente; **~ly populated** a bassa densità di popolazione

pasm /'spæzm/ n spasmo m. **~odic** adj spasmodico

pat /spæt/ ▸**spit**[1]

pate /speɪt/ n (series) successione f; **be in full ~** essere in piena

patial /'speɪʃl/ adj spaziale

patter /'spætə(r)/ vt schizzare

pawn /spɔ:n/ n uova fpl (di pesci, rane, ecc.) •vi deporre le uova •vt fig generare

peak /spi:k/ v (pt **spoke**, pp **spoken**) •vi parlare (**to** a); **~ing!** (Teleph) sono io! •vt dire; **~ one's mind** dire quello che si pensa. □ **~ for** vi parlare a nome di. □ **~ up** vi parlare più forte; **~ up for oneself** parlare per se stesso

peaker /'spi:kə(r)/ n parlante mf; (in public) oratore, -trice mf; (of stereo) cassa f

pear /spɪə(r)/ n lancia f

pecial /'speʃl/ adj speciale. **~ist** n specialista mf. **~ity** n specialità f inv

pecial|ize /'speʃəlaɪz/ vi specializzarsi. **~ly** adv specialmente; (particularly) particolarmente

pecies /'spi:ʃi:z/ n specie f inv

pecific /spə'sɪfɪk/ adj specifico. **~ally** adv in modo specifico

pecify /'spesɪfaɪ/ vt (pt/pp **-ied**) specificare

pecimen /'spesɪmən/ n campione m

peck /spek/ n macchiolina f; (particle) granello m

pecs /speks/ npl [!] occhiali mpl

pectacle /'spektəkl/ n (show) spettacolo m. **~s** npl occhiali mpl

pectacular /spek'tækjʊlə(r)/ adj spettacolare

pectator /spek'teɪtə(r)/ n spettatore, -trice mf

pectre /'spektə(r)/ n spettro m

pectrum /'spektrəm/ n (pl **-tra**) spettro m; fig gamma f

peculat|e /'spekjʊleɪt/ vi speculare. **~ion** n speculazione f. **~ive** adj speculativo. **~or** n speculatore, -trice mf

ped /sped/ ▸**speed**

peech /spi:tʃ/ n linguaggio m; (address) discorso m. **~less** adj senza parole

speed /spi:d/ n velocità f inv; (gear) marcia f; **at ~** a tutta velocità •vi (pt/pp **sped**) andare veloce; (pt/pp **speeded**) (go too fast) andare a velocità eccessiva. □ **~ up** (pt/pp **speeded up**) vt/i accelerare

speed: ~boat n motoscafo m. **~ camera** n Autovelox® m inv. **~ dating** n speed dating m. **~ limit** n limite m di velocità

speedometer /spi:'dɒmɪtə(r)/ n tachimetro m

speed|y /'spi:dɪ/ adj (**-ier, -iest**) rapido. **~ily** adv rapidamente

spell[1] /spel/ n (turn) turno m; (of weather) periodo m

spell[2] v (pt/pp **spelled, spelt**) •vt **how do you ~...?** come si scrive...?; **could you ~ that for me?** me lo può compitare?; **~ disaster** essere disastroso •vi **he can't ~** fa molti errori d'ortografia

spell[3] n (magic) incantesimo m. **~bound** adj affascinato

spelling /'spelɪŋ/ n ortografia f

spelt /spelt/ ▸**spell**[2]

spend /spend/ vt/i (pt/pp **spent**) spendere; passare (time)

sperm /spɜ:m/ n spermatozoo m; (semen) sperma m

spew /spju:/ vt/i vomitare

spher|e /sfɪə(r)/ n sfera f. **~ical** adj sferico

spice /spaɪs/ n spezia f; fig pepe m

spick /spɪk/ adj **~ and span** lindo

spicy /'spaɪsɪ/ adj piccante

spider /'spaɪdə(r)/ n ragno m

spik|e /spaɪk/ n punta f; (Bot, Zool) spina f; (on shoe) chiodo m. **~y** adj (plant) pungente

spill /spɪl/ v (pt/pp **spilt** or **spilled**) •vt versare (blood) •vi rovesciarsi

spin /spɪn/ v (pt/pp **spun**, pres p **spinning**) •vt far girare; filare (wool); centrifugare (washing) •vi girare; (washing machine:) centrifugare •n rotazione f; (short drive) giretto m. □ **~ out** vt far durare

spinach /'spɪnɪdʒ/ n spinaci mpl

spin-'drier n centrifuga f

spine /spaɪn/ n spina f dorsale; (of

book) dorso m; (Bot, Zool) spina f. ~**less** adj fig smidollato

'**spin-off** n ricaduta f

spiral /'spaɪrəl/ adj a spirale •n spirale f •vi (pt/pp **spiralled**) formare una spirale. ~ '**staircase** n scala f a chiocciola

spire /'spaɪə(r)/ n guglia f

spirit /'spɪrɪt/ n spirito m; (courage) ardore m; ~**s** pl (alcohol) liquori mpl; **in good ~s** di buon umore; **in low ~s** abbattuto

spirited /'spɪrɪtɪd/ adj vivace; (courageous) pieno d'ardore

spiritual /'spɪrɪtjʊəl/ adj spirituale •n spiritual m. ~**ism** n spiritismo m. ~**ist** n spiritista mf

spit[1] /spɪt/ n (for roasting) spiedo m

spit[2] n sputo m •vt/i (pt/pp **spat**, pres p **spitting**) sputare; (cat:) soffiare; (fat:) sfrigolare; **it's ~ting [with rain]** pioviggina; **the ~ting image of** il ritratto spiccicato di

spite /spaɪt/ n dispetto m; **in ~ of** malgrado •vt far dispetto a. ~**ful** adj indispettito

spittle /'spɪtl/ n saliva f

splash /splæʃ/ n schizzo m; (of colour) macchia f; (!: drop) goccio m •vt schizzare; ~ **sb with sth** schizzare qcno di qcsa •vi schizzare. □ ~ **about** vi schizzarsi. □ ~ **down** vi (spacecraft:) ammarare

splendid /'splendɪd/ adj splendido

splendour /'splendə(r)/ n splendore m

splint /splɪnt/ n (Med) stecca f

splinter /'splɪntə(r)/ n scheggia f •vi scheggiarsi

split /splɪt/ n fessura f; (quarrel) rottura f; (division) scissione f; (tear) strappo m •v (pt/pp **split**, pres p **splitting**) •vt spaccare; (share, divide) dividere; (tear) strappare •vi spaccarsi; (tear) strapparsi; (divide) dividersi; ~ **on sb** ! denunciare qcno •adj **a ~ second** una frazione f di secondo. □ ~ **up** vt dividersi •vi (couple:) separarsi

splutter /'splʌtə(r)/ vi farfugliare

spoil /spɔɪl/ n ~**s** pl bottino msg •v (pt/pp **spoilt** or **spoiled**) •vt rovinare; viziare (person) •vi andare a male. ~**sport** n guastafeste mf inv

spoke[1] /spəʊk/ n raggio m

spoke[2], **spoken** /'spəʊkn/ ▸**speak**

'**spokesman** n portavoce m inv

sponge /spʌndʒ/ n spugna f •vt pulire (con la spugna) •vi ~ **on** scroccare da. ~**-cake** n pan m di Spagna

sponsor /'spɒnsə(r)/ n garante m; (Radio, TV) sponsor m inv; (god-parent) padrino m, madrina f; (for membership) socio, -a mf garante •vt sponsorizzare. ~**ship** n sponsorizzazione f

spontaneous /spɒn'teɪnɪəs/ adj spontaneo

spoof /spu:f/ n ! parodia f

spooky /'spu:kɪ/ adj (**-ier, -iest**) ! sinistro

spool /spu:l/ n bobina f

spoon /spu:n/ n cucchiaio m •vt mettere col cucchiaio. ~**-feed** vt (pt/pp **-fed**) fig imboccare. ~**ful** n cucchiaiata f

sporadic /spə'rædɪk/ adj sporadico

sport /spɔ:t/ n sport m inv •vt sfoggiare. ~**ing** adj sportivo; ~**ing chance** possibilità f inv

sports: ~**car** n automobile f sportiva. ~**man** n sportivo m. ~**woman** n sportiva f

spot /spɒt/ n macchia f; (pimple) brufolo m; (place) posto m; (in pattern) pois m inv; (of rain) goccia f; (of water) goccio m; ~**s** pl (rash) sfogo msg; **a ~ of** ! un po' di; **a ~ of bother** qualche problema; **on the ~** sul luogo; (immediately) immediatamente; **in a [tight] ~** ! in difficoltà •vt (pt/pp **spotted**) macchiare; (!: notice) individuare

spot: ~ '**check** n (without warning) controllo m a sorpresa; **do a ~ check on sth** dare una controllata a qcsa. ~**less** adj immacolato. ~**light** n riflettore m

spotted /'spɒtɪd/ adj (material) a pois

spotty /'spɒtɪ/ adj (**-ier, -iest**) (pimply) brufoloso

spouse /spaʊz/ n consorte mf

spout /spaʊt/ n becco m •vi zampillare (**from** da)

sprain /spreɪn/ n slogatura f •vt slogare

sprang /spræŋ/ ▸**spring**[2]

ray /spreɪ/ n spruzzo m; (preparation) pray m inv; (container) spruzzatore m ıv • vt spruzzare. **~-gun** n pistola f a pruzzo

read /spred/ n estensione f; (of sease) diffusione f; (paste) crema f; [!]: feast) banchetto m • v (pt/pp **pread**) • vt spargere; spalmare outter, jam); stendere (cloth, arms); iffondere (news, disease); dilazionare oayments); **~ sth with** spalmare csa di • vi spargersi; (butter:) palmarsi; (disease:) diffondersi. **-sheet** n (Comput) foglio m lettronico. □ **~ out** vt sparpagliare vi sparpagliarsi

ree /spri:/ n [!] **go on a ~** far aldoria; **go on a shopping ~** fare pese folli

rightly /'spraɪtlɪ/ adj (**-ier, -iest**) ivace

ring¹ /sprɪŋ/ n primavera f • attrib rimaverile

ring² n (jump) balzo m; (water) orgente f; (device) molla f; (elasticity) lasticità f inv • v (pt **sprang**, pp **prung**) • vi balzare; (arise) provenire **from** da) • vt **he just sprang it on ne** me l'ha detto a cose fatte ompiuto. □ **~ up** balzare; fig puntare

ring: ~board n trampolino m. **-time** n primavera f

rinkl|e /'sprɪŋkl/ vt (scatter) pruzzare (liquid); spargere (flour, ocoa); **~ sth with** spruzzare qcsa di liquid); cospargere qcsa di (flour, ocoa). **~er** n sprinkler m inv; (for lawn) rrigatore m. **~ing** n (of liquid) pruzzatina f; (of pepper, salt) pizzico ı; (of flour, sugar) spolveratina f; (of nowledge) infarinatura f; (of people) ugno m

rint /sprɪnt/ n sprint m inv • vi fare ıno sprint; (Sport) sprintare. **~er** n printer mf inv

rout /spraʊt/ n germoglio m; **Brussels**] **~s** pl cavolini mpl di ruxelles • vi germogliare

rung /sprʌŋ/ ▸**spring²** • adj nolleggiato

ud /spʌd/ n [!] patata f

un /spʌn/ ▸**spin**

ur /spɜ:(r)/ n sperone m; (stimulus) timolo m; (road) svincolo m; **on the ~ of the moment** su due piedi • vt (pt/pp **spurred**) **~ [on]** fig spronare [a]

spurn /spɜ:n/ vt sdegnare

spurt /spɜ:t/ n getto m; (Sport) scatto m; **put on a ~** fare uno scatto • vi sprizzare; (increase speed) scattare

spy /spaɪ/ n spia f • v (pt/pp **spied**) • vi spiare • vt ([!]: see) spiare. □ **~ on** vi spiare

squabble /'skwɒbl/ n bisticcio m • vi bisticciare

squad /skwɒd/ n squadra f; (Sport) squadra

squadron /'skwɒdrən/ n (Mil) squadrone m; (Aeron), (Naut) squadriglia f

squalid /'skwɒlɪd/ adj squallido

squalor /'skwɒlə(r)/ n squallore m

squander /'skwɒndə(r)/ vt sprecare

square /skweə(r)/ adj quadrato; (meal) sostanzioso; ([!]: old-fashioned) vecchio stampo; **all ~** [!] pari • n quadrato m; (in city) piazza f; (on chessboard) riquadro m • vt (settle) far quadrare; (Math) elevare al quadrato • vi (agree) armonizzare

squash /skwɒʃ/ n (drink) spremuta f; (sport) squash m; (vegetable) zucca f • vt schiacciare; soffocare (rebellion)

squat /skwɒt/ adj tarchiato • n [!] edificio m occupato abusivamente • vi (pt/pp **squatted**) accovacciarsi; **~ in** occupare abusivamente. **~ter** n occupante mf abusivo, -a

squawk /skwɔ:k/ n gracchio m • vi gracchiare

squeak /skwi:k/ n squittio m; (of hinge, brakes) scricchiolio m • vi squittire; (hinge, brakes:) scricchiolare

squeal /skwi:l/ n strillo m; (of brakes) cigolio m • vi strillare; [✖] spifferare

squeamish /'skwi:mɪʃ/ adj dallo stomaco delicato

squeeze /skwi:z/ n stretta f; (crush) pigia pigia m inv • vt premere; (to get juice) spremere; stringere (hand); (force) spingere a forza; ([!]: extort) estorcere (**out of** da). □ **~ in/out** vi sgusciare dentro/fuori. □ **~ up** vi stringersi

squid /skwɪd/ n calamaro m

squiggle /'skwɪgl/ n scarabocchio m

squint /skwɪnt/ n strabismo m • vi essere strabico

squirm /skwɜːm/ vi contorcersi; (feel embarrassed) sentirsi imbarazzato

squirrel /'skwɪrəl/ n scoiattolo m

squirt /skwɜːt/ n spruzzo m; ([!]: person) presuntuoso m • vt/i spruzzare

St abbr (Saint) S; abbr Street

stab /stæb/ n pugnalata f, coltellata f; (sensation) fitta f; ([!]: attempt) tentativo m • vt (pt/pp **stabbed**) pugnalare, accoltellare

stability /stə'bɪlətɪ/ n stabilità f inv

stabilize /'steɪbɪlaɪz/ vt stabilizzare • vi stabilizzarsi

stable[1] /'steɪbl/ adj stabile

stable[2] n stalla f; (establishment) scuderia f

stack /stæk/ n catasta f; (of chimney) comignolo m; (chimney) ciminiera f; ([!]: large quantity) montagna f • vt accatastare

stadium /'steɪdɪəm/ n stadio m

staff /stɑːf/ n (stick) bastone m; (employees) personale m; (teachers) corpo m insegnante; (Mil) Stato m Maggiore • vt fornire di personale. **~-room** n (Sch) sala f insegnanti

stag /stæg/ n cervo m

stage /steɪdʒ/ n palcoscenico m; (profession) teatro m; (in journey) tappa f; (in process) stadio m; **go on the ~** darsi al teatro; **by** or **in ~s** a tappe • vt mettere in scena; (arrange) organizzare

stagger /'stægə(r)/ vi barcollare • vt sbalordire; scaglionare (holidays etc); **I was ~ed** sono rimasto sbalordito • n vacillamento m. **~ing** adj sbalorditivo

stagnant /'stægnənt/ adj stagnante

stagnat|e /stæg'neɪt/ vi fig [ri]stagnare. **~ion** n fig inattività f

'stag party n addio m al celibato

staid /steɪd/ adj posato

stain /steɪn/ n macchia f; (for wood) mordente m • vt macchiare; (wood) dare il mordente a; **~ed glass** vetro m colorato; **~ed-glass window** vetrata f colorata. **~less** adj senza macchia; (steel) inossidabile. **~ remover** n smacchiatore m

stair /steə(r)/ n gradino m; **~s** pl sc[ale] fpl. **~case** n scale fpl

stake /steɪk/ n palo m; (wager) post[a] (Comm) partecipazione f; **at ~** in gioco • vt puntellare; (wager) scommettere

stale /steɪl/ adj stantio; (air) viziato (uninteresting) trito [e ritrito]. **~ma[te]** n (in chess) stallo m; (deadlock) situazione f di stallo

stalk[1] /stɔːk/ n gambo m

stalk[2] vt inseguire • vi camminare impettito

stall /stɔːl/ n box m inv; (in market) bancarella f; **~s** pl (Theat) platea f (engine:) spegnersi; fig temporeggia[re] • vt far spegnere (engine); tenere a bada (person)

stallion /'stæljən/ n stallone m

stalwart /'stɔːlwət/ adj fedele

stamina /'stæmɪnə/ n [capacità f in[v] di] resistenza f

stammer /'stæmə(r)/ n balbettio m • vt/i balbettare

stamp /stæmp/ n (postage) francobollo m; (instrument) timbro [m]; fig impronta f • vt affrancare (letter) timbrare (bill); battere (feet). □ **~ out** vt spegnere; fig soffocare

stampede /stæm'piːd/ n fuga f precipitosa; [!] fuggi-fuggi m • vi fuggire precipitosamente

stance /stɑːns/ n posizione f

stand /stænd/ n (for bikes) rastrellie[ra] f; (at exhibition) stand m inv; (in marke[t]) bancarella f; (in stadium) gradinata [f] inv; fig posizione f • v (pt/pp **stood**) [•] stare in piedi; (rise) alzarsi [in pie[di]] (be) trovarsi; (be candidate) essere candidato (**for** a); (stay valid) rimanere valido; **~ still** non muoversi; **I don't know where I ~** non so qual'è la mia posizione[;] **~ firm** fig tener duro; **~ together** essere solidali; **~ to lose/gain** rischiare di perdere/vincere; **~ to reason** essere logico • vt (withstand) resistere a; (endure) sopportare; (place) mettere; **~ a chance** avere una possibilità; **~ one's ground** tener duro; **~ the test of time** superare la prova del tempo; **~ s[omebody] a beer** offrire una birra a qcno. □ **~ by** vi stare a guardare; (be ready) essere pronto • vt (support) appoggiare. ▫ ~ **down** vi (retire) ritirarsi. ▫ ~ **for** vt (mean) significare; (tolerate) tollerare. ▫ ~ **in for** vt sostituire. ▫ ~ **out** vi spiccare. ▫ ~ **up** vi alzarsi [in piedi]. ▫ ~ **up for** vt prendere le difese di; ~ **up for oneself** farsi valere. ▫ ~ **up to** vt affrontare

standard /'stændəd/ adj standard; **be ~ practice** essere pratica corrente • n standard m inv; (Techn) norma f; (level) livello m; (quality) qualità f inv; (flag) stendardo m; **~s** pl (morals) valori mpl; **~ of living** tenore m di vita. **~ize** vt standardizzare

'standard lamp n lampada f a stelo

'stand-by n riserva f; **on ~** (at airport) in lista d'attesa

'stand-in n controfigura f

standing /'stændɪŋ/ adj (erect) in piedi; (permanent) permanente • n posizione f; (duration) durata f. **~ 'order** n addebitamento m diretto. **~-room** n posti mpl in piedi

stand: ~point n punto m di vista. **~still** n **come to a ~still** fermarsi; **at a ~still** in un periodo di stasi

stank /stæŋk/ ▸**stink**

staple[1] /'steɪpl/ n (product) prodotto m principale

staple[2] n graffa f • vt pinzare. **~r** n pinzatrice f, cucitrice f

star /stɑ:(r)/ n stella f; (asterisk) asterisco m; (Cinema, Sport, Theat) divo, -a mf, stella f • vi (pt/pp **starred**) essere l'interprete principale

starboard /'stɑ:bəd/ n tribordo m

starch /stɑ:tʃ/ n amido m • vt inamidare. **~y** adj ricco di amido; fig compito

stare /steə(r)/ n sguardo m fisso • vi **it's rude to ~** è da maleducati fissare la gente; **~ at** fissare; **~ into space** guardare nel vuoto

'starfish n stella f di mare

stark /stɑ:k/ adj austero; (contrast) forte • adv completamente; **~ naked** completamente nudo

starling /'stɑ:lɪŋ/ n storno m

starry /'stɑ:rɪ/ adj stellato

start /stɑ:t/ n inizio m; (departure) partenza f; (jump) sobbalzo m; **from the ~** [fin] dall'inizio; **for a ~** tanto per cominciare; **give sb a ~** (Sport) dare un vantaggio a qcno • vi [in]cominciare; (set out) avviarsi; (engine, car:) partire; (jump) trasalire; **to ~ with,...** tanto per cominciare,... • vt [in]cominciare; (cause) dare inizio a; (found) mettere su; mettere in moto (car); mettere in giro (rumour). **~er** n (Culin) primo m [piatto m]; (in race: giving signal) starter m inv; (participant) concorrente mf; (Auto) motorino m d'avviamento. **~ing-point** n punto m di partenza

startle /'stɑ:tl/ vt far trasalire; (news:) sconvolgere

starvation /stɑ:'veɪʃn/ n fame f

starve /stɑ:v/ vi morire di fame • vt far morire di fame

state /steɪt/ n stato m; (grand style) pompa f; **~ of play** punteggio m; **be in a ~** (person:) essere agitato; **lie in ~** essere esposto • attrib di Stato; (Sch) pubblico; (with ceremony) di gala • vt dichiarare; (specify) precisare. **~less** adj apolide

stately /'steɪtlɪ/ adj (**-ier, -iest**) maestoso. **~ 'home** n dimora f signorile

statement /'steɪtmənt/ n dichiarazione f; (Jur) deposizione f; (in banking) estratto m conto; (account) rapporto m

'statesman n statista mf

static /'stætɪk/ adj statico

station /'steɪʃn/ n stazione f; (police) commissariato m • vt appostare (guard); **be ~ed in Germany** essere di stanza in Germania. **~ary** adj immobile

'station-wagon n Am familiare f

statistic|al /stə'tɪstɪkl/ adj statistico. **~s** n & pl statistica f

statue /'stætju:/ n statua f

stature /'stætʃə(r)/ n statura f

status /'steɪtəs/ n condizione f; (high rank) alto rango m. **~ symbol** n status symbol m inv

statut|e /'stætju:t/ n statuto m. **~ory** adj statutario

staunch /stɔ:ntʃ/ adj fedele. **~ly** adv fedelmente

stave /steɪv/ vt **~ off** tenere lontano

stay /steɪ/ n soggiorno m • vi restare, rimanere; (reside) alloggiare; **~ the**

night passare la notte; ~ **put** non muoversi •vt ~ **the course** resistere fino alla fine. ▫ ~ **away** vi stare lontano. ▫ ~ **behind** vi non andare con gli altri. ▫ ~ **in** vi (at home) stare in casa; (Sch) restare a scuola dopo le lezioni. ▫ ~ **up** vi stare su; (person:) stare alzato

stead /sted/ n **in his** ~ in sua vece; **stand sb in good** ~ tornare utile a qcno. ~**fast** adj fedele; (refusal) fermo

steadily /ˈstedɪlɪ/ adv (continually) continuamente

steady /ˈstedɪ/ adj (**-ier, -iest**) saldo, fermo; (breathing) regolare; (job, boyfriend) fisso; (dependable) serio

steak /steɪk/ n (for stew) spezzatino m; (for grilling, frying) bistecca f

steal /stiːl/ v (pt **stole**, pp **stolen**) •vt rubare (**from** da). ▫ ~ **in**/**out** vi entrare/uscire furtivamente

stealth /stelθ/ n **by** ~ di nascosto. ~**y** adj furtivo

steam /stiːm/ n vapore m; **under one's own** ~ [!] da solo •vt (Culin) cucinare a vapore •vi fumare. ▫ ~ **up** vi appannarsi

ˈ**steam-engine** n locomotiva f

steamer /ˈstiːmə(r)/ n piroscafo m; (saucepan) pentola f a vapore

ˈ**steamroller** n rullo m compressore

steamy /ˈstiːmɪ/ adj appannato

steel /stiːl/ n acciaio m •vt ~ **oneself** temprarsi

steep[1] /stiːp/ vt (soak) lasciare a bagno

steep[2] adj ripido; ([!]: price) esorbitante. ~**ly** adv ripidamente

steeple /ˈstiːpl/ n campanile m. ~**chase** n corsa f ippica a ostacoli

steer /stɪə(r)/ vt/i guidare; ~ **clear of** stare alla larga da. ~**ing** n (Auto) sterzo m. ~**ing-wheel** n volante m

stem[1] /stem/ n stelo m; (of glass) gambo m; (of word) radice f •vi (pt/pp **stemmed**) ~ **from** derivare da

stem[2] vt (pt/pp **stemmed**) contenere

stench /stentʃ/ n fetore m

step /step/ n passo m; (stair) gradino m; ~**s** pl (ladder) scala f portatile; **in** ~ al passo; **be out of** ~ non stare al passo; ~ **by** ~ un passo alla volta •vi (pt/pp **stepped**) ~ **into** entrare in; ~ **out of** uscire da; ~ **out of line** sgarrare. ▫ ~ **down** vi fig dimettersi. ▫ ~ **forward** vi farsi avanti. ▫ ~ **in** vi fig intervenire. ▫ ~ **up** vt (increase) aumentare

step: ~**brother** n fratellastro m. ~**daughter** n figliastra f. ~**father** n patrigno m. ~**-ladder** n scala f portatile. ~**mother** n matrigna f

ˈ**stepping-stone** n pietra f per guadare; fig trampolino m

step: ~**sister** n sorellastra f. ~**son** n figliastro m

stereo /ˈsterɪəʊ/ n stereo m; **in** ~ in stereofonia. ~**phonic** adj stereofonico

stereotype /ˈsterɪətaɪp/ n stereotipo m. ~**d** adj stereotipato

steril|e /ˈsteraɪl/ adj sterile. ~**ity** n sterilità f inv

sterling /ˈstɜːlɪŋ/ adj fig apprezzabile; ~ **silver** argento m pregiato •n sterlina f

stern[1] /stɜːn/ adj severo

stern[2] n (of boat) poppa f

stethoscope /ˈsteθəskəʊp/ n stetoscopio m

stew /stjuː/ n stufato m; **in a** ~ [!] agitato •vt/i cuocere in umido; ~**ed fruit** frutta f cotta

steward /ˈstjuːəd/ n (at meeting) organizzatore, -trice mf; (on ship, aircraft) steward m inv. ~**ess** n hostess f inv

stick[1] /stɪk/ n bastone m; (of celery, rhubarb) gambo m; (Sport) mazza f

stick[2] v (pt/pp **stuck**) •vt (stab) [con]ficcare; (glue) attaccare; ([!]: put) mettere; ([!]: endure) sopportare •vi (adhere) attaccarsi (**to** a); (jam) bloccarsi; ~ **to** attenersi a (facts); mantenere (story); perseverare in (task); ~ **at it** [!] tener duro; ~ **at nothing** [!] non fermarsi di fronte a niente; **be stuck** (vehicle, person:) essere bloccato; (drawer:) essere incastrato; **be stuck with sth** [!] farsi incastrare con qcsa. ▫ ~ **out** vi (project) sporgere; ([!]: catch the eye) risaltare •vt [!] fare (tongue). ▫ ~ **up for** vt [!] difendere

sticker /ˈstɪkə(r)/ n autoadesivo m

ˈ**sticking plaster** n cerotto m

stickler /'stɪklə(r)/ n **be a ~ for** tenere molto a

sticky /'stɪkɪ/ adj (**-ier, -iest**) appiccicoso; (adhesive) adesivo; (fig: difficult) difficile

stiff /stɪf/ adj rigido; (brush, task) duro; (person) controllato; (drink) forte; (penalty) severo; (price) alto; **bored ~** [!] annoiato a morte; **~ neck** torcicollo m. **~en** vt irrigidire • vi irrigidirsi. **~ness** n rigidità f inv

stifl|e /'staɪfl/ vt soffocare. **~ing** adj soffocante

still¹ /stɪl/ n distilleria f

still² adj fermo; (drink) non gasato; **keep/stand ~** stare fermo • n quiete f; (photo) posa f • adv ancora; (nevertheless) nondimeno, comunque; **I'm ~ not sure** non sono ancora sicuro

stillborn adj nato morto

still 'life n natura f morta

stilted /'stɪltɪd/ adj artificioso

stilts /stɪlts/ npl trampoli mpl

stimulant /'stɪmjʊlənt/ n eccitante m

stimulat|e /'stɪmjʊleɪt/ vt stimolare. **~ion** n stimolo m

stimulus /'stɪmjʊləs/ n (pl **-li** /-laɪ/) stimolo m

sting /stɪŋ/ n puntura f; (from nettle, jellyfish) sostanza f irritante; (organ) pungiglione m • v (pt/pp **stung**) • vt pungere; (jellyfish:) pizzicare • vi (insect:) pungere. **~ing nettle** n ortica f

stingy /'stɪndʒɪ/ adj (**-ier, -iest**) tirchio

stink /stɪŋk/ n puzza f • vi (pt **stank**, pp **stunk**) puzzare

stipulat|e /'stɪpjʊleɪt/ vt porre come condizione. **~ion** n condizione f

stir /stɜ:(r)/ n mescolata f; (commotion) trambusto m • v (pt/pp **stirred**) • vt muovere; (mix) mescolare • vi muoversi

stirrup /'stɪrəp/ n staffa f

stitch /stɪtʃ/ n punto m; (in knitting) maglia f; (pain) fitta f; **have sb in ~es** [!] far ridere qcno a crepapelle • vt cucire

stock /stɒk/ n (for use or selling) scorta f, stock m inv; (livestock) bestiame m; (lineage) stirpe f; (Fin) titoli mpl; (Culin) brodo m; **in ~** disponibile; **out of ~** esaurito; **take ~** fig fare il punto • adj solito • vt (shop:) vendere; approvvigionare (shelves). □ **~ up** vi far scorta (**with** di)

stock: ~broker n agente m di cambio. **S~ Exchange** n Borsa f Valori

stocking /'stɒkɪŋ/ n calza f

stock: ~pile vt fare scorta di • n riserva f. **~-'still** adj immobile. **~-taking** n (Comm) inventario m

stocky /'stɒkɪ/ adj (**-ier, -iest**) tarchiato

stodgy /'stɒdʒɪ/ adj indigesto

stoke /stəʊk/ vt alimentare

stole¹ /stəʊl/ n stola f

stole², stolen /'stəʊln/ ▹**steal**

stomach /'stʌmək/ n pancia f; (Anat) stomaco m • vt [!] reggere. **~-ache** n mal m di pancia

stone /stəʊn/ n pietra f; (in fruit) nocciolo m; (Med) calcolo m; (weight) 6,348 kg • adj di pietra; (wall, Age) della pietra • vt snocciolare (fruit). **~-cold** adj gelido. **~-'deaf** adj [!] sordo come una campana

stony /'stəʊnɪ/ adj pietroso; (glare) glaciale

stood /stʊd/ ▹**stand**

stool /stu:l/ n sgabello m

stoop /stu:p/ n curvatura f • vi stare curvo; (bend down) chinarsi; fig abbassarsi

stop /stɒp/ n (break) sosta f; (for bus, train) fermata f; (Gram) punto m; **come to a ~** fermarsi; **put a ~ to sth** mettere fine a qcsa • v (pt/pp **stopped**) • vt fermare; arrestare (machine); (prevent) impedire; **~ sb doing sth** impedire a qcno di fare qcsa; **~ doing sth** smettere di fare qcsa; **~ that!** smettila! • vi fermarsi; (rain:) smettere • int fermo!. □ **~ off** vi fare una sosta. □ **~ up** vt otturare (sink); tappare (hole). □ **~ with** vi ([!]: stay with) fermarsi da

stop: ~gap n palliativo m; (person) tappabuchi m inv. **~-over** n sosta f; (Aeron) scalo m

stoppage /'stɒpɪdʒ/ n ostruzione f; (strike) interruzione f; (deduction) trattenute fpl

stopper /'stɒpə(r)/ n tappo m

S

stop-watch n cronometro m

storage /'stɔ:rɪdʒ/ n deposito m; (in warehouse) immagazzinaggio m; (Comput) memoria f

store /stɔ:(r)/ n (stock) riserva f; (shop) grande magazzino m; (depot) deposito m; **in ~** in deposito; **what the future has in ~ for me** cosa mi riserva il futuro; **set great ~ by** tenere in gran conto •vt tenere; (in warehouse, (Comput)) immagazzinare. **~-room** n magazzino m

storey /'stɔ:rɪ/ n piano m

stork /stɔ:k/ n cicogna f

storm /stɔ:m/ n temporale m; (with thunder) tempesta f •vt prendere d'assalto. **~y** adj tempestoso

story /'stɔ:rɪ/ n storia f; (in newspaper) articolo m

stout /staʊt/ adj (shoes) resistente; (fat) robusto; (defence) strenuo

stove /stəʊv/ n stufa f; (for cooking) cucina f [economica]

stow /stəʊ/ vt metter via. **~away** n passeggero, -a mf clandestino, -a

straggl|e /'strægl/ vi crescere disordinatamente; (dawdle) rimanere indietro. **~er** n persona f che rimane indietro. **~y** adj in disordine

straight /streɪt/ adj diritto, dritto; (answer, question, person) diretto; (tidy) in ordine; (drink, hair) liscio •adv diritto, dritto; (directly) direttamente; **~ away** immediatamente; **~ on** or **ahead** diritto; **~ out** fig apertamente; **go ~** ! rigare diritto; **put sth ~** mettere qcsa in ordine; **sit/stand up ~** stare diritto

straighten /'streɪtn/ vt raddrizzare •vi raddrizzarsi; **~ [up]** (person:) mettersi diritto. □ **~ out** vt fig chiarire (situation)

straight'forward adj franco; (simple) semplice

strain[1] /streɪn/ n (streak) vena f; (Bot) varietà f inv; (of virus) forma f

strain[2] n tensione f; (injury) stiramento m; **~s** pl (of music) note fpl •vt tirare; sforzare (eyes, voice); stirarsi (muscle); (Culin) scolare •vi sforzarsi. **~ed** adj (relations) teso. **~er** n colino m

strait /streɪt/ n stretto m; **in dire ~s** in serie difficoltà. **~-jacket** n camicia f di forza. **~-'laced** adj puritano

strand[1] /strænd/ n (of thread) gugliata f; (of beads) filo m; (of hair) capello m

strand[2] vt **be ~ed** rimanere bloccato

strange /streɪndʒ/ adj strano; (not known) sconosciuto; (unaccustomed) estraneo. **~ly** adv stranamente; **~ly enough** curiosamente. **~r** n estraneo, -a mf

strangle /'stræŋgl/ vt strangolare; fig reprimere

strap /stræp/ n cinghia f (to grasp in vehicle) maniglia f; (of watch) cinturino m; (shoulder **~**) bretella f, spallina f •vt (pt/pp **strapped**) legare; **~ in** or **down** assicurare

strategic /strə'ti:dʒɪk/ adj strategico

strategy /'strætədʒɪ/ n strategia f

straw /strɔ:/ n paglia f; (single piece) fuscello m; (for drinking) cannuccia f; **the last ~** l'ultima goccia

strawberry /'strɔ:bərɪ/ n fragola f

stray /streɪ/ adj (animal) randagio •n randagio m •vi andarsene per conto proprio; (deviate) deviare (**from** da)

streak /stri:k/ n striatura f; (fig: trait) vena f •vi sfrecciare. **~y** adj striato; (bacon) grasso

stream /stri:m/ n ruscello m; (current) corrente f; (of blood, people) flusso m; (Sch) classe f •vi scorrere. □ **~ in/out** vi entrare/uscire a fiotti

streamer /'stri:mə(r)/ n (paper) stella f filante; (flag) pennone m

'streamline vt rendere aerodinamico; (simplify) snellire. **~d** adj aerodinamico

street /stri:t/ n strada f. **~car** n Am tram m inv. **~lamp** n lampione m

strength /streŋθ/ n forza f; (of wall, bridge etc) solidità f inv; **~s** punti mpl forti; **on the ~ of** grazie a. **~en** vt rinforzare

strenuous /'strenjʊəs/ adj faticoso; (attempt, denial) energico

stress /stres/ n (emphasis) insistenza f; (Gram) accento m tonico; (mental) stress m inv; (Mech) spinta f •vt (emphasize) insistere su; (Gram) mettere l'accento [tonico] su. **~ed**

adj (mentally) stressato. **~ful** adj stressante

tretch /stretʃ/ n stiramento m; (period) periodo m di tempo; (of road) estensione f; (elasticity) elasticità f inv; **at a ~** di fila; **have a ~** stirarsi • vt tirare; allargare (shoes, arms etc); (person:) allungare • vi (become wider) allargarsi; (extend) estendersi; (person:) stirarsi. **~er** n barella f

trict /strɪkt/ adj severo; (precise) preciso. **~ly** adv severamente; **~ly speaking** in senso stretto

tride /straɪd/ n [lungo] passo m; **take sth in one's ~** accettare qcsa con facilità • vi (pt **strode**, pp **stridden**) andare a gran passi

trident /'straɪdənt/ adj stridente; (colour) vistoso

trife /straɪf/ n conflitto m

trike /straɪk/ n sciopero m; (Mil) attacco m; **on ~** in sciopero • v (pt/pp **struck**) • vt colpire; accendere (match); trovare (oil, gold); (delete) depennare; (occur to) venire in mente a; (Mil) attaccare • vi (lightning:) cadere; (clock:) suonare; (Mil) attaccare; (workers:) scioperare; **~ lucky** azzeccarla. □ **~ off, strike out** vt eliminare. □ **~ up** vt fare (friendship); attaccare (conversation). **~-breaker** n persona f che non aderisce a uno sciopero

triker /'straɪkə(r)/ n scioperante mf

triking /'straɪkɪŋ/ adj impressionante; (attractive) affascinante

tring /strɪŋ/ n spago m; (of musical instrument, racket) corda f; (of pearls) filo m; (of lies) serie f; **the ~s** (Mus) gli archi; **pull ~s** [!] usare le proprie conoscenze • vt (pt/pp **strung**) (thread) infilare (beads). **~ed** adj (instrument) a corda

tringent /'strɪndʒnt/ adj rigido

trip /strɪp/ n striscia f • v (pt/pp **stripped**) • vt spogliare; togliere le lenzuola da (bed); scrostare (wood, furniture); smontare (machine); (deprive) privare (**of** di) • vi (undress) spogliarsi. **~ cartoon** n striscia f. **~ club** n locale m di strip-tease

tripe /straɪp/ n striscia f; (Mil) gallone m. **~d** adj a strisce

strip-'tease n spogliarello m, strip-tease m inv

strive /straɪv/ vi (pt **strove**, pp **striven**) sforzarsi (**to** di); **~ for** sforzarsi di ottenere

strode /strəʊd/ ▸**stride**

stroke[1] /strəʊk/ n colpo m; (of pen) tratto m; (in swimming) bracciata f; (Med) ictus m inv; **~ of luck** colpo m di fortuna; **put sb off his ~** far perdere il filo a qcno

stroke[2] vt accarezzare

stroll /strəʊl/ n passeggiata f • vi passeggiare. **~er** n (Am: push-chair) passeggino m

strong /strɒŋ/ adj (**-er** /-gə(r)/, **-est** /-gɪst/) forte; (argument) valido

strong: ~hold n roccaforte f. **~ly** adv fortemente. **~-room** n camera f blindata

stroppy /'strɒpɪ/ adj scorbutico

strove /strəʊv/ ▸**strive**

struck /strʌk/ ▸**strike**

structural /'strʌktʃərəl/ adj strutturale. **~ly** adv strutturalmente

structure /'strʌktʃə(r)/ n struttura f

struggle /'strʌgl/ n lotta f; **without a ~** senza lottare • vi lottare; **~ for breath** respirare con fatica; **~ to do sth** fare fatica a fare qcsa; **~ to one's feet** alzarsi con fatica

strum /strʌm/ vt/i (pt/pp **strummed**) strimpellare

strung /strʌŋ/ ▸**string**

strut[1] /strʌt/ n (component) puntello m

strut[2] vi (pt/pp **strutted**) camminare impettito

stub /stʌb/ n mozzicone m; (counterfoil) matrice f • vt (pt/pp **stubbed**) **~ one's toe** sbattere il dito del piede (**on** contro). □ **~ out** vt spegnere (cigarette)

stubb|le /'stʌbl/ n barba f ispida. **~ly** adj ispido

stubborn /'stʌbən/ adj testardo; (refusal) ostinato

stuck /stʌk/ ▸**stick[2]**. **~-'up** adj [!] snob

stud[1] /stʌd/ n (on boot) tacchetto m; (on jacket) borchia f; (for ear) orecchino m [a bottone]

stud[2] n (of horses) scuderia f

student /'stju:dənt/ n studente m, studentessa f; (school child) scolaro, -a mf. ~ **nurse** n studente, studentessa infermiere, -a

studio /'stju:dɪəʊ/ n studio m

studious /'stju:dɪəs/ adj studioso; (attention) studiato

study /'stʌdɪ/ n studio m •vt/i (pt/pp **studied**) studiare

stuff /stʌf/ n materiale m; ([!]: things) roba f •vt riempire; (with padding) imbottire; (Culin) farcire; ~ **sth into a drawer/one's pocket** ficcare qcsa alla rinfusa in un cassetto/in tasca. ~**ing** n (padding) imbottitura f; (Culin) ripieno m

stuffy /'stʌfɪ/ adj (**-ier, -iest**) che sa di chiuso; (old-fashioned) antiquato

stumbl|e /'stʌmbl/ vi inciampare; ~**e across** or **on** imbattersi in. ~**ing-block** n ostacolo m

stump /stʌmp/ n ceppo m; (of limb) moncone m. ~**ed** adj [!] perplesso •**stump up** vt/i [!] sganciare

stun /stʌn/ vt (pt/pp **stunned**) stordire; (astonish) sbalordire

stung /stʌŋ/ ▸**sting**

stunk /stʌŋk/ ▸**stink**

stunning /'stʌnɪŋ/ adj [!] favoloso; (blow, victory) sbalorditivo

stunt[1] /stʌnt/ n [!] trovata f pubblicitaria

stunt[2] vt arrestare lo sviluppo di. ~**ed** adj stentato

stupendous /stju:'pendəs/ adj stupendo. ~**ly** adv stupendamente

stupid /'stju:pɪd/ adj stupido. ~**ity** n stupidità f. ~**ly** adv stupidamente

stupor /'stju:pə(r)/ n torpore m

sturdy /'stɜ:dɪ/ adj (**-ier, -iest**) robusto; (furniture) solido

stutter /'stʌtə(r)/ n balbuzie f •vt/i balbettare

sty, stye /staɪ/ n (pl **styes**) (Med) orzaiolo m

style /staɪl/ n stile m; (fashion) moda f; (sort) tipo m; (hair~) pettinatura f; **in** ~ in grande stile

stylish /'staɪlɪʃ/ adj elegante. ~**ly** adv con eleganza

stylist /'staɪlɪst/ n stilista mf; (hair-~) parrucchiere, -a mf. ~**ic** adj stilistico

stylus /'staɪləs/ n (on record player) puntina f

suave /swɑ:v/ adj dai modi garbati

sub'conscious /sʌb-/ adj subcosciente •n subcosciente m. ~**ly** adv in modo inconscio

'**subdivi|de** vt suddividere. ~**sion** n suddivisione f

subject[1] /'sʌbdʒɪkt/ adj ~ **to** soggetto a; (depending on) subordinato a; ~ **to availability** nei limiti della disponibilità •n soggetto m; (of ruler) suddito, -a mf; (Sch) materia f

subject[2] /səb'dʒekt/ vt (to attack, abuse) sottoporre; assoggettare (country)

subjective /səb'dʒektɪv/ adj soggettivo. ~**ly** adv soggettivamente

subjunctive /səb'dʒʌŋktɪv/ adj & n congiuntivo m

sublime /sə'blaɪm/ adj sublime. ~**ly** adv sublimamente

subma'rine n sommergibile m

submerge /səb'mɜ:dʒ/ vt immergere; **be** ~**d** essere sommerso •vi immergersi

submiss|ion /səb'mɪʃn/ n sottomissione f. ~**ive** adj sottomesso

submit /səb'mɪt/ v (pt/pp **-mitted**, pres p **-mitting**) •vt sottoporre •vi sottomettersi

subordinate /sə'bɔ:dɪneɪt/ vt subordinare (**to** a)

subscribe /səb'skraɪb/ vi contribuire; ~ **to** abbonarsi a (newspaper); sottoscrivere (fund); fig aderire a. ~**r** n abbonato, -a mf

subscription /səb'skrɪpʃn/ n (to club) sottoscrizione f; (to newspaper) abbonamento m

subsequent /'sʌbsɪkwənt/ adj susseguente. ~**ly** adv in seguito

subside /səb'saɪd/ vi sprofondare; (ground:) avvallarsi; (storm:) placarsi

subsidiary /səb'sɪdɪərɪ/ adj secondario •n ~ [**company**] filiale f

subsid|ize /'sʌbsɪdaɪz/ vt sovvenzionare. ~**y** n sovvenzione f

substance /'sʌbstəns/ n sostanza f

sub'standard adj di qualità inferiore

substantial /səb'stænʃl/ adj solido;

(meal) sostanzioso; (considerable) notevole. **~ly** adv notevolmente; (essentially) sostanzialmente

substitut|e /'sʌbstɪtju:t/ n sostituto m • vt **~e A for B** sostituire B con A • vi **~e for sb** sostituire qcno. **~ion** n sostituzione f

subterranean /sʌbtə'reɪnɪən/ adj sotterraneo

'subtitle n sottotitolo m

sub|tle /'sʌtl/ adj sottile; (taste, perfume) delicato. **~tlety** n sottigliezza f. **~tly** adv sottilmente

subtract /səb'trækt/ vt sottrare. **~ion** n sottrazione f

suburb /'ʃʌbɜ:b/ n sobborgo m; **in the ~s** in periferia. **~an** adj suburbano. **~ia** n i sobborghi mpl

subversive /səb'vɜ:sɪv/ adj sovversivo

'subway n sottopassagio m; (Am: railway) metropolitana f

succeed /sək'si:d/ vi riuscire; (follow) succedere a; **~ in doing** riuscire a fare • vt succedere a (king). **~ing** adj successivo

success /sək'ses/ n successo m; **be a ~** (in life) aver successo. **~ful** adj riuscito; (businessman, artist etc) di successo. **~fully** adv con successo

succession /sək'seʃn/ n successione f; **in ~** di seguito

successive /sək'sesɪv/ adj successivo. **~ly** adv successivamente

successor /sək'sesə(r)/ n successore m

succulent /'ʃʌkjʊlənt/ adj succulento

succumb /sə'kʌm/ vi soccombere (**to** a)

such /sʌtʃ/ adj tale; **~ a book** un libro di questo genere; **~ a thing** una cosa di questo genere; **~ a long time ago** talmente tanto tempo fa; **there is no ~ thing** non esiste una cosa così; **there is no ~ person** non esiste una persona così • pron **as ~** come tale; **~ as** chi; **and ~** e simili; **~ as it is** così com'è. **~like** pron 🅸 di tal genere

suck /ʃʌk/ vt succhiare. □ **~ up** vt assorbire. □ **~ up to** vt 🅸 fare il lecchino con

sucker /'ʃʌkə(r)/ n (Bot) pollone m; (🅸: person) credulone, -a mf

suction /'sʌkʃn/ n aspirazione f

sudden /'sʌdn/ adj improvviso • n **all of a ~** all'improvviso. **~ly** adv improvvisamente

sue /su:/ vt (pres p **suing**) fare causa a (**for** per) • vi fare causa

suede /sweɪd/ n pelle f scamosciata

suet /'su:ɪt/ n grasso m di rognone

suffer /'sʌfə(r)/ vi soffrire (**from** per) • vt soffrire; subire (loss etc); (tolerate) subire. **~ing** n sofferenza f

suffice /sə'faɪs/ vi bastare

sufficient /sə'fɪʃənt/ adj sufficiente. **~ly** adv sufficientemente

suffix /'sʌfɪks/ n suffisso m

suffocat|e /'sʌfəkeɪt/ vt/i soffocare. **~ion** n soffocamento m

sugar /'ʃʊgə(r)/ n zucchero m • vt zuccherare. **~ basin**, **~-bowl** n zuccheriera f. **~y** adj zuccheroso; fig sdolcinato

suggest /sə'dʒest/ vt suggerire; (indicate, insinuate) fare pensare a. **~ion** n suggerimento m; (trace) traccia f. **~ive** adj allusivo. **~ively** adv in modo allusivo

suicidal /su:ɪ'saɪdl/ adj suicida

suicide /'su:ɪsaɪd/ n suicidio m; (person) suicida mf; **commit ~** suicidarsi

suit /su:t/ n vestito m; (woman's) tailleur m inv; (in cards) seme m; (Jur) causa f; **follow ~** fig fare lo stesso • vt andar bene a; (adapt) adattare (**to** a); (be convenient for) andare bene per; **be ~ed to** or **for** essere adatto a; **~ yourself!** fa' come vuoi!

suitabl|e /'su:təbl/ adj adatto. **~y** adv convenientemente

'suitcase n valigia f

suite /swi:t/ n suite f inv; (of furniture) divano m e poltrone fpl assortiti

sulk /sʌlk/ vi fare il broncio. **~y** adj imbronciato

sullen /'sʌlən/ adj svogliato

sulphur /'sʌlfə(r)/ n zolfo m. **~ic acid** n acido m solforico

sultana /sʌl'tɑ:nə/ n uva f sultanina

sultry /'sʌltrɪ/ adj (**-ier, -iest**) (weather) afoso; fig sensuale

sum /sʌm/ n somma f; (Sch) addizione f • **~ up** (pt/pp **summed**) vi riassumere •vt valutare

summar|ize /'sʌməraɪz/ vt riassumere. **~y** n sommario m •adj sommario; (dismissal) sbrigativo

summer /'sʌmə(r)/ n estate f. **~-house** n padiglione m. **~time** n (season) estate f

summery /'sʌmərɪ/ adj estivo

summit /'sʌmɪt/ n cima f. **~ conference** n vertice m

summon /'sʌmən/ vt convocare; (Jur) citare. ▫ **~ up** vt raccogliere (strength); rievocare (memory)

summons /'sʌmənz/ n (Jur) citazione f •vt citare in giudizio

sumptuous /'sʌmptjʊəs/ adj sontuoso. **~ly** adv sontuosamente

sun /sʌn/ n sole m •vt (pt/pp **sunned**) **~ oneself** prendere il sole

sun: ~bathe vi prendere il sole. **~burn** n scottatura f (solare). **~burnt** adj scottato (dal sole)

Sunday /'sʌndeɪ/ n domenica f

'**sunflower** n girasole m

sung /sʌŋ/ ▹**sing**

'**sun-glasses** npl occhiali mpl da sole

sunk /sʌŋk/ ▹**sink**

sunken /'sʌŋkn/ adj incavato

'**sunlight** n [luce f del] sole m

sunny /'sʌnɪ/ adj (**-ier, -iest**) assolato

sun: ~rise n alba f. **~-roof** n (Auto) tettuccio m apribile. **~set** n tramonto m. **~shine** n [luce f del] sole m. **~stroke** n insolazione f. **~-tan** n abbronzatura f. **~-tan oil** n olio m solare

super /'su:pə(r)/ adj ⓘ fantastico

superb /sʊ'p3:b/ adj splendido

supercilious /su:pə'sɪlɪəs/ adj altezzoso

superficial /su:pə'fɪʃl/ adj superficiale. **~ly** adv superficialmente

superfluous /sʊ'p3:flʊəs/ adj superfluo

super'human adj sovrumano

superintendent /su:pərɪn'tendənt/ n (of police) commissario m di polizia

superior /su:'pɪərɪə(r)/ adj superiore •n superiore, -a mf. **~ity** n superiorità f

superlative /su:'p3:lətɪv/ adj eccellente •n superlativo m

'**supermarket** n supermercato m

super'natural adj soprannaturale

'**superpower** n superpotenza f

supersede /su:pə'si:d/ vt rimpiazzare

super'sonic adj supersonico

superstiti|on /su:pə'stɪʃn/ n superstizione f. **~ous** adj superstizioso

supervis|e /'su:pəvaɪz/ vt supervisionare. **~ion** n supervisione f. **~or** n supervisore m

supper /'sʌpə(r)/ n cena f

supple /'sʌpl/ adj slogato

supplement /'sʌplɪmənt/ n supplemento m •vt integrare. **~ary** adj supplementare

supplier /sə'plaɪə(r)/ n fornitore, -trice mf

supply /sə'plaɪ/ n fornitura f; (in economics) offerta f; **supplies** pl (Mil) approvvigionamenti mpl •vt (pt/pp **-ied**) fornire; **~ sb with sth** fornire qcsa a qcno

support /sə'pɔ:t/ n sostegno m; (base) supporto m; (keep) sostentamento m •vt sostenere; mantenere (family); (give money to) mantenere finanziariamente; (Sport) fare il tifo per. **~er** n sostenitore, -trice mf; (Sport) tifoso, -a mf. **~ive** adj incoraggiante

suppose /sə'pəʊz/ vt (presume) supporre; (imagine) pensare; **be ~d to do** dover fare; **not be ~d to** ⓘ non avere il permesso di; **I ~ so** suppongo di sì. **~dly** adv presumibilmente

suppress /sə'pres/ vt sopprimere. **~ion** n soppressione f

supremacy /su:'preməsɪ/ n supremazia f

supreme /su:'pri:m/ adj supremo

sure /ʃʊə(r)/ adj sicuro, certo; **make ~** accertarsi; **be ~ to do it** mi raccomando di farlo •adv Am ⓘ certamente; **~ enough** infatti. **~ly** adv certamente; (Am: gladly) volentieri

surety /'ʃʊərətɪ/ n garanzia f; **stand ~ for** garantire

surf /s3:f/ n schiuma f •vt (Comput) ~

S

the Net surfare in Internet

ırface /'sɜ:fɪs/ n superficie f; **on the ~** fig in apparenza •vi (emerge) ɛmergere. **~ mail** n **by ~ mail** per ɔosta ordinaria

urfboard n tavola f da surf

ırfing /'sɜ:fɪŋ/ n surf m inv

ırge /sɜ:dʒ/ n (of sea) ondata f; (of nterest) aumento m; (in demand) impennata f; (of anger, pity) impeto m •vi riversarsi; **~ forward** buttarsi in avanti

ırgeon /'sɜ:dʒən/ n chirurgo m

ırgery /'sɜ:dʒərɪ/ n chirurgia f; (place, consulting room) ambulatorio m; (hours) ore fpl di visita; **have ~** subire un'intervento [chirurgico]

ırgical /'sɜ:dʒɪkl/ adj chirurgico

ırly /'sɜ:lɪ/ adj (**-ier, -iest**) scontroso

ırmise /sə'maɪz/ vt supporre

ırmount /sə'maʊnt/ vt sormontare

ırname /'sɜ:neɪm/ n cognome m

ırpass /sə'pɑ:s/ vt superare

ırplus /'sɜ:pləs/ adj d'avanzo •n sovrappiù m

ırpris|e /sə'praɪz/ n sorpresa f •vt sorprendere; **be ~ed** essere sorpreso (**at** da). **~ing** adj sorprendente. **~ingly** adv sorprendentemente

ırrender /sə'rendə(r)/ n resa f •vi ırrendersi •vt cedere

ırreptitious /sʌrəp'tɪʃəs/ adj & adv di nascosto

ırround /sə'raʊnd/ vt circondare. **~ing** adj circostante. **~ings** npl dintorni mpl

ırveillance /sə'veɪləns/ n sorveglianza f

ırvey[1] /'sɜ:veɪ/ n sguardo m; (poll) sondaggio m; (investigation) indagine f; (of land) rilevamento m; (of house) perizia f

ırvey[2] /sə'veɪ/ vt esaminare; fare un rilevamento di (land); fare una perizia di (building). **~or** n perito m; (of land) topografo, -a mf

ırvival /sə'vaɪvl/ n sopravvivenza f; (relic) resto m

ırviv|e /sə'vaɪv/ vt sopravvivere a •vi sopravvivere. **~or** n superstite mf; **be a ~or** ⓘ riuscire sempre a cavarsela

susceptible /sə'septəbl/ adj influenzabile; **~ to** sensibile a

suspect[1] /sə'spekt/ vt sospettare; (assume) supporre

suspect[2] /'sʌspekt/ adj & n sospetto, -a mf

suspend /sə'spend/ vt appendere; (stop, from duty) sospendere. **~er belt** n reggicalze m inv. **~ders** npl giarretiere fpl; (Am: braces) bretelle mpl

suspense /sə'spens/ n tensione f; (in book etc) suspense f

suspension /sə'spenʃn/ n (Auto) sospensione f. **~ bridge** n ponte m sospeso

suspici|on /sə'spɪʃn/ n sospetto m; (trace) pizzico m; **under ~on** sospettato. **~ous** adj sospettoso; (arousing suspicion) sospetto. **~ously** adv sospettosamente; (arousing suspicion) in modo sospetto

sustain /sə'steɪn/ vt sostenere; mantenere (life); subire (injury)

swab /swɒb/ n (Med) tampone m

swagger /'swægə(r)/ vi pavoneggiarsi

swallow[1] /'swɒləʊ/ vt/i inghiottire. □ **~ up** vt divorare; (earth, crowd:) inghiottire

swallow[2] n (bird) rondine f

swam /swæm/ ▸**swim**

swamp /swɒmp/ n palude f •vt fig sommergere. **~y** adj paludoso

swan /swɒn/ n cigno m

swap /swɒp/ n ⓘ scambio m •vt (pt/pp **swapped**) ⓘ scambiare (**for** con) •vi fare cambio

swarm /swɔ:m/ n sciame m •vi sciamare; **be ~ing with** brulicare di

swarthy /'swɔ:ðɪ/ adj (**-ier, -iest**) di carnagione scura

swat /swɒt/ vt (pt/pp **swatted**) schiacciare

sway /sweɪ/ n fig influenza f •vi oscillare; (person:) ondeggiare •vt (influence) influenzare

swear /sweə(r)/ v (pt **swore**, pp **sworn**) •vt giurare •vi giurare; (curse) dire parolacce; **~ at sb** imprecare contro qcno; **~ by** ⓘ credere ciecamente in. **~-word** n parolaccia f

sweat /swet/ n sudore m •vi sudare

sweater /'swetə(r)/ n golf m inv

swede /swi:d/ n rapa f svedese

Swed|e n svedese mf. **~en** n Svezia f. **~ish** adj svedese

sweep /swi:p/ n scopata f, spazzata f; (curve) curva f; (movement) movimento m ampio; **make a clean ~** fig fare piazza pulita •v (pt/pp **swept**) •vt scopare, spazzare; (wind:) spazzare •vi (go swiftly) andare rapidamente; (wind:) soffiare. ▫ **~ away** vt fig spazzare via. ▫ **~ up** vt spazzare

sweeping /'swi:pɪŋ/ adj (gesture) ampio; (statement) generico; (changes) radicale

sweet /swi:t/ adj dolce; **have a ~ tooth** essere goloso •n caramella f; (dessert) dolce m. **~ corn** n mais m

sweeten /'swi:tn/ vt addolcire. **~er** n dolcificante m

sweetheart n innamorato, -a mf; **hi, ~** ciao, tesoro

swell /swel/ •v (pt **swelled**, pp **swollen** or **swelled**) •vi gonfiarsi; (increase) aumentare •vt gonfiare; (increase) far salire. **~ing** n gonfiore m

swept /swept/ ▹**sweep**

swerve /swɜ:v/ vi deviare bruscamente

swift /swɪft/ adj rapido. **~ly** adv rapidamente

swig /swɪg/ n ! sorso m •vt (pt/pp **swigged**) ! scolarsi

swim /swɪm/ n **have a ~** fare una nuotata •v (pt **swam**, pp **swum**) •vi nuotare; (room:) girare; **my head is ~ming** mi gira la testa •vt percorrere a nuoto. **~mer** n nuotatore, -trice mf

swimming /'swɪmɪŋ/ n nuoto m. **~-baths** npl piscina fsg. **~ costume** n costume m da bagno. **~-pool** n piscina f. **~ trunks** npl calzoncini mpl da bagno

'swim-suit n costume m da bagno

swindle /'swɪndl/ n truffa f •vt truffare. **~r** n truffatore, -trice mf

swine /swaɪn/ n ! porco m

swing /swɪŋ/ n oscillazione f; (shift) cambiamento m; (seat) altalena f; (Mus) swing m; **in full ~** in piena attività •v (pt/pp **swung**) •vi oscillare; (on swing, sway) dondolare; (dangle) penzolare; (turn) girare •vt oscillare; far deviare (vote). **~-'do**[or] n porta f a vento

swipe /swaɪp/ n ! botta f •vt ! colpire; (steal) rubare; far passare nella macchinetta (credit card); **~ card** n pass m inv magnetico

Swiss /swɪs/ adj & n svizzero, -a mf; **the ~** pl gli svizzeri. **~ 'roll** n rotol[o] m di pan di Spagna ripieno di marmellata

switch /swɪtʃ/ n interruttore m; (change) mutamento m •vt cambiar[e]; (exchange) scambiare •vi cambiare; **to** passare a. ▫ **~ off** vt spegnere. ▫ **~ on** vt accendere

switchboard n centralino m

Switzerland /'swɪtsələnd/ n Svizzera f

swivel /'swɪvl/ v (pt/pp **swivelled**) • girare •vi girarsi

swollen /'swəʊlən/ ▹**swell** •adj gonfio. **~-'headed** adj presuntuos[o]

swoop /swu:p/ n (by police) incursio[ne] f •vi **~ [down]** (bird:) piombare; fig fare un'incursione

sword /sɔ:d/ n spada f

swore /swɔ:(r)/ ▹**swear**

sworn /swɔ:n/ ▹**swear**

swot /swɒt/ n ! sgobbone, -a mf •v[i] (pt/pp **swotted**) ! sgobbare

swum /swʌm/ ▹**swim**

swung /swʌŋ/ ▹**swing**

syllable /'sɪləbl/ n sillaba f

syllabus /'sɪləbəs/ n programma m [dei corsi]

symbol /'sɪmbl/ n simbolo m (**of** di). **~ic** adj simbolico. **~ism** n simbolismo m. **~ize** vt simboleggiare

symmetr|ical /sɪ'metrɪkl/ adj simmetrico. **~y** n simmetria f

sympathetic /sɪmpə'θetɪk/ adj (understanding) comprensivo; (showing pity) compassionevole. **~ally** adv co[n] comprensione/compassione

sympathize /'sɪmpəθaɪz/ vi capire; (in grief) solidarizzare; **~ with sb** capire qcno/solidarizzare con qcno. **~r** n (Pol) simpatizzante mf

sympathy /'sɪmpəθɪ/ n comprensione f; (pity) compassione f; (condolences) condoglianze fpl; **in ~**

vith (strike) per solidarietà con

mphony /'sɪmfənɪ/ n sinfonia f

mptom /'sɪmptəm/ n sintomo m. **~atic** adj sintomatico (**of** di)

nagogue /'sɪnəgɒg/ n sinagoga f

nchronize /'sɪŋkrənaɪz/ vt sincronizzare

ndicate /'sɪndɪkət/ n gruppo m

nonym /'sɪnənɪm/ n sinonimo m. **~ous** adj sinonimo

syntax /'sɪntæks/ n sintassi f inv

synthesize /'sɪnθəsaɪz/ vt sintetizzare. **~r** n (Mus) sintetizzatore m

synthetic /sɪn'thetɪk/ adj sintetico •n fibra f sintetica

syringe /sɪ'rɪndʒ/ n siringa f

syrup /'sɪrəp/ n sciroppo m; *treacle* tipo m di melassa

system /'sɪstəm/ n sistema m. **~atic** adj sistematico

Tt

b /tæb/ n linguetta f; (with name) etichetta f; **keep ~s on** [!] sorvegliare; **pick up the ~** [!] pagare il conto

ble /'teɪbl/ n tavolo m; (list) tavola f; **at** [**the**] **~** a tavola; **~ of contents** tavola f delle materie •vt proporre. **~-cloth** n tovaglia f. **~spoon** n cucchiaio m da tavola. **~spoon**[**ful**] n cucchiaiata f

blet /'tæblɪt/ n pastiglia f; (slab) lastra f; **~ of soap** saponetta f

able tennis n tennis m da tavolo; (everyday level) ping pong m

bloid /'tæblɔɪd/ n [giornale m formato] tabloid m inv; pej giornale m scandalistico

boo /tə'bu:/ adj tabù inv •n tabù m inv

cit /'tæsɪt/ adj tacito

citurn /'tæsɪtɜ:n/ adj taciturno

ck /tæk/ n (nail) chiodino m; (stitch) imbastitura f; (Naut) virata f; fig linea f di condotta •vt inchiodare; (sew) imbastire •vi (Naut) virare

ckle /'tækl/ n (equipment) attrezzatura f; (football etc) contrasto m, tackle m inv •vt affrontare

cky /'tækɪ/ adj (paint) non ancora asciutto; (glue) appiccicoso; fig pacchiano

ct /tækt/ n tatto m. **~ful** adj pieno di tatto; (remark) delicato. **~fully** adv con tatto

tactic|al /'tæktɪkl/ adj tattico. **~s** npl tattica fsg

tactless /'tæktlɪs/ adj privo di tatto. **~ly** adv senza tatto. **~ness** n mancanza f di tatto; (of remark) indelicatezza f

tadpole /'tædpəʊl/ n girino m

tag[1] /tæg/ n (label) etichetta f •vt (pt/pp **tagged**) attaccare l'etichetta a. □ **~ along** vi seguire passo passo

tag[2] n (game) acchiapparello m

tail /teɪl/ n coda f; **~s** pl (tailcoat) frac m inv •vt ([!]: follow) pedinare. □ **~ off** vi diminuire

tail light n fanalino m di coda

tailor /'teɪlə(r)/ n sarto m. **~-made** adj fatto su misura

taint /teɪnt/ vt contaminare

take /teɪk/ n (Cinema) ripresa f •v (pt **took**, pp **taken**) •vt prendere; (to a place) portare (person, object); (contain) contenere (passengers etc); (endure) sopportare; (require) occorrere; (teach) insegnare; (study) studiare (subject); fare (exam, holiday, photograph, walk, bath); sentire (pulse); misurare (sb's temperature); **~ sb prisoner** fare prigioniero qcno; **be ~n ill** ammalarsi; **~ sth calmly** prendere con calma qcsa •vi (plant:) attecchire. □ **~ after** vt assomigliare a. □ **~ away** vt (with one) portare via; (remove) togliere; (subtract) sottrarre; **'to ~ away'** 'da asporto'. □ **~ back** vt riprendere; ritirare (statement);

(return) riportare [indietro]. □ ~ **down** vt portare giù; (remove) tirare giù; (write down) prendere nota di. □ ~ **in** vt (bring indoors) portare dentro; (to one's home) ospitare; (understand) capire; (deceive) ingannare; riprendere (garment); (include) includere. □ ~ **off** vt togliersi (clothes); (deduct) togliere; (mimic) imitare; ~ **time off** prendere delle vacanze; ~ **oneself off** andarsene • vi (Aeron) decollare. □ ~ **on** vt farsi carico di; assumere (employee); (as opponent) prendersela con. □ ~ **out** vt portare fuori; togliere (word, stain); (withdraw) ritirare (money, books); ~ **out a subscription to sth** abbonarsi a qcsa; ~ **it out on sb** 🅘 prendersela con qcno. □ ~ **over** vt assumere il controllo di (firm) • vi ~ **over from sb** sostituire qcno; (permanently) succedere a qcno. □ ~ **to** vt (as a habit) darsi a; **I took to her** (liked) mi è piaciuta. □ ~ **up** vt portare su; accettare (offer); intraprendere (profession); dedicarsi a (hobby); prendere (time); occupare (space); tirare su (floor-boards); accorciare (dress); ~ **sth up with sb** discutere qcsa con qcno • vi ~ **up with sb** legarsi a qcno

take: ~**-off** n (Aeron) decollo m. ~**-over** n rilevamento m

takings /ˈteɪkɪŋz/ npl incassi mpl

tale /teɪl/ n storia f; pej fandonia f

talent /ˈtælənt/ n talento m. ~**ed** adj [ricco] di talento

talk /tɔːk/ n conversazione f; (lecture) conferenza f; (gossip) chiacchere fpl; **make small** ~ parlare del più e del meno • vi parlare • vt parlare di (politics etc); ~ **sb into sth** convincere qcno di qcsa. □ ~ **over** vt discutere

talkative /ˈtɔːkətɪv/ adj loquace

tall /tɔːl/ adj alto. ~**boy** n cassettone m. ~ **order** n impresa f difficile. ~ ˈ**story** n frottola f

tally /ˈtælɪ/ n conteggio m; **keep a** ~ **of** tenere il conto di • vi coincidere

tambourine /tæmbəˈriːn/ n tamburello m

tame /teɪm/ adj (animal) domestico; (dull) insulso • vt domare. ~**ly** adv docilmente. ~**r** n domatore, -trice mf

tamper /ˈtæmpə(r)/ vi ~ **with** manomettere

tampon /ˈtæmpɒn/ n tampone m

tan /tæn/ adj marrone rossiccio • n marrone m rossiccio; (from sun) abbronzatura f • v (pt/pp **tanned**) • vt conciare (hide) • vi abbronzarsi

tang /tæŋ/ n sapore m forte; (smell) odore m penetrante

tangent /ˈtændʒənt/ n tangente f

tangible /ˈtændʒɪbl/ adj tangibile

tangle /ˈtæŋgl/ n groviglio m; (in hair) nodo m • vt ~[**up**] aggrovigliare • vi aggrovigliarsi

tango /ˈtæŋgəʊ/ n tango m inv

tank /tæŋk/ n contenitore m; (for petrol) serbatoio m; (fish ~) acquario m; (Mil) carro m armato

tanker /ˈtæŋkə(r)/ n nave f cisterna; (lorry) autobotte f

tantrum /ˈtæntrəm/ n scoppio m d'ira

tap /tæp/ n rubinetto m; (knock) colpo m; **on** ~ a disposizione • (pt/pp **tapped**) • vt dare un colpetto a; sfruttare (resources); mettere sotto controllo (telephone) • vi picchiettare. ~**-dance** n tip tap m • vi ballare il tip tap

tape /teɪp/ n nastro m; (recording) cassetta f • vt legare con nastro; (record) registrare

tape-measure n metro m [a nastro]

taper /ˈteɪpə(r)/ n candela f sottile • **taper off** vi assottigliarsi

tape recorder n registratore m

tapestry /ˈtæpɪstrɪ/ n arazzo m

tar /tɑː(r)/ n catrame m • vt (pt/pp **tarred**) incatramare

target /ˈtɑːgɪt/ n bersaglio m; fig obiettivo m

tarnish /ˈtɑːnɪʃ/ vi ossidarsi • vt ossidare; fig macchiare

tart[1] /tɑːt/ adj aspro; fig acido

tart[2] n crostata f; (individual) crostatina f; (🅧: prostitute) donnaccia f • **tart up** vt 🅘 ~ **oneself up** agghindarsi

tartan /ˈtɑːtn/ n tessuto m scozzese, tartan m inv • attrib di tessuto scozzese

ask /tɑːsk/ n compito m; **take sb to ~** riprendere qcno. **~ force** n (Pol) commissione f; (Mil) task-force f inv

assel /'tæsl/ n nappa f

aste /teɪst/ n gusto m; (sample) assaggio m; **get a ~ of sth** fig assaporare il gusto di qcsa • vt sentire il sapore di; (sample) assaggiare • vi sapere (**of** di); **it ~s lovely** è ottimo. **~ful** adj di [buon] gusto. **~fully** adv con gusto. **~less** adj senza gusto. **~lessly** adv con cattivo gusto

asty /'teɪstɪ/ adj (**-ier, -iest**) saporito

at /tæt/ ▸**tit²**

atter|ed /'tætəd/ adj cencioso; (pages) stracciato. **~s** npl **in ~s** a brandelli

attoo¹ /tæ'tuː/ n tatuaggio m • vt tatuare

attoo² n (Mil) parata f militare

atty /'tætɪ/ adj (**-ier, -iest**) (clothes, person) trasandato; (book) malandato

aught /tɔːt/ ▸**teach**

aunt /tɔːnt/ n scherno m • vt schernire

aurus /'tɔːrəs/ n Toro m

aut /tɔːt/ adj teso

ax /tæks/ n tassa f; (on income) imposte fpl; **before ~** (price) tasse escluse; (salary) lordo • vt tassare; fig mettere alla prova; **~ with** accusare di. **~able** adj tassabile. **~ation** n tasse fpl. **~ evasion** n evasione f fiscale. **~-free** adj esentasse. **~ haven** n paradiso m fiscale

axi /'tæksɪ/ n taxi m inv • vi (pt/pp **taxied**, pres p **taxiing**) (aircraft:) rullare. **~ driver** n tassista mf. **~ rank** n posteggio m per taxi

axpayer n contribuente mf

ea /tiː/ n tè m inv. **~-bag** n bustina f di tè. **~-break** n intervallo m per il tè

each /tiːtʃ/ vt/i (pt/pp **taught**) insegnare; **~ sb sth** insegnare qcsa a qcno. **~er** n insegnante mf; (primary) maestro, -a mf. **~ing** n insegnamento m

eacup n tazza f da tè

eam /tiːm/ n squadra f; fig équipe f inv • **team up** vi unirsi

team-work n lavoro m di squadra; fig lavoro m d'équipe

'teapot n teiera f

tear¹ /teə(r)/ n strappo m • v (pt **tore**, pp **torn**) • vt strappare • vi strappare; (material:) strapparsi; (run) precipitarsi. □ **~ apart** vt (fig: criticize) fare a pezzi; (separate) dividere. □ **~ away** vt **~ oneself away** andare via; **~ oneself away from** staccarsi da (television). □ **~ open** vt aprire strappando. □ **~ up** vt strappare; rompere (agreement)

tear² /tɪə(r)/ n lacrima f. **~ful** adj (person) in lacrime; (farewell) lacrimevole. **~fully** adv in lacrime. **~gas** n gas m lacrimogeno

tease /tiːz/ vt prendere in giro (person); tormentare (animal)

tea: ~-set n servizio m da tè. **~spoon** n cucchiaino m [da tè]

teat /tiːt/ n capezzolo m; (on bottle) tettarella f

'tea-towel n strofinaccio m [per i piatti]

technical /'teknɪkl/ adj tecnico. **~ity** n tecnicismo m; (Jur) cavillo m giuridico. **~ly** adv tecnicamente; (strictly) strettamente

technician /tek'nɪʃn/ n tecnico, -a mf

technique /tek'niːk/ n tecnica f

technological /teknə'lɒdʒɪkl/ adj tecnologico

technology /tek'nɒlədʒɪ/ n tecnologia f

tedious /'tiːdɪəs/ adj noioso

tedium /'tiːdɪəm/ n tedio m

teem /tiːm/ vi (rain) piovere a dirotto; **be ~ing with** (full of) pullulare di

teenage /'tiːneɪdʒ/ adj per ragazzi; **~ boy/girl** adolescente mf. **~r** n adolescente mf

teens /tiːnz/ npl **the ~** l'adolescenza fsg; **be in one's ~** essere adolescente

teeny /'tiːnɪ/ adj (**-ier, -iest**) piccolissimo

teeter /'tiːtə(r)/ vi barcollare

teeth /tiːθ/ ▸**tooth**

teeth|e /tiːð/ vi mettere i [primi] denti. **~ing troubles** npl fig difficoltà fpl iniziali

telecommunications /telɪkəmjuːnɪ'keɪʃnz/ npl

t

telecomunicazioni fpl

telegram /'telɪgræm/ n telegramma m

telepathy /tɪ'lepəθɪ/ n telepatia f

telephone /'telɪfəʊn/ n telefono m; **be on the ~** avere il telefono; (be telephoning) essere al telefono •vt telefonare a •vi telefonare

telephone: ~ booth n, **~ box** n cabina f telefonica. **~ directory** n elenco m telefonico

telephonist /tɪ'lefənɪst/ n telefonista mf

telescop|e /'telɪskəʊp/ n telescopio m. **~ic** adj telescopico

televise /'telɪvaɪz/ vt trasmettere per televisione

television /'telɪvɪʒn/ n televisione f; **watch ~** guardare la televisione. **~ set** n televisore m

teleworking /'telɪwɜːkɪŋ/ n telelavoro m

telex /'teleks/ n telex m inv

tell /tel/ vt (pt/pp **told**) dire; raccontare (story); (distinguish) distinguere (**from** da); **~ sb sth** dire qcsa a qcno; **~ the time** dire l'ora; **I couldn't ~ why...** non sapevo perché... •vi (produce an effect) avere effetto; **time will ~** il tempo ce lo dirà; **his age is beginning to ~** l'età comincia a farsi sentire [per lui]; **you mustn't ~** non devi dire niente. □ **~ off** vt sgridare

teller /'telə(r)/ n (in bank) cassiere, -a mf

telling /'telɪŋ/ adj significativo; (argument) efficace

telly /'telɪ/ n [!] tv f inv

temp /temp/ n [!] impiegato, -a mf temporaneo, -a

temper /'tempə(r)/ n (disposition) carattere m; (mood) umore m; (anger) collera f; **lose one's ~** arrabbiarsi; **be in a ~** essere arrabbiato; **keep one's ~** mantenere la calma

temperament /'temprəmənt/ n temperamento m. **~al** adj (moody) capriccioso

temperate /'tempərət/ adj (climate) temperato

temperature /'temprətʃə(r)/ n temperatura f; **have a ~** avere la febbre

temple[1] /'templ/ n tempio m

temple[2] n (Anat) tempia f

tempo /'tempəʊ/ n ritmo m; (Mus) tempo m

temporar|y /'tempərərɪ/ adj temporaneo; (measure, building) provvisorio. **~ily** adv temporaneamente; (introduced, erected) provvisoriamente

tempt /tempt/ vt tentare; sfidare (fate); **~ sb to** indurre qcno a; **be ~ed** essere tentato (**to** di); **I am ~ed by the offer** l'offerta mi tenta. **~ation** n tentazione f. **~ing** adj allettante; (food, drink) invitante

ten /ten/ adj dieci

tenaci|ous /tɪ'neɪʃəs/ adj tenace. **~ty** n tenacia f

tenant /'tenənt/ n inquilino, -a mf; (Comm) locatario, -a mf

tend vi **~ to do sth** tendere a far qcsa

tendency /'tendənsɪ/ n tendenza f

tender[1] /'tendə(r)/ n (Comm) offerta f; **be legal ~** avere corso legale •vt offrire; presentare (resignation)

tender[2] adj tenero; (painful) dolorante. **~ly** adv teneramente. **~ness** n tenerezza f; (painfulness) dolore m

tendon /'tendən/ n tendine m

tennis /'tenɪs/ n tennis m. **~-court** n campo m da tennis. **~ player** n tennista mf

tenor /'tenə(r)/ n tenore m

tense[1] /tens/ n (Gram) tempo m

tense[2] adj teso •vt tendere (muscle). □ **~ up** vi tendersi

tension /'tenʃn/ n tensione f

tent /tent/ n tenda f

tentacle /'tentəkl/ n tentacolo m

tentative /'tentətɪv/ adj provvisorio; (smile, gesture) esitante. **~ly** adv timidamente; (accept) provvisoriamente

tenterhooks /'tentəhʊks/ npl **be on ~** essere sulle spine

tenth /tenθ/ adj decimo •n decimo, -a mf

tenuous /'tenjʊəs/ adj fig debole

tepid /'tepɪd/ adj tiepido

term /tɜːm/ n periodo m; (Sch, Univ)

trimestre m; (expression) termine m; **~s** pl (conditions) condizioni fpl; **~ of office** carica f; **in the short/long ~** a breve/lungo termine; **be on good/bad ~s** essere in buoni/cattivi rapporti; **come to ~s with** accettare (past, fact); **easy ~s** facilità f di pagamento

terminal /ˈtɜːmɪn(ə)l/ adj finale; (Med) terminale • n (Aeron) terminal m inv; (Rail) stazione f di testa; (of bus) capolinea m; (on battery) morsetto m; (Comput) terminale m. **~ly** adv **be ~ly ill** essere in fase terminale

terminat|e /ˈtɜːmɪneɪt/ vt terminare; rescindere (contract); interrompere (pregnancy) • vi terminare; **~e in** finire in. **~ion** n termine m; (Med) interruzione f di gravidanza

terminology /tɜːmɪˈnɒlədʒɪ/ n terminologia f

terrace /ˈterəs/ n terrazza f; (houses) fila f di case a schiera; **the ~s** (Sport) le gradinate. **~d house** n casa f a schiera

terrain /teˈreɪn/ n terreno m

terrible /ˈterəbl/ adj terribile

terrific /təˈrɪfɪk/ adj ! (excellent) fantastico; (huge) enorme. **~ally** adv ! terribilmente

terri|fy /ˈterɪfaɪ/ vt (pt/pp **-ied**) atterrire; **be ~fied** essere terrorizzato. **~fying** adj terrificante

territorial /terɪˈtɔːrɪəl/ adj territoriale

territory /ˈterɪtərɪ/ n territorio m

terror /ˈterə(r)/ n terrore m. **~ism** n terrorismo m. **~ist** n terrorista mf. **~ize** vt terrorizzare

terse /tɜːs/ adj conciso

test /test/ n esame m; (in laboratory) esperimento m; (of friendship, machine) prova m; (of intelligence, aptitude) test m inv; **put to the ~** mettere alla prova • vt esaminare; provare (machine)

testament /ˈtestəmənt/ n testamento m; **Old/New T~** Antico/Nuovo Testamento m

testicle /ˈtestɪkl/ n testicolo m

testify /ˈtestɪfaɪ/ vt/i (pt/pp **-ied**) testimoniare

testimonial /testɪˈməʊnɪəl/ n lettera f di referenze

testimony /ˈtestɪmənɪ/ n testimonianza f

ˈ**test: ~ match** n partita f internazionale. **~-tube** n provetta f

tether /ˈteðə(r)/ n **be at the end of one's ~** non poterne più

text /tekst/ n testo m. **~book** n manuale m

textile /ˈtekstaɪl/ adj tessile • n stoffa f

text message n sms m inv, breve messaggio m di testo

texture /ˈtekstʃə(r)/ n (of skin) grana f; (of food) consistenza f; **of a smooth ~** (to the touch) soffice al tatto

Thames /temz/ n Tamigi m

than /ðən/, accentato /ðæn/ conj che; (with numbers, names) di; **older ~ me** più vecchio di me

thank /θæŋk/ vt ringraziare; **~ you [very much]** grazie [mille]. **~ful** adj grato. **~fully** adv con gratitudine; (happily) fortunatamente. **~less** adj ingrato

thanks /θæŋks/ npl ringraziamenti mpl; **~!** ! grazie!; **~ to** grazie a

that /ðæt/

• adj & pron (pl **those**) quel, quei pl; (*before s + consonant, gn, ps and z*) quello, quegli pl; (*before vowel*) quell' mf, quegli mpl, quelle fpl; **~ woman** quella donna; **I don't like those** quelli non mi piacciono; **~ is** cioè; **is ~ you?** sei tu?; **who is ~?** chi è?; **what did you do after ~?** cosa hai fatto dopo?; **like ~** in questo modo, così; **a man like ~** un uomo così; **~ is why** ecco perché; **~'s it!** (*you've understood*) ecco!; (*I've finished*) ecco fatto!; (*I've had enough*) basta così!; (*there's nothing more*) tutto qui!; **~'s ~!** (*with job*) ecco fatto!; (*with relationship*) è tutto finito!; **and ~'s ~!** punto e basta! **all ~ I know** tutto quello che so

• adv così; **it wasn't ~ good** non era poi così buono

• rel pron che; **the man ~ I spoke to** l'uomo con cui ho parlato; **the day ~ I saw him** il giorno in cui l'ho visto; **all ~ I know** tutto quello che so

• conj che; **I think ~...** penso che...

t

thaw /θɔː/ n disgelo m ●vt fare scongelare (food) ●vi (food:) scongelarsi; **it's ~ing** sta sgelando

the /ðə/, *di fronte a una vocale* /ðiː/
● def art il, la f; i mpl, le fpl; (*before s + consonant, gn, ps and z*) lo, gli mpl; (*before vowel*) l' mf, gli mpl, le fpl; **at ~ cinema/station** al cinema/alla stazione; **from ~ cinema/station** dal cinema/dalla stazione
● adv **~ more ~ better** più ce n'è meglio è; (*with reference to* pl) più ce ne sono, meglio è; **all ~ better** tanto meglio

theatre /'θɪətə(r)/ n teatro m; (Med) sala f operatoria

theatrical /θɪ'ætrɪkl/ adj teatrale; (showy) melodrammatico

theft /θeft/ n furto m

their /ðeə(r)/ adj il loro m, la loro f, i loro mpl, le loro fpl; **~ mother/father** la loro madre/il loro padre

theirs /ðeəz/ poss pron il loro m, la loro f, i loro mpl, le loro fpl; **a friend of ~** un loro amico; **friends of ~** dei loro amici; **those are ~** quelli sono loro; (as opposed to ours) quelli sono i loro

them /ðem/ pron (direct object) li m, le f; (indirect object) gli, loro fml; (after prep: with people) loro; (after preposition: with things) essi; **we haven't seen ~** non li/le abbiamo visti/viste; **give ~ the money** dai loro or dagli i soldi; **give it to ~** daglielo; **I've spoken to ~** ho parlato con loro; **it's ~** sono loro

theme /θiːm/ n tema m. **~ park** n parco m a tema. **~ song** n motivo m conduttore

them'selves pron (reflexive) si; (emphatic) se stessi; **they poured ~ a drink** si sono versati da bere; **they said so ~** lo hanno detto loro stessi; **they kept it to ~** se lo sono tenuti per sé; **by ~** da soli

then /ðen/ adv allora; (next) poi; **by ~** (in the past) ormai; (in the future) per allora; **since ~** sin da allora; **before ~** prima di allora; **from ~ on** da allora in poi; **now and ~** ogni tanto; **there and ~** all'istante ●adj di allora

theoretical /θɪə'retɪkl/ adj teorico

theory /'θɪərɪ/ n teoria f; **in ~** in teoria

therapeutic /θerə'pjuːtɪk/ adj terapeutico

therap|ist /'θerəpɪst/ n terapista mf. **~y** n terapia f

there /ðeə(r)/ adv là, lì; **down/up ~** laggiù/lassù; **~ is/are** c'è/ci sono; **~ he/she is** eccolo/eccola ●int **~, ~!** dai, su!

there: ~abouts adv **[or] ~abouts** (roughly) all'incirca. **~fore** /-fɔː(r)/ adv perciò

thermometer /θə'mɒmɪtə(r)/ n termometro m

thermostat /'θɜːməstæt/ n termostato m

thesaurus /θɪ'sɔːrəs/ n dizionario m dei sinonimi

these /ðiːz/ ▸**this**

thesis /'θiːsɪs/ n (pl **-ses** /-siːz/) tesi f inv

they /ðeɪ/ pron loro; **~ are tired** sono stanchi; **we're going, but ~ are not** noi andiamo, ma loro no; **~ say** (generalizing) si dice; **~ are building a new road** stanno costruendo una nuova strada

thick /θɪk/ adj spesso; (forest) fitto; (liquid) denso; (hair) folto; (!: stupid) ottuso; (!: close) molto unito; **be 5 mm ~** essere 5 mm di spessore ●adv densamente ●n **in the ~ of** nel mezzo di. **~en** vt ispessire (sauce) ●vi ispessirsi; (fog:) infittirsi. **~ly** adv densamente; (cut) a fette spesse. **~ness** n spessore m

thief /θiːf/ n (pl **thieves**) ladro, -a mf

thigh /θaɪ/ n coscia f

thimble /'θɪmbl/ n ditale m

thin /θɪn/ adj (**thinner, thinnest**) sottile; (shoes, sweater) leggero; (liquid) liquido; (person) magro; (fig: excuse, plot) inconsistente ●adv = **thinly** ●v (pt/pp **thinned**) ●vt diluire (liquid) ●vi diradarsi. ▫ **~ out** vi diradarsi. **~ly** adv (populated) scarsamente; (disguised) leggermente; (cut) a fette sottili

thing /θɪŋ/ n cosa f; **~s** pl (belongings) roba fsg; **for one ~** in primo luogo; **the right ~** la cosa giusta; **just the ~!** proprio quel che ci vuole!; **how are ~s?** come vanno le cose?;

the latest ~ [!] l'ultima cosa; **the best ~ would be** la cosa migliore sarebbe; **poor ~!** poveretto!

ink /θɪŋk/ vt/i (pt/pp **thought**) pensare; (believe) credere; **I ~ so** credo di sì; **what do you ~?** (what s your opinion?) cosa ne pensi?; **~ of/about** pensare a; **what do you ~ of it?** cosa ne pensi di questo?. ▫ **~ over** vt riflettere su. ▫ **~ up** vt escogitare

ird /θɜ:d/ adj & n terzo, -a mf. **~ly** adv terzo. **~-rate** adj scadente

irst /θɜ:st/ n sete f. **~ily** adv con sete. **~y** adj assetato; **be ~y** aver sete

irteen /θɜ:'ti:n/ adj tredici. **~th** adj tredicesimo

irtieth /'θɜ:tɪɪθ/ adj trentesimo

irty /'θɜ:tɪ/ adj trenta

is /ðɪs/ adj (pl **these**) questo; **~ man/woman** quest'uomo/questa donna; **these men/women** questi uomini/queste donne; **~ one** questo; **~ morning/evening** stamattina/stasera •pron (pl **these**) questo; **we talked about ~ and that** abbiamo parlato del più e del meno; **like ~** così; **~ is Peter** questo è Peter; (Teleph) sono Peter; **who is ~** chi è?; (Teleph) chi parla? •adv così; **~ big** così grande

istle /'θɪsl/ n cardo m

orn /θɔ:n/ n spina f. **~y** adj spinoso

orough /'θʌrə/ adj completo; (knowledge) profondo; (clean, search, training) a fondo; (person) scrupoloso

orough: ~bred n purosangue m inv. **~fare** n via f principale; **'no ~fare'** 'strada non transitabile'

orough|ly /'θʌrəlɪ/ adv (clean, search, know sth) a fondo; (extremely) estremamente. **~ness** n completezza f

ose /ðəʊz/ ▹**that**

ough /ðəʊ/ conj sebbene; **as ~** come se •adv [!] tuttavia

ought /θɔ:t/ ▹**think** •n pensiero m; (idea) idea f. **~ful** adj pensieroso; (considerate) premuroso. **~fully** adv pensierosamente; (considerately) premurosamente. **~less** adj (inconsiderate) sconsiderato. **~lessly** adv con noncuranza

ousand /'θaʊznd/ adj **one/a ~** mille m inv •n mille m inv; **~s of** migliaia fpl di. **~th** adj millesimo •n millesimo, -a mf

thrash /θræʃ/ vt picchiare; (defeat) sconfiggere. ▫ **~ out** vt mettere a punto

thread /θred/ n filo m; (of screw) filetto m •vt infilare (beads); **~ one's way through** farsi strada fra. **~bare** adj logoro

threat /θret/ n minaccia f

threaten /'θretn/ vt minacciare (**to do** di fare) •vi fig incalzare. **~ing** adj minaccioso; (sky, atmosphere) sinistro

three /θri:/ adj tre. **~fold** adj & adv triplo. **~some** n trio m

threshold /'θreʃəʊld/ n soglia f

threw /θru:/ ▹**throw**

thrift /θrɪft/ n economia f. **~y** adj parsimonioso

thrill /θrɪl/ n emozione f; (of fear) brivido m •vt entusiasmare; **be ~ed with** essere entusiasta di. **~er** n (book) [romanzo m] giallo m; (film) [film m] giallo m. **~ing** adj eccitante

thrive /θraɪv/ vi (pt **thrived** or **throve**, pp **thrived** or **thriven** /'θrɪvn/) (business:) prosperare; (child, plant:) crescere bene; **I ~ on pressure** mi piace essere sotto tensione

throat /θrəʊt/ n gola f; **sore ~** mal m di gola

throb /θrɒb/ n pulsazione f; (of heart) battito m •vi (pt/pp **throbbed**) (vibrate) pulsare; (heart:) battere

throes /θrəʊz/ npl **in the ~ of** fig alle prese con

throne /θrəʊn/ n trono m

throng /θrɒŋ/ n calca f

throttle /'θrɒtl/ n (on motorbike) manopola f di accelerazione •vt strozzare

through /θru:/ prep attraverso; (during) durante; (by means of) tramite; (thanks to) grazie a; **Saturday ~ Tuesday** Am da sabato a martedì incluso •adv attraverso; **~ and ~** fino in fondo; **wet ~** completamente bagnato; **read sth ~** dare una lettura a qcsa; **let ~** lasciar passare (sb) •adj (train) diretto; **be ~** (finished) aver finito; (Teleph) avere la comunicazione

throughout /θru:'aʊt/ prep per tutto

•adv completamente; (time) per tutto il tempo

throw /θrəʊ/ n tiro m •vt (pt **threw**, pp **thrown**) lanciare; (throw away) gettare; azionare (switch); disarcionare (rider); ([!]: disconcert) disorientare; [!] dare (party). □ ~ **away** vt gettare via. □ ~ **out** vt gettare via; rigettare (plan); buttare fuori (person). □ ~ **up** vt alzare •vi (vomit) vomitare

thrush /θrʌʃ/ n tordo m

thrust /θrʌst/ n spinta f •vt (pt/pp **thrust**) (push) spingere; (insert) conficcare; ~ [**up**]**on** imporre a

thud /θʌd/ n tonfo m

thug /θʌg/ n deliquente m

thumb /θʌm/ n pollice m; **as a rule of** ~ come regola generale; **under sb's** ~ succube di qcno •vt ~ **a lift** fare l'autostop. ~**-index** n indice m a rubrica. ~**tack** n Am puntina f da disegno

thump /θʌmp/ n colpo m; (noise) tonfo m •vt battere su (table, door); battere (fist); colpire (person) •vi battere (**on** su); (heart:) battere forte. □ ~ **about** vi camminare pesantemente

thunder /'θʌndə(r)/ n tuono m; (loud noise) rimbombo m •vi tuonare; (make loud noise) rimbombare. ~**clap** n rombo m di tuono. ~**storm** n temporale m. ~**y** adj temporalesco

Thursday /'θɜ:zdeɪ/ n giovedì m inv

thus /ðʌs/ adv così

thwart /θwɔ:t/ vt ostacolare

Tiber /'taɪbə(r)/ n Tevere m

tick /tɪk/ n (sound) ticchettio m; (mark) segno m; ([!]: instant) attimo m •vi ticchettare. □ ~ **off** vt spuntare; [!] sgridare. □ ~ **over** vi (engine:) andare al minimo

ticket /'tɪkɪt/ n biglietto m; (for item deposited, library) tagliando m; (label) cartellino m; (fine) multa f. ~**-collector** n controllore m. ~**-office** n biglietteria f

tick|le /'tɪkl/ n solletico m •vt fare il solletico a; (amuse) divertire •vi fare prurito. ~**lish** adj che soffre il solletico

tide /taɪd/ n marea f; (of events) corso m; **the** ~ **is in/out** c'è alta/bassa marea •**tide over** vt ~ **sb over** aiutare qcno a andare avanti

tidily /'taɪdɪlɪ/ adv in modo ordinato

tidiness /'taɪdɪnɪs/ n ordine m

tidy /'taɪdɪ/ adj (**-ier, -iest**) ordinato; ([!]: amount) bello •vt (pt/pp **-ied**) ~ [**up**] ordinare; ~ **oneself up** mettersi in ordine

tie /taɪ/ n cravatta f; (cord) legaccio m; (fig: bond) legame m; (restriction) impedimento m; (Sport) pareggio m •v (pres p **tying**) •vt legare; fare (knot); **be** ~**d** (in competition) essere in parità •vi pareggiare. □ ~ **in with** corrispondere a. □ ~ **up** vt legare; vincolare (capital); **be** ~**d up** (busy) essere occupato

tier /tɪə(r)/ n fila f; (of cake) piano m; (in stadium) gradinata f

tiger /'taɪgə(r)/ n tigre f

tight /taɪt/ adj stretto; (taut) teso; ([!]: drunk) sbronzo; ([!]: mean) spilorcio; ~ **corner** [!] brutta situazione f •adv strettamente; (hold) forte; (closed) bene

tighten /'taɪtn/ vt stringere; avvitare (screw); intensificare (control) •vi stringersi

tight: ~**-'fisted** adj tirchio. ~**ly** adv strettamente; (hold) forte; (closed) bene. ~**rope** n fune f (da funamboli)

tights /taɪts/ npl collant m inv

tile /taɪl/ n mattonella f; (on roof) tegola f •vt rivestire di mattonelle (wall)

till[1] /tɪl/ prep & conj = **until**

till[2] n cassa f

tilt /tɪlt/ n inclinazione f; **at full** ~ a tutta velocità •vt inclinare •vi inclinarsi

timber /'tɪmbə(r)/ n legname m

time /taɪm/ n tempo m; (occasion) volta f; (by clock) ora f; **two** ~**s four** due volte quattro; **at any** ~ in qualsiasi momento; **this** ~ questa volta; **at** ~**s, from** ~ **to** ~ ogni tanto; ~ **and again** cento volte; **two at a** ~ due alla volta; **on** ~ in orario; **in** ~ in tempo; (eventually) col tempo; **in no** ~ **at all** velocemente; **in a year's** ~ fra un anno; **behind** ~ in ritardo; **behind the** ~**s** antiquato; **for the** ~ **being** per il momento; **what is the** ~**?** che ora è?; **by the** ~ **we arrive** quando arriviamo; **did you have a nice** ~**?** ti sei

t

divertito?; **have a good ~!** divertiti! • vt scegliere il momento per; cronometrare (race); **be well ~d** essere ben calcolato

ime: ~ bomb n bomba f a orologeria. **~ly** adj opportuno. **~-table** n orario m

imid /'tɪmɪd/ adj (shy) timido; (fearful) timoroso

in /tɪn/ n stagno m; (container) barattolo m • vt (pt/pp **tinned**) inscatolare. **~ foil** n [carta f] stagnola f

tinge /tɪndʒ/ n sfumatura f • vt **~d with** fig misto a

tingle /'tɪŋgl/ vi pizzicare

tinker /'tɪŋkə(r)/ vi armeggiare

tinkle /'tɪŋkl/ n tintinnio m; (!: phone call) colpo m di telefono • vi tintinnare

tinned /tɪnd/ adj in scatola

'tin opener n apriscatole m inv

tint /tɪnt/ n tinta f • vt tingersi (hair)

tiny /'taɪnɪ/ adj (**-ier, -iest**) minuscolo

tip¹ /tɪp/ n punta f

tip² n (money) mancia f; (advice) consiglio m; (for rubbish) discarica f • v (pt/pp **tipped**) • vt (tilt) inclinare; (overturn) capovolgere; (pour) versare; (reward) dare una mancia a • vi inclinarsi; (overturn) capovolgersi. □ **~ off** vt **~ sb off** (inform) fare una soffiata a qcno. □ **~ out** vt rovesciare. □ **~ over** vt capovolgere • vi capovolgersi

tipped /tɪpt/ adj (cigarette) col filtro

tipsy /'tɪpsɪ/ adj ! brillo

tiptoe /'tɪptəʊ/ n **on ~** in punta di piedi

tiptop /tɪp'tɒp/ adj ! in condizioni perfette

tire /'taɪə(r)/ vt stancare • vi stancarsi. **~d** adj stanco; **~d of** stanco di; **~d out** stanco morto. **~less** adj instancabile. **~some** adj fastidioso

tiring /'taɪərɪŋ/ adj stancante

tissue /'tɪʃu:/ n tessuto m; (handkerchief) fazzolettino m di carta. **~-paper** n carta f velina

tit¹ /tɪt/ n (bird) cincia f

tit² n **~ for tat** pan per focaccia

title /'taɪtl/ n titolo m. **~-deed** n atto m di proprietà. **~-role** n ruolo m principale

to /tu:/, *atono* /tə/

• prep a; (*to countries*) in; (*towards*) verso; (*up to, until*) fino a; **I'm going to John's/the butcher's** vado da John/dal macellaio; **come/go to sb** venire/andare da qcno; **to Italy/Switzerland** in Italia/Svizzera; **I've never been to Rome** non sono mai stato a Roma; **go to the market** andare al mercato; **to the toilet/my room** in bagno/camera mia; **to an exhibition** a una mostra; **to university** all'università; **twenty/quarter to eight** le otto meno venti/un quarto; **5 to 6 kilos** da 5 a 6 chili; **to the end** alla fine; **to this day** fino a oggi; **to the best of my recollection** per quanto mi possa ricordare; **give/say sth to sb** dare/dire qcsa a qcno; **give it to me** dammelo; **there's nothing to it** è una cosa da niente

• *verbal constructions* **to go** andare; **learn to swim** imparare a nuotare; **I want to/have to go** voglio/devo andare; **it's easy to forget** è facile da dimenticare; **too ill/tired to go** troppo malato/stanco per andare; **you have to** devi; **I don't want to** non voglio; **live to be 90** vivere fino a 90 anni; **he was the last to arrive** è stato l'ultimo ad arrivare; **to be honest,...** per essere sincero,...

• adv **pull to** chiudere; **to and fro** avanti e indietro

toad /təʊd/ n rospo m. **~stool** n fungo m velenoso

toast /təʊst/ n pane m tostato; (drink) brindisi m • vt tostare (bread); (drink a ~ to) brindare a. **~er** n tostapane m inv

tobacco /tə'bækəʊ/ n tabacco m. **~nist's [shop]** n tabaccheria f

toboggan /tə'bɒgən/ n toboga m • vi andare in toboga

today /tə'deɪ/ adj & adv oggi m; **a week ~** una settimana a oggi; **~'s paper** il giornale di oggi

toddler /'tɒdlə(r)/ n bambino, -a mf ai primi passi

t

toe /təʊ/ n dito m del piede; (of footwear) punta f; **big ~** alluce m • vt **~ the line** rigar diritto. **~nail** n unghia f del piede

toffee /ˈtɒfɪ/ n caramella f al mou

together /təˈgeðə(r)/ adv insieme; (at the same time) allo stesso tempo; **~ with** insieme a

toilet /ˈtɔɪlɪt/ n (lavatory) gabinetto m. **~ paper** n carta f igienica

toiletries /ˈtɔɪlɪtrɪz/ npl articoli mpl da toilette

toilet roll n rotolo m di carta igienica

token /ˈtəʊkən/ n segno m; (counter) gettone m; (voucher) buono m • attrib simbolico

told /təʊld/ ▸**tell** • adj **all ~** in tutto

tolerabl|e /ˈtɒl(ə)rəbl/ adj tollerabile; (not bad) discreto. **~y** adv discretamente

toleran|ce /ˈtɒl(ə)r(ə)ns/ n tolleranza f. **~t** adj tollerante. **~tly** adv con tolleranza

tolerate /ˈtɒləreɪt/ vt tollerare

toll¹ /təʊl/ n pedaggio m; **death ~** numero m di morti

toll² vi suonare a morto

tomato /təˈmɑːtəʊ/ n (pl **-es**) pomodoro m. **~ ketchup** n ketchup m. **~ purée** n concentrato m di pomodoro

tomb /tuːm/ n tomba f

ˈ**tombstone** n pietra f tombale

tomorrow /təˈmɒrəʊ/ adj & adv domani m; **~ morning** domani mattina; **the day after ~** dopodomani; **see you ~!** a domani!

ton /tʌn/ n tonnellata f (= 1,016 kg.); **~s of** 🅸 un sacco di

tone /təʊn/ n tono m; (colour) tonalità f inv • **tone down** vt attenuare. ▫ **~ up** vt tonificare (muscles)

tongs /tɒŋz/ npl pinze fpl

tongue /tʌŋ/ n lingua f; **~ in cheek** (say) ironicamente. **~-twister** n scioglilingua m inv

tonic /ˈtɒnɪk/ n tonico m; (for hair) lozione f per i capelli; fig toccasana m inv; **~ [water]** acqua f tonica

tonight /təˈnaɪt/ adv stanotte; (evening) stasera • n questa notte f; (evening) questa sera f

tonne /tʌn/ n tonnellata f metrica

tonsil /ˈtɒnsl/ n (Anat) tonsilla f. **~litis** n tonsillite f

too /tuː/ adv troppo; (also) anche; **~ many** troppi; **~ much** troppo; **~ little** troppo poco

took /tʊk/ ▸**take**

tool /tuːl/ n attrezzo m

tooth /tuːθ/ n (pl **teeth**) dente m

tooth: ~ache n mal m di denti. **~brush** n spazzolino m da denti. **~paste** n dentifricio m. **~pick** n stuzzicadenti m inv

top¹ /tɒp/ n (toy) trottola f

top² n cima f; (Sch) primo, -a mf; (upper part or half) parte f superiore; (of page, list, road) inizio m; (upper surface) superficie f; (lid) coperchio m; (of bottle) tappo m; (garment) maglia f; (blouse) camicia f; (Auto) marcia f più alta; **at the ~** fig al vertice; **at the ~ of one's voice** a squarciagola; **on ~/on ~ of** sopra; **on ~ of that** (besides) per di più; **from ~ to bottom** da cima a fondo • adj in alto; (official, floor) superiore; (pupil, musician etc) migliore; (speed) massimo • vt (pt/pp **topped**) essere in testa a (list); (exceed) sorpassare; **~ped with ice-cream** ricoperto di gelato. ▫ **~ up** vt riempire

top: ~ ˈfloor n ultimo piano m. **~ hat** n cilindro m. **~-heavy** adj con la parte superiore sovraccarica

topic /ˈtɒpɪk/ n soggetto m; (of conversation) argomento m. **~al** adj d'attualità

topless adj & adv topless

topple /ˈtɒpl/ vt rovesciare • vi rovesciarsi. ▫ **~ off** vi cadere

top-ˈsecret adj segretissimo, top secret inv

torch /tɔːtʃ/ n torcia f [elettrica]; (flaming) fiaccola f

tore /tɔː(r)/ ▸**tear¹**

torment¹ /ˈtɔːment/ n tormento m

torment² /tɔːˈment/ vt tormentare

torn /tɔːn/ ▸**tear¹** • adj bucato

tornado /tɔːˈneɪdəʊ/ n (pl **-es**) tornado m inv

torpedo /tɔːˈpiːdəʊ/ n (pl **-es**) siluro m • vt silurare

torrent /'tɒrənt/ n torrente m. **~ial** adj (rain) torrenziale

tortoise /'tɔːtəs/ n tartaruga f

torture /'tɔːtʃə(r)/ n tortura f •vt torturare

Tory /'tɔːrɪ/ adj & n [!] conservatore, -trice mf

toss /tɒs/ vt gettare; (into the air) lanciare in aria; (shake) scrollare; (horse:) disarcionare; mescolare (salad); rivoltare facendo saltare in aria (pancake); **~ a coin** fare testa o croce •vi **~ and turn** (in bed) rigirarsi; **let's ~ for it** facciamo testa o croce

tot[1] /tɒt/ n bimbetto, -a mf; ([!]: of liquor) goccio m

tot[2] vt (pt/pp **totted**) **~ up** [!] fare la somma di

total /'təʊtl/ adj totale •n totale m •vt (pt/pp **totalled**) ammontare a; (add up) sommare

totalitarian /təʊtælɪ'teərɪən/ adj totalitario

totally /'təʊtəlɪ/ adv totalmente

totter /'tɒtə(r)/ vi barcollare; (government:) vacillare

touch /tʌtʃ/ n tocco m; (sense) tatto m; (contact) contatto m; (trace) traccia f; (of irony, humour) tocco m; **get/be in ~** mettersi/essere in contatto •vt toccare; (lightly) sfiorare; (equal) eguagliare; (fig: move) commuovere •vi toccarsi. □ **~ down** vi (Aeron) atterrare. □ **~ on** vt fig accennare a. **touch up** vt ritoccare (painting). **~ing** adj commovente. **~screen** n touch screen m inv. **~-tone** adj a tastiera. **~y** adj permaloso; (subject) delicato

tough /tʌf/ adj duro; (severe, harsh) severo; (durable) resistente; (resilient) forte

toughen /'tʌfn/ vt rinforzare. □ **~ up** vt rendere più forte (person)

tour /tʊə(r)/ n giro m; (of building, town) visita f; (Theat), (Sport) tournée f inv; (of duty) servizio m •vt visitare •vi fare un giro turistico; (Theat) essere in tournée

touris|m /'tʊərɪzm/ n turismo m. **~t** n turista mf •attrib turistico. **~t office** n ufficio m turistico

tournament /'tʊənəmənt/ n torneo m

tousle /'taʊzl/ vt spettinare

tout /taʊt/ n (ticket **~**) bagarino m; (horse-racing) informatore m •vi **~ for** sollecitare

tow /təʊ/ n rimorchio m; **'on ~'** 'a rimorchio'; **in ~** [!] al seguito •vt rimorchiare. □ **~ away** vt portare via col carro attrezzi

toward[s] /tə'wɔːd(z)/ prep verso (with respect to) nei riguardi di

towel /'taʊəl/ n asciugamano m. **~ling** n spugna f

tower /'taʊə(r)/ n torre f •vi **~ above** dominare. **~ block** n palazzone m. **~ing** adj torreggiante; (rage) violento

town /taʊn/ n città f inv. **~ 'hall** n municipio m

toxic /'tɒksɪk/ adj tossico

toy /tɔɪ/ n giocattolo m. **~shop** n negozio m di giocattoli. □ **~ with** vt giocherellare con

trace /treɪs/ n traccia f •vt seguire le tracce di; (find) rintracciare; (draw) tracciare; (with tracing-paper) ricalcare

track /træk/ n traccia f; (path, (Sport)) pista f; (Rail) binario m; **keep ~ of** tenere d'occhio •vt seguire le tracce di. □ **~ down** vt scovare

tracksuit n tuta f da ginnastica

tractor /'træktə(r)/ n trattore m

trade /treɪd/ n commercio m; (line of business) settore m; (craft) mestiere m; **by ~** di mestiere •vt commerciare; **~ sth for sth** scambiare qcsa per qcsa •vi commerciare. □ **~ in** vt (give in part exchange) dare in pagamento parziale

'trade mark n marchio m di fabbrica

trader /'treɪdə(r)/ n commerciante mf

trades 'union n sindacato m

tradition /trə'dɪʃn/ n tradizione f. **~al** adj tradizionale. **~ally** adv tradizionalmente

traffic /'træfɪk/ n traffico m •vi (pt/pp **trafficked**) trafficare

traffic: ~ circle n Am isola f rotatoria. **~ jam** n ingorgo m. **~ lights** npl semaforo msg. **~ warden** n vigile m [urbano]; (woman) vigilessa f

tragedy /'trædʒədɪ/ n tragedia f

tragic /'trædʒɪk/ adj tragico. **~ally** adv tragicamente

trail /treɪl/ n traccia f; (path) sentiero m •vi strisciare; (plant:) arrampicarsi; ~ [**behind**] rimanere indietro; (in competition) essere in svantaggio •vt trascinare

trailer /'treɪlə(r)/ n (Auto) rimorchio m; (Am: caravan) roulotte f inv; (film) presentazione f (di un film)

train /treɪn/ n treno m; ~ **of thought** filo m dei pensieri •vt formare professionalmente; (Sport) allenare; (aim) puntare; educare (child); addestrare (animal, soldier) •vi fare il tirocinio; (Sport) allenarsi. **~ed** adj (animal) addestrato (**to do** a fare)

trainee /treɪ'ni:/ n apprendista mf

train|er /'treɪnə(r)/ n (Sport) allenatore, -trice mf; (in circus) domatore, -trice mf; (of dog, race-horse) addestratore, -trice mf; **~ers** pl scarpe fpl da ginnastica. **~ing** n tirocinio m; (Sport) allenamento m; (of animal, soldier) addestramento m

trait /treɪt/ n caratteristica f

traitor /'treɪtə(r)/ n traditore, -trice mf

tram /træm/ n tram m inv. **~-lines** npl rotaie fpl del tram

tramp /træmp/ n (hike) camminata f; (vagrant) barbone, -a mf; (of feet) calpestio m •vi camminare con passo pesante; (hike) percorrere a piedi

trample /'træmpl/ vt/i ~ [**on**] calpestare

trampoline /'træmpəli:n/ n trampolino m

trance /trɑ:ns/ n trance f inv

tranquil /'træŋkwɪl/ adj tranquillo. **~lity** n tranquillità f

tranquillizer /'træŋkwɪlaɪzə(r)/ n tranquillante m

transatlantic /trænzət'læntɪk/ adj transatlantico

transcend /træn'send/ vt trascendere

transfer¹ /'trænsfɜ:(r)/ n trasferimento m; (Sport) cessione f; (design) decalcomania f

transfer² /træns'fɜ:(r)/ v (pt/pp **transferred**) •vt trasferire; (Sport) cedere •vi trasferirsi; (when travelling) cambiare. **~able** adj trasferibile

transform /træns'fɔ:m/ vt trasformare. **~ation** n trasformazione f. **~er** n trasformatore m

transfusion /træns'fju:ʒn/ n trasfusione f

transient /'trænzɪənt/ adj passeggero

transistor /træn'zɪstə(r)/ n transistor m inv; (radio) radiolina f a transistor

transit /'trænzɪt/ n transito m; **in** ~ (goods) in transito

transition /træn'zɪʃn/ n transizione f. **~al** adj di transizione

transitive /'trænzɪtɪv/ adj transitivo

translat|e /trænz'leɪt/ vt tradurre. **~ion** n traduzione f. **~or** n traduttore, -trice mf

transmission /trænz'mɪʃn/ n trasmissione f

transmit /trænz'mɪt/ vt (pt/pp **transmitted**) trasmettere. **~ter** n trasmettitore m

transparen|cy /træn'spærənsɪ/ n (Phot) diapositiva f. **~t** adj trasparente

transplant¹ /'trænsplɑ:nt/ n trapianto m

transplant² /træns'plɑ:nt/ vt trapiantare

transport¹ /'trænspɔ:t/ n trasporto m

transport² /træn'spɔ:t/ vt trasportare. **~ation** n trasporto m

trap /træp/ n trappola f; ([!]: mouth) boccaccia f •vt (pt/pp **trapped**) intrappolare; schiacciare (finger in door). **~'door** n botola f

trapeze /trə'pi:z/ n trapezio m

trash /træʃ/ n robaccia f; (rubbish) spazzatura f; (nonsense) schiocchezze fpl. **~can** n Am secchio m della spazzatura. **~y** adj scadente

travel /'trævl/ n viaggi mpl •v (pt/pp **travelled**) •vi viaggiare; (to work) andare •vt percorrere (distance). ~ **agency** n agenzia f di viaggi. ~ **agent** n agente mf di viaggio

traveller /'trævələ(r)/ n viaggiatore, -trice mf; (Comm) commesso m viaggiatore; **~s** pl (gypsies) zingari mpl. **~'s cheque** n traveller's cheque m inv

awler /'trɔ:lə(r)/ n peschereccio m

'ay /treɪ/ n vassoio m; (for baking) teglia f; (for documents) vaschetta f sparticarta; (of printer, photocopier) vassoio m

'eacher|ous /'tretʃərəs/ adj traditore; (weather, currents) pericoloso. **~y** n tradimento m

'eacle /'tri:kl/ n melassa f

'read /tred/ n andatura f; (step) gradino m; (of tyre) battistrada m inv • v (pt **trod**, pp **trodden**) • vi (walk) camminare. □ **~ on** vt calpestare (grass); pestare (foot)

reason /'tri:zn/ n tradimento m

reasure /'treʒə(r)/ n tesoro m • vt tenere in gran conto. **~r** n tesoriere, -a mf

reasury /'treʒərɪ/ n **the T~** il Ministero del Tesoro

reat /tri:t/ n piacere m; (present) regalo m; **give sb a ~** fare una sorpresa a qcno • vt trattare; (Med) curare; **~ sb to sth** offrire qcsa a qcno

reatise /'tri:tɪz/ n trattato m

reatment /'tri:tmənt/ n trattamento m; (Med) cura f

reaty /'tri:tɪ/ n trattato m

:reble /'trebl/ adj triplo • n (Mus: voice) voce f bianca • vt triplicare • vi triplicarsi. **~ clef** n chiave f di violino

:ree /tri:/ n albero m

trek /trek/ n scarpinata f; (as holiday) trekking m inv • vi (pt/pp **trekked**) farsi una scarpinata; (on holiday) fare trekking

tremble /'trembl/ vi tremare

tremendous /trɪ'mendəs/ adj (huge) enorme; ([!]: excellent) formidabile. **~ly** adv (very) straordinariamente; (adj lot) enormemente

tremor /'tremə(r)/ n tremito m; [**earth**] **~** scossa f [sismica]

trench /trentʃ/ n fosso m; (Mil) trincea f. **~ coat** n trench m inv

trend /trend/ n tendenza f; (fashion) moda f. **~y** adj (**-ier, -iest**) [!] di or alla moda

trepidation /trepɪ'deɪʃn/ n trepidazione f

trespass /'trespəs/ vi **~ on** introdursi abusivamente in; fig abusare di. **~er** n intruso, -a mf

trial /'traɪəl/ n (Jur) processo m; (test, ordeal) prova f; **on ~** in prova; (Jur) in giudizio; **by ~ and error** per tentativi

triang|le /'traɪæŋgl/ n triangolo m. **~ular** adj triangolare

tribe /traɪb/ n tribù f inv

tribulation /trɪbjʊ'leɪʃn/ n tribolazione f

tribunal /traɪ'bju:nl/ n tribunale m

tributary /'trɪbjʊtərɪ/ n affluente m

tribute /'trɪbju:t/ n tributo m; **pay ~** rendere omaggio

trick /trɪk/ n trucco m; (joke) scherzo m; (in cards) presa f; **do the ~** [!] funzionare; **play a ~ on** fare uno scherzo a • vt imbrogliare

trickle /'trɪkl/ vi colare

trick|ster /'trɪkstə(r)/ n imbroglione, -a mf. **~y** adj (**-ier, -iest**) adj (operation) complesso; (situation) delicato

tricycle /'traɪsɪkl/ n triciclo m

tried /traɪd/ ▸**try**

trifl|e /'traɪfl/ n inezia f; (Culin) zuppa f inglese. **~ing** adj insignificante

trigger /'trɪgə(r)/ n grilletto m • vt **~** [**off**] scatenare

trim /trɪm/ adj (**trimmer, trimmest**) curato; (figure) snello • n (of hair, hedge) spuntata f; (decoration) rifinitura f; **in good ~** in buono stato; (person) in forma • vt (pt/pp **trimmed**) spuntare (hair etc); (decorate) ornare; (Naut) orientare. **~ming** n bordo m; **~mings** pl (decorations) guarnizioni fpl; **with all the ~mings** (Culin) guarnito

trinket /'trɪŋkɪt/ n ninnolo m

trio /'tri:əʊ/ n trio m

trip /trɪp/ n (excursion) gita f; (journey) viaggio m; (stumble) passo m falso • v (pt/pp **tripped**) • vt far inciampare • vi inciampare (**on**/**over** in). □ **~ up** vt far inciampare

tripe /traɪp/ n trippa f; ([x]: nonsense) fesserie fpl

triple /'trɪpl/ adj triplo • vt triplicare • vi triplicarsi

triplets /'trɪplɪts/ npl tre gemelli mpl

triplicate /'trɪplɪkət/ n **in ~** in triplice copia

t

tripod /'traɪpɒd/ n treppiede m inv

trite /traɪt/ adj banale

triumph /'traɪʌmf/ n trionfo m •vi trionfare (**over** su). **~ant** adj trionfante. **~antly** adv (exclaim) con tono trionfante

trivial /'trɪvɪəl/ adj insignificante. **~ity** n banalità f inv

trolley /'trɒlɪ/ n carrello m; (Am: tram) tram m inv. **~ bus** n filobus m inv

trombone /trɒm'bəʊn/ n trombone m

troop /tru:p/ n gruppo m; **~s** pl truppe fpl •vi **~ in/out** entrare/uscire in gruppo

trophy /'trəʊfɪ/ n trofeo m

tropic /'trɒpɪk/ n tropico m; **~s** pl tropici mpl. **~al** adj tropicale

trot /trɒt/ n trotto m •vi (pt/pp **trotted**) trottare

trouble /'trʌbl/ n guaio m; (difficulties) problemi mpl; (inconvenience, (Med) disturbo m; (conflict) conflitto m; **be in ~** essere nei guai; (swimmer, climber:) essere in difficoltà; **get into ~** finire nei guai; **get sb into ~** mettere qcno nei guai; **take the ~ to do sth** darsi la pena di far qcsa •vt (worry) preoccupare; (inconvenience) disturbare; (conscience, old wound:) tormentare •vi **don't ~!** non ti disturbare!. **~-maker** n **be a ~-maker** seminare zizzania. **~some** adj fastidioso

trough /trɒf/ n trogolo m; (atmospheric) depressione f

troupe /tru:p/ n troupe f inv

trousers /'traʊzəz/ npl pantaloni mpl

trout /traʊt/ n inv trota f

trowel /'traʊəl/ n (for gardening) paletta f; (for builder) cazzuola f

truant /'tru:ənt/ n **play ~** marinare la scuola

truce /tru:s/ n tregua f

truck /trʌk/ n (lorry) camion m inv

trudge /trʌdʒ/ n camminata f faticosa •vi arrancare

true /tru:/ adj vero; **come ~** avverarsi

truffle /'trʌfl/ n tartufo m

truly /'tru:lɪ/ adv veramente; **Yours ~** distinti saluti

trump /trʌmp/ n (in cards) atout m inv

trumpet /'trʌmpɪt/ n tromba f. **~er** trombettista mf

truncheon /'trʌntʃn/ n manganello m

trunk /trʌŋk/ n (of tree, body) tronco m (of elephant) proboscide f; (for travelling, storage) baule m; (Am: of car) bagagliaio m; **~s** pl calzoncini mpl da bagno

truss /trʌs/ n (Med) cinto m erniario

trust /trʌst/ n fiducia f; (group of companies) trust m inv; (organization) associazione f; **on ~** sulla parola •vt fidarsi di; (hope) augurarsi •vi **~ in** credere in; **~ to** affidarsi a. **~ed** adj fidato

trustee /trʌs'ti:/ n amministratore, -trice mf fiduciario, -a

'**trust|ful** /'trʌstfl/ adj fiducioso. **~ing** adj fiducioso. **~worthy** adj fidato

truth /tru:θ/ n (pl **-s** /tru:ðz/) verità f inv. **~ful** adj veritiero. **~fully** adv sinceramente

try /traɪ/ n tentativo m, prova f; (in rugby) meta f •v (pt/pp **tried**) •vt provare; (be a strain on) mettere a dura prova; (Jur) processare (person); discutere (case); **~ to do sth** provare a fare qcsa •vi provare. □ **~ on** vt provarsi (garment). □ **~ out** vt provare

trying /'traɪɪŋ/ adj duro; (person) irritante

T-shirt /'ti:-/ n maglietta f

tub /tʌb/ n tinozza f; (carton) vaschetta f; (bath) vasca f da bagno

tuba /'tju:bə/ n (Mus) tuba f

tubby /'tʌbɪ/ adj (**-ier, -iest**) tozzo

tube /tju:b/ n tubo m; (of toothpaste) tubetto m; (Rail) metro f

tuberculosis /tju:bɜ:kjʊ'ləʊsɪs/ n tubercolosi f

tubular /'tju:bjʊlə(r)/ adj tubolare

tuck /tʌk/ n piega f •vt (put) infilare. □ **~ in** vt rimboccare; **~ sb in** rimboccare le coperte a qcno •vi (!: eat) mangiare con appetito. □ **~ up** vt rimboccarsi (sleeves); (in bed) rimboccare le coperte a

Tuesday /'tju:zdeɪ/ n martedì m inv

tuft /tʌft/ n ciuffo m

tug /tʌg/ n strattone m; (Naut)

rimorchiatore m •v (pt/pp **tugged**) •vt tirare •vi dare uno strattone. **~ of war** n tiro m alla fune

tuition /tjuːˈɪʃn/ n lezioni fpl

tulip /ˈtjuːlɪp/ n tulipano m

tumble /ˈtʌmbl/ n ruzzolone m •vi ruzzolare. **~down** adj cadente. **~-drier** n asciugabiancheria f

tumbler /ˈtʌmblə(r)/ n bicchiere m (senza stelo)

tummy /ˈtʌmɪ/ n [!] pancia f

tumour /ˈtjuːmə(r)/ n tumore m

tumult /ˈtjuːmʌlt/ n tumulto m. **~uous** adj tumultuoso

tuna /ˈtjuːnə/ n tonno m

tune /tjuːn/ n motivo m; **out of/in ~** (instrument) scordato/accordato; (person) stonato/intonato; **to the ~ of** [!] per la modesta somma di •vt accordare (instrument); sintonizzare (radio, TV); mettere a punto (engine). □ **~ in** vt sintonizzare •vi sintonizzarsi (**to** su). □ **~ up** vi (orchestra:) accordare gli strumenti

tuneful /ˈtjuːnfl/ adj melodioso

tuner /ˈtjuːnə(r)/ n accordatore, -trice mf; (Radio, TV) sintonizzatore m

tunic /ˈtjuːnɪk/ n tunica f; (Mil) giacca f; (Sch) ≈ grembiule m

tunnel /ˈtʌnl/ n tunnel m inv •vi (pt/pp **tunnelled**) scavare un tunnel

turban /ˈtɜːbən/ n turbante m

turbine /ˈtɜːbaɪn/ n turbina f

turbulen|ce /ˈtɜːbjʊləns/ n turbolenza f. **~t** adj turbolento

turf /tɜːf/ n erba f; (segment) zolla f erbosa •**turf out** vt [!] buttar fuori

Turin /tjuːˈrɪn/ n Torino f

Turk /tɜːk/ n turco, -a mf

turkey /ˈtɜːkɪ/ n tacchino m

Turk|ey n Turchia f. **~ish** adj turco

turmoil /ˈtɜːmɔɪl/ n tumulto m

turn /tɜːn/ n (rotation, short walk) giro m; (in road) svolta f, curva f; (development) svolta f; (Theat) numero m; ([!]: attack) crisi f inv; **a ~ for the better/ worse** un miglioramento/ peggioramento; **do sb a good ~** rendere un servizio a qcno; **take ~s** fare a turno; **in ~** a turno; **out of ~** (speak) a sproposito; **it's your ~** tocca a te •vt girare; voltare (back, eyes); dirigere (gun, attention) •vi girare; (person:) girarsi; (leaves:) ingiallire; (become) diventare; **~ right/left** girare a destra/sinistra; **~ sour** inacidirsi; **~ to sb** girarsi verso qcno; fig rivolgersi a qcno. □ **~ against** vi diventare ostile a •vt mettere contro. □ **~ away** vt mandare via (people); girare dall'altra parte (head) •vi girarsi dall'altra parte. □ **~ down** vt piegare (collar); abbassare (heat, gas, sound); respingere (person, proposal). □ **~ in** vt ripiegare in dentro (edges); consegnare (lost object) •vi ([!]: go to bed) andare a letto; **~ into the drive** entrare nel viale. □ **~ off** vt spegnere; chiudere (tap, water) •vi (car:) girare. □ **~ on** vt accendere; aprire (tap, water); ([!]: attract) eccitare •vi (attack) attaccare. □ **~ out** vt (expel) mandar via; spegnere (light, gas); (produce) produrre; (empty) svuotare (room, cupboard) •vi (transpire) risultare; **~ out well/badly** (cake, dress:) riuscire bene/male; (situation:) andare bene/male. □ **~ over** vt girare •vi girarsi; **please ~ over** vedi retro. □ **~ round** vi girarsi; (car:) girare. □ **~ up** vt tirare su (collar); alzare (heat, gas, sound, radio) •vi farsi vedere

turning /ˈtɜːnɪŋ/ n svolta f. **~-point** n svolta f decisiva

turnip /ˈtɜːnɪp/ n rapa f

turn: ~over n (Comm) giro m d'affari; (of staff) ricambio m. **~pike** n Am autostrada f. **~stile** n cancelletto m girevole. **~table** n piattaforma f girevole; (on record-player) piatto m (di giradischi). **~-up** n (of trousers) risvolto m

turquoise /ˈtɜːkwɔɪz/ adj (colour) turchese •n turchese m

turret /ˈtʌrɪt/ n torretta f

turtle /ˈtɜːtl/ n tartaruga f acquatica

tusk /tʌsk/ n zanna f

tussle /ˈtʌsl/ n zuffa f •vi azzuffarsi

tutor /ˈtjuːtə(r)/ n insegnante mf privato, -a; (Univ) insegnante mf universitario, -a che segue individualmente un ristretto numero di studenti. **~ial** n discussione f col tutor

tuxedo /tʌkˈsiːdəʊ/ n Am smoking m inv

TV n abbr (television) tv f inv, tivù f inv

twang /twæŋ/ n (in voice) suono m

nasale •vt far vibrare

tweezers /'twi:zəz/ npl pinzette fpl

twelfth /twelfθ/ adj dodicesimo

twelve /twelv/ adj dodici

twentieth /'twentɪɪθ/ adj ventesimo

twenty /'twentɪ/ adj venti

twice /twaɪs/ adv due volte

twiddle /'twɪdl/ vt giocherellare con; ~ **one's thumbs** fig girarsi i pollici

twig[1] /twɪg/ n ramoscello m

twig[2] vt/i (pt/pp **twigged**) [!] intuire

twilight /'twaɪ-/ n crepuscolo m

twin /twɪn/ n gemello, -a mf •attrib gemello. ~ **beds** npl letti mpl gemelli

twine /twaɪn/ n spago m •vi intrecciarsi; (plant:) attorcigliarsi •vt intrecciare

twinge /twɪndʒ/ n fitta f; ~ **of conscience** rimorso m di coscienza

twinkle /'twɪŋkl/ n scintillio m •vi scintillare

twirl /twɜ:l/ vt far roteare •vi volteggiare •n piroetta f

twist /twɪst/ n torsione f; (curve) curva f; (in rope) attorcigliata f; (in book, plot) colpo m di scena •vt attorcigliare (rope); torcere (metal); girare (knob, cap); (distort) distorcere; ~ **one's ankle** storcersi la caviglia •vi attorcigliarsi; (road:) essere pieno di curve

twit /twɪt/ n [!] cretino, -a mf

twitch /twɪtʃ/ n tic m inv; (jerk) strattone m •vi contrarsi

twitter /'twɪtə(r)/ n cinguettio m •vi cinguettare; (person:) cianciare

two /tu:/ adj due

two: ~**-faced** adj falso. ~**-piece** adj (swimsuit) due pezzi m inv; (suit) completo m. ~**-way** adj (traffic) a doppio senso di marcia

tycoon /taɪ'ku:n/ n magnate m

tying /'taɪɪŋ/ ▸**tie**

type /taɪp/ n tipo m; (printing) carattere m [tipografico] •vt scrivere a macchina •vi scrivere a macchina. ~**writer** n macchina f da scrivere. ~**written** adj dattiloscritto

typical /'tɪpɪkl/ adj tipico. ~**ly** adv tipicamente; (as usual) come al solito

typify /'tɪpɪfaɪ/ vt (pt/pp **-ied**) essere tipico di

typing /'taɪpɪŋ/ n dattilografia f

typist /'taɪpɪst/ n dattilografo, -a mf

tyrannical /tɪ'rænɪkl/ adj tirannico

tyranny /'tɪrənɪ/ n tirannia f

tyrant /'taɪrənt/ n tiranno, -a mf

tyre /'taɪə(r)/ n gomma f, pneumatico m

Uu

udder /'ʌdə(r)/ n mammella f (di vacca, capra ecc)

ugly /'ʌglɪ/ adj (**-ier, -iest**) brutto

UK n abbr United Kingdom

ulcer /'ʌlsə(r)/ n ulcera f

ultimate /'ʌltɪmət/ adj definitivo; (final) finale; (fundamental) fondamentale. ~**ly** adv alla fine

ultimatum /ʌltɪ'meɪtəm/ n ultimatum m inv

ultra'violet adj ultravioletto

umbrella /ʌm'brelə/ n ombrello m

umpire /'ʌmpaɪə(r)/ n arbitro m •vt/i arbitrare

umpteen /ʌmp'ti:n/ adj [!] innumerevole. ~**th** adj [!] ennesimo; **for the** ~**th time** per l'ennesima volta

UN n abbr (United Nations) ONU f

un'able /ʌn-/ adj **be** ~ **to do sth** non potere fare qcsa; (not know how) non sapere fare qcsa

unac'companied adj non accompagnato; (luggage) incustodito

unac'customed adj insolito; **be** ~ **to** non essere abituato a

un'aided adj senza aiuto

unanimous /juːˈnænɪməs/ adj unanime. **~ly** adv all'unanimità

un'armed adj disarmato; **~ combat** n lotta f senza armi

unat'tended adj incustodito

una'voidable adj inevitabile

una'ware adj **be ~ of sth** non rendersi conto di qcsa. **~s** adv **catch sb ~s** prendere qcno alla sprovvista

un'bearabl|e adj insopportabile. **~y** adv insopportabilmente

unbeat|able /ʌnˈbiːtəbl/ adj imbattibile. **~en** adj imbattuto

unbe'lievable adj incredibile

un'biased adj obiettivo

un'block vt sbloccare

un'bolt vt togliere il chiavistello di

un'breakable adj infrangibile

un'button vt sbottonare

uncalled-for /ʌnˈkɔːldfɔː(r)/ adj fuori luogo

un'canny adj sorprendente; (silence, feeling) inquietante

un'certain adj incerto; (weather) instabile; **in no ~ terms** senza mezzi termini. **~ty** n incertezza f

un'charitable adj duro

uncle /ˈʌŋkl/ n zio m

un'comfortabl|e adj scomodo; imbarazzante (silence, situation); **feel ~e** fig sentirsi a disagio. **~y** adv (sit) scomodamente; (causing alarm etc) spaventosamente

un'common adj insolito

un'compromising adj intransigente

uncon'ditional adj incondizionato. **~ly** adv incondizionatamente

un'conscious adj privo di sensi; (unaware) inconsapevole; **be ~ of sth** non rendersi conto di qcsa. **~ly** adv inconsapevolmente

uncon'ventional adj poco convenzionale

un'cork vt sturare

uncouth /ʌnˈkuːθ/ adj zotico

un'cover vt scoprire; portare alla luce (buried object)

unde'cided adj indeciso; (not settled) incerto

undeniabl|e /ʌndɪˈnaɪəbl/ adj innegabile. **~y** adv innegabilmente

under /ˈʌndə(r)/ prep sotto; (less than) al di sotto di; **~ there** lì sotto; **~ repair/construction** in riparazione/costruzione; **~ way** fig in corso • adv (~ water) sott'acqua; (unconscious) sotto anestesia

'undercarriage n (Aeron) carrello m

'underclothes npl biancheria fsg intima

under'cover adj clandestino

'undercurrent n corrente f sottomarina; fig sottofondo m

'underdog n perdente m

under'done adj (meat) al sangue

under'estimate vt sottovalutare

under'fed adj denutrito

under'foot adv sotto i piedi; **trample ~** calpestare

under'go vt (pt **-went**, pp **-gone**) subire (operation, treatment); **~ repair** essere in riparazione

under'graduate n studente, -tessa mf universitario, -a

under'ground¹ adv sottoterra

'underground² adj sotterraneo; (secret) clandestino • n (railway) metropolitana f. **~ car park** n parcheggio m sotterraneo

'undergrowth n sottobosco m

'underhand adj subdolo

under'lie vt (pt **-lay**, pp **-lain**, pres p **-lying**) fig essere alla base di

under'line vt sottolineare

under'lying adj fig fondamentale

under'mine vt fig minare

underneath /ʌndəˈniːθ/ prep sotto; **~ it** sotto • adv sotto

under'paid adj mal pagato

'underpants npl mutande fpl

'underpass n sottopassaggio m

under'privileged adj non abbiente

under'rate vt sottovalutare

'undershirt n Am maglia f della pelle

under'stand vt (pt/pp **-stood**) capire; **I ~ that...** (have heard) mi risulta che... • vi capire. **~able** adj comprensibile. **~ably** adv comprensibilmente

under'standing adj comprensivo • n

U

comprensione f; (agreement) accordo m; **on the ~ that** a condizione che

'understatement n understatement m inv

under'take vt (pt **-took**, pp **-taken**) intraprendere; **~ to do sth** impegnarsi a fare qcsa

'undertaker n impresario m di pompe funebri; [**firm of**] **~s** n impresa f di pompe funebri

under'taking n impresa f; (promise) promessa f

'undertone n fig sottofondo m; **in an ~** sottovoce

under'value vt sottovalutare

'underwater[1] adj subacqueo

under'water[2] adv sott'acqua

'underwear n biancheria f intima

under'weight adj sotto peso

'underworld n (criminals) malavita f

unde'sirable adj indesiderato; (person) poco raccomandabile

un'dignified adj non dignitoso

un'do vt (pt **-did**, pp **-done**) disfare; slacciare (dress, shoes); sbottonare (shirt); fig, (Comput) annullare

un'doubted adj indubbio. **~ly** adv senza dubbio

un'dress vt spogliare; **get ~ed** spogliarsi •vi spogliarsi

un'due adj eccessivo

un'duly adv eccessivamente

un'earth vt dissotterrare; fig scovare; scoprire (secret). **~ly** adj soprannaturale; **at an ~ly hour** [!] a un'ora impossibile

uneco'nomic adj poco remunerativo

unem'ployed adj disoccupato •npl **the ~** i disoccupati

unem'ployment n disoccupazione f. **~ benefit** n sussidio m di disoccupazione

un'ending adj senza fine

un'equal adj disuguale; (struggle) impari; **be ~ to a task** non essere all'altezza di un compito

unequivocal /ʌnɪ'kwɪvəkl/ adj inequivocabile; (person) esplicito

un'ethical adj immorale

un'even adj irregolare; (distribution) ineguale; (number) dispari

unex'pected adj inaspettato. **~ly** adv inaspettatamente

un'fair adj ingiusto. **~ly** adv ingiustamente. **~ness** n ingiustizia f

un'faithful adj infedele

unfa'miliar adj sconosciuto; **be ~ with** non conoscere

un'fasten vt slacciare; (detach) staccare

un'favourable adj sfavorevole; (impression) negativo

un'feeling adj insensibile

un'fit adj inadatto; (morally) indegno; (Sport) fuori forma; **~ for work** non in grado di lavorare

un'fold vt spiegare; (spread out) aprire; fig rivelare •vi (view:) spiegarsi

unfore'seen adj imprevisto

unforgettable /ʌnfə'getəbl/ adj indimenticabile

unforgivable /ʌnfə'gɪvəbl/ adj imperdonabile

un'fortunate adj sfortunato; (regrettable) spiacevole; (remark, choice) infelice. **~ly** adv purtroppo

un'founded adj infondato

unfurl /ʌn'fɜːl/ vt spiegare

ungainly /ʌn'geɪnlɪ/ adj sgraziato

un'grateful adj ingrato. **~ly** adv senza riconoscenza

un'happy adj infelice; (not content) insoddisfatto (**with** di)

un'harmed adj incolume

un'healthy adj poco sano; (insanitary) malsano

un'hurt adj illeso

unification /juːnɪfɪ'keɪʃn/ n unificazione f

uniform /'juːnɪfɔːm/ adj uniforme •n uniforme f. **~ly** adv uniformemente

unify /'juːnɪfaɪ/ vt (pt/pp **-ied**) unificare

uni'lateral /juːnɪ-/ adj unilaterale

uni'maginable adj inimmaginabile

unim'portant adj irrilevante

unin'habited adj disabitato

unin'tentional adj involontario.

~ly adv involontariamente

nion /'ju:nɪən/ n unione f; (trade ~) sindacato m. **U~ Jack** n bandiera f del Regno Unito

nique /ju:'ni:k/ adj unico. **~ly** adv unicamente

nison /'ju:nɪsn/ n **in ~** all'unisono

nit /'ju:nɪt/ n unità f inv; (department) reparto m; (of furniture) elemento m

nite /ju:'naɪt/ vt unire •vi unirsi

nity /'ju:nətɪ/ n unità f; (agreement) accordo m

niversal /ju:nɪ'vɜ:sl/ adj universale. **~ly** adv universalmente

niverse /'ju:nɪvɜ:s/ n universo m

niversity /ju:nɪ'vɜ:sətɪ/ n università f •attrib universitario

n'just adj ingiusto

n'kind adj scortese. **~ly** adv in modo scortese. **~ness** n mancanza f di gentilezza

n'known adj sconosciuto

n'lawful adj illecito, illegale

nleaded /ʌn'ledɪd/ adj senza piombo

n'leash vt fig scatenare

nless /ən'les/ conj a meno che; **~ I am mistaken** se non mi sbaglio

n'like adj (not the same) diversi •prep diverso da; **that's ~ him** non è da lui; **~ me, he...** diversamente da me, lui...

n'likely adj improbabile

n'limited adj illimitato

n'load vt scaricare

n'lock vt aprire (con chiave)

n'lucky adj sfortunato; **it's ~ to...** porta sfortuna...

n'married adj non sposato. **~ 'mother** n ragazza f madre

n'mask vt fig smascherare

nmistakabl|e /ʌnmɪ'steɪkəbl/ adj inconfondibile. **~y** adv chiaramente

n'natural adj innaturale; pej anormale. **~ly** adv in modo innaturale; pej in modo anormale

n'necessar|y adj inutile. **~ily** adv inutilmente

n'noticed adj inosservato

nob'tainable adj (product) introvabile; (phone number) non ottenibile

unob'trusive adj discreto. **~ly** adv in modo discreto

unof'ficial adj non ufficiale. **~ly** adv ufficiosamente

un'pack vi disfare le valigie •vt svuotare (parcel); spacchettare (books); **~ one's case** disfare la valigia

un'paid adj da pagare; (work) non retribuito

un'pleasant adj sgradevole; (person) maleducato. **~ly** adv sgradevolmente; (behave) maleducatamente. **~ness** n (bad feeling) tensioni fpl

un'plug vt (pt/pp **-plugged**) staccare

un'popular adj impopolare

un'precedented adj senza precedenti

unpre'dictable adj imprevedibile

unpre'pared adj impreparato

unpro'fessional adj non professionale; **it's ~** è una mancanza di professionalità

un'profitable adj non redditizio

un'qualified adj non qualificato; (fig: absolute) assoluto

un'questionable adj incontestabile

unravel /ʌn'rævl/ vt (pt/pp **-ravelled**) districare; (in knitting) disfare

un'real adj irreale; [!] inverosimile

un'reasonable adj irragionevole

unre'lated adj (fact) senza rapporto (**to** con); (person) non imparentato (**to** con)

unre'liable adj inattendibile; (person) inaffidabile, che non dà affidamento

un'rest n fermenti mpl

un'rivalled adj ineguagliato

un'roll vt srotolare •vi srotolarsi

unruly /ʌn'ru:lɪ/ adj indisciplinato

un'safe adj pericoloso

unsatis'factory adj poco soddisfacente

un'savoury adj equivoco

unscathed /ʌn'skeɪðd/ adj illeso

un'screw vt svitare

un'scrupulous adj senza scrupoli

un'seemly adj indecoroso

un'selfish adj disinteressato

un'settled adj in agitazione; (weather) variabile; (bill) non saldato

unshakeable /ʌn'ʃeɪkəbl/ adj categorico

unshaven /ʌn'ʃeɪvn/ adj non rasato

unsightly /ʌn'saɪtlɪ/ adj brutto

un'skilled adj non specializzato. ~ **worker** n manovale m

un'sociable adj scontroso

unso'phisticated adj semplice

un'sound adj (building, reasoning) poco solido; (advice) poco sensato; **of ~ mind** malato di mente

un'stable adj instabile; (mentally) squilibrato

un'steady adj malsicuro

un'stuck adj **come ~** staccarsi; (!: project) andare a monte

unsuc'cessful adj fallimentare; **be ~** (in attempt) non aver successo. **~ly** adv senza successo

un'suitable adj (inappropriate) inadatto; (inconvenient) inopportuno

unthinkable /ʌn'θɪŋkəbl/ adj impensabile

un'tidiness n disordine m

un'tidy adj disordinato

un'tie vt slegare

until /ən'tɪl/ prep fino a; **not ~** non prima di; **~ the evening** fino alla sera; **~ his arrival** fino al suo arrivo •conj finché, fino a quando; **not ~ you've seen it** non prima che tu l'abbia visto

un'told adj (wealth) incalcolabile; (suffering) indescrivibile; (story) inedito

un'true adj falso; **that's ~** non è vero

unused[1] /ʌn'ju:zd/ adj non [ancora] usato

unused[2] /ʌn'ju:st/ adj **be ~ to** non essere abituato a

un'usual adj insolito. **~ly** adv insolitamente

un'veil vt scoprire

un'wanted adj indesiderato

un'welcome adj sgradito

un'well adj indisposto

unwieldy /ʌn'wi:ldɪ/ adj ingombrante

un'willing adj riluttante. **~ly** adv malvolentieri

un'wind v (pt/pp **unwound**) •vt svolgere, srotolare •vi svolgersi, srotolarsi; (!: relax) rilassarsi

un'wise adj imprudente

un'worthy adj non degno

un'wrap vt (pt/pp **-wrapped**) scartare (present, parcel)

un'written adj tacito

up /ʌp/ adv su; (not in bed) alzato; (road) smantellato; (theatre curtain, blinds) alzato; (shelves, tent) montato; (notice) affisso; (building) costruito; **prices are up** i prezzi sono aumentati; **be up for sale** essere in vendita; **up here/there** quassù/lassù; **time's up** tempo scaduto; **what's up?** ! cosa è successo?; **up to** (as far as) fino a; **be up to** essere all'altezza di (task); **what's he up to?** ! cosa sta facendo?; (plotting) cosa sta combinando?; **I'm up to page 100** sono arrivato a pagina 100; **feel up to it** sentirsela; **be one up on sb** ! essere in vantaggio su qcno; **go up** salire; **lift up** alzare; **up against** fig alle prese con •prep su; **the cat ran/is up the tree** il gatto è salito di corsa/è sull'albero; **further up this road** più avanti su questa strada; **row up the river** risalire il fiume; **go up the stairs** salire su per le scale; **be up the pub** ! essere al pub; **be up on** or **in sth** essere bene informato su qcsa •n **ups and downs** npl alti mpl e bassi

'upbringing n educazione f

up'date[1] vt aggiornare

'update[2] n aggiornamento m

up'grade vt promuovere (person); modernizzare (equipment)

upheaval /ʌp'hi:vl/ n scompiglio m

up'hill adj in salita; fig arduo •adv in salita

up'hold vt (pt/pp **upheld**) sostenere (principle); confermare (verdict)

upholster /ʌp'həʊlstə(r)/ vt tappezzare. **~er** n tappezziere, -a mf. **~y** n tappezzeria f

u

ıpkeep n mantenimento m

p-'market adj di qualità

ıpon /ə'pɒn/ prep su; ~ **arriving home** una volta arrivato a casa

pper /'ʌpə(r)/ adj superiore • n (of shoe) tomaia f

ıpper class n alta borghesia f

ıpright adj dritto; (piano) verticale; (honest) retto • n montante m

ıprising n rivolta f

ıproar n tumulto m; **be in an ~** essere in trambusto

ıp'set¹ vt (pt/pp **upset**, pres p **upsetting**) rovesciare; sconvolgere (plan); (distress) turbare; **get ~ about sth** prendersela per qcsa; **be very ~** essere sconvolto; **have an ~ stomach** avere l'intestino disturbato

upset² n scombussolamento m

upshot n risultato m

ıpside 'down adv sottosopra; **turn ~ ~** capovolgere

ıp'stairs¹ adv [al piano] di sopra

upstairs² adj del piano superiore

upstart n arrivato, -a mf

ıp'stream adv controcorrente

uptake n **be slow on the ~** essere lento nel capire; **be quick on the ~** capire le cose al volo

ıp-to-'date adj moderno; (news) ultimo; (records) aggiornato

upturn n ripresa f

ıpward /'ʌpwəd/ adj verso l'alto, in su; ~ **slope** salita f • adv ~[**s**] verso l'alto; **~s of** oltre

ıranium /jʊ'reɪnɪəm/ n uranio m

ırban /'ɜːbən/ adj urbano

urge /ɜːdʒ/ n forte desiderio m • vt esortare (**to** a). □ ~ **on** vt spronare

urgen|cy /'ɜːdʒənsɪ/ n urgenza f. **~t** adj urgente

urinate /'jʊərɪneɪt/ vi urinare

urine /'jʊərɪn/ n urina f

us /ʌs/ pron ci; (after prep) noi; **they know us** ci conoscono; **give us the money** dateci i soldi; **give it to us** datecelo; **they showed it to us** ce l'hanno fatto vedere; **they meant us, not you** intendevano noi, non voi; **it's us** siamo noi; **she hates us** ci odia

US[A] n[pl] abbr (**United States** [**of America**]) U.S.A. mpl

usage /'juːsɪdʒ/ n uso m

use¹ /juːs/ n uso m; **be of ~** essere utile; **be of no ~** essere inutile; **make ~ of** usare; (exploit) sfruttare; **it is no ~** è inutile; **what's the ~?** a che scopo?

use² /juːz/ vt usare. □ ~ **up** vt consumare

used¹ /juːzd/ adj usato

used² /juːst/ pt **be ~ to sth** essere abituato a qcsa; **get ~ to** abituarsi a; **he ~ to live here** viveva qui

useful /'juːsfl/ adj utile. **~ness** n utilità f

useless /'juːslɪs/ adj inutile; ([!]: person) incapace

user /'juːzə(r)/ n utente mf. **~-'friendly** adj facile da usare

usher /'ʌʃə(r)/ n (Theat) maschera f; (Jur) usciere m; (at wedding) persona f che accompagna gli invitati a un matrimonio ai loro posti in chiesa • **usher in** vt fare entrare

usherette /ʌʃə'ret/ n maschera f

usual /'juːʒʊəl/ adj usuale; **as ~** come al solito. **~ly** adv di solito

utensil /juː'tensl/ n utensile m

utilize /'juːtɪlaɪz/ vt utilizzare

utmost /'ʌtməʊst/ adj estremo • n **one's ~** tutto il possibile

utter¹ /'ʌtə(r)/ adj totale. **~ly** adv completamente

utter² vt emettere (sigh, sound); proferire (word). **~ance** n dichiarazione f

U-turn /'juː-/ n (Auto) inversione f a U; fig marcia f indietro

Vv

vacan|cy /'veɪk(ə)nsɪ/ n (job) posto m vacante; (room) stanza f disponibile. **~t** adj libero; (position) vacante; (look) assente

vacate /və'keɪt/ vt lasciare libero

vacation /və'keɪʃn/ n vacanza f

vaccinat|e /'væksɪneɪt/ vt vaccinare. **~ion** n vaccinazione f

vaccine /'væksi:n/ n vaccino m

vacuum /'vækjʊəm/ n vuoto m •vt passare l'aspirapolvere in/su. **~ cleaner** n aspirapolvere m inv. **~ flask** n thermos® m inv. **~-packed** adj confezionato sottovuoto

vagina /və'dʒaɪnə/ n (Anat) vagina f

vague /veɪg/ adj vago; (outline) impreciso; (absent-minded) distratto; **I'm still ~ about it** non ho ancora le idee chiare in proposito. **~ly** adv vagamente

vain /veɪn/ adj vanitoso; (hope, attempt) vano; **in ~** invano. **~ly** adv vanamente

valentine /'væləntaɪn/ n (card) biglietto m di San Valentino

valiant /'vælɪənt/ adj valoroso

valid /'vælɪd/ adj valido. **~ate** vt (confirm) convalidare. **~ity** n validità f

valley /'vælɪ/ n valle f

valour /'vælə(r)/ n valore m

valuable /'væljʊəbl/ adj di valore; fig prezioso. **~s** npl oggetti mpl di valore

valuation /væljʊ'eɪʃn/ n valutazione f

value /'vælju:/ n valore m; (usefulness) utilità f •vt valutare; (cherish) apprezzare. **~ 'added tax** n imposta f sul valore aggiunto

valve /vælv/ n valvola f

vampire /'væmpaɪə(r)/ n vampiro m

van /væn/ n furgone m

vandal /'vændl/ n vandalo, -a mf. **~ism** n vandalismo m. **~ize** vt vandalizzare

vanilla /və'nɪlə/ n vaniglia f

vanish /'vænɪʃ/ vi svanire

vanity /'vænətɪ/ n vanità f. **~ bag** or **case** n beauty-case m inv

vapour /'veɪpə(r)/ n vapore m

variable /'veərɪəbl/ adj variabile; (adjustable) regolabile

variance /'veərɪəns/ n **be at ~** essere in disaccordo

variant /'veərɪənt/ n variante f

variation /veərɪ'eɪʃn/ n variazione f

varied /'veərɪd/ adj vario; (diet) diversificato; (life) movimentato

variety /və'raɪətɪ/ n varietà f inv

various /'veərɪəs/ adj vario

varnish /'vɑ:nɪʃ/ n vernice f; (for nails) smalto m •vt verniciare; **~ one's nails** mettersi lo smalto

vary /'veərɪ/ vt/i (pt/pp **-ied**) variare. **~ing** adj variabile; (different) diverso

vase /vɑ:z/ n vaso m

vast /vɑ:st/ adj vasto; (difference, amusement) enorme. **~ly** adv (superior) di gran lunga; (different, amused) enormemente

vat /væt/ n tino m

VAT /vi:eɪ'ti:/, /væt/ n abbr (value added tax) I.V.A. f

vault¹ /vɔ:lt/ n (roof) volta f; (in bank) caveau m inv; (tomb) cripta f

vault² n salto m •vt/i **~ [over]** saltare

VDU n abbr (visual display unit) VDU m

veal /vi:l/ n carne f di vitello •attrib di vitello

veer /vɪə(r)/ vi cambiare direzione; (Auto, Naut) virare

vegetable /'vedʒtəbl/ n (food) verdura f; (when growing) ortaggio m •attrib (oil, fat) vegetale

vegetarian /vedʒɪ'teərɪən/ adj & n vegetariano, -a mf

vehicle /'vi:ɪkl/ n veicolo m; (fig: medium) mezzo m

veil /veɪl/ n velo m •vt velare

vein /veɪn/ n vena f; (mood) umore m; (manner) tenore m. **~ed** adj venato

velocity /vɪ'lɒsətɪ/ n velocità f

velvet /'velvɪt/ n velluto m. **~y** adj vellutato

vendetta /ven'detə/ n vendetta f

vending-machine /'vendɪŋ-/ n distributore m automatico

veneer /və'nɪə(r)/ n impiallacciatura f; fig vernice f. **~ed** adj impiallacciato

venereal /vɪ'nɪərɪəl/ adj **~ disease** malattia f venerea

Venetian /və'ni:ʃn/ adj & n veneziano, -a mf. **v~ blind** n persiana f alla veneziana

vengeance /'vendʒəns/ n vendetta f; **with a ~** [!] a più non posso

venison /'venɪsn/ n (Culin) carne f di cervo

venom /'venəm/ n veleno m. **~ous** adj velenoso

vent[1] /vent/ n presa f d'aria; **give ~ to** fig dar libero sfogo a • vt fig sfogare (anger)

vent[2] n (in jacket) spacco m

ventilat|e /'ventɪleɪt/ vt ventilare. **~ion** n ventilazione f; (installation) sistema m di ventilazione. **~or** n ventilatore m

ventriloquist /ven'trɪləkwɪst/ n ventriloquo, -a mf

venture /'ventʃə(r)/ n impresa f • vt azzardare • vi avventurarsi

venue /'venju:/ n luogo m (di convegno, concerto, ecc.)

veranda /və'rændə/ n veranda f

verb /vɜ:b/ n verbo m. **~al** adj verbale

verdict /'vɜ:dɪkt/ n verdetto m; (opinion) parere m

verge /vɜ:dʒ/ n orlo m; **be on the ~ of doing sth** essere sul punto di fare qcsa • **verge on** vt fig rasentare

verify /'verɪfaɪ/ vt (pt/pp **-ied**) verificare; (confirm) confermare

vermin /'vɜ:mɪn/ n animali mpl nocivi

versatil|e /'vɜ:sətaɪl/ adj versatile. **~ity** n versatilità f

verse /vɜ:s/ n verso m; (of Bible) versetto m; (poetry) versi mpl

versed /vɜ:st/ adj **~ in** versato in

versus /'vɜ:səs/ prep contro

vertebra /'vɜ:tɪbrə/ n (pl **-brae** /-bri:/) (Anat) vertebra f

vertical /'vɜ:tɪkl/ adj & n verticale m

vertigo /'vɜ:tɪgəʊ/ n (Med) vertigine f

verve /vɜ:v/ n verve f

very /'verɪ/ adv molto; **~ much** molto; **~ little** pochissimo; **~ many** moltissimi; **~ few** pochissimi; **~ probably** molto probabilmente; **~ well** benissimo; **at the ~ most** tutt'al più; **at the ~ latest** al più tardi • adj **the ~ first** il primissimo; **the ~ thing** proprio ciò che ci vuole; **at the ~ end/beginning** proprio alla fine/ all'inizio; **that ~ day** proprio quel giorno; **the ~ thought** la sola idea; **only a ~ little** solo un pochino

vessel /'vesl/ n nave f

vest /vest/ n maglia f della pelle; (Am: waistcoat) gilè m inv. **~ed interest** n interesse m personale

vestige /'vestɪdʒ/ n (of past) vestigio m

vet /vet/ n veterinario, -a mf • vt (pt/pp **vetted**) controllare minuziosamente

veteran /'vetərən/ n veterano, -a mf

veterinary /'vetərɪnərɪ/ adj veterinario. **~ surgeon** n medico m veterinario

veto /'vi:təʊ/ n (pl **-es**) veto m • vt proibire

vex /veks/ vt irritare. **~ation** n irritazione f. **~ed** adj irritato; **~ed question** questione f controversa

via /'vaɪə/ prep via; (by means of) attraverso

viable /'vaɪəbl/ adj (life form, relationship, company) in grado di sopravvivere; (proposition) attuabile

viaduct /'vaɪədʌkt/ n viadotto m

vibrat|e /vaɪ'breɪt/ vi vibrare. **~ion** n vibrazione f

vicar /'vɪkə(r)/ n parroco m (protestante). **~age** n casa f parrocchiale

vice[1] /vaɪs/ n vizio m

vice[2] n (Techn) morsa f

vice versa /vaɪsɪ'vɜ:sə/ adv viceversa

vicinity /vɪ'sɪnətɪ/ n vicinanza f; **in the ~ of** nelle vicinanze di

vicious /'vɪʃəs/ adj cattivo; (attack)

brutale; (animal) pericoloso. ~ **'circle** n circolo m vizioso. **~ly** adv (attack) brutalmente

victim /'vɪktɪm/ n vittima f. **~ize** vt fare delle rappresaglie contro

victor /'vɪktə(r)/ n vincitore m

victor|ious /vɪk'tɔ:rɪəs/ adj vittorioso. **~y** n vittoria f

video /'vɪdɪəʊ/ n video m; (cassette) videocassetta f; (recorder) videoregistratore m • attrib video • vt registrare

video: ~ recorder n videoregistratore m. **~-tape** n videocassetta f

vie /vaɪ/ vi (pres p **vying**) rivaleggiare

view /vju:/ n vista f; (photographed, painted) veduta f; (opinion) visione f; **look at the ~** guardare il panorama; **in my ~** secondo me; **in ~ of** in considerazione di; **on ~** esposto; **with a ~ to** con l'intenzione di • vt visitare (house); (consider) considerare • vi (TV) guardare. **~er** n (TV) telespettatore, -trice mf; (Phot) visore m

view: ~finder n (Phot) mirino m. **~point** n punto m di vista

vigilan|ce /'vɪdʒɪləns/ n vigilanza f. **~t** adj vigile

vigorous /'vɪgərəs/ adj vigoroso

vigour /'vɪgə(r)/ n vigore m

vile /vaɪl/ adj disgustoso; (weather) orribile; (temper, mood) pessimo

village /'vɪlɪdʒ/ n paese m. **~r** n paesano, -a mf

villain /'vɪlən/ n furfante m; (in story) cattivo m

vindicate /'vɪndɪkeɪt/ vt (from guilt) discolpare; **you are ~d** ti sei dimostrato nel giusto

vindictive /vɪn'dɪktɪv/ adj vendicativo

vine /vaɪn/ n vite f

vinegar /'vɪnɪgə(r)/ n aceto m

vineyard /'vɪnjɑ:d/ n vigneto m

vintage /'vɪntɪdʒ/ adj (wine) d'annata • n (year) annata f

viola /vɪ'əʊlə/ n (Mus) viola f

violat|e /'vaɪəleɪt/ vt violare. **~ion** n violazione f

violen|ce /'vaɪələns/ n violenza f. **~t** adj violento

violet /'vaɪələt/ adj violetto • n (flower) violetta f; (colour) violetto m

violin /vaɪə'lɪn/ n violino m. **~ist** n violinista mf

VIP n abbr (very important person) vip mf

virgin /'vɜ:dʒɪn/ adj vergine • n vergine f. **~ity** n verginità f

Virgo /'vɜ:gəʊ/ n Vergine f

viril|e /'vɪraɪl/ adj virile. **~ity** n virilità f

virtual /'vɜ:tjʊəl/ adj effettivo. **~ reality** n realtà f virtuale. **~ly** adv praticamente

virtue /'vɜ:tju:/ n virtù f inv; (advantage) vantaggio m; **by** or **in ~ of** a causa di

virtuous /'vɜ:tjʊəs/ adj virtuoso

virulent /'vɪrʊlənt/ adj virulento

virus /'vaɪərəs/ n virus m inv

visa /'vi:zə/ n visto m

visibility /vɪzə'bɪlətɪ/ n visibilità f

visibl|e /'vɪzəbl/ adj visibile. **~y** adv visibilmente

vision /'vɪʒn/ n visione f; (sight) vista f

visit /'vɪzɪt/ n visita f • vt andare a trovare (person); andare da (doctor etc); visitare (town, building). **~ing hours** npl orario m delle visite. **~or** n ospite mf; (of town, museum) visitatore, -trice mf; (in hotel) cliente mf

visor /'vaɪzə(r)/ n visiera f; (Auto) parasole m

visual /'vɪzjʊəl/ adj visivo. **~ aids** npl supporto m visivo. **~ dis'play unit** n visualizzatore m. **~ly** adv visualmente; **~ly handicapped** non vedente

visualize /'vɪzjʊəlaɪz/ vt visualizzare

vital /'vaɪtl/ adj vitale. **~ity** n vitalità f. **~ly** adv estremamente

vitamin /'vɪtəmɪn/ n vitamina f

vivaci|ous /vɪ'veɪʃəs/ adj vivace. **~ty** n vivacità f

vivid /'vɪvɪd/ adj vivido. **~ly** adv in modo vivido

vocabulary /və'kæbjʊlərɪ/ n vocabolario m; (list) glossario m

vocal /'vəʊkl/ adj vocale; (vociferous) eloquente. **~ cords** npl corde fpl vocali

vocalist /'vəʊkəlɪst/ n vocalista mf

vocation /və'keɪʃn/ n vocazione f. **~al** adj di orientamento professionale

vociferous /və'sɪfərəs/ adj vociante

vogue /vəʊg/ n moda f; **in ~** in voga

voice /vɔɪs/ n voce f •vt esprimere. **~mail** n posta f elettronica vocale

void /vɔɪd/ adj (not valid) nullo; **~ of** privo di •n vuoto m

volatile /'vɒlətaɪl/ adj volatile; (person) volubile

volcanic /vɒl'kænɪk/ adj vulcanico

volcano /vɒl'keɪnəʊ/ n vulcano m

volley /'vɒlɪ/ n (of gunfire) raffica f; (Tennis) volée f inv

volt /vəʊlt/ n volt m inv. **~age** n (Electr) voltaggio m

volume /'vɒlju:m/ n volume m; (of work, traffic) quantità f inv. **~ control** n volume m

voluntar|y /'vɒləntərɪ/ adj volontario. **~y work** n volontariato m. **~ily** adv volontariamente

volunteer /vɒlən'tɪə(r)/ n volontario, -a mf •vt offrire volontariamente (information) •vi offrirsi volontario; (Mil) arruolarsi come volontario

vomit /'vɒmɪt/ n vomito m •vt/i vomitare

voracious /və'reɪʃəs/ adj vorace

vot|e /vəʊt/ n voto m; (ballot) votazione f; (right) diritto m di voto; **take a ~e on** votare su •vi votare •vt **~e sb president** eleggere qcno presidente. **~er** n elettore, -trice mf. **~ing** n votazione f

vouch /vaʊtʃ/ vi **~ for** garantire per. **~er** n buono m

vow /vaʊ/ n voto m •vt giurare

vowel /'vaʊəl/ n vocale f

voyage /'vɔɪɪdʒ/ n viaggio m [marittimo]; (in space) viaggio m [nello spazio]

vulgar /'vʌlgə(r)/ adj volgare. **~ity** n volgarità f inv

vulnerable /'vʌlnərəbl/ adj vulnerabile

vulture /'vʌltʃə(r)/ n avvoltoio m

vying /'vaɪɪŋ/ ▸**vie**

Ww

wad /wɒd/ n batuffolo m; (bundle) rotolo m. **~ding** n ovatta f

waddle /'wɒdl/ vi camminare ondeggiando

wade /weɪd/ vi guadare; **~ through** [!] procedere faticosamente in (book)

wafer /'weɪfə(r)/ n cialda f, wafer m inv; (Relig) ostia f

waffle¹ /'wɒfl/ vi [!] blaterare

waffle² n (Culin) cialda f

waft /wɒft/ vt trasportare •vi diffondersi

wag /wæg/ v (pt/pp **wagged**) •vt agitare •vi agitarsi

wage¹ /weɪdʒ/ vt dichiarare (war); lanciare (campaign)

wage² n, & **~s** npl salario msg. **~ packet** n busta f paga

waggle /'wægl/ vt dimenare •vi dimenarsi

wagon /'wægən/ n carro m; (Rail) vagone m merci

wail /weɪl/ n piagnucolio m; (of wind) lamento m; (of baby) vagito m •vi piagnucolare; (wind:) lamentarsi; (baby:) vagire

waist /weɪst/ n vita f. **~coat** n gilè m inv; (of man's suit) panciotto m. **~line** n vita f

wait /weɪt/ n attesa f; **lie in ~ for** appostarsi per sorprendere •vi aspettare; **~ for** aspettare •vt **~ one's turn** aspettare il proprio turno. □ **~ on** vt servire

waiter /'weɪtə(r)/ n cameriere m

waiting: ~-list n lista f d'attesa. **~-room** n sala f d'aspetto

waitress /'weɪtrɪs/ n cameriera f

waive /weɪv/ vt rinunciare a (claim); non tener conto di (rule)

wake[1] /weɪk/ n veglia f funebre •v (pt **woke**, pp **woken**) ~ [**up**] •vt svegliare •vi svegliarsi

wake[2] n (Naut) scia f; **in the ~ of** fig nella scia di

Wales /weɪlz/ n Galles m

walk /wɔ:k/ n passeggiata f; (gait) andatura f; (path) sentiero m; **go for a ~** andare a fare una passeggiata •vi camminare; (as opposed to drive etc) andare a piedi; (ramble) passeggiare •vt portare a spasso (dog); percorrere (streets). □ **~ out** vi (husband, employee:) andarsene; (workers:) scioperare. □ **~ out on** vt lasciare

walker /'wɔ:kə(r)/ n camminatore, -trice mf; (rambler) escursionista mf

walk-out n sciopero m

wall /wɔ:l/ n muro m; **go to the ~** [!] andare a rotoli; **drive sb up the ~** [!] far diventare matto qcno •**wall up** vt murare

wallet /'wɒlɪt/ n portafoglio m

wallop /'wɒləp/ n [!] colpo m •vt (pt/pp **walloped**) [!] colpire

wallow /'wɒləʊ/ vi sguazzare; (in self-pity, grief) crogiolarsi

'**wallpaper** n tappezzeria f •vt tappezzare

walnut /'wɔ:lnʌt/ n noce f

waltz /wɔ:lts/ n valzer m inv •vi ballare il valzer

wand /wɒnd/ n (magic ~) bacchetta f [magica]

wander /'wɒndə(r)/ vi girovagare; (fig: digress) divagare. □ **~ about** vi andare a spasso

wane /weɪn/ n **be on the ~** essere in fase calante •vi calare

wangle /'wæŋgl/ vt [!] rimediare (invitation, holiday)

want /wɒnt/ n (hardship) bisogno m; (lack) mancanza f •vt volere; (need) aver bisogno di; **~ [to have] sth** volere qcsa; **~ to do sth** voler fare qcsa; **we ~ to stay** vogliamo rimanere; **I ~ you to go** voglio che tu vada; **it ~s painting** ha bisogno d'essere dipinto; **you ~ to learn to swim** bisogna che impari a nuotare •vi **~ for** mancare di. **~ed** adj ricercato. **~ing** adj **be ~ing** mancare; **be ~ing in** mancare di

WAP /wæp/ n abbr (wireless application protocol) WAP m inv

war /wɔ:(r)/ n guerra f; fig lotta f (**on** contro); **at ~** in guerra

ward /wɔ:d/ n (in hospital) reparto m; (child) minore m sotto tutela •**ward off** vt evitare; parare (blow)

warden /'wɔ:dn/ n guardiano, -a mf

warder /'wɔ:də(r)/ n guardia f carceraria

wardrobe /'wɔ:drəʊb/ n guardaroba m

warehouse /'weəhaʊs/ n magazzino m

war: ~fare n guerra f. **~head** n testata f

warm /wɔ:m/ adj caldo; (welcome) caloroso; **be ~** (person:) aver caldo; **it is ~** (weather) fa caldo •vt scaldare. □ **~ up** vt scaldare •vi scaldarsi; fig animarsi. **~-hearted** adj espansivo. **~ly** adv (greet) calorosamente; (dress) in modo pesante. **~th** n calore m

warn /wɔ:n/ vt avvertire. **~ing** n avvertimento m; (advance notice) preavviso m

warp /wɔ:p/ vt deformare; fig distorcere •vi deformarsi

warped /wɔ:pt/ adj fig contorto; (sexuality) deviato; (view) distorto

warrant /'wɒrənt/ n (for arrest, search) mandato m •vt (justify) giustificare; (guarantee) garantire. **~y** n garanzia f

warrior /'wɒrɪə(r)/ n guerriero, -a mf

'**warship** n nave f da guerra

wart /wɔ:t/ n porro m

'**wartime** n tempo m di guerra

war|y /'weərɪ/ adj (**-ier, -iest**) (careful) cauto; (suspicious) diffidente

was /wɒz/ ▸**be**

wash /wɒʃ/ n lavata f; (clothes) bucato m; (in washing machine) lavaggio m; **have a ~** darsi una lavata •vt lavare; (sea:) bagnare; **~ one's hands** lavarsi le mani •vi lavarsi. □ **~ out** vt sciacquare (soap);

sciacquarsi (mouth). □~ **up** vt lavare • vi lavare i piatti; Am lavarsi

washable /ˈwɒʃəbl/ adj lavabile

wash-basin n lavandino m

washer /ˈwɒʃə(r)/ n (Techn) guarnizione f; (machine) lavatrice f

washing /ˈwɒʃɪŋ/ n bucato m. **~-machine** n lavatrice f. **~-powder** n detersivo m. **~-ˈup** n **do the ~-up** lavare i piatti. **~-ˈup liquid** n detersivo m per i piatti

wash: ~-out n disastro m. **~-room** n bagno m

wasp /wɒsp/ n vespa f

waste /weɪst/ n spreco m; (rubbish) rifiuto m; **~ of time** perdita f di tempo • adj (product) di scarto; (land) desolato; **lay ~** devastare • vt sprecare. □~ **away** vi deperire

waste: ~-diˈsposal unit n eliminatore m di rifiuti. **~ful** adj dispendioso. **~-ˈpaper basket** n cestino m per la carta [straccia]

watch /wɒtʃ/ n guardia f; (period of duty) turno m di guardia; (timepiece) orologio m; **be on the ~** stare all'erta • vt guardare (film, match, television); (be careful of, look after) stare attento a • vi guardare. □~ **out** vi (be careful) stare attento (**for** a). □~ **out for** vt (look for) fare attenzione all'arrivo di (person)

watch: ~-dog n cane m da guardia. **~man** n guardiano m

water /ˈwɔːtə(r)/ n acqua f • vt annaffiare (garden, plant); (dilute) annacquare • vi (eyes:) lacrimare; **my mouth was ~ing** avevo l'acquolina in bocca. □~ **down** vt diluire; fig attenuare

water: ~-colour n acquerello m. **~cress** n crescione m. **~fall** n cascata f

watering-can n annaffiatoio m

water: ~-lily n ninfea f. **~ logged** adj inzuppato. **~proof** adj impermeabile. **~-skiing** n sci m nautico. **~tight** stagno; fig irrefutabile. **~way** n canale m navigabile

watery /ˈwɔːtərɪ/ adj acquoso; (eyes) lacrimoso

watt /wɒt/ n watt m inv

wave /weɪv/ n onda f; (gesture) cenno m; fig ondata f • vt agitare; **~ one's hand** agitare la mano • vi far segno; (flag:) sventolare. **~length** n lunghezza f d'onda

waver /ˈweɪvə(r)/ vi vacillare; (hesitate) esitare

wavy /ˈweɪvɪ/ adj ondulato

wax¹ /wæks/ vi (moon:) crescere; (fig: become) diventare

wax² n cera f; (in ear) cerume m • vt dare la cera a. **~works** n museo m delle cere

way /weɪ/ n percorso m; (direction) direzione f; (manner, method) modo m; **~s** pl (customs) abitudini fpl; **be in the ~** essere in mezzo; **on the ~ to Rome** andando a Roma; **I'll do it on the ~** lo faccio mentre vado; **it's on my ~** è sul mio percorso; **a long ~ off** lontano; **this ~** da questa parte; (like this) così; **by the ~** a proposito; **by ~ of** come; (via) via; **either ~** (whatever we do) in un modo o nell'altro; **in some ~s** sotto certi aspetti; **in a ~** in un certo senso; **in a bad ~** (person) molto grave; **out of the ~** fuori mano; **under ~** in corso; **lead the ~** far strada; fig aprire la strada; **make ~** far posto (**for** a); **give ~** (Auto) dare la precedenza; **go out of one's ~** fig scomodarsi (**to** per); **get one's [own] ~** averla vinta • adv **~ behind** molto indietro. **~ˈin** n entrata f

wayˈlay vt (pt/pp **-laid**) aspettare al varco (person)

way ˈout n uscita f; fig via f d'uscita

way-ˈout adj [!] eccentrico

we /wiː/ pron noi; **we're the last** siamo gli ultimi; **they're going, but we're not** loro vanno, ma noi no

weak /wiːk/ adj debole; (liquid) leggero. **~en** vt indebolire • vi indebolirsi. **~ling** n smidollato, -a mf. **~ness** n debolezza f; (liking) debole m

wealth /welθ/ n ricchezza f; fig gran quantità f. **~y** adj (**-ier, -iest**) ricco

weapon /ˈwepən/ n arma f; **~s of mass destruction** pl armi mpl di distruzione di massa

wear /weə(r)/ n (clothing) abbigliamento m; **for everyday ~**

da portare tutti i giorni; ~ [**and tear**] usura f •v (pt **wore**, pp **worn**) •vt portare; (damage) consumare; ~ **a hole in sth** logorare qcsa fino a fare un buco; **what shall I ~?** cosa mi metto? •vi consumarsi; (last) durare. □ ~ **off** vi scomparire; (effect:) finire. □ ~ **out** vt consumare [fino in fondo]; (exhaust) estenuare •vi estenuarsi

wear|y /ˈwɪərɪ/ adj (**-ier, -iest**) sfinito •v (pt/pp **wearied**) •vt sfinire •vi **~y of** stancarsi di. **~ily** adv stancamente

weather /ˈweðə(r)/ n tempo m; **in this ~** con questo tempo; **under the ~** [!] giù di corda •vt sopravvivere a (storm)

weather: ~-beaten adj (face) segnato dalle intemperie. ~ **forecast** n previsioni fpl del tempo

weave[1] /wi:v/ vi (pt/pp **weaved**) (move) zigzagare

weave[2] n tessuto m •vt (pt **wove**, pp **woven**) tessere; intrecciare (flowers etc); intrecciare le fila di (story etc). **~r** n tessitore, -trice mf

web /web/ n rete f; (spider's) ragnatela f. **W~** (Comput) Web m inv, Rete f. **~bed feet** npl piedi mpl palmati. **~cam** n webcam f inv. ~ **master** n webmaster m inv. ~ **page** n pagina f web. ~ **site** n sito m web

wed /wed/ vt (pt/pp **wedded**) sposare •vi sposarsi. **~ding** n matrimonio m

wedding: ~ cake n torta f nuziale. **~-ring** n fede f

wedge /wedʒ/ n zeppa f; (for splitting wood) cuneo m; (of cheese) fetta f •vt (fix) fissare

Wednesday /ˈwenzdeɪ/ n mercoledì m inv

wee[1] /wi:/ adj [!] piccolo

wee[2] vi [!] fare la pipì

weed /wi:d/ n erbaccia f; ([!]: person) mollusco m •vt estirpare le erbacce da. □ ~ **out** vt fig eliminare

ˈ**weed-killer** n erbicida m

weedy /ˈwi:dɪ/ adj [!] mingherlino

week /wi:k/ n settimana f. **~day** n giorno m feriale. **~end** n fine settimana m

weekly /ˈwi:klɪ/ adj settimanale •n settimanale m •adv settimanalmente

weep /wi:p/ vi (pt/pp **wept**) piangere

weigh /weɪ/ vt/i pesare; ~ **anchor** levare l'ancora. □ ~ **down** vt fig piegare. □ ~ **up** vt fig soppesare; valutare (person)

weight /weɪt/ n peso m; **put on/lose ~** ingrassare/dimagrire. **~ing** n (allowance) indennità f inv

weight-lifting n sollevamento m pesi

weir /wɪə(r)/ n chiusa f

weird /wɪəd/ adj misterioso; (bizarre) bizzarro

welcome /ˈwelkəm/ adj benvenuto; **you're ~!** prego!; **you're ~ to have it/to come** prendilo/vieni pure •n accoglienza f •vt accogliere; (appreciate) gradire

weld /weld/ vt saldare. **~er** n saldatore m

welfare /ˈwelfeə(r)/ n benessere m; (aid) assistenza f. **W~ State** n Stato m assistenziale

well[1] /wel/ n pozzo m; (of staircase) tromba f

well[2] adv (**better, best**) bene; **as ~** anche; **as ~ as** (in addition) oltre a; ~ **done!** bravo!; **very ~** benissimo •adj **he is not ~** non sta bene; **get ~ soon!** guarisci presto! •int beh!; ~ **I never!** ma va!

well-behaved adj educato

well: ~-known adj famoso. **~-off** adj benestante. **~-to-do** adj ricco

Welsh /welʃ/ adj & n gallese; **the ~** pl i gallesi. **~man** n gallese m. ~ **rabbit** n toast m inv al formaggio

went /went/ ▹**go**

wept /wept/ ▹**weep**

were /wɜ:(r)/ ▹**be**

west /west/ n ovest m; **to the ~ of** a ovest di; **the W~** l'Occidente m •adj occidentale •adv verso occidente; **go ~** [!] andare in malora. **~erly** adj verso ovest; occidentale (wind). **~ern** adj occidentale •n western m inv

West: ~ ˈ**Indian** adj & n antillese mf. ~ ˈ**Indies** /ˈɪndɪz/ npl Antille fpl

ˈ**westward[s]** /-wəd[z]/ adv verso ovest

wet /wet/ adj (**wetter, wettest**) bagnato; fresco (paint); (rainy) piovoso; (⊡: person) smidollato; **get ~** bagnarsi •vt (pt/pp **wet, wetted**) bagnare. ~ '**blanket** n guastafeste mf inv

whack /wæk/ n ⊡ colpo m •vt ⊡ dare un colpo a. ~**ed** adj ⊡ stanco morto. ~**ing** adj (⊡: huge) enorme

whale /weɪl/ n balena f; **have a ~ of a time** ⊡ divertirsi un sacco

wham /wæm/ int bum

wharf /wɔːf/ n banchina f

what /wɒt/ pron che, [che] cosa; **~ for?** perché?; **~ is that for?** a che cosa serve?; **~ is it?** (what do you want) cosa c'è?; **~ is it like?** com'è?; **~ is your name?** come ti chiami?; **~ is the weather like?** com'è il tempo?; **~ is the film about?** di cosa parla il film?; **~ is he talking about?** di cosa sta parlando?; **he asked me ~ she had said** mi ha chiesto cosa ha detto; **~ about going to the cinema?** e se andassimo al cinema?; **~ about the children?** (what will they do) e i bambini?; **~ if it rains?** e se piove? •adj quale, che; **take ~ books you want** prendi tutti i libri che vuoi; **~ kind of a** che tipo di; **at ~ time?** a che ora? •adv che; **~ a lovely day!** che bella giornata! •int **~!** [che] cosa!; **~?** [che] cosa?

what'ever adj qualunque •pron qualsiasi cosa; **~ is it?** cos'è?; **~ he does** qualsiasi cosa faccia; **~ happens** qualunque cosa succeda; **nothing ~** proprio niente

whatso'ever adj & pron = **whatever**

wheat /wiːt/ n grano m, frumento m

wheel /wiːl/ n ruota f; (steering) volante m; **at the ~** al volante •vt (push) spingere •vi (circle) ruotare; **~ [round]** ruotare

wheel: ~barrow n carriola f. **~chair** n sedia f a rotelle. **~-clamp** n ceppo m bloccaruote

wheeze /wiːz/ vi ansimare

when /wen/ adv & conj quando; **the day ~** il giorno in cui; **~ swimming/reading** nuotando/leggendo

when'ever adv & conj in qualsiasi momento; (every time that) ogni volta che; **~ did it happen?** quando è successo?

where /weə(r)/ adv & conj dove; **the street ~ I live** la via in cui abito; **~ do you come from?** da dove vieni?

whereabouts[1] /weərə'baʊts/ adv dove

'**whereabouts**[2] n **nobody knows his ~** nessuno sa dove si trova

where'as conj dal momento che; (in contrast) mentre

wher'ever adv & conj dovunque; **~ is he?** dov'è mai?; **~ possible** dovunque sia possibile

whet /wet/ vt (pt/pp **whetted**) aguzzare (appetite)

whether /'weðə(r)/ conj se; **~ you like it or not** che ti piaccia o no

which /wɪtʃ/ adj & pron quale; **~ one?** quale?; **~ one of you?** chi di voi?; **~ way?** (direction) in che direzione? •rel pron (object) che; **~ he does frequently** cosa che fa spesso; **after ~** dopo di che; **on/in ~** su/in cui

which'ever adj & pron qualunque; **~ it is** qualunque sia; **~ one of you** chiunque tra voi

while /waɪl/ n **a long ~** un bel po'; **a little ~** un po' •conj mentre; (as long as) finché; (although) sebbene **•while away** vt passare (time)

whilst /waɪlst/ conj see **while**

whim /wɪm/ n capriccio m

whimper /'wɪmpə(r)/ vi piagnucolare; (dog:) mugolare

whine /waɪn/ n lamento m; (of dog) guaito m •vi lamentarsi; (dog:) guaire

whip /wɪp/ n frusta f; (Pol: person) parlamentare mf incaricato, -a di assicurarsi della presenza dei membri del suo partito alle votazioni •vt (pt/pp **whipped**) frustare; (Culin) sbattere; (snatch) afferrare; (⊡: steal) fregare. □ **~ up** vt (incite) stimolare; ⊡ improvvisare (meal). **~ped 'cream** n panna f montata

whirl /wɜːl/ n (movement) rotazione f; **my mind's in a ~** ho le idee confuse •vi girare rapidamente •vt far girare rapidamente. **~pool** n vortice m. **~wind** n turbine m

whirr /wɜː(r)/ vi ronzare

whisk /wɪsk/ n (Culin) frullino m •vt

(Culin) frullare. ▫ ~ **away** vt portare via

whisker /'wɪskə(r)/ n ~**s** (of cat) baffi mpl; (on man's cheek) basette fpl; **by a ~** per un pelo

whisky /'wɪskɪ/ n whisky m inv

whisper /'wɪspə(r)/ n sussurro m; (rumour) diceria f •vt/i sussurrare

whistle /'wɪsl/ n fischio m; (instrument) fischietto m •vt fischiettare •vi fischiettare; (referee) fischiare

white /waɪt/ adj bianco; **go ~** (pale) sbiancare •n bianco m; (of egg) albume m; (person) bianco, -a mf

white: ~ 'coffee n caffè m inv macchiato. **~-'collar worker** n colletto m bianco

white 'lie n bugia f pietosa

whiten /'waɪtn/ vt imbiancare •vi sbiancare

'whitewash n intonaco m; fig copertura f •vt dare una mano d'intonaco a; fig coprire

Whitsun /'wɪtsn/ n Pentecoste f

who /hu:/ inter pron chi •rel pron che; **the children, ~ were all tired,...** i bambini, che erano tutti stanchi,...

who'ever pron chiunque; **~ he is** chiunque sia; **~ can that be?** chi può mai essere?

whole /həʊl/ adj tutto; (not broken) intatto; **the ~ truth** tutta la verità; **the ~ world** il mondo intero; **the ~ lot** (everything) tutto; (pl) tutti; **the ~ lot of you** tutti voi •n tutto m; **as a ~** nell'insieme; **on the ~** tutto considerato; **the ~ of Italy** tutta l'Italia

whole: ~-'hearted adj di tutto cuore. **~meal** adj integrale

'wholesale adj & adv all'ingrosso; fig in massa. **~r** n grossista mf

wholesome /'həʊlsəm/ adj sano

wholly /'həʊlɪ/ adv completamente

whom /hu:m/ rel pron che; **the man ~ I saw** l'uomo che ho visto; **to/with ~** a/con cui •inter pron chi; **to ~ did you speak?** con chi hai parlato?

whooping cough /'hu:pɪŋ/ n pertosse f

whore /hɔ:(r)/ n [!] puttana f

whose /hu:z/ rel pron il cui; **people ~ name begins with D** le persone i cui nomi cominciano con la D •inter pron di chi; **~ is that?** di chi è quello? •adj **~ car did you use?** di chi è la macchina che hai usato?

why /waɪ/ adv (inter) perché; **the reason ~** la ragione per cui; **that's ~** per questo •int diamine

wick /wɪk/ n stoppino m

wicked /'wɪkɪd/ adj cattivo; (mischievous) malizioso

wicker /'wɪkə(r)/ n vimini mpl •attrib di vimini

wide /waɪd/ adj largo; (experience, knowledge) vasto; (difference) profondo; (far from target) lontano; **10 cm ~** largo 10 cm; **how ~ is it?** quanto è largo? •adv (off target) lontano dal bersaglio; **~ awake** del tutto sveglio; **~ open** spalancato; **far and ~** in lungo e in largo. **~ly** adv largamente; (known, accepted) generalmente; (different) profondamente

widen /'waɪdn/ vt allargare •vi allargarsi

'widespread adj diffuso

widow /'wɪdəʊ/ n vedova f. **~ed** adj vedovo. **~er** n vedovo m

width /wɪdθ/ n larghezza f; (of material) altezza f

wield /wi:ld/ vt maneggiare; esercitare (power)

wife /waɪf/ n (pl **wives**) moglie f

wig /wɪg/ n parrucca f

wiggle /'wɪgl/ vi dimenarsi •vt dimenare

wild /waɪld/ adj selvaggio; (animal, flower) selvatico; (furious) furibondo; (applause) fragoroso; (idea) folle; (with joy) pazzo; (guess) azzardato; **be ~ about** (keen on) andare pazzo per •adv **run ~** crescere senza controllo •n **in the ~** allo stato naturale; **the ~s** pl le zone fpl sperdute

wilderness /'wɪldənɪs/ n deserto m; (fig: garden) giungla f

'wildfire n **spread like ~** allargarsi a macchia d'olio

wild: ~-'goose chase n ricerca f inutile. **~life** n animali mpl selvatici

will¹ /wɪl/ v aux **he ~ arrive tomorrow** arriverà domani; **I won't tell him** non glielo dirò; **you ~ be back soon, won't you?** tornerai presto, no?; **he ~ be there, won't he?** sarà là, no?; **she ~ be there by now** sarà là ormai; **~ you go?** (*do you intend to go*) pensi di andare?; **~ you go to the baker's and buy...?** puoi andare dal panettiere a comprare...?; **~ you be quiet!** vuoi stare calmo!; **~ you have some wine?** vuoi del vino?; **the engine won't start** la macchina non parte

will² n volontà f inv; (document) testamento m

willing /ˈwɪlɪŋ/ adj disposto; (eager) volonteroso. **~ly** adv volentieri. **~ness** n buona volontà f

willow /ˈwɪləʊ/ n salice m

will-power n forza f di volontà

wilt /wɪlt/ vi appassire

win /wɪn/ n vittoria f; **have a ~** riportare una vittoria •v (pt/pp **won**; pres p **winning**) •vt vincere; conquistare (fame) •vi vincere. ▫ **~ over** vt convincere

wince /wɪns/ vi contrarre il viso

winch /wɪntʃ/ n argano m

wind¹ /wɪnd/ n vento m; (breath) fiato m; (!: flatulence) aria f; **get/have the ~ up** ! aver fifa; **get ~ of** aver sentore di; **in the ~** nell'aria •vt **~ sb** lasciare qcno senza fiato

wind² /waɪnd/ v (pt/pp **wound**) •vt (wrap) avvolgere; (move by turning) far girare; (clock) caricare •vi (road:) serpeggiare. ▫ **~ up** vt caricare (clock); concludere (proceedings); ! prendere in giro (sb)

windfall /ˈwɪndfɔːl/ n fig fortuna f inaspettata

wind farm n centrale f eolica

winding /ˈwaɪndɪŋ/ adj tortuoso

wind: ~ instrument n strumento m a fiato. **~mill** n mulino m a vento

window /ˈwɪndəʊ/ n finestra f; (of car) finestrino m; (of shop) vetrina f

window: ~-box n cassetta f per i fiori. **~-sill** n davanzale m

windscreen n, Am **ˈwindshield** n parabrezza m inv. **~ washer** n getto m d'acqua. **~-wiper** n tergicristallo m

wine /waɪn/ n vino m

wine: ~glass n bicchiere m da vino. **~-list** n carta f dei vini

ˈwine-tasting n degustazione f di vini

wing /wɪŋ/ n ala f; (Auto) parafango m; **~s** pl (Theat) quinte fpl. **~er** n (Sport) ala f

wink /wɪŋk/ n strizzata f d'occhio; **not sleep a ~** non chiudere occhio •vi strizzare l'occhio; (light:) lampeggiare

winner /ˈwɪnə(r)/ n vincitore, -trice mf

wint|er /ˈwɪntə(r)/ n inverno m. **~ry** adj invernale

wipe /waɪp/ n passata f; (to dry) asciugata f •vt strofinare; (dry) asciugare. ▫ **~ off** vt asciugare; (erase) cancellare. ▫ **~ out** vt annientare; eliminare (village); estinguere (debt). ▫ **~ up** vt asciugare (dishes)

wire /ˈwaɪə(r)/ n fil m di ferro; (electrical) filo m elettrico

wiring /ˈwaɪərɪŋ/ n impianto m elettrico

wisdom /ˈwɪzdəm/ n saggezza f; (of action) sensatezza f. **~ tooth** n dente m del giudizio

wise /waɪz/ adj saggio; (prudent) sensato. **~ly** adv saggiamente; (act) sensatamente

wish /wɪʃ/ n desiderio m; **make a ~** esprimere un desiderio; **with best ~es** con i migliori auguri •vt desiderare; **~ sb well** fare tanti auguri a qcno; **I ~ you every success** ti auguro buona fortuna; **I ~ you could stay** vorrei che tu potessi rimanere •vi **~ for sth** desiderare qcsa. **~ful** adj **~ful thinking** illusione f

wistful /ˈwɪstfl/ adj malinconico

wit /wɪt/ n spirito m; (person) persona f di spirito; **be at one's ~s' end** non saper che pesci pigliare

W

witch /wɪtʃ/ n strega f. **~craft** n magia f. **~-hunt** n caccia f alle streghe

with /wɪð/ prep con; (fear, cold, jealousy etc) di; **I'm not ~ you** ! non ti seguo; **can I leave it ~ you?** (task) puoi occupartene tu?; **~ no regrets/money** senza rimpianti/ soldi; **be ~ it** [!] essere al passo coi tempi; (alert) essere concentrato

with'draw v (pt **-drew**, pp **-drawn**) • vt ritirare; prelevare (money) • vi ritirarsi. **~al** n ritiro m; (of money) prelevamento m; (from drugs) crisi f inv di astinenza; (Psych) chiusura f in se stessi. **~al symptoms** npl sintomi mpl da crisi di astinenza

with'drawn ▹**withdraw** • adj (person) chiuso in se stesso

wither /'wɪðə(r)/ vi (flower:) appassire

with'hold vt (pt/pp **-held**) rifiutare (consent) (**from** a); nascondere (information) (**from** a); trattenere (smile)

with'in prep in; (before the end of) entro; **~ the law** legale • adv all'interno

with'out prep senza; **~ stopping** senza fermarsi

with'stand vt (pt/pp **-stood**) resistere a

witness /'wɪtnɪs/ n testimone mf • vt autenticare (signature); essere testimone di (accident). **~-box** n, Am **~-stand** n banco m dei testimoni

witticism /'wɪtɪsɪzm/ n spiritosaggine f

witty /'wɪtɪ/ adj (**-ier, -iest**) spiritoso

wives /waɪvz/ ▹**wife**

wizard /'wɪzəd/ n mago m. **~ry** n stregoneria f

wobb|le /'wɒbl/ vi traballare. **~ly** adj traballante

woe /wəʊ/ n afflizione f

woke, woken /wəʊk/, /'wəʊkn/ ▹**wake**[1]

wolf /wʊlf/ n (pl **wolves** /wʊlvz/) lupo m; ([!]: womanizer) donnaiolo m • vt **~ [down]** divorare. **~ whistle** n fischio m • vi **~-whistle at sb** fischiare dietro a qcno

woman /'wʊmən/ n (pl **women**) donna f. **~izer** n donnaiolo m. **~ly** adj femmineo

womb /wu:m/ n utero m

women /'wɪmɪn/ ▹**woman**. **W~'s Libber** n femminista f. **W~'s Liberation** n movimento m femminista

won /wʌn/ ▹**win**

wonder /'wʌndə(r)/ n meraviglia f; (surprise) stupore m; **no ~!** non c'è da stupirsi!; **it's a ~ that...** è incredibile che... • vi restare in ammirazione; (be surprised) essere sorpreso; **I ~** è quello che mi chiedo; **I ~ whether she is ill** mi chiedo se è malata?. **~ful** adj meraviglioso. **~fully** adv meravigliosamente

wood /wʊd/ n legno m; (for burning) legna f; (forest) bosco m; **out of the ~** fig fuori pericolo; **touch ~!** tocc ferro!

wood: ~ed /-ɪd/ adj boscoso. **~en** adj di legno; fig legnoso. **~ wind** n strumenti mpl a fiato. **~work** n (wooden parts) parti fpl in legno; (craft falegnameria f. **~worm** n tarlo m. **~y** adj legnoso; (hill) boscoso

wool /wʊl/ n lana f • attrib di lana. **~len** adj di lana. **~lens** npl capi mpl di lana

woolly /'wʊlɪ/ adj (**-ier, -iest**) (sweate di lana; fig confuso

word /wɜ:d/ n parola f; (news) notizi f; **by ~ of mouth** a viva voce; **have a ~ with** dire due parole a; **have ~s** bisticciare; **in other ~s** in altre parole. **~ing** n parole fpl. **~ processor** n programma m di videoscrittura, word processor m in

wore /wɔ:(r)/ ▹**wear**

work /wɜ:k/ n lavoro m; (of art) opera f; **~s** pl (factory) fabbrica fsg; (mechanism) meccanismo msg; **at ~** a lavoro; **out of ~** disoccupato • vi lavorare; (machine, ruse:) funzionare; (study) studiare • vt far funzionare (machine); far lavorare (employee); far studiare (student). □ **~ off** vt sfogare (anger); lavorare per estinguere (debt); fare sport per smaltire (weight). □ **~ out** vt elaborare (plan); risolvere (problem); calcolare (bill); **I ~ed out how he did it** ho capito come l'ha fatto • vi evolvere. □ **~ up** vt **I've ~ed up an appetite** mi è venuto appetito; **don't get ~ed up** (anxious) non farti prendere dal panico; (angry) non arrabbiarti

vorkable /ˈwɜːkəbl/ adj (feasible) fattibile

vorker /ˈwɜːkə(r)/ n lavoratore, -trice mf; (manual) operaio, -a mf

vorking /ˈwɜːkɪŋ/ adj (clothes etc) da lavoro; (day) feriale; **in ~ order** funzionante. **~ class** n classe f operaia. **~-class** adj operaio

vork: ~man n operaio m. **~manship** n lavorazione f. **~shop** n officina f; (discussion) dibattito m

vorld /wɜːld/ n mondo m; **a ~ of difference** una differenza abissale; **out of this ~** favoloso; **think the ~ of sb** andare matto per qcno. **~ly** adj materiale; (person) materialista. **~-ˈwide** adj mondiale • adv mondialmente

vorm /wɜːm/ n verme m • vt **~ one's way into sb's confidence** conquistarsi la fiducia di qcno in modo subdolo. **~-eaten** adj tarlato

vorn /wɔːn/ ▹**wear** • adj sciupato. **~-out** adj consumato; (person) sfinito

vorried /ˈwʌrɪd/ adj preoccupato

vorr|y /ˈwʌrɪ/ n preoccupazione f • v (pt/pp **worried**) • vt preoccupare; (bother) disturbare • vi preoccuparsi. **~ing** adj preoccupante

vorse /wɜːs/ adj peggiore • adv peggio • n peggio m

vorsen /ˈwɜːsn/ vt/i peggiorare

vorship /ˈwɜːʃɪp/ n culto m; (service) funzione f; **Your/His W~** (to judge) signor giudice/il giudice • v (pt/pp **-shipped**) • vt venerare • vi andare a messa

vorst /wɜːst/ adj peggiore • adv peggio [di tutti] • n **the ~** il peggio; **get the ~ of it** avere la peggio; **if the ~ comes to the ~** nella peggiore delle ipotesi

vorth /wɜːθ/ n valore m; **£10 ~ of petrol** 10 sterline di benzina • adj **be ~** valere; **be ~ it** fig valerne la pena; **it's ~ trying** vale la pena di provare; **it's ~ my while** mi conviene. **~less** adj senza valore. **~while** adj che vale la pena; (cause) lodevole

vorthy /ˈwɜːðɪ/ adj degno; (cause, motive) lodevole

would /wʊd/ v aux **I ~ do it** lo farei; **~ you go?** andresti?; **~ you mind if I opened the window?** ti dispiace se apro la finestra?; **he ~ come if he could** verrebbe se potesse; **he said he ~n't** ha detto di no; **~ you like a drink?** vuoi qualcosa da bere?; **what ~ you like to drink?** cosa prendi da bere?; **you ~n't, ~ you?** non lo faresti, vero?

wound¹ /wuːnd/ n ferita f • vt ferire

wound² /waʊnd/ ▹**wind²**

wrangle /ˈræŋgl/ n litigio m • vi litigare

wrap /ræp/ n (shawl) scialle m • vt (pt/pp **wrapped**) **~ [up]** avvolgere; (present) incartare; **be ~ped up in** fig essere completamente preso da • vi **~ up warmly** coprirsi bene. **~per** n (for sweet) carta f [di caramella]. **~ping** n materiale m da imballaggio. **~ping paper** n carta f da pacchi; (for gift) carta f da regalo

wrath /rɒθ/ n ira f

wreak /riːk/ vt **~ havoc with sth** scombussolare qcsa

wreath /riːθ/ n (pl **~s** /-ðz/) corona f

wreck /rek/ n (of ship) relitto m; (of car) carcassa f; (person) rottame m • vt far naufragare; demolire (car). **~age** n rottami mpl; fig brandelli mpl

wrench /rentʃ/ n (injury) slogatura f; (tool) chiave f inglese; (pull) strattone m • vt (pull) strappare; slogarsi (wrist, ankle etc)

wrestl|e /ˈresl/ vi lottare corpo a corpo; fig lottare. **~er** n lottatore, -trice mf. **~ing** n lotta f libera; (all-in) catch m

wretch /retʃ/ n disgraziato, -a mf. **~ed** adj odioso; (weather) orribile; **feel ~ed** (unhappy) essere triste; (ill) sentirsi malissimo

wriggle /ˈrɪgl/ n contorsione f • vi contorcersi; (move forward) strisciare; **~ out of sth** [!] sottrarsi a qcsa

wring /rɪŋ/ vt (pt/pp **wrung**) torcere (sb's neck); strizzare (clothes); **~ one's hands** torcersi le mani; **~ing wet** inzuppato

wrinkle /ˈrɪŋkl/ n grinza f; (on skin) ruga f • vt/i raggrinzire. **~d** adj (skin, face) rugoso; (clothes) raggrinzito

wrist /rɪst/ n polso m. **~-watch** n orologio m da polso
writ /rɪt/ n (Jur) mandato m
write /raɪt/ vt/i (pt **wrote**, pp **written**, pres p **writing**) scrivere. □ **~ down** vt annotare. □ **~ off** vt cancellare (debt); distruggere (car)
'**write-off** n (car) rottame m
writer /'raɪtə(r)/ n autore, -trice mf; **she's a ~** è una scrittrice
writhe /raɪð/ vi contorcersi
writing /'raɪtɪŋ/ n (occupation) scrivere m; (words) scritte fpl; (handwriting) scrittura f; **in ~** per iscritto. **~-paper** n carta f da lettera
written /'rɪtn/ ▸**write**
wrong /rɒŋ/ adj sbagliato; **be ~** (person:) sbagliare; **what's ~?** cosa c'è che non va? • adv (spelt) in modo sbagliato; **go ~** (person:) sbagliare; (machine:) funzionare male; (plan:) andar male • n ingiustizia f; **in the ~** dalla parte del torto; **know right from ~** distinguere il bene dal male • vt fare torto a. **~ful** adj ingiusto. **~ly** adv in modo sbagliato (accuse, imagine) a torto; (informed) male
wrote /rəʊt/ ▸**write**
wrought'iron /rɔ:t-/ n ferro m battuto • attrib di ferro battuto
wrung /rʌŋ/ ▸**wring**
wry /raɪ/ adj (**-er, -est**) (humour, smile) beffardo

Xmas /'krɪsməs/ n [!] Natale m
'**X-ray** n (picture) radiografia f; **have an ~** farsi fare una radiografia • vt passare ai raggi X

yacht /jɒt/ n yacht m inv; (for racing) barca f a vela. **~ing** n vela f
yank /jæŋk/ vt [!] tirare
Yank n [!] americano, -a mf
yap /jæp/ vi (pt/pp **yapped**) (dog:) guaire
yard¹ /jɑ:d/ n cortile m; (for storage) deposito m
yard² n iarda f (= 91,44 cm). **~stick** n fig pietra f di paragone
yarn /jɑ:n/ n filo m; ([!]: tale) storia f
yawn /jɔ:n/ n sbadiglio m • vi sbadigliare. **~ing** adj **~ing gap** sbadiglio m
yeah /jeə/ adv sì
year /jɪə(r)/ n anno m; (of wine) annata f; **for ~s** [!] da secoli. **~-book** n annuario m. **~ly** adj annuale • adv annualmente
yearn /jɜ:n/ vi struggersi. **~ing** n desiderio m struggente
yeast /ji:st/ n lievito m
yell /jel/ n urlo m • vi urlare
yellow /'jeləʊ/ adj & n giallo m

elp /jelp/ n (of dog) guaito m •vi (dog:) guaire

es /jes/ adv sì •n sì m inv

esterday /'jestədeɪ/ adj & adv ieri m inv; **~'s paper** il giornale di ieri; **the day before ~** l'altroieri

et /jet/ adv ancora; **as ~** fino ad ora; **not ~** non ancora; **the best ~** il migliore finora •conj eppure

ield /ji:ld/ n produzione f; (profit) reddito m •vt produrre; fruttare (profit) •vi cedere; Am (Auto) dare la precedenza

oga /'jəʊgə/ n yoga m

oghurt /'jɒgət/ n yogurt m inv

oke /jəʊk/ n giogo m; (of garment) carré m inv

okel /'jəʊkl/ n zotico, -a mf

olk /jəʊk/ n tuorlo m

you /ju:/ pron (*subject*) tu, voi pl; (*formal*) lei, voi pl; (*direct/indirect object*) ti, vi pl; (*formal: direct object*) la; (*formal: indirect object*) le; (*after* prep) te, voi pl; (*formal: after* prep) lei;

> **!** **tu** is used when speaking to friends, children and animals. **lei** is used to speak to someone you do not know. **voi** is used to speak to more than one person. Note that *you* is often not translated when it is the subject of the sentence

~ are very kind (sg) sei molto gentile; (*formal*) è molto gentile; (pl & formal pl) siete molto gentili; **~ can stay, but he has to go** (sg) tu puoi rimanere, ma lui deve andarsene; (pl) voi potete rimanere, ma lui deve andarsene; **all of ~** tutti voi; **I'll give ~ the money** (sg) ti darò i soldi; (pl) vi darò i soldi; **I'll give it to ~** (sg) te/(pl) ve lo darò; **it was ~!** (sg) eri tu!; (pl) eravate voi!; **~ have to be careful** (*one*) si deve fare attenzione

young /jʌŋ/ adj giovane •npl (animals) piccoli mpl; **the ~** (people) i giovani mpl. **~ lady** n signorina f. **~ man** n giovanotto. **~ster** n ragazzo, -a mf; (child) bambino, -a mf

your /jɔ:(r)/ adj il tuo m, la tua f, i tuoi mpl, le tue fpl; (formal) il suo m, la sua f, i suoi mpl, le sue fpl; (pl & formal pl) il vostro m, la vostra f, i vostri mpl, le vostre fpl; **~ mother/father** tua madre/tuo padre; (formal) sua madre/suo padre; (pl & formal pl) vostra madre/vostro padre

yours /jɔ:z/ poss pron il tuo m, la tua f, i tuoi mpl, le tue fpl; (formal) il suo m, la sua f, i suoi mpl, le sue fpl; (pl & formal pl) il vostro m, la vostra f, i vostri mpl, le vostre fpl; **a friend of ~** un tuo/suo/vostro amico; **friends of ~** dei tuoi/vostri/suoi amici; **that is ~** quello è tuo/vostro/suo; (as opposed to mine) quello è il tuo/il vostro/il suo

your'self pron (reflexive) ti; (formal) si; (emphatic) te stesso; (formal) sé, se stesso; **do pour ~ a drink** versati da bere; (formal) si versi da bere; **you said so ~** lo hai detto tu stesso; (formal) lo ha detto lei stesso; **you can be proud of ~** puoi/può essere fiero di te/di sé; **by ~** da solo

your'selves pron (reflexive) vi; (emphatic) voi stessi; **do pour ~ a drink** versatevi da bere; **you said so ~** lo avete detto voi stessi; **you can be proud of ~** potete essere fieri di voi; **by ~** da soli

youth /ju:θ/ n (pl **youths** /-ðːz/) gioventù f inv; (boy) giovanetto m; **the ~** (young people) i giovani mpl. **~ful** adj giovanile. **~ hostel** n ostello m [della gioventù]

Yugoslav /'ju:gəslɑ:v/ adj & n jugoslavo, -a mf

Yugoslavia /-'slɑ:vɪə/ n Jugoslavia f

Zz

zeal /zi:l/ n zelo m

zealous /'zeləs/ adj zelante. ~**ly** adv con zelo

zebra /'zebrə/ n zebra f. ~-'**crossing** n passaggio m pedonale, zebre fpl

zero /'zɪərəʊ/ n zero m

zest /zest/ n gusto m

zigzag /'zɪgzæg/ n zigzag m inv •vi (pt/pp **-zagged**) zigzagare

zilch /zɪltʃ/ n [!] zero m assoluto

zinc /zɪŋk/ n zinco m

zip /zɪp/ n ~ [**fastener**] cerniera f [lampo] •vt (pt/pp **zipped**) ~ [**up**] chiudere con la cerniera [lampo]

'**Zip code** n Am codice m postale

zipper /'zɪpə(r)/ n Am cerniera f [lampo]

zodiac /'zəʊdɪæk/ n zodiaco m

zombie /'zɒmbɪ/ n [!] zombi mf inv

zone /zəʊn/ n zona f

zoo /zu:/ n zoo m inv

zoolog|ist /zəʊ'ɒlədʒɪst/ n zoologo, -a mf. ~**y** zoologia f

zoom /zu:m/ vi sfrecciare. ~ **lens** n zoom m inv

Grammar and Verbs

Summary of Italian grammar

Nouns

Gender

All Italian nouns are either masculine or feminine. As a general rule, nouns ending in **-o** are usually masculine.

il ragazzo *boy* **un treno** *train* **un albero** *tree*
lo sbaglio *mistake* **l'amico** *friend* **uno specchio** *mirror*

Nouns ending in **-a** are usually feminine.

la ragazza *girl* **una sorella** *sister* **un'amica** *friend*
l'arancia *orange* **la scuola** *school* **una zia** *aunt*

Nouns ending in **-e** can be either masculine or feminine.

il nome *name* **la stazione** *station*
una ragione *reason* **un giornale** *newspaper*

Plural forms

Masculine nouns ending in **-o** change to **-i** in the plural:

i ragazzi *boys* **gli amici** *friends* **gli sbagli** *mistakes*

Feminine nouns ending in **-a** change to **-e**:

le ragazze *girls* **le scuole** *schools* **le amiche** *friends*

All nouns ending in **-e** change to **-i**:

i genitori *parents* **le stazioni** *stations*

Nouns ending in accented vowels do not change in the plural.

il caffè *coffee* **i caffè** *coffees*
la città *city* **le città** *cities*
la virtù *virtue* **le virtù** *virtues*

Nouns ending in a consonant (imported from other languages) do not change in the plural.

il computer **i computer**
lo sport **gli sport**
l'autobus **gli autobus**

The definite article

Masculine forms before:

	singular	plural	
most consonants	**il**	**i**	**il treno**, **i treni**
a, e, i, o, u	**l'**	**gli**	**l'albero**, **gli alberi**
gn, ps, z, s+consonant	**lo**	**gli**	**lo studente**, **gli studenti**

Feminine forms before:

	singular	plural	
any consonant	**la**	**le**	**la camera**, **le camere**
a, e, i, o, u	**l'**	**le**	**l'arancia**, **le arance**

The indefinite article

Masculine forms before:

	singular	
vowel or most consonants	**un**	**un ombrello**, **un caffè**
gn, ps, z, s+consonant	**uno**	**uno zoo**

Feminine forms before:

	singular	
any consonant	**una**	**una stanza**
a, e, i, o, u	**un'**	**un'aspirina**

Adjectives

Adjectives agree in number and gender with the noun to which they refer. Italian adjectives end in either **-o** or **-e**.

	singular	plural	
masculine	**pigr*o***	**pigr*i***	*lazy*
	felice	**felic*i***	*happy*

	singular	plural	
feminine	**pigr*a***	**pigr*e***	*lazy*
	felice	**felic*i***	*happy*

When you have a mixture of masculine and feminine nouns, the adjective ending is masculine.

Max e Anna sono **pigri**/**gentili**.
Max and Anna are lazy/kind.

Position

Adjectives are usually placed after the noun they describe.

Ho letto **un libro interessante**.
I've read an interesting book.

There are, however, a few common adjectives, such as **bello**, **brutto**, **buono**, **cattivo**, **piccolo**, **grande**, **giovane**, **vecchio**, **nuovo**, which can be placed before the noun.

Ho visto **un bel film**.
I have seen a lovely film.

Possessive adjectives

In Italian, the possessive adjective agrees in gender and number with what is possessed and not with the possessor. The possessive adjective is generally preceded by the definite article: **il mio ufficio**.

	singular	
	masculine	feminine
my	**il mio**	**la mia**
your [informal]	**il tuo**	**la tua**
his/her; your [formal]	**il suo**	**la sua**
our	**il nostro**	**la nostra**
your [plural]	**il vostro**	**la vostra**
their	**il loro**	**la loro**

	plural	
	masculine	feminine
my	**i miei**	**le mie**
your [informal]	**i tuoi**	**le tue**
his/her; your [formal]	**i suoi**	**le sue**
our	**i nostri**	**le nostre**
your [plural]	**i vostri**	**le vostre**
their	**i loro**	**le loro**

Except with **loro**, the definite article is dropped when the noun refers to single immediate family members – **mia sorella**, **tuo fratello**, but **le mie sorelle**, **i tuoi fratelli**; **la loro sorella**, **i loro fratelli**.

Questo and *quello*

Questo and **quello** can be used both as adjectives ('this'/'that') and pronouns ('this one'/'that one'). **Questo** takes the usual adjective endings (**-o/-a/-i/-e**) whether it is used as an adjective or a pronoun. **Quello** also takes these endings when used as a pronoun; however, when it comes before a noun, it takes the same endings as the definite article.

singular	**quel, quello, quell', quella**	**quella casa quell'amico**
plural	**quei, quegli, quelle**	**quegli amici quelle case**

Subject pronouns

In Italian, subject pronouns are generally omitted (unless you want to place emphasis on them): the subject is shown in the verb ending.

io	I	**noi**	we
tu	you [informal]	**voi**	you [plural]
lui	he	**loro**	they
lei	she		
lei	you [formal]		

The **tu** form is used when speaking to a child or someone you know well; the **lei** form when speaking to an adult you don't know well.

Object pronouns

Direct object pronouns

mi	me	**ci**	us
ti	you	**vi**	you
lo	him/it [m]	**li**	them [m]
la	her/it [f]	**le**	them [f]
la	you [formal]		

Indirect object pronouns

mi	to (etc.) me	**ci**	to us
ti	to you	**vi**	to you
gli	to him/to it [m]	**gli**	to them [m/f]
le	to her/to it [f]		
le	to you [formal]		

Indirect object pronouns are used with verbs which are normally followed by a preposition, such as **telefonare a** ('to telephone') and **dare a** ('to give to').

Anna telefona a Maria. Anna **le** telefona.
Anna telefona a Mario. Anna **gli** telefona.

The position of direct and indirect object pronouns

Both direct and indirect object pronouns come before the verb (or before **avere/essere** in the perfect tense). When both appear in a sentence, the indirect comes before the direct pronoun: the indirect pronoun may also change form (see below).

Ti offro un caffè.
I'll buy you a coffee.

Le scrivo domani.
I'll write to her tomorrow.

Mi piacciono quegli stivali. **Li** compro!
I like those boots. I'll buy them!

Me lo avete comprato.
You bought it for me.

When there are two verbs, and the second is an infinitive, the pronoun comes either before the first verb or combines with the infinitive.

Ti vorrei incontrare.
I'd like to meet you.

Vorrei incontrar**ti**.
I'd like to meet you.

Before a direct object pronoun, the indirect object pronouns **mi**, **ti**, **ci**, and **vi** change respectively to **me**, **te**, **ce**, and **ve**.

Ti abbiamo già dato il libro.
We have already given the book to you.

Te lo abbiamo già dato.
We have already given it to you.

Vi mando la lettera domani.
I'll send the letter to you tomorrow.

Ve la mando domani.
I'll send it to you tomorrow.

The third person indirect pronouns – **le** and **gli** – change to **glie-** and combine with **lo, la**, **li**, and **le** to form one word.

Mando un biglietto d'auguri ai nonni. **Glielo** mando.
I'll send a card to our grandparents.
I'll send it to them.

These forms come before the verb or can be joined to an infinitive.

Glielo dovrei dare.
I should give it to him/her/them.

Dovrei dar**glielo**.
I should give it to him/her/them.

Disjunctive pronouns

me	me	**noi**	us
te	you [informal]	**voi**	you [plural]
lui	him	**loro**	them
lei	her		
lei	you [formal]		

Disjunctive pronouns are used for emphasis and after prepositions, such as **di**, **a**, **da**, **con**, etc.:

Conosco **lui**.
I know him.

Lo fa per **me**.
He does it for me.

Mario gioca con **noi**.
Mario plays with us.

Viene con **te**?
Is he coming with you?

Possessive pronouns

These have the same form as the possessive adjectives.

Questa è la mia bicicletta.
That's my bike.

E quella è **la mia**.
And that's mine.

The definite article is used with family members in the singular.

Mia nonna abita a Roma.
My grandmother lives in Rome.

La mia abita a Napoli.
Mine lives in Naples.

Demonstratives

ci

ci is also used to refer to location. It is used to mean 'here' or 'there', although in some instances its meaning in English is understood rather than translated. It usually comes before the verb.

Siete mai stati a Parigi? Sì, **ci** siamo andati molte volte.
Have you ever been to Paris? Yes, we've been there many times.

Quando andate a Roma? **Ci** andiamo venerdì.
When are you going to Rome? We're going (there) on Friday.

ne

ne can mean *'of it/him/her'*, *'about it/him/her'*, etc., or *'of them'*, *'about them'*, etc. In some instances it isn't translated, but it must be included.

Vorrei delle banane.
I would like some bananas.

Quante **ne** vuole?
How many (of them) do you want?

Maria parlerà delle sue vacanze.
Maria will talk about her holidays.

Maria **ne** parlerà.
Maria will talk about them.

Prepositions

In addition to the general meanings of the prepositions the following uses are particularly worth noting.

a with cities

Abito **a** Parma.
I live in Parma.

Vado **a** Parigi.
I am going to Paris.

in with countries and regions

Vivono **in** Italia/**in** Toscana.
They live in Italy/in Tuscany.

di to express possession

la mamma **di** Federica.
Federica's mum

da + name of a person means 'to or at their house, shop, etc.'

Vai **da** Paola?
Are you going to Paola's?

Andate **dal** giornalaio?
Are you going to the newsagent's?

Sei già stato **dal** dentista?
Have you already been to the dentist's?

da + present tense to describe an action which began in the past and which continues in the present ('for', 'since')

È malato **da** due giorni.
He has been ill for two days.

Lavorano qui **dal** 1975.
They have worked here since 1975.

Prepositions and articles

When the prepositions **a** ('to'), **da** ('from'), **di** ('of'), **in** ('in'), and **su** ('on') are followed by the definite article, the words combine as follows.

	singular				plural		
	il	lo	l'	la	i	gli	le
a	**al**	**allo**	**all'**	**alla**	**ai**	**agli**	**alle**
da	**dal**	**dallo**	**dall'**	**dalla**	**dai**	**dagli**	**dalle**
di	**del**	**dello**	**dell'**	**della**	**dei**	**degli**	**delle**
in	**nel**	**nello**	**nell'**	**nella**	**nei**	**negli**	**nelle**
su	**sul**	**sullo**	**sull'**	**sulla**	**sui**	**sugli**	**sulle**

La sveglia è **sul** comodino.
The alarm clock is on the bedside cabinet.

I pantaloni sono **nell'**armadio.
The trousers are in the wardrobe.

Adverbs

Regular adverbs

Most adverbs are formed by adding **-mente** to the feminine form of the adjective.

lento *slow* **lenta*mente*** *slowly*
vero *true* **vera*mente*** *truly*

Adjectives ending in **-e** in the singular simply add **-mente**.

triste *sad* **triste*mente*** *sadly*
semplice *simple* **semplice*mente*** *simply*

However, if the adjective ends in **-re** or **-le**, the **-e** is dropped:

normale *normal* **normalmente** *normally*
regolare *regular* **regolarmente** *regularly*

The comparative and superlative

Comparative

più ... di	Lui è **più** giovane **di** lei. *He is younger than she is.*
meno ... di	Lui è **meno** vivace **di** lei. *He is less lively than she is.*
(tanto) ... quanto/come	Lui è alto **quanto** lei. *He's as tall as she is.*

Superlative

To say 'the most ...' in Italian is **il** / **la** / **i / le più**; 'the least ...' is **il / la / i / le meno**.

Mara è **la più** giovane.
Mara is the youngest.

Franco è **il più** alto.
Franco is the tallest.

After a superlative 'in' is translated by **di**.

È **la ragazza più** intelligente **della** classe.
She is the cleverest girl in her class.

È **l'albergo più** costoso **di** Venezia.
It is the most expensive hotel in Venice.

Irregular forms

Some adjectives have two different forms of the comparative and superlative. The distinctions in meaning are slight and best learnt in context.

	singular	plural
buono (good)	**più buono / migliore**	**il/la più buono / a il/la migliore**
cattivo (bad)	**più cattivo / peggiore**	**il/la più cattivo / a il/la peggiore**

Expressing quantities

di + *article*

Ordino **del** vino?
Shall I order some wine?

Preferisco **dell'**acqua.
I'd prefer some water.

Compra **dei** pomodori.
Buy some tomatoes.

Hai **delle** aspirine?
Do you have any aspirins®?

qualche

qualche is always followed by a singular noun.

Ho **qualche amico** a Roma.
I have some friends in Rome.

Asking questions

There are two ways of asking questions: (a) you keep the same wording as the sentence, but use a rising intonation; (b) you use a question word – then the verb and the subject change places.

È inglese?	**Dove lavora Roberta?**
Are you English?	*Where does Roberta work?*

Negatives

To make a sentence negative, you simply put **non** in front of the verb.

Sono americano.	**Non sono** americano.
I'm American.	*I'm not American.*

Numbers

1 **uno**
2 **due**
3 **tre**
4 **quattro**
5 **cinque**
6 **sei**
7 **sette**
8 **otto**
9 **nove**
10 **dieci**
11 **undici**
12 **dodici**
13 **tredici**
14 **quattordici**
15 **quindici**
16 **sedici**
17 **diciassette**
18 **diciotto**
19 **diciannove**
20 **venti**
21 **ventuno**
22 **ventidue**
23 **ventitré**
30 **trenta**
40 **quaranta**
50 **cinquanta**
60 **sessanta**
70 **settanta**
71 **settantuno**
72 **settantadue**
73 **settantatré**
74 **settantaquattro**, etc.
80 **ottanta**
81 **ottantuno**
82 **ottantadue**, etc.
90 **novanta**
91 **novantuno**
92 **novantadue**, etc.
100 **cento**
101 **centouno**
102 **centodue**
200 **duecento**
202 **duecentodue**
999 **novecentonovantanove**
1000 **mille**
2000 **duemila**
2001 **duemilauno**

Verbs

The infinitive

Dictionaries and glossaries usually list verbs in the infinitive form, which in Italian has three different endings: **-are, -ere**, or **-ire** (apart from a few irregular forms in **-rre**). Regular verbs within each group take the same endings.

Reflexive verbs

Reflexive verbs can easily be identified by the additional **si** which appears at the end of the infinitive (**chiamars*i***): they end in **-arsi**, **-ersi**, or **-irsi**, taking the endings for **-are**, **-ere**, and **-ire** verbs respectively. They just add the reflexive pronouns **mi**, **ti**, **si**, **ci**, **vi**, and **si** in front of the verb.

	alzars*i* – to get up	**divertirs*i*** – to enjoy oneself
(io)	***mi* alzo**	***mi* diverto**
(tu)	***ti* alzi**	***ti* diverti**
(lui/lei)	***si* alza**	***si* diverte**
(noi)	***ci* alziamo**	***ci* divertiamo**
(voi)	***vi* alzate**	***vi* divertite**
(loro)	***si* alzano**	***si* divertono**

Non **si alzano** mai prima delle otto.
They never get up before eight.

Si divertirà senz'altro.
He will definitely enjoy himself.

The imperative

The imperative is used to give orders, instructions, and advice. Irregular imperative forms are covered in the verb tables on pages 616–624.

The ***tu*** form of the imperative is used to address children or people you know well. The ***voi*** form is used to address a group of people. Except for the ***tu*** form of the **-are** verbs, the other forms are the same as the ***tu*** form of the present tense.

	parlare	**credere**	**sentire**	**finire**
(tu)	**parl*a***	**credi**	**senti**	**finisci**
(voi)	**parlate**	**credete**	**sentite**	**finite**

The imperative also has a ***noi*** form, translated 'let's …'. This is the same as the ***noi*** form of the present tense.

	parlare	**credere**	**sentire**	**finire**
(noi)	**parliamo**	**crediamo**	**sentiamo**	**finiamo**

The ***lei*** form of the imperative is used with adults you don't know.

	parlare	**credere**	**sentire**	**finire**
(lei)	**parli**	**creda**	**senta**	**finisca**

The imperative and object pronouns

Direct and indirect object pronouns come *before the **lei** imperative*.

La guardi meglio. È tutta sporca!
Look at it more closely. It's all dirty!

Non **lo ascolti**! Scherza.
Don't listen to him. He's joking.

However, they are added to the *end of the **tu**, **voi**, and **noi** imperatives*.

Telefonate**gli** al più presto.
Ring him very soon.

Alziamoci alle sette.
Let's get up at seven o'clock.

Non parliamo**ne** più.
Let's not speak about it any more.

When you add a pronoun to the ***tu*** imperative forms of **andare**, **fare**, **dare**, **dire**, and **stare**, the first letter of the pronoun is doubled. The only exception to this is **gli**.

Di*mmi* la verità!
Tell me the truth!

Da***lle*** questo.
Give her this.

Digli che arrivo domani.
Tell him I'll be arriving tomorrow.

The negative imperative

tu form	**non** + infinitive	**Non fumare**, per favore. *Please don't smoke.*
other forms	**non** + imperative	**Non fumate**, per favore. *Please don't smoke.*

In the negative, object pronouns come *before the **lei** imperative*.

Non **lo** dica!
Don't say it!

They can either come before the ***tu***, ***voi***, and ***noi*** imperatives or be added on to the end of it. In the negative **tu** form, the final **-e** of the infinitive is dropped when an object pronoun is added on.

Non **dirlo**!/Non **lo dire**!
Don't say it!

The present tense

The single present tense in Italian has a wider use than its English equivalent: **io lavoro** can be translated as either 'I work' or 'I am working', according to context. Besides expressing actions which relate to the immediate present, it can also be used to express:

– actions which are done regularly

Ogni mattina **faccio** una passeggiata.
Every morning I go for a walk.

– actions which relate to a future intention.

Fra un mese **andiamo** in Spagna.
In a month we're going to Spain.

For the forms of the present tense, see the verb tables on pages 616–624.

The progressive forms

The progressive forms are used to say what is or was happening at the moment of speaking. These forms are less common in Italian than in English, because it is perfectly normal to use the simple present tense to convey the same idea.

The progressives are formed by combining the verb **stare** with the gerund, the form of the verb which ends with **-ando** or **-endo**. The present tense and the imperfect tense of **stare** are used respectively to talk about the present and the past.

parlare	prendere	dormire
sto/ stavo parlando	**sto/ stavo prendendo**	**sto/ stavo dormendo**
stai/ stavi parlando	**stai/ stavi prendendo**	**stai/ stavi dormendo**
sta/ stava parlando	**sta/ stava prendendo**	**sta/ stava dormendo**
stiamo/ stavamo parlando	**stiamo/ stavamo prendendo**	**stiamo/ stavamo dormendo**
state/ stavate parlando	**state/ stavate prendendo**	**state/ stavate dormendo**
stanno/ stavano parlando	**stanno/ stavano prendendo**	**stanno/ stavano dormendo**

Sta piovendo.
It is raining.

Che **stavi facendo**?
What were you doing?

The perfect tense

The perfect tense is used to describe a single completed event or action which took place in the past. It can be translated in one of two ways, depending on the context: for example, **ho parlato** can mean either 'I spoke' or 'I have spoken'. It is formed with the present tense of **avere** or **essere** + the past participle of the verb required. For regular verbs this is formed as follows: **-are** verbs → **-ato**, **-ere** verbs → **-uto**, and **-ire** verbs → **-ito**.

parl*ato* **cred*uto*** **sent*ito***

With *avere*

Most transitive verbs form the perfect tense with **avere**.

Ho mangiato troppo.
I've eaten too much.

Non **ha avuto** molta fortuna.
She didn't have much luck.

When **avere** is used, the past participle must agree with any direct object which comes before the verb. Note that **lo** and **la** shorten to **l'**; **li** and **le** don't.

Ho comprato una macchina. **L'**ho comprat**a** ieri.
I bought a car. I bought it yesterday.

Hai visto Maria e Carla? Sì, **le** ho vist**e** ieri.
Did you see Maria and Carla? Yes, I saw them yesterday.

With *essere*

Most intransitive verbs, all reflexive verbs, and a few others (such as **essere**, **piacere**, **sembrare**, etc.) form the perfect tense with **essere**. When this happens, the past participle acts like an adjective: it agrees with the subject in gender and number.

Maria **è andat***a* a Roma molte volte.
Maria has been to Rome many times.

Ci siamo annoiat*i* molto.
We got really bored.

La serata **è stat***a* veramente piacevole.
The evening was very pleasant.

Irregular past participles

* indicates a verb forming the perfect with **essere**

infinitive	past participle	infinitive	past participle
aprire (to open)	**aperto**	**piacere*** (to please)	**piaciuto**
bere (to drink)	**bevuto**	**prendere** (to take)	**preso**
chiedere (to ask)	**chiesto**	**rimanere*** (to stay)	**rimasto**
chiudere (to close)	**chiuso**	**scegliere** (to choose)	**scelto**
crescere* (to grow)	**cresciuto**	**scrivere** (to write)	**scritto**
decidere (to decide)	**deciso**	**stare*** (to stay, to be situated)	**stato**
dire (to say)	**detto**	**succedere*** (to happen)	**successo**
essere* (to be)	**stato**	**trascorrere** (to spend)	**trascorso**
fare (to do)	**fatto**	**vedere** (to see)	**visto**
leggere (to read)	**letto**	**venire*** (to come)	**venuto**
mettere (to put)	**messo**	**vincere** (to win)	**vinto**
morire* (to die)	**morto**	**vivere*** (to live)	**vissuto**
nascere* (to be born)	**nato**		
perdere (to lose)	**perso**		

The imperfect tense

The imperfect tense is used:

1 to describe something which used to happen frequently or regularly in the past.

Andavamo a scuola a piedi.
We walked/We used to walk to school.

2 to describe what was happening or what the situation was when something else happened.

Dormivo quando Sergio **è arrivato**.
I was sleeping when Sergio arrived.

Aveva sei anni quando **è nata** Carla.
He was six when Carla was born.

3 to express an emotional or physical state in the past and to refer to time, age, or the weather.

Ieri sera Beatrice **era** stanca.
Beatrice was tired.

Aveva i capelli biondi.
She had blonde hair.

Erano le sette.
It was seven o'clock.

Era una bella giornata.
It was a lovely day.

Quando **eravamo** piccoli, ci piaceva andare al mare.
When we were little, we used to like going to the seaside.

The imperfect tense is formed by adding the following endings to the stem.

	parlare	**credere**	**sentire**
(io)	**parl*avo***	**cred*evo***	**sent*ivo***
(tu)	**parl*avi***	**cred*evi***	**sent*ivi***
(lui/lei; lei)	**parl*ava***	**cred*eva***	**sent*iva***
(noi)	**parl*avamo***	**cred*evamo***	**sent*ivamo***
(voi)	**parl*avate***	**cred*evate***	**sent*ivate***
(loro)	**parl*avano***	**cred*evano***	**sent*ivano***

See the verb tables for details of verbs which are irregular in the imperfect.

Use of the perfect and the imperfect

The perfect is used to describe a completed or single action in the past; the imperfect describes a continuing, repeated, or habitual action. When they are used together, the imperfect is the tense that sets the scene, while the perfect is used to move the action forward.

Ho visto Marco giovedì.
I saw Marco on Thursday.

Andavo in piscina il giovedì.
I used to go swimming on Thursdays.

Poiché **faceva** caldo, **siamo andati** tutti al mare.
Because it was hot, we all went to the seaside.

The past historic tense

The past historic is a tense that refers to something that happened in the past, generally in the relatively distant past. It is formed by adding a set of endings to the verb. Before adding the endings, the infinitive ending (**-are**, **-ere**, or **–ire**) is dropped. For some **-ere** verbs there is a choice of endings for some forms; both sets of endings are commonly used. A large number of verbs form their past historic in irregular ways.

	parlare	vendere	dormire
(io)	**parlai**	**vendei** or **vendetti**	**dormii**
(tu)	**parlasti**	**vendesti**	**dormisti**
(lui/lei; lei)	**parlò**	**vendé** or **vendette**	**dormì**
(noi)	**parlammo**	**vendemmo**	**dormimmo**
(voi)	**parlaste**	**vendeste**	**dormiste**
(loro)	**parlarono**	**venderono** or **vendettero**	**dormirono**

Pagò il conto e se **ne andò**.
He paid the bill and left.

La città **fu fondata** nel 500 a.C.
The city was founded in 500 BC.

The pluperfect tense

The pluperfect tense is used to talk about events that happened *before* the event that is the main focus of attention. Like the perfect tense, it uses a form of **avere** or **essere** with the past participle: the past tense of **avere** (or **essere** if the verb forms its compound tenses with **essere**) is followed by the past participle. If the verb uses **essere** as an auxiliary, the past participle agrees with the subject (see the section on the perfect tense).

Li **avevo visti** l'estate prima.
I had seen them the summer before.

Ci **eravamo** già **conosciuti**.
We had already met.

The future tense

In Italian, the future can be expressed in different ways.

1 You can use the present tense with an appropriate time expression when talking about plans (as in English):

Non **sono** libero domani.
I'm not/I won't be available tomorrow.

Partiamo per le vacanze lunedì prossimo.
We're going on holiday next Monday.

2 You can use the future tense – especially when making predictions (as in weather forecasts or horoscopes) or stating a fact about the future.

Avrete molto successo.
You will have great success.

Balleranno tutta la notte.
They'll dance all night.

Domani **nevicherà**.
Tomorrow it will snow.

The future tense is formed by dropping the final **-e** of the infinitive and adding the future endings. In **-are** verbs, the **a** in the infinitive changes to **e.**

	parlare	prendere	dormire
(io)	**parler*ò***	**prender*ò***	**dormir*ò***
(tu)	**parler*ai***	**prender*ai***	**dormir*ai***
(lui/lei; lei)	**parler*à***	**prender*à***	**dormir*à***
(noi)	**parler*emo***	**prender*emo***	**dormir*emo***
(voi)	**parler*ete***	**prender*ete***	**dormir*ete***
(loro)	**parler*anno***	**prender*anno***	**dormir*anno***

Stasera Elio **parlerà** con il padre.
Tonight Elio will talk to his father.

Non lo **lascerà** mai.
She'll never leave him.

Verbs ending in **-care** and **-gare** add an **h** before the endings to keep the hard sound of the stem.

Gli spie**gheremo** tutto noi.
We will explain everything to him.

Cer**cherete** subito lavoro?
Will you be looking for work straight away?

For irregular future forms, see the verb tables on pages 616–624.

The conditional

In Italian the conditional is used for polite requests and suggestions, and to express a wish or a probable action. The endings are the same for all conjugations and, like the future tense, are added to the infinitive minus the final **-e** (or, if irregular, to the same stem used for the future tense).
As with the future, the **a** in **-are** verbs changes to **e**. The rules affecting the spelling of **cercare**, **spiegare**, etc. also apply: see above.

	parlare	prendere	dormire
(io)	**parler*ei***	**prender*ei***	**dormir*ei***
(tu)	**parler*esti***	**prender*esti***	**dormir*esti***
(lui/lei; lei)	**parler*ebbe***	**prender*ebbe***	**dormir*ebbe***
(noi)	**parler*emmo***	**prender*emmo***	**dormir*emmo***
(voi)	**parler*este***	**prender*este***	**dormir*este***
(loro)	**parler*ebbero***	**prender*ebbero***	**dormir*ebbero***

Potremmo venire con te.
We could come with you.

Dovresti andare a letto presto.
You should go to bed early.

Non **vivrebbero** mai all'estero.
They'd never live abroad.

Saresti il primo a saperlo.
You'd be the first to know.

Vorrebbe fare una partita a tennis?
Would you like to have a game of tennis?

The subjunctive

The subjunctive is a special form of the verb that expresses doubt, unlikelihood, or desire. The subjunctive is not very common in modern English, and often forms with *let*, *should*, etc. do the same job. In Italian the subjunctive is very common, and is obligatory in certain circumstances. The subjunctive is commonly used to show that what is being said is not a concrete fact, for example to indicate doubt or necessity, or after verbs of ordering, requiring, or persuasion. It contrasts with the *indicative*, the normal form of the verb, which always implies a greater degree of certainty. The subjunctive is sometimes translated by an infinitive in English.

The present subjunctive is generally used when the main verb in the sentence is in the present; the past subjunctive is used when the main verb is in the past, or in order to talk about hypothetical situations.

For the forms of the subjunctive, see the verb tables on pages 616–624.

Credo che tu **abbia** ragione.
I think you're right.

Spero che questo problema si **risolva**.
I hope this problem is solved.

Bisogna che tu **legga** tutto.
It's necessary for you to read it all.

Voglio che tu mi **aiuti**.
I want you to help me.

Volevo che mi **aiutassi**.
I wanted you to help me.

Regular verbs -are

parlare – to speak (past participle **parlato**)

	present	future	conditional	perfect	imperfect
io	parlo	parlerò	parlerei	ho parlato	parlavo
tu	parli	parlerai	parleresti	hai parlato	parlavi
lui/lei; lei	parla	parlerà	parlerebbe	ha parlato	parlava
noi	parliamo	parleremo	parleremmo	abbiamo parlato	parlavamo
voi	parlate	parlerete	parlereste	avete parlato	parlavate
loro	parlano	parleranno	parlerebbero	hanno parlato	parlavano

	pluperfect	past historic	present subjunctive	past subjunctive	imperative
io	avevo parlato	parlai	parli	parlassi	
tu	avevi parlato	parlasti	parli	parlassi	parla
lui/lei; lei	aveva parlato	parlò	parli	parlasse	parli
noi	avevamo parlato	parlammo	parliamo	parlassimo	parliamo
voi	avevate parlato	parlaste	parliate	parlaste	parlate
loro	avevano parlato	parlarono	parlino	parlassero	

Verbs ending in **-care** and **-gare**, such as **cercare**, ('to look for') or **spiegare** ('to explain'), add an **h** before **i** or **e**.

Cerchiamo un posto tranquillo. We're looking for a quiet place.
Ti spieghiamo tutto domani. We'll explain everything tomorrow.

Regular verbs -ere

credere – to believe (past participle **creduto**)

	present	future	conditional	perfect	imperfect
io	credo	crederò	crederei	ho creduto	credevo
tu	credi	crederai	crederesti	hai creduto	credevi
lui/lei; lei	crede	crederà	crederebbe	ha creduto	credeva
noi	crediamo	crederemo	crederemmo	abbiamo creduto	credevamo
voi	credete	crederete	credereste	avete creduto	credevate
loro	credono	crederanno	crederebbero	hanno creduto	credevano

	pluperfect	past historic	present subjunctive	past subjunctive	imperative
io	avevo creduto	credei *or* credetti	creda	credessi	
tu	avevi creduto	credesti	creda	credessi	credi
lui/lei; lei	aveva creduto	credé *or* credette	creda	credesse	creda
noi	avevamo creduto	credemmo	crediamo	credessimo	crediamo
voi	avevate creduto	credeste	crediate	credeste	credete
loro	avevano creduto	crederono *or* credettero	credano	credessero	

Regular verbs -ire (1)

sentire – to hear (past participle **sentito**)

	present	future	conditional	perfect	imperfect
io	sento	sentirò	sentirei	ho sentito	sentivo
tu	senti	sentirai	sentiresti	hai sentito	sentivi
lui/lei; lei	sente	sentirà	sentirebbe	ha sentito	sentiva
noi	sentiamo	sentiremo	sentiremmo	abbiamo sentito	sentivamo
voi	sentite	sentirete	sentireste	avete sentito	sentivate
loro	sentono	sentiranno	sentirebbero	hanno sentito	sentivano

	pluperfect	past historic	present subjunctive	past subjunctive	imperative
io	avevo sentito	sentii	senta	sentissi	
tu	avevi sentito	sentisti	senta	sentissi	senti
lui/lei; lei	aveva sentito	sentì	senta	sentisse	senta
noi	avevamo sentito	sentimmo	sentiamo	sentissimo	sentiamo
voi	avevate sentito	sentiste	sentiate	sentiste	sentite
loro	avevano sentito	sentirono	sentano	sentissero	

Regular verbs -ire (2)

Some verbs ending in **-ire** insert **-isc-** between the stem and the ending in the three singular forms and in the 3rd person plural form of the present tense.

finire – to finish (past participle **finito**)

	present	future	conditional	perfect	imperfect
io	finisco	finirò	finirei	ho finito	finivo
tu	finisci	finirai	finiresti	hai finito	finivi
lui/lei; lei	finisce	finirà	finirebbe	ha finito	finiva
noi	finiamo	finiremo	finiremmo	abbiamo finito	finivamo
voi	finite	finirete	finireste	avete finito	finivate
loro	finiscono	finiranno	finirebbero	hanno finito	finivano

	pluperfect	past historic	present subjunctive	past subjunctive	imperative
io	avevo finito	finii	finisca	finissi	
tu	avevi finito	finisti	finisca	finissi	finisci
lui/lei; lei	aveva finito	finì	finisca	finisse	finisca
noi	avevamo finito	finimmo	finiamo	finissimo	finiamo
voi	avevate finito	finiste	finiate	finiste	finite
loro	avevano finito	finirono	finiscano	finissero	

Irregular verbs

avere – to have (past participle avuto)

	present	future	conditional	perfect	imperfect
io	ho	avrò	avrei	ho avuto	avevo
tu	hai	avrai	avresti	hai avuto	avevi
lui/lei; lei	ha	avrà	avrebbe	ha avuto	aveva
noi	abbiamo	avremo	avremmo	abbiamo avuto	avevamo
voi	avete	avrete	avreste	avete avuto	avevate
loro	hanno	avranno	avrebbero	hanno avuto	avevano

	pluperfect	past historic	present subjunctive	past subjunctive	imperative
io	avevo avuto	ebbi	abbia	avessi	
tu	avevi avuto	avesti	abbia	avessi	abbi
lui/lei; lei	aveva avuto	ebbe	abbia	avesse	abbia
noi	avevamo avuto	avemmo	abbiamo	avessimo	abbiamo
voi	avevate avuto	aveste	abbiate	aveste	abbiate
loro	avevano avuto	ebbero	abbiano	avessero	

essere* – to be (past participle stato)

	present	future	conditional	perfect	imperfect
io	sono	sarò	sarei	sono stato/stata	ero
tu	sei	sarai	saresti	sei stato/stata	eri
lui/lei; lei	è	sarà	sarebbe	è stato/stata	era
noi	siamo	saremo	saremmo	siamo stati/state	eravamo
voi	siete	sarete	sareste	siete stati/state	eravate
loro	sono	saranno	sarebbero	sono stati/state	erano

	pluperfect	past historic	present subjunctive	past subjunctive	imperative
io	ero stato/stata	fui	sia	fossi	
tu	eri stato/stata	fosti	sia	fossi	sii
lui/lei; lei	era stato/stata	fu	sia	fosse	sia
noi	eravamo stati/state	fummo	siamo	fossimo	siamo
voi	eravate stati/state	foste	siate	foste	siate
loro	erano stati/state	furono	siano	fossero	

Irregular verbs cont.

andare* – to go (past participle **andato**)

	present	future	conditional	perfect	imperfect
io	vado	andrò	andrei	sono andato/andata	andavo
tu	vai	andrai	andresti	sei andato/andata	andavi
lui/lei; lei	va	andrà	andrebbe	è andato/andata	andava
noi	andiamo	andremo	andremmo	siamo andati/andate	andavamo
voi	andate	andrete	andreste	siete andati/andate	andavate
loro	vanno	andranno	andrebbero	sono andati/andate	andavano

	pluperfect	past historic	present subjunctive	past subjunctive	imperative
io	ero andato/andata	andai	vada	andassi	
tu	eri andato/andata	andasti	vada	andassi	va'
lui/lei; lei	era andato/andata	andò	vada	andasse	vada
noi	eravamo andati/andate	andammo	andiamo	andassimo	andiamo
voi	eravate andati/andate	andaste	andiate	andaste	andate
loro	erano andati/andate	andarono	vadano	andassero	

bere – to drink (past participle **bevuto**)

	present	future	conditional	perfect	imperfect
io	bevo	berrò	berrei	ho bevuto	bevevo
tu	bevi	berrai	berresti	hai bevuto	bevevi
lui/lei; lei	beve	berrà	berrebbe	ha bevuto	beveva
noi	beviamo	berremo	berremmo	abbiamo bevuto	bevevamo
voi	bevete	berrete	berreste	avete bevuto	bevevate
loro	bevono	berranno	berrebbero	hanno bevuto	bevevano

	pluperfect	past historic	present subjunctive	past subjunctive	imperative
io	avevo bevuto	bevvi *or* bevetti	beva	bevessi	
tu	avevi bevuto	bevesti	beva	bevessi	bevi
lui/lei; lei	aveva bevuto	bevve *or* bevette	beva	bevesse	beva
noi	avevamo bevuto	bevemmo	beviamo	bevessimo	beviamo
voi	avevate bevuto	beveste	beviate	beveste	bevete
loro	avevano bevuto	bevvero *or* bevettero	bevano	bevessero	

Irregular verbs cont.

dare – to give (past participle **dato**)

	present	future	conditional	perfect	imperfect
io	do	darò	darei	ho dato	davo
tu	dai	darai	daresti	hai dato	davi
lui/lei; lei	dà	darà	darebbe	ha dato	dava
noi	diamo	daremo	daremmo	abbiamo dato	davamo
voi	date	darete	dareste	avete dato	davate
loro	danno	daranno	darebbero	hanno dato	davano

	pluperfect	past historic	present subjunctive	past subjunctive	imperative
io	avevo dato	diedi *or* detti	dia	dessi	
tu	avevi dato	desti	dia	dessi	da'
lui/lei; lei	aveva dato	diede *or* dette	dia	desse	dia
noi	avevamo dato	demmo	diamo	dessimo	diamo
voi	avevate dato	deste	diate	deste	date
loro	avevano dato	diedero *or* dettero	diano	dessero	

dire – to say (past participle **detto**)

	present	future	conditional	perfect	imperfect
io	dico	dirò	direi	ho detto	dicevo
tu	dici	dirai	diresti	hai detto	dicevi
lui/lei; lei	dice	dirà	direbbe	ha detto	diceva
noi	diciamo	diremo	diremmo	abbiamo detto	dicevamo
voi	dite	direte	direste	avete detto	dicevate
loro	dicono	diranno	direbbero	hanno detto	dicevano

	pluperfect	past historic	present subjunctive	past subjunctive	imperative
io	avevo detto	dissi	dica	dicessi	
tu	avevi detto	dicesti	dica	dicessi	di'
lui/lei; lei	aveva detto	disse	dica	dicesse	dica
noi	avevamo detto	dicemmo	diciamo	dicessimo	diciamo
voi	avevate detto	diceste	diciate	diceste	dite
loro	avevano detto	dissero	dicano	dicessero	

Irregular verbs cont.

dovere – to have to (past participle **dovuto**)

	present	future	conditional	perfect	imperfect
io	devo	dovrò	dovrei	ho dovuto	dovevo
tu	devi	dovrai	dovresti	hai dovuto	dovevi
lui/lei; lei	deve	dovrà	dovrebbe	ha dovuto	doveva
noi	dobbiamo	dovremo	dovremmo	abbiamo dovuto	dovevamo
voi	dovete	dovrete	dovreste	avete dovuto	dovevate
loro	devono	dovranno	dovrebbero	hanno dovuto	dovevano

	pluperfect	past historic	present subjunctive	past subjunctive
io	avevo dovuto	dovetti	deva	dovessi
tu	avevi dovuto	dovesti	deva	dovessi
lui/lei; lei	aveva dovuto	dovette	deva	dovesse
noi	avevamo dovuto	dovemmo	dobbiamo	dovessimo
voi	avevate dovuto	doveste	dobbiate	doveste
loro	avevano dovuto	dovettero	devano	dovessero

fare – to do, to make (past participle **fatto**)

	present	future	conditional	perfect	imperfect
io	faccio	farò	farei	ho fatto	facevo
tu	fai	farai	faresti	hai fatto	facevi
lui/lei; lei	fa	farà	farebbe	ha fatto	faceva
noi	facciamo	faremo	faremmo	abbiamo fatto	facevamo
voi	fate	farete	fareste	avete fatto	facevate
loro	fanno	faranno	farebbero	hanno fatto	facevano

	pluperfect	past historic	present subjunctive	past subjunctive	imperative
io	avevo fatto	feci	faccia	facessi	
tu	avevi fatto	facesti	faccia	facessi	fa'
lui/lei; lei	aveva fatto	fece	faccia	facesse	faccia
noi	avevamo fatto	facemmo	facciamo	facessimo	facciamo
voi	avevate fatto	faceste	facciate	faceste	fate
loro	avevano fatto	fecero	facciano	facessero	

Irregular verbs cont.

potere – to be able to (past participle **potuto**)

	present	future	conditional	perfect	imperfect
io	posso	potrò	potrei	ho potuto	potevo
tu	puoi	potrai	potresti	hai potuto	potevi
lui/lei; lei	può	potrà	potrebbe	ha potuto	poteva
noi	possiamo	potremo	potremmo	abbiamo potuto	potevamo
voi	potete	potrete	potreste	avete potuto	potevate
loro	possono	potranno	potrebbero	hanno potuto	potevano

	pluperfect	past historic	present subjunctive	past subjunctive	imperative
io	avevo potuto	potei	possa	potessi	
tu	avevi potuto	potesti	possa	potessi	
lui/lei; lei	aveva potuto	poté	possa	potesse	
noi	avevamo potuto	potemmo	possiamo	potessimo	
voi	avevate potuto	poteste	possiate	poteste	
loro	avevano potuto	poterono	possano	potessero	

sapere – to know (a fact, how to do something) (past participle **saputo**)

	present	future	conditional	perfect	imperfect
io	so	saprò	saprei	ho saputo	sapevo
tu	sai	saprai	sapresti	hai saputo	sapevi
lui/lei; lei	sa	saprà	saprebbe	ha saputo	sapeva
noi	sappiamo	sapremo	sapremmo	abbiamo saputo	sapevamo
voi	sapete	saprete	sapreste	avete saputo	sapevate
loro	sanno	sapranno	saprebbero	hanno saputo	sapevano

	pluperfect	past historic	present subjunctive	past subjunctive	imperative
io	avevo saputo	seppi	sappia	sapessi	
tu	avevi saputo	sapesti	sappia	sapessi	sappi
lui/lei; lei	aveva saputo	seppe	sappia	sapesse	sappia
noi	avevamo saputo	sapemmo	sappiamo	sapessimo	sappiamo
voi	avevate saputo	sapeste	sappiate	sapeste	sappiate
loro	avevano saputo	seppero	sappiano	sapessero	

Irregular verbs cont.

stare* – to stay (past participle **stato**)

	present	future	conditional	perfect	imperfect
io	sto	starò	starei	sono stato/stata	stavo
tu	stai	starai	staresti	sei stato/stata	stavi
lui/lei; lei	sta	starà	starebbe	è stato/stata	stava
noi	stiamo	staremo	staremmo	siamo stati/state	stavamo
voi	state	starete	stareste	siete stati/state	stavate
loro	stanno	staranno	starebbero	sono stati/state	stavano

	pluperfect	past historic	present subjunctive	past subjunctive	imperative
io	ero stato/stata	stetti	stia	stessi	
tu	eri stato/stata	stesti	stia	stessi	sta'
lui/lei; lei	era stato/stata	stette	stia	stesse	stia
noi	eravamo stati/state	stemmo	stiamo	stessimo	stiamo
voi	eravate stati/state	steste	stiate	steste	state
loro	erano stati/state	stettero	stiano	stessero	

uscire* – to go out (past participle **uscito**)

	present	future	conditional	perfect	imperfect
io	esco	uscirò	uscirei	sono uscito/uscita	uscivo
tu	esci	uscirai	usciresti	sei uscito/uscita	uscivi
lui/lei; lei	esce	uscirà	uscirebbe	è uscito/uscita	usciva
noi	usciamo	usciremo	usciremmo	siamo usciti/uscite	uscivamo
voi	uscite	uscirete	uscireste	siete usciti/uscite	uscivate
loro	escono	usciranno	uscirebbero	sono usciti/uscite	uscivano

	pluperfect	past historic	present subjunctive	past subjunctive	imperative
io	ero uscito/uscita	uscii	esca	uscissi	
tu	eri uscito/uscita	uscisti	esca	uscissi	esci
lui/lei; lei	era uscito/uscita	uscì	esca	uscisse	esca
noi	eravamo usciti/uscite	uscimmo	usciamo	uscissimo	usciamo
voi	eravate usciti/uscite	usciste	usciate	usciste	uscite
loro	erano usciti/uscite	uscirono	escano	uscissero	

Irregular verbs cont.

venire* – to come (past participle **venuto**)

	present	future	conditional	perfect	imperfect
io	vengo	verrò	verrei	sono venuto/venuta	venivo
tu	vieni	verrai	verresti	sei venuto/venuta	venivi
lui/lei; lei	viene	verrà	verrebbe	è venuto/venuta	veniva
noi	veniamo	verremo	verremmo	siamo venuti/venute	venivamo
voi	venite	verrete	verreste	siete venuti/venute	venivate
loro	vengono	verranno	verrebbero	sono venuti/venute	venivano

	pluperfect	past historic	present subjunctive	past subjunctive	imperative
io	ero venuto/venuta	venni	venga	venissi	
tu	eri venuto/venuta	venisti	venga	venissi	vieni
lui/lei; lei	era venuto/venuta	venne	venga	venisse	venga
noi	eravamo venuti/venute	venimmo	veniamo	venissimo	veniamo
voi	eravate venuti/venute	veniste	veniate	veniste	venite
loro	erano venuti/venute	vennero	vengano	venissero	

volere – to want (past participle **voluto**)

	present	future	conditional	perfect	imperfect
io	voglio	vorrò	vorrei	ho voluto	volevo
tu	vuoi	vorrai	vorresti	hai voluto	volevi
lui/lei; lei	vuole	vorrà	vorrebbe	ha voluto	voleva
noi	vogliamo	vorremo	vorremmo	abbiamo voluto	volevamo
voi	volete	vorrete	vorreste	avete voluto	volevate
loro	vogliono	vorranno	vorrebbero	hanno voluto	volevano

	pluperfect	past historic	present subjunctive	past subjunctive
io	avevo voluto	volli	voglia	volessi
tu	avevi voluto	volesti	voglia	volessi
lui/lei; lei	aveva voluto	volle	voglia	volesse
noi	avevamo voluto	volemmo	vogliamo	volessimo
voi	avevate voluto	voleste	vogliate	voleste
loro	avevano voluto	vollero	vogliano	volessero